UNIVERSITY CASEBOOK SERIES

CASES AND MATERIALS

BUSINESS PLANNING

FOURTH EDITION

by

FRANKLIN A. GEVURTZ
Distinguished Professor and Scholar
University of the Pacific, McGeorge School of Law
Sacramento, California

395 Hudson Street

New York, NY 10014

Phone Toll Free 1–877–888–1330

Fax (212) 367–6799

foundation–press.com

Printed in the United States of America

ISBN 978–1–59941–149–1

To Carmen, Sara, Marvin and Manya

*

PREFACE TO FOURTH EDITION

This fourth edition of Business Planning reflects a commitment to try to keep this book as current as humanly possible in a field as expansive and as changing as business planning. Unlike the third edition, there is no major rethinking of any chapter in the book. Instead, changes to keep the material up to date are scattered throughout. (Perhaps I am settling into a pattern in which odd numbered editions will reflect a more substantial rethinking of major parts of the book, while even numbered editions reflect just a general updating.) For me, the highlights (or, in some sense, the low-lights) of the new materials consist of a number of new cases that illustrate the manifold ways in which attorneys and parties can mess up business transactions and from which our students (hopefully) can learn. As this suggests, I remain convinced that there is no substitute for reading cases if one wishes to learn how to be a transactional attorney.

A number of individuals deserve some thanks for contributing to this edition of the book. I received helpful unsolicited comments from Kevin Outterson and Matthew Ward on the prior edition. My research assistant, Jim Bothwell, provided invaluable help.

*

PREFACE TO FIRST EDITION

The essence of business planning (from a business as opposed to a legal standpoint) is identifying a need in the market and filling it. Simply put, that is what this book is all about. It seeks to provide an up-to-date text for use in teaching this advanced elective course.

There are two facets to providing an up-to-date text. The more obvious is the need to incorporate the constant changes in statutory, regulatory and case law governing the applicable field. This is particularly challenging in the area of business planning. For one thing, the course involves a cross-section of substantive areas, which multiplies the number of relevant changes. Moreover, Congress and the administration seem to have become addicted to the notion that the tax code ought to change every year.

An equally, if not more important, aspect to providing an up-to-date text is to incorporate new thinking, both in matters of substance and pedagogy. For example, changes in the tax law necessitate a reconsideration of what this course should cover. When Professor Herwitz and the Harvard Law School originated the business planning course in the 1960s, a corporation was generally the vehicle of choice for all but professional firms and the unsophisticated. The current tax laws make this no longer true. Accordingly, this book provides careful consideration of the choice of entity question and a comprehensive exploration of both the tax and general aspects of forming partnerships and limited partnerships. The chapters dealing with forming partnerships, limited partnerships and corporations follow a four-part parallel structure so that students can make comparisons between the entities.

A relatively recent (or recently revived) stream of thought is that law schools should do more to develop their students into professionals. This means different things to different people and there is substantial debate as to what extent law schools can (or even should try to) produce graduates who immediately possess the skills of a practitioner. Still, it may be highly appropriate to encourage law students to reflect upon the various demands they will soon face as members of the profession, and a course in business planning seems a particularly good vehicle for this task. Accordingly, this book provides materials addressing the role of the business attorney in various transactions and the ethical issues he or she faces. Also, the problem set accompanying the book seeks to raise such questions at every opportunity.

Modern financial and economic theories also make their demands. By and large, the book deliberately attempts to avoid the use of economics jargon; at the same time, the text seeks to have the students understand the basic business and economic aspects of various transactions. One area of this course heavily impacted by changing financial theory is valuation. The subject has become increasingly mathematical and hence more intimidating to most law students. In response, the book disperses the valuation materials throughout its chapters in the hope that returning to the subject from slightly different angles, or in an increasingly more sophisticated manner, will prevent the "sensory overload" students might otherwise experience if they must deal with the subject of valuation all at once.

While making these changes, this book retains the central idea of the business planning course; that is, to provide a problem method, planning oriented course which will cross traditional legal subject matter boundaries. Indeed, the book attempts to build upon this foundation with several evolutionary steps. The chapters follow a structure which seeks to more closely integrate considerations of corporate, tax, securities, general business and other considerations together as the text guides the reader step-by-step through various transactions. Also, both the text (particularly through case selection) and the problem set try to have students appreciate the human, as opposed to just the technical, aspects of planning business transactions. In addition, the problem set follows the same business through various stages—specifically, forming a partnership at the start-up, incorporating and financing the business facing significant money needs, a corporate buy-out, recapitalization and split-off, and finally, the sale of a mature business. Following the same business in this manner can often provide interesting opportunities for students to "experience" the impact of their earlier planning decisions.

Of course, a primary business objective is to satisfy the needs of as many users of one's product as possible. Hence, this book is designed with the idea of flexibility. Business planning courses in different law schools run from 30 to 80 hours long. Some schools require as a prerequisite for taking business planning that students have completed a course in corporate income tax and even Federal securities regulation; others merely require completion of basic corporate law and individual income tax courses. Different instructors prefer to emphasize different aspects of the subject matter: Some focus more on tax; others emphasize securities and financing issues; still others give more attention to general business considerations. Many instructors (this writer included) believe the heart of the course lies in the small business formation and financing issues which are the "bread and butter" of most business attorneys' (especially new attorneys') practices. Many others, however, find the sophisticated downstream corporate transactions to hold greater interest. Given these parameters, the best the writer can do is to provide treatment of all aspects of the subject (within reasonable page limitations), and leave it to each individual instructor to cover the material which fits his or her situation.

Finally, some words of gratitude are in order. The late F. Hodge O'Neal, Andrew Demetriou, of Jones, Day, Reavis and Pogue in Los Angeles, and especially Philip Wile, Director of Graduate Tax and Business Programs at the McGeorge School of Law, graciously gave of their time to review all or portions of this book. My colleague Claude Rohwer originally suggested I undertake this project. During the years, a number of research assistants helped on various phases of this book; most recently and most especially thanks go to Blaine Wanke. Of course, appreciation must be extended to Jo-Carol Arisman, Irma Johnson and the other secretaries who turned countless yellow pads of semi-legible scrawl into neatly typed manuscript. Last, but by no means least, much thanks go to the numerous students since 1983 who served as guinea pigs for various editions of this book.

*

ACKNOWLEDGEMENTS

The following individuals or organizations kindly gave permission to reprint excerpts from their copyrighted works:

New York University

Cornell, Tax Planning, Teaching and Practice, 22 Tax L.Rev. 221 (1967)

Eustice, Subchapter S Corporations and Partnerships: A Search for the Pass Through Paradigm (Some Preliminary Proposals), 39 Tax L.Rev. 345 (1984)

John Wiley & Sons, Inc.

Schollhammer & Kuriloff, Entrepreneurship and Small Business Management (1979)

Foundation Press

Klein & Coffee, Business Organization and Finance: Legal and Economic Principles (4th ed. 1990)

Pacific Law Journal

Committee on Corporations of the Business Law Section of the State Bar of California, Report Regarding Legal Opinions in Business Transactions, 14 Pac.L.J. 1001 (1983)

Gevurtz, California's New Limited Liability Company Act: A Look at the Good, the Bad and the Ambiguous, 27 Pac.L.J. 261 (1996).

University of Southern California Institute on Federal Taxation

Smith, Tax Rulings—Their Use and Abuse, 1970 U.So.Cal. Tax Inst. 163

American Bar Association

Model Rules of Professional Conduct

Formal Opinions of the Committee on Professional Ethics

Llewellyn & Umbrucht, No Choice of Entity After Check-the-Box 52 Tax Law 1 (1998).

Nebraska Law Review

Hazen, The Decision to Incorporate, 58 Neb.L.Rev. 627 (1979)

Clark, Boardman Callaghan

O'Neal's Oppression of Minority Shareholders (1989)

Warren, Gorham & Lamont, Inc.

Bittker, Federal Taxation of Income, Estates and Gifts (1981). Copyright 1981 and 1989 by Warren, Gorham & Lamont, Inc. 210 South Street, Boston, MA 02111. Reprinted with permission. All rights reserved

Handbook of Modern Finance (1984). Copyright 1984 by Warren, Gorham & Lamont, Inc. Reprinted with permission. All rights reserved

Harvard Law Review

Herwitz, Allocation of Stock Between Services and Capital in the Organization of a Close Corporation, 70 Harv.L.Rev. 1098 (1962)

Boston University Journal of Tax Law

Apelbaum, The Accumulated Earnings Tax and the Personal Holding Company Tax: Problems and Proposals, 3 Boston U.J. Tax L. 53 (1985)

Matthew Bender & Co., Inc.

Cavitch, Tax Planning for Shareholders and Corporations (1990). Copyright 1990 by Matthew Bender & Co., Inc. and reprinted with permission

Douglas Walter

An Overview of Compensation Techniques Following TRA '86, 13 J.Corp. Tax 139 (1987)

Michael Newmark and Dudley Lang

The Subchapter S Revision Act of 1982, 37 Tax Law. 93 (1986)

Deloitte & Touche

Raising Venture Capital (1982)

Strategies for Going Public (1983)

North American Securities Administrators Association

Statements of Policy

Uniform Limited Offering Exemption

Carl Schneider, Joseph Manko, and Robert Kant

Going Public—Practice, Procedure and Consequences, 27 Vill.L. Rev. 1 (1981), as updated by the authors through May 1988

Journal of Corporation Law

Brandi, Securities Practitioners and Blue Sky Laws: A Survey of Comments and a Ranking of States by Stringency of Regulation, 10 J.Corp.L. 689 (1985). Reprinted with the permission of the Journal of Corporation Law, Copyright 1985

University of Baltimore Law Review

Davidow, Limitations Imposed by the Tax Reform Act of 1986 on a Corporation's Use of Net Operating Loss Carryovers After an Ownership Change, 17 U.Balt.L.Rev. 331 (1988)

Frank Curci

Curci, Protecting Your Trademarks, Copyrights, Patents and Trade Secrets Overseas, 15 Trans. Law. 15 (2001)

West Group

Gevurtz, Corporation Law (2000)

Susan Hamill

Stover & Hamill, The LLCVersusLLP Conundrum: Advice for Businesses Contemplating the Choice, 50 Ala. L. Rev. 813 (1999)

Washington University Law Quarterly

Gevurtz, Squeeze-Outs and Freeze-Outs in Limited Liability Companies, 73 Wash. U.L.Q. 497 (1995)

Journal of Small & Emerging Business Law

Langevoort, Angels on the Internet: The Elusive Promise of "Technological Disintermediation" for Unregistered Offerings of Securities, 2 J. Small & Emerging Bus. L. 1 (1998)

Joseph W. Bartlett

Bartlett, Venture Capital: Law, Business Strategies, and Investment Planning

*

SUMMARY OF CONTENTS

PREFACE TO FOURTH EDITION ---------- v
PREFACE TO FIRST EDITION ---------- vii
ACKNOWLEDGEMENTS ---------- xi
TABLE OF CASES ---------- xxix

CHAPTER I. Introduction to Business Planning ---------- 1

A. The Lawyer as a Planner ---------- 1
B. Ethical Considerations for the Business Attorney ---------- 26
C. Overcoming the Fear of Numbers: An Introduction to Valuation ---------- 52

CHAPTER II. Choice of Business Entity ---------- 58

A. Traditional Non–Tax Considerations ---------- 58
B. Separate Taxpaying Entity Versus Pass–Through Treatment ---------- 69
C. Choosing Between Pass–Through Forms ---------- 87
D. Multientity Structures ---------- 100

CHAPTER III. Forming a Partnership, Limited Partnership, Limited Liability Partnership, or Limited Liability Company ---------- 113

A. Contributions ---------- 119
B. Profit and Loss ---------- 168
C. Management ---------- 246
D. Dissolution and Changes in Ownership ---------- 269

CHAPTER IV. Forming a Corporation ---------- 359

A. Contributions ---------- 361
B. Profit and Loss ---------- 437
C. Management ---------- 494
D. Dissolution and Changes in Ownership ---------- 528

CHAPTER V. Financing ---------- 576

A. Assessing Financial Needs ---------- 576
B. Determining the Nature and Worth of the Investments Offered ---------- 577
C. Targeting the Appropriate Investors ---------- 608

CHAPTER VI. Corporate Restructuring Transactions ---------- 721

A. Restructuring Through Buy–Outs ---------- 722
B. Restructuring Through Stock Dividends and Recapitalizations ---------- 806
C. Restructuring Through Divisions and Contractions ---------- 858

CHAPTER VII. Purchase and Sale of a Business 890

A. Preliminary Considerations 890
B. Structuring the Acquisition 1006
C. Follow–Up Transactions 1123

APPENDIX 1149
INDEX 1173

TABLE OF CONTENTS

PREFACE TO FOURTH EDITION ---- v
PREFACE TO FIRST EDITION ---- vii
ACKNOWLEDGEMENTS ---- xi
TABLE OF CASES ---- xxix

CHAPTER I. Introduction to Business Planning ---- 1

Sec.
A. The Lawyer as a Planner ---- 1
Corneel, Tax Planning: Teaching and Practice ---- 1
Schollhammer & Kuriloff, Entrepreneurship and Small Business Management ---- 5
Klein & Coffee, Business Organization & Finance, Legal & Economic Principles ---- 17
Committee on Corporations of the Business Law Section of the State Bar of California, Report of the Committee on Corporations Regarding Legal Opinions in Business Transactions ---- 18
Smith, Tax Rulings—Their Use and Abuse ---- 22
B. Ethical Considerations for the Business Attorney ---- 26
1. Typical Conflict of Interest Problems ---- 27
American Bar Association Model Rules of Professional Conduct 27
American Bar Association Model Rules of Professional Conduct 30
American Bar Association Model Rules of Professional Conduct 33
Notes ---- 33
2. The Limits of Zeal ---- 35
American Bar Association Standing Committee on Ethics and Professional Responsibility, Formal Opinion 85–352, Tax Return Advice; Reconsideration of Formal Opinion 314 ---- 36
Note ---- 38
3. Expertise ---- 39
American Bar Association Model Rules of Professional Conduct 39
Note ---- 39
Waggoner v. Snow, Becker, Kroll, Klaris & Krauss ---- 40
Notes ---- 44
Curci, Protecting Your Intellectual Property Rights Overseas ---- 45
C. Overcoming the Fear of Numbers: An Introduction to Valuation ---- 52
Small Business Administration Management Aid for Small Manufacturers No. 166 ---- 52
Note ---- 57

CHAPTER II. Choice of Business Entity ---- 58

Sec.
A. Traditional Non–Tax Considerations ---- 58
Hazen, The Decision to Incorporate ---- 58
Notes ---- 62
Gevurtz, Corporation Law ---- 68

Sec.

B. Separate Taxpaying Entity Versus Pass–Through Treatment 69
 Llewellyn & Umbrecht, No Choice of Entity After Check–the–Box 69
 Notes 74
 Pope & Talbot, Inc. v. Commissioner of Internal Revenue 80
 Notes 84
C. Choosing Between Pass–Through Forms 87
 1. S Corporation Versus Partnership Tax Treatment 87
  Eustice, Subchapter S Corporations and Partnerships: A Search for the Pass Through Paradigm (Some Preliminary Proposals) 88
  Note 92
 2. Choosing Among Non–Corporate Forms 94
  Stover & Hamill, The LLC Versus LLP Conundrum: Advice for Businesses Contemplating the Choice 94
  Notes 97
D. Multientity Structures 100
 1. Corporations (or Other Entities) as Partners 100
  Revenue Ruling 94–43 100
  Notes 100
 2. Corporations With Common Ownership 102
  Wolter Construction Co. v. Commissioner of Internal Revenue 102
  Notes 106

CHAPTER III. Forming a Partnership, Limited Partnership, Limited Liability Partnership, or Limited Liability Company 113

Sec.

A. Contributions 119
 1. Special Problems With Non–Cash Contributions 120
  a. In General 120
   McConnell v. Hunt Sports Enterprises 120
   Notes 126
   Schymanski v. Conventz 129
   Notes 132
  b. Tax Aspects 135
   Johnston v. Commissioner of Internal Revenue 135
   Notes 140
   Revenue Procedure 93–27 142
   Revenue Procedure 2001–43 147
 2. Alternatives to Capital Contributions 155
  DeShazo v. Clayton 155
  Notes 159
 3. Later Contributions 166
B. Profit and Loss 168
 1. In General 168
  a. Allocating Profit 168
   Five Star Concrete, L.L.C. v. Klink, Inc. 168
   Notes 170

Sec.

1. In General—Continued
b. Allocating Losses 180
Richert v. Handly 180
Richert v. Handly 183
Notes 185
2. Tax Aspects 191
a. The Conduit Principle in Operation 191
Bittker, Federal Taxation of Income, Estates & Gifts 191
b. Uses and Abuses of the Conduit Principle 196
(i) Special Allocations 196
PNRC Limited Partnership v. Commissioner of Internal Revenue 196
Notes 199
(ii) Basis, Leverage and At–Risk Limits 213
IPO II v. Commissioner of Internal Revenue 213
Notes 217
(iii) Passive Losses 222
Mordkin v. Commissioner of Internal Revenue 222
Note 230
3. Alternatives to Profit Shares 233
a. In General 233
Levy v. Leavitt 233
Notes 236
b. Tax Aspects 238
Gaines v. Commissioner of Internal Revenue 238
Notes 241
C. Management 246
1. Simple Direct Governance 246
Summers v. Dooley 246
Note 248
2. More Complex Management Schemes 249
Broyhill v. DeLuca 249
Notes 253
VGS, Inc. v. Castiel 258
Notes 261
Gevurtz, California's New Limited Liability Company Act: A Look at the Good, the Bad and the Ambiguous 262
Gevurtz, California's New Limited Liability Company Act: A Look at the Good, the Bad, and the Ambiguous 266
D. Dissolution and Changes in Ownership 269
1. Consequences Absent Any Planning 269
Page v. Page 270
Notes 272
Horning v. Horning Construction, LLC 276
Notes 281
2. Planning for a Buy–Out 285
a. Triggering Events 285
CCD, L.C. v. Millsap 285
Notes 290
b. Price 293
Curtis v. Campbell 293
Note 296

Sec.
2. Planning for a Buy–Out—Continued
c. Funding 299
Block v. Mylish 299
Notes 303
d. Tax Aspects 307
Foxman v. Commissioner of Internal Revenue 307
Notes 312
3. Planning for Liquidation 318
Cude v. Couch 318
Notes 320
4. Planning for Individual New Owners 326
a. In General 326
Rapoport v. 55 Perry Co. 326
Notes 328
In re Ehmann v. Fiesta Investments 331
Note 336
Holdeman v. Epperson 337
Notes 340
b. Tax Aspects 340
Estate of Dupree v. United States 340
Notes 342
5. Mergers and the Like Involving Non–Corporate Entities 346
a. In General 346
Gevurtz, Squeeze–Outs and Freeze–Outs in Limited Liability Companies 350
Note 351
b. Tax Aspects 353
Revenue Ruling 95–37 353
Note 354
Notice of Proposed Rulemaking and Notice of Public Hearing, Partnership Mergers and Divisions Reg–111119–99 355
Note 358

CHAPTER IV. Forming a Corporation 359

Sec.
A. Contributions 361
1. Special Problems With Non–Cash Contributions 362
a. In General 362
Herwitz, Allocation of Stock Between Services and Capital in the Organization of a Close Corporation 362
Notes 364
b. Tax Aspects 365
(i) Receipt of Stock for Property or Services 365
James v. Commissioner of Internal Revenue 365
Notes 369
(ii) Incorporating a Going Business 381
Revenue Ruling 80–198 381
Notes 384
Revenue Ruling 84–111 389
Note 392
Prizant v. Commissioner of Internal Revenue 394
Notes 397

Sec.
2. Alternatives to Purchasing Stock ---- 400
a. In General ---- 400
Costello v. Fazio ---- 400
Notes ---- 405
b. Tax Aspects ---- 408
Bradshaw v. United States ---- 408
Notes ---- 413
Bauer v. Commissioner of Internal Revenue ---- 419
Notes ---- 423
Revenue Ruling 55–540 ---- 429
3. Later Stock Purchases ---- 431
Katzowitz v. Sidler ---- 431
Note ---- 434
B. Profit and Loss ---- 437
1. Dividends ---- 437
a. In General ---- 437
Gottfried v. Gottfried ---- 437
Notes ---- 442
b. Tax Aspects ---- 458
(i) Taxation of Distributions ---- 458
Bittker, Federal Taxation of Income, Estates and Gifts ---- 458
Note ---- 461
(ii) Taxation of Accumulations ---- 462
Apelbaum, The Accumulated Earnings Tax and the Personal Holding Company Tax: Problems and Proposals ---- 462
2. Alternatives to Dividends ---- 466
Menard, Inc. v. Commissioner of Internal Revenue ---- 466
Notes ---- 472
Cavitch, Tax Planning for Shareholders and Corporations ---- 476
Walter, An Overview of Compensation Techniques Following TRA '86 ---- 479
Notes ---- 481
3. Subchapter S ---- 481
a. The Election ---- 481
Newmark & Lang, The Subchapter S Revision Act of 1982 ---- 482
b. Operation ---- 484
(i) Generally ---- 484
Bittker, Taxation of Income, Estates and Gifts ---- 484
(ii) Uses and Abuses ---- 486
Estate of Leavitt v. Commissioner of Internal Revenue ---- 489
Notes ---- 491
C. Management ---- 494
Wilkes v. Springside Nursing Home, Inc. ---- 494
Note ---- 499
1. Ensuring Positions on the Board of Directors ---- 500
Ringling Bros.–Barnum & Bailey Combined Shows, Inc. v. Ringling ---- 500
Notes ---- 506

Sec.
2. Controlling Specific Decisions ---- 514
Blount v. Taft ---- 514
Notes ---- 522
D. Dissolution and Changes in Ownership ---- 528
1. Share Transfer Restrictions ---- 528
Zidell v. Zidell, Inc. ---- 528
Rafe v. Hindin ---- 531
Notes ---- 534
a. Drafting Problems ---- 537
Earthman's Inc. v. Earthman ---- 537
Notes ---- 540
Rainwater v. Milfeld ---- 543
Note ---- 547
b. Tax Aspects ---- 548
Robinson v. Commissioner of Internal Revenue ---- 548
Notes ---- 552
Alves v. Commissioner of Internal Revenue ---- 554
Notes ---- 557
2. Dissolution for Deadlock or Oppression: A Postscript Re Failed Planning ---- 560
Gidwitz v. Lanzit Corrugated Box Co. ---- 560
Note ---- 564
O'Neal & Thompson, O'Neal's Oppression of Minority Shareholders ---- 566
Note ---- 574

CHAPTER V. Financing ---- 576

Sec.
A. Assessing Financial Needs ---- 576
Deloitte & Touche, Raising Venture Capital ---- 576
Note ---- 577
B. Determining the Nature and Worth of the Investments Offered ---- 577
1. Some Further Details on Interests in a Business ---- 577
2. Valuation Revisited ---- 583
W. Bauman & J. Komarynsky, Chapter 16: Security Analysis, Handbook of Modern Finance ---- 583
Note ---- 594
3. The Definition of a Security: Entering the Realm of Securities Regulation ---- 595
Robinson v. Glynn ---- 595
Reves v. Ernst & Young ---- 601
Notes ---- 606
C. Targeting the Appropriate Investors ---- 608
1. Going Public ---- 608
a. Business Considerations ---- 608
Deloitte & Touche, Strategies For Going Public ---- 608
Notes ---- 616

Sec.

1. Going Public—Continued
   - b. Federal Registration 617
     - *Schneider, Manko & Kant, Going Public—Practice Procedures & Consequences* 617
     - Notes 628
     - *Escott v. BarChris Construction Corporation* 628
     - *In re Donald J. Trump Casino Securities Litigation—Taj Mahal Litigation* 639
     - Notes 645
   - c. State Securities Laws 647
     - *Benjamin v. Cablevision Programming Investments* 647
     - Notes 651
     - *Brandi, Securities Practitioners and Blue Sky Laws: A Survey of Comments and a Ranking of States By Stringency of Regulation* 654
     - *Statement of Policy Regarding Promoter's Equity Investment* 656
     - *Statement of Policy Regarding Promotional Shares* 657
     - NASDAQ Listing Requirement 661
     - *Statement of Policy Regarding Underwriting Expenses, Underwriter's Warrants, Selling Expenses and Selling Security Holders* 657
2. Alternatives to Going Public 664
   - a. Availability of Venture Capital 664
     - *Bartlett, Venture Capital, Law, Business Strategies, and Investment Planning* 664
     - Notes 668
     - *Mcilwraith, The Outlook for the Private Equity Market* 669
   - b. Exemptions from the Registration Requirement 673
     - (i) Private Offerings 673
       - *Doran v. Petroleum Management Corp.* 673
       - Notes 680
     - (ii) Regulation D 684
       - *Securities Act Release No. 33–6455* 685
       - Note 693
       - *Langevoort, Angels on the Internet: The Elusive Promise of "Technological Disintermediation" for Unregistered Offerings of Securities* 695
       - Notes 698
     - (iii) Intrastate Offerings 698
       - *Securities Act Release No. 5450* 699
       - Notes 705
     - (iv) Exemptions From State Blue Sky Laws 705
       - Uniform Limited Offering Exemption 707
       - Note 711
     - (v) The Resale Problem 712
       - *Securities Act Release No. 5223* 713
       - Notes 716
     - (vi) The Attorney's Role 717
       - *Opinions of the Committee on Professional Ethics of the American Bar Association, Formal Opinion 335* 717
       - Note 720

CHAPTER VI. Corporate Restructuring Transactions 721

Sec.
A. Restructuring Through Buy–Outs 722
  1. Cross–Purchases 722
    a. Corporate and Securities Law Aspects 722
      Rochez Bros., Inc. v. Rhoades 722
      Note 726
    b. Tax Aspects 726
      Garber Industries v. Commissioner of Internal Revenue 726
      Notes 729
  2. Redemptions 730
    a. Corporate and Securities Law Aspects 731
      (i) Funds Available 731
        Neimark v. Mel Kramer Sales, Inc. 731
        Notes 737
      (ii) Fiduciary Obligations and Securities Law Concerns 741
        Kaplan v. Goldsamt 741
        Donahue v. Rodd Electrotype Company of New England, Inc. 753
        Zahn v. Transamerica Corporation 759
        Notes 762
    b. Tax Aspects 767
      (i) Treatment of the Selling Shareholder 767
        David Metzger Trust v. Commissioner of Internal Revenue 767
        Notes 776
      (ii) Treatment of the Corporation 787
        Lamark Shipping Agency, Inc. v. Commissioner of Internal Revenue 787
        Notes 797
      (iii) Treatment of the Remaining Shareholders 800
        Revenue Ruling 69–608 800
        Revenue Ruling 78–60 802
        Notes 804
B. Restructuring Through Stock Dividends and Recapitalizations 806
  1. Stock Dividends and Stock Splits 806
    a. Corporate and Securities Law Aspects 806
    b. Tax Aspects 810
      (i) Treatment Upon Receipt 810
        Revenue Ruling 76–258 810
        Note 811
      (ii) Treatment Upon Disposition 813
        Fireoved v. United States 814
        Notes 821
  2. Recapitalizations 823
    a. Corporate and Securities Law Aspects 823
      Honigman v. Green Giant Company 823
      Notes 828

Sec.
2. Recapitalizations—Continued
b. Tax Aspects 838
(i) Treatment Upon the Exchange 838
Dean v. Commissioner of Internal Revenue 838
Notes 842
(ii) Treatment Upon Disposition 854
Notes 856
C. Restructuring Through Divisions and Contractions 858
1. Dividing the Business 858
Coady v. Commissioner of Internal Revenue 858
Notes 862
2. Shrinking the Business 882
a. Corporate Law Aspects 882
Katz v. Bregman 882
Notes 884
b. Tax Aspects 885
Revenue Ruling 74–296 886
Notes 887

CHAPTER VII. Purchase and Sale of a Business 890

Sec.
A. Preliminary Considerations 890
1. To Sell or Not to Sell 890
Paramount Communications, Inc. v. Time Incorporated 890
Notes 898
1992 Department of Justice and Federal Trade Commission Horizontal Merger Guidelines 908
Note 916
2. Negotiating the Basic Deal 918
a. Price 918
Piemonte v. New Boston Garden Corporation 918
Gilbert v. MPM Enterprises, Inc. 923
Notes 928
b. Type and Source of Payment 935
Wieboldt Stores, Inc. v. Schottenstein 936
Notes 947
c. The Negotiation Process 952
Jewel Companies, Inc. v. Pay Less Drug Stores Northwest, Inc. 952
Notes 959
AES Corp. v. The Dow Chemical Company 964
Notes 969
3. Preacquisition Transactions 970
a. Toehold Share Purchases 970
Brown v. Halbert 970
Note 974
Wellman v. Dickinson 976
Notes 989
b. Bootstrap Transactions and Disposing of Unwanted Assets 994
Commissioner of Internal Revenue v. Morris Trust 994
Notes 998
Revenue Ruling 75–360 1003
Note 1004

Sec.
B. Structuring the Acquisition ---- 1006
1. Corporate Mechanics ---- 1006
Hariton v. Arco Electronics, Inc. ---- 1006
Notes ---- 1008
Kirschner Brothers Oil, Inc. v. Natomas Company ---- 1016
Notes ---- 1020
2. Acquirer's Rights and Liabilities ---- 1023
PPG Industries, Inc. v. Guardian Industries Corporation ---- 1023
Note ---- 1026
Ramirez v. Amsted Industries, Inc. ---- 1028
Note ---- 1035
National Labor Relations Board v. Burns International Security Services ---- 1038
Notes ---- 1045
Pension Benefit Guaranty Corporation v. Ouimet Corporation ---- 1047
Notes ---- 1051
3. Securities Law Aspects ---- 1052
a. Registration Requirements Resulting from Issuing Shares to Buy the Business ---- 1052
Securities Act Release No. 5463 ---- 1054
b. Restrictions on Acquisitions of Shares ---- 1061
4. Tax Aspects ---- 1064
a. Recognition Upon the Exchange ---- 1064
(i) The Taxable Sale of Assets Transaction ---- 1064
(ii) The Taxable Sale of Stock Transaction ---- 1067
(iii) The Tax–Free Sale of Assets Transaction ---- 1070
Revenue Ruling 57–518 ---- 1070
Note ---- 1072
Revenue Ruling 73–102 ---- 1072
Notes ---- 1074
(iv) The Tax–Free Sale of Stock Transaction ---- 1078
Chapman v. Commissioner of Internal Revenue ---- 1078
Notes ---- 1084
(v) The Statutory Merger ---- 1090
J.E. Seagram Corp. v. Commissioner of Internal Revenue ---- 1090
Notes ---- 1099
(vi) Triangular Transactions ---- 1105
b. Carryover of Tax Attributes ---- 1108
(i) Generally ---- 1108
(ii) Uses, Abuses and Limitations ---- 1111
Briarcliff Candy Corp. v. Commissioner of Internal Revenue ---- 1111
Notes ---- 1115
C. Follow–Up Transactions ---- 1123
1. Liquidating the Selling Corporation Following a Sale of Assets 1123
a. In General ---- 1123
Pacific Scene, Inc. v. Penasquitos, Inc. ---- 1124
Notes ---- 1128
b. Tax Aspects ---- 1129

Sec.

2. Dealing With the Subsidiary and Non–Selling Shareholders Following a Sale of Stock Transaction ---- 1133
   a. In General ---- 1133
      Alpert v. 28 Williams St. Corp. ---- 1133
      Notes ---- 1137
   b. Tax Aspects ---- 1144

APPENDIX ---- 1149
INDEX ---- 1173

*

TABLE OF CASES

Principal cases are in bold type. Non-principal cases are in roman type. References are to Pages.

Abelow v. Midstates Oil Corp., 41 Del.Ch. 145, 189 A.2d 675 (Del.Supr.1963), 1139

Abercrombie v. Davies, 36 Del.Ch. 371, 130 A.2d 338 (Del.Supr.1957), 511

Abry Partners V, L.P. v. F & W Acquisition LLC, 891 A.2d 1032 (Del.Ch.2006), 969

ACE Ltd. v. Capital Re Corp., 747 A.2d 95 (Del.Ch.1999), 961

Adler v. Svingos, 80 A.D.2d 764, 436 N.Y.S.2d 719 (N.Y.A.D. 1 Dept.1981), 526

AES Corp. v. Dow Chemical Co., 325 F.3d 174 (3rd Cir.2003), **964,** 969

Allen v. Biltmore Tissue Corp., 161 N.Y.S.2d 418, 141 N.E.2d 812 (N.Y.1957), 536

Alpert v. 28 Williams Street Corp., 483 N.Y.S.2d 667, 473 N.E.2d 19 (N.Y.1984), 764, **1133,** 1138, 1139, 1141, 1142

Alterman Foods, Inc. v. United States, 505 F.2d 873 (5th Cir.1974), 474

Alumax Inc. v. Commissioner, 165 F.3d 822 (11th Cir.1999), 109

Alves v. Commissioner, 734 F.2d 478 (9th Cir.1984), **554**

Amalgamated Sugar Co. v. NL Industries, Inc., 644 F.Supp. 1229 (S.D.N.Y.1986), 902

American General Ins. Co. v. Equitable General Corp., 493 F.Supp. 721 (E.D.Va.1980), 765

Anadarko Petroleum Corp. v. Panhandle Eastern Corp., 545 A.2d 1171 (Del. Supr.1988), 865

Anderson v. Wilder, 2003 WL 22768666 (Tenn.Ct.App.2003), 291

Applebaum v. Avaya, Inc., 812 A.2d 880 (Del. Supr.2002), 1140

Applestein v. United Board & Carton Corp., 60 N.J.Super. 333, 159 A.2d 146 (N.J.Super.Ch.1960), 1014

Application of (see name of party)

Armstrong v. Phinney, 394 F.2d 661 (5th Cir.1968), 246

Arnold v. Phillips, 117 F.2d 497 (5th Cir. 1941), 407

Aron v. Gillman, 309 N.Y. 157, 128 N.E.2d 284 (N.Y.1955), 297

Arpadi v. First MSP Corp., 68 Ohio St.3d 453, 628 N.E.2d 1335 (Ohio 1994), 29

Arrowsmith v. Commissioner, 344 U.S. 6, 73 S.Ct. 71, 97 L.Ed. 6 (1952), 1132

Astronics Corp. v. Protective Closures Co., 561 F.Supp. 329 (W.D.N.Y.1983), 1063

Automotriz Del Golfo De California v. Resnick, 47 Cal.2d 792, 306 P.2d 1 (Cal.1957), 407

Badanes v. Commissioner, 39 T.C. 410 (Tax Ct.1962), 880

Bailes v. Colonial Press, Inc., 444 F.2d 1241 (5th Cir.1971), 365

Balafas v. Balafas, 263 Minn. 267, 117 N.W.2d 20 (Minn.1962), 162

Bancroft–Whitney Co. v. Glen, 64 Cal.2d 327, 49 Cal.Rptr. 825, 411 P.2d 921 (Cal.1966), 128

Banghart v. Hollywood General Partnership, 902 F.2d 805 (10th Cir.1990), 607

Barr v. Wackman, 368 N.Y.S.2d 497, 329 N.E.2d 180 (N.Y.1975), 975

Barrett v. Denver Tramway Corporation, 53 F.Supp. 198 (D.Del.1943), 831

Basic Inc. v. Levinson, 485 U.S. 224, 108 S.Ct. 978, 99 L.Ed.2d 194 (1988), 962

Bath Industries, Inc. v. Blot, 427 F.2d 97 (7th Cir.1970), 990

Bauer v. Commissioner, 748 F.2d 1365 (9th Cir.1984), **419,** 423, 424, 425, 426

Bausch & Lomb Optical Co. v. Commissioner, 267 F.2d 75 (2nd Cir.1959), 1077, 1078, 1086, 1148

Bazley v. Commissioner, 331 U.S. 737, 67 S.Ct. 1489, 91 L.Ed. 1782 (1947), 853

Beatrice Co. v. State Bd. of Equalization, 25 Cal.Rptr.2d 438, 863 P.2d 683 (Cal.1993), 868

Beaver Bolt, Inc. v. Commissioner, T.C. Memo. 1995-549 (U.S.Tax Ct.1995), 1066

Benintendi v. Kenton Hotel, 294 N.Y. 112, 60 N.E.2d 829 (N.Y.1945), 526

Benjamin v. Cablevision Programming Investments, 114 Ill.2d 150, 102 Ill.Dec. 296, 499 N.E.2d 1309 (Ill.1986), **647,** 651, 681, 706

Benjamin v. Commissioner, 592 F.2d 1259 (5th Cir.1979), 780

Bennett v. Propp, 41 Del.Ch. 14, 187 A.2d 405 (Del.Supr.1962), 763, 899

Bentsen v. Phinney, 199 F.Supp. 363 (S.D.Tex.1961), 1100

Berckmans v. Commissioner, 20 T.C.M. (CCH) 458 (Tax Ct.1961), 372

Bhada v. Commissioner, 89 T.C. 959 (U.S.Tax Ct.1987), 786
Bleily & Collishaw, Inc. v. Commissioner, 72 T.C. 751 (U.S.Tax Ct.1979), 780
Block v. Mylish, 351 Pa. 611, 41 A.2d 731 (Pa.1945), **299,** 303, 304, 305
Blount v. Commissioner, 425 F.2d 921 (2nd Cir.1969), 779
Blount v. Taft, 295 N.C. 472, 246 S.E.2d 763 (N.C.1978), **514,** 522, 523, 524, 525, 526, 547
Bobsee Corp. v. United States, 411 F.2d 231 (5th Cir.1969), 1116
Boca Investerings Partnership v. United States, 314 F.3d 625 (D.C.Cir.2003), 211, 212
Boeing Co. v. International Ass'n of Machinists, 504 F.2d 307 (5th Cir.1974), 1047
Bohannan v. Corporation Commission, 82 Ariz. 299, 313 P.2d 379 (Ariz.1957), 508
Bolding v. Commissioner, 117 F.3d 270 (5th Cir.1997), 492
Bond v. Atlantic Terra Cotta Co., 137 A.D. 671, 122 N.Y.S. 425 (N.Y.A.D. 1 Dept. 1910), 510
Borg v. International Silver Co., 11 F.2d 147 (2nd Cir.1925), 437
Borge v. Commissioner, 405 F.2d 673 (2nd Cir.1968), 1117
Borland v. John F. Sass Printing Co., 95 Colo. 53, 32 P.2d 827 (Colo.1934), 527
Boss v. Boss, 98 R.I. 146, 200 A.2d 231 (R.I. 1964), 543
Botts, People v., 376 Ill. 476, 34 N.E.2d 403 (Ill.1941), 512
Bove v. Community Hotel Corp., 105 R.I. 36, 249 A.2d 89 (R.I.1969), 832
Bradshaw v. United States, 231 Ct.Cl. 144, 683 F.2d 365 (Ct.Cl.1982), **408,** 413, 414, 416, 417, 423, 425
Brake & Elec. Sales Corp. v. United States, 185 F.Supp. 1 (D.Mass.1960), 425
Brascan Ltd. v. Edper Equities Ltd., 477 F.Supp. 773 (S.D.N.Y.1979), 992
Brazen v. Bell Atlantic Corp., 695 A.2d 43 (Del.Supr.1997), 961
Briarcliff Candy Corp. v. Commissioner, 54 T.C.M. (CCH) 667 (U.S.Tax Ct.1987), **1111,** 1115, 1116, 1117, 1122
British Motor Car Distributors, Commissioner v., 278 F.2d 392 (9th Cir.1960), 1116
Broad v. Rockwell Intern. Corp., 642 F.2d 929 (5th Cir.1981), 451
Brooke v. Mt. Hood Meadows Oreg., Ltd., 81 Or.App. 387, 725 P.2d 925 (Or.App.1986), 177
Brountas v. Commissioner, 692 F.2d 152 (1st Cir.1982), 221
Brown v. Halbert, 271 Cal.App.2d 252, 76 Cal.Rptr. 781 (Cal.App. 1 Dist.1969), 898, **970,** 974, 975, 976, 1015, 1023
Brown v. Kleen Kut Mfg. Co., 238 Kan. 642, 714 P.2d 942 (Kan.1986), 1037
Brown, In re, 242 N.Y. 1, 150 N.E. 581 (N.Y. 1926), 164
Brown Shoe Co. v. United States, 370 U.S. 294, 82 S.Ct. 1502, 8 L.Ed.2d 510 (1962), 916
Broyhill v. DeLuca, 194 B.R. 65 (Bkrtcy. E.D.Va.1996), **249,** 253, 254, 255, 256, 257, 329, 336, 337, 536
Bryson v. Bryson, 62 Cal.App. 170, 216 P. 391 (Cal.App. 2 Dist.1923), 512
Burkle v. Burkle, 46 Cal.Rptr.3d 562 (Cal. App. 2 Dist.2006), 116
Burnett v. Word, Inc., 412 S.W.2d 792 (Tex. Civ.App.-Waco 1967), 522
Busick v. Stoetzl, 264 Cal.App.2d 736, 70 Cal.Rptr. 581 (Cal.App. 5 Dist.1968), 236

Calumet Industries, Inc. v. MacClure, 464 F.Supp. 19 (N.D.Ill.1978), 510
Canaveral International Corp. v. Commissioner, 61 T.C. 520 (U.S.Tax Ct.1974), 1117
Caplan, Petition of, 20 A.D.2d 301, 246 N.Y.S.2d 913 (N.Y.A.D. 1 Dept.1964), 975
Carlberg v. United States, 281 F.2d 507 (8th Cir.1960), 1087
Carlson v. Ringgold County Mut. Tel. Co., 252 Iowa 748, 108 N.W.2d 478 (Iowa 1961), 547
Carolina Transformer Co., United States v., 978 F.2d 832 (4th Cir.1992), 1037
Carter v. Muscat, 21 A.D.2d 543, 251 N.Y.S.2d 378 (N.Y.A.D. 1 Dept.1964), 975
Case v. New York Cent. R. Co., 256 N.Y.S.2d 607, 204 N.E.2d 643 (N.Y.1965), 110, 1142
CCD, L.C. v. Millsap, 116 P.3d 366 (Utah 2005), **285,** 291
Central Bank of Denver, N.A. v. First Interstate Bank of Denver, N.A., 511 U.S. 164, 114 S.Ct. 1439, 128 L.Ed.2d 119 (1994), 645
Cerone v. Commissioner, 87 T.C. 1 (U.S.Tax Ct.1986), 782
Chaplin v. Magic Woods, Inc., 794 P.2d 1176 (Kan.App.1990), 541
Chapman v. Commissioner, 618 F.2d 856 (1st Cir.1980), 994, **1078,** 1086, 1087, 1108
Childs Co., In re, 69 F.Supp. 856 (S.D.N.Y. 1946), 832
Chilson, In re, 19 Del.Ch. 398, 168 A. 82 (Del.Ch.1933), 510
Cicone v. URS Corp., 183 Cal.App.3d 194, 227 Cal.Rptr. 887 (Cal.App. 5 Dist.1986), 964
Citron v. Commissioner, 97 T.C. 200 (U.S.Tax Ct.1991), 318
C & J Builders and Remodelers, LLC v. Geisenheimer, 249 Conn. 415, 733 A.2d 193 (Conn.1999), 350
Clagett v. Hutchison, 583 F.2d 1259 (4th Cir.1978), 975
Clark v. Dodge, 269 N.Y. 410, 199 N.E. 641 (N.Y.1936), 523
Clark, Commissioner v., 489 U.S. 726, 109 S.Ct. 1455, 103 L.Ed.2d 753 (1989), 1077

Clarke Memorial College v. Monaghan Land Co., 257 A.2d 234 (Del.Ch.1969), 512
Clark's Will, In re, 131 Misc. 151, 226 N.Y.S. 141 (N.Y.Sup.1928), 449
C–Lec Plastics, Inc. v. Commissioner, 76 T.C. 601 (U.S.Tax Ct.1981), 417
Coady v. Commissioner, 33 T.C. 771 (Tax Ct.1960), **858,** 862, 863, 864, 868D, 869, 870, 871, 871, 876, 880
Coggins v. New England Patriots Football Club, Inc., 397 Mass. 525, 492 N.E.2d 1112 (Mass.1986), 1142
Cohen, Application of, 183 Misc. 1034, 52 N.Y.S.2d 671 (N.Y.Sup.1944), 565
Cole v. National Cash Credit Ass'n, 18 Del. Ch. 47, 156 A. 183 (Del.Ch.1931), 1011
Consolidated Film Industries v. Johnson, 22 Del.Ch. 407, 197 A. 489 (Del.Supr.1937), 831
Cooper v. Isaacs, 448 F.2d 1202 (D.C.Cir. 1971), 284, 292
Costello v. Fazio, 256 F.2d 903 (9th Cir. 1958), **400,** 405, 406, 407, 423, 425
Cottrell v. Pawcatuck Co., 36 Del.Ch. 169, 128 A.2d 225 (Del.Supr.1956), 1012
Cowan v. Salt Lake Hardware Co., 118 Utah 300, 221 P.2d 625 (Utah 1950), 831
Craftmatic Securities Litigation v. Kraftsow, 890 F.2d 628 (3rd Cir.1989), 646
Craig v. Hamilton, 213 Kan. 665, 518 P.2d 539 (Kan.1974), 133
Cramer v. Commissioner, 101 T.C. 225 (U.S.Tax Ct.1993), 557
Crocker v. Waltham Watch Co., 315 Mass. 397, 53 N.E.2d 230 (Mass.1944), 454
Cross v. Communication Channels, Inc., 116 Misc.2d 1019, 456 N.Y.S.2d 971 (N.Y.Sup. 1982), 1142
Crowder, State ex rel. v. Sperry Corp., 41 Del. 84, 15 A.2d 661 (Del.Super.1940), 511
C–T of Virginia, Inc., In re, 958 F.2d 606 (4th Cir.1992), 949
CTS Corp. v. Dynamics Corp. of America, 481 U.S. 69, 107 S.Ct. 1637, 95 L.Ed.2d 67 (1987), 992
Cude v. Couch, 588 S.W.2d 554 (Tenn. 1979), 274, **318,** 320, 321
Culbertson, Commissioner v., 337 U.S. 733, 69 S.Ct. 1210, 93 L.Ed. 1659 (1949), 209, 210, 211, 212, 488
Culligan Water Conditioning of Tri–Cities, Inc. v. United States, 567 F.2d 867 (9th Cir.1978), 380
Curtis v. Campbell, 336 S.W.2d 355 (Ky. 1960), **293,** 297, 298

Dalton v. American Inv. Co., 490 A.2d 574 (Del.Ch.1985), 1023
D'Angelo Associates, Inc. v. Commissioner, 70 T.C. 121 (U.S.Tax Ct.1978), 380
Dan River, Inc. v. Icahn, 701 F.2d 278 (4th Cir.1983), 903
Darcy v. Brooklyn & N.Y. Ferry Co., 196 N.Y. 99, 89 N.E. 461 (N.Y.1909), 1128
Darcy v. Brooklyn & N.Y. Ferry Co., 127 A.D. 167, 111 N.Y.S. 514 (N.Y.A.D. 2 Dept. 1908), 864
Datapoint Corp. v. Plaza Securities Co., 496 A.2d 1031 (Del.Supr.1985), 900
David Metzger Trust v. Commissioner, 693 F.2d 459 (5th Cir.1982), **767,** 776, 777, 780, 781, 782
Davis v. Commissioner, 64 T.C. 1034 (U.S.Tax Ct.1975), 488
Davis v. Louisville Gas & Electric Co., 16 Del.Ch. 157, 142 A. 654 (Del.Ch.1928), 832
Davis, United States v., 397 U.S. 301, 90 S.Ct. 1041, 25 L.Ed.2d 323 (1970), 777, 886
Davis, United States v., 370 U.S. 65, 82 S.Ct. 1190, 8 L.Ed.2d 335 (1962), 845
Day v. Sidley & Austin, 394 F.Supp. 986 (D.D.C.1975), 248, 255, 347
Day & Zimmermann, Commissioner v., 151 F.2d 517 (3rd Cir.1945), 1145
Dean v. Commissioner, 10 T.C. 19 (Tax Ct.1948), 829, 830, **838,** 842, 843, 853
DeBaun v. First Western Bank & Trust Co., 46 Cal.App.3d 686, 120 Cal.Rptr. 354 (Cal. App. 2 Dist.1975), 974, 975
Dees v. Commissioner, 21 T.C.M. (CCH) 833 (Tax Ct.1962), 372
Delaney v. Fidelity Lease Limited, 526 S.W.2d 543 (Tex.1975), 101
DeShazo v. Estate of Clayton, 2006 WL 1794735 (D.Idaho 2006), **155,** 160, 161, 162, 163, 321
DeWitt Truck Brokers, Inc. v. W. Ray Flemming Fruit Co., 540 F.2d 681 (4th Cir. 1976), 476
Diamond v. Commissioner, 492 F.2d 286 (7th Cir.1974), 141
Diamond v. Parkersburg–Aetna Corp., 146 W.Va. 543, 122 S.E.2d 436 (W.Va.1961), 513
Diamond Parking, Inc. v. Frontier Bldg. Ltd. Partnership, 72 Wash.App. 314, 864 P.2d 954 (Wash.App. Div. 1 1993), 330
Disotell v. Stiltner, 100 P.3d 890 (Alaska 2004), 273
Ditty v. CheckRite, Ltd., Inc., 973 F.Supp. 1320 (D.Utah 1997), 64, 119
Donahue v. Rodd Electrotype Co. of New England, Inc., 367 Mass. 578, 328 N.E.2d 505 (Mass.1975), 524, **753,** 762, 763
Donald J. Trump Casino Securities Litigation–Taj Mahal Litigation, In re, 7 F.3d 357 (3rd Cir.1993), **639,** 645, 646
Donovan v. Bierwirth, 680 F.2d 263 (2nd Cir.1982), 904
Doran v. Petroleum Management Corp., 545 F.2d 893 (5th Cir.1977), **673,** 681, 682, 683, 705
Drashner v. Sorenson, 75 S.D. 247, 63 N.W.2d 255 (S.D.1954), 176, 292
Dunn v. Commissioner, 615 F.2d 578 (2nd Cir.1980), 783

Dupree, Estate of v. United States, 391 F.2d 753 (5th Cir.1968), **340,** 343, 346
Dwyer v. United States, 622 F.2d 460 (9th Cir.1980), 1132

Earthman's, Inc. v. Earthman, 526 S.W.2d 192 (TexCivApp.-Hous (1 Dist.) 1975), **537,** 540
Ederer v. Gursky, 9 N.Y.3d 514, 851 N.Y.S.2d 108, 881 N.E.2d 204 (N.Y.2007), 190
Ehmann v. Fiesta Investments, 319 B.R. 200 (Bkrtcy.D.Ariz.2005), **331,** 336
E. I. Du Pont de Nemours & Co. v. United States, 200 Ct.Cl. 391, 471 F.2d 1211 (Ct. Cl.1973), 374
Elf Atochem North America, Inc. v. Jaffari, 727 A.2d 286 (Del.Supr.1999), 118
Eli Lilly & Company v. Commissioner, 84 T.C. 996 (U.S.Tax Ct.1985), 384
Elkhorn Coal Co., Helvering v., 95 F.2d 732 (4th Cir.1937), 1004, 1005
Elko Realty Co. v. Commissioner, 29 T.C. 1012 (Tax Ct.1958), 1123
Ellis v. Mihelis, 60 Cal.2d 206, 32 Cal.Rptr. 415, 384 P.2d 7 (Cal.1963), 162
Ellis & Marshall Associates, Inc. v. Marshall, 16 Ill.App.3d 398, 306 N.E.2d 712 (Ill.App. 1 Dist.1973), 128
Emeloid Co. v. Commissioner, 189 F.2d 230 (3rd Cir.1951), 799
Emerson v. Arnold, 92 Mich.App. 345, 285 N.W.2d 45 (Mich.App.1979), 297
Englander v. Osborne, 261 Pa. 366, 104 A. 614 (Pa.1918), 447
Enron Corp. Securities, Derivative & ERISA Litigation, In re, 235 F.Supp.2d 549 (S.D.Tex.2002), 645
Ernst & Ernst v. Hochfelder, 425 U.S. 185, 96 S.Ct. 1375, 47 L.Ed.2d 668 (1976), 683
Escott v. BarChris Const. Corp., 283 F.Supp. 643 (S.D.N.Y.1968), **628,** 645, 683
Estate of (see name of party)
Eureka VIII LLC v. Niagara Falls Holdings LLC, 899 A.2d 95 (Del.Ch.2006), 330
Everett Trust & Sav. Bank, State ex rel. v. Pacific Waxed Paper Co., 22 Wash.2d 844, 157 P.2d 707 (Wash.1945), 510
Exacto Spring Corp. v. Commissioner, 196 F.3d 833 (7th Cir.1999), 473

Fairfield Steamship Corp. v. Commissioner, 157 F.2d 321 (2nd Cir.1946), 1145
Fairway Development Co. v. Title Ins. Co., 621 F.Supp. 120 (N.D.Ohio 1985), 274
Falstaff Brewing Corp., United States v., 410 U.S. 526, 93 S.Ct. 1096, 35 L.Ed.2d 475 (1973), 917
Farris v. Glen Alden Corp., 393 Pa. 427, 143 A.2d 25 (Pa.1958), 1013, 1022
Fawkes v. Farm Lands Inv. Co., 112 Cal.App. 374, 297 P. 47 (Cal.App. 4 Dist.1931), 446
Fayard v. Fayard, 293 So.2d 421 (Miss.1974), 535
F. & D. Rentals, Inc. v. Commissioner, 365 F.2d 34 (7th Cir.1966), 1052
Feit v. Leasco Data Processing Equipment Corp., 332 F.Supp. 544 (E.D.N.Y.1971), 1058, 1062
Ferguson v. Williams, 670 S.W.2d 327 (Tex. App.-Austin 1984), 186
Field v. Lamson & Goodnow Mfg. Co., 162 Mass. 388, 38 N.E. 1126 (Mass.1894), 454
Field v. Trump, 850 F.2d 938 (2nd Cir.1988), 994
Fink, Commissioner v., 483 U.S. 89, 107 S.Ct. 2729, 97 L.Ed.2d 74 (1987), 417
Fireoved v. United States, 462 F.2d 1281 (3rd Cir.1972), **814,** 821, 822
Five Star Concrete, L.L.C. v. Klink, Inc., 693 N.E.2d 583 (Ind.App.1998), **168,** 171, 172, 173, 174, 176, 177, 178, 180, 306
Flanagan v. Flanagan, 273 A.D. 918, 77 N.Y.S.2d 682 (N.Y.A.D. 2 Dept.1948), 536
Flynn v. Bass Bros. Enterprises, Inc., 744 F.2d 978 (3rd Cir.1984), 1015, 1058, 1062
Foremost–McKesson, Inc. v. Provident Securities Co., 423 U.S. 232, 96 S.Ct. 508, 46 L.Ed.2d 464 (1976), 994
Forward Communications Corp. v. United States, 608 F.2d 485 (Ct.Cl.1979), 1066
Fox v. Ehrmantraut, 167 Cal.Rptr. 595, 615 P.2d 1383 (Cal.1980), 1061
Foxman v. Commissioner, 41 T.C. 535 (Tax Ct.1964), **307,** 313, 314, 315
Francis v. United Jersey Bank, 87 N.J. 15, 432 A.2d 814 (N.J.1981), 908
Francis I. duPont & Co. v. Universal City Studios, Inc., 312 A.2d 344 (Del.Ch.1973), 1010
Frandsen v. Jensen–Sundquist Agency, Inc., 802 F.2d 941 (7th Cir.1986), 540
Frank Lyon Co. v. United States, 435 U.S. 561, 98 S.Ct. 1291, 55 L.Ed.2d 550 (1978), 429
Frazell, United States v., 335 F.2d 487 (5th Cir.1964), 393
Frieda Popkov Corp. v. Stack, 198 Misc. 826, 103 N.Y.S.2d 507 (N.Y.Sup.1950), 102
Frigidaire Sales Corp. v. Union Properties, Inc., 88 Wash.2d 400, 562 P.2d 244 (Wash. 1977), 101
Frontier Chevrolet Co. v. Commissioner, 329 F.3d 1131 (9th Cir.2003), 798

GAF Corp. v. Milstein, 453 F.2d 709 (2nd Cir.1971), 990
Gaines v. Commissioner, 45 T.C.M. (CCH) 363 (U.S.Tax Ct.1982), **238,** 241, 242, 243
Gallagher v. Lambert, 549 N.Y.S.2d 945, 549 N.E.2d 136 (N.Y.1989), 541
Galler v. Galler, 32 Ill.2d 16, 203 N.E.2d 577 (Ill.1964), 523
Garber Industries, Inc. v. Commissioner, 435 F.3d 555 (5th Cir.2006), **726,** 729, 730, 799, 1117
Gazda v. Kolinski, 91 A.D.2d 860, 458 N.Y.S.2d 387 (N.Y.A.D. 4 Dept.1982), 526

Gazette Pub. Co. v. Self, 103 F.Supp. 779 (E.D.Ark.1952), 799
Gearing v. Kelly, 227 N.Y.S.2d 897, 182 N.E.2d 391 (N.Y.1962), 527
Gelder Medical Group v. Webber, 394 N.Y.S.2d 867, 363 N.E.2d 573 (N.Y.1977), 128
General Time Corp. v. Talley Industries, Inc., 403 F.2d 159 (2nd Cir.1968), 991
General Utilities & Operating Co. v. Helvering, 296 U.S. 200, 56 S.Ct. 185, 80 L.Ed. 154 (1935), 84
Generes, United States v., 405 U.S. 93, 92 S.Ct. 827, 31 L.Ed.2d 62 (1972), 428
Gentry v. Credit Plan Corp., 528 S.W.2d 571 (Tex.1975), 107
George L. Riggs, Inc. v. Commissioner, 64 T.C. 474 (U.S.Tax Ct.1975), 1144
Gerdes v. Reynolds, 28 N.Y.S.2d 622 (N.Y.Sup.1941), 908, 975
Gerlach's Estate, In re, 364 Pa. 207, 72 A.2d 271 (Pa.1950), 162
Gershkowitz v. Commissioner, 88 T.C. 984 (U.S.Tax Ct.1987), 218
G. Eugene England Foundation v. First Federal Corp., 663 F.2d 988 (10th Cir.1973), 681
Gidwitz v. Lanzit Corrugated Box Co., 20 Ill.2d 208, 170 N.E.2d 131 (Ill.1960), **560,** 564
Gilbert v. Commissioner, 248 F.2d 399 (2nd Cir.1957), 426
Gilbert v. MPM Enterprises, Inc., 709 A.2d 663 (Del.Ch.1997), 57, **923,** 928, 929, 930, 934, 1010
Golden State Bottling Co., Inc. v. N.L.R.B., 414 U.S. 168, 94 S.Ct. 414, 38 L.Ed.2d 388 (1973), 1045, 1046
Goldman v. Postal Telegraph, 52 F.Supp. 763 (D.Del.1943), 831, 1129
Gonzalez v. Chalpin, 564 N.Y.S.2d 702, 565 N.E.2d 1253 (N.Y.1990), 101
Gooding Amusement Co. v. Commissioner, 236 F.2d 159 (6th Cir.1956), 426
Goodwin v. Elkins & Co., 730 F.2d 99 (3rd Cir.1984), 565
Gordon v. Commissioner, 424 F.2d 378 (2nd Cir.1970), 889
Gottfried v. Gottfried, 73 N.Y.S.2d 692 (N.Y.Sup.1947), 238, **437,** 442, 445, 452, 453, 454, 475, 500, 857
Gray v. Harris Land & Cattle Co., 227 Mont. 51, 737 P.2d 475 (Mont.1987), 535
Gregg v. United States, 186 F.Supp.2d 1123 (D.Or.2000), 231
Grogan v. Grogan, 315 S.W.2d 34 (Tex.Civ. App.-Beaumont 1958), 512
Grumman Corp. v. LTV Corp., 527 F.Supp. 86 (E.D.N.Y.1981), 1061
Guinand v. Walton, 25 Utah 2d 253, 480 P.2d 137 (Utah 1971), 330
Gulf Oil/Cities Service Tender Offer Litigation, In re, 725 F.Supp. 712 (S.D.N.Y. 1989), 962
Gulf & Western Industries, Inc. v. Great Atlantic & Pac. Tea Co., Inc., 476 F.2d 687 (2nd Cir.1973), 903
Guttmann v. Illinois Cent. R. Co., 189 F.2d 927 (2nd Cir.1951), 446

Haldeman v. Haldeman, 176 Ky. 635, 197 S.W. 376 (Ky.1917), 509, 510
Haley v. Talcott, 864 A.2d 86 (Del.Ch.2004), 306
Hall v. Hall, 506 S.W.2d 42 (Mo.App.1974), 527
Hambuechen v. Commissioner, 43 T.C. 90 (Tax Ct.1964), 166
Hamilton v. United States, 231 Ct.Cl. 517, 687 F.2d 408 (Ct.Cl.1982), 202
Hampton v. Tri–State Finance Corp., 30 Colo.App. 420, 495 P.2d 566 (Colo.App. 1972), 514
Hamrick v. Commissioner, 43 T.C. 21 (Tax Ct.1964), 380
Hankin v. Hankin, 507 Pa. 603, 493 A.2d 675 (Pa.1985), 321
Hanson Trust PLC v. SCM Corp., 774 F.2d 47 (2nd Cir.1985), 991, 994
Harff v. Kerkorian, 324 A.2d 215 (Del.Ch. 1974), 458
Hariton v. Arco Electronics, Inc., 41 Del. Ch. 74, 188 A.2d 123 (Del.Supr.1963), **1006,** 1008, 1012, 1013, 1124
Harris v. Curtis, 8 Cal.App.3d 837, 87 Cal. Rptr. 614 (Cal.App. 5 Dist.1970), 362
Harvard Industries, Inc. v. Tyson, 1986–87 Fed. Sec. L. Rep. ¶ 93064 (E.D.Mich.1986), 902
Haynes v. Monson, 301 Minn. 327, 224 N.W.2d 482 (Minn.1974), 1027
Hazel Atlas Glass Co. v. Van Dyk & Reeves, 8 F.2d 716 (2nd Cir.1925), 446
Heady v. Commissioner, 162 F.2d 699 (7th Cir.1947), 843
Healey v. Catalyst Recovery of Pennsylvania, Inc., 616 F.2d 641 (3rd Cir.1980), 1143
Heckmann v. Ahmanson, 168 Cal.App.3d 119, 214 Cal.Rptr. 177 (Cal.App. 2 Dist.1985), 905
Hega Knitting Mills, Inc., Application of, 124 N.Y.S.2d 115 (N.Y.Sup.1953), 536
Heintz v. Commissioner, 25 T.C. 132 (Tax Ct.1955), 1102, 1103
Helvering v. ★★★★★★★D (see opposing party)
Hendler, United States v., 303 U.S. 564, 58 S.Ct. 655, 82 L.Ed. 1018 (1938), 385
Hendley v. Lee, 676 F.Supp. 1317 (D.S.C. 1987), 565
Henry T. Patterson Trust v. United States, 729 F.2d 1089 (6th Cir.1984), 778
Henshaw v. Kroenecke, 656 S.W.2d 416 (Tex. 1983), 167
Herculite Protective Fabrics Corp. v. Commissioner, 387 F.2d 475 (3rd Cir.1968), 1117

Hermes Consol., Inc. v. United States, 14 Cl.Ct. 398 (Cl.Ct.1988), 374, 1115
Herring v. Offutt, 266 Md. 593, 295 A.2d 876 (Md.1972), 135
Hesse, Estate of v. Commissioner, 74 T.C. 1307 (U.S.Tax Ct.1980), 316
Heverly v. Commissioner, 621 F.2d 1227 (3rd Cir.1980), 1086
Hillman v. I.R.S., 250 F.3d 228 (4th Cir. 2001), 244
Hillsboro Nat. Bank v. Commissioner, 460 U.S. 370, 103 S.Ct. 1134, 75 L.Ed.2d 130 (1983), 385
H.K. Porter Co., Inc. v. Commissioner, 87 T.C. 689 (U.S.Tax Ct.1986), 1147
H.M. Byllesby & Co. v. Doriot, 25 Del.Ch. 46, 12 A.2d 603 (Del.Ch.1940), 513
Holbrook v. Commissioner, 34 T.C.M. (CCH) 1283 (U.S.Tax Ct.1975), 315
Holdeman v. Epperson, 111 Ohio St.3d 551, 857 N.E.2d 583 (Ohio 2006), **337,** 340
Holsey v. Commissioner, 258 F.2d 865 (3rd Cir.1958), 805
Home Sav. & Loan Ass'n v. United States, 514 F.2d 1199 (9th Cir.1975), 1104
Honigman v. Commissioner, 466 F.2d 69 (6th Cir.1972), 474
Honigman v. Green Giant Co., 208 F.Supp. 754 (D.Minn.1961), **823,** 828, 829, 830, 831, 832
Horne v. Peckham, 97 Cal.App.3d 404, 158 Cal.Rptr. 714 (Cal.App. 3 Dist.1979), 44
Horning v. Horning Const., LLC, 816 N.Y.S.2d 877 (N.Y.Sup.2006), **276,** 281, 282, 283, 284, 285
Horn's Crane Service v. Prior, 182 Neb. 94, 152 N.W.2d 421 (Neb.1967), 163
Howard Johnson Co. v. Detroit Local Joint Executive Bd., 417 U.S. 249, 94 S.Ct. 2236, 41 L.Ed.2d 46 (1974), 1046, 1047
Humphrys v. Winous Co., 165 Ohio St. 45, 133 N.E.2d 780 (Ohio 1956), 508
Hurst v. Commissioner, 124 T.C. 16 (U.S.Tax Ct.2005), 784
Hyman v. Velsicol Corp., 342 Ill.App. 489, 97 N.E.2d 122 (Ill.App. 1 Dist.1951), 436

Illinois Tool Works Inc. v. Commissioner, 355 F.3d 997 (7th Cir.2004), 1066
In re (see name of party)
Insuranshares Corp. v. Northern Fiscal Corp., 35 F.Supp. 22 (E.D.Pa.1940), 975
Inter Mountain Ass'n of Credit Men v. Villager, Inc., 527 P.2d 664 (Utah 1974), 1036
Intermountain Lumber Co. v. Commissioner, 65 T.C. 1025 (U.S.Tax Ct.1976), 379
International Broth. of Teamsters v. Daniel, 439 U.S. 551, 99 S.Ct. 790, 58 L.Ed.2d 808 (1979), 608
International Ins. Co. v. Johns, 874 F.2d 1447 (11th Cir.1989), 1047
International Inv. Corp. v. Commissioner, 11 T.C. 678 (Tax Ct.1948), 1145
Internet Law Library, Inc. v. Southridge Capital Management, LLC, 223 F.Supp.2d 474 (S.D.N.Y.2002), 450
IPO II v. Commissioner, 122 T.C. 295 (U.S.Tax Ct.2004), **213,** 217, 218, 220
Ireland v. United States, 621 F.2d 731 (5th Cir.1980), 474
Itek Corp. v. Chicago Aerial Industries, Inc., 248 A.2d 625 (Del.Supr.1968), 959

Jack's Maintenance Contractors, Inc. v. Commissioner, 703 F.2d 154 (5th Cir.1983), 474
Jackson v. Hooper, 75 A. 568 (N.J.Err. & App.1910), 522
Jackson Inv. Co., Commissioner v., 346 F.2d 187 (9th Cir.1965), 314
Jacobs v. Commissioner, 41 T.C.M. (CCH) 951 (U.S.Tax Ct.1981), 804
Jaffe Commercial Finance Co. v. Harris, 119 Ill.App.3d 136, 74 Ill.Dec. 722, 456 N.E.2d 224 (Ill.App. 1 Dist.1983), 476
James v. Commissioner, 53 T.C. 63 (Tax Ct.1969), **365,** 369, 370, 374, 375, 393
Jedwab v. MGM Grand Hotels, Inc., 509 A.2d 584 (Del.Ch.1986), 1023
Jefferson County v. Barton–Douglas Contractors, Inc., 282 N.W.2d 155 (Iowa 1979), 564
J.E. Seagram Corp. v. Commissioner, 104 T.C. 75 (U.S.Tax Ct.1995), **1090,** 1099, 1101, 1102, 1103, 1104, 1105, 1107
Jewel v. Boxer, 156 Cal.App.3d 171, 203 Cal. Rptr. 13 (Cal.App. 1 Dist.1984), 320
Jewel Companies, Inc. v. Pay Less Drug Stores Northwest, Inc., 741 F.2d 1555 (9th Cir.1984), **952,** 959, 960, 961
John A. Nelson Co. v. Helvering, 296 U.S. 374, 56 S.Ct. 273, 80 L.Ed. 281 (1935), 1102
John Kelley Co. v. Commissioner, 326 U.S. 521, 326 U.S. 698, 66 S.Ct. 299, 90 L.Ed. 278 (1946), 426
Johnson v. Buck, 540 S.W.2d 393 (TexCiv-App.-Corpus Christi 1976), 298
Johnson v. Commissioner, 74 T.C. 1316 (U.S.Tax Ct.1980), 542
Johnson v. Fuller, 121 F.2d 618 (3rd Cir. 1941), 830
Johnson v. Spartanburg County Fair Ass'n, 210 S.C. 56, 41 S.E.2d 599 (S.C.1947), 509
Johnson Trust v. Commissioner, 71 T.C. 941 (U.S.Tax Ct.1979), 778
Johnston v. Commissioner, T.C. Memo. 1995-140 (U.S.Tax Ct.1995), **135,** 140, 141, 346, 369
John Wiley & Sons, Inc. v. Livingston, 376 U.S. 543, 84 S.Ct. 909, 11 L.Ed.2d 898 (1964), 1046
Joseph M. Grey Public Accountant, P.C. v. Commissioner, 119 T.C. 121 (U.S.Tax Ct.2002), 492
JTB Enterprises v. D & B Venture, 194 B.R. 79 (Bkrtcy.E.D.Va.1996), 254, 255, 256

Jutkowitz v. Bourns, Inc., No. CA 000268 (Cal.Super.1975), 1140

Kaczmarek v. Commissioner, 21 T.C.M. (CCH) 691 (Tax Ct.1962), 378
Kamborian, Estate of v. Commissioner, 469 F.2d 219 (1st Cir.1972), 378
Kamena v. Janssen Dairy Corporation, 31 A.2d 200 (N.J.Ch.1943), 831, 832
Kaplan v. Goldsamt, 380 A.2d 556 (Del.Ch. 1977), **741,** 762, 763, 765, 831, 904, 1011
Karfunkel v. United StatesLIFE Corp., 116 Misc.2d 841, 455 N.Y.S.2d 937 (N.Y.Sup. 1982), 763
Kass v. Commissioner, 60 T.C. 218 (U.S.Tax Ct.1973), 1148
Katcher v. Ohsman, 26 N.J.Super. 28, 97 A.2d 180 (N.J.Super.Ch.1953), 526
Katt v. Titan Acquisitions Ltd., 244 F.Supp.2d 841 (M.D.Tenn.2003), 991
Katz v. Bregman, 431 A.2d 1274 (Del.Ch. 1981), 863, **882,** 884, 1012
Katzowitz v. Sidler, 301 N.Y.S.2d 470, 249 N.E.2d 359 (N.Y.1969), **431,** 434, 435, 436, 437
Keller v. Wilson & Co., 21 Del.Ch. 391, 190 A. 115 (Del.Supr.1936), 831
Kellogg v. Georgia–Pacific Paper Corp., 227 F.Supp. 719 (W.D.Ark.1964), 1139
Kennerson v. Burbank Amusement Co., 120 Cal.App.2d 157, 260 P.2d 823 (Cal.App. 1 Dist.1953), 528
Kimbell–Diamond Milling Co. v. Commissioner, 14 T.C. 74 (Tax Ct.1950), 1146
King v. Commissioner, 458 F.2d 245 (6th Cir.1972), 875
King Enterprises, Inc. v. United States, 189 Ct.Cl. 466, 418 F.2d 511 (Ct.Cl.1969), 1148
Kirschner Brothers Oil, Inc. v. Natomas Co., 185 Cal.App.3d 784, 229 Cal.Rptr. 899 (Cal.App. 1 Dist.1986), **1016,** 1020, 1021, 1022, 1023
Klang v. Smith's Food and Drug Centers, Inc., 702 A.2d 150 (Del.Supr.1997), 456
Knutson v. Lauer, 627 P.2d 66 (Utah 1981), 236
Kovacik v. Reed, 49 Cal.2d 166, 315 P.2d 314 (Cal.1957), 185
Kresser v. Commissioner, 54 T.C. 1621 (U.S.Tax Ct.1970), 202
Kupetz v. Wolf, 845 F.2d 842 (9th Cir.1988), 948, 949

Labovitz v. Dolan, 189 Ill.App.3d 403, 136 Ill.Dec. 780, 545 N.E.2d 304 (Ill.App. 1 Dist.1989), 177
Lacos Land Co. v. Arden Group, Inc., 517 A.2d 271 (Del.Ch.1986), 831
Lamark Shipping Agency, Inc. v. Commissioner, 42 T.C.M. (CCH) 38 (U.S.Tax Ct.1981), 424, 542, **787,** 798, 799, 899
Lambert v. Fishermen's Dock Co-op., Inc., 61 N.J. 596, 297 A.2d 566 (N.J.1972), 547
Landreth Timber Co. v. Landreth, 471 U.S. 681, 105 S.Ct. 2297, 85 L.Ed.2d 692 (1985), 607, 1061
Langness v. O Street Carpet Shop, Inc., 217 Neb. 569, 353 N.W.2d 709 (Neb.1984), 132
Lansburgh v. Commissioner, 92 T.C. 448 (U.S.Tax Ct.1989), 221
Lash v. Lash Furniture Co. of Barre, Inc., 130 Vt. 517, 296 A.2d 207 (Vt.1972), 542
Lawlis v. Kightlinger & Gray, 562 N.E.2d 435 (Ind.App. 4 Dist.1990), 291
Leavitt, Estate of v. Commissioner, 90 T.C. 206 (U.S.Tax Ct.1988), **489,** 491
Lebold v. Inland Steel Co., 125 F.2d 369 (7th Cir.1941), 764
Lehrman v. Cohen, 43 Del.Ch. 222, 222 A.2d 800 (Del.Supr.1966), 513
Lerner v. Lerner, 306 Md. 771, 511 A.2d 501 (Md.1986), 808
Lessinger v. Commissioner, 872 F.2d 519 (2nd Cir.1989), 386
Le Tulle v. Scofield, 308 U.S. 415, 60 S.Ct. 313, 84 L.Ed. 355 (1940), 1102
Levy v. American Beverage Corp., 265 A.D. 208, 38 N.Y.S.2d 517 (N.Y.A.D. 1 Dept. 1942), 974
Levy v. Leavitt, 257 N.Y. 461, 178 N.E. 758 (N.Y.1931), **233,** 236
Libson Shops, Inc. v. Koehler, 353 U.S. 382, 77 S.Ct. 990, 1 L.Ed.2d 924 (1957), 1122
Likins–Foster Honolulu Corp. v. Commissioner, 840 F.2d 642 (9th Cir.1988), 1131
Lisle v. Commissioner, 35 T.C.M. (CCH) 627 (U.S.Tax Ct.1976), 784
Litarowich v. Wiederkehr, 170 N.J.Super. 144, 405 A.2d 874 (N.J.Super.L.1979), 1037
Livens v. William D. Witter, Inc., 374 F.Supp. 1104 (D.Mass.1974), 683
Local Lodge No. 1266, IAM v. Panoramic Corp., 668 F.2d 276 (7th Cir.1981), 1047
Lockwood's Estate v. Commissioner, 350 F.2d 712 (8th Cir.1965), 876
Louisiana Weekly Pub. Co. v. First Nat. Bank of Commerce, 483 So.2d 929 (La.1986), 540
Lowenschuss v. Kane, 520 F.2d 255 (2nd Cir.1975), 994
L.P. Acquisition Co. v. Tyson, 772 F.2d 201 (6th Cir.1985), 1063
Luckenbach S.S. Co. v. W.R. Grace & Co., 267 F. 676 (4th Cir.1920), 408
Luedecke v. Des Moines Cabinet Co., 140 Iowa 223, 118 N.W. 456 (Iowa 1908), 1037
Lydia E. Pinkham Medicine Co. v. Gove, 305 Mass. 213, 25 N.E.2d 332 (Mass.1940), 527
Lynch v. Commissioner, 801 F.2d 1176 (9th Cir.1986), 782
Lynch v. Commissioner, 83 T.C. 597 (U.S.Tax Ct.1984), 783
Lynch Multimedia Corp. v. Carson Communications, L.L.C., 102 F.Supp.2d 1261 (D.Kan.2000), 168

Macht v. Merchants Mortgage & Credit Co., 22 Del.Ch. 74, 194 A. 19 (Del.Ch.1937), 509

Maddock v. Vorclone Corporation, 17 Del.Ch. 39, 147 A. 255 (Del.Ch.1929), 508

Maffia v. American Woolen Co, 125 F.Supp. 465 (S.D.N.Y.1954), 885

Maguire, Estate of v. Commissioner, 50 T.C. 130 (Tax Ct.1968), 1133

Marshall v. Harris, 276 Or. 447, 555 P.2d 756 (Or.1976), 706

Mason v. Pewabic Min. Co., 133 U.S. 50, 10 S.Ct. 224, 33 L.Ed. 524 (1890), 1139

Mather's Estate, In re, 410 Pa. 361, 189 A.2d 586 (Pa.1963), 541

Matter of (see name of party)

Matteson v. Zicbarth, 40 Wash.2d 286, 242 P.2d 1025 (Wash.1952), 1140

Maxwell Hardware Co. v. Commissioner, 343 F.2d 713 (9th Cir.1965), 1122

McCallum v. Asbury, 238 Or. 257, 393 P.2d 774 (Or.1964), 248

McConnell v. Hunt Sports Ent., 132 Ohio App.3d 657, 725 N.E.2d 1193 (Ohio App. 10 Dist.1999), **120,** 126, 127, 166

McDonald v. Commissioner, 52 T.C. 82 (Tax Ct.1969), 1005

McDonald's Restaurants of Illinois, Inc. v. Commissioner, 688 F.2d 520 (7th Cir. 1982), 1102, 1103

McLaulin v. Commissioner, 276 F.3d 1269 (11th Cir.2001), 879

McQuade v. Stoneham, 263 N.Y. 323, 189 N.E. 234 (N.Y.1934), 522

McShain v. Commissioner, 71 T.C. 998 (U.S.Tax Ct.1979), 414

Mease v. Warm Mineral Springs, Inc., 128 So.2d 174 (Fla.App. 2 Dist.1961), 534

Meehan v. Shaughnessy, 404 Mass. 419, 535 N.E.2d 1255 (Mass.1989), 128

Meinhard v. Salmon, 249 N.Y. 458, 164 N.E. 545 (N.Y.1928), 168

Menard, Inc. v. Commissioner, T.C. Memo. 2004-207, 2004 WL 2066599 (U.S.Tax Ct.2004), **466,** 472, 473, 474, 475, 476, 493

Merlo v. Commissioner, T.C. Memo. 2005-178 (U.S.Tax Ct.2005), 554

Michelson v. Duncan, 407 A.2d 211 (Del. Supr.1979), 475

Mid–Continent Tel. Corp. v. Home Tel. Co., 319 F.Supp. 1176 (N.D.Miss.1970), 959

Miller–Wohl Co., State ex rel. Waldman v., 42 Del. 73, 28 A.2d 148 (Del.Super.1942), 452

Mills v. Commissioner, 331 F.2d 321 (5th Cir.1964), 1087

Mills v. Electric Auto–Lite Co., 396 U.S. 375, 90 S.Ct. 616, 24 L.Ed.2d 593 (1970), 1011

Mills Acquisition Co. v. Macmillan, Inc., 559 A.2d 1261 (Del.Supr.1989), 904

Minnesota Tea Co., Helvering v., 296 U.S. 378, 56 S.Ct. 269, 80 L.Ed. 284 (1935), 1102

Minton v. Cavaney, 56 Cal.2d 576, 15 Cal. Rptr. 641, 364 P.2d 473 (Cal.1961), 362

Minute Maid Corp. v. United Foods, Inc., 291 F.2d 577 (5th Cir.1961), 58

Misko v. Commissioner, T.C. Memo. 2005-166 (U.S.Tax Ct.2005), 245

Model, Roland & Co. v. Industrial Acoustics Co., 261 N.Y.S.2d 896, 209 N.E.2d 553 (N.Y.1965), 526

Mohawk Carpet Mills v. Delaware Rayon Co., 35 Del.Ch. 51, 110 A.2d 305 (Del.Ch. 1954), 449

Monin v. Monin, 785 S.W.2d 499 (Ky.App. 1989), 128

Monson v. Commissioner, 79 T.C. 827 (U.S.Tax Ct.1982), 1000

Moran v. Household Intern., Inc., 500 A.2d 1346 (Del.Supr.1985), 902

Mordkin v. Commissioner, 71 T.C.M. (CCH) 2796 (U.S.Tax Ct.1996), **222,** 230

Morris Trust, Commissioner v., 367 F.2d 794 (4th Cir.1966), **994,** 998, 999, 1001, 1002, 1004

Mundy v. Holden, 42 Del.Ch. 84, 204 A.2d 83 (Del.Supr.1964), 296

Nachman Corp. v. Pension Ben. Guaranty Corp., 446 U.S. 359, 100 S.Ct. 1723, 64 L.Ed.2d 354 (1980), 1051

Nash v. United States, 398 U.S. 1, 90 S.Ct. 1550, 26 L.Ed.2d 1 (1970), 385

National Tea Co. v. Commissioner, 793 F.2d 864 (7th Cir.1986), 1122

National Tile & Terrazzo Co., Matter of, 537 F.2d 329 (9th Cir.1976), 740

NCR Corp. v. AT & T, 761 F.Supp. 475 (S.D.Ohio 1991), 904

Neidert v. Neidert, 637 S.W.2d 296 (Mo.App. S.D.1982), 499

Neimark v. Mel Kramer Sales, Inc., 102 Wis.2d 282, 306 N.W.2d 278 (Wis.App. 1981), **731,** 737, 739, 740, 741

Neustadt's Trust, Commissioner v., 131 F.2d 528 (2nd Cir.1942), 853

Neville Coke & Chemical Co. v. Commissioner, 148 F.2d 599 (3rd Cir.1945), 853

Newark Morning Ledger Co. v. United States, 507 U.S. 546, 113 S.Ct. 1670, 123 L.Ed.2d 288 (1993), 1065

New York v. Shore Realty Corp., 759 F.2d 1032 (2nd Cir.1985), 1037

Nicholes v. Hunt, 273 Or. 255, 541 P.2d 820 (Or.1975), 120, 273

Nickolopoulos v. Sarantis, 141 A. 792 (N.J.Err. & App.1928), 509

Nielsen v. Commissioner, 61 T.C. 311 (U.S.Tax Ct.1973), 876

Nixon v. Blackwell, 626 A.2d 1366 (Del. Supr.1993), 500, 763

N.L.R.B. v. Band–Age, Inc., 534 F.2d 1 (1st Cir.1976), 1046

N.L.R.B. v. Burns Intern. Sec. Services, Inc., 406 U.S. 272, 92 S.Ct. 1571, 32 L.Ed.2d 61 (1972), **1038,** 1045, 1046

N.L.R.B. v. Fall River Dyeing & Finishing Corp., 775 F.2d 425 (1st Cir.1985), 1046

Northern Bank & Trust Co. v. Day, 83 Wash. 296, 145 P. 182 (Wash.1915), 808

Northway, Inc. v. TSC Industries, Inc., 512 F.2d 324 (7th Cir.1975), 975

Obre v. Alban Tractor Co., 228 Md. 291, 179 A.2d 861 (Md.1962), 405

O'Brien v. Socony Mobil Oil Co., 207 Va. 707, 152 S.E.2d 278 (Va.1967), 831

Odman v. Oleson, 319 Mass. 24, 64 N.E.2d 439 (Mass.1946), 523

Oglesby–Barnitz Bank & Trust Co. v. Clark, 112 Ohio App. 31, 175 N.E.2d 98 (Ohio App. 1 Dist.1959), 304

Old Dominion Copper Mining & Smelting Co. v. Bigelow, 203 Mass. 159, 89 N.E. 193 (Mass.1909), 361

Old Dominion Copper Mining & Smelting Co. v. Lewisohn, 210 U.S. 206, 28 S.Ct. 634, 52 L.Ed. 1025 (1908), 361

O'Melveny & Myers v. F.D.I.C., 512 U.S. 79, 114 S.Ct. 2048, 129 L.Ed.2d 67 (1994), 44

Omnicare, Inc. v. NCS Healthcare, Inc., 818 A.2d 914 (Del.Supr.2003), 960

Orzeck v. Englehart, 41 Del.Ch. 361, 195 A.2d 375 (Del.Supr.1963), 1014

Oswald v. Commissioner, 49 T.C. 645 (Tax Ct.1968), 473

Outwater v. Public Service Corp., 143 A. 729 (N.J.Ch.1928), 1140

Pacific Scene, Inc. v. Penasquitos, Inc., 250 Cal.Rptr. 651, 758 P.2d 1182 (Cal. 1988), 1035, **1124,** 1128, 1129

Pacific Waxed Paper Co., State ex rel. Everett Trust & Sav. Bank v., 22 Wash.2d 844, 157 P.2d 707 (Wash.1945), 510

Page v. Page, 55 Cal.2d 192, 10 Cal.Rptr. 643, 359 P.2d 41 (Cal.1961), **270,** 272, 273, 274, 275, 281, 285, 764

Pahl v. Commissioner, 67 T.C. 286 (U.S.Tax Ct.1976), 473

Panepucci v. Honigman Miller Schwartz, Cohn, LLP, 408 F.Supp.2d 374 (E.D.Mich. 2005), 99

Panter v. Marshall Field & Co., 646 F.2d 271 (7th Cir.1981), 908

Paramount Communications Inc. v. QVC Network Inc., 637 A.2d 34 (Del. Supr.1994), 905

Paramount Communications, Inc. v. Time Inc., 571 A.2d 1140 (Del. Supr.1989), **890,** 898, 899, 900, 905, 907, 960, 961

Paramount Publix Corporation, In re, 90 F.2d 441 (2nd Cir.1937), 527

Pargas, Inc. v. Empire Gas Corp., 423 F.Supp. 199 (D.Md.1976), 949

Parshelsky's Estate v. Commissioner, 303 F.2d 14 (2nd Cir.1962), 872

Patterson v. Durham Hosiery Mills, 214 N.C. 806, 200 S.E. 906 (N.C.1939), 830

Paulsen v. Commissioner, 469 U.S. 131, 105 S.Ct. 627, 83 L.Ed.2d 540 (1985), 1102

Paxton v. McDonald, 72 Ariz. 240, 233 P.2d 450 (Ariz.1951), 128, 167

Pelton Steel Casting Co. v. Commissioner, 28 T.C. 153 (Tax Ct.1957), 799

Penn Central Securities Litigation, In re, 367 F.Supp. 1158 (E.D.Pa.1973), 1021

Pension Ben. Guaranty Corp. v. Ouimet Corp., 630 F.2d 4 (1st Cir.1980), **1047,** 1051

Pension Ben. Guar. Corp. v. Anthony Co., 537 F.Supp. 1048 (N.D.Ill.1982), 1051

People ex rel. v. ______ (see opposing party and relator)

Perlman v. Feldmann, 219 F.2d 173 (2nd Cir.1955), 975

Petition of (see name of party)

Piemonte v. New Boston Garden Corp., 377 Mass. 719, 387 N.E.2d 1145 (Mass. 1979), 57, **918,** 928, 929, 930, 1010

Pilch v. Milikin, 200 Cal.App.2d 212, 19 Cal. Rptr. 334 (Cal.App. 2 Dist.1962), 324

Pinter v. Dahl, 486 U.S. 622, 108 S.Ct. 2063, 100 L.Ed.2d 658 (1988), 681

Pioneer Specialties, Inc. v. Nelson, 161 Tex. 244, 339 S.W.2d 199 (Tex.1960), 527

Pipelife Corp. v. Bedford, 37 Del.Ch. 467, 145 A.2d 206 (Del.Ch.1958), 365

Pittsburgh Terminal Corp. v. Baltimore & Ohio R.R. Co., 680 F.2d 933 (3rd Cir. 1982), 864

Plantation Patterns, Inc. v. Commissioner, 462 F.2d 712 (5th Cir.1972), 428

PNRC Ltd. Partnership v. Commissioner, 66 T.C.M. (CCH) 265 (U.S.Tax Ct.1993), **196,** 199, 200, 203, 217

Polikoff v. Levy, 132 Ill.App.2d 492, 270 N.E.2d 540 (Ill.App. 1 Dist.1971), 321

Pope & Talbot, Inc. v. Commissioner, 162 F.3d 1236 (9th Cir.1999), **80,** 84, 85, 86

Potter Elec. Signal & Mfg. Co. v. Commissioner, 286 F.2d 200 (8th Cir.1961), 474

Powers v. Baker–Perkins, Inc., 92 Mich.App. 645, 285 N.W.2d 402 (Mich.App.1979), 1038

PPG Industries, Inc. v. Guardian Industries Corp., 597 F.2d 1090 (6th Cir. 1979), 933, **1023,** 1026, 1027, 1028

Pratt v. American Bell Tel. Co., 141 Mass. 225, 5 N.E. 307 (Mass.1886), 450

Pratt v. Ballman–Cummings Furniture Co., 254 Ark. 570, 495 S.W.2d 509 (Ark.1973), 1023

Pratt v. Commissioner, 550 F.2d 1023 (5th Cir.1977), 243, 245

Pratt v. Commissioner, 64 T.C. 203 (U.S.Tax Ct.1975), 245

Prizant v. Commissioner, 30 T.C.M. (CCH) 817 (U.S.Tax Ct.1971), **394,** 398, 399

Pullman Const. Industries Inc., In re, 107 B.R. 909 (Bkrtcy.N.D.Ill.1989), 930

Quickturn Design Systems, Inc. v. Shapiro, 721 A.2d 1281 (Del.Supr.1998), 902
Quillen v. Titus, 172 Va. 523, 2 S.E.2d 284 (Va.1939), 236

Radtke v. United States, 712 F.Supp. 143 (E.D.Wis.1989), 94, 474, 492
Rafe v. Hindin, 29 A.D.2d 481, 288 N.Y.S.2d 662 (N.Y.A.D. 2 Dept.1968), **531,** 534, 535
Rafferty v. Commissioner, 452 F.2d 767 (1st Cir.1971), 872, 875
Rainwater v. Milfeld, 485 S.W.2d 831 (Tex-CivApp.-Corpus Christi 1972), **543,** 547
Ramirez v. Amsted Industries, Inc., 86 N.J. 332, 431 A.2d 811 (N.J.1981), 933, **1028,** 1035, 1036, 1037, 1038, 1087
Randall v. Bailey, 288 N.Y. 280, 43 N.E.2d 43 (N.Y.1942), 456
Rapoport v. 55 Perry Co., 50 A.D.2d 54, 376 N.Y.S.2d 147 (N.Y.A.D. 1 Dept.1975), **326,** 328, 329, 330, 331
Rath v. Commissioner, 101 T.C. 196 (U.S.Tax Ct.1993), 398
Rathborne v. Rathborne, 508 F.Supp. 515 (E.D.La.1980), 867
Raynor v. Commissioner, 50 T.C. 762 (Tax Ct.1968), 490
Real Estate Capital Corp. v. Thunder Corp., 31 Ohio Misc. 169, 287 N.E.2d 838 (Ohio Com.Pl.1972), 948
Redding v. Commissioner, 630 F.2d 1169 (7th Cir.1980), 880
Reilly v. Rangers Management, Inc., 727 S.W.2d 527 (Tex.1987), 166
Reilly Oil Co. v. Commissioner, 189 F.2d 382 (5th Cir.1951), 1102
Reiner v. Washington Plate Glass Co., 711 F.2d 414 (D.C.Cir.1983), 740
Reiss v. Financial Performance Corp., 738 N.Y.S.2d 658, 764 N.E.2d 958 (N.Y.2001), 450
Remillong v. Schneider, 185 N.W.2d 493 (N.D.1971), 540
Reves v. Ernst & Young, 494 U.S. 56, 110 S.Ct. 945, 108 L.Ed.2d 47 (1990), **601,** 607, 608
Revlon, Inc. v. MacAndrews & Forbes Holdings, Inc., 506 A.2d 173 (Del.Supr.1985), 905, 907, 962
Richert v. Handly, 53 Wash.2d 121, 330 P.2d 1079 (Wash.1958), **183,** 185, 186, 187, 188, 189, 190
Richert v. Handly, 50 Wash.2d 356, 311 P.2d 417 (Wash.1957), **180**
Rickey v. United States, 592 F.2d 1251 (5th Cir.1979), 782
Riedel, United States v., 126 F.2d 81 (7th Cir.1942), 833
Ringling Bros.-Barnum & Bailey Combined Shows v. Ringling, 29 Del.Ch. 610, 53 A.2d 441 (Del.Supr.1947), **500,** 506, 507, 508, 509, 510, 536
Roberts v. Roberts–Wicks Co., 184 N.Y. 257, 77 N.E. 13 (N.Y.1906), 885
Roberts v. Whitson, 188 S.W.2d 875 (Tex.Civ. App.-Dallas 1945), 509
Robinson v. Commissioner, 805 F.2d 38 (1st Cir.1986), **548,** 552, 553, 554
Robinson v. Glynn, 349 F.3d 166 (4th Cir. 2003), **595,** 606, 607
Rochez Bros., Inc. v. Rhoades, 491 F.2d 402 (3rd Cir.1973), **722,** 726, 764, 765, 765
Rooney v. United States, 305 F.2d 681 (9th Cir.1962), 384
Rothschild Intern. Corp. v. Liggett Group Inc., 474 A.2d 133 (Del.Supr.1984), 1140
Roxbury State Bank v. The Clarendon, 129 N.J.Super. 358, 324 A.2d 24 (N.J.Super.A.D.1974), 948
Ruetz v. Topping, 453 S.W.2d 624 (Mo.App. 1970), 475
Ruth v. Crane, 392 F.Supp. 724 (E.D.Pa. 1975), 115

Sanders v. Cuba Railroad Co., 21 N.J. 78, 120 A.2d 849 (N.J.1956), 446
Sankin v. 5410 Connecticut Ave. Corp., 281 F.Supp. 524 (D.D.C 1968), 509
Santa Fe Industries, Inc. v. Green, 430 U.S. 462, 97 S.Ct. 1292, 51 L.Ed.2d 480 (1977), 1143
Schaefer v. Bork, 413 N.W.2d 873 (Minn.App. 1987), 132
Schaefer's Estate, In re, 72 Wis.2d 600, 241 N.W.2d 607 (Wis.1976), 113
Schenker v. E. I. du Pont de Nemours & Co., 329 F.2d 77 (2nd Cir.1964), 864
Schneider v. Commissioner, 65 T.C. 18 (U.S.Tax Ct.1975), 1132
Schneider, Estate of v. Commissioner, 855 F.2d 435 (7th Cir.1988), 785
Schnitzer v. Commissioner, 13 T.C. 43 (Tax Ct.1949), 425
Schreiber v. Burlington Northern, Inc., 472 U.S. 1, 105 S.Ct. 2458, 86 L.Ed.2d 1 (1985), 1063
Schwartz v. Marien, 373 N.Y.S.2d 122, 335 N.E.2d 334 (N.Y.1975), 436, 437
Schymanski v. Conventz, 674 P.2d 281 (Alaska 1983), **129,** 132, 133, 185, 364
Scientific Instrument Co. v. Commissioner, 17 T.C. 1253 (Tax Ct.1952), 377
Scriptomatic, Inc. v. United States, 555 F.2d 364 (3rd Cir.1977), 426
Seattle Trust & Sav. Bank v. McCarthy, 94 Wash.2d 605, 617 P.2d 1023 (Wash.1980), 437
SEC v. Carter Hawley Hale Stores, Inc., 760 F.2d 945 (9th Cir.1985), 991
SEC v. Central–Illinois Securities Corp., 338 U.S. 96, 69 S.Ct. 1377, 93 L.Ed. 1836 (1949), 832, 833
SEC v. Continental Tobacco Co., 463 F.2d 137 (5th Cir.1972), 682

SEC v. Datronics Engineers, Inc., 490 F.2d 250 (4th Cir.1973), 863, 866, 867
SEC v. Edwards, 540 U.S. 389, 124 S.Ct. 892, 157 L.Ed.2d 813 (2004), 608
SEC v. Georgia–Pacific Corp., Fed.Sec.L.Rep. (CCH) ¶ 91680 (1966), 932
SEC v. Holschuh, 694 F.2d 130 (7th Cir. 1982), 682
SEC v. McDonald Inv. Co., 343 F.Supp. 343 (D.Minn.1972), 705
SEC v. Ralston Purina Co., 346 U.S. 119, 73 S.Ct. 981, 97 L.Ed. 1494 (1953), 682
SEC v. Texas Gulf Sulphur Co., 401 F.2d 833 (2nd Cir.1968), 962
SEC v. W.J. Howey Co., 328 U.S. 293, 66 S.Ct. 1100, 90 L.Ed. 1244 (1946), 607, 608
Securities Industry Ass'n v. Connolly, 883 F.2d 1114 (1st Cir.1989), 564
Seggerman Farms, Inc. v. Commissioner, 308 F.3d 803 (7th Cir.2002), 386
Seide v. Commissioner, 18 T.C. 502 (Tax Ct.1952), 853
Service Co. v. Commissioner, 165 F.2d 75 (8th Cir.1948), 1145
Shamrock Holdings, Inc. v. Polaroid Corp., 559 A.2d 257 (Del.Ch.1989), 904
Shanik v. White Sewing Mach. Corp., 25 Del. Ch. 371, 19 A.2d 831 (Del.Supr.1941), 830
Shannon v. Samuel Langston Co., 379 F.Supp. 797 (W.D.Mich.1974), 1037
Sharon Steel Corp. v. Chase Manhattan Bank, 691 F.2d 1039 (2nd Cir.1982), 1036
Silva v. Coastal Plywood & Timber Co., 124 Cal.App.2d 276, 268 P.2d 510 (Cal.App. 3 Dist.1954), 547
Simas v. Quaker Fabric Corp., 6 F.3d 849 (1st Cir.1993), 1047
Sinclair Oil Corp. v. Levien, 280 A.2d 717 (Del.Supr.1971), 1138
Skyline Memorial Gardens, Inc. v. Commissioner, 50 T.C.M. (CCH) 360 (U.S.Tax Ct.1985), 1001
Slappey Drive Indus. Park v. United States, 561 F.2d 572 (5th Cir.1977), 426
Smith v. Atlantic Properties, Inc., 12 Mass. App.Ct. 201, 422 N.E.2d 798 (Mass.App. Ct.1981), 527
Smith v. Dravo Corp., 203 F.2d 369 (7th Cir.1953), 963
Smith v. Good Music Station, Inc., 36 Del.Ch. 262, 129 A.2d 242 (Del.Ch.1957), 975, 976
Smith v. Van Gorkom, 488 A.2d 858 (Del. Supr.1985), 900, 929, 970, 1011
Smith–Shrader Co. v. Smith, 136 Ill.App.3d 571, 91 Ill.Dec. 1, 483 N.E.2d 283 (Ill.App. 1 Dist.1985), 128
Smoot Sand & Gravel Corp. v. Commissioner, 241 F.2d 197 (4th Cir.1957), 424
Solon v. Kaplan, 398 F.3d 629 (7th Cir.2005), 99
Southland Ice Co. v. Commissioner, 5 T.C. 842 (Tax Ct.1945), 1075
Southwest Consol. Corp., Helvering v., 315 U.S. 194, 62 S.Ct. 546, 86 L.Ed. 789 (1942), 842, 1074, 1090
Speca v. Commissioner, 630 F.2d 554 (7th Cir.1980), 488
Speed v. Transamerica, 235 F.2d 369 (3rd Cir.1956), 764
Sperry Corp., State ex rel. Crowder v., 41 Del. 84, 15 A.2d 661 (Del.Super.1940), 511
Spratt v. Paramount Pictures, 178 Misc. 682, 35 N.Y.S.2d 815 (N.Y.Sup.1942), 450
Staffin v. Greenberg, 672 F.2d 1196 (3rd Cir. 1982), 765, 962
Staklinski v. Pyramid Elec. Co., 188 N.Y.S.2d 541, 160 N.E.2d 78 (N.Y.1959), 565
Starring v. American Hair & Felt Co., 21 Del.Ch. 380, 191 A. 887 (Del.Ch.1937), 451
State ex rel. v. _____ (see opposing party and relator)
State of (see name of state)
St. Charles Inv. Co. v. Commissioner, 232 F.3d 773 (10th Cir.2000), 85
Steinberg v. Amplica, Inc., 233 Cal.Rptr. 249, 729 P.2d 683 (Cal.1986), 1011, 1141
Stephenson v. Drever, 69 Cal.Rptr.2d 764, 947 P.2d 1301 (Cal.1997), 548
Sterling Industries v. Ball Bearing Pen Corporation, 298 N.Y. 483, 84 N.E.2d 790 (N.Y.1949), 527
Stevens v. Commissioner, 46 T.C. 492 (Tax Ct.1966), 213
Stewart v. Robinson, 115 N.Y. 328, 26 N.Y.St. Rep. 117, 22 N.E. 160 (N.Y.1889), 331
St. Louis Southwestern Ry. Co. v. Loeb, 318 S.W.2d 246 (Mo.1958), 447
Stockton Harbor Indus. Co. v. Commissioner, 216 F.2d 638 (9th Cir.1954), 1075
Stoddard v. Commissioner, 141 F.2d 76 (2nd Cir.1944), 1075
Stoiber v. Miller Brewing Co., 257 Wis. 13, 42 N.W.2d 144 (Wis.1950), 475
Stokes v. Continental Trust Co., 186 N.Y. 285, 78 N.E. 1090 (N.Y.1906), 436
Stone v. Auslander, 28 Misc.2d 384, 212 N.Y.S.2d 777 (N.Y.Sup.1961), 508
Stratton v. Garvey Intern., Inc., 9 Kan. App.2d 254, 676 P.2d 1290 (Kan.App. 1984), 1037
Stroh v. Blackhawk Holding Corp., 48 Ill.2d 471, 272 N.E.2d 1 (Ill.1971), 514
Summers v. Dooley, 94 Idaho 87, 481 P.2d 318 (Idaho 1971), **246,** 248, 249, 253
Superior Coach of Florida, Inc. v. Commissioner, 80 T.C. 895 (U.S.Tax Ct.1983), 1103
Swann v. Mitchell, 435 So.2d 797 (Fla.1983), 321
Systematics, Inc. v. Mitchell, 253 Ark. 848, 491 S.W.2d 40 (Ark.1973), 541

Tabor Court Realty Corp., United States v., 803 F.2d 1288 (3rd Cir.1986), 948, 949
Taft Realty Corp. v. Yorkhaven Enterprises, Inc., 146 Conn. 338, 150 A.2d 597 (Conn. 1959), 512

Tallant v. Executive Equities, Inc., 232 Ga. 807, 209 S.E.2d 159 (Ga.1974), 436
Tanzer v. International General Industries, Inc., 379 A.2d 1121 (Del.Supr.1977), 1141
Tanzer Economic Associates, Inc. v. Universal Food Specialties, Inc., 87 Misc.2d 167, 383 N.Y.S.2d 472 (N.Y.Sup.1976), 832, 1142
Taylor v. Standard Gas & Elec. Co., 306 U.S. 307, 59 S.Ct. 543, 83 L.Ed. 669 (1939), 405
Technalysis Corp. v. Commissioner, 101 T.C. 397 (U.S.Tax Ct.1993), 463
Telefest, Inc. v. VU–TV, Inc., 591 F.Supp. 1368 (D.N.J.1984), 948
Television Industries, Inc. v. Commissioner, 284 F.2d 322 (2nd Cir.1960), 999
Terry v. Penn Central Corp., 668 F.2d 188 (3rd Cir.1981), 1021
Teschner v. Chicago Title & Trust Co., 59 Ill.2d 452, 322 N.E.2d 54 (Ill.1974), 764
Texaco, Inc. v. Pennzoil, Co., 729 S.W.2d 768 (Tex.App.-Hous. (1 Dist.) 1987), 959
Theis v. Spokane Falls Gaslight Co., 34 Wash. 23, 74 P. 1004 (Wash.1904), 1139
Theophilos v. Commissioner, 85 F.3d 440 (9th Cir.1996), 557, 558
Thom v. Baltimore Trust Co., 158 Md. 352, 148 A. 234 (Md.1930), 437
Thomas Branch & Co. v. Riverside & Dan River Cotton Mills, 139 Va. 291, 123 S.E. 542 (Va.1924), 437
Thompson v. Campbell, 353 F.2d 787 (5th Cir.1965), 385
Thompson v. Fairleigh, 300 Ky. 144, 187 S.W.2d 812 (Ky.1945), 451
Thorpe v. CERBCO, Inc., 676 A.2d 436 (Del. Supr.1996), 976
Timberline Equipment Co. v. Davenport, 267 Or. 64, 514 P.2d 1109 (Or.1973), 360
Transamerica Corp. v. United States, 7 Cl.Ct. 441 (Cl.Ct.1985), 429
Treadway Companies, Inc. v. Care Corp., 638 F.2d 357 (2nd Cir.1980), 905
Tribble v. J.W. Greer Co., 83 F.Supp. 1015 (D.Mass.1949), 444
Triple Five of Minnesota, Inc. v. Simon, 404 F.3d 1088 (8th Cir.2005), 127
True, Estate of v. Commissioner, 390 F.3d 1210 (10th Cir.2004), 297
Tryon v. Smith, 191 Or. 172, 229 P.2d 251 (Or.1951), 976
Tufts, Commissioner v., 461 U.S. 300, 103 S.Ct. 1826, 75 L.Ed.2d 863 (1983), 202, 343

United Housing Foundation, Inc. v. Forman, 421 U.S. 837, 95 S.Ct. 2051, 44 L.Ed.2d 621 (1975), 607
United Paperworkers Intern. Union v. Penntech Papers, Inc., 439 F.Supp. 610 (D.Me. 1977), 1046
United States v. ______ (see opposing party)
United States Shelter Corp. v. United States, 13 Cl.Ct. 606 (Cl.Ct.1987), 1116, 1117
Unocal Corp. v. Mesa Petroleum Co., 493 A.2d 946 (Del.Supr.1985), 899, 904, 907

Validation Review Associates, Inc., In re, 223 A.D.2d 134, 646 N.Y.S.2d 149 (N.Y.A.D. 2 Dept.1996), 565
Van Gemert v. Boeing Co., 520 F.2d 1373 (2nd Cir.1975), 452
Van Ruiten v. Van Ruiten, 268 Cal.App.2d 619, 74 Cal.Rptr. 186 (Cal.App. 5 Dist. 1969), 237
Van Wyk v. Commissioner, 113 T.C. 440 (U.S.Tax Ct.1999), 492
Vaughn v. Teledyne, Inc., 628 F.2d 1214 (9th Cir.1980), 765
VGS, Inc. v. Castiel, 2000 WL 1277372 (Del.Ch.2000), **258,** 351
Vogel, Application of, 25 A.D.2d 212, 268 N.Y.S.2d 237 (N.Y.A.D. 1 Dept.1966), 565

Waggoner v. Snow, Becker, Kroll, Klaris & Krauss, 991 F.2d 1501 (9th Cir.1993), **39,** 44
Waldman, State ex rel. v. Miller–Wohl Co., 42 Del. 73, 28 A.2d 148 (Del.Super.1942), 452
Walkovszky v. Carlton, 276 N.Y.S.2d 585, 223 N.E.2d 6 (N.Y.1966), 107
Walter J. Schloss Associates v. Arkwin Industries, Inc., 472 N.Y.S.2d 605, 460 N.E.2d 1090 (N.Y.1984), 1141
Ward v. City Drug Co., 235 Ark. 767, 362 S.W.2d 27 (Ark.1962), 536
Warren v. United States, 145 Ct.Cl. 571, 171 F.Supp. 846 (Ct.Cl.1959), 1131
Warsaw Photographic Associates v. Commissioner, 84 T.C. 21 (U.S.Tax Ct.1985), 1066
Waterman Steamship Corp. v. Commissioner, 430 F.2d 1185 (5th Cir.1970), 1000
Weinberger v. UOP, Inc., 457 A.2d 701 (Del. Supr.1983), 1010, 1141, 1142
Weiss v. Commissioner, 956 F.2d 242 (11th Cir.1992), 318
Welch v. Via Christi Health Partners, Inc., 281 Kan. 732, 133 P.3d 122 (Kan.2006), 352
Wellman v. Dickinson, 475 F.Supp. 783 (S.D.N.Y.1979), **976,** 989, 990, 991, 992, 993, 1063
Wells Fargo Bank v. Desert View Bldg. Supplies, Inc., 475 F.Supp. 693 (D.Nev.1978), 456
Western Federal Corp. v. Erickson, 739 F.2d 1439 (9th Cir.1984), 683
Western Foundry Co. v. Wicker, 403 Ill. 260, 85 N.E.2d 722 (Ill.1949), 830
West Shore Fuel, Inc. v. United States, 453 F.Supp. 956 (W.D.N.Y.1978), 1104
White v. Hickey, 8 Ark.App. 264, 651 S.W.2d 467 (Ark.App.1983), 304
Whitley v. Klauber and Alagna, 435 N.Y.S.2d 568, 416 N.E.2d 569 (N.Y.1980), 307

Wieboldt Stores, Inc. v. Schottenstein, 94 B.R. 488 (N.D.Ill.1988), **936,** 947, 948, 949, 999

Wilderman v. Wilderman, 315 A.2d 610 (Del. Ch.1974), 238, 475

Wilkes v. Springside Nursing Home, Inc., 370 Mass. 842, 353 N.E.2d 657 (Mass.1976), 238, **494,** 499, 523, 524, 526, 527, 534

Williamson v. Tucker, 645 F.2d 404 (5th Cir. 1981), 606, 608

Wilson, Commissioner v., 353 F.2d 184 (9th Cir.1965), 871, 872

Wolf Envelope Co. v. Commissioner, 17 T.C. 471 (Tax Ct.1951), 843

Wolter Const. Co. v. Commissioner, 634 F.2d 1029 (6th Cir.1980), **102,** 106, 107, 109, 110, 111, 112, 1122

Wortham Machinery Co. v. United States, 521 F.2d 160 (10th Cir.1975), 1100

Wright v. United States, 482 F.2d 600 (8th Cir.1973), 778

Yanow v. Teal Industries, Inc., 178 Conn. 262, 422 A.2d 311 (Conn.1979), 1141

Yasik v. Wachtel, 25 Del.Ch. 247, 17 A.2d 309 (Del.Ch.1941), 437

Yelencsics v. Commissioner, 74 T.C. 1513 (U.S.Tax Ct.1980), 804

Yoc Heating Corp. v. Commissioner, 61 T.C. 168 (U.S.Tax Ct.1973), 1103

Zahn v. Transamerica Corp., 162 F.2d 36 (3rd Cir.1947), 451, **759,** 763, 764, 1023, 1141

Zaist v. Olson, 154 Conn. 563, 227 A.2d 552 (Conn.1967), 107

Zannis v. Lake Shore Radiologists, Ltd., 73 Ill.App.3d 901, 29 Ill.Dec. 569, 392 N.E.2d 126 (Ill.App. 1 Dist.1979), 528

Zetlin v. Hanson Holdings, Inc., 421 N.Y.S.2d 877, 397 N.E.2d 387 (N.Y.1979), 974

Zidell v. Zidell, Inc., 277 Or. 413, 560 P.2d 1086 (Or.1977), 500

Zidell v. Zidell, Inc., 277 Or. 423, 560 P.2d 1091 (Or.1977), **528,** 534, 726

*

BUSINESS PLANNING

*

CHAPTER I

INTRODUCTION TO BUSINESS PLANNING

SECTION A. THE LAWYER AS A PLANNER

Studies in law school tend to center around litigation—the resolution of disputes between two or more parties growing out of past events. In part, this reflects the fact that appellate court opinions, as a primary source of law, constitute a major portion of law school reading. In part, it reflects the traditional perception of an attorney as the champion of his or her client's cause in court. Yet, many attorneys will go through their careers rarely, if ever, seeing the inside of a courtroom. These practitioners are concerned with planning future transactions rather than litigating over past ones. This book deals with one particular area of such planning—that involving the formation, operation and disposition of business enterprises. Before delving into the substance of business planning, however, it may be useful to briefly consider several aspects of the planning process itself. The following article addresses the specific area of tax planning. Nevertheless, the insights it provides into the planning process are applicable to all fields of legal advice.

Corneel, Tax Planning: Teaching and Practice

22 Tax L.Rev. 221, 228–234 (1967).

* * *

Analyzing the Problem

While traditional solutions and the tax avoidance principles which gave rise to them must always be kept in mind in the selection of alternatives to be given more detailed review, they are not likely by themselves to provide answers in particular situations. Therefore, a third branch of the study of tax planning is the method of selecting the best approach to individual problems. * * * [I]t seems best to state these rules in homely admonitions which are more easily remembered than formulae of symbolic logic.

* * *

1. *What is the end sought? State the problem simply.* Clients tend to state their problems not in terms of their basic objectives, but in terms of a particular technique they have devised. A lawyer will overlook many useful alternatives if he does not first cut through to the true economic end to be

achieved. If he does this, he may find that there are a number of substantially different ways that will achieve the desired end.

* * *

4. *Look for the least change: It never hurts to read the code.* While any number of alterations in a plan can reduce the tax burden, if the changes are sufficiently substantial or numerous they may well mean that the client will miss his general economic objective. What the tax adviser should seek then is the very least change necessary to produce the desired improvement in the tax situation. Because the Code draws such fine lines, sometimes based on purely formal differences, a word by word analysis of the relevant Code sections, no matter how well they are already known, will often reveal the least change necessary.

Example: The owners of a large property decide for business reasons to incorporate their property. The market value of the property is substantially less than the owners' cost and they would like to deduct their loss on incorporation.

If the tax adviser "knows" that under section 351 the transferors of property to a corporation cannot deduct their loss if they own 80 per cent of the stock, he may advise his clients to transfer their property to an existing corporation of such size that the present shareholders will have more than 20 per cent of the continuing company and the former owners of the loss property less than 80 per cent. This, of course, would mean a very substantial change in the business picture, since it requires finding a suitable corporation and negotiating with its owners.

If section 351 and section 368(c) to which it refers are read carefully it will be seen that nonrecognition of the loss occurs only if the persons transferring the property own "stock possessing at least 80 per cent of the total combined voting power of all classes of stock entitled to vote and at least 80 per cent of the total number of shares of all other classes of stock of the corporation."

Reading the statutory language carefully may bring to mind the possibility, previously overlooked, of creating in addition to the normal voting common stock another class of nonvoting stock, and giving this second class of stock to persons who are not transferring property to the corporation, but merely rendering services such as employees, promoters, lawyers or accountants. This solution which was brought to mind only on a thoughtful reading of the law, is certainly closer to the original intent than the solution requiring dealings with an existing unrelated corporation.

5. *Seek the most flexible plan.* * * * [I]n tax practice as in other aspects of life it is important not to cross bridges too soon, not to eliminate options until the last moment.

* * *

Preventing Mistakes

So far we have dealt only with the vital first step which consists of devising a plan. * * * [T]his is only the first step and that there is an equally important second step, namely to determine whether the plan is sound. * * * A study of aborted plans led to the following check list:

1. *Note and check each assumption.* Almost every tax plan involves the making of a large number of assumptions as to the treatment of the transactions and entities involved. Unless each of these assumptions is separately noted and checked, the plan is unreliable.

* * *

2. *Understand the general setting of the problem.* One of the most frightening aspects of tax practice is that because of the enormous variety of rules and of the fact patterns made pertinent by these rules it is exceedingly easy to overlook either a rule or a fact which entirely alters the result.

* * *

Perhaps the best way to avoid these dreadful surprises is to get more facts and study more law than appear at first glance necessary to a solution of the particular problem. One probably should not advise any corporate client without having looked at the last annual report or tax return, learned something about its business and property, its shareholders and the relationship among them. None of these may be relevant, but often some seeming irrelevancy will bring to mind a half forgotten rule or cause the trained nose to detect a scent of danger otherwise not noticed. In checking the applicable law, the tax adviser should not confine himself to the precise point at issue, but should review generally the rules in this area of the law, read an article or two and check the index of his tax service with respect to the taxable entity, property and type of transaction involved.

3. *How can the Internal Revenue Service attack your plan?* No plan is complete until the adviser has placed himself in the position of an intelligent, ambitious Internal Revenue agent examining the plan in the light of all of the facts that diligent inquiry might reveal. * * *

While relatively simple plans, particularly if they have some business justification, may survive the imaginary agent's inspection, exceedingly complicated and involved schemes rarely will. There are two reasons for this: In the first place, these Rube Goldberg structures are most easily subject to the attack that in substance they are something else. In the second place, it is a mathematical truth that the larger the number of steps involved in a given process, the greater is the chance of failure somewhere along the line. A tax lawyer would not be doing his clients a disservice if he made it a rule to counsel against all plans which involved doing in twenty steps what might have been done in one.

4. *Compute the results of your plan.* No plan should ever be adopted until its results and those of other promising alternatives have been

carefully computed on the basis of the actual facts, and, if assumptions are needed, they should be supplied by the client and not the lawyer. In such computations account should be taken not only of the person for whom the plan is devised, but of all who will be affected. Such detailed computations may bring to light aspects which had previously been overlooked. Computation is also necessary because many of the grand principles of tax avoidance do not in fact produce tax savings when applied to a particular situation. For instance, it is usually good to defer income, but not when the particular taxpayer has a loss carryover which is expiring unused.

* * *

Several other aspects of the planning process are worth mentioning. In litigation, the events have transpired and the existence of dispute is a given. In planning, the attorney must anticipate what events might occur in the future and seek to avoid those events leading to costly disputes and litigation. This difference, in turn, creates a divergence in what the planning attorney and the litigator look for in reading judicial opinions. The litigator (and traditionally law school discussion) focus on who won (or should have won), who lost, and why. The planner, however, not only asks what facts must occur to ensure a favorable result if matters reach the stage of litigation, but also asks what the parties could have done differently to avoid reaching this stage altogether. Under this approach, reported cases become warning signs of dangers to be anticipated and avoided, rather than simply exercises in applying law to existing facts.

Another factor to consider when dealing with planning becomes apparent as one starts to think about the implications of Professor Corneel's first rule—identifying the client's ultimate goal(s). As the attorney begins thinking broadly in terms of obtaining general objectives, rather than just narrowly in terms of addressing specific legal issues, the question inevitably arises as to when he or she has gone beyond the appropriate role or expertise of an attorney. Specifically, in the context of this course, the question is to what extent a lawyer should become involved in helping his or her clients make business decisions.

An example illustrates the problem. Suppose a client requests an attorney to draft a partnership agreement or the papers to incorporate a new business venture the client wishes to enter. Should the attorney probe into the client's business plan to determine whether the enterprise is thought through and viable? The following excerpt suggests some questions which an entrepreneur would do well to answer before starting a new venture. Is it the attorney's role to pose these questions to his or her client?

Schollhammer & Kuriloff, Entrepreneurship and Small Business Management

53–83 (1979).

Evaluating New Venture Opportunities

Every year many millions of dollars are spent in starting new enterprises. Many of these newly established businesses vanish within a year or two, and only a very few are eventually successful. One study, "Why New Products Fail," gives evidence that the factors underlying the failure of new ventures are in most cases within the control of the entrepreneur. This study also lists as the major reasons for the failure of new ventures the following shortcomings:

- *Inadequate market knowledge.* This deficiency includes a lack of information about the demand potential for the product or service, the present and future size of the market, the market share that can realistically be expected, and appropriate distribution methods.
- *Faulty product performance.* Frequently new products do not perform properly because of hastily taken shortcuts in production development and product testing, or inadequate quality control.
- *Ineffective marketing and sales efforts.* Poor results often indicate inadequate or misdirected promotional efforts and a lack of appreciation of the problems involved in selling to, or servicing of, unfamiliar markets.
- *Inadequate awareness of competitive pressures.* New ventures often fail because the entrepreneur did not take into account the possible reactions of competitors, such as severe price cuts or special discounts to retailers.
- *Rapid product obsolescence.* The economic life of new products tends to get shorter; in many industries technological advances are so rapid as to make a new product obsolescent shortly after it is launched.
- *Poor timing for the start of the new venture.* Choosing the wrong time to launch a new venture often leads to commercial failure. A new product or service may be introduced before a real market interest or technological need for it exists, or it may be placed on the market too late, when consumer interest is waning.
- *Undercapitalization, unforeseen operating expenses, excessive investments in fixed assets, and related financial difficulties.* These financial problems are also among the major causes of new venture failures.

A comprehensive and systematic feasibility analysis should identify these dangers, if they exist, and indicate ways of controlling them.

* * * The essence of a feasibility analysis for an intended new venture is thus to find reasonably conclusive answers to some very basic but also very difficult questions: What will it take to implement the new venture idea? Will it sell? What will it cost? Will it show a profit?

* * *

TECHNICAL FEASIBILITY ANALYSIS

Every entrepreneurial idea—be it the production of a product or the provision of a service—has technical aspects that should be carefully analyzed before any effort toward implementation of the idea is undertaken. The two most important steps in this process are 1) identifying the critical technical specifications, and 2) testing the product or service to find out whether it meets performance specifications.

Identifying Critical Technical Specifications

The evaluation of a new venture idea should start with identifying the technical requirements that are market critical and thus mandatory to satisfying the expectations of potential customers. Although a wide range of requirements may be critical, the more important technical requirements are:

- functional design of the product and attractiveness in appearance
- flexibility, permitting ready modification of the external features of the product to meet customer demands or technological and competitive changes
- durability of the materials from which the product is made
- reliability, ensuring performance as expected under normal operating conditions
- product safety, posing no potential dangers under normal operating conditions
- reasonable utility—an acceptable rate of obsolescence
- ease and low cost of maintenance
- standardization through elimination of unnecessary variety among potentially interchangeable parts
- ease of processing, or manufacture
- ease in handling and use.

This list shows the broad range of technical requirements that must be analyzed. The results of this investigation provide a basis for deciding whether a new venture idea is really feasible from a technical point of view. However, in conducting a technical analysis along these lines, the entrepreneur must realize from the outset that there are trade-offs between technical excellence and associated cost.

* * *

Developing and Testing the Product

Product development and testing may include engineering studies, laboratory testing, evaluation of alternative materials, and the fabrication of various breadboard models and prototypes for field testing. At every stage the positive and negative results of the investigation must be carefully weighed and the necessary adjustments made.

* * *

ASSESSING MARKET OPPORTUNITIES

Assembling, screening, and analyzing relevant information about the market and the marketability of its product are basic in judging the potential success of an intended new venture. Three major aspects to this procedure are:

1. investigating market potential and identifying potential customers (or users)
2. analyzing the extent to which the new enterprise might exploit a potential market
3. determining the actual market opportunities and risks through market testing.

Analysis of Market Potential

* * *

Unfortunately, many budding entrepreneurs are so enamored of their new venture idea that they neglect to probe for the existence of a market or they conduct market research simply to validate their beliefs. In contrast, wise entrepreneurs spend considerable effort in identifying the actual market potential. They will guard against slanting the market research design through personal bias.

Identifying the Market Potential

The market potential is an expression of the maximum sales opportunities for a particular product or service during a stated period of time, for example, one year. An estimation of the market potential should ideally involve both the current demand for the product and a projection of future market trends. Although the literature recommends a variety of guidelines for identifying and estimating the market potential of a new venture, there is no one approach that is clearly superior to others. In general it is advisable to follow three steps:

1. identify the specific end-users of the product or service
2. identify the major market segments, that is, relatively homogeneous customer categories
3. determine or estimate the potential volume of purchases within each market segment and the summation of all segments.

The first step, identifying potential customers or end-users, may in some cases be fairly easy, because the product makes it obvious who would want it. For example, the maker of electronic micro chips to be used solely in minicalculators has a clearly defined potential customer base. In other cases much investigation may be required to identify potential users. For example, a producer of electronic minicircuits with a wide range of applications may find it difficult to determine who the most promising customers might be. Answers to the following questions should be sought to identify potential users:

Who are the potential buyers of the product? In the case of a consumer product, what are the personal characteristics of the customers, such as age, sex, income level, educational background? In the case of an industrial product, what are the characteristics of the industry that may use this product, such as the size of the industry, number of firms, and geographical dispersion?

Where are the potential buyers located?

Why would customers want to buy this product? What are their buying habits? How often do they buy? What is the size of the average order?

What is the total monthly or annual demand for this product?

How cyclical is the demand?

What is the potential growth of this market?

Once the likely customers have been identified, the second step is to classify them into relatively homogeneous categories—each having similar, identifiable characteristics. Typical significant characteristics are the potential customers' physical location, their demographic characteristics, the channels of distribution by which they can best be reached, and the advertising media to which they seem to be most responsive. This categorization of potential users is critical because it later enables the new venture organization to select specific categories, or market segments, by matching its own capabilities against what is needed to attract and gain the loyalty of these customer groups.

The third step involves estimating the potential consumption of the new product or service by each market segment immediately and in future periods. This task is obviously the most crucial aspect in any attempt to determine the market potential of a new venture. One way to get information is to select a representative test market, a geographically limited market area in which the new product is actually marketed. From the results of this market test the total market potential may be estimated.

A less time consuming and less costly approach is to investigate relatively constant, measurable relationships—so-called ratios of usage—between the use of the new product and some statistical measure that is known or that can be reliably estimated. For example, the market potential of a new, optional antismog device for passenger automobiles is clearly related to new car production and the number of cars currently in use. * * *

These three steps indicate the complexity of estimating the market potential of a new product. But in spite of the difficulties, an attempt should be made to get a reasonably reliable appraisal of the market potential. The essential aim is to find out whether the market or some segment of it would be large enough to support the new entry. In addition, the entrepreneur ultimately needs to know the rate of penetration of the market that the new company might realistically achieve over a given period of time. * * * With this awareness the new company's short-and long-term potential sales volume, the attendant costs, and finally the profits that might be realized from a given level of sales, can be appraised.

Estimating Price (Cost)–Volume Relationships

Once the total market potential of a new product has been established by summing the potential volume of purchases per market segment, the impact of strategic factors such as pricing and promotion on the total volume of sales revenues must be considered. The entrepreneur will want to know, for example, how various price levels or differences in the amount of promotional support may affect the total volume of sales. The total volume of sales, in turn, will have an effect on the cost structure. Assuming certain economies of scale, unit costs would be reduced by increasing the total volume of output. However, a higher level of output may find a market only at lower prices. For this reason it is important to find out how much the prospective consumers are willing to pay for the new product or service. It must not be overlooked that the price should represent the value of the product in the mind of the consumer and not simply the sum of all costs plus a desired profit margin. The pricing strategy of a firm cannot ignore the customers' concept of value. The entrepreneur should therefore find out how specific customer groups will respond to specific prices. * * *

The economies of scale should also be determined: How would the costs per unit of output change with a higher or lower level of production? To answer this question the entrepreneur should try to determine total costs for various levels of production and the resultant unit costs. This effort will also give some idea about the optimum size of the enterprise. The optimum size is defined as one that obtains, in a given state of technology, the lowest average unit cost of production and distribution. It may be that the entrepreneur does not command the financial resources to establish a business of the optimum size. However, a significant difference between the actual size of the firm and the ideal optimum size will probably increase the competitive pressures with which the firm will have to cope.

The estimates developed to this point should be modified by factors reflecting confidence in their reliability. * * *

The data obtained by analyzing the market potential and the impact of marketing strategy decisions should preferably be summarized in the form of a preliminary projected income statement as shown in Table 3–2.

TABLE 3–2. PROJECTED INCOME STATEMENT

		Periods*				
	Calculation	1	2	3	4	● ● ● n
(1) Potential unit sales						
(2) Average unit price						
(3) Potential sales revenue	(1) × (2)					
(4) Unit manufacturing costs						

	Calculation	Periods* 1	2	3	4	● ● ●	n
(5) Cost of goods sold	(1) × (4)						
(6) Other costs							
(7) Profit before tax	(3) − (5 + 6)						
(8) Tax							
(9) Net profit (or loss)	(7) − (8)						

On the basis of an assessment of the market potential, the entrepreneur can project the physical volume of sales during future periods. * * * Multiplying the average unit price by the projected unit sales gives the projected sales revenue. Deducting from this figure the manufacturing, distribution, and other cost items, and the taxes to be paid, gives the projected net profit (or loss). That is the essential criterion for assessing the economic (market) feasibility of a prospective new venture.

Sources of Market Information

The preceding sections have dealt with categories of information that must be investigated to evaluate the existing and future market opportunities for a new venture. The purpose of this section is to describe major sources of information for such an analysis.

The entrepreneur will rarely find existing market data that relate directly to the new product or service. Two approaches may be taken to obtain desired data: 1) Conduct a survey that is specifically designed to gather information on a particular project. Information generated in this way is referred to as *primary data.* 2) Locate relevant data published by organizations such as the U.S. Bureau of the Census (for example, Census of Manufacturers), other government agencies, trade associations, chambers of commerce, and university bureaus of business research. Information of this kind is referred to as *secondary data.*

Gathering primary data is usually much more costly and time consuming than accumulating secondary data. Secondary data may have the drawback of not quite meeting the specific requirements of the entrepreneur. It is wise, however, to start by looking for secondary data. If the required information cannot be obtained in this way, a specifically designed market research study should be conducted.

* * *

The Role of Market Testing

A systematic assessment of the market opportunities and an evaluation of the likely success of a new venture usually requires a market test.

Market testing requires that the new product be scrutinized and evaluated by potential buyers. Among the preferred methods are displaying the product at trade shows, selling it in a limited number of selected areas, and using test markets where the receptivity of prospective buyers may be closely observed and analyzed. A market test can give the following important information: 1) the likely sales volume and profitability when the new product is marketed on a larger scale, 2) an indication of the sales volume at different price levels, 3) an indication of the soundness of the chosen market strategy, and 4) information about the key influences that would make people want to buy. Market testing also gives clues to opportunities in marketing, distribution, and servicing. The testing process may reveal unsuspected weaknesses or shortcomings that require drastic alteration or even scrapping of the new venture idea. In such a case, market testing becomes a means for limiting losses and liabilities.

The entrepreneur should be aware of the drawbacks as well as the advantages of market testing. The time consumed by the procedure may cause delay in the realization of the new venture idea. The new product or service may be prematurely exposed to competitors, which would give them time to organize a counter-strategy. Market testing can be relatively expensive. The small business owner should use ingenuity to mount an adequate market testing program without straining customarily limited financial resources.

As has been implied, market testing must be carefully planned to produce reliable results. The desired data should be sought only after clearly specifying the critical variables. Particular attention must be paid to the selection of test areas, length of the test period, and the techniques for gathering and analyzing the test data.

* * *

FINANCIAL FEASIBILITY ANALYSIS

A financial feasibility analysis is basic to determining the financial resources required for a particular level of activity and the profits that can be expected. The financial requirements and the returns can vary considerably, depending upon the selection of alternatives that exist for most new ventures. For example, an entrepreneur may have the component parts of a new product manufactured in-house, which requires investment in production machinery and perhaps buildings. In contrast, manufacture of the new product may be subcontracted to outside suppliers; here the firm becomes essentially a warehousing and marketing operation with little investment in fixed assets. In this case the profit margin of the firm might prove smaller. However, the total return on invested capital could be higher than in the case of a fully integrated operation. * * *

* * * These examples show that the financial feasibility of a new venture depends to a large extent on the alternatives chosen for starting it. One way of launching an entrepreneurial idea may turn out to be financially infeasible; an alternate approach may very well lead to financially acceptable results.

The analysis of the financial feasibility of a new venture requires probing various alternatives for implementation. The analytical approach to this problem focuses on four essential steps:

1. Determining the total financial requirement by itemizing the operationally necessary funds.

2. Determining the available financial resources and their costs, which implies examining sources of funds and cost of capital.

3. Determining the future cash flow that can be expected from the operation by means of a cash flow analysis at relatively short intervals, preferably monthly.

4. Determining the expected return through a return-on-investment analysis.

The Total Financial Requirement

The first step in a financial feasibility calculation is a detailed analysis of all the financial obligations and pay-out requirements that the new venture would be expected to meet over the foreseeable future. This information can be accumulated and organized in a variety of ways. The scheme shown in Table 3–4 is one guide for the development of a financial requirement statement. In a new venture it is imperative to project the financial requirements—preferably on a month-by-month basis—as far into the future as can be done with reasonable accuracy, as Table 3–4 shows.

The estimates for each category of expenditure should be as detailed as possible for each period and should carefully take into account when payments become due. In making these forecasts of the expected financial requirements it must always be kept in mind that environmental dynamics such as price increases may raise start-up and operating expenditures considerably. Also, as the firm grows it is likely to require more cash to cover investments in inventories and fixed assets and to experience a lag in collecting increasingly larger receivables.

* * *

TABLE 3–4. FINANCIAL REQUIREMENTS STATEMENT

	Period 1	. . . Period 2	. . . Period *n*
Start-up expenses			
Product (business) development expenses (expenditures associated with the conceptual development of the venture idea)			
Legal expenses (expenditures for all legal matters including patent search and registration procedures)			
Product testing expenses (expenditures associated with the development and testing of models and prototypes)			
Expenditures for market opportunity analyses			
Expenditures for other feasibility analyses			
Miscellaneous business development and start-up expenditures (such as expenditures for materials, test equipment, and salaries and wages during the start-up phase)			

	Period 1	. . . Period 2	. . . Period *n*
Required fixed investments			
Buildings			
Equipment and machinery			
Office equipment			
Expenditures for the installation of equipment and machinery			
Operating expenses			
Material and other supplies			
Wages, salaries			
Marketing and promotion expenditures			
General administrative expenditures			
Rent			
Interest payments			
Repayments on loans			
Insurance			
Expenditures for utilities			
Taxes			
Contingency funds			
Funds to cover expenditures caused by unforeseen developments or by changes in the venture implementation strategy			
Total required payments per period			

Available Financial Resources and Their Costs

The second essential step in the financial feasibility analysis is projecting the financial resources available and the funds that would be generated by operations. * * *

In determining potentially available financial resources, one should distinguish between short-, intermediate-, and long-term sources of financing. Short-term sources of funds are generally those scheduled for repayment within one year. Two major sources are trade credit from suppliers, represented by accounts payable, and short-term loans from banks or other lending institutions. * * *

Intermediate-term sources of finance are those available for one to three years, or in some cases up to five years. The major categories are term loans from commercial banks or insurance companies, sales contracts, and lease financing. * * *

Long-term sources of finance are long-term loans from investment banks, equity that can be raised, and eventually reinvested earnings. The cost of long-term loans is, as in other loans, the interest rate that has to be paid. The cost of equity is more difficult to determine; it is essentially the rate of return on equity that the entrepreneur expects. Reinvested earnings should also be considered to cost at least the same rate as equity capital.

* * *

Anticipated Cash Flows

When projected sales, the associated financial requirements, and the available financial resources are known, it is possible to determine the anticipated cash flow and the ways in which a negative cash flow may be countered. Table 3–6 shows a breakdown of the information needed for cash flow planning.

As the table indicates, it is important to determine systematically, for a series of time periods, the anticipated operating inflows, outflows, and resultant net cash flow. Every business requires, in addition, a minimum cash balance to meet emergencies. A negative cash flow plus the desired minimum cash balance gives the amount that must be financed. The next step is to identify the sources of funds to meet the financial requirements at every period.

The net cash flow of a new venture tends to be highly negative in the beginning. Eventually it must turn positive and yield a profit if the venture is to be successful. A detailed cash flow and financial analysis along the lines shown in Table 3–6 is fundamental to assessing the feasibility of a new venture. The final step in this analysis is determining the return on investment the venture will yield.

Anticipated Return on Investment

The ultimate test of the feasibility of a new venture is whether it will yield a satisfactory return on the invested capital. One way of calculating the rate of return is to relate the average earnings expected over a given period of time either to the total amount of investment (return on investment) or the net worth of the organization (return on equity). Both ratios are then compared with the potential yield from alternative investment opportunities. The entrepreneur can judge from this comparison whether the expected return from a new venture would be acceptable. * * *

TABLE 3–6. CASH FLOW PLANNING

Cash Flow and Financing Transactions	Period 1	. . . Period 2	. . . Period *n*
(I) *Cash outflows*			
Start-up expenses			
•			
•			
•			
Fixed investments			
•			
•			
•			
Operating expenses			
•			
•			
•			
Total cash outflow			

Cash Flow and Financing Transactions	1	2	n
(II) *Cash inflows*			
Cash sales			
Accounts receivable			
Total operating inflows			
(III) *Net cash flow* [(II)–(I)]			
(IV) *Desired minimum cash balance*			
(V) *Total amount of funds required* [(III), if negative, + (IV)]			
(VI) *Sources of funds to meet financing requirements*			
Short-term			
Net trade credit			
Commercial loans			
Intermediate-term			
Term loans			
Conditional sales contracts			
Long-term			
Long-term loans			
Equity			
Total financing			

Projecting financial results of a planned venture requires certain assumptions about market and cost behavior. Every assumption reflects a degree of uncertainty and risk. To arrive at an explicit appreciation of the risk factor in a financial feasibility analysis one must indicate the degree of probability associated with each important variable, such as the expected market potential, the selling price, and the operating costs.

* * *

ASSESSING ORGANIZATIONAL CAPABILITIES

Every business enterprise requires people with various skills and talents to work cooperatively toward accomplishing a common organizational objective. Even though the new product may be superior and the financial resources ample, it is nevertheless people who are the organization's source of vitality; it is people whose activities bring its success. An accurate evaluation of the total personnel requirements and especially of the required managerial talent is an indispensable part of a feasibility analysis of a new venture. This analysis requires that three questions be answered:

1. What personnel skills and talents are available and what organization structure, if any, already exists?

2. What kind of organization and what talents will be needed initially for the effective implementation of the new venture?

3. What skills and talents will be required once the new venture starts to succeed and grow?

* * * Experience has shown that it is important to distinguish between questions 2 and 3. The successful launching of a new venture requires the initiative and drive of an entrepreneur. Unfortunately this person frequent-

ly does not have the skill, or the patience, for managing routine day-to-day affairs of a business that has grown past some critical size. * * *

The entrepreneur faces some problems in staffing the new business. The capabilities of people already available to the new firm tend to be overestimated and the difficulty of attracting new people with the skills needed tends to be underestimated. Qualified people who have clearly demonstrated their competence are not easily persuaded to join a new organization with an uncertain future. * * * For these reasons the personnel requirements for the new business should be estimated and planned with as much care as its financial requirements.

ANALYSIS OF THE COMPETITION

Practically all business enterprises in a market economy face intelligent competition. A new enterprise cannot survive unless it offers and maintains competitive advantages such as a superior product, better service, shorter delivery time, or a relatively lower price.

* * * The feasibility studies for a new venture should therefore include an analysis of competitive pressures and of the actions competitors might take against it. This analysis should be done separately from the market feasibility analysis, although the issues are obviously interrelated.

Every business generally has to contend with two major types of competitive pressures: 1) direct competition from products or services very similar to its own that appeal to approximately the same market, and 2) indirect competition from substitutes. It is important to recognize both types of competitive pressures and to judge how their impact on the new venture may change over time.

A pragmatic approach to the analysis of competitive pressures focuses on three tasks:

1. identifying major potential competitors

2. identifying the various strategies and tactics the competitors can employ and their potential impact on the operation of the planned venture

3. identifying the specific competitive advantages the planned venture offers and developing a strategy based on the consistent emphasis of these advantages.

* * *

Whether or not the attorney gets deeply involved in matters of business judgment, he or she may raise questions which cause the clients to realize some of the difficulties with their plans. This often leads to the complaint the attorney is ruining the deal. Must the attorney take heed of this complaint, or is it an inevitable by-product of his or her doing a thorough job?

Klein & Coffee, Business Organization & Finance, Legal & Economic Principles

61–63 (9th ed. 2004).

E. "SPOILING THE DEAL"

One of the interesting and significant aspects of the process of drafting partnership agreements (and other business agreements as well) has to do with the concern often expressed by experienced lawyers that their efforts might "spoil the deal." One of the most important functions of the lawyer is to look beyond the days of heady optimism and mutual good will that may characterize the initiation of a business venture. The lawyer must bear in mind that as the needs of the parties and the nature of the business change, as the partners encounter issues of business strategy on which they cannot agree, as the firm confronts the often harsh vicissitudes of business existence, the rules that are laid down in the partnership agreement may become critical. There are choices about how these rules should be drafted and many lawyers consider that they should explain those choices to their clients. But this gets tricky, for if the would-be partners start worrying too much about the problems that might arise and become excessively concerned about the difficulty of solving them, they may become overly anxious and walk away from a venture that would have been good for them. Moreover, the parties may reasonably believe that they can trust each other to reach a fair and equitable resolution of any potential conflicts as they arise and that focusing on such problems at the outset may send a bad message about expectations of trust, cooperation, and fairness.

Suppose, for example, that all the partners expect to work in the business and to participate fully in management decisions. At the outset they may be in complete accord on who should do what and how the business should be operated. Given this state of mind, they may have ignored the question of what rules should apply in the event of disagreement. The lawyer might think that it is precisely his or her function to make the client or clients aware of that potential issue (among others). The lawyer might want the parties to choose between, say, a majority voting rule and a unanimity rule for resolving certain kinds of disputes. As the partners begin to focus on the choice, they may, for the first time, begin to be fully aware of the potential difficulties of co-ownership. One issue leads to another. Suppose, for example, that the parties agree on control by majority vote. They might then begin to worry about whether there should be some provision for allowing a dissatisfied dissenter to withdraw and, if so, at what price. (A lawyer may, by the way, represent more than one potential partner, and sometimes may represent all of them—for the obvious reason that hiring a separate lawyer for each partner would be too costly. This kind of role creates special problems for the lawyer in defining his obligations to people whose interest may conflict, who may at some future time want his help in seeking an advantage over other partner-clients, etc.)

Some lawyers think it is their responsibility not only to try to raise all the significant issues with which their clients may be confronted in the future but also to be sure that the clients understand those issues. Others will tend to pay less attention to such matters, fearing, as suggested, that it is too easy for the parties, because of their unfamiliarity with the law, or with business, to exaggerate the significance of the problems and, consequently, to forgo a business opportunity that the lawyer thinks they ought not to forgo. This kind of lawyer may express the idea by saying that he did not want to "spoil the deal." Other lawyers will tend more often to think that if raising issues and pointing to problems kills a deal then it deserves to die. Obviously there are no formulas to tell the lawyer how to act with respect to this basic issue of client-handling strategy. No two deals, no two sets of clients, and no two lawyers are alike. There is no widely agreed upon "correct" approach. What does seem plain, however, and what is most significant for our purposes, is that the phenomenon of widespread lawyer concern with the possibility of frustrating worthwhile business ventures reveals, first, the difficulty and complexity of the problems of organization of joint economic activity and, in turn, a belief by some experienced practitioners that excessive anxieties and antagonisms may be aroused by efforts to cope with such difficulties and complexities.

Attempting to anticipate and plan for future events raises a further judgment question beyond the concern with "spoiling the deal." Preparing a document which tries to cope with every possible contingency, no matter how remote, is a costly proposition. Moreover, keep in mind Professor Corneel's admonition about the need to preserve a certain degree of flexibility. Presumably, the planner must seek a balance.

Another problem for the planning attorney occurs when clients ask him or her for an opinion on the legal consequences of a proposed transaction. Among the first things every law student discovers is that the law does not always provide clear cut answers. This reality of uncertainty may be comfortable to the litigator, since his or her job is to make the best argument for a result favorable to the client. (While prediction of outcome is necessary to litigation and settlement strategy, uncertainty is simply part of the equation—indeed it may provide the major impetus for compromise.) In the planning context, however, such uncertainty is frustrating, and no time is it more so than when clients ask the attorney for a formal opinion upon which they plan to predicate a transaction involving large sums of money. What should the attorney do? What dangers exist if the attorney's opinion turns out to be wrong?

Committee on Corporations of the Business Law Section of the State Bar of California, *Report of the Committee on Corporations Regarding Legal Opinions in Business Transactions*

14 Pac.L.J. 1001, 1004–1007, 1009–1011, 1013–1015 (1983).

* * *

II. DEFINITION AND PURPOSE OF A LEGAL OPINION

The term "legal opinion" has received varying definitions from commentators depending upon the context in which it is used. In the context of business transactions, a legal opinion can be more accurately defined as a formal writing prepared by a lawyer, expressing the lawyer's informed understanding of the legal principles generally applicable to a specific transaction or applicable to a particular aspect of such a transaction.

Legal opinions in business transactions are frequently prepared either at the request of the lawyer's client in order to furnish the client with information regarding the probable legal consequences of a contemplated action or transaction. More commonly, they are prepared in order to satisfy a requirement to the transaction's closing which has been imposed through negotiation by the parties to the transaction and their counsel. A client may also request a formal legal opinion, not for the client's own guidance, but rather for delivery to a government agency or presentation to third parties, either directly or in a prospectus or annual financial report.

The following are several of the more common reasons for the preparation and delivery of a legal opinion.

1. To provide assurance that an intended course of action is lawful or that certain acceptable legal consequences will follow from an intended course of action (or, conversely, that certain unacceptable legal consequences will not result from the proposed course of action);

2. To confirm that certain legal relationships exist or have been created;

3. To provide a warning to the recipient that there are certain legal risks in proceeding with the transaction;

4. To resolve disputes or uncertainties (*e.g.*, an opinion expressed as to the meaning of particular language in a contract);

5. To satisfy contractual requirements (*e.g.*, an opinion given by issuer's counsel pursuant to a stock purchase or bank loan agreement);

6. To satisfy regulatory requirements (*e.g.*, an opinion given in connection with the qualification of securities under the California Corporate Securities Law of 1968 or their registration under the Securities Act of 1933);

7. To provide a basis upon which a regulatory body may rely in its own interpretation of a fact situation (*e.g.*, an opinion relied on by the staff of the Securities and Exchange Commission in issuing a "no-action" letter);

8. To resolve a question raised by other professionals and to provide an authoritative basis for statements, reports and opinions with respect to matters on which other professionals are not competent to make judgments, or for which they are unwilling to assume responsibility (*e.g.*, an opinion provided on local law for a general counsel); and

9. To provide a defense to allegations of wrongful conduct or assessment of penalties through reliance in good faith on an opinion of counsel.

III. LEGAL STANDARDS APPLICABLE TO PREPARATION OF AN OPINION

* * * Generally speaking, a lawyer is expected to be well informed and to exercise "such skill, prudence and diligence as lawyers of ordinary skill and capacity commonly possess and exercise in the performance of the tasks which they undertake." In addition, a lawyer is expected to discover "rules of law which, although not commonly known, may readily be found by standard research techniques." When a matter falls within a recognized area of legal specialty, a more stringent "prudent expert rule" is generally applied.

There is little case law that specifically involves errors in rendering legal opinions, but the same or similar legal standards no doubt apply. An attorney should afford ample time to research and interpret applicable legal principles, investigate the facts which underlie the opinion and identify areas of uncertainty, if any, in the interpretation and application of legal principles. Early research and investigation will also afford the attorney a greater opportunity to isolate potential problem areas and to negotiate an appropriate form of the opinion.

IV. PREPARATION OF THE OPINION

* * *

B. Problem Areas and Inappropriate Subjects for Opinion

* * *

2. Factual Opinions

The lawyer should always bear in mind that the function of his or her legal opinion is to present informed judgments and analysis regarding matters of law, not factual statements which the parties are, no doubt, in a better position to verify.

* * *

[W]hen an attorney is asked to render opinions of mixed law and fact, the attorney should state clearly those facts upon which the conclusions of law are based, particularly when reasonable attorneys might differ as to the conclusions.

* * *

3. Opinions Regarding Issues of Legal Uncertainty

A third area of disagreement involves requested opinions concerning legal issues that may be appropriate for inclusion in an opinion but are subject to a generally recognized and substantial legal uncertainty. If the uncertainty extends only to a portion of the matter covered by the opinion, the question is frequently resolved by a "qualification" to the opinion expressed. The "qualification" may be a statement that the particular opinion does not cover the effect of a certain law or laws.

* * *

The situation is different when the uncertainty goes to the principal subject of the opinion. In such cases the lawyer requesting the opinion is often seeking legal "insurance" rather than legal "assurance."

* * * [A] lawyer should not render an opinion when there is a substantial legal uncertainty regarding an issue. If there is disagreement regarding the existence or degree of the legal uncertainty, a compromise is sometimes reached, and a "reasoned" opinion is rendered. In such an opinion, the lawyer does not merely render a legal conclusion; instead, the lawyer presents a discussion of statutory and judicial authorities, indicates that the matter is uncertain or "not free from doubt," and states a prediction of the likely judicial resolution of the matter if the issue is appropriately presented to a court.

* * *

D. The Form and Elements of the Opinion

There is no prescribed form for a legal opinion. Opinions, however, have developed a certain uniformity because of their continued use in similar business transactions, such as business acquisitions, secured and unsecured loan transactions, and securities issuances. The legal opinion in general will cover (1) certain introductory matter, such as the date, the identity of the recipient of the opinion, the role of the lawyer giving the opinion and the purpose for which the opinion is given, (2) a general or specific recitation of the factual and legal matters reviewed by the lawyer, including in some instances a statement of certain factual assumptions, and the reliance of the lawyer upon such matters of fact and law, (3) the legal conclusions covered by the opinion, and any qualifications to these legal conclusions not covered by the opinion, (4) special matters peculiar to the particular opinion, such as matters relative to opinions of local counsel in other jurisdictions, specific limitations on the use of the opinion, and the lawyer's qualification with respect to his willingness to pass upon matters of law in jurisdictions other than those in which the lawyer is licensed, and (5) the form of signature.

1. Introductory Matters

* * *

Addressee. The opinion is normally addressed to a specified party to the business transaction in an individual capacity, to a party as representative of a larger group, or to an identified class of persons.

* * *

The Committee's view is that the only person or persons entitled to rely upon an opinion are the person or persons to whom the opinion is specifically addressed and that no additional limitation need be expressed in the opinion. Many firms, however, as a matter of caution include a sentence at the conclusion of the opinion to the following effect:

> This opinion is rendered solely for your information and assistance in connection with the above transaction, and may not be relied upon by any other person or for any other purpose without our prior written consent.

There are instances in which the opinion is to be relied upon by other persons or legal counsel, such as an opinion delivered to an underwriter concerning the validity of a proposed stock issuance which is also to be relied upon by the issuer's transfer agent and registrar, or an opinion rendered by a local counsel in a transaction when the lawyers principally involved will rely on the opinion to render their own opinion. In such cases, the opinion should specifically describe who, in addition to the addressee, may rely on the opinion.

The foregoing discussion does not deal with situations in which the opinion is being rendered to a client, and the lawyer knows or has reason to believe that the client will be utilizing the opinion in dealing with third parties. In such cases, the lawyer's responsibility probably extends to these additional persons, and limitations expressed in the opinion will likely have little legal effect. For this reason the potential liability of the opining lawyer is greater and therefore the issuance of such an opinion should be considered carefully, particularly with respect to the need for greater qualification of the advice given.

* * *

What can be done if there is a need for greater certainty than provided by an attorney's opinion? One possibility, if a government agency administers the law in question, is to seek guidance from the agency. For example, if the issue concerns the federal tax consequences of a proposed transaction, one may attempt to obtain a ruling from the I.R.S.

Smith, Tax Rulings—Their Use and Abuse

1970 U.So.Cal.Tax Inst. 663–684.

* * *

RULING LETTERS

There are several kinds of "rulings" issued by the Service: an information letter, a determination letter, a closing agreement, a technical advice letter, and a ruling letter.

An information letter is a statement issued either by the National Office or by the District Director that refers only to well-established interpretations of the tax law without dealing with a specific set of facts. It is issued where the request seeks general information on a subject matter. In some situations, it may be a useful substitute for a ruling letter, particularly where time is of the essence. * * *

A determination letter is a statement issued by a District Director in response to an inquiry involving those principles or precedents previously announced by the National Office. It will be issued only where the specific facts of the particular transaction are set forth in the request. A determination letter is requested, for example, in the matter of the qualification of pension and profit-sharing plans.

A closing agreement is an agreement between the Commissioner of Internal Revenue, or his delegate, and a taxpayer with respect to specific issues entered into pursuant to the authority provided by Section 7121. Quite often, it is based on a ruling signed by the Commissioner or his delegate and will be a final and conclusive determination of the specific tax issues except upon a showing of fraud, malfeasance, or misrepresentation of a material fact.

Technical advice is a statement issued by the National Office to the District Director concerning the interpretation and application of the tax laws to a specific set of facts. It is a means of assisting Service personnel, establishing positions, and maintaining consistency in applying the law. * * *

A ruling letter is a statement issued by the National Office that interprets and applies the tax laws to a specific set of facts. In most instances, a ruling letter deals either with a prospective transaction or a transaction which is completed but which is not yet reflected in a tax return. It is this type of ruling with which this article is principally concerned.

The issuance of any of the above statements by the Service is entirely discretionary.

* * *

PRELIMINARIES TO PREPARATION OF RULING REQUEST

It should first be ascertained whether the issue is one on which the Service will rule. Because of the inherent factual nature of some issues, the Service may decline to issue a ruling. Most of the "no ruling areas" and "ordinarily no ruling areas" are published in Revenue Procedure 69–6.* The Service will also refuse to issue a ruling involving issues which the Service is litigating or issues with respect to which litigation policy is not resolved. In addition, the Service will decline to rule where the transaction is not iminent [sic], where the transaction lacks a bona fide business purpose, or where the principal purpose is the reduction of federal taxes.

In addition to the "no ruling areas," the National Office will not rule where returns already have been filed and the transaction is within the

* [More recently see Rev. Proc. 2007–3, 2007–1 I.R.B. 108. Ed.]

jurisdiction of the District Director. It may, however, be possible to obtain a waiver of jurisdiction from the District Director so that the National Office can rule, or it may be possible to obtain technical advice after the fact.

In addition, the Service will sometimes decline to issue a ruling where the matter involves recently enacted legislation and no regulations have been promulgated. Where the legislation appears clear, however, the Service may rule. In certain instances, a ruling involving recently enacted legislation may simply contain a caveat to the effect that the ruling is without effect if regulations, when issued, conflict with its holding.

* * *

Pros and cons for requesting a ruling

Where the ruling is not required to satisfy statutory requirements, it does not automatically follow that a ruling should nonetheless be sought. On the one hand, an advance ruling will give the parties practical assurance that the transaction will be treated as determined therein unless the facts vary materially from those submitted in the request. The Service's policy is to honor its rulings where relied upon in good faith by the taxpayer, even though the Service's position may have changed.

Also, in some instances, the Service personnel will recommend changes in the proposed transaction which will aid in reaching the desired tax result. In a complicated tax matter, an experienced tax law specialist, because of his familiarity with administrative precedents, can be of great help.

Another benefit in requesting a ruling is that it enables the parties, if questions arise concerning the proposed handling of the transaction, to make required changes; this obviously cannot be done in consummated transactions.

A further benefit in seeking a ruling is to settle the issue before it is examined by a revenue agent who, by the nature of his position, has a more general knowledge of the income tax law and may not be familiar with the specific provisions of the Code involved in a particular transaction.

Since the proposed transaction may not clearly be within the statute or the Regulations, a ruling letter could thus prevent drawn-out confrontations with revenue agents and eliminate the hazards and expense of litigation.

However, other factors may argue against requesting a ruling. Are the parties in a position to wait four to six months before the ruling is issued? Has the National Office already taken an adverse position? Are there related issues where the Service's attitude is known to be adverse and which could be raised by applying for a ruling?

It should be kept in mind that the Service will rule adversely on some related matters, even if rulings on such points were not requested. * * * The National Office will often take a stricter approach to an issue than the revenue agent. This is due to the reluctance of the Service to rule in advance where the conclusion is not entirely clear because of the facts involved and because the facts are presented only by the taxpayer.

It is possible, of course, that a transaction is so clearly within the Code and the Regulations that it can be consummated without requesting and receiving a ruling. The cost and delay involved in getting a ruling would, in such situations, argue against applying for one.*

PREPARING THE REQUEST FOR RULING

The initial step in preparing a request for ruling should be to become familiar with Revenue Procedure 69–1, which describes the requirements for an acceptable ruling application.** It is about as important to understand the procedural niceties involved in requesting a ruling as it is to understand the substantive tax laws involved.

Also, in recent years the Service has published guidelines to aid practitioners in requesting rulings in certain specific areas.

* * *

THE EFFECT OF THE RULING

A private ruling letter is a confidential communication which applies only to the particular taxpayer with respect to the transaction described therein. It has no precedent value * * *.

A ruling which is found to be in error or is no longer in accord with a position of the Service may be modified or revoked. However, if the taxpayer has relied upon the ruling and the error was not of his making, the National Office will normally not modify or revoke the ruling letter retroactively. In the exceptional case where the Service considers retroactive revocation, it will examine all relevant factors to determine if there has been any material misrepresentation or misstatement of fact, whether the facts subsequently developed are materially different from the facts on which the ruling was based, and whether there has been any change in applicable law. The Service will also make a determination with respect to the good-faith nature of the reliance upon the ruling. If a ruling is issued covering a continuous action or a series of actions and it is determined that the ruling is in error or no longer in accord with the position of the National Office, the Assistant Commissioner (Technical) ordinarily would limit the retroactivity of the modification or revocation to a date not earlier than that on which the original ruling was modified or revoked. In this type of situation, the taxpayer will be able to rely upon the ruling until the date of revocation. Any further action with respect to the transaction will be subject to the then applicable position of the Service.

* * *

Published revenue rulings, as distinguished from private rulings, are administrative precedents only. They may be safely relied upon by the tax practitioner only to the extent that his particular situation is substantially

* [The Internal Revenue Service also charges a user fee (the amount of which varies depending upon the nature and subject matter of the ruling) for rulings. Rev. Proc. 2001–1, 2007–1 I.R.B. 1 (Appendix A). Ed.]

** [More recently see Rev. Proc. 2007–1, 2007–1 I.R.B. 1. Ed.]

the same as that in the revenue ruling and only then where the holding is unimpaired by subsequent legislation, regulations, court decisions, or other revenue rulings. Where a published revenue ruling is revoked by the Internal Revenue Service, the effect of the revoked or modified revenue ruling ordinarily will not be retroactive unless the later revenue ruling specifically includes a statement indicating that it is to be applied retroactively. Under Section 7805(b), the Commissioner can provide that revenue rulings will not be applied retroactively.

SOME ABUSES OF THE RULING PROCESS

* * *

The major abuse of the rulings process is the use of such process as a substitute for homework and self-reliance by practitioners. Although maximum assurance is admittedly important in tax and business planning, in many instances such assurance can be given without using the ruling process. An example would be a transaction the tax consequences of which are plainly and unquestionably dealt with in a published revenue ruling. It is difficult to perceive the need for a private ruling under such circumstances, yet there are many such applications. * * *

A second abuse of the rulings process lies in the failure of the practitioner properly to prepare the ruling request. Although Revenue Procedures published by the Service clearly indicate what the Service expects a proper rulings request to contain, the rules of these procedures are honored as much in the breach as in the observance. Particularly is this true with respect to the statement of the grounds for issuing the rulings that have been requested. Failure to include a discussion of the applicable authorities requires the tax law specialist who is handling the request to do the basic research for the practitioner. This is not fair to the tax law specialist or to the Service generally, and it is not fair to other taxpayers whose applications are thereby further delayed.

Another area of abuse is the sometime failure of the practitioner to describe adequately the relevant transactions. Whether consciously or otherwise, it is a too frequent occurrence that the critical parts of a transaction, so far as the tax consequences are concerned, are not stated in the request itself and can be found by the tax law specialist only by a detailed examination of the documents accompanying the ruling request. Again, this requires a tax law specialist to do the practitioner's work. It delays not only the application involved but other applications pending on his desk.

* * *

SECTION B. ETHICAL CONSIDERATIONS FOR THE BUSINESS ATTORNEY

Professional responsibility concerns pervade every area of legal practice. Business planning is no exception. While many of the ethical problems faced by business attorneys are no different either in their nature or frequency than for other practitioners, several problems tend to present a continuing challenge particularly to lawyers in this field.

1. Typical Conflict of Interest Problems

One of the most common ethics problems faced by business attorneys is the recurrent request that they represent several parties involved in a given transaction. For example, parties going into business may ask an attorney to draft the documents (such as a partnership agreement or articles of incorporation) needed to get the venture started. Later, parties involved in a business may wish an attorney to draft an agreement for some of them to buy out the others. Is there any potential conflict between the interests of the parties in these situations? If so, can the attorney still represent all the parties? One safe solution is for separate counsel to represent each party. The parties, however, typically will not be sympathetic to the extra costs entailed in this solution. What other solutions are available?

American Bar Association Model Rules of Professional Conduct

(2004).

RULE 1.7 CONFLICT OF INTEREST: CURRENT CLIENTS

(a) Except as provided in paragraph (b), a lawyer shall not represent a client if the representation involves a concurrent conflict of interest. A concurrent conflict of interest exists if:

(1) the representation of one client will be directly adverse to another client; or

(2) there is a significant risk that the representation of one or more clients will be materially limited by the lawyer's responsibilities to another client, a former client or a third person or by a personal interest of the lawyer.

(b) Notwithstanding the existence of a concurrent conflict of interest under paragraph (a), a lawyer may represent a client if:

(1) the lawyer reasonably believes that the lawyer will be able to provide competent and diligent representation to each affected client;

(2) the representation is not prohibited by law;

(3) the representation does not involve the assertion of a claim by one client against another client represented by the lawyer in the same litigation or other proceeding before a tribunal; and

(4) each affected client gives informed consent, confirmed in writing.

Comment

* * *

Identifying Conflicts of Interest: Material Limitation

[8] Even where there is no direct adverseness, a conflict of interest exists if there is a significant risk that a lawyer's ability to consider, recommend or carry out an appropriate course of action for the client will be materially limited as a result of the lawyer's other responsibilities or interests. For example, a lawyer asked to represent several individuals seeking to form a joint venture is likely to be materially limited in the lawyer's ability to recommend or advocate all possible positions that each might take because of the lawyer's duty of loyalty to the others. The conflict in effect forecloses alternatives that would otherwise be available to the client.

* * *

Nonlitigation Conflicts

* * *

[28] Whether a conflict is consentable depends on the circumstances. For example, a lawyer may not represent multiple parties to a negotiation whose interests are fundamentally antagonistic to each other, but common representation is permissible where the clients are generally aligned in interest even though there is some difference in interest among them. Thus, a lawyer may seek to establish or adjust a relationship between clients on an amicable and mutually advantageous basis; for example, in helping to organize a business in which two or more clients are entrepreneurs * * *. The lawyer seeks to resolve potentially adverse interests by developing the parties' mutual interests. Otherwise, each party might have to obtain separate representation, with the possibility of incurring additional cost, complication or even litigation. Given these and other relevant factors, the clients may prefer that the lawyer act for all of them.

Special Considerations in Common Representation

[29] In considering whether to represent multiple clients in the same matter, a lawyer should be mindful that if the common representation fails because the potentially adverse interests cannot be reconciled, the result can be additional cost, embarrassment and recrimination. Ordinarily, the lawyer will be forced to withdraw from representing all of the clients if the common representation fails. In some situations, the risk of failure is so great that multiple representation is plainly impossible. For example, a lawyer cannot undertake common representation of clients where contentious litigation or negotiations between them are imminent or contemplated. Moreover, because the lawyer is required to be impartial between commonly represented clients, representation of multiple clients is improper when it is unlikely that impartiality can be maintained. Generally, if the relationship between the parties has already assumed antagonism, the

possibility that the clients' interests can be adequately served by common representation is not very good. Other relevant factors are whether the lawyer subsequently will represent both parties on a continuing basis and whether the situation involves creating or terminating a relationship between the parties.

* * *

[31] As to the duty of confidentiality, continued common representation will almost certainly be inadequate if one client asks the lawyer not to disclose to the other client information relevant to the common representation. This is so because the lawyer has an equal duty of loyalty to each client, and each client has the right to be informed of anything bearing on the representation that might affect that client's interests and the right to expect that the lawyer will use that information to that client's benefit. See Rule 1.4. The lawyer should, at the outset of the common representation and as part of the process of obtaining each client's informed consent, advise each client that information will be shared and that the lawyer will have to withdraw if one client decides that some matter material to the representation should be kept from the other. In limited circumstances, it may be appropriate for the lawyer to proceed with the representation when the clients have agreed, after being properly informed, that the lawyer will keep certain information confidential. For example, the lawyer may reasonably conclude that failure to disclose one client's trade secrets to another client will not adversely affect representation involving a joint venture between the clients and agree to keep that information confidential with the informed consent of both clients.

[32] When seeking to establish or adjust a relationship between clients, the lawyer should make clear that the lawyer's role is not that of partisanship normally expected in other circumstances and, thus, that the clients may be required to assume greater responsibility for decisions than when each client is separately represented. * * *

[33] Subject to the above limitations, each client in the common representation has the right to loyal and diligent representation and the protection of Rule 1.9 concerning the obligations to a former client. The client also has the right to discharge the lawyer as stated in Rule 1.16.

* * *

An alternative to representing multiple parties or acting as an intermediary might be to represent the business entity (the partnership or corporation). This raises several questions. Can the entity be the client before it comes into legal existence (as would be the situation if the attorney is asked to aid in the formation)? Is a partnership an entity capable of being the client, or is it simply a group of individuals? *Compare* American Bar Ass'n Formal Ethics Opinion 91–361 (July 12, 1991), *with Arpadi v. First MSP Corp.,* 68 Ohio St.3d 453, 628 N.E.2d 1335 (1994). More fundamentally, does representation of the business entity avoid conflicts of interest, or does it create a new one: the possible conflict between the entity's interest and the interest of those running it?

American Bar Association Model Rules of Professional Conduct

(2004).

RULE 1.13 ORGANIZATION AS CLIENT

(a) A lawyer employed or retained by an organization represents the organization acting through its duly authorized constituents.

(b) If a lawyer for an organization knows that an officer, employee or other person associated with the organization is engaged in action, intends to act or refuses to act in a matter related to the representation that is a violation of a legal obligation to the organization, or a violation of law that reasonably might be imputed to the organization, and that is likely to result in substantial injury to the organization, then the lawyer shall proceed as is reasonably necessary in the best interest of the organization. Unless the lawyer reasonably believes that it is not necessary in the best interest of the organization to do so, the lawyer shall refer the matter to higher authority in the organization, including, if warranted by the circumstances to the highest authority that can act on behalf of the organization as determined by applicable law.

(c) Except as provided in paragraph (d), if

(1) despite the lawyer's efforts in accordance with paragraph (b) the highest authority that can act on behalf of the organization insists upon or fails to address in a timely and appropriate manner an action, or a refusal to act, that is clearly a violation of law, and

(2) the lawyer reasonably believes that the violation is reasonably certain to result in substantial injury to the organization,

then the lawyer may reveal information relating to the representation whether or not Rule 1.6 permits such disclosure, but only if and to the extent the lawyer reasonably believes necessary to prevent substantial injury to the organization.

(d) Paragraph (c) shall not apply with respect to information relating to a lawyer's representation of an organization to investigate an alleged violation of law, or to defend the organization or an officer, employee or other constituent associated with the organization against a claim arising out of an alleged violation of law.

(e) A lawyer who reasonably believes that he or she has been discharged because of the lawyer's actions taken pursuant to paragraphs (b) or (c), or who withdraws under circumstances that require or permit the lawyer to take action under either of those paragraphs, shall proceed as the lawyer reasonably believes necessary to assure that the organization's highest authority is informed of the lawyer's discharge or withdrawal.

(f) In dealing with an organization's directors, officers, employees, members, shareholders or other constituents, a lawyer shall explain the identity of the client when the lawyer knows or reasonably should know that the organization's interests are adverse to those of the constituents with whom the lawyer is dealing.

(g) A lawyer representing an organization may also represent any of its directors, officers, employees, members, shareholders or other constituents, subject to the provisions of Rule 1.7. If the organization's consent to the dual representation is required by Rule 1.7, the consent shall be given by an appropriate official of the organization other than the individual who is to be represented, or by the shareholders.

Comment

The Entity as the Client

[1] An organizational client is a legal entity, but it cannot act except through its officers, directors, employees, shareholders and other constituents. * * * The duties defined in this Comment apply equally to unincorporated associations. "Other constituents" as used in this Comment means the positions equivalent to officers, directors, employees and shareholders held by persons acting for organizational clients that are not corporations.

* * *

[3] When constituents of the organization make decisions for it, the decisions ordinarily must be accepted by the lawyer even if their utility or prudence is doubtful. Decisions concerning policy and operations, including ones entailing serious risk, are not as such in the lawyer's province. Paragraph (b) makes clear, however, that when the lawyer knows that the organization is likely to be substantially injured by action of an officer or other constituent that violates a legal obligation to the organization or is in violation of law that might be imputed to the organization, the lawyer must proceed as is reasonably necessary in the best interest of the organization. As defined in Rule 1.0(f), knowledge can be inferred from circumstances, and a lawyer cannot ignore the obvious.

[4] In determining how to proceed under paragraph (b), the lawyer should give due consideration to the seriousness of the violation and its consequences, the responsibility in the organization and the apparent motivation of the person involved, the policies of the organization concerning such matters, and any other relevant considerations. Ordinarily, referral to a higher authority would be necessary. In some circumstances, however, it may be appropriate for the lawyer to ask the constituent to reconsider the matter; for example, if the circumstances involve a constituent's innocent misunderstanding of law and subsequent acceptance of the lawyer's advice, the lawyer may reasonably conclude that the best interest of the organization does not require that the matter be referred to higher authority. If a constituent persists in conduct contrary to the lawyer's

advice, it will be necessary for the lawyer to take steps to have the matter reviewed by a higher authority in the organization. If the matter is of sufficient seriousness and importance or urgency to the organization, referral to higher authority in the organization may be necessary even if the lawyer has not communicated with the constituent. Any measures taken should, to the extent practicable, minimize the risk of revealing information relating to the representation to persons outside the organization. * * *

[5] Paragraph (b) also makes clear that when it is reasonably necessary to enable the organization to address the matter in a timely and appropriate manner, the lawyer must refer the matter to higher authority, including, if warranted by the circumstances, the highest authority that can act on behalf of the organization under applicable law. The organization's highest authority to whom a matter may be referred ordinarily will be the board of directors or similar governing body. However, applicable law may prescribe that under certain conditions the highest authority reposes elsewhere, for example, in the independent directors of a corporation.

Conflicts between the interests of the business entity and of those managing it can become most acute with the introduction of passive investors (shareholders or limited partners). To what extent does the attorney for the business owe a duty to protect the interests of such investors? What about prospective investors? If an attorney is concerned about the conduct of those in management which might be harmful to a company and those who invested in it, should he or she go "over the head" of management to the shareholders?

Massive fraudulent financial reporting at companies such as Enron and Worldcom led Congress and the Securities Exchange Commission, in 2002 and 2003, to address the duty of attorneys to protect investors. Specifically, Congress, in Section 307 of the Sarbanes–Oxley Act, directed the Securities Exchange Commission to issue rules that, at a minimum, required attorneys to report violations of securities laws, or breaches of fiduciary duty, by their corporate client, or any of its agents, to appropriate officers within the corporation, or to the highest authority within the corporation if the report to lower level officials did not result in an appropriate response. Carrying out this directive, the Securities Exchange Commission adopted a rule requiring attorneys to engage in such "up-the-ladder" reporting of wrongdoing within the corporation. In addition, and far more controversially, the Securities Exchange Commission proposed, but has deferred action on, requiring attorneys to withdraw from representation, and to notify the Commission of their withdrawal (so-called "noisy withdrawal"), if the board of directors itself did not act appropriately. This reporting requirement only reaches wrongdoing at public companies, and attorneys who appear and practice before the Securities Exchange Commission; albeit the Commission has interpreted broadly the concept of appear and practice to encompass not only attorneys who communicate with the Commission on behalf of their clients, but also attorneys who advise clients with respect to Federal securities law requirements. Sec. Act Release 33–8185 (February 6, 2003).

Another conflict of interest problem results if, as is sometimes the case, the client(s) offer the attorney the opportunity to "get in on the ground floor" by receiving an interest in the venture. Can the attorney take the opportunity (assuming he or she wants it)?

American Bar Association Model Rules of Professional Conduct

(2004).

RULE 1.8 CONFLICT OF INTEREST: CURRENT CLIENTS: SPECIFIC RULES

(a) A lawyer shall not enter into a business transaction with a client or knowingly acquire an ownership, possessory, security or other pecuniary interest adverse to a client unless:

(1) the transaction and terms on which the lawyer acquires the interest are fair and reasonable to the client and are fully disclosed and transmitted in writing in a manner that can be reasonably understood by the client;

(2) the client is advised in writing of the desirability of seeking and is given a reasonable opportunity to seek the advice of independent legal counsel on the transaction; and

(3) the client gives informed consent, in a writing signed by the client, to the essential terms of the transaction and the lawyer's role in the transaction, including whether the lawyer is representing the client in the transaction.

* * *

NOTES

1. Recall, as well, that Rule 1.7 (dealing with conflicts of interest in general) refers not only to conflicts between the representation of different clients, but also to potential conflicts between the client's and the lawyer's own interests. Hence Rule 1.7 also applies to business dealings with a client.

While neither of these rules completely preclude an attorney from having an interest in a client's business venture, opinions vary as to the wisdom of the practice. One distinguished member of the New York bar held the view

> that in most cases the client is best advised by a lawyer who maintains an objective point of view and that such objectivity may be impeded by any financial interest in the client's business or any participation in its

> management. Accordingly, he made it the policy of the firm that neither its partners nor its associates should hold equity securities of any client, or serve as a director of a corporate client, or have a financial interest, direct or indirect, in any transaction in which the firm was acting as counsel. Occasionally, more frequently in recent years, clients have insisted upon exceptions permitting partners to occupy directorships and own qualifying equity securities, but the exceptions have been few.

II R.T. Swaine, *The Cravath Firm and Its Predecessors: 1819–1948,* 9–10 (1948). Other practitioners have been of a very different mind:

> Rosati says his firm does not accept stock in lieu of fees, a rule followed by many mainstream firms. "But generally our [clients] want us to invest because it makes them look more credible. Some of those deals have worked out very nicely."
>
> * * *
>
> Wilson, Sonsini is one of the few firms that admits to accepting founders' shares. "I've never felt that because the firm has an investment in a company it's made me do anything different one way or the other," says Rosati. "Except to be real happy when they go public."

Weber. *Venture Capital, "It's Not Form–Book Practice,"* 4 Cal.Law. No. 8, at 41, 44 (August 1984). Is it true, as Mr. Rosati claims, that a lawyer who owns stock in a client is not influenced? What if the client asked Mr. Rosati for advice on whether to go public with its stock? During the bull market for high technology stocks in the late 1990s, the practice of investing in clients spread from firms like Wilson, Sonsini to many more traditional firms. This, in turn, led to increased debate about the practice. *Compare* Dzienkowski & Peroni, *The Decline in Lawyer Independence: Lawyer Equity Investments in Clients*, 81 Tex. L. Rev. 401, 413–414 (2002):

> Beginning in 1995, several bar associations, ultimately including the ABA in 2000, issued ethics opinions that basically place their stamp of approval on lawyers obtaining equity interests in clients, subject to a few exceptions and provided that they meet certain requirements. Lawyers throughout the country have used these opinions to justify aggressive and even arrogant demands for client equity in standard corporate practice. These opinions have completely reversed the traditional view of the organized bar that such practices should be severely restricted. * * *
>
> This Article challenges the tacit approval that the organized bar has given these modern arrangements in which lawyers invest in their clients. Even in situations in which the exceptions and requirements set forth in these ethics opinions are met, the current practice of allowing equity investments in clients continues to severely undercut many time-honored ideals of the legal profession. How can lawyers exercise independent professional judgment and offer unbiased legal advice to their clients if they have an ownership interest at stake in the venture? How can lawyers fulfill their function as gatekeepers of the

> securities laws if their personal equity interests in the venture will be injured by disclosure of negative information concerning the client? How can a client exercise its right to discharge a law firm, with or without cause, if that law firm has an investment in the client? Furthermore, in today's climate of legal malpractice and expansion of lawyers' fiduciary duties, equity investments expose lawyers to potentially serious liability if the parties suffer harm by reason of a lawyer's judgment colored by an equity investment.

with Langevoort, *When Lawyers and Law Firms Invest In Their Corporate Clients' Stock*, 80 Wash. U.L.Q. 569, 570 (2002):

> I will state my conclusion at the outset. I am not convinced that lawyers' investments in clients in lieu of fees are problematic enough from a conflicts standpoint that the rules of professional responsibility should treat them as presumptively inconsistent with the lawyer's fiduciary responsibility. Lawyers' investments in their clients do raise interesting and unsettling issues, but these issues are not qualitatively different from issues raised by many other norms or practices within the legal profession that also threaten lawyerly objectivity. Indeed, in contrast to some other practices, these fee arrangements can, in some respects, enhance objectivity, or at least balance out some of the agency-cost problems that otherwise infect attorney-client relationships in the corporate setting. If so, broadly banning these fee arrangements in the name of fiduciary responsibility makes little sense.

2. A closely related question is whether an attorney should serve on the board of directors of a corporate client. The practice is both widespread and often criticized. *E.g., Panel Discussion, Lawyers as Directors,* 30 Bus.Law 41 (1975). The commentary to Rule 1.7 of the Model Rules of Professional Conduct provides the following guidance on this subject:

> A lawyer for a corporation or other organization who is also a member of its board of directors should determine whether the responsibilities of the two roles may conflict. The lawyer may be called on to advise the corporation in matters involving actions of the directors. Consideration should be given to the frequency with which such situations may arise, the potential intensity of the conflict, the effect of the lawyer's resignation from the board and the possibility of the corporation's obtaining legal advice from another lawyer in such situations. If there is material risk that the dual role will compromise the lawyer's independence of professional judgment, the lawyer should not serve as a director.

For a further discussion of the ethical issues faced by attorneys who serve as directors of their corporate clients, and suggested guidelines for attorneys in this situation, see *The Lawyer as Director of a Client: Report and Recommendations of the Committee on Lawyer Business Ethics of the ABA Section of Business Law*, 57 Bus. Law. 385 (2001).

2. THE LIMITS OF ZEAL

Much of business planning concerns ways to minimize taxes and avoid regulatory impediments to the client's objectives. Is there anything immoral, in and of itself, about attempting to achieve such goals? Assuming not, how far can the attorney go in such counseling?

American Bar Association Standing Committee on Ethics and Professional Responsibility, Formal Opinion 85–352, Tax Return Advice; Reconsideration of Formal Opinion 314

July 7, 1985.

The Committee has been requested by the Section of Taxation of the American Bar Association to reconsider the "reasonable basis" standard in the Committee's Formal Opinion 314 governing the position a lawyer may advise a client to take on a tax return.

Opinion 314 (April 27, 1965) was issued in response to a number of specific inquiries regarding the ethical relationship between the Internal Revenue Service and lawyers practicing before it. The opinion formulated general principles governing this relationship, including the following:

> [A] lawyer who is asked to advise his client in the course of the preparation of the client's tax returns may freely urge the statement of positions most favorable to the client just as long as there is a *reasonable basis* for this position. (Emphasis supplied).

The Committee is informed that the standard of "reasonable basis" has been construed by many lawyers to support the use of any colorable claim on a tax return to justify exploitation of the lottery of the tax return audit selection process. This view is not universally held, and the Committee does not believe that the reasonable basis standard, properly interpreted and applied, permits this construction.

However, the Committee is persuaded that as a result of serious controversy over this standard and its persistent criticism by distinguished members of the tax bar, IRS officials and members of Congress, sufficient doubt has been created regarding the validity of the standard so as to erode its effectiveness as an ethical guideline. For this reason, the Committee has concluded that it should be restated. Another reason for restating the standard is that since publication of Opinion 314, the ABA has adopted in succession the Model Code of Professional Responsibility (1969, revised 1980) and the Model Rules of Professional Conduct (1983). * * *

This opinion reconsiders and revises only that part of Opinion 314 that relates to the lawyer's duty in advising a client of positions that can be taken on a tax return. It does not deal with a lawyer's opinion on tax shelter investment offerings, which is specifically addressed by this Committee's Formal Opinion 346 (Revised), and which involves very different considerations, including third party reliance.

The ethical standards governing the conduct of a lawyer in advising a client on positions that can be taken in a tax return are no different from those governing a lawyer's conduct in advising or taking positions for a client in other civil matters. Although the Model Rules distinguish between the roles of advisor and advocate, both roles are involved here, and the ethical standards applicable to them provide relevant guidance. In many cases a lawyer must realistically anticipate that the filing of the tax return may be the first step in a process that may result in an adversary relationship between the client and the IRS. This normally occurs in situations when a lawyer advises an aggressive position on a tax return, not when the position taken is a safe or conservative one that is unlikely to be challenged by the IRS.

Rule 3.1 of the Model Rules, which is in essence a restatement of DR 7–102(A)(2) of the Model Code, states in pertinent part:

> A lawyer shall not bring or defend a proceeding, or assert or controvert an issue therein, unless there is a basis for doing so that is not frivolous, which includes a good faith argument for an extension, modification or reversal of existing law.

Rule 1.2(d), which applies to representation generally, states:

> A lawyer shall not counsel a client to engage, or assist a client, in conduct that the lawyer knows is criminal or fraudulent, but a lawyer may discuss the legal consequences of any proposed course of conduct with a client and may counsel or assist a client to make a good faith effort to determine the validity, scope, meaning or application of the law.

On the basis of these rules and analogous provisions of the Model Code, a lawyer, in representing a client in the course of the preparation of the client's tax return, may advise the statement of positions most favorable to the client if the lawyer has a good faith belief that those positions are warranted in existing law or can be supported by a good faith argument for an extension, modification or reversal of existing law. A lawyer can have a good faith belief in this context even if the lawyer believes the client's position probably will not prevail. However, good faith requires that there be some realistic possibility of success if the matter is litigated.

This formulation of the lawyer's duty in the situation addressed by this opinion is consistent with the basic duty of the lawyer to a client, recognized in ethical standards since the ABA Canons of Professional Ethics, and in the opinions of this Committee: zealously and loyally to represent the interests of the client within the bounds of the law.

Thus, where a lawyer has a good faith belief in the validity of a position in accordance with the standard stated above that a particular transaction does not result in taxable income or that certain expenditures are properly deductible as expenses, the lawyer has no duty to require as a condition of his or her continued representation that riders be attached to the client's tax return explaining the circumstances surrounding the transaction or the expenditures.

In the role of advisor, the lawyer should counsel the client as to whether the position is likely to be sustained by a court if challenged by the IRS, as well as of the potential penalty consequences to the client if the position is taken on the tax return without disclosure. Section 6661 of the Internal Revenue Code imposes a penalty for substantial understatement of tax liability which can be avoided if the facts are adequately disclosed or if there is or was substantial authority for the position taken by the taxpayer. Competent representation of the client would require the lawyer to advise the client fully as to whether there is or was substantial authority for the position taken in the tax return. If the lawyer is unable to conclude that the position is supported by substantial authority, the lawyer should advise the client of the penalty the client may suffer and of the opportunity to avoid such penalty by adequately disclosing the facts in the return or in a statement attached to the return. If after receiving such advice the client decides to risk the penalty by making no disclosure and to take the position initially advised by the lawyer in accordance with the standard stated above, the lawyer has met his or her ethical responsibility with respect to the advice.

In all cases, however, with regard both to the preparation of returns and negotiating administrative settlements, the lawyer is under a duty not to mislead the Internal Revenue Service deliberately, either by misstatements or by silence or by permitting the client to mislead. Rules 4.1 and 8.4(c); DRs 1–102(A)(4), 7–102(A)(3) and (5).

In summary, a lawyer may advise reporting a position on a return even where the lawyer believes the position probably will not prevail, there is no "substantial authority" in support of the position, and there will be no disclosure of the position in the return. However, the position to be asserted must be one which the lawyer in good faith believes is warranted in existing law or can be supported by a good faith argument for an extension, modification or reversal of existing law. This requires that there is some realistic possibility of success if the matter is litigated. In addition, in his role as advisor, the lawyer should refer to potential penalties and other legal consequences should the client take the position advised.

NOTE

Opinion 85–352 refers to Section 6661 of the Internal Revenue Code. This section provided a penalty in case of a substantial underpayment of tax, but created an exception if the underpayment resulted from treating an item in a way either for which the taxpayer had substantial authority or else disclosed. This penalty is now found in Section 6662. Also, disclosure no longer is sufficient to avoid a penalty, unless the taxpayer has at least a reasonable basis (even if not substantial authority) for the position the taxpayer is taking. I.R.C. § 6662(d)(2)(B)(ii). For certain so-called "reportable transactions", however, Section 6662A imposes a penalty unless the transaction is both reported in the taxpayer's return, *and* the taxpayer has substantial authority, as well as a reasonable belief in the likelihood of prevailing, for the taxpayer's position. I.R.C. § 6664(d).

Later, Chapter V will explore some of the limits on zealous representation which exist when attorneys advise clients concerning obligations under the securities laws.

3. EXPERTISE

As one delves into the substance of business planning, it becomes evident the subject involves a number of areas of special expertise, including tax and securities law. Can the general business attorney be competent in all aspects of these fields? When must he or she bring in specialists?

American Bar Association Model Rules of Professional Conduct

(2004).

RULE 1.1 COMPETENCE

A lawyer shall provide competent representation to a client. Competent representation requires the legal knowledge, skill, thoroughness and preparation reasonably necessary for the representation.

Comment

Legal Knowledge and Skill

In determining whether a lawyer employs the requisite knowledge and skill in a particular matter, relevant factors include the relative complexity and specialized nature of the matter, the lawyer's general experience, the lawyer's training and experience in the field in question, the preparation and study the lawyer is able to give the matter and whether it is feasible to refer the matter to, or associate or consult with, a lawyer of established competence in the field in question. In many instances, the required proficiency is that of a general practitioner. Expertise in a particular field of law may be required in some circumstances.

A lawyer need not necessarily have special training or prior experience to handle legal problems of a type with which the lawyer is unfamiliar. * * * A lawyer can provide adequate representation in a wholly novel field through necessary study. Competent representation can also be provided through the association of a lawyer of established competence in the field in question.

* * *

A lawyer may accept representation where the requisite level of competence can be achieved by reasonable preparation.

* * *

NOTE

In addition to exposing an attorney to professional discipline, lack of competence may expose him or her to civil liability. The issues of who the attorney represents and the consequences of incompetence often overlap as the following case illustrates.

Waggoner v. Snow, Becker, Kroll, Klaris & Krauss

991 F.2d 1501 (9th Cir.1993).

■ SNEED, CIRCUIT JUDGE:

* * *

I. FACTS AND PRIOR PROCEEDINGS

Thomas Waggoner is a cofounder of STAAR Surgical Company (Staar), a publicly held company incorporated in California in 1982. Until 1989, he was also its Chief Executive Officer and a member of its Board of Directors (Board). Waggoner hired defendant Elliot Lutzker as counsel for Staar in 1984.[2] In April of 1986, Lutzker supervised Staar's reincorporation to Delaware.

From 1982 to 1986, Staar was principally engaged in the manufacture and sale of a patented soft intraocular lens (IOL) used in treating cataracts. In 1986 Staar expanded into other markets. In July 1987, however, finding the company short of capital, Staar negotiated a line of credit from the Bank of New York (BONY), secured primarily by accounts receivable and inventory. By September of 1987, BONY determined that Staar was under-collateralized and over-advanced on its credit line by almost $2 million. BONY threatened to discontinue the credit line and initiate foreclosure proceedings unless Staar's officers would personally guarantee the outstanding loans.

On December 13, 1987, the Staar Board convened to discuss the company's options. During the course of that meeting, Waggoner declared that he was willing to guarantee $3.5 million of BONY debt and $2.8 million of other debt in exchange for voting control of Staar for as long as his personal guarantees were outstanding. Lutzker was at the meeting and reminded everyone there that he was present only in his capacity as counsel for Staar.

On December 16, 1987, BONY informed Waggoner that he had only three days in which to provide the Bank with a written personal guarantee of the overdrawn line of credit. Staar's directors convened an emergency telephone meeting on December 17, 1987. At that meeting, Waggoner explained Staar's financial straits to the directors and advised them that he was the only person who could afford to guarantee personally Staar's debt. The Board then adopted a resolution transferring 100 shares of Class A Preferred Stock to Waggoner in exchange for his guarantee. One of those shares was to be convertible into 2 million shares of common stock after January 16, 1988, if Waggoner's guarantees were still outstanding.

2. At the time, Lutzker was a lawyer with the New York based firm of Bachner, Tally, Polevoy, Misher & Brinberg (Bachner Tally). In 1985, Lutzker left Bachner Tally in order to become a partner at Snow, Becker, Kroll, Klaris & Krauss, P.C. (Snow Becker), another New York based firm. Nevertheless, Lutzker retained his position as Staar's counsel. Lutzker and Staar apparently never signed a written retainer agreement.

Following that meeting, at the Board's direction, Lutzker drew up the Shareholders Agreement and the Certificate of Designation, the papers necessary to transfer voting control of the company to Waggoner. Waggoner had the documents reviewed by Staar's California patent counsel, Frank Frisenda, and on December 24, 1987, Waggoner personally guaranteed Staar's debt and pledged his Staar stock to BONY. Although Staar's directors tried to obtain financing in order to replace Waggoner's guarantees in the month that followed, they were not successful. Consequently, on January 19, 1988, after consulting with Lutzker, Waggoner converted one of his Preferred shares in exchange for 2 million shares of common stock.

* * *

[In August 1989, the Board] voted to remove Waggoner from his positions as president, CEO, and director of Staar. In response, Waggoner called Lutzker to ascertain if his preferred stock empowered him to remove the other directors from the Board and create a new Board. Lutzker informed Waggoner that he knew of nothing to hinder Waggoner from using his voting power in that manner. Thus, after voting to remove the other directors from the Board, Waggoner named a new Board consisting of himself, his wife and one vacancy. Waggoner sent his written consent regarding the removal of the other directors to Lutzker, who informed the other Board members what had transpired.

The Board members sought relief in court, filing two suits in Delaware. As a result of the ensuing litigation, Waggoner lost his position in and control over Staar. He also lost ownership of the common stock which he had allegedly derived from the convertible preferred stock.[3]

On August 23, 1990, Waggoner filed this diversity action for legal malpractice against Lutzker and Snow Becker. Waggoner alleged that the defendants breached their duty of care because Lutzker: negligently failed to include the power to fix voting rights among the Board of Directors' powers when Staar was reincorporated in Delaware; failed to advise Waggoner that the Board did not have the power to fix voting rights; and knew or should have known that the Board lacked that power. Waggoner further alleged that Lutzker was aware that Waggoner would rely on his advice, that Waggoner did in fact rely on that advice, and that Waggoner suffered damage as a result. On September 12, 1991, the district court granted summary judgment for the defendants.

* * *

3. The Delaware Supreme Court found that the Board's transfer of preferred stock endowed with voting rights was invalid on the ground that it was ultra vires, or beyond the Board's powers, because Staar's Certificate of Incorporation did not expressly allow the Board to create a class of preferred stock with voting rights. The Delaware Supreme Court further found that Waggoner's attempt to convert one of his preferred shares into common stock was invalid. See Waggoner v. Laster, 581 A.2d 1127 (Del.1990); STAAR Surgical Co. v. Waggoner, 588 A.2d 1130 (Del.1991).

Waggoner timely appealed.

* * *

III. DISCUSSION

A. *Attorney–Client Relationship*

Waggoner first contends that Lutzker and Snow Becker are liable to him for Lutzker's negligence because Lutzker was acting as Waggoner's attorney during the preferred stock transaction.[4] New York and California treat the formation of an attorney-client relationship similarly. An attorney-client relationship is formed when an attorney renders advice directly to a client who has consulted him seeking legal counsel. * * * A formal contract is not necessary to show that an attorney-client relationship has been formed. * * * The court may look to the intent and conduct of the parties to determine whether the relationship was actually formed. * * *

To support his allegation that Lutzker acted as his counsel during the preferred stock transaction, Waggoner emphasizes that: (1) Lutzker informed him by telephone between the December 13th and December 17th meetings in 1987 that Delaware law did not prevent Staar from transferring preferred stock with a conversion feature to Waggoner; (2) the Board approved of the transaction only after Lutzker represented to all the Board members, including Waggoner, that the Board was authorized to issue super majority voting stock in exchange for Waggoner's guarantees; (3) Lutzker sent Waggoner the documents regarding the voting stock exchange for review and advised Waggoner that they complied with all the necessary laws and regulations; (4) Lutzker reassured Waggoner that the voting rights were valid in January, 1988 and in the summer of 1988; (5) Lutzker assured Waggoner that he could exercise his voting rights should the need arise, and advised him on the procedure involved; and (6) Lutzker did not advise him to seek outside counsel until the summer of 1989. While Lutzker does not contest that he spoke with Waggoner on these occasions, Lutzker contends that any advice he rendered to Waggoner was only in his role as corporate counsel for Staar.

Despite Waggoner's allegations, the intent and conduct of the parties supports the district court's finding that Waggoner and Lutzker were not in an attorney-client relationship. As noted above, it is undisputed that Lutzker informed everyone at the Board meeting on December 13, 1987, including Waggoner, that Lutzker was only present as counsel for Staar

4. Waggoner initially contends that he and Lutzker had an on-going attorney-client relationship based on several instances in which he sought and received legal counsel from Lutzker on personal matters. As the district court properly pointed out, however, the issue here is whether Lutzker and Waggoner had an attorney-client relationship during the transactions giving rise to this malpractice suit: Lutzker's drafting and filing of the documents reincorporating Staar from California to Delaware, and Lutzker's drafting of the documents ostensibly transferring preferred stock to Waggoner in exchange for his personal guarantees. We need only focus on the transaction involving preferred stock, because all parties concede Lutzker was acting solely on behalf of Staar at the time Staar was reincorporated.

and that he did not represent Waggoner. Waggoner's claim is further undermined by his own repeated references to Lutzker as corporate counsel and to Rick Love as his personal counsel. * * *

B. Choice of Law

Waggoner argues, alternatively, that the district court erred by granting summary judgment for defendants because there is a genuine issue regarding Lutzker's liability to Waggoner as a third party.

* * *

In the instant case, there is a clear conflict between the laws of California and New York: California allows a third party to recover from an attorney in situations where New York generally precludes it. Under California law, attorneys may be liable to a third party where the third party "was an intended beneficiary of the attorney's services, or where it was reasonably foreseeable that negligent service or advice to or on behalf of the client could cause harm to others." Fox v. Pollack, 181 Cal.App.3d 954, 960, 226 Cal.Rptr. 532, 535 (1986).

Under New York law, by contrast, attorneys are not liable to a party for economic injury arising from negligent misrepresentation unless there was privity between the injured party and the attorney, or unless there was "a relationship so close as to approach that of privity." Prudential Ins. Co. v. Dewey, Ballantine, Bushby, Palmer & Wood, 80 N.Y.2d 377, 590 N.Y.S.2d 831, 833, 605 N.E.2d 318 (1992).

* * *

[The court then concluded that the district court properly followed California conflict of law rules in deciding to apply New York instead of California law to the issue of Lutzker's liability to a non-client.]

New York's interest in this litigation is significant because of its numerous contacts with the events giving rise to the litigation. In fact, the wealth of transactions and events which occurred in New York demonstrate that the reasonable expectations of the parties can only have been that New York law would apply to a dispute between them. * * * Lutzker has been a New York resident since 1976. He has been licensed to practice law in New York since 1979, and he is a partner in a New York law firm. He has never been licensed to practice law in California. In addition, it was Staar which originally retained the New York firm of Bachner Tally for its corporate counsel and which decided to retain Lutzker as its corporate counsel when he left Bachner Tally to become a partner at Snow Becker. Neither Bachner Tally nor Snow Becker have ever had offices outside of New York. Moreover, almost all of the transactions relevant to this litigation took place in New York: Lutzker prepared the Certificate of Incorporation, reincorporating Staar in Delaware, in New York; the December 13, 1987 meeting of Staar's Board was held at Snow Becker's offices in New York; Lutzker prepared the Shareholders Agreement and the Certificate of Designation in New York; and each time Waggoner contacted Lutzker regarding these and other transactions, it was at Lutzker's office in New York.

* * *

C. Summary Judgment

We must next determine whether the district court erred by granting summary judgment for the defendants. As noted above, New York law, with few exceptions, requires privity before a lawyer can be held liable by a party not his client in the absence of fraud, collusion, or a malicious or tortious act. "The fact that an attorney represents a corporation does not thereby make that attorney counsel to the individual officers and directors thereof." * * * On the contrary, attorneys are specifically required by the New York Code of Professional Responsibility, Ethical Consideration 5–18, to act in the interests of the entity they represent, rather than on behalf of the officers of that entity. * * *

Unless the attorney for a corporation or partnership affirmatively assumes a duty toward an officer or partner, the lawyer is not liable to a partner or director who relied on his advice. * * * In the instant case, Lutzker's duty as counsel for Staar lay with the corporation, not with its officers and directors individually. In addition, the record reveals no sign that Lutzker affirmatively adopted Waggoner as a client during the transfer of preferred stock. Thus, the district court did not err by granting summary judgment for the defendants.

* * *

Affirmed.

NOTES

1. *Waggoner* illustrates the need for clarity (and the potential for confusion) over who the corporate attorney represents, as well as the divided authority concerning the attorney's obligations toward third parties. Putting aside obvious questions about the justice of the court's decision, the facts in *Waggoner* also show that the business attorney's blunder can impact real people, not just corporations. While Lutzker and his partners avoided liability for what was an elementary error in corporate law, there are other non-legal sanctions for sloppiness—such as the impact on one's professional reputation or even on one's ability to sleep at night.

How far does the notion that the attorney for the corporation owes his or her duty of care to the entity, not the individuals running the entity, go? For example, can a corporation's attorney be liable for negligently failing to protect the company from fraud committed by those in charge of it? See, *O'Melveny & Myers v. F.D.I.C.*, 512 U.S. 79 (1994) (defendants argued that they could not be liable, because state law imputed the corporate officers' knowledge of their own fraud to the corporation).

2. On the specific question of when an attorney may be liable for not bringing in a specialist, consider the following jury instruction approved by

the court in *Horne v. Peckham,* 97 Cal.App.3d 404, 414, 158 Cal.Rptr. 714, 720 (1979):

> It is the duty of an attorney who is a general practitioner to refer his client to a specialist or recommend the assistance of a specialist if under the circumstances a reasonably careful and skillful practitioner would do so.
>
> If he fails to perform that duty and undertakes to perform professional services without the aid of a specialist, it is his further duty to have the knowledge and skill ordinarily possessed, and exercise the care and skill ordinarily used by specialists in good standing in the same or similar locality and under the same circumstances. A failure to perform any such duty is negligence.

Unfortunately, sometimes a general business attorney might neglect to bring in a specialist when appropriate, not because the general business attorney overestimates his or her own abilities, but rather because the general business attorney did not recognize until too late that the situation raised any legal issue in the specialized area. As an illustration of this potential hazard, consider the issues raised in following article, which was written to introduce business persons to the need to consult attorneys familiar with the protection of intellectual property for firms doing business overseas.

Curci, Protecting Your Intellectual Property Rights Overseas

15 Transnat'l Law. 15 (2002).

I. Introduction

While legal protections for fundamental intellectual property rights are well established in the United States, the development of, and philosophical basis for, the enactment and enforcement of intellectual property law differs widely from nation to nation. Accordingly, as American companies increasingly expand their business globally, these companies should also become aware of the best methods of protecting their intellectual property rights overseas. The key intellectual property rights covered by this article are: (1) trademarks/service marks, (2) copyrights, (3) patents, and (4) trade secrets. * * *

II. Trademarks

Under the laws of the United States, a trademark or service mark, commonly called a "mark(s)," is generally defined as a word, name, symbol, device or any other combination thereof used on goods or associated with services to distinguish the source of those goods or services from those of others. While marks in the United States can be protected through asserting common law rights and state registrations, federal registration with the United States Patent & Trademark Office (PTO) provides greater protection. While the PTO allows submission of an application to register a mark based only on the applicant's bona fide intent to use the mark in interstate or international commerce, United States law, contrary to the practice in many other nations, prohibits the PTO's registration of that mark if the applicant fails to ultimately prove use of that mark in such commerce. Once a mark is registered, the United States, again in contrast to the practice in many other nations, requires registrants to prove use of a mark in commerce at various stages, including one year prior to each renewal, in order to maintain the registration.

In contrast to the "first-to-use" registration system in the United States, many other nations have a "first-to-file" registration system, which provides that the first applicant who files an application for a mark will be granted an appropriate registration for that mark. In most "first-to-file" nations, an applicant need not submit evidence of use of the mark at either the application or registration stage, and will typically have to submit relatively minimal, if any, evidence of use to maintain the registration.

The "first-to-file" system presents both benefits and burdens to American companies doing business overseas. On a positive side, this system allows an American company to register a mark in certain foreign nations before beginning to actually use the mark in those nations. This advantage allows the company to begin the process of protecting company marks before incurring the significant capital expense of actually selling or distributing goods or providing services in association with that mark in that particular nation.

On the negative side, however, an American company's mark may already be registered in a particular foreign nation by a third party, possibly by a competitor, because the "first-to-file" system fosters registration of marks that a registrant may not actually use. * * * Thus, for American companies intending to do business overseas, it is prudent to first analyze appropriate overseas protection of marks and consider registering certain marks in "first-to-file" nations before actually doing business in those nations to avoid the possibility of another entity, such as a competitor, acquiring prior registration rights in that mark.

With the exception of the European Union's Community Trade Mark (CTM) registration process, there is currently no truly centralized method available to American companies for registering a mark in multiple nations around the world. Thus, American companies generally must submit mark applications in each nation in which the company seeks a registration. American companies doing business in the European Union should, however, analyze the benefits of obtaining a CTM, which provides for the registration of one mark to cover all European Union nations. * * *

While efforts to create a centralized worldwide filing system for mark applications have had limited success, there are other international conventions and agreements that provide benefits to American entities seeking to protect their marks overseas. For example, all American companies contemplating multinational trademark applications should be aware of the benefits of the International Convention for the Protection of Industrial Property (Paris Convention). The Paris Convention, which has numerous member nations, including the United States, provides that if a national of a member nation files a mark application in any member nation, any subsequent application in a Paris Convention nation filed within six months of the first application will enjoy (as a "priority date") the filing date of the original application.

* * *

Despite additional efforts to harmonize global trademark law and practice, such as the Agreement on Trade–Related Aspects of Intellectual Property Rights (TRIPs) and the World Intellectual Property Organization's (WIPO) Trademark Law Treaty, differences, in addition to those noted above, still exist from nation to nation. For example, "use" requirements, treatment of service marks, and duration and renewal procedures may vary.

III. Copyrights

In the United States, an original work of authorship fixed in a tangible medium of expression is protected under the federal copyright statute. Protected works include literary works, musical works, dramatic works, computer programs, sound recordings and sculptural works. Copyright owners are granted certain exclusive "economic rights," including the exclusive right to the public performance of a work; public display of a work; distribution of copies of a work by sale, lease, rental, lending or otherwise; reproduction of a work in copies; and preparation of derivative works.

The United States is a member of the Berne Convention for the Protection of Literary and Artistic Works (Berne Convention). All Berne Convention nations must recognize certain fundamental copyright principles set forth in the Berne Convention. One key principle is the notion that a copyright comes into existence upon the creation of the original work of authorship, and that Berne Convention nations cannot impose prerequisites to obtaining that copyright, including such pre-creation formalities as registration or providing copyright notice. However, the Berne Convention does permit member nations to impose certain post-creation formalities on works that originate within that particular member nation. This is why United States copyright law provides that a "United States work" must first be registered with the U.S. Copyright Office before the copyright owner of such work can institute an infringement action in United States courts. Additionally, registration with the U.S. Copyright Office within specified time periods is necessary before the owner of a "United States work" can take full advantage of certain statutory damages and statutory attorney's fees in an infringement action. However, such post-creation "formalities" do not apply to works originating from other Berne Convention nations seeking copyright protection in the United States as long as such works are not otherwise deemed to be a "United States work."

While the Berne Convention has harmonized copyright standards among Berne Convention nations more than any other international treaty has done for other intellectual property rights, the scope or degree of copyright protection can still vary in Berne Convention nations. Additionally, variations can exist nation to nation concerning copyright duration, the criteria for determining independent creation of a work, the criteria for determining fair use, how a nation's laws interpret "expression," which is protected by copyright, compared with mere ideas, and how a nation's laws treat the ownership of works created by an employee within the scope of employment or by a commissioned third party. Accordingly, one should understand the degree of protection truly available overseas before releasing valuable works that could migrate to a foreign nation.

Although the Berne Convention does not require it, some American companies should consider obtaining a copyright registration in select foreign nations to obtain a tangible certificate of ownership in that nation. Tangible registration certificates can help American companies in their efforts to combat copyright infringement in certain foreign nations, particularly when working with foreign customs officials. Also, while United States' adherence to the Berne Convention technically eliminated the "formality" of mandating a copyright notice as a condition precedent to protection in the United States, use of copyright notice is still the best practice. Current U.S. law only provides that copyright notice "may be placed on publicly distributed copies" rather than providing for the mandatory language previously contained in the statute. Nonetheless, copyright notice is desirable to counter a defense of innocent infringement and may still be needed to obtain protection under certain copyright conventions other than the Berne Convention.

In addition to the "economic rights" outlined above, the Berne Convention also requires its member nations to recognize the "moral rights" of the original author of a work. The original author's moral rights, which can survive the transfer of the work to subsequent owners, include the "right of attribution," which is the right of the original author to always claim authorship, and the "right of integrity," which includes the original author's right to prevent any distortion, mutilation, modification or any other derogatory actions in relation to that work if such actions are prejudicial to the original author. The level to which nations have amended their laws to respect these moral rights greatly varies. Many European Union nations, such as France, have longstanding and significant moral rights protections. The United States, on the other hand, has been criticized by other Berne Convention nations, particularly those in the European Union, for not adequately amending its laws to truly adhere to the moral rights obligations of the Berne Convention. Thus, the owner of a work who is not the original author should verify the extent of moral rights laws in a particular nation before making any alterations or modifications to a work.

IV. Patents

The United States patent system grants a monopoly to an inventor for a certain number of years in exchange for the inventor's public disclosure of the details of his invention. The invention becomes public domain once the patent registration expires. To obtain a utility patent—the most common type of patent in the United States—the inventor must file an application with the United States PTO and establish that the invention is of the type covered by statute, is "non-obvious" and "novel" in relation to prior inventions, and is "useful."

There are a number of international agreements and treaties that can assist an American entity in its efforts to seek patent protection in multiple nations. For example, all American companies contemplating multinational patent applications should be aware of the benefits of the Paris Convention. Pursuant to this multinational convention, if a national of a Paris Convention member nation files a patent application in any member nation, any subsequent applications in a Paris Convention member nation filed within twelve months of the first application will enjoy (as a "priority date") the filing date of the original application. * * *

The benefits of the Patent Cooperation Treaty (PCT), an agreement administered by WIPO, is also available to Paris Convention member nations. Pursuant to the PCT, the WIPO, along with the patent agencies of certain nations, coordinates the simultaneous filing of patent applications in PCT member nations, allowing the same filing date (i.e., "priority date") in all of those nations. Thus, the PCT provides significant benefits to invention owners because it provides a simplified procedure to simultaneously file patent applications in several nations. * * *

Notwithstanding the harmonization efforts of the Paris Convention and the PCT, American companies seeking overseas protection of their inventions must be keenly aware of patent practices that, while common in many foreign nations, may greatly differ from practices in the United States. For example, contrary to the practice in many other nations, United States law still adheres to the "first-to-invent" registration system, which mandates that only the inventor who first conceived the idea for a particular invention and reduced it to practice will be entitled to a patent. Indeed, most other nations adhere to the "first-to-file" registration system, which grants patent rights to the first person who files a patent application for a particular invention, even if the applicant was not the first person to conceive the idea for that invention.

Also, many foreign nations deny a patent for an invention that is not "absolutely novel" prior to the filing of the patent application, and offer very limited exceptions to this harsh rule. Indeed, the actions of the inventor prior to submitting the patent application could destroy the "absolute novelty" of that invention. For example, under Japan's Patent Law, if prior to filing a patent application, the invention is publicly known or used in Japan or abroad, if it is described in a printed publication and distributed, or if it became publicly available through electric telecommunications in Japan or abroad, the Japanese Patent Office (JPO) will deny registration of the patent because the invention is no longer "absolutely novel." Inventors submitting applications in the United States, on the other hand, can take advantage of a more liberal U.S. rule that permits the inventor to file for a patent within one year of publication or other use of the invention without destroying the invention's "novelty" under U.S. Patent Act. However, U.S. inventors must understand that most other nations do not recognize the United States' more liberal exceptions to "novelty." Therefore, while "novelty" may not be destroyed in the United States pursuant to this more liberal exception, "novelty" could be destroyed in many other nations.

Several foreign nations officially "lay-open," or release to the public, the contents of a patent application within eighteen months of the filing date. The theoretical purpose of this practice is to encourage the general public of that nation to inform the nation's patent examiners of prior inventions which could be the basis for denying a patent for an applied invention. Unfortunately, in several nations, particularly in developing nations, the practical effect of this procedure is to hand over the details of an invention to the inventor's competitors. Additionally, if the patent is ultimately denied, the inventor will normally also lose trade secret protections.

The United States has traditionally viewed the patent prosecution process as a confidential process. Until U.S. patent law was amended in November 1999, the U.S. patent prosecution process was completely confidential. Consequently, the United States did not adhere to the international trend of publishing patent applications after a specific period of time. However, section 122 of the Patent Act was amended to allow the publication of U.S. patent applications after the expiration of the eighteen-month period from the application date. One significant exception to the statute provides that a U.S. patent application shall not be published after the expiration of the above mentioned eighteen month period if the applicant makes a request upon filing not to publish that application, provided such request contains a certification that the invention disclosed in the U.S. application has not, and will not, be the subject of an application filed in another country or under a multilateral international agreement that requires publication of applications eighteen months after filing. Pursuant to the U.S. Patent Act, if a request is made for non-publication but the applicant subsequently files an application in a foreign country or under a multilateral treaty that publishes applications, the applicant must notify the PTO no later than forty-five days after the date of filing the application in the foreign country or international organization. Failure to notify the PTO within that forty-five day period will result in the U.S. patent application being deemed abandoned, unless one can demonstrate to the satisfaction of the PTO Director that the delay in submitting the notice was unintentional.

* * *

Finally, many nations have strong "compulsory licensing" laws which can force a patent owner to license his patent to a third party if the patent has not been "adequately worked" in that nation for a time period specified by statute. Accordingly, any American company with an invention which may be sold or distributed overseas should formulate the company's domestic and international strategy for maximizing all protections for such invention before disclosing, distributing, or otherwise using that invention.

V. Trade Secrets

In the United States, trade secrets are generally considered confidential, proprietary information of an owner which is used in the owner's business to provide an economic value or advantage to that owner because the information is not generally known to the public—and under circumstances where the owner has taken reasonable measures to keep the information secret. Trade secrets can include confidential formulas, customer lists, patterns, methods, techniques, and processes. A key element differentiating trade secrets from trademarks, copyrights, and patents is that trade secrets are not necessarily filed or registered with any governmental entity, but are primarily protected by efforts of the owner through contract, and by otherwise taking measures to keep the information secret. Thus, if an owner does not want to make a formal intellectual property filing or registration for some proprietary know-how because that know-how will, as a result of such filing or registration, become public knowledge, the trade secret can potentially be protected under varied common law principles and trade secret statutes of the applicable state. The Coca–Cola formula is likely the most famous example of proprietary know-how that has been protected merely by trade secret protection, and not by any formal intellectual property filings or registrations (such as a patent for the formula).

While recent international treaties, including TRIPs, have recognized the significance of international trade secret protection, and while a growing number of nations have adopted laws protecting trade secrets, the ability of American companies to effectively protect trade secrets overseas continues to be a significant problem. For example, while many developing nations have begun to adopt Western style intellectual property laws as a result of TRIPs, such laws are often not effectively enforced or are simply ignored. American entities must also be wary of relying solely on the protections provided by the trade secrets laws of certain developed nations, such as Japan, due to the difficulty of effectively enforcing those rights in the courts of such nations. Accordingly, every American entity must fully analyze all risks associated with revealing any trade secrets to overseas contacts, including the entity's own overseas employees, even if that overseas contact has agreed to sign a confidentiality agreement.

VI. Conclusion: Mechanisms For Protecting Intellectual Property Rights Overseas

* * *

[I]t is incumbent upon every American entity doing business overseas to fully investigate the level of intellectual property protection in a nation and, particularly, the risk of piracy, before doing business in that nation. Additionally, an American entity can take practical steps to enhance the protection of its own rights by: (1) conducting intellectual property audits to determine the value of its intellectual property rights and the status of protection; (2) limiting disclosure of intellectual property rights within the corporation and its foreign distributors, licensees, and other contacts; (3) learning the law, bureaucracy and customs of all nations in which the corporation does business; and (4) developing strategic alliances with local people in order to discourage piracy.

SECTION C. OVERCOMING THE FEAR OF NUMBERS: AN INTRODUCTION TO VALUATION

One of the recurrent problems in transactions involving business enterprises, from formation through final disposition, is to determine the value of the business or an interest in the business. The reader has already confronted a foretaste of this subject in the Schollhammer and Kuriloff piece on evaluating new venture opportunities, which was reprinted earlier in this chapter. The result of such an evaluation is to create a projection of income from the new venture and of the capital necessary to produce this income, thereby allowing one to determine the return on investment. Investors can then evaluate the risks of the new venture not producing the projected income and assess whether the rate of return is acceptable for this level of risk.

Turning from start-ups to going businesses, the Small Business Administration has provided a high readable, and highly simplified, explanation of valuation methods.

Small Business Administration Management Aid for Small Manufacturers No. 166

By G.H.B. Gould and Dean C. Coddington.
(August 1964).

HOW DO YOU KNOW WHAT YOUR BUSINESS IS WORTH?

Corporations whose stocks are actively traded on the major exchanges are valued continuously by the investing public. But how do owner-managers of small closely held companies determine how much their business is worth when they, for instance, seek outside financing?

Or how do you value a business for situations such as those involving estate and gift taxes? And what about the value of a company which you may purchase in order to strengthen your own business?

NO SET FORMULA FOR VALUATION

Various methods can be used for computing a company's worth, but no set formula exists. Keep in mind that the buyer, or investor, wants an answer to one question: What percent of return can I get on my investment? Or said another way: What is the value of the future earning power of this company?

The best way to answer that question is by using the capitalized earnings method for evaluating the worth of a company. But first, look at two other commonly used methods: (1) asset valuation, and (2) market valuation.

• Asset Valuation

Companies are often evaluated by their assets as reflected in book value, reproduction value, and liquidation value. However, assets are significant only as they enable a company to manufacture and sell products, or services, that will generate profits.

Book Value. Sometimes a company's book value does not hold up in the market place. One company, for example, sold for $300,000 even though its net worth or book value was $600,000. The reason: a large part of the assets was tied up in specialized equipment and slow-moving inventory, sales volume was down, and the company's net income after taxes was only $30,000. The purchasers decided that the company to them was worth only 10 times earnings, or $300,000.

Another disadvantage of valuing a company on its net worth is that book value can be high because of retained earnings over a long period of time. The company can still be a poor investment because its current earnings are down and prospects for increased future earnings are dim.

Reproduction Value. Many small businessmen value their companies in terms of reproduction value—the current cost of reproducing the assets of the business. They reason like this: The cost of duplicating my business will be higher than what is shown on my balance sheet because many items have been depreciated. Also inflation has increased the prices of certain pieces of machinery.

A disadvantage of reproduction value is that it tends to set a high asking price on a business. Often a man can start a new one with less capital than it takes to buy a company on its reproduction value.

Liquidation value is the amount that would be available to the common stockholders in the event that a small business is liquidated. In liquidation, time is often a factor; outside pressures demand action; and the business is sold at a sacrifice. However, this method has some use in placing a floor under the value of a company—determining the minimum asking price.

• Market Value

Quoted prices on stock exchanges constitute market value of common stock. Usually such prices in a broad and active market can be considered the current value of a company. But even so a company is sometimes merged or sold at quite a different value from the current value of its marketable common stocks.

Market value can be subjected for example, to short-term swings caused by rumors, opinions, and other factors. The fickleness of over-the-counter stock prices tends to be even greater than that of the major stock exchanges. For example, the announcement of potential contracts often raises the over-the-counter value of the stock of an electronics company out of proportion to its real value.

Where thin, limited markets exist, differences between the current value and market price of a company's stock are apt to be great. For example, a company with 300,000 shares outstanding might sell at 5 to 10 times earnings and under book value per share because demand for the stock is slight. The industry is highly competitive, the company's sales are down, and profits have been declining. At the same time, another company with 300,000 shares outstanding—but with strong earnings and growth prospects—might sell at 30 to 50 times earnings and many times book value.

Capitalized Earnings Value

Whether you buy or sell a small company you need to know about the company's ability to earn profits—especially future profits. The capitalized earning approach considers a business as a living, changing organism which uses its assets to produce the greatest possible return on investment.

Two steps are used in capitalizing earnings. First, you find a company's true earning power, based on both its past experience and future probabilities. Second, you capitalize these earnings at a rate which is realistic for the risks involved.

- Finding a Company's Earnings

A company's *past earnings* record gives a buyer, or investor, an indication of what he might reasonably expect in the future. He learns about this record from past income statements. Looking at them for a 5–year period helps him to see trends.

The buyer should make adjustments to the income statement for: (1) nonrecurring items that a buyer should not expect to encounter in the future, (2) unusually large bad debts, (3) inventory write-offs, (4) excessive salaries, (5) low salaries that might have to be raised in order to get qualified assistants, and (6) nonbusiness ventures.

The kind of accounting procedure used can also have a direct effect on reported earnings. For example, one company may charge the cost of tools and dies as expense items in the year in which they were bought. Another may amortize the cost of such equipment over a period of years and thereby increase earnings.

When a potential buyer adjusts for nonrecurring items and for varying accounting practices, he is trying to judge what future earnings might be under his ownership. His return on investment has to come from possible *future earnings*.

Therefore, the buyer needs income statement projections based on what he thinks he can do with the company. Often an independent study of the company's prospects for sales helps to give a sound basis for earnings projections.

Even though selling may be your last thought at this point, it is a good idea to look ahead. Make sure that your accounting system records the information necessary for making realistic earnings projections. Thus you can base your negotiations on facts should you ever decide to sell. Also, don't buy, or sell, without having an independent audit of the company's books.

Finally, from the 5-year period, you have to pick one annual earnings figure as the true *earning power* of the business. If the company has a proven record, current earnings can often be used. In well-established companies, *proven past profits* and *projected income* for the current year usually go together to make the true earnings figure. However, when a company is fairly new but with good potential, future earnings estimates are weighed heavily.

• What Capitalization Rate Should Be Used?

The rate at which you capitalize a company's average earning power depends on the risks involved. The higher the risk of generating projected earnings—and thus creating a return on the buyer's investment—the lower the capitalization rate.

Suppose, for example, that the earning power of two companies is the same—$100,000. Suppose further that Company A has a proven record of profits and a very substantial annual earnings growth rate. With highly favorable prospects for the future, Company A might be capitalized at 20 times earnings for a value of $2 million. At the start, the investor would get 5 percent return on investment, and the proven growth of earnings would increase his possibility for a greater return in the future.

However, keep in mind that valuation is also subjective—what the buyer thinks the business is worth to him. Some may be willing to pay a much lower multiple of earnings for a closely held company even though the present owners have built an outstanding record for growth and prospects appear favorable.

On the other hand, Company B is relatively small and in a highly competitive industry. The company is growing but has not established itself. A buyer would need a high percentage return—20 percent or more—on investment. If he needed 20 percent, earnings could be capitalized at 5 times for a value of $500,000.

• External Influences

When determining the proper capitalization rate, or price-earnings multiple, external influences have to be weighed. Some of them are:

(1) *Economy.* What effect will the state of business and the regional and national economic outlook have on the company?

(2) *Industry.* Do industry factors—such as competitive structure, cyclical, seasonal and Governmental influences, and industry glamour—make the company attractive to investors? Unattractive?

(3) *Company position.* How does the company compare with its competitors in size, growth, margins, order backlog, suppliers, patents, and freight advantages?

(4) *Financial strength.* How do the company's balance sheets and income statement ratios compare with competitors and with credit statistics for the industry as a whole? A debt-free company, of course, can borrow capital for expansion and diversification.

(5) *Management.* Is the company's management strong? Does its past performance indicate that it can maintain and increase profits in the future?

(6) *Character of investment.* In a closely held company—one person or a small group owning more than half the stock—the price-earnings multiple will be lower because of the nonmarketability of the investment.

• Factors Which The Buyer Injects

In addition to these external influences, the price-earnings multiple is often determined by factors which the buyer, or investor, may throw into the situation. Some examples are:

(1) *Buyer's price-earnings multiple.* If an investing company can buy a company at a price-earnings multiple below its own, its stockholder's position is not diluted. For example, if a buying company's stock is selling at 15 times earnings, it can afford to issue stock with a value up to—but not more than—15 times earnings for an acquisition. However, if the buying company pays more than 15 times earnings, its stockholders will earn less per share on the combined earnings.

(2) *Competitive investments.* When buying for investment, the return on the purchase price of a company must compare favorably with other things—such as stocks, bonds, real estate, or savings deposits—for which the buyer could spend his money.

(3) *Job money.* Companies are often sold to buyers who want to take over active management, and such a buyer may be willing to pay a little more.

(4) *Buyer's needs.* Another company might pay a higher price than an individual buyer in order to fill needs such as management, products, brands, patents, franchises, or licensing agreements.

(5) *Method of payment.* Tax factors have to be considered. Acquisitions effected through merger, sale of stock, or sale of assets for either cash or stock depend on tax factors involved with the corporation's assets and net worth as well as each stockholder's personal position.

(6) *Minority stockholders.* The value of a minority ownership position in a closely held company is not as great as a majority stockholder because of the additional risks associated with lack of control.

(7) *Cash flow.* Cash flow—net profits after taxes plus non-cash charges, such as depreciation, depletion, and amortization, has become an important factor in valuation. The cash generated from operations can be

used for capital expenditures, reduction of debt, payment of dividends, and expansion. So a company may be sold at a very high multiple of earnings yet at a reasonable ratio to cash flow. This cash "payout" often determines the ultimate value of a business and is becoming increasingly important.

APPLICATION OF METHODS

When determining how much your company is worth, keep in mind that its marketable value may vary according to what you are planning to do.

If you set a value in order to get *public financing,* bear in mind that a public underwriting of securities should be priced so that the investment will be attractive in comparison with stocks of other companies in your industry. Such pricing should also give the stock room to rise after the issue has been floated.

The situation is somewhat different if you seek *private financing.* When buying non-marketable securities, an investor needs a higher return. Usually private venture capital sources seek investments which will double in value and be marketable within 3 years.

In a *private sale* to one individual, he buys on what he thinks he can earn from the company. If he plans to operate the company himself, he may pay more for the intangible benefits of having managerial responsibilities.

Above all, in buying or selling, keep in mind that value varies with individuals. The worth of a going company is largely a subjective matter—what a person thinks the business is worth to him. But even so, the capitalized earnings approach embodies facts which can be used to arrive at a realistic value.

The capitalized earnings method helps you to: (1) find the true earning power of a business and (2) then find the investment necessary to earn a rate of return that is in line with the risks involved. This method also considers all of the external influences—such as the economy and industry conditions—which bear on a company's prospects.

NOTE

The above discussion is simply "the camel's nose under the tent" to introduce a subject to which this book will repeatedly return. Specifically, in dealing with raising financing in Chapter V, it will be necessary to explore in some mathematical detail the methods by which securities analysts evaluate the worth of investments. Valuation discussions in more "legal" contexts—i.e., judicial opinions and revenue rulings—occur in Chapter II (*Pope & Talbot v. Commissioner* (difference in value between assets held by a limited partnership and the aggregate value of the limited partnership interests), Chapter III (*e.g., Curtis v. Campbell* (dispute over price term in a partnership buy-out agreement)), Chapter VI (*e.g., Kaplan v. Goldsamt* (challenge to price paid to redeem dissident stockholder's shares); Revenue Ruling 83–120 (valuation of shares exchanged in a recapitalization)), and Chapter VII (*e.g., Piemonte v. New Boston Garden Corp.* and *Gilbert v. MPM Enterprises, Inc.* (appraisal proceedings following a merger)).

CHAPTER II

CHOICE OF BUSINESS ENTITY

SECTION A. TRADITIONAL NON-TAX CONSIDERATIONS

For the most part, individuals in the United States operate businesses in one of six forms: the sole proprietorship, the partnership, the limited partnership, the corporation, and, more recently, the limited liability company (or "LLC"), or the limited liability partnership (or "LLP"). The sole proprietorship is the simplest of these forms. There is one owner who receives all the profits or bears all the losses and who has ultimate control. If the business requires services beyond what the owner can perform, he or she hires employees or contracts the work out. If the firm requires additional capital, the owner borrows. The sole proprietor obtains needed property through purchase or lease.

Individuals who supply capital, services or property to a business often desire a share of the profits and control. At some point, it may make economic sense to accede to such desires rather than pay more interest, wages and rents. The result can be to create a partnership—an association of persons who carry on as co-owners of a business for profit. Uniform Partnership Act ("U.P.A.") § 6; Revised Uniform Partnership Act ("R.U.P.A.") § 202(a). Indeed, a partnership might be the result of a sharing of profits and control even if the parties never so intended. *E.g., Minute Maid Corp. v. United Foods, Inc.,* 291 F.2d 577 (5th Cir.1961).

The proprietorship and partnership as forms of business possess certain real or perceived disadvantages. Traditionally, the primary disadvantage has been unlimited personal liability of the owner(s) for obligations arising out of the enterprise. Avoiding such liability or other perceived disadvantages led to the development of the corporation, the limited partnership, and, recently, the limited liability company and limited liability partnership.

Hazen, The Decision to Incorporate

58 Neb. L. Rev. 627 (1979).

* * *

The nontax disadvantages to incorporation such as the increased formality and expenses of operation speak for themselves. It is easy to see how they must fit into the calculus of the incorporation decision. Not as clear, however, is the extent to which the advantages of incorporation may be illusory. The discussion that follows is directed towards pointing out some of the pitfalls in relying too heavily upon the supposed advantages. It will become clear that although the corporate form is preferable in a large number of situations, it should not be routinely and mechanically adopted.

A. Limited Liability

Common and preferred shares in corporations are nonassessable and accordingly the shareholders' exposure to liability is generally considered to be limited to their initial investment. It follows that any business planner is well versed in the general black-letter-law proposition that shareholders of a corporation enjoy limited liability. However, such generalities are overboard and may wane when applied to specific situations; this is especially true in the context of the closely-held concern.

To begin with, as a practical matter a shareholder's potential liability will go further. When a small incorporated concern decides to raise funds by borrowing, prudent creditors will require the major shareholders to personally guarantee corporate obligations. Similarly, third parties contracting with the corporation will often require performance bonds or individual guarantees by the shareholders. Accordingly, at least until the enterprise becomes well established and sufficiently stable in the eyes of outsiders, limited liability will be limited in application to insulating the shareholders against tort judgments.

In addition to the demands of the market place, there are various judicially created doctrines that may be applied to extinguish the shareholders' limited liability. Application of these doctrines can work extreme harshness since the lack of predictability of result makes this an extremely difficult risk to anticipate and guard against.

Although the courts have exhibited great reluctance to apply the doctrine, thin capitalization may be the basis for piercing the veil of limited liability. For example, in Minton v. Cavaney[23], Justice Traynor, speaking for the California Supreme Court, held that shareholders of a corporation operating a swimming pool could be held personally liable for a tort judgment against the corporation due to their failure to adequately capitalize the business and thereby provide a cushion to absorb the foreseeable risks of the enterprise.

Another basis for piercing through the corporation to the shareholders' personal assets is a finding by the court that the shareholders disregarded the corporate entity by operating the corporation as their "alter ego." In applying the alter ego analysis, the courts look to such factors as the failure to segregate funds, the failure to keep separate books, and the absence of arm's-length dealings between the principal shareholders and the corporation. Other activities that fall into this category include the failure to follow corporate formalities such as keeping minutes of the required shareholder and director meetings. * * * It follows that the diligence required to * * * [avoid the alter ego problem] is a significant burden of corporate form. * * *

23. 56 Cal.2d 576, 364 P.2d 473, 15 Cal.Rptr. 641 (1961).

The foregoing discussion should not be taken to indicate that limited liability is too easily lost. This is not the case, as the corporate veil is a benchmark of corporate life. On the other hand, piercing the veil is a risk which should not be minimized. When this risk is coupled with the likelihood that creditors and other third parties will often require personal guarantees before dealing with the corporation, it would be a mistake to give limited liability too much weight in deciding whether or not to incorporate.

A final point to be kept in mind in deciding whether to incorporate is the alternative availability of the limited partnership form of operation. * * * The primary drawbacks of this form are (1) the limited partners' inability to actively participate in management and (2) the general partner's unlimited personal exposure to liability. Accordingly, the limited partnership interest represents a passive investment which may not meet the participants' objectives if they desire some control over their investment. The unlimited liability of the general managing partner may be minimized by incorporation of the general partner. * * *

Another factor in evaluating the importance of limited liability is the availability and cost of insurance to cover the risks of the enterprise. While it is impossible to insure against a general business failure, many of the risks are insurable. For example, any business involving the use of motor vehicles will want adequate liability insurance, as would any business owning real property. The nature of the business and the potential exposure of the owners to liability will necessarily be factors, but in many instances insurance may make even the general partnership a viable business form despite its lack of limited liability protection.

B. Continuity of Existence

Under * * * current corporate chartering statutes, * * * corporate duration is perpetual unless a shorter period is provided for in the articles. This possibility of immortality contrasts to the black letter common law rule that a partnership dissolves whenever a general partner ceases to hold that position whether it be by virtue of death, [or] withdrawal * * *.

A reading of the current statutory provisions governing partnerships makes it clear that a corporation's perpetual existence is not unique. * * * [T]he partners may in essence provide for perpetual existence. * * *

An additional factor in evaluating the importance of perpetual existence in selecting the corporate form is the fact that a corporation may be subject to involuntary dissolution. * * * [I]nvoluntary dissolution may be obtained at the behest of a disgruntled shareholder. This may be even more of a factor in the future to the extent that courts become more willing to decree involuntary dissolution upon a shareholder petition in order to accommodate the flexibility and needs of the incorporated partnership. As a result of this unpredictability, the planned duration of the enterprise may not always be a significant factor in deciding whether to adopt the corporate rather than partnership form.

C. Free Transferability

As is the case with continuity of existence, in most situations the partnership form's limitations on the free transferability of ownership interests need no longer be a significant factor in the planner's decision to opt for the corporate form. The partnership is not as restrictive as it once was. * * *

Conversely, the increasing recognition of special treatment for closely held corporations has led the courts to be extremely tolerant of share transfer restrictions. The types of transfer restrictions on corporate shares are many and can be readily adopted to meet the needs of a particular situation.

* * *

D. Flexibility in Structuring Management

* * *

Another divergence between the corporate and general partnership form is the centralization of management. The directors manage the affairs of the corporation and these directors, who are elected by the shareholders, in turn appoint the corporate officers over whom the shareholders have no direct control. In contrast, the members of a general partnership are all co-managers. For example, any partner has both the apparent and implied authority to bind the partnership in dealings with third parties. Of course, utilization of the limited partnership form provides for the same type of management centralization that exists with the corporation. However, this is true only to a limited degree insofar as in the limited partnership the management is not highly stratified as readily as it may be in the corporation, * * *.

Certainly, to the extent that the enterprise in question requires a sophisticated, stratified management structure, the corporate form is preferable. However, the need for a sophisticated structure is not typical, especially for the small business, but rather is a situation that may occur in a relative handful of situations.

E. Flexibility in Capitalization

The final corporate advantage to be discussed is, standing alone, probably the most utilitarian and hence the most significant in selecting the form of operation. The partnership basically provides for one type of equity or ownership interest with the one variation presented by the limited partnership form. Intrapartnership agreements can, of course, define relative priorities in profit sharing with even more flexibility than is available with the corporate form. However, planners may be reluctant to rely on such contractual definitions because of unfamiliarity. The various types of share classification and senior securities that are available in the corporate form are expressly sanctioned by the corporate statutes and have been subject to much judicial scrutiny, thus providing guidelines. The absence of statutes and case law in the partnership setting gives more flexibility but provides a lesser degree of certainty. This certainty in the partnership context can only be provided by the far-thinking planner who is able to anticipate and then draft provisions to cover all contingencies with respect to the desired preferences.

* * *

III. CONCLUSION

It has been admonished: "When in doubt, don't incorporate." This advice is well taken. Indiscriminate use of the corporate form will frequently result in a counter-productive situation in which the expense, time and formality will far outweigh any benefit to the enterprise. In deciding which form to adopt the planner should take cognizance of the oft-times illusory nature of the advantages discussed above. When viewed in the appropriate perspective and when properly balanced against the known disadvantages, the optimal form of enterprise will be chosen through an informed rather than a mechanical selection process.

NOTES

1. Professor Hazen states that the increased expense and formality of corporate operation is a factor weighing against incorporation. Before accepting this or any other such generalization at face value, however, one should ask just exactly how much extra expense and formality one is dealing with. One expense and formality comes from the requirement that parties file a document (generally called either a certificate or articles of incorporation) with a state official in order to form a corporation. Similar filing requirements exist to form limited partnerships, LLPs and LLCs. This requirement can impose two types of expense—the legal fees to prepare the document, and the filing fees and franchise taxes imposed by the state for the privilege of forming and maintaining a corporation (or other statutory entity). Chapters III and IV will look at the contents of such formation documents. For now, however, it is useful to note that the contents of such documents need not be extensive, and, accordingly, might not entail significant legal expense to prepare (especially in comparison with the complexity and expense entailed in drafting documents, like a partnership agreement, to govern the internal relationship of the participants in the venture). Fees and franchise taxes vary from state to state and between the various business forms, making generalization difficult and specific inquiry necessary.

Professor Hazen also notes the possible burden posed by complying with so-called corporate formalities in order to avoid a court "piercing the corporate veil." Actually, the notion that courts pierce the corporate veil based upon the failure to follow formalities with respect to shareholders' and directors' meeting might be the legal equivalent of an "old wives' tale." *E.g.*, Gevurtz, *Piercing Piercing: An Attempt to Lift the Veil of Confusion Surrounding the Doctrine of Piercing the Corporate Veil*, 76 Ore. L. Rev. 853, 866–67 (1997). Even if not, how much of a burden will it really be in a corporation with few shareholders to get the shareholders together once a year for a shareholders' meeting to elect themselves as directors, and thereafter to have the occasional directors' meeting? There probably is more realistic significance to financial formalities—segregating corporate from personal funds, keeping corporate financial records, and the like—when it comes to piercing. Yet, it is a little difficult to tell corporate creditors that they can only look to corporate funds for repayment, and, at the same time, expect that one need not keep corporate funds separate from one's own.

2. Discussion of piercing the corporate veil brings one to the broader topic of limited liability. Limited liability traditionally is viewed as the primary advantage of the corporation over the ordinary partnership—any of whose members can be called upon to pay the entire debt of the firm. U.P.A. § 15; R.U.P.A. § 306. As Professor Hazen points out, several factors undermine this advantage. The significance of these factors varies with the type of debt a business might face. The demand that shareholders sign personal guarantees, for instance, is a phenomenon of negotiated contracts claims, less typical of debts to trade creditors, and not a concern with obligations arising by virtue of the firm's torts. Conversely, insurance is largely a protection against tort claims rather than against the inability to pay contracts creditors due to general business failure. Moreover, the utility of insurance varies inversely with the prospects for catastrophic losses which could exceed reasonable policy limits. This makes it necessary for the planner to evaluate the nature of the anticipated debts of the specific business in order to assess the importance of incorporating to obtain limited liability. It is also useful to consider the particular owners involved. How much do they stand to lose if worse comes to worse and they must declare a personal bankruptcy?

Professor Hazen points to use of a limited partnership as an alternative for obtaining limited liability—at least for those whose role is that of limited partner. Note the two disadvantages he points out. These disadvantages arose because the traditional rationale underlying limited partnership statutes was to allow a trade-off: some owners (the limited partners) would obtain limited liability in exchange for relinquishing all control to other owners (the general partners), who would have unlimited personal liability for the firm's debts. By contrast, corporate law allows the owners of a corporation (the shareholders) to enjoy limited liability even if they elect themselves as directors, appoint themselves to be officers, and thereby to manage the company. As Professor Hazen mentions, forming a corporation to act as the general partner is a common way to avoid any individual (as opposed to a corporation) being liable for the debts of the limited partnership. Moreover, having the individuals, who wish to run the business, act as the directors and officers of the corporate general partner might allow individuals to control a limited partnership without fear of personal liability. Even without use of a corporate general partner, the law concerning limited partnerships has changed substantially since Professor Hazen wrote his article. As will be discussed in Chapter III, a revised version of the Uniform Limited Partnership Act promulgated in 1976, and amended in 1985, both expanded the scope of activities that a limited partner can undertake without being deemed to participate in control and narrowed the range of circumstances in which a limited partner's participation in control will lead to personal liability. Yet a newer revised edition of the Uniform Limited Partnership Act promulgated in 2001 completely eliminates the rule that limited partners forfeit limited liability if they participate in control.

Far more significantly, new non-corporate forms of business, which provide limited liability to all of the owners, have come into existence since Professor Hazen wrote his article. The first of these new forms is the limited liability company. Wyoming enacted the first LLC statute in 1977. It was not until after a favorable 1988 pronouncement by the Internal Revenue Service concerning the tax treatment of LLCs, however, that other states enacted statutes allowing for this form of business entity. By the mid–1990s, every state had adopted an LLC statute. Under these statutes, owners of an LLC (without regard to their role in management) enjoy the same limited liability as shareholders in a corporation. *E.g.*, Cal. Corp. Code § 17101(a); Del. Code Ann. Title 6 § 18–303; N.Y. Ltd. Liab. Co. Law § 609. In 1991, Texas pioneered another new limited liability business form, the limited liability partnership. Almost all of the states now have statutes providing for LLPs. (Some states now even have begun to allow the creation of limited liability *limited* partnerships. This, however, may be getting silly, since, as discussed later, it is usually difficult to understand what advantage parties would gain by forming a limited liability limited partnership rather than just an LLP or LLC.) Partners in an LLP generally enjoy the same limited liability as owners of an LLC or shareholders of a corporation. *E.g.*, Cal. Corp. Code § 16306(c); Del. Code Ann. Chap. 15 § 1515(b); NY Partnership Law § 26(b).

Incidentally, even those who conduct their business as partners in an ordinary partnership sometimes can obtain a certain degree of self-help limited liability to the extent the partnership's creditors agree to look only to the firm's assets for repayment. This is known as a non-recourse loan. Creditors might be willing to agree to a non-recourse loan when they obtain a security interest in some property used by the business.

On the flip side, recall that Professor Hazen pointed out that limited liability in a corporation can be lost if the court pierces the corporate veil. The conventional wisdom concerning this subject has been that piercing is rare. An empirical study of over 1500 piercing cases found, however, that courts pierce very closely held corporations to impose liability upon individuals who are shareholders at almost the percentage that would result if one were flipping a coin. Thompson, *Piercing the Corporate Veil: An Empirical Study*, 76 Cornell L. Rev. 1036 (1991). Courts also have held that owner(s) of an LLC can be liable for the firm's debts under similar standards applied to pierce the corporate veil. *E.g., Ditty v. CheckRite, Ltd., Inc.*, 973 F.Supp. 1320 (D.Utah 1997).

Finally, it is important to keep in mind that limited liability only deals with debts of the firm; each owner still remains liable for his or her own debts. This includes any liability the owner personally faces because he or she committed a tort, even if done in the scope of his or her employment for the company. Put differently, the doctrine of vicarious liability—which makes the company liable for the torts of its employees in the scope of their employment—only adds a defendant (the company); it does not relieve the employee of personal liability.

3. Continuity of existence and free transferability are really flip sides of the same phenomenon: what happens when an owner departs the venture, either through death, personal bankruptcy or simply the desire to withdraw. This subject is quite extensive and occupies an entire section in both Chapters III and IV (dealing with non-corporate forms of business and corporations respectively). For present purposes, however, it may be useful to think of partnerships as generally following a buy-out model, under which, essentially, if the remaining partners of the firm wish to continue the venture in these circumstances, they must purchase the departing partner's interest. This is also the basic model followed for LLPs, limited partnerships (albeit with some differences in mechanics), and, under the original statutes, for LLCs. Recently, however, LLC statutes in many states have switched to a lock-in approach, under which, absent contrary agreement, LLC members can neither sell their complete interest (including management rights) to whomever they choose, nor demand that the other owners buy them out. A 2001 revision of the Uniform Limited Partnership Act follows this lock-in approach as well. Still, it is relatively straightforward to contract for the buy-out model in an LLC or a limited partnership. With a certain degree of planning, corporations can also follow a buy-out model. Without such planning, corporations follow a free transfer model, under which what happens to one owner does not directly impact the other owners' ability to carry on the business through the corporation; instead, the departing owner conveys his or her shares to whomever he or she wishes. (As discussed later in this book, however, the lack of willing buyers for minority shareholder interests in a closely held corporation may effectively mean that such corporations follow, in reality, a lock-in model.) It is legally possible to create the equivalent of a free-transfer model by agreement in a partnership or other non-corporate entity; yet, other rules applicable to non-corporate entities (such as unlimited personal liability for any transferee who becomes a partner in an ordinary partnership) may pose practical impediments to freely transferring interests in such entities.

Overall, the choice of entity impact depends upon which model the owners wish to follow. In a closely held business (in other words, one with few owners), the owners often prefer the buy-out model. This is not only because such owners want to limit who are their associates in the venture, but also because free transfer often does not provide a very happy solution when there is no outsider interested in buying into a closely held business (which, as just mentioned, effectively turns the free transfer approach into a de facto lock-in). One result of locking co-owners into a soured business relationship is to produce litigation, such as mentioned by Professor Hazen, in which a shareholder seeks judicial dissolution of the corporation (which, in turn, normally leads to a buy-out). The buy-out model is equally available in all of the forms for conducting business, and, accordingly, renders the continuity of existence and free transferability factors irrelevant to choice of entity. In the widely held business (in other words, one with many owners), the free transfer approach works nicely—as exemplified by the activities of the stock exchanges every day. Selection of the free transfer regime favors corporations.

4. As Professor Hazen points out, corporation statutes contemplate a sort of republican management structure: the owners (the shareholders) elect directors to be in overall charge of the corporation, while the directors appoint officers to run the day-to-day affairs of the company. By contrast, partnership law follows a direct (or Athenian) democracy approach to governance. The uniform partnership acts make (barring other agreement) all partners co-managers. The laws governing LLPs and LLCs (typically) follow the partnership law approach. Limited partnership statutes follow yet a third model; that of a sort of dictatorship under which some partners (the general partners) possess the exclusive right to control without (unlike corporate directors) being subject to periodic election (at least barring contrary agreement). As explained earlier, traditionally, this management structure reflected the notion that limited partners must relinquish control to the general partners as the quid pro quo for limited liability. While the 2001 revision of the Uniform Limited Partnership Act eliminates the requirement that limited partners abstain from control in order to retain limited liability, the 2001 Act still leaves exclusive control (barring other agreement) in the hands of the designated general partner(s). Indeed, much of the purpose for continuing to have a limited partnership statute, according to the drafters of the 2001 revision, is to provide for a form of business under which investors would have even less control than shareholders enjoy under the republican model of corporate law.

In any event, deviations from the basic governance models for these forms of business are common. One partner or a management committee often rules large partnerships, while the shareholders of small corporations typically all take part in running the business. The only limit, which partners cannot contract around, on partnerships employing a corporate-type management structure is the greater apparent authority of partners than of shareholders to bind the firm to transactions beyond one's actual authority. As discussed in Chapter III, LLC statutes in some states provide a means to avoid even this apparent authority problem. As discussed in Chapter IV, during the evolution of corporate law, courts sometimes blocked efforts by shareholders in closely held corporations to follow partnership style management. Now, however, parties exercising a modicum of legal skill in the application of corporate law can avoid falling victim to this judicial attitude, to the extent it still exists. Hence, owners of a closely held business can pretty much contract for the type of management structure they desire regardless of the form of business they choose.

5. While the various types of share classifications and senior securities give corporate capital structures great flexibility in achieving desired allocations of profits and rights to return of invested capital, skilled planners possess theoretically unbounded flexibility in this regard when preparing a partnership agreement (or an agreement governing a limited partnership,

LLP or LLC). Why then does Professor Hazen give the edge to corporations in this area? The answer lies not in flexibility, but in familiarity. Corporate preferred stock and debt securities represent long established means of obtaining often desired allocations of profits and of distributions on liquidation, regarding which an attorney can find more "law" than when attempting to achieve the same sort of allocations through a partnership agreement.

This rationale, in turn, raises a broader question whose impact permeates all of business planning (and, indeed, much of human endeavor): Why should one sacrifice optimum flexibility by sticking to the familiar? Normally, it is because one assumes what is familiar is safer. A widely used technique presumably has worked and has the "bugs" worked out, whereas with a new or less used approach, the planner may more easily overlook something which will torpedo his or her efforts. Moreover, the very effort of thinking through all the potential problems with a more creative approach and embodying the approach in original documents, in itself, adds to the cost of the transaction. Yet, there are a couple of countervailing considerations. One is obvious. Creating a structure which more optimally achieves a client's objectives than does slavish adherence to the familiar is often what separates the leaders of a profession from the pedestrian practitioner. A second factor is less obvious. Consider what it is in the legal context which makes a technique more familiar to attorneys. Professor Hazen gives a hint when he states that corporate securities have been subject to much judicial scrutiny. While this provides the planner useful guidelines, might the presence of considerable "law" (judicial opinions) regarding a technique suggest something else about the approach?

6. The upshot of much of Professor Hazen's article, as well as of the last three notes, is that specific planning, rather then choice of entity, can govern the relations between the participants in the venture—in other words, allocations of profit, management and dealing with departure problems. This is why these factors often become choice of entity neutral. (Contrast this with limited liability, where third party rights are involved.) In an ideal world, the participants will completely plan out their relationship at the inception. As noted in Chapter I, however, in the real world this is impractical if not impossible. Statutes governing corporations, partnerships, limited partnerships, LLPs and LLCs are in large part composed of rules (often referred to as gap filling or default rules) to apply in situations for which the parties did not plan. As indicated by the discussion so far, and as developed in much greater detail by Chapters III and IV, these rules differ in the different entities. Could this provide a basis for choosing one type of entity over another? Perhaps one form better deals with situations parties do not anticipate. For example, perhaps one form will better protect minority interests from oppressive actions by the majority.

While this sounds good, it suffers from one obvious problem. In order to consider rationally which statute better handles unplanned for events, one seemingly needs to anticipate the events, determine how the parties wish to deal with them, and compare that with the statutory schemes. Of course, if one has done all that, one might as well go ahead and specify the parties' plans in an appropriate agreement. Is there any other way to make this comparison? Perhaps one might ask in which statute's drafters does one have greater confidence. A possible answer could be a statute whose drafters focused more on a business of the nature one is dealing with.

Gevurtz, Corporation Law

§ 1.1.2*d* (2000).

* * *

To understand why, it is useful to introduce the concept of "coherence," by which we mean that all the terms governing the business venture work together in a sensible fashion.[24] To illustrate, return to the fact that corporations normally follow a free transfer model to deal with departure of owners. This norm, in turn, makes possible active trading markets in corporate stock. The liquidity provided by such markets encourages investment in the publicly held corporation. Why has this not happened to anywhere near the same extent for partnerships and other non-corporate forms?

The answer is not that partnerships and other non-corporate forms legally cannot follow a free transfer model. On the contrary, we saw earlier that partnerships and other forms could provide this by contract. Rather, the answer is that the practicality of free transfer depends on a lot more than simply the exit rules. We already noted one example: Unlimited personal liability will put a damper on trading ownership interests which would make the purchaser a partner.

Governance also plays a role. The republican model of corporate governance in which shareholders elect directors by voting in proportion to their stockholding is well suited to the firm with free transfer of ownership. Because stockholders, as such, do not directly participate in managing the corporation, they can trade their stock without disrupting the running of the company. At the same time, the liquidity from being able to sell in an active trading market makes the shareholders more willing not to participate directly in management. On the other hand, the fact stock carries proportionate voting rights gives the purchaser of a majority of the stock the power to replace management. The fact that the purchaser of a majority of the stock also gets most of the economic worth of the corporation gives the purchaser an incentive for responsible action in selecting management. This creates some discipline over those in charge of the corporation.

Finally, the fact that corporate law both assumes the norm of, and provides for, ownership interests based upon fungible shares of stock encourages active trading. Purchasers can buy in small quantities. Current shareholders can sell portions of their holdings. There is no need to amend, or even for the buyer to read, any agreement setting out the profit shares or management rights of all the owners of the corporation. The bottom line

24. For a development of this concept see Larry E. Ribstein, *Statutory Forms for Closely Held Firms: Theories and Evidence from LLCs,* 73 Wash. U. L. Q. 369, 381–382 (1995).

is that a variety of corporate law rules work together to make public ownership and trading in corporate shares attractive.

By contrast, unlimited personal liability is likely to make partners particularly insistent on being able to protect themselves through a direct role in management and by having the right to veto extraordinary decisions. This, in turn, suggests the desirability of following a buy-out, rather than a free-transfer, approach to owner departure, since free transfer can lead to problems when there is direct management by, and a veto for, all owners. On the other hand, the availability of a buy-out makes direct management and veto powers more tolerable than if there was no exit for dissatisfied partners. Also, as we shall see later in this book, it is much more straightforward and less prone to unintended consequences for a few owners to specify their economic and management rights expressly in a contract, than it is to attempt to achieve the same results by playing with the distribution of stock. Hence, partnership rules also interrelate.

These interrelationships create the hazard that parties and their attorneys will underestimate the impact of deviations from statutory norms. Often more dangerous, parties risk overlooking some of the terms they should agree to in order to achieve coherence when they choose a form of business organization which the legislature established with a very different type of ownership in mind.

For example, later in this book, we will look at situations in which the majority owner(s) of a closely held corporation squeeze a minority shareholder out from sharing in the profits of the business. This is a frequent problem in closely held corporations, but rarely comes up in partnerships. Why? Because various provisions in partnership law work together to prevent the phenomenon. Corporations statutes, drafted with the widely held business in mind, have different provisions. Unfortunately, many times, neither the parties putting together a closely held corporation, nor their attorney, recognize the significance of all of the different provisions until after a problem arises and it is too late for contracting.

* * *

SECTION B. SEPARATE TAXPAYING ENTITY VERSUS PASS-THROUGH TREATMENT

Llewellyn & Umbrecht, No Choice of Entity After Check-the-Box

52 Tax Law. 1 (1998).

I. TAX CLASSIFICATION UNDER CHECK-THE-BOX

A. The Old Entity Classification Regulations

The Code divides business entities into two general categories: C corporations and pass-through entities, the latter category being further divided between S corporations and partnership-type entities governed under subchapter K. The sole proprietorship falls on the pass-through entity side of this watershed.

C corporation and pass-through entity are tax law designations that do not necessarily correlate with familiar state law entities. For incorporated entities, C corporation tax status is the Code's default. Disregarding special purpose entities subject to special taxing schemes (such as RICs, REITs, REMICs, DISCs and FSCs), an entity that is a corporation for state law purposes is automatically classified as a corporation for federal income tax purposes, and is automatically a C corporation unless an S election is made. * * *

C corporation tax status also attaches to any unincorporated entity (such as a partnership or LLC) classified as an "association" taxable as a corporation under section 7701(a)(3). Regulations under this section (the "classification regulations") sought for decades to classify unincorporated entities as either associations or pass-through entities on the basis of their supposed similarity to or difference from state law corporations, as determined by the presence or absence of certain specified corporate characteristics. Under this approach, an unincorporated entity could be classified as a corporation for federal tax purposes by reason of structural factors making it more like a corporation than not. In practice, the threat of C corporation status was more apparent than real. The regulations were interpreted and applied so mechanically by the courts that entities could evade association status through drafting talismans and cosmetic structural changes while retaining functional equivalence to "real" corporations. * * *

B. The New Entity Classification Regulations

A new era in tax planning began last year with the publication of revised final regulations under section 7701(a)(3), generally effective January 1, 1997. Under these new entity classification regulations, the treatment of incorporated entities is unchanged: as before, incorporated entities are always taxable as corporations, with no tax election to this effect required or permitted. The treatment of unincorporated entities, however, is profoundly changed. The new entity classification regulations abandon any pretense to theory and make the federal tax treatment of unincorporated entities explicitly optional. Hence their nickname, the "check-the-box" regulations. Under the "check-the-box" scheme, a domestic unincorporated entity with multiple owners may choose to be taxed either as a C corporation or as a pass-through entity, and if the latter, either as a partnership under subchapter K or, if it qualifies and elects, as an S corporation. A domestic entity with a single individual owner may choose to be treated either as a "disregarded entity" (sole proprietorship), as an S corporation if it qualifies and elects, or, if it does not, as a C corporation. Substantially similar rules apply to foreign entities and entities with corporate owners.

* * *

In the absence of a check-the-box election, the federal income tax treatment of a partnership, LLC or any other unincorporated domestic entity is automatically governed under subchapter K (or the sole proprietorship provisions in the case of an LLC with a single individual owner).

* * *

II. THE SUPERIORITY OF PASS-THROUGH TREATMENT

A. Explanation

Under current law, a C corporation is a taxpayer in its own right separate from its shareholders and its current earnings and realized capital appreciation are taxable both in its hands and (if and when distributed as dividends) in theirs. Losses and deductions of a C corporation can be used, if at all, only to offset corporate income and gain. Except for an S corporation that was once a C, a pass-through entity or sole proprietorship is tax-exempt in its own right and its current earnings and realized capital appreciation are taxable (whether or not distributed as dividends) only in the hands of its owners. Losses and deductions derived at the entity level pass through to the owners and, subject to limitations, can be used to offset an owner's income and gain from other sources.

The contrast was not always so stark, nor the choice of pass-through treatment so compelling. Under the pre-1986 *General Utilities* doctrine, corporate capital appreciation could be passed to C corporation shareholders in liquidation without the realization of corporate-level gain. Furthermore, the C corporation tax rates were at times sufficiently lower than individual rates to allow the effect of the double tax exposure to be eliminated through short-term deferral of dividend distributions. With the repeal of *General Utilities* and the narrowing of the rate gap, pass-through treatment will in most circumstances produce better tax results than taxation as a C corporation.

* * *

C. Ineffectiveness of C for Low-Rate Accumulation

For a C corporation to produce better tax results than an S corporation or partnership [due to lower income tax rates on corporate, as opposed to individual, income], it would be necessary to retain earnings and gain on inside appreciation in corporate solution long enough that, on a present value basis, the * * * additional tax cost on distribution to shareholders * * * is less than the [tax saved by having the income initially taxed at lower corporate income tax rates]. * * * This strategy only works, however, if there is indeed lag time between the realization and the recognition of income by the shareholder. * * * [G]iven the narrow range of rates, the lag time might need to be so long (depending on discount rate and other factors) as to be unacceptable from an economic standpoint and/or invite accumulated earnings or personal holding company tax.

* * *

D. A C Corporation Can Be the Only Choice for Publicly–Traded Entities

If equity interests in a business are to be "publicly traded" within the rather broad definition given in section 7704, then C corporation tax status is probably mandatory regardless of which state law entity is the chosen vehicle for conduct of the business. If the chosen vehicle is a state law business corporation, it will automatically be classified as a corporation under the check-the-box regulations. If the chosen vehicle is a partnership or LLC, then unless its income is predominantly the "passive-type income" described in section 7704(c) and (d), it will be "publicly traded partnership" (PTP) automatically treated as a corporation for federal tax purposes under section 7704. In either case, it will probably not qualify for S status because of the [one hundred] shareholder limitation.

If, by reason of public trading, C corporation tax status cannot be avoided, section 7704 should probably be avoided by operating in corporate form. From the federal income tax standpoint, operating in noncorporate form could entail chronic problems of interpretation of subchapter C, which was designed with corporations and stock in mind, not partnerships and partnership interests. * * * Moreover, using a PTP instead of a "real" corporation introduces the classification uncertainty of section 7704 itself, entailing as it does the possibility of an inadvertent deemed liquidation (and the attendant tax liability) in the event that the entity unexpectedly ceases to be PTP, either because public trading ceases or because of a change in the entity's mix of passive and active income. * * *

E. Utility of C to Avoid the Passive Activity Loss Restrictions

If an individual owner (sole proprietor or partner) does not "materially participate" in a business activity, the activity is a "passive activity" as to that owner and the owner generally can use losses from that passive activity only to offset income from other passive activities (and not to offset active or portfolio income) until such time as the loss activity is disposed of. A C corporation is subject to no participation-based restriction on the utilization of losses unless it is a "personal service corporation" or a "closely held C corporation," as those terms are defined in the Code. A personal service corporation is subject to the passive loss rules to the same extent as an individual. A closely held C corporation that is not a personal service corporation is subject to a modified version of the passive loss rules: it can use passive losses to offset "active" income, but not portfolio income.

If a business enterprise (other than a personal service business) is expected to engage in at least two separate business "activities" within the meaning of the passive loss rules, and it can be anticipated that the activities will throw off both active income and net passive losses, then a C corporation might be preferable to a pass-through from the standpoint of loss utilization. * * *

F. Residual Utility of the Zeroed–Out C for Service Businesses

* * * Corporate-level tax exposure on current income can be reduced or eliminated by distributing the earnings of the corporation to shareholders

in the form of compensation (which is deductible) rather than dividends (which are not), a technique known as "zeroing out" because of its effect of reducing the taxable income of the corporation to or close to zero.

The tax advantage of a "zeroed-out" C corporation lies in the treatment of some fringe benefits paid to employee-shareholders. Unless a C corporation is a "personal service corporation" within the meaning of section 269A, most fringe benefits paid to its employee-shareholders are treated in accordance with the rules governing employees generally, without regard to the stock ownership of the recipient. Subject to some nondiscrimination requirements, C corporation employee-shareholders generally are eligible to exclude a particular fringe benefit from income if and to the extent the exclusion would be available to an employee who does not own stock. For example, health insurance premiums paid by a C corporation for the benefit of an employee-shareholder are deductible by the corporation under section 162(a)(1) and excludable from the employee-shareholder's income under section 106(b). Similarly, the exclusions available under section 132 for a laundry list of fringe benefits generally are available to employee-shareholders.

Some of the same fringe benefits would be taxable if the employer were a pass-through entity. Under the partnership rules (applicable to S corporations through section 1372), fringe benefits paid to an employee-owner as compensation for services are excludable from income only to the extent they would be excludable if paid to or for the benefit of a self-employed person. * * *

Another advantage of selecting a C corporation to conduct an enterprise arises when a shareholder who is a qualified retirement plan participant wants to borrow money from the plan. No prohibition other than those under the constraints of section 72(p) exists for such borrowing. Any partner who has a significant (more than ten percent) capital or profit interest in the partnership or any S shareholder who owns a significant number of outstanding shares (more than 5 percent) is prohibited by section 4975 from borrowing from the plan. Sole proprietorships are subject to the same prohibition under section 4975 with respect to such borrowing.

* * * [T]he tax savings from excluding fringe benefits would be too small in many cases to justify the significant comparative disadvantages of [choosing to do business as a C corporation].

* * *

There are other disadvantages to the use of a zeroed-out C corporation. Shareholders would need to work for the corporation rather than to derive income from the corporation strictly in their capacities as shareholders. Depending on the type of business involved, the reasonableness of compensation paid to employee-shareholders (and its corollary, the lack of dividend distributions) could be called into question.

* * *

NOTES

1. Professors Llewellyn and Umbrecht focus on the tax consequences of choosing between pass-through and C corporation treatment for a business earning money. After all, few people go into business in order to lose money. Nevertheless, the owners of many (if not most) new ventures expect to go through a period of losses before the enterprise becomes profitable. Moreover, some businesses may generate deductions (such as depreciation) which produce tax losses despite the business achieving a positive cash flow and no real economic loss. Traditionally, parties have viewed pass-through entities as the more desirable form for a business expected to generate tax deductible losses. *But see* Bankman, *The Structure of Silicon Valley Start-ups*, 41 U.C.L.A. L. Rev. 1737 (1994) (finding that high tech start-ups generally have not employed pass-through forms despite incurring losses). By using a pass-through form, the owners may be able to claim an immediate deduction of the losses to offset against the owners' other income, whereas a C corporation would carry such losses forward to use against future (and maybe never realized) income. Indeed, this is the basis of what is often referred to as a tax shelter.

In the Tax Reform Act of 1986, Congress sought to curb the use of tax shelters. The act expanded the reach of Section 465 of the Internal Revenue Code, which limits the ability of a business' owner to claim deductions for losses in excess of the amount the owner faces personal liability to pay. More significantly, Congress added a new section to the tax code (Section 469), which precludes a taxpayer from deducting so-called passive activity losses against non-passive activity income. Chapter III will explore both Sections 465 and 469 in some detail. For present purposes, however, the question is to what extent do these changes alter the traditional view of pass-through entities as the vehicle of choice for a loss generating business.

There are three answers to this question, depending upon the circumstances. The first answer is in some circumstances the 1986 changes will not matter because Sections 465 and 469 will not prevent the owners from taking an immediate deduction for losses generated by the business. This is easy to see for Section 465. This section only limits deductions beyond the amount the owner is at risk to pay, but still leaves him or her able to take deductions equal to his or her investment. Section 469's impact is more complicated. In brief, however, Section 469 will not prevent those who actively participate in the venture—Chapter III will discuss the criteria for sufficient participation—from gaining an immediate deduction for the business' losses. The practical problem here, however, is that those who actively participate in a loss venture often do not have large outside incomes to offset by deductions; perhaps because they are busy running a loss venture. Alternately, passive investors may still be able to use deductions from the pass-through entity if they have other passive activity income (since Section 469 only prevents use of passive activity losses against non-passive activity income). In this regard, however, it is important to note that portfolio income (such as dividends and interest from stocks and bonds) is not passive activity income. I.R.C. § 469(e)(1)(A).

In other circumstances, Sections 465 and 469 might completely reverse the former thinking and, as explained by Professors Llewellyn and Umbrecht, favor the formation of C corporations for a business expected to incur losses. This is because these sections do not apply, with certain exceptions, to C corporations. I.R.C. §§ 465(a)(1)(B), 469(a)(2). The primary difficulty here, however, is that if all a C corporation's activities generate losses, the company cannot gain any immediate tax advantage from the losses regardless of Sections 465 and 469. Hence, the way to gain an immediate tax advantage is to pair income producing and loss generating activities in a C corporation (or else have an income producing C corporation be an owner of a pass-through loss generating entity). The *Wolter Construction* case, reprinted later in this chapter, provides an example where parties could have tried this. Yet, the approach of pairing income producing and loss generating activities in a C corporation may have only limited potential. As a practical matter, a start-up business often will not have, or be able to create, immediate income producing activities which can mop up its losses. Moreover, if the offsetting income producing activity would constitute a passive activity for the business' owners, then Section 469 would not prevent the owners from offsetting losses against this income on the owner level if they conduct the business in a pass-through entity. On the other hand, the types of income which cause a problem under Section 469 to offset on the owner level—income from the owner's personal services, and portfolio income—also can cause a problem for a C corporation. Section 469 applies to personal service corporations—defined generally as companies whose primary business is having employees who are also owners (and who own more than 10 percent of its stock) perform services. I.R.C. § 469(a)(2)(C),(j)(2). It also prevents closely-held C corporations from netting passive activity losses against their portfolio income. I.R.C. § 469(a)(2)(B),(e)(2),(j)(1). In addition, the at-risk rules of Section 465 apply to such closely-held C corporations—defined as companies in which five or fewer shareholders hold over 50 percent of the stock. I.R.C. § 465(a)(1)(B). This type of ownership is likely to be typical of start up businesses.

The third possibility is that these sections (especially Section 469) will render losses not immediately useable no matter what the choice of entity. This, in turn, has two impacts on the choice of entity question. One is to raise the question of whether the unused loss carryovers would be more valuable on the owner or entity level. If the business does well, a C corporation could use the loss carryovers to offset its future income. I.R.C. § 172. On the other hand, so might passive owners of a pass-through entity, since they now have passive income. *See* I.R.C. § 469(b) (allowing carry-forwards of unused passive losses). *Cf.* I.R.C. § 465(a)(2) (allowing carry-forwards of losses in excess of the at-risk limit). What if the business does not do well? Perhaps the business will need substantial infusions of additional cash. If a C corporation must give a majority of shares to obtain the cash, Section 382 may substantially curtail the company's ability to use the loss carryovers. (Chapter VII contains a detailed discussion of Section 382.) This section does not apply to loss carryovers on the owner level. *But see* Lockhart, *Do Loss–Trafficking Limitations Apply to S Corporations?* 79 J.Tax. 242 (1993) (open issue as to whether Section 382 applies to loss carryovers from an S corporation, when Section 465 limited the owners' use of the losses). Worse yet, the business could fail. Disposition of the owner's interest in a passive activity—including through the interest becoming worthless—allows the owner to use the previously unused passive activity losses against non-passive activity income. I.R.C. § 469(g)(1). Loss on worthless stock from a C corporation, however, as explained in Chapter IV, generally is a capital loss of limited utility. *But see* I.R.C. § 1244 (allowing a limited amount of ordinary loss treatment for worthless stock).

The other corollary to the lack of immediate use of losses is to force greater attention to what is the best form to handle an income producing business—which one hopes ultimately to have. Here, Section 469 produces an interesting twist on the choice of entity question. Since investors can deduct passive activity losses against passive activity income, Section 469 can put a premium on obtaining such income, as opposed to dividend or interest income, from investments. This, in turn, favors use of pass-through entities (which generate passive activity income for their passive owners), over C corporations, which do not produce such income.

2. Looking beyond the possible impact of Section 469, what choice of entity is best from a tax standpoint for a business which is producing income? Answering this question involves some complex tradeoffs outlined by Professors Llewellyn and Umbrecht.

The tradeoffs between separate taxpaying entity versus pass-through treatment for a business earning money begin with the fact that corporate tax rates often differ from individual tax rates. Throughout most of the history of the income tax, corporate tax rates have been lower than individual tax rates. Hence, at the time Professors Llewellyn and Umbrecht wrote, the corporate tax rate was 35 percent on income over $10 million, and 34 percent on income between $75,000 and $10 million, while individuals paid tax at a rate of 39.6 percent on income over $250,000. This created the prospect of an immediate tax savings by paying tax at the corporate, rather than the individual, tax rate. In 2001 and 2003, however, Congress reduced tax rates on individual, but not corporate, income. As a result, the top rate for both corporate and individual income is now, as a general matter, 35 percent; seemingly removing the immediate advantage of taxing income at corporate rates. I.R.C. §§ 1, 11.

Yet, the differential between corporate and individual rates is far more complicated than suggested by a simple comparison of the basic top rates. For one thing, there are rate differentials at lower levels of income to consider. Specifically, the corporate rate of 34 percent on income below $10 million has a slight advantage over the 35 percent maximum individual rate. Making the calculation even more complicated, various provisions in the tax code can result in an effective marginal tax rate above the nominal rate. For example, corporate income between $100,000 and $335,000 faces an effective 39 percent marginal tax rate because of the phase-out of lower-rate brackets for corporations making over $100,000. In addition, the fact that lower levels of either corporate or individual income generally are taxed at lower rates (the idea behind a progressive income tax) means it also may be necessary to consider the impact of choice of entity on the number of taxpayers: The more taxpayers who split a given amount of income, the more income might be taxed at lower rates (depending upon how much other income the taxpayers make). At first glance, this might suggest an advantage for pass-through forms, which can split the income from the business among their owners, as opposed to a C corporation, which is a single taxpayer. Finally, just to throw the whole calculation into a "never-never-land" of uncertainty, tax rates have been anything but stable. Indeed, the 2001 and 2003 reduction in the maximum individual tax rate, barring further action by Congress, will expire in 2010—at which point the numbers will return to give the corporation an approximately five percent advantage.

In addition to this comparison of income tax rates generally, it is worth noting that both corporations and individuals can face alternative minimum taxes if their taxable income reflects too much advantage from favorable Code provisions. I.R.C. §§ 55–59. The alternative minimum tax essentially requires a taxpayer to pay an additional tax equal to the amount by which a tax on the taxpayer's "alternative minimum taxable income" exceeds the taxpayer's regular tax liability. Alternative minimum taxable income, in turn, represents a sum derived from making various adjustments and additions to taxable income; the notion behind which is to determine an amount which more nearly reflects real economic earnings. A comparison between potential pass-through and corporate alternative minimum tax liability is complex because of differing adjustments—for instance, corporations must take into account so-called adjusted current earnings in computing their alternative minimum taxable income, whereas individuals need not. I.R.C. § 56(c)(1). Nevertheless, it may be worth noting that the corporate alternative minimum tax rate is 20 percent, while the rate for individuals is 26 or 28 percent (depending upon the level of alternative minimum taxable income). I.R.C. § 55(b)(1). In addition, corporations which averaged gross receipts of less than $7.5 million for the proceeding three years (or less than $5 million for the corporation's first three years, or what portion thereof the corporation has existed) do not face the alternative minimum tax. I.R.C. § 55(e).

The analysis, however, cannot stop simply with a comparison of tax rates, or even the possible impact of the alternate minimum tax. Instead, underlying Professors Llewellyn and Umbrecht's claim for the superiority of pass-through treatment is the need to ask how the owners are going to see any benefit from money made by the business. In a pass-through form, distributions of earnings to the owners are generally tax-free. (Chapters III and IV contain discussions of the mechanics of this.) In contrast, if a C corporation declares a dividend from its after-tax earnings, the recipients will receive taxable income. I.R.C. § 61(a)(7). The result is a so-called "double tax" on corporate income: one tax on the corporation when the company earns money, and a second tax on the shareholders when they receive dividends. In 2003, Congress reduced this double tax by lowering the maximum rate on dividend income received by individuals to fifteen percent. (This rate reduction will expire in 2008, however, barring further action by Congress.) While this action decreased the double tax, this comes, as mentioned above, during a period in which there is little difference between the top corporate and individual income tax rates, and so even the reduced double tax is a significant disadvantage for the corporate form of business.

The article by Professors Llewellyn and Umbrecht notes a couple of ways to avoid this double tax. Payments to owners which produce a deduction for the corporation—as, for example, with salaries or interest on loans—will lead to taxation of earnings only once, on the owner's level. Of course, if the company pays out all its earnings in this manner, this would destroy any advantage of having income taxed at potentially lower corporate rates. In essence, all one has done is to create a self-help pass-through entity—at least as far as earnings rather than losses—this being the business which zeros out its taxable income through deductible payments to its owners. Another problem with salaries and interest payments to owners is that the Internal Revenue Service may seek to deny deductions for an unreasonable salary and to recharacterize salary or interest payments as non-deductible dividends. Chapter IV will address this subject in some detail.

As this discussion makes clear, avoiding the double tax—particularly if the objective is to gain an advantage from potentially lower corporate income tax rates—may require leaving the money in the corporation. More precisely, the owners might take out money they need immediately through a salary and leave the rest in the company. Indeed, splitting the income generated by the corporation between salary payments to the owners and the earnings remaining in the company could result in more income taxed at lower rates. *E.g.*, Lee, *A Populist Political Perspective of the Business Tax Entities Universe*, 78 Tex. L. Rev. 885, 909 (2000). Yet, accumulating earnings in the corporation creates a couple of problems. To begin with, as Professors Llewellyn and Umbrecht mention, it may trigger penalty taxes designed to prevent precisely this sort of effort at tax savings through accumulating corporate earnings. Chapter IV contains a further discussion of these penalty taxes. More fundamentally, how does leaving money in the corporation do any good for the owners? The answer, of course, is that the value of their stock should increase with the retained earnings. Yet, won't the taxation of the gain on the ultimate sale of their stock bring one back to the same double-tax problem? Here is where the calculus becomes even more complicated.

To begin with, there is the aspect of deferral. The company has had the opportunity to reinvest the money, while the owners put off, perhaps for many years, the second tax on their sale of stock. Whether this deferral, in itself, is worth the double tax depends, as discussed by Professors Llewellyn and Umbrecht, upon the differential between corporate and individual tax rates, the rate of return the firm achieves on reinvesting the money, and how long the owners plan to hold their stock. This makes deferral more valuable in a rapidly growing business, which not only provides a better return, but also has the sort of reasonable need for accumulated earnings that can avoid penalty taxes. (Of course, in a pass-through entity, the firm might theoretically reinvest all its earnings, since the owners, not it, pay the tax. As a practical matter, however, the pass-through firm normally will distribute to its owners at least enough money to cover their taxes on the income from the firm. Otherwise, the owners effectively would be investing additional money in the firm equal to the taxes they pay with their own funds.)

Next, one needs to factor in the normally capital gains treatment of income made on the owner's sale of stock. The maximum rate on capital gains made by individuals is now generally 15 percent. I.R.C. § 1(h). It is useful to note, however, that dividends are now taxed at the same rate as capital gains, thereby removing the advantage of selling stock, versus receiving dividends, as a means of minimizing double taxation of accumulated corporate income. It is also useful to note that the reduction in the tax rate on capital gains to 15 percent will expire, barring further action by Congress, at the end of 2008; at which point the top rate on capital gains will still be a favorable, but not quite as favorable, 20 percent.

Of course, this discussion assumes the owners plan to benefit through sale of their stock. They might, instead, plan to "benefit" by holding their stock until death in order to build up an estate. (Whether this really benefits the decedent, we will leave to the philosophers.) Tax-wise, the impact has been to increase the basis of the shares to their fair market value at the time of death (I.R.C. § 1014), thereby preventing the double-tax. Potentially offsetting this advantage, a larger estate has meant more estate taxes. Still, this assumes the law will remain what it currently is at the time one dies. Unfortunately, from the standpoint of planning, while death is certain, the future tax implications of death are not. Congress has enacted legislation that phases out the estate tax—albeit only to return unless Congress makes the phase out permanent. The elimination of the estate tax, however, will come at the cost of repealing the stepped up basis for property in a decedent's estate under Section 1014.

Finally, one type of shareholder has much less worry when it comes to double tax of corporate earnings distributed as dividends. This is a shareholder which is itself a C corporation. Section 243 of the Internal Revenue Code provides C corporations with a deduction equal to 70 or 80 percent of the dividends the corporation receives from other domestic corporations (depending upon whether the recipient corporation owns 20 percent or more of the dividend payer's outstanding stock).

3. The discussion thus far has focused on income from operations. What about income from appreciating property? If a pass-through entity sells property entitled to capital gains treatment, the owners will face tax at a top rate currently of 15 percent (20 percent after 2008, barring further action by Congress). In contrast, the rate on capital gains made by a corporation generally is the same as the corporate rate on ordinary income (*see* I.R.C. §§ 11(b), 1201); which means a top rate of 35 percent. Add to

this the second tax faced by the owners on distribution of the money or sale of their stock and one can see a serious disadvantage potentially created by having appreciating property in a C corporation.

Is there a way around this problem? Perhaps the corporation could distribute appreciated assets to its shareholders.

Pope & Talbot, Inc. v. Commissioner of Internal Revenue

162 F.3d 1236 (9th Cir.1999).

I

BACKGROUND

Pope & Talbot is a publicly held Delaware corporation. * * * During 1985, Pope & Talbot's Board of Directors and shareholders approved a "Plan of Distribution" ("the Plan") to transfer 71,363 acres of its timberlands, timber, land development, and resort businesses in the State of Washington (together, "the Washington Properties") to Pope Resources, a newly formed Delaware limited partnership ("the Partnership"). Although Pope & Talbot was not to become a partner in the Partnership, the Plan included the formation of two new Delaware corporations—Pope MGP, Inc. and Pope EGP, Inc.—to serve, respectively, as the managing general partner and the standby general partner. Both of these new corporations were owned initially by two principal shareholders of Pope & Talbot, who were to have exclusive authority for managing the Partnership. The Plan required that when Pope & Talbot transferred the Washington Properties to the Partnership, the Partnership would issue limited partnership interests to Pope MGP, Inc., which in turn would distribute the limited partnership units pro rata to the Pope & Talbot shareholders. The holders of the limited partnership units were to have no management power and only limited voting rights.

* * *

The Partnership paid no consideration for the Washington Properties. The limited partnership units in the Partnership were distributed to the approximately 6,000 shareholders of Pope & Talbot, each shareholder receiving one limited partnership unit for every five shares of Pope & Talbot's common stock.

Two weeks before the effective date of the distribution, approximately 1.2 million limited partnership units of the Partnership began trading on the Pacific Stock Exchange on a "when issued" basis. A "when issued" transaction is a conditional transaction in which the buyer indicates a desire to buy the security when it is authorized for sale. The weighted average trading price of the partnership units between December 6, 1985, and January 7, 1996, was approximately $11.50 per unit.

When Pope & Talbot filed its tax returns, it computed the fair market value of the distributed property by using the aggregate value of all the limited partnership units, which individually were valued at $11.50 per unit. The Commissioner disputed this valuation and determined that additional tax was due. Pope & Talbot eventually filed suit in the tax court challenging the Commissioner's deficiency determination.

The tax court granted the Commissioner's motion for partial summary judgment, holding that, under 26 U.S.C. § 311(d)(1), the appropriate methodology to compute Pope & Talbot's gain on the distribution of the appreciated Washington Properties was to treat the properties as if they had been sold by Pope & Talbot for their fair market value on the day of distribution and "not by reference to the property interest received by each shareholder."

A trial then ensued to determine the fair market value of the Washington Properties, using the methodology determined by the tax court in its partial summary judgment. The tax court reviewed extensive expert witness reports and testimony about the fair market value of each of the Washington Properties. Based on this review, the court determined that the valuation range for the combined Properties was between $46.7 million and $59.7 million. The court then considered the aggregate value of the trading price of the limited partnership units, but only as evidence of the fair market value of the Properties. Concluding that the aggregate value of the units warranted valuation toward the low end of the valuation range, the court found the fair market value of the Washington Properties to be $48.5 million.

In this appeal, Pope & Talbot challenges the methodology by which the tax court valued the distribution of the Washington Properties, as well as the value placed on those properties.

II

ANALYSIS

To determine the correct methodology to be used in calculating the fair market value of appreciated property a corporation distributes to its shareholders, we must interpret 26 U.S.C. § 311(d)(1).

The version of 26 U.S.C. § 311(d)(1) ("section 311(d)(1)") in effect when this distribution occurred provides:

I. Distributions of Appreciated Property.—

(1) In General.—If—

(A) a corporation distributes property (other than an obligation of such corporation) to a shareholder in a distribution to which subpart A applies, and

(B) the fair market value of such property exceeds its adjusted basis (in the hands of the distributing corporation), then a gain shall be recognized to the distributing corporation in an amount equal to such excess as if the property distributed had been sold at the time of distribution.

26 U.S.C. § 311(d)(1) (1984).

* * *

The statute's focus is on gain to the corporation. The final clause of the statute provides that a distributing corporation is required to recognize such gain "in an amount equal to [the excess of fair market value over adjusted basis] as if the property distributed had been sold at the time of distribution." 26 U.S.C. § 311(d)(1)(1984). This clause unambiguously requires that the distributed property be valued as if the corporation had sold it. The plain reference is to the corporation's property. * * *

We conclude that the plain meaning of section 311(d)(1) requires that the gain recognized by Pope & Talbot be valued as if the corporation had sold the Washington Properties at the time of distribution, not by aggregating the value of the individual limited partnership units.

The legislative history supports this conclusion. Since 1969 Congress has passed several income tax measures that have progressively repealed the controversial holding of the Supreme Court in *General Utilities & Operating Co. v. Helvering,* 296 U.S. 200, 56 S.Ct. 185, 80 L.Ed. 154 (1935). * * * In *General Utilities,* the Supreme Court held that a corporation was not required to recognize gain when it distributed appreciated property to its shareholders. *General Utilities,* 296 U.S. at 206, 56 S.Ct. 185.

* * *

Congress continued its repeal of the *General Utilities* doctrine with the Deficit Reduction Act of 1984. * * * The legislative history of the 1984 amendment again points to Congress's purpose:

Reasons for Change

* * * The committee believes that under a double-tax system, the distributing corporation generally should be taxed on any appreciation in value of any property distributed in a non-liquidating distribution. *For example, had the corporation sold the property and distributed the proceeds, it would have been taxed. The result should not be different if the corporation distributes the property to its shareholders and the shareholders then sell it....*

Explanation of Provisions

Under the bill, gain (but not loss) is generally recognized to the distributing corporation on any ordinary, non-liquidating distribution * * * *as if such property had been sold by the distributing corporation for its fair market value rather than distributed.* * * *

Regardless of the legislative history, Pope & Talbot argues that section 311(d)(1) must be read symmetrically with 26 U.S.C. sections 301 and 302.[3] Such a reading, Pope & Talbot contends, yields the conclusion that the "fair market value" of the property distributed by a corporation necessarily equals the "fair market value" of the property in the form it is received by the shareholders. We disagree with this reading of these sections. Sections 301 and 302 focus on shareholders' tax liability. Cases interpreting these sections usually concern to what extent shareholders receiving distributions should be taxed. *See, e.g., Cordner v. United States,* 671 F.2d 367 (9th Cir.1982) (holding that gold coins distributed to shareholders were "property" to be taxed at fair market value for purposes of section 301). However, if the corporation distributes one form of property and the shareholders receive another, there is no "symmetry." That was the case here. The corporation did not distribute gold coins to shareholders who received gold coins. The corporation distributed the Washington Properties to the Partnership, and the shareholders received individual limited partnership interests. We conclude the tax court used the proper methodology to determine the fair market value of the distributed property.

We next consider the tax court's actual valuation of the Washington Properties. Pope & Talbot argues that even if the value is to be determined by reference to the value of the distributed property in the hands of the corporation, the tax court erred in not finding that value to be the aggregate dollar amount of the limited partnership units on the date of distribution. That value, Pope & Talbot argues, is the true value placed on the Washington Properties by the market in actual sales of partnership units, not on some hypothetical sale conjured up for valuation purposes.

* * *

The success of Pope & Talbot's argument depends on applying to this case the general rule that, when one is valuing securities on a stock exchange, "the average exchange price quoted on the valuation date furnishes the most accurate, as well as the most readily ascertainable, measure of fair market value." *Amerada Hess Corp. v. Commissioner,* 517 F.2d 75, 83 (3d Cir.1975)* * *. We are unpersuaded that this general rule applies to the Pope & Talbot distribution before us.

The rule in *Amerada Hess* applies to the valuation of stocks, not to the valuation of the underlying assets of a publicly traded entity.

* * *

3. Section 301 sets forth how a shareholder receiving a distribution of property should be taxed, specifically requiring that the "amount of any distribution shall be the amount of money received, plus the fair market value of the other property received." Under section 302, a redemption transaction is treated either as an exchange whereby section 1001 applies or as a distribution of property whereby section 301 applies. If it is treated as an exchange, section 1001 requires that the amount realized be the sum of any money received plus the "fair market value of the property received." * * *

Common sense also dictates that the value of an entire interest in property, such as the Washington Properties, is greater than the sum of its fractional parts. * * *

* * * The Pope & Talbot shareholders who received limited partnership units in the Partnership received fractional parts of the whole. These fractional parts also bore some burdens. As the tax court found, the limited partners had no management powers, limited voting rights, and significant limitations on their power to remove the managing general partner.

In addition, the limited partnership interests were newly issued. This circumstance made the units difficult to value. According to a report prepared by Kidder, Peabody & Co. prior to the distribution, once the limited partnership units were placed on the market, the units would be "very undervalued relative to the market value of the Partnership's underlying assets" because of "low cash distribution," "the complexity of tax issues," "uncertainty over future tax law changes," and "small market capitalization of the units." Kidder, Peabody believed that a trading value of $5 to $7 per unit was possible, but estimated that "the underlying asset value could be around $26 a unit."

Finally, in Pope & Talbot's proxy statement to its shareholders, Pope & Talbot stated that the corporation was transferring the Washington Properties to the Partnership because it believed that the market value of the properties was not fully reflected in the trading price of Pope & Talbot's stock. * * *

Because market valuation based on sales of the individual limited partnership units would not accurately value the Washington Properties, the tax court properly turned to expert appraisals. The court heard extensive valuation testimony, finally determining a valuation range for the Washington Properties of between $46.7 million and $59.7 million. It also considered the aggregate trading price of the partnership units and ultimately found the fair market value of the Washington Properties on the date of distribution to be $48.5 million. The tax court did not err in making this finding.

* * *

NOTES

1. As *Pope & Talbot* illustrates, a corporation's distribution of appreciated property to the company's shareholders not only can constitute a taxable dividend to the shareholders, but, in addition, the Code generally treats such a distribution as if the corporation sold the assets at fair market value. I.R.C. §§ 311(b)(1), 336(a). (When Pope & Talbot made its distribution, the *General Utilities* doctrine still applied to prevent taxation of the corporation which distributed appreciated assets as part of a liquidation of the company. The next year, Congress completed the repeal of the doctrine by requiring corporate recognition of gain even on liquidation.) Hence, getting appreciated assets out of a corporation means paying a double tax. (The oddity which created the issue in *Pope & Talbot* was that the property

distributed by the corporation was not the same as the property which the shareholders received. This, in turn, led to the valuation question as to whether interests in a limited partnership could have a different worth than the assets held by the limited partnership. Was there any way in which Pope & Talbot could have structured this transaction so that it distributed limited partnership interests rather than the Washington properties? Consider this question after reading the material on partnership formation in Chapter III.)

One way to avoid the double tax problem of having potentially appreciating property in a C corporation, despite the decision to operate in such a form, would be to have the corporation lease rather than own assets expected to appreciate substantially. Chapter IV will explore this possibility. Notice, however, the effect of owners leasing assets to a C corporation is to call essentially for a separate leasing business in a pass-through form.

2. *Pope & Talbot* has an important corollary for the choice of entity question. Circumstances could change so that the optimum choice at one point might not be the best choice later. This could reflect not only changes in the business—such as going from losing money to profitability (or the other way) or reaching a point when the firm no longer has good use for retained earnings—but also changes in the tax law (such as an increase in corporate tax rates over individual rates). How easy is it to go from pass-through to C corporation or from C corporation to pass-through?

Pope & Talbot shows the double tax potential if a C corporation with appreciated assets distributes the assets in order have its owners operate the business through a partnership (or its owner operate through a sole proprietorship). *See also* Treas. Reg. § 301.7701–3(g)(1)(ii)(a business which changes its election under the "check-the-box" regulation from taxation as an association (corporation) to taxation as a partnership is treated as if it is a liquidating corporation for purposes of income tax). In contrast, Chapter IV will show that incorporating a business operated as a partnership, sole proprietorship or other non-corporate form is generally tax-free.

Chapter IV also explores election and revocation of S corporation status. Without discussing this subject now in detail, it is worth noting for present purposes that one generally can go tax-free from C to S or from S to C corporation. *But see* I.R.C. § 1363(d) (a C corporation which uses LIFO inventory accounting must recapture the excess of the inventory's FIFO over its LIFO value upon electing S status). Nevertheless, the Code contains provisions designed to prevent parties from using S elections essentially to rectify the past. Specifically, an S corporation cannot shed any double tax inherent in earnings accumulated, or property which appreciated, while it was a C corporation. I.R.C. §§ 1368(c), 1374. Nor can an S election allow the owners to take advantage of net operating loss carryovers from a company's former C corporation years. I.R.C. § 1371(b)(1). *But see St. Charles Investment Co. v. Commissioner*, 232 F.3d 773 (10th Cir.2000) (Section 469(b) carryover survives changing from C to S corporation). Also, there are limits on passive income (defined differently than under Section 469) that an S corporation, which formerly operated as a C corporation, can earn. I.R.C. §§ 1362(d)(3), 1375.

3. As Professors Llewellyn and Umbrecht discussed in the article reprinted earlier, publicly traded firms are doomed to C corporation tax treatment and so may as well be a corporation under state law. Why then did Pope & Talbot decide to form a limited partnership for the Washington properties? The answer is that this transaction pre-dated Congress' amendment of the tax code to treat publicly traded partnerships as corporations for income tax purposes. Even now, however, publicly traded partnerships for oil and gas and rental businesses remain eligible for pass through treatment.

Normally, businesses do not begin life as publicly traded. Hence, at first glance, the tax treatment of publicly traded firms would seem irrelevant to the initial choice of entity of a start-up venture. Yet, suppose the founders of the venture optimistically plan to go public within a few years of beginning the business. Should they form a corporation from the beginning? As the discussion above indicates, incorporating a pass-through entity is generally tax-free. What non-tax costs, however, might the parties incur when incorporating a business previously operating as pass-through entity? How are these costs likely to compare to any lost tax advantages from not starting life in the pass-through form? See Bankman, *The Structure of Silicon Valley Start-ups*, 41 U.C.L.A. L. Rev. 1737 (1994) (tax savings lost by virtue of incorporating the surveyed high tech companies from their inception significantly outweighed the added non-tax costs of waiting to incorporate until actually going public).

4. Suppose, instead of the corporation selling its appreciated assets, the shareholders sell all their stock in the company to the person who wanted the property. This would appear to avoid the double tax problem. A full exploration of such a transaction must await Chapter VII, which deals with the sale of a business. For now, however, it is sufficient to note a couple of practical problems with suggesting that this idea makes a C corporation a more desirable vehicle for conducting a business with appreciating assets. To begin with, what happens if the prospective buyer only wants some of the corporation's properties, such as the Washington properties in *Pope & Talbot*? Moreover, such a sale of stock means that the assets held by the purchased corporation will not gain an increased basis reflecting the purchase price—which is not an outcome buyers like.

In one situation, however, having appreciated property in a corporation actually can have an advantage when it comes to tax treatment upon the sale of a business. This is during a transaction in which another corporation seeks to acquire the assets in exchange for stock rather than cash. As discussed in Chapter VII, it is possible to structure such a transaction so as to be tax free to all concerned. By contrast, unless the owners of a pass-through entity were to receive 80 percent of stock in the corporation acquiring the property, they would need to recognize income upon the pass-through entity's transfer of the property in exchange for stock in the acquiring corporation. (Could a quick tax-free incorporation work to allow parties to gain the advantage of such a tax-free sale of corporate assets for stock? Unfortunately, as discussed in Chapter VII, such an incorporation immediately followed by a merger or other such reorganization risks running afoul of the step transaction doctrine.)

5. Certain types of taxpayers have particular reasons to disfavor pass-through taxation. Tax-exempt entities, such as pension funds and university endowments, are one such type of taxpayer. Such entities do not have to pay tax on investment income (such as dividends from a C corporation), but must pay tax on so-called unrelated business taxable income. A tax exempt entity's share of ordinary income from a pass-through entity would constitute unrelated business taxable income. I.R.C. §§ 511(a), 512(b)(1), (c)(1).

6. Professors Llewellyn and Umbrecht mentioned in the article reprinted earlier that various fringe benefits might be more available to owners working for their corporations than for owners working for non-corporate entities. This difference flows from the traditional conception that partners who work for their firm are simply "self employed", whereas shareholders who work for their corporation work for a separate legal person. Over the years, various tax code changes have sought to reduce this difference, either by extending some favorable tax treatment for retirement plans or the like to self employed persons, or by reducing the favorable tax treatment for fringe benefits received by shareholder employees of a corporation. Still, there remain some gaps mentioned by Professors Llewellyn and Umbrecht. Chapter IV will discuss in more detail some of the advantages and limitations on corporate fringe benefits.

The different conception of partners versus shareholder employees can manifest itself in other ways as well. One example comes from the deduction available for domestic manufacturing activities under Section 199. This deduction is available both for corporations and for owners of businesses conducted in pass-through forms. Yet, there can be a difference in the amount of the deduction. This is because the deduction is limited by the amount of the W–2 wages paid by the firm—meaning the more W–2 wages paid by the firm, the more the deduction. Partners, unlike shareholder employees, apparently cannot receive W–2 compensation from a partnership. *See, e.g.,* Rev. Rul. 69–184, 1969–1 C.B. 256. Hence, a firm in which the work by owners constitutes a significant amount of the labor costs could have a substantially different deduction under Section 199 depending upon whether it is a corporation or a firm taxed as a partnership.

SECTION C. CHOOSING BETWEEN PASS-THROUGH FORMS

1. S CORPORATION VERSUS PARTNERSHIP TAX TREATMENT

As Professors Llewellyn and Umbrecht discuss, the Internal Revenue Code contains two separate pass-through regimes: Subchapter K for non-corporate entities electing to be treated as partnerships for federal income tax purposes, and Subchapter S for corporations electing the optional pass-through treatment available to companies which meet certain eligibility requirements. This chapter earlier explored the traditional non-tax factors which influence the choice between corporate and non-corporate forms. What tax factors influence the choice between using Subchapter S and Subchapter K?

Eustice, Subchapter S Corporations and Partnerships: A Search for the Pass Through Paradigm (Some Preliminary Proposals)

39 Tax L. Rev. 345 (1984).

* * *

Continuing Discontinuities Between Subchapters S and K: In General

* * *

Eligibility Limitations

Number of Owners Limitation

A partnership can have an unlimited number of owners, while S corporations have always been limited in the number of permissible owners. Initially, only ten shareholders were allowed; subsequent amendments raised the number to 15, then 25, and finally to 35.[77] [Presently, S corporations can have 100 unrelated shareholders. Ed.]

* * *

Eligible Owner Limitations

Any type of entity (a corporation, trust, estate, or other partnership) can be a partner in a partnership. Even an S corporation can be a partner without forfeiting its qualified status. An S corporation, by contrast, cannot have a corporation or a partnership as a shareholder and most types of trusts do not qualify as S corporation shareholders.*

* * *

Foreign Owner Limitation

A partnership can have foreign owners, but an S corporation cannot.

Capital Structure Limitations

The partnership rules permit the creation of varied economic interests in partnerships. Section 704(b) allows partnership income and loss to be

77. I.R.C. § 1361(b)(1)(A). Husband and wife count as only one shareholder, even if they bought stock individually. I.R.C. § 1361(a)(1). [Even more radically, Section 1361(c)(1) now allows family members traceable to a common ancestor up to six generations removed to receive treatment as a single shareholder for purposes of the 100 shareholder limit. Ed.]

* [Wholly owned subsidiaries of S corporations now can avoid treatment as C corporations, and tax exempt charities and employee benefit plans (including ESOPs) can be shareholders in an S corporation. Ed.]

allocated among the distributive shares of the partners by agreement in any way that has substantial economic effect. Special allocations of particular items of income and deduction are permitted, and allocations of bottom line income and loss can vary from year to year and from the partners' proportionate interests in capital. Each share of the stock of an S corporation, by contrast, must have the same economic interest in the corporation. An S corporation cannot issue preferred stock (even proportionately to the common shareholdings), while partnerships can issue preferred partner interests.

The partnership form thus allows significantly greater flexibility in structuring varied economic interests. * * * This disparity is one of the principal disadvantages of an S corporation as compared to a partnership.

* * * The point is illustrated by the confusion that arises when the debt-equity classification problem enters the S corporation scene. Traditional debt-equity stakes ordinarily do not exist in the context of subchapter S, especially the new version. There are, however, important stakes peculiar to subchapter S. If purported debt of an S corporation is held to be equity for tax purposes, the corporation's election can be terminated because (1) the debt deemed equity may be a second class of stock, (2) the purported debt may be held by a person who cannot be a shareholder of an S corporation, or (3) the shareholder number limitation may be exceeded when the debt holder is counted as a shareholder. The first of these possibilities has received the most attention.

* * *

[S]ection 1361(c)(5) * * * provides a straight debt safe harbor * * *. Under this provision, straight debt is not considered a second class of stock, even if it is reclassified as equity for other purposes. Straight debt is a fixed written obligation to pay a sum certain on demand or on a specified due date which (1) bears interest not contingent as to rate or timing, (2) is not convertible into stock (directly or indirectly), and (3) is held only by persons who can be shareholders of an S corporation. * * * Classification of non-safe harbor debt, say the committee reports, will be made under the usual tax law principles (the Joint Committee staff explanation added "applicable to Subchapter S corporations").

* * *

Status Electivity Aspects

* * *

Owner Consents

Since partnership status is automatic, partners do not have to affirmatively consent. Subchapter S, however, requires unanimous shareholder consent to an S election.

* * *

Entity Level Treatment

Entity Taxability

Partnerships are not taxed on their income. Section 1363(a) generally tracks the partnership model by exempting S corporations from the corporate taxes of sections 11, 531, and 541. An S corporation, however, is taxed in [several] situations [which involve S corporations that had previously conducted operations as a C corporation].

* * *

Ordinary Distributions

Current distributions of cash generally have no effect at the entity level for either S corporations or partnerships. * * *

* * * [A] major discontinuity [exists, however,] between S corporations and partnerships with respect to the treatment of appreciated property distributions. * * * [A]n S corporation that distributes to a shareholder property worth more than its basis must recognize gain as though it sold the property at its fair market value[; albeit, the taxable income flows through to the owners].

* * *

When partnerships distribute property to partners, typically, neither the partnerships nor the partners recognize gain or loss. Instead, the partners usually take the partnerships' bases for the property.

* * *

Inside Asset Basis Adjustments

The bases of an S corporation's assets are determined only by events at the corporate level. They are not affected by sales of the corporation's stock. Nor does a distribution of property affect an S corporation's bases for its remaining assets. Partnership distributions and sales of partnership interests likewise do not usually affect the basis of partnership property. The bases of partnership and S corporation assets are thus determined by rules premised on an entity view of S corporations and partnerships. * * *

Subchapter K contains an alternative regime, however, which is a modified version of the aggregate approach. If a partnership makes an election under section 754, adjustments to partnership basis are made whenever an interest in the partnership is sold or exchanged and on some distributions. On a sale or exchange of an interest, partnership basis is increased or decreased, in the aggregate, by the difference between the buyer's basis for the interest and his proportionate share of partnership basis before the adjustments. The aggregate adjustment is allocated among the partnership's assets, and the adjustment for each asset is used solely for the benefit of (or applied solely to the detriment of) the new partner. Immediately after the adjustments are made, the new partner's proportionate share of partnership basis (including the adjustments) equals the basis for his interest.

* * *

Owner Level Treatment

Owner Taxability: Conduit System in General

* * * Subchapters S and K now have virtually indistinguishable rules governing the timing and taxability of entity items in the hands of the owners.

Under section 1366(a), income, losses, deductions, and credits of an S corporation pass through currently to the shareholders, independently of distributions. Each item is allocated pro rata to the shareholders on a per share, per day basis, and retains its entity level character in the hands of the shareholders. * * * An S shareholder reports his ratable share of each separately stated item and of nonseparately computed income or loss. Section 704—which provides that partnership items are generally allocated among partners as they agree—has no analogue in subchapter S.

An S shareholder's deduction for his share of corporate losses is limited to the sum of the bases of his stock and debt obligations of the corporation. A partner can deduct partnership losses only to the extent of the basis of his partnership interest.

* * *

Outside Basis

In General. Sections 1367 and 705 provide substantially identical rules for adjusting the basis of S stock and partnership interests for items passed through to shareholders and partners. Basis is increased for income items (taxable and tax exempt) and is reduced for deductions, losses, nondeductible expenses, and distributions.

* * *

Effect of Entity Debt

One critical discontinuity between S corporations and partnerships [is that] * * * [u]nder section 752, a partner's basis for his partnership interest includes his share of the partnership's debts to third parties. An S shareholders's basis for his stock, by contrast, is not affected by corporate debt. Assume P contributes $100 for a 50% interest in a newly organized entity, and the entity uses the $200 received from its owners and $800 of borrowed money to buy property for $1,000. If the entity is a partnership, P's basis for his partnership interest is initially $500 (that is, the sum of the $100 he paid plus his half of the partnership liability). If the entity is a corporation, even an S corporation, P's basis for his stock is only $100. P can thus deduct losses of the entity up to $500 if the entity is a partnership or $100 if the entity is an S corporation.

* * *

Ordinary Distributions

* * * In general, distributions by S corporations are now treated much like partnership distributions. A distribution by either form of entity is usually treated as a tax-free recovery of the owner's basis. If the distribution exceeds the owner's basis, the excess is taxable gain from the sale of the owner's interest.

* * *

NOTE

Professor Eustice points out that one difference between an S corporation and a partnership lies in the limitation of how many shareholders an S corporation can have (presently, no more than 100 unrelated individuals). While there is no absolute limit on the permissible number of partners, as pointed out earlier, the Internal Revenue Code taxes certain "publicly traded partnerships" as corporations. I.R.C. § 7704. A partnership is publicly traded if interests in it are traded on an established securities market, or readily tradable on a secondary market or the equivalent. I.R.C. § 7704(b). (An exception to taxation as a corporation exists for publicly traded partnerships making over 90% of their gross income from passive sources (such as interest, dividends and the like). I.R.C. § 7704(c),(d).) The Internal Revenue Service has issued regulations interpreting the publicly traded partnership provision. These regulations contain a safe harbor which excludes partnerships from the status of publicly traded, without regard to other criteria, so long as the partnership never sold interests through an offering registered under federal securities laws and has less than 100 partners. Treas. Reg. § 1.7704–1(h). Hence, as a practical matter, there may not be too great a difference between S corporations and partnerships in regard to the number of owners.

Professor Eustice states that one of the primary advantages of the partnership over the S corporation lies in the partnership's greater flexibility in creating varied economic interests without running afoul of the eligibility requirements for pass-through treatment. There is some disagreement, however, as to whether this is really an advantage in all cases—as witnessed by the following exchange among practitioners over the Internet:

> **Lemke:** * * * Drafting the allocation and distribution provisions of LLC agreements [to comply with I.R.C. § 704(b) and (c)], for example, can be daunting for the lawyer who is not a tax specialist. It is certainly daunting to try and explain them in plain English to a client. I think Subchapter S is more easily understood and applied by the nontax specialist than Subchapter K [the portion of the Internal

Revenue Code governing partnerships]. Clients seem to comprehend Subchapter S more easily as well.

* * *

Schedler: * * * In the typical "straight splits" LLC, one can easily draft a less than one-page allocation provision to comply with the regulatory "partners' interests in the partnership" test. While there are a few cases in which the regulatory safe harbor-type allocation provisions may be necessary, in the vast majority of cases, such provisions do more to confuse the client than add any substance to the agreement. In my experience, the cost difference between a vanilla S corporation and a similar LLC is almost entirely attributable to the fact that the LLC operating agreement typically contains the equivalent of a basic shareholders' agreement. If you compared the costs of forming an S corporation with a shareholders' agreement to an LLC, the costs to form an LLC might be less.

Symposium, Check-the-Box and Beyond: The Future of Limited Liability Entities, 52 Bus. Law. 605, 630–31 (1997).

Several other income tax provisions can bear upon the choice between partnerships and S corporations in specialized cases. For example, there is somewhat more potential for recognition of gain with the transfer of services or property to an S corporation in exchange for stock, than there is with the contribution of services or property to an entity treated as a partnership for income tax purposes. Chapters III and IV will explore the reasons for this. On the other hand, owners of an S corporation might be able to trade their stock for stock in a bigger corporation through a tax-free merger or acquisition, whereas owners of a firm treated as a partnership for income tax purposes might need to recognize gain on such a transaction. Chapter VII will explore the requirements for tax-free corporate mergers and acquisitions.

A difference between S corporations and partnerships involves the ability of a corporation to hire its owners as "employees", while, by contrast, partners who work for the firm are simply considered "self employed". This distinction is not as important as it could have been because, as pointed out in the article by Professors Llewellyn and Umbrecht reprinted earlier, Section 1372 generally treats shareholder employees of S corporations the same as partners when it comes to the tax treatment of fringe benefits. Nevertheless, some other advantages to the treatment of shareholder employees versus partners remain with S corporations. For example, this difference can allow S corporations to obtain a greater deduction for domestic manufacturing activities than can a partnership, since, as explained earlier, this deduction is limited to a portion of the W–2 wages paid by the firm, and amounts received by a partner apparently cannot constitute W–2 wages. Also, the fact that shareholder employees are not self employed means that the amount of their Social Security taxes depends upon the amount of their salary; whereas the fact that partners are "self employed" means that the amount of money they choose to call salary and the amount they choose to call a distribution of profit is irrelevant to their Social Security tax. This creates the prospect that owners of an S corporation (unlike partners) can reduce Social Security taxes by reducing their salaries, and taking more of their income from the firm through dividends. *But see Radtke v. United States,* 712 F.Supp. 143 (E.D.Wis.1989) (recharacterized dividend as a salary).

State taxes can also affect the choice between using an S corporation versus an entity treated as a partnership for federal income tax purposes. For instance, some states impose an income tax on S corporations, meaning double taxation of corporate income by the state. *See* Cal. Rev. & Tax. Code § 23802 (taxing S corporations on their income, albeit at a lower rate than C corporations). On the other hand, some states impose significant fees on LLCs in order to make up for the loss of state tax revenue which the owners saved by virtue of pass-through treatment.

2. Choosing Among Non-Corporate Forms

Stover & Hamill, The LLC Versus LLP Conundrum: Advice for Businesses Contemplating the Choice

50 Ala. L. Rev. 813 (1999).

* * *

III. CHOOSING BETWEEN THE LLC AND LLP ON A PRACTICAL LEVEL

While the LLP and LLC are similar in many respects and often difficult to distinguish, there are many situations in which the LLC clearly represents the better choice for a business. * * * [B]ecause the LLP offers no statutory mechanism for formally centralizing management, the manager-managed LLC will be the best choice when the participants truly desire a centralized management structure. Such businesses include high-risk, leveraged real estate or natural resource ventures and other businesses in which the majority of the capital is contributed by passive investors. * * * Because these investment-oriented business ventures typically engage in adequate business planning, including having a detailed operating agreement, the potential traps hidden in the LLC default provisions should not cause any negative effects for these businesses. These potential traps include the ambiguous standard for authorizing salaries, the writing requirement for operating agreements, the default profit sharing ratio, and the absence of dissociation rights.

The LLC is also the better choice for family businesses where the participants have estate and gift tax planning as a major goal. Apparently, the goal of making LLCs suitable for gift and estate tax planning for family businesses constituted a major reason for eliminating dissociation rights in the LLC statute. In order to qualify for discounted valuation for gifts and bequests among family members, the business interest, pursuant to federal law, must be nontransferable and non-liquid as a matter of state law.

Therefore, because LLPs preserve the absolute right of the partners to dissociate and have their interests redeemed by the partnership, LLP interests will never qualify for discounted valuation if transferred among family members in the gift and estate tax context. Because estate planning normally involves a fair amount of legal advice, family businesses that choose LLCs, in order to qualify for discounted valuation of gifted or bequeathed interests, will not likely be caught by the traps hidden in the LLC's default provisions.

The third type of business for which the LLC is clearly the better choice is one in which the participants desire a business form as close to the corporate structure as possible. Often these will include small, active businesses or joint ventures that want a formal centralized management structure, even if they use the operating agreement to undercut it. Often these businesses desire the corporate form to avoid the liquidity problems that sometimes result from dissociation rights or simply for the intangible reason of familiarity. Corporations have been around since America's beginnings, and for most of the twentieth century they have held their place as the dominant business form. The LLC represents the most logical choice for such businesses because the* * * LLC, with the elimination of dissociation rights and the presence of capital-based economic sharing default rules, more closely resembles a corporation than any other business form.

Conversely, the LLP probably represents the preferred choice for business participants who have traditionally used general partnerships. Law and accounting firms are the prime examples of entities that have historically organized as general partnerships, thus making them good candidates for LLP registration. Typically, these firms make an effort to centralize management through the use of internal management committees. The fact that such internal governance rules do not affect third parties has not been a concern of law firms and other professional organizations. Usually law firms do not experience the problems that arise when a partner conducts transactions beyond the scope of his authority. Sophisticated expulsion agreements will normally discourage partners from violating the internal management committee structure agreed upon. As a result, there is no need for these firms and other professional organizations, which customarily organize as general partnerships, to move to an entirely new business form. The expectations of the owners make the LLP, which is, in effect, a general partnership, the better choice.

Unsophisticated businesses that either cannot afford the transaction costs of completing an elaborate operating agreement or have not even considered entering into a written agreement will typically be better off choosing the LLP. Such businesses include those that consist of a small amount of capital and few participants, all or most of whom are heavily involved in the business. Some owners may contribute services to the business because they are unable to contribute capital. The prototype of this business encompasses the classic closely held corporation.

The closely held corporation evolved during the last half of the twentieth century as an alternative to the general partnership. Before the development of the LLC and the LLP, the only option for a small business wanting to secure limited liability was to incorporate and operate as a closely held corporation. Because the default rules of the corporate statutes largely failed to conform to the expectations of small businesses, many close corporation shareholders experienced significant problems, especially with freeze-outs. The ability of a general partnership to register as a LLP provides small businesses, which would have otherwise used a close corporation, the opportunity to combine partnership business characteristics with limited liability. Because the LLC's business characteristics have gravitated more toward the corporate side, the LLP offers a better choice over the LLC for these small businesses.

The following hypothetical business illustrates how the technical differences between LLCs and LLPs in Alabama may significantly impact the participants:

A, B, C, D, and E are all old college friends who decide to open a video rental and sales store together. A and B agree to contribute seventy-five percent and twenty-five percent, respectively, of the capital needed for the business, but will not work in the store. C, D, and E decide to devote their full time to running the business.

The group agrees to share profits equally, but fails to put the agreement in writing. Because they are sure that the business will be successful, they do not discuss losses. The group also decides to designate A as the tax matters partner, but all five owners participate in and vote on other matters affecting the operation of the business.

In the first three years of operation, due largely to start-up expenditures, the entity experiences an overall loss. In year four, the entity breaks even. In years five through seven, the entity realizes a profit, which increases yearly. Because they feel that the profitability of the entity is due entirely to their efforts, C, D, and E become dissatisfied with their profit share in year 8 and demand that A and B, who have not been contributing services to the business, take a smaller share of the profits.

There are many problems that may arise if the entity discussed in the hypothetical were formed as a LLC. The parties' oral agreement to share profits equally may not be enforceable because the Alabama LLC Act requires that operating agreements be in writing. If the statutory default profit sharing ratio applies, C, D, and E, the members who only contributed services, could be denied any portion of the profits because the default ratio reflects the percentage of capital contributed. The capital contributors (A and B) would be entitled to seventy-five and twenty-five percent of the profits, respectively, an unconscionably harsh result for the service-contributors (C, D, and E).

* * *

Because C, D, and E constitute a "corporate majority" on a per capita basis, those three may be able to suspend all distributions and authorize salary for themselves while excluding A and B from receiving any current return on their investment. Because members of Alabama LLCs do not possess dissociation rights and A and B have not entered into a buy/sell agreement, A and B (the minority members * * * from a vote perspective[)], are vulnerable to the squeeze-out techniques very commonly seen in close corporations.

While the Alabama LLC form proved to be problematic for the hypothesized business, the LLP form, although not perfect, will more likely result in consequences that are fair to all five owners. Under RUPA the oral agreement to share profits equally will be enforceable, thus protecting the service-contributors far better than the LLC. Moreover, the default provisions of RUPA addressing governance and voting provide much better protection for the capital-contributors who, as a group, possess less voting strength than the service-contributors. Although the majority group (C, D, and E) controls all ordinary business decisions of the partnership, C, D, and E must obtain A and B's consent for all extraordinary business decisions, including the authorization of salary payments. By requiring all five partners to agree to authorize a salary payment or a distribution that varies from the profit sharing ratio, the LLP statute contains powerful safeguards preventing the squeeze-out techniques so common among close corporations and now a serious risk for LLC members. Because all partners of LLPs have the right to dissociate, A and B, or any of the other partners who are not satisfied with their share of the profits, will be able to withdraw from the partnership.

* * *

NOTES

1. Selecting among the various non-corporate forms for conducting business brings one back to the traditional choice-of-entity factors discussed in the first section of this chapter—albeit now no longer with the focus on comparing corporations to partnerships. Ms. Stover and Professor Hamill did not discuss limited liability as a factor in choosing between LLCs and LLPs. This is because Alabama, like almost all states, provides equivalent limited liability for all of the owners of both types of firms. Limited liability is a potentially much more significant factor when it comes to non-corporate forms other than LLCs and LLPs. For example, unlimited personal liability remains the rule for sole proprietorships and ordinary partnerships. Moreover, as noted earlier in this chapter, limited partnerships only provide limited liability for limited, but not for general, partners, of which the limited partnership must have at least one. Interestingly, a few states have recognized a limited liability limited partnership in which the general partner(s) of the limited partnership enjoy limited liability. Yet, given the existence of LLCs and LLPs, what could be the point of this?

Ms. Stover and Professor Hamill focus on the impact of differences concerning management, sharing of profits and distributions, and member departure, between the Alabama statutes governing LLCs and LLPs. Most of the differences they discuss are differences in default rules which parties can contract around. This is one reason why Ms. Stover and Professor Hamill find LLCs appropriate for businesses with more sophisticated participants (or with more sophisticated legal representation), who will have drafted a detailed operating agreement to avoid some of the problems the authors see in the LLC statute, and, conversely, why they recommend an LLP for businesses with less sophisticated owners. One irony here, however, is how are unsophisticated owners, without sophisticated legal advice, supposed to figure out that an LLP is their better choice? On the other hand, since the reader of this book is learning to engage in sophisticated business planning, should any of this discussion about default rules as a factor in choosing a business form have any relevance to the reader? Recall the earlier material about the burdens and dangers of contracting around statutory default rules designed with a different sort of business in mind. Could this be relevant to the choice between LLCs and LLPs, even when the participants hire a sophisticated attorney? Recall, as well, the discussion of the potential advantages presented by using a form which is more familiar. Notice, in this regard, that Ms. Stover and Professor Hamill suggest an advantage here for LLCs, because of provisions in the LLC statute which follow corporate law principles. On the other hand, LLP statutes are simply an add on to the state's uniform partnership act. This means that the default rules with respect to the LLP owners' relationship to each other, for the most part, follow the long familiar rules of partnership law. By contrast, LLC statutes are entirely new, and represent an attempt to blend provisions copied from partnership, limited partnership and corporation statutes. Might such an attempt to mix and match statutory provisions designed for very different business forms create problems? In any event, Chapter III will provide detailed discussion of LLC and LLP default rules, which should clarify some of the distinctions discussed by Ms. Stover and Professor Hamill.

Turning to the differences between LLCs and LLPs, which did not involve default rules, Ms. Stover and Professor Hamill note the advantage of LLCs for firms which desire only some owners to have control over management. As discussed earlier, and, indeed, as Ms. Stover and Professor Hamill recognize, partnerships or LLPs can have agreements which give some partners complete control over the firm. So what is the difference? The answer is that, under many LLC statutes, such as Alabama's, the parties can provide for management of the LLC by so-called managers. Doing so will deprive the other owners of the LLC of apparent authority to bind the LLC to transactions for which the non-managing owner has no actual authority. By contrast, all partners in an LLP, just as all partners in an ordinary partnership, have apparent authority to bind the firm to transactions for apparently carrying on the firm in the usual way. Of course, the significance of this distinction depends upon how likely it is for an owner, who agreed to remain passive, to suddenly run amok and bind the firm to some contract with an uninformed third party. In this regard, is there any empirical basis for Ms. Stover's and Professor Hamill's sanguine dismissal of this danger in law and other professional firms, while, at the same time, suggesting passive investors in capital intensive ventures might take it into their heads to start entering contracts for the firm? The other distinction pointed to by Ms. Stover and Professor Hamill is the requirement in Alabama's LLC statute for certain terms to be in a written operating agreement in order to avoid the default rules. This sort of requirement exists in a number of LLC statutes. Presumably, however, parties represented by an attorney in establishing their business should not have any problem in complying with such formal requirements—at least one hopes.

2. A number of other factors can impact the choice of which non-corporate form to use for the parties' venture. These factors could be as simple as laws which prevent certain types of businesses from using certain forms for conducting their operations. For example, California does not allow law or accounting firms to conduct business as an LLC. Instead, law and accounting firms—but not most other types of businesses—may form LLPs in California. Cal. Corp. Code § 16101(8)(A). Some jurisdictions, similarly to California, allow only professional firms to use LLPs; even when the jurisdiction (unlike California) allows professional firms also to form LLCs. *E.g.*, N.Y. Ltd. Liab. Co. Law § 1203(a); N.Y. Partnership Law § 121–1500(a). Can parties avoid these restrictions on the permissible type of business by forming their LLC or LLP in a state other than where they intend to conduct business? See, *e.g.*, Cal. Corp. Code § 16101(6)(A)(foreign limited liability partnerships are limited to professional services); Del. Code Ann. Title 6 § 18–901(b)(foreign limited liability company is subject to the same limitation on permissible business as a domestic limited liability company); New York Ltd. Liab. Co. Law § 805(b)(same).

An explanation sometimes given for the widespread preference of professional firms for LLPs over LLCs, where such firms have a choice, lies in age discrimination laws. Age discrimination laws typically only cover "employees." Partners, it is commonly argued, are "employers", rather than "employees", thereby allowing professional firms to insist on mandatory retirement for partners. Some legal advisors have worried that it might be more difficult to make this "employer" not "employee" argument for "members" in an LLC. Actually, however, this rationale may be a case of putting undue weight on a label. It is not the label of "partner" that avoids classification as an employee; rather, the facts involving the individual's control over the venture and the like dictate the classification. *Compare Solon v. Kaplan*, 398 F.3d 629 (7th Cir.2005), *with Panepucci v. Honigman Miller Schwartz, Cohn, LLP*, 408 F.Supp.2d 374 (E.D.Mich. 2005). Hence, it is not clear how much difference the label "member" in an LLC, rather than "partner" in a partnership, would make to the applicability of discrimination laws. Still, there may be situations in which labels might matter. For example, denomination of an owner as a limited partner could avoid questions about self-employment tax. *See* I.R.C. § 1402(a)(13) (excluding the distributive share of firm income allocated to a limited partner from self-employment income—except for guaranteed payments for services rendered). This might explain some parties' desire to use limited liability limited partnerships.

SECTION D. MULTIENTITY STRUCTURES

1. CORPORATIONS (OR OTHER ENTITIES) AS PARTNERS

Revenue Ruling 94–43

1994–2 C.B. 198.

In Rev. Rul. 77–220, 1977–1 C.B. 263, thirty unrelated individuals entered into the joint operation of a single business. The individuals divided into three equal groups of ten individuals and each group formed a separate corporation. The three corporations then organized a partnership for the joint operation of the business. The principal purpose for forming three separate corporations instead of one corporation was to avoid the 10 shareholder limitation of § 1371 of the Internal Revenue Code of 1954 (the predecessor of § 1361) and thereby allow the corporations to elect to be treated as S corporations under Subchapter S.

Rev. Rul. 77–220 concluded that the three corporations should be considered to be a single corporation, solely for purposes of making the election, because the principal purpose for organizing the separate corporations was to make the election. Under this approach, there would be 30 shareholders in one corporation and the election made by this corporation would not be valid because the 10 shareholder limitation would be violated.

The Service has reconsidered Rev. Rul. 77–220 and concluded that the election of the separate corporations should be respected. The purpose of the number of shareholders requirement is to restrict S corporation status to corporations with a limited number of shareholders so as to obtain administrative simplicity in the administration of the corporation's tax affairs. * * * [T]he fact that several S corporations are partners in a single partnership does not increase the administrative complexity at the S corporation level. As a result, the purpose of the number of shareholders requirement is not avoided by the structure in Rev. Rul. 77–220 and, therefore, the election of the corporations should be respected.

NOTES

1. The previous sections of this chapter operated under the assumption that only one entity (a sole proprietor, a partnership, a limited partnership, an LLP, an LLC, or a corporation) would conduct whatever business the parties were setting up. Often, however, more than one entity will be involved. For example, Revenue Ruling 94–43 illustrates how multiple corporations under different ownership might form a partnership in order to carry on one common business. In some instances, the fact that a corporation, rather than an individual, is a partner (or limited partner, or member of an LLC) simply reflects the interest of a pre-existing corporation in participating in the venture. For example, a software corporation

might enter into a partnership with a computer company in order to develop a new product. Revenue Ruling 94–43, however, dealt with new corporations set up solely to act as partners in carrying on the new venture. There are a number of advantages parties might hope to gain by the use of such a structure.

Revenue Ruling 94–43 illustrates the use of partnerships composed of S corporations, rather than individuals, to circumvent the limitations contained in Subchapter S. One suspects that the Internal Revenue Service's new-found liberality in Revenue Ruling 94–43 may have more to do the growing availability of LLCs and LLPs than with the rationale expressed. Be this as it may, can partnerships composed of S corporations avoid other limitations on eligibility for S elections? For example, one of the disadvantages of S corporations relative to partnerships pointed out by Professor Eustice is the requirement that the corporation issue only one class of stock. Could parties create a partnership of S corporations in order to establish more complex allocations of profits, losses and rights on liquidation than they could using one S corporation limited to one class of stock?

Professor Hazen's article at the beginning of this chapter mentioned a much more common use of corporations as partners. This is for a corporation to act as the general partner in a limited partnership. In this manner, no individual need be exposed to unlimited personal liability. One significant problem with this approach existed under the 1916 version of the Uniform Limited Partnership Act. Suppose some of the participants wanted both to be limited partners and to take an active role in running the business. Could the participants achieve this goal by becoming directors and officers of the corporate general partner, as well as being limited partners? Courts were divided on this issue under the 1916 act. *Compare Frigidaire Sales Corp. v. Union Properties, Inc.*, 88 Wash.2d 400, 562 P.2d 244 (1977)*, with Delaney v. Fidelity Lease Ltd.*, 526 S.W.2d 543 (Tex.1975). A revised version of the Uniform Limited Partnership Act promulgated in 1976, and amended in 1985, (the "U.L.P.A.") explicitly allows limited partners to act as officers, directors and shareholders of a corporate general partner without losing their limited liability. U.L.P.A. § 303(b)(1). Keep in mind, however, that to come within this provision, the limited partner's conduct must be that of an officer, director or shareholder of a corporate general partner. *Compare Frigidaire Sales, supra* (the court noted that the limited partners "scrupulously separated their actions on behalf of the corporation from their personal actions") *with Gonzalez v. Chalpin*, 77 N.Y.2d 74, 565 N.E.2d 1253 (1990) (limited partner failed to prove his actions were solely in his capacity as an officer of the corporate general partner when, for example, he signed partnership checks in his own name and without naming the corporation or indicating that he was signing in a representative capacity). The 2001 revision of the U.L.P.A. ("U.L.P.A. 2001") removes the whole problem, by allowing limited partners to participate in control without concern about incurring liability merely from having done so.

Incidentally, Sections 2 and 6(1) of the Uniform Partnership Act—defining a partnership as an association of "persons," and including corporations in the definition of "persons"—suggest there is no problem with corporate partners as a matter of partnership law. *See also* R.U.P.A. §§ 101(6), 202(a); U.L.P.A. § 101(5), (6), (11); U.L.P.A.(2001) § 102(11), (14). While, at one time, a number of court opinions held that entering a partnership—especially one to undertake all the company's activities—violates the statutory corporate law requirement that the board of directors manage the company, or is otherwise *ultra vires* (*e.g., Frieda Popkov Corp. v. Stack,* 198 Misc. 826, 103 N.Y.S.2d 507 (1950)), modern corporate statutes typically empower corporations to enter partnerships. *E.g.,* Cal. Corp. Code § 207(h); Del. Gen. Corp. Law § 122(11); N.Y. Bus. Corp. Law § 202(a)(15); M.B.C.A. § 3.02(9).

2. In addition to having corporations as partners, parties occasionally structure partnerships, some of whose partners consist of other partnerships. (This is often referred to as a tiered partnership). Sometimes this might represent a convenient way of obtaining the profit and management allocation desired. For instance, when an existing partnership wishes to enter into a side venture with outside partners, it may be easier to make the existing partnership the partner, rather than drafting an agreement making all the individuals partners. For some years, planners also sought to use tiered partnerships to gain certain subtle tax advantages. Congress responded by enacting a number of provisions which, for the most part, remove any tax advantages for tiered partnerships. *E.g.,* I.R.C. §§ 706(d)(3) (preventing the use of tiered partnerships to create retroactive allocations of income or loss items to incoming partners), 734(b) (preventing a partnership from obtaining a basis adjustment pursuant to a Section 754 election, if the partnership distributes to its members an interest in another partnership which did not make a Section 754 election), 751(f) (preventing partners avoiding Section 751 treatment by holding Section 751 assets in a lower tier partnership).

2. Corporations With Common Ownership

Wolter Construction Co. v. Commissioner of Internal Revenue

634 F.2d 1029 (6th Cir.1980).

■ CELEBREZZE, CIRCUIT JUDGE.

* * *

I.

Wolter Construction Company, Inc. (taxpayer) appeals from a decision of the United States Tax Court.

* * *

Wolter Construction, a corporation engaged in a general contracting business, was organized on July 12, 1968. From July 15, 1968 through 1970 and 1971, the taxable years in question, its issued and outstanding stock consisted of 250 shares of common stock. Brent F. Peacher owned 200 of these shares, and Theodore T. Finneseth, Mr. Peacher's brother-in-law, owned the remaining 50 shares.

River Hills Golf Club, Inc. (River Hills), a corporation engaged in the business of operating a golf course located in California, Kentucky, was organized on September 5, 1968. From September 20, 1968, until October 23, 1969, River Hills' issued and outstanding stock consisted of 587 shares of common stock and 226 shares of preferred stock. Mr. Peacher and Mr. Finneseth each held 270 shares of common stock. The remaining 47 common shares were owned by Luella Peacher, Mr. Peacher's mother and Mr. Finneseth's mother-in-law. Luella Peacher also owned all 226 shares of River Hills' preferred stock, which was nonvoting and limited and preferred as to dividends.

On October 24, 1969, * * * River Hills issued 360 shares of its Treasury common stock to taxpayer in consideration of taxpayer's cancellation of $18,000 in obligations owed by River Hills to Wolter for construction work performed by the latter. * * *

Not quite five months later, on March 2, 1970, River Hills issued an additional 1,988 shares of Treasury common stock to taxpayer. This was done in consideration of taxpayer's cancellation of another $90,000 owed by River Hills to Wolter for construction work performed by the latter and taxpayer's cancellation of $27,400 in promissory notes given by River Hills to Wolter for sums advanced by the latter. As a result of the March 2 transaction, taxpayer increased the total number of River Hills' common shares held by it to 2,348 or 80 percent of the 2,935 shares issued and outstanding. Having become an affiliated group under Section 1504(a) of the Internal Revenue Code of 1954 by virtue of taxpayer's acquisition of 80 percent of River Hills' common stock, taxpayer and River Hills filed consolidated income tax returns for 1970 and 1971, as they were permitted to do under Section 1501 of the Internal Revenue Code. On these returns deductions totaling $125,255.43 were claimed for net operating losses reported by River Hills on its separate income tax returns for 1968, 1969, and the short taxable year January 1, through March 31, 1970. After an audit, the Commissioner of Internal Revenue determined that the carry-over of River Hills' net operating losses for the period prior to the time that it and taxpayer became affiliated was limited to the income produced by River Hills during the consolidated return years in question. Since River Hills had no income in these years, the Commissioner disallowed in full the net operating loss deductions claimed on the consolidated returns.

* * *

II.

Section 1501 of the Internal Revenue Code (Code) allows an "affiliated group" of corporations to file a consolidated income tax return for a taxable year instead of filing separate income tax returns.* An "affiliated group" of corporations, as defined in Section 1504(a) of the Code, consists of a common parent corporation and one or more other corporations. Each corporation in the "affiliated group," except the common parent, must be 80 percent directly owned by another corporation in the group.** The common parent corporation must directly own a minimum of 80 percent of at least one of the other corporations in the group. On March 2, 1970, Wolter and River Hills became an affiliated group eligible to file a consolidated return by virtue of Wolter's acquisition of 80 percent of the common stock of River Hills.***

The calculus for computing the consolidated income for an affiliated group and the corresponding income tax is not spelled out within the Code. Rather, Congress in § 1502 of the Code has authorized the Secretary of the Treasury to promulgate regulations that outline the requisites for and effects of filing a consolidated income tax return. * * *

Reg. 1.1502–21(b)(1) is concerned with the use of net operating losses on a consolidated return. That regulation permits an affiliated group to use net operating losses sustained by any members of the group in "separate return years" if the losses could be carried over pursuant to the general principles of § 172 of the Code. A "separate return year" is defined as any year in which a company filed a separate return or in which it joined in the filing of a consolidated return by another group. Reg. 1.1502–1(e).

* * * An important exception to this rule is found in Reg. 1.1502–21(c). That section provides that the net operating loss of a member of an affiliated group arising in a "separate return *limitation* year" which may be included in the consolidated net operating loss deduction of the group shall not exceed the amount of consolidated taxable income contributed by the loss-sustaining member for the taxable year at issue. The term "separate return limitation year" is defined in Reg. 1.1502–1(f), in essence, as a separate return year in which the member of the group (except, with qualifications, the common parent) was either: 1) not a member of the group for its entire taxable year; or 2) a member of the group for its entire taxable year, that enjoyed the benefits of multiple surtax exemptions. In summary, losses incurred by a brother or sister corporation or by a corporation which is unrelated at the time of its losses to its subsequent

* The following are the major advantages usually associated with filing a consolidated return: 1) deferral of gain on intercompany transactions; 2) offsetting gains and losses; 3) tax-free intercompany dividends; 4) greater utilization of NOL and capital loss carryovers; 5) greater utilization of unused investment credits; 6) greater utilization of excess charitable contribution deductions; 7) reduction in gain on sale of a subsidiary; 8) minimizing the minimum tax. * * *

** Direct ownership entails ownership of at least 80 percent of the voting power of the owned corporation's voting stock, and at least 80 percent of each class of nonvoting stock. The term "stock" as used in § 1504(a) does not encompass nonvoting stock which is limited and preferred as to dividends.

*** River Hills' other outstanding class of stock was nonvoting preferred stock which was limited and preferred as to dividends. Since this was not "stock" within the definition of § 1504(a), it was not necessary for Wolter to directly own 80 percent of this preferred stock to qualify for affiliated group status.

affiliates, before it becomes a member of an affiliated group filing a consolidated return, can only be carried forward and used on the consolidated return to the extent that the corporation that incurred the losses has current income reflected on the consolidated return.

* * *

III.

Wolter's principal argument is that the net operating loss (NOL) carryover should be allowed under the Common Parent rule of Reg. 1.1502–1(f)(2) since Wolter and River Hills were commonly controlled when the losses were sustained. In the alternative taxpayer contends that Section 1.1502–2(c) of the Treasury Regulations is invalid to the extent that it prohibits the carryforward of River Hills' net operating losses from separate return limitation years.

* * *

Notwithstanding th[e] general restriction on the carryover of NOL's arising in a separate return limitation year, Reg. 1.1502–1(f)(2) provides that a separate return year for the corporation which is the *common parent* of the affiliated companies for the consolidated return year is not generally considered a separate return limitation year (the so-called "lonely parent" rule). Accordingly, a NOL sustained in a separate return year by the common parent of an affiliated group is not subject to the limitation of Reg. 1.1502–21(c). The net effect is to allow pre-affiliation NOL's of the common parent to be used to offset post-affiliation profits of any member of the group.

Were the relationship between Wolter and River Hills different in a few critical respects, the regulations would allow the River Hills' losses to be employed to offset Wolter's income. For instance, if Wolter had possessed 80 percent control of River Hills when the losses were incurred, but a consolidated return was not filed, River Hills could have carried forward those losses to the consolidated return years. Similarly, if the losses in question were losses incurred by Wolter (which is now the "parent" of the affiliated group) in pre-affiliation years, the losses could be carried forward onto the consolidated return regardless of Wolter's current income. Both of these hypothetical situations would exempt the early net operating loss years from the definition of "separate return limitations year," and it is only those losses from separate return limitation years which cannot be carried forward to consolidated return years unless the corporation which incurred the losses has sufficient consolidated return income to offset them.

* * *

To conclude that River Hills is entitled to an exemption from the SRLY restriction would require us to make a leap that we are unwilling to take. First, it would require an assumption that an exception to the SRLY rule for commonly controlled brother-sister corporations was inadvertently omitted from the consolidated return regulations. Second, it would require us to overrule a legislative regulation so as to permit a deduction based only upon a generalized policy distilled from the regulations and symbiotic Code provisions. Even if we were to assume that the instant transaction was indistinguishable, as a matter of economic reality, from the common parent exception, we would not be required to recognize a claimed deduction for the carryover of River Hills' net operating losses. "The propriety of a deduction does not turn upon general equitable considerations, such a demonstration of effective economic and practical equivalence. Rather, it depends upon legislative grace; and only as there is clear provision therefore can any particular deduction be allowed." * * * Reg. 1.1502–21(c) is a clear expression that a particular deduction is limited; conspicuously absent from the Code is any clear provision which allows the deduction in full.

* * *

The decision of the Tax Court is Affirmed.

NOTES

1. In contrast with Revenue Ruling 94–43, in which several corporations under different ownership carried on just one business, *Wolter Construction* involved two corporations under similar ownership, which carried on different businesses. Corporations under common ownership may be brother-sister companies (in other words, the same people own all or most of both firms' outstanding stock)—which was the situation in *Wolter Construction* before 1969—or they may have a parent-subsidiary relationship (one corporation owns all or most of the stock in another corporation), as was the situation in *Wolter Construction* after 1969.

A number of factors—some legitimate, some arguably abusive—motivate the use of multiple corporations despite the corporations having substantially common ownership. Perhaps the simplest is the desire, despite the substantial overlap in ownership, to have somewhat different ownership interests in the different businesses. In this regard, notice the apparent desire of the two brothers-in-law in *Wolter Construction* to own different percentages of the construction business and the golf course—as well as the apparent desire of the mother/mother-in-law to own stock in the golf course company. Many times, the disparity in ownership reflects the desire to allow an employee working in one line of business to buy shares just in that venture as an incentive. A variation on this theme occurs when a corporation wishes to establish an overseas operation in a country whose laws require any business operating in that county to have a certain percentage of ownership by that country's citizens.

Another factor sometimes leading to the use of multiple corporations is the existence of statutes or regulations which prevent certain types of companies from engaging in other lines of businesses which the firm's owners or managers might find attractive. For example, for many years, federal law prohibited banking corporations from underwriting securities. Yet another reason often claimed for establishing multiple corporations is the possibly greater efficiency achieved by keeping the management of various operations separate. For example, in this manner it is easier to see which operations are not pulling their weight. On the other hand, it is not clear why use of unincorporated divisions could not just as well accomplish this goal. Moreover, this goal seems inapposite to the typically informal management practices prevalent among closely held firms such as Wolter Construction.

A very common ground for operating different businesses in different corporations is the desire to insulate the assets of one venture from liabilities incurred in another. Indeed, both the construction business and the golf course in *Wolter Construction* are businesses in which owners might worry about potentially large tort claims. *Walkovszky v. Carlton,* 18 N.Y.2d 414, 276 N.Y.S.2d 585, 223 N.E.2d 6 (1966), provides a classic example of using separate corporations for purposes of confining liabilities. The defendant (Carlton) owned ten corporations, each operating one or two taxicabs with the minimum liability insurance. The claim by the plaintiff in *Walkovszky* points out a problem with carrying this strategy too far. Creditors of one corporation unable to pay them may urge a court to disregard the separate corporate entities, thereby holding the other companies, and possibly even their owner(s), liable. Avoiding this danger suggests the importance of the owners and managers themselves respecting the separate status of the corporations (particularly, by not shuttling funds between the companies, by not having one company undertake transactions solely for the benefit of another, and by not confusing creditors as to which company they are dealing with or what assets that company, as opposed to related companies, owns). *E.g., Zaist v. Olson,* 154 Conn. 563, 227 A.2d 552 (1967). This lack of flexibility, however, is one of the disadvantages of using multiple corporations. Moreover, to avoid courts disregarding the separate corporations, it is probably helpful for the owners to adequately capitalize each corporation to carry out its respective business. *E.g., Gentry v. Credit Plan Corp.,* 528 S.W.2d 571 (Tex.1975). In addition, it would seem that each corporation should undertake a viable business on its own, rather than carrying on what is really just a fragment of one enterprise. *E.g.,* Berle, *The Theory of Enterprise Entity,* 47 Colum. L. Rev. 343 (1947).

With the growth of non-corporate entities, such as LLCs, which provide limited liability, the use of multiple firms under common ownership as a strategy to compartmentalize liabilities has spread beyond the corporation. Delaware, joined by a number of other states, has sought to facilitate this development by allowing the creation of so-called series LLCs. *E.g.*, Del. Code Ann. Title 6 § 18–215. Under the Delaware statute, an LLC agreement can provide for a series of separate members, managers and interests, which can have separate rights and duties with regard to specified property and liabilities of the firm. This allows the parties to divide their LLC into separate pieces, each of which can have its own business purpose, management, profit and loss allocation and rights to distributions, and rules governing entry and exit of members. If the statute had stopped with the rights of the LLC members vis-a-vis each other, then such a series LLC would do nothing more than parties could have done by agreement even in the absence of such a statute. What is significant about the statute is that it allows for subdividing the LLC's liabilities such that the property dedicated to one series cannot be seized to pay the debts of another series. The quid pro quo for this treatment is to keep separate and distinct records that account for the assets of each series, and to provide notice of the division of liabilities in the certificate filed to form the LLC. Also, each series must comply individually with the limits on distributions from an LLC to its members, which the Delaware statute imposes for the protection of creditors.

How useful is a series LLC? After all, as discussed above with corporations, parties can isolate liabilities by forming multiple LLCs; so why have a series LLC? If state franchise fees were per LLC, and the state did not charge more for a series LLC, then there might be some cost savings. This, however, does not appear to be the principal motivation. Rather, the notion is that courts might pierce the "corporate" veil of multiple LLCs under common ownership and this risk can be avoided by using a series LLC. Indeed, the reference in the Delaware statute to the ability of a series LLC to compartmentalize liabilities "notwithstanding anything to the contrary ... under other applicable law" seems designed to produce this impact. Still, it is not entirely clear to what extent parties can avoid a risk of piercing the corporate veil through the use of series LLCs, which they realistically faced by use of multiple LLCs. For example, to the extent, as suggested above, that a common ground for piercing the corporate veil of separate companies is the owners' shuttling funds between firms, would such conduct with a series LLC mean the failure to comply with the statutory requirement of separate and distinct records presumably in order to keep separate property separate? To the extent a common ground for piercing the corporate veil is conduct that misleads creditors, does the series LLC statute trump liability for fraud? To the extent jurisdictions pierce the corporate veil for inadequate capitalization, will such jurisdictions view Delaware's statute as precluding piercing if a Delaware series LLC operating without liability insurance or much other assets causes an accident in that jurisdiction?

Turning to tax concerns, for many years, tax advantages promoted the use of multiple corporations under common ownership. In particular, splitting income between a number of companies would result in taxing more of the total income at the lower end of the progressive rate scale. Sections 1561 and 1563 of the Internal Revenue Code largely put a stop to this. These sections limit the ability of a controlled group of corporations to take advantage of the graduated corporate rate structure. A controlled group is defined, in turn, as a group of corporations in which five or fewer stockholders, who are individuals, estates or trusts, own stock possessing over 50 percent of the total combined voting power, or over 50 percent of the total value, of the outstanding stock of each of the corporations, taking only into account the stock owned in identical proportions among all the corporations.

Nevertheless, some possible tax advantages remain for multiple corporations under common ownership. For example, this may facilitate the future sale of one line of business without facing a double tax. (Chapter VII, dealing with the purchase and sale of incorporated businesses, will develop the reasoning behind this.) Alternately, separate corporations may allow for different tax elections, such as S corporation status, for different business activities. In seeking any tax advantages through multiple corporations, however, one must keep in mind Sections 269 and 482 (discussed in Chapters IV and VII), as well as the fact that other tax code sections sometimes also use a controlled group approach to prevent abuse through multiple companies. *E.g.,* I.R.C. § 414(b) (involving qualification for tax advantaged pension plans).

2. *Wolter Construction* shows one potential disadvantage of multiple corporations—the inability to offset losses from one venture against taxable income from another—and the possible use of consolidated returns to solve this problem. Section 1504(a) specifies the requirements for two or more corporations to constitute an affiliated group eligible under Section 1501 to file such a return. The link which binds the individual members of the group together is the parent-subsidiary relationship in which the parent owns enough stock in the subsidiary to possess at least 80 percent of the total voting power and 80 percent of the total value of all the subsidiary's outstanding shares. I.R.C. § 1504(a)(2). Preferred shares which are non-voting, non-participating and non-convertible (such as those owned by the mother in *Wolter Construction*) do not count in determining this 80 percent. I.R.C. § 1504(a)(4). On the other hand, regulations issued by the Internal Revenue Service pursuant to Section 1504(a)(5) treat options to acquire or sell stock as if already exercised (in determining whether the parent owns the requisite 80 percent) when the options are reasonably certain to be exercised and when issuing options rather than stock otherwise would have resulted in substantial tax savings. Treas.Reg. § 1.1504–4. Determining whether the parent has 80 percent of the voting power is not always simply a matter of whether the parent owns 80 percent of the voting shares or can elect 80 percent of the directors. *See, e.g., Alumax Inc. v. Commissioner*, 165 F.3d 822 (11th Cir.1999) (the 80 percent test was not met where the minority shareholders had an effective veto on major corporate decisions and were entitled to a disproportionate amount of annual dividends). More than two corporations (one parent, one subsidiary) can, of course, be members of the same affiliated group. There could exist a chain of parent-subsidiary relations—in other words, a subsidiary, in turn, may be the parent of another corporation. There even can exist multiple chains, so long as they all trace back to a common parent company; for example, one parent has two subsidiaries, which each have two subsidiaries, and so on. Note, however, Section 1504 excludes some types of corporations—such as tax exempt and most foreign corporations—from eligibility to be part of an affiliated group. (This means these companies also cannot serve as a link in the chain of eligible companies.)

Consolidated reporting is entirely elective. In fact, each company in the group must consent. I.R.C. § 1501. Given the relationship between the firms in the group, obtaining unanimous concurrence usually is not difficult; albeit the governing parent should keep in mind its fiduciary obligations to minority shareholders. *See, e.g., Case v. New York Central R. Co.*, 15 N.Y.2d 150, 204 N.E.2d 643, 256 N.Y.S.2d 607 (1965). A problem with obtaining consent could occur if a company starting the tax year in the group changes hands during the tax year, as Section 1501 still requires its acceptance. Moreover, each firm in the group must participate in the consolidated return; in other words, the parties cannot pick and choose which affiliated firms will join in the return, and which will not. *See* Treas. Reg. § 1.1502–75(e). Once the group makes the election, the firms cannot change back to separate returns without the Internal Revenue Service's consent. Treas. Reg. § 1.1502–75(c). (Companies might get around this rule by breaking the eligibility requirements for filing consolidated returns. Section 1504(a)(3) responds by establishing a five-year waiting period for a company, which lost eligibility, to rejoin in a consolidated return with its former group.)

The court in *Wolter Construction* briefly noted the advantages of electing to file a consolidated return. The primary benefits fall into three broad camps. The first involves the treatment of various intercompany transactions. Normally, as companies engage in buying and selling goods and services to one another, they must recognize taxable income (or loss). *But see* I.R.C. § 267(f) (limiting recognition of losses on sales between related companies). Moreover, when a subsidiary pays dividends to its parent, this can produce taxable income for both the parent and the subsidiary. Specifically, distributions in excess of earnings and profits are not dividends for tax purposes and so do not qualify for the dividends received deduction of Section 243. *See* I.R.C. § 316. Instead, they produce taxable gain if in excess of the recipient's basis in its stock. I.R.C. § 301(c). Also, if the distribution consists of appreciated property, the subsidiary must recognize gain, just as if it sold the property. I.R.C. § 311(b). The consolidated return regulations largely eliminate these sources of income.

With respect to commercial transactions between affiliated corporations (such as a purchase and sale), the regulations seek to approximate the results which would occur if the two corporations were simply two divisions of one corporation, instead of separate companies. Treas. Reg. § 1.1502–13(a). The regulations accomplish this, in part, by matching the timing of the selling company's recognition of income, with the purchasing company's taking of a deduction, so the two items cancel out and result in no gain on the consolidated return. Treas. Reg. § 1.1502–13(c). For example, if the sale consists of depreciable property, the regulations suspend the seller's recognition of gain and allow the seller to recognize the suspended gain in stages as the buyer takes its deductions. Suppose, however, the purchasing corporation resells the item to someone outside the group. In this event, the regulations trigger immediate recognition of the suspended gain by the company which sold the property in the earlier intragroup transaction. *Id.* Needless to say, in this event, there is no offsetting deduction. This is appropriate, because the group as a whole has now made or lost money by selling an item to an outsider. (If the price paid by the outside buyer exceeds the price earlier paid by the intragroup buyer, then the intragroup buyer also will recognize income.) Moreover, following the approach of approximating the results which would occur if the original sale only involved a transaction between divisions of the same corporation, the nature of the intragroup buyer's use of the property will dictate the type of income (ordinary income versus capital gains) recognized by the intragroup seller. This sometimes could result in the intragroup seller recognizing as ordinary income what otherwise would have been capital gain.

Treatment of intercorporate distributions among the group (in other words, dividends) is reminiscent of the pattern followed by S corporations. Such distributions are tax-free to the recipient corporation (Treas. Reg. § 1.1502–13(f)), and, instead, reduce the recipient company's basis in its shares in the subsidiary (Treas. Reg. § 1.1502–32(b)(3)(iv)). If the distribution exceeds the parent's basis in its shares in the subsidiary, the excess is added to the parent's "excess loss account" (which works much like a negative basis). Treas. Reg. § 1.1502–32(a)(3). Note, as well, the regulations defer the distributing company's recognition of gain from the distribution of appreciated property in the same manner as if the distributing company sold the property to its parent. Treas. Reg. § 1.1502–13(f)(2).

Also reminiscent of the treatment accorded S corporations and their shareholders are the "investment basis adjustments" provided by the consolidated return regulations. Generally, the regulations call for the parents in an affiliated group to increase their basis in their stock in the subsidiaries to reflect the subsidiaries' taxable and tax exempt income for the year, and to decrease their basis to reflect the subsidiaries' tax losses and noncapital, nondeductible expenses. Treas. Reg. § 1.1502–32(b)(3). These adjustments may allow the parent to lessen its tax upon the sale of a profitable subsidiary—the second principal advantage from consolidated returns—albeit the adjustment may increase the parent's gain upon the sale of an unprofitable subsidiary.

The third area of advantage from filing consolidated returns is the one involved in *Wolter Construction*. An affiliated group filing a consolidated return can receive a current tax benefit from net operating losses, capital losses, and charitable contributions, which the individual company incurring the item could not immediately have obtained. *See* Treas. Reg. §§ 1.1502–21–1.1502–24. The problem in *Wolter Construction* was the golf course corporation incurred losses prior to being in an affiliated group with the construction firm. The consolidated return regulations generally limit a group's use of pre-affiliation net operating loss carryovers to the amount of income subsequently generated by the corporation which originally incurred the loss. The purpose is to prevent companies buying other corporations in order to use their loss carryovers. Chapter VII will look more generally at the purchase of corporations to exploit their loss carryovers, and especially the limitation created by Section 382 on a corporation's ability to use its loss carryovers after an "ownership change" (generally speaking, a change in the ownership of at least 50 percent of the outstanding stock). Under changes in the regulations since *Wolter Construction*, the limitation in Section 382, when it applies, trumps the limitation in the regulation discussed in *Wolter Construction*. In any event, what is important for present purposes is that *Wolter Construction* illustrates the need for those who operate through multiple corporations to consider what relationship these companies should have to each other. Because the two brothers-in-law originally owned both the construction company and the golf course corporation directly, large net operating loss carryovers generated by the golf course went unused. On the other hand, had the construction company owned the golf course corporation from the start, then the construction company could have used the NOLs (even if they did not immediately elect to file a consolidated return). One possible difficulty is that this would have meant somewhat different economic interests for the two brothers-in-law (as well as the mother), as their ownership in the construction company was not the same as their relative holdings in the golf course. Consider, however, the potential of non-voting, non-participating preferred stock (which does not count under Section 1504(a)) or shareholder loans—subjects explored in Chapter IV—to create the desired economic relationship without upsetting eligibility as an affiliated group.

Balanced against the benefits of consolidated returns are several possible disadvantages. The companies in the group must use the same tax year (Treas. Reg. § 1.1502–76(a)(1)), albeit they can use different accounting methods. Treas. Reg. § 1.1502–17(a). They must share a single graduated rate bracket, accumulated earnings tax credit, and any other special exemption or credit limits. *See* Treas. Reg. § 1.1502–2. (Section 1561(a), however, would compel this result anyway.) The investment basis adjustments, as mentioned above, can occasionally increase the parent's gain, while the regulations often prevent the parent from recognizing any loss, on the disposition of stock in a subsidiary. Treas. Reg. §§ 1.337(d)–2T, 1.1502–20T (loss disallowed unless parent establishes that the loss was not attributable to a built-in gain reflected in the basis of the subsidiary stock at time of acquisition). Characterizing the income recognized by an intragroup seller of property, based upon a later sale by the intragroup buyer, could result in turning into ordinary income what otherwise would have been capital gains. Perhaps worst is simply the burden of complying with the complex set of regulations governing such returns.

3. As stated earlier, an S corporation cannot have another corporation as a shareholder. Something of an exception to this rule exists for a corporation which is a wholly owned subsidiary of an S corporation. If the subsidiary is not among the special types of corporations which are ineligible to make an S election, then the subsidiary may elect treatment as a "qualified Subchapter S subsidiary" (a "QSSS"). In this event, the subsidiary is not treated as a corporation separate from its parent for income tax purposes. I.R.C. § 1361(b)(3). The regulations spell out the procedures and consequences of both electing to be a QSSS and the termination of such an election. Treas. Reg. §§ 1361–3–1361–5. Of potential significance, the effect of terminating a QSSS election is to create a new C corporation (for tax purposes), while the effect of making a QSSS election can be to destroy (for tax purposes) an existing C corporation. This, in turn, can trigger provisions of the tax code governing contribution of assets to, or distribution of assets from, a C corporation.

CHAPTER III

Forming a Partnership, Limited Partnership, Limited Liability Partnership, or Limited Liability Company

This chapter explores the formation of partnerships, limited partnerships, limited liability partnerships (also referred to as "LLPs") and limited liability companies (also referred to as "LLCs")—put differently, this chapter explores the establishment of the various non-corporate forms commonly used in the United States to conduct businesses having more than one owner. There are a couple of reasons for considering the formation of these types of business entities together with each other and in a separate chapter from considering the formation of corporations. As discussed in the previous chapter, these various non-corporate forms can, and typically do, choose to be subject to the federal income tax rules governing partnerships rather than corporations. Hence, the income tax rules, which significantly impact (as much of this chapter will attest) planning for the formation of such business entities, are, for most part, the same regardless of which non-corporate form the parties employ to conduct their venture.

There is a second overarching manner in which planning for the formation of partnerships, limited partnerships, LLPs, and LLCs is the same among these various business forms, and differs from planning for the establishment of a corporation. This has to do with the basic activity involved in forming a partnership, limited partnership, LLP or LLC. Generally, no formalities are necessary to establish a partnership. *But see In re Schaefer's Estate,* 72 Wis.2d 600, 241 N.W.2d 607 (1976) (minority view that partnership agreement to engage in purchase or sale of real estate falls within the statute of frauds). As a number of the cases reprinted in this chapter illustrate, however, forming a partnership based upon little more than a handshake may lead to problems among the partners later. Therefore, well-advised prospective partners often seek an attorney's help in drafting an agreement among themselves to govern their relationship. Suppose, however, the partners do not enter such an agreement, or their agreement neglects to cover a particular issue. In this event, the uniform partnership acts, which codify the law governing partnerships, provide gap-filling (or "default") rules. (The reason for referring to the uniform partnership *acts* is because some states still have as part of their statutes the original 1914 version of the Uniform Partnership Act (the

"U.P.A."), while other states have adopted a new version of the uniform partnership act, promulgated in the 1990s (the Revised Uniform Partnership Act or "R.U.P.A.").) Significantly, both the U.P.A. and the R.U.P.A. expressly make the vast bulk of the statutes' rules subject to contrary provision in the partners' agreement. *E.g.*, U.P.A. §§ 18, 19, 27, 31, 37, 38, 40, 42; R.U.P.A. § 103. Hence, planning for the formation of a partnership basically involves the drafting of a contract among the partners (which, for obvious reasons, commonly is called a partnership agreement).

By contrast, while parties forming a corporation might enter into a contract among themselves, much of rules governing their relationship will not be found in such a shareholders agreement. Instead, as Chapter IV of this book will detail, much of the rights of the owners of a corporation vis-a-vis each other are encapsulated in the allocation of stock among the participants, and in various provisions of the relevant state's corporations statute. Moreover, unlike the U.P.A. and the R.U.P.A., state corporations statutes often are persnickety as to the manner and extent to which owners of the business can agree to follow rules different from those provided in the statute. Hence, planning for the relationship among the owners of a corporation involves the employment of different tools than used in planning a partnership.

What about limited partnerships, LLPs and LLCs? The governing statute for limited partnerships in virtually every state is one or another edition of the Uniform Limited Partnership Act (the "U.L.P.A."). (As with the uniform partnership acts, there has been more than one iteration of the Uniform Limited Partnership Act. The original U.L.P.A. was promulgated in 1916. A revised U.L.P.A., promulgated in 1976, and amended in 1985, supplanted the 1916 U.L.P.A. in pretty much every state. Yet a new version of the U.L.P.A. ("U.L.P.A. (2001)") was promulgated in 2001. It is useful to note, however, that, under the pre–2001 versions of the U.L.P.A., the uniform partnership acts still might provide the applicable gap-filling rule even for a limited partnership to the extent that the U.L.P.A. does not address an issue. U.L.P.A. § 1105). In contrast with partnerships and limited partnerships, the governing statutes for limited liability companies lack the degree of uniformity in which states generally follow some version of the uniform acts. By the time the Uniform Limited Liability Company Act (the "U.L.L.C.A.") was promulgated, virtually every state already had adopted its own limited liability company statute, and states have generally seen no reason to switch to the U.L.L.C.A. (Undissuaded by this lack of interest, a revised U.L.L.C.A. was promulgated at the end of 2006.) Limited liability partnerships follow yet a different statutory pattern. The state statutes establishing this form for conducting business typically contain only a few sections, which commonly are located within the state's version of the uniform partnership act. These sections largely deal with the steps necessary to form a limited liability partnership and issues of liability to creditors and creditor protection. *See, e.g.*, Cal. Corp. Code §§ 16101(6)(A.), 16306(c), 16951–16959; Del. Code. Ann. Title 6 §§ 15–306(c), 15–309(b), 15–807, 15–1001–15–1105; N.Y. Partnership :Law §§ 26(b)–(f), 121–1500–121–1506. As far as the rights of the partners in an LLP vis-a-vis each other, as mentioned in Chapter II, provisions in the U.P.A. or R.U.P.A for the most part govern limited liability partnerships.

At first glance, forming a limited partnership, LLP or LLC might appear more similar to forming a corporation than to forming an ordinary partnership. This is because, like corporations, and unlike ordinary partnerships, formation of a limited partnership, an LLP or an LLC requires filing a statutorily prescribed document with a state agency. Specifically, to form a limited partnership, the parties must file a "certificate of limited partnership" with the state official designated by the statute (typically the Secretary of State). U.L.P.A. § 201. U.L.P.A. (2001) § 201. Failure to file this certificate can result in the would-be limited partners losing their limited liability. *E.g.*, *Ruth v. Crane*, 392 F.Supp. 724 (E.D.Pa.1975). *But see* U.L.P.A. § 304 (allowing persons who erroneously thought they were limited partners to avoid liability to creditors—so long as the creditor was not confused as to the would-be limited partner's status—by belatedly filing the certificate of limited partnership or withdrawing from the firm). U.L.P.A. (2001) § 306 (same). Along similar lines, formation of a limited liability company requires filing a document, variously referred to as the "articles of organization" or "certificate of formation," with a designated state official. *E.g.*, Cal. Corp. Code § 17050; Del. Code Ann. Title 6 § 18–201; N.Y. Ltd. Liab. Co. Law § 203. As in the case of limited partnerships, failure to file the necessary document to form an LLC can lead to loss of the expected limited liability. *E.g.*, Wyo. Stat. § 17–15–133. Finally, in order to have an LLP, rather than an ordinary partnership with unlimited personal liability, the partners typically must file a document, variously referred to as a "registration," "application," "statement of qualification," or the like, with a designated state official. *E.g.*, Cal. Corp. Code § 16953, Del. Code Ann. Title 6 § 15–1001; N.Y. Partnership Law § 121–1500. All told, the consequences of failing to file the required document to form a limited partnership, an LLP or an LLC are sufficiently grave to call for a certain amount of care. For example, cautious participants might demand to see proof of the necessary filing before allowing the venture to engage in any business activities.

The requirement of filing with a state official might lead one to ask in which state should such a filing take place. Typically, one's immediate answer to this question is to file in the state where the parties plan to conduct their business. Yet, suppose the parties will conduct their business in more than one state. In this event, it might be necessary for the participants to file appropriate documents in the various states in which they will conduct business. *E.g.*, U.L.P.A. § 902 (foreign limited partnerships must register before transacting business in the state); U.L.P.A. (2001) § 902 (foreign limited partnerships may apply for a certificate of authority to transact business within the state); Cal. Corp. Code §§ 16959, 17451 (foreign LLPs and LLCs must register before transacting business in the state); Del Code Ann. Title 6 §§ 15–1102, 18–902 (same); N.Y. Ltd Liab. Co. Law § 802 (same for foreign LLCs); N.Y. Partnership Law § 121–1502 (same for foreign LLPs). More significantly, when dealing with corporations, it has long been common to file the necessary document to form the corporation in a state other than the one(s) in which the parties plan to conduct business. The purpose for this practice, as discussed in Chapter IV, is to have this state's presumably more desirable corporations statute govern the internal affairs of the corporation. When dealing with business forms in which uniform laws dominate, such choice-of-law considerations, while relevant insofar as states may have older or newer versions of the acts, and state courts might have different interpretations of the law, nevertheless might not have overwhelming significance. The greater disparity among limited liability company statutes, however, provides more incentive to form an LLC under the law of a state other than where the parties intend to conduct business. *See, e.g.*, Cal. Corp. Code § 17450; Del. Code Ann. Title 6 § 18–901; N.Y. Ltd. Liab. Co. Law § 801(a) (all generally allowing the law of the state of organization to govern the internal affairs and member liability of foreign LLCs doing business in the state). *See also* U.L.P.A. § 901; U.L.P.A. (2001) § 901 (same for limited partnerships). *But see Burkle v. Burkle*, 141 Cal.App.4th 1029, 46 Cal.Rptr.3d 562 (2006) (applying Cal. Corp. Code § 17453, which states that "[i]f the members of a foreign limited liability company residing in this state represent 25 percent or more of the voting interests of members of that limited liability company, those members shall be entitled to all information and inspection rights provided in Section 17106").

Still, the amount of planning entailed in complying with the filing requirements to form a limited partnership, LLP or LLC is rather trivial. This is because the required document generally does not contain much of anything significant. For example, under the U.L.P.A., the certificate of limited partnership must contain the name of the limited partnership. To protect against creditor confusion, the name must include the words "limited partnership," and, under the pre–2001 version of the U.L.P.A., the firm's name ordinarily cannot include the name of a limited partner (since this historically implied a person was a general partner). U.L.P.A. § 102. *But see* U.L.P.A. (2001) § 108(no limitation on using the names of limited partners in the name of a limited partnership, and providing for different suffixes to identify limited liability limited partnerships). Also, for obvious reasons, the name must not be the same or deceptively similar to another firm's name. In addition to the firm's name, the certificate of limited partnership must contain the address of the limited partnership's office, and the name and address of an agent to receive service of process on the limited partnership. The certificate also must include the name and business address of each general partner, and, under the pre–2001 version of the U.L.P.A., the latest date on which the limited partnership is to dissolve (which presumably could be infinitely far in the future). U.L.P.A. § 201(a). *But see* U.L.P.A. (2001) § 201(a)(no longer must include duration, which, under Section 104(c), is perpetual). The certificate also can include any other matters the general partners decide to place in the certificate. Yet, because the certificate is a public document, and because there is no advantage to placing anything else in the certificate, partners typically prefer not to include in the certificate any matters beyond the minimum required.

Along the same lines, the registration document for a limited liability partnership typically must provide its name (which must include language, such as "LLP," to identify for creditors the firm as a limited liability partnership), an office address, a name and address of an agent for service of process, and, under some statutes, a brief description of the firm's business or the number of partners. *E.g.*, Cal. Corp. Code §§ 16952, 16953; Del. Code Ann. Title 6 §§ 15–108(b), 15–1001; N.Y. Partnership Law § 121–1500. Again, while the partners might include additional material in the registration document, there seems little reason to do so.

Limited liability company statutes deviate from this pattern in one potentially significant manner. Once again, there is a requirement to set out the name of the firm, which must include language, such as "LLC," to let prospective creditors know what sort of entity they are dealing with. *E.g.*, Cal. Corp. Code § 17052; Del. Code Ann. Title 6 § 18–102; N.Y. Ltd. Liab. Co. Law. § 204. Naturally, the articles of organization must give an address for the firm's office and a name and address of an agent to receive service of process on the firm. *E.g.*, Del. Code Ann. Title 6 § 18–201. *See also* N.Y. Ltd. Liab. Co. Law § 203(e)(designate secretary of state as agent to receive service of process). Some statutes also might require a statement of purpose (such as "any lawful activity"), and the latest date the company will dissolve (which presumably might be some time in the infinitely distant future). *E.g.*, Cal. Corp. Code § 17051. These requirements do not provide too much of significance with respect to planning for the participants' future relationship. The one item of such potential significance in the articles of organization of an LLC arises if the participants decide that only some owners ought to be involved in running the company. As discussed later in this Chapter, limited liability company statutes commonly allow the owners of an LLC (who the statutes call "members") to provide that one or more persons (called "managers") shall be in charge of the company. What is relevant for present purposes is to note that many of the limited liability company statutes require that if the participants in the LLC wish to have managers rather than members be in charge of the company, they must state this in the articles of organization. *E.g.*, Cal. Corp. Code § 17051(a)(6). Beyond this, however, the articles of organization of a limited liability company need not encapsulate much planning regarding the details of the parties' relationship, and, while it is possible to include other provisions in an LLC's articles of organization, there appears little advantage to publicly filing the details of what otherwise would be a private agreement.

So, if the formally filed document to create a limited partnership, LLP or LLC does not encapsulate much of the planning for the participants' future relationship, where does such planning manifest itself? The typical answer is the same as used in the ordinary partnership—an agreement among the parties. In an LLP or a limited partnership, this still typically is referred to as a partnership agreement. The term often used by limited liability company statutes for such an agreement among the owners of an LLC is an "operating agreement" (*e.g.*, Cal. Corp. Code § 17001(ab); N.Y. Ltd. Liab. Co. Law § 102(u)), albeit some statutes just refer to this as a limited liability company agreement (*e.g.*, Del. Code Ann. Title 6 § 18–101(7)). Moreover, the statutory rules governing the partners' or LLC members' relationships vis-a-vis each other in a limited partnership, an LLC or an LLP, for the most part, are expressly subject to contrary provisions in the partners' or members' agreement. *E.g.*, U.L.P.A. §§ 301, 302, 401, 403, 405, 502, 503, 504, 601, 603, 604, 605, 702, 704, 801, 803, 804; Cal. Corp. Code § 17005. U.L.P.A. (2001) § 110. Hence, planning for a limited partnership, an LLP or an LLC, like planning for an ordinary partnership, essentially revolves around drafting an agreement among the owners. This said, however, a conceptual difference arises with respect to agreements among the parties as one moves beyond the ordinary partnership. Since the common law traditionally viewed a partnership as simply a group of partners, there was no basis at common law for arguing that the partnership, as a firm, was not bound by the partnership agreement. What happens, however, with new forms of business, or even with partnerships under the modern view codified in the R.U.P.A., which the law considers to be entities separate from their owners, with their own rights and liabilities? Does this mean that an owner might assert rights on behalf of the firm and claim that an agreement among the owners does not apply because the firm was not formally a party to the agreement—perhaps because the agreement predated the actual formation of the firm, or because the parties never even thought about the need to have the firm expressly enter the agreement? See R.U.P.A. § 103(a) (partnership agreement governs relations between partners and the partnership); U.L.P.A. (2001) § 110(a) (same); Cal. Corp. Code § 17005(a) (operating agreement governs relations between members and the limited liability company); *Elf Atochem N.A., Inc. v. Jaffari*, 727 A.2d 286 (Del. 1999)(Delaware LLC could not avoid operating agreement provision calling for arbitration in California by arguing that the firm, itself, had not entered the agreement).

Drafting a contract to cover a long-term relationship among parties, such as a partnership or an LLC operating agreement, is a challenging undertaking. No doubt, before going to an attorney, the parties will have reached an agreement on the basic terms of their undertaking, such as their respective profit shares. How can the attorney aid his or her clients to make sure they have not overlooked other terms upon which they should reach advance agreement? One source is to examine the default rules in the relevant statute—the U.P.A. or R.U.P.A., the U.L.P.A., or the governing limited liability company statute. By reviewing such provisions, an attorney can get some idea of topics with which to be concerned. Another resource an attorney can use is the experience of other lawyers as embodied in various forms. Use of a form, however, should not be a substitute for the attorney's own judgment as to how best to meet his or her clients' particular needs. With this in mind, the cases and materials in the following sections illustrate some of the problems which the attorney will want to consider in drafting a partnership or an LLC operating agreement and some of the alternate approaches his or her clients may wish to use in dealing with potential problems. These sections are organized to parallel the life cycle of a firm—formation, operation and termination. Each stage should be considered in the partnership or LLC operating agreement. The principal concern regarding formation is what the partners or members will contribute to the business. This is the subject of Section A. The concerns during operation are essentially the allocation of wealth (profit and loss) and power (management). These are the subjects of Sections B and C respectively. At the termination of the relationship, the problems revolve around dissolution and changes in ownership. Section D covers this subject.

SECTION A. CONTRIBUTIONS

Probably the first thing any group of prospective co-venturers consider is what each participant can contribute to the proposed business. After all, except where there are motivations based on friendship or family, the very reason for gathering a number of individuals together into a business association is to obtain an advantage from a combination of ideas (or other intangibles), services, property and cash which is greater than what each individual possesses on his or her own.

Of the various types of contributions, cash presents the least planning difficulty. The principal question which the parties must address is how much money each will invest. The answer to this question requires an assessment of the needs of the business and the resources of the prospective participants. Unfortunately, it is far from rare to discover some gap between these figures. Indeed, one of the common causes of business failure noted in the Schollhammer and Kuriloff excerpt in Chapter I is inadequate initial financing. Given this reality, should the attorney drafting the partnership or LLC operating agreement do more than simply write down the amounts the parties promise to contribute? In any event, if the parties form a limited liability partnership, then they must ensure that the firm has sufficient cash to maintain the minimum insurance which some statutes require in order to register as an LLP. *E.g.*, Cal. Corp. Code § 16959. Moreover, as mentioned in Chapter II, LLCs, like corporations, might be subject to piercing to hold the members liable for company debts. One of the possible grounds for such piercing is inadequate capitalization. *See, e.g., Ditty v. CheckRite, Ltd., Inc.*, 973 F.Supp. 1320 (D.Utah 1997). This, in turn, leads to the question of what is inadequate capitalization for purposes of piercing. Unfortunately, as discussed in Chapter IV (since the only authority exists in the corporate context), the answer to this question is far from clear.

Often a business requires further financing as it develops over time. Thus, it may be necessary to consider what cash the participants have an obligation to put in after their initial investments. In addition, the participants must decide on nature of their investment—in other words, will their money be a loan or a capital contribution. These two issues, however, are in large part common to all of the various types of contributions. Therefore, consideration of these two issues will await an exploration of the unique complexities introduced when the parties are to contribute property, services and intangibles.

1. Special Problems With Non-Cash Contributions

a. *In General*

The first task in drafting a partnership or an LLC operating agreement calling for non-cash contributions is to describe them. The description of tangible property is relatively straightforward. Services or intangibles (such as ideas, business contacts, goodwill or the like) may present much greater difficulty.

When dealing with services, the drafter might either provide for a specific obligation—a commitment of so much time or a given result—or a more general responsibility such as "best efforts." These provisions can be important since one of the common maladies suffered by partnerships is the complaint by some partners that others are "not carrying their load." *See, e.g., Nicholes v. Hunt,* 273 Or. 255, 541 P.2d 820 (1975). On the other hand, to what extent can provisions specifying required services really eliminate this problem? The drafter also should consider whether partners or members must devote their exclusive efforts to the firm or whether instead they may engage in outside business activities. If partners or members may work in other businesses, should this extend to those that compete with the firm?

McConnell v. Hunt Sports Enterprises

132 Ohio App.3d 657, 725 N.E.2d 1193 (1999).

■ Tyack, Judge.

On June 17, 1997, John H. McConnell and Wolfe Enterprises, Inc. filed a complaint for declaratory judgment in the Franklin County Court of Common Pleas against * * * Hunt Sports Group, L.L.C. ("Hunt Sports Group"), and Columbus Hockey Limited ("CHL"). CHL was a limited liability company formed under R.C. Chapter 1705 [(Ohio's limited liability company statute)]. A brief background of the events leading up to the formation of CHL and the subsequent discord among certain of its members follows.

In 1996, the National Hockey League ("NHL") determined it would be accepting applications for new hockey franchises. In April 1996, Gregory S. Lashutka, the mayor of Columbus, received a phone call from an NHL representative inquiring as to Columbus's interest in a hockey team. As a result, Mayor Lashutka asked certain community leaders who had been involved in exploring professional sports in Columbus to pursue the possibility of applying for an NHL hockey franchise. Two of these persons were Ronald A. Pizzuti and McConnell.

Pizzuti began efforts to recruit investors in a possible franchise. Pizzuti approached Lamar Hunt, principal of Hunt Sports Group, as to Hunt's interest in investing in such a franchise for Columbus. Hunt was already the operating member of the Columbus Crew, a professional soccer team whose investors included Hunt Sports Group, Pizzuti, McConnell, and

Wolfe Enterprises, Inc. Hunt expressed an interest in participating in a possible franchise. The deadline for applying for an NHL expansion franchise was November 1, 1996.

On October 31, 1996, CHL was formed when its articles of organization were filed with the secretary of state pursuant to R.C. 1705.04. The members of CHL were McConnell, Wolfe Enterprises, Inc., Hunt Sports Group, Pizzuti Sports Limited, and Buckeye Hockey, L.L.C. Each member made an initial capital contribution of $25,000. CHL was subject to an operating agreement that set forth the terms between the members. Pursuant to section 2.1 of CHL's operating agreement, the general character of the business of CHL was to invest in and operate a franchise in the NHL.

On or about November 1, 1996, an application was filed with the NHL on behalf of the city of Columbus. In the application, the ownership group was identified as CHL, and the individuals in such group were listed as Pizzuti Sports Limited, McConnell, Wolfe Enterprises, Inc., and Hunt Sports Group. A $100,000 check from CHL was included as the application fee. Also included within the application package was Columbus's plan for an arena to house the hockey games. There was no facility at the time, and the proposal was to build a facility that would be financed, in large part, by a three-year countywide one-half percent sales tax. The sales tax issue would be on the May 1997 ballot.

On May 6, 1997, the sales tax issue failed. The day after, Mayor Lashutka met with Hunt, and other opportunities were discussed. The mayor also spoke with Gary Bettman, commissioner of the NHL, and they discussed whether an alternate plan for an arena was possible. Also on May 7, 1997, Dimon McPherson, chairman and chief executive officer of Nationwide Insurance Enterprise ("Nationwide"), met with Hunt, and they discussed the possibility of building the arena despite the failure of the sales tax issue. * * * On or about May 9, 1997, the mayor spoke with Bettman and let him know that alternate plans would be pursued, and Mr. Bettman gave Columbus until June 4, 1997 to come up with a plan.

By May 28, 1997, Nationwide had come up with a plan to finance an arena privately and on such date, Nationwide representatives met with representatives of Hunt Sports Group. Hunt Sports Group did not accept Nationwide's lease proposal. [Hunt objected to the terms under which Nationwide would lease the new arena to the hockey team.] * * *

On May 30, 1997, McPherson called McConnell and requested that they meet and discuss "where [they] were on the arena." * * * McConnell stated that if Hunt would not step up and lease the arena and, therefore, get the franchise, McConnell would. * * *

* * * On Monday, June 2, 1997, City Council passed the resolution that set forth the terms for Nationwide to build an arena downtown. Also on June 2, 1997, McPherson met with Bettman and told him that Nationwide would be building an arena in downtown Columbus. McPherson also

told Bettman that if need be, McConnell would purchase the franchise on his own.

* * *

On June 5, 1997, the NHL sent Hunt a letter requesting that he let the NHL know by Monday, June 9, 1997 whether he was going forward with his franchise application. In a June 6, 1997 letter to the NHL, Hunt responded that CHL intended to pursue the franchise application. Hunt informed the NHL that he had arranged a meeting with the members of CHL to be held on June 9, 1997. Hunt indicated that the application was contingent upon entering into an appropriate lease for a hockey facility.

[At the June 9 meeting, Hunt continued to object to Nationwide's proposed lease terms, whereupon McConnell, Pizzuti and Wolfe agreed to accept the franchise for themselves.] * * *

On June 17, 1997, the NHL expansion committee recommended to the NHL board of governors that Columbus be awarded a franchise with McConnell's group as owner of the franchise. On the same date, the complaint in the case at bar was filed. On or about June 25, 1997, the NHL board of governors awarded Columbus a franchise with McConnell's group as owner.[2]

* * *

In their complaint, McConnell and Wolfe Enterprises, Inc. requested a declaration that section 3.3 of the CHL operating agreement allowed members of CHL to compete with CHL. Specifically, McConnell and Wolfe Enterprises, Inc. sought a declaration that under the operating agreement, they were permitted to participate in COLHOC and obtain the franchise.

* * *

On June 23, 1997, Hunt Sports Group filed an answer and counterclaim on its behalf and on behalf on CHL. The counterclaim was asserted against McConnell and alleged breach of contract, breach of fiduciary duty, and interference with prospective business relationships.

On July 3, 1997, McConnell and Wolfe Enterprises, Inc. filed a motion for summary judgment. * * * On October 31, 1997, the trial court rendered a decision, granting summary judgment in favor of McConnell and Wolfe Enterprises, Inc. on count one of the first amended complaint and on counts one and three of the counterclaim. Specifically, the trial court found that section 3.3 of the operating agreement was clear and unambiguous and allowed McConnell and Wolfe Enterprises, Inc. to compete against CHL and obtain the NHL franchise. In addition, the trial court found McConnell did not breach the operating agreement by competing against CHL. * * * Therefore, the claims that remained were count two of the first amended complaint (judicial dissolution of CHL) and counts two, four, five, six,

2. The ownership group is now formally known as COLHOC Limited Partnership ("COLHOC"). * * *

seven, and eight of the counterclaim (breach of fiduciary duty and interference with prospective business relationships).

A jury trial was held in May 1998 on counts three and four of the second amended complaint. * * * [After both sides rested], the trial court [granted] * * * McConnell and Wolfe Enterprises, Inc.'s motion for directed verdicts on counts three and four of the second amended complaint.

* * *

In its first assignment of error, appellant contends the trial court erred in granting summary judgment in favor of McConnell and Wolfe Enterprises, Inc. ("appellees") on count one of the first amended complaint and on counts one and three of appellant's counterclaim. These counts each involve provisions of the operating agreement and will be addressed separately.

* * *

As indicated above, count one of the first amended complaint sought a declaration that section 3.3 of CHL's operating agreement allowed members to compete against CHL to obtain an NHL franchise. Appellees contend section 3.3 is plain and unambiguous and allows what occurred here—COLHOC competing for and obtaining the NHL franchise. Appellant asserts, in part, that the trial court's interpretation of section 3.3 was incorrect and that section 3.3 is ambiguous and subject to different interpretations. Therefore, appellant contends extrinsic evidence should have been considered, and such evidence would have shown the parties did not intend section 3.3 to mean members could compete against CHL and take away CHL's only purpose.

* * *

Section 3.3 of the operating agreement states:

"Members May Compete. Members shall not in any way be prohibited from or restricted in engaging or owning an interest in any other business venture of any nature, including any venture which might be competitive with the business of the Company."

Appellant emphasizes the word "other" in the above language and states, in essence, that it means any business venture that is different from the business of the company. Appellant points out that under section 2.1 of the operating agreement, the general character of the business is "to invest in and operate a franchise in the National Hockey League." Hence, appellant contends that members may only engage in or own an interest in a venture that is not in the business of investing in and operating a franchise with the NHL.

Appellant's interpretation of section 3.3 goes beyond the plain language of the agreement and adds words or meanings not stated in the provision. Section 3.3, for example, does not state "[m]embers shall not be prohibited from or restricted in engaging or owning an interest in any other business venture that is different from the business of the company."

Rather, section 3.3 states: "any other business venture of *any nature.*" (Emphasis added.) It then adds to this statement: "including any venture which might be competitive with the business of the Company." The words "any nature" could not be broader, and the inclusion of the words "any venture which might be competitive with the business of the Company" makes it clear that members were not prohibited from engaging in a venture that was competitive with CHL's investing in and operating an NHL franchise. Contrary to appellant's contention, the word "other" simply means a business venture other than CHL. The word "other" does not limit the type of business venture in which members may engage.

Hence, section 3.3 did not prohibit appellees from engaging in activities that may have been competitive with CHL, including appellees' participation in COLHOC. Accordingly, summary judgment in favor of appellees was appropriate, and appellees were entitled to a declaration that section 3.3 of the operating agreement permitted appellees to request and obtain an NHL hockey franchise to the exclusion of CHL.

Appellant next contends that the trial court erred in granting summary judgment in favor of appellees on counts one and three of appellant's counterclaim. Count one of the counterclaim alleged McConnell breached the operating agreement by forming COLHOC for the sole purpose of competing directly with CHL's application for an NHL franchise. Count three avers McConnell breached the operating agreement in refusing to call for additional capital to fund CHL.

We have already determined that section 3.3 permitted appellees to request and obtain an NHL franchise. Appellant points to section 4.1(c)(v) of the operating agreement in further support of its argument that McConnell breached the operating agreement in forming COLHOC and in failing to call for additional capital. Section 4.1 states:

> "Approval by Members. * * *[N]o Member shall take any action *on behalf of the Company* unless such actions are approved by a vote of the specified number of Members:
>
> "* * *
>
> "(c) The following actions require the approval of Members owning all of the Units allocated to the Members:
>
> "* * *
>
> "(v) do any other act that would make it impossible to carry on the ordinary business of the Company[.]" (Emphasis added.)

As to any argument that McConnell breached section 4.1(c)(v) in forming COLHOC and competing against CHL, there is no genuine issue of material fact, and appellees are entitled to judgment as a matter of law. The voting requirements in section 4.1 apply only to actions taken "on behalf of the Company." In forming COLHOC and in obtaining the NHL franchise, McConnell was obviously not taking action on behalf of CHL. Therefore, McConnell did not breach section 4.1(c)(v) in failing to obtain the vote of all CHL members prior to taking such action.

Appellant averred in count three of its counterclaim that McConnell further breached section 4.1(c)(v) by refusing to call for additional capital to fund CHL. In an affidavit filed in support of appellant's memorandum contra the motion for summary judgment, Hunt stated that at the June 9, 1997 meeting, McConnell informed the other members of CHL that he would attempt to block any effort to raise capital that would allow CHL to obtain an NHL expansion franchise. However, a reading of other sections of the operating agreement shows that McConnell did not breach the operating agreement in allegedly blocking or threatening to block any call for additional capital to fund CHL.

Section 4.1(c)(viii) of the operating agreement requires the approval of all the members of CHL to call for additional capital as provided in section 5.2. Section 5.2 states:

> "If at any time or times the Members determine that additional capital is required to preserve and maintain the business of the Company, the Members shall have the opportunity *but not the obligation* to provide such additional capital in proportion to their Percentage Interests." (Emphasis added.)

Further, section 5.1 of the operating agreement states:

> "The Members shall have no obligation to make additional capital contributions to the Company."

Hence, McConnell was not obligated to call for or provide additional capital to fund CHL.

* * *

We now address the substance of the trial court's granting of appellees' motion for a directed verdict on count three of the second amended complaint. The trial court found, in essence, that the evidence did not show appellees interfered with appellant's prospective business relationships with Nationwide or the NHL. As to the fiduciary duty issue, the trial court found, in part, that appellees had not engaged in any kind of willful misconduct, misrepresentation, or concealment. Therefore, the trial court concluded that appellees had not breached any fiduciary duty in seeking and obtaining the NHL franchise and in negotiating with Nationwide concerning the arena lease. For the reasons that follow, we conclude that a directed verdict on count three of the second amended complaint was appropriate.

* * *

Before we can review the propriety of the directed verdict in this case, the law on fiduciary duty and interference with a prospective business relationship must be addressed. The term "fiduciary relationship" has been defined as a relationship in which special confidence and trust is reposed in the integrity and fidelity of another, and there is a resulting position of superiority or influence acquired by virtue of this special trust. * * * In the case at bar, a limited liability company is involved which, like a partnership, involves a fiduciary relationship. Normally, the presence of such a relationship would preclude direct competition between members of the company. However, here we have an operating agreement that by its very terms allows members to compete with the business of the company. Hence, the question we are presented with is whether an operating agreement of a limited liability company may, in essence, limit or define the scope of the fiduciary duties imposed upon its members. We answer this question in the affirmative.

* * *

The operating agreement constitutes the undertaking of the parties herein. In becoming members of CHL, appellant and appellees agreed to abide by the terms of the operating agreement, and such agreement specifically allowed competition with the company by its members. As such, the duties created pursuant to such undertaking did not include a duty not to compete. Therefore, there was no duty on the part of appellees to refrain from subjecting appellant to the injury complained of herein.

We find further support for our conclusion in case law concerning close corporations and partnerships.

* * *

Given the above, we conclude as a matter of law that it was not a breach of fiduciary duty for appellees to form COLHOC and obtain an NHL franchise to the exclusion of CHL. In so concluding, we are not stating that no act related to such obtainment could be considered a breach of fiduciary duty. In general terms, members of limited liability companies owe one another the duty of utmost trust and loyalty. However, such general duty in this case must be considered in the context of members' ability, pursuant to operating agreement, to compete with the company.

[For similar reasons the court held that there was no tortious interference with a prospective business relationship.]

* * *

NOTES

1. As the court in *McConnell* points out, barring contrary agreement, partners cannot compete with their firm. *E.g.*, R.U.P.A. § 404(b)(3). Working by analogy, the court in *McConnell* states that the same is normally true for members in an LLC. *See also* Cal. Corp. Code §§ 17150 (members who manage an LLC have the same obligations as managers), 17153 (managers in an LLC owe the same fiduciary duties as partners). Hence, one contribution each partner or, presumably, LLC member normally makes by virtue of entering into the partnership or limited liability company is an implied promise not to compete. (Notice, however, under a limited liability company statute such as California's, it is possible to argue that members who lack any management role also lack any obligation not to compete. Similarly, one might argue that limited partners who are merely passive investors would not be subject to the prohibition on competing with the firm. Indeed, the 2001 revision of the U.L.P.A. provides that

limited partners have no fiduciary duties solely by reason of being limited partners. U.L.P.A. (2001) § 305(a).) The restriction on the ability to compete, the court in *McConnell* explains, is, in turn, part of a partner's or LLC member's fiduciary duty to his or her fellow partners or members. While not the sort of contribution which parties typically focus on at the time they form a partnership or limited liability company, assuming such a fiduciary duty toward one's fellow owners is itself a potentially important contribution each partner or LLC member implicitly agrees to make.

The court in *McConnell* holds that the duty not to compete, as well presumably as other fiduciary duties, are subject to contrary provisions in a partnership or limited liability company operating agreement. There is, however, authority to the contrary. *E.g.*, Triple Five of Minnesota, Inc. v. Simon, 404 F.3d 1088 (8th Cir.2005). Indeed, the extent to which partners or members in limited liability companies can contract out of fiduciary duties is a subject upon which there is considerable debate and legal uncertainty, and, hence, one which the planning attorney must research carefully in the relevant jurisdiction, and approach with some caution in the absence of binding authority. The R.U.P.A and some limited liability company statutes contain provisions which address the owners' ability to contract vis-a-vis fiduciary duties; albeit, such provisions, not surprisingly, often lack perfect clarity regarding their scope. *E.g.*, R.U.P.A. § 103(b)(3)–(5); Cal. Corp. Code § 17005(d); Del. Code Ann. Title 6 § 18–1101(c). *See also* U.L.P.A. (2001) § 110(b)(5)-(7) (containing provisions similar to the R.U.P.A.). In any event, even if it is legally permissible to contract out of fiduciary duties, does this mean it is wise to do so? Looking at the events in *McConnell* in hindsight, is it likely that the parties really intended to allow competition to obtain the sole hockey franchise for Columbus? If so, what was the point of forming the LLC? If not, what did they have in mind and how did a provision drafted with such broad language end up in their contract? Is it possible that this language had come from partnership or LLC agreements involving other lines of business (say development of a piece of real property) in which broad language allowing competition might make sense (insofar as investors in real estate development might invest in several real estate ventures that ultimately compete for tenants)?

The scope of fiduciary duty is itself a subject of considerable uncertainty. For example, the court in *McConnell* found that McConnell did not breach the operating agreement in allegedly announcing that he would block any efforts to raise additional financing. Could such an action, however, constitute a breach of fiduciary duty? True, the agreement stated that McConnell was under no obligation to contribute additional capital; but what if McConnell, in order to gain a competitive advantage over the company, used his contractual power as a tool to block efforts to raise money for the company from other sources? We shall see in various contexts that at least some courts have held that the exercise of contractual and statutory powers is potentially subject to fiduciary and good faith limits.

While the normal rule is that partners or, presumably, members of limited liability companies cannot compete so long as one is a partner or a member of the company, this obligation generally ends upon one's ceasing to be a partner or a member of the firm. *See, e.g., Meehan v. Shaughnessy*, 404 Mass. 419, 535 N.E.2d 1255 (1989). *But see Monin v. Monin*, 785 S.W.2d 499 (Ky.App.1989). Indeed, covenants not to compete following a partner's departure from the firm are unenforceable unless the covenant is reasonable—particularly with respect to the duration and scope of the covenant. *See, e.g., Gelder Medical Group v. Webber*, 41 N.Y.2d 680, 363 N.E.2d 573, 394 N.Y.S.2d 867 (1977). Unfortunately, there is an inherent tension between the rule that current partners or other fiduciaries cannot compete with their current firm, and the rule that former partners or other fiduciaries can compete with their former firm. Typically, partners or other participants in a firm do not terminate their association one day, wake up the next day, and then decide to go into competition with their former firm. Rather, the decision to go into competition commonly occurs before one quits. As a result, numerous courts have faced the question as to how far fiduciaries can go to prepare a competing venture without crossing the line and engaging in impermissible competition before the fiduciary quits. Incorporating the new business and lining up its finances and facilities seem okay. *E.g., Meehan, supra*. Soliciting the firm's clients or customers before departure is unacceptable. *See, e.g., Smith–Shrader Co. v. Smith*, 136 Ill.App.3d 571, 483 N.E.2d 283 (1985). Borderline questions involve soliciting employees to leave and join the new venture (*See, e.g., Bancroft–Whitney Co. v. Glen*, 64 Cal.2d 327, 411 P.2d 921, 49 Cal.Rptr. 825 (1966)), and notifying clients or customers of the fiduciary's intentions, without soliciting their business. *See, e.g., Ellis & Marshall Associates, Inc. v. Marshall*, 16 Ill.App.3d 398, 306 N.E.2d 712 (1973). To what extent is this a subject upon which participants in a business might wish to have advance agreement?

2. The difficulties in describing contributions of intangibles in a partnership or LLC operating agreement are as manifold as the types of intangibles which exist. For example, suppose a partner or LLC member will contribute a "secret process" to the firm. Will that contribution encompass processes which are derivative of the one originally developed? This obviously may depend upon precisely how the agreement describes the idea given to the firm. *Cf. Paxton v. McDonald,* 72 Ariz. 240, 233 P.2d 450 (1951). The failure of a partnership or LLC operating agreement to specify obligations with respect to such derivative ideas can leave the parties arguing over whether a partner or LLC member breached his or her fiduciary duty by taking such an idea for him-or herself.

3. Unlike traditional corporations statutes which, as discussed in the next chapter, restrict the acceptable non-cash consideration corporations can receive in exchange for issuing stock, the uniform partnership and limited partnership acts and typical limited liability company statutes do not restrict the types of contributions that partners, limited partners or LLC members can make in exchange for an interest in the firm. *E.g.*, U.L.P.A.

§ 501; U.L.P.A. (2001) § 501; Cal. Corp. Code § 17200(a); Del. Code Ann. Title 6 § 18–501; N.Y. Ltd. Liab. Co. Law § 501.

4. Once the agreement describes the non-cash contribution, the next question is its value. Is there a need to establish an initial value for non-cash contributions? The R.U.P.A., the U.L.P.A., and some limited liability company statutes seem to require (at least barring a contrary agreement) such a valuation. *E.g.*, R.U.P.A. § 401(a)(1) (the contributing partner's account must be credited with the value of the contributed property, barring other agreement); U.L.P.A. § 105(a)(5)(i) (barring a contrary agreement, a limited partnership must keep at its office a writing setting out the agreed value of the property and services contributed by each partner); U.L.P.A. (2001) § 111(9)(A) (unless contained in a partnership agreement, a limited partnership must keep at its office a record stating a description and agreed value of the benefits other than cash that each partner agrees to contribute); Del. Code Ann. Title 6 § 18–305(a)(5) (LLC members have a right to demand information showing the agreed value of property and services contributed by the LLC's members). Before agreeing on a value of the various non-cash contributions (or agreeing not to establish any such valuation), however, it might be a good idea to ask what practical impact such a valuation can have.

Schymanski v. Conventz

674 P.2d 281 (Alaska 1983).

■ SERDAHELY, JUDGE.

This is an appeal from a decree of the trial court ordering the dissolution of a partnership formed to construct and operate a fishing lodge. Appellants challenge (1) the lower court's determination to treat appellee's personal services as non-cash capital contributions, and/or as services for which appellees were entitled to special remuneration; (2) the specific valuations given by the court to such services; * * *. For the reasons set forth below, we reverse and remand the case for further proceedings in connection with the personal services/non-cash contribution issue.

FACTUAL BACKGROUND

Appellants Wolfgang and Renate Schymanski and Minna Huss (Schymanskis), and appellees Klaus and Christa Conventz (Conventz), entered into an oral partnership agreement for the purpose of building and operating a fishing lodge at Lake Illiamna. The partnership was on a 50–50 basis as between the two groups. Initially, the two groups were to contribute equal shares of cash and, in addition, each group was to contribute personal services according to their respective expertise—Conventz through supervising the construction of the lodge and advertising in Alaska; the Schymanskis by handling the promotional campaign in Germany.

On May 24, 1980, the partners signed two agreements drafted by Conventz. Conventz' contend that these documents reflect a modification of the original agreement whereby they would play a more significant role in construction and would manage the lodge for the first season in lieu of making further cash contributions. * * *

The lodge building project suffered delays. The costs of construction ran higher than anticipated and misunderstandings and disagreements arose between the partners. * * *

On September 2, 1980, Conventz expressed his desire to terminate the partnership in a letter to the Schymanskis. * * *

On September 9, 1980, the Schymanskis brought suit. * * *

After a bench trial, the lower court found that the total amount paid out by the partnership for the construction of the lodge was $173,496.64. Of that amount, the trial court further found that the Schymanski group had contributed $133,838.06 in cash and that Conventz had contributed $39,658.48 in money and property plus $70,000 of non-cash contributions, consisting of $50,000 worth of architectural services and $20,000 worth of managerial services, for a total of $109,658.48. The court further declared the partnership dissolved as of September 1, 1980, due to constant disagreement between the partners rather than to any wrongful conduct by any partner, and ordered the lodge to be either sold to a third party who had made an offer for $350,000 or listed with a real estate agent for $400,000. Partnership proceeds were to be divided so that the Schymanskis would receive the first $24,179.48 with the remainder of the sales proceeds being split equally. * * *

This appeal ensued with the Schymanskis challenging the trial court's determination to treat Conventz' architectural and managerial services as a $70,000 non-cash capital contribution to the partnership. * * *

CONVENTZ' NON-CASH CAPITAL CONTRIBUTION

* * *

Appellants argue that the record fails to support any finding that the parties had agreed to treat Conventz' personal services as non-cash capital contributions or to otherwise remunerate him for such services. Appellants also argue that the evidence fails to support the trial court's valuation finding of $70,000 regarding Conventz' personal services.

* * *

This court has previously noted that under appropriate circumstances, personal services of a partner also may constitute a capital contribution to the partnership. Thus, in Coleman v. Lofgren, 633 P.2d 1365 (Alaska 1981), this court noted, in a footnote accompanying a discussion regarding non-cash capital contributions to a partnership, that:

> Contribution by parties to a partnership enterprise need not always be in the form of tangible assets or capital. Partnerships are often formed

where one party provides the money and the other party provides labor or services.

The general rule is that, in the absence of an agreement to such effect, a partner contributing only personal services is ordinarily not entitled to any share of partnership capital pursuant to dissolution. * * * Personal services may, however, qualify as capital contributions to a partnership where an express or implied agreement to such effect exists. * * * Thus, in *Craig v. Hamilton,* [213 Kan. 665, 518 P.2d 539 (1974)] * * * a provision of a written partnership agreement expressly referred to two partners' "contributions" to the partnership in the form of "equipment, technical knowledge, skill and experience" and one partner's "contribution" in the form of cash. Id. at 542.

To be distinguished from non-cash capital contributions to a partnership is compensation or remuneration for a partner's personal services performed in the course of day-to-day affairs of the partnership. In the absence of an agreement to provide for such compensation, remuneration for a partner's services performed in the course of partnership affairs is prohibited by statute. Specifically, Alaska's Partnership Act, AS 32.05.130(6) [U.P.A. § 18(f)] provides:

> [N]o partner is entitled to remuneration for acting in the partnership business, except that a surviving partner is entitled to reasonable compensation for his services in winding up the partnership affairs.

The distinction between non-cash capital contributions and remuneration for ordinary services was recognized in *Thompson v. Beth*, 14 Wis.2d 271, 111 N.W.2d 171 (1961), where the Wisconsin Supreme Court analyzed an identical provision of the Wisconsin partnership statute:

> Sec. 123.15(6), Stats., [U.P.A. § 18(f)] applies where a partner has been active in contributing his skill and labor toward the affairs of the partnership on a day-to-day basis. There, his labor is compensated for by a share in the partnership profits. This section does not apply where the skill and labor of the partner are his contribution to the capital assets of the partnership, as in the instant case. The return of such contribution on liquidation is not remuneration, but a return of capital investment.
>
> *Id.* at 175. * * *

In the instant case, it is unclear whether the trial court found an express or implied agreement between the partners to treat Conventz' architectural and managerial services as capital contributions, as services performed in the ordinary course of partnership affairs for which remuneration was required, or both. No specific finding of fact to such effect was made.

Likewise, it is unclear from the lower court's findings what evidentiary basis existed for the court's valuation determination, * * * that Conventz' architectural services were worth $50,000 and that his managerial and operational services were worth $20,000. Again, no specific finding or reference was made regarding the foundation for these valuation findings.

In view of the foregoing, we are unable to determine whether the trial court's findings on this issue are clearly erroneous and must be set aside. Accordingly, this aspect of the case must be remanded to the lower court for additional findings, and/or evidentiary proceedings, as may be appropriate, to specifically determine (1) whether an express or implied agreement existed to treat Conventz' personal services as partnership capital, and/or to specifically remunerate him for such services, and if so, (2) the value of such services based on the evidentiary record herein.

* * *

NOTES

1. *Schymanski* illustrates that dealing with non-cash contributions not only requires asking what obligations do owners of the firm have to make such contributions, but also requires asking what rights in the firm do the contributing parties obtain by virtue of making the contributions. Sections 18(a) and 40(b) of the U.P.A., and 401(a)(1) and 807(b) of the R.U.P.A., provide (barring contrary agreement) that partners, upon liquidation of the partnership, are entitled to return of their contributions to the firm's capital, before splitting anything else as profits (or making up for any shortfall as losses). Applying this default rule seems simple enough when dealing with cash contributions, but becomes more difficult with non-cash contributions.

For example, suppose a partner contributes an item of property worth $100,000 at the time of its contribution to the partnership. What happens if, at the time the partnership dissolves, the property is worth $200,000: Is the contributor entitled to return of the actual property? To $100,000? To $200,000? See R.U.P.A. §§ 401(a)(1), 807(b) (upon liquidation, barring other agreement, the contributing partner receives back an amount equal to the agreed value of the property at the time of the contribution, with the remainder treated as profit to be shared); *Langness v. "O" Street Carpet Shop, Inc.,* 217 Neb. 569, 353 N.W.2d 709 (1984) (treating appreciation in the value of contributed property as part of profit to be shared). *But see Schaefer v. Bork,* 413 N.W.2d 873 (Minn.App.1987). Suppose, upon liquidation, the contributed property is worth only $50,000; now what result? Notice the implications of this default rule upon the question of whether partners need to value property upon its contribution to the partnership and the impact of the value upon which they agree. Suppose (as might be the case with a contribution of intangible items such as some intellectual property) the property is difficult to value upon its contribution: Are there approaches the parties might take to avoid problems of attempting to value property of highly speculative worth in order to establish their rights for a later liquidation?

Schymanski deals with contributions of services rather than property. The trial court treated Conventz' services as a contribution to capital with a value of $70,000. This entitled the Schymanskis to return of the $133,838.06 of cash they contributed, and the Conventz to return of the $109,658.48 of cash, the value of the property, and the value of the services, they contributed, before splitting equally the remaining proceeds from selling the lodge. Notice that without counting the services as a contribution to capital with a value of $70,000, the Schymanskis would be entitled to return of $133,838.06, but the Conventz would only be entitled to return of the $39,658.48 of cash and the value of the property they contributed, before splitting the rest of the sale proceeds equally.

As the Alaska Supreme Court's opinion explains, most courts do not treat services as a contribution to the capital of an ordinary partnership, requiring repayment on liquidation, unless the partners specifically agreed to do so. Why should this be so? Is this fair to the partner performing services? What does he or she then get for the services rendered? Would there be unfairness to other partners from treating services as a contribution to capital requiring repayment? What happens if the firm dissolves before the partner performs the services? As just mentioned, contributions of property to an ordinary partnership normally constitute a contribution to capital requiring repayment on liquidation, in the absence of contrary agreement. *E.g.*, R.U.P.A. § 401(a)(1). What justifies the difference in treatment from services?

In any event, the *Craig* decision discussed in *Schymanski* shows how courts might interpret language in a partnership agreement referring to "contributions" of services as showing an intent to treat services as a contribution to capital entitling the contributor to repayment on liquidation. If the parties wish to specify in their agreement an obligation to provide services, but do not wish a court to treat those services as a contribution to capital requiring repayment on liquidation, how can the parties avoid ambiguity on this issue?

2. The situation in *Schymanski* would have been even more complicated had the case involved a limited partnership or an LLC, instead of an ordinary partnership. To begin with, one can read the language in the pre–2001 U.L.P.A. to suggest that, in a limited partnership, services count as a contribution to capital requiring repayment on liquidation, unless the partners agree to the contrary. *See* U.L.P.A. § 105(a)(5)(i). *But see* U.L.P.A. (2001) § 111(9)(A)(no longer referring to keeping a record of the agreed value of "services", but just of the agreed value of "other benefits" besides cash, that partners contribute to the limited partnership).

Moreover, the U.L.P.A. increases the potential impact of the valuation of property or services agreed to by the partners. Under the pre–2001 version of the U.L.P.A., just as under the uniform partnership acts, each partner is entitled to receive back, upon liquidation, his or her contribution to capital. U.L.P.A. § 804(3). Presumably, as under the uniform partnership acts, the measure of this right would be the value of any non-cash contribution at the time of the contribution. This measure is particularly likely in light of the obligation under the U.L.P.A. to keep a record of the agreed value of any non-cash contribution (U.L.P.A. § 105(a)(5)(i). Adding to the impact of the valuation, the relative values of the partners' contributions establishes, under the pre–2001 version of the U.L.P.A., the profit allocation in the absence of other agreement. U.L.P.A. § 503. Of course, this is not likely to be too significant, since typically the parties will have reached an agreement on their profit shares, rather than fall into the statutory default rule. The 2001 version probably yields the same results. It no longer establishes, barring other agreement, a right to return of contributions upon liquidation, nor does it mention allocation of profits. However, it gets to the same point (in the absence of any agreement on the topic) by making rights to distributions, upon liquidation or otherwise, proportional to the agreed value of the partners' contributions. U.L.P.A. (2001) § 503, 812(b).

There are a couple of other impacts of the agreed valuation under the U.L.P.A. One arises if a partner fails to make the agreed non-cash contribution. In this event, the U.L.P.A. creates a potential liability of the defaulting partner to the limited partnership (or even to creditors of the limited partnership) in the amount of the agreed valuation of the non-cash contribution. U.L.P.A. § 502; U.L.P.A. (2001) § 502. A somewhat related impact involves liability for return of a partner's agreed contribution. Section 608 of the pre–2001 U.L.P.A. imposes a liability upon a partner who receives a return of his or her contribution, if the limited partnership is, within a specified period of time after the distribution, unable to pay its debts. *But see* U.L.P.A. (2001) § 508(b) (not establishing liability for a partner who receives a return of his or her contribution). Whether a distribution constitutes a return of a partner's contribution depends upon whether the partner's share of the fair market value of the partnership's assets after the distribution at least equals the partner's agreed contribution—which, in turn, depends upon the agreed valuation for any non-cash contributions.

This discussion of the U.L.P.A can be also apropos to LLCs, since many limited liability company statutes have copied various of the provisions of the U.L.P.A. that are relevant to non-cash contributions. Hence, many limited liability company statutes seem to suggest that services count as a capital contribution requiring repayment on liquidation, barring other agreement. *See, e.g.*, Cal Corp. Code § 17200(a); Del. Code Ann. Title 6 § 18–501; N.Y. Ltd. Liab. Co. Law § 501(a). Most LLC statutes call for return of capital upon liquidation (*e.g.*, Cal. Corp. Code § 17353; Del. Code Ann. Title 6 § 18–804(a)(3); N.Y. Ltd. Liab. Co. Law § 704(c))—which presumably, just as under the uniform partnership acts and the U.L.P.A., bases this right upon the value of any non-cash contributions. Most LLC statutes make the allocation of profit depend upon the relative values of contributions, barring other agreement *E.g.*, Cal. Corp. Code § 17106; Del. Code Ann. Title 6 § 18–503; N.Y. Ltd. Liab. Co. Law § 503. Also, many LLC statutes measure liability for failing to make an agreed non-cash contribution by the agreed value of the contribution. *E.g.*, Cal. Corp. Code § 17201(a)(2); Del. Code Ann. Title 6 § 18–502; N.Y. Ltd. Liab. Co. Law § 502(a). *See also* Del. Code Ann. Title 6 § 15–207(a) (creating similar liability in an LLP).

3. Whether or not partners or LLC members set an explicit value on their non-cash contributions, there typically will be some discussions between them prior to forming the firm as to the nature and worth of their

respective inputs. What obligations of candor do the prospective partners or LLC members owe each other during these discussions? The Maryland Court of Appeals addressed this issue for an ordinary partnership in *Herring v. Offutt,* 266 Md. 593, 295 A.2d 876, 879 (1972):

> The partnership relationship is of a fiduciary character which carries with it the requirements of utmost good faith and loyalty and the obligation of each member of the partnership to make full disclosure of all known information that is significant and material to the affairs or property of the partnership. * * *
>
> Moreover, "the principle of utmost good faith covers not only dealings and transactions occurring during the partnership but also those taking place during the negotiations leading to the formation of the partnership." * * * See also *The Uniform Partnership Act,* Sec. 21, which provides, in pertinent part:
>
> > "21. Partner accountable as a fiduciary.
> >
> > (1) Every partner must account to the partnership for any benefit, and hold as trustee for it any profits derived by him without the consent of the other partners from any transaction *connected with the formation,* conduct, or liquidation *of the partnership* or from any use by him of its property." (Emphasis added.)

Does the R.U.P.A. change this result? See R.U.P.A. § 404(b)(1) (eliminating any reference to a partner having a duty to account for profits he or she made in connection with the formation of the partnership). *See also* U.L.P.A. (2001) § 408(b)(1) (same).

b. *Tax Aspects*

Johnston v. Commissioner of Internal Revenue

T.C. Memo. 1995–140.

The issues for decision are:

(1) Do petitioners have gross income for 1982 as a result of the receipt by petitioner Robert Johnston of an interest in a partnership known as Maple Village Associates? We hold that they do.

* * *

FINDINGS OF FACT

* * *

[P]etitioner Robert Johnston (Mr. Johnston) [was] * * * a broker/dealer in securities * * *. Sometime in the summer of 1982, * * * Eccelston Properties, Ltd. (Eccelston), a sponsor of real estate limited partnerships, approached Mr. Johnston to ascertain whether he would be interested in participating in the organization of a real estate limited partnership that was to acquire, own, and operate Maple Village shopping center (Maple Village property or shopping center) in the Detroit area and that was to be known as Maple Village Associates (Maple Village partnership or Partnership). * * * Mr. Johnston agreed to participate in the formation of the Partnership and to serve as its general partner. * * *

On or about September 2, 1982, Maple Village partnership was formed under the laws of Michigan as a limited partnership. Its initial capital was $100, $90 of which was paid by Mr. Johnston in return for a 90–percent interest as a general partner and $10 of which was paid by another individual (original limited partner) in return for a 10–percent interest as a limited partner. The original limited partner was to withdraw as a limited partner from the Partnership and receive a return of his $10 capital contribution upon the admission as limited partners in Maple Village partnership of those investors who agreed to purchase the limited partnership interests that were to be offered for sale.

Subsequent to the formation of Maple Village partnership, 40 units of limited partnership interests were offered for sale at $200,000 per unit. Each such unit entitled the investor to a 2.475–percent limited partnership interest in Maple Village partnership. Pursuant to Federal securities laws, an offering document entitled "Confidential Private Placement Memorandum, Maple Village Associates" (placement memorandum) was prepared by Eccelston for distribution to potential purchasers of the limited partnership interests. * * *

The placement memorandum * * * provided that Mr. Johnston was to serve as the general partner of Maple Village partnership. It also stated in part:

> The General Partner will make no contribution to the capital of the Partnership but will own one (1%) percent of the capital, profits and losses of the Partnership. * * *
>
> * * *
>
> The General Partner will receive a 1% interest in the profits, losses and distributions of the Partnership. This compensation will be received despite no capital contribution by him. He will also receive a one-time organization [sic] fee of $30,000.

The amended limited partnership agreement for Maple Village partnership (amended partnership agreement) that was attached to the placement memorandum also provided that the general partner was entitled to one percent of the profits, losses, and distributions of Maple Village partnership, including any liquidating distribution.

The placement memorandum set forth certain organizational services for which Mr. Johnston, as general partner, was responsible. * * *

The placement memorandum further indicated that "Robert Johnston, the General Partner, will manage and control the affairs of the Partnership."

* * *

Eccelston was responsible for negotiating the purchase of the Maple Village property on behalf of Maple Village partnership. * * *

[The Maple Village partnership entered contracts to sell the 40 units of limited partnership interests to investors, who would become limited partners, for $8 million.] All of the contributions made by the investors to Maple Village partnership in return for their limited partnership interests therein were held in escrow pending the closing of the purchase of the Maple Village property. Prior to that closing in late December 1982, the Partnership had no control over those escrowed amounts, and those contributions to the Partnership remained contingent upon whether it in fact closed the purchase of the shopping center. The investors did not receive their limited partnership interests in, and were not admitted as limited partners of, Maple Village partnership until that closing in late December 1982.

* * *

After having purchased the Maple Village property, Maple Village partnership leased it to Eccelston. Eccelston agreed to be responsible for the management and maintenance of the shopping center in return for a fee from the Partnership. Mr. Johnston had no interest in Eccelston and did not assist Eccelston in carrying out its management contract for the Maple Village property.

* * *

OPINION

* * *

Respondent determined in the notice that the one-percent capital interest in Maple Village partnership that Mr. Johnston received in 1982 had a fair market value of $80,808 that is includible in petitioners' gross income upon receipt.

Section 721 provides that neither a partnership nor any of its partners are to recognize gain or loss in the case of a contribution of property to a partnership in exchange for an interest in that partnership. * * *

To the extent that a partner relinquishes any part of his or her right to be repaid contributions of capital in favor of another partner as compensation for services such other partner provides, section 721 does not apply. * * * In that event, pursuant to section 1.721–1(b)(1), Income Tax Regs., the receipt of an interest in the capital[3] of a partnership is income to the partner who provides the services (service partner). That regulation further provides in part:

3. A capital interest is to be distinguished from a profits interest. A capital interest is an interest that includes the right to share in the capital of a partnership upon liquidation. A profits interest is a right to share in the profits and losses of a partnership, but not to share in its capital. * * *

> The amount of such income is the fair market value of the interest in capital so transferred, either at the time the transfer is made for past services, or at the time the services have been rendered where the transfer is conditioned on the completion of the transferee's future services.* * *

Section 1.721–1(b)(1), Income Tax Regs., specifically states that it applies regardless whether the shift of capital from a partner to a service partner occurs at the time the partnership is formed or subsequent thereto.

* * *

To determine whether such a shift in capital has occurred, we must examine the effects of a hypothetical liquidation of the partnership occurring immediately after the partners receive their partnership interests. * * * If the service partner is entitled upon liquidation to a share of the capital contributed by other partners, a shift in capital has occurred, and the service partner has received an interest in the capital of the partnership for which he did not make a contribution of property.

* * *

Since the limited partners did not receive their interests in Maple Village partnership until the closing of the purchase of the shopping center in late December 1982, that closing date is the appropriate date on which to determine whether the limited partners shifted part of their capital to Mr. Johnston in return for services. * * * As of that date, * * *Mr. Johnston * * * received a one-percent interest in the profits, losses, and capital of the Partnership that entitled him to one percent of the assets of Maple Village partnership upon liquidation. If the Partnership had been liquidated as of that time, the Partnership would have had a total of $8,000,000 [contributed by the limited partners] * * *. Of that amount, each limited partner would have been entitled to a 2.475–percent share, i.e., a total of $198,000 * * *, and Mr. Johnston would have been entitled to a one-percent share, i.e., a total of $80,000 * * *. Thus, each limited partner shifted $2,000 of his or her capital contribution to Mr. Johnston. * * *

Contrary to petitioners' position, Mr. Johnston did not hold his one-percent capital interest in Maple Village partnership on December 31, 1982, as a result of his having made a capital contribution to that Partnership in September 1982 when he contributed $90 to the Partnership in return for a 90–percent interest therein. The total capitalization of the Partnership immediately after it was formed under State law on or about September 2, 1982, was only $100. Thus, if Maple Village partnership had been liquidated after Mr. Johnston contributed $90 of capital to it but before the limited partners' capital contributions were released from escrow to the Partnership in late December 1982, Mr. Johnston would have been entitled to only the $90 he contributed to it in September 1982. In contrast, if the Partnership had been liquidated in late December 1982, after the limited partners shifted to Mr. Johnston $80,000 of their capital, Mr. Johnston would have been entitled to a one-percent share or $80,000. In this connection, it is noteworthy that the placement memorandum informed potential limited partners of Maple Village partnership that a dilution of their investment would occur as a result of their giving Mr. Johnston a one-percent interest in the capital of the Partnership without his making a capital contribution.

Petitioners appear to contend that even if the Court were to hold that in late December 1982 the limited partners did shift to Mr. Johnston, and he did receive, a one-percent capital interest in the Partnership, such interest was not transferred to him as compensation for services. They assert that the $30,000 organizational fee that Mr. Johnston received pursuant to the placement memorandum represented full compensation for any services he provided to Maple Village partnership. Mr. Johnston testified that the $30,000 fee was to compensate him for assuming as general partner unlimited liability for the debts of the Partnership. His testimony does not establish that the $30,000 fee was intended to be his total compensation for services to the Partnership. Indeed, the placement memorandum makes it clear that the reason the limited partners shifted to Mr. Johnston part of their capital interest in Maple Village partnership was to compensate him and that he was to receive that capital interest in addition to the $30,000 organizational fee.

* * *

Although it was anticipated that Mr. Johnston would devote only minimal time to the affairs of the Partnership, this in no way changes the fact that he was expected to, and did, perform some services for it.

* * *

We shall now determine the income tax consequences to petitioners from our finding. To determine those consequences, we must decide when the fair market value of that interest is to be determined and what the fair market value of that interest was on that valuation date.

* * *

Under section 1.721–1(b)(1), Income Tax Regs., the amount of income that petitioners must recognize is the fair market value of the interest transferred to Mr. Johnston, either at the time the transfer is made for his past services or at the time the services are performed if the transfer is conditioned on the completion of future services by Mr. Johnston. * * *

We turn now to whether the transfer by the limited partners to Mr. Johnston in late December 1982 of a one-percent capital interest in the Partnership was conditioned on the completion of future services by him. If we find that it was, section 1.721–1(b)(1), Income Tax Regs., requires that the fair market value of that interest be determined at the time such services are rendered by Mr. Johnston. Although Mr. Johnston was obligated to perform some minimal future services after the limited partners transferred to him in late December 1982 a one-percent capital interest in the Partnership, petitioners do not argue, and we find that the record does not establish, that the transfer of that interest was conditioned on the performance of future services by him.

* * *

Respondent determined in the notice that when the limited partners transferred to Mr. Johnston a one-percent capital interest in the Partnership its fair market value was $80,808.[8] In determining that value, respondent reasoned that since each limited partner was willing to purchase a 2.475–percent interest in the capital of Maple Village partnership for $200,000, a willing buyer would pay $80,808 for a one-percent capital interest in that Partnership (1%/2.475% x $200,000).

Petitioners appear to contend that respondent's determination of the fair market value of the interest received by Mr. Johnston is erroneous. They assert that respondent's valuation ignores the fact that Mr. Johnston was a general partner, and not a limited partner. They appear to argue that a willing buyer would not pay the same amount for an interest as a general partner exposed to unlimited liability that he or she would pay for an interest as a limited partner not exposed to unlimited liability. * * *

Although petitioners' arguments may have some theoretical appeal, petitioners failed to offer any evidence, and we have found none in the record, that would provide us with an informed, reasoned basis on which to find that the fair market value of the one-percent capital interest transferred to Mr. Johnston by the limited partners in late December 1982 is an amount different from the value determined by respondent. * * *

Based on our review of the entire record in this case, we sustain respondent's determination that petitioners must include in their gross income for 1982 the fair market value, as determined by her, of the one-percent capital interest in Maple Village partnership that the limited partners transferred to Mr. Johnston in late December of that year.

* * *

NOTES

1. A partner, limited partner or LLC member who contributes services ultimately hopes for compensation by receiving a share of the firm's profits when made, and possibly some portion of the firm's assets upon liquidation of the business or the service contributor's withdrawal from the firm. As *Johnston* illustrates, recognition of taxable income by a partner contributing services may not wait, however, until the partnership makes a profit, or liquidation or withdrawal takes place. The *right* to future profits or distribution of assets (the partner's interest in the partnership) is itself an

8. The fair market value of that interest is not necessarily the same as the amount of capital to which Mr. Johnston could have been entitled if Maple Village partnership had been liquidated immediately after the limited partners shifted that interest to him. This is because of factors that might exist which could affect fair market value, such as anticipated gains and/or losses of the Partnership and material restrictions on transferability of the Partnership interests.

item of property which the partner generally obtains immediately upon entry into the partnership in compensation for his or her past or prospective work. Of course the same is true for limited partners or LLC members who contribute services in exchange for interests in limited partnerships or in limited liability companies that elect to be treated as partnerships for purposes of federal income taxation.

To determine how much, if any, taxable income the services contributor must recognize upon entry into the firm, the approach applied by the court in *Johnston* begins by asking what is the nature of the interest received in exchange for services. To answer this question, it is necessary to consider what would happen if the firm liquidated immediately following entry of the services contributor. As the court points out in *Johnston*, if the party contributing services would receive any of the proceeds of such an immediate liquidation (over and above the amount of any cash and the value of any property he or she also contributed), then the services contributor obtained a capital interest in exchange for his or her work. *See* Treas. Reg. § 1.721–1(b)(1). In essence, the other owners transferred to the services contributor a share in the cash or property they contributed. Such a transfer is what happened in *Johnston*—albeit, in an ultimately irrelevant twist, the transfer in *Johnston* took place when the limited partners entered the firm, rather than upon the somewhat earlier entry of the services contributor. It is apparent that such a share in the firm's existing assets possesses an immediate and ascertainable value and, as *Johnston* makes clear, receipt of such an interest in exchange for services constitutes taxable income.

A more complex situation is presented when the services contributor is only entitled to share in future profits (including proceeds upon liquidation which are in excess of the contributions of all of the owners). This is referred to as a profits interest. *See* Treas. Reg. § 1.721–1(b)(1). In *Diamond v. Commissioner*, 492 F.2d 286 (7th Cir.1974), a partner received a profits interest in exchange for services, and then sold the interest soon after its receipt. In light of this prompt sale, the court in *Diamond* concluded that the profits interest had a present and ascertainable value and its receipt in exchange for services constituted taxable income. Normally, however, such a prompt sale will not occur. In this event, the recipient might argue the profits interest has such a speculative and unascertainable value that its receipt should not be subject to immediate taxation. Moreover, consider the practical impact of a rule under which persons entering partnerships in which they contribute services in exchange for their right to future profits—as is invariably the case with professional firms—must recognize income immediately upon their entry into the partnership. Would lawyers and other professionals enter into partnerships if they must immediately recognize taxable income just for having done so? Yielding to such practicality concerns, the Internal Revenue Service came to the following helpful conclusion regarding receipt of profits interests for services:

Revenue Procedure 93–27

1993–2 C.B. 343.

* * *

SEC. 2. DEFINITIONS

The following definitions apply for purposes of this revenue procedure.

.01 A capital interest is an interest that would give the holder a share of the proceeds if the partnership's assets were sold at fair market value and then the proceeds were distributed in a complete liquidation of the partnership. This determination generally is made at the time of receipt of the partnership interest.

.02 A profits interest is a partnership interest other than a capital interest.

* * *

SEC. 4. APPLICATION

.01 Other than as provided below, if a person receives a profits interest for the provision of services to or for the benefit of a partnership in a partner capacity or in anticipation of being a partner, the Internal Revenue Service will not treat the receipt of such an interest as a taxable event for the partner or the partnership.

.02 This revenue procedure does not apply:

(1) If the profits interest relates to a substantially certain and predictable stream of income from partnership assets, such as income from high-quality debt securities or a high-quality net lease;

(2) If within two years of receipt, the partner disposes of the profits interest; or

(3) If the profits interest is a limited partnership interest in a "publicly traded partnership" within the meaning of section 7704(b) of the Internal Revenue Code.

As the court in *Johnston* discusses, the taxable receipt of a capital interest in a partnership (or an entity electing income tax treatment as a partnership) raises questions both as to the amount, and as to the timing, of the tax. The issue as to the amount of tax liability involves valuing the interest. What was the basis for the court's valuation of the capital interest received by Mr. Johnston? Notice, while the court discussed what Mr. Johnston would have received upon a liquidation immediately after the limited partners' entry (in order to establish that Mr. Johnston received a capital interest), this was not the basis for the valuation of his interest. At least one court, however, has measured the tax based upon the liquidation value of a partnership interest received for services. *St. John v. United*

States, 84–1 U.S.T.C. (CCH) ¶ 9158 (C.D.Ill.1983). A major significance of using liquidation value would be to preclude taxation of a profits interest regardless of Revenue Procedure 93–27—since a profits interest, by definition, has a liquidation value of zero. Instead of liquidation value, the court in *Johnston* measured the value based upon what the limited partners paid for their interests. Yet, why were the limited partners willing to pay more than liquidation value for their interests? The answer, of course, is because of the potential future profits from the shopping center (plus perhaps some tax shelter benefits). This means that, in basing the valuation upon what the limited partners were willing to pay, the court in *Johnston* was valuing both Mr. Johnston's capital interest and his profits interest. Does this seem contrary to Revenue Procedure 93–27? Moreover, what about the point argued by Mr. Johnston as to the difference in worth between limited and general partnership interests? In contrast to *Johnston*, the court of appeals in *Campbell v. Comm'r*, 943 F.2d 815 (8th Cir.1991), rejected a valuation based upon the sale price of other partnership interests (as well as upon the discounted present value of expected future earnings (and other benefits) from owning the partnership interests). Perhaps, instead of valuing Mr. Johnston' interest based upon what other partners paid for their interests, is there a way to value Mr. Johnston's interest based upon what he paid for his interest? See *Hensel Phelps Construction Co. v. Commissioner*, 74 T.C. 939 (1980) (holding that the value of an interest received for services equals the value of the services).

Beyond the question of how much tax is due, there is also the question of when recognition must occur. The court states that, if Mr. Johnston would have lost his interest in the event of non-performance of his services, this threat of forfeiture would have delayed recognition until Mr. Johnston's performance. While the court cites, in support of this proposition, the tax regulation dealing with the receipt of a partnership capital interest for services, it also seems to follow from Section 83 of the Internal Revenue Code. Under Section 83, if property received in connection with the performance of services is both subject to a substantial risk of forfeiture and nontransferable, then, barring an election by the taxpayer under Section 83(b), the taxpayer does not recognize income until either of the restrictions lapse. Notice, while this is a conjunctive requirement—delay only exists so long as there is both a restriction on transfer and a risk of forfeiting the property—Section 83(c)(2) treats a risk of forfeiture, which follows the property into the hands of any new owner, as a transfer restriction. Hence, just as the court discussed under the regulation, the key to the timing of recognition under Section 83 is the existence of a risk of forfeiture. A common example of such a risk of forfeiture—both expressly mentioned in Section 83 and the focus of the regulation relied on by the court—is to condition retention of the interest on the performance of the services. Chapter IV will consider other examples of forfeiture risk, and will explore in some detail the criteria for when interests are subject to a substantial risk of forfeiture within the meaning of Section 83.

2. So, what is the practical impact of all this for the attorney drafting a partnership or LLC operating agreement? The problem for Mr. Johnston

was that he faced immediate recognition of taxable income, yet he had not received anything which he readily could use to pay the tax. This suggests that receiving an interest in partnership capital in exchange for services is generally a bad idea from a tax standpoint. Indeed, the negative tax consequences for the partner receiving the capital interest for services, coupled with the negative economic consequences (as illustrated by what the trial court did in *Schymanski*) for the partner who contributes cash or property and who sees the value of some of his or her contributions transferred to the partner providing services, suggests that avoiding receipt of capital interests for services is something on which all partners (or limited partners or LLC members) normally can agree.

Of course, if the partner (or person taxed as a partner) providing services to the firm will not receive a capital interest in exchange for the services, what will he or she receive? Mr. Johnston received a $30,000 fee; albeit, he also received a one percent interest in partnership capital and profits. Whether or not Mr. Johnston should have been satisfied just with the flat fee, would such a flat fee be adequate compensation for partners in a professional or personal service partnership? For example, how many lawyers would agree to work as a partner in a law firm solely in exchange for a flat fee? Here is where Revenue Procedure 93–27, quoted above, is so useful, since it allows the tax free receipt of a profits interest in a partnership (or other entity treated as a partnership for income tax purposes). Indeed, this means there is no automatic reason to fear partners (persons taxed as partners) receiving interests in the firm in exchange for their services—as is done every day—so long as they receive profits interests, not capital interests.

Before assuming, however, that only individuals who are too greedy can end up facing a tax upon contributing services for an interest in the partnership, it is useful to review carefully Revenue Procedure 93–27. It contains several exceptions to the rule of non-recognition for partners who receive a profits interest in exchange for services. The exceptions for partnerships with a predictable steady stream of income, and for publicly traded partnerships, will not be a problem upon formation for most firms. On the other hand, can there be greater significance to the exception for disposing of a profits interest within two years of its receipt? Of course, selling the interest would be a taxable event in any case. Consider, however, the possible impact of this exception on both the type (ordinary income versus capital gains) and timing (when received versus when sold) of income recognized as a result of selling the profits interest within two years. Incidentally, can disposing of an interest for purposes of this exception include gifts, transfers on death, or incorporating the partnership in a Section 351 transaction?

Next, read carefully the definition of a profits interest in Revenue Procedure 93–27. What impact does this definition create for the valuation of property contributed to a partnership (including any entity which elects to be treated as a partnership for purposes of income taxation)? For example, suppose one owner receives an interest for services, while another receives an interest for contributing property. What is the impact under Revenue Procedure 93–27 if the parties unrealistically undervalue the property upon its contribution, so that an immediate liquidation would result in money going to the services providing partner?

So far, nothing explains why the parties drafted the agreement to give Mr. Johnston an interest in capital in exchange for his services. Notice that the agreement granted Mr. Johnston a one percent share in all economic interests in the firm—capital, profits and distributions. In fact, the reason the parties in *Johnston* probably structured the deal to give Mr. Johnston a one-percent interest in capital, as well as profits, is because giving at least a one percent interest in capital and profits to the general partner formerly helped ensure treatment of the limited partnership as a partnership for tax purposes—a motive which is no longer relevant with the "check the box" regulation. Nevertheless, the common desire for simplicity often tempts partners (or parties taxed as partners) to draft their agreement so each partner holds a percentage share in the firm, rather than a share in profits which differs from his or her share in the firm's capital. This was the structure of the agreement in *Johnston*. As *Johnston* illustrates, when one or more partners contribute services, while other partners contribute cash or property, granting to each partner a simple percentage interest in the firm means granting to the partner(s) contributing services an interest in the capital contributed by the partner(s) contributing cash or property—in other words, granting the service contributor(s) an immediately taxable capital interest.

Suppose a partner (or a person taxed as a partner) contributes both services and capital (either cash or property) to a firm electing partnership tax treatment. In this event, receiving a capital interest in exchange for the capital contribution would not be receiving a capital interest for services. Is there any limit on the amount of the capital interest, which the recipient partner might claim he or she received for his or her capital contribution? Consider, in this regard, Mr. Johnston's argument that he received his capital interest in exchange for money ($90), not services. Why did this argument fail? Does it make any sense to suppose that Mr. Johnston really could purchase an interest worth $80,000 for just $90? Broadening this example, does this suggest a danger for partners (or persons taxed as partners), who contribute both services and capital (i.e. cash or property). If they obtain an interest in firm capital with a value greater than the amount of cash and value of property they contribute, is not the logical conclusion that they received some of their interest in capital in exchange for services? Indeed, Section 83(a) seems to speak to this issue. It requires a person, who receives property in connection with the performance of services, to recognize, as taxable income, the difference between the fair market value of the property received, and the amount of money and value of property the recipient paid for the property. On the other hand, does this mean any time later investors pay a higher amount for their interests in a venture than the founders had paid, that the founders received interests at a bargain price as compensation for services? Suppose something good happened to the business between the time the founders bought in and the time later investors purchased their interests, and this made interests in the business more valuable? In this event, would there have been any transfer of a capital interest in exchange for services? Why could such an argument not work in *Johnston*? Chapter IV will return to this subject when exploring the sale of bargain shares to those performing services for a corporation.

3. Things become more complicated if, unlike the situation in *Johnston*, the interest received (whether in capital or profits) is contingent upon completion of the services, or is otherwise subject to a substantial risk of being forfeited by the recipient partner. On the positive side, as discussed above, this can delay recognition of income for the partner who receives a capital interest in exchange for services. Specifically, there is no need to recognize income until the risk of forfeiture lapses (for example, the services are performed). Lest one be tempted to overly exploit this rule by providing for a permanent risk of forfeiture, however, Section 83(a) denies delay based upon a risk of forfeiture, which, by its terms, never lapses. Treas. Reg. § 1.83–3(c)(1).

The delay in recognition provided by Section 83 does not come without negative consequences. As just mentioned, Section 83(a) requires a person, who receives any sort of property in connection with the performance of services, to recognize, as taxable income, the difference between the fair market value of the property received, and the amount of money and value of property, if any, the recipient paid for the property. If a risk of forfeiture allows the recipient of property to delay recognition until the risk lapses, the question becomes whether one measures the taxable income based upon the fair market value of the property when it was received, or when recipient recognizes the income. The answer provided by Section 83(a) is to measure the taxable income based upon the fair market value of the received property *on the date of recognition*—in other words, the date the risk of forfeiture lapsed. Consider what this means if the property received by the services provider appreciates in worth prior to the lapse of a risk of forfeiture—which, naturally, is what one hopes to happen when receiving an interest in a business. Of course, if one plans to sell the interest as soon as the risk of forfeiture lapses, the seller would face recognition of this appreciation anyway. A difficulty is that the lapse might occur after significant appreciation, but well before the recipient wishes to sell out—thereby exacerbating the problem of recognition without getting anything to pay the tax. Far worse, delay in recognition turns this appreciation into ordinary income rather than capital gains.

A second downside to delaying recognition under Section 83(a) results from Treasury Regulation § 1.83–1(a). This regulation states that property received in connection with the performance of services will not be regarded as owned, for tax purposes, by the transferee until the lapse of any substantial risk of forfeiture. If applied to the restricted transfer of a partnership interest to a services contributor, the consequences could be to deprive that individual and the firm of any tax benefits associated with his or her partner (for tax purposes) status—as, for example, being able to take advantage of loss deductions from the partnership. A third negative consequence of delaying recognition of income pursuant to Section 83 is that the partnership (or entity electing income tax treatment as a partnership) is not entitled to a deduction (for paying for the services by giving the interest) until the services contributor recognizes income. I.R.C. § 83(h).

Given these tradeoffs, a recipient of an interest in partnership capital in exchange for services might wish to recognize tax immediately, even if the interest is subject to a risk of forfeiture (say for non-performance of the services). In fact, Section 83(b) allows persons receiving property subject to a risk of forfeiture to elect immediate taxation, thereby avoiding the tradeoffs imposed upon those who delay recognition. Of course, a person making this election may regret having done so if he or she then forfeits the property. Chapter IV will look at this as part of its exploration of Section 83. For now, however, note that partners, who make a Section 83(b) election, may not only have paid tax on receiving the interest they forfeited, but also may have paid tax on partnership income they recognized and now also might forfeit.

Just to make things even more complicated, suppose the interest subject to a risk of forfeiture is a partnership profits, rather than a capital, interest. At first glance, one may be tempted to assume that Section 83 is irrelevant, because Revenue Procedure 93–27 makes the receipt solely of a profits interest for services not taxable—assuming the three caveats in the Procedure do not apply—even without the interest being subject to a risk of forfeiture. Yet, what happens when the risk of forfeiture lapses: Is there still no taxable income, or does the normal rule under Section 83 require the recipient to pay a tax based upon the fair market value of the interest at the time of the lapse? Of course, the recipient partner might have tried to avoid this concern—assuming his or her attorney was alert to the problem—by making an election under Section 83(b) to recognize, despite the risk of forfeiture, income immediately upon receiving the profits interest; but then the question becomes whether the recipient partner could still invoke Revenue Procedure 93–27 to avoid recognition upon the initial receipt of the interest. Fortunately, the Internal Revenue Service has taken a helpful position:

Revenue Procedure 2001–43

2001–2 C.B. 191.

* * *

SECTION 3. SCOPE

This revenue procedure clarifies Rev. Proc. 93–27 by providing that the determination under Rev. Proc. 93–27 of whether an interest granted to a service provider is a profits interest is, under the circumstances described below, tested at the time the interest is granted, even if, at that time, the interest is substantially nonvested (within the meaning of § 1.83–3(b) of the Income Tax Regulations)[–in other words, subject to a substantial risk of forfeiture and non-transferable]. Accordingly, where a partnership grants a profits interest to a service provider in a transaction meeting the requirements of this revenue procedure and Rev. Proc. 93–27, the Internal Revenue Service will not treat the grant of the interest or the event that causes the interest to become substantially vested (within the meaning of § 1.83–3(b) of the Income Tax Regulations) as a taxable event for the partner or the partnership. Taxpayers to which this revenue procedure applies need not file an election under section 83(b) of the Code.

SECTION 4. APPLICATION

This revenue procedure clarifies that, for purposes of Rev. Proc. 93–27, where a partnership grants an interest in the partnership that is substantially nonvested to a service provider, the service provider will be treated as receiving the interest on the date of its grant, provided that:

.01 The partnership and the service provider treat the service provider as the owner of the partnership interest from the date of its grant and the service provider takes into account the distributive share of partnership income, gain, loss, deduction, and credit associated with that interest in computing the service provider's income tax liability for the entire period during which the service provider has the interest;

.02 Upon the grant of the interest or at the time that the interest becomes substantially vested, neither the partnership nor any of the partners deducts any amount (as wages, compensation, or otherwise) for the fair market value of the interest; and

.03 All other conditions of Rev. Proc. 93–27 are satisfied.

* * *

Notice that this Revenue Procedure allows—indeed requires—partners receiving profits interests subject to a risk of forfeiture to be treated as partners for purposes of allocating partnership income and losses; thereby trumping Treas. Reg. § 1.83–1(a), which, as stated above, normally does not consider the transferee to own (for tax purposes) property subject to a risk of forfeiture until the lapse of the restriction. Helpful however as this Revenue Procedure is, questions remain. For example, what about a situation, as in *Johnston*, in which the partner receives both a profits and a capital interest in exchange for services, but, unlike *Johnston*, the interests are subject to a substantial risk of forfeiture: Can the partner still take advantage of Revenue Procedure 2001–43 for the profits interest and only face the Section 83 tradeoff for any appreciation in the value of the capital interest prior to the lapse of the risk of forfeiture? See Banoff, *First IRS Ruling on Unvested Partnership Profits Interests: No Income Recognized but Questions Remain*, 99 J. Tax. 133 (2003) (citing a private letter ruling apparently allowing bifurcation of profits and capital interests).

4. Having explored the analysis under current law, the reader should be warned that the law in this area threatens to change. The I.R.S. issued proposed regulations in 2005 that would junk the distinction between receipt of capital and profits interests for services and the helpful Revenue Procedures 93–27 and 2001–43. Prop. Reg. §§ 1.83–3(e), (*l*), 1.721–1(b). Instead, the proposed regulations take the view that receipt, in connection with the performance of services, of any interest in a partnership (or entity electing tax treatment as a partnership) falls within the scope of Section 83—thereby requiring recognition of the difference between the fair market value of the interest received and whatever cash and property the recipient paid for the interest. Fortunately, the proposed regulations—and an accompanying proposed revenue procedure (Prop. Rev. Proc. 2005–43, 2005–1 C.B. 1221)—contain a safe harbor that produces much the same result as current law. If the partnership and all of its partners elect the safe harbor, then the I.R.S. will deem the fair market value of any interest in the partnership received for services to equal the liquidation value of the interest. As noted above, the liquidation value of a profits interest is, by definition, zero. Hence, the safe harbor ends up only producing tax upon the receipt of a capital interest, as in *Johnston*. Further paralleling current law, the safe harbor election under the regulations only applies to a so-called "safe harbor partnership interest"—the definition of which excludes roughly the same three sort of profits interests that Revenue Procedure 93–27 excluded from its protective reach.

So, if the proposed regulations, with their safe harbor provision, simply bring one back largely to the same results as the present law, what will be the significance if the regulations actually take effect? One critical impact from a planning standpoint will be to require an affirmative election of the safe harbor by the partnership and all of the partners—either through a provision in the partnership or LLC operating agreement, or otherwise. Moreover, in contrast to the approach of Revenue Procedure 2001–43, recipients of a profits interest, which is subject to a risk of forfeiture, must affirmatively make an election under Section 83(b) if they wish to avoid the disadvantages Section 83 imposes when recognition is delayed. Presumably, such elections will be the norm in the case of a profits interest received for services—since, in that event, there is no income to recognize in case of a Section 83(b) election if the partnership also elects the safe harbor. On the other hand, for those who make the Section 83(b) election and then forfeit their interest, there will be consequences (which the proposed regulations address) as far as income and losses allocated to the partner contributing services before the forfeiture. Also, the safe harbor election removes some of the disadvantage for those who do not make a Section 83(b) election, since they need only recognize, when the risk of forfeiture lapses, the increase in the liquidation value of the firm's assets—as opposed to recognizing an increased valuation based the improvement in the firm's future profit expectations as the business develops.

5. *Johnston* dealt with the tax effects on the partner contributing services. There are also effects on the partnership (or entity electing tax treatment as a partnership) and hence all the partners (or limited partners or LLC

members). Treasury Regulation § 1.721–1(b)(2) treats the transfer of a capital interest in exchange for services to the firm as a guaranteed payment under Internal Revenue Code Section 707(c). As a result, the firm (which is, in essence, paying for services rendered) may be entitled either to a deduction pursuant to Section 162 or to capitalize the value of the interest and add it to the basis of its assets under Sections 195, 263 and 709. On the other hand, Revenue Procedure 2001–43 makes it clear that the quid pro quo for non-recognition under Revenue Procedure 93–27 for a partner receiving a profits interest for services is that neither the partnership nor the other partners can claim a deduction. Currently, there is some dispute about another possible consequence of treating the transfer of a capital interest as a Section 707(c) guaranteed payment. Specifically, must the partnership (or entity electing tax treatment as a partnership) recognize a gain or loss equal to any difference between the basis and value of the capital interest. *Compare* W. McKee, W. Nelson & R. Whitmire, *Federal Taxation of Partnerships and Partners* ¶ 5.07[2] (1977), *with* A. Gunn, *Partnership Income Taxation* 29 (1991). (As discussed below, such a difference between the basis and value of a capital interest is common due to the firm's retention of the contributor's basis in any property contributed to the firm.) The proposed regulations side with those who argue that there should be no recognition by the partnership. Prop. Reg. §§ 1.83–6(b), 1.721–1(b)(1).

This discussion, in turn, leads to the question of how to allocate among the partners (or limited partners or LLC members) any deduction or increased basis obtained by the partnership (or entity electing tax treatment as a partnership) as a result of the transaction. (As will be explored in Section B, the Internal Revenue Code allows the owners of a firm treated as a partnership for income tax purposes wide latitude in determining which of their number will receive the tax benefit or detriment of firm gains, losses, deductions or credits.) At first thought, one may be tempted to allocate to the services contributor any deduction obtained by the firm as a result of its "paying" for his or her work with a capital interest. In this manner, assuming payment for the work is all immediately deductible under Section § 162 (rather than capitalized under Sections 195, 263 or 709), this deduction would offset exactly the taxable income to the services contributor. One problem with this neat solution is that parties giving up an interest in their capital to a service contributor might feel themselves entitled to any deduction this creates. Another problem is that the I.R.S. takes the position that Section 706(d)(1)—which deals with the impact on partnership allocations of changes in the ownership of the firm during a tax year—requires such a deduction go to partners in the firm prior to the entry of the partner receiving the interest for services. 70 Fed. Reg. 29675 (May 23, 2005).

6. Fortunately, the tax issues raised by contributing property to a partnership (or firm electing tax treatment as a partnership) are generally not as difficult as the tax issues raised by contributing services. At first, one might be worried about taxable income upon the contribution of property in exchange for an interest in the partnership, because parties exchanging

property normally must recognize as gain (or loss) the difference between their basis in the property surrendered and the value of the property received. I.R.C. § 1001. Does this apply to the contribution of property to a partnership, where, in essence, the partner receives an interest in the firm in exchange for his or her contribution (and the partnership receives the contribution in exchange for the interest)? The answer is no. Instead, as stated by the court in *Johnston*, Section 721 of the Internal Revenue Code provides that neither the partners nor the partnership recognize gain or loss upon a contribution of property in exchange for an interest in the firm. (Naturally, Section 721 also applies to any firm, such as a limited partnership, an LLP or an LLC, electing income tax treatment as a partnership.) As a corollary to non-recognition, Section 723 provides generally that the firm will retain the same basis in the contributed property as previously possessed by the contributing party. Section 722 provides generally that the contributing party's basis in the interest he or she receives in the firm will be the same as the basis he or she had in the contributed property, plus the amount of any money he or she also contributed. In this manner, the tax code avoids tax upon the contribution, but preserves for the future the recognition of the pre-contribution gain (or loss) on the contributed property. Incidentally, while Section 721 provides non-recognition from federal income tax, could the exchange of property for a partnership interest equal a sale for purposes of state sales taxes? See 18 Cal.Code Regs. § 1595(b)(4) (exempting a transfer of property to a commencing partnership solely in exchange for an interest in the partnership from California sales tax).

Several fairly common types of property contributions introduce additional complexities. To begin with, suppose a prospective partner or LLC member creates rights or assets through his or her efforts; is this a contribution of services or can this fall within Section 721 as property? See *United States v. Frazell,* 335 F.2d 487 (5th Cir.1964), *cert. denied,* 380 U.S. 961 (1965) (maps, possibly made by the taxpayer, were property under Section 721). On which side of the line does technical know-how fall? See Rev. Rul. 64–56, which is reprinted in Chapter IV. Along this line, what exactly were the services which Mr. Johnston provided for the limited partnership, given the fact that Eccelston purchased and ran the shopping center for the partnership? The court notes that Johnston served as general partner with unlimited personal liability. Is an agreement to provide one's personal credit in this manner a contribution of property or services?

Another issue that arises with the contribution of intangibles (such as intellectual property) to the firm involves the ability of the firm to claim amortization deductions. Section 197 allows a deduction based upon amortizing intangible assets over a 15 year period. Suppose, however, the contributor had created the intangible. Section 197(c)(2) denies amortization for self-created intangibles (in other words, intangibles created by the taxpayer claiming the deduction). Will transferring the intangible to the partnership (or firm electing tax treatment as a partnership) avoid this restriction (since the firm did not create the intangible)? See I.R.C. § 197(f)(2) (suggesting that, in a non-recognition transaction such as a Section 721 contribution, the transferee of the intangible steps into the shoes of the transferor). Of course, typically there would be little or no carryover basis for the firm to amortize anyway in the case of such a self-created intangible contributed by one of the owners. As discussed later, however, allocations under Section 704(c) could provide some significance to the issue of whether the firm is treated as if it created the intangible in question.

Often, property contributed to a partnership (or entity electing tax treatment as a partnership) is subject to a liability. In this event, the Internal Revenue Code treats the liability as if assumed by the firm to the extent the liability does not exceed the fair market value of the property at the time of the contribution. I.R.C. § 752(c); Treas. Reg. § 1.752–1(c). This has important effects upon the partners (or parties treated as partners for tax purposes) under Section 752 of the Code. Section 752(a) (working in conjunction with Section 722), increases the other partners' bases in their interests in the firm by their share of the firm's liabilities. Section 752(b) treats the assumption by the firm of the contributor's liability as a distribution of money to the contributor. The result is to reduce (but not below zero) the basis of the contributor's interest in the firm by the amount of the liability allocated to the other partners. *See* I.R.C. § 733; Treas. Reg. § 1.722–1, Ex. 1. If the amount of the liability allocated to the other partners exceeds the contributor's basis in his or her interest in the firm, the excess is taxable, presumably as capital gain. *See* I.R.C. §§ 731(a)(1), 741; Treas. Reg. § 1.722–1, Ex.2; Rev. Rul. 84–15, 1984–1 C.B. 158. The contributor who faces such recognition of income may wish to contribute additional cash or property to increase his or her basis in the firm. Alternately, the contributor could refrain from having the debts assumed by the firm. While Section 752(c) seems to indicate that transfer of encumbered property automatically equals an assumption of the debt by the partnership, the regulations suggest that the partnership can decline to assume the debt. Wile, *Partnership Contributions of Encumbered Property Revisited*, 84 Tax Notes 1181, 1184 (1999). Indeed, given that the contributor normally will remain at least secondarily liable on the original debt despite its assumption by the partnership, and that the contributor could always use distributions from the partnership to discharge the debt without normally paying a tax on the distribution (as with distributions from a corporation), a contributor might want to think twice about having the partnership to assume a debt attached to the contributed property.

Debts which produce a deduction only when paid—such as the accounts payable of a cash basis taxpayer, or certain obligations under environmental laws to clean up hazardous waste found on land contributed to the partnership—do not count as a liability for purposes of Section 752. Treas. Reg. § 1.752–1(a); Rev. Rul. 88–77, 1988–2 C.B. 128. This nicely removes the prospective problem under Section 752, discussed above, of having the partnership (or entity treated as a partnership for tax purposes) assume such a liability along with the contributed property. In addition—showing that in tax law no good deed goes unabused—it has produced schemes designed to achieve immediate tax reduction. The schemes typically involved having the partnership assume such obligations, which, because the partnership was stuck with the burden to pay a future claim, lowered the economic value of the partnership interest received in the Section 721 exchange. At the same time, because the obligation did not count as a "liability" under Section 752, the assumption did not lower the transferor's basis in the partnership interest the transferor received. The resulting gap between the economic value of the partnership interest received, versus the partner's basis in this interest, produced a built-in loss for tax purposes, which the transferor could quickly recognize by selling the interest. Later, the partnership would claim a deduction upon paying off the assumed obligation. The Internal Revenue Service has promulgated complex regulations in order to address this problem through the application of Section 704(c)—which is discussed later in this chapter. Treas. Reg. § 1.752–7.

Suppose, instead of a partnership (or an entity treated as a partnership for tax purposes) assuming debt as part of a contribution of property, an existing creditor of the firm agrees to cancel the firm's debt in exchange for an interest in the firm. Could this constitute a contribution of property within the meaning of Section 721? See I.R.C. § 108(e)(8) (not a contribution under Section 721; but rather the partnership must recognize cancellation of indebtedness income).

Sometimes partners, limited partners or LLC members may contribute to the firm rights they possess to profits or distributions from other sources. If that occurs, does Section 721 override the assignment-of-income doctrine? See H.R. Rep. No. 98–861, 98th Cong. 2d Sess. 857 (1984) (suggesting the doctrine might apply under circumstances outlined, for example, by Revenue Ruling 80–198—which is reprinted in Chapter IV); *Schneer v. Commissioner,* 97 T.C. 643 (1991) (transfer of referral and consulting fees to a partnership did not fall within assignment of income doctrine).

Normally, the contribution of cash or property in exchange for an interest in the partnership is a one-step process in which the arms-length nature of the transaction should lead to an equivalence between the amount of cash or value of the property transferred to the partnership, and the value of the interest in the partnership received by the transferor. The growing use of option contracts involving partnership interests (copying from the common issuance of stock options) creates the prospect, however, of two-step transactions between partners and the partnership (or entity treated as a partnership for tax purposes). The first step is the firm's sale of a contract giving to a partner (or prospective partner) the option to buy an interest in the firm at a set price. The second step is the partner's (or person treated as a partner) exercise of the option—in which the partner will receive an interest in the firm presumably of greater value at the time of exercise than the amount of cash or value of property exchanged for the interest (which generally is why one exercises a call option). Will Section 721 cover either or both of these steps? See Prop. Treas. Reg. § 1.721–2 (Section 721 applies and prevents recognition upon the exercise of a non-compensatory option to purchase a partnership interest for cash or property, with the cash or property received by the partnership both for the option and in exercising the option treated as contributed to the partnership in the Section 721 exchange; but Section 721 does not apply to the original purchase of the option—meaning possible recognition if appreciated property is used to purchase the option; nor does Section 721 apply to holder's allowing the option to lapse unexercised—meaning the consideration for selling the option is then income to the partnership, rather than a Section 721 contribution). Notice that the proposed regulation only addresses non-compensatory options—as opposed to options issued to partners in exchange for performing services. Chapter IV will discuss the tax treatment of stock options issued in exchange for services.

Suppose the contributed property consists of unrealized receivables or inventory that would produce ordinary income if the contributor had sold the property him- or herself. Alternately, suppose the contributed property is worth less than the contributor's basis in the property so that sale by the contributor would have produced a capital loss. Might parties attempt to use such contributions to transform ordinary income into capital gains, or capital losses into ordinary losses, if the firm is able to change the manner in which the assets are used? Section 724 is designed to prevent this from occurring. It requires the firm to recognize ordinary income on the disposition of any contributed unrealized receivables or on any contributed inventory items sold within five years of the contribution. It also requires the firm, if it sells contributed property (assuming the property consists of a capital asset) at a loss within five years of the contribution, to treat as a capital loss the difference between the basis and the fair market value of the contributed property at the time of its contribution.

Finally, suppose an individual contributes property to a partnership (or entity electing income tax treatment as a partnership), and shortly thereafter the firm distributes to him or her money or other property worth about the same as his or her contribution. Could the I.R.S. attack such a transaction as really constituting a not-too cleverly disguised sale? See I.R.C. § 707(a)(2)(B); Treas. Reg. §§ 1.707–3; 1.707–4 (outlining when distributions coinciding with contributions constitute sale proceeds for tax purposes). Not surprisingly, while finding a disguised sale depends upon a number of factors, the timing of the two events may be the most telling—in fact, the regulations create a rebuttable presumption that distributions within two years of a contribution constitute disguised sale payments, while distributions more than two years apart from a contribution do not. Treas. Reg. § 1.707–3(c), (d). Another important factor is whether the distributions simply reflect payment to the property contributor of his or her share of the firm's earnings from ordinary operations. The regulations encompass this notion by creating a rebuttable presumption that "operating cash flow distributions" are not disguised sale proceeds. Treas. Reg. § 1.707–4(b). Moreover, distributions to which the recipient was entitled even without the property contribution would not be disguised sale proceeds. Treas. Reg. § 1.707–3(b)(1)(i). Note, by the way, that the disguised sale may not always take the form of a distribution equal in amount to the value of the contributed property. There could be a partial sale and partial contribution. Treas. Reg. § 1.707–3(f) Ex. 1. Also, suppose the contributor mortgaged the property in contemplation of a transfer in which the firm assumes the liability. See Treas. Reg. § 1.707–5 (laying out rules for when the assumption of debts upon the contribution of property will be treated as sale proceeds).

7. In addition to the partnership agreement, the court in *Johnston* quoted from a so-called confidential private placement memorandum. What is this document? As the court alludes to, the parties prepared this document in order to comply with securities law requirements involving disclosure to individuals asked to invest in businesses. Chapter V will explore such securities law requirements in detail.

2. ALTERNATIVES TO CAPITAL CONTRIBUTIONS

DeShazo v. Clayton

2006 WL 1794735 (D.Idaho 2006).

* * *

I.

BACKGROUND

The present action arises out of Paul Clayton's purchase of property in Eagle, Idaho (the "Property"). Clayton obtained title to the Property in his name as an "unmarried man" by Warranty Deed from Kathryn H. Mauritz on May 4, 2001. Almost three years later, in May of 2004, Clayton created the Paul B. Clayton Trust (the "Trust") and, on May 5, 2004, transferred the Property to the Trust.

Plaintiffs claim that Clayton purchased the Property on behalf of Berkshire West, an association created by Paul Clayton, Robert DeShazo, and Douglas Landwer (collectively "Members") for the purpose of developing the Property. At the time Clayton purchased the Property, DeShazo held an "Exclusive Purchase Agreement" for the Property. DeShazo entered into this agreement with the Property owner, Kathryn Mauritz, on November 24, 2000, before Berkshire West was organized. The agreement recites that Mauritz agreed to accept three non-refundable payments of $2,000 each "for the exclusive right of Robert DeShazo to purchase [the] property" for the sum of $330,500.00. The $2,000 payments were to be applied to the purchase price.

DeShazo's agreement with Mauritz was amended on April 10, 2001, in order to allow additional time for DeShazo to obtain Eagle city's approval of a proposed subdivision on the Property before closing on the purchase. DeShazo ultimately made $8,000 in payments to retain his exclusive right of purchase, and these payments were credited toward the purchase price when Clayton purchased the Property.

* * * Clayton purchased the Property * * * in May of 2001. Thereafter, on August 2, 2001, Clayton, DeShazo, and Landwer signed Articles of

Organization for Berkshire West, LLC, ("Berkshire West" or "LLC") and a Limited Liability Company Management Operating Agreement ("Operating Agreement") for Berkshire West.

Both the Articles of Organization and the Operating Agreement listed the period of duration for Berkshire West as that necessary to develop the Property until the subdivision was either built out or all the lots were sold. The Operating Agreement also set forth the Members' cash, property, and service contributions. According to the Operating Agreement, each Member, including Clayton, contributed only $1.00 to the LLC. In addition, although the Members of the LLC had been associated since January of 2001, the Operating Agreement entered into in August of 2001 specified that it "replaced and supersedes all prior written and oral agreements among any and all members." Finally, the Operating Agreement stated that "the members do not consider each other partners . . . with any other member of this LLC for any purpose other than federal and state tax purposes."

Plaintiffs initiated the present action * * * on April 19, 2005 after Clayton died and the Trust began developing the Property without Plaintiffs' assistance. * * * Plaintiffs assert twenty-nine (29) causes of action in their Amended Complaint. Plaintiffs' claims can be grouped into six general categories: (1) breach of contract claims; (2) tortious interference claims; (3) estoppel/reliance equitable claims; (4) claims for creation of a trust; (5) fraud claims; and (6) claims related to the creation and dissolution of an alleged partnership. * * * Defendants have moved for summary judgment on all claims.

* * *

II.

DEFENDANTS' MOTION FOR SUMMARY JUDGMENT

* * *

B. The Operating Agreement

The primary issue in the present action is whether Clayton purchased the Property on behalf of Berkshire West or otherwise agreed to contribute the Property to Berkshire West. Key to resolving this issue is whether parol evidence can be considered in determining what the parties agreed to.

Although Clayton, DeShazo, and Landwer began a relationship with each other relative to the Property in January of 2001, in August of 2001 they entered into a written Operating Agreement to govern their relationship. This Operating Agreement contains a clause stating that it "represents the entire agreement among the members of this LLC, and it shall not be amended, modified, or replaced except by a written instrument executed by all the parties to this agreement." The Agreement goes on to state that it "replaced and supersedes all prior written and oral agreements among any and all members of this LLC."[9] Thus, as a matter of law, the Operating Agreement is an integrated agreement. In Idaho, "extrinsic evidence of prior or contemporaneous negotiations or conversations" (i.e., parol evidence) is not admissible to contradict, vary, alter, add to, or detract from the terms of an integrated agreement.

The Operating Agreement sets forth the members' total "cash, *property,*" and service contributions. According to the Agreement, each member, including Clayton, contributed only $1.00 to Berkshire West. The Agreement does not mention any contribution of the Property to the LLC, despite the fact that Clayton had purchased the Property approximately three months before the Members formed the LLC. The Members also did nothing after finalizing the LLC to change the capital contributions listed in the Operating Agreement.

Moreover, the Operating Agreement provides for the holding of property in a manner directly contrary to that asserted by Plaintiffs. Pursuant to the Agreement, a member is not allowed to hold property in his own name for the LLC, but rather "all personal and real property of [the] LLC shall be held in the name of the LLC, not in the names of individual members or managers." Clayton held the Property in his name, individually, with no mention of Berkshire West.

Plaintiffs, however, allege that the Members agreed in May of 2001 that the Property "would be acquired by Paul Clayton obtaining legal title to the real property in trust for the benefit of the 'partners and/or managing members' and/or the limited liability company to be created and/or in trust for the benefit of all parties." This evidence of a capital contribution structure different than that set forth in the Operating Agreement would contradict, vary, alter or add to the terms of the Operating Agreement. For this reason, and because the Operating Agreement is an integrated agreement and Plaintiffs' allegation is based on extrinsic

9. This statement sets forth the intent of the Members to dissolve their informal partnership and convert it into a limited liability company. The Agreement also expressly recites that the Members "do not consider each other partners ... with any other member of this LLC." Accordingly, Plaintiffs' claims for breach of contract based on an alleged oral partnership agreement fail because any partnership ended in August of 2001 and Clayton's transfer of the Property to the Trust did not occur until almost three years later when the partnership no longer existed. As a result, there was no partnership contract, oral or otherwise, for Clayton to breach by transferring the Property to the Trust.

Moreover, the Uniform Partnership Act relied on by Plaintiffs provides that property acquired by a partner is partnership property only if acquired in the name of the partnership or in the name of a partner or if the property is transferred to the partnership in its name. *[R.U.P.A. §]204(a), (b).* Property acquired in the name of a partner, without an indication in the instrument transferring title to the property of the person's capacity as a partner or of the existence of a partnership, "is presumed to be separate property, even if used for partnership purposes." *Id.* at *204(d).* That is the case here. Clayton acquired the Property in his own name, with no mention of Berkshire West or his capacity as a partner. Thus, even under partnership law, Plaintiffs have no ownership claim to the Property. For this reason, the Court recommends that summary judgment be granted to Defendants on Counts Twenty and Twenty–Six of the Amended Complaint, both of which allege a breach of a partnership agreement.

evidence of prior conversations (i.e., parol evidence), the evidence offered by Plaintiffs is not admissible.

Because the evidence necessary to show breach of contract is not admissible, the District Court should grant summary judgment in favor of Defendants on Plaintiffs' breach of contract claims (Counts One, Six, and Seven). Furthermore, because Clayton owned the Property individually and was not required by the Operating Agreement to contribute it to the LLC, his transfer of the Property to the Trust did not breach a fiduciary duty to Plaintiffs. Therefore, it is recommended that the District Court grant summary judgment to Defendants on Plaintiffs' breach of fiduciary duty claim (Count Nineteen) and on Plaintiffs' fraudulent conveyance claim (Count Twenty–Three). Consequently, this conclusion leaves no basis for the specific performance requested by Plaintiffs, and it is also recommended that the District Court grant summary judgment to Defendants on Plaintiffs' request for specific performance (Count Twenty–One) seeking transfer of the Property from the Trust to Plaintiffs.

As explained above, the Operating Agreement did not set forth a promise by Clayton to hold the Property for the benefit of Plaintiffs or to transfer the Property to the LLC, so the parties' Agreement cannot be the basis for a quasi-estoppel claim. Thus, the recommendation is to grant summary judgment on Plaintiffs' quasi-estoppel claim (Count Six), which is based on Plaintiffs' claim that they relied to their detriment on the contract terms and conditions.

Additionally, because Clayton's transfer of the Property to the Trust and the Trust's development of the Property did not violate any term in the Operating Agreement, Defendants' request for summary judgment on Plaintiffs' tortious interference claims should be granted (Counts Two and Three). * * *

C. The Idaho Limited Liability Company Act

The Idaho Limited Liability Company Act (the "Act") provides an additional reason for granting summary judgment to Defendants on Plaintiffs' breach of contract, fraud, and tortious interference claims. The Act provides that any promise by an LLC member to contribute property to the LLC "is not enforceable unless set forth in a writing signed by the member." Plaintiffs have not provided any writing setting forth a promise by Clayton to contribute the Property to Berkshire West that would satisfy the plain language of *Section 53–627*.

* * *

F. Plaintiffs' Remaining Claims

* * *

[U]njust enrichment is the measure of recovery under a contract implied in law.[10] "A contract implied in law, or quasi-contract, is not a

10. Recovery under an unjust enrichment theory is limited to the amount by which Defendants were unjustly enriched.

contract at all, but an obligation imposed by law for the purpose of bringing about justice and equity without reference to the intent of the agreement of the parties, and, in some cases, in spite of an agreement between the parties." None of Defendants' arguments would preclude Plaintiffs from recovering restitution damages under an implied in law contract theory. There is ample evidence in the record that Plaintiffs DeShazo and Berkshire West expended funds to secure the right to purchase the Property and in developing the Property. Plaintiffs also paid taxes, insurance, and other incidental fees for the Property and Plaintiff DeShazo's company paid Landwer for his time working on the Property development. Thus, Defendants' request for summary judgment on Counts Eight and Nine should be denied.

* * *

NOTES

1. According to the court's interpretation of the parties' operating agreement, Clayton, DeShazo and Landwer had formed an LLC to subdivide and develop real property, with only three dollars (one dollar from each of the three members) of contributed cash and without even the intent for the LLC to own the property it would develop. Does this make any sense? In defense of the court, it did not write the agreement. One might suspect that the written operating agreement—perhaps drafted by an attorney and never read by the members before executing it—did not match what the members, in fact, had agreed. Nevertheless, it is worth asking whether there were any alternatives, within the confines of an agreement calling for contributions of just three dollars in cash and nothing else, that would have allowed the company to carry out its objectives.

2. DeShazo personally spent $8000 to secure the right to purchase the property at issue in the case—which the seller of the property credited toward the purchase price—while both DeShazo and the LLC expended funds to develop the property, and to pay taxes, insurance, and other incidental fees for the property. How can one reconcile this with the fact that the LLC operating agreement only obligated DeShazo to contribute one dollar to the firm, and only called for three dollars in total cash contributions from all members? As mentioned earlier, partners, limited partners or LLC members, who put cash into the venture, might make either a contribution to capital or a loan. Perhaps the additional money represented loans from DeShazo to the LLC. If so, what are the practical implications of a partner, limited partner or LLC member loaning, rather than contributing, funds to the firm?

One potential effect of loaning versus contributing cash to a partnership or an LLP is found in Section 18(c) and (d) of the U.P.A. and Section 401(d) and (e) of the R.U.P.A. These provisions indicate that a partner making a capital contribution is generally not entitled to interest on the money put in, whereas a partner making a loan is entitled to interest. The provisions of U.P.A. Section 18 and R.U.P.A. Section 401, however, are subject to any agreement between the partners. Section 40(b) of the U.P.A. and Section 807(a) of the R.U.P.A. create a second apparent effect. These provisions give amounts owing to partners "other than for capital and profits," in other words, as creditors, a priority in payment on liquidation over amounts owing to partners in respect of capital. This too, is subject to agreement by the partners to the contrary. Moreover, there may be less significance to this priority than meets the eye, at least in an ordinary partnership. Sections 40(d) and 18(a) of the U.P.A. and Section 807(c) of the R.U.P.A. obligate partners to contribute sums sufficient to ensure a return of capital if the proceeds from liquidating the partnership's property are insufficient for this purpose.

There can be more significance to the loan versus capital contribution distinction, however, when it comes to limited partnerships, LLPs and LLCs. To begin with, loans in lieu of capital contributions could have a negative impact on the lending party's profit share under the U.L.P.A. and LLC statutes which tie the profit allocation to the relative amounts of the owners' contributions. Of course, this only applies if the parties do not have an agreement on their profit shares—which does not seem too likely. Interestingly, the U.L.P.A. and typical LLC statutes do not mention any right to interest on owner loans, barring other agreement—albeit, in this instance, uniform partnership acts provide the gap filler for a limited partnership under the pre–2001 U.L.P.A. The court in *DeShazo* does not address whether DeShazo was entitled to interest under any sort of implied contract claim.

More significantly, limited liability in limited partnerships, LLPs and LLCs means that there can be a real impact to the priority which repayment of loans enjoys on liquidation over repayment of contributions. The U.L.P.A. and typical limited liability company statutes follow the pattern of the uniform partnership acts in calling for the repayment of loans—including loans made by partners, limited partners or LLC members—prior to distributing any assets during liquidation to return capital contributions. *E.g.*, U.L.P.A. § 804; U.L.P.A. (2001) § 812; Cal. Corp. Code § 17353(a); Del. Code Ann. Title 6 § 18–804(a); N.Y. Ltd. Liab. Law § 704. With limited liability—which means the owners do not need to pony up whatever it takes to pay all of the firm's debts and return capital contributions—this priority can impact the rights of the owners both vis-a-vis each other and vis-a-vis outside creditors. Specifically, limited partners or LLC members, who make loans instead of capital contributions, can obtain an advantage over their fellow owners who made capital contributions, in the event there are not enough assets left to repay all of the loans and capital contributions. Moreover, by making loans instead of larger capital contributions, limited partners or LLC members might be able to share in whatever assets are left in a failed firm on a par with outside creditors, rather than only taking what, if anything, is left after the outside creditors get paid. *See, e.g.*, U.L.P.A. § 107; U.L.P.A. (2001) § 112; Cal. Corp. Code § 17004; Del. Code Ann. Title 6 § 18–107; N.Y. Ltd. Liab. Co. Law § 611 (all allowing partner or member loans the same treatment as loans to outside creditors).

Indeed, the impact of owner loans versus capital contributions on outside creditors can create an interesting temptation. Why not have all of the owners loan virtually all of their investment, and thereby maximize the amount the owners might pull out of a failed venture on a par with, rather than subordinate to, outside creditors? Indeed, perhaps this may have been the thinking (such as there was) behind the provision in the LLC operating agreement in *DeShazo* to have the members only contribute three dollars. Before succumbing to this temptation, however, consider how prospective creditors might react to such a tactic in deciding whether to extend credit to the firm. Also, Chapter IV will examine judicial hostility to this sort of tactic in the corporate context (where it often has occurred).

The impact of partner loans versus capital contributions becomes a bit more complicated in the limited liability partnership. This is because not only might partner loans impact who gets whatever money is left over in an insolvent LLP, but such loans might also impact obligations of the partners to put in additional money in the event of a business failure. Specifically, LLP statutes typically speak of partners not bearing any personal liability for "debts, obligations, or liabilities of or chargeable to the partnership." *E.g.*, Cal. Corp. Code § 16306(c); NY Partnership Law § 26(b). *See also* Del Code. Ann. Title 18 § 15–306(c) ("obligation of a partnership"). Does the right of a partner upon liquidation to receive a return of his or her contribution constitute a "debt, obligation or liability" of the partnership within the meaning of the LLP statutes? Section 40(b) of the U.P.A. suggests this might be the case, but the R.U.P.A. seems less clear. If return of capital does not constitute such a debt, obligation or liability, then partners in a limited liability partnership could need to contribute in order to reimburse capital contributions, whereas they would not need to contribute in order to pay off the same money put in as a loan from the partner.

3. The dispute in *DeShazo* involved the obligation to contribute property, not cash. In fact, partners, limited partners or LLC members owning property of use to the firm may contribute the property outright, so it becomes property owned by the firm, or instead may simply loan (or lease) the property to the firm, in which case the firm only obtains the use of the property (as evidently occurred under the court's interpretation of the contract in *DeShazo*). Yet another alternative is for the partner, limited partner or LLC member to sell the property to the firm. The obvious lesson from *DeShazo*—where it is impossible to tell from the agreement what the members actually intended—is the need for the agreement to address the issue in a manner that is both clear and consistent with what the parties to the contract had in mind. Yet, before drafting a clear statement of the parties' agreement, it may be useful to consider just what impact there will be if the partners, limited partners or LLC members agree to contribute property, or else agree just allow the firm to use the property.

DeShazo involves the impact of this choice on the rights of a partner or LLC member, and the rights of the firm, to use and sell the property in question. Because the court found that the agreement let Clayton own the property, he could transfer it to the trust he established, which, in turn, evidently planned to take over development and sell off the property. This also meant that, after three years of "using" the property—at least insofar as the LLC was trying to develop the property and was paying taxes, insurance and fees on the property—the firm would be not be able to benefit by completing development and selling the property. *See, e.g., Ellis v. Mihelis,* 60 Cal.2d 206, 384 P.2d 7, 32 Cal.Rptr. 415 (1963) (partner could not bind partnership to sell property the firm used but did not own). By contrast, if the property had belonged to the LLC, then the firm could have continued to develop and sell the property, while Clayton could not have transferred any right to the property itself to the trust he created, nor could the trust have undertaken to develop and sell the property. *See, e.g.*, Cal. Corp. Code § 17300; Del. Code Ann. Title 6 § 18–701; N.Y. Ltd. Liab. Co. Law § 601 (under all, members have no interest in specific items of company property, but rather have an interest in the company). The same rules would have applied if the property had belonged to the partnership that the three individuals allegedly formed before forming the LLC. U.P.A. §§ 25(2)(a) (partners may use firm assets for partnership purposes, but may not, without the consent of the other partners, make personal use of them), 25(2)(b) (partners cannot assign their interest in specific firm property except as part of a sale by the firm of the asset); R.U.P.A. §§ 401(g) (partners may only use partnership property for firm purposes without consent of the other partners), 501 (partners may not sell an interest in specific firm assets). Presumably, the same rules would apply to a limited partnership—especially under the pre–2001 U.L.P.A., which looks to the uniform partnership acts to fill any gaps in the U.L.P.A.'s provisions. So what do these differences suggest as far as the most sensible agreement? The outcome in *DeShazo* suggests that the firm, rather than an individual participant in the venture, should own the property. Yet, is this always the case, or was there something particular about the intended use of the property in *DeShazo* that made it critical for the LLC to own the property if the venture was to succeed at all?

Interestingly, it was Clayton's death, rather than his earlier transfer of the property to the trust he created, that precipitated the dispute in *DeShazo*. Suppose Clayton had died while still owning the property himself. In fact, contributing versus lending property to a firm can have important consequences in the event the partner's, limited partner's or LLC member's death. In large measure, the difference is simply a corollary to the difference in the rights to use and transfer discussed above, only in this instance with a heir being involved. Occasionally, however, there can be an additional impact on who economically benefits from the death. *E.g., In re Gerlach's Estate,* 364 Pa. 207, 72 A.2d 271 (1950) (the deceased partner left his personal property (which included his interest in the partnership) to a different beneficiary from the recipient of his realty, thereby triggering a dispute over whether the decedent had contributed real property to the partnership); *Balafas v. Balafas,* 263 Minn. 267, 117 N.W.2d 20 (1962) (the title to property used by the partnership described the partners as "joint tenants", thereby triggering a dispute over whether the surviving partner obtained the property by right of survivorship without having to pay anything for it).

Suppose Clayton had contributed the property to the LLC. If the firm sold the property and dissolved, would all the proceeds be shared among the LLC owners, since the property belonged to the firm? In fact, as discussed earlier when considering the need to value non-cash contributions, partners, limited partners and LLC members, who contribute property to their firm, are entitled (in the absence of agreement to the contrary) to receive, upon liquidation, repayment of their capital contribution based upon the value of the property when contributed. Given that the value of the property in *DeShazo* presumably increased upon its development, who would have received the benefit of this appreciation had Clayton agreed to contribute the property to the LLC? By comparison, who received the benefit of any increase in the value of the property as a result of the court's decision? True, the court allowed the claim for unjust enrichment, based upon the money spent by DeShazo and the LLC on the property; but what is the measure of recovery on this claim?

Finally, the status of property employed in the business also can affect significantly the rights of creditors. Creditors of the individual partners, limited partners or LLC members have no right to levy on firm property, but, instead, must seek a charging order against the partner's, limited partner's or LLC member's interest in the firm. *E.g.*, U.P.A. §§ 25(2)(c), 28; R.U.P.A. §§ 501, 504; U.L.P.A. §§ 605, 701, 703; U.L.P.A. (2001) §§ 506, 701, 703; Cal. Corp. Code §§ 17300, 17302; Del. Code Ann. Title 6 §§ 18–701, 18–703; N.Y. Ltd. Liab. Co. Law §§ 601, 607. Consider the implications of this rule if a partner, limited partner or LLC member runs into personal financial difficulties. Compare the result under the court's view of the contract in *DeShazo* had Clayton run into financial difficulties. On the other hand, suppose it is the partnership, limited partnership, LLP or LLC that runs into financial problems. Under the R.U.P.A. and a minority view under the U.P.A., partnership creditors must first exhaust the assets of the firm before executing upon the separate property of the partners. R.U.P.A. § 307(d); *Horn's Crane Service v. Prior,* 182 Neb. 94, 152 N.W.2d 421 (1967). Of course, insofar as partners in an ordinary partnership, and general partners in a limited partnership, are personally liable for the firm's debts, this exhaustion rule only provides a partial shield for assets that the partners loan, rather than contribute, to the firm. Notice, however, a critical difference when dealing with limited partners in a limited partnership, or owners of an LLP or an LLC. Here, because of limited liability, property which is only loaned (or leased) by limited partners to a limited partnership, or by partners to an LLP, or by members to an LLC, may not be subject to sale to pay the claims of the firm's creditors—unlike any property contributed to the LLC, LLP or limited partnership. Indeed, perhaps this notion may have been in the mind of whomever drafted the agreement in *DeShazo*. There are, however, a couple of caveats to this possible advantage for not having a limited partnership, LLP or LLC own the property that the firm uses—beyond, of course, the obvious problem this created in *DeShazo*. For one thing, creditors of the firm may be able to levy upon whatever leasehold or other rights the firm had to use the property—indeed, contract clauses which purport to cut off a lease or other contract rights in the event of bankruptcy might not be valid. 11 U.S.C. § 365. More ominously, the willingness of courts to apply "piercing the corporate veil" analysis to LLCs (as discussed in Chapter II) creates a danger if LLC members decide to lease or loan (rather than contribute) too many assets to an LLC. The result could be to create the basis for an argument that the LLC is undercapitalized and the court should pierce.

4. It also may be useful to consider whether various intangibles should belong to the firm or to the individual members. This is a particularly common problem in personal service or professional firms where members may join with favorable reputations and where both the firm and its members may develop further goodwill over time. This goodwill may be the most valuable asset upon dissolution, and, therefore, without advance agreement, there is the potential for dispute over how much, if any, of it belongs to the firm as opposed to the individual owners. *E.g., In re Brown,* 242 N.Y. 1, 150 N.E. 581 (1926).

5. Tax consequences also may influence the choice of whether to loan or sell, versus contribute, money or property to an entity electing income tax treatment as a partnership. A full exploration of these consequences must await discussion of the tax aspects of allocating partnership profit and loss and of alternatives to profit shares later in this chapter. For now, it is useful to see an overview of these impacts.

To begin with, suppose property that a partner, limited partner or LLC member might contribute to the firm is worth more than the prospective contributor's basis in the property. As noted earlier, with a contribution from a partner (or person taxed as a partner), the firm will retain the contributor's basis in the property. As this chapter will explore later, the result can be to trigger some fairly complex tax provisions designed to deal with the fact that gain and deductions for tax purposes (which depend upon the property's basis) will differ, in this event, from the firm's economic gain or expenses (which depend upon the property's value when contributed to the firm). One way to avoid dealing with such complexity is for the property's owner to loan or sell, rather than to contribute, the property to the firm. Moreover, sale of appreciated property to the business provides the firm with the advantages of an increased basis. *See* I.R.C. § 707(a)(1). Of course, the partner, limited partner or LLC member selling the property must recognize income from the transaction, thereby usually more than offsetting any advantages of an increased basis. One case in which such a trade-off might make sense is if selling the property to the partnership could produce capital gains for the selling partner (or limited partner or LLC member), yet a higher basis would later save the firm (and hence the persons taxed as partners in the firm) from ordinary income (perhaps by producing greater depreciation deductions or because the property will be sold as part of the firm's trade or business). Here, however, one faces tax code provisions under which a partner (or party taxed as a partner) selling depreciable property or inventory to his or her firm must treat his or her gain on the sale as ordinary income, rather than capital gains, if the seller owns a majority interest in the firm. I.R.C. §§ 707(b)(2), 1239(a).

Now, suppose a partner (or party treated as a partner for income tax purposes) owns property needed by the firm, which has declined in value since the partner bought the property. Can the partner sell the property to the firm and thereby recognize an immediate tax loss? See I.R.C. § 707(b)(1) (not if owns a majority interest in the firm). Beyond the question of immediate loss recognition, however, there are tax disadvantages to contributing such property. These disadvantages result from the collateral impacts of a statutory provision (Section 707(c)(1)(C)) designed to prevent non-contributing partners from benefitting (tax wise) from the pre-contribution decline in a contributed property's value, and will be discussed later in this chapter.

Under Section § 707(a)(1), lease or interest payments to a partner (or person considered a partner for tax purposes) leasing property or loaning money to the firm constitute income to the partner and create a deduction for the firm. The party leasing property might also take deductions (such as depreciation under Section 167) associated with owning income producing property. Whether this provides the possibility for creative tax planning depends upon whether partners (or parties treated as partners for tax purposes) can just as easily achieve the same results by virtue of the conduit principle of partnership taxation and the ability of partners, as discussed later in this chapter, to specially allocate items of income, loss, gain, deduction or credit. Also discussed later in this chapter are possible advantages or disadvantages to such lease or interest payments under the passive activity loss limits of Section 469.

Leasing, loaning or selling property, or loaning money, rather than contributing it to the firm, may create several tax problems. First, a loan of property in exchange for an interest in the firm might not come within Section 721, meaning the lending party will immediately recognize income. *See* Treas.Reg. § 1.721–1(a).

In addition, a sale, lease or loan of property, or a loan of money, will not provide the partner (or party treated as a partner for income tax purposes) with a basis in his or her interest in the firm, as does a contribution. *See* I.R.C. § 722. Rather than increasing the contributing partner's basis, money loaned to the firm will increase, under Section 752, the various partners' basis in the firm by their share of this liability. I.R.C. §§ 722, 752(a); Treas. Reg. §§ 1.707–1(a), 1.752–2(c)(1). This chapter will discuss later the determination of each partner's share of liabilities for purposes of Section 752. For now, however, it is sufficient to note that this potential shift in which partner (or person taxed as a partner) gains the basis as a result of a loan, versus a contribution, of money may have undesirable or desirable consequences depending upon the specific circumstances. Even if the impact on basis is not undesirable, however, the impact on the amount by which participants in the business are "at risk" will be disadvantageous. As discussed later, Section 465 limits loss deductions to the amount by which a taxpayer (such as a partner) is at risk in the venture. Loans from partners (or persons taxed as partners) do not (unlike a contribution) increase the amount by which any of the partners are at risk for purposes of Section 465. I.R.C. § 465(b)(3); Treas. Reg. §§ 1.465–8, 1.465–20. Incidentally, sometimes what partners may designate as a "loan" could, in fact, be a capital contribution. For example, a court may conclude that a so-called loan from a partner is really a capital contribution, when there is no obligation to pay interest, no fixed maturity date and the loan is unsecured and subordinated to outside creditors. *See, e.g., Hambuechen v. Commissioner,* 43 T.C. 90 (1964).

A practical difficulty with selling property to the firm is the need to raise the purchase price. Perhaps the party selling the property could first contribute sufficient cash to cover the amount. This seems to raise difficulties, however, with the step transaction doctrine. Alternately, the firm may pay the price over time, thereby making the selling partner also a creditor of the firm and bringing into play the discussion above concerning the tax impact of debts owed to partners (or parties taxed as partners).

3. Later Contributions

Often, a firm will find itself in need of funds beyond those initially contributed by the founders. This may be the result of a deliberate choice by the founders to contribute money to the firm only when actually needed, or it may be the result of the firm's needs exceeding original expectations. (It may also be the result of the firm's expected needs exceeding the resources of its founders. The problem of obtaining outside financing, however, will be deferred until Chapter V.) In any case, the result without advance planning could be a crisis.

Owners of a business may possess unequal capability and willingness to provide additional funding. If some owners are unable to make additional contributions, those upon whom the burden falls might view themselves entitled to a greater share of firm profits (or even control) as compensation. *See, e.g., Reilly v. Rangers Management, Inc.,* 727 S.W.2d 527 (Tex.1987). While from the standpoint of the contributing owners such a demand may seem perfectly reasonable, the owners unable to contribute may feel this is an oppressive attempt to exploit an advantage. Even where all owners are able to provide further funds, some may be unwilling to do so. This might be the result of differing assessments as to whether it is worthwhile to pump additional money into the venture, or could constitute an attempt to obtain a "free ride" on funds put up by the more willing owners.

Planning for additional cash contributions requires answering some basic questions. First, how much additional funds is each owner obligated to contribute? There may be a set limit beyond which the owner has no further obligations without renegotiation, or there could be an unlimited obligation. Recall in *McConnell,* the LLC operating agreement stated that members had no further obligation to contribute. Closely related to the question of how much additional funds owners have an obligation to provide is the need to decide under what circumstances owners must make additional contributions. This means either the agreement must set forth criteria under which the obligation becomes due or else state who decides when and what additional contributions are required. Moreover, one should decide which owners are obligated to contribute how much of any given call for additional funds. Next, what, if any, impact will additional contributions have on the allocation of profit and control among the owners? To the extent there is a favorable impact, this may necessitate consideration of limits on voluntary additional contributions. Finally, the owners might consider how to enforce obligations to make further contributions. For example, will unwillingness or inability to provide additional funding result in removal of an owner or a lowering of his or her profit share? Given the attitude of courts toward contractual penalties, are there limits on such enforcement provisions? *See, e.g., Henshaw v. Kroenecke,* 656 S.W.2d 416 (Tex.1983) (liquidated damages provision must be a reasonable forecast of just compensation for harm, and not a penalty). Interestingly, a number of LLC statutes expressly validate provisions in the operating agreement which impose penalties upon members for failure to make promised contributions. *E.g.*, Cal. Corp. Code § 17201(a)(3); Del. Code Ann. Title 6 § 18–502(c); N.Y. Ltd. Liab. Co. Law § 502(c). *See also* Del. Code Ann. Title 6 § 15–207(b) (same for LLPs). Of course, valid or not, a penalty for failing to contribute still leaves the question of where the funds will come from to make up for the breach. Moreover, note that the impact of a forfeiture is to shift a greater interest in the firm to the non-forfeiting owners. Could this constitute taxable income for them? See Schneider & O'Connor, *LLC Capital Shifts: Avoiding Problems When Applying Corporate Principles*, 92 J. Tax. 13, 25 (2000) (suggesting an affirmative answer).

An alternate source of additional funds may be for the firm to borrow. Since ordinary partners are personally liable for partnership debts, such borrowing could circumvent any limitations on later contributions. The partners might wish to keep this fact in mind when considering how to make decisions which increase the indebtedness of the firm. The same general notion might also be kept in mind when considering the ability of partners to make voluntary advances or contributions to the firm which all partners could be obligated to repay.

The existence of firm creditors creates a different problem when it comes to owner promises of additional contributions in a limited partnership or LLC. Suppose the partnership or LLC operating agreement obligates limited partners or LLC members to make additional contributions to the firm. Can the partners or members all later agree to waive the obligation? See U.L.P.A. § 502(c) (creditor who acted in reliance on the original commitment can enforce it despite compromise agreed to by the partners); U.L.P.A. (2001) § 502(c)(same); Cal. Corp. Code § 17201(b)(2); Del. Code Ann. Title 6 § 18–502 (b); N.Y. Ltd. Liab. Law § 502(b) (all providing a similar rule for LLCs).

Controversy also can arise over additional non-cash inputs. For example, an owner might invent something of use to the firm. *See Paxton v. McDonald,* 72 Ariz. 240, 233 P.2d 450 (1951), opinion modified on rehearing 72 Ariz. 378, 236 P.2d 364 (1951). Similarly, an owner might be presented with a business opportunity which could be profitably exploited either by the firm or the individual. *See Meinhard v. Salmon,* 249 N.Y. 458, 164 N.E. 545 (1928). A well drafted provision expressing the parties' intent as to the extent of each owner's obligation to present to the firm any opportunities, inventions and the like, might avoid litigation if such events occur—albeit, preparing a well-drafted provision may be more difficult than one thinks. *See Lynch Multimedia Corp. v. Carson Communications, L.L.C.*, 102 F. Supp. 2d 1261 (D. Kan. 2000) (dispute over whether a provision in an LLC operating agreement, which required that an opportunity to purchase cable television systems "shall be first offered to the company," was satisfied when a member simply notified the other members that the opportunity existed, and then took the opportunity for himself).

SECTION B. PROFIT AND LOSS

1. IN GENERAL

a. *Allocating Profit*

Five Star Concrete, L.L.C. v. Klink, Inc.

693 N.E.2d 583 (Ind.App.1998).

■ STATON, JUDGE.

* * *

On June 14, 1994, Klink[, Inc. ("Klink")] and four other corporations, all engaged in supplying ready-mix concrete, formed Five Star [Concrete, L.L.C. ("Five Star")], a limited liability company ("LLC"), in order to furnish concrete to large construction projects. Klink contributed $38,500.00, 12.5% of the initial total capitalization, and was issued 12.5 ownership units.

In a letter dated October 13, 1995, Klink formally notified Five Star of its intent to withdraw from membership effective October 10, 1995.[2] The remaining members decided to purchase Klink's ownership units and to continue the business. To accomplish this end, Five Star members met on October 23, 1995 and agreed that Klink would receive $61,047.22 for the value of its "units."

After Five Star's fiscal year ended December 31, 1995, Klink was allocated $31,889.02 of income, representing its share of the LLC's profits for the approximate ten-month period of 1995 when Klink was a member. The allocation did not result in a monetary distribution to Klink. Instead,

2. Unless a written operating agreement provides that a member may not withdraw by voluntary act, a member may withdraw from a[n Indiana] limited liability company "at any time by giving thirty (30) days written notice to the other members.... " Ind.Code § 23–18–6–6 (1993). * * *

the allocation was made only for the purpose of properly determining Klink's tax liability. After receiving notification of the allocation, Klink filed a complaint against Five Star claiming that it was entitled to a distribution of cash in the sum of $31,889.02. Klink moved for summary judgment on its claim, and Five Star responded with its own motion for summary judgment, asserting that Klink had already been paid for its entire interest. Following a hearing, the trial court granted Klink's motion, finding that Klink had a legal right to receive a distribution of $31,889.02. The court also denied Five Star's cross-motion. Five Star appeals both rulings.

* * *

Five Star first contends that the trial court improperly entered summary judgment in favor of Klink on the basis that Klink had the legal right to an actual distribution of $31,889.02, the amount allocated for taxation purposes. At the outset, we recognize that LLCs offer the same limited liability as the corporate form of business organization, but they are treated by federal and state taxing bodies in the same way as partnerships, that is, income "passes through" the entity and is taxed to the member, an owner of an interest in the company. * * * Limited liability companies are also governed by the Indiana Business Flexibility Act (the "Act"). * * * The Act empowers members to make and amend operating agreements for managing the business and regulating the LLC's affairs, as long as these are not inconsistent with state law or the LLC's articles of organization. * * *

Here, there is no dispute that the allocation, Klink's portion of Five Star's income, was proper. Five Star was being taxed as a "pass-through" entity, and the allocation was required by tax law as well as by the Operating Agreement. However, Klink insists that when there is an allocation to a dissociating member there is a corresponding obligation to make a cash distribution of income equal to the allocation. We do not agree.

Nowhere does the Act provide that allocation of income to members for income tax purposes creates an automatic legal right to receive a distribution in the amount of that income, even when a member is withdrawing from the LLC. Indeed, there are times that such a distribution would be unlawful.[4] * * *

The Operating Agreement is also silent regarding the timing and amount of distributions; thus, under the Act, these decisions are to be made by the majority of the members. * * * The evidence construed in favor of Five Star shows that Five Star made a distribution to all members in July of 1995; Klink's share was approximately $12,500.00. However,

4. A distribution may not be made [under Indiana's limited liability company statute] if after giving effect to the distribution: (1) the limited liability company would not be able to pay its debts as the debts become due in the usual course of business; or (2) the limited liability company's total assets would be less than the sum of its total liabilities plus, unless the operating agreement permits otherwise, the amount that would be needed if the affairs of the limited liability company were to be wound up at the time of the distribution to satisfy any preferential rights that are superior to the rights of members receiving the distribution. * * *

neither this distribution nor any other was made based upon the amount of income allocated to a member. Further, since that date no distributions were made to any members.

Conduit treatment under income tax law means that allocations occur regardless of the magnitude or timing of distributions. * * * We conclude that the allocation of profits for tax reporting purposes did not provide Klink with a legal right under either the Act or the Operating Agreement to receive a distribution in the same amount. Summary judgment in favor of Klink was improvidently granted.

It does not follow, however, that Klink's interest in Five Star's profits for the ten-month period of 1995 should be ignored. Here, the member's share of Five Star's profits and losses is part of the total economic interest transferred in the buy-sell agreement. However, in this case, we cannot value that interest as a matter of law. [The court held that the trial court properly denied summary judgment on Five Star's claim that, in the buy-out, Klink received payment for all of Klink's interest in Five Star, including Klink's share of the profits for the ten month period of 1995.]

* * *

NOTES

1. One of the continuing routines in the last of the Bob Hope and Bing Crosby "Road" movies was the comic pair, although facing imminent physical danger, arguing over whether their partnership shares would be equal or "60–40." This illustrates, with slight exaggeration, that the division of profit is likely to be a subject of considerable negotiation between the owners of any business. There are a number of ways in which to allocate profits among owners. Barring contrary agreement, Section 18(a) of the U.P.A. and 401(b) of the R.U.P.A. (which govern both ordinary partnerships and LLPs on this issue) provide for an equal sharing. Notice this disconnects relative contributions from the allocation of profits, making, for example, a partner who contributes nine thousand dollars or does ninety percent of the work entitled to no greater share than another partner who contributed only one thousand dollars or does ten percent of the work. By contrast, Section 503 of the U.L.P.A. allocates profit—in the absence of a profit allocation in the partnership agreement—on the basis of the relative values which the parties agreed to place on their various contributions. This apparently reflects the rather odd expectation that parties forming a limited partnership might forget to agree on their profit sharing, but would remember to agree on the valuation of each of their contributions. Most limited liability company acts generally follow the U.L.P.A. in allocating profit and loss (unless otherwise agreed) in proportion to contributions (*e.g.*, Cal. Corp. Code § 17202; Del. Code Ann. Title 6 § 18–503; N.Y. Ltd. Liab. Co. Law § 503.), albeit some acts follow the U.P.A. and R.U.P.A. scheme of equal sharing barring other agreement. *See, e.g.*, U.L.L.C.A. § 405(a). The 2001 revision of the U.L.P.A. takes a somewhat different approach—albeit, as discussed later, this may just be a different way of reaching the same end result. The 2001 version no longer

refers to an allocation of profit or loss in the absence of other agreement. Rather, it only refers to the allocation of distributions in the absence of agreement.

These statutory provisions allocating profit are subject to the partnership or LLC operating agreement, which can provide for any other division. The division will often, implicitly if not explicitly, reflect the nature of the business, and the parties' assessment of the relative worth of their various contributions. For example, in a firm primarily dependent on capital, the partners might agree to share profits in proportion to their capital accounts. When the contributions are of different natures, deciding upon a division of profits can become quite complicated—as, for instance, in a law firm, where the partners must decide how to reward attraction of clients versus generation of billable hours. In a start-up venture combining cash with a promising idea, the cash contributor(s) may demand a greater share of the first profits (to compensate for the larger concrete risk), but be willing to share a larger portion of later profits (by which point the intangibles will have proven their worth). Another factor the owners may consider is the value they place on more certainty of return. Those who place greater value on certainty of return (or, put another way, have a greater aversion to risk) may wish to obtain a larger percentage of the first earnings of the business, in exchange for giving all or most of any further earnings beyond this amount to those more willing to gamble. This is the idea behind the concept of leverage. In any event, the parties typically have reached a basic agreement on profit shares, being at the heart of their deal, prior to the coming to an attorney. This raises the question of what, if anything, the attorney should do if he or she doubts the equity of the arrangement.

2. *Five Star* illustrates that it is not enough for a partnership or a limited liability company operating agreement to set out a formula for allocating profits. Rather, one must consider what will be the actual impact of such an allocation. The facts in *Five Star* involved the two potential impacts. One impact, which roiled the water, is that Klink had to pay tax on its share of the LLC's taxable income. The other potential impact, which was the issue in the litigation, involved Klink's right to obtain any distribution of money based upon the allocation of this income. Hence, partnership or LLC operating agreements commonly contain terms addressing the allocation of profits, taxable income, and rights to distributions. The failure of these terms to coordinate with each other can produce problems.

To begin with, Klink paid tax on over $31,000 of Five Star's income. If Klink never received the benefit of this income, then Klink will have paid tax on income which some other owner(s) of Five Star, in fact, enjoyed. This would seem to be unfair to Klink (which presumably is why Klink sued). It also presents the opportunity for some abusive tax planning, if, for example, parties allocate more of the firm's taxable income to an owner in a lower tax bracket in order to reduce the net tax owed, but this low-bracket owner does not, in fact, receive any extra money. The tax code and regulations contain rules, which this chapter shall discuss in detail later, to prevent such abuse.

For now, let us focus on the non-tax, or economic, impact of the allocation of profit. Stepping back to view the big picture, notice that the owners of any business must agree in some manner as to how they will divide among themselves the basic incidents of ownership, these being the right to obtain the wealth of the business and the right to exercise control over the venture. There are two ways to conceptualize dividing the right to obtain the wealth of the business. The bottom line question is what claims the various owners will have to any given distribution of money or property from the business. Such a distribution might occur during the ongoing course of the venture (which is often referred to as a current distribution), upon the venture's termination (which is generally referred to as a liquidating distribution), or, as in *Five Star*, upon the firm's buying out the interest of an owner who withdraws from the venture. Generally speaking, the two ultimate sources of these distributions are the profits made by the business, and the capital which the owners invested in the business. (This ignores the prospect of funding distributions by loans which the firm never repays.) Hence, if the provisions of a partnership or an LLC operating agreement which govern distributions do not mesh, when all is said and done, with provisions governing the economic source of such distributions (the allocation of profits and the rights to the return of invested capital), the result can be a litigation producing inconsistency in the terms of the contract.

To explore approaches one can take to coordinate provisions allocating profits with those governing distributions, let us start with a simple hypothetical. Suppose three prospectors form a partnership to search for gold in the Sierra Madre mountain range. One prospector contributes $500 to purchase supplies, and the three agree to split profits equally. The prospectors go off to the mountains, and some months later return with their mules laden with gold dust. Under the U.P.A. scheme, if the prospectors decide to dissolve their partnership after selling off the gold and any left over supplies, they should pay $500 to the one prospector in return of his capital contribution, and distribute the remainder of the money (which represents the profits of the venture) equally. U.P.A. § 18(a). Hence, in the short-term venture with only a liquidating distribution, the U.P.A. provides a straightforward method for coordinating profit shares and distributions. Complexity arises, however, because most owners expect their business to continue for years, during which time the owners will receive current distributions. In this event, how might one coordinate distribution rights with the allocation of profits (and the right to return of invested capital)?

A simple-minded approach to coordinate profit shares and distributions might be to distribute all profits, promptly as made, in proportion to the agreed profit allocation. There are several problems, however, with this approach. To begin with, unlike the simple hypothetical in which the prospectors can determine their profit by subtracting the $500 they started with from the money they obtained when they sold all of the firm's gold dust and other assets, determining how much profit an ongoing business made during a specified period of time involves choosing among a number of accounting conventions. For example, should the firm consider revenues as made and expenses as incurred when the sums become due, or when the firm actually pays or receives the money (in other words, should the firm compute its profits in accordance with the accrual versus the cash method of accounting)? Beyond the accounting issues involved in computing the profit for the period, the idea of distributing all profit as made may still be unsatisfactory. For one thing, owners who contribute capital might feel that they should be entitled to return of their investment prior to distributions of profits. Most fundamentally, it might be necessary or desirable to retain some earnings in the firm as a reserve or for expansion.

Once the owners rule out the simple-minded approach of distributing all profits as made, the need arises for a method to keep score so that, at least by the time the venture terminates, the total distributions match the agreed profit shares and agreed rights to return of invested capital. The method accountants devised for keeping such score in a partnership is to divide the equity section of a partnership's balance sheet into accounts representing each partner's share of the total equity. In fact, the R.U.P.A. expressly calls for the use of such accounts as the means to keep track of each partner's share of contributions, profits and losses. R.U.P.A. § 401(a), (b). These entries on the balance sheet are referred to as the partner's capital accounts. (Keep in mind these accounts represent simply paper balances and not any segregated fund of money.) At the outset of the business, the total equity is simply the sum of the capital contributions made by the partners, and each partner's capital account normally equals the value of his or her contribution. (This presupposes each partner is entitled under the partnership agreement to return of his or her capital contribution, rather than having transferred a capital interest, for example, to a services partner.) As the business goes on, additional contributions normally are credited to the capital accounts of the partners making them. At the end of every accounting period, each partner's share of undistributed profits is added to his or her capital account (or each partner's share of the firm's losses is subtracted from his or her capital account). If a partner received distributions during the period in excess of his or her share of profits, the excess is deducted from his or her capital account. Critically, since these capital accounts represent the total of each partner's contributions and share of profits (less the total of each partner's share of losses and prior distributions), if, at the termination of the venture, the firm distributes its assets according to the balances in the capital accounts, the end result will be that the total distributions over the life of the venture will match the agreed profit allocation and rights to return of invested capital. As we shall discuss later when dealing with liquidation, this sort of "day of reckoning" approach to ensure that total distributions ultimately match the agreed profit allocation and rights to return of invested capital is the implicit or explicit default rule under the U.P.A. and R.U.P.A.

Unfortunately, as *Five Star* illustrates, the day of reckoning scheme embedded in the U.P.A. and R.U.P.A. does not always allow the drafter of a partnership or an LLC operating agreement to ignore the coordination of profit allocations and distributions. In *Five Star*, the problem stemmed from the fact that the day of reckoning between the members occurred in a buy-out rather than in a liquidation. Under these circumstances, it was not clear whether the distribution made by Five Star to buy out Klink's interest either had included in fact, or should include under the parties' agreement, the $31,000 in taxable income allocated to Klink. This, in turn, illustrates a broader point. The day of reckoning scheme embedded in the U.P.A. and R.U.P.A. is subject to contrary provisions in the partnership agreement. Hence, it is always possible to include provisions in the agreement which undercut, often inadvertently, the coordination of profit shares and total distributions. Finally, even if the day of reckoning scheme embedded in the U.P.A. and R.U.P.A. works well for partnerships and LLPs in the absence of other agreement, what about limited partnerships and LLCs, for whom the U.P.A. and R.U.P.A. do not provide the applicable default rules? In fact, as discussed later in this chapter, there is some ambiguity in the U.L.P.A., and in the LLC statutes which have borrowed distribution provisions from the U.L.P.A., with respect to the allocation (in the absence of specific agreement) of distributions on liquidation of a limited partnership or an LLC.

Actually, there is a very different way to deal with the problem of coordinating the right to receive distributions, with the allocation of profit. One could simply not worry about allocating profit, and just have an agreement specifying the partners' rights to receive distributions. After all, as discussed above, profit sharing only has an actual economic impact insofar as it affects the participants' rights to receive distributions. Indeed, as discussed in Chapter IV, this sort of bottom line approach is the way corporations work. Breaking with tradition, the 2001 revision of the U.L.P.A. adopts this bottom line approach for limited partnerships. This new version of the U.L.P.A. contains a rule allocating the partners' rights to distributions in the absence of other agreement, but no rule directly allocating profits. There are, however, a couple problems with this approach. To begin with, while it works well enough for an agreement that completely ignores the whole issue—albeit, how realistic is this—what happens when, as is more likely, an agreement follows the traditional approach of specifying the partners' profit shares, but fails to address distributions? Moreover, as suggested by the facts in *Five Star*, and as discussed in detail later, partners must recognize their shares of the firm's taxable income, rather than just their receipt of actual distributions from the partnership—which means that an agreement simply allocating distributions may leave the parties somewhat adrift when it comes time to report their taxable income from the firm.

Incidentally, since the owners' rights to distributions depend upon figures in the firm's books, it is common for partnership or limited liability company operating agreements to contain terms regarding the maintenance of such books and records. Moreover, since trust has its limits, the owners of a firm generally wish access to the firm's books and records. The uniform partnership and limited partnership acts and most LLC statutes provide for such access. *E.g.*, U.P.A. § 19; R.U.P.A. § 403; U.L.P.A. § 305(2); U.L.P.A. (2001) § 304(b); Cal. Corp. Code § 17106; Del. Code Ann. Title 6 § 18–305; N.Y. Ltd. Liab. Co. Law § 1102(b). To what extent is this subject to contrary agreement? See R.U.P.A. § 103(b)(2) (cannot "unreasonably" restrict access to books and records); U.L.P.A. (2001) § 110(b)(4) (cannot unreasonably restrict the right to information); Cal. Corp. Code § 17005(b) (LLC operating agreement cannot vary information rights).

3. The use of capital accounts, and the requirement that liquidating distributions match the sums in the capital accounts, only serves to ensure that, by the end of the venture, distributions match the parties' agreed allocation of profits and rights to return of invested capital. Such a final reckoning, however, might be years or even decades away. In the meantime, disputes might arise among the owners over current distributions.

To begin with, the owners might get into a dispute about what proportion of a given distribution should go to each owner. For example, suppose the owners of a business made unequal capital contributions, and agreed to profit shares which are not proportionate to their capital contributions. In this event, should distributions from the firm be equal, proportionate to capital accounts, or proportionate to profit shares? The U.P.A. and R.U.P.A. are silent on this question. By contrast, Section 504 of the U.L.P.A., and limited liability company statutes which have copied Section 504 (*e.g.*, Del. Code Ann. Title 6 § 18–504; N.Y. Ltd. Liab. Co. § 504), call, in the absence of specific agreement, for a distribution in proportion to the relative values of the owners' contributions which have not been returned. The drafters of Section 504 presumably had in mind coordinating distributions with the profit allocation in Section 503—which is also proportionate to the relative values of the parties' contributions in the absence of agreement by the owners. Yet, how well would Section 504 work if the owners did not agree to profit shares in proportion to the values of their contributions? For example, say one owner of a two-person firm contributed $10,000, while the other owner made no capital contribution (but, instead, performs services which the parties decide not to treat as a capital contribution). Assume also that the parties agree to share profits equally, and the firm made $40,000. At this point, the cash contributor's capital account is at $30,000 (the $10,000 contribution plus $20,000 share of the profit), while the other owner's account is at $20,000 (representing his or her share of the profit). If the parties then decide to have the firm distribute $40,000, which party is entitled to how much under the default rule of distributions in proportion to unreturned contributions? If the result in this example is either open to dispute (i.e. does the first or the latter part of the distribution to the cash contributor constitute a return of capital?) or does not make sense (suppose all distributions go to the capital contributor until his or her capital account reaches zero, at which point the remaining distributions are shared equally), what is the lesson for the drafter of a partnership or an LLC operating agreement? Other LLC statutes have avoided this problem. *E.g.*, Cal. Corp. Code § 17250 (distributions that are not a return of capital shall be made in proportion to the allocation of profits). By contrast, the drafters of the 2001 revision of the U.L.P.A. may have only made things worse by providing that distributions are, in the absence of other agreement, shared in proportion to the contributions the firm has received from each partner. U.L.P.A. (2001) § 503. Notice how, in the example above, this might enable the cash contributor to claim all distributions, and thereby completely negate the profit sharing agreement.

Another dispute concerning current distributions arises if owners disagree over whether to retain earnings in the firm or distribute the earnings to the firm's owners. There are several reasons for such disagreements. Sometimes, one or more owners might have personal needs for immediate money from the venture, while other owners have sources of income outside of the firm. *See, e.g,, Drashner v. Sorenson*, 75 S.D. 247, 63 N.W.2d 255 (1954). Alternately, owners might simply disagree on how much the company will benefit from the retention of funds for a reserve or for expansion. Disagreement about the wisdom of reserves is particularly likely if (as in a limited partnership) some owners face personal liability in the event of the firm's failure, while other owners do not. Disagreement about the wisdom of expansion becomes more likely if profit shares among the owners shift so that some owners get an increased share of the profits at higher levels of firm income. Finally, if some owners extract income from the venture in the form of salaries and fees, these owners might lack an incentive for the firm to make a distribution which would go to all of the owners.

The court in *Five Star* states that, absent a provision in the operating agreement, decisions about distributions from an Indiana limited liability company are subject to majority rule. Whether this is the case for partnerships, limited partnerships, LLPs, or for limited liability companies outside of Indiana, is unclear. Specifically, both the U.P.A. and R.U.P.A. (which govern both ordinary and limited liability partnerships on this issue) are silent regarding a partner's right to demand immediate distribution of the firm's earnings. Presumably, in the absence of a provision in the partnership agreement, the issues then become whether the decision to retain rather than distribute earnings is one concerning an ordinary matter—making it subject to majority rule under the uniform partnership acts—and, if not, whether the failure to reach a unanimous decision on the question results in requiring distribution or requiring retention. The various versions of the U.L.P.A. are also somewhat Delphic on the topic. Section 601 of the pre–2001 U.L.P.A. makes the partnership agreement control the timing and extent of pre-withdrawal distributions from a limited partnership—leaving the question of what happens when the agreement is silent on the subject. The 2001 revision of the U.L.P.A. simply provides that partners have no rights to distributions before liquidation unless the limited partnership decides to make such a distribution—which one might guess means that, in the absence of other agreement, the general partners will decide the matter under their general power to decide "any matter related to the activities of the limited partnership." U.L.P.A. (2001) §§ 406(a), 504. Curiously, there have been only a few court opinions filing this gap in the uniform acts. *See, e.g., Brooke v. Mt. Hood Meadows Oregon, Ltd.*, 81 Or.App. 387, 725 P.2d 925 (1986) (holding, in the absence of a provision in the partnership agreement, that the general partner in a limited partnership has the same discretion over distributions, which the directors of a corporation have over declaring dividends). Limited liability company statutes vary widely concerning decisions over distributions. Many statutes, like the Indiana statute involved in *Five Star*, expressly provide for majority rule on the question in the absence of contrary provision in the operating agreement. Some of the most prominent jurisdictions, such as California (Cal. Corp. Code § 17251), Delaware (Del. Code Ann. Title 6, § 18–601) and New York (N.Y. Ltd. Liab. Co. Law § 507) follow the pre–2001 U.L.P.A. approach and make the timing and extent of distributions subject to the operating agreement—ignoring the question of what rights exist if there is no provision in the agreement on this issue. Still other limited liability company statutes are like the uniform partnership acts on this question and fail to address at all the timing and extent of distributions.

Incidentally, the fact that partners, or persons taxed as partners, must pay tax on their share of the firm's income, even if the firm does not distribute the money, suggests that such parties might wish to ensure that the firm distributes enough of the firm's income to cover the partners' or owners' tax. *See, e.g., Labovitz v. Dolan,* 189 Ill.App.3d 403, 545 N.E.2d 304 (1989) (court held that a general partner, who had discretion under the partnership agreement to determine distributions, breached his fiduciary duty in refusing to distribute enough money to cover the limited partners' tax obligations, in order to induce the limited partners to sell out).

4. The preceding discussion viewed current distributions as a means by which the owners obtained money corresponding to their shares of the firm's profits. Sometimes, however, current distributions might not be limited to the recipient's share of the firm's profits (or even to return of capital contributions). For example, owners dependent upon the firm as their principal source of income might not be able to wait for distributions until the computation of their profits at the close of an accounting period (especially if this period is one year). Indeed, such owners might need to receive distributions even if the firm did not make sufficient profits during the period to cover the sum. As a result, owners might agree to allow distributions (often referred to as "draws") prior to the computation (or even the making) of profits.

Providing for draws, in turn, raises the question of what to do if an owner's share of profits turns out to be less than he or she drew out of the firm: Must the owner repay the difference or should the sum be a withdrawal of capital? This, in turn, raises the broader issue of when owners may withdraw any portion of their capital contribution from the firm. Without some limits on such an ability, obligations to contribute could lose much of their effect. Even worse, suppose an owner draws out of the firm an amount that not only exceeds his or her share of accumulated profits, but also exceeds his or her capital contribution: What danger does this create? How might an agreement deal with the danger?

Interestingly, neither the U.P.A. nor the R.U.P.A. contain any provisions limiting current distributions to partners. One reason for this silence is that distributions to partners in an ordinary partnership, for the most part, cannot prejudice the ability of creditors or other partners to obtain payments to which the creditors or other partners are due. Because partners have unlimited personal liability, creditors and other partners can go after a partner's assets if distributions from the partnership to the partner leave insufficient assets in the firm to pay any claims. (Of course, if the partner receiving a distribution squandered the money and is judgment-proof, then the creditors or other partners will have a problem collecting on their claims against this partner. Yet, for the same reason, it might be impossible to enforce (other than by jail time) a prohibition on such a partner taking money out of the partnership.) The lack of prejudice to creditors and other owners from distributions changes with a limited partnership, an LLP or an LLC. This is because in these forms of business the owners no longer automatically have personal liability for whatever it takes to pay claims against the firm. For this reason, the U.L.P.A. and typical LLC statutes (as noted by the court in *Five Star*) contain financial limits on distributions from the firm to its owners. Curiously, however, some of the statutes establishing LLPs have overlooked this problem. *But see* Cal. Corp. Code § 16957(a); Del. Code Ann. Title 6 § 15–309.

The U.L.P.A. and the LLC (and similar LLP) statutes take two somewhat different approaches to limiting distributions. The LLC (and similar LLP) statutes typically contain the least restrictive limit. These statutes tend to copy from distribution limits contained in the Model Business Corporations Act (which Chapter IV will discuss). For example, California's LLP and LLC statutes prohibit distributions from the firm to its owners unless the firm is able to pay its bills as due and the assets remaining in the firm after the distribution are at least equal to the firm's debts plus any priorities which some owners may have over other owners to receive distributions on dissolution. Cal. Corp. Code §§ 16957(a), 17254(a). (Interestingly, as discussed in Chapter IV, California's corporations statute contains a more restrictive limit on distributions from a California corporation.) At first glance, Delaware's LLP and LLC statutes and New York's LLC statute seem even less demanding than California's. Specifically, these statutes prohibit distributions only if the remaining assets are insufficient to cover the firm's liabilities (other than non-recourse secured debts, and other than liabilities to partners or members on account of their LLP or LLC interests). Del. Code Ann. Title 6 §§ 15–309(a), 18–607(a); N. Y. Ltd. Liab. Co. Law § 508(a). On the other hand, a distribution which left an LLC or LLP with insufficient liquid assets to pay its bills when due—even though the firm's total assets exceeded its total liabilities—would probably constitute a fraudulent conveyance, and so would be subject to challenge even without a prohibition in the LLC or LLP statute. There is one other difference between Delaware's and New York's statutes and the LLC and

LLP statutes which copy the Model Business Corporation Act. Delaware's and New York's statutes are not clear as to whether the post-distribution assets must exceed both debts and the partners' or members' rights to return of their capital contributions (as opposed to the members' or partner's interests in undistributed profits).

Notice one common feature of the typical LLC (and similar LLP) statutes is that, as a general proposition, they do not prohibit distributions which constitute the return of the owners' capital contributions. This creates the prospect that owners of such firms might make contributions to the firm, obtain credit for the firm, and then yank back the contributions upon which creditors might have relied in deciding to extend credit. As discussed earlier in this chapter, creditors of an LLC, who relied upon a member's promise to make a contribution, might be able to enforce the obligation to contribute despite all the members' agreement to waive the obligation. It is by no means clear, however, whether the provisions of the LLC statutes giving creditors this right apply to distributions that withdraw contributions, rather than only to the failure to make the contributions in the first place. In any event, the pre–2001 U.L.P.A. takes a different approach to the withdrawal of contributions. Specifically, Section 607 of the U.L.P.A., like the LLC and similar LLP statutes, prohibits distributions which leave the limited partnership with less assets than debts. Significantly, however, Section 608 of the U.L.P.A. goes beyond this to create an obligation for partners to pay back any distributions which constitute a return of the partner's contribution, if, within a year of the distribution, the limited partnership is unable to pay debts incurred during the time the firm held the contribution. (Whether a distribution constitutes a return of a partner's contribution does not depend upon any tracing of the funds, but, rather, depends upon whether the partner's equity in the firm after the distribution at least equals the agreed value of the partner's contribution.) Still, it is uncertain how much longer the disparity between limited partnerships versus LLCs and LLPs will remain with respect to distributions that return contributions. The 2001 revision of the U.L.P.A. eliminates the potential obligation, which Section 608 of the earlier version of the U.L.P.A. had created, to return such distributions—albeit, the 2001 revision to the U.L.P.A. restricts distributions that would leave insufficient assets to pay, not only the firm's debts, but also any priorities some partners may have over others to distributions on liquidation. U.L.P.A. § 508.

One feature of all of these limits on distributions is that they depend upon a comparison of the value of the firm's assets with its liabilities. This, in turn, raises the question of how to value the firm's assets. Specifically, must the parties rely on the book value of the assets—in other words, the price the firm paid for the property, less, in appropriate cases, depreciation—or can the parties argue that some assets have increased in worth and thereby justify larger distributions? Chapter IV shall return to this question in the corporate context (in which there is more authority). Many LLC statutes address this question. *E.g.*, Cal. Corp. Code § 17254(b) (allowing "a fair valuation" for purposes of distributions from an LLC);

Del. Code Ann. Title 6 §§ 15–309(a), 18–607(a) (referring to "fair value"); N.Y. Ltd. Liab. Co. Law § 508(a) (same). The U.L.P.A. and some LLC and LLP statutes, however, are silent on the issue. *See, e.g.*, U.L.P.A. §§ 607, 608; Cal. Corp. Code § 16957 (dealing with LLPs).

These statutory limits obviously impact the parties at the time the firm makes distributions. What, however, is the impact of these limits upon the drafting of a partnership or LLC operating agreement? Many drafters like to restate the relevant statutory limit as a provision in the agreement. Other than adding to the length of the contract, what purpose can restating statutory requirements serve? Some attorneys believe this might alert the parties, who are unlikely to read the relevant statutes, of the requirements imposed by the statutes. Of course, this assumes the parties will read the agreement before they act. Beyond restating the statutory requirements, what might the agreement do? Since these statutes exist largely for the protection of creditors, they are not subject to watering down by contrary provisions in the partnership or LLC operating agreement. Nothing in these statutes, however, prevents the participants from agreeing to even more stringent limitations on distributions. Is there any reason the participants might wish to go beyond the statutes in restricting distributions? As just discussed, some of these statutes seemingly allow a distribution, despite the distribution leaving insufficient assets in the firm to return capital contributions (as opposed to paying debts). Might parties making larger capital contributions wish to limit distributions which leave the firm with less assets than the amount of unreturned capital (except, perhaps, if the distributions are made in proportion to the capital contributions)? Also, even if the firm is not an ordinary partnership, some owners nevertheless might be personally liable for some or all of the firm's unpaid debts. This includes general partners in a limited partnership, and owners of an LLP or LLC, who committed the tort (such as malpractice) which led to the firm's liability or who personally guaranteed loans to the firm. Might such participants be concerned about distributions which increase the chance that the firm might not have the assets to pay its debts? Finally, this chapter later will explore the possible difficulties which statutory distribution restrictions may create in drafting provisions in partnership or LLC operating agreements dealing with the buy-out of departing owners (as in *Five Star*).

b. *Allocating Losses*

Richert v. Handly

50 Wash.2d 356, 311 P.2d 417 (1957).

■ ROSELLINI, JUSTICE.

This is an action for an accounting, wherein the plaintiff alleged that he entered into a partnership agreement with the defendant * * * under the terms of which he, the plaintiff, was to purchase a stand of timber and the defendant was to log it, using his equipment, and the two were to share equally in the profits or losses resulting from the venture. He further alleged that the undertaking was unsuccessful; that after the payment of all operating expenses, the partnership suffered a loss * * *; that he had advanced $26,842 but had been repaid only $10,000 for his advances; and that he was entitled to $16,842 less * * * one half of the net loss. * * * In his amended answer, the defendant admitted that the parties had contracted with each other, but alleged that "there was no settled agreement between the partners as to recovery by the plaintiff for loss upon his capital contribution, nor as to the priority of any right to recover upon his capital contribution." In addition, he claimed certain offsets and asked that the complaint be dismissed.

The cause was tried to the court, which found in favor of the defendant in the amount of $1,494.51, plus costs.

* * *

The facts found by the trial court are as follows:

* * *

"II During the month of April 1953 plaintiff Richert advised defendant Handly that he had available for purchase according to his cruise 1,700,000 feet of timber in the State of Oregon, that he, Richert proposed to purchase said timber with his funds and requested Handly to log said timber on the basis that the two of them would share the profit or loss on the transaction.

* * *

"IV The plaintiff Richert purchased the timber for a price of $24,300.00 after the parties had inspected it as aforesaid, and Handly proceeded to log the same under an oral working agreement. The essential elements of this agreement were as follows: Handly was to furnish a tractor for which he was to be paid rental at the rate of $13.00 per hour and was to haul the logs on his trucks at the rate of $8.00 per thousand. * * * The profit or loss resulting from this single logging venture was to be borne equally. There was no requirement that Handly contribute to Richert for the purchase price of the timber in the event of loss.

"V The tract involved yielded between 800,000 and 900,000 feet of timber and the transaction resulted in a loss.

* * *

"VII The gross receipts of the venture amounted to $41,629.83. * * *

"VIII Handly drew from the proceeds of the sale of the timber the sum of $7,016.88. Richert received from the proceeds of the sale of the timber the sum of $10,000.00.

"IX There was no agreement express or implied on the part of Handly to repay Richert for his investment in the timber.

* * *

"XI The $10,000.00 received by Richert and the $7,016.88 drawn by Handly are unexpended gross revenues of the undertaking."

Upon these facts, the court entered the following conclusions of law:

* * *

"II The defendant Handly is in no way responsible for plaintiff's loss on the purchase of the timber involved.

"III Of the total amount of $17,016.88 heretofore identified as unexpended gross revenue of the undertaking each party hereto is entitled to $8,508.44. Richert has been overpaid in the amount of $1491.56, and Handly is entitled to judgment against him in the amount of $1491.56 * * *."

* * *

[I]t is manifest that the findings are inadequate to support the judgment entered, or any other judgment. There is a finding that the parties to the contract had agreed to share the profits or losses equally; but there is a further finding that the defendant had not agreed to contribute to the plaintiff for his investment in the timber in the event of loss; in other words, that they had not agreed to share the losses equally. Aside from the finding that the profit or loss was to be borne equally, which is inconsistent with the further finding that the defendant was not to contribute to the plaintiff for the purchase price of the timber in the event of loss, the findings are silent as to the basis on which the profit or loss was to be shared, whether proportionately to the contribution of each party, or otherwise. The mere fact that the defendant was not to be personally liable to the plaintiff for his losses does not mean that the plaintiff was not to be reimbursed out of the proceeds of the venture.

The findings also fail to reveal whether there was an understanding that the defendant was to be compensated for his services in managing the operation, apart from his share in the profits, and if so, in what amount. * * * [Y]et inherent in the court's disposition of the matter is a finding that these services were worth the full amount of the plaintiff's investment, or $26,842; for the court treated all of the "unexpended gross revenues" as profits and divided them equally between the parties, one of whom had lost nothing * * * while the other had lost an investment of $26,842.

The court appears to have lost sight of the fact that there could be no profits until the expenses of the operation were paid, including the cost of the timber. The conclusion that all of the "unexpended gross revenues" were to be divided equally between the parties could only be reached if it had been agreed that the plaintiff would not be reimbursed for his contribution. Such an intention cannot be inferred from any of the findings entered.

Since the findings are inadequate to support the conclusions and judgment, or any judgment on the matter in question, the cause must be remanded with directions to make findings regarding the basis on which the parties agreed that the losses were to be shared and whether the claims of one partner were to take priority over the claims of the other; the amount contributed by each (including cost of timber, and equipment rental, and also including services if there was an agreement that the defendant was to be compensated for his services, in addition to his share in the profits, if any); the total receipts and the authorized disbursements; the amount which each of the parties has received to date; and the amount due each on the basis of their agreement.

The judgment is reversed and the cause is remanded with directions to enter findings indicated above, conclusions, and judgment based thereon.

* * *

Richert v. Handly

53 Wash.2d 121, 330 P.2d 1079 (1958).

■ HUNTER, JUSTICE.

* * *

At the hearing on this matter pursuant to the remittitur, counsel for the respective parties agreed that no additional proof would be produced. Therefore, the trial court, after hearing argument of counsel, entered the following additional findings of fact in compliance with the remittitur:

> "XII The parties *did not agree upon or specify the basis* upon which losses were to be shared, nor whether the claims of *one partner* were to take priority over the claims of *the other.*
>
> "XIII Richert * * * contributed a total of $26,842 for cost of timber and incidental advancements. Handly * * * used his own tractor, as agreed by the parties, and was paid $9,240 for this service. *There was no agreement that Handly was to be compensated for his services, in addition to his share in the profits, if any, (and except for the equipment and tractor services as last hereinbefore stated), and the accounting between the parties does not disclose any such compensation.*
>
> "XIV The gross receipts from the sale of logs were $41,629.83. The disbursements were hauling (as per Finding XIII), $8,673.84; falling and bucking, $3,474.21; tractor (as per Finding XIII), $9,240.00; payroll and taxes, $4,786.56; right of way, $200.00; cruising, $35.00; commission, $500.00; paid to Richert, $10,000.00; withdrawn by Handly, $7,016.88; Total, $43,926.49.
>
> "XV *There was no agreement* of the parties as to how a loss of the capital contributed by Richert in the amount of $26,842.00 was to be borne, and *accordingly it cannot be determined the amount due each on the basis of their agreement.* (Italics ours.)

On the basis of such findings, the court concluded neither party was entitled to judgment against the other, that the complaint should be dismissed, * * *.

Mr. Richert has again appealed to this court from the judgment entered.

Since the trial court found that the parties had not agreed upon or specified the basis upon which losses were to be shared, or whether the claims of one partner were to take priority over the claims of the other, the provisions of the uniform partnership act are controlling. RCW 25.04.180 [U.P.A. § 18] provides:

> "The rights and duties of the partners in relation to the partnership shall be determined, *subject to any agreement between them,* by the following rules;
>
> "(1) *Each partner shall be repaid his contributions, whether by way of capital or advances to the partnership property and share equally in the profits and surplus remaining after all liabilities,* including those to partners, are satisfied; *and must contribute toward the losses, whether of capital or otherwise, sustained by the partnership according to his share in the profits.*
>
> * * *
>
> "(6) *No partner is entitled to remuneration for acting in the partnership business,* except that a surviving partner is entitled to reasonable compensation for his services in winding up the partnership affairs * * *." (Italics ours.)

* * *

Therefore, applying the statute to the additional facts found by the trial court, to which no error was assigned, we find the following account established:

Capital Contribution:	
Appellant Richert	$26,842.00
Respondent Handly	None
Gross Receipts From Sale of Timber	41,629.83
Expenses:	
Tractor	9,240.00
Hauling	8,673.84
Falling & Bucking	3,474.21
Payroll & Taxes	4,786.56
Cruising	35.00
Right of Way	200.00
Commission	500.00
	$26,909.61
Gross Receipts	41,629.83
Less Expenses	26,909.61
Net Receipts	$14,720.22
Appellant's Capital Contribution	26,842.00
Less Net Receipts	14,720.22
Net Loss	$12,121.78
Appellant has received $10,000 from the venture leaving a balance due on his Capital Contribution of	$16,842.00
LESS ½ OF NET LOSS ($12,121.78)	6,060.89
Amount respondent must reimburse appellant for loss resulting from logging venture	$10,781.11

It follows that the judgment of the trial court is incorrect, as a matter of law, under the facts found. Therefore, the judgment is reversed, and the cause remanded with directions to enter judgment in favor of the appellant in accordance with the views expressed herein.

NOTES

1. Individuals typically enter business ventures expecting ultimately to make, not lose, money (albeit tax considerations occasionally complicate such expectations). As a result, they may give only limited thought to allocating losses. Mr. Handly discovered this could be a mistake, especially when parties make different types of contributions.

Reducing the case to its essentials, *Richert* presents the classic situation where one owner put up all the cash, while the other did the work. When the dust settled, the firm had lost money during the life of the business, resulting in insufficient funds left to reimburse the cash contributor for his entire contribution. Had they thought about it in advance, what would the parties most probably plan to do in this situation: split the remaining cash equally between themselves (as essentially first ordered by the trial court); give what was left to the cash contributor and leave it at that; or give what was left to the cash contributor and also require the services contributor to pay the cash contributor half the losses, as the Washington Supreme Court ordered? The Supreme Court's order carried out the literal language of Section 18(a) of the U.P.A.—that partners, in the absence of agreement, share losses in the same proportion as they share profits (in other words, equally if the partners follow the default rule of equal profit sharing). *But see Kovacik v. Reed,* 49 Cal.2d 166, 315 P.2d 314 (1957). The result remains the same under the R.U.P.A. R.U.P.A. § 401(b). On the other hand, would this be the result expected by the parties if they had considered the situation in advance? If not, what might they do in drafting their agreement?

Perhaps the problem with the U.P.A. approach as carried out in *Richert* is it ignores the contribution of the services partner. Maybe the solution, therefore, is to agree to credit the services partner's capital account with the value of his or her prospective efforts. *See Schymanski v. Conventz,* reprinted earlier in this chapter. What outcome would this yield under the *Richert* facts (assuming Handly's uncompensated services were worth the same as Richert's cash)? Is it reasonable for Handly to get any of the left-over cash? Recall as well the tax problem which treating services as a capital contribution creates. An alternate approach is to deviate from the U.P.A. method of allocating losses in order to recognize that when one owner puts up cash against another's contribution of services (or other intangibles), the cash contributor often may expect to bear all dollar losses up to the amount of his or her contribution. Indeed, the U.L.P.A. and most LLC statutes allocate losses (as well as profits), in the absence of contrary agreement, in proportion to the agreed value of the owner's contributions. *E.g.*, U.L.P.A. § 503; Cal. Corp. Code § 17202; Del. Code Ann. Title 6 § 18–503; N.Y. Ltd. Liab. Co. Law § 503. If the partnership agreement allocates losses in proportion to capital contributions, what would be the result in *Richert* (assuming the agreement did not treat Handly's services as a capital contribution)? (Interestingly, the 2001 revision of the U.L.P.A. seemingly avoids the whole issue by removing any reference to sharing losses. While this works well enough for limited partners, whose obligation should be limited to their investment, suppose there are multiple general partners.)

Suppose the parties in *Richert* had agreed for Richert to bear a greater share of losses corresponding to his greater capital contribution, but, in recognition of Handly's work, still had agreed to share profits equally. What, if any, problems might allocating losses in different proportions from profits create? For example, assume, much as in *Richert*, a firm has two owners: One contributes $10,000, the other contributes his services. They agree to split profits equally, but, unlike *Richert*, to have the cash contributor bear the first $10,000 in losses. What would happen if during the first year of operation the firm lost $10,000 (all borne by the cash contributor), while during the second year the firm made $10,000 (split equally between the two owners)? How might the parties adjust the profit allocation in order to reach what might be a more reasonable result?

Another situation where owners might allocate losses other than in proportion to profits is when one owner causes the loss. For example, suppose a partner in a law firm commits malpractice, thereby making the partnership liable. Alternately, suppose an owner forgets to lock up the business premises one night, resulting in the robbery of valuable business assets. Or, suppose a majority of the owners make a business decision over the objection of other owners, and the decision turns out to lose money for the firm. As between themselves, should the owners share these losses in the same proportion they share any other? *Compare Ferguson v. Williams,* 670 S.W.2d 327 (Tex.App.1984) (partners cannot be liable to fellow partners for negligent operation of the partnership), *with* R.U.P.A. § 404(c) (imposing liability for gross negligence). The owners of a firm may wish to agree to rules clarifying and perhaps expanding or contracting the range of losses borne by the owner causing them.

2. Recall, in discussing the allocation of profits, how it was important to consider the actual impact of the allocation. The same is true in considering the allocation of losses. As with profits, one potential impact involves income taxes—in this instance, the ability of persons treated as partners for income tax purposes to obtain deductions based upon their share of firm losses. Naturally, it might be both unfair and an abuse of tax laws if some owners reduced their taxable income based upon firm generated losses, while other owners, in fact, bore the economic burden of such losses. This chapter will return to the tax issue shortly. For now, let us focus on the economic impact of firm losses on the owners.

When dealing with the allocation of profits, the bottom line economic impact occurs when owners receive greater distributions at some point in time as a reflection of their individual shares of the profits. When dealing with the allocation of losses, one bottom line economic impact similarly occurs if the allocation impacts rights to distributions from the firm—in this case, by owners receiving smaller distributions as a reflection of their shares of the losses. This brings one back to the earlier discussion of partners' capital accounts. As explained then, each partner's share of firm losses is subtracted at the close of every accounting period from the partner's capital account. As a result, if each partner receives on liquidation a distribution equal to the balance in his or her capital account, then each partner's share of firm losses decreases the total of the distributions he or she ultimately receives. The effect of the losses on the cash contributor in *Richert* illustrates this sort of impact. Even with Richert's recovery against Handly, Richert did not get back all of the cash Richert contributed to the firm.

Richert also illustrates that there can be another economic impact to a loss allocation. As Handly discovered, partners might find themselves forced to pony up more money to cover their share of the losses. Again, capital accounts provide the customary computational mechanism for coordinating the partners' agreed loss allocation with this impact. Specifically, as one subtracts losses from a partner's capital account, eventually the account will become a negative number. (Handly reached this point right away, because he made no capital contributions. Richert would have reached this point after his share of the losses exceeded his capital contribution.) If, at least upon liquidation, each partner with a negative balance must pay the balance, then each partner will have borne his or her share of the firm's losses, as called for under the default rule in the U.P.A. and R.U.P.A. This essentially is what happened to Handly.

This discussion of negative capital accounts suggests yet another possible approach for partners who wish to contract out of the result in *Richert v. Handly*. Why not have a term in the partnership agreement which states that partners are not required to pay off deficits in their capital accounts upon liquidation? Before taking this step, however, one might want consider several potential problems. To begin with, absent careful drafting, such a term can introduce an inconsistency in the partnership agreement. For example, suppose Richert and Handly had made a partnership agreement which expressly stated that the partners would share losses equally, but also stated that neither partner has an obligation to pay a negative balance in his capital account. If Handly does not pay the negative balance in his capital account, will the partners share the losses equally? If not, what happens if the contract is not clear as to which term trumps? Moreover, suppose the negative balance in a partner's capital account did not result from firm losses, but rather from distributions or withdrawals. In this case, might any partners with positive balances in their accounts have a different attitude about requiring payment of negative balances? Beyond these problems, a major difficulty with a provision removing the obligation of partners to pay deficits in their capital accounts lies in the income tax regulations. This is a very complex subject to which this chapter will return. Finally, it is important to keep in mind the difference between affecting the rights of the partners *inter se* and affecting the rights of third party creditors. While partners are at liberty to agree between themselves as to which of their number will bear responsibility for any losses or liabilities, such an agreement does not affect the rights of creditors under Section 15 of the U.P.A. and 306 of the R.U.P.A. to demand complete satisfaction of the creditors' claims from any ordinary or general partner. Hence, a term in the partnership agreement relieving partners of the obligation to pay deficits in their capital accounts is no protection against claims for payment by the partnership's creditors.

3. Of course, if the firm is a limited partnership, an LLP, or an LLC, then some or all of the owners might not be subject to claims by the firm's creditors. At first glance, one might think that this simplifies the task of dealing with losses in the partnership or LLC operating agreement. In fact, however, limited liability can introduce some new complexities.

One complexity arises from grafting together partnership and corporate approaches to dealing with losses. As seen in *Richert*, in an ordinary partnership, the allocation of losses in the partnership agreement (or the statutory default rule in the absence of agreement) dictates the rights of the partners vis-a-vis each other in the event of firm losses. By contrast, in a corporation, there is no express agreement among the owners allocating losses. Instead, each stockholder's loss depends upon how much the stockholder paid for his or her shares, and the relative rights of his or her shares to receive anything back on liquidation. If worse comes to worse, the essence of limited liability is that the stockholders simply can walk away from the company having lost all of their investment. The U.L.P.A. and the statutes creating LLPs and LLCs mush together the two approaches. As with corporations, the U.L.P.A. and the LLP and LLC statutes speak of limited liability under which owners are not personally liable for debts or obligations of the firm. At the same time, however, like a partnership, the statutes call for an allocation of losses pursuant to the partnership or LLC operating agreement, or under a default rule in the absence of agreement. The result is a potential conflict along the lines just discussed in considering contract provisions relieving partners of the obligation to pay negative balances in their capital accounts. Actually, the existence of a conflict depends upon the agreed loss allocation. If the allocation is proportional to contributions—which is the default rule under the U.L.P.A. and most LLC statutes—then losses generally should not produce a situation in which some owners have positive and some owners have negative capital accounts. In this event, allowing owners simply to walk away generally will not lead to a conflict with the loss sharing agreement. Suppose, however, the partnership or LLC operating agreement allocates losses other than in proportion to contributions. For example, the agreement might allocate losses equally despite unequal contributions (as is the default rule applicable to LLPs—where the U.P.A. or R.U.P.A. governs). In this event, as *Richert* illustrates, there is a conflict between equal loss sharing and the lack of any obligation for an owner to pay sums beyond his or her agreed contribution.

How do the various statutes dealing with limited partnerships, LLCs and LLPs reconcile this possible conflict between an agreed allocation of losses, and liability limited to one's agreed contribution? Section 303 of the U.L.P.A. (both before and after the 2001 revision) states that limited partners are not liable for "obligations of the limited partnership." Does this mean that a partner with a positive capital account cannot call upon a limited partner with a negative capital account to pay the agreed share of the losses which produced the imbalance in the accounts? The U.L.P.A. is not clear. It is at least arguable that the claim against the limited partner in this instance would not be for an obligation of the limited partnership, but, rather, would be based upon enforcement of the agreed loss sharing. The heading of the pre–2001 version of Section 303—"Liability to Third Parties"—certainly reinforces this interpretation; while the removal of this heading in the 2001 revision perhaps suggests a contrary intent. Should it matter how the capital account imbalance arose? For example, suppose the reason the partners did not bear losses in the agreed proportions was because the general partner personally had to pay off the limited partnership's creditors. If the general partner then could turn around and recover part of this sum from the limited partner, the result would seem to undermine the notion of limited liability for third party claims.

As seen before, LLC statutes often copy language from the U.L.P.A. and thereby pick up whatever ambiguities the U.L.P.A. contains. Along this line, typical LLC statutes state that members of an LLC are not liable for "debts, obligations and liabilities of a limited liability company" solely by reason of being a member of the LLC. Cal. Corp. Code § 17101(a); Del. Code Ann. Title 6 § 18–303; N.Y. Ltd. Liab. Co. Law § 609(a). Again, however, the question arises as to whether a claim asserted by other members based upon an agreed loss sharing falls outside the ambit of a debt, liability or obligation of the LLC, the obligation to pay which would be solely the result of being a member.

LLP statutes create limited liability by adding language to the state's version of Section 15 of the U.P.A. or Section 306 of the R.U.P.A. Typical language states that a partner is not liable, either directly or indirectly, by way of indemnification, contribution, assessment or otherwise, for any debt, obligation or other liability of or chargeable to the partnership or another partner. *E.g.*, Cal. Corp. Code § 16306(c); N.Y. Partnership Law § 26(b). *See also* Del. Code Ann. Title 6 § 15–306(c) (not liable for obligation of the partnership). The language about indirect liability by way of contribution and the like makes clear one point that the U.L.P.A. left open to doubt: a partner in an LLP called upon to pay personally a claim involving the LLP—perhaps because this partner committed the malpractice upon which the claim arose, or because this partner gave a personal guarantee for the contract creating this claim—cannot turn around and seek recovery from the other partners in the LLP. Yet, what about the *Richert* situation in which losses have left insufficient funds to return a partner's capital account? Specifically, does application of the loss sharing agreement in a situation such as *Richert* constitute liability for a debt, obligation or other liability of the partnership, or is this simply enforcement of the contract between the partners? Since Section 15 of the U.P.A. and Section 306 of the R.U.P.A. are concerned with partners' liabilities to third parties, one certainly could argue that the limitation of each partner's liability in an LLP does not alter the outcome in a *Richert* situation. Indeed, it is Sections 18(a) and 40(d) of the U.P.A., and 401(a) and 807(b) of the R.U.P.A., rather than Sections 15 and 306, respectively, which deal with the partners' obligations to pay their shares of the firm's losses. Some LLP statutes have modified the sections dealing with partners' obligations to contribute toward losses. For example, in 1996, the drafters of the R.U.P.A. added provisions to accommodate LLPs. Section 807(b) of the R.U.P.A., as amended in 1996, requires a partner to contribute to the partnership the amount equal to a negative balance in his or her capital account, but excludes from the calculation of this balance charges attributable to obligations for which there is limited liability under Section 306. Yet, such language simply forces one back to the ambiguity in Section 306. By comparison, California's version of Section 807(b) (Cal. Corp. Code § 16807(b)) avoids the ambiguity of referring back to charges for which liability is limited under Section 306. Instead, the California version simply excludes an LLP from the stated obligation of partners to pay negative balances in their capital accounts. This appears to mean that, barring other agreement, loss sharing for a California LLP stops at the zero capital account edge. By contrast, a recent decision in New York holds that the limited liability provisions in New York's LLP act do not trump claims between partners in an LLP based upon their rights under the partnership agreement. *Ederer v. Gursky*, 9 N.Y. 3d 514, 881 N.E. 2d 204 (2007).

Another complication introduced by limited liability in limited partnerships, LLPs and LLCs arises from the prospect that some partners or members might face personal liability for some claims, while other partners or members might face personal liability for other claims. For example, an individual who commits malpractice remains liable for his or her own tort even though he or she is a partner in a limited liability partnership. Since this means that the tortfeasor partner will end up paying whatever portion of the judgment the partnership does not cover, the tortfeasor partner has a strong incentive to see that the partnership pays the tort claim. On the other hand, other partners in the LLP might be liable if the LLP does not pay its other debts. This might occur, for example, because some partners personally guaranteed some of the firm's debts or because the partnership incurred some liabilities before registering as an LLP (*see, e.g.*, Cal. Corp. Code § 16306(b); Del. Code Ann. Title 6 § 15–306(b); N.Y. Partnership Law § 26(b) (under all, limited liability only applies to debts incurred while the firm is registered as an LLP)). As a result, the non-tortfeasor partners might prefer to apply the partnership's assets to the payment of the firm's other debts. Who decides which debts to pay first?

Parties in a limited partnership, LLP or LLC might leave questions as to the impact of limited liability on their rights vis-a-vis each other for judicial statutory interpretation. To avoid being called upon as the persons to fund such interpretation (by engaging in expensive litigation), perhaps the partners might prefer to include answers in their partnership or LLC operating agreement.

2. TAX ASPECTS

a. *The Conduit Principle in Operation*

Bittker, Federal Taxation of Income, Estates & Gifts

¶ ¶ 86.1–86.3 (1981).

¶ 86.1 PARTNERSHIP INCOME AND CURRENT DISTRIBUTIONS

¶ 86.1.1 Introductory

Although a partnership is a conduit whose receipts and expenses are allocated to its partners and accounted for on their separate tax returns rather than a taxable entity, IRC § 703(a) refers to "the taxable income of a partnership" and prescribes rules for its computation. At first blush, this term seems self-contradictory; but on analysis it proves to be a method of centralizing a host of decisions that must be made uniformly for all partners, such as whether particular items received by the partnership constitute income or the return of capital, whether expenditures qualify as ordinary and necessary expenses of conducting the firm's business, and so on. In effect, the partnership is treated as an entity in analyzing the financial results of its operations, since these ingredients determine the chemical composition of the liquid that is channeled through the partnership to the partners. In furtherance of this unifying function, the partnership has its own taxable year, and elections affecting the computation of taxable income are ordinarily made by the partnership as an entity, rather than separately by the partners in their individual capacities. Summarizing the applicable rules, the Supreme Court observed in *United States v. Basye* that "partnerships are entities for purposes of calculating and filing informational returns but * * * are conduits through which the taxpaying obligation passes to the individual partners in accord with their distributive shares." As will be seen, however, there are important exceptions to these general principles.

¶ 86.1.2 Partnership Taxable Income

Section 703(a) provides that the taxable income of a partnership shall be computed in the same manner as an individual's taxable income, except that (1) the items described in IRC § 702(a) must be separately stated and (2) certain deductions are not allowed.

1. *Separately stated items.* Section 703(a) requires the items described in IRC § 702(a) to be separately stated. These items, which must be segregated so they can be properly accounted for on each partner's return, include short-and long-term capital gains and losses; gains and losses

entering into the IRC § 1231 hotchpot; charitable contributions; foreign income taxes; and numerous other receipts and expenditures that are subject to special tax rates, to percentage or dollar limits, or to other provisions resulting in a different income tax liability for the partner than if they were drowned in a sea of undifferentiated "income" or "loss."* [number with *] For example, it is not possible to decide at the partnership level whether a long-term capital loss incurred by a partnership is currently deductible or not, since each partner's share of the loss must be amalgamated with the partner's other long-term capital losses (whether incurred in a personal capacity or attributed to the partner from trusts, estates, and other partnerships), and the resulting aggregate amount must then be applied against the partner's long term capital gains and ordinary income to the extent allowable.

2. *Nondeductible Items.* Section 703(A)(2) provides that partnerships may not deduct foreign income taxes, charitable contributions, net operating losses, or depletion. This prohibition's bark is worse than its bite, however, since the relevant data flow through to the partners, who combine the partnership's items with their own in preparing their separate income tax returns. Section 703(A)(2) also disallows certain deductions whose nondeductibility by an artificial entity is virtually self-evident, such as personal and dependency exemptions, medical expenses, and alimony.

* * *

¶ 86.1.3 Partnership Elections

To avoid chaos, IRC § 703(b) provides that, with minor exceptions, all elections affecting the computation of a partnership's taxable income shall be made by the partnership.

* * *

¶ 86.1.4 Partnership Taxable Year

In computing his taxable income for any taxable year, a partner takes into account his distributive share of the partnership's income, gains, losses, deductions, and credits for the taxable year of the partnership that ends with or within his own taxable year. For example, in computing taxable income for 1980, a calendar year partner takes into account all relevant partnership items for the partnership's taxable year ending on any day in 1980.

By treating partnership items as received by the partners on the last day of the partnership's taxable year, IRC § 706(a) sets the stage for a deferral of partnership income (or, conversely, losses) if the partnership's taxable year differs from its partners' years. If, for example, the partners report on a calendar year basis but the partnership's taxable year ends on

* [The 1997 Taxpayer Relief Act, however, allows partnerships with at least 100 partners to elect special treatment which, among other things, reduces the number of specific items that each partner must report separately instead of included within the partner's overall income or loss from the partnership. I.R.C. §§ 771–777. Ed.]

January 31, the partnership's income for eleven months of 1980 and one month of 1981 will be reported by the partners on their returns for the calendar year 1981.

To forestall tax-motivated deferrals of this type, IRC § 706(b) [limits the ability of the partnership to select a different taxable year from its partners.*]

* * *

¶ 86.2 DISTRIBUTIVE SHARES OF PARTNERSHIP INCOME AND OTHER ITEMS

¶ 86.2.1 In General

Section 702(a) requires each partner to take his "distributive share" of various partnership items into account in determining his own income tax liability, and IRC § 704(a) provides that the partner's distributive share of the partnership's income, gains, losses, deductions and credits shall be determined by the partnership agreement.

* * *

The distributive share rules ordinarily presuppose that items whose status depends on their function, purpose, or motivation are to be characterized at the partnership level, rather than partner by partner, and that each partner's distributive share of the item retains its partnership-level classification. This message is conveyed, albeit murkily, by IRC § 702(b). Partnership-level classification is obviously appropriate in deciding such issues as (1) whether property is "held by the taxpayer primarily for sale to customers in the ordinary course of his trade or business" (IRC § 1221(1), relating to capital assets); [and] (2) the period "for which the taxpayer has held property" (IRC § 1223, relating to the holding period for capital gain and loss purposes) * * *—even though partnerships are not taxpayers. On the other hand, it seems more appropriate to classify some items at the individual level or to subject them to the statutory test at both levels; and deductibility, as distinguished from classification, is ordinarily determined partner by partner.

* * *

As used by IRC §§ 702(a) and 704(a), the term "distributive share" refers to amounts that are *allocable* to the partner, without implying that the amounts have been or will be *distributed* to him; indeed, it embraces deductions and credits, although they cannot be "distributed" in the way

* [As amended in 1986, Section 706(b) provides that, unless the partnership can show to the satisfaction of the IRS a business purpose for having a different taxable year, it must use the same taxable year used by its partners holding a majority of the profits and capital interest in the firm; or, if partners holding a majority of interest use different years, it must use the year used by all the principal partners (holders of a 5% or greater interest); or, if they use different years, it must look to the regulations as to the choice of taxable year. Section 444 creates a minor exception by allowing limited use of different tax years in exchange for paying an extra tax for obtaining any deferral. Ed.]

that cash and property can be paid out. Moreover, a partner's distributive share of income as determined by the partnership agreement must be taken into account even if litigation, embezzlement, bankruptcy, or other calamities prevent him from getting amounts to which he is entitled, since the shortage will ordinarily be reflected at the proper time by a deduction under IRC § 165, relating to losses. As the Supreme Court has observed, "few principles of partnership taxation are more firmly established than that no matter the reason for nondistribution each partner must pay taxes on his distributive share."

¶ 86.2.2 Special Allocations

In the first instance, a partner's distributive share of the partnership's income, gains, losses, deductions, and credits is determined by the partnership agreement. Some agreements deal with this matter in detail; but if the agreement is silent or the allocation is devoid of substantial economic effect, IRC § 704(b), as amended in 1976, provides that the distributive share shall be determined "in accordance with the partner's interest in the partnership (determined by taking into account all facts and circumstances)."

* * *

¶ 86.2.3 Distributive Shares, Distributions, and Basis of Partnership Interests

Because partners must take their distributive shares of partnership income into account on their separate returns even if the firm's earnings are retained and reinvested, it is necessary to protect them against a second tax on the same amount if a partnership interest is sold or the firm is liquidated. Similarly, if a partnership receives but retains tax-exempt interest, the partners should not be taxed on this amount when it is realized by a liquidation of the partnership or a sale of partnership interests. Conversely, partners who have deducted their distributive shares of partnership losses should not be allowed to offset their original investments against the amount realized on liquidation or sale without adjustments for the amount already deducted.

To achieve these objectives, IRC § 705(a) provides that the adjusted basis of a partnership interest is its original basis (determined under IRC § 722 if acquired by contributions to the partnership or under IRC § 742 if acquired by purchase, etc.) *increased* by the partner's distributive share of partnership taxable income and exempt income and *decreased* (but not below zero) by distributions (as provided by IRC § 733) and the partner's distributive share of partnership losses. The increase in basis for the partner's distributive share of "income of the partnership exempt from tax under this title" is intended to avoid a later tax on distributions of exempt receipts such as tax-exempt interest and should not be construed to encompass realized income qualifying for nonrecognition, where tax liability is deferred rather than excused. In making these adjustments, it should be remembered that increases and decreases in a partner's share of partnership liabilities and in certain individual liabilities of the partner are treated as contributions or distributions of money, as the case may be, by IRC § 752.

* * *

¶ 86.3 CURRENT DISTRIBUTIONS

¶ 86.3.1 Gain, Loss, and Basis of Distributed Property

Under IRC §§ 731(a)(1) and 731(a)(2), partners do not recognize gain or loss on current distributions by their partnerships except for (a) distributions of money [or marketable securities] in excess of the adjusted basis of the partner's interest in the partnership, which usually generates capital gain, * * * (b) distributions altering a partner's interest in Section 751 property (unrealized receivables and substantially appreciated inventory, as defined, whose tax consequences are described below), [or (c) distributions which might allow partners to escape the consequences of a Section 704(c) allocation (ed.)]. This nonrecognition principle applies even if the partner receives property (other than money) whose fair market value exceeds the adjusted basis of the partnership interest; in effect, the distribution is viewed as a continuation of ownership rather than as a settlement of accounts between the firm and the partner. As to losses, the nonrecognition principle rests on an independent foundation: Since the partner's interest in the firm is not terminated by the distribution, it is too early to determine whether a loss has been realized.

In keeping with the nonrecognition principle embodied in IRC § 731(a), the partnership's adjusted basis for the distributed assets carries over to the distributee partner, except that the assets' aggregate basis may not exceed the adjusted basis for the partner's interest in the partnership reduced by any money received in the same transaction. [IRC § 732(a)]

* * *

So far as the partnership is concerned, IRC § 731(b) establishes a seemingly unqualified nonrecognition principle: No gain or loss is recognized on a distribution of partnership property, including money, to a partner. This basic rule, however, is subject to three important exceptions: (1) a statutory exception, set out in IRC § 731(c), for distributions changing the partners' proportionate shares of Section 751(b) property (relating to unrealized receivables and substantially appreciated inventory items); (2) a qualification set out in the regulations, involving distributions used to effect an exchange of property between the firm's partners or between the firm and one or more partners; and (3) an exception arising, under a basic principle of income tax law, for transactions purporting to be distributions of property followed by sale of the property by the distributing partner, if in substance the transaction is a sale of the property by the partnership coupled with a distribution of the proceeds to the partner.

* * *

¶ 86.3.2 Distributions by Partnerships With Unrealized Receivables or Substantially Appreciated Inventory

The rules ordinarily applicable to current distributions of money and other property * * * are altered by IRC § 751(b) if the distribution alters the partner's interest in so-called Section 751 property—"unrealized receivables" and "inventory items which have appreciated substantially in value." These two categories of partnership assets are segregated for special treatment because they often have a high "ordinary income" component * * *.

If a current distribution to a partner has the effect of increasing his pro rata share of Section 751 property and correspondingly decreasing his share of non-Section 751 property, the transaction is treated in part as though the partner had received a current distribution of part or all of his share of the partnership's non-Section 751 property and then immediately exchanged it with the partnership for the excess Section 751 property actually received by him, resulting in gain or loss to both parties to the constructive exchange. The remaining portion of the current distribution of Section 751 property (i.e., the portion not in excess of the partner's share) is subject to the regular distribution rules.

* * *

In the converse situation, where a partner receives a current distribution of *less* than his share of Section 751 property, a similar constructive exchange is mandated by IRC § 751(b)(1)(B), which views the partner as selling part or all of his share of the Section 751 property for the excess non-section 751 property actually received by him.

The function of the constructive sale mandated by IRC § 751(b) is evidently to prevent shifting the ordinary-income component of Section 751 property from high-bracket partners to their low-bracket compatriots. * * *

b. *Uses and Abuses of the Conduit Principle*

(i) Special Allocations

PNRC Limited Partnership v. Commissioner of Internal Revenue

66 T.C.M. (CCH) 265 (1993).

LARO, Judge: Respondent issued petitioner a notice of final partnership administrative adjustment * * * on behalf of PNRC Limited Partnership (PNRC LP) asserting that its losses for the taxable years 1983, 1984, 1985, and 1986 were disproportionately distributed between the general partner and the limited partner. * * * The issue for decision is whether petitioner's allocation of its losses 99 percent to the limited partner and 1 percent to the general partner has substantial economic effect. We find for respondent and hold that the partnership's losses must be reallocated in accordance with the partners' interests in the partnership.

FINDINGS OF FACT

* * *

PNRC LP is a partnership between Peter D. Carlino (Carlino) as limited partner and PNRC [Corporation (PNRC)] as general partner. Carlino organized both PNRC and PNRC LP in December 1982 * * *. During the years at issue, PNRC was wholly owned by the Carlino Family Partnership (CFP), a limited partnership controlled by Carlino and his family.

* * *

The PNRC LP partnership agreement (the Agreement) allocates losses 1 percent to the general partner, PNRC, and 99 percent to the limited partner, Carlino. [Carlino had substantial income and stood to obtain a tax benefit from the allocation of losses to him, whereas PNRC did not.] * * * The Agreement * * * provide[s] for an allocation of 60 percent of any profits to the general partner and 40 percent to the limited partner. The Agreement does not reflect the parties' capital contributions.

The Agreement further provides that upon termination of the partnership, the general partner shall either sell the partnership's assets and distribute the net proceeds or distribute the partnership property to the partners in proportion to their percentage interests. The Agreement provides that any reference to a partner's percentage interest is to his interest in net profits. PNRC LP sustained losses in all of the years at issue, which it allocated as follows:

Year	Loss	General Partner— PNRC Corporation 1%	Limited Partner— Peter Carlino 99%
1983	($194,355)	($1,944)	($192,411)
1984	($831,909)	($8,319)	($823,590)
1985	($227,431)	($2,274)	($225,157)
1986	($526,976)	($5,270)	($521,706)

PNRC LP was initially capitalized with $420,000. The partnership information returns and financial statements for 1982 and 1983 reflect that the general partner, PNRC, contributed $300,000 (71.4 percent of the initial capital) and the limited partner, Carlino, contributed $120,000 (28.6 percent of the initial capital). Carlino loaned the partnership $358,346 in 1984. This loan was reclassified on the books of the partnership as additional capital. Because of this additional capital contribution, the partnership's capital for 1985 and 1986 was allocable 38.6 percent to PNRC and 61.4 percent to Carlino. * * *

OPINION

Although the facts of this case are complicated, the issue for decision is straightforward: Did the allocation of 99 percent of the losses of PNRC LP to Carlino, the limited partner, have substantial economic effect? * * *

Section 704(a) generally provides that a partner's distributive share of any item of income, gain, loss, deduction, or credit is determined by the partnership agreement. Section 704(b) provides that a partner's share of any such item is determined according to the partner's interest in the partnership, taking into account all the facts and circumstances, if the allocation of the item under the partnership agreement does not have "substantial economic effect". Sec. 704(b).

Section 1.704–1(b), Income Tax Regs., provides a process for determining if an allocation has "substantial economic effect". * * *

To have substantial economic effect, the allocation must have "economic effect" and such economic effect must be "substantial". Sec. 1.704–1(b)(2)(i), Income Tax Regs.[13] In order to have economic effect under the basic test, the partnership agreement must provide, throughout the full term of the partnership: (1) For the determination and maintenance of the partners' capital accounts in accordance with the provisions of section 1.704–1(b)(2)(iv), Income Tax Regs.; (2) that upon liquidation of the partnership, all liquidating distributions must be made in accordance with the positive capital account balances of the partners; and (3) that if a partner has a deficit balance in his capital account following liquidation of his interest in the partnership, he is unconditionally obligated to restore the amount of this deficit balance by the end of the taxable year or within 90 days after the date of such liquidation, whichever is later. Sec. 1.704–1(b)(2)(ii)(b), Income Tax Regs. The Agreement does not have these provisions. In fact, the Agreement expressly provides that the general partner shall never be obligated to pay the limited partner or the partnership the amount of any deficit in its capital account. Thus, the allocation does not pass the basic test for economic effect.

The regulation also provides an alternate test for economic effect, contingent on satisfaction of items (1) and (2) above, which PNRC LP does not satisfy.[14] Sec. 1.701–1(b)(2)(ii)(d), Income Tax Regs. Thus, the loss allocation fails the alternate test for economic effect.

Allocations that lack economic effect under the provisions discussed above may nevertheless be deemed to have economic effect if, as of the end of each taxable year, a liquidation of the partnership would produce the same economic results to the partners as if the requirements of the basic test for economic effect were met, regardless of the performance of the partnership. Sec. 1.704–1(b)(2)(ii)(i), Income Tax Regs. Because the Agree-

13. Different rules may apply to allocations attributable to nonrecourse deductions. PNRC LP treated all its outstanding debt obligations as recourse, and as respondent conceded this issue in her briefs, we assume no loss allocations in issue are attributable to nonrecourse debt.

14. In addition, the agreement must contain a "qualified income offset" provision. A "qualified income offset" is where a partnership agreement provides that a partner who unexpectedly receives certain adjustments, allocations, or distributions will be allocated items of income and gain in an amount and manner so as to eliminate his deficit balance as quickly as possible. Sec. 1.704–1(b)(2)(ii)(d), Income Tax Regs. The PNRC LP agreement does not contain a qualified income offset provision.

ment provides that upon termination of the partnership, partnership property will be distributed to the partners in proportion to their interests in net profits, that is, 60 percent to the general partner and 40 percent to the limited partner, even a liquidation after one year of operation would not produce the same results to the partners as if the Agreement met the basic test for economic effect. That is, partly because the general partner contributed 71.4 percent of the initial capital and the limited partner contributed 28.6 percent, liquidating distributions to each partner will not equal the balance each has in his capital account. Thus, the allocation fails this "economic effect equivalence" test as well.

* * *

We have considered petitioner's other arguments and find them similarly to be without merit. Thus, the allocation of 99 percent of PNRC LP's losses to Carlino lacks substantial economic effect. Accordingly, section 704(b) requires the losses to be reallocated in accordance with the partners' respective interests in the partnership. This is a facts and circumstances inquiry. Among the factors to consider in determining the partners' interests in a partnership are the partners' relative contributions to the partnership, their respective interests in profits and losses, if different from taxable income and loss, cash flow, and their distribution rights upon liquidation. * * * In this case, the partners' contributions to the partnership are the most indicative of their interests in the partnership.

* * *

NOTES

1. Under Section 704(a), the partnership (or LLC operating) agreement normally determines each partner's (or party treated as a partner for income tax purposes) distributive share of income, gains, losses, deductions or credits. This ability of partners (or limited partners or LLC members) to allocate who shall bear the burden or enjoy the benefit of recognizing various items of the firm's income and expense provides a powerful tax planning tool—and also carries a great potential for abuse. For example, in *PNRC* there existed the common situation where the limited partner had significant income from activities outside the firm. He sought to "shelter" this income from tax by receiving 99 percent of the losses generated by the firm. The general partner had no taxable income from outside sources and thus would obtain no immediate tax benefit from any partnership losses.

Allocations of losses, deductions or credits to one or more parties often might provide an incentive for them to invest. To the extent these parties ultimately fund or bear the burden of the losses or expenses generating these tax items, there is no abuse: The allocation of tax items corresponds to the underlying economic realities. Similarly, allocation of more taxable income or gain to parties with less outside income entails no abuse where those individuals obtain the ultimate benefit of the income or gain. This is the principle the court in *PNRC* worked from when it searched the parties' arrangement to determine whether the allocation had a "substantial economic effect."

How can one determine whether a given allocation has an economic effect independent of tax consequences when, as with the losses in *PNRC,* it involves an item which has no immediate dollar impact on any party? Conventional accounting practice, as discussed earlier, keeps track of the impact of undistributed profits or losses on each partner's equity in the firm by crediting or debiting the partner's capital account with his or her share of such profits or losses. Consider the effect this would have had on the capital accounts of the partners in *PNRC.* By the end of 1986, the limited partner's capital account would have had credited to it contributions totaling $478,346, and debited losses totaling $1,762,864, for a net balance of *minus* $1,284,518. The general partner's account, by contrast, would stand at *plus* $282,193 ($300,000 contribution, minus $17,807 in losses). At this point, however, the effect exists only on paper. What must happen for the crediting or debiting of capital accounts to have an actual dollar impact on the partners? Suppose the business ended in 1987 and the partners liquidated it by selling its assets at book value. If the limited partner was obligated to make up the deficit in his capital account, while the general partner was entitled to receive the sum represented in the general partner's capital account, then the allocation would indeed have an effect independent of its tax consequences. (Recall the discussion earlier in this chapter of the "day of reckoning" approach under the U.P.A. and R.U.P.A.) It was the partnership agreement's failure to provide for such upon eventual liquidation that doomed the allocation.

This suggests a three part test (which the regulations discussed in *PNRC* set forth) to determine if a special allocation has an economic effect:

> (1) The partnership (or entity electing treatment as a partnership for income tax purposes) must keep capital accounts in accordance with the regulations;
>
> (2) Proceeds from liquidating the partnership must be distributed in accordance with the positive balances in the capital accounts; and
>
> (3) Any partner (or owner treated as a partner for income tax purposes) with a negative account must be obligated to make up the deficit upon liquidation.

Treas. Reg. § 1.704–1(b)(2)(ii)(b). As stated in *PNRC* and in the regulations, the partnership (or LLC operating) agreement must specify these three obligations; albeit, the lack of agreement is not fatal if state law default rules reach the same result (Treas. Reg. § 1.704–1(b)(5) Ex. (4)(ii)).

Note that it is possible to have a partially valid and partially invalid allocation. For example, if an allocation of losses is reflected in capital accounts which are used as the basis for distributing assets upon liquidation, but parties are not obligated to restore deficits in their accounts, then the allocation would be valid except for that portion which creates a negative capital account. Treas. Reg. § 1.704–1(b)(2)(ii)(d). (This is the alternate test referred to in *PNRC.*) There are a couple of caveats to this conclusion. To begin with, a party might have an obligation to restore a deficit under certain conditions—a so-called limited deficit restoration obligation. In this event, allocations creating a negative capital account can be valid to the extent of this limited obligation. An example of such a limited deficit restoration obligation is the liability which state law imposes on ordinary partners to pay creditors of the partnership if the firm cannot, despite any provision in the partnership agreement waiving obligations to pay deficits in a partner's capital account. To calculate the amount of this obligation, the Internal Revenue Service considers how much of the partnership's existing liabilities could not be paid based upon the assumption that the firm's assets are worth their book value. Rev. Rul. 97–38, 1997–2 C.B. 69. In addition, suppose the firm distributes to an owner, who has no obligation to restore a negative capital account, a sufficient amount of cash or property to put his or her account into the red. What would be the effect on a prior loss allocation to this owner, which otherwise would have been valid as the allocation itself did not create a negative account? See Treas. Reg. § 1.704–1(b)(2)(ii)(d) (if a distribution, which will create a negative capital account, is reasonably expected at the time of the loss allocation, then must take it into account in determining the validity of the loss allocation; if the subsequent distribution was unexpected, then the partnership agreement must allocate later income to this owner to make up the deficit as quickly as possible (in tax jargon, the agreement must provide a "qualified income offset")).

In a number of situations, testing the effect of a special allocation solely by using capital accounts as outlined above is not wholly satisfactory. For example, suppose a partnership or LLC operating agreement allocates a certain amount of capital gains to an owner with capital losses from another source, while allocating an equal amount of ordinary income to another owner. Such an allocation may be reflected in the capital accounts of the two owners, yet it still lacks any real effect independent of its tax consequences. *See* Treas. Reg. § 1.704–1(b)(5) Exs. (5), (6) and (7). The regulations treat this as a situation where the economic effect is not "substantial".

Similar problems occur when the partnership or LLC operating agreement contains chargeback or "flip-flop" provisions. A common example of a chargeback occurs when a partnership or LLC operating agreement allocates to some owners the depreciation deductions generated by the firm's property, but also provides that any gain on the sale of the property will go to those owners to the extent of the depreciation previously allocated to them. This means if the property does not in fact decrease in value, the gain upon sale will offset the special allocation of depreciation deductions and the net effect would simply be to postpone tax. Nevertheless, the regulations indicate that such an allocation is acceptable, since at the time the parties agreed to the allocation they could not tell that the property would not decrease in value thereby creating an effect independent of tax consequences. *See* Treas. Reg. § 1.704–1(b)(2)(iii)(c). (While depreciation rates under the tax code often are designed more to provide an incentive for capital investment than a realistic estimate of the property's decline in value, the regulations deem that the fair market value of firm property will decline with its adjusted basis for the purpose of concluding that such allocations are likely to create a real economic effect.) In a "flip-flop," the partnership or LLC operating agreement calls for a shift of profit and loss shares at some point in time. For example, when one owner provides more capital to a new venture, the parties might agree to allocate more income and losses to that owner until the firm is on its feet and he or she regains the amount invested. Thereafter, they may change the allocation to give the other owners a greater share of profits and losses. If all goes well, later profits will offset the losses and deductions allocated to the capital provider. Nevertheless, as in the case of the chargeback for depreciation above, one should not conclude there is no substantial effect to the allocation of losses in this instance, since at the time of the allocation there is no guarantee of later profits. *See Hamilton v. United States,* 687 F.2d 408 (Ct.Cl.1982). On the other hand, consider the situation in a well-established business which makes a predictably steady income. Allocating all income to one owner who has large tax losses from other activities during one year, with the agreement that the same amount will be allocated to the other owners during the succeeding years, might well lack any substantial effect since it is reasonably certain the firm will continue to achieve the same level of income. *See Kresser v. Commissioner,* 54 T.C. 1621 (1970). Under the regulations, the key factor in such "transitory" allocations is whether there is a "strong likelihood" that the offsetting allocation will occur and the only effect will be to save tax. Treas. Reg. § 1.704–1(b)(2)(iii).

If a firm acquires property through non-recourse financing, the lender bears the risk that the property will decrease in value beyond the amount of any cash the firm put down. As a result, it is difficult to see how an allocation of depreciation deductions in excess of the firm's cash investment could have a substantial economic effect. On the other hand, taxable income eventually will offset such depreciation deductions, either as the firm makes money which it uses to repay the lender or when disposal of the property relieves the liability. *See Commissioner v. Tufts,* 461 U.S. 300 (1983). This creates the argument that an allocation of depreciation deductions financed through non-recourse debt should be valid if the party allocated the deductions also reports the taxable income from discharging the debt. Extrapolating from this notion, the regulations allow allocations of items attributable to non-recourse financing if the partnership (or LLC operating) agreement contains a provision establishing so-called "minimum gain chargebacks". Under such a provision, the firm allocates any income or gain associated with a reduction in the amount by which the firm's non-recourse debt exceeds its basis in the property securing the debt—for example, the cancellation of indebtedness income realized by the firm upon foreclosure of the mortgage on the property, or the income the firm uses to pay off the debt—under guidelines designed to ensure that the partners recognize the income in an amount that offsets their prior tax benefit from the non-recourse financed deductions. In addition, the allocation must be reasonably consistent with other allocations, which have substantial economic effect, involving the property securing the non-recourse loan, and the firm must follow the capital account regulations discussed above designed to ensure allocations generally have substantial economic effect. Treas. Reg. § 1.704–2.

The allocation of losses financed with loans in which the lender lacks any recourse against the firm's owners becomes both more pervasive and subject to less guidance with the introduction of the limited liability company and limited liability partnership. In an ordinary or limited partnership, the quid pro quo for letting the partners or general partners off the hook from personal liability is almost invariably for creditors to demand that the firm to put up collateral. By contrast, LLC and LLP statutes relieve all members or partners from personal liability on loans to the firm unless the members or partners agree to guarantee the loan. Hence, the normal unsecured credit extended to an LLC or an LLP is, in effect, a non-recourse loan as far as the owners of the LLC or LLP are concerned. What this means is that unsecured non-recourse loans will be financing much of the losses of an LLC or an LLP once the losses exceed the amount of the owner's capital contributions. Unfortunately, the treatment of such losses under the Section 704(b) regulations is not entirely clear. The problem is that these regulations predate the widespread use of LLCs and LLPs, and, hence, the Internal Revenue Service never gave much thought about unsecured non-recourse loans. Of course, lamenting the lack of foresight in the regulations does not answer the practical question of what the drafter of an LLC operating agreement or a partnership agreement for an LLP is supposed to do about allocating losses in excess of the members' or partners' contributions when the losses do not come from the depreciation of property securing a loan to the firm. One guess is to follow the parties' profit allocation, since, as discussed later, this corresponds to the way in which the regulations interpreting Section 752 deal with the impact of non-recourse liabilities on each owner's basis in his or her interest in the firm when those liabilities match neither depreciation on property securing the non-recourse debt nor the recognition called for under Section 704(c) on the disposition of appreciated property contributed to the firm. This also corresponds to the underlying notion that the party entitled to take the loss financed through non-recourse loans is the one who will recognize the corresponding income, and, with an unsecured non-recourse loan, the corresponding income would seem to be the firm's profits—as this is the only source to pay off such a loan.

Finally, recall from the earlier discussion that capital accounts reflect not only each owner's share of income or loss, but also contributions from, and distributions to, the owners. This, in turn, raises the question of what impact contributions and distributions of property, rather than cash, might have on the substantial economic effect test. For example, suppose the limited partner in *PNRC* had attempted to discharge the deficit in his capital account by contributing property on which the partners (who, after all, were essentially family) agreed to place a highly inflated value (or, thinking ahead, the limited partner had puffed up his account at the inception of the partnership by contributing property with such an inflated valuation). To prevent parties from avoiding the economic consequences of allocations in this manner, the regulations require capital accounts to reflect any contributed or distributed property's fair market value. Treas. Reg. § 1.704–1(b)(2)(iv)(d)(1),(e)(1). (Normally, however, the adverse interests of the parties will lead the Service to respect the value the parties set. Treas. Reg. § 1.704–1(b)(2)(iv)(h).) Remember the question raised earlier in this Chapter as to whether and why the owners must value contributed property: Does this provide a further answer?

2. Contributing property to a partnership (or an entity treated as a partnership for tax purposes) raises issues under Section 704 beyond simply the need to have capital accounts reflect the fair market value of the contributions. As discussed earlier in this Chapter, the basis the firm will obtain in property to the firm is the same as the basis the contributor had in the property before the contribution. This means the firm often will obtain a basis for the contributed property which differs from the property's value upon contribution and, hence, from the value reflected in the owners' capital accounts. This, in turn, leads to situations in which the firm must allocate tax items—such as taxable gain upon the sale of the property—whose amounts do not correspond to the items' economic effect upon the owners.

To illustrate, assume two individuals agree to be equal partners. One contributes $10,000 in cash, while the other contributes property with a fair market value of $10,000, but a basis of only $4,000 (perhaps because the contributor purchased the property several years earlier for $4,000 and the property appreciated in value since then). Suppose the firm sells the property for $10,000. From an ordinary accounting standpoint there is no profit, and each partner's capital account remains at $10,000 (which reflects the amount or value of each partner's initial contribution). However, for tax purposes the partnership must report $6,000 gain (the difference between the $10,000 received in the sale and the property's basis of $4000). Since the two individuals are equal partners, they might (incorrectly it turns out) assume each should recognize $3,000. Would this result be fair to the partner who contributed cash and still only possesses the same 50 percent interest in a partnership worth $20,000? Moreover, the partner contributing cash might have grounds for complaint even if the firm retains the property. Depreciation deductions generated by the property are limited by its basis ($4,000 in this example), whereas if the firm uses the cash in this example to buy depreciable property, it measures depreciation against a $10,000 basis.

Is there any way to mitigate these effects? One approach is to allocate the firm's gain or depreciation to offset the impact of contributions with basis unequal to fair market value at the time of contribution; for instance, have the partner who contributed the appreciated property recognize the entire $6,000 taxable gain upon sale of the contributed property in the above example. In fact, the Internal Revenue Code mandates this result. Section 704(c)(1)(A) requires allocations of income, gain, loss and deduction between partners (or limited partners or LLC members when their firm elects income tax treatment as a partnership) to take into account the difference between the basis and fair market value of contributed property. Such allocations improve equities. (Congress enacted Section 704(c) less to achieve fairness between parties, however, than to prevent parties shifting income between themselves in order to lower their net tax.) Such allocations also increase the accounting burden on the firm, which must now deal with the built-in gain of various items of contributed property. The problem is two-fold. First, of course, one must establish the amount of built-in gain (or loss) on each item of contributed property. (Does this provide a further answer to the question raised earlier as to whether and why owners need to value non-cash contributions?) Next, one must allocate tax items to reflect this built-in gain or loss. When dealing with the sale of property, as in the example above, this is rather straightforward. But what happens with depreciation? In 1993, the Internal Revenue Service issued regulations addressing such questions.

Under the regulations, partners (or parties treated as partners for income tax purposes) can use any method of allocating tax items to take into account built-in gain or loss so long as the method is reasonable rather than designed to shift the consequences of the built-in gain or loss off the contributor in order to save net taxes. Treas. Reg. § 1.704–3(a)(1), (10). The regulations expressly sanction three methods (unless they yield an unreasonable result in a specific case). The first is the so-called traditional method, which allocates to the non-contributing party all depreciation deductions generated by the contributed property up to his or her "book depreciation" (in other words, the amount of depreciation he or she would get under the partnership or LLC operating agreement if the property's basis equaled its fair market value). Anything left goes to the contributor. Treas. Reg. § 1.704–3(b)(1). The regulations give the following example:

> A and B form partnership AB and agree that each will be allocated a 50 percent share of all partnership items and that AB will make allocations under Section 704(c) using the traditional method under paragraph (b) of this section. A contributes depreciable property with an adjusted tax basis of $4,000 and a book value of $10,000, and B contributes $10,000 cash. * * *
>
> The property is depreciated using the straight-line method over a 10–year recovery period. Because the property depreciates at an annual rate of 10 percent, B would have been entitled to a depreciation deduction of $500 per year for both book and tax purposes if the adjusted tax basis of the property equaled its fair market value at the time of contribution. Although each partner is allocated $500 of book depreciation per year, the partnership is allowed a tax depreciation deduction of only $400 per year (10 percent of $4,000). The partnership can allocate only $400 of tax depreciation under the ceiling rule of paragraph (b)(1) of this section, and it must be allocated entirely to B. * * * At the end of that year, the book value of the property is $9,000 ($10,000 less the $1,000 book depreciation deduction), and the adjusted tax basis is $3,600 ($4,000 less the $400 tax depreciation deduction).

> A's built-in gain with respect to the property decreases to $5,400 ($9,000 book value less $3,600 adjusted tax basis).

Treas. Reg. § 1.704–3(b)(2) Ex 1.

Notice a couple of potentially important aspects to this example. To begin with, A's built-in gain declined. Suppose, however, the property does not, in fact, decline in value to match the decrease in its book value, and the partnership is able to sell the property after one year for $10,000. Could this provide a tool for shifting pre-contribution gain off the contributing partner (since B will recognize $500 of the gain (corresponding to his share of the book gain) even though he only received $400 in depreciation deductions)? See Treas. Reg. § 1.704–3(b)(2) Ex.2 (using an extreme version of this as an example of an unreasonable use of the traditional method). In fact, this shift is part of a broader phenomenon. The property in the example did not generate enough depreciation deductions to cover the non-contributing partner's book depreciation. This brought into play the "ceiling rule" under which the non-contributing party cannot take a larger depreciation deduction than the property generates. Not only can the ceiling rule shift pre-contribution gain, but it can also produce counter-intuitive (if not downright unfair) depreciation allocations, as illustrated by the following example in the regulations:

> G and H form partnership GH and agree that each will be allocated a 50 percent share of all partnership items * * *. G contributes property G1, with an adjusted tax basis of $3,000 and a fair market value of $10,000, and H contributes property H1, with an adjusted tax basis of $6,000 and a fair market value of $10,000. Both properties have 5 years remaining on their cost recovery schedules and are depreciable using the straight-line method. * * * [Property] G1 generates $600 of tax depreciation and $2,000 of book depreciation for each of 5 years. [Property] H1 generates $1,200 of tax depreciation and $2,000 of book depreciation for each of 5 years. * * * G and H are each allocated $1,000 of book depreciation for each property. Under the traditional method of paragraph (b) of this section, G would be allocated $0 of tax depreciation for G1 and $1,000 for H1, and H would be allocated $600 of tax depreciation for G1 and $200 for H1.

Treas. Reg. § 1.704–3(c)(4) Ex. 2. In this example, H contributed property with a large enough basis to cover G's book depreciation. The property from G, in contrast, did not have a sufficient basis to cover H's book depreciation. As a result, H ends up getting less tax depreciation deductions than G, even though H contributed the property which generates more of the deductions. Is there any way to avoid such a outcome?

Suppose the GH partnership allocates to H enough of the depreciation generated by the property H contributed to overcome the shortfall caused by the ceiling rule. Similarly, suppose the partnership in the AB example used the contributed cash to buy other depreciable property; could the cash partner take an extra share of that depreciation in order to offset the shortfall caused by the ceiling rule? In fact, these are examples of the second method expressly sanctioned by the regulations—the so-called traditional method with curative allocation. Treas. Reg. 1.704–3(c). With this method, depreciation is not the only tax item the firm may use in order to offset the ceiling rule. Treas. Reg. § 1.704–3(c)(4) Ex. 1 (allocating extra taxable, but not book, income to the contributing rather than the non-contributing partner). However, the regulations require the offsetting item (unless it involves the disposition of the contributed property) to have substantially the same tax impact as the item limited by the ceiling rule. Treas. Reg. § 1.704–3(c)(3)(iii). Subject to the general reasonableness versus tax avoidance limit, the firm may use different methods for different pieces of property (although it cannot switch methods, once chosen, on any given property). Treas. Reg. § 1.704–3(a)(2).

In addition to the traditional and curative allocation methods, the regulations sanction a third method—the so-called remedial method. Treas. Reg. § 1.704–3(d). This method works like a physics equation, allowing partners (or parties treated as partners for income tax purposes) to create out of a taxable nil set equal and opposite taxable income and deduction. Specifically, the non-contributing party can claim all of his or her book depreciation as a deduction despite the fact that the property is not generating this much tax depreciation deductions (in other words, despite the ceiling rule). The quid pro quo is that the contributor must recognize offsetting income in equal amount and type. Interestingly enough, this method even can allow the non-contributing party to claim a loss for tax purposes on the sale of property for less than its book value (even if the sale price is more than the property's basis). Treas. Reg. § 1.704–3(d)(7) Ex. 2.

Suppose the contributed property constitutes an intangible within the meaning of Section 197 (such as some intellectual property). In this event, the question becomes how to allocate under Section 704(c) the 15 year amortization allowed by Section 197. If the contributor had purchased the intangible and contributed it to the firm, then the application of Section 704(c) to the firm's amortization under Section 197 is no different than discussed in dealing with depreciation of normal assets. A difference, however, arises if the contributor had created the intangible. Section 197(c)(2) denies amortization for so-called self-created intangibles (in other words, intangibles created by the taxpayer claiming the deduction). As discussed earlier in dealing with contributions, the general approach of Section 197 to non-recognition transactions, such as a contribution under Section 721, is for the transferee to step into the shoes of the transferor—meaning that the firm cannot claim an amortization of what was a self-created intangible for the contributor. Accordingly, the regulations take the position that the firm cannot make a curative allocation to the non-contributing owners in order to make up for the gap between the basis and fair market value of what was a self-created intangible for the contributor. On the other hand, the regulations allow the parties to agree to make a remedial allocation, under which the non-contributing owners can gain amortization deductions for what was a self-created intangible by the contributor, so long as the contributor recognizes offsetting income. Treas. Reg. § 1.197–2(g)(4). (The rationale for what otherwise would seem to be an inexplicable distinction is that, unlike a curative allocation, a remedial allocation effectively constitutes the equivalent of a sale of the contributed asset to the extent of the income recognized by the contributor; thereby avoiding the conclusion that self-created status follows property transferred in a non-recognition transaction.)

As these examples illustrate, allocations to meet Section 704(c) can be complex and lead to unintended consequences. Moreover, picking allocation methods to save net taxes risks being labeled unreasonable. Is there any way to avoid the need for such accounting? If the total disparity between the basis and value of all properties contributed by a partner (or party treated as a partner for income tax purposes) during a year is small enough (less than both 15 percent and $20,000), then the regulations allow the parties, if they wish, either to ignore Section 704(c) for such properties or to defer the application of Section 704(c) until the property is disposed of—thus avoiding the complexity of reflecting Section 704(c) in computation of depreciation. Treas. Reg. § 1.704–3(e)(1).

Suppose, instead of selling property subject to a Section 704(c) allocation, the firm distributes the property to a partner (or person taxed as a partner), who did not contribute the property. Could this circumvent the goal of Section 704(c) to ensure that the contributing partner ultimately recognizes any pre-contribution appreciation (or depreciation)? Section 704(c)(1)(B) exists to prevent this. Under this section, partners, who contribute property with built-in gain or loss to a partnership, recognize gain or loss if the partnership distributes the property to another partner within seven years of the contribution. Reinforcing this result, Section 737 taxes partners, who contribute appreciated property to a partnership, and, within seven years of the contribution, receive other property from the partnership. Under Section 737, the recipient partner must recognize the lesser of the difference between the fair market value of the distributed property and the partner's basis in the firm, or the amount which the partner would have recognized under Section 704(c)(1)(B) had the firm distributed all appreciated property it received from that partner within seven years to another partner.

The discussion thus far has focused on appreciated property contributed to the partnership (or firm electing partnership tax treatment). Suppose a partner (or a person treated as a partner for tax purposes) contributes property with a fair market value less than its basis. Section 704(c)(1)(C) is designed to ensure that only the contributing partner recognizes the pre-contribution loss on the firm's sale or other disposition of the property. The section works by capping the carryover basis of property contributed to a partnership (or firm treated as a partnership for tax purposes) at the property's fair market value at the time of the contribution for purposes of computing gain or loss for the non-contributing partners on the disposition of the property. For example, if the contributed property had a basis of $2000, but a fair market value upon contribution of only $1000, the non-contributing partners' gain or loss on the disposition of this property by the partnership would be calculated by treating the basis of the property as

$1000, rather than the $2000 carryover basis the partnership received under Section 723. This works simply enough if the partnership sells the property at a price equal to, or less than, the property's fair market value at the date of the contribution—albeit, the partnership or LLC operating agreement had better allocate all of the pre-contribution loss to the contributing partner as the only person who can recognize it. What happens, however, if the property appreciates in value after its contribution? This could lead to the rather odd result of the non-contributing partners recognizing gain on a transaction in which the property sold for an amount equal to the contributor's basis on the date of the contribution—meaning zero gain for the partnership as a whole. Moreover, since Section 704(c)(1)(C) does not speak to the basis of the property for purposes of computing gain or loss to the contributing partner, it is not clear that the contributing partner could recognize a loss offsetting the gain recognized by the non-contributing partners in this situation. Further, if the contributing partner leaves prior to the firm selling or otherwise disposing of the property, the pre-contribution loss will be lost for anyone, since the transferee of the contributing partner is treated as another non-contributing partner. As mentioned earlier in this chapter, these results may counsel against contributing (as opposed to selling, leasing or loaning) to a partnership (or firm electing partnership tax treatment) property whose value at the time of contribution is less than the contributor's basis.

3. The ability to allocate tax items among partners (or persons taxed as partners) sometimes tempts persons to bring into a firm "partners", whose function is solely to serve as a receptacle into which to shift taxable income. One common example of this involves "family partnerships." Individuals with substantial taxable income stemming from their services, capital or both, often take in as partners (or limited partners or LLC members) close relatives who have lower outside income. When these "partners" contribute neither significant services nor capital to the venture, the suspicion is strong that the only reason for the "partnership" is tax avoidance through shifting of income to lower bracket taxpayers. Such suspicions may still exist where the low income individuals contribute capital previously given to them by the high income family member. The I.R.S. has repeatedly attacked such schemes using the anticipatory assignment of income doctrine. *See, e.g., Commissioner v. Culbertson,* 337 U.S. 733 (1949).

In *Culbertson,* the court provided the following guidance as to when so-called family partnerships are vulnerable to attack:

> The question is * * * whether, considering all the facts—the agreement, the conduct of the parties in execution of its provisions, their statements, the testimony of disinterested persons, the relationship of the parties, their respective abilities and capital contributions, and actual control of income and the purposes for which it is used, and any other facts throwing light on their true intent—the parties in good faith and acting with a business purpose intended to join together in the present conduct of the enterprise.

* * *

> Unquestionably a court's determination that the services contributed by a partner are not "vital" and that he has not participated in "management and control of the business" or contributed "original capital" has the effect of placing a heavy burden on the taxpayer to show the bona fide intent of the parties to join together as partners. But such a determination is not conclusive. * * * If, upon a consideration of all the facts, it is found that the partners joined together in good faith to conduct a business having agreed that the services or capital to be contributed presently by each is of such value to the partnership that the contributor should participate in the distribution of profits, that is sufficient.
>
> * * *
>
> We did not say that the donee of an intra-family gift could never become a partner through investment of the capital in the family partnership * * *. The facts may indicate, on the contrary, that the amount thus contributed and the income therefrom should be considered the property of the donee for tax, as well as general law, purposes. In the *Tower* and *Lusthaus* cases this Court * * * found that the purported gift, whether or not technically complete, had made no substantial change in the economic relation of members of the family to the income. In each case the husband continued to manage and control the business as before, and income from the property given to the wife and invested by her in the partnership continued to be used in the business or expended for family purposes. We characterized the results of the transactions entered into between husband and wife as "a mere paper reallocation of income among the family members," noting that "The actualities of their relation to the income did not change." * * * This, we thought, provided ample grounds for the finding that no true partnership was intended; that the husband was still the true earner of the income.
>
> * * *
>
> The fact that transfers to members of the family group may be mere camouflage does not, however, mean that they invariably are. The *Tower* case recognized that one's participation in control and management of the business is a circumstance indicating an intent to be a bona fide partner despite the fact that the capital contributed originated elsewhere in the family. If the donee of property who then invests it in the family partnership exercises dominion and control over that property—and through that control influences the conduct of the partnership and the disposition of its income—he may well be a true partner. 337 U.S. at 742–47.

Congress enacted Section 704(e) after *Culbertson* to provide further guidance in this area. Section 704(e)(1) creates a safe harbor by considering individuals to be partners, even if they obtain their interest by gift, so long as they own a capital interest in a partnership (or entity electing income tax treatment as a partnership) where capital is a material income-producing factor. If capital is not a material income-producing factor (such as in a law firm), or a purported partner does not own a capital interest, then the guidelines set forth in *Culbertson* remain relevant. Section 704(e)(2) attempts to prevent income shifting in partnerships where an interest was created by gift by requiring any allocation of income to give reasonable compensation for the donor's services to the firm and not to give the donee a disproportionate return on capital.

Income shifting among family members is not the only circumstance in which nominal partners may enter into partnerships (or entities electing income tax treatment as partnerships) whose purpose is tax avoidance. For example, consider the following scheme described by the court in *Boca Investerings Partnership v. United States*, 314 F.3d 625, 626–27 (D.C. Cir.2003):

> In 1990, American Home Products (AHP), sold a subsidiary, Boyle–Midway, for a capital gain of more than $605 million. Just before the sale, Merrill Lynch approached AHP with an investment plan which would enable AHP to claim paper tax losses of a comparable amount, while generating only about $8 million in actual losses. * * *
>
> The plan require[d] the formation of a partnership between a United States corporation and a foreign corporation not subject to United States tax, combined with a series of investment transactions that exploit the terms of Temp. Treas. Reg. § 15A.453–1(c)(3)(I). That regulation provides a tax accounting rule for contingent installment sales. * * * The partnership formed between the domestic entities and the foreign entities takes advantage of this regulation by first buying, then immediately selling a debt instrument on an installment basis.
>
> [A]lthough the transaction is basically a wash, generating hardly any economic gain or loss, Merrill Lynch's lawyers' interpretation of the relevant provisions allows the partnership to claim a massive tax gain, which is allocated to the foreign partner, and a massive tax loss, which the U.S. corporation keeps for itself. This * * * essentially describes the transactions in which AHP * * * and its foreign partners, Addiscombe and Syringa[, two Netherlands Antilles special purpose corporations created for this partnership], engaged after forming the Boca partnership. The massive loss AHP was able to claim for tax purposes was then used to offset the tax gain it realized from the sale of its subsidiary, Boyle–Midway.

In *Boca Inverterings*, the court applied *Culbertson* to prevent AHP from recognizing this so-called loss:

> Boca argues that the district court made the finding that the parties "intended to, and did, organize Boca as a partnership to share the income, expenses, gains and losses from Boca's investments." This finding, contrary to the appellee's assertion, does not satisfy the legal test for recognition of this type of partnership for tax purposes * * *. In order to satisfy the legal test for this type of partnership, the district court must have found a non-tax business purpose need for the

partnership in order to accomplish the goals of the partners. In this case, there is no evidence of any need for AHP to enter into the Boca partnership with the newly-minted Addiscombe and Syringa in order to invest in the [debt instruments purchased and resold by the partnership]. Nor is there even evidence of any non-tax purpose in the use of the partnerships. The only logical explanation then, for the partnership's formation was the exploitation of Temp. Treas. Reg. § 15A.453–1(c)(3)(I) and the gain of a paper tax loss to absorb its enormous capital gains. * * *

* * * We do not of course suggest that in every transaction using a partnership a taxpayer must justify that to[sic] form, but * * * where taxpayers use an "elaborate partnership" with entities created solely for the purpose of the questioned transaction, "the absence of a non-tax business purpose" is fatal to the recognition of the entity for the tax purposes. * * *. 314 F.3d at 632.

As an alternative to challenging the bona fides of the overall partnership under judicially created doctrines as in *Culbertson* and *Boca Investerings*, the Internal Revenue Service promulgated a partnership "anti-abuse" regulation. Treas. Reg. § 1.701–2. Under this regulation, the Service can challenge transactions which have a principal purpose of tax reduction in a manner inconsistent with the intent of the partnership tax code provisions. While this appears to be a rather broad and vague standard, the examples in the regulation suggest a narrower focus on transactions involving nominal partners, or involving partnerships which do not carry on a bona fide business. By contrast, the regulation does not appear to condemn the normal desire of parties engaged in business to select and operate their form of business with an eye toward minimizing taxes. (The regulation also sets out the Internal Revenue Service's position that certain limitations in the tax code apply directly to partners, rather than treating partnerships as entities.)

4. The discussion thus far has considered the limits imposed on parties who are aware of and attempt to exploit fully their ability to allocate various items of income, gain, loss, deduction and credit. What happens to parties who omit planning in this regard? If the partnership or LLC operating agreement fails to allocate income, gain, loss, deduction or credit (or any item thereof), or if the allocation lacks substantial economic effect, Section 704(b) determines the partners' (or parties treated as partners for income tax purposes) distributive shares in accordance with their interests in the firm. Among the factors useful in defining the parties' interests in the firm for purposes of Section 704(b) are:

(i) The parties' relative contributions to the firm;

(ii) The interests of the parties in economic profits and losses (if different from that in taxable income or loss);

(iii) The interest of the parties in cash flow and other distributions; and

(iv) The rights of the parties to distributions of capital and other property upon liquidation. Treas. Reg. § 1.704–1(b)(3)(ii).

This "interests in the firm" criteria works well enough in a very simple situation in which partners (or parties taxed as partners) agree to share all economic interests in the firm (profits, losses, distributions) in proportion to their contributions to capital. Indeed, as mentioned in Chapter II, some practitioners feel they can leave out of the partnership or LLC operating agreement, for such a simple firm, the capital accounting provisions called for under the regulations interpreting Section 704(b), and rely on this "interests in the firm" standard to support reporting tax items in the same ratio. Yet, the approach of having partners share all interests in the firm in proportion to their contributions to capital will not always work well—as, for example, when some partners contribute services, while other contribute capital. In that event, application of this "interest in the partnership" standard creates uncertainty.

Partnership or LLC operating agreements commonly provide for an allocation of "profit," "net profit," "income," "net income," "loss" or "net loss" rather than specifying the various tax items listed in Section 702(a). In this event, the allocation in the agreement controls the allocation of taxable income or loss as well as the other items listed in Section 702(a). *See* S. Rep. No. 938, 94th Cong. 2d Sess. 100 (1976). Notice that if the agreement divides net profits in a different ratio from net losses, various individually reported items of loss, deduction or credit will be allocated according to the profit ratios if the firm makes a net profit, while various income and gain items will be allocated according to the net loss ratios if the firm suffers a net loss. *See* H. Rep. No. 1337, 83d Cong. 2d Sess. A223 (1954); S. Rep. No. 1622, 83d Cong. 2d Sess. 379 (1954). If this is not a desired result, the agreement must allocate specific items. Why might this result ever create a problem?

Often an owner personally pays certain expenses of the firm. Unless there is a special allocation of such expenses to that party, he or she can only deduct the portion of expenses which corresponds to his or her share of firm losses. (The IRS considers the payment to be a contribution to firm capital). *See Stevens v. Commissioner,* 46 T.C. 492 (1966), *aff'd per curiam,* 388 F.2d 298 (6th Cir.1968). Parties anticipating personal payment of expenses might, therefore, do well to include a provision in their partnership or LLC operating agreement specifying their intent in this area.

(ii) Basis, Leverage and At–Risk Limits

IPO II v. Commissioner of Internal Revenue

122 T.C. 295 (2004).

* * *

After concessions,[1] the issue for decision is whether any of the recourse liability incurred by IPO II with respect to the purchase of an aircraft is allocable to Indeck Power Overseas Ltd. (Indeck Overseas).

1. * * * [R]espondent conceded that IPO II correctly reported ordinary losses from [its airplane charter leasing] activity of $1,385,457 in 1998 and $752,824 in 1999.

Background

* * *

IPO II is a limited liability company organized in 1996 under the *Illinois Limited Liability Company Act.* * * *

IPO II was treated as a partnership for Federal income tax purposes for the years in issue. The members of IPO II are Mr. Forsythe and Indeck Overseas. Indeck Overseas is an S corporation in which Mr. Forsythe owned 100 percent of the outstanding shares during the years in issue. The members' interests in the profits and losses of IPO II were allocated during the years in issue, and are currently allocated, as follows: Indeck Overseas, 99 units; Mr. Forsythe, 1 unit.

[The IPO II operating agreement disavowed any liability of members to third parties or to make capital contributions to the company, and provided that profits and losses were allocated in proportion to units.]

* * *

On December 27, 1996, IPO II purchased a Cessna Citation VII aircraft. The total purchase price of the aircraft ($9,406,175) was funded by a loan from Nationsbanc Leasing Corp. of North Carolina (Nationsbanc).

To secure the loan, IPO II and Nationsbanc entered into an Aircraft Loan and Security Agreement (the loan and security agreement) on December 27, 1996. * * *

In connection with the loan, Mr. Forsythe [and two other corporations in which Mr. Forsythe was the majority shareholder] * * * each entered into a guaranty agreement with Nationsbanc [to pay the aircraft loan if IPO II defaulted].

* * * On July 12, 2002, * * * respondent determined * * * that 100 percent of the recourse liability shown on the Schedules K–1 [of IPO II's partnership tax returns for the years in question] * * * was allocable to Mr. Forsythe, and, therefore, none of the liability was allocable to Indeck Overseas. [This apparently resulted in Indeck Overseas being unable to utilize the loss deductions allocated to it from IPO II's aircraft chartering business.]

On September 11, 2002, petitioner filed a Petition for Readjustment of Partnership Items * * * with the Court * * *. Petitioner alleged, inter alia, that respondent erred in the determination that the liability shown on the respective Schedules K-1 for the years in issue is fully allocable to Mr. Forsythe, and in no part to Indeck Overseas.

Discussion

* * *

II. Allocation of Recourse Liability

A partner's distributive share of partnership loss is allowed only to the extent of the adjusted basis of the partner's interest in the partnership at the end of the partnership year in which such loss occurred. *Sec. 704(d).* As relevant here, the partner's adjusted basis in the partnership interest is the basis of such interest determined under *section 722*, increased or decreased by the partner's distributive share of income, loss, and applicable expenditures. *Sec. 705(a)(1)* and *(2).* The basis of an interest in a partnership acquired by a contribution of property, including money, is the amount of money and the adjusted basis of such property to the partner at the time of contribution, increased by the amount of any gain recognized under *section 721(b)* at the time. *Sec. 722.* Any increase in a partner's share of liabilities of the partnership is considered a contribution by such partner to the partnership, and, consequently, increases the basis of the partner's interest in the partnership. *Sec. 752(a).*

The regulations guide our allocation of the instant partnership recourse liability. *Section 1.752–1(a)(1),* Income Tax Regs., defines a partnership liability as a recourse liability "to the extent that any partner or related person bears the economic risk of loss for that liability under *section 1.752–2.*" *Section 1.752–2,* Income Tax Regs., provides the test for determining whether a partner or related person bears the economic risk of loss. The determination to be made is whether, if the partnership were constructively liquidated, the partner or related person would be obligated to make a payment when the liability became due and payable. *Sec. 1.752–2(b)(1),* Income Tax Regs.

In a constructive liquidation, the regulations provide that the following events are deemed to occur:

(i) All of the partnership's liabilities become payable in full;

(ii) With the exception of property contributed to secure a partnership liability, all of the partnership's assets, including cash, have a value of zero;

(iii) The partnership disposes of all of its property in a fully taxable transaction for no consideration (except relief from liabilities for which the creditor's right to repayment is limited solely to one or more assets of the partnership);

(iv) All items of income, gain, loss, or deduction are allocated among the partners; and

(v) The partnership liquidates.

Sec. 1.752–2(b)(1)(i)-(v), Income Tax Regs.

In a constructive liquidation, the determination of which partner or related person has an obligation to make a payment is "based on the facts and circumstances at the time of the determination." *Sec. 1.752–2(b)(3),* Income

Tax Regs. Such facts and circumstances take into account all statutory and contractual obligations relating to the partnership liability, including contractual obligations outside of the partnership agreement such as guaranties. Id. Further, the regulations assume that all partners and related persons who have obligations actually perform those obligations, "unless the facts and circumstances indicate a plan to circumvent or avoid the obligation." *Sec. 1.752–2(b)(6)*, Income Tax Regs.

Initially, we must determine whether Indeck Overseas, as a member of IPO II, was required by statute, by IPO II's operating agreement, or by any other contractual arrangements it entered into to directly pay the Nationsbanc loan or any other obligations of IPO II. The Illinois Limited Liability Company Act (LLC Act) provides, in relevant part:

> *section 10–10*. Liability of members and managers.
>
> (a) Except [if provided to the contrary in the LLC's articles] * * *, the debts, obligations, and liabilities of a limited liability company, whether arising in contract, tort, or otherwise, are solely the debts, obligations, and liabilities of the company. A member or manager is not personally liable for a debt, obligation, or liability of the company solely by reason of being or acting as a member or manager.

* * *

Section 2.4 of the [IPO II] operating agreement * * * provides that no member or manager of IPO II is obligated for any debts, obligations, or liabilities of IPO II. Moreover, the LLC Act does not establish a statutory obligation on the part of Indeck Overseas to contribute to IPO II to meet IPO II's obligations, either during its operation or upon its liquidation and dissolution, unless a promise is otherwise made by Indeck Overseas to contribute. The record is devoid of any evidence of a promise by Indeck Overseas to contribute to IPO II or to otherwise directly become responsible for IPO II's debts, obligations, or liabilities including the Nationsbanc loan. Indeck Overseas did not guarantee the Nationsbanc loan. Consequently, there is no evidence that in a constructive liquidation Indeck Overseas would directly bear the economic risk of loss for the Nationsbanc loan.

* * *

Mr. Forsythe bore the economic risk of loss with regard to the recourse liability because he personally guaranteed the full amount of the Nationsbanc loan and had no rights to "reimbursement, contribution, exoneration or indemnity (or any similar right)". See *sec. 1.752–2(b)(3)(i)*, Income Tax Regs. * * * Mr. Forsythe and Indeck Overseas, as common owners of interests in IPO II, may not [under the regulations] be treated as related persons for purposes of all determinations of economic risk of loss. Therefore, Mr. Forsythe's economic risk of loss as guarantor cannot be attributed to Indeck Overseas, as conceded by petitioner. [Because Indeck Overseas would only be related to the other corporation guaranteeing the loan through the common ownership of both corporations by Mr. Forsythe, and because Mr. Forsythe's common ownership is disregarded due to the fact he also was an owner of IPO II, the court rejected the contention that the guarantee by the other corporation should be attributed to Indeck Overseas as a related party.]

* * *

Therefore, we hold that none of the recourse liability incurred by IPO II with respect to the purchase of the aircraft is allocable to Indeck Overseas.

* * *

NOTES

1. In *IPO II*, just as in *PNRC*, a partner to whom the agreement allocated 99 percent of the firm's losses apparently was unable to deduct the losses. Here, however, the problem came from Section 704(d), rather than Section 704(b). As the court points out, Section 704(d) allows loss deductions only to the extent of the partner's (or person taxed as a partner) basis in the firm at the end of the year during which the loss occurred. The IPO II operating agreement allocated 99 percent of the firm's losses to Indeck Overseas; but Indeck Overseas apparently lacked sufficient basis in its interest in IPO II to take advantage the losses under Section 704(d). By contrast, Mr. Forsythe, the party to whom the IPO II agreement allocated only 1 percent of the losses, had plenty of basis in his interest in the firm to have been able to use all of the firm's losses. Instead of the unused losses going to Forsythe, however, Indeck Overseas is entitled to carry the losses forward and use them at such time as it obtains additional basis in the firm—if it ever does. *See* Treas. Reg. 1.704–1(d)(1). Ironically—and making one wonder about the competence of whomever put this deal together—Indeck Overseas was itself an S corporation owned entirely by Forsythe, meaning that the objective was to flow the losses through to Forsythe anyway.

How can a partner (or LLC member taxed as a partner, like Indeck Overseas) increase the partner's basis in the firm in order to utilize more deductions? One way is to make additional contributions. I.R.C. §§ 705(a), 722. Coming up with additional contributions, however, may not be a desirable option. Undistributed firm income also increases basis (I.R.C. § 705(a)), but, if the firm is generating undistributed income, one would not be dealing with a firm generating tax deductible net losses. Most significantly for much tax planning, and at the heart of the dispute in *IPO II*, liabilities of the firm increase the owners' bases.

2. Section 752(a) treats any increase in a partner's (or a party treated as a partner for income tax purposes) share of the firm's liabilities as a contribution of money by that party. As stated before, contributions of money increase basis. One way in which to increase the amount of firm liabilities that is each partner's (or party treated as a partner for tax purposes) share is for the firm to incur more debt—as IPO II did when it borrowed money to buy the airplane. The other way to increase a partner's (or party treated as a partner for tax purposes) share of firm liabilities is to increase the

fraction of the firm's total liabilities which is that partner's share—which is the issue in *IPO II*. In either event, the practical problem with use of debt to increase basis is that loans presumably must be repaid. The owners hope, of course, to repay the loans out of later business profits. This creates the problem sometimes referred to as "phantom income": the fact that the parties treated as partners for income tax purposes must report their distributive share of the firm's taxable income even though the firm uses the income to repay liabilities. *See* I.R.C. § 702. Moreover, there is always the risk that the business will not generate sufficient profits to repay the debt. If the firm thereupon obtains a release from its liabilities, this constitutes taxable income to the partners (or parties taxed as partners). *E.g., Gershkowitz v. Commissioner,* 88 T.C. 984 (1987). Worse, if partners in an ordinary partnership cannot obtain a release, they are personally liable.

Several methods exist to reduce a partner's risk from firm debt. These include agreements by another owner to pay the debt, limited partner status, forming an LLP or an LLC, and the use of non-recourse loans. As illustrated by *IPO II*, reducing exposure to firm debt (as Indeck Overseas did by being a member in an LLC) can reduce one's share of the firm's liabilities for purposes of Section 752—in Indeck Oversea's case to zero percent of the debt incurred to buy the airplane. Is there a way to square the circle and both reduce one's exposure to debt, but still have the debt count as one's share of the firm's liabilities for purposes of Section 752?

To answer this question, one must ask what exactly does Section 752 mean by each partner's "share" of liabilities. As noted earlier, each partner in an ordinary partnership is potentially liable for the entire debt of the firm. Nevertheless, each partner cannot claim the entire amount of firm debt as his or her share of liabilities, since that would mean the partners together would claim more than 100 percent of the debt. Instead, the partners must take into account that upon liquidation they have rights of indemnity and obligations to contribute, until each bears his or her agreed share of the firm's losses. U.P.A. §§ 18(a), 40(d); R.U.P.A. § 807(b). Hence, share of liabilities for purposes of Section 752 normally means that portion of the firm's liabilities for which the partner bears what the tax regulations refer to as the "economic risk of loss"—i.e. the amount of debt he or she could be called upon to pay either directly to the creditor or through contributions to the partnership, without claim for reimbursement by the firm or other partners. Treas. Reg. § 1.752–2(a), (b). The regulations test this risk by asking what would happen under the parties' agreement(s) in the event of an immediate liquidation of the partnership in which all the property sells for nothing (except for relief from non-recourse debt), there is no cash left and all the debts became due. The regulations expressly ignore the prospect that a partner may be unable to pay his or her agreed share of the debt. Treas. Reg. § 1.752–2(b)(6).

In a simple partnership, the partners' capital contributions and loss sharing agreement dictate their share of the liabilities, since upon a liquidation each partner would need to pony up his or her share of the firm's losses, less whatever he or she already contributed. *See* Treas. Reg. § 1.752–2(f) Ex. 2. If one thinks about the matter for awhile, one realizes that, if the agreement in such a partnership allocates losses in proportion to contributions, the partners' percentage shares of liabilities are the same as their shares of losses. Calculating which party bears the "economic risk of loss", however, may be less than straightforward in cases where the loss allocation does not follow simple ratios, or where the ratios change over time or upon the occurrence of certain events. Notice, along these lines, since loss allocations impact each party's share of liabilities, changes in loss allocations may alter the owners' shares in the liabilities of the firm, resulting in a decrease in some shares. Under Section 752(b), a decrease in a partner's (or party treated as a partner for income tax purposes) share of the firm's liabilities constitutes a distribution to that party. This raises the disturbing prospect that such shifts in loss ratios could trigger recognition of income. *See* I.R.C. §§ 731, 751.

Turning from the simple partnership, various techniques for reducing exposure to debt decrease the risk of loss and hence affect the partner's (or the party treated as a partner for income tax purposes) share of liabilities. Hence, under the regulations, a partner does not share in liabilities which another owner has agreed to pay without claim for reimbursement. Treas. Reg. § 1.752–2(b)(1), (5). Because a limited partner is not personally liable for debts beyond the amount he or she agreed to contribute, a limited partner's share of liabilities normally cannot exceed the additional amount, if any, he or she promised to put in beyond that already contributed. (What happens, however, if the limited partner promised to make an additional contribution, but that obligation is contingent upon future events (such as a discretionary call by the general partners)? See Treas. Reg. § 1.752–2(b)(4) (disregard if unlikely that the obligation ever will be discharged or is too uncertain).) The critical point to notice is that the limitation on one partner's or limited partner's exposure to liability in these examples shifts a greater share of the liabilities for purposes of Section 752 to other partners.

Suppose, however, no partner faces any risk of personal liability for a debt owed by the firm. Historically, in ordinary and limited partnerships, this happened when creditors agreed to make non-recourse loans secured by some collateral. More recently, state laws creating limited liability for the owners of LLCs and LLPs mean that even ordinary unsecured creditors of such entities have no recourse against the members or partners—at least barring a personal guarantee or a promise by LLC members to make additional contributions. If no partner (or party treated as a partner for income tax purposes) faces an economic risk of loss beyond his or her existing investment, one might assume that no partner has a share of the liabilities for purposes of Section 752. This assumption, however, turns out to be wrong. Critically, under Section 752, liabilities of a partnership (or an entity electing income tax treatment as a partnership) increase the owners' basis in their interests in the firm even though no owner has personal liability for the debt.

Yet, if no partner (or party treated as a partner for income tax purposes) bears an economic risk of loss corresponding to the liability, how can one determine which owners have what share of such a liability? The answer provided by the regulations is to allocate so-called non-recourse debts—defined as a debt for which no partner has personal liability—among all partners (or parties treated as partners for income tax purposes) first in proportion to the gain the partners would recognize by virtue of either Section 704(b) or (c) upon immediate disposition of all property securing non-recourse loans in satisfaction of the loans and for no other consideration, and whatever is left according to the ratio in which the partners share firm profits. Treas. Reg. § 1.752–3. The rationale is to coordinate with the rules governing allocations under Section 704, albeit, as discussed earlier, the rules governing allocations under Section 704(b) do not contemplate losses financed through unsecured non-recourse loans. The regulations call for determining the partners' shares of firm profits by considering all of the facts and circumstances, but allow partners to allocate profits specifically for purposes of allocating non-recourse liabilities so long as the allocation is reasonably consistent with allocations that have substantial economic effect, or that take into account any gain recognizable under Section 704(c) upon the disposition of property securing a non-recourse loan for more than the amount of the loan. Incidentally, since profit allocations impact each partner's share of non-recourse liabilities, changes in the profit allocation under the agreement can produce a decrease in a partner's share of liabilities—which Section 752 treats as a distribution of cash to the partner. This creates the ironic situation in which a decrease (not an increase) in a partner's profit share could produce taxable income for that partner.

This brings the discussion to the issue in *IPO II*. Because IPO II was a limited liability company, normally both Forsythe and Indeck Overseas would not have faced any personal liability from the debt incurred by the company to buy the airplane. The debt would have been a non-recourse loan, as defined by the regulations, and allocated, for purposes of Section 752, 99 percent to Indeck Overseas (reflecting the LLC operating agreement's allocation of 99 percent of profits and losses to Indeck Overseas). The problem arose because the lender (showing understandable caution) required Forsythe to personally guarantee the loan. The result, under the regulations, is to treat the debt as a recourse loan, with the risk of loss on the guaranteeing party (Forsythe). Treas. Reg. § 1.752–2(f) Ex. 5.

Finally, issues occasionally can arise as to what constitutes a liability for purposes of Section 752. The general standard is that a liability is an obligation that (1) creates or increases basis of any of the obligor's assets (including cash), (2) gives rise to an immediate deduction, or (3) gives rise to an expense that is not deductible nor properly chargeable to capital. Treas. Reg. § 1.752–1(a)(4)(i). While this seems very expansive, there are obligations it does not pick up—for example, accounts payable of a cash basis taxpayer (since these are deductible expenses, but only later when paid). *See also* Rev. Rul. 88–77, 1988–2 C.B. 128. The I.R.S. also has taken the position on occasions when the price of the securing property is inflated or the security is otherwise grossly inadequate, or where there are other indications the debtor never intends to repay, that non-recourse loans are too contingent or illusory to be liabilities. *See, e.g., Brountas v. Commissioner*, 692 F.2d 152 (1st Cir.1982).

3. The impact of increasing basis by non-recourse debt is to allow parties treated as partners for income tax purposes to avoid the risk of personal liability and still obtain tax benefits in excess of the amount invested. Section 465, however, puts a damper on such efforts to "have one's cake and eat it too." This section limits the amount of any loss that a taxpayer (including, but limited to, a person taxed as a partner) may deduct in connection with a business to the amount by which the taxpayer is at risk in the business at the close of the taxable year in which the loss occurs.

The key concept behind this limitation is, of course, "at risk." Section 465 generally deems a taxpayer to be "at risk" for the amount of cash, and the adjusted basis of other property, he or she contributed to the venture (such as the partnership). I.R.C. § 465(b)(1)(A). In addition, the taxpayer is at risk for amounts borrowed for use in the venture to the extent the taxpayer has personal liability for those debts. I.R.C. § 465(b)(2)(A). By contrast, loans providing funding for the venture, for which the taxpayer has no personal liability, generally do not increase the amount by which the taxpayer is at risk.

Of course, tax rules are never this simple, and various contractual arrangements can impact the amount by which a taxpayer is at risk. For example, if the taxpayer uses some of his or her personal property to secure what is otherwise a non-recourse loan to the business, this increases the amount by which the taxpayer is at risk up to the fair market value of the property. I.R.C. § 465(b)(2)(B). On the other hand, a taxpayer will not be "at risk" for money contributed to the venture to the extent that a contract—such as insurance against business losses (as opposed to casualty or liability insurance), or an indemnity agreement—protects the taxpayer against loss of the contribution. I.R.C. § 465(b)(4). Significantly, loans by other persons interested in the venture (except as a creditor), or who are related to the taxpayer (within the meaning of Section 267(b)), do not count in a taxpayer's amount at risk. I.R.C. § 465(b)(3); Treas. Reg. §§ 1.465–8, 1.465–20. Hence, loans by partners (or parties treated as partners for income tax purposes) to the firm generally count as liabilities for purposes of Section 752, but do not count for the at risk limits of Section 465. As mentioned earlier in discussing loans by partners, limited partners or LLC members to their firm, this could be a significant tax disadvantage for such loans—as opposed to contributions of money to the firm.

If the venture makes money, the undistributed income of the partnership (or entity electing partnership tax treatment) increases the partner's amount at risk (even if used to pay off non-recourse loans). *E.g., Lansburgh v. Commissioner*, 92 T.C. 448 (1989). If the venture loses money, the amount of any loss which Section 465 allowed the taxpayer to use for the year reduces the taxpayer's amount at risk. I.R.C. 465(b)(5). If the venture loses more money than the taxpayer has at risk, the taxpayer may carry forward the suspended losses to use in a future year when he or she increases his or her amount at risk. I.R.C. § 465(a)(2).

(iii) Passive Losses

Mordkin v. Commissioner of Internal Revenue

71 T.C.M. (CCH) 2796 (1996).

* * *

Petitioner Arnold P. Mordkin is an attorney * * * who specialized during all relevant periods in personal injury and medical malpractice matters. * * *

In March 1982 and October 1985, petitioner purchased unit no. 2303 and unit no. 2301, respectively, at a condominium development known as Crestwood Condominiums (Crestwood) that is located in Snowmass Village, Colorado (Snowmass Village). During the years at issue, Crestwood had 141 condominium units that were owned by various persons.

During all relevant periods, Crestwood Condominium Association, Inc. (Crestwood Association), a membership association whose members consisted of all the Crestwood condominium owners, was responsible for the operations at Crestwood. During those periods, Crestwood Association had a nine-member board of directors (board) that was elected by the members of that association and that oversaw, and made policy regarding, its operations.

During all relevant periods, Crestwood Association ran two separate and distinct operations: (1) Those operations affecting all Crestwood condominium owners that involved providing services to, and fulfilling the obligations of, those owners, including maintaining and repairing Crestwood's common areas and building structures * * * and (2) those operations affecting only those Crestwood condominium owners who desired to rent their condominium units that involved marketing and managing the rental of those units for short-term periods and providing extensive hotel-type services to the patrons of such rental operations.

* * *

During the years at issue, petitioner rented both of his condominium units. The average period of customer use for petitioner's condominium units was less than seven days.

* * *

During the years at issue, Crestwood Association maintained a full-time nonmanagement staff of 40 to 85 employees (Crestwood staff) and a full-time management staff of six to eight employees (Crestwood management staff). The Crestwood staff and the Crestwood management staff ran the daily Crestwood Association owners' operations and lodge operations.

* * *

During 1989 and 1990, petitioner was president of Crestwood Association, chairperson of the board of Crestwood Association, and chairperson of the executive committee of that board (executive committee) that was vested with the authority of the board and was to act in the absence of a meeting of the board. On April 7, 1990, petitioner was appointed chairperson of the management compensation committee of the board (management compensation committee). Petitioner received no compensation during the years at issue for serving in any of those positions.

* * *

During each of the years at issue, petitioner attended the three board meetings that were held at Crestwood in the months of January, April, and September, and, as chairperson of the board, presided over those meetings.

* * *

In preparation for an upcoming board meeting during each of the years 1989 and 1990, petitioner met with * * * the Crestwood management employees to obtain their perspectives on issues that were to be raised at the upcoming board meeting, and worked with those employees to prepare information packets offered to board members and owners.

* * *

OPINION

* * *

The General Framework of Section 469 and the Regulations Thereunder and the Positions of the Parties

Pursuant to section 469(a), a passive activity loss of an individual for the taxable year is generally not allowed as a deduction for such year. For this purpose, the passive activity loss for the taxable year is generally the amount, if any, by which the passive activity deductions for the taxable year exceed the passive activity gross income for such year. Sec. 469(d)(1) * * *.

As pertinent here, section 469(c) defines the term "passive activity" to include: (1) Any activity which involves the conduct of any trade or business and in which the taxpayer does not materially participate, sec. 469(c)(1), and (2) any rental activity without regard to whether or not the taxpayer materially participates in the activity, sec. 469(c)(2), (4).

For purposes of section 469(c)(1), the term "trade or business" is defined in section 469(c)(6) to include any activity in connection with a trade or business or any activity with respect to which expenses are allowable as a deduction under section 212.

For purposes of section 469(c)(2), the term "rental activity" is defined in section 469(j)(8) as any activity where payments are principally for the use of tangible property. However, an activity involving the use of tangible property is not a rental activity for a taxable year, inter alia, if for such taxable year the average period of customer use for such property is seven days or less. Sec. 1.4691T(e)(3)(i) and (ii)(A), Temporary Income Tax Regs.

In the instant case, the parties have stipulated that the average period of customer use of petitioner's condominiums at Crestwood was less than seven days during each of the years at issue. Respondent concedes on brief, and the parties thus agree, that, consequently, petitioner's rental activity at Crestwood during each such year is not a rental activity as defined in section 469(j)(8) and the regulations thereunder and thus is not a passive activity under section 469(c)(2). * * *

The parties do not dispute that petitioner's rental activity at Crestwood during each year at issue constitutes an activity that is treated as a trade or business under section 469(c)(6). Consequently, petitioner's rental activity at Crestwood will constitute a passive activity under section 469(c)(1) for each of those years if he did not materially participate in that activity during each such year.

Section 469(h)(1) provides that generally an individual shall be treated as materially participating in an activity only if he or she is involved in the operations of the activity on a basis that is regular, continuous, and substantial. Congress expressly authorized the Secretary of the Treasury (Secretary) to prescribe such regulations as may be necessary or appropriate to carry out the provisions of section 469, including regulations that specify what constitutes material participation.

Both temporary and final regulations relating to the meaning of the terms "participation" and "material participation" have been promulgated under section 469. With respect to the term "participation", final regulations issued under section 469 provide that generally "any work done by an individual (without regard to the capacity in which the individual does the work) in connection with an activity in which the individual owns an interest at the time the work is done shall be treated for purposes of this section as participation of the individual in the activity." Sec. 1.469–5(f)(1), Income Tax Regs. Temporary regulations issued under section 469 provide certain exceptions to that definition of participation. As pertinent here, section 1.469–5T(f)(2)(ii)(A), Temporary Income Tax Regs., * * * provides that work done by an individual in such individual's capacity as an investor in an activity shall not be treated as participation by the individual in the activity unless the individual is involved in the day-to-day management or operations of the activity. For this purpose, work done by an individual in such individual's capacity as an investor in an activity includes:

> (1) Studying and reviewing financial statements or reports on operations of the activity;
>
> (2) Preparing or compiling summaries or analyses of the finances or operations of the activity for the individual's own use; and
>
> (3) Monitoring the finances or operations of the activity in a non-managerial capacity. * * *

Temporary regulations relating to the meaning of the term "material participation" in section 469(h)(1) provide that, in general, an individual shall be treated, for purposes of section 469 and the regulations thereunder, as materially participating in an activity for the taxable year if and only if—

(1) The individual participates in the activity for more than 500 hours during such year;

(2) The individual's participation in the activity for the taxable year constitutes substantially all of the participation in such activity of all individuals (including individuals who are not owners of interests in the activity) for such year;

(3) The individual participates in the activity for more than 100 hours during the taxable year, and such individual's participation in the activity for the taxable year is not less than the participation in the activity of any other individual (including individuals who are not owners of interests in the activity) for such year;

(4) The activity is a significant participation activity (within the meaning of paragraph (c) of this section) for the taxable year, and the individual's aggregate participation in all significant participation activities during such year exceeds 500 hours;

(5) The individual materially participated in the activity (determined without regard to this paragraph (a)(5)) for any five taxable years (whether or not consecutive) during the ten taxable years that immediately precede the taxable year;

(6) The activity is a personal service activity (within the meaning of paragraph (d) of this section), and the individual materially participated in the activity for any three taxable years (whether or not consecutive) preceding the taxable year; or

(7) Based on all of the facts and circumstances (taking into account the rules in paragraph (b) of this section), the individual participates in the activity on a regular, continuous, and substantial basis during such year.

* * *

Certain Preliminary Issues

Before turning our attention to the regulatory provisions on which petitioners rely to establish that petitioner materially participated during each of the years at issue in his rental activity at Crestwood, we shall address two preliminary issues.

The first preliminary issue we address is whether respondent is correct in contending that the work done by petitioner in connection with the operations of Crestwood Association was work done in his capacity as an investor in Crestwood under section 1.469–5T(f)(2)(ii)(B), Temporary Income Tax Regs., * * * that does not constitute participation for purposes of section 469 because it is excluded by section 1.4695–T(f)(2)(ii)(A), Temporary Income Tax Regs., *supra*. Our answer is no. During 1989 and 1990, as president of Crestwood Association, chairperson of the board of Crestwood

Association, chairperson of the executive committee, and chairperson of the management compensation committee, petitioner spent time dealing with a wide range of issues relating to the operations of Crestwood Association. By way of illustration, petitioner dealt with issues relating to the installation of the fire protection system at Crestwood, the proposal by the town of Snowmass Village for terminating its ownership of the Crestwood roads and parking lots, employee housing, quality assurance, and management compensation. The work done by petitioner in his capacity as a board member and an officer of Crestwood Association was work he did in the management of the operations of Crestwood Association and was not the type of work that is considered investor participation within the meaning of section 1.469–5T(f)(2)(ii)(B), Temporary Income Tax Regs., *supra*.

The second preliminary issue we address is whether petitioner's involvement as a board member and an officer in the operations of Crestwood Association constitutes participation by petitioner in his rental activity at Crestwood within the meaning of section 1.469–5(f)(1), Income Tax Regs. We note that, in those capacities during the years at issue, petitioner dealt with a wide range of issues that affected not only the two Crestwood condominium units he owned, but also all other Crestwood condominium units. At trial and on brief, petitioners assume, with no discussion or explanation of the basis for such an assumption, that all of the work done by petitioner during the years at issue in his capacity as a board member and an officer of Crestwood Association in connection with the operations of Crestwood Association constitutes work done by him in connection with his rental activity at Crestwood that satisfies the definition of the term "participation" in section 1.469–5(f)(1), Income Tax Regs. Respondent does not dispute, or even address, that assumption. Therefore, we shall proceed on the same assumption, although we are in no way deciding herein that it is a correct assumption.

* * *

Petitioners' Challenge to the Validity of Section 1.469–5T(a)(1), Temporary Income Tax Regs.

Although their argument is not altogether clear, as we understand it, petitioners contend that section 1.469–5T(a)(1), Temporary Income Tax Regs., * * * is invalid because, by requiring an individual to participate in an activity for more than 500 hours during a taxable year in order to be treated as materially participating in that activity for such year, that regulation is quantitative, rather than qualitative, in nature, and, consequently, it is an unreasonable interpretation of section 469(h)(1).

* * *

Based on our examination of section 469 and its legislative history, and section 1.469–5T(a)(1), Temporary Income Tax Regs., * * * we reject petitioners' argument that, because that regulation is quantitative in nature, it is an unreasonable interpretation of section 469(h)(1) and thus is invalid. We conclude that that regulation implements section 469(h)(1) in a reasonable manner by providing as one of seven alternative ways for an individual to satisfy the material participation test of section 469(h)(1) that an individual shall be treated as materially participating in an activity for a taxable year if he or she participates in the activity for more than 500 hours during such year. Accordingly, we hold that regulation to be valid.

Application of * * * *Temporary Income Tax Regs.*

Petitioners claim that petitioner should be treated as having materially participated in his rental activity at Crestwood for each of the years at issue under section 1.469–5T(a)(1), Temporary Income Tax Regs., *supra*, because he was involved in that activity for more than 500 hours during each of those years. * * *

Based on our examination of the entire record before us, we find that petitioners have failed to establish through any reasonable means as required by section 1.469–5T(f)(4), Temporary Income Tax Regs., * * * (1988),[23] that, during each of the years at issue, petitioner's participation in his rental activity at Crestwood exceeded 500 hours. On that record, we have found as a fact that, during each of those years, petitioner spent a total of at least 75, but no more than 135, hours in attending to matters relating to the operations of Crestwood Association and in attending to matters relating exclusively to his two Crestwood condominium units.

* * *

Petitioners claim that petitioner should be treated as having materially participated in his rental activity at Crestwood for each of the years at issue under section 1.469–5T(a)(6), Temporary Income Tax Regs., * * * because his rental activity at Crestwood was a personal service activity and he materially participated in that activity for the three taxable years preceding each of the taxable years at issue. Respondent disagrees with petitioners' contention.

Section 1.469–5T(d), Temporary Income Tax Regs., *supra*, defines the term "personal service activity" as follows:

23. Sec. 1.469–5T(f)(4), Temporary Income Tax Regs., * * * sets forth the manner in which an individual may prove the degree of his or her participation in an activity. It provides that although a taxpayer is not required to maintain contemporaneous daily time reports, logs, or similar documents, the taxpayer must substantiate the level of his or her participation through reasonable means. Reasonable means include, but are not limited to, "the identification of services performed over a period of time and the approximate number of hours spent performing such services during such period, based on appointment books, calendars, or narrative summaries." Sec. 1.469–5T(f)(4), Temporary Income Tax Regs., *supra*.

Our finding that petitioner spent during each year at issue a total of at least 75, but no more than 135, hours on matters relating to the operations of Crestwood Association and on matters relating exclusively to his two Crestwood condominium units is based on the actual amount of time spent by him on such matters as established by the record and our estimate of the time spent by him on such matters where the record does not establish the actual amount of time spent, but contains sufficient evidence from which we were able to estimate the amount of such time.

> (d) Personal service activity. An activity constitutes a personal service activity * * * if such activity involves the performance of personal services in—
>
> (A) The fields of health, law, engineering, architecture, accounting, actuarial science, performing arts, or consulting; or
>
> (B) Any other trade or business in which capital is not a material income-producing factor.

* * *

On the instant record, we find that petitioner's rental activity at Crestwood is not a personal service activity within the meaning of section 1.469–5T(d), Temporary Income Tax Regs., *supra*, even though it involved the furnishing of certain hotel-type services to patrons (e.g., on-site management, daily housekeeping service, and 24–hour switchboard service). Petitioner's rental activity at Crestwood did not involve the performance of personal services in the fields that are specifically identified in that regulation. We further find on the record before us that that activity necessarily employed capital as a substantial, material income-producing factor. In other words, a substantial portion of the gross income of petitioner's rental activity at Crestwood was attributable to his capital investment in his two condominium units, the furnishings in those units, and the common elements of Crestwood consisting of the land, buildings, and other physical facilities of Crestwood.

* * *

Petitioners claim that petitioner should be treated as having materially participated in his rental activity at Crestwood for each of the years at issue under section 1.469–5T(a)(7), Temporary Income Tax Regs., *supra* (facts and circumstances test) because, based on all of the facts and circumstances, he was involved in that activity on a regular, continuous, and substantial basis during each such year. * * *

In advancing their claim that petitioner materially participated in his rental activity at Crestwood under the facts and circumstances test, petitioners disregard the following limitations with respect to the applicability of that test that are set forth in section 1.469–5T(b)(2)(ii) and (iii), Temporary Income Tax Regs., *supra*:

> (ii) Certain management activities. An individual's services performed in the management of an activity shall not be taken into account in determining whether such individual is treated as materially participating in such activity for the taxable year under paragraph (a)(7) of this section unless, for such taxable year—
>
> (A) No person (other than such individual) who performs services in connection with the management of the activity receives compensation described in section 911(d)(2)(A) in consideration for such services; and

(B) No individual performs services in connection with the management of the activity that exceed (by hours) the amount of such services performed by such individual.

(iii) Participation less than 100 hours. If an individual participates in an activity for 100 hours or less during the taxable year, such individual shall not be treated as materially participating in such activity for the taxable year under paragraph (a)(7) of this section.

* * *

We have found as a fact that during each of the years at issue petitioner spent a total of at least 75, but no more than 135, hours in attending to matters relating to the operations of Crestwood Association and in attending to matters relating exclusively to his two Crestwood condominium units. If during either of the years at issue petitioner were involved in his rental activity at Crestwood for 100 hours or less, pursuant to section 1.469–5T(b)(2)(iii), Temporary Income Tax Regs., *supra*, petitioner would not be treated under the facts and circumstances test as having materially participated in that activity for either year.

Assuming arguendo that petitioner were [sic] involved in his rental activity at Crestwood for more than 100 hours during each of the years at issue, petitioner nonetheless could not be treated under the facts and circumstances test as having materially participated in that activity for either of those years because of the limitations set forth in section 1.469–5T(b)(2)(ii)(A) and (B), Temporary Income Tax Regs. * * *. During 1989 and 1990, petitioner was involved in his rental activity at Crestwood almost exclusively through the performance of management services in connection with the operations of Crestwood Association. During each of those years, individuals other than petitioner, including Mr. Dempsey, vice president, chief operating officer, and general manager of Crestwood Association, and Ms. Gahm, assistant general manager of Crestwood Association, participated in petitioner's rental activity at Crestwood by performing management services in connection with the operations of Crestwood Association. Since Mr. Dempsey, Ms. Gahm, and others were compensated during each of the years at issue for the performance of management services in connection with petitioner's rental activity at Crestwood, pursuant to section 1.469–5T(b)(2)(ii)(A), Temporary Income Tax Regs., *supra,* the performance of management services by petitioner cannot be taken into account for the purpose of determining whether petitioner is to be treated under the facts and circumstances test as having materially participated in that activity for each of those years.

In addition, the performance of management services during each of the years at issue in connection with petitioner's rental activity at Crestwood by individuals other than petitioner exceeded, by hours, the performance of management services by petitioner in connection with that activity. Consequently, pursuant to section 1.469–5T(b)(2)(ii)(B), Temporary Income Tax Regs., *supra,* the performance of management services by petitioner cannot be taken into account for the purpose of determining whether petitioner is to be treated under the facts and circumstances test as having materially participated in that activity for each of those years.

On the record before us, we find that petitioners have failed to establish that petitioner is to be treated as having materially participated during each of the years at issue in his rental activity at Crestwood under section 1.469–5T(a)(7), Temporary Income Tax Regs., *supra*.

* * *

NOTE

As Mr. Mordkin found out, Section 469 puts a significant crimp on the ability of taxpayers to utilize losses generated by one business activity (in Mordkin's case, ownership of a couple of condominium units) to offset taxable income generated by other activities (in Mordkin's case, his law practice). Actually, Section 469 does not specifically concern partnerships—indeed, *Mordkin* did not involve a partnership. Instead, the section addresses the ability of taxpayers (which includes partners rather than partnerships) to take advantage of business losses, such as the losses flowed through to the owners of a business treated as a partnership for income tax purposes. Interestingly, however, as noted when discussing choice of business entity in Chapter II, Section 469 excludes from its reach many C corporations. For present purposes, the significance of this exclusion is that partners, limited partners or LLC members, which themselves are C corporations, often do not need to worry about Section 469.

As *Mordkin* demonstrates, the key issue in applying Section 469 is to determine whether one is dealing with a passive activity. A passive activity, as the court explained, is either an activity involving the conduct of a trade or business in which the taxpayer does not materially participate or a rental activity. Actually, it is a little odd to state what the trade or business was in *Mordkin*. Mordkin did not rent out his condominiums enough days to constitute a rental activity under Section 469. Yet, the only business use Mordkin made of the condominiums was as a rental. In any event, as the court states, the definition of a trade or business under Section 469 is whether the activity produces expenses allowable as a business deduction—presumably based upon the logical notion that if the activity does not produce tax deductible business expenses, there will not be any tax deductible business losses to worry about limiting. One other aspect of the trade or business activity concept is worth noting. The focus is not on business entities, but rather on business activities. Hence, if Mordkin had put together his two condominiums and his law practice into one business entity—such as an LLC—this, in and of itself, would not have allowed him to use the losses from the condominiums to offset the income from the law practice. Needless to say, it may not always be clear whether an individual or firm is conducting only one activity or two separate activities.

The actual issue in *Mordkin* was whether Mordkin's condominium activity was passive—or, more precisely, whether Mordkin "materially participated" in the activity. Section 469, itself, gives virtually no guidance as what it takes to materially participate in an activity. All the section says is that the participation must be "regular, continuous and substantial." I.R.C. § 469(h)(1). The section does create, however, two, more or less, per se rules regarding what is a passive activity. As originally enacted, the section made rental activities passive without regard to material participation. In 1993, however, Congress ended the per se characterization of rental activities as passive for individuals who perform most of their personal services in real property trades or businesses (and who put in over 750 hours per year in those real property activities in which they materially participate). I.R.C. § 469(c)(2), (7).

The other ostensibly per se passive category is for limited partners. I.R.C. § 469(h)(2). This presumably comes from the notion that traditionally state law required limited partners to be passive investors if they were to retain their limited liability. Section 469, however, allows the Internal Revenue Service to issue regulations creating an exception to the per se categorization of limited partners as passive. Using this authority, the regulations create an exception where the limited partner devotes (or has devoted over a number of prior years) over 500 hours to the activity, or where a limited partner is also a general partner. Temp. Treas. Reg. § 1.469–5T(e)(2), (3)(ii). One point worth noting about Section 469's treatment of limited partners is that this is one of the few places in the Internal Revenue Code which expressly distinguishes limited partners from other parties treated as partners for income tax purposes. This, in turn, creates the question of whether LLC members are partners or limited partners for purposes of Section 469. *See Gregg v. United States*, 186 F. Supp. 2d 1123 (D.Or.2000) (court rejected the argument that limited liability meant that LLC members should be treated as limited partners for purposes of Section 469, and instead looked at actual participation of LLC members to apply the material participation test).

Given the lack of guidance in Section 469 itself as to the meaning of material participation, the main authority on this question has become the regulations quoted and applied by the court in *Mordkin*. Probably, Mordkin's law practice involved contingency fees, and so he lacked the sort of billable hour mentality which might have served him better in coping with the quantitative approach taken by the regulations. In a nutshell, under the regulations, working over 500 hours in an activity during the year constitutes material participation (Temp. Treas. Reg. § 1.469–5T(a)(1)), while less than 100 hours generally does not. *See* Temp. Treas. Reg. § 1.469–5T(a)(3),(4), (b)(2)(iii), (c)(2). (One exception to the 100 hour minimum is when the taxpayer is essentially the only participant in the activity. Temp. Treas. Reg. § 1.469–5T(a)(2)). In between 100 and 500 hours, the regulations find material participation if the taxpayer participates at least as much as any other individual involved (Temp. Treas. Reg. § 1.469–5T(a)(3)), when he or she participates over 100 hours in a number of activities aggregating over 500 hours (Temp. Treas. Reg. § 1.469–5T(a)(4)), or if otherwise justified by all the facts and circumstances (Temp. Treas. Reg. § 1.469–5T(a)(7)). (What were the problems Mordkin faced with the facts and circumstances test?) The regulations also find material participation despite insufficient involvement during the present year if a specified history of material participation existed in prior years. Temp. Treas. Reg. § 1.469–5T(a)(5), (6). "Participation" includes any work done by an owner of an activity regardless of the capacity in which he or she acts, except work not customarily done by an owner does not count if its principal purpose was to avoid section 469, nor does simply monitoring one's investment in a non-managerial capacity. Temp. Treas. Reg. § 1.469–5T(f)(1), (2). (Notice, incidentally, the Service's failure to challenge how much of Mordkin's work on behalf of the condominium association constituted participation in Mordkin's activity of owning his two condominiums.)

Given the conclusion that Mordkin's condominiums constituted a passive activity, what, if anything, could Mordkin do with the losses this activity generated? Section 469 precludes a taxpayer's use of his or her "net passive activity loss" (or "net passive activity credit") for the year. I.R.C. § 469(a). A net passive activity loss is the amount by which all of the losses for the year from all of a taxpayer's passive activities exceed all of the income for the year from all of this taxpayer's passive activities. I.R.C. § 469(d). (A net passive activity credit is similar.) What this means is that Section 469 allows a taxpayer to use losses from a passive activity to offset taxable income from any other passive activity—including activities carried out by entirely different partnerships (or entities electing income treatment as partnerships) in which the taxpayer is a partner. Hence, if Mordkin had income from a partnership in which he was a passive investor, he could have offset the condominium losses against that income in computing his taxes for the year. Mordkin's problem was that his income came from his law practice—hardly a passive activity. Unfortunately, much of what most people would label as passive income does not, in fact, constitute income from a passive activity. This is because Section 469(e)(1)(a) excludes income from interest, dividends, annuities or royalties that does not come from a trade or business conducted by the taxpayer—often referred to as portfolio income—from the category of passive activity income. (Put differently, the Code deems portfolio income to involve situations in which the taxpayer's involvement is so passive as to not even count as an activity.) Incidentally, Section 469 contains an exception of significant, albeit focused, practical importance. This is when losses come from working interests in oil and gas investments. I.R.C. § 469(a)(3)(A).

Since Mordkin could not use the losses in the year in which he incurred them, what could he do? Section 469(b) allows the taxpayer to carry forward any unutilized losses. If, at some year in the future, Mordkin had obtained passive income—whether from the condominiums or from any other activity—then he could offset the carried over losses. Moreover, if the condominiums had started turning a profit, then Mordkin could have used the carried over losses even if he had increased his participation to the point where the condominiums no longer constituted a passive activity. I.R.C. § 469(f). Alternately, once a taxpayer disposes of his interest in the activity which produced the passive losses—as, for instance, if Mordkin sold the condominiums—then the taxpayer can offset the carried over losses from this passive activity against non-passive income from other sources. I.R.C. 469(g)(1).

From a planning standpoint, while Section 469 makes passive activity losses (sometimes referred to by the acronym "PALs") less desirable, the section also makes income from passive activity sources (sometimes called passive income generators or "PIGs") highly desirable. In other words, it is nice to have PIGs against which to offset one's PALs. (In any event, Section 469 imposes no disadvantage on passive activity income which is in excess of passive activity losses; so PIGs are never a bad thing.) Unfortunately, several of the temporary regulations limit efforts to "PIG out." For example, the regulations recharacterize income from certain otherwise passive activities as not passive. Temp. Treas. Reg. § 1.469–2T(f). This includes, for example, activities in which the taxpayer participates between 100 and 500 hours, but does not meet the criteria for material participation (Temp. Treas. Reg. § 1.469–2T(f)(2)), and situations where the taxpayer conveniently might convert normally active income into rental, and, hence, passive income (such as by leasing property to a business in which the taxpayer materially participates). Treas. Reg. § 1.469–2(f)(6). Notice that these recharacterizations apply only to income, not losses.

3. ALTERNATIVES TO PROFIT SHARES

a. *In General*

Levy v. Leavitt

257 N.Y. 461, 178 N.E. 758 (1931).

■ LEHMAN, J.

In June, 1919, the plaintiff agreed to assume a 20 percent interest in the purchase for resale of a large quantity of bacon which the United States government offered for sale. The plaintiff paid the defendant the sum of $50,000 and received a letter from the defendant stating: 'This is to acknowledge receipt of your check for $50,000 as part payment on the purchase of approximately 2,500,000 pound of bacon. It is understood that you are to receive twenty per cent. of the net profits or stand twenty per cent. of the net loss should there be any loss.' No formal contract was made. Indeed, the record does not show that the parties agreed as to how the purchase should be financed or how the joint venture should be conducted, but the evidence shows, and the trial court has in effect found, that the parties agreed that the joint venture should be managed by the defendant, and that the plaintiff was not obligated to perform any services or to make any further capital contributions.

The parties, undoubtedly, anticipated large profits to be derived from a quick resale of the bacon. Their anticipations were defeated through obstacles unexpectedly interposed by the United States government. Claiming that the defendant was violating the "Act to provide further for the national security and defense" commonly known as the "Lever Act" (40

Stat. 276), it procured an indictment against the defendant and libeled the bacon purchased by the joint venture. The defendant could not deliver to purchasers the bacon which had been taken from his possession. By the time that the defendant succeeded in obtaining a judicial determination in his favor, the bacon had so deteriorated that it was no longer readily salable.

The defendant than made extraordinary efforts to sell the bacon. He traveled through Europe in the hope that there he might find a purchaser for bacon which was not merchantable here. His efforts were fruitless. The bacon had then become unfit for human consumption and was seized and destroyed by the public authorities.

Through the destruction of the bacon the joint venture had irretrievably lost the entire purchase price of the bacon, amounting to about $700,000, augmented by expenses incurred in the conduct of the venture and offset only by payments for the small proportion of the bacon which had already been sold and delivered. Indemnification for such loss might still be obtained from the United States government if its executive, legislative, and judicial branches could all be convinced that the loss was occasioned by unfounded charges of the government, and that a moral duty rested on the government to make good such loss. The defendant succeeded in convincing the President and General Dawes, the Director of the Budget, that a favorable report should be made to Congress; he succeeded in convincing Congress that a statute should be enacted permitting the submission of the claim for indemnification to the Court of Claims, and his attorneys succeeded in convincing the court that the claim should be allowed with few deductions. For the plaintiff's share of the moneys received or expended by the defendant in the joint venture, the defendant must now account.

Upon the accounting, the defendant has been denied the right to charge as an expense of the joint venture or partnership the reasonable value of any services rendered by the defendant, and interest on any moneys which he loaned or furnished to the venture in the conduct of its business. * * *

We consider first whether a charge may be made for services rendered. * * * In the business of a partnership the services of a partner are rendered for the common benefit in the performance of an obligation created by the partnership agreement, and the resultant benefit is divided pro rata as provided in the partnership contract. Those profits constitute, in the absence of other agreement, the stipulated reward for services to be rendered, and there is no right to other compensation based on the reasonable value of the services actually rendered. Inequality in the value of services rendered, even the fact that the services were extraordinary and that, at the time the contract was made, the parties did not contemplate that such services would be required in the course of the partnership business, would not alone justify the award of compensation outside the share of profits accruing to the partner rendering the services.

* * *

Under the general rule which is applicable here, the defendant is entitled to special compensation for services only if the parties did in fact agree that such compensation should be allowed, and not otherwise. [The court then holds there was sufficient evidence to support the trial court's finding that no agreement existed to compensate the defendant for his extraordinary services]

* * *

The defendant's right to charge against the plaintiff's share in the partnership funds, interest on moneys furnished by the defendant, like his right to charge compensation for his services, depends upon the contract made between the parties. True, the Partnership Law * * * [U.P.A. § 18] has provided statutory rules for determining the rights and duties of partners "subject to any agreement between them." These rules provide (* * * [§ 18(c)]) "A partner, who in aid of the partnership makes any payment or advance beyond the amount of capital which he agreed to contribute, shall be paid interest from the date of the payment or advance." And (* * * [§ 18(e)]) "No partner is entitled to remuneration for acting in the partnership business, except that a surviving partner is entitled to reasonable compensation for his services in winding up the partnership affairs." Such rules, by the terms of the statute, are not intended to supersede or override an agreement, whether expressed in words or implied in fact. * * * Under these "working rules," as at common law, where the express contract of partnership fails to provide for payment of special compensation for services rendered, the burden of proving that the parties intended such payment rests upon the person claiming such compensation. Where the express contract fails to provide for payment of interest on moneys furnished by a partner beyond the amount which he agreed to contribute, the burden of proving that the parties intended that no such interest should be paid rests upon the other partners. To that extent only, the question of the right to interest bears a different aspect.

* * *

There is no finding and no evidence that the defendant assumed any obligation to contribute to the partnership capital the remainder of the moneys necessary to pay the purchase price of the bacon, and other expenses. * * * [E]ven though the defendant as managing partner may have anticipated that the venture would be financed without further contribution of capital from the plaintiff, it does not follow that he impliedly agreed to assume an obligation to contribute to the capital fund the moneys required to finance the venture. The trial judge has not so found, and the evidence does not support such an inference. * * * [T]he defendant, in behalf of the joint venture, might borrow the moneys necessary to finance the venture, and * * * the plaintiff's 20 percent interest in the venture could be charged with interest on a proportionate share after deducting the plaintiff's contribution. Indeed, the plaintiff does not seriously contend otherwise, but insists that since the defendant borrowed the money on his own behalf and then furnished the borrowed money to the venture, it must be regarded as a capital contribution. There is no basis for the contention, since the defendant was under no obligation to contribute that money to the capital, but was at liberty to finance the venture by loans. Under the express terms of the statute, if not at common law, the defendant is entitled to interest upon the amount so contributed, and the plaintiff's share in the venture must be charged with interest on the balance of his proportionate share of the moneys furnished after deducting the plaintiff's capital contribution.

The judgment should be modified in accordance with this opinion and as modified affirmed, without costs.

NOTES

1. The R.U.P.A. generally provides the same rules as the U.P.A. concerning a partner's rights to a salary or interest without an agreement. R.U.P.A. § 401(e), (h). Thinking in terms of an agreement, under what circumstances should a partnership pay salaries to its partners? One possibility, which existed in *Levy,* is when some partners do more work than others. Indeed, some courts eagerly imply an agreement to grant a salary in such an event. *See Busick v. Stoetzl,* 264 Cal.App.2d 736, 70 Cal.Rptr. 581 (1968). On the other hand, unequal contribution of services may offset unequal contributions to capital (as where one partner agrees to put up all the cash, while the other does the work). Alternately, the parties might reward disproportionate efforts by altering the share of profits going to each partner. So long as the partnership is making a profit, is there any difference between providing a partner with a salary and giving him or her the same amount in extra profit share? If, however, the firm is not making a profit, what is the effect of providing a partner with a salary? See *Knutson v. Lauer,* 627 P.2d 66 (Utah 1981) (lack of profit made by partnership is irrelevant to its obligation to pay an agreed salary not specifically made contingent on earning a profit). Partners relying on the partnership for income may desire a salary in order to ensure they receive a regular flow of funds. As discussed earlier in this chapter, draws also can serve this function. Unlike a salary, however, a draw normally refers to an advance which will either reduce later profit distributions, lower a partner's capital account or require repayment.

2. Providing a salary to a partner raises several questions. What happens if circumstances change so that the partner performs either more or less work than originally anticipated? For example, a crisis in the business could, as occurred in *Levy,* force one partner to undertake a substantial increase in efforts. Alternately, illness or disability might curtail the amount of work a partner can perform. Changing circumstances are not grounds for an adjustment of salary in the absence of agreement. *Quillen v. Titus,* 172 Va. 523, 2 S.E.2d 284 (1939). How can partners reach an advance agreement on such contingencies?

Another question relates to the accounting treatment of the salary. Should the partners consider it a partnership expense (thereby reducing the profit distributed to all partners), deduct it entirely from the non-recipient partners' share of profits, or deduct it entirely from the recipient partner's share of profits (thereby largely obliterating the distinction between salaries and draws)? See *Van Ruiten v. Van Ruiten,* 268 Cal.App.2d 619, 74 Cal.Rptr. 186 (1969) (a salary is normally treated as a partnership expense). Partnership agreements occasionally specify that salaries are an expense against partnership income in order to avoid any question on this subject.

Finally, what happens if the partnership lacks the assets to pay an agreed salary? See U.P.A. § 40(d); R.U.P.A. § 807(b). Should the partners treat the salary as any other debt of the firm? What alternatives are there?

3. The default rules in the U.P.A. and R.U.P.A. regarding salary and interest payments to partners also govern LLPs and limited partnerships. (Since nothing in the pre–2001 U.L.P.A. addresses the subject, the U.P.A. or R.U.P.A. becomes applicable under the pre–2001 version of the U.L.P.A., which incorporates the partnership acts whenever the limited partnership statute is silent. While the 2001 version of the U.L.P.A. no longer incorporates the uniform partnership acts to fill gaps in the limited partnership statute, the 2001 version of the U.L.P.A. contains a provision, like the uniform partnership acts, barring, unless otherwise agreed, remuneration of general partners for services (U.L.P.A. (2001) § 406(f)), so the end result is the same.) On the other hand, the uniform partnership acts do not provide the fallback statute for LLCs, so one can look only to the LLC statutes (supplemented perhaps by judicial notions of implied agreement) for the default rules regarding salaries and interest payments to limited liability company members. A few LLC statutes expressly follow the partnership scheme of denying members salaries barring an agreement by all of the members. *E.g.*, Cal. Corp. Code § 17004(b). A few go in the opposite direction and explicitly allow members who are managers to vote themselves a salary. *E.g.*, Minn. Stat. Ann. § 322B.623. The vast majority of LLC statutes, however, are silent on the question of salaries and interest to LLC members. In this event, the issue becomes whether provisions in the operating agreement or the statute, which govern general management decisions, also govern decisions for some members to receive a salary or other compensation. If so, then compensation decisions generally would be subject to majority vote, rather than unanimous consent (as under the partnership scheme).

What, if any, problems can result from allowing the managers of an LLC, or a majority of the LLC's members, to vote compensation for themselves without the consent of all members? Such a vote entails an evident conflict-of-interest. Perhaps dissenting members might file a lawsuit asserting that the salary or other compensation constitutes a breach of the managers' or majority members' fiduciary duty. Indeed, there have been numerous cases in which minority shareholders have brought lawsuits challenging compensation voted by corporate directors. (By contrast, the inability of a majority of partners to vote themselves a salary without the agreement of all partners means that partners rarely would need to challenge, based upon a fiduciary duty argument, compensation paid to another partner.) Given the absence of authority dealing specifically with salaries in LLCs (because of their short history), one might expect courts to apply corporate law by analogy. Chapter IV will look at judicial review of compensation voted by a corporation's directors. In brief, however, if the compensation involves a conflict-of-interest for the directors (they are the recipients) and there is no disinterested approval (from non-recipient directors or shareholders), then the burden is on the recipients to prove to the court the fairness of the salary or other compensation. *E.g.*, *Wilderman v. Wilderman*, 315 A.2d 610 (Del.Ch.1974). Does the prospect of judicial review for fairness provide an adequate solution for any problems created by allowing managers or majority LLC members to vote themselves a salary? What costs might such litigation impose, and how will a court decide if compensation is fair? For an illustration of many of the factors which might be relevant to such a judicial review—albeit, in the context of a dispute over the tax deductibility of compensation paid by a corporation—see the *Menard* opinion reprinted in Chapter IV. Even if managers or the majority of members do not vote to pay themselves salaries so large that a court would find the salaries to be unfair, might a problem still result from the managers' or majority of members' receipt of salaries not shared by all members? Recall the discussion earlier in this chapter concerning distributions from an LLC. What incentive might the receipt of salaries or other compensation by managers or a majority of members create as far as the willingness of managers or a majority of members to vote for distributions from the LLC to all members? What are the implications of this incentive on planning for distributions and compensation in an LLC? Reconsider the answer to this question after reading the *Gottfried* and *Wilkes* opinions in Chapter IV.

b. *Tax Aspects*

Gaines v. Commissioner of Internal Revenue

45 T.C.M. (CCH) 363 (1982).

* * *

Issue No. 2: Guaranteed Payments

Findings of Fact

On their partnership returns for the year 1973, Lincoln Manor, Brookwood, Gaines Realty, and Riverbend each claimed as deductions certain guaranteed payments to [Gaines Properties] * * *. Gaines Properties was a general partner in each of these partnerships. The amounts claimed by the limited partnerships as deductions for guaranteed payments to partners and Gaines Properties' share of those guaranteed payments were as follows:

Partnership	Amount Claimed	Gaines Properties' Share
Lincoln Manor	$ 74,131.26	$ 23,750.00
Brookwood	109,666.00	88,666.00
Gaines Realty	125,881.00	91,006.00
Riverbend	216,087.00	104,168.50

Each of the four limited partnerships accrued and claimed deductions for these guaranteed payments. Lincoln Manor, Brookwood, Gaines Realty, and Riverbend all used the accrual method of accounting on their 1973 partnership returns. Gaines Properties reported its income using the cash receipts and disbursements method of accounting. Gaines Properties never received any of the guaranteed payments and did not report them in its income.

Respondent determined that Gaines Properties should have reported as income the guaranteed payments accrued and deducted by the four limited partnerships. Respondent, however, disallowed portions of the deductions that the four limited partnerships claimed for these guaranteed payments, on the ground that some portions were capital expenditures and not currently deductible.

Issue No. 2: Guaranteed Payments

Opinion

* * * Notwithstanding this partial disallowance of deductions at the partnership level, respondent determined that the *entire amount* of the guaranteed payments to Gaines Properties, including the portion disallowed as deductions at the partnership level, should be included in Gaines Properties' income. Petitioners argue that the guaranteed payments that Gaines Properties did not receive, or at least such payments to the extent that the deductions therefor were disallowed at the partnership level, were not includable in Gaines Properties' income. Respondent argues that Gaines Properties' share of these guaranteed payments were includable in its income regardless of the fact that the deduction was partially disallowed at the partnership level and regardless of the fact that Gaines Properties, which used the cash method of accounting, never received the payments. We agree with respondent.

Section 707(c), as in effect in 1973, provided:

> To the extent determined without regard to the income of the partnership, payments to a partner for services or the use of capital shall be considered as made to one who is not a member of the partnership, but only for the purposes of section 61(a) (relating to gross income) and section 162(a) (relating to trade or business expenses).

This case does in fact involve "guaranteed payments" to a partner within the meaning of section 707(c) of the Code. The fact that no actual payments were made does not affect the status of these transactions as section 707(c) guaranteed payments. "[D]espite the use of the word "payments" in both § 707(c) and the Regulations thereunder, it is clear that no actual payment need be made; if the partnership deducts the amount under its method of accounting, the "recipient" partner must include the amount in income in the appropriate year." W. McKee, W. Nelson and R. Whitmire, Federal Taxation of Partnerships and Partners (hereinafter McKee, Nelson and Whitmire), par. 13.03[2], pp. 13–16. * * * The parties stipulated that each of the four limited partnerships deducted "guaranteed payments." The partnership agreements of Brookwood and Gaines Realty expressly stated that certain payments to partners "shall constitute guaranteed payments within the meaning of section 707(c) of the Code." While the descriptions of such payments in the partnership agreements are not binding upon us, * * * the payments referred to in those two partnership agreements are clearly fixed sums determined without regard to partnership income. See Sec. 707(c); Sec. 1.707–1(c), Income Tax Regs. Furthermore, it is equally clear that the payments to the partners were for services in their capacities as partners.[25] Respondent in his notices of deficiency determined that these payments were in fact guaranteed payments under section 707(c), and petitioners did not dispute this determination. Accordingly, we hold that the payments here were guaranteed payments within the meaning of section 707(c).

The statutory language of section 707(c) addresses only the character of the guaranteed payments and not the timing. Respondent's regulation under section 707(c), section 1.707–1(c), Income Tax Regs., addresses the timing question, as follows:

> Payments made by a partnership to a partner for services or for the use of capital are considered as made to a person who is not a partner, to the extent such payments are determined without regard to the income of the partnership. However, a partner must include such payments as ordinary income for his taxable year within or with which ends the partnership taxable year in which the partnership deducted such payments as paid or accrued under its method of accounting. See section 706(a) and paragraph (a) of 1.706–1.

As the regulation makes clear, the statutory authority for the timing of the inclusion of these guaranteed payments is section 706(a), which provides:

> In computing the taxable income of a partner for a taxable year, the inclusions required by section 702 and section 707(c) with respect to a partnership shall be based on the income, gain, loss, deduction, or credit of the partnership for any taxable year of the partnership ending within or with the taxable year of the partner.

The separate reference of section 707(c) guaranteed payments in the timing provisions of section 706(a) was explained by the Senate Report as simply—

25. Transactions between a partner and his partnership when the partner is not acting in his capacity as a partner are governed by section 707(a), not section 707(c). * * *

> to make clear that payments made to a partner for services or for the use of capital are includable in his income at the same time as his distributive share of partnership income for the partnership year when the payments are made or accrued.... (S. Rept. No. 1622, to accompany H.R. 8300 (Pub. L. No. 591), 83d Cong., 2d Sess. 385 (1954)).

In *Cagle v. Commissioner* * * *, 63 T.C. 86 (1974), affd., * * * 539 F.2d 409 (5th Cir.1976), we held that includability and deductibility of guaranteed payments are two separate questions, and specifically that guaranteed payments are not automatically deductible simply by reason of their being included in the recipient's income. * * * We have found nothing in the statutory language, regulations, or legislative history to indicate that includability in the recipient partner's income was intended to be dependent upon deductibility at the partnership level.

Petitioners seem to argue that there is a patent unfairness in taxing them on nonexistent income, namely income that they have neither received nor benefitted from (*e.g.* through a tax deduction at the partnership level). Their argument has a superficial appeal to it, but on closer analysis must fail. Except for certain very limited purposes, guaranteed payments are treated as part of the partner's distributive share of partnership income and loss. Sec. 1.707–1(c), Income Tax Regs. For timing purposes guaranteed payments are treated the same as distributive income and loss. Sec. 706(a); sec. 1.706–1(a) and sec. 1.707–1(c), Income Tax Regs. A partner's distributive share of partnership income is includable in his taxable income for any partnership year ending within or with the partner's taxable year. Sec. 706(a). As is the case with a partner's ordinary distributive share of partnership income and loss, any unfairness in taxing a partner on guaranteed payments that he neither receives nor benefits from results from the conduit theory of partnerships, and is a consequence of the taxpayer's choice to do the business in the partnership form. We find no justification in the statute, regulations, or legislative history to permit these petitioners to recognize their income pro rata as deductions are allowed to the partnership. * * * We hold for respondent on the guaranteed payments issue.

* * *

NOTES

1. As the partners discovered in *Gaines,* salaries, interest, rent and similar payments to members of a firm treated as a partnership for income tax purposes can have significant tax effects which should be understood before providing for them. Instead of taxation under the conduit principle established for partnership income (by Sections 702 and 704) and distributions (by Section 731), such payments follow the alternate principles established by Section 707(a)(1) or (c). Section 707(a)(1) deals with transactions between a partnership (or any entity electing income tax treatment as a partnership) and a partner (or a party treated as a partner for income tax purposes), when the party is acting other than in his or her role as a partner or owner of the firm. The section treats the transaction as if the

transaction took place between the firm and a stranger. Thus, if a partner performs work for the firm in a capacity other than as a partner, loans money to the firm, or leases property to it, the salary, interest or rent is taxable income to the partner under the general principles of Section 61(a), and may generate a deduction in accordance with the principles established in Section 162(a) or be capitalized per Section 263. Section 707(c) governs payments to a partner (or to a party treated as a partner for income tax purposes) for services in his or her capacity as a partner or owner of the firm or for use of his or her capital contribution, but only to the extent the payment is determined without regard to the income of the firm. Section 707(c) treats such guaranteed payments as if made to a stranger for purposes of Sections 61(a), 162(b) and 263. In most other respects, however, Section 707(c) guaranteed payments, unlike Section 707(a) payments, follow the conduit principles of partnership taxation.

The actual effects of the difference between the conduit approach, the separate entity approach of Section 707(a)(1), and the hybrid approach of Section 707(c) are subtle and depend upon the circumstances. First, there may be different consequences to the party receiving the payment. Under Section 707(a)(1) or (c), payments of salaries, interest and rent constitute ordinary income for the recipient. If the firm makes ordinary income adequate to cover the proposed payment, there will be no difference if, instead of a salary (for example), the partnership or LLC operating agreement allocates an equal amount of the firm's profits to the partner or member as part of his or her distributive share. On the other hand, if the firm does not make any taxable income, the choice between a salary and a draw has significant tax consequences. If treated as a distribution under Section 731, money paid as a draw constitutes a tax-free return of capital up to the amount of the recipient's basis in the firm, and thereafter (except insofar as Section 751 applies) capital gain. To the extent the draw constitutes a bona fide loan from the firm, which the recipient must repay, there should be no tax consequences for the recipient. *See* Treas. Reg. 1.731–1(a)(1)(ii) and (c)(2).

There also may be consequences to the firm and the other owners. Allocating a distributive share to one partner or owner lowers the distributive shares recognized by other owners of the firm. Payment of salaries, interest or rent only accomplishes the same result if the payment generates an immediate deduction. To the extent, as in *Gaines,* the payment is not immediately deductible (perhaps because it must be capitalized under Sections 263 or 709), there is a clear tax disadvantage to a salary or other such payment. Notice the impact this created in *Gaines*. The recipient partner had to recognize taxable income even though the partnership gained no offsetting deduction—a result which working with profit allocations rather than guaranteed payments might have avoided. Fortunately, changes in the tax regulations since *Gaines* decrease the frequency with which this problem will result. Specifically, regulations interpreting Section 263 now provide that employee compensation—including a guaranteed payment to partners—that facilities that acquisition or creation of intangible assets need not be capitalized as part of the cost of the intangible asset.

Treas. Reg. § 1.263(a)–4(e)(4)(i), (ii). In any event, suppose the salary is deductible. Can there be a tax advantage over conduit treatment? If the firm does not generate taxable income, then the deduction resulting from paying a salary must be compared with the fact that a distribution under Section 731 (or a loan under Section 707(a)(1)) has no effect on firm income. The tax advantage to the non-recipient owners in this case is the flip-side of the tax detriment noted above of such a payment to the recipient. Given this trade-off, under what, if any, circumstances is there a net tax savings?

Additional differences exist in the timing of recognition. Before 1984, the accounting system of the firm determined when a deduction generated by a Section 707(a) payment could be recognized, while the recipient's method of accounting dictated when he or she recognized the payment as income. This created the interesting possibility, if the firm was on the accrual system, while its owners operated on a cash basis, of the firm taking a deduction for a payment not yet recognized by the recipient. *See Pratt v. Commissioner,* 550 F.2d 1023 (5th Cir.1977). This result cannot occur under Section 707(c) (contrary the bumbling claim of the taxpayers in *Gaines*), since the recipient must recognize a guaranteed payment, like a distributive share, in the tax year in which ends the partnership year when the firm treats the item as paid or accrued. I.R.C. § 706(a). Notice, in *Gaines*, this meant that the recipient partner had to recognize the income in the year in which the partnership accrued the expense under the partnership's accounting system, even though the partner did not receive the sum that year (or apparently ever), and even though the partnership had to capitalize, rather than immediately deduct, much of the payment. In any event, Section 267(a)(2) and (e) now preclude the firm from taking a deduction before recognition by the recipient of a payment covered by Section 707(a)(1). What timing difference does this leave between a Section 707(a)(1) and a Section 707(c) payment? (Examine whose accounting system in each case determines the point of recognition.)

Next, suppose the partnership uses property to make a Section 707(a)(1) or a Section 707(c) payment. If the fair market value of the property is greater than the partnership's basis, the partnership (and hence the partners) will need to recognize gain, just as if the firm sold the property. Rev. Rul. 2007–40, 2007–25 I.R.B. 1426. By contrast, Section 731(b) precludes recognition on a distribution of property to a partner.

The passive activity loss limitation of Section 469 creates yet another impact to the choice between distributive shares and Section 707 payments. Distributive shares of income (other than portfolio income made by the firm) to partners (or parties taxed as partners) constitute passive or non-passive activity income depending upon the partner's participation in the activity generating the income. Temp. Treas. Reg. § 1.469–2T(e)(1). What about salary payments? A salary constitutes non-passive activity income regardless of the extent of the recipient's overall level of participation in the activity. *See* I.R.C. § 469(e)(3); Temp. Treas. Reg. § 1.469–2T(c)(4)(i)(A) and (e)(2). Consider the result if a partner (or person taxed as a partner) receives a salary or similar compensation, but nevertheless does not put in enough hours to meet the material participation test. *Hillman v. Commissioner*, 250 F.3d 228 (4th Cir.2001), illustrates the consequences. There, an S corporation received management fees from partnerships, and the owner of the S corporation had to recognize these management fees as income. The owner of the S corporation was also a partner in the firms paying the fees, and the partnership agreements allocated to him some of the deductions generated by paying these fees. Regrettably for the owner, however, he was unable to offset these deductions against this taxable income, since his participation in the individual partnerships was insufficient to constitute material participation for purposes of Section 469. Compare the result if the owner or his S corporation had simply received a greater distributive share of the partnerships' income equal to the difference between the planned fees and the portion of the fee expense allocated to the recipient.

Suppose, instead of dealing with a salary, the alternative to profit shares involves interest on a loan or rental payments on a lease. Interest payments normally constitute portfolio income. *See* I.R.C. § 469(e)(1)(A); Temp. Treas. Reg. § 1.469–2T(e)(2). In the case of a loan from a partner (or person taxed as a partner) to a firm in which he or she does not materially participate, this would seem to create the same problem under Section 469 as a salary (since losses from a passive activity cannot be offset against portfolio income). Fortunately, in this case, Treas. Reg. § 1.469–7 steps in to treat such "self-charged interest" as passive activity income, rather than portfolio income, to the extent of the interest expense deduction allocated to the recipient partner. Rental payments on a lease, by contrast, are normally considered passive activity income, meaning such payments could actually have an advantage in regards to Section 469 when compared with a greater distributive share of partnership income. As discussed previously, however, the regulations prevent a partner from increasing passive activity income through the receipt of lease payments. Specifically, the regulations characterize such payments as active income when the rent comes from a partnership in which the recipient materially participates. Treas. Reg. § 1.469–2(f)(6). Suppose, on the other hand, the rental payments are insufficient to offset the expenses, such as depreciation, realized by a party holding back and renting needed property to the firm in which he or she is an owner. Here, the normal characterization of rental activities as passive works against the owner. Of course, if the owner did not materially participate in the activity, it hardly matters that the activity also gets slapped with a rental label. If, by comparison, the owner materially participates in the firm using the property, the lesson is to illustrate the tax disadvantages, discussed earlier, of holding back from contributing property needed by the firm. Even if the owner held back the property, all may not be lost, however, as the regulations allow parties to avoid rental characterization if the rental is simply incidental to a taxpayer's trade or business. Temp. Treas. Reg. § 1.469–1T(e)(3)(vi)(C)(1)-(3). To fall within this exception, the property must be used predominantly in the taxpayer's trade or business during the taxable year or during at least two of the five immediately preceding taxable years, and the gross rental income from the property for the taxable year must be less than two percent of the lesser of (i) the unadjusted basis of the property or (ii) the fair market value of the property. *See also Misko v. Commissioner*, T.C. Memo. 2005–166 (applying this regulation). Notice, in this instance, the importance of not charging too much rent.

2. What limits the partners' ability to control the tax effects dependant on the differences between distributive shares, Section 707(a) payments, and Section 707(c) payments, by changing the label of a given payment? For example, if they agree that a party performing services will receive a certain sum, can the parties alter the tax consequences simply by labeling the sum as a salary for services other than in the role of a partner, as a guaranteed payment, or as a distributive share of firm profits? Regrettably, at least from the taxpayers' standpoint, the answer is no. For a salary to come within Section 707(a)(1), it, in fact, must be for services other than in the recipient's role as a partner or owner of the firm. If a payment is for services as a partner or owner of the firm, then, whatever the label, it falls under Section 707(c) if fixed without regard to partnership income; otherwise it is a distributive share. (Suppose a payment for services as a partner or owner is set as a percentage of gross, rather than net, income. Is such a payment a guaranteed payment or a distributive share? *Compare Pratt v. Commissioner,* 64 T.C. 203 (1975), *aff'd in part and rev'd in part*, 550 F.2d 1023 (5th Cir.1977), *with* Rev.Rul. 81–300, 1981–2 C.B. 143.) The inability to rely on labels raises the question of just how one can tell whether or not services are performed in the role of a partner or owner of the firm. See *Pratt v. Commissioner,* 550 F.2d 1023 (5th Cir.1977) (finding management activities, work extending over a considerable period of time, and efforts specified in the partnership agreement to be services performed in the role of partner). In a similar vein, interest on bona fide loans falls under Section 707(a)(1), while a fixed return on capital contributions comes within Section 707(c). *See* Treas. Reg. § 1.707–1(a). This distinction creates the potential for controversy over whether a sum advanced to a firm represents a loan versus a portion of the firm's equity. Lease payments come within Section 707(a)(1) only so long as the lessor retains title to the property. Treas. Reg. § 1.707–1(a).

Section 707(a)(2) contains a further limit on the parties' ability to characterize payments to firm members. This provision empowers the Internal Revenue Service to promulgate regulations preventing partners (or parties treated as partners for income tax purposes) from avoiding undesirable effects of salary treatment (principally because the salary would be capitalized under Sections 263 or 709) by labeling the payment a distributive share. While the Service has yet to issue these regulations, the legislative history suggests that parties will not be able to obtain distributive share treatment of payments to owners who perform services unless there is an appreciable risk as to whether, and in what amount, the owners will receive payments. *See* Staff of the Joint Committee on Taxation, General Explanation of the Revenue Provisions of the Deficit Reduction Act of 1984, 98th Cong., 2d Sess. 226–229 (1984). Regulations issued pursuant to Section 707(a)(2)(B) also may recast payments received from a partnership (or an entity electing income tax treatment as a partnership) to be something other than what the parties chose to label them. As discussed earlier, these regulations deal with sales of property disguised to appear as a contribution and later distribution. Under the regulations, for example, an unreasonable guaranteed payment for capital could be reclassified as sale proceeds. Treas. Reg. § 1.707–4.

3. Beyond Section 707(a), to what extent does the tax code allow treatment of partners as employees? *Compare Armstrong v. Phinney,* 394 F.2d 661 (5th Cir.1968) (I.R.C. § 119, which excludes from taxable income certain living expenses paid for employees, applied to a partner performing work as an employee), *with* Rev. Rul. 70–411, 1970–2 C.B. 91 (stating that partners are not employees for purposes of I.R.C. § 401 retirement plan provisions).

4. One form of compensation often used in the corporate context is to grant stock options. Similarly, participants in partnerships and LLCs (particularly in high technology ventures) might agree to grant parties, who are working for the firm, options to purchase interests in the venture at a fixed price. In part, this might give an incentive to those in charge of the venture to act in a manner in which the worth of the venture increases. Such options also provide compensation with no immediate out-of-pocket cost for the firm. (On the other hand, simply providing a profits interest accomplishes both of these goals.) From a tax standpoint, providing options returns the discussion to the subject of the receipt of partnership interests in exchange for services. If the option is simply to purchase a profits interest in the firm, then, under Revenue Procedure 93–27, there generally should be no recognition. If, however, exercising the option will mean purchasing a capital interest in the firm in excess of the option price, then, as seen in *Johnston*, there will be recognition of income. As discussed in Chapter IV, receipt of the option itself is generally not considered to be taxable income on the ground that the worth of the option is too speculative.

SECTION C. MANAGEMENT

1. SIMPLE DIRECT GOVERNANCE

Summers v. Dooley

94 Idaho 87, 481 P.2d 318 (1971).

■ DONALDSON, JUSTICE.

This lawsuit, tried in the district court, involves a claim by one partner against the other for $6,000. The complaining partner asserts that he has been required to pay out more than $11,000 in expenses without any reimbursement from either the partnership funds or his partner. The expenditure in question was incurred by the complaining partner * * * for the purpose of hiring an additional employee. The trial court denied him any relief except for ordering that he be entitled to one-half $966.72 which it found to be a legitimate partnership expense.

The pertinent facts leading to this lawsuit are as follows. Summers entered a partnership agreement with Dooley * * * in 1958 for the purpose of operating a trash collection business. * * * In July, 1966, Summers approached his partner Dooley regarding the hiring of an additional employee but Dooley refused. Nevertheless, on his own initiative, Summers hired the man and paid him out of his own pocket. Dooley, upon discovering that Summers had hired an additional man, objected, stating that he did not feel additional labor was necessary and refused to pay for the new employee out of the partnership funds. Summers continued to operate the business using the third man and in October of 1967 instituted suit in the district court for $6,000 against his partner, the gravamen of the complaint being that Summers has been required to pay out more than $11,000 in expenses incurred in the hiring of the additional man, without any reimbursement from either the partnership funds or his partner. After trial before the court, sitting without a jury, Summers was granted only partial relief and he has appealed. He urges in essence that the trial court erred by failing to conclude that he should be reimbursed for expenses and costs connected in the employment of extra help in the partnership business.

* * *

The issue presented for decision by this appeal is whether an equal partner in a two man partnership has the authority to hire a new employee in disregard of the objection of the other partner and then attempt to charge the dissenting partner with the costs incurred as a result of his unilateral decision.

* * *

An application of the relevant statutory provisions and pertinent case law of the factual situation presented by the instant case indicates that the trial court was correct in its disposal of the issue since a majority of the partners did not consent to the hiring of the third man. I.C. § 53–318(8) [U.P.A. § 18(h)] provides:

> "Any difference arising as to ordinary matters connected with the partnership business may be decided by a *majority of the partners* * * *." (emphasis supplied)

* * *

A careful reading of the statutory provision indicates that subsection 5 bestows equal rights in the management and conduct of the partnership business upon all of the partners. The concept of equality between partners with respect to management of business affairs is a central theme and recurs throughout the Uniform Partnership law, which has been enacted in this jurisdiction. Thus the only reasonable interpretation of I.C. § 53–318(8) is that business differences must be decided by a majority of the partners provided no other agreement between the partners speaks to the issues.

A noted scholar has dealt precisely with the issue to be decided.

> "* * * if the partners are equally divided, those who forbid a change must have their way." Walter B. Lindley, A Treatise on the Law of Partnership, Ch. II, § III, ¶ 24–8, p. 403 (1924).

* * *

In the case at bar one of the partners continually voiced objection to the hiring of the third man. He did not sit idly by and acquiesce in the actions of his partner. Under these circumstances it is manifestly unjust to permit recovery of an expense which was incurred individually and not for the benefit of the partnership but rather for the benefit of one partner.

Judgment affirmed. * * *

NOTE

Many partners or LLC members, if asked to describe decision-making in their firms, are likely to speak about "reaching a consensus." They also might explain that if a person anticipates irreconcilable disagreements with his or her prospective fellow owners, perhaps the person ought to reconsider the whole idea of entering the venture. Nevertheless, as *Summers* illustrates, differences of opinion can arise and prospective co-owners might anticipate how to handle such events.

What different approaches can owners of a business take to allocate management powers? Section 18(e) of the U.P.A. and 401(f) of the R.U.P.A.—which apply to both ordinary partnerships and LLPs—provide, in the absence of agreement to the contrary, that partners have equal rights in management. The concept of equal rights has a couple of connotations. First, it means that all partners have the right to participate in making decisions. Recall, Chapter II contrasted this sort of direct (or Athenian) democracy mode of partnership governance with the representative structure of corporate governance. In addition, paralleling the uniform partnership acts' default rule for allocating profits, the default rule of equal rights in management divorces the voting power of partners from the relative size of their contributions. The partner who contributes one thousand dollars is entitled to no greater say than the partner who puts in one dollar. Section 18(h) of the U.P.A. and 401(j) of the R.U.P.A. provide that, barring other agreement, a majority vote resolves disagreements among the partners as to ordinary matters. Extraordinary matters in a partnership or LLP require a unanimous vote. (This is implicit in the U.P.A. and explicit in the R.U.P.A.) In a number of cases, the uniform partnership acts avoid any question as to whether an action is ordinary or extraordinary by specifically requiring a unanimous vote. U.P.A. §§ 9(3), 18(g); R.U.P.A. § 401(i). Partners can lessen the unanimity requirements by agreement. *E.g., Day v. Sidley & Austin,* 394 F.Supp. 986 (D.D.C.1975). *But see McCallum v. Asbury,* 238 Or. 257, 393 P.2d 774 (1964).

What problems exist with this relatively simple scheme of management that might lead prospective co-owners to contract for different rules? For example, how satisfactory was the uniform partnership acts' approach for the two-person partnership in *Summers*? What about for a four or six-person partnership? How can co-owners deal with the possibility of deadlock? Perhaps arbitration is the answer. Are there any problems, however, with having an outsider make decisions for the firm? Might this depend upon the nature and frequency of the disputes? *Summers* illustrates the consequences which can flow from the fact that, as a practical matter, even ordinary business decisions in the two-person partnership require (barring other agreement) a unanimous vote. Does this suggest a problem with the uniform partnership acts' requirement of unanimous approval for extraordinary decisions? Consider, moreover, with a two-person partnership, how many persons must agree in order to make a decision. If a decision requires unanimity and there are one hundred partners, how many persons must see eye-to-eye on the matter? If unanimity requirements create a practical problem, is there some reason nevertheless to have them for certain decisions? If so, are there any other decisions beyond those specified in the uniform partnership acts where owners might wish to deviate from majority rule and require all to concur? Turning to the idea of equal rights in management, should a party who contributes one thousand dollars to a venture expect no greater vote than a party who contributes only one dollar? Even if everyone contributes equally, how satisfactory is the direct democracy approach for managing the day-to-day operation of a large firm with scores of owners, such as some accounting and law firms? Does appointing a managing partner or committee provide a better approach? If so, do the non-managing owners need any protections?

2. MORE COMPLEX MANAGEMENT SCHEMES

Broyhill v. DeLuca

194 B.R. 65 (Bkrtcy.E.D.Va.1996).

In this action, the plaintiffs, Joel T. Broyhill and Northern Virginia Realty, Inc. Profit Sharing Trust seek a declaration that the defendants, Robert and Marilyn DeLuca, were properly removed as the managers of D & B Countryside, L.L.C., and that Joel T. Broyhill was properly appointed as the successor manager. * * *

D & B Countryside, L.L.C., ("D & B Countryside") is a Virginia limited liability company that was formed on April 12, 1994 to develop a shopping center and office development in Sterling, Virginia, known as Parc City Centre. * * * The original members of the company were Joel T. Broyhill ("Broyhill") and Robert and Marilyn DeLuca ("the DeLucas"). The organization of the company was set forth in an Operating Agreement dated April 12, 1994 ("the operating agreement"), signed by Broyhill and the DeLucas. Under the terms of the operating agreement, Broyhill and the DeLucas were each 50% members, and the DeLucas were named as joint managing members. The operating agreement stated that the manager of the company must be appointed by unanimous vote but was silent on removal of a manager. The operating agreement further required written consent of the other members for the assignment or pledge of a member's interest.

* * *

In July 1994, the DeLucas solicited Theodore Boinis ("Boinis"), the president of Northern Virginia Realty, Inc. ("NVRI") and trustee of its profit sharing plan, to become a member and offered him a 15% interest in the company in exchange for a $600,000 investment. * * * NVRI agreed to the proposal and wire-transferred the $600,000 to D & B Countryside's bank account on July 22, 1994. Within a week, $594,300 of those funds had been transferred to other DeLuca-related entities or Robert DeLuca personally. Sometime later (apparently in September), Boinis and the DeLucas signed an Amended and Restated Operating Agreement dated "as of July 22, 1994" ("the amended operating agreement"), which assigned to the NVRI Profit Sharing Trust a 7.5% portion of the DeLucas' interest in the company and a 7.5% portion of Broyhill's interest. Although the DeLucas told Boinis that the amended operating agreement would be sent to Broyhill for signature, it never was, and was never signed by Broyhill. Broyhill testified at trial that, although he had not seen the amended operating agreement until approximately mid-January, 1995, he had no objection to any of its provisions except for language in one paragraph acknowledging his having "received all amounts and other consideration due . . . on account of this membership assignment." * * *

Beginning in September or October 1994, the relationship between the DeLucas and Broyhill soured, largely because the DeLucas did not respond to a number of requests by Broyhill for information concerning his investment. After Broyhill learned that almost all of the $600,000.00 invested by Boinis had been immediately transferred out of D & B Countryside and that the DeLucas had placed a $3,000,000.00 deed of trust against D & B Countryside's property without his knowledge, Broyhill and NVRI Profit Sharing Trust executed a document on April 14, 1995, purporting to remove the DeLucas as D & B Countryside's managers and electing Broyhill as manager. No notice was given to the DeLucas of the meeting of Broyhill and Boinis at which the document was signed. Written notice was sent to the DeLucas that same date, however, that the action had been taken. In addition, notice was also sent that same date to the attorney who was representing the DeLucas * * * advising him that the DeLucas had been removed as managers and that he had no authority to represent D & B Countryside or to make any filings for D & B Countryside in the United States Bankruptcy Court. On May 5, 1995, the DeLucas filed a voluntary chapter 11 petition in this court, and on May 9, 1995, they caused D & B Countryside to file a voluntary chapter 11 petition. Subsequent to the DeLucas' petition, Broyhill and NVRI Profit Sharing Trust executed a document in which they elected to continue the business and confirmed the election of Broyhill as the new manager.

* * *

There are two major issues raised by the complaint and the evidence. The first is whether the April 28, 1995 action by Broyhill and NVRI was effective to remove the DeLucas as the managers of D & B Countryside and to appoint Broyhill as the successor manager. If not, the second issue is whether the chapter 11 filing by the DeLucas terminated their right to act as manager and permitted Broyhill and NVRI Profit Sharing Trust to elect to continue the business with Broyhill as the manager. Each of these issues will be discussed in turn.

A. Whether the April 28, 1995 action was effective to remove the DeLucas as managers.

* * *

In order to determine whether the April 28, 1995 action by Broyhill and NVRI was effective to remove the DeLucas as managers, it is necessary first to resolve just who the members of D & B Countryside were. The DeLucas, in their pleadings and through counsel, have denied that NVRI became a member of the company because the operating agreement required unanimous consent to assign a membership interest or to admit a new member and Broyhill never signed the amended operating agreement which assigned a portion of Broyhill's and the DeLucas' membership interest to NVRI and recognized NVRI as a member.

* * *

The DeLucas, by signing the Amended and Restated Operating Agreement, effectively (1) assigned a 7.5% portion of their own membership interest to NVRI and (2) consented to an assignment of a 7.5% portion of Broyhill's interest to NVRI. Although Broyhill never executed a writing explicitly assigning the 7.5% portion of his interest or consenting to the assignment of a similar portion of the DeLuca's interest, he testified at trial that he consented in fact to both actions, that he had never been sent the amended operating agreement to sign, and that the only reason he would not now sign the amended operating agreement was because of the language acknowledging that he had received all amounts to which he was due on account of the assignment. The requirement in the original operating agreement that any assignment and consent to assignment be in writing is clearly for the protection and benefit of the party whose interest would be adversely affected by the assignment, and that party is free to waive, as Broyhill has done in this case, the requirement of a writing. Accordingly, the court concludes that Broyhill's failure to sign the amended operating agreement did not, under the facts of this case, prevent NVRI from becoming a 15% member of D & B Countryside and that NVRI is in fact the holder of a 15% membership interest.

As discussed above, the original operating agreement required that the manager of the company be elected by unanimous vote of the members but was silent on removal of an existing manager. The plaintiffs argue, and the court concurs, that where the operating agreement is silent, resort must be had to the statute. In this connection, § 13.1–1024(F), Va.Code Ann. provides,

> All managers or any lesser number may be removed in the manner provided in the articles of organization or an operating agreement. *If the articles of organization or an operating agreement does not provide for the removal of managers, then all managers or any lesser number may be removed with or without cause by a majority vote of the members.*

(emphasis added). Since Broyhill's 42.5% interest and NVRI's 15% interest clearly constituted a majority of the membership interest, their joint action removing the DeLucas as managers was, under the plain language of the statute, effective to accomplish its stated purpose. The court rejects the DeLucas' argument that, because the operating agreement required *election* of a manager to be unanimous, *removal* likewise necessarily had to be unanimous. That result simply does not follow. The obvious purpose of the operating agreement was to prevent a manager from being elected who did not enjoy the unanimous support of the members. By April 28, 1995, the DeLucas not only no longer had the unanimous support of the members, their continued retention in office was actively opposed by the majority of the members. Thus, their removal from office by the majority, pursuant to the statute, was not at all inconsistent with the requirement of the operating agreement that a manager had to be elected by unanimous vote.

At the same time, the requirement in the operating agreement for a unanimous vote in order to elect a manager presents an obvious practical difficulty. Since the manager may be removed by a majority, but less than unanimous, vote, the company could well find itself in the difficult and untenable position of having removed a manager but being unable to elect a new one, thereby leaving the company essentially paralyzed. If that were to occur, the only apparent remedy would be a judicial winding up under § 13.1–1047, Va.Code Ann.[16] That potentially is the situation that exists in the present case. Although the April 28, 1995 action was effective to remove the DeLucas as the managers of D & B Countryside, since the plain language of the operating agreement requires a unanimous vote to elect a manager, NVRI and Broyhill could not, by their sole act, elect Broyhill as the new manager, *unless*, as argued by NVRI and Broyhill, the DeLucas' subsequent chapter 11 filing in effect terminated their membership and gave NVRI and Broyhill the right under the operating agreement to elect to continue the business of the company and select a new manager. It is to that question that we must now turn. [The remainder of the opinion is reprinted later in this chapter.]

* * *

16. "On application by or for a member, the circuit court of the locality in which the registered office of the limited liability company is located may decree dissolution of a limited liability company if it is not reasonably practicable to carry on the business in conformity with the articles of organization and any operating agreement."

NOTES

1. In contrast to the apparently informal partnership in *Summers*, the parties in *Broyhill* formed an LLC, entered a lengthy agreement which addressed issues of management, and employed a management structure involving governance by so-called managers rather than all members. To what extent did this improve the situation when the parties got into a dispute? If all of this evident planning effort did not produce a swift and easy resolution, is the lesson that planning for management is useless, or did the parties in *Broyhill* make specific mistakes, which undermined the effectiveness of their efforts and from which later planners can learn?

2. To answer the broad questions posed above, it might be helpful to begin with a much narrower focus: Was it clear that there had been a majority vote to remove Mr. and Mrs. DeLuca as managers? After all, Mr. Broyhill and the NVRI Trust were only two of the four members of the limited liability company—Mr. and Mrs. DeLuca being the other two members. The answer is that the court weighed the votes according to the members' interests in the limited liability company (rather than the one-person-one-vote partnership law default rule). While the court never explained its basis for counting votes in this manner, a related case gives some insight into the court's thinking. In that action, Mr. Broyhill, essentially, also attempted to remove the DeLuca's as managers of another real estate development limited liability company he co-owned with them. (Actually, both sides in that case held their respective membership interests through other LLCs, instead of personally being members.) Mr. Broyhill again claimed to have a majority for this vote. In this instance, the court rejected the claim:

> JTB [the limited liability company through which Broyhill held his interest] asserts that because its capital account balance ($1,488,369) was greater than that of R & M Kiln Creek [the limited liability company through which the DeLucas held their interest] ($647,146) * * * JTB had the right to remove R & M Kiln Creek as manager, since (1) under § 13.1–1024(F), Va. Code Ann., "If the articles of organization or an operating agreement of a limited liability company does not provide for the removal of managers, then all managers or any lesser number may be removed with or without cause *by a majority vote of the members*" (emphasis added), and (2) under § 13.1–1022, Va.Code Ann.,
>
> > Unless otherwise provided in the articles of organization or an operating agreement, the members of a limited liability company *shall vote in proportion to their contributions to the limited liability company*, as adjusted from time to time to reflect any additional contributions or withdrawals, and *a majority vote of the members of a limited liability company shall consist of the vote or other approval of members having a majority share of the voting power of all members.*
>
> (emphasis added). R & M Kiln Creek disputes that JTB had the larger capital account, but the issue is not one which need be resolved, since

the provision of § 13.1–1022 that members "shall vote in proportion to their contributions" only applies in the absence of contrary provisions in the articles of organization or operating agreement. Under the terms of the amended operating agreement for D & B Venture, "membership interest" was not tied to the level of capital contributions. * * * The amended operating agreement clearly treats membership interest as distinct both from capital accounts and distribution rights and provides separate treatment for each. While the amended operating agreement never explicitly states how votes are to be counted in connection with what are described as "Major Decisions" by the company requiring member vote (¶ 6.2),[12] the clear implication is that each of the members has an equal vote. Accordingly, the court concludes that JTB, as the holder of a 50% membership interest, could not under the amended operating agreement cast "a majority vote of the members" to remove R & M Kiln Creek as manager notwithstanding that JTB may have had the larger capital account.

*JTB Enterprises, L.C. v. D & B Venture, L.C.,*194 B.R. 79, 86–87 (Bkrtcy. E.D.Va.1996).

Why was there any room for doubt as to the allocation of voting power in *JTB Enterprises*? Was it clear that the parties had contracted for a different measure of voting power than provided by the Virginia statute? Specifically, why might the limited liability company operating agreement in *JTB Enterprises* have specified "membership interests" if not for purposes of votes? Is it possible that the parties meant to decouple their profits interests from their relative contributions, but not to decouple their voting power from their relative contributions? Is one drafting lesson that parties need to be careful when using terms like "membership interests," which might refer to interests in profits, voting or capital? Is another drafting lesson that if a contract calls for votes on "major decisions," the agreement needs to specify the answer to questions such as what is the voting power of the parties and what vote is required?

Is the lesson simply to use clear terms in drafting an agreement, or was there another problem with the agreements in both *Broyhill* and *JTB Enterprises* as well? Notice how the court in both cases reached its result by blending together provisions of the operating agreement with statutory default rules. To what extent did this lead to undesirable results? For example, consider the impact of combining the default rule allowing a majority vote to remove managers, with the operating agreement provision requiring unanimity to elect managers. Was this result what the drafter of the agreement anticipated? If not, how can the drafter avoid such potentially unpleasant surprises?

Incidentally, like the Virginia LLC statute involved in *Broyhill* and *JTB Enterprises,* most LLC statutes do not follow the one-owner-one-vote

12. While not directly raised as an issue in this adversary proceeding, it is clear that the decision to file a chapter 11 petition was a "major decision" that required the vote of the members and that R & M Kiln Creek had no authority, solely in its capacity as manager, to file a chapter 11 petition on behalf of D & B Venture. * * *

default rule of the U.P.A. or R.U.P.A. Instead, LLC statutes typically provide for allocating voting power in proportion to contributions (as in Virginia) or profits (*e.g.*, Cal. Corp. Code § 17103(a)(1); Del. Code Ann. Title 6 § 18–402; N.Y. Ltd. Liab. Co. Law § 402(a)). *But see* U.L.L.C.A. § 407(b)(2). Notice the dispute which voting in proportion to contributions might have created in *JTB Enterprises* had the court not interpreted the agreement to call for voting in proportion to so-called interests in the LLC. Besides possible disputes regarding the amount or value of each party's contribution, could voting in proportion to contributions lead to any other problems? Consider the impact under the Virginia LLC statute of either distributions or additional contributions. On the other hand, might there be some problem with voting in proportion to profits interests in circumstances in which the profit allocation does not follow simple ratios, but perhaps changes at various levels of firm income?

3. LLC statutes normally follow the partnership law scheme insofar as they provide, in the absence of any agreement to the contrary, for direct governance by all of the members of the LLC. *E.g.*, Cal. Corp. Code § 17150; Del. Code Ann. Title 6 § 18–402; N.Y. Ltd. Liab. Co. Law § 401(a). *But see* Tex. Rev. Civ. Stat. Ann. Art. 1528n. art. 2.12 (governed by managers rather than all members unless otherwise agreed). *Broyhill* illustrates, however, that LLC statutes typically also contain provisions explicitly allowing the members to empower one or more "managers" (who may or may not be members) to run the company. Of course, there is no reason that partners cannot provide in their partnership agreement for such centralized management despite the fact that neither the U.P.A. nor R.U.P.A. explicitly say anything about "managers." Indeed, larger law and accounting firms commonly have management committees or managing partners to whom the partnership agreement delegates significant power. *See, e.g., Day v. Sidley & Austin,* 394 F.Supp. 986 (D.D.C.1975). So what is the practical significance of the fact that LLC statutes contain special provisions allowing the members to opt for governance by managers? One possible impact is to create an extra hoop the parties must jump through if they wish to have managers, rather than all members, run the business. As mentioned at the start of this chapter, some states' LLC statutes require the LLC's articles, rather than just the operating agreement, to set forth this election. *E.g.*, Cal. Corp. Code § 17151(b); N.Y. Ltd. Liab. Co. Law § 401(a). A second impact, illustrated by *Broyhill*, is that the LLC statutes often contain various specific rules dealing with governance by managers. *E.g.*, Cal. Corp. Code §§ 17152, 17153, 17156; N.Y. Ltd. Liab. Co. Law §§ 408–411, 413–416, 419, 420. On the positive side, such rules can deal with contingencies the parties might overlook in deciding upon governance by managers—such as the possible need to remove managers who, like the DeLucas, turn out to be crooks. On the negative side, *Broyhill* illustrates the potential that more particularized statutory default rules might not mesh well with provisions of the parties' agreement unless the drafter of the agreement is familiar with the statutory default rules.

When does it make sense to provide for management of a partnership by a management committee or a managing partner, or for management of an LLC by managers? The obvious answer is when there are too many owners to allow for efficient decision-making by the entire group of owners. As mentioned in Chapter II, this is one reason why the corporate management scheme works for widely held businesses. In *Broyhill*, however, there were only four owners, and in *JTB Enterprises* there were only two owners (which themselves were only owned by a total of three individuals). So why did Broyhill and the DeLucas go to all of the trouble of entering an agreement calling for managers? Perhaps Broyhill did not wish to be active in running the venture. If so, could the DeLucas unilaterally have made decisions in their roles as members (rather than making anyone managers) so long as Broyhill agreed that they could act without consulting him? Would it make such an understanding simpler or more complex to designate the DeLucas as managers? Alternately, perhaps the DeLucas did not want Broyhill involved in management. Could this have been a tipoff as to their trustworthiness, or are there legitimate reasons to exclude an equal owner from management? Perhaps there are some reasons to designate managers of an LLC, which go beyond the relationships of the members vis-a-vis each other. We shall return to this idea shortly.

Designating a management committee or a managing partner to run a partnership, or electing some members as managers to run a limited liability company, creates issues not confronted when using the simple approach of direct governance by all of the owners. For example, notice how the agreement in *JTB Enterprises* specified that "major decisions" required a member vote, rather than being within the managers' power to decide. This illustrates that central management schemes call for careful thought as to what, if any, decisions should be beyond the power of the managers without approval from the partners or members. More broadly, suppose the statute governing the LLCs in *Broyhill* and *JTB Enterprises* had not contained a default rule allowing removal of managers by majority vote. How are members to protect themselves from dishonest managers like the DeLucas, or even from managers who are simply inept? To the extent that a primary protection lies in the ability to select and remove managers, what sort of questions must an agreement address about this process?

Incidentally, as discussed in Chapter II, the idea of empowering only some owners to manage the firm is central to the structure of a limited partnership. Traditionally, this reflected the notion that relinquishing control was the quid pro quo for limited liability. The 2001 revision of the U.L.P.A. abandoned this notion—which already had been extremely watered down by revisions to the U.L.P.A. in the 1970s and 1980s—instead viewing the role of the limited partnership simply as providing a structure for those desiring a firm in which some owners have sole control. (Evidently, the drafters of the 2001 revision viewed the options of partners or LLC members granting some owners sole control by agreement to be insufficient.) Consistent with the goal of providing this structure of management, the 2001 revision of the U.L.P.A. vests exclusive power to control the firm in the general partners, except insofar as otherwise provided in the partnership agreement, and except for certain fundamental decisions upon which limited partners exercise a veto. U.L.P.A. (2001) § 406(a). Under either version of the U.L.P.A., in the absence of other agreement, general partners in a limited partnership have equal rights in management, and most decisions are subject to majority rule in the event of disagreement among the general partners. U.L.P.A. § 403; U.L.P.A. (2001) § 406(a).

4. Notice that the operating agreement in *Broyhill* required a unanimous vote to elect a manager. The agreement also effectively required all of the members to consent to the entry of a new member, such as the NVRI Trust, into the company. These are examples of the sort of unanimous vote requirements which, as noted earlier, are the default rule under the uniform partnership acts for extraordinary decisions. As under the partnership law scheme for ordinary decisions, LLC statutes typically contain provisions establishing a general principle of majority rule. *E.g.*, Cal. Corp. Code § 17103(a)(3); Del. Code Ann. Title 6 § 18–402; N.Y. Ltd. Liab. Co. Law §§ 402(f), 408(b). In contrast with the partnership scheme, however, many LLC statutes allow a majority (barring other agreement) to undertake extraordinary actions—potentially even including amendment of the operating agreement. *See, e.g.*, N.Y. Ltd. Liab. Co. Law § 402(c), (d). *But see* Cal. Corp. Code § 17103(a)(2)(C). What problems might this create?

> * * *LLC statutes vary on th[e] question [of whether a majority of the members can amend the operating agreement]. Many, if not most, acts require unanimity to amend the operating agreement, unless the parties have otherwise agreed. Numerous other acts, however, allow amendment on a majority (or, under some statutes, two-thirds) vote. Still other acts fail to address the question—leaving for litigation the issue of whether the statutes' general majority rule provisions trump the normal rule requiring the consent of all parties in order to modify a contract.
>
> The obvious problem with amendment by majority vote is that it enables the majority to alter the fundamental division of power and profit in ways the parties would never have agreed to allow. For example, the abuse is evident if a party with fifty-one percent of the profits and voting power could simply amend the agreement to increase his or her profit share to ninety-nine percent (particularly if he or she made no added contributions). To address this problem, New York's statute will not allow a bare majority, barring other agreement, to remove a supermajority voting requirement in the agreement. Nor will the New York statute allow the majority to alter agreed contributions, tax item allocations, or distributions over the opposition of prejudiced members. Such provisions, however, are largely unique to New York. They also risk ambiguities and gaps. As an illustration, New York's statute only indirectly, if at all, prevents the alteration of profit shares in the abusive manner described above. Since the New York statute refers only to profit allocations for tax purposes, the prejudiced minority member would need to argue that the act also prohibits changing the allocation of economic profits because this would render any unchanged allocation of profits for tax purposes of questionable validity under I.R.C. section 704(b)'s "substantial economic effect" require-

> ment. Yet, what about the majority voting itself generous salaries? This could certainly upset the allocation of economic benefits from the firm. Nevertheless, it is unclear if New York's law would prevent such an amendment.

Gevurtz, *Freeze-outs and Squeeze-outs in Limited Liability Companies*, 73 Wash. U.L.Q. 497, 511–12 (1995). More challenging from the standpoint of the drafter trying to anticipate possible problems from the default rules is the fact that sometimes the default rule allowing majority actions such as amending the operating agreement might be hidden in the statute. *See, e.g.*, Del. Code Ann. Title 6 § 18–209(f) (allowing amendment of a limited liability company operating agreement through a merger of LLCs). Indeed, the potential laying in Section 18–209(f) of Delaware's LLC statute has not been ignored.

VGS, Inc. v. Castiel

2000 WL 1277372 (Del. Ch.).

■ STEELE, V.C.

I. Facts

David Castiel formed Virtual Geosatellite LLC (the "LLC") on January 6, 1999 in order to pursue a Federal Communications Commission ("FCC") license to build and operate a satellite system which its proponents claim could dramatically increase the "real estate" in outer space capable of transmitting high speed internet traffic and other communications. When originally formed, it had only one Member—Virtual Geosatellite Holdings, Inc. ("Holdings"). On January 8, 1999, Ellipso, Inc. ("Ellipso") joined the LLC as its second Member. Several weeks later, on January 29, 1999, Sahagen Satellite Technology Group LLC ("Sahagen Satellite") became the third Member of the LLC. David Castiel controls both Holdings and Ellipso. Peter Sahagen, an aggressive and apparently successful venture capitalist, controls Sahagen Satellite.

Pursuant to the LLC Agreement, Holdings received 660 units (representing 63.46% of the total equity in the LLC), Sahagen Satellite received 260 units (representing 25%), and Ellipso received 120 units (representing 11.54%). The founders vested management of the LLC in a Board of Managers. As the majority unitholder, Castiel had the power to appoint, remove, and replace two of the three members of the Board of Managers. Castiel, therefore, had the power to prevent any Board decision with which he disagreed. Castiel named himself and Tom Quinn to the Board of Managers. Sahagen named himself as the third member of the Board.

Not long after the formation of the LLC, Castiel and Sahagen were at odds. Castiel contends that Sahagen wanted to control the LLC ever since he became involved, and that Sahagen repeatedly offered, unsuccessfully, to buy control of the LLC. Sahagen maintains that Castiel ran the LLC so poorly that its mission had become untracked, additional necessary capital could not be raised, and competent managers could not be attracted to join the enterprise. Further, Sahagen claims that Castiel directed LLC assets to Ellipso in order to prop up a failing, cash-strapped Ellipso. At trial, these issues and other similar accusations from both sides were explored in great detail. For our purposes here, all that need be concluded is the unarguable fact that Castiel and Sahagen had very different ideas about how the LLC should be managed and operated.

Sahagen ultimately convinced Quinn that Castiel must be ousted from leadership in order for the LLC to prosper. As a result, Quinn (Castiel's nominee) covertly "defected" to Sahagen's camp, and he and Sahagen decided to wrest control of the LLC from Castiel. Many LLC employees and even some of Castiel's lieutenants testified that they believed it to be in the LLC's best interest to take control from Castiel.

On April 14, 2000, without notice to Castiel, Quinn and Sahagen acted by written consent to merge the LLC under Delaware law into VGS, Inc. ("VGS"), a Delaware corporation. Accordingly, the LLC ceased to exist, its assets and liabilities passed to VGS, and VGS became the LLC's legal successor-in-interest. VGS's Board of Directors is comprised of Sahagen, Quinn, and Neel Howard. Of course, the incorporators did not name Castiel to VGS's Board.

On the day of the merger, Sahagen executed a promissory note to VGS in the amount of $10 million plus interest. In return, he received two million shares of VGS Series A Preferred Stock. VGS also issued 1,269,200 shares of common stock to Holdings, 230,800 shares of common stock to Ellipso, and 500,000 shares of common stock to Sahagen Satellite. Once one does the math, it is apparent that Holdings and Ellipso went from having a 75% controlling combined ownership interest in the LLC to having only a 37.5% interest in VGS. On the other hand, Sahagen and Sahagen Satellite went from owning 25% of the LLC to owning 62.5% of VGS.

There can be no doubt why Sahagen and Quinn, acting as a majority of the LLC's board of managers did not notify Castiel of the merger plan. Notice to Castiel would have immediately resulted in Quinn's removal from the board and a newly constituted majority which would thwart the effort to strip Castiel of control. Had he known in advance, Castiel surely would have attempted to replace Quinn with someone loyal to Castiel who would agree with his views. Clandestine machinations were, therefore, essential to the success of Quinn and Sahagen's plan.

II. Analysis

A. The Board of Managers did have authority to act by majority vote

The LLC Agreement does not expressly state whether the Board of Managers must act unanimously or by majority vote. Sahagen and Quinn contend that because a number of provisions would be rendered meaningless if a unanimous vote was required, a majority vote is implied. * * *

Section 8.01(b)(i) of the LLC Agreement states that, "[t]he Board of Managers shall initially be composed of three (3) Managers." Sahagen Satellite has the right to designate one member of the initial board, and if the Board of Managers increased in number, Sahagen Satellite could "designate a number of representatives on the Board of Managers that is less than Sahagen's then current Percentage Interest." If unanimity were required, the number of managers would be irrelevant–Sahagen, and his minority interest, would have veto power in any event. The existence of language in the LLC Agreement discussing expansion of the Board is therefore quite telling.

Also persuasive is the fact that Section 8.01(c) of the LLC Agreement, entitled "Matters Requiring Consent of Sahagen," provides that Sahagen's approval is needed for a merger, consolidation, or reorganization of the LLC. If a unanimity requirement indeed existed, there would have been no need to expressly list matters on which Sahagen's minority interest had veto power.

* * *

B. By failing to give notice of their proposed action, Sahagen and Quinn failed to discharge their duty of loyalty to Castiel in good faith

Section 18–404(d) of the LLC Act states in pertinent part:

> Unless otherwise provided in a limited liability company agreement, on any matter that is to be voted on by managers, the managers may take such action without a meeting, *without prior notice* and without a vote if a consent or consents in writing, setting forth the action so taken, shall be signed by the managers having not less than the minimum number of votes that would be necessary to authorize such action at a meeting (emphasis added).

Therefore, the LLC Act, read literally, does not require notice to Castiel before Sahagen and Quinn could act by written consent. The LLC Agreement does not purport to modify the statute in this regard.

Those observations cannot complete the analysis of Sahagen and Quinn's actions, however. Sahagen and Quinn knew what would happen if they notified Castiel of their intention to act by written consent to merge the LLC into VGS, Inc. Castiel would have attempted to remove Quinn, and block the planned action. Regardless of his motivation in doing so, removal of Quinn in that circumstance would have been within Castiel's rights as the LLC's controlling owner under the Agreement.

Section 18–404(d) has yet to be interpreted by this Court or the Supreme Court. Nonetheless, it seems clear that the purpose of permitting action by written consent without notice is to enable LLC managers to take quick, efficient action in situations where a minority of managers could not block or adversely affect the course set by the majority even if they were notified of the proposed action and objected to it. The General Assembly never intended, I am quite confident, to enable two managers to deprive, clandestinely and surreptitiously, a third manager representing the majority interest in the LLC of an opportunity to protect that interest by taking an action that the third manager's member would surely have opposed if he had knowledge of it. My reading of Section 18–404(d) is grounded in a classic maxim of equity—"Equity looks to the intent rather than to the form." In this hopefully unique situation, this application of the maxim requires construction of the statute to allow action without notice only by a *constant or fixed majority.* It can not apply to an illusory, will-of-the wisp majority which would implode should notice be given. Nothing in the statute suggests that this court of equity should blind its eyes to a shallow, too clever by half, manipulative attempt to restructure an enterprise through an action taken by a "majority" that existed only so long as it could act in secrecy.

Sahagen and Quinn each owed a duty of loyalty to the LLC, its investors and Castiel, their fellow manager. Castiel or his entities owned a majority interest in the LLC and he sat as a member of the board representing entities and interests empowered by the Agreement to control the majority membership of the board. The majority investor protected his equity interest in the LLC through the mechanism of appointment to the board rather than by the statutorily sanctioned mechanism of approval by members owning a majority of the LLC's equity interests. It may seem somewhat incongruous, but this Agreement allows the action to merge, dissolve or change to corporate status to be taken by a simple majority vote of the board of managers rather than rely upon the default position of the statute which requires a majority vote of the equity interest. Instead the drafters made the critical assumption, known to all the players here, that the holder of the majority equity interest has the right to appoint and remove two managers, ostensibly guaranteeing control over a three member board. When Sahagen and Quinn, fully recognizing that this was Castiel's protection against actions adverse to his majority interest, acted in secret, without notice, they failed to discharge their duty of loyalty to him in good faith. They owed Castiel a duty to give him prior notice even if he would have interfered with a plan that they conscientiously believed to be in the best interest of the LLC.

* * *

NOTES

1. Notice how Sahagen had protected himself from the same sort of action he took against Castiel. Suppose Sahagen had not had this veto power in the agreement; how much would the court's approach have done to protect a minority owner like him? More broadly, notice the type of transaction Sahagen and Quinn used to amend the control and economic arrangement between Sahagen and Castiel. Suppose an LLC operating agreement, or the governing statute, has a provision requiring unanimity for amending an operating agreement; could mergers or other transactions still allow a majority of the membership to amend?

Gevurtz, California's New Limited Liability Company Act: A Look at the Good, the Bad and the Ambiguous

27 Pac. L.J. 261, 291–294 (1996).

Given this requirement of unanimity to amend the operating agreement, the question becomes can a majority in a California LLC circumvent this rule? One common technique for altering the financial interests of shareholders in a corporation (including amending the organic documents of the company) is through a merger with a shell company, the impact of which is not really to combine different firms, but, rather, to alter the rights within one corporation. Could a voting majority in an LLC use this technique? In fact, in some jurisdictions, most notably Delaware, the answer is yes. To their credit, the drafters of California's LLC statute recognized this danger and attempted to deal with it. Unfortunately, ambiguity mars the attempt.

The pertinent language is in Section 17551(e) of the California Corporations Code:

> An agreement of merger approved in accordance with subdivision (a) may effect any amendment to the operating agreement of any constituent limited liability company or effect the adoption of a new operating agreement for a constituent limited liability company if it is the surviving limited liability company in the merger. * * * Notwithstanding the above provisions of this subdivision, if a greater number of members is required to approve an amendment to the operating agreement of the constituent limited liability company than is required to approve the agreement of merger pursuant to subdivision (a), and the number of members that approve the agreement of merger is less than the number of members required to approve an amendment to the operating agreement of the constituent limited liability company, any amendment to the operating agreement or adoption of a new operating agreement of the surviving limited liability company made pursuant to the first sentence of this subdivision shall be effective only if the agreement of merger is approved by the number of members required to approve an amendment to the operating agreement of the constituent limited liability company.

At first glance, the meaning of this provision, despite its rather convoluted language, seems simple enough: Mergers receiving less than unanimous approval cannot effect an amendment of the operating agreement of a constituent LLC (unless the agreement expressly allowed amendment on less than unanimous vote). Yet, this leaves questions unanswered. To begin with, * * *

* * * when does a merger [effect an] amendment of an operating agreement? A simple hypothetical illustrates the problem. Suppose there are two LLCs, each of which has three members, and the

operating agreement of each of which calls for each member to receive an equal one-third share of the firm's profits. Would a merger between the two firms under an agreement which calls for each member to receive an equal one-sixth profit share effect any amendment of the operating agreements? If one focuses on the equal sharing aspect of the original agreements, then there appears to be no alteration. If, however, one focuses on the one-third share aspect of the original agreements, then the conclusion is to the contrary. In deciding which interpretation to adopt, a court naturally may be inclined to look to language differences: Did the agreements refer to "equal shares" or "one-third shares?" The problem is that from the standpoint of the drafters of the original agreements, this language was substantially equivalent and, therefore, the words chosen could have been largely accidental. (The same ambiguity can exist if the agreement follows the statutory default rule of profit sharing in proportion to contributions, since it may be quite common in drafting such an agreement to specify the actual percentage of profit interests in order to avoid disputes later as to what was the ratio of contributions and, hence, profits.)

Faced with this problem, one temptation may be to read Section 17551(e) narrowly so as to avoid eclipsing the majority rule principle of Section 17551(a). For example, a court might interpret the "effect any amendment" language not to encompass the alteration of profit shares virtually inevitable upon merging two LLCs together. More broadly, one might assert that the merger of one LLC into another, under a plan which leaves the surviving LLC's operating agreement unchanged, does not effect any amendment despite whatever changes this means for the rights of members of the disappearing LLC. (The basis for this construction lies in Section 17551(e)'s references to the "surviving limited liability company.") Yet, the impact of the latter construction is to create a huge disparity in the voting rights of the members of two merging LLCs, depending upon the artificial distinction of which firm receives the label of survivor. * * * Moreover, reading Section 17551(e) narrowly opens dangerous prospects for abuse. A hypothetical illustrates why. Suppose A, B and C are equal members of an LLC. A and B feel they should receive an increase in their profit shares. C demurs. A and B cannot amend the operating agreement (barring a contrary provision in the document) to increase their shares over C's objection. Yet, if Section 17551(e) does not apply, what would stop A and B from forming a new LLC owned by themselves, which they then merge with the existing LLC, thereby increasing their profit shares?

One further ambiguity in Section 17551(e) may prove even more telling. Suppose a California LLC merges into a foreign LLC so the foreign LLC is the survivor; does this "effect any amendment" of the California LLC's operating agreement? After all, changing the law governing the LLC could significantly change the rights of the parties. For example, the majority voting interest in a Delaware LLC (as mentioned earlier) may amend the operating agreement by merger—

something the majority could not do (barring other agreement) in California. Hence, unless one interprets Section 17551(e) to apply to a merger which changes the governing law for a California LLC, majorities can circumvent the statute by merging into a shell Delaware LLC, which then merges again with another shell LLC in order to effect an amendment.

* * *

Beyond mergers, a sale of substantially all assets to a new LLC in exchange for interests in the new firm, followed by a dissolution of the old firm and a distribution of the new interests, could serve as a tool to amend an operating agreement. This suggests again the need for California's LLC act to address sales of substantially all assets[, since California's LLC act does not indicate what the required vote is for such an action].

Interestingly, among the decisions requiring a unanimous vote under the 2001 revision of the U.L.P.A. (in the absence of contrary agreement) are amendments of the partnership agreement, sales of substantially all assets, and mergers. U.L.P.A. (2001) §§ 406(b)(1), (3), 1107(a).)

2. While the court's objection to the lack of notice saved Castiel, the court in *Broyhill* ignored the fact that Mr. Broyhill and the NVRI Trust never gave the DeLucas advance notice of the meeting at which Mr. Broyhill and the NVRI Trust voted to remove the DeLucas as managers. Is such notice something that the operating agreement should have called for, or would this just create a meaningless formality, which, if neglected, could produce legal uncertainties? If the parties do not want to require such formalities, does this mean the operating agreement can ignore the question? See, *e.g.*, Cal. Corp. Code § 17104(c) (requiring notice of meetings unless otherwise provided in the operating agreement); N.Y. Ltd. Liab. Co. Law § 405 (same).

3. External Constraints

So far, the focus in discussing management has been on the rights among the owners of the venture. For example, the litigation about hiring the employee in *Summers* arose from the effort of one partner to claim reimbursement from the partnership for compensation this partner personally had paid to the employee. Suppose, however, the employee in *Summers* had not been paid. Could he successfully sue the partnership and the partner who was opposed to his employment? To ask this question is to illustrate that planning for management entails considering factors other than simply the relationship of the owners towards each other.

In fact, if the partner's action in *Summers* appeared to be for carrying on in the usual way the partnership business, then the employee would have prevailed in suing the firm and the other partner—regardless of whether the partnership agreement, or the uniform partnership acts in the absence of agreement, denied the hiring partner the right to decide whether the firm should hire an employee. U.P.A. § 9(1); R.U.P.A. § 301. How might one limit the ability of partners to bind the firm to transactions beyond their actual authority? Will a purposes clause in the partnership agreement help? Is a party dealing with a partner going to see such a clause? In addition to the danger of unauthorized contracts, partners might also be concerned with the unauthorized expenditure of partnership funds. Does this explain the attention partnership agreements often give to the question of who must sign partnership checks? What concrete step can the partnership take to ensure that the partnership's bank acts consistently with a provision in the partnership agreement concerning signatures on partnership checks? Section 303 of the R.U.P.A. allows partnerships to file a "statement of authority" with an appropriate state official. This document can specify limitations on the authority of partners to enter a transaction on behalf of the firm. Will parties dealing with a partner see this document? If not, are such parties deemed to know of its contents? See R.U.P.A. § 303(e), (f) (if filed in the office in which one would record the transfer of real property held by the partnership, then can cut off the unauthorized attempt to transfer that real property; otherwise the statement of authority generally does not provide constructive notice of limitations of a partner's authority).

What about unauthorized actions in a limited partnership or an LLC? In fact, the discussion of unauthorized actions brings one back to the utility of designating managers, rather than members, to run a limited liability company. Some LLC statutes curtail the apparent authority of non-manager members for those companies who choose to be run by managers rather than members. *E.g.*, Cal. Corp. Code § 17157(b)(1); N.Y. Ltd. Liab. Co. Law § 412(b)(1). Similarly, one residual utility of the limited partnership is to curtail the apparent authority of limited partners to bind the firm. U.L.P.A. § 302.

Introducing limited partners and the limited partnership brings up a second external constrain on the owners' structuring management. Traditionally, the tradeoff for limited partners maintaining their limited liability was to avoid taking part in control of the business. Indeed, read literally, the 1916 version of the U.L.P.A. would deny limited liability if there was any management activity by limited partners. Yet, even if limited partners are content to remain for the most part as passive investors, they may need some control in order to protect their interests. Moreover, limited partners may have ideas and management skills which would be useful to the venture.

The danger that limited partners would lose limited liability if they took part in control underwent a major decline with revisions to the U.L.P.A in the 1970s and 1980s. Specifically, the drafters of the revisions replaced the simple rule that limited partners would not be liable unless they took part in control, with an elaborate provision (Section 303), which sought to provide both greater clarity and liberality. From a planning perspective, Section 303(b) of the U.L.P.A. as revised in 1976, and amended in 1985, is of particular utility, since it provides a safe harbor of enumerated activities that limited partners may undertake. These include acting as agent of the firm or of its general partner, consulting with or advising the general partner, and voting on certain matters (such as admission or removal of partners, incurrence of extraordinary debt, sale of substantially all assets, dissolving or changing the nature of the business and amending the agreement). Indeed, under the 1985 amendments to Section 303, this safe harbor includes voting on anything the agreement specifies. In addition, the second sentence of Section 303(a), to some extent as revised in 1976, and particularly as amended in 1985, protects limited partners who overstep the permissible bounds of control, but do not thereby mislead creditors into believing they are general partners. Still, while helpful in defending litigation, how much utility does the second sentence of Section 303(a) have from a planning perspective? After all, are limited partners participating in control always going to remember to make sure a third party understands their role? Moreover, is it clear whether the second sentence of Section 303(a) applies to tort claimants? See Buxbaum, *Understanding California's New Limited Partnership Act,* 4 Cal.Law. No. 5, p. 13 (May 1984) (stating it does not).

More dramatically, the 2001 revision of the U.L.P.A. seemingly shatters the whole concern that limited partners might lose their limited liability by participating in control. Section 303, as revised in 2001, flatly states that a limited partner is not liable for obligations of the firm, without any caveat about control. Suppose, however, that a creditor of the limited partnership claims that a limited partner's participation in control confused the creditor into thinking that the limited partner was, in fact, a general partner, and, hence, had unlimited liability. See *Antonic Rigging and Erecting, Inc. v. Foundry East Ltd. Partnership*, 773 F. Supp. 420 (S.D. Ga. 1991) (in applying Georgia's version of the U.L.P.A.—which, as early as 1989, eliminated liability for limited partners who participated in control—the court held open the possibility of liability based upon estoppel if a limited partner leads a creditor to believe the limited partner is a general partner; but the court did not find facts to support such a claim in the case before it).

A different concern with management and the loss of limited liability in an LLC arises from so-called management formalities. It is often said that the disregard of so-called corporate formalities, such as the failure to hold shareholders' and directors' meetings, is a factor that might influence a court to pierce the corporate veil and make shareholders personally liable for corporate debts. To what extent is the non-observance of similar formalities regarding meetings of members and managers a factor which might lead to members of an LLC facing personal liability for the firm's debts? If this is a concern, is it better for the LLC operating agreement to provide for more meetings and other such formalities, or less?

Gevurtz, California's New Limited Liability Company Act: A Look at the Good, the Bad, and the Ambiguous

27 Pac. L.J. 261, 299–301 (1996).

Section 17101(b) of California's new LLC [limited liability company] act imports the doctrine of piercing into the LLC context. It states that an LLC member shall be personally liable generally to the same extent as a shareholder may be liable for the debt of a corporation. * * *

Section 17101(b) contains one special direction. It states that:

> [T]he failure to hold meetings of members or managers or the failure to observe formalities pertaining to the calling or conduct of meetings shall not be considered a factor tending to establish that the members have personal liability for any debt, obligation, or liability of the limited liability company where the articles of organization or operating agreement do not expressly require the holding of meetings of members or managers.

At first glance, this provision appears eminently sensible. The failure to hold, or the informal handling of, meetings for which there is no legal requirement in the first place should hardly be a factor for piercing. A difficulty, however, lies in the possible negative implication of this provision. Will the failure to hold meetings called for in the articles or operating agreement be a ground for piercing? Concern that this could be the case has already led some writers to suggest that members not include in their articles or operating agreements any specific requirement for member or manager meetings.

This is an unfortunate development. In LLCs with more than several members, and especially those choosing governance by managers, specifying in a written agreement when there will be meetings (for example, to elect managers) might be handy to avoid later disputes among the membership. Why then should the failure to observe meeting requirements intended for the benefit of the owners in their relationship with each other be a factor against them when it comes to liability to outsiders?

This raises the question of whether this caveat was really necessary. Section 17101(b) appears to be based upon section 300(e) of California's Corporation Code. Section 300(e) provides that

> The failure of a close corporation to observe corporate formalities relating to meetings of directors or shareholders in connection with the management of its affairs, pursuant to an agreement authorized by subdivision (b), shall not be considered a factor tending to establish that the shareholders have personal liability for corporate obligations.

The logic behind section 300(e) is not difficult to comprehend. Section 300(b) validates shareholders agreements respecting the management of a statutory close corporation in California against the claim that they are contrary to public policy because they interfere with the statutory power of the board of directors to manage the corporation. Ultra-cautious parties might not take advantage of this provision, however, for fear that the failure to follow management formalities pursuant to a shareholders agreement could be a factor leading to piercing. To allay this fear and ensure that the statutory close corporation provision did not become a trap leading to personal liability, the legislature included section 300(e).

Yet, is it really true that the failure to observe formalities respecting meetings of directors or shareholders is a factor leading to piercing? This belief is the critical assumption behind section 300(e) and, in turn, section 17101(b). While getting beyond the scope of this article, a careful examination of corporate piercing cases suggests that this may be the legal equivalent of an "old wives' tale." Admittedly, numerous court opinions and writers list lack of management formalities as a factor for piercing. It is a challenge to find a decision, however, in which the absence of *meeting* formalities actually yielded a decision to pierce, which the observance of such formalities would have changed. Instead, this "factor" seems at most to be a make-weight used to justify further a result already reached on other grounds. In fact, there is no reason for formalities regarding meetings to be a factor in piercing. Their presence is hardly likely to benefit creditors, nor their absence to harm them. (In this regard, it is important to distinguish informalities regarding meetings from informalities regarding finances; i.e. failure to issue stock, commingling funds, and typically unfair as well as poorly documented self-dealing transactions.)

From the standpoint of counseling clients, the caveat at the end of the excerpt above is of critical importance. Numerous piercing the corporate veil cases find their real justification, not in the failure to hold shareholder or director meetings, but rather in abusive transactions by the owner with the corporation's assets. To avoid charges of such abusive dealings, the owner should document that any assets or other benefits he or she received from the company were either in exchange for fair consideration—for example, as a salary equal to what the company would have paid if dealing with one who was not in control—or constituted a distribution which complied with statutory limits on distributions from a company to its owners. Creating documentation contemporaneously with the transaction to show that the transaction entailed such a fair exchange, or statutory compliance, is the sort of "formality" that can help avoid piercing. *E.g.*, Gevurtz, *Piercing Piercing: An Attempt to Lift the Veil of Confusion Surrounding the Doctrine of Piercing the Corporate Veil*, 76 Ore. L. Rev. 853, 879–880 (1997). This sort of "formality" is just as relevant to limited liability companies as it is to corporations.

Strangely enough, taxes also can become a factor in structuring management. Specifically, designating managers for an LLC might save the non-managing members from the need to pay self-employment taxes. Section 1401 of the Internal Revenue Code imposes two taxes on net earnings from self-employment: a 12.4 percent Social Security tax on such income (up to a limit), and a 2.9 percent Medicare tax on all self-employment income (without any maximum). In defining self-employment income, Section 1402 of the Internal Revenue Code generally includes the distributive share of a partner in a partnership, but generally excludes the distributive share of a limited partner. In which camp do members in a limited liability company fit? The Internal Revenue Service proposed a regulation in 1997 to answer this question. The proposed regulation generally places all owners of entities taxed as partnerships into the camp of limited partners unless the owner either (1) has personal liability as a partner for debts of the firm; (2) has authority to contract on behalf of the firm; or (3) participates over 500 hours during the year in the firm's business. Prop. Treas. Reg. § 1.1402(a)–2(h). Of course, this was only a proposed regulation, and the 1997 Taxpayer Relief Act contained a provision postponing the regulation's coming into effect. Nevertheless, if apparent authority makes an LLC member subject to self-employment tax, avoiding such taxes can provide a reason to opt for governance by managers rather than members (thereby cutting off the apparent authority of the non-managing members).

Estate tax concerns also can impact permissible control in limited partnerships and LLCs—at least until the repeal of the estate tax takes full effect in 2010, and assuming Congress does not allow reinstatement of the tax in 2011. The problem arises from Section 2036(a) of the Internal Revenue Code. Normally, if a person transfers property before his or her death, the property would not be part of his or her estate for purposes of estate tax. Hence, if an elderly person transfers various business assets into a limited partnership or an LLC, and then gives interests in the limited partnership or LLC to his or her children, the value of the business assets and the value of the interests received by the children normally would not be subject to estate tax when the transferor dies. Limited partnerships (or even LLCs) set up for this purpose often are referred to as family limited partnerships. Section 2036(a), however, treats property transferred by a decedent as still part of the decedent's estate if the decedent retains for his or her life either the possession or enjoyment of, or the right to income from, the property, or the right to designate the person who shall possess or enjoy the property or the income from the property. Of course, the mere fact that the elderly transferor may have power to manage the limited partnership does not mean he or she possesses or enjoys the firm's assets or his or her children's interests in the firm. Managing a business, particularly if one has fiduciary obligations to other owners, is different from possessing or enjoying property for one's personal benefit. On the other hand, if the elderly transferor has the power to use the limited partnership as a personal piggy bank to cover living expenses, or as a vehicle to hold title to his or her residence, or the like, then Section 2036(a) can apply. *Compare Estate of Strangi v. Commissioner*, T.C.M. 2003–145, *with Estate of Kimball v. Commissioner*, 371 F.3d 257 (5th Cir. 2004).

SECTION D. DISSOLUTION AND CHANGES IN OWNERSHIP

1. CONSEQUENCES ABSENT ANY PLANNING

The prior three sections of this chapter dealt with areas in which the need for advance agreement seems fairly obvious. After all, the subject of contributions goes to the very reason the parties decided to join together, and involves, in large part, actions to occur at the outset of the business. The allocation of profits and control lie at the heart of the deal. By contrast, in considering dissolution and changes in ownership, one is planning for events which may be far off in the future and might never occur. Accordingly, the participants might take the view that they should "cross that bridge when they get there." What, if any, problems might result from such an approach?

Page v. Page

55 Cal.2d 192, 10 Cal.Rptr. 643, 359 P.2d 41 (1961).

■ TRAYNOR, JUSTICE.

Plaintiff and defendant are partners in a linen supply business in Santa Maria, California. Plaintiff appeals from a judgment declaring the partnership to be for a term rather than at will.

The partners entered into an oral partnership agreement in 1949. Within the first two years each partner contributed approximately $43,000 for the purchase of land, machinery, and linen needed to begin the business. From 1949 to 1957 the enterprise was unprofitable, losing approximately $62,000. The partnership's major creditor is a corporation, wholly owned by plaintiff, that supplies the linen and machinery necessary for day-to-day operation of the business. This corporation holds a $47,000 demand note of the partnership. The partnership operations began to improve in 1958. The partnership earned $3,824.41 in that year and $2,282.30 in the first three months of 1959. Despite this improvement plaintiff wishes to terminate the partnership.

The Uniform Partnership Act provides that a partnership may be dissolved "By the express will of any partner when no definite term or particular undertaking is specified." Corp. Code, § 15031, subd. (1)(b) [U.P.A. § 31(1)(b)]. The trial court found that the partnership is for a term, namely, "such reasonable time as is necessary to enable said partnership to repay from partnership profits, indebtedness incurred for the purchase of land, building, laundry and delivery equipment and linen for the operation of such business. * * * "Plaintiff correctly contends that this finding is without support in the evidence.

Defendant testified that the terms of the partnership were to be similar to former partnerships of plaintiff and defendant, and that the understanding of these partnerships was that "we went into partnership to start the business and let the business operation pay for itself, put in so much money, and let the business pay itself out." * * *

* * * He nevertheless concedes that there was no understanding as to the term of the present partnership in the event of losses. He was asked: "[W]as there any discussion with reference to the continuation of the business in the event of losses?" He replied, "Not that I can remember." He was then asked, "did you have any understanding with Mr. Page, your

brother, the plaintiff in this action, as to how the obligations were to be paid if there were losses?" He replied, "Not that I can remember. I can't remember discussing that at all. We never figured on losing, I guess."

Viewing this evidence most favorably for defendant, it proves only that the partners expected to meet current expenses from current income and to recoup their investment if the business were successful.

Defendant contends that such an expectation is sufficient to create a partnership for a term under the rule of Owen v. Cohen, 19 Cal.2d 147, 150, 119 P.2d 713. In that case we held that when a partner advances a sum of money to a partnership with the understanding that the amount contributed was to be a loan to the partnership and was to be repaid as soon as feasible from the prospective profits of the business, the partnership is for the term reasonably required to repay the loan. It is true that Owen v. Cohen, supra, and other cases hold that partners may impliedly agree to continue in business until certain sum of money is earned (Mervyn Investment Co. v. Biber, 184 Cal. 637, 641–642, 194 P. 1037), or one or more partners recoup their investments (Vangel v. Vangel, 116 Cal.App.2d 615, 625, 254 P.2d 919), or until certain debts are paid (Owen v. Cohen, supra, 19 Cal.2d at page 150, 119 P.2d at page 714), or until certain property could be disposed of on favorable terms (Shannon v. Hudson, 161 Cal.App.2d 44, 48, 325 P.2d 1022). In each of these cases, however, the implied agreement found support in the evidence.

* * *

In the instant case, however, defendant failed to prove any facts from which an agreement to continue the partnership for a term may be implied. The understanding to which defendant testified was no more than a common hope that the partnership earnings would pay for all the necessary expenses. Such a hope does not establish even by implication a "definite term or particular undertaking" as required by section 15031, subdivision (1)(b) of the Corporations Code. All partnerships are ordinarily entered into with the hope that they will be profitable, but that alone does not make them all partnerships for a term and obligate the partners to continue in the partnerships until all of the losses over a period of many years have been recovered.

Defendant contends that plaintiff is acting in bad faith and is attempting to use his superior financial position to appropriate the now profitable business of the partnership. Defendant has invested $43,000 in the firm, and owing to the long period of losses his interest in the partnership assets is very small. The fact that plaintiff's wholly-owned corporation holds a $47,000 demand note of the partnership may make it difficult to sell the business as a going concern. Defendant fears that upon dissolution he will receive very little and that plaintiff, who is the managing partner and knows how to conduct the operations of the partnership, will receive a business that has become very profitable because of the establishment of Vandenberg Air Force Base in its vicinity. Defendant charges that plaintiff has been content to share the losses but now that the business has become profitable he wishes to keep all the gains.

There is no showing in the record of bad faith or that the improved profit situation is more than temporary. In any event these contentions are irrelevant to the issue whether the partnership is for a term or at will. Since, however, this action is for a declaratory judgment and will be the basis for future action by the parties, it is appropriate to point out that defendant is amply protected by the fiduciary duties of co-partners.

Even though the Uniform Partnership Act provides that a partnership at will may be dissolved by the express will of any partner (Corp. Code, § 15031, subd. (1)(b)), this power, like any other power held by a fiduciary, must be exercised in good faith.

* * *

A partner at will is not bound to remain in a partnership, regardless of whether the business is profitable or unprofitable. A partner may not, however, by use of adverse pressure "freeze out" a co-partner and appropriate the business to his own use. A partner may not dissolve a partnership to gain the benefits of the business for himself, unless he fully compensates his co-partner for his share of the prospective business opportunity. In this regard his fiduciary duties are at least as great as those of a shareholder of a corporation.

* * *

Likewise in the instant case, plaintiff has the power to dissolve the partnership by express notice to defendant. If, however, it is proved that plaintiff acted in bad faith and violated his fiduciary duties by attempting to appropriate to his own use the new prosperity of the partnership without adequate compensation to his co-partner, the dissolution would be wrongful and the plaintiff would be liable as provided by subdivision (2)(a) of Corporations Code, § 15038 [U.P.A. § 38(2)(a)] (rights of partners upon wrongful dissolution) for violation of the implied agreement not to exclude defendant wrongfully from the partnership business opportunity.

The judgment is reversed.

NOTES

1. *Page* illustrates the consequences for partnerships (as well as LLPs) in which the partners have done no planning concerning how to conclude their relationship. In this event, each partner can dissolve the firm at will. *See also* R.U.P.A. § 801(a). *But see* Cal. Corp. Code § 16801(a) (takes at least half the partners to dissolve a partnership at will). The case also shows that some partners may be upset with this result. Before assuming, however, that the partnership agreement automatically should do something to change this outcome, it is useful to ask what exactly will happen upon dissolution and why, if at all, does this pose a problem. In fact, it is a mistake to assume, as often done, that the impact of dissolution upon the

business conducted by the partnership is much the same as pouring water on the "Wicked Witch of the West."

Following dissolution—assuming no other agreement—the partnership's assets must be sold, its debts paid and the remaining cash, if any, distributed to the partners. U.P.A. § 38(1); R.U.P.A. § 807(a). *But see Disotell v. Stiltner*, 100 P.3d 890 (Alaska 2004). Writers often warn that such a liquidation can be ruinous. *See, e.g.,* Bromberg, *Partnership, Dissolution—Causes, Consequences and Cures,* 43 Tex. L. Rev. 631, 647 (1965). What might be the reasoning behind this assertion? Recall the materials in Chapter I on valuing businesses. If the partnership assets must be sold piecemeal, what is the likely result? Perhaps, however, an outsider will offer to buy the business as a going concern. But in a partnership heavily dependent on the services of its members and about which outsiders have no readily available information, is a sale to an outsider likely to bring top dollar? On the other hand, is there any reason why partners who wish to keep operating the venture (assuming some do) cannot purchase all the assets following dissolution and thereupon continue the business? Indeed, this is precisely what the defendant in *Page* suspected his brother would do. Given the availability of this alternative, what is wrong with liquidation so as to require any advance planning?

In *Page,* the two partners wished to continue the business, but not, at least as far as one was concerned, together. In a liquidation, what decides which partner purchases the firm's assets? Is competitive bidding a fair approach? What would that have led to in *Page*? The court in *Page* warned that dissolving in bad faith to freeze out a partner can result in liability. (Whether the R.U.P.A. alters this result is unclear. *Compare* R.U.P.A. § 404(d) (partners must exercise any rights in good faith), *with* § 602(b) (limiting the definition of wrongful dissociation).) What risks does the *Page* warning create for an individual who simply no longer gets along with his or her partner, dissolves and thereupon bids for the firm's assets? See Hillman, *The Dissatisfied Participant in the Solvent Business Venture: A Consideration of the Relative Permanence of Partnerships and Close Corporations,* 67 Minn. L. Rev. 1, 31 (1982) (risks allegations that he or she acted in bad faith). Other courts have held that, instead of competitive bidding, they will decide which partner is more entitled to the business. *E.g., Nicholes v. Hunt,* 273 Or. 255, 541 P.2d 820 (1975). Is this a satisfactory solution? Can advance planning provide a better answer to deciding which partner should get to keep the business when partners do not get along?

If one or more partners are content to leave the business, what concern will they still have about a sale of the firm's assets to the remaining partners? Is there a legitimate concern that the sale may occur at less than a fair price, especially given the typical lack of outside buyers? One protection against this possibility is for all partners to bid on the assets. Another safeguard is found in the reminder by the court in *Page* that each partner owes a fiduciary duty to the other partners, which a partner might violate by paying an unfairly low price. Are there limits, however, on the effectiveness of these two protections? Can advance planning help assure a fair price?

Next, consider the situation from the standpoint of the partners who wish to continue the business. Might they face some difficulty in coming up with the necessary funds to buy the assets in a liquidation sale, especially if the event causing dissolution occurs without much advance warning? Is there any danger, albeit infrequent, they may lose the business in such a sale to an outsider willing to pay more? Might they be unable to acquire some properties critical to the business—perhaps because the property belongs to the departing partner who only loaned it to the firm (*see Cude v. Couch*, reprinted later in this chapter), or because the property consists of rights which are not assignable upon dissolution? *Cf. Fairway Development v. Title Ins. Co.,* 621 F.Supp. 120 (N.D.Ohio 1985). What other administrative difficulties does continuing the business by purchasing its assets in a liquidation sale entail? Once again, can advance planning help avoid these problems? If so, how?

2. One apparent solution, suggested by the court's opinion in *Page,* is to agree that the partnership shall continue for a "definite term or particular undertaking." U.P.A. § 31(1)(b). Does this require specifying a set number of years or an identifiable task? What about specifying the term as until all (or a majority of the partners) vote to dissolve? If partners agree to a term, how effective is this in preventing dissolution under the original Uniform Partnership Act if one partner wants out? See U.P.A. § 31(2) (partner can still dissolve, albeit in contravention of the agreement). Moreover, what happens under the U.P.A. if a partner in a partnership for a term dies or goes bankrupt? See U.P.A. § 31(4), (5).

The upshot of this discussion is that even agreeing to a term cannot prevent dissolution upon a partner's departure under the original Uniform Partnership Act. This follows from the Act's definition of dissolution as "the change in relation of the partners caused by any partner ceasing to be associated in the carrying on * * * of the business." U.P.A. § 29. If it cannot prevent dissolution, what might an agreement do?

Notice, partners only have the right to demand liquidation under Section 38(1) of the U.P.A. "unless otherwise agreed." This means the partners can consent to allow some of their number to continue the business after dissolution without the necessity of buying the assets in a liquidation sale. *See also* U.P.A. § 41. Since it is unlikely any partner would wish to give up the liquidation right without some offsetting compensation, providing for the continuation of the firm normally means agreeing to a buy-out of the withdrawing partner's interest. In fact, Section 38 explicitly substitutes a buy-out for liquidation in a pair of events: (1) dissolution in contravention of an agreement providing a term (wrongful dissolution)—in which event, Section 38(2) gives the partners not dissolving wrongfully the option to continue the business by paying off the interest of the wrongfully dissolving partner (but without paying for goodwill and less damages, and with the option to pay only at the end of the term); and (2) the expulsion of a partner under an agreement which allows some partners to expel others from the firm—in which event, the expelled partner gets paid for his or her interest. Moreover, Section 42 of the U.P.A. provides for a buy-out whenever the business is continued without liquidation. Given this scheme, what is left for the partnership agreement to address? Specifically, do these U.P.A. provisions adequately deal with the various problems—such as ensuring a fair price and available funding—which can occur in a liquidation sale?

3. The R.U.P.A. changes the U.P.A. scheme with respect to the concept and consequences of dissolution. To begin with, the revised act introduces a new term, "dissociation," which essentially means the same thing as "dissolution" did under the U.P.A. Specifically, under the R.U.P.A., a partner's withdrawal or expulsion from the partnership, or death or bankruptcy, causes a dissociation, but not necessarily a "dissolution." R.U.P.A. §§ 601, 603(a), 801. If there is a dissociation without a dissolution, the R.U.P.A. provides for a buy-out of the departing partner's interest (R.U.P.A. § 701), whereas a dissolution leads to winding up and liquidation barring other agreement. R.U.P.A. §§ 803, 807. The practical impact is to conform the legal meaning of "dissolution" more closely with lay usage of the term. This, in turn, might prevent the confusion which otherwise occurs when a partnership agreement inartfully attempts to prevent a partner's departure from the firm leading to "dissolution"—which, as seen above, is a terminological impossibility under the U.P.A.—when what the drafter meant was to prevent the departure leading to a winding up and liquidation. This change might also avoid problems when the firm enters contracts with third parties which are non-assignable or terminate upon the partnership's dissolution. (Notice, the only way under the U.P.A. to deal with the problem of non-assignable contracts, or contracts which terminate upon dissolution, is to make sure all contracts the partnership enters have a provision which allows their assignment to successors of the partnership.)

Beyond semantics, the R.U.P.A. alters the U.P.A.'s scheme by possibly narrowing the list of circumstances in which a partner's departure will lead to liquidation barring other agreement. Under both acts, partners can agree not to liquidate the partnership upon departure in various situations—either explicitly or by agreeing to a partnership for a term or to an expulsion clause. *See* U.P.A. § 38(1) and (2); R.U.P.A. §§ 103, 603(a), 801. Section 38(1) of the U.P.A. is unclear, however, as whether those who obtain a partner's interest (as opposed to the remaining partners) can force liquidation upon a partner's death or bankruptcy. The R.U.P.A. answers this question in the negative. *See* R.U.P.A. § 801(1), (2). (Why docs Section 801(6) not apply in this situation? See R.U.P.A. § 801 Comments 4, 8.)

To what extent do these changes in the R.U.P.A. remove the need for advance planning regarding a partner's departure? For example, as indicated above, the R.U.P.A. does not change the outcome in a situation like *Page* in which the partners have made absolutely no agreement respecting the duration of the partnership or their departure from the firm. R.U.P.A. § 801(1). Even when the R.U.P.A. cuts back on the rule of liquidation barring contrary agreement—as, for example, upon death of a partner—

does it ensure an acceptable price for the departing partner's interest, available funds for the continuing partners to afford the buy-out and optimal tax treatment? See R.U.P.A. § 701(a) (stating that the partnership "shall cause" the purchase, which leaves the option open as to whether the partnership or the other partners pay for the interest, which, in turn, impacts tax treatment), (b) (buy-out price based upon hypothetical sale), (h) (only authorizing deferred payment in case of wrongful dissolution), and (i) (court determines the buy-out price if the parties cannot agree).

Horning v. Horning Construction, LLC

12 Misc.3d 402, 816 N.Y.S.2d 877 (2006).

This is a petition by Horning for a judgment to dissolve Horning Construction LLC. Horning Construction LLC is a limited liability company organized under the laws of New York in December 2001. There is no operating agreement.

According to petitioner, he formed the business originally as Horning Construction Company, Inc. in July 1984. It was, and is, a commercial construction company. He asserts that it has grown to become a major construction company in Monroe County. * * * Petitioner asserts that, by 2001, the corporation had between 10 and 15 million dollars in annual sales. However, petitioner states, by December 2001, he felt he had to take on partners in order to lessen his crushing workload. Therefore, he offered two of his employees, respondents Klimowski and Holdsworth, an interest in a new company, Horning Construction LLC.

Petitioner details the arrangement offered to each respondent, which was basically that they would take over some of the day-to-day responsibilities of the business in return for a 1/3 interest each in the LLC.* * * [P]etitioner states that all business was transitioned from Horning Inc. to Horning LLC, presumably at his direction. * * *

Petitioner contends that respondents never assumed their anticipated duties to relieve petitioner of his workload, but they did realize substantial financial gain because petitioner nevertheless treated them as partners. Because the parties could not agree on an operating agreement, by 2005, petitioner offered to sell the LLC to respondents. Petitioner maintains that the offer was a fair one and that independent business advisors have so opined. On the other hand, respondents assert that the agreement is not fair in that it gives too much to petitioner. Alternative proposals were exchanged, but the parties cannot agree on a resolution.

Petitioner contends further that, as a result of the inability to agree on a sales proposal, the relationship between the three of them has deteriorated to the point that they cannot work together. He asserts that the animosity is "palpable." Petitioner maintains that this status has reached a critical stage because they cannot put together competitive bids on projects because of this strain. Petitioner attaches a letter from Klimowski, which contains profanity, to demonstrate the level of animosity which exists between the parties. * * * He concludes that the LLC must be dissolved pursuant to *§ 702 of the Limited Liability Company Law* ("LLCL"). * * *

Respondents Position

Respondents oppose the petition and ask that petitioner be enjoined from engaging in activities inimical to the LLC's interests, which respondents characterize as a breach of fiduciary duties to the LLC.

Klimowski stated that he worked for Horning, Inc. since 1989. In early 2001, he was approached by petitioner to gauge his interest in forming a LLC with his own ownership interest. According to Klimowski, petitioner did this because * * * Klimowski was the only person at Horning who could manage projects in excess of $5,000,000.00. Klimowski agreed to join. Holdsworth's states that he came from a separate company and would only consider joining the LLC if he was a part owner. He also asserts that Horning, Inc. could not bid for larger projects which is another reason why the LLC was formed. * * * Holdsworth asserts that there was no condition that, if the LLC was formed, he would assume "administrative duties." The LLC was formed in December 2001, with each member getting a 1/3 ownership interest. Respondents state that the LLC began doing business in March 2002, and since then has maintained steady progress with revenues capping out at approximately $25 million in 2005. Respondents contend that they accounted for the generation of between 73 and 80 percent of the LLC's gross profits in 2004 and 2005 respectively.

Respondents point out that the LLC continues to employ more than 40 people, that it meets all of its financial obligations, and that it is fully solvent. Respondents contend that there is no reason to believe that the LLC can no longer function. Klimowski admits that he demonstrated "pique" in his recent letter to petitioner, but it was based upon frustration engendered by petitioner's constant condescending behavior towards him. He asserts that petitioner fails to acknowledge that the is a 1/3 owner instead of a mere employee. Respondents maintain that petitioner is not "frozen out" of the business, that petitioner continues to receive his $120,000.00 yearly salary, which is greater than the salary of respondents, that the company is not deadlocked, that it is simply run by a majority rule, and that under the circumstances, it is unnecessary and unjust to dissolve the LLC which would place in jeopardy the livelihood of the 40+ employees. There is no impediment to the LLC's continuation because all bids only require the approval of two of the members.

Holdsworth states that petitioner has not generated much business of late and has been allowed to take more vacation than other members. Holdsworth acknowledges petitioner's stated wish to retire coupled with petitioner's offer of a buy-out under which the LLC would pay him $358,000 for 12 years with 2 ½ percent yearly escalators. According to Holdsworth, petitioner indicated that he would shut down the business unless the other two agreed to the deal. Negotiations continued throughout 2005. Holdsworth maintains that respondents made petitioner a reasonable offer based upon his 1/3 interest in the business and that it is disingenuous for petitioner to say otherwise.

* * *

Respondents also filed an affidavit of Fagan, the contract administrator for the LLC. She asserts that she was approached by petitioner in December 2005, who stated that he had made a big mistake in offering respondents an ownership interest in the LLC. According to Fagan, petitioner told her that he had funding and personnel to transfer the business of the LLC back to Horning, Inc., and that she would have a job waiting for her after the dissolution of the LLC. * * *

Respondents also filed an affidavit of Bowers, the superintendent of the LLC. * * * Bowers * * * asserts that petitioner told him that he could freeze the LLC's assets while the dissolution was taking place. This, according to petitioner, would allow him to starve the respondents out while he used the LLC's assets to restart Horning, Inc.

* * *

Petitioner's Reply

In its reply affidavit, petitioner relies mainly on the failure of the members since inception in December 2001 to agree on an operating agreement defining the job duties of each. * * * Although petitioner stresses that "parties ... unable to agree on their fundamental terms of operation ... can not fairly and sensibly operate without them," he maintains that he "generally handles the administrative work in the office and Klimowski and Holdsworth continue to do their jobs in the field."

Petitioner takes issue with other aspects of respondents' affidavits, but the only real allegation that the business of the LLC is failing comes from his contention that it "continues either to fail to bid or not to bid well on projects that we normally would bid on and often times win." * * * The concern about bidding was included in the initial papers filed with the petition, but in neither petitioner's reply or in these original papers are any examples given. Furthermore, they fly in the face of the substantial growth of the company from the time of its inception in 2001. At bottom, petitioner requests dissolution on the ground that Klimowski despises him, Holdsworth resents him, neither of them trust petitioner, and "that it is Klimowski's and Holdsworth's intention to defeat an involuntary dissolution and make my remaining time with Horning, LLC so unbearable that I will relent and give them for a pittance the remainder of the company for which they have paid nothing to date."

Analysis

Petitioner has asked for an order directing dissolution of the LLC pursuant to *LLCL §§ 702, 703*, and *704*. *Section 702* allows for a judicial decree of dissolution, "whenever it is not reasonably practicable to carry on the business in conformity with the articles of organization or operating agreement." Further, pursuant to *LLCL § 703*, the court may appoint a receiver or "liquidating trustee" to wind up the LLC's affairs. *Section 704* mandates that, in the event of dissolution, a dissolution order be issued under which the assets shall be distributed, beginning with all creditors.

Under petitioner's view, [the decision of the court in] *Spires v. Casterline, 4 Misc 3d 428, 778 N.Y.S.2d 259 (Sup. Ct. Monroe Co. 2004)*, stands for the proposition that, whenever presented with a member's "expressed desire to sever his relationship with ... [the] LLC," due to "untenable circumstances," *§ 606(a)* requires dissolution if there is no operating agreement. *Spires*, however, does not stand for that proposition nor could it in the face of *§ 701(b)*. Indeed, the LLCL was designed to protect members from such disruptions and expressly avoids such a result. While *§ 606(a)* requires dissolution and winding up upon withdrawal of a member, withdrawal is not available just for the asking, especially if there is no operating agreement. Instead, *§ 701(b)* insists that the "death, retirement, expulsion, bankruptcy, or dissolution of any member or the occurrence of any other event that terminates the continued membership of any member *shall not cause the limited liability company to be dissolved or its affairs to be wound up*, and upon the occurrence of any such event, the limited liability company *shall be continued without dissolution*" except in the event of a majority vote (not applicable here). *LLCL § 701(b)*(emphasis supplied). Thus, instead of triggering dissolution upon announced intention to withdraw, the LLCL provides for just the opposite. Dissolution in the absence of an operating agreement can only be had upon satisfaction of the standard of *§ 702*, i.e., "whenever it is not reasonably practicable to carry on the business."

Given this statutory standard, the very real dilemma faced by petitioner, foreseen in the excellent article by Peter A. Mahler, *When Limited Liability Companies Seek Judicial Dissolution, Will the Statute Be Up to the Task?* 74 N.Y.S. Bar Ass'n J. 8 (June 2002), readily can be seen. As Mahler ably explains, dissolution under the LLCL is not as easy as [obtaining a dissolution or buy-out] under the [Business Corporation Law]. With the 1999 amendments, the previous default dissolution rules under *§ 701*, which required dissolution upon the withdrawal of a member unless the remaining members voted to continue, "was eliminated" in favor of the provision quoted above. The 1999 amendments, with respect to *§ 606(a)* and *§ 701*, "jettisoned the partnership model in favor of the corporate model, but left *LLCL § 702* untouched." Because of the "relative ease of exit under partnership law," *§ 702* was not problematic before 1999. But when the more rigorous requirements of the current *§ 701* were enacted, eliminating dissolution rights upon a member's withdrawal in favor of the solitary *§ 702* "not reasonably practicable to carry on business" standard, LLC members such as petitioner were, and are, left at the mercy of other members' conduct which does not in the circumstances create the statutory standard for judicial dissolution in *§ 702*, particularly in view of the fact that there is no buy out provision in the LLCL * * *.

Retention of *§ 702* in unaltered form (i.e., originally designed for compatibility with the very flexible pre–1999 partnership default dissolution rules but now applied to the more restrictive corporate model default dissolution rules) appears not to have been an oversight. *Section 702*, according to Mahler, "closely tracts the language in § 902 of the ABA Prototype LLC Act," which contains commentary "suggesting a deliberate avoidance of the typical grounds for dissolution found in corporate dissolution statutes, on the ground that disgruntled members' of an LLC would be encouraged to make this sort of allegation in limited liability company breakups." Mahler predicted that the tension between amended *§ 606* and *§ 701*, on the one hand, and unaltered *§ 702*, on the other hand, would create litigation in a case like this:

> The most likely candidates are post-amendment LLC's without operating agreements and therefore governed by the LLCL's new default rules. A member of such an LLC has no right to withdraw and no right to receive fair value for his or her interest. An action for judicial dissolution may be the only way out.

* * *

The foregoing analysis was echoed in a comprehensive survey, Douglas F. Moll, *Minority Oppression & The Limited Liability Company: Learning (Or Not) From Close Corporation History, 40 Wake Forest L. Rev. 883, 925–40 (2005)*, which shows beyond peradventure that the limitations imposed by the new default withdrawal and dissolution provisions * * * were intentional and designed for estate and gift tax purposes "[t}o minimize the tax value of an ownership interest]" in an LLC * * *. "While perhaps accomplishing an estate tax goal, the elimination of default and dissolution rights leaves minority members vulnerable to oppressive majority actions since the minority can no longer easily exit the venture with the value of its investment."

Given the statutory standard for involuntary dissolution of an LLC without an operating agreement, petitioner fails to meet his burden to raise a material issue of fact warranting a trial under *CPLR 410*.

* * *

One certainly can sympathize with petitioner's plight. In 2001, he had a thriving corporation and wished to reduce his work schedule. Whether for estate and gift tax reasons, or otherwise, he brought in two trusted men and gave them each one third ownership of a new venture set up as a LLC. But he did this without prior or contemporaneous execution of an operating agreement giving him fair exit rights in the event of future disharmony. Moreover, during the next few years, despite having failed to secure an operating agreement to protect him, he transferred the business of his corporation to the LLC (something he did not have to do if he was dissatisfied with the parties' arrangements), and the LLC grew substantially even in relation to the corporation's previous level of business. Despite petitioner's stated frustration with the failure of the members to reach terms on an operating agreement, he was happy to keep doing business through the LLC until he unsuccessfully proposed a buyout to respondents in 2005, the company's most successful year. Only then did he seek dissolution. The company continues to thrive in the ups and downs of the construction business.

Even in the corporate context, with the more liberal involuntary dissolution standards designed to protect minority interests, courts have rejected dissolution petitions in similar circumstances (or even worse scenarios from petitioner's perspective).

A fortiori, petitioner's showing under the more stringent standard of *LLCL § 702* is insufficient here.

* * *

NOTES

1. The New York limited liability company law rules applied in *Horning*, which govern dissolution and the departure of members from a limited liability company in the absence of contrary agreement, take an approach at the opposite extreme from the partnership law rules involved in *Page*. Did these rules obviate the need for advance agreement in *Horning* any more than did the partnership law rules in *Page*? Are the rules for LLCs formed outside of New York likely to be better? What about for limited partnerships? In fact, as discussed by the court in *Horning*, there has been an evolution in LLC acts—which has been influenced by, and influenced, versions of the Uniform Limited Partnership Act.

The court focuses on an evolution in the rules regarding dissolution of the entity. In the early LLC statutes, there was a tendency to follow partnership style dissolution provisions under which, at least barring contrary agreement, the LLC would dissolve upon a member's departure. The motivation for this, however, had less to do with picking a rule best designed to deal with the problem of member departure, then it did with picking a rule designed to have the I.R.S. treat LLCs for tax purposes like a partnership. With greater liberality on this issue by the I.R.S., culminating in the "check-the-box" regulation, the rules regarding entity dissolution changed in most states. As in New York, the death, bankruptcy, expulsion, resignation or other termination of a member in a limited liability company typically does not trigger dissolution of an LLC. Instead, LLC statutes now generally allow the remaining members to continue the company without dissolution, unless otherwise called for by the operating agreement, or unless a majority of the members vote to dissolve. *E.g.*, Cal. Corp. Code § 17350(d); Del. Code Ann. Title 6 § 18–801(a)(3), (b). There has been a parallel evolution in the U.L.P.A. Under the pre–2001 U.L.P.A., the remaining general partner(s) may continue the business without dissolution following a general partner's departure from a limited partnership—by virtue of death, bankruptcy, a decision to withdraw, or the like—only if there is a right granted in the partnership agreement (or in the certificate of limited partnership), or with the consent of all the general and limited partners. U.L.P.A. § 801(4). Under the 2001 revision of the U.L.P.A., it is no longer necessary to have an advance agreement, or the agreement of all partners, to continue after the departure of a general partner. Instead, barring other agreement, the limited partnership can continue unless there is a majority vote of the partners to dissolve. U.L.P.A. (2001) § 801(3). (If there is no remaining general partner, limited partners can consent to continue with a new general partner. U.L.P.A. § 801(4)(with unanimous consent); U.L.P.A. (2001) § 801(3)(B)(with majority consent).) Note, however, under either version of the U.L.P.A., the death, bankruptcy or withdrawal of a limited (as opposed to a general) partner does not trigger dissolution. *See* U.L.P.A. § 801; U.L.P.A. (2001) § 801.

Actually, the more profound evolution in the statutes governing LLCs and limited partnerships does not involve entity dissolution. Instead, it involves what happens to the interest of a member or partner (or of his or her successor-in-interest) when the entity does not dissolve, but the member, or partner, or successor-in-interest, wants out. The earlier statutes tended to follow what Chapter II referred to as a "buy-out model." For example, absent other agreement, the pre–2001 U.L.P.A. gives general partners (or their estate) the right to demand that the limited partnership pay them the fair value of their interest when their withdrawal does not result in dissolution, and gives limited partners the right to withdraw and receive similar payment from the limited partnership upon six months notice. U.L.P.A. §§ 603, 604. Older LLC statutes copied this buy-out right for departing members in an LLC—sometimes requiring six months or other advance notice, and sometimes without any notice requirement. *E.g.*, Gevurtz, *Squeeze-outs and Freeze-outs in Limited Liability Companies*, 73 Wash. U.L.Q. 497, 514 n. 95 (1995).

Horning involves an example of the newer type of LLC statute. They follow what Chapter II refers to as a "lock-in model." Under these LLC statutes, members or their successors-in-interest have no right to force the company to cash out their interest unless the operating agreement gives members this right. *E.g.*, Cal. Corp. Code § 17252; Del. Code Ann. Title 6 §§ 18–603, 604; N.Y. Ltd. Liab. Co. Law §§ 509, 606. Moreover, just to bring things full circle, the 2001 revision of the U.L.P.A. copied from these LLC acts to deprive both general and limited partners, or the transferees of their interests, of any right to force a cash out of their interests, unless the partnership agreement so provides. U.L.P.A. (2001) § 505.U.L.P.A. (2001) §§ 505 (no right to distribution on dissociation), 602(a)(3) (dissociated limited partner treated as the transferee of a transferable interest), 605(a)(5) (same for dissociated general partner), 702(b) (transferee only receives the same rights to distributions that the transferor had).

2. As the court mentions in *Horning*, a major impetus for this legislative evolution apparently came from a concern with estate taxes. Under Internal Revenue Code Section 2704, and the regulations issued pursuant to that section, state law default rules establish the minimum value for computing estate tax on interests in a family controlled business held in a decedent's estate. In other words, if state law provides, barring other agreement, members in a limited liability company with the right to cash out at fair market value, then the minimum value of an interest in a family controlled LLC for estate tax purposes is the fair market value that the

decedent's estate hypothetically would have received if the estate exercised this cash-out right, even though the actual LLC operating agreement denied or otherwise limited such a cash-out right. Such a denial, of course, means that the estate could not, in fact, cash out at the statutory fair market value and this, in turn, presumably lowers the real value of the interest. Hence, by reducing the rights to withdraw and cash out in the absence of agreement, these newer LLC statutes can lower the estate tax payable for those family controlled limited liability companies whose operating agreements provide poor terms for a deceased member's interest.

From a planning standpoint, the change in state law rules regarding the right to withdraw and cash out in the absence of other agreement opens up the prospect for saving on estate taxes by providing, in the operating agreement, the estate or heir poor economic terms—either a low price buy-out, or, as under the default rules applied in *Horning*, no right to withdraw altogether. On the other hand, can there be a danger in letting the tax "tail"—especially one, like the estate tax, that may be phased out by the time the member dies—wag the economic "dog"? For example, what will be the likely future relations between the parties if the person inheriting a member's interest (say a widow) is unable to cash out at a satisfactory price, lacks control over the venture, and receives skimpy distributions? Moreover, what danger exists if, as in *Horning*, prior to a member's death, the members are unable to get along?

This, in turn, raises a broader observation about default rules. How did the estate tax concerns of business owners in family controlled LLCs become the basis for rules to govern persons, like Horning, for whom this was a far less important concern (if, indeed, it was a concern at all) than being able to exit amicably from an untenable business relationship? The capture of the legislative drafting process by attorneys with a particular focus, as illustrated by this example, raises, of course, profound policy questions. From the standpoint of a course in Business Planning, however, there is another, more immediately practical, lesson: one should not automatically assume that the drafters of statutory default rules were even attempting to reach a sensible result for most situations likely to confront one's clients.

3. As the court in *Horning* points out, the inability of a departing member either to dissolve the firm, or to compel the firm to purchase one's interest, follows a corporate, rather than a partnership, model. Hence, had Horning taken Klimowski and Holdsworth into his original corporation, instead of forming a new LLC, Horning could not have demanded the corporation buy-out his interest or dissolve, any more than he could demand this of the LLC. One the other hand, with a corporation, Horning have sold his stock to whomever he desired, and the purchaser would have had all the rights to vote for directors and the like that Horning had possessed as a stockholder. The same would follow upon Horning's death or bankruptcy. This free transfer approach, at least theoretically, makes more palatable the departing shareholder's inability to compel dissolution or a buy-out by the corporation. Of course, as Chapter IV will discuss, the lack of willing buyers

for minority interests in closely held corporations undermines this rationale as a practical matter. Yet, as will be discussed later in this chapter, the situation is worse under typical default rules in LLC statutes. Under these rules, a member in an LLC (barring contrary agreement) can transfer his or her economic interest in the firm, but the transferee will not become a new member with the transferor's management rights. As discussed later, the same is true in a limited partnership. Without any management rights—for example, to veto actions requiring unanimous vote of the members or partners—how many persons would wish to be the assignee of an economic interest in an LLC or a limited partnership?

4. *Horning* illustrates both the legal and extra-legal strategies often followed by owners trapped in a bad business marriage. Horning's legal strategy was to sue in order to force dissolution. As the court explains, the judicial dissolution provision in New York's LLC statute copied from the involuntary dissolution provisions in the uniform partnership acts. *See also* Del Code Ann. Title 6 § 802. Other LLC statutes have copied from the provisions in corporations statutes allowing judicial dissolution for cause, or have blended corporate and partnership standards together. *E.g.*, Cal. Corp. Code § 17351 (member can petition a court to order dissolution if not reasonably practical to carry on in conformity with the operating agreement, or if reasonably necessary to protect the interest of the complaining member). The court in *Horning* asserts that the standard for judicial dissolution in partnership law is more difficult to meet than the corporate law standard for judicial dissolution. Some courts, however, have taken a fairly liberal view of the grounds for judicial dissolution of a partnership. *E.g., Cooper v. Isaacs*, 448 F.2d 1202 (D.C.Cir.1971) (irreconcilable differences can be grounds for judicial dissolution under the U.P.A.). In either event, how satisfactory is leaving things to a judicially ordered dissolution as an escape valve for business owners who cannot get along? Was Horning entirely without fault in the falling out? What about Klimowski and Holdsworth? In general, how difficult might it often be to figure out which side caused a business relationship to go sour? To the extent the standard focuses on the impact of the dissension on the business, or even the impact on a minority owner's enjoyment of the fruits of the business, what problems of prediction might this create? How much money will the parties need to spend on litigation costs in order to figure out who insulted whom first, and what the impact of the dissension really is?

Is litigation likely to be the only, or indeed even the worst, manifestation of a dispute between feuding owners locked into business relationship? Horning accused Klimowski and Holdsworth of following an extra-legal strategy of making his life at the firm so miserable that he would be forced to sell out cheap. No doubt Klimowski and Holdsworth might accuse Horning of making their lives miserable in order to force them to buy him out at a high price. (As an extreme example of an extra-legal strategy, a distant cousin of this book's author made the newspapers some years back when he was arrested for allegedly hiring someone to "take care of" his partner.)

A famous study of the aftermath of corporate dissolution litigation found, when the business was viable, almost invariably one side bought out the interest of the other side regardless of whether the court ordered dissolution; the litigation presumably served simply as an effort to gain leverage in negotiating the price. Hetherington & Dooley, *Illiquidity and Exploitation: A Proposed Statutory Solution to the Remaining Close Corporation Problem*, 63 Va. L. Rev. 1 (1977). Indeed, what does one suspect happened after the court's decision in *Horning*, or would have happened if the court held the other way? If this is all about one side buying out the other, is there a way for advance planning to avoid litigation costs, or to avoid the human costs from extra-legal strategies? Is there a lesson from prenuptial agreements drafted by family law attorneys?

2. Planning for a Buy-Out

The bottom line of the discussion above is that partners or LLC members who wish to continue the business despite a partner's or LLC member's voluntary or involuntary departure normally end up buying out the departing individual's interest in the firm—which was in all likelihood the end result in *Page* and *Horning*. The impact of the various default rules is on the terms of the buy-out and on how much hassle it takes to reach this disposition. Presumably, the least hassle occurs if the parties reach their own agreement on the terms for a buy-out. Parties might make such an agreement in advance—typically as part of the partnership or LLC operating agreement—or after the event precipitating the departure occurs. Conventional wisdom holds that it is better to seek agreement at the former point rather than the latter. This is because, at the former point, the parties cannot know for sure who will be the buyer and who will be the seller. Note the incentives this ignorance creates in deciding upon the terms for the buy-out. Nevertheless, drafting an advance buy-out agreement is no simple task, as the failed efforts encountered in the following cases attest.

a. *Triggering Events*

CCD, L.C. v. Millsap

116 P.3d 366 (Utah 2005).

Christopher Millsap challenges a district court determination that he was lawfully expelled as a member of the limited liability company from which he had diverted money for his own use. We affirm.

FACTUAL AND PROCEDURAL BACKGROUND

Messrs. Craig Newman, Doug Stanley, and Christopher Millsap formed CCD, a limited liability company, in 1997. The company operated United Title Services of Southern Utah, a title company located in St. George, Utah. Mr. Millsap acted as the manager in St. George. Messrs. Newman and Stanley oversaw marketing in Salt Lake County.

All title companies are required by law to set up trust accounts to hold the money from the closings of real estate transactions and any other funds held by the company when acting as an escrow agent. In March 2000, Messrs. Newman and Stanley discovered that Mr. Millsap had misappropriated $625,000 from CCD's trust account to finance his personal interest in Pheasant Meadow Subdivision in Washington County.

Mr. Millsap admitted to his partners that he took the money. To remedy the situation, CCD's members entered into an amended operating agreement. Under its terms, Mr. Millsap agreed not to access the trust account or write company checks. Mr. Newman consented to lend Mr. Millsap $493,965 to help replace the trust money. * * * The amended agreement provided that Mr. Millsap's status as a full member in CCD would be restored one year after he timely repaid the loan.

Shortly after the amended agreement was made, at the request of the Utah State Insurance Department, Mr. Newman investigated the source of the funds that Mr. Millsap used to repay the trust account. He discovered that Mr. Millsap had continued to misappropriate trust account funds by using CCD customer file numbers to disguise the transfer of funds obtained in connection with property sales to Mr. Millsap's own company, Gren Development. The second episode of defalcation resulted in trust fund misappropriations totaling $11,540.06.

The parties dispute what happened next. Mr. Millsap says the other members of CCD presented him with what amounted to an extortionate ultimatum: accept a buy-out or face disclosure of his crimes to authorities. Mr. Millsap claims that he refused the buy-out and reported his crimes to the insurance commission, an act that led to his being charged with thirteen counts of unlawful dealing of property by a fiduciary and his pleading guilty to five counts.

Messrs. Newman and Stanley tell a different story. They claim that after they discovered Mr. Millsap's misuse of the trust account, CCD terminated Mr. Millsap's employment. In support of their account, they cite a letter CCD sent to Mr. Millsap, less than a week after his new misappropriations were discovered, advising him that his employment and benefits had been terminated. * * *

Mr. Millsap contends that * * * he fulfilled the amended operating agreement conditions, refused the buy-out, and could not be terminated as a member of CCD. According to Mr. Millsap, he had satisfied all of the amended operating agreement conditions for reinstatement as a member of CCD and was, therefore, eligible to retire from the company and enjoy the rights extended to a retiring member under the original operating agreement. Consistent with this understanding, Mr. Millsap wrote CCD a letter giving formal notice of his desire to retire as a member of the company. After receiving the request for an appraisal of Mr. Millsap's interest in CCD in anticipation of retirement, CCD sued Mr. Millsap. The company alleged multiple grounds for relief. Only its claim that it was entitled to a decree expelling Mr. Millsap from CCD concerns us here.

Mr. Millsap and CCD each sought to support their disparate positions by turning to the Utah Limited Liability Act and CCD's operating agreement. * * *

Specifically, the operating agreement specified that: "no member may be expelled from the Company by act or desire of the remaining members"; and that "no member, without the majority consent of the members, shall: use the name, credit or property of the Company for any purposes other than a proper Company purpose." The operating agreement further forbade any member from "any act detrimental to the Company business ... which would make it impossible to carry on business" and in the event of a violation provides that the "member shall become liable to the Company for the amount of the claim incurred by the Company in connection with said violation of the restriction." Upon the retirement of a member, the operating agreement authorized CCD to acquire the retiring member's interest in the company. If CCD did not elect to purchase the member's interest, the remaining members could acquire the interest. If neither CCD nor the remaining members acquired the interest, then CCD would dissolve and all remaining properties would be distributed in liquidation.

Mr. Millsap moved for summary judgment on CCD's expulsion claim. He argued that since he was "retired" and no longer a member of CCD, he could not be expelled from CCD. * * *

CCD responded to Mr. Millsap's motion with a cross-motion for summary judgment claiming that it was entitled to expel Mr. Millsap as a matter of law. The district court granted CCD's motion.

* * *

ANALYSIS

This appeal presents us with a variation on the well-worn rhetorical volley between employer and employee: "You're fired!" "You can't fire me, I quit." * * *

A. Under the Language and Policy Considerations of the Revised Limited Liability Company Act, Mr. Millsap was Ineligible for Retirement

No one disputes that by misappropriating some $625,000 from the trust account of CCD, Mr. Millsap was eligible for expulsion from CCD. Still, if the CCD operating agreement contained the sole grant of authority to members of CCD to respond to the misdeeds of other members, it would be unlikely that CCD could have expelled Mr. Millsap. Section 13 of the agreement imposes an absolute bar to expulsions stating, "no member may be expelled from the Company by act or desire of the remaining members." This contractual prohibition is superceded, however, by *section 48–2c–120* of [Utah's limited liability company] Act, which prohibits an operating agreement from "varying the right to expel a member based on any event specified in *subsection 48–2c–710(3)*." Mr. Millsap's conduct could reasonably be interpreted to satisfy one or more of these statutory events. *Section 48–20–710* identifies the relevant events and explains the procedure for expulsion this way:

(3) on application by the company or another member, by judicial determination that the member:

(a) has engaged in wrongful conduct that adversely and materially affected the company's business;

(b) has willfully or persistently committed a material breach of the articles of organization or operating agreement or of a duty owed to the company or to the other members under Section 48–2c–807; or

(c) has engaged in conduct relating to the company's business which makes it not reasonably practicable to carry on the business with the member.

Although entitled to expel Mr. Millsap for his first episode of misdeeds, Messrs. Newman and Stanley elected instead to extend to Mr. Millsap what they have described as a "second chance." * * * Mr. Millsap insists that, his relapse into converting trust account monies for his own use notwithstanding, he met the conditions imposed by the amended operating agreement. Having had his membership rights restored and having declared his intention to retire, Mr. Millsap contends that the Act renders him immune from expulsion and requires CCD to treat him as a retiring member under the terms of CCD's initial operating agreement.

Mr. Millsap labors to coax this result from a plain language interpretation of selected provisions of the Act. First, he asserts that the Act supports his contention that by declaring an intent to retire, he terminated his membership in CCD. *Section 48–2c–709* (2001) of the Act authorizes members to withdraw upon the happening of events specified in an operating agreement. Because CCD's operating agreement specifically permitted retirement of a member, Mr. Millsap insists that he was permitted to withdraw pursuant to section 709. Next, he asserts that CCD's attempt to expel him was a nullity because section 709 [*sic*] of the Act expressly limits expulsion to members, and at the time CCD filed suit to expel him, he had retired and was no longer a member. We do not read the Act as mandating this result.

Of course, there is a logical tie between the status of membership and the act of being expelled from that status. Mr. Millsap's argument neatly reduces to this syllogism: only members of limited liability companies may be expelled; Mr. Millsap was not a member; therefore, Mr. Millsap could not be expelled. There exists, however, no legal principle that requires legislative enactments to be leashed to Aristotelian logic. While it is true that nonmembership generally moots the necessity of expulsion, it is not always so. We think this is apparent from the language and structure of the Act that the cessation of membership in a limited liability company does not inevitably foreclose expulsion.

Mr. Millsap's plain language reading of the Act strips away from its text all policy considerations associated with limited liability company membership and expulsion and replaces them with a bare mechanical application driven exclusively by considerations of chronology

* * *

The drafters of the Act deemed expulsion authority to be so important that, despite acknowledging the power of limited liability company members to govern their affairs by contract, they expressly barred members from bargaining for expulsion rules that varied from those set out in section 710.

These legitimate policy aims would be frustrated if a member whose conduct made him eligible for expulsion could block expulsion by voluntarily ceasing to be a member, a move that under the terms of the retirement provision of CCD's operating agreement could threaten a forced liquidation of the company. Where the Act takes pains to preserve the statutory expulsion provisions against erosion through the terms of operating agreements, we decline to read its provisions in a manner that sanctions by indirection what the Act directly prohibits. Yet this is precisely what an interpretation of section 710 that conditions expulsion on membership status would do.

The absence of textual guidance on the relationship between membership status and the right to expel does not, in our view, support Mr. Millsap's plain language interpretation. To the contrary, if the drafters of the Act had intended that its provisions be interpreted in a way that imposed a substantial burden on a limited liability company's right to expel a member based solely on the timing considerations tied to the member's voluntary secession from membership, they would reasonably have been expected to have been more attentive to setting out the substantive and procedural parameters of membership secession and expulsion. Were we to adopt Mr. Millsap's chronology-driven interpretation, we would be compelled to engraft onto the Act timing benchmarks of our making that would permit us to determine whether CCD expelled Mr. Millsap before he terminated his membership. The alternative is to construe the meaning of the Act in a manner consonant with its policy objectives. Faced with these choices, we elect to interpret the Act in light of its underlying policy rather than an artificial construction unrelated to the Act's purpose.

In Mr. Millsap's view, any policy-based interpretation of the Act that would permit the expulsion of a retired or withdrawn member targets the wrong source of potential mischief. According to Mr. Millsap, the Act should be interpreted in a manner that best protects a member like himself from a company's bad faith expulsion efforts. The prospect that such abuse can occur assumes that courts are either incapable or unwilling to make informed and impartial judgments about the merits of expulsion actions brought under section 710. * * * The requirement that expulsions be made by judicial determination affords members like Mr. Millsap, through the intervention of a neutral and impartial fact finder, the most reliable safeguard against inequitable treatment available in our society.

Indeed, the greater risk of overreaching would arise from Mr. Millsap's preferred interpretation. A member who has engaged in wrongdoing that would expose him to expulsion would command unjustifiable leverage were he to be able to force a dissolution of the company by withdrawing as a member before the company could obtain a judicial determination that he should be expelled.

Moreover, we are wary of embracing statutory interpretations that confer legal rights based on victories in races to the courthouse. The proper focus of inquiry should be on the merits of claims concerning a limited liability company members's conduct and not on reviewing the results of photo finishes to the courthouse door. Accordingly, we reject the premise that underlies Mr. Millsap's argument that because his announced retirement predated the judicial determination of his expulsion, he could not be expelled as a member of CCD.

* * *

Having determined that CCD's right to seek the expulsion of Mr. Millsap survived his attempts to retire, we now take up Mr. Millsap's challenge to the district court's determination that CCD established through undisputed facts sufficient grounds to expel Mr. Millsap as a member of CCD.

* * *

According to Mr. Millsap's view of the Act, expulsion is permitted only in response to an ongoing threat to the company. [A]ccording to Mr. Millsap, * * * the district court permitted Mr. Millsap to be expelled for stale misdeeds that, as a matter of law, could no longer adversely and materially affect CCD's business. * * * We disagree.

It is undisputed that Mr. Millsap misappropriated trust account funds totaling at least $11,540.06 for his personal use after the amended operating agreement was signed. It is difficult for us to find justification for reversing the district court's conclusion that this behavior merited expulsion. Mr. Millsap's misconduct continued the pattern of behavior that resulted in losses to the company of $625,000. It took place after Mr. Millsap's prior wrongdoing had been discovered and after CCD had assented to permit Mr. Millsap to atone for his misdeeds by fulfilling the terms of the amended operating agreement.

* * *

NOTES

1. How might the parties better drafted the CCD agreement to deal with the problem that arose? Perhaps, they never anticipated the need to expel a dishonest member. Alternately, perhaps they felt they could rely on the statutory expulsion provision to deal with a dishonest member, without anticipating the possibility of a preemptive retirement by such a member. In either event, the moral is to illustrate how defining the precise events that trigger a buy-out—be that a voluntary departure through retirement, an involuntary departure through expulsion, or something else entirely—entails a challenging exercise in imagination. As a help in this exercise, one might look for lists of events to consider. Here is where consulting a number of agreements or forms might be handy. In addition, one might

examine various statutory sections, which list events that might cause, or not cause, dissolution or dissociation for partnerships, limited partnerships and LLCs. *E.g.*, U.P.A. §§ 31, 32; R.U.P.A. § 601; U.L.P.A. §§ 402, 801, 802; U.L.P.A. (2001) §§ 601, 603, 801, 802; Cal. Corp. Code § 17350; Del. Code Ann. Title 6 § 18–801; N.Y. Ltd. Liab. Co. Law § 701.

Listing possible events that might trigger a buy-out is only the beginning of the process. Next, the attorney drafting the agreement must consider whether, and when, such events should trigger a buy-out. For example, why did the CCD agreement provide for a buy-out upon retirement? Was there something about the nature of CCD's business, and the members' roles in the venture, that would make a member no longer wish to continue as a member, or would make active members no longer wish to have another member continue as a member, after the member retires from actively working for the firm? Suppose a partner's or member's essential role in a venture is to provide capital: in that case, should retirement trigger a buy-out? Might this same distinction apply to other circumstances, such as death of a partner or member? Or, might there be a difference with death—particularly if the deceased partner or member had rights in the management of the venture?

Alternately, why did the CCD agreement expressly disclaim the power of the other members to expel a member from the firm? Why did the court conclude that judicially ordered expulsion would avoid the concerns about abuse by the majority that presumably motivated the disclaimer of this power in the CCD agreement? While Millsap's conduct seems rather extreme, does he have at least a colorable argument that stale misdeeds did not show an ongoing danger—particularly since he was retiring anyway? If the court had decided that Millsap's argument was sufficient at least to avoid summary judgment, how much time and expense would litigating over expulsion in court have entailed? Is there a way in the agreement to avoid such time and expense? Might an agreement seek to avoid litigation over grounds for expulsion by allowing a majority to expel partners or members without cause? See *Lawlis v. Kightlinger & Gray*, 562 N.E.2d 435 (Ind.App.1990) (court reviewed good faith of expulsion). To the extent such a provision avoids judicial review, could it lead to abuse? See *Anderson v. Wilder*, 2003 WL 22768666 (Tenn.Ct.App.)(LLC member claimed in an affidavit that he was expelled because he had refused to go along with a scheme to expel other members in order to turn around and sell their interests to an outsider at a greater price than expelled members would receive).

2. Since Millsap was going to leave the firm in any event, why was there litigation over whether the departure resulted from a retirement or an expulsion? Might there have been some difference in what he received from the firm depending upon which event triggered the buy-out? Is there some broader drafting lesson here—specifically, as an alternative to drafting prescient and unambiguous triggering events provisions, could one attempt to minimize the incentives for parties to argue over whether the buy-out will take place (or, as in *CCD*, under which provision the buy-out will take

place)? For example, might the drafter of the CCD agreement have had the three prospective members consider, before the dispute occurred and emotions were running high, whether it was really important to have less favorable buy-out terms upon expulsion as opposed to retirement? In this light, consider the wisdom of the following provisions:

(1) Including a covenant not to compete by the departing partner or member. What purpose can such a covenant serve? What incentives, however, does it create for a party, who faces such a provision? See *Cooper v. Isaacs*, 448 F.2d 1202 (D.C.Cir.1971)(partner sought judicial dissolution, rather than retire and be subject to a non-competition clause).

(2) Setting a term for the partnership without providing a buy-out. In this case, under the U.P.A. the partner who wants out faces the sanctions established by Section 38(2). These include the prospect of paying damages, exclusion of goodwill from the valuation of his or her interest in the partnership, and the option of the continuing partner(s) to indefinitely delay payment by posting a bond. Why might one wish to penalize the dissatisfied partner in such a manner? On the other hand, what might a desperate partner do to avoid Section 38(2) treatment? See *Drashner v. Sorenson,* 75 S.D. 247, 63 N.W.2d 255 (1954) (each partner charged the other with wrongful dissolution). The R.U.P.A., by contrast, allows the court to consider goodwill in valuing a wrongfully departing partner's interest and gives the court power to require payment before expiration of the term if early payment will not cause undue hardship to the partnership. R.U.P.A. § 701(b), (h). Do these changes remove the incentives for dispute over whether a partner is wrongfully causing a dissociation? Notice, the wrongful partner is still liable for damages. R.U.P.A. § 702(b).

3. Interestingly, Utah's expulsion for cause provisions were not subject to contrary agreement. This illustrates that there legal constraints on what events can (or cannot) trigger a buy-out agreement. As another example with respect to expulsion, California's LLC statute will not allow expulsion pursuant to an agreement if the expelled member can establish that the expulsion terms were unreasonable under the circumstances in which they were made. Cal. Corp. Code § 17100(c).

Presumably, these limits on expulsion agreements are designed to protect members from the consequences of their own agreements. A different problem exists if a buy-out agreement impacts parties who did not sign agreement. For example, partners or LLC members might agree to trigger a buy-out upon the transfer of an interest pursuant to a divorce. Alternately, partners or LLC members commonly agree to trigger a buy-out upon a partner's or member's filing bankruptcy. In either event, there may be a strong temptation to set buy-out terms which are highly unfavorable to the spouse or creditors. The legal issues this raises will be considered later in this chapter, when dealing with the transfer of a partner's or LLC member's interest.

4. The agreement also must specify who chooses whether or not to carry out the buy-out upon the happening of a triggering event: the remaining owners, the departing owner or both. (Indeed, this became a minor issue in

the *Curtis v. Campbell* decision reprinted *infra.*) What are the relevant considerations in drafting this portion of the agreement? Who is a buy-out agreement intended to protect? Who then should have the option? Notice how the CCD agreement handled this question. Incidentally, using mandatory language in the buy-out agreement gives both parties the option to force the sale, since only if both sides agree can they abrogate the contract. Also, consider the decision-making impact of giving the option to the firm. Can the departing partner or member vote on whether to exercise the option in such event?

b. *Price*

Curtis v. Campbell

336 S.W.2d 355 (Ky.1960).

■ CLAY, COMMISSIONER.

This suit was brought by three business partners against the executrix and heirs of a deceased partner to have the rights of the parties declared in the settlement of partnership interests. * * * The Chancellor decided all questions favorably to plaintiff appellees.

* * *

In 1900 the mercantile business of "T. H. Campbell & Bros." was established. * * * As of January 1, 1945, * * * a new partnership was formed among the three appellees (all of whom as Campbells) and Jennie Campbell. Each had a one-fourth interest in the partnership, although the latter took no active part in its affairs.

In 1952 Jennie Campbell died and since that time the three appellees have continued to operate this business. The settlement of the partnership accounts have been delayed for many reasons.

* * *

The pertinent provisions of the partnership agreement are as follows:

> "IX. *At the time of the dissolution of this partnership* regardless of how dissolution is effected, there shall be prepared *a true and final account* of all partnership transactions, showing *the true and correct financial condition of this partnership as of that date.* A true and correct copy of this financial statement shall be given to each of the partners, or if the dissolution is caused by the death of one of the partners, then the executor, administrator or personal representative of the deceased partner shall receive a copy of the aforesaid financial statement.
>
> "Each of the partners or their heirs, executors, administrators or personal representatives agree that in the event of dissolution of this partnership from any cause whatsoever, that if any one or more of the partners wish to continue that partnership business, that the partner wishing to withdraw and dissolve the partnership, or the executor,

administrator *or personal representative of the deceased partner shall first offer* the interest of the partner wishing to withdraw, or *the personal representative of the deceased partner, shall offer such interest* to any one or more of the partners who may wish to buy, and the partners wishing to continue the business or the surviving partners shall have *the unqualified first right to purchase such interest.*

"The purchase price of said partnership interest shall be based upon the *value of the partners' interest as shown upon the last financial statement,* plus the proportional part of the earnings accrued since the preparation of the balance sheet and *including a fair allowance for good will,* to be determined by the parties at the time any such sale and purchase is effected." (Emphasis added.)

These provisions are rather awkwardly drawn and are in some respects ambiguous. The wording of the second paragraph of Article IX above quoted gives rise to appellant's contention that until she first offered to sell the interest of Jennie Campbell appellees could not terminate the estate's rights in the partnership. In spite of the somewhat reverse wording of this paragraph, since the partnership was automatically dissolved at the death of Jennie Campbell and since the personal representative had no authority to participate as a partner, this provision of the agreement must be construed as giving the surviving partners an absolute option to buy the deceased partner's interest and continue the business. They have properly and timely exercised the option.

The real nub of this controversy is the basis upon which the value of the deceased partner's interest shall be fixed. The first paragraph of Article IX provides the 'true and final account' shall be based upon 'the true and correct financial condition' of the partnership at the date of Jennie Campbell's death. In view of the purpose for which this accounting is required, clearly it was intended to reflect *the fair value of the business property.*

The last paragraph of Article IX is confusing. It recites "the purchase price of said partnership interest shall be based upon the value of the partner's interest as shown upon the last financial statement" (plus accrued earnings and an allowance for good will). This seems to assume that the partnership agreement provided for periodical financial statements which would show the value of each partner's interest. It did not do so. Article VII had provided for a biannual 'financial statement of operations,' but even this periodical accounting had been discontinued. It may be that whoever drafted this instrument anticipated that the value of each partner's interest would be shown on the books of the partnership, which could be a proper basis of settlement. However, the language used wholly failed to accomplish this purpose and the books did not fairly show the value of any partner's interest. * * * If there was any doubt concerning the proper method of determining the value of Jennie Campbell's interest, it should be resolved in her favor.

We must bear in mind that partners are obligated to deal with each other in utmost good faith and fairness. This is particularly true when one partner seeks to purchase the interest of another partner. * * * If there is an ambiguity in the agreement, it should be construed in favor of the estate of the deceased partner. * * * It will also be construed against the party who prepared the instrument, who in this case was one of the surviving partners. * * *

Appellees, the surviving partners, made no attempt to determine the fair value of Jennie Campbell's interest in this partnership. No witness for appellees testified that the amount they offered for the purchase of her interest represented the fair value of that interest. Nor did the Chancellor make such a finding.

As of the day after her death the accountant for the partnership, who is also appellees' counsel in this litigation, prepared a "balance Sheet" which he made up from the books and the records of the partnership. This gave a "book value" of the partnership business, which is not generally regarded as being fair value. * * * That the two are quite disparate is evidenced in this case by some of the computations shown on the "Balance Sheet."

This financial statement lists the real property at a value of approximately $134,000, which is slightly more than its valuation shown on the original balance sheet of January 1, 1945. The books of the company disclose that this valuation is an arbitrary figure based upon cost computations which do not represent either actual cost or present value. At least two of appellant's witnesses estimated the fair market value of this real property substantially in excess of the figure shown on the "Balance Sheet."

For the purposes for which this financial statement should have been prepared, the next item seems wholly illusory. The "balance Sheet" shows that there has been deducted from the book value of the fixed assets (principally the real estate) an item of $56,000 for "Reserve for depreciation." This reduces the book value of those assets to approximately $86,000. There was evidence the real estate alone had a market value in excess of $150,000.

For certain purposes, such as the preparation of income tax returns, the accounting method shown on the "Balance Sheet" may have been perfectly proper. However, we cannot understand how this item of depreciation may be used to reduce the value of any partner's interest. * * * This rather arbitrary deduction substantially distorts the true financial condition of the business insofar as the fair value of each partner's interest is concerned.

There are other questioned items on the "Balance Sheet" which we do not believe it necessary to discuss. It is evident, however, that the figures upon which appellees proposed to settle the deceased partner's interest do not reflect the "true and correct financial condition" of the partnership as of the date of Jennie Campbell's death. Appellees have assumed throughout that the value of such interest has been continuously shown on the books of the company, which is not provided for in the partnership agreement and does not conform to the facts. We are therefore of the opinion the

Chancellor erred in accepting the "Balance Sheet" as conclusive of the value of Jennie Campbell's interest.

The next important item involved in this controversy is the good will of the business. The partnership agreement specifically provides for "a fair allowance for good will." Since this provision of the contract is qualified by the words "to be determined by the parties at the time any such sale and purchase is effected," appellees have taken the position that they have the sole authority to determine whether or not to allow anything on this item. (Here again we find ambiguity, but it must be resolved in favor of fair dealing.) In addition, their accountant and counsel testified that no value could be placed upon the good will of this partnership.

On the face of it, it seems rather unusual that this highly successful business enterprise should have no good will value whatsoever. As a matter of fact, the surviving partners admitted that the business had some good will, but insist that it was attributable to their participation in the business. (If the good will was a partnership asset, each partner had a right to share in it.)

We recognize that fixing the cash value of good will is a difficult problem and there are different acceptable methods of determining it. However, the partnership agreement in at least two places refers to the good will of the business and the enterprise has proven quite successful. It has shown a gross profit of $333,000 on a relatively small capitalization in its seven and one-half years of existence.

The record shows that for inheritance tax purposes the estate of Jennie Campbell was assessed with an inheritance tax based upon a good will valuation of $69,000. This valuation was confirmed by two witnesses, one of whom was a disinterested reputable certified public accountant. We believe the Chancellor erred in his finding that no value could be attributed to good will.

* * *

In our opinion the judgment must be reversed in part and further proceedings are required to determine the fair value of Jennie Campbell's interest in this partnership at the date of her death. To the extent the parties do not agree on the items of account, the Chancellor may permit the introduction of further proof.

The judgment is affirmed in part and reversed in part for further proceedings consistent with this opinion.

NOTE

A variety of approaches exist to set a buy-out price. The simplest is to specify a fixed price in the agreement. Can such a fixed price, however, accurately reflect the value of a partnership, limited partnership or LLC interest over the course of years? See *Mundy v. Holden,* 42 Del.Ch. 84, 204 A.2d 83 (1964). An agreement could provide for periodic adjustments. What happens, however, if the partners or members forget to make the adjustment or are unable to reach agreement (perhaps after one partner or member becomes seriously ill)? See *Emerson v. Arnold,* 92 Mich.App. 345, 285 N.W.2d 45 (1979) (required a judicial determination of value). On the other hand, is there any situation in which a partner or member may be unconcerned with (or even disadvantaged by) receiving a buy-out price which increased over time to reflect appreciation of the business? Suppose there was a partnership between parent and child. Could the parties save estate taxes by "freezing" the value of the parent's interest in the business through a fixed price, which effectively transfers any appreciation to the child? See I.R.C. § 2703 (disregarding in valuing property for purposes of estate tax any contract to sell property at less than fair market value in an effort to transfer property to members of the decedent's family at less than full and adequate consideration); *Estate of True v. Commissioner*, 390 F.3d 1210 (10th Cir.2004) (disregarding, in valuing a partnership interest for estate tax purposes, a buy-out agreement price based upon tax book value, when the court found that the decedent's intent was to pass the partnership interest to his heirs at less than full consideration).

In *Curtis,* the continuing partners argued for a price equal to the value the last balance sheet showed for the deceased partner's interest (in other words, his or her capital account). This is often referred to as "book value." The court, however, seemed only too eager to find an ambiguity in the agreement and to resolve it against the use of book value. Is there something about the use of book value the court regarded as unfair? Recall the material in Chapter I on valuing businesses. The problems with relying on book value appear well illustrated by the facts in *Curtis.* The value shown on the balance sheet in *Curtis* for certain real property (which, by accounting custom, is based on cost less a reserve for depreciation) apparently diverged substantially from the fair market value of the property at the time of dissolution. Moreover, the balance sheet failed to show (again following accepted accounting principles) any added worth inherent in a going business (i.e. goodwill). Recall as well from Chapter I that book value can be very different depending upon what generally accepted accounting principles parties employ in keeping their books—thereby setting the stage for possible disputes over the book value of a departing owner's interest. *See Aron v. Gillman,* 309 N.Y. 157, 128 N.E.2d 284 (1955). An added problem in *Curtis* was the partners evidently did not keep up the books. Nevertheless, is there anything to be said for using book value? How much more complexity did the court's interpretation of the agreement introduce in order to value the deceased partner's interest? What difficulty exists when one must value intangibles such as goodwill, especially when one of the owners running the business just died? Is there any tax reason to follow capital accounts in setting a price? Recall the discussion of substantial economic effect and specifically how the regulations under Section 704(b) require liquidating distributions to follow capital accounts. Yet, is a buy-out the same as a liquidation? If not, does this mean partners (or parties treated as partners for income tax purposes) can agree to a buy-out price which completely ignores their capital accounts? For example, how much real dollar impact will allocation of income and loss have if the partnership agreement in a two-person partnership calls for one partner to buy the other out at an unchanging price fixed in the initial contract? (Assume this partnership is far more likely to terminate through a buy-out than through a liquidation.) On the other hand, if a buy-out is equivalent to a liquidation for Section 704(b) purposes, does this mean the buy-out price must reflect the book value of the departing owner's capital account without any adjustments? See Treas. Reg. § 1.704–1(b)(2)(iv)(f)(5)(ii) (allowing adjustments in capital accounts to reflect the fair market value of the firm's assets if done for a non-tax business purpose in connection with a buy-out).

Using appraisers (or arbitrators) is a third approach to set the price. Since appraisal can be expensive, the agreement should specify who will pay. The agreement must also specify the manner in which the parties select the appraisers or arbitrators. Finally, the parties must consider what instructions to give the appraisers if, for example, the appraisers ask whether they should take goodwill into account. This suggests (as the *Block* opinion reprinted *infra* further illustrates) that providing for appraisal may not completely avoid the need to consider the basis for valuing an owner's interest.

The material in Chapter I pointed out that parties often value businesses based upon expected future earnings. Could an agreement set a price using this approach? On the other hand, how accurate can a prediction of future earnings be, especially when one or more owners leave the firm? In addition, consider the possible effect of a valuation using this method on the ability of the buyers to fund the purchase (since future earnings do not provide current cash). Is there any way to provide some compensation based upon future earnings and yet avoid both of these problems? What if a withdrawing owner (or his or her estate) receives a percentage of firm profits for a number of years?

Still other methods of setting the price may work in specialized circumstances. For example, if the desire of one owner to sell to a third party triggers the buy-out, the other owners might have the right of first-refusal to buy the interest at the same price as the third party offered. Another method exists when two partners or LLC members cannot get along. One party may set the price, while giving the other the option either to buy or sell at that price. Are there any problems with either of these approaches? For example, how effective is the latter approach in setting a fair price if one of the two parties cannot afford the purchase? See *Johnson v. Buck,* 540 S.W.2d 393 (Tex.Civ.App.1976).

Finally, consider the court's interpretation of the partnership agreement in *Curtis* as calling for a price equal to a "fair value." Is there anything wrong with the partnership or LLC operating agreement simply providing "fair value" as the price—after all, what could be fairer than the fair value? Under such an agreement, who determines what is the fair value and how will this determination be made? If the answer is to go to court, what is the practical impact of going through a trial in order to obtain a price based upon a battle of expert testimony? Incidentally, while many statutes, such as the pre–2001 U.L.P.A., have provided default rules calling for buy-outs at fair value, notice the approach used by the R.U.P.A. Under the R.U.P.A.'s buy-out provision, if the parties cannot agree, the court sets a price based upon a hypothetical sale at the greater of liquidation or going concern value. R.U.P.A. § 701(b), (i). Does this provide any significant improvement? How does a court determine what price would result in a hypothetical sale at going concern value?

c. *Funding*

Block v. Mylish

351 Pa. 611, 41 A.2d 731 (1945).

■ JONES, JUSTICE.

This appeal arises out of a declaratory judgment proceeding instituted to settle a controversy between surviving partners and the personal representative of a deceased partner concerning the proceeds of insurance carried by the partnership on the life of the deceased partner.

In 1923, the firm of Mylish, Mann and Drucker, composed of Isaac D. Mylish, Alfred Mann and Jerome J. Drucker, took out a separate policy of insurance on the life of each of the partners in principal sums of $10,000 and, in 1930, took out three additional like policies for $50,000 each, making in all two policies for an aggregate amount of $60,000 of insurance on the life of each partner. The partnership was named beneficiary in all of the policies and, at all times, paid the premiums thereon with partnership funds, as business expenses.

The partnership endured until June 4, 1943. Throughout its existence, the three partners had equal interests in the partnership and shared equally its profits and losses. On December 29, 1941, the partners entered into a written agreement continuing the partnership until December 31, 1943, and thereafter, from year to year, until any of the partners should give specified notice in writing to the other of his intention to terminate the agreement at the end of the then current term. This agreement conferred on the surviving partners an option to purchase a deceased partner's interest in the business upon a basis and terms as provided for in the agreement to which further reference will hereinafter be made.

* * *

Mann died on June 4, 1943, leaving a last will of which Gordon A. Block is executor. * * * Following his death, the insurance companies paid the sums due under the policies on his life, in an aggregate amount of $60,077.70. * * *

Mylish and Drucker duly exercised their option to purchase Mann's interest in the business pursuant to the provisions of the partnership agreement, but a dispute arose among the interested parties with respect to the extent to which the value of the business should be affected on account of the policies of insurance on Mann's life. His executor maintained that the life insurance proceeds became an asset of the partnership contemporaneously with Mann's death and should, therefore, be reflected in toto in a valuation of the business, while Mylish and Drucker contended that only the cash surrender value of the policies on Mann's life was a partnership asset at the date of his death and that the proceeds of the insurance were available to them under the partnership agreement for their personal use in purchasing Mann's interest in the business. The learned judge of the court below decided the controversy in favor of the deceased partner's estate and entered judgment accordingly from which the surviving partners have appealed.

The matter in dispute is to be determined in accordance with the intent and purpose of the partnership agreement.

* * *

The presently material portions of the partnership agreement are contained in paragraph 7 thereof and the three ensuing unnumbered paragraphs from which the following excerpts or summaries are taken:

In paragraph 7 it is provided that "In the event of the termination of the partnership by the death of any one of the partners, a complete inventory of the assets of the business shall be ascertained as soon after the death of said partner as possible, * * * "by appraisers to be selected as provided in the agreement.[2]

The next succeeding paragraph provides that "From the gross assets of the business so ascertained, the liabilities shall be deducted which shall show the net worth of the business. The surviving partners shall have the right and are hereby granted the option of purchasing the deceased partner's interest in the partnership for the sum so arrived at as to his share (good-will not to be included), * * * ". The same paragraph specifies the terms of payment for the deceased partner's interest, viz., $5,000 in cash at the time the surviving partners exercise their option to purchase, fifty per cent of the balance within six months of the date of death of the deceased partner, twenty-five per cent within nine months of the same date and the remaining twenty-five per cent within one year.

The next paragraph provides that "In the event that the proceeds of life insurance on the deceased partner's life shall be paid to the copartnership and is free and clear, or is partially so, then in that event the entire proceeds, or such portion thereof as is free and clear of the said life insurance, shall be turned over and paid by said partnership on account of the purchase price and applied against the above payments insofar as it can be."

2. The partnership agreement provides that "the action of the appraisers in arriving at the figures (in the inventory of the assets of the business) shall be binding on the partners and the estate of the deceased partner." While an appraisal was had, as contemplated by the partnership agreement, upon the exercise by Mylish and Drucker of their option to purchase Mann's interest in the business, the appraisers purposely left open for judicial determination the question involved in this case concerning the proceeds of the partnership insurance on Mann's life.

Then follows a paragraph which provides that the surviving partners should give promissory notes in accordance with the terms of payment (bearing interest at four per cent per annum) for the unpaid balance of the purchase price for the deceased partner's interest. The remaining portions of the partnership agreement are not material to the question here involved.

The appellants base their claim to the proceeds of the insurance on Mann's life upon the clause above quoted to the effect, in material part, that "the entire proceeds (of the insurance on the deceased partner's life), or such portion thereof as is free and clear * * *, shall be turned over and paid by said partnership on account of the purchase price; for the deceased partner's share of the business." Because of this provision, which relates to the type of payments to be made in discharge of the liability for the purchase of the deceased partner's interest rather than to the valuation of the assets of the business, the surviving partners would have the agreement interpreted so as to mean that the proceeds of the insurance on the life of a deceased partner were to be the property of the surviving partners in their individual and personal right and not the property of the partnership. Such a construction is not admissible under any fair interpretation of the written agreement.

That the insurance policies on the lives of the partners were assets of the business, and as such partnership property, is not open to reasonable dispute. That the parties themselves so considered the insurance is equally clear. The provision in paragraph 7 that "a complete inventory of the assets of the business" should be ascertained as soon as possible after the death of a partner did not contemplate the exclusion of the insurance. Likewise, in the next paragraph, which conferred on the surviving partners the option to purchase a deceased partner's interest in the business, the agreement specified as the price to be paid therefor "the sum so arrived at as to his share (good-will not to be included);" i.e., according to "the complete inventory of the (cashable) assets of the business." Thus, in the portions of the agreement concerned with the ascertainment of the value of the business and the basis for computing the sum to be paid for a deceased partner's interest there is neither mention nor intimation that the insurance on the lives of the partners was not to be appraised as an asset of the business. Under the well known rule of construction (*Expressio unius est exclusio alterius*), any thought that the insurance was not to be included was still further negatived by the express and sole exclusion of good-will from a valuation of thc assets of the business. * * *

The purpose and intent of the provision respecting the use to be made of the proceeds of the insurance is readily apparent. Under the immediately preceding paragraph of the agreement, the surviving partners were required to make but a relatively small cash payment upon exercising their option to purchase a deceased partner's interest. Payment of the balance of the purchase price was deferred and was to be made in installments over the year succeeding the partner's death. The reason for that provision is obvious. It was designed to save the surviving partners from the necessity of converting partnership assets, to the possible impairment or disruption of the business, in order to pay the purchase price in cash forthwith. Immediately following the provision about the use of the proceeds of the insurance, the agreement provides that the surviving partners' deferred liability for the balance of the purchase price should be evidenced by no more than their promissory notes. It is in connection with those provisions (as to the deferred payment and the notes) that the agreement requires that "the entire proceeds (of the life insurance), or such portion thereof as is free and clear * * *, shall be turned over and paid by said partnership on account of the purchase price (for the deceased partner's interest) and applied against the above (deferred) payments insofar as it can be." In short, to the extent of the insurance money received by the partnership upon the death of a partner, his representatives were to receive (on account of the purchase price for his interest in the business) cash instead of notes of the surviving partners. That is the clearly expressed meaning of the provision. It was not intended to advantage the surviving partners pecuniarily at the expense of their deceased associate.

The element of wager, based upon the fortuity of survivorship, which the appellants' construction of the agreement would introduce, could serve to deny the right of the partners to a reciprocal insurable interest in the life of each other. * * * Under the present appellants' contention, a partner's expectation of benefit or advantage could lie not in the continuance of the lives of his partners but rather in the possibility of their deaths prior to his own. The impeachment of the basis for the insurance which the appellants' construction would thus inject would require that the contention be discountenanced. * * *

The unreasonableness of the appellants' contention is further apparent. The construction of the partnership agreement, which they advocate, would not furnish a rule uniformly applicable. For example, had the surviving partners declined to exercise their option to purchase Mann's interest, then, under further terms of the partnership agreement, liquidation would have ensued. In that event, the value of the deceased partner's interest would have been fixed as of the date of the dissolution of the partnership. * * * Mann's death worked a dissolution of the partnership. Act of March 26, 1915, P.L. 18, Part VI, § 31, 59 P.S. § 93 [U.P.A. § 31]. And, at the instant of dissolution, the cash proceeds of the matured policies on Mann's life forthwith became part of the partnership assets. The fact that the policies were not paid by the insurance companies for several weeks thereafter, pending the filing of required proofs, did not constitute the insurance a subsequently accruing asset. * * *

Furthermore, there was no basis for including in the assets of the business merely the cash surrender value of the policies on Mann's life. Yet, that is the sole alternative proffered by the appellants. Their position would have been more consistent had they contended that, upon their exercise of the option to purchase Mann's interest (the proceeds of the insurance on his life being free from encumbrance), nothing on account of the insurance was to be included in the assets of the business. It is anachronous to treat with cash surrender value in respect of policies which, at once, have become liabilities of the insurer for the net proceeds of the face value of the insurance. The fact is that the partnership policies on the lives of all of the partners had asset value—cash surrender while they lived—face value (less any encumbrances) as to any of them who died. Consequently, at the instant of Mann's death, the life insurance assets on the books of the partnership would properly show the net proceeds payable on the matured policies on Mann's life and the cash surrender value of the policies on Mylish and Drucker.

The judgment is affirmed. * * *

NOTES

1. The agreement in *Block* anticipated the problems continuing owners often face in paying for the departing owner's interest and provided both classic responses: insurance and installment payments. Unfortunately, the agreement failed to answer all the questions raised by these techniques.

Providing insurance first requires deciding who buys and pays for the policies. There are three obvious possibilities: (1) the firm, (2) each owner for insurance on the life of the other owner(s), or (3) each owner for insurance on his or her own life. (A less obvious, but occasionally used, alternative is to have a trustee buy the policies.) To decide what makes the most sense, consider who benefits from insurance proceeds used to fund the purchase of the deceased owner's interest. Since the proceeds ultimately go to the deceased owner's heirs or beneficiaries, one may be tempted to conclude the insurance is for their benefit. The deceased owner, however, did not need a buy-out agreement in order to obtain life insurance for his or her heirs. Moreover, without the insurance, the remaining owners must pay for the decedent's interest out of their own pockets (either directly if they purchase the decedent's interest, or indirectly through diminution in the value of the firm if the firm makes the purchase). This suggests the insurance exists to benefit the surviving owners, and each owner should, therefore, buy and pay for insurance on the lives of the others. On the other hand, if the firm is large (say 100 partners or members) consider the proliferation of policies necessitated by each owner buying a policy on every other owner. Why not, for convenience, simply have the firm buy and pay for the policies? Yet, if the owners are different ages, what effect will this have on insurance premiums and, in turn, on the fairness of having the firm rather than the individual owners pay the premiums? Similarly, what is the effect if the owners have unequal interests in the firm—meaning the owner with the larger interest effectively pays more and benefits less from policies maintained by the firm. On the other hand, if the firm maintains the policies, must the parties allocate this expense in accordance with their general sharing of profit and loss, rather than in accordance with which owners benefit from which policies?

The next question is who should be the beneficiary of the policy: the firm, the members of the firm, or the heirs of the deceased owner. The choice between the firm or surviving owners depends upon who purchases the decedent's interest, a subject considered below. Naming the heirs can create a couple of problems. It risks confusion as to whether the proceeds constitute payment for the decedent's interest. *See White v. Hickey,* 8 Ark.App. 264, 651 S.W.2d 467 (1983). Also, the proceeds may become part of the estate of the decedent for estate tax purposes (albeit, the alternative, if the proceeds go to the firm, may be simply to have a more valuable interest in the firm included in the estate). *See* Rev. Rul. 82–85, 1982–1 C.B. 137. Incidentally, in either case, will the payoff of the policy, itself, constitute taxable income to the firm or to the individuals who receive the insurance payout? See I.R.C. § 101(a), (j) (not if certain coverage, notice and consent requirements are satisfied).

Naming the firm as beneficiary leads to the issue raised in *Block*: Should the proceeds count as part of the firm's assets in determining the value of the decedent's interest? What were the court's reasons for determining they should? On the other hand, is there a problem created by counting the proceeds in valuing the decedent's interest? If the agreement includes the proceeds in the valuation, what must the owners do in order to provide adequate insurance to fund the entire purchase? Will this become something like a cat chasing its tail? Yet another problem with insurance proceeds and price occurs when agreements are ambiguous as to whether the proceeds might constitute the entire payment for the interest regardless of whether they are greater or less than its value. *See Oglesby—Barnitz Bank & Trust Co. v. Clark,* 112 Ohio App. 31, 175 N.E.2d 98 (1959).

2. Allowing installment payments also raises a number of questions. For example, what, if any, compensation does the withdrawing partner or member receive for accepting delay in payment? Section 42 of the U.P.A. provides, in the absence of agreement to the contrary, that the withdrawing partner, who is not yet paid for his or her interest, is entitled to either interest on or profits made from the amount owed. The R.U.P.A., however, provides only for interest. R.U.P.A. § 701(b), (h). By and large, LLC statutes ignore the question. Typically, buy-out agreements specifically cover this subject rather than leave things to any statutory scheme. A further question is how to secure the departing owner's payment against a reversal in the firm's fortunes. How much leeway do the partners possess in this regard—specifically, to what extent can a former partner compete for payment out of the firm's assets with creditors whose claims predate his or her departure? See U.P.A. § 41(8). (The R.U.P.A., however, contains no similar restriction, and the personal liability of a departing partner for predissolution debts might render the question somewhat academic.)

3. This, in turn, raises broader questions about the impact of the liabilities of the firm upon the buy-out. Notice that neither dissolution nor dissociation relieves the departing partner in an ordinary partnership of liability for debts the partnership incurred before his or her leaving. *See* U.P.A. § 36(1). R.U.P.A. § 703(b). What then should happen to the ordinary partnership's existing debts upon the buy-out? The U.P.A. provides a different scheme depending upon what triggers the buy-out. If the remaining partners wish to buy out a wrongfully dissolving partner under Section

38(2), they must agree to indemnify the departing partner for any present (or future) liabilities and may need to secure this obligation with a bond. Upon expulsion of a partner pursuant to an agreement allowing for such, Section 38(1) requires the remaining partners either to pay off all the liabilities or to get the creditors to let the expelled partner off the hook. If the buy-out occurs pursuant to any other agreement, the U.P.A. is silent. The R.U.P.A. is broader—if there is a buy-out rather than dissolution, the partnership must indemnify the departing partner against all known (as well as future) liabilities. R.U.P.A. § 701(d). These provisions, however, are implicitly, if not explicitly, subject to contrary agreement (R.U.P.A. § 103), which makes the important question for planning purposes what should the partners agree.

To answer this question, one must ask what are the available options and what practical impact separates them. The parties could leave the departing partner responsible to pay off his or her share of the existing liabilities, or else the remaining partners (or the firm) could agree to take care of the debts. The impacts of this choice occur largely in the areas of price, funding and assurance of performance. (There are also some tax impacts discussed later.)

Notice the agreement in *Block* called for subtracting the partnership's liabilities from the value of its assets in order to determine the net worth of the business and hence the buy-out price. This reflects the fact that if the partnership or remaining partners assume the liabilities (as no doubt occurred in *Block*), this should lower the price to an amount equal to the departing partner's equity in the business, whereas if the price equals the departing partner's share of the firm's assets without considering its liabilities, then presumably the continuing partners will insist that the departing partner pays his or her share of the firm's debts. This suggests that the question of what to do about liabilities becomes something of a wash, since the price simply will change so that the parties end up in the same place regardless. This certainly works for liabilities whose existence and amounts are known to the partners at the time of dissolution; but what if the firm becomes liable for pre-dissolution torts whose consequences only come home to roost after dissolution? How can the parties adjust the price if the firm agrees to assume the departing partner's share of this sort of debt? Does this explain why the R.U.P.A. (in the absence of other agreement) does not call upon the firm to assume unknown liabilities?

If the price must go up because the firm or remaining partners do not assume all the debts, what is the impact of this upon funding the buy-out? Does this explain, in part, why buy-out agreements typically call for the assumption of debts? In this regard, notice a funding advantage of any buy-out arrangement over purchasing assets in a liquidation sale—assuming the firm's debts will not all by their terms require immediate payment upon dissolution or dissociation. In a buy-out, the continuing partners only need to come up with enough money to pay off the net value of the departing partner's interest.

Next, consider the impact of non-performance by whoever assumes the contractual obligation for the debts. If the continuing partners agree to assume the debts, the former partner stands as surety for their payment unless the creditors agree to a novation. *See* U.P.A. § 36(2); R.U.P.A. § 703(c). Conversely, the firm and continuing partners remain on the hook for all the liabilities, even if the departing partner agreed to take care of his or her share. *See*, U.P.A. § 15, R.U.P.A. § 306. Hence, unless the creditors agree to release someone, the parties to the buy-out face a risk if whoever agreed to take care of the liabilities fails to do so. Does this fact impact who should assume the primary obligation? Specifically, does relying on payment by one versus the other side to the buy-out present a greater likelihood of non-performance and more difficulties in enforcement? If so, which side? Of course, if the departing partner is too concerned about the firm defaulting on a debt for which he or she will remain secondarily liable, this may render the whole idea of a buy-out impractical. *See Haley v. Talcott*, 864 A.2d 86 (Del. Ch.2004) (LLC member's personal guarantee of a major debt owed by the LLC rendered the buy-out provision in the LLC operating agreement an insufficient solution to a deadlock between the two members of the LLC).

What about the future as opposed to the existing debts of the firm? The answer here is to ensure that those who do business with the firm receive appropriate notice of the withdrawal, in order to cut off claims for new debts incurred by the continuing partnership. *See* U.P.A. § 35(1)(b); R.U.P.A. § 703(b). The revised act helpfully authorizes the filing of a statement of dissociation in order to deal with the creditor notice problem (R.U.P.A. § 704) and, in any event, cuts off claims based upon transactions more than two years after dissociation. R.U.P.A. § 703(b).

Suppose, instead of dealing with ordinary partners, the buy-out involves limited partners, partners in an LLP or LLC members. In these instances, the departing party does not have any personal liability for the firm's debts (unless there was some personal guarantee or liability for one's own tort). Without such liability, would it make any sense for the departing party to agree to assume any of the firm's debts?

Notice that the impact of buying out an owner who enjoys limited liability is to remove money which otherwise might have been available to the firm's creditors. What legal issues does this create? As mentioned when dealing with allocation of profit earlier in this chapter, statutes governing limited liability entities commonly contain restrictions on distributions from the firm to its owners. Accordingly, the court in the *Five Star* opinion, reprinted earlier in this chapter, noted that LLC statutes could impact payments made to buy out an LLC member's interest. The basic limit under the U.L.P.A., typical LLC statutes, and many LLP statutes, is that the firm cannot legally distribute money to buy out a limited partner, an LLC member, or a partner in an LLP, unless the firm's assets after the payment exceed its debts. The pre–2001 U.L.P.A. contains an additional limit. To the extent the payment returns the limited partner's contribution—as a buy-out by the firm will—the limited partner may need to return the money if necessary within a year to pay debts owed at the time of the buy-out.

What impact do these restrictions have upon drafting a partnership or an LLC operating agreement? To begin with, might these restrictions impact the choice of who should undertake a buy-out: the firm or the remaining owners? Reading carefully, one sees that the U.L.P.A., and similar LLC and LLP provisions, limit distributions *from the limited partnership, LLC or LLP. E.g.*, U.L.P.A. § 607; U.L.P.A. (2001) § 508; Cal. Corp. Code §§ 16957(a), 17254(a); Del. Code Ann. Title 6 §§ 15–309,18–607; N.Y. Ltd. Liab. Co. Law § 508. Hence, on their face, do these sections apply to buy-outs in which the remaining owners, rather than the firm, are the purchasers? *But see Whitley v. Klauber and Alagna*, 51 N.Y.2d 555, 435 N.Y.S.2d 568, 416 N.E.2d 569 (1980) (holding that the sale of limited partnership interests to a new general partner constituted a return of the limited partners' contributions within the meaning of Section 608 of the 1916 version of the U.L.P.A., thereby making the recipients liable for the amounts received when the partnership could not pay its debts).

As noted above, a common solution if a firm presently lacks the money to buy out a departing owner is to provide for installment payments. In this event, when does one measure the firm's condition against the financial limits contained in the U.L.P.A., or in LLC or LLP statutes: at the time the firm buys out the departing owner in exchange for an IOU, at the time the firm makes each payment on the IOU, or at both times? See U.L.P.A. (2001) § 508(d)(1) (measure at the date the debt was incurred); Cal. Corp. Code § 17254(c), (d) (measure at the date of authorization if distribution occurs within 120 days of authorization, or at the date of payment if later than 120 days from authorization; and, in calculating the firm's total debt, disregard debts to members conditioned on meeting, at the time of payment, the financial tests for distributions). Neither the pre–2001 U.L.P.A. nor many LLC or LLP statutes, however, expressly address the question. A later chapter in this book will return to this issue in the context of buy-outs by corporations.

d. *Tax Aspects*

Foxman v. Commissioner of Internal Revenue

41 T.C. 535 (1964), *aff'd*, 352 F.2d 466 (3d Cir.1965).

FINDINGS OF FACT

* * *

* * * Abbey Record Manufacturing Co. was a partnership * * * engaged in the business of custom manufacturing of phonograph records * * *. [A]s a result of certain agreements dated February 1, 1955, and January 26, 1956, Foxman, Grenell, and Jacobowitz became equal partners in Abbey, each with a one-third interest.

* * *

A related venture commenced by Jacobowitz, Foxman, and Grenell, individually, was represented by Sound Plastics, Inc., a corporation in which each owned one-third of the stock; it was engaged in the business of manufacturing "biscuits" or vinyl forms used in the making of records.

* * *

Notwithstanding Abbey's success there was considerable disharmony among and between the partners. As a result there were discussions during the spring of 1956 relating to the withdrawal of Jacobowitz from Abbey. These negotiations did not lead to any agreement and the partners continued to work and to quarrel. * * * [D]iscussions were resumed again in March 1957. It was at about this time that Foxman offered Jacobowitz $225,000 in cash, an automobile which was in Abbey's name, and Foxman's and Grenell's interest in Sound Plastics, Inc., for Jacobowitz's interest in Abbey. * * *

The negotiations of the three partners culminated in an agreement dated May 21, 1957, for the "sale" of Jacobowitz's partnership interest * * *.

Relevant portions of the May 21, 1957, agreement are as follows:

> AGREEMENT, made this 21st day of May 1957, between NORMAN B. JACOBOWITZ, hereinafter referred to as the "First Party", and HORACE W. GRENELL, and DAVID A. FOXMAN, individually, jointly and severally, hereinafter referred to as the "Second Parties" and ABBEY RECORD MFG. CO., hereinafter referred to as the "Third Party," WITNESSETH:
>
> * * *
>
> NOW, THEREFORE, IT IS MUTUALLY AGREED AS FOLLOWS:
>
> FIRST: The second parties hereby purchase all the right, title, share and interest of the first party in ABBEY and the first party does hereby sell, transfer, convey and assign all of his right, title, interest and share in ABBEY and in the moneys in banks, trade names, accounts due, or to become due, and in all other assets of any kind whatsoever, belonging to said ABBEY, for and in consideration of the following:
>
> A) The payment of TWO HUNDRED FORTY TWO THOUSAND FIVE HUNDRED & FIFTY ($242,550.00) DOLLARS, payable as follows:
>
> * * *
>
> B) In addition to the payments required under paragraph "A" hereof, the second parties hereby transfer, convey and assign all of their right, title and interest in SOUND PLASTICS, INC. to the first party. * * *
>
> C) In addition to the payments required under paragraph "A" hereof and the transfer of stock referred to in paragraph "B" hereof,

the second parties hereby transfer, convey and assign all of their right, title and interest in and to one, 1956 Chrysler New Yorker Sedan, as evidenced by the transfer of registration thereof, duly executed herewith, the receipt of which by the first party is hereby acknowledged.

* * *

Samuel Feldman, a New York City attorney who represented Foxman and Grenell, drafted the agreement of May 21, 1957; at Feldman's suggestion, Abbey was added as a party to the agreement. An earlier draft of the proposed agreement did not include Abbey as a party. During the negotiations leading to the May 21, 1957, agreement, the words "retirement" or "liquidation of a partner's interest" were not mentioned. There was no specific undertaking by the third party (Abbey) any place in the instrument. A sale of a partnership interest was the only transaction ever discussed.

* * *

OPINION

RAUM, Judge:

* * * On May 21, 1957, Jacobowitz's status as a partner in Abbey came to an end pursuant to an agreement executed on that day. The first issue before us is whether Jacobowitz thus made a "sale" of this partnership interest to Foxman and Grenell within section 741 of the 1954 Code, as contended by him, or whether the payments to him required by the agreement are to be regarded as "made in liquidation" of his interest within section 736, as contended by Foxman and Grenell. Jacobowitz treated the transaction as constituting a "sale," and reported a capital gain thereon in his return for 1957. Foxman and Grenell, on the other hand, treated the payments as having been "made in liquidation" of Jacobowitz's interest under section 736, with the result that a substantial portion thereof reduced their distributive shares of partnership income for the fiscal year ending February 28, 1958.

The Commissioner, in order to protect the revenues, took inconsistent positions. In Jacobowitz's case, his determination proceeded upon the assumption that there was a section 736 "liquidation" with the result that payments thereunder were charged to Jacobowitz for the partnership fiscal year ending February 28, 1958, thus not only attributing to Jacobowitz additional income for his calendar year 1958 but also treating it as ordinary income rather than capital gain. In the cases of Foxman and Grenell, the Commissioner adopted Jacobowitz's position that there was a section 741 "sale" on May 21, 1957, to Foxman and Grenell, thus disallowing the deductions in respect thereof from the partnership's income for its fiscal year ending February 28, 1958; as a consequence, there was a corresponding increase in the distributive partnership income of Foxman and Grenell for that fiscal year which was reflected in the deficiencies determined for the calendar year 1958 in respect of each of them.

As is obvious, the real controversy herein is not between the various petitioners and the Government, but rather between Jacobowitz and his two former partners. We hold, in favor of Jacobowitz, that the May 21, 1957, transaction was a "sale" under section 741.

* * *

That a partnership interest may be "sold" to one or more members of the partnership within section 741 is not disputed by any of the parties. Indeed, the Income Tax Regulations, section 1.741–1(b), explicitly state:

> Section 1.741–1 Recognition and character of gain or loss on sale or exchange.
>
> (b) Section 741 shall apply whether the partnership interest is sold to one or more members of the partnership or to one or more persons who are not members of the partnership. * * *

And it is clear that in such circumstances, sections 736 and 761(d), do not apply. See regulations, sec. 1.736–1(a)(1)(i):

> Sec. 1.736–1 Payments to a retiring partner or a deceased partner's successor in interest.
>
> (a) Payments considered as distributive share or guaranteed payment.
>
> (1)(i) Section 736 and this section apply only to payments made to a retiring partner or to a deceased partner's successor in interest in liquidation of such partner's entire interest in the partnership. See section 761(d). * * * Section 736 and this section apply only to payments made by the partnership and not to transactions between the partners. Thus, a sale by partner A to partner B of his entire one-fourth interest in partnership ABCD would not come within the scope of section 736.

Did Jacobowitz sell his interest to Foxman and Grenell, or did he merely enter into an arrangement to receive "payments * * * in liquidation of (his) * * * interest" from the partnership? We think the record establishes that he sold his interest.

At first blush, one may indeed wonder why Congress provided for such drastically different tax consequences, depending upon whether the amounts received by the withdrawing partner are to be classified as the proceeds of a "sale" or as "payments * * * in liquidation" of his interest.[7]

7. If the transaction were a "sale" under section 741, Jacobowitz's gain would be taxed as capital gain (there being no section 751 problem in respect of unrealized receivables or inventory items which have appreciated substantially in value), and would be reportable in 1957 rather than in 1958. On the other hand, if the transaction were a section 736 "liquidation," the amounts received by him (to the extent that they were not for his "interest * * * in partnership property" pursuant to section 736(b)(1)) would be taxable as ordinary income and would be reportable by him in 1958, rather than in 1957. The tax liabilities of the remaining partners, Foxman and Grenell, would be affected accordingly, depending upon whether section 736 or 741 governed the transaction.

For, there may be very little, if any, difference in ultimate economic affect between a "sale" of a partnership interest to the remaining partners and a "liquidation" of that interest. * * * In the case of a sale the remaining partners may well obtain part or all of the needed cash to pay the purchase price from the partnership assets, funds borrowed by the partnership or future earnings of the partnership. * * * Yet the practical difference between such transaction and one in which the withdrawing partner agrees merely to receive payments in liquidation directly from the partnership itself would hardly be a meaningful one in most circumstances.[8] Why then the enormous disparity in tax burden, turning upon what for practical purposes is merely the difference between Tweedledum and Tweedledee, and what criteria are we to apply in our effort to discover that difference in a particular case? The answer to the first part of the questions is to be found in the legislative history of subchapter K, and it goes far towards supplying the answer to the second part.

In its report on the bill which became the 1954 Code the House Ways and Means Committee stated that the then "existing tax treatment of partners and partnerships is among the most confused in the entire tax field"; that "Partners * * * cannot form, operate, or dissolve a partnership with any assurance as to tax consequences"; that the proposed statutory provisions (subchapter K) represented the "first comprehensive statutory treatment of partners and partnerships in the history of the income tax laws"; and that "principal objectives have been simplicity, flexibility, and equity as between the partners." H. Rept. No. 1337, 83d Cong., 2d Sess., p.65. Like thoughts were expressed in virtually identical language by a the Senate Finance Committee. S. Rept. No. 1622, 83d Cong., 2d Sess., p. 89.

Although there can be little doubt that the attempt to achieve "simplicity" has resulted in utter failure, the new legislation was intended to and in fact did bring into play an element of "flexibility." Tax law in respect of partners may often involve a delicate mechanism, for a ruling in favor of one partner may automatically produce adverse consequences to the others. Accordingly, one of the underlying philosophic objectives of the 1954 Code was to permit the partners themselves to determine their tax burdens inter sese to a certain extent, and this is what the committee reports meant when they referred to "flexibility." The theory was that the partners would take their prospective tax liabilities into account in bargaining with one another.

* * *

Recurring to the problem immediately before us, this policy of "flexibility" is particularly pertinent in determining the tax consequences of the withdrawal of a partner. Where the practical differences between a "sale"

8. The only difference suggested by counsel for Foxman and Grenell, for the first time in their reply brief, is that in the event of bankruptcy of the partnership the liability to the withdrawing partner might be subject to a different order of priority depending upon whether there is involved the liability of the partnership itself, as in the case of a "liquidation," or the liability of the purchasing partners, as in the case of a "sale." * * *

and a "liquidation" are, at most, slight, if they exist at all, and where the tax consequences to the partners can vary greatly, it is in accord with the purpose of the statutory provisions to allow the partners themselves, through arm's-length negotiations, to determine whether to take the "sale" route or the "liquidation" route, thereby allocating the tax burden among themselves. And in the case the record leaves no doubt that they intended to and in fact did adopt the "sale" route.

The agreement of May 21, 1957, indicates a clear intention on the part of Jacobowitz to sell, and Foxman and Grenell to purchase, Jacobowitz's partnership interest. * * * [T]he agreement explicitly states not only that the "second parties (Foxman and Grenell) hereby purchase * * * the * * * interest of * * * (Jacobowitz) * * * in Abbey," but also that "the first party (Jacobowitz) does hereby sell" his interest in Abbey. Thus, Foxman and Grenell obligated themselves individually to purchase Jacobowitz's interest. Nowhere in the agreement was there any obligation on the part of Abbey to compensate Jacobowitz for withdrawing from the partnership. Indeed, a portion of the consideration received by him was the Sound Plastics stock, not a partnership asset at all. That stock was owned by Foxman and Grenell as individuals and their undertaking to turn it over to Jacobowitz as part of the consideration for Jacobowitz's partnership interest reinforces the conclusion that they as individuals were buying his interest, and that the transaction represented a "sale" of his interest to them rather than a "liquidation" of that interest by the partnership.

* * *

The fact that they utilized partnership resources to discharge their own individual liability * * * can hardly convert into a section 736 "liquidation" what would otherwise qualify as a section 741 "sale." It is important to bear in mind the object of "flexibility" which Congress attempted to attain, and we should be slow to give a different meaning to the arrangement which the partners entered into among themselves than that which the words of their agreement fairly spell out. Otherwise, the reasonable expectations of the partners in arranging their tax burdens inter sese would come to naught, and the purpose of the statute would be defeated. * * * We hold that the Commissioner's determination in respect of this issue was in error in Jacobowitz's case but was correct in the cases involving Foxman and Grenell.

* * *

NOTES

1. As the Court's opinion points out, there is little economic difference in an ordinary partnership between the firm purchasing the withdrawing partner's interest or the continuing partners doing so—at least so long as they buy in proportion to their current ownership. What might be the effect, however, if the continuing owners do not buy the withdrawing owner's interest in proportion to their current shares? Can this lead to any problems? Consider the impact in a firm in which voting power is propor-

tionate to interests. How might the buy-out agreement deal with this prospect? Also, as discussed earlier, the introduction of limited liability with the limited partnership, LLP and LLC creates greater non-tax significance to the question of whether the firm, versus the other owner(s), acts as the purchaser of a departing owner's interest. Specifically, statutory limits on distributions from a limited partnership, LLP or LLC to the firm's owners (including in a buy-out) will apply if the firm is the purchaser, but generally should not apply if the other owners act as purchasers.

2. Foxman shows how Section 741 treats the sale of the interest of a departing partner (or a person treated as a partner for income tax purposes) to the remaining owners. Except insofar as the interest encompasses the departing owner's interest in Section 751 assets, Section 741 treats the transaction as the sale of a capital asset. This results in no income to the departing owner except for that portion of the purchase price in excess of his or her basis in the firm. This excess receives capital gains treatment (again, except payment for the Section 751 assets). The result of the transaction also can be to increase the remaining owners' bases in their interests in the firm. *See* I.R.C. § 742. (If there is only one remaining owner, then the basis impact is on the assets of the former firm. See Rev. Rul. 99–6, 1999–1 C.B. 432 (treating one owner who buys out the other owner of a two-person LLC as if he or she purchased the firm's assets).) The remaining owners, however, obviously would much prefer to immediately deduct the payments made to the departing owner. Suppose the buy-out agreement includes a covenant not to compete. What is the tax impact on the remaining owners of any portion of the buy-out price earmarked as compensation for the covenant? See I.R.C. § 197 (buyer may obtain a deduction based upon a 15 year amortization for intangibles, including a covenant not to compete entered into in connection with the acquisition of an interest in a trade or business). Is there an offsetting tax disadvantage to the withdrawing owner? Note the type of income represented by payments on a covenant not to compete. More significantly, as evident from *Foxman,* Section 736 potentially provides the remaining owners favorable treatment. It comes into play if the firm is the purchaser (or, to use the tax parlance, if there is a "liquidation of a retired partner's interest"). Section 736, however, calls for different treatment depending upon what "interest" of the retired owner the payment is for.

3. Section 736 establishes two regimes governing payments made by a partnership (or any entity electing income tax treatment as a partnership) to buy out an owner's interest. Payments coming within Section 736(b) are treated as distributions by the firm to the owner. This brings into play the rules set out in Sections 731 and 732, which were discussed in the general description of the taxation of partnership profit and loss earlier in this chapter. (Because a Section 736(b) distribution is in liquidation of an owner's interest, however, there are two differences—one dealing with the ability to recognize losses, and the other with the basis of any distributed assets—from the treatment of non-liquidating distributions described previously. *See* I.R.C. §§ 731(a)(2); 732(b).) Treating payments as distributions generally favors (much as the result under Section 741) the departing

owner, who, barring problems under Sections 737 or 751(b), need recognize no income except insofar as he or she receives cash in excess of the basis or his or her interest in the firm, and then the income is capital gain. I.R.C. § 731(a). As with distributions generally, unless there is a basis impact under Section 734 or a disproportionate handling of Section 751 assets or assets subject to Section 704(c), a Section 736(b) payment has no tax effect on the firm or the other owners. *See* I.R.C. §§ 731(b), 734. Compare these results with the results for a purchase by the other partners (or parties treated as partners for tax purposes): How significant does the difference appear to be so far between treatment under Sections 741 and 736(b)?

Section 736(a), however, establishes a very different scheme. Payments coming under it are treated as a distributive share if determined by income of the firm; otherwise they are guaranteed payments. The result is that the entire payment constitutes income to the departing owner—ordinary income in the case of a guaranteed payment (*see* I.R.C. § 707(c); Treas. Reg. § 1.736–1(a)(4)) and usually (depending upon the character of the firm's revenues) for a distributive share as well. *Cf* I.R.C. § 702(b). Against the disadvantage to the departing owner, however, stands the treatment of the remaining owners. Payments characterized as a distributive share decrease the portion of income of the firm left for them to recognize. Amounts considered a guaranteed payment provide them a deduction. Treas. Reg. § 1.736–1(a)(4).

The court in *Foxman* appeared to assume the tax disadvantage to the departing owner under Section 736(a) more or less completely offsets the tax advantage to the remaining owners. Is this necessarily true? If parties can save on net tax through Section 736(a), is there a way to let the withdrawing owner share in the good fortune?

4. While partners (or parties treated as partners for income tax purposes) seemingly have complete flexibility in choosing between Section 741 and Section 736 treatment, they are more constrained as between Section 736(a) and (b). Section 736 expressly addresses three items the firm may pay for when it buys out an owner. Payments made for an interest in the firm's property (ignoring for a moment unrealized receivables and goodwill) come within Section 736(b). I.R.C. § 736(b)(1). Prior to 1993, payments for unrealized receivables came within Section 736(a), while the parties could pretty well choose which provision governed payments for goodwill. *E.g., Commissioner v. Jackson Investment Co.,* 346 F.2d 187 (9th Cir.1965). In 1993, however, Congress ended Section 736(a) treatment for unrealized receivables and goodwill for partnerships (or entities treated as partnerships for income tax purposes) in which capital is a material income-producing factor, as well as for buying limited partners out from any firm. I.R.C. § 736(b)(3). For such partnerships and limited partners, all payments for any interest in the property of the firm now come within Section 736(b). This confines the impact focused on in *Foxman* from a buy-out's coming within Section 736 instead of 741 to personal service firms. For them, the pre–1993 rules regarding unrealized receivables and goodwill still apply. There remains a couple of ambiguities. To begin with, historically,

the regulations have recognized that a firm might make buy-out payments, not for any interest in the firm's property, but as a sort of mutual insurance. These payments would come within Section 736(a). Treas.Reg. § 1.736–1(a)(2). Whether this remains true after 1993 for firms in which capital is a material income-producing factor and for limited partners is unclear. In addition, it is unclear whether LLC members constitute partners or limited partners for purposes of Section 736.

5. While the difference between Sections 736(a) and 741 treatment that lead to the dispute in *Foxman* is now largely confined to personal service firms, other more subtle differences exist between Section 736 and Section 741 treatment of a buy-out. First, as apparent from the facts in *Foxman,* the choice affects when the departing owner recognizes income, if any, from the transaction. Section 741 brings into play the timing rules applicable to sales of property generally. *See Holbrook v. Commissioner,* 34 T.C.M. (CCH) 1283 (1975). This includes dealing with Section 453 if the departing owner receives payment in installments. Rev. Rul. 76–483, 1976–2 C.B. 131. (Section 453 will not apply, however, to the portion of the income on the sale attributable to Section 751 assets. Rev.Rul. 89–108, 1989–2 C.B. 100.) In contrast, payments coming under Section 736 follow timing principles uniquely part of the conduit approach of partnership taxation. Section 736(a) payments follow the rules controlling distributive shares and guaranteed payments. Treas. Reg. § 1.736–1(a)(5). Section 736(b) payments follow the timing principle implicit in their treatment as distributions, which only yield income under Section 731 at such time as the amount of cash received exceeds the recipient's basis. This means the departing owner receiving installment Section 736(b) payments need not recognize income until after the total of installments received recapture his or her basis. Treas. Reg. § 1.736–1(b)(6), (7) Ex. (1). (Compare this delay to the proportionate recognition of gain in each installment provided for by Section 453(c). The recipient of Section 736(b) payments can, however, elect to recognize gain (or, more desirably, loss) proportionately in each installment. Treas.Reg. § 1.736–1(b)(6).) The parties can decide how much of each deferred Section 736 payment represents a 736(a) versus a 736(b) payment—so long, of course, as the total of each type follows the rules discussed above. Treas. Reg. § 1.736–1(b)(5)(iii).

A second difference comes about by virtue of Section 708. Section 708(b)(1)(B) "terminates" a partnership (or any entity electing income tax treatment as a partnership) for tax purposes whenever the firm's owners sell within a twelve-month period fifty percent or more of the total interests in profits and capital. A sale under Section 741 by the departing owner to the continuing owners will trigger such a termination if the departing owner's interest is sufficiently large. *See* Treas. Reg. § 1.708–1(b)(1)(ii). (This becomes more likely if there is more than one departing owner.) Section 708(b)(1)(B) does not apply to a liquidation of a party's interest under Section 736. Treas. Reg. § 1.708–1(b)(1)(ii). (Suppose, however, only one person remains to carry on the business. In this event, a sale under Section 741 will terminate the partnership regardless of the size of the selling partner's interest. *See, e.g.,* Rev. Rul. 99–6, 1999–1 C.B. 432

(dealing with one owner of an LLC buying out the other, thereby converting the firm from a partnership to a sole proprietorship for income tax purposes). By contrast, when dealing with a Section 736 liquidation, Section 708(b)(1)(A) treats the partnership as terminated if there is only one owner left, but only after the last Section 736 payment. *See* Treas. Reg. § 1.736–1(a)(6).) In any event, the effect of a partnership termination under Section 708 is to close the tax year of the old firm, and to conjure a pair of constructive transactions in which tax law pretends that the "old firm" transferred its assets to the "new firm" (assuming there will be a continuing partnership rather than a sole proprietorship) in exchange for interests in the new firm, following which the old firm distributed the interests in the new firm to the parties continuing their ownership in the firm. Treas. Reg. § 1.708–1(b)(3)(ii), (4). What, if any, problems might a Section 708 termination create for the continuing owners? Notice that the two constructive transfers normally should be tax free under Sections 721 and 731, respectively.

Section 706(c)(2)(A) creates a third distinction, which involves the partnership tax year for departing owner. A Section 741 sale immediately closes the partnership tax year with respect to the selling owner, whereas, with one important exception, a Section 736 liquidation does not close the partnership tax year for the departing owner until receipt of the last Section 736 payment. *See* Treas. Reg. § 1.736–1(a)(6). The exception, under which Section 706(c)(2)(A) immediately closes the partnership tax year even in the case of a Section 736 liquidation, occurs upon a partner's (or a party treated as a partner for income tax purposes) death. Congress generously created this exception to avoid the problem which occurred in *Estate of Hesse v. Commissioner,* 74 T.C. 1307 (1980). In *Hesse*, the failure to close the partnership tax year for a deceased partner on the date of his death meant that partnership losses for the year of death flowed to the estate—which could neither use them, nor carry them back to reduce the deceased partner's tax liability for the years preceding his death. The impact of now closing the deceased partner's tax year on the date of death, even in the case of a Section 736 liquidation, is to remove what had been a significant incentive to utilize a Section 741 sale, rather than a Section 736 liquidation, in the event of a buy-out following a partner's death.

Section 751 creates a fourth potential distinction between sale and 736 liquidation treatment. In both cases, the objective of Section 751 is the same—to turn amounts received by the departing partner (or person treated as a partner for income tax purposes) in exchange for his or her share of the firm's inventory and unrealized receivables (sometimes called Section 751 assets) into ordinary income—but the scope, mechanics and precise impact of this transformation is different. A sale under Section 741 triggers Section 751(a)—which simply turns into ordinary income the portion of the purchase price attributable to the seller's interest in the firm's inventory and unrealized receivables. (Section 751 (a) is discussed in more detail later when the Chapter explores the sale of partnership interests generally.) Section 751(a) has no effect on the continuing owners. Section 736(b) payments, in contrast, since they are treated as a distribution, can trigger Section 751(b). As discussed earlier when outlining the tax treatment of distributions from a firm treated as a partnership for income tax purposes, Section 751(b) creates a hypothetical exchange between the firm and the recipient whenever there is a disproportionate distribution of either Section 751 or of non-Section 751 assets. (In the typical cash buy-out from a firm owning Section 751 assets, there is a disproportionate distribution of non-Section 751 assets (cash) to the withdrawing owner. In such a case, Section 751(b) will pretend that the firm distributed to the withdrawing owner his or her share of the firm's Section 751 assets, which the withdrawing owner then sold back to the firm for cash.) Notice that this hypothetical exchange can impact the remaining owners. On the positive side, it can increase the firm's basis in Section 751 assets (which would otherwise not occur without a Section 754 election). On the negative side, it can result in recognition of income if the payment to the withdrawing owner consists of appreciated property rather than cash. Moreover, as a result of an amendment in 1997, Section 751(a) reaches a broader set of assets than Section 751(b). Specifically, Section 751(a) covers the selling owner's interest in all of the firm's inventory, whereas, for purposes of Section 751(b), the only inventory which counts as a Section 751 asset is so-called substantially appreciated inventory.

The presence of assets subject to Section 704(c)—in other words, contributed property whose basis differed from its fair market value upon the date of contribution—triggers a fifth difference in a buy-out governed by Sections 736 and 741. A distribution under Section 736(b) can trigger recognition under Sections 704(c)(1)(B) or 737 (discussed earlier in dealing with the tax aspects of the allocation of profit and loss), whereas a purchase under Section 741 would not.

Finally, there can be a difference in the basis of the firm's remaining assets following the buy-out (even aside from the possible impact of Section 751 discussed above). A purchase by the other partners (or parties taxed as partners) under Section 741 gives the purchasers a basis in their partnership interests reflective of the purchase price. This, however, does not change the firm's basis in its assets. I.R.C. § 743(a). As discussed later in dealing with the sale of partnership interests generally, however, Section 754 gives a firm treated as a partnership for tax purposes the option to elect, in advance, to have the basis in its assets adjusted pursuant to Section 743(b) to reflect the purchase price paid by a person purchasing a partnership interest from another partner. This basis adjustment would be good in the case of a purchase price that reflected the firm's ownership of appreciated assets. At first glance, the basis impact of a Section 736 distribution seems similar. Normally, a distribution of cash or property to the bought out partner (or party taxed as a partner) does not impact the firm's basis in its remaining assets. I.R.C. § 734(a). Yet, an election under Section 754 can trigger an adjustment in the basis of the firm's assets—albeit, in this case, under Section 734(b). Here, however, is where the difference arises. The operation of Section 734(b) is not the same as the operation of Section 743(b). Among other things, Section 743(b) measures the basis adjustment by purchaser's basis in the acquired interest, whereas

Section 734(b) measures the adjustment by the gain recognized by the bought out partner. These may be different, for example, if the bought out partner, him- or herself, had purchased the interest from another partner. Incidentally, lest firms decline to make Section 754 elections in order to avoid downward, as opposed to upward, basis adjustments, Sections 734(b) and 743(b) require negative basis adjustments whenever the optional adjustments would have been over $250,000.

6. Under either Section 741 or 736, if the seller suffers a loss on the buy-out, it will be a capital loss. Suppose a partner (or person treated as a partner for income tax purposes) simply walks away from his or her interest, figuring it is worthless. See *Citron v. Commissioner*, 97 T.C. 200 (1991) (abandonment of a partnership interest without receiving any consideration produces an ordinary loss). What if the party treated as a partner for income tax purposes, however, is also able to walk away from his or her share of the firm's liabilities? See Rev. Rul. 93–80, 1993–2 C.B. 239 (a deemed distribution under Section 752 resulting from lowering a partner's share of liabilities prevents the transaction from equaling an abandonment entitled to ordinary rather than capital loss treatment).

7. Mention of liabilities raises a broader concern. Regardless of whether the transaction is a sale under Section 741 or a liquidation under Section 736, the amount realized by the departing owner includes not only the payments he or she receives, but also the amount of his or her share of the firm's liabilities assumed by the other owners. *See* I.R.C. § 752(b), (d). This can create confusion if the parties' agreement or the applicable state law is unclear as to whether a departing partner is relieved from a liability. *See Weiss v. Commissioner*, 956 F.2d 242 (11th Cir.1992).

3. Planning for Liquidation

Cude v. Couch

588 S.W.2d 554 (Tenn.1979).

■ Cooper, Justice.

This case presents the single question of whether, in purchasing certain assets of a partnership upon its liquidation, Nathan Couch breached the duty that he owed to his partner, J.R. Cude. We conclude, as did both courts below, that he did not.

* * *

The partnership in question was formed by Couch and Cude in 1965 for the purpose of operating a laundromat. The partnership rented space for the business, on a month-to-month basis, from Couch, in a building that housed Couch's car dealership. In 1973, Couch filed an action seeking to have the partnership dissolved. A receiver was appointed, and operated the laundry for several months. On court order, and after advertisement, the assets of the partnership, which consisted of the equipment of the laundry, were sold at public sale. At the time of the sale, Couch indicated that he would not lease the building to anyone who might want to continue to operate the laundry there, and thus the purchaser of the equipment would have to remove it from the premises. The equipment was ultimately purchased by one Louis Platkin for $800.00. Although it was not revealed at the time of the sale, Platkin was an agent of Couch. Couch and his son have continued to operate the laundromat at the same location.

Cude moved to set aside the sale, or in the alternative for damages, contending in essence that Couch had purchased the equipment clandestinely, at a value artificially depressed by his refusal to permit others to lease the premises, and that in doing so he had gained an unfair advantage in a transaction with the partnership, breaching his fiduciary duty to Cude. After a hearing, the trial judge denied the motion. * * *

We agree with the several judges who have considered this case previously that Cude's claim is without merit. We do not question that partners owe each other a fiduciary duty in all matters pertaining to the partnership, and that this duty continues while the partnership is being liquidated. See T.C.A. § 61–120 [U.P.A. § 21]. We simply do not believe that, on the facts shown here, Couch breached his duty to Cude. There is no doubt but that Couch had an inherent advantage throughout the dealing in question, as a result of his ownership of the property on which the laundromat operated. However, the record does not show that he used this advantage to force Cude out of the partnership. Absent such a showing, neither Couch's refusal to permit others to lease the premises, nor the manner and price of his purchase of the equipment—which together form the basis of the petitioner's complaint—can be termed improper. From the beginning of the partnership, Couch made it clear that he would not permit a lease of the property, in part to insure that the operation of the laundromat would not interfere with that of his car dealership, operating in the same building. The proof also shows that, at the time of the dissolution, Couch's determination in this regard was strengthened by his belief that he might need to put the space to use for other purposes on short notice, either to expand his dealership, or to provide office space for his son's medical practice. Under these circumstances, we cannot conceive that Couch's admitted duty to his partner would require that he lease the premises against his own best interests, despite the fact that the laundry could not be sold as a going business without a lease. As to the manner in which Couch purchased the equipment, while we agree with the petitioner that it would have been better had Platkin disclosed his agency, there is no suggestion in the record that his failure to do so, of itself, prejudiced either the partnership or Cude. Neither can we find anything objectionable in the price that Couch paid for the equipment. It was greater than the amount that Cude, who also bid on the equipment owned by the partnership, deemed prudent to offer. There were no other bidders, which would seem to suggest that the value of the property on the open market was minimal. The price offered at a public sale is the best indication of an item's worth. * * * Unquestionably, Couch had an advantage, divorced from the partnership, that made it more practicable for him to carry on the business of the partnership after dissolution than for others. However, the fact that Couch benefitted from that circumstance harmed neither Cude nor the partnership, and breached his duty to neither. * * *

The decision of the Court of Appeals is affirmed.

HENRY, Justice, dissenting.

* * *

The laundry was purchased by Nathan Couch and his employee of twenty-six years, Robert Cude, without a lease, on September 9, 1975, for the sum of $7,000.00. They changed the name from the "Washtime Laundrymat" to the "C & C Laundrymat" and continued to operate it without a lease and in the same location. They replaced all machines with new ones. After owning and operating it for seven years and seven months, it was sold for $800.00. The written appraisal of record shows the same laundry, the same or newer equipment, at the same location, and the same operation without a lease to have been worth $10,000.00.

* * *

NOTES

1. As the parties discovered in *Cude*, it is useful to give some advance thought concerning how to liquidate the firm. This requires addressing a number of questions. First, who should wind up the business? Unless agreed otherwise, under the U.P.A. or R.U.P.A., all partners not wrongfully causing dissolution (or the representative of the last surviving partner) have a right to undertake this task or may petition the court to do so. U.P.A. § 37; R.U.P.A. § 803. Reflecting the different management structure of a limited partnership, absent other agreement, the U.L.P.A. grants normally the power to wind up to the general partners. U.L.P.A. § 803 (all general partners not wrongfully causing dissolution may wind up; only if there are no general partners, do the limited partners obtain this power); U.L.P.A. §§ 406(a), 605(a)(1), 803(c), (d), 804(a) (general partners, who have not dissociated from the firm, may wind up, unless no general partner is left, or a court orders otherwise). LLC statutes commonly reflect a similar breakdown with respect to role of managers versus members. *E.g.*, Cal. Corp. Code § 17352; Del. Code Ann. Title 6 § 18–803. *But see* N.Y. Ltd Liab. Co. Law § 703(a) (members may wind up). Is there any reason for the agreement to specify who has the responsibility for winding up? Is there any problem with doing so, especially when one does not know in advance which participant in the venture may die, become disabled or quit? Incidentally, do partners have any duty to aid in winding up—for example, upon the break-up of a law firm where they may need to finish off on-going cases? See *Jewel v. Boxer*, 156 Cal.App.3d 171, 203 Cal.Rptr. 13 (1984) (giving an affirmative answer).

Next, what, if any, compensation should the person(s) charged with winding up receive? Section 18(f) of the U.P.A. mandates such compensation for a surviving partner unless otherwise agreed. Section 401(h) of the

R.U.P.A. mandates compensation (barring other agreement) for partners winding up whether or not they are surviving partners. The results under the pre–2001 U.L.P.A. are the same, since the pre–2001 U.L.P.A. defaults to the uniform partnership acts on the issue; however, the 2001 revision seemingly denies general partners compensation for winding up. U.L.P.A. (2001) § 406(f). LLC statutes may or may not address the issue. *Compare* Cal. Corp. Code § 17352 (c), *with* Del. Code Ann. Title 6 § 18–803; N.Y. Ltd. Liab. Co. Law § 703.

As explained earlier, under the uniform partnership acts, winding up requires (barring a contrary agreement) selling the firm's assets. If the partners are unable to agree upon another arrangement, a judicially supervised sale is necessary. *Polikoff v. Levy,* 132 Ill.App.2d 492, 270 N.E.2d 540 (1971). *But see* R.U.P.A. § 803(c). Is there any problem with this? Should the agreement allow the person(s) in charge of winding up to negotiate private sales? Would it matter who the buyer is?

Questions also might arise regarding what the firm can sell. Tangible assets raise little difficulty, but what about intangibles such as goodwill? A buyer of goodwill may want to use the firm name and even to restrict competition by the former owners. Parties who wish to carry on in a similar business obviously will have difficulty accepting this.

This gets to the problem in *Cude*. What prevents a party with a lock on a key intangible—for example, by owning the building in a business where location is critical, or by having gained the confidence of clients in a personal service firm—from obtaining the firm's goodwill following liquidation without paying compensation? One way to have handled the problem in *Cude* would have been for the firm to own the property, as discussed earlier in this chapter. Yet, in contrast to the property to be developed in the *DeShazo* case earlier in the chapter, was it really necessary for the Cude and Couch partnership to own the property on which the laundromat operated—at least so long as Couch was willing to allow use of the property? Was there some legitimate reason why Couch would be reluctant to have the partnership own a piece of the property he might need to use later for his car dealership? Besides, can some critical items—such as the client relationships established by individual partners—really be owned by the firm? Perhaps the answer on liquidation is to require a party to pay for any goodwill he or she is able to appropriate. While some courts might recognize such a claim without an agreement (*e.g., Swann v. Mitchell,* 435 So.2d 797 (Fla.1983)), can advance planning help avoid litigation?

Another concern with liquidating the firm's assets is how long the person(s) charged with selling the assets can take to accomplish the task. Forcing a hasty sale may lessen the price obtained. On the other hand, parties on occasion have been known to dawdle, especially when they would like to continue the business without buying out those who departed. *See, e.g., Hankin v. Hankin,* 507 Pa. 603, 493 A.2d 675 (1985). Notice how Section 42 of the U.P.A. may eliminate the incentive for such conduct. (The R.U.P.A. and typical LLC statutes, however, contain no equivalent to U.P.A. § 42 which might force a dawdling party to pay off departing partners with interest or profits and forgo liquidation.) Is this an area where advance agreement can help, or is it more important to preserve flexibility?

Once the assets are sold, the question becomes how to distribute the proceeds. Section 40(b) and (c) of the U.P.A. provides that the proceeds go first to repay creditors, then to repay debts owned partners other than for capital and profits, next to return of capital contributions, and finally to pay each partner's share of undistributed profits. How does the system of partnership accounting discussed earlier fit in with this scheme of distribution? As the partnership sells its assets (either individually or as a going business), the difference between the amount received and the book value of the assets is profit or loss, and, barring agreement to the contrary, each partner's capital account will be credited or debited with his or her share of this profit or loss. As a result, the amount of cash remaining after the firm liquidates all its assets equals the sum of the debts owed to outside creditors, the debts owed to partners other than for capital and profits, and the total of the partners' capital accounts (which can be a negative sum). (Remember, assets (the cash) must, by definition, equal debts plus equity (the capital accounts).) Since the capital account of each partner represents the sum of his or her contributions to capital (less any withdrawals) plus his or her share of undistributed profits (less his or her share of firm losses), distributing to each partner the amount shown in his or her capital account exactly carries out the command of Section 40(b) and (c). (Of course, this was the whole purpose of keeping capital accounts.)

Suppose, however, one or more partners have a negative balance in their capital account. (This will be reflected in an inability of the proceeds to cover all the payments specified in Section 40(b). If the total of the partners' capital accounts is a negative balance, the proceeds will be insufficient to pay all the creditors. If the total is positive, there will be enough funds to pay all the creditors, but not all the amounts owed to partners for their capital and profits.) Section 40(d) requires partners to contribute their share (as dictated by the allocation of losses) of the amount necessary to satisfy all the payments listed in Section 40(b) (including amounts owed to partners for capital and profits). Since each partner's capital account reflects his or her share of losses, repayment of the negative balance carries out the command of Section 40(d). What happens, however, if a partner is insolvent or refuses to make up a deficit in his or her account? In that event, Section 40(d) requires the remaining partners to make up the shortfall in the same ratio as they share profits. (In a partnership where the partners agree to share losses in a different ratio from profits, should they also agree to change the treatment of such shortfalls?)

Several additional points are worth noting about Section 40. To begin with, since Section 40(d) obligates partners to contribute amounts sufficient to make the distribution called for under Section 40(b), does the priority of distribution really make any difference? Next, note that Section 40 is subject to contrary agreement. (Can this prejudice outside creditors?)

As mentioned earlier in this chapter, sometimes partners may agree simply to ignore capital accounts and split equally the proceeds remaining after payment of creditors. Another possibility is to agree that (at least after payment of outside creditors) partners with negative capital accounts need not make up the deficit. Recall the earlier discussion of the tax and other problems such an agreement might produce. Finally, as noted before, Sections 18(a) and 40(b) tie partners' rights to liquidating distributions to the amount of their contributions. Recall the need this creates for partners to value property contributed to the firm, and the resulting problem if they over- or under-value the property.

The R.U.P.A. provides generally the same results as U.P.A. § 40 in a more direct manner. Section 401(a) of the revised act commands the partners to keep capital accounts and Section 807(b) calls for partners to receive the positive balances (the excess of credits over charges) or pay the negative balances (the excess of charges over credits) in their accounts. Section 807(b) also calls for crediting or debiting to the partners' accounts the profits or losses resulting from liquidating the firm's assets, while Section 807(a) calls for paying debts, including those owed to partners, first. Section 103 makes these provisions subject to contrary agreement (unless such agreement restricts third party rights). One slight change under the R.U.P.A. is that partners must contribute to shortfalls in meeting firm obligations in accordance with their share of losses, not profits. R.U.P.A. § 807(c).

Curiously, while the R.U.P.A. marked an increase in clarity with respect to coordinating profit and loss allocation with the liquidating distributions, the U.L.P.A. and many limited liability company statutes contain provisions which are not all that clear. Specifically, Section 804(3) of the pre–2001 U.L.P.A. calls for the final distributions on liquidation to go first in return of the partners' contributions, and then "respecting their partnership interests, in the proportions in which partners share in distributions." This, in turn, seems to trigger Section 504 of the U.L.P.A., which provides, in the absence of agreement, that the partners share in distributions in proportion to the value of their contributions not yet returned. Does this mean that all liquidating distributions in excess of the parties' capital contributions go to the parties equally—since, after the firm has returned all contributions, each partner or limited partner has the same zero unreturned contribution? What problem does this create if the partnership agreement did not allocate profits equally? No doubt, this is not what the drafters of the U.L.P.A. had in mind. Yet, what planning attorney wants his or her clients to be the ones to fund—by engaging in expensive litigation—the court opinion which will clarify the point? Moreover, since many of the limited liability company statutes have copied their distribution provisions from the U.L.P.A., this same lack of clarity exists in many of the LLC statutes as well. *E.g.*, Del. Code. Ann. Title 6 §§ 18–504, 18–804(a)(3); N.Y. Ltd. Liab. Co. Law §§ 504, 704(c). *But see* Cal. Corp. Code §§ 17250, 17353(a)(3) (distributions after return of capital, including final distributions on liquidation, go in proportion to profit shares). At first glance, the 2001 revision of the U.L.P.A. tries to improve things by providing simply that any surplus left after paying the partnership's debts goes to the partners as a distribution, and that all distributions go to the partners (barring other agreement) in proportion to their contributions. U.L.P.A. (2001) §§ 503, 812(b). There are problems, however, with this simplicity. Suppose the partners wish to share profits in a different proportion from the value their of tangible contributions, and wish to ensure that the values of the tangible contributions are returned first on liquidation before a distribution which follows the profit sharing formula. So long as the partnership agreement calls for liquidating distributions that carry out this plan, there is no problem. How well, however, does the default rule under the 2001 revision of the U.L.P.A. work if there are any gaps in the parties' agreement?

An alternative to selling assets is for the parties to agree to distribution in kind. In contrast to the approach under the uniform partnership acts, the pre–2001 U.L.P.A. and typical LLC statutes imply that, while members have no right to demand an in-kind distribution, those in charge of winding up might have the option to force members to take assets of the LLC in-kind rather than getting cash—at least if there is a pro-rata distribution of the assets in question. *See, e.g.,* U.L.P.A. § 605; Cal. Corp. Code § 17253; Del. Code Ann. Title 6 § 18–605; N.Y. Ltd. Liab. Co. Law § 505. *But see* U.L.P.A. (2001) § 812 (b) (must distribute in cash). Are there some circumstances or some types of assets (say ones that might be particularly difficult to sell) for which it may make sense to agree in advance to an in-kind distribution? Conversely, should the agreement deprive those in charge of the power to have an in-kind distribution they might otherwise possess under the governing statutory default rule?

One evident problem with an in-kind distribution is determining who gets what. One simple solution was described as follows:

> "We argued [sic] between ourselves that we would draw high card for any item that we chose, the man who drew high card, if there were two items of the same kind the man with the high card, he would have the pick or if there was one specific item, the man who drew the high card for that, he had the item. We divided all the equipment on that basis. * * *"

Pilch v. Milikin, 200 Cal.App.2d 212, 217, 19 Cal.Rptr. 334, 337 (1962). Many parties will wish, however, for a more quantitative approach. This raises the need to value the various assets. One could look at their value on the firm's books, but, as noted before, book value often diverges from present fair market value. If the parties revalue assets upon their distribution, should this effect their capital accounts?

2. What is the tax impact of liquidating a partnership (or an entity electing income tax treatment as a partnership)? As the firm sells its assets, the owners of the firm recognize gain or loss, and adjust their basis, under the conduit principle discussed earlier. I.R.C. §§ 701, 702, 705(a). Each recipient of a liquidating distribution also must recognize gain to the extent the subsequent distribution of cash exceeds his or her basis in the firm. I.R.C. § 731(a)(1). Unlike the situation with non-liquidating distributions,

the recipients of liquidating distributions may recognize a loss if they receive only money on liquidation the total of which is less than their basis in the firm. I.R.C. § 731(a)(2). The Code treats this gain or loss as gain or loss from the sale of a capital asset. I.R.C. §§ 731(a), 741.

What if the partnership (or entity electing income tax treatment as a partnership) distributes some or all of its assets in kind? Generally, there is no recognition of gain or loss. I.R.C. § 731(a). Section 704(c)(1)(B) creates an exception. As mentioned before, Section 704(c)(1)(B) triggers recognition if the firm distributes property, which was contributed with a built-in gain or loss, to a party who did not contribute the item. This only applies, however, if the distribution takes place within seven years of the contribution. Along similar lines, as mentioned earlier, Section 737 can require recognition when the contributor of appreciated property receives other property from the firm within seven years of the contribution. A different sort of exception exists if the firm distributes unrealized receivables or inventory. The recipient who receives only such assets (or only such assets and cash) recognizes a loss if his or her basis in the firm is greater than the sum of the cash and the firm's basis in the receivables and inventory that he or she received. I.R.C. § 731(a)(2). (Why might the recipient have preferred not to recognize this loss? Notice the basis these assets otherwise would receive as discussed below.) Also, if the firm distributes inventory and receivables disproportionately among the owners, Section 751(b) comes into play. Rev. Rul. 77–412, 1977–2 C.B. 223. An important difference between current and liquidating distributions lies in the basis the assets obtain in the hands of the recipient. Under Section 732(b), the basis in a liquidating distribution equals the recipient's basis in his or her interest in the firm less the amount of any cash received. This is allocated first to unrealized receivables and inventory in an amount equal to the firm's basis in such items and then to the other assets taking into account the assets' unrealized appreciation and relative fair market values as well as the basis the firm had in each piece of property. I.R.C. § 732(c). Overall, given this tax treatment, note the incentives for parties treated as partners for income tax purposes to take assets from the firm in kind.

Often in professional firms, the parties liquidating a partnership split up into new firms. In this event, Section 708(b)(2)(B) deems either of the emerging firms to be a continuation of the prior partnership if the members of the prior partnership have an interest of greater than 50 percent in the capital and profits in the emerging firm. In this event, since the partnership does not terminate, the provisions in Sections 731 and 732 dealing with current rather than liquidating partnership distributions presumably govern. Moreover, the fact that the assets of the original firm end up in partnerships, rather than sold or distributed among the owners, triggers application of Sections 721, 722 and 723. In this regard, does it matter how the partners characterize the transfer of assets into the emerging partnerships—for example, whether they characterize this as a transfer from the original partnership to the two emerging partnerships, or whether they characterize this as a transfer first to the individual partners and then from the individual partners to the two emerging partnerships?

Reconsider this question after reading the materials on partnership mergers later in this chapter.

4. Planning for Individual New Owners

a. *In General*

Rapoport v. 55 Perry Co.

50 A.D.2d 54, 376 N.Y.S.2d 147 (1975).

■ TILZER, JUSTICE.

In 1969, Simon, Genia and Ury Rapoport entered into a partnership agreement with Morton, Jerome and Burton Parnes, forming the partnership known as 55 Perry Company. Pursuant to the agreement, each of the families owned 50% of the partnership interests. In December of 1974 Simon and Genia Rapoport assigned a 10% interest of their share in the partnership to their adult children, Daniel and Kalia. The Parnes defendants were advised of the assignment and an amended partnership certificate was filed in the County Clerk's Office indicating the addition of Daniel and Kalia as partners. However, when the plaintiffs, thereafter, requested the Parnes defendants to execute an amended partnership agreement to reflect the above changes in the partnership, the Parnes refused, taking the position that the partnership agreement did not permit the introduction of new partners without consent of all the existing partners. Thereafter, the plaintiffs Rapoport brought this action seeking a declaration that Simon and Genia Rapoport had an absolute right to assign their interests to their adult children without consent of the defendants and that such assignment was authorized pursuant to Paragraph 12 of the partnership agreement. * * * After joinder of issue plaintiffs moved for summary judgment. * * *

On the motion for summary judgment both parties agreed that there were no issues of fact and that there was only a question of the interpretation of the written documents which should be disposed of as a matter of law by the Court. Nevertheless, the Court below found that the agreement was ambiguous and that there was a triable issue with respect to the intent of the parties. We disagree and conclude that the agreement is without ambiguity and that the pursuant to the terms of the agreement and of the Partnership Law, consent of the Parnes defendants was required in order to admit Daniel Rapoport and Kalia Shalleck to the partnership.

Plaintiffs, in support of their contention that they have an absolute right to assign their interests in the partnership to their adult children and that the children must be admitted to the partnership as partners rely on Paragraph 12 of the partnership agreement which provides as follows:

> "No partner or partners shall have the authority to transfer, sell ... assign or in any way dispose of the partnership realty and/or personalty and shall not have the authority to sell, transfer, assign ... his or their share in this firm, nor enter into any agreement as a result of

which any person shall become interested with him in this firm, unless the same is agreed to in writing by a majority of the partners as determined by the percentage of ownership . . . , except for members of his immediate family who have attained majority, in which case no such consent shall be required."

As indicated, plaintiffs argue that the above provision expressly authorizes entry of their adult children into the partnership. Defendants, on the other hand, maintain that Paragraph 12 provides only for the right of a partner to assign or transfer a share of the profits in the partnership. We agree with that construction of the agreement.

A reading of the partnership agreement indicates that the parties intended to observe the differences, as set forth in the Partnership Law, between assignees of a partnership interest and the admission into the partnership itself of new partners. The Partnership Law provides that subject to any contrary agreement between the partners, "(n)o person can become a member of a partnership without the consent of all the partners." ([New York] Partnership Law § 40(7) [U.P.A. § 18(g)].) [New York] Partnership Law § 53 [U.P.A. § 27] provides that an assignee of an interest in the partnership is not entitled "to interfere in the management or administration of the partnership business" but is merely entitled to receive "the profits to which the assigning partner would otherwise be entitled." * * * Additionally, [New York] Partnership Law § 50 [U.P.A. § 24] indicates the differences between the rights of an assignee and a new partner. That section states that the "property rights of a partner are (a) his rights in specific partnership property, (b) his interest in the partnership, and (c) his right to participate in the management." On the other hand, as already indicated above, an assignee is excluded in the absence of agreement from interfering in the management of the partnership business and from access to the partnership books and information about partnership transactions. * * *

The effect, therefore, of the various provisions of the Partnership Law, above discussed, is that unless the parties have agreed otherwise, a person cannot become a member of a partnership without consent of all the partners whereas an assignment of a partnership interest may be made without consent, but the assignee is entitled only to receive the profits of the assigning partner. And, as already stated, the partnership agreement herein clearly took cognizance of the differences between an assignment of an interest in the partnership as compared to the full rights of a partner as set forth in Partnership Law § 50 [U.P.A. § 24]. Paragraph 12 of the agreement by its language has reference to Partnership Law § 53 [U.P.A. § 27] dealing with an "assignment of partner's interest." It (Paragraph 12) refers to assignments, encumbrances and agreements "as a result of which any person shall become interested with (the assignor) in this firm." That paragraph does not contain language with respect to admitting a partner to the partnership with all rights to participate in the management of its affairs. Moreover, interpretation of Paragraph 12 in this manner is consistent with other provisions of the partnership agreement. For example, in Paragraph 15 of the agreement, the following is provided:

> "In the event of the death of any partner the business of this firm shall continue with the heir, or distributee providing he has reached majority, or fiduciary of the deceased partner having the right to succeed the deceased partner with the same rights and privileges and the same obligations, pursuant to all of the terms hereof."

In that paragraph, therefore, there is specific provision to succeed to all the privileges and obligations of a partner—language which is completely absent from paragraph 12.

Accordingly, it appears that contrary to plaintiffs' contention that Paragraph 12 was intended to give the parties the right to transfer a full partnership interest to adult children, without consent of all other partners, (an agreement which would vary the rights otherwise existing pursuant to Partnership Law § 40(7) [U.P.A. § 18(g)]) that paragraph was instead intended to limit a partner with respect to his right to assign a partnership interest as provided for under Partnership Law § 53 [U.P.A. § 27] (i.e., the right to profits)—to the extent of prohibiting such assignments without consent of other partners except to children of the existing partners who have reached majority. Therefore, it must be concluded that pursuant to the terms of the partnership agreement, the plaintiffs could not transfer a full partnership interest to their children and that the children only have the rights as assignees to receive a share of the partnership income and profits of their assignors.

* * *

NOTES

1. As explained in *Rapoport,* Section 27 of the U.P.A. deals with assignment of a partner's interest in the partnership. A partner may assign his or her right to receive firm profits, but, barring agreement to the contrary, the assignee does not become a partner with any rights to manage (or even obtain information about) the business. On the contrary, admission of a new partner (absent other agreement) requires unanimous consent of the current members. U.P.A. § 18(g). These rules—which apply to LLPs as well as ordinary partnerships—remain the same under the R.U.P.A. R.U.P.A. §§ 401(i), 502, 503. Limited partnerships generally follow the same approach. U.L.P.A. §§ 301(b)(1), 401, 702, 704(a); U.L.P.A. (2001) §§ 301, 402. 701, 702.

Limited liability company statutes typically start by following the partnership model in allowing assignment of a member's financial interest, but not allowing the assignee any management rights. *E.g.*, Cal. Corp. Code § 17301; Del. Code Ann. Title 6 § 18–702; N.Y. Ltd. Liab. Co. Law § 603. The statutes differ, however, in the consent required for entry of a new member (who either might be an assignee or a person seeking to purchase an interest directly from the LLC). Some states follow the partnership law scheme of requiring unanimous consent of the existing members. *E.g.*, Del.

Code Ann. Title 6 §§ 18–301(b)(1),18–704. Other states, however, only require consent of the majority. *E.g.,* Cal. Corp. Code § 17100(a)(1), 17303; N.Y. Ltd. Liab. Co. Law §§ 602(b)(1), 604(a). Of course, all of this typically is subject to contrary agreement.

Upon what rules regarding transfer of interests and entry of new owners might it make sense for partners, limited partners or LLC members to agree? To answer this question, consider what concerns owners of a business might have about allowing in new owners without their approval. Might such concerns depend upon the size of the firm, and the role new owners will play? For example, compare the impact a new partner would have on a large law firm, with the impact of an additional partner on the partnership of Summers & Dooley encountered earlier. In this regard, recall the impact which the entry of the NVRI Trust into the limited liability company eventually had in the *Broyhill* case reprinted earlier in this chapter. One caveat, however, is that even if a new partner does not upset the balance of power within the firm, each partner possesses a certain degree of apparent authority to bind the partnership. U.P.A. § 9(1); R.U.P.A. § 301. Recall, on the other hand, that members of an LLC run by managers might not have any apparent authority.

Conversely, when might partners, limited partners or LLC members wish to limit each other's right to assign a share of profits? (This is what the agreement in *Rapoport* awkwardly tried to do.) Might there be a concern with management decisions by a person who no longer has a financial stake in the decisions he or she makes? In this regard, it is worth noting that the uniform partnership and limited partnership acts, and many LLC statutes, allow the remaining owners to force out an owner who has assigned away all of his or her interest in the firm. *See, e.g.,* U.P.A. § 31(1)(c) (if a partner has assigned away all of his or her interest in the firm, the other partners (if they all agree) can dissolve even before the term is up); R.U.P.A. § 601(4)(ii) (a transfer of substantially all of a partner's interest in the firm creates a dissociation); U.L.P.A. § 702 (except as provided in the partnership agreement, a partner ceases to be a partner upon assignment of all of his or her interest in the firm); U.L.P.A. (2001) §§ 603(b)(4)(B), 603(4)(B) (allowing the remaining partners, by unanimous vote, to expel general or limited partners who have assigned away substantially all of their transferable interest); Del. Code Ann. Title 6 § 18–702(b)(3) (same for LLC members); N.Y. Ltd. Liab. Co. Law § 603(4) (same). *But see* Cal. Corp. Code § 17301(a)(4) (assignor retains membership in LLC and voting power until assignee becomes a member). On the other hand, does removal of an owner who has assigned all of his or her interest completely solve the loss of incentives problem? For example, what if an irreplaceable partner or member assigned away most or all of his or her interest in firm profits; what incentives would he or she have left to carry out responsibilities to the firm? Keep in mind, however, that assignment of all of an owner's interest does not terminate any contractual obligation of the assignor to make additional contributions. *See, e.g.,* U.L.P.A. § 704(c); U.L.P.A. (2001) § 702(d). Does this suggest a practical reason to distinguish between assignments by owners obligated to contribute additional cash, and assignments by owners obligated to perform further services? One right an assignee possesses in an ordinary partnership or an LLP, which could pose a problem, is to obtain dissolution of a partnership which is at will or for which the term is up. U.P.A. § 32(2); R.U.P.A. § 801(b). Is this a reason to restrict assignment? After all, what could a partner in a partnership at will do in response to a restriction on assignment, if this partner is desperate to cash out?

Suppose, instead of having individuals as partners or members, the partners or members themselves are entities (such as corporations, partnerships, LLCs or trusts). In this event, what happens if the ownership or management of the entity, which itself is a partner or member of the firm, changes hands? How might the partnership or LLC operating agreement address this? See *Eureka VIII LLC v. Niagara Falls Holdings LLC*, 899 A.2d 95 (Del.Ch.2006) (LLC agreement restricted changes in control or ownership of a member in the LLC, which was itself an LLC established by an individual who had a critical role in carrying out the venture).

As an alternative to buying the interest of a current owner, an individual may seek entry by contributing to the firm in exchange for a newly created interest. Does such new entry create any different concerns from allowing an assignee to become a partner or member? See *Diamond Parking, Inc. v. Frontier Bldg. Ltd. Partnership,* 72 Wash.App. 314, 864 P.2d 954 (1993) (limited partner found his interest diluted from 10% to 0.65% by virtue of the interests going to the new entrants). Will the fruits of the added capital not offset the decrease in one's percentage interest in the firm—or, put metaphorically, will the larger pie not offset the additional slices cut from the pie? How could one measure this (for businesses, not pies)?

One final concern with the transfer of partnership, limited partnership, and LLC interests arises by virtue of Federal and state securities laws. Chapter V will explore this.

2. *Rapoport* is symptomatic of the confusion possible when an agreement inartfully speaks of an assignment of "interests" or "shares" in a partnership or other non-corporate entity. (This could occur in an LLC operating or a partnership agreement, as in *Rapoport,* specifying the rights of the parties to transfer their interests, or an agreement actually granting an interest in the firm.) The interest assigned may be simply the interest in profits referred to by U.P.A. Section 27, it could be the interest in profits and management that the assignee would possess as a new partner or member, or it might even refer to an interest in the underlying capital of the firm thereby giving the assignee a right to share the proceeds of the existing assets upon liquidation. *See Guinand v. Walton,* 25 Utah 2d 253, 480 P.2d 137 (1971). Indeed, the variations in the definition of a partnership (or LLC) interest found in different statutes illustrate what a malleable term this is. *Compare* R.U.P.A. § 101(9) ("partnership interest" means all of a partner's interests in the partnership, including the transferable interest in the partner's share of profits and losses and right to receive distributions, and all management and other rights), *with* U.L.P.A.

§ 101(10) ("partnership interest" means the partner's share of profits and losses and right to receive distributions); U.L.P.A. (2001) § 102(22) ("transferable interest" means a partner's rights to distributions). Del. Code Ann. Title 6 § 18–101(8) (same definition for "limited liability company interest"); N.Y. Ltd. Liab. Co. Law § 102 ("membership interest" means the member's shares of profits and losses and right to receive distributions and right to vote and participate in management). *See also* Cal. Corp. Code § 17001(n), (z) (distinguishing "economic interest" from "membership interest"). Recall the similar drafting problem confronted in dealing with the litigation between Broyhill and the DeLucas earlier in this chapter.

3. If a new partner, limited partner or LLC member does not receive any interest in the existing assets of the firm, how should the capital accounts reflect this? Is it enough simply to give the new participant a capital account of zero (or whatever he or she contributes to capital)? Suppose at the time the new participant enters the firm, its assets are worth more or less than the value shown on the books. What will happen if the capital accounts of the existing owners (along with the values shown for the assets) are not revised to reflect this fact?

4. In addition to questions concerning the rights of an incoming party, there may also be questions concerning his or her liabilities—at least in an ordinary partnership. Section 17 of the U.P.A. and 309 of the R.U.P.A. make a new partner liable for pre-existing debts of the firm, but only to the extent of his or her interest in partnership property.

5. Interestingly, the agreement in *Rapoport* called for the transfer of the deceased partner's entire ownership interest (including management rights) to his or her heir following the death of a partner. How viable a solution is this to deal with a partner's or member's death, bankruptcy or desire to depart? In addition to the concerns, noted above, which the remaining owners might have about a new owner, are there any problems with the free transfer solution from the standpoint of the departing owner or his or her successors-in-interest? Are such concerns limited to the prospect of personal liability if the transferee becomes a new partner in an ordinary partnership? What other risks does the recipient of an ownership interest face if he or she lacks control over the venture, including the power to force distributions? Incidentally, can a partnership or LLC operating agreement force successors-in-interest to become partners or members? See *Stewart v. Robinson,* 115 N.Y. 328, 22 N.E. 160 (1889) (no).

6. Are there legal limits on the ability of a partnership or LLC operating agreement to restrict transfers of interests upon death, bankruptcy or divorce? After all, such transfers are not voluntary.

In re Ehmann v. Fiesta Investments

319 B.R. 200 (Bankr.D.Ariz.2005).

The Court here concludes that because the operating agreement of a limited liability company imposes no obligations on its members, it is not an executory contract. Consequently when a member who is not the manager files a Chapter 7 case, his trustee acquires all of the member's rights and interests pursuant to Bankruptcy Code §§ 541(a) and (c)(1), and the limitations of §§ 365(c) and (e) do not apply.

Procedural Background

Plaintiff Louis A. Movitz ("Trustee") is the Chapter 7 Trustee for the estate of Debtor Gregory L. Ehmann ("Debtor"). The Trustee has sued Defendant Fiesta Investments, LLC ("Defendant" or "Fiesta"), an Arizona limited liability company of which the Debtor was a member when his bankruptcy case was filed. The Trustee's suit seeks a declaration that the Trustee has the status of a member in Fiesta, a determination that the assets of Fiesta are being wasted, misapplied or diverted for improper purposes, and an order for dissolution and liquidation of Fiesta or the appointment of a receiver for Fiesta.

Fiesta has moved to dismiss the complaint * * * arguing essentially that the Trustee has no rights with respect to Fiesta other than the right to receive a distribution that might have been made to the Debtor if and when Fiesta decides to make such a distribution. Such a motion to dismiss should be granted only if the Court concludes that the Trustee could prove no set of facts that would entitle him to any remedy other than simply waiting to see if Fiesta should ever decide to make a distribution.

Background Facts

The Trustee's complaint identifies Fiesta as an Arizona limited liability company that was formed in approximately 1998 by the Debtor's parents, Anthony and Alice Ehmann. At the time it was formed, it had two assets, a 17% interest in City Leasing Co. Ltd. and 25% interest in Desert Farms LLC. Shortly after this bankruptcy case was filed, however, City Leasing was liquidated and as a result of that liquidation Fiesta received cash distributions in the amount of approximately $837,000 in the summer of 2000. Fiesta is still receiving regular quarterly distributions of cash from its other asset, Desert Farms.

The Trustee's complaint stems from the fact that although no formal distributions have been declared or paid to members, and certainly not to the Debtor, substantial amounts of cash have flowed out of Fiesta to or for the benefit of other members, including $374,500 in loans to members or to corporations owned or controlled by members, a $42,500 payment to one member, and $124,000 paid to another member to redeem his interest. In response to the Trustee's demand for information and distributions, the managing member of Fiesta, the Debtor's father, responded that he had created "Fiesta a few years ago to remove assets from our estate for estate tax purposes, and to accumulate investments for the benefit of our children after our deaths.... [W]e see no reason to accede to the wishes of any member or assignee of any member which runs contrary to our original goals." Yet the outflow of over half a million dollars does not seem to be consistent with the original goal "to accumulate investments for the benefit of our children after our deaths."

The Parties' Arguments

While the parties disagree on several relevant legal principles, a dispute that is absolutely central to the motion to dismiss is whether the Trustee's rights are governed by Bankruptcy Code § 541(c)(1) or by § 365(e)(2). In a very general sense, the latter provision, if applicable, permits the enforcement of state and contract law restrictions on the Trustee's rights and powers, whereas the former provision, if applicable, would render such restrictions and conditions unenforceable as against the Trustee. Because § 541 applies generally to all property and rights that the Trustee acquires, whereas § 365 applies more specifically to executory contract rights, the answer to this question hinges on whether the Trustee is asserting a property right or an executory contract right.

* * * In its motion to dismiss, Fiesta relies heavily on various provisions of the Fiesta Operating Agreement which provide that in the event a trustee acquires a member's interests, such action shall not dissolve the company or entitle "any such assignee to participate in the management of the business and affairs of the company or to exercise the right of a Member unless such assignee is admitted as a Member.... " Operating Agreement ¶ 7.2. "Such an assignee that has not become a Member is only entitled to receive to the extent assigned the share of distributions ... to which such Member would otherwise be entitled with respect to the assigned interest." *Id.* Fiesta further notes that such limitations on the rights of assignees of members' interests in LLCs are specifically authorized by state law, Arizona Revised Statutes ("A.R.S.") § 29–732(A). Fiesta also argues that the Trustee is akin to a judgment creditor, and that A.R.S. § 29–655(c) provides that a charging order is the exclusive remedy by which a judgment creditor of a member may satisfy a judgment out of the member's interest in an LLC. * * *

In response, the Trustee argues that he is not a mere assignee of the Debtor's membership interest, but rather acquired **all** of the Debtor's right, title and interest pursuant to § 541(a). He argues, further, that the Trustee took the Debtor's rights free of certain conditions and restrictions that would otherwise devalue the asset in the hands of any other assignee, pursuant to § 541(c)(1).

In reply, Fiesta relies on § 365(e) to maintain that the state and contract law restrictions are enforceable against the Trustee notwithstanding § 541(c)(1). * * * [T]he very case that Fiesta cites after making that assertion itself concluded that a partnership relationship may include both an executory contract and a nonexecutory property interest in the profits and surplus.

If a partnership relation entails both executory contract rights and nonexecutory property rights, then it would seem to necessitate a threshold determination of which kind of rights are at issue for the particular kind of relief a Trustee seeks with respect to a partnership or LLC. Before reaching that issue, however, it may be fruitful first to examine whether the Fiesta Operating Agreement even includes any executory contract rights.

Legal Analysis

Although the Bankruptcy Code contains no definition of an executory contract, the Ninth Circuit has adopted the "Countryman Test": "[A] contract is executory if 'the obligations of both parties are so far unperformed that the failure of either party to complete performance would constitute a material breach and thus excuse the performance of the other.' "

While Fiesta undoubtedly owes many obligations to its members pursuant to the Operating Agreement, for the contract to be executory there would also have to be some material obligation owing to the company by the member. Moreover, such member's obligation must be so material that if the member did not perform it, Fiesta would owe no further obligations to that member.

[I]n its briefing on the motion to dismiss Fiesta has not attempted to demonstrate that the Operating Agreement is in fact an executory contract, much less to demonstrate exactly what material obligation is owed to the company by its members. Moreover, the founding member's statement of the purposes for which the company was formed suggests that it is very likely there are no such obligations. The purpose was twofold: to remove assets from the parents' estates for estate tax purposes, and to accumulate investments for the benefit of their children after their deaths. One would certainly not expect the children-members to have any obligations with respect to satisfaction of that first goal, which was a unilateral act by the parents, and it is highly unlikely the children-members undertook any obligations with respect to the second goal, any more than would an ordinary prospective heir.

This suspicion is borne out by a close reading of the Operating Agreement itself. It imposes many obligations on the managers, but as noted above the manager is the Debtor's father, not the Debtor. Article V is entitled "Rights and Obligations of Members," but in fact it identifies only rights and no obligations. It (1) limits members' liability for company debts, (2) grants members the right to obtain a list of other members, (3) grants members the right to approve by majority vote the sale, exchange or other disposition of all or substantially all of the company's assets, (4) grants the members rights to inspect and copy any documents, (5) grants members the same priority as to return of capital contributions or to profits and losses, and (6) grants the permissible transferee of a member's interests the right to require the company to adjust the basis of the company's property and the capital account of the affected member. In short, the Article of the Operating Agreement that is partially titled "Obligations of Members" reveals that members have no obligations to the company.

In the entire Agreement, the only provision where members, who are not managers, agree to do anything is Article 7.4, which provides in part that "Each member agrees not to voluntarily withdraw from the company as a member. . . . " It is now questionable in the Ninth Circuit whether such an agreement merely to refrain from acting is sufficient, standing alone, to create an executory contract. But we need not go that far to resolve this issue, because the sentence in which each member agrees not to voluntarily withdraw goes on to say: "[A]nd each Member further agrees that if he attempts to withdraw from the Company in violation of the provisions of this paragraph, he shall receive One Dollar ($1.00) in payment of his interest in the Company and the remaining portion of such Member's interest shall be retained by the Company as liquidated damages." This reveals that what at first may have appeared as a mandatory obligation is in fact merely an option, which gives each member the option of withdrawing if he is willing to accept $1.00 for his interest. But * * * such an unexercised option is not an executory contract.

* * *

[I]t is facile to assume that all partnership agreements are executory contracts. Closer analysis reveals that if there are no material obligations that must be performed by the members of a limited liability company or the limited partners in a limited partnership, then the contract is not executory and is not governed by Code § 365. This case is therefore unlike others that have expressly found "an obligation to contribute capital" and other "continuing fiduciary obligations among the partners that make this [Partnership] Agreement an executory contract."

* * *

Moreover, not only do there not appear to be *any* obligations imposed upon members by the Fiesta Operating Agreement, but there are certainly none with respect to either receipt of a distribution or proper management of the company by its managers. Members do not have to do anything to be entitled to proper management of the company by the managers. The Trustee's complaint does not involve the Debtor's lone arguable obligation not to voluntarily withdraw.

Because there are no obligations imposed on members that bear on the rights the Trustee seeks to assert here, the Trustee's rights are not controlled by the law of executory contracts and Bankruptcy Code § 365. Consequently the Trustee's rights are controlled by the more general provision governing property of the estate, which is Bankruptcy Code § 541.

Code § 541(c)(1) expressly provides that an interest of the debtor becomes property of the estate notwithstanding any agreement or applicable law that would otherwise restrict or condition transfer of such interest by the debtor. All of the limitations in the Operating Agreement, and all of the provisions of Arizona law on which Fiesta relies, constitute conditions and restrictions upon the member's transfer of his interest. Code § 541(c)(1) renders those restrictions inapplicable. This necessarily implies the Trustee has all of the rights and powers with respect to Fiesta that the Debtor held as of the commencement of the case.

It therefore appears that the Trustee may be able to prove a set of facts that would entitle the Trustee to some remedy. The appropriate remedy might include a declaration of the Trustee's rights, redemption of the Debtor's interest, appointment of a receiver to operate the partnership in accordance with its purposes and the members' rights, or dissolution, wind up and liquidation. Consequently Fiesta's motion to dismiss must be denied.

NOTE

Looking at the situation from the standpoint of the parents who had established the LLC in *Ehmann*, it is easy to understand why the transfer of their bankrupt son's interest to the bankruptcy trustee was undesirable. Whereas the son seemingly had been content to allow his parents and siblings to use the LLC as a personal piggy-bank, the trustee was not so amenable. (Incidentally, as discussed earlier, such actions by the parents probably would frustrate their efforts to reduce estate taxes.) The result in *Ehmann* illustrates, however, that there are legal limits on the ability of parties to a partnership, limited partnership or LLC operating agreement to restrict transfers of interests.

Suppose the LLC operating agreement had simply stated that members could not transfer any interest, or, more narrowly, could not transfer an interest to a bankruptcy trustee. Alternately, suppose the agreement stated that filing bankruptcy triggered the provision requiring the member to sell his or her interest back to the LLC for $1.00. In fact, the members of the Fiesta LLC—or most any LLC, partnership, limited partnership or LLP—have little incentive to oppose such provisions in their agreement. After all, the negative impact of such provisions falls upon future creditors of the members; and who cares about them. It is precisely for this reason that Section 541(c)(1) of the Bankruptcy Code, as discussed by the court, invalidates provisions in agreements—often referred to as ipso facto provisions—that attempt to restrict the rights of the trustee appointed when a party to such an agreement files bankruptcy.

On the other hand, suppose the son had significant financial or managerial obligations under the LLC operating agreement. He could hardly be counted on to perform the financial obligations after declaring bankruptcy, and would anyone want either him (with a cavalier attitude once his economic interest in the firm is used to pay creditors), or the bankruptcy trustee, to manage the firm? It is because of these sort of concerns that Section 365 makes restrictions in an "executory contract" binding upon the bankruptcy trustee. As *Ehmann* shows, deciding whether the trustee is asserting rights under an executory contract subject to Section 365, or claiming an interest in property subject to Section 541(c)(1), is often very difficult when dealing with partnerships, limited partnerships, LLPs and LLCs. Indeed, the *Broyhill* decision found earlier in this chapter (in a portion of the opinion not reprinted in this book) held the LLC operating agreement in that case to be an executory contract. While, at first glance, this result seems entirely consistent with *Ehmann*—since the bankrupt party in *Broyhill* had been the managing LLC member—the court reached this result despite the removal of the bankrupt member as manager. This was because the court in *Broyhill* focused less on the obligations of the bankrupt member than on the powers that the bankrupt member retained even after removal as a manager.

Bankruptcy is not the only situation in which involuntary transferees might avoid restrictions in an agreement to which they were not parties.

Holdeman v. Epperson

857 N.E.2d 583 (Ohio 2006).

In this case, * * * we are asked to determine what rights an executor of the estate of a deceased member of a limited liability company is entitled to exercise. Louise Epperson and Daniel Holdeman formed Holdeman–Eros, L.L.C., a limited liability company, by filing articles of organization with the Ohio Secretary of State on May 3, 2002. They also executed an operating agreement that set forth their respective ownership interests and management authority for the business. Pursuant to the agreement, Daniel Holdeman was a member and director and held a 51 percent interest in the company and Louise Epperson, the other member and director, held a 49 percent interest in the company.

Shortly after the company was formed, Holdeman died, and his widow, Jo Ann Holdeman, was appointed executor of his estate. As the executor, pursuant to Section 12 of the operating agreement, Mrs. Holdeman became Holdeman's successor-in-interest. Under the agreement's terms, a successor-in-interest shall be admitted as a member only upon the written consent of the company. When Mrs. Holdeman asked for consent to become a member, Epperson refused.

Mrs. Holdeman then filed a declaratory-judgment action against Epperson and the company, requesting a declaration that she should be given all the rights of a member during the estate's administration. Epperson and the company counterclaimed, seeking a declaration that because Holdeman ceased to be a member of the company when he died, Mrs. Holdeman, though the assignee of his membership interest, was not a member.

The Clark County Court of Common Pleas awarded a declaratory judgment to Mrs. Holdeman, holding that she, as executor of her husband's estate and successor-in-interest, should be accorded all rights as a member of the company, including, but not limited to, the full rights of profits and distributions, full access to all business records, and full rights of operation and control of the company "with due regard for and with the purpose of timely administering the estate."

The Second District Court of Appeals affirmed the judgment of the trial court * * *. In concluding that "Mrs. Holdeman is entitled to exercise all the member rights that Daniel Holdeman possessed before his death," the court of appeals stressed that Mrs. Holdeman could exercise her member rights only during the period of administration of the estate, for purposes of settling the estate.

* * *

The Operating Agreement

* * *

The provision of specific interest in resolving the issue before us is Section 11, entitled "Death of a Member." This section states that when a member dies, the successor-in-interest of the deceased member "shall immediately succeed to the interest of such member in the Company. Such Successor-in-Interest shall not become a Member of the Company unless admitted as a Member in accordance with Section 10 of this Agreement." A successor-in-interest is defined in Section 12 as "such person as the Member shall, from time to time, have designated in a notice to the Company * * *. In the event that a Member has failed to designate a Successor in Interest, or if the person designated is not then living or for any reason renounces, disclaims or is unable to succeed to such interest, the Successor in Interest shall be the executor or administrator of the deceased Member's estate, who shall hold or distribute such interest in accordance with applicable fiduciary law." The section also directs that a successor-in-interest shall not become a full member unless the company consents.

Since Daniel Holdeman never executed a notice to the company designating a successor-in-interest, his widow, as executor of his estate, automatically became the successor-in-interest pursuant to Section 12. Mrs. Holdeman could not become a full member of the company without consent from the company, which the company declined to give. Thus, the language of the operating agreement implicitly restricted Mrs. Holdeman to a membership interest rather than the status of a member of the company.

Typically, once an operating agreement is reviewed and it appears that the terms of the contract dictate the status of the parties, the inquiry ends. * * * Nevertheless, in this case, both the trial court and the court of appeals examined R.C. Chapter 1705 and found that the General Assembly has preempted this area by enacting R.C. 1705.21(A).

Statutory Provisions

R.C. 1705.21(A) provides, "If a member who is an individual dies or is adjudged an incompetent, his executor, administrator, guardian, or other legal representative may exercise all of his rights as a member for the purpose of settling his estate or administering his property, including any authority that he had to give an assignee the right to become a member."

In examining this statute, both the trial court and appellate court looked at the definitions of "member" and "membership interest" set forth in the Limited Liability Company Act, R.C. Chapter 1705. "Member" is defined as a "person whose name appears on the records of the limited liability company as the owner of a membership interest in that company."

R.C. 1705.01(G). A "membership interest" is defined as "a member's share of the profits and losses of a limited liability company and the right to receive distributions from that company." R.C. 1705.01(H).

The terms are distinguishable in that a "member" possesses management rights, and one holding merely a "membership interest" possesses limited, economic rights. R.C. 1705.22 gives members the right to obtain "[t]rue and full information" regarding the status of the business and financial condition of the company, while R.C. 1705.18 limits the assignee of a membership interest to receiving profits, losses, and allocations of the company and specifically directs that the assignee is not "to become or to exercise any rights of a member."

The appellants contend that the company's operating agreement explicitly limits a member's successor-in-interest to possession of an economic interest in the company unless consent is given. Nevertheless, while it is true that the operating agreement restricts Mrs. Holdeman as the successor-in-interest to economic rights only, R.C. 1705.21(A) expressly grants the executor of an estate the right to exercise "*all of [the decedent's] rights as a member* for the purposes of settling his estate." (Emphasis added.)

* * *

Statutory Precedence

* * *

Because this section does not state "except as otherwise provided in the operating agreement," we can infer that the General Assembly did not intend R.C. 1705.21(A) to be restricted by contrary language within an operating agreement.

Furthermore, as the court of appeals so aptly remarked, "R.C. 1705.21(A) refers to member rights in the past tense. In this regard, the statute specifically says that an executor may exercise all the decedent's rights as a member, 'including any authority he [the decedent] *had* to give an assignee the right to become a member.' * * * If the legislature intended to restrict executors to member rights that a decedent possesses after death, the legislature would have used the present tense.

In enacting R.C. 1705.21(A), the General Assembly ensured that the legal representative of a decedent's estate has the ability to carry out an executor's fiduciary obligations to the estate's beneficiaries. The membership rights granted are limited in time and in purpose for settlement of the estate.

Accordingly, we affirm the judgment of the Clark County Court of Appeals and hold that an executor of the estate of a deceased member of a limited liability company has all rights that the member had prior to death, for the limited purpose of settling the member's estate or administering his property.

NOTES

1. Given that the Ohio statute trumped the LLC agreement, was there anything that the parties could have done to have avoided the executor potentially assuming control of the business in *Holdeman*? Maybe there is no reason to worry about this result. After all, the ability of the executor to assume the powers of a member is limited to the duration of the estate administration and only for the purpose of administering the estate. Yet, how long might the estate administration take, and who defines what exercise of power as a member might be necessary for administering the estate? The language in the Ohio statute is very common. *E.g.*, Cal. Corp. Code § 17304(a); Del. Code Ann. Title 6 § 18–705); N.Y. Ltd. Liab. Co. Law § 608. Nevertheless, the Court of Appeals, in its opinion in *Holdeman*, noted that legislatures in some other states had changed the language in their LLC statutes so as to not reach the result called for by the Ohio statute. Is this something to consider when deciding in which state to organize one's LLC? Alternately, suppose the LLC operating agreement calls for an immediate buy-out of the decedent's interest. While this might not trump the executor's rights under the statute, could such a provision limit the duration and extent to which the executor can legitimately argue that the exercise of the decedent member's rights are necessary for the administration of the estate?

2. Suppose the involuntary transfer is occasioned by a divorce. Is there something drafters of a partnership or LLC operating agreement can do to prevent a divorcing spouse from asserting rights in the firm?

b. *Tax Aspects*

Estate of Dupree v. United States

391 F.2d 753 (5th Cir.1968).

■ YOUNG, DISTRICT JUDGE:

The estate of Robert B. Dupree, deceased taxpayer, seeks a refund of income taxes paid by the deceased prior to his death for the year 1960.

In 1947, a limited partnership known as "Stroud's Motor Courts" was organized under the laws of Missouri for the purpose of operating the Park Plaza Motor Court, a motel in St. Louis, Missouri. * * *

The taxpayer and his wife, Katherine P. Dupree, owned as their community property, a 15% limited interest in the partnership. On September 25, 1957, Katherine P. Dupree died, leaving her one-half of the 15% partnership interest to her son, Robert P. Dupree. Thereafter, the taxpayer, Robert B. Dupree, and his son, Robert P. Dupree, each owned a 7½% interest in the partnership. The taxpayer, upon the death of his wife, obtained a new basis for his 7½% of the partnership interest pursuant to 26 U.S.C.A. Section 1014(b)(6).[1] An audit completed in December, 1960, of

1. Sec. 1014(a) "* * * the basis of property in the hands of a person acquiring the property from a decedent or to whom the property passed from a decedent shall * * *

Mrs. Dupree's estate tax return resulted in a determination by the Internal Revenue Service that the fair market value of the Dupree 15% interest in the partnership as of the date of her death was $142,500.00, so that the taxpayer's new basis in his 7 partnership interest as of September 25, 1957, was $71,250.00.

On August 1, 1960, the motel was sold. * * * The sale was reported in the final partnership return for its fiscal year ending March 31, 1961, as a capital gain and $52,441.31 was attributed to the taxpayer as his share of the gain.

* * *

An audit of the final partnership return resulted in a determination by Internal Revenue on March 19, 1962, that the partnership terminated in 1960, and not in 1961 as claimed on the return. A subsequent and related audit of taxpayer's individual return for the year 1960, resulted in a deficiency assessment of $17,388.77 additional tax based on a $52,441.31 capital gain by taxpayer from his share of the sale of the motel properties. The additional tax was paid and is the basis for this suit.

* * *

Subsequent to the audit of taxpayer's individual 1960 return, an amended partnership return was filed in September 1963, * * * which sought to exercise an election by the partnership under the provision of Section 754 of the 1954 Internal Revenue Code to adjust the basis of partnership property under Section 734(b) and 743(b) of the Code for the taxable year ending December 31, 1960.

* * *

At the conclusion of the plaintiff's case-in-chief the Court granted the government's motion for directed verdict.

* * *

When the taxpayer received a stepped-up basis in the value of his partnership interest as a result of the death of his wife in 1957, the basis of his partnership interest became considerably larger than his proportionate share of the adjusted basis of the partnership property ($71,250.00 vs. $14,973.27). Ordinarily, the fact that a taxpayer received a stepped-up basis in his partnership interest by virtue of a transfer on the death of a partner, does not affect the basis of the partnership property. However, Section 743(b) of the Code * * * permits an adjustment in [sic] the partnership makes an election under Section 754 of the Code. The adjustment to the basis of the partnership's assets is for the benefit of the transferee partner

be the fair market value of the property at the date of decedent's death * * *.

Sec. 1014 (b) "* * * For purposes of subsection (a), the following property shall be considered to have been acquired from or to have passed from a decedent: * * * if at least one-half of the whole of the community interest in such property was includable in determining the value of the decedent's gross estate * * *."

only, and the special basis adjustment is measured by the difference between the transferee's basis for his partnership interest and his proportionate share of the partnership's basis for its assets at the time of the transfer.

In the case before us the transfer giving rise to a right of an election under Section 754, was that occasioned by the death of Mrs. Dupree in 1957. If a valid election had been effected, the taxpayer would have been entitled to a special basis adjustment by an increase of the basis of his proportionate share of partnership assets, in the amount of $56,276.73 (the difference between $71,250.00 and $14,973.27). Instead of a $52,441.31 capital gain he would have had a $3,834.42 loss on the sale of the motel properties. Although an election was attempted by the partnership, the validity of that election is in issue. The partnership in filing its original return on July 15, 1961, for the 1960 tax year, did not make the Section 754 election, but instead separately stated the taxpayer's distributive share of the gain realized from the sale of its assets without employing any special adjustment for his benefit. Subsequently, on September 24, 1963, as previously noted herein, the partnership filed an amendment to its 1960 return for the sole purpose of making the election under Section 754, for the 1960 tax year.

The government contends the election was too late to be effective. Assuming that an election could have been made for the first time for the 1960 taxable year (which position the government disputes), the government insists the election could not be by an amendment filed over two years after the original return for 1960 was due. We agree. Cases involving elections under other sections of the Internal Revenue Code have permitted an election to be validly exercised only in an original return or in a timely amendment, with "timely amendment" meaning if filed within the period provided by the statute for filing the original return. * * * We conclude that for a valid election to have been made for the taxable year 1960, it should have been timely made in the original return or by an amended return filed within the statutory time for filing the original return.

In view of our conclusion that the election was made too late to be valid, it is unnecessary to consider and decide the second defense of the government that an election could be made for the first time only in the year of the transfer—1957.

* * *

Affirmed.

* * *

NOTES

1. Section 741, encountered earlier, dictates the tax impact on the partner (or anyone treated as a partner for income tax purposes) who sells his or her interest in the firm. It treats such a transfer as the sale or exchange of a capital asset. An exception exists by virtue of Section 751(a), which

removes from capital gains or loss treatment the portion of the purchase price received in exchange for the seller's interest in either inventory or "unrealized receivables." Section 751(c) defines "unrealized receivables." The term encompasses not only that which one would normally think of as an unrealized receivable—*i.e.* rights to payment for goods sold or services rendered, which were not yet recognized as income under the firm's accounting system—but a host of other items whose common feature is that they normally yield ordinary income. To determine the amount of the purchase price which the selling partner received in exchange for his or her interest in Section 751 assets, the regulations ask how much income from such assets would have been allocated under the partnership agreement to the selling partner had the firm sold all of its property at fair market value immediately prior to the selling partner's transfer of his or her interest. Treas. Reg. § 1.751–1(a)(2). In order to compute the selling partner's gain or loss on the sale of his or her overall interest in the firm, the selling partner subtracts the sum attributable to his or her share in the firm's Section 751 assets from the total purchase price he or she received in exchange for the partnership interest. Notice that this creates the disturbing prospect of the selling party recognizing both ordinary income and a capital loss on the same transaction.

Note, incidentally, following principles applicable to the sale of encumbered property generally, the amount realized by the selling partner (or party treated as a partner for income tax purposes) includes the amount of his or her share of the firm's liabilities from which he or she is relieved. *See* I.R.C. § 752(d); *Commissioner v. Tufts,* 461 U.S. 300 (1983). Also, as stated earlier, Section 453 may apply if the buyer pays in installments (except insofar as the payment is for Section 751 assets). Rev. Rul. 76–483, 1976–2 C.B. 131; Rev.Rul. 89–108, 1989–2 C.B. 100.

2. Following principles applicable to the purchase of property generally, the buyer of an interest in a firm treated as a partnership for income tax purposes obtains a basis in the interest equal to his or her cost. *See* I.R.C. §§ 742, 1012. Along the same lines, an individual who inherits an interest in a firm treated as a partnership for income tax purposes obtains a basis equal to the fair market value of the interest on the date of the former owner's death. *See* I.R.C. §§ 742, 1014. (If the estate tax repeal scheduled for 2010 actually takes place, however, then the stepped up basis provided by Section 1014 also will be repealed.) Under the general rule of Section 743(a), however, the firm does not adjust the basis of its property upon the transfer of an interest in the firm. *Dupree* illustrates the result if the firm's property increased in value between its acquisition by the firm and the transfer of the interest. The incoming owner must recognize his or her distributive share of the firm's income if and when the firm sells the property, even though (in the case of a buyer paying fair market value) the incoming owner made nothing and the seller already recognized the gain resulting from the pre-transfer appreciation. Because the recognition increases the new owner's basis in his or her interest in the firm (I.R.C. § 705(a)(1)(A)), the new owner later may realize an offsetting loss. Still, the sale or liquidation necessary to trigger such recognition may be years

off, and will produce only a capital loss of often limited utility. *See* I.R.C. §§ 731(a), 741. Section 754 provides a possible remedy. If the partnership (or firm treated as a partnership for income tax purposes) elects this option, the firm adjusts the transferee's share of the firm's basis in the firm's assets to reflect the difference between what otherwise would be the firm's basis in the firm's property and the transferee's basis in his or her interest in the firm. I.R.C. § 743(b). In addition, under this election, the partnership (or firm treated as a partnership for income tax purposes) adjusts the basis of the firm's assets if a distribution to any of the firm's owners creates an inequality between the firm's basis in its assets and the owners' basis in their interests in the firm. I.R.C. § 734(b). (Section 755 dictates how to allocate the basis adjustment among the firm's assets, while Treas. Reg. §§ 1.743–1 and 1.755–1 contain detailed rules for computing these adjustments.)

Before assuming the universal desirability of a Section 754 election, notice that its adjustment cuts both ways. If the firm's assets have decreased in value, their basis will go down under Section 743(b). Unfortunately, the firm must obtain the Internal Revenue Service's approval to revoke a Section 754 election. Treas. Reg. § 1.754–1(c). Avoiding potential decreases in basis is not an acceptable ground for such approval. While this suggests some ground for hesitation before making a Section 754 election, declining to make the election in order to avoid downward basis adjustments only works to a limited extent anyway. Section 743(b) requires negative basis adjustments whenever the optional adjustments would have been over $250,000. A different sort of problem with a Section 754 election lies in the record keeping and accounting burdens it imposes. These disadvantages for a Section 754 election can create conflicting interests between the owners when one desires to sell out. If the firm's assets have appreciated, a prospective buyer may demand the firm make the 754 election. The remaining owners, however, gain nothing by the election in this context (since the basis adjustment under Section 743(b) applies only to the transferee). Should the partnership or LLC operating agreement attempt to avoid later conflict by speaking to whether the firm will make a Section 754 election? (If the firm does not make a Section 754 election, the transferee may opt to adjust his or her basis in any property distributed by the firm to the new entrant within two years of his or her acquisition of the interest. I.R.C. § 732(d). This, of course, is of far less utility than a Section 743(b) adjustment.)

3. In addition to questions of basis, an individual who purchases an interest during the middle of the firm's tax year may be concerned with what portion of the year's income, gains, losses, deductions or credits will be included in his or her distributive share. Section 706(c)(2)(A)(i) closes the partnership taxable year for the owner who sells his or her entire interest in the firm. If the owner does not sell his or her entire interest, the partnership taxable year does not close. I.R.C. § 706(c)(B). Nevertheless, Section 706(d)(1) commands that each partner's (or person treated as a partner for income tax purposes) distributive share take into account the varying interests of the owners during the year. Parties may comply with

the requirements of Section 706(c)(2)(A)(i) and (d)(1) through an interim closing of the books whereby they attempt to trace in which portion of the year the firm incurred various items of income, gain, loss, deduction or credit. Alternately, they simply can prorate each item, assuming, for example, the firm incurred one-twelfth of all income, gains, losses, deductions or credits for the year during each month. Treas. Reg. § 1.706–1(c)(2)(ii). Section 706(d)(2), however, contains a special rule designed to prevent cash basis firms shifting deductions to incoming owners by postponing the payment of expenses.

4. What tax impact may the transfer of an interest in a firm treated as a partnership for income tax purposes have on the non-selling owners? As explained earlier when dealing with the tax aspects of buy-outs, Section 708(b)(1)(B) terminates for tax purposes a partnership (or any firm electing income tax treatment as a partnership) whenever the owners sell or exchange 50 percent or more of the total interests in profits and capital within a twelve month period. (This can occur by virtue of a number of independent sales. Treas. Reg. § 1.708–1(b)(1)(ii). Resale of the same interest within twelve months, however, does not count. Neither, by the way, does the sale of interests by the firm rather than by an owner. Rev.Rul. 75–423, 1975–2 C.B. 260.) What can parties do to prevent such terminations? Is this a reason for altering the rule allowing partners, limited partners or LLC members, in the absence of agreement to the contrary, to assign their interests in profits? Before assuming an affirmative answer to these questions, it is important to examine the consequences of a termination for tax purposes of a firm treated under tax law as partnership. In fact, the effect of a termination under Section 708 is to close the tax year of the old firm and to pretend that the "old firm" transferred its assets to the "new firm" in exchange for interests in the new firm, following which the old firm distributed these interests to the parties continuing as owners in the new firm. Treas. Reg. § 1.708–1(b)(3)(ii), (4). Notice that the hypothetical transfer of assets to the new firm, and distribution of interests in the new firm to the continuing owners, normally will be tax-free under Sections 721 and 731. Moreover, the regulations provide that the deemed distribution resulting from a Section 708 termination will not trigger application of Sections 704(c) or 737. Treas. Reg. §§ 1.704–3(a)(3)(i), 1.737–2(d)(1). Given all that, how important is it to avoid Section 708 terminations?

One other impact can occur if the new entrant assumes some of the existing owners' shares of the firm's liabilities. This triggers constructive distribution treatment under Section 752(b), which, in turn, could trigger a hypothetical exchange under Section 751(b). Rev.Rul. 84–102, 1984–2 C.B. 119.

5. As discussed earlier, owners commonly revalue the firm's assets upon entry of a party who acquires his or her interest from the firm (rather than from another owner), in order to avoid unintended transfers of interests in the existing capital. Is there any tax impact to this? Suppose a new owner enters the firm in exchange for services to the firm. If, in setting capital

accounts, the parties do not revalue the firm's existing assets to reflect their current fair market value, what problem may exist under Revenue Procedure 93–27 reprinted in the notes following *Johnston*? Also, such revaluations create a disparity between tax and book value of the firm's assets, thereby triggering the need for Section 704(c) allocations. Treas. Reg. 1.704–3(a)(6). Such revaluations, properly done, will not create any problem with the substantial economic effect test under Section 704. Treas. Reg. § 1.704–1(b)(2)(iv)(f). By the way, if the revalued assets are Section 197 intangibles, then the allocation of any deductions from amortizing the assets will follow the same principles discussed earlier when exploring Section 704(c) and contributed Section 197 intangibles. Rev. Rul. 2004–49, 2004–1 C.B. 939.

6. Is there any tax significance to the choice between merely assigning a profit interest versus making the transferee a new partner, limited partner or LLC member? Can a mere assignee take full advantage of the various tax attributes of being a partner (for tax purposes)? For example, is the optional basis treatment of Section 743(b) available? See 2 W. McKee, W. Nelson & R. Whitmore, *Federal Taxation of Partnerships and Partners,* ¶ 24.03[2] (2d ed. 1990) (law unclear).

7. Suppose a single member LLC, which is treated as a sole proprietorship for income tax purposes, lets in a new member, thereby becoming a partnership for income tax purposes. See Rev. Rul 99–5, 1999–1 C.B. 434 (if the existing owner sells part of his or her interest and keeps the proceeds, the transaction is treated as a sale of an interest in all of the LLC's assets followed by a deemed contribution by both parties of these assets to a new partnership; if the LLC sells the new interest and keeps the proceeds, then the original member is treated as if he or she contributed all of the assets formerly owned by the LLC to a new partnership with the new owner). Suppose both owners of a two-person LLC sell out to a new owner, thereby going from a partnership to a sole proprietorship for tax purposes. See Rev. Rul. 99–6, 1999–1 C.B. 432 (considering the new owner to have purchased the assets, while the selling owners are considered to have sold their partnership interests).

8. *Dupree* also illustrates one non-tax concern. How did Mr. Dupree obtain his partnership interest? What additional planning is necessary for dissolution and changes in ownership in a community property state?

5. MERGERS AND THE LIKE INVOLVING NON-CORPORATE ENTITIES

a. *In General*

Traditionally, mergers of business entities brings to mind transactions involving corporations. Indeed, the final chapter of this book is devoted to mergers and sales of corporations. By contrast, the U.P.A. never specifically addresses the merger of partnerships. Suppose, however, two partnerships decide to join together to make one larger firm (as has become a growing phenomenon among law and accounting firms). Under the U.P.A., the parties can handle this either as the formation of a new partnership or as the admission of new partners into one of the existing partnerships. In either case, this transaction raises a number of questions: (i) What will be the rights of the partners in the emerging partnership? (ii) What partners must approve the transaction? (iii) What happens to the assets of the two original partnerships? and (iv) What happens to the debts of the two original partnerships? (Incidentally, while this discussion generally assumes that the partners will enter into the new or expanded firm as individuals, the parties could structure the combination as a transaction in which the one or both of the existing partnerships enter into the new or expanded firm as the partners—in other words, there would be a tiered partnership in which some or all of the partners themselves are partnerships.)

Even though the U.P.A. does not specifically address mergers, one still can answer these questions under the U.P.A. The rights of the partners in the partnership emerging from the combination will be whatever the partnership agreement of this firm provides. This will be a new agreement in the event of a new partnership, or the existing agreement of the absorbing partnership (probably amended) if the parties structure the transaction as the entry of new partners into an existing firm. In negotiating their relative interests in the emerging partnership, the bargaining power each partner brings to the table depends upon the relative worth of the two combining firms, the relative interests each partner has in his or her former firm, any additional contributions (such as services, or loaned property) which each partner will make to the emerging firm, as well as each partner's ability to veto the transaction.

The required approval of the partners for the transaction depends upon the provisions of the two firms' existing partnership agreements. *See, e.g., Day v. Sidley & Austin,* 394 F.Supp. 986 (D.D.C.1975) (partnership agreement allowed merger through admission of new partners and amendment of partnership agreement based upon a majority vote of the partners). Assuming, however, that the partnership agreements of the joining firms do not contain provisions which deviate from the U.P.A., then all of the partners of both firms would need to approve the transaction. This is because, as discussed earlier, the U.P.A. default rules require unanimous approval for admission of new partners, decisions outside of ordinary business, and alteration of a partnership agreement. *See* U.P.A. § 18(g), (h). Alternately, if the parties structure the transaction as the individual action of partners joining together into a new firm, then all of the partners individually must consent to join the new firm. There is one caveat to the requirement of unanimous approval. The partners who desire the combination could form a partnership which excludes the partners who dissent from the combination. This would entail dissolving the existing partnerships and forming a new partnership after the dissolution. The practicality of this scheme presupposes that the partners desiring the combination will be able to acquire the critical assets of the partnerships in the liquidation following dissolution.

Assuming there is no need to deal with dissenting partners, then it is fairly straightforward for the emerging firm to acquire the assets of the partnership(s) ceasing to exist. This could occur by virtue of a transfer of assets from the terminating partnership(s) to the emerging firm. Alternately, the partners individually could transfer their interests in the terminating partnership(s) to the emerging firm, which thereupon can dissolve the terminating partnership(s) and obtain the assets. Yet a third option would be to have the terminating partnership(s) transfer the assets to the partners, who then transfer the assets to the emerging partnership. In any event, recording the transfer of title to all of the assets could be a bit of a chore. Moreover, if any of the assets (such as contract rights) are non-assignable, there could be problems.

Sections 17, 36 and 41 of the U.P.A. address liabilities. As discussed earlier, Section 17 makes new partners who enter an existing partnership liable for debts incurred before their entry, but only to the extent of the new partners' interests in partnership property. Section 36 leaves partners from a dissolved partnership still liable for the debts incurred before their departure, barring a novation agreed to by the creditors. Section 41 deals with the rights of the pre-combination creditors against the continuing firm. Not surprisingly, the partnership which continues without liquidation following the entry of new partners is still liable for the debts the partnership incurred before the entry of the new partners. All told then, creditors of the pre-combination partnerships will have their rights to pursue the partners of those firms, and pre-combination creditors of the partnership which continues to exist after the combination still have their rights against that partnership. Creditors of a partnership which ceases to exist as a result of the transaction, however, only would have rights against the emerging partnership (as opposed to the former partners) if the firm agrees to assume the debts. U.P.A. § 41(4).

The R.U.P.A. contains provisions paralleling the U.P.A. with respect to admission of new partners and the like. R.U.P.A. §§ 306(b), 401(i), (j), 703. The drafters of the R.U.P.A. were not content, however, with the options for combining partnerships and limited partnerships available under the U.P.A. Instead, they decided to add the option of employing a statutory merger procedure, which borrowed from corporate law. R.U.P.A. §§ 905–908. By and large, this merger procedure yields the same answers to the four questions about mergers of partnerships as the U.P.A. yielded without any merger provisions. The only differences are that the continuing partnership automatically obtains all of the assets and assumes all of the debts of the terminating partnership (regardless of any agreement to assume or not assume those debts). R.U.P.A. § 906(a). A possible advantage of this merger procedure is presumably to save the need to record individual asset transfers, and it might—albeit, as Chapter VII will address in the corporate context, this is by no means certain—avoid problems with non-assignable assets.

The idea of combining firms either by having one firm absorb members of the other firm as new members in itself, or by having the members of the two firms form a new firm in which they become owners, can be used not only with partnerships, but also with any type of non-corporate business. Indeed, there is no reason why these techniques cannot allow marriages between different types of non-corporate entities—say an ordinary partnership combining with a limited partnership. Combinations involving limited partnerships, LLPs and LLCs, however, confront a couple of additional concerns. The first is a simple matter of filing. Because limited partnerships, LLPs and LLCs come into existence by virtue of a filing with the state, the creation of a new limited partnership, LLP or LLC, the alteration of an existing limited partnership, LLP or LLC with the admission of new owners, and the dissolution of one or both of the preexisting limited partnerships, LLPs or LLCs, can require filing the appropriate document. *See, e.g.,* U.L.P.A. §§ 201–203; U.L.P.A. (2001) §§ 201–203; Cal. Corp. Code §§ 16953, 17050, 17356; Del. Code Ann. Title 6 §§ 15–1001,18–201–18–203; N.Y. Ltd. Liab. Co. Law §§ 203; N.Y. Partnership Law § 121–1500.

The second concern involves the rights of creditors of a limited partnership, LLP or LLC that might dissolve as part of the combination. Since partners in an ordinary partnership remain liable for all of the firm's debts, the U.P.A. does not require the partners to pay off the firm's debts with the firm's assets following dissolution. Instead, if all of the partners agree, they could transfer all of the assets to a new firm (albeit, if the former partners then end up insolvent and cannot pay the debts, creditors might argue there was a fraudulent conveyance). By contrast, the U.L.P.A. provision requiring payment of creditors upon the dissolution of a limited partnership (U.L.P.A. § 804; U.L.P.A. (2001) § 812(a).) is not on its face subject to the contrary agreement among just the partners. Hence, the parties either must discharge the debts of the dissolving limited partnership or else they must obtain the creditors' agreement to allow the continuing firm to assume the dissolving limited partnership's liabilities in lieu of immediate payment. The same is true upon dissolution of an LLP or LLC. *See, e.g.,* Cal. Corp. Code §§ 16807(a), 17353(a); Del. Code Ann. Title 6 §§ 15–807(h), 18–804; N.Y. Ltd. Liab. Co. Law § 704.

These additional concerns with combinations involving limited partnerships, LLPs and LLCs increase the utility of a statutory merger. While the pre–2001 U.L.P.A., like the U.P.A., does not contain any provisions addressing mergers—albeit the R.U.P.A. may then become applicable as the gap filler—the 2001 revision contains provisions authorizing mergers involving limited partnerships. U.L.P.A. §§ 1101, et. seq. Limited liability company statutes also commonly contain provisions allowing limited liability companies to merge with other firms. *E.g.,* Cal. Corp. Code §§ 17550 *et seq.*; Del. Code Ann. Title 6 § 18–209; N.Y. Ltd. Liab. Co. Law §§ 1001, *et seq.* These provisions allow combinations in which the surviving firm obtains the assets of the disappearing firm(s) by operation of law, and the surviving firm assumes the liabilities of the disappearing firm(s), rather than requiring the discharge of these liabilities.

Mergers between different forms of business are not only potentially handy to marry different businesses, but also could be used to convert a single business into a different form (without the hassles of individual asset transfers and dealing with liabilities). All the owners would need to do is to merge their existing firm with a shell firm with the desired form. Short circuiting the need to undertake such mergers, however, statutes such as R.U.P.A., contain provisions allowing conversions of various business forms into other forms—for instance, partnerships into limited partnerships, and limited partnerships into partnerships—by a simple filing. *E.g.*, R.U.P.A. §§ 902–904. *See also* Cal. Corp. Code §§ 1150–1160 (allowing conversions between corporate and other forms); Del. Gen. Corp. Law §§ 265, 266 (same); M.B.C.A. §§ 9.50–9.56 (same). As an example of the utility of such conversion statutes, see *C & J Builders and Remodelers, LLC v. Geisenheimer*, 249 Conn. 415, 733 A.2d 193 (1999) (in which the court relied on a conversion statute, which provided that when a partnership or limited partnership converts into an LLC, the LLC succeeds by operation of law to the partnership's or limited partnership's assets, to hold that an LLC, into which a sole proprietor had converted his business, could enforce a contract between the sole proprietor and another party—even though the statute did not apply to such a conversion of a sole proprietorship).

Handy as these statutory merger provisions can be, their existence might lead to unexpected problems unless anticipated in the operating agreement.

Gevurtz, Squeeze–Outs and Freeze–Outs in Limited Liability Companies

73 Wash. U.L.Q. 497 (1995).

* * *

b. *Freeze–Outs in Corporations*

* * * [U]nless partners expressly agree to give a majority the right to expel members, the majority of partners have no power, simply by virtue of being the majority, to freeze other partners out of the firm. True, the majority (or even a minority) might dissolve a partnership which is at will and attempt to acquire the business in the ensuing liquidation. But majority status does not dictate who succeeds to the business in this event; rather, the willingness and ability to pay more does. Corporate law has evolved in a different direction. Significantly, this evolution has not occurred by virtue of provisions in the corporations statutes that have as their explicit objective allowing majority shareholders to expel the minority. Instead, majority shareholders have discovered ways to use provisions directed toward other ends in order to achieve this power.

* * *

The most popular freeze-out technique * * * is through a cash-out merger [in which the majority forms a shell corporation to merge with the existing company under a plan of merger which gives the minority cash instead of shares in the surviving firm].

* * *

c. *Whither Limited Liability Companies, Again?*

* * *

Wyoming's ground-breaking LLC statute originally lacked any provision allowing the merger of LLCs with other LLCs or with other business entities. As LLC statutes spread to other jurisdictions, drafters began to include merger provisions in the acts. Now, such provisions are common. Two aspects of these provisions are critical to the potential for freeze-out mergers: (1) What vote do they require to approve a merger?; and (2) Can the merger agreement force members of a merged LLC to take consideration other than an ownership interest in the surviving entity?

The LLC statutes vary in terms of the vote required for a merger (at least in the absence of other agreement). A couple are silent—preferring perhaps to leave the question to litigation. Some require unanimity. This requirement, of course, will prevent freeze-out mergers for LLCs formed under the laws of those jurisdictions. Many others, however, including such important jurisdictions as Delaware, New York, and California, call for majority (or at least less than unanimous) approval.

Still, if consideration in a merger must consist of an ownership interest in the new LLC, then even a majority vote could not turn the key for a freeze-out merger. Yet, most of the jurisdictions that allow majority approval of mergers also allow nonequity consideration. Other acts are silent or ambiguous, thereby inviting litigation. At least one important jurisdiction, California, recognizing that the combination of majority vote and nonequity consideration allows for freeze-out mergers, limits the use of such consideration (unless all members consent) when an LLC merges with an entity owned by the majority of ownership in the LLC.

* * *

At any event, even if majority [vote] expulsion is the better default rule, it should be explicit in the statute rather than hidden in merger provisions. * * * The problem lies * * * with * * * parties who seek assistance of counsel, but whose counsel does not realize the hidden significance of merger provisions in the LLC statute. Is this likely to be a large group? Given the fact that a review of many of the articles to date discussing the LLC statutes, as well as the available treatise on the acts, found no mention of the possibility of freeze-out mergers, the answer must be yes.

* * *

NOTE

For an example of a merger used to reduce the economic interest and controlling power of one member in an LLC, see *VGS, Inc. v. Castiel*, reprinted earlier in this Chapter. Recall that the court in *VGS* came to the rescue by finding a breach of fiduciary duty. A decision by the Kansas Supreme Court in *Welch v. Via Christi Health Partners*, 281 Kan. 732, 133 P.3d 122 (2006), illustrates, however, that frozen out owners should not always expect judicial assistance. *Welch* involved a merger of a limited partnership into an LLC pursuant to a Kansas statute allowing mergers between different business forms. The limited partners received cash for their interests under the merger plan. Interestingly, while the controlling partner in the limited partnership remained the controlling owner in the LLC surviving the business, it brought in new minority investors in the LLC so that actual percentage interest of the controlling party declined. The court rejected breach of fiduciary duty challenges to the majority owner's action, holding that the frozen out limited partners failed to prove specific acts of fraud, misrepresentation, or misconduct sufficient to shift the burden of proof to the defendants to establish the fairness of the transaction. Moreover, the merger statute did not provide any appraisal rights for the limited partners dissenting from the merger. As a result, the limited partners were consigned to receiving a price for their interests, which was based upon a valuation undertaken by a firm selected by the controlling party, without any judicial review of the price.

The moral for the planning attorney is that one cannot always count on legislative default rules, or judicial review, to protect one's clients from arguably oppressive actions by co-owners of their business. Understanding precisely how majority (or sometimes even minority) owners can obtain unexpected advantages over their fellow owners under the statutory rules should arm the attorney in drafting a partnership or LLC operating agreement hopefully to prevent the actions which the parties did not mean to allow—which is what planning attorneys get paid to do. Indeed, it is useful to note that mergers are not the only mechanism for a majority to expel the minority from an LLC. The majority could vote to sell the LLC's operating assets for cash to another entity owned only by themselves and then dissolve the LLC. Partnership law would preclude this because a transaction outside the ordinary course of business, such as the sale of substantially all assets, requires a unanimous vote (barring other agreement). LLC statutes differ on this requirement. A few follow the partnership law rule and require a unanimous vote. *E.g.*, U.L.L.C.A. § 404(c)(4)(A). Many, however, explicitly allow a sale of substantially all assets on less than unanimous vote. *E.g.*, N.Y. Ltd. Liab. Co. Law § 402(d)(2). Still others (such as California and Delaware) do not specifically address the issue—which may leave the matter open to majority rule by default. Alternately, recall the discussion earlier in this chapter about LLC statutes which allow amendment of the operating agreement with less than unanimous vote. What is to prevent the majority with such a power from amending an operating agreement to add an expulsion clause which allows the majority to kick out the minority? Interestingly, the limited partnership agreement in the *Welch* case discussed above had required a unanimous vote to approve a merger. It also, however, contained a provision allowing the majority owner to amend the agreement—which the majority owner did to reduce the requirement for approving a merger. Incidentally, one other consequence of a merger involving LLCs is potentially to introduce new members into the firm. If the LLC statute or operating agreement requires unanimous consent for entry of new members, what problem does it create when, at the same time, the statute allows mergers based upon majority vote?

b. *Tax Aspects*

As under the U.P.A., the Internal Revenue Code contains almost no provisions explicitly addressing mergers of partnerships (or other non-corporate entities electing income tax treatment as partnerships). Nor does the Internal Revenue Code contain any provisions dealing explicitly with conversions of partnerships to limited partnerships, LLPs or LLCs. Accordingly, figuring out the tax consequences of such transactions is a matter of applying the various provisions in the Internal Revenue Code dealing with partnerships.

Revenue Ruling 95–37

1995–1 C.B. 130.

* * *

In Rev. Rul. 84–52, a general partnership formed under the Uniform Partnership Act of State M proposed to convert to a limited partnership under the Uniform Limited Partnership Act of State M. Rev. Rul. 84–52 generally holds that (1) under § 721 of the Internal Revenue Code, the conversion will not cause the partners to recognize gain or loss under §§ 741 or 1001, (2) unless its business will not continue after the conversion, the partnership will not terminate under § 708 because the conversion is not treated as a sale or exchange for purposes of § 708, (3) if the partners' shares of partnership liabilities do not change, there will be no change in the adjusted basis of any partner's interest in the partnership, (4) if the partners' shares of partnership liabilities change and cause a deemed contribution of money to the partnership by a partner under § 752(a), then the adjusted basis of such a partner's interest will be increased under § 722 by the amount of the deemed contribution, (5) if the partners' shares of partnership liabilities change and cause a deemed distribution of money by the partnership to a partner under § 752(b), then the basis of such a partner's interest will be reduced under § 733 (but not below zero) by the amount of the deemed distribution, and, gain will be recognized by the partner under § 731 to the extent the deemed distribution exceeds the adjusted basis of the partner's interest in the partnership, and (6) under § 1223(1), there will be no change in the holding period of any partner's total interest in the partnership.

The conversion of an interest in a domestic partnership into an interest in a domestic LLC that is classified as a partnership for federal tax purposes is treated as a partnership-to-partnership conversion that is subject to the principles of Rev. Rul. 84–52.

* * *

NOTE

The bottom line of the ruling is that the conversion of an ordinary partnership to a limited partnership, LLP or LLC only creates an immediate tax impact if changing some partners into limited partners, partners in an LLP, or LLC members alters the parties' relative shares of the partnership's existing liabilities. (Changing the shares of future liabilities leads to a future tax impact.) Whether such an alteration will occur is not as obvious as it initially might seem. Changing into a limited partner, a partner in an LLP or an LLC member cannot let one off the hook for partnership debts existing before the change; but, for tax purposes, this is not the issue anyway. Rather, as explained earlier in this chapter, the question is whether the partners agreed, as part of the conversion, to change who is to bear the economic risk of loss for such liabilities. Treas. Reg. § 1.752–2(a),(b).

More broadly, the ruling indicates that conversions, and also combinations, of partnerships (or entities electing treatment for income tax purposes as partnerships) can trigger a number of provisions in the Internal Revenue Code. For example, Section 721 covers the transfer of the assets of the disappearing firm(s) to the emerging partnership (or entity treated for income tax purposes as a partnership) in exchange for interests in the emerging firm. As discussed earlier in this chapter, the substituted basis rules of Section 722 and 723 tag along in any transaction covered by Section 721. This is why the ruling can conclude (ignoring the impact of liabilities) there will be no recognition of income or change in any basis. One difficulty with this conclusion, however, is whether it is subject to how the parties characterize the steps involved in the conversion or combination. Specifically, as stated above, to transfer assets to the emerging firm, the parties could have the disappearing firm(s) transfer assets to the emerging firm, or the parties might accomplish the same result by transferring their interests in the disappearing firm(s) to the emerging firm, which then obtains the assets upon the liquidation of the disappearing firm(s), or the parties could have the disappearing firm(s) transfer the assets to the partners or members, who then transfer the assets to the emerging firm. Will these different forms lead to any different results (say under Section 732 if there is a difference between a disappearing firm's basis in its assets and the owners' basis in their interests in the disappearing firm)? Also, in a conversion of a partnership into a limited partnership, an LLP or an LLC, all of the partners retain their same interests in the emerging firm. Hence, it was not too difficult for the I.R.S. to conclude that there is no termination for purposes of Section 708. What happens, however, with a combination between two firms?

Notice of Proposed Rulemaking and Notice of Public Hearing, Partnership Mergers and Divisions Reg–111119–99

2000–5 I.R.B. 455.

Partnership Mergers

Background

Section 708(b)(2)(A) provides that in the case of a merger or consolidation of two or more partnerships, the resulting partnership is, for purposes of section 708, considered the continuation of any merging or consolidating partnership whose members own an interest of more than 50 percent in the capital and profits of the resulting partnership. Section 1.708–1(b)(2)(i) of the Income Tax Regulations provides that if the resulting partnership can be considered a continuation of more than one of the merging partnerships, the resulting partnership is the continuation of the partnership that is credited with the contribution of the greatest dollar value of assets to the resulting partnership. If none of the members of the merging partnerships own more than a 50 percent interest in the capital and profits of the resulting partnership, all of the merged partnerships are considered terminated, and a new partnership results. The taxable years of the merging partnerships that are considered terminated are closed under section 706(c).

Although section 708 and the applicable regulations provide which partnership continues when two or more partnerships merge, the statute and regulations do not prescribe a form for the partnership merger. (Often, state merger statutes do not provide a particular form for a partnership merger.) In revenue rulings, however, the IRS has prescribed the form of a partnership merger for Federal income tax purposes.

In Rev. Rul. 68–289 (1968–1 C.B.314), three existing partnerships (P1, P2,and P3) merged into one partnership with P3 continuing under section 708(b)(2)(A). The revenue ruling holds that P1 and P2, the two terminating partnerships, are treated as having contributed all of their respective assets and liabilities to P3, the resulting partnership, in exchange for a partnership interest in P3. P1 and P2 are considered terminated and the partners of P1 and P2 receive interests in P3 with a basis under section 732(b) in liquidation of P1 and P2 (Assets–Over Form). * * *

Explanation of Provisions

A. Form of a Partnership Merger

The IRS and Treasury are aware that taxpayers may accomplish a partnership merger by undertaking transactions in accordance with jurisdictional laws that follow a form other than the Assets–Over Form. For example, the terminating partnership could liquidate by distributing its assets and liabilities to its partners who then contribute the assets and liabilities to the resulting partnership (Assets–Up Form). In addition, the partners in the terminating partnership could transfer their terminating partnership interests to the resulting partnership in exchange for resulting partnership interests, and the terminating partnership could liquidate into the resulting partnership (Interest–Over Form).

Under the Assets–Up Form, partners could recognize gain under sections 704(c)(1)(B) and 737 (and incur state or local transfer taxes) when the terminating partnership distributes the assets to the partners. However, under the Assets–Over Form, gain under sections 704(c)(1)(B) and 737 is not triggered. * * * Additionally, under the Assets–Up Form, because the adjusted basis of the assets contributed to the resulting partnership is determined first by reference to section 732 (as a result of the liquidation) and then section 723 (by virtue of the contribution), in certain circumstances, the adjusted basis of the assets contributed may not be the same as the adjusted basis of the assets in the terminating partnership. These circumstances occur if the partners' aggregate adjusted basis of their interests in the terminating partnership does not equal the terminating partnership's adjusted basis in its assets.

Under the Assets–Over Form, because the resulting partnership's adjusted basis in the assets it receives is determined solely under section 723, the adjusted basis of the assets in the resulting partnership is the same as the adjusted basis of the assets in the terminating partnership.

The regulations propose to respect the form of a partnership merger for Federal income tax purposes if the partnerships undertake, pursuant to the laws of the applicable jurisdiction, the steps of either the Assets–Over Form or the Assets–Up Form. (This rule applies even if none of the merged partnerships are treated as continuing for Federal income tax purposes.) Generally, when partnerships merge, the assets move from one partnership to another at the entity level, or in other words, like the Assets–Over Form. However, if as part of the merger, the partnership titles the assets in the partners' names, the proposed regulations treat the transaction under the Assets–Up Form. If partnerships use the Interest–Over Form to accomplish the result of a merger, the partnerships will be treated as following the Assets–Over Form for Federal income tax purposes.

* * *

The Assets–Over Form generally will be preferable for both the IRS and taxpayers. For example, when partnerships merge under the Assets–Over Form, gain under sections 704(c)(1)(B)and 737 is not triggered. Moreover, the basis of the assets in the resulting partnership is the same as the basis of the assets in the terminating partnership, even if the partners' aggregate adjusted basis of their interests in the terminating partnership does not equal the terminating partnership's adjusted basis in its assets.

If partnerships merge under applicable law without implementing a form, the proposed regulations treat the partnerships as following the Assets–Over Form. * * *

B. *Adverse Tax Consequences of the Assets–Over Form*

The IRS and Treasury are aware that certain adverse tax consequences may occur for partnerships that merge in a transaction that will be taxed in accordance with the Assets–Over Form. These proposed regulations address some of the adverse tax consequences regarding section 752 liability shifts and buyouts of exiting partners.

1. Section 752 Revisions

If a highly leveraged partnership (the terminating partnership) merges with another partnership (the resulting partnership), all of the partners in the terminating partnership could recognize gain because of section 752 liability shifts. Under the Assets–Over Form, the terminating partnership becomes a momentary partner in the resulting partnership when the terminating partnership contributes its assets and liabilities to the resulting partnership in exchange for interests in the resulting partnership. If the terminating partnership (as a momentary partner in the resulting partnership) is considered to receive a deemed distribution under section 752 (after netting increases and decreases in liabilities under § 1.752–1(f)) that exceeds the terminating partnership's adjusted basis of its interests in the resulting partnership, the terminating partnership would recognize gain under section 731. The terminating partnership's gain then would be allocated to each partner in the terminating partnership under section 704(b). In this situation, a partner in the terminating partnership could recognize gain even though the partner's adjusted basis in its resulting partnership interest or its share of partnership liabilities in the resulting partnership is large enough to avoid the recognition of gain * * *.

The proposed regulations clarify that when two or more partnerships merge under the Assets–Over Form, increases or decreases in partnership liabilities associated with the merger are netted by the partners in the terminating partnership and the resulting partnership to determine the effect of the merger under section 752. The IRS and Treasury consider it appropriate to treat the merger as a single transaction for determining the net liability shifts under section 752. Therefore, a partner in the terminating partnership will recognize gain on the contribution under section 731 only if the net section 752 deemed distribution exceeds that partner's adjusted basis of its interest in the resulting partnership.

2. Buyout of a Partner

Another adverse tax consequence may occur when a partner in the terminating partnership does not want to become a partner in the resulting partnership and would like to receive money or property instead of an interest in the resulting partnership. Under the Assets–Over Form, the terminating partnership will not recognize gain or loss under section 721 when it contributes its property to the resulting partnership in exchange for interests in the resulting partnership. However, if, in order to facilitate the buyout of the exiting partner, the resulting partnership transfers money or other consideration to the terminating partnership in addition to the resulting partnership interests, the terminating partnership may be treated as selling part of its property to the resulting partnership under section 707(a)(2)(B). Any gain or loss recognized by the terminating partnership generally would be allocated to all the partners in the terminating partnership even though only the exiting partner would receive the consideration.

The IRS and Treasury believe that, under certain circumstances, when partnerships merge and one partner does not become a partner in the resulting partnership, the receipt of cash or property by that partner should be treated as a sale of that partner's interest in the terminating partnership to the resulting partnership, not a disguised sale of the terminating partnership's assets. Accordingly, the proposed regulations provide that if the merger agreement (or similar document) specifies that the resulting partnership is purchasing the exiting partner's interest in the terminating partnership and the amount paid for the interest, the transaction will be treated as a sale of the exiting partner's interest to the resulting partnership. This treatment will apply even if the resulting partnership sends the consideration to the terminating partnership on behalf of the exiting partner, so long as the designated language is used in the relevant document.

* * *

NOTE

The proposed regulations dealing with partnership mergers discussed in the Notice have become final. Treas. Reg. §§ 1.708–1(c), (d), 1.752–1(g) Ex.2. A major advantage of assets-over mergers according to the Notice is that they will not trigger recognition upon the merger under Sections 704(c)(1)(B) and 737. As discussed earlier in the Chapter, these sections can trigger recognition by a partner who contributed appreciated property to a partnership, when the partnership, within seven years of the contribution, either distributes the appreciated property to another partner or distributes other property to this partner. What might happen, however, if the partnership, within seven years after an assets-over merger, distributes property to any partners? In Revenue Ruling 2004–43, 2004–1 C.B. 842, the I.R.S. held that, should a merged partnership later distribute assets from the pre-merger firms, Sections 704(c)(1)(B) and 737 can apply to the newly created Section 704(c) gain caused by the deemed contribution of assets by the disappearing partnership in a partnership assets-over merger, but not to any Section 704(c) gain resulting from the revaluation of assets of the surviving partnership incident to the merger. Consider the impact of the differentiation drawn by Revenue Ruling 2004–43 in the case in which the merging partnerships have flexibility in deciding which firm will be the survivor for tax purposes. While the I.R.S. subsequently revoked Revenue Ruling 2004–43 (Rev. Rul. 2005–10, 2005–7 I.R.B. 492), proposed regulations follow the approach of Revenue Ruling 2004–43, except where the subsequent distribution of property is part of the plan of merger. Prop. Reg. § 1.704–4(c)(4).

CHAPTER IV

FORMING A CORPORATION

Creating a corporation might occur at the inception of a venture or may involve a business that has been functioning for some time in a non-corporate form. In either case, the first question is in what state to incorporate. For a business planning to operate in one state, the cheapest answer is to incorporate in that state. Otherwise, the company will need to pay taxes both to its state of incorporation and to the state in which it must qualify to do business, as well as to pay the cost of maintaining an office and a resident agent in the state of incorporation. In addition, incorporating in a state other than where the company does business subjects it to suit in both jurisdictions. Nevertheless, it is possible to incorporate in a state other than where the company will operate (and, of course, if the firm operates in more than one state, it must conduct at least some business outside its state of incorporation). The motivation for incorporating in a state other than where the firm does business is that the law of the state of incorporation governs the company's internal affairs. *But see* Cal. Corp. Code § 2115 (attempting to subject companies to certain sections of California's corporations code if the companies meet tests establishing a dominant relationship with California); N.Y. Bus. Corp. Law §§ 1317–1320 (applying certain sections of New York's corporations statute to foreign corporations doing business in New York).

How can one decide what corporate law is more favorable than another? There are a number of criteria to consider. Most obvious is flexibility: In other words, what states allow the parties to do the things they desire in setting up and running the company? Delaware has a favorable reputation in this regard; albeit one must examine the specific issues the parties are concerned with. A less obvious criteria is gap filling: To the extent the participants do not plan for a contingency (either through inadvertence or the impossibility of covering everything), does the code provide workable answers which protect the interests of the various individuals? In this regard, the best statute to choose may not be that which provides the most freedom of action for directors and majority shareholders. A practical problem with applying this criteria, however, is the difficulty of asking what statute best handles items one has overlooked. Yet another criteria is predictability: Are there judicial or other authoritative interpretations of the statute's various sections available to take the guess work and risk out of dealing with the statute? Delaware again has an advantage here. A frequently employed criteria (at least for small corporations) probably is familiarity: Which state's corporation law is the attorney most knowledgeable of? This is typically his or her home state. (Before assuming this last criteria is completely crass and unprofessional, consider the costs—ultimately borne by the client—of conducting an extensive 50 state survey applying the other three criteria, as well as the expense, and risk of error, in applying a statute less familiar to the attorney.) These materials will focus on four statutes: California, Delaware, New York and the Model Business Corporation Act (the M.B.C.A., which a number of states have adopted in whole or part). By comparing how these statutes handle various issues to arise in forming and operating a corporation, one can make a more informed choice.

Having selected the state of incorporation, the parties must comply with the organizational requirements set forth in this state's statute. This invariably means, at a minimum, drafting and filing articles or a certificate of incorporation (different names used by different statutes for the same document). Cal. Corp. Code §§ 200, 202; Del. Gen. Corp. Law §§ 101, 102; N.Y. Bus. Corp. Law §§ 401, 402; M.B.C.A. §§ 2.01–2.02. As with limited partnerships, LLCs and LLPs, failure to follow the required formalities can result in personal liability for the participants. *E.g., Timberline Equip. Co. v. Davenport,* 267 Or. 64, 514 P.2d 1109 (1973). For this reason, cautious participants in the business might wish to see written evidence of filing before they begin corporate operations.

A bare bones articles under many acts requires little more than a corporate name (which should include a word such "Inc." to identify the corporation as such), an address and agent for service of process, the number and (except in California and under the M.B.C.A.) par value, if any, of the shares of stock the company may issue, and (except under the Model Act) a statement of purpose. The last item may be as broad as "any lawful business," thereby avoiding the need to amend the articles, or interpretation questions, should the company confront opportunities tangential or entirely foreign to its original line of endeavor. All told, such a minimal job should not take long to do—the most time will probably go into checking whether another company has already taken the desired name. During the course of this chapter, however, the reader will encounter a number of optional provisions which parties may wish to put into the articles (such as preemptive rights, multiple classes of stock, and various items regarding the management of the corporation). Hence, the stripped down articles are often unsatisfactory.

Once the incorporators file the articles, they need to appoint the initial directors (unless named in the articles), who can then adopt bylaws and issue shares. The bylaws set out the various operational rules. They cover topics such as: (i) shareholders' meetings (including time and place of the annual meeting, who can call special meetings, requirements as to notice and quorum); (ii) recordkeeping with respect to stock transfers and certificates (including guidance for recording transfers, issuing new certificates, and setting a record date to determine who is entitled to vote at a meeting or receive dividends); (iii) directors and directors' meetings (including number and qualifications, if any, method of filling vacancies, who can call a meeting, requirements as to notice and quorum), and (iv) officers (including positions, job duties and authority, appointment and removal).

SECTION A. CONTRIBUTIONS

Even before preparing the articles of incorporation and the bylaws, it is reasonable to begin, just as in forming a non-corporate business, by considering what each party will put into the enterprise. Instead of referring to contributions to capital, however, one now speaks of the purchase of stock (putting aside, for the present, the alternate possibilities of loans, leases, and sales of property to the corporation for cash). This difference marks a critical distinction in planning for a corporation versus a partnership, limited partnership, LLP or LLC. In these various non-corporate entities, the rights of the parties flow from the partnership or LLC operating agreement, and planning essentially involves drafting this agreement. The parties can allocate their rights to profits and control independently of any other factor—especially, the right to return of their contribution. In the corporation, all rights normally flow from and in proportion to stock holdings. This may result in a relationship between rights to return of invested capital, rights to profits, and rights to control, different from what the parties desire. Much of this chapter is devoted to ways of modifying this relationship.

The fact that capital contributions to a corporation come through the purchase of stock creates one other technical difference. Instead of the owners agreeing directly between themselves (as in a partnership or LLC operating agreement) who will contribute what, in exchange for what, now the agreement (often referred to as a subscription agreement) is ultimately between the purchasers of stock and the corporation, acting through its board of directors. This difference can raise a couple of questions not faced in the non-corporate setting. Does it mean individuals planning to form a corporation must spend the time and money necessary to bring the company into existence without any legally binding assurance against a party with a key contribution backing out of the deal? See Del. Gen. Corp. Law § 165 (pre-incorporation subscription agreement is irrevocable for six months from its date unless otherwise agreed); M.B.C.A. § 6.20(a) (same); N.Y. Bus. Corp. Law § 503(a) (irrevocable for three months). In addition, if all the initial participants agree who puts in what for how much stock, does the board of directors have any duty to the corporation as an independent entity possibly to demand more for its stock? *Compare Old Dominion Copper Mining & Smelting Co. v. Lewisohn,* 210 U.S. 206 (1908), *with Old Dominion Copper Mining & Smelting Co. v. Bigelow,* 203 Mass. 159, 89 N.E. 193 (1909).

As was true with non-corporate forms, inputs of cash to a corporation present the least planning difficulty. The initial question again is how much should each party put in. An added factor beyond those considered in an ordinary partnership is that inadequate capitalization may not only doom the venture to failure, but could also result in the loss of the shareholders' limited liability. *E.g., Minton v. Cavaney,* 56 Cal.2d 576, 15 Cal.Rptr. 641, 364 P.2d 473 (1961). *But see Harris v. Curtis,* 8 Cal.App.3d 837, 87 Cal.Rptr. 614 (1970) (inadequate capitalization is not enough by itself to impose personal liability upon shareholders). How much money do shareholders need to put in to avoid the danger of personal liability? See Gevurtz, *Piercing Piercing: An Attempt to Lift the Veil of Confusion Surrounding the Doctrine of Piercing the Corporate Veil*, 76 Ore. L. Rev. 853, 888–896 (1997) (court decisions on what constitutes inadequate capital for purposes of piercing the corporate veil are in hopeless conflict and provide little guidance; but owners of corporations should ensure that their corporations have adequate insurance to cover foreseeable tort liability, and should not have their companies incur debts when the state of their corporations' finances has made it clear to the owners that their companies will default on the obligations). In addition, the parties must determine how many shares of stock they will receive for cash (in other words, the price per share). This is a matter of negotiation. The board possesses the statutory authority to set the price of shares, subject to the limit that the corporation must not sell shares for which the articles specify a par value below the amount specified as par. *E.g.,* Del. Gen. Corp. Law 153(a), (b); N.Y. Bus. Corp. Law § 504(c), (d). *But see* Cal. Corp. Code § 409(a)(1) (eliminating any reference to par value); M.B.C.A. § 6.21(c) (same).

1. Special Problems With Non-Cash Contributions

a. *In General*

As with non-corporate forms, contributing property or services, instead of cash, to a corporation introduces substantial complications. To begin with, many statutes limit the types of consideration for which a company can issue its stock. Specifically, more traditional statutes exclude future services and promissory notes as types of consideration acceptable for shares. *E.g.,* Cal. Corp. Code § 409(a)(1). *But see* Del. Gen. Corp. Law § 152; N.Y. Bus. Corp. Law § 504(a); M.B.C.A. § 6.21(b). What planning problems do these restrictive statutes create?

Herwitz, Allocation of Stock Between Services and Capital in the Organization of a Close Corporation

75 Harv. L. Rev. 1098 (1962).

It is a familiar rule under corporate law that stock may not be issued for future services. Various aspects of the federal tax laws may also serve to discourage such transactions. Despite this apparent disfavor, it is submitted that the issuance of stock primarily on account of future services is a desirable and even necessary element in many business situations, particularly those involving the organization of a close corporation. To take a fairly typical illustration, assume that S is a person who has little or no capital but does have special service skills * * *. C is a person with substantial capital to invest in new enterprises, but his time is fully occupied in his own business affairs. C and S decide that a combination of C's capital and S's services could produce a profitable business operation. Certainly such a proposed enterprise would hold little attraction for S if he were expected to become a mere employee of the new organization. And S has good reason to insist upon some substantial proprietary interest. When viewed from the point of view of sound planning and practical business judgment, the ultimate profits of a small business based upon a combination of capital and services should be shared by those who contribute necessary service skills, rather than be allocated exclusively to the contributors of capital. The same is true of the power to control the operations of the new business. So if the new venture took the form of a partnership, S would expect the partnership agreement to give him a substantial share in the future profits of the business, as well as a considerable voice in the management of its affairs, regardless of the amount of capital which he could personally contribute to the enterprise.

If instead the parties chose to form a corporation, S would be no less eager to obtain a reasonable share of the future profits, as well as a right to participate in control. But under the corporate form, control and the right to profits inhere in the stock of the corporation, particularly the basic equity stock. Thus S could satisfy his desires only by obtaining a substantial portion of that stock. But if S could make no more than a nominal capital investment, most of his stock would be received essentially on account of his future service, and thus run head-on into the corporate and tax obstacles. The object of this paper is to demonstrate how sound planning may nevertheless accommodate the justifiable interests of the parties in such circumstances.

* * *

Typically, the corporate bar against issuing stock for services has been based upon some provision of the corporation statute such as "no corporation shall issue shares of stock except for money, labor done or property." * * *

* * * Consequently, in the simple illustration above, where S and C want to combine their services and capital respectively to form a new corporation, S could not receive any stock avowedly on account of his agreement to render future services without subjection himself to some danger of cancellation of his stock as well as some risk of liability to creditors in the event the enterprise fails.

* * *

Actually, however, the rule forbidding the issuance of stock for future services amounts to little more than a trap for the unwary, in view of the ease with which it can be circumvented. One who is to receive stock primarily on account of future services or other doubtful consideration can validate his stock under the statute dealing with eligible consideration merely by contributing some modest amount of qualified property. The fact that other parties pay a substantially higher price for their shares is of no concern, for there is normally no requirement in the corporation statutes that stock be issued for the same consideration, even when it is issued at the same time. To be sure, an arbitrary sale of stock at different prices to different shareholders at the same time may be actionable. But where there are practical business reasons for such differences in prices and all the shareholders consent with full knowledge, there would seem to be no valid objection to this procedure.

* * *

As a practical matter, however, this approach does not normally provide a very satisfactory resolution of the problem. When stock is issued to S for a nominal consideration compared to that paid by C for his stock, there is in effect an immediate transfer by C to S of an undivided pro rata interest in the capital contributed by C. For example, S would be entitled from the outset to one-half of the income earned on C's capital even if it were deposited in a savings bank and S's services contributed in no way to that income. Moreover, upon a subsequent liquidation of the enterprise S would be entitled to one-half of the total net assets even though they represented primarily the capital contributed by C.

* * *

What is needed, then, is both a recognition of C's superior rights in the capital contributed by him, particularly in the event of a liquidation, and a senior return upon such capital before determination of the profits to be divided between S and C. These two requirements are the very essence of a senior security. Thus C might receive debt securities with their automatic asset preference and senior return, or preferred stock with a cumulative dividend and a liquidation preference, or some combination of the two, in the total amount of his capital contribution. * * *

The important corollary of interposing senior securities representing C's capital contribution is that the common stock, while still retaining all of its control features, is nevertheless reduced to a basic equity security representing solely the prospective profits in excess of a reasonable return on the capital invested in the enterprise. In view of its extremely speculative character such stock would quite appropriately be issued for purely nominal consideration. Hence it becomes quite simple to allocate the stock between the parties in accordance with whatever bargain is reached as to the division of profits and control.

NOTES

1. Does the ability to issue shares in exchange for future services under newer or amended statutes like Delaware, New York and the Model Act eliminate any need to use senior securities because of such contributions? What is the impact of issuing shares for services upon the right of those paying for shares with cash or tangible property to receive back their investment upon liquidation? Does this problem strike a familiar chord? Recall the impact of treating services as a capital contribution to a partnership. *See Schymanski v. Conventz,* reprinted in Chapter III. Perhaps

the company could issue the shares as the work is done. (Labor done is acceptable consideration for shares. *E.g.,* Cal. Corp. Code § 409(a)(1). *See also* N.Y. Bus. Corp. Law § 504(j) (authorizing corporations to place shares in escrow for payment to a party as he or she completes work); M.B.C.A. § 6.21(e) (same). What problems might this entail (particularly from the standpoint of the service provider)? Finally, as discussed before, it is not always easy to tell the difference between services and intangible property created by an individual's effort.

2. Beyond the problem of providing an acceptable type of consideration, non-cash contributions also raise questions of valuation. In the non-corporate context, such valuation directly impacted the parties' rights to return of the worth of their contributions upon liquidation, and indirectly affected their other rights insofar as the relative worth of contributions dictates the various parties' bargaining positions. In the corporation, all the impact is normally indirect (unless there is a liquidation preference tied to the shares' purchase price), since the purchase price of stock, in itself, dictates no rights. Still, the statutes typically implicitly, if not explicitly, require the board to place a value on property received for stock (*e.g.,* Cal. Corp. Code § 409(e); Del. Gen. Corp. Law § 152; N.Y. Bus. Corp. Law § 504(a); *but see* M.B.C.A. § 6.21(c)), and later purchasers of stock and creditors might rely on this figure. This reliance might, in turn, both tempt the board to place a high value upon the property, and create liability for the directors if they do so. *E.g., Bailes v. Colonial Press, Inc.,* 444 F.2d 1241 (5th Cir.1971) (imposing liability for violating Rule 10b–5 and Section 10(b) of the 1934 Securities Exchange Act). Suppose the board is merely mistaken as to the value of the assets received (rather than deliberately puffing them up)? See, *e.g.,* Cal. Corp. Code § 409(b); Del. Gen. Corp. Law § 152; N.Y. Bus. Corp. Law § 504(a) (all making the board's determination conclusive barring fraud). *But see Pipelife Corp. v. Bedford,* 37 Del.Ch. 467, 145 A.2d 206 (1958) (in an action to cancel shares directors issued to themselves for property, the court held the statute making their judgment conclusive barring fraud was inapplicable).

b. *Tax Aspects*

(i) Receipt of Stock for Property or Services

James v. Commissioner of Internal Revenue

53 T.C. 63 (1969).

■ SIMPSON, JUDGE.

* * *

The issue for decision is whether the transaction by which Mr. James and Mr. Talbot acquired stock in a corporation was taxable or whether such transaction was tax free under section 351 of the Internal Revenue Code of 1954. The answer to the question thus posed with respect to each person depends on the determination of whether Mr. James received his stock in exchange for a transfer of property or as compensation for services.

FINDINGS OF FACT

* * *

For many years, Mr. James was a builder, real estate promoter and developer. * * *

On January, 12, 1962 Mr. and Mrs. Talbot entered into an agreement with Mr. James for the promotion and construction of a rental apartment project * * *. The agreement provided that on completion of the project the parties would form a corporation to take title to the project. The voting stock in such corporation was to be distributed one-half to the Talbots and one-half to Mr. James * * *. The Talbots agreed to transfer to the corporation the land on which the apartment project was to be built, such land to be the only asset contributed by the Talbots to the venture. Mr. James agreed "to promote the project * * * and * * * (to) be responsible for the planning, architectural work, construction, landscaping, legal fees, and loan processing of the entire project." * * *

After the execution of the January 12 agreement, Mr. James began negotiations to fulfill his part of the contract. He made arrangements with an attorney and an architectural firm to perform the work necessary to meet FHA requirements—development of legal documents, preparation of architectural plans, and the like; he obtained from United Mortgagee Service Corp. (United Mortgagee), a lender, its agreement to finance the project and a commitment by FHA to insure the financing. * * * The attorney's and architect's fees were not paid by Mr. James but were paid out of the proceeds of the construction loan to the corporation subsequently established.

* * *

On November 5, 1963, Chicora Apartments, Inc. (Chicora), was granted, upon application of Messrs. Talbot and James, a corporate charter, stating its authorized capital stock to consist of 20 no-par common shares. On the same date, the land on which the apartment project was to be constructed was conveyed to Chicora by Mrs. Talbot in consideration for 10 shares of stock. * * * Chicora's board of directors determined that on the date of this conveyance the value of the real property so transferred was $44,000. Also on November 5, 1963, 10 shares of stock were issued to Mr. James. The minutes of a meeting of Chicora's board of directors held on that date state that those 10 shares were issued to Mr. James in consideration of his "transfer" to the corporation of the "following described property":

> 1. FHA Commitment issued pursuant to Title 2, Section 207 of the National Housing Act, whereby the FHA agrees to insure a mortgage loan in the amount of $850,700.00, on a parcel of land in Myrtle Beach, South Carolina * * *.

2. Commitment from United Mortgagee Servicing Corp., agreeing to make a mortgage loan on said property in the amount of $850,700.00 and also commitment from said mortgagee to make an interim construction loan in an identical amount.

3. Certain contracts and agreement which W.A. James over the past two years have (sic) worked out and developed in connection with the architectural and construction services required for said project.

4. The use of the finances and credit of W.A. James during the past two years (and including the construction period) in order to make it possible to proceed with the project.

Thus, as a result of these transactions, Chicora had outstanding all 20 of its authorized shares of stock.

* * *

Both Mr. and Mrs. James and Mr. and Mrs. Talbot deemed their receipt of Chicora common stock to be in return for a transfer of property to a controlled corporation under Section 351. Accordingly, neither family reported any income from such receipt on their respective income tax returns for 1963. In his statutory notice of deficiency, the respondent determined that Mr. James received such stock, with a value of $22,000, for services rendered and not in exchange for property, and thus received taxable income in that amount. He further determined that the Talbot's transfer of property to Chicora did not meet the requirements of Section 351, with the result that they should have recognized a long-term capital gain of $14,675—the difference between $7,325, the basis of the land transferred, and $22,000, the value of the stock received.

OPINION

The first, and critical, issue for our determination is whether Mr. James received his Chicora stock in exchange for the transfer of property or as compensation for services. The petitioners argue that he received such stock in consideration of his transfer to Chicora of the FHA and United Mortgagee commitments and that such commitments constituted "property" within the meaning of Section 351. The respondent does not appear to challenge the petitioners' implicit assertion that Mr. James was not expected to render future services to the corporation in exchange for the issuance of stock to him. Although the accuracy of this assertion is subject to some question, the state of the record is such that we must decide the issues as the parties have presented them. Thus, the sole question on this issue is whether Mr. James' personal services, which the petitioners freely admit were rendered, resulted in the development of a property right which was transferred to Chicora, within the meaning of Section 351.

* * *

According to the petitioners' argument, Mr. James, as a result of the services performed by him, acquired certain contract rights which constituted property and which he transferred to Chicora. The fact that such rights resulted from the performance of personal services does not, in their view, disqualify them from being treated as property for purposes of Section 351. In support of this position, the petitioners refer to situations involving the transfer of patents and secret processes. * * *

It is altogether clear that for purposes of Section 351, not every right is to be treated as property. The second sentence of such section indicates that, whatever may be considered as property for purposes of local law, the performances of services, or the agreement to perform services, is not to be treated as a transfer of property for purposes of Section 351. Thus, if in this case we have merely an agreement to perform services in exchange for stock of the corporation to be created, the performance of such services does not constitute the transfer of property within the meaning of Section 351.

Although patents and secret processes—the product of services—are treated as property for purposes of Section 351, we have carefully analyzed the arrangement in this case and have concluded that Mr. James did not transfer any property essentially like a patent or secret process; he merely performed services for Chicora. In January of 1962, he entered into an agreement to perform services for the corporation to be created. He was to secure the necessary legal and architectural work and to arrange for the financing of the project, and these were the services performed by him. Although he secured the services of the lawyer and the architect, they were paid for by the corporation. He put in motion the wheels that led to the FHA commitment, but it was not a commitment to him—it was a commitment to United Mortgagee to insure a loan to Chicora, a project sponsored by Mr. James. It was stipulated that under the FHA regulations, a commitment would not be issued to an individual, but only to a corporation. Throughout these arrangements, it was contemplated that a corporation would be created and that the commitment would run to the corporation. The petitioners rely heavily on the claim that Mr. James had a right to the commitment, that such right constituted property, and that such right was transferred to the corporation in return for his stock. However, the commitment was not his to transfer; he never acquired ownership of the commitment—he could not and did not undertake to acquire such ownership. The evidence as to the commitment by United Mortgagee to make a loan for the construction of the project is somewhat incomplete, but since all the parties knew that a corporation was to be formed and that the FHA commitment would be made to that corporation, it seems clear that there was no commitment to loan to Mr. James the funds necessary for the construction of the project. Thus, throughout these arrangements, Mr. James never undertook to acquire anything for himself; he was, in accordance with his agreement with the Talbots, making the preliminary arrangements for the construction of the apartment project. The enterprise would be operated, once the initial steps were completed, by a corporation, Chicora, and everything that was done by him was done on behalf of the contemplated corporation. In these circumstances, it seems clear that Mr. James received his share of the stock in the corporation in return for the services performed by him and that he did not transfer any property, within the meaning of Section 351, to the corporation. * * *

The facts of this case are substantially similar to those in *United States v. Frazell,* 335 F.2d 487 (C.A.5, 1964), rehearing denied 339 F.2d 885 (C.A.5, 1964), certiorari denied 380 U.S. 961 (1965). In that case, the taxpayer, a geologist, investigated certain oil and gas properties to be acquired by a joint venture, and he was to receive an interest in the joint venture. However, before any transfer was made to him, a corporation was formed to take over the assets of the joint venture, and part of the stock was transferred to the taxpayer. It was not clear whether the taxpayer acquired an interest in the joint venture which was then exchanged for his share of the stock or whether he acquired the stock directly in exchange for the services performed by him. The court found that, in either event, the taxpayer received compensation for his services. If he received the stock in return for the services performed by him, such stock was taxable as compensation; and he did not transfer any property to the corporation within the meaning of Section 351. * * *

The next question is whether the Talbots are taxable on the gain realized from the exchange of their land for Chicora stock. Section 351(a) applies only if immediately after the transfer those who transferred property in exchange for stock owned at least 80 percent of Chicora's stock. Section 368(c). Since Mr. James is not to be treated as a transferor of property, he cannot be included among those in control for purposes of this test. * * * The transferors of property, the Talbots, did not have the required 80–percent control of Chicora immediately after the transfer, and therefore, their gain must be recognized. * * *

Decisions will be entered for the respondent.

NOTES

1. The issue in *James* may remind the reader of the *Johnston* case encountered earlier when dealing with contributions of services to a firm treated as a partnership for income tax purposes. In the corporate, as in the partnership setting, the tax code must confront the question of whether to treat as a taxable event the contribution of services or property in exchange for an interest in the venture. For partnerships, the critical code section is 721, which provides that neither the partnership nor partners recognize income or loss upon the contribution of property to the firm. For corporations, separate sections address the effect on the contributor and the company. Section 1032 precludes recognition by the corporation which sells its shares (either newly issued or treasury) for cash or property. In contrast to this simple rule, Section 351 only precludes recognition by contributors when they transfer property to the company solely in exchange for its stock, and when they are in "control" of the company immediately after the exchange. As evident from even this one-sentence description, applying Section 351 requires both a re-examination of issues raised by Section 721, as well as surmounting hurdles not faced in forming a partnership.

2. One area where Section 351 parallels 721 is in excluding stock received for services from non-recognition. (Section 351(d) removes any question on this subject by expressly stating that stock obtained in exchange for services is not considered received for property.) As a result, individuals, like Mr. James, who obtain shares for services must recognize ordinary income equal to the fair market value of the stock (less any cash and the value of any property they also gave for the shares). I.R.C. § 83(a).

James illustrates, however, that ambiguities can arise over whether a taxpayer received stock in exchange for services. This occurs in two circumstances. The first is the situation in *James,* where the question is whether the stated consideration for the shares constitutes services or property, albeit property created by the taxpayer's efforts. The problem often occurs in dealing with secret processes, ideas or technical know-how. Here, the Internal Revenue Service provides the following guidance.

Revenue Ruling 64–56

1964–1 (Part 1) C.B. 133.

* * *

The Internal Revenue Service has received inquiries whether technical "know-how" constitutes property which can be transferred, without recognition of gain or loss, in exchange for stock * * * under Section 351 of the Internal Revenue Code of 1954.

The issue has been drawn to the attention of the Service, particularly in cases in which a manufacturer agrees to assist a newly organized foreign corporation to enter upon a business abroad of making and selling the same kind of product as it makes. The transferor typically grants to the transferee rights to use manufacturing processes in which the transferor has exclusive rights by virtue of process patents or the protection otherwise extended by law to the owner of a process. The transferor also often agrees to furnish technical assistance in the construction and operation of the plant and to provide on a continuing basis technical information as to new developments in the field.

Some of this consideration is commonly called "know-how." In exchange, the transferee typically issues to the transferor all or part of its stock.

* * *

Since the term "know-how" does not appear in Section 351 of the Code, its meaning is immaterial in applying this section, and the Service will look behind the term in each case to determine to what extent, if any, the items so called constitute "property * * * transferred to a corporation * * * in exchange for stock."

The term "property" for purposes of Section 351 of the Code will be held to include anything qualifying as "secret processes and formulas'' within the meaning of Sections 861(a)(4) and 862(a)(4) of the Code and any other secret information as to a device, process, etc., in the general nature of a patentable invention without regard to whether a patent has been applied for, * * * and without regard to whether it is patentable in the patent law sense * * *. Other information which is secret will be given consideration as ''property'' on a case-by-case basis.

The fact that information is recorded on paper or some other physical material is not itself an indication that the information is property. See, for example, *Harold L. Regenstein, et ex, v. Commissioner,* 35 T.C. 183 (1960), where the fact that a program for providing group life insurance to Federal Government employees was transmitted in the form of a written plan did not preclude a finding that the payment for the plan was a payment for personal services.

It is assumed for the purpose of this Revenue Ruling that the country in which the transferee is to operate affords to the transferor substantial legal protection against the unauthorized disclosure and use of the process, formula, or other secret information involved.

Once it is established that ''property'' has been transferred, the transfer will be tax-free under Section 351 even though services were used to produce the property. Such is generally the case where the transferor developed the property primarily for use in its own manufacturing business. However, where the information transferred has been developed specially for the transferee, the stock received in exchange for it may be treated as payment for services rendered. * * *

Where the transferor agrees to perform services in connection with a transfer of property, tax-free treatment will be accorded if the services are merely ancillary and subsidiary to the property transfer. Whether or not services are merely ancillary and subsidiary to a property transfer is a question of fact. Ancillary and subsidiary services could be performed, for example, in promoting the transaction by demonstrating and explaining the use of the property, or by assisting in the effective ''starting-up'' of the property transferred, or by performing under a guarantee relating to such effective starting-up. * * * Where both property and services are furnished as consideration, and the services are not merely ancillary and subsidiary to the property transfer, a reasonable allocation is to be made.

* * *

The transfer of all substantial rights in property of the kind hereinbefore specified will be treated as a transfer of property for purposes of Section 351 of the Code. The transfer will also qualify under Section 351 of the Code if the transferred rights extend to all of the territory of one or more countries and consist of all substantial rights therein, the transfer being clearly limited to such territory, notwithstanding that rights are retained as to some other country's territory. * * *

> The property right in a formula may consist of the method of making a composition and the composition itself, namely the proportions of its ingredients, or it may consist of only the method of making the composition. Where the property right in the secret formula consists of both the composition and the method of making it, the unqualified transfer in perpetuity of the exclusive right to use the formula, including the right to use and sell the products made from and representing the formula, within all the territory of the country will be treated as the transfer of all substantial rights in the property in that country. * * *

The second situation in which the Internal Revenue Service may claim a taxpayer received stock for services involves bargain purchases. Suppose a promoter for the corporation, or one of its directors, officers or employees, purchases shares from the company at a price less than that paid by individuals who perform no work for the firm. (Recall the Herwitz article excerpted above explored this option as one method whereby a party providing services could obtain profit and control in a corporation equal to another party providing cash or property.) It takes little imagination for the I.R.S. to argue that the discount represents compensation for work performed. *E.g., Dees v. Commissioner,* 21 T.C.M. (CCH) 833 (1962). In fact, Section 83(a) requires one receiving property (such as stock) "in connection with the performance of services" to recognize immediately (assuming no risk of forfeiture) as ordinary income the difference between the fair market value of the property and the price the recipient paid for it.

What responses may the taxpayer make to such an attack? Suppose some time elapsed between the low price purchase by those working for the company and the higher priced purchase by those who do not. The recipients of the low price stock might argue they paid fair market value at the moment of their purchase. Thereafter, they would attempt to show that the company rose in value (resulting in the higher price later paid for its stock) once it met various milestones establishing decreased risk and increased profitability. *See, e.g., Berckmans v. Commissioner,* 20 T.C.M. (CCH) 458 (1961). Alternately, suppose the low price stock purchased by those working for the company lacks some of the rights of the high price stock purchased by those not employed. For example, the high price stock might enjoy dividend or liquidation preferences, or the low price shares might be subject to a permanent restriction on transfer. In this event, the recipients of the low price shares may assert the differential in price simply reflects a difference in the worth of the stock, rather than constituting compensation for their efforts. (Section 83(a), however, precludes making this argument based upon temporary restrictions affecting shares received for services.) Finally, suppose those working for the company pay for their shares with property rather than cash. Here, they may claim they paid the same price as other buyers. This obviously creates the potential for dispute with the I.R.S. over the value of the property transferred for the shares.

What impact does issuing stock for services have on the corporation? Unlike the result which might sometimes occur with partnerships, a corporation will not recognize any income or loss upon issuing stock for services. Treas. Reg. § 1.1032–1(a) (considering services as property for purposes of I.R.C. § 1032). The company may, however, obtain a deduction under the principles generally governing payment for services (I.R.C. § 162(a)(1)) even though it pays in stock rather than cash. Rev. Rul. 62–217, 1962–2 C.B. 59. (Recall this deduction will not flow through to the owners except in an S corporation, and the shareholders in an S corporation lack the ability to specially allocate the deduction. *See* I.R.C. § 1366(a). Hence, this deduction does not provide a means to cancel out the taxable income otherwise reported by the party receiving stock for services, as it might in the partnership context.)

What planning lessons flow from the taxation of stock received for services? As in the partnership setting, the recipient faces tax without having received the means of its payment—unless he or she is both willing and able to sell some of the stock. This may suggest parties avoid issuing stock for services. The problem then becomes what can the service provider give for his or her desired share of stock, and what will the company give in exchange for his or her work. Notice how the Herwitz article excerpted above handled the former question.

On the other hand, if one decides to give stock for services, is there a way to delay recognition? Recall, from a similar discussion dealing with contribution of services to a partnership, how Section 83 treats property obtained in connection with performing services when the property is non-transferable and subject to a substantial risk of forfeiture. The section allows the recipient to delay recognition until either of these restrictions lapse. (The material on share transfer restrictions later in this chapter will consider what it means under Section 83 for stock to be non-transferable and subject to a substantial risk of forfeiture.) Keep in mind, however, the price Section 83(a) exacts for this delay in cases where the stock appreciates in value prior to the lapse of a restriction—since the section measures the amount of ordinary income by the value of the property on the date of recognition. Of course, the recipient of the shares would face tax upon their appreciation in any event when he or she sells them. The problem created by Section 83(a) is that the recognition event may occur after the shares have substantially appreciated, but well before their recipient plans to dispose of them, thereby increasing the problem of taxable income without receiving money to pay the tax. Even worse, post-receipt appreciation will be taxable at ordinary income rather than capital gains rates. One should also note the provision in the regulations, which refuses to recognize a party receiving restricted property as the owner for tax purposes until recognition. Treas. Reg. § 1.83–1(a). This could be especially important in an S corporation. (On the other hand, the fact that restricted shares are not considered outstanding could avoid eligibility problems for an S corporation. *See* Treas. Reg. 1.1361–1(b)(3).) Finally, the corporation does not receive a deduction until the recipient recognizes income. I.R.C. § 83(h). Here, however, there may actually be a net tax savings due to delay. Specifically, to the extent the stock appreciates, delay will produce a larger deduction for the company (since the company's deduction is measured by the recipient's income). If the corporation pays tax at the highest rate (35 percent), then the tax the company saves by a larger deduction will exceed the extra tax faced by the recipient of the stock, who must recognize ordinary income rather than capital gain on the appreciation.

As yet another approach to the stock for services problem, one may wish to give stock for services, and accept immediate recognition, but seek to minimize the amount of tax. In this regard, notice Section 83(a) allows the taxpayer to take cognizance of permanent (but not temporary) transfer restrictions in valuing property received for services. (In other words, permanent restrictions impact value rather than delaying recognition.) In fact, Section 83(d)(1) makes the price set in a transfer restriction which forever prevents the recipient from selling for any other amount, prima facie evidence that the value of the property is the price. Hence, by accepting the disadvantage of an agreement obligating him or her to resell shares to the corporation at a low price, an individual might enjoy the control and dividends associated with share ownership while lowering the tax on stock received for services. *But see* Treas.Reg. § 1.83–5(a) (I.R.S. may challenge self-evidently unrealistic prices as not equaling fair market value).

3. Suppose, instead of transferring ownership of property to the corporation in exchange for stock, an individual pays for the stock by simply giving the company the right to use the property. Such a transaction raises two questions under Section 351: Does a license (either exclusive or non-exclusive) constitute property, and, even if so, is there a transfer within the meaning of the section? See, *e.g., E.I. Du Pont de Nemours & Co. v. United States,* 471 F.2d 1211 (Ct.Cl.1973) (answering both questions in the affirmative). *But see* Rev. Rul. 71–564, 1971–2 C.B. 179. Compare the treatment by the regulations of this issue under Section 721. Treas. Reg. § 1.721–1(a).

4. One area where Section 351 differs significantly from Section 721 is in Section 351's requirement that the transferors of property be in control of the corporation immediately after the exchange. Section 368(c) defines control for this purpose as owning stock possessing at least 80 percent of the total combined voting power of all classes entitled to vote and at least 80 percent of the total number of shares of all other classes. If the company issues only one class of stock, this simply means owning at least 80 percent of the shares. See Treas. Reg. § 1.351–1(a)(2) Ex.(3). The issue becomes complicated when the company issues several classes of voting stock with differing rights. How does one then ascertain "total combined voting power"? See *Hermes Consolidated, Inc. v. United States,* 14 Cl.Ct. 398 (1988) (determining voting power for purposes of Section 269). As to non-voting shares, the Internal Revenue Service takes the position that the transferors of property must own at least 80 percent of each separate class of such stock, rather than 80 percent of the aggregate total of all non-voting shares. Rev. Rul. 59–259, 1959–2 C.B. 115.

The control requirement creates difficulty primarily in two situations. The first area of concern, as illustrated in *James,* arises when the company issues shares to an individual who gives the corporation in return something other than property (which means this person's shares may not count in determining whether the transferors of property own the required 80 percent). Money is considered property for this purpose. *E.g.*, Rev. Rul. 69–357, 1969–1 C.B. 101. Hence, the problem occurs upon an exchange of services for shares. (Section 351(d) also excludes cancellation of the corporation's indebtedness (including accrued interest) which is not evidenced by a security from the category of a transfer of property.) Consider the impact this had in *James*. Not only did Mr. James' receipt of 50 percent of the stock in exchange for his services trigger recognition for him, it also meant the Talbots, who received only 50 percent of the shares in return for their property, fell outside the ambit of Section 351. As a result, under the general rule governing exchanges of property, they had to recognize gain equal to the difference between the value of the stock they received and their basis in the land they gave up. I.R.C. § 1001.

What would happen, however, if an individual provides cash or property in addition to services for his or her shares? A careful reading of Sections 351(a) and 368(c) reveals that all they literally require is for those persons who transfer property for stock to own the requisite percentage of shares immediately after the exchange. They do not say such persons cannot *also* have transferred services for stock. (Keep in mind, this discussion deals only with what shares count toward control. Shares received for services still produce taxable income for the recipient.) More importantly, these sections do not say how or when the persons transferring property must have acquired *all* of their 80 percent. Hence, so long as an individual transfers some property for stock, every share owned by that person after the exchange, including shares previously owned or shares acquired for services, counts toward control. Treas. Reg. § 1.351–1(a)(2) Ex. (3); Rev. Rul. 73–473, 1973–2 C.B. 115. Does this mean Mr. James could have saved the Talbots merely by paying one dollar (or some other token amount) in addition to his services? See Treas. Reg. § 1.351–1(a)(1)(ii) ("stock * * * issued for property which is of relatively small value in comparison to the value of the stock * * * already owned (or to be received for services) by the person who transferred such property, shall not be treated as having been issued in return for property if the primary purpose of the transfer is to qualify under this section the exchanges of property by other persons transferring property.") *See also* Rev. Proc. 77–37, 1977–2 C.B. 568 (providing guidelines for what interests are large enough not to be disregarded under this regulation).

The second situation creating problems with the control requirement is when there are successive transfers. This may be a series of sales by the corporation of its shares, or resales by those who originally acquired shares from the corporation of the shares they acquired. The following revenue ruling looked at a series of sales by the corporation.

Revenue Ruling 78–294

1978–2 C.B. 141.

Advice has been requested regarding the effect of a sale of stock by an underwriter to the general public on the control requirement of Section 351 of the Internal Revenue Code of 1954 * * *.

A is a person who conducted business in a noncorporate form. The business needed additional capital. A decided to incorporate the business to increase its capital through a public offering of stock. Therefore, A sought the assistance of U, an underwriter of corporate stock * * *. In accordance with the plan, A organized a new corporation, Z. Z had capital stock of 1,000 authorized but unissued shares upon its formation.

* * *

Pursuant to an agreement among A, U, and Z, A transferred all of A's business property to Z in exchange for 500 shares of Z stock. U agreed to use its best efforts as Z's agent to sell the 500 unissued shares of Z stock to the general public at $200 per share. U succeeded in selling the 500 shares within two weeks of the initial offering with no change in the terms of the offering.

* * *

Section 351(a) of the Code provides, in part, that no gain or loss will be recognized if property is transferred to a corporation by one or more persons solely in exchange for stock * * * in such corporation and, immediately after the exchange, the transferors are in control (as defined in Section 368(c)) of the corporation.

* * *

Section 1.351–1(a)(1) of the Income Tax Regulations states that the phrase "immediately after the exchange" does not necessarily require simultaneous exchanges by two or more persons, but comprehends a situation where the rights of the parties have been previously defined and the execution of the agreement proceeds with an expedition consistent with orderly procedure.

* * *

In [the situation described,] the business needed additional capital so that the public stock offering was integral to A's plan to incorporate the going business. In such circumstances it is appropriate to treat the incorporation and subsequent public offering as elements in a single transaction that may be tested for qualification under Section 351 of the Code. * * *

Furthermore, the charter and bylaws of the issuing corporation as well as various public documents required to be filed with governmental agencies in connection with a public offering of stock set forth the rights of the parties to the offering. Thus, the rights of the parties * * * are previously defined as required by Section 1.351–1(a)(1) of the regulations.

Finally, the sale of stock to the public * * * took place in a short period of time with no change in the terms of the offering. These facts indicate that the transfers * * * occurred with an expedition consistent with orderly procedure within the meaning of Section 1.351–1(a)(1) of the regulations.

Therefore, the public investors * * * should be treated, along with A, as transferors for purposes of Section 351 of the Code.

Accordingly, * * * the transferors are in control of Z immediately after the exchange within the meaning of Section 1.351–1(a)(1) of the regulations.

* * *

Since the person in the ruling (A), who transferred his business assets to the new corporation, ended up with only 50 percent of the stock, how could he have met the control requirement, which calls for the transferors of property to end up with at least 80 percent of the stock? The answer is that the ruling considered the transferors for purposes of Section 351 to include the public investors as well as A, and this meant that the transferors ended up with 100 percent of the stock. Implicit in reaching this result are three conclusions. The first, as mentioned earlier, is that cash counts as property. Hence, the fact that the public investors paid cash for their stock still meant that they transferred property. Next, persons need not have had any prior connection to each other, nor be acting in concert, in order to count together as transferors for purposes of Section 351. All that was necessary was that there was a plan for the corporation to issues shares to A, and shares to the public investors, for both to count toward control. Finally, and the focus of the discussion in the ruling, transfers need not be simultaneous in order for the transferors to be included in determining if the control requirement is met. So long as the rights of the transferors have been previously defined and the transfers proceed expeditiously, they can be grouped together for purposes of the control requirement.

What would have happened in the ruling, however, if the I.R.S. treated this as two separate exchanges? Interestingly, the answer is that the result would been entirely the same. Since A went first, if his transfer of business assets for stock had been considered a separate exchange, then, after A's exchange, he would hold 100 percent of the outstanding stock. This means his exchange still meets the control requirement for Section 351 to apply. The subsequent dilution of his interest is irrelevant, because Section 351(a) measures control "immediately after" the exchange under review, which is now assumed to be only A's purchase. *See, e.g., Scientific Instrument Co. v. Commissioner,* 17 T.C. 1253 (1952), *aff'd,* 202 F.2d 155 (6th Cir.1953). Hence, it does not matter how one characterizes this series of sales: A obtains tax-free treatment under Section 351 whether one treats the exchange as ended after A purchased his stock, or whether one treats the exchange as over only once the public investors buy in. In addition, it does not matter for the public investors whether they count as transferors along with A, because they paid cash for their shares. Buying stock from the corporation for cash is not a taxable event even without Section 351.

So, why for purposes of Section 351 should one care whether a series of stock transfers by the corporation are a single exchange or constitute separate exchanges? Suppose the order of the transactions in Revenue Ruling 78–294 was reversed: in other words, the public investors bought first and then A bought his stock. In this event, if the public investors' purchase was considered a separate exchange from A's later purchase, then the shares earlier purchased by the public investors would not count in determining whether A's transfer met the control requirement, because the public investors were not transferors in A's later exchange. *E.g., Estate of Kamborian v. Commissioner,* 469 F.2d 219 (1st Cir.1972). As a result, the transferors in A's exchange (just A in this event) would only own 50 percent of the stock immediately after his purchase, and A must recognize any gain. Treas. Reg. § 1.351–1(a)(2) Ex. (2). Hence, had A gone second, then whether the transfers are treated as separate or lumped together becomes critical. By the way, sometimes considering transfers to be separate can actually save Section 351 treatment. Specifically, suppose later purchasers buy over 20 percent of the stock and pay for their shares by performing services. In this event, characterizing transactions as separate may save earlier buyers, who obtain shares for property, from recognizing income. *See Kaczmarek v. Commissioner,* 21 T.C.M. (CCH) 691 (1962). This analysis can be generalized to suggest the importance of the one exchange or separate exchanges discussion any time there are a series of stock sales by the corporation, and (unlike Revenue Ruling 78–294) the later sales involve non-cash consideration.

The excerpt from Revenue Ruling 78–294 reprinted above dealt with a situation in which the underwriter simply acted as an agent for the corporation in selling shares to the public (commonly referred to as a best efforts underwriting). In an omitted portion of the ruling, the I.R.S. addressed the situation in which the underwriter purchases shares from the corporation for resale. (This is known as a firm commitment underwriting, since the underwriter keeps any shares it does not resell.) A subsequent regulation rendered this part of the ruling obsolete. The regulation ignores the transitory ownership of the shares by the underwriter in a firm commitment underwriting, and thereby treats a firm commitment underwriting the same as a best efforts underwriting. Treas. Reg. § 1.351–1(a)(3). There is a caveat, however. The regulation only ignores the underwriter's purchase, and treats the public investors as if they bought directly from the corporation, so long as the underwriter's ownership is transitory. Yet, suppose a firm commitment underwriter's ownership is not transitory. Presumably, in this case, one would test who has control "immediately after the exchange" based upon ownership after the underwriter acquires the shares, but before the underwriter resells them. This, however, simply means performing the same analysis as before, but substituting the underwriter for the public investors as the transferor. Since the underwriter has paid cash for the stock, this makes no difference.

So far, it does not seem to matter how one characterizes the transactions in Revenue Ruling 78–294—firm commitment or best efforts; one continuous exchange or two separate exchanges. So long as A goes first, there will be no recognition. Why then did the I.R.S. even bother with Revenue Ruling 78–294 or with amending the regulations to treat a firm commitment underwriting with transitory ownership the same as a best efforts underwriting? The answer comes from asking what would happen if the I.R.S. had insisted on respecting the fact that the underwriter, in a firm commitment underwriting, is the party who purchases the stock from the corporation (while the public investors buy their stock from the underwriter). If the I.R.S. had insisted on respecting this fact, the public investors would not be persons transferring property *to the corporation*, since they would have paid money to the underwriter, who was reselling stock the underwriter purchased from the corporation. As a result, the shares owned by the public investors would then not count toward meeting control. (Remember, Section 351 requires persons transferring property to the corporation to own the requisite 80 percent after the exchange. Persons, who buy stock from a prior shareholder, are not transferring property to the corporation.)

This would not matter if one tested control right after the underwriter buys, but before it resells (which was the approach taken in the omitted portion of Revenue Ruling 78–294). Ignoring the subsequent resale to the public investors, however, is inconsistent with the approach of the ruling to the best efforts underwriting—where the ruling does not consider the exchange over until the public investors bought in—as well as with the general standards for testing what is "immediately after the exchange". The upshot is, unless the I.R.S. was willing to bend the rules, the incorporation of a business, followed by a public offering pursuant to a firm commitment underwriting of over 20 percent of the corporation's stock, would have been a taxable event for someone like "A" in the ruling. This would have inhibited incorporation and capital formation, and so the I.R.S. decided to ignore the precise legal nature of a firm commitment underwriting.

What about situations, other than a firm commitment underwriting, in which persons buy stock from a corporation with the intent of quickly turning around and reconveying the shares? Here, it becomes critical to determine whether the reconveyance is part of the exchange under review, since persons obtaining their stock from a prior shareholder did not transfer property to the corporation, and so their shares will not count in determining whether the transferors of property to the corporation own the requisite 80 percent. *See, e.g.,* Rev. Rul. 79–70, 1979–1 C.B. 144. One instance where the line is clearly crossed, and resales become part of the exchange, is when the initial buyer was already under a binding obligation to convey the shares to a third party at the time he or she purchased them from the corporation. *E.g., Intermountain Lumber Co. v. Commissioner,* 65 T.C. 1025 (1976). *But see* Rev. Rul. 2003–51, 2003–1 C.B. 938 (a binding commitment to transfer stock did not preclude the transferor from having control immediately after the exchange for purposes of Section 351, when the transfer pursuant to the binding commitment was itself a transaction that qualified for non-recognition under Section 351). Absent such a binding commitment, the law becomes murkier. Some courts have so focused on whether there is a binding contract that they have refused to consider gifts of shares by the initial transferor part of the exchange—even when the transferor instructed the corporation to issue the shares directly to his donee—on the grounds that the transferor in the case of a gift retains the right to direct who receives the shares. *E.g., D'Angelo Associates, Inc. v. Commissioner,* 70 T.C. 121 (1978). Conversely, other decisions express a willingness to integrate resales with the original purchase—despite the lack of a binding obligation—simply when the initial purchase would not have occurred without the intention to make the subsequent sale. *Culligan Water Conditioning of Tri–Cities, Inc. v. United States,* 567 F.2d 867 (9th Cir.1978). In one context, Section 351 itself avoids the need to resolve the issue. When one corporation transfers property to another in exchange for the other corporation's stock, the transferor may distribute the shares to its own stockholders without failing the control requirement. I.R.C. § 351(c).

One final point should be noted concerning successive transfers. Shares already owned by a person, who transfers property in exchange for more shares, still count toward control. *E.g.,* Rev. Rul. 73–473, 1973–2 C.B. 115. Hence, if an earlier owner buys more stock at the same time another individual transfers property for shares, this may help the latter individual avoid recognition. Similarly, if a person buying shares from a prior purchaser, also buys shares directly from the corporation, that person becomes a transferor to the corporation. As a result, all of his or her shares (even those acquired from the prior purchaser) count toward control. Rev. Rul. 79–194 1979–1 C.B. 145. Keep in mind, however, that the regulations call for disregarding token transfers to the corporation made for achieving these effects. Treas. Reg. § 1.351–1(a)(1)(ii).

5. Section 351 precludes recognition only to the extent the transferor receives stock. The regulations exclude warrants (options to buy additional shares) from the category of "stock." Treas. Reg. § 1.351–1(a)(1). Hence, receipt of options in exchange for property is potentially taxable. Receipt of stock options in compensation for services gets more complicated, and will be dealt with later in this chapter. In contrast to options, contingent rights to receive future shares without additional payment (for example, under an earn-out clause) count as stock for purposes of Section 351. *E.g., Hamrick v. Commissioner,* 43 T.C. 21 (1964). (For the Internal Revenue Service's requirements for a favorable advance ruling on an earn-out, see Rev.Proc. 84–42, reprinted in Chapter VII.)

Certain types of preferred stock do not count as "stock" which persons can receive tax-free under Section 351. Specifically, Section 351(g) states that "nonqualified preferred stock" constitutes "other property," as opposed to stock. Essentially, nonqualified preferred stock is stock which has a right to receive dividends before other classes of stock, but the shares lack either the right to receive dividends beyond a set amount, or other rights, which give the shares a chance to participate in corporate growth. This chance to participate in growth must have a real and meaningful likelihood—for example, if based upon participation in dividends, the company must have some intent to declare dividends if it can. In addition, to constitute nonqualified preferred stock, either the corporation must have the right to redeem the shares and must be more likely than not to exercise this right, or the owners must have the right to force the corporation to redeem the shares. The redemption must be exercisable within 20 years and not subject to a contingency which renders the likelihood of redemption remote. Redemption rights which can occur only on the death or incapacity of the owner, or the termination of employment of a shareholder who received the preferred for services, do not count toward making the preferred nonqualified for non-publicly traded corporations. Alternately, even if there is no disqualifying redemption right, if the dividend preference varies with interest rates, commodity prices or the like, the shares still will be nonqualified preferred. One uncertainty regarding Section 351(g) is whether nonqualified preferred stock constitutes property other than stock for all purposes under Section 351, or whether nonqualified preferred stock is still stock for purposes other than tax-free receipt. For example, can receipt of nonqualified preferred stock, even though taxable to the recipient, count toward meeting the control requirement? The legislative history of Section 351(g) suggests that receipt of nonqualified preferred stock in exchange for property makes the recipient a transferor whose stock ownership counts toward control.

Later, in considering alternatives to purchasing stock, this chapter will return to explore the tax impact of receiving consideration other than stock in exchange for transferring property to the corporation.

6. Can the transfer of property to a new corporation in exchange for stock constitute a sale for state sales tax purposes? See 18 Cal. Code. Regs. § 1595(b)(4) (exempting a transfer of property to a commencing corporation in exchange solely for the first issue of stock from California sales tax).

(ii) Incorporating a Going Business

Revenue Ruling 80–198

1980–2 C.B. 113.

ISSUE

Under the circumstances described below, do the nonrecognition of gain or loss provisions of Section 351 of the Internal Revenue Code apply to a transfer of the operating assets of an ongoing sole proprietorship (including unrealized accounts receivable) to a corporation in exchange solely for the common stock of a corporation and the assumption by the corporation of the proprietorship liabilities?

FACTS

Individual A conducted a medical practice as a sole proprietorship, the income of which was reported on the cash receipts and disbursements method of accounting. A transferred to a newly organized corporation all of the operating assets of the sole proprietorship in exchange for all of the stock of the corporation, plus the assumption by the corporation of all of the liabilities of the sole proprietorship. The purpose of the incorporation was to provide a form of business organization that would be more conducive to the planned expansion of the medical services to be made available by the business enterprise.

The assets transferred were tangible assets having a fair market value of $40,000 and an adjusted basis of $30,000 and unrealized trade accounts receivable having a face amount of $20,000 and an adjusted basis of zero. The liabilities assumed by the corporation consisted of trade accounts payable in the face amount of $10,000. The liabilities assumed by the corporation also included a mortgage liability, related to the tangible property transferred, of $10,000. A had neither accumulated the accounts receivable nor prepaid any of the liabilities of the sole proprietorship in a manner inconsistent with normal business practices in anticipation of the incorporation. If A had paid the trade accounts payable liabilities, the amounts paid would have been deductible by A as ordinary and necessary business expenses under Section 162 of the Code. The new corporation continued to utilize the cash receipts and disbursements method of accounting.

LAW AND ANALYSIS

The applicable section of the Code is Section 351(a), which provides that no gain or loss shall be recognized when property is transferred to a corporation in exchange solely for stock * * * and the transferor is in control (as defined by Section 368(c)) of the transferee corporation immediately after the transfer.

In *Hempt Bros., Inc. v. United States,* 490 F.2d 1172 (3d Cir. 1974), cert. denied, 419 U.S. 826 (1974), the United States Court of Appeals for the Third Circuit held, as the Internal Revenue Service contended, that a cash basis transferee corporation was taxable on the monies it collected on accounts receivable that had been transferred to it by a cash basis partnership in a transaction described in Section 351(a) of the Code. The corporate taxpayer contended that it was not obligated to include the accounts receivable in income; rather the transferor partnership should have been taxed on the stock the partnership received under the assignment of income doctrine which is predicted on the well established general principle that income be taxed to the party that earned it.

The court in *Hempt Bros.* solved the conflict between the assignment of income doctrine and the statutory nonrecognition provisions of Section 351 of the Code by reasoning that if the cash basis transferor were taxed on the transfer of the accounts receivable, the specific congressional intent reflected in Section 351(a) that the incorporation of an ongoing business should be facilitated by making the incorporation tax free would be frustrated.

The facts of the instant case are similar to those in *Hempt Bros.* in that there was a valid business purpose for the transfer of the accounts receivable along with all of the assets and liabilities of A's proprietorship to a corporate transferee that would continue the business of the transferor.

Further, A had neither accumulated the accounts receivable nor paid any of the account payable liabilities of the sole proprietorship in anticipation of the incorporation, which is an indication that, under the facts and circumstances of the case, the transaction was not designed for tax avoidance.

HOLDING

The transfer by A of the operating assets of the sole proprietorship (including unrealized accounts receivable) to the corporation in exchange solely for the common stock of the corporation and the assumption by the corporation of the proprietorship liabilities (including accounts payable) is an exchange within the meaning of Section 351(a) of the Code. Therefore, no gain or loss is recognized to A with respect to the property transferred, including the accounts receivable. * * * [T]he assumption of the trade accounts payable that would give rise to a deduction if A had paid them is not, pursuant to Section 357(c)(3), considered as an assumption of a liability for purposes of Section 357(c)(1) and 358(d). * * * The corporation, under the cash receipts and disbursements method of accounting, will report in its income the account receivables as collected and will be allowed deductions under Section 162 for the payments it makes to satisfy the assumed trade accounts payable when such payments are made.

* * *

LIMITATIONS

Section 351 of the Code does not apply to a transfer of accounts receivable which constitute an assignment of an income right in a case such as *Brown v. Commissioner,* 40 B.T.A. 565 (1939), aff'd. 115 F.2d 337 (2d Cir.1940). In *Brown,* an attorney transferred to a corporation, in which he was the sole owner, a one-half interest in a claim for legal services performed by the attorney and his law partner. In exchange, the attorney received additional stock of the corporation. The claim represented the corporation's only asset. Subsequent to the receipt by the corporation of the proceeds of the claim, the attorney gave all of the stock of the corporation to his wife. The United States Court of Appeals for the Second Circuit found that the transfer of the claim for the fee to the corporation had no purpose other than to avoid taxes and held that in such a case the intervention of the corporation would not prevent the attorney from being liable for the tax on the income which resulted from services under the assignment of income rule of *Lucas v. Earl,* 281 U.S. 111 (1930). Accordingly, in a case of a transfer to a controlled corporation of an account receivable in respect of services rendered where there is a tax avoidance purpose for the transaction (which might be evidenced by the corporation not conducting an ongoing business), the Internal Revenue Service will continue to apply assignment of income principles and require that the transferor of such a receivable include it in income when received by the transferee corporation.

Likewise, it may be appropriate in certain situations to allocate income, deductions, credits, or allowances to the transferor or transferee under Section 482 of the Code when the timing of the incorporation improperly separates income from related expenses. *See Rooney v. United States,* 305 F.2d 681 (9th Cir.1962), where a farming operation was incorporated in a transaction described in Section 351(a) after the expenses of the crop had been incurred but before the crop had been sold and income realized. The transferor's tax return contained all the expenses but none of the farming income to which the expenses related. The United States Court of Appeals for the Ninth Circuit held that the expenses could be allocated under Section 482 to the corporation, to be matched with the income to which the expenses related. Similar adjustments may be appropriate where some assets, liabilities, or both, are retained by the transferor and such retention results in the income of the transferor, transferee, or both, not being clearly reflected.

NOTES

1. Transferring to a corporation assets commonly found in a going business can raise additional questions under Section 351. The revenue ruling above considers one concern encountered when a taxpayer, who uses the cash method of accounting, transfers his or her accounts receivable. Such a conveyance might fall within the assignment of income doctrine. While the ruling indicates this is normally not a problem, notice the caveat expressed by the Service when there is a tax avoidance rather than legitimate business purpose for the transfer. The ruling also expressed concern about the transfer of assets—such as crops or receivables—to the extent the proprietor has already deducted the expenses of producing the asset, but now the corporation will make the income from selling, using or collecting upon it. As indicated in the ruling, the I.R.S. might use Section 482 to match these expense deductions with the resulting income (for example, by having the corporation take the expense, or the transferor report the income). Yet, the incorporation of a going business will often entail some separation of expense from associated income. Moreover, Chapter II indicated it often might be desirable to operate a start-up business in a flow-through form in order to let the owners take advantage of the tax losses and then incorporate when the business achieves profitability. Will Section 482 apply in every one of these situations? If not, when will the section apply? See *Eli Lilly & Co. v. Commissioner,* 84 T.C. 996 (1985), *aff'd on this issue,* 856 F.2d 855 (7th Cir.1988) (The court rejected an I.R.S. attempt to apply Section 482 to tax a parent corporation on income made by its subsidiary's manufacturing and selling a product, the patent for which the parent had developed and transferred to the subsidiary in a Section 351 transaction. The court distinguished the farm incorporation cases (like the *Rooney* decision discussed in the revenue ruling above) as involving the sale of the actual property (the crops) transferred to the corporation, rather than the use of the transferred property in the business (as with the patents transferred to the subsidiary); and also as involving the matching of expenses and income incurred within the same year, rather than separated over a number of years.) Finally, the tax benefit rule may force the transferor to recognize as income the previously deducted amount on the

grounds the deduction is no longer justified when the transferor will not report the associated income. This depends upon the unresolved question as to what extent Section 351 overrides the tax benefit rule. *Compare Hillsboro Nat. Bank v. Commissioner* and *United States v. Bliss Dairy, Inc.*, 460 U.S. 370 (1983), *with Nash v. United States,* 398 U.S. 1 (1970).

2. Proprietors incorporating a going business typically plan not only to transfer the assets used by the venture to the corporation, but also to have the company assume personal liabilities previously incurred in connection with the enterprise. The ruling above shows two typical examples. The new corporation agreed to cover the accounts payable of the proprietorship. It also assumed the mortgage debt on one of the transferred assets. (Having the corporation assume a liability attached to a contributed asset may often occur, of course, in contexts other than the incorporation of a going business.) Normally, relief from liabilities constitutes taxable income, and, hence, the transferor will have received something other than the stock allowed without recognition by Section 351. *United States v. Hendler,* 303 U.S. 564 (1938). Section 357(a) provides, however, that a corporation's assumption of liabilities as part of a Section 351 exchange is tax free. There are two exceptions. Section 357(b) creates an exception when the corporation assumes the liability for either a tax avoidance or other non-business purpose. (For example, the transferor has the company assume liabilities having nothing to do with the transferred business. *E.g., Thompson v. Campbell, Jr.,* 353 F.2d 787 (5th Cir.1965).) Section 357(c) requires the transferor to recognize gain to the extent the liabilities assumed exceed the transferor's basis in the property transferred. The reason for this exception, as explained later, is to prevent the transferor from ending up with a negative basis in his or her stock. Incidentally, Section 357(d) is designed to deal with possible ambiguities and double counting when it comes to what liabilities a corporation, in fact, has assumed–as might arise, for example, if more than one party has agreed to satisfy a recourse liability, or if a non-recourse loan is secured both by property which is transferred to the corporation and by other property which the transferor retains.

Section 357(c) can sometimes create problems when incorporating a going business. At first glance, one might assume this problem principally occurs when the transferred business is insolvent (its liabilities exceed the value of its assets). In fact, however, the I.R.S. takes the position that a transfer, in which the amount of liabilities assumed exceeds the value of the assets transferred, does not fall into Section 351 at all (since, in such a case, there really is nothing transferred for the stock). Prop. Reg. § 1.351–1(a)(1)(iii)(A). Instead, the problem occurs when the liabilities assumed exceed the basis, not the fair market value, of the transferred assets. For example, as the ruling indicates, the accounts receivable of a taxpayer using the cash method of accounting have a basis of zero. Other assets (particularly those created by the taxpayer, rather than purchased) may have little basis relative to their fair market value. Hence, a solvent business whose principal assets consist of accounts receivable or other low basis property could easily find its liabilities exceed the owner's basis in its assets. Fortunately, as the ruling indicates, Section 357(c)(3) provides some relief.

It allows the taxpayer not to count liabilities which will give rise to a deduction when paid—unless the liability created or increased the basis of the transferred property—in determining how much, if at all, the liabilities assumed exceed the taxpayer's basis in the transferred assets. Thus, for example, the accounts payable in the ruling above would not count for purposes of Section 357(c). This exclusion also extends to the assumption by the corporation of an obligation to make Section 736(a) payments to a former partner. I.R.C. § 357(c)(3)(A)(ii). Otherwise, to avoid recognition under Section 357(c), the transferor might lessen the amount of liabilities assumed by the corporation, or contribute more property in exchange for stock. Suppose the transferred assets include an I.O.U. from the transferor in an amount equal to the difference between his or her basis in the transferred assets, and the total of the debts assumed. See *Lessinger v. Commissioner,* 872 F.2d 519 (2d Cir.1989) (avoided recognition under Section 357(c)). On the other hand, personally guaranteeing the corporation's performance on the liabilities the corporation assumes does not either decrease the amount of liability assumed by the corporation, or constitute a contribution to the corporation, and hence will not avoid the impact of Section 357(c). *Seggerman Farms, Inc. v Commissioner*, 308 F.3d 803 (7th Cir.2002).

Application of Section 357(c) creates a couple of questions. Suppose, instead of the liability producing a deduction when paid, the corporation must capitalize the expenditure it incurs upon paying the liability—can Section 357(c)(3) apply? Alternately, suppose the corporation assumes liabilities whose amount, or even existence, is contingent upon later events—will such liabilities fit within Section 357(c)? The Internal Revenue Service took a helpful view of the former question—thereby avoiding dealing with the later question—in the following revenue ruling:

Revenue Ruling 95–74

1995–2 C.B. 36.

* * *

FACTS

Corporation *P* is an accrual basis, calendar-year corporation engaged in various ongoing businesses, one of which includes the operation of a manufacturing plant (the Manufacturing Business). The plant is located on land purchased by *P* many years before. The land was not contaminated by any hazardous waste when *P* purchased it. However, as a result of plant operations, certain environmental liabilities, such as potential soil and groundwater remediation, are now associated with the land.

In Year 1, for bona fide business purposes, *P* engages in an exchange to which § 351 of the Internal Revenue Code applies by transferring substantially all of the assets associated with the Manufacturing Business, including the manufacturing plant and the land on which the plant is located, to a newly formed corporation, *S,* in exchange for all of the stock of *S* and for *S's* assumption of the liabilities associated with the Manufacturing Business, including the environmental liabilities associated with the land. *P* has no plan or intention to dispose of (or have *S* issue) any *S* stock.

* * *

P did not undertake any environmental remediation efforts in connection with the land transferred to *S* before the transfer and did not deduct or capitalize any amount with respect to the contingent environmental liabilities associated with the transferred land.

In Year 3, *S* undertakes soil and groundwater remediation efforts relating to the land transferred in the § 351 exchange and incur costs * * * as a result of those remediation efforts. Of the total amount of costs incurred, a portion would have constituted ordinary and necessary business expenses that are deductible under § 162 and the remaining portion would have constituted capital expenditures under § 263 if there had not been a § 351 exchange and the costs for remediation efforts had been incurred by *P*.

* * *

LAW AND ANALYSIS

Issue 1: * * * Congress concluded that including in the § 357(c)(1) determination liabilities that have not yet been taken into account by the transferor results in an overstatement of liabilities of, and potential inappropriate gain recognition to, the transferor because the transferor has not received the corresponding deduction or other corresponding tax benefit. * * * To prevent this result, Congress enacted § 357(c)(3)(A) to exclude certain deductible liabilities from the scope of § 357(c), as long as the liabilities had not resulted in the creation of, or an increase in, the basis of any property (as provided in § 357(c)(3)(B).

* * *

While § 357(c)(3) explicitly addresses liabilities that give rise to deductible items, the same principle applies to liabilities that give rise to capital expenditures as well. Including in the § 357(c)(1) determination those liabilities that have not yet given rise to capital expenditures (and thus have not yet created or increased basis) with respect to the property of the transferor prior to the transfer also would result in an overstatement of liabilities. Thus, such liabilities also appropriately are excluded in determining liabilities for purposes of § 357(c)(1).

* * *

In this case, the contingent environmental liabilities assumed by *S* had not yet been taken into account by *P* prior to the transfer (and therefore had neither given rise to deductions for *P* nor resulted in the creation of, or increase in, basis in any property of *P*). As a result, the contingent environmental liabilities are not included in determining whether the amount of the liabilities assumed by *S* exceeds the adjusted basis of the property transferred by *P* pursuant to § 357(c)(1).

Due to the parallel constructions and interrelated function and mechanics of §§ 357 and 358, liabilities that are not included in the determination under § 357(c)(1) also are not included in the § 358 determination of the transferor's basis in the stock received in the § 351 exchange. * * * Therefore, the contingent environmental liabilities assumed by *S* are not treated as money received by *P* under § 358 for purposes of determining *P's* basis in the stock of *S* received in the exchange.

Issue 2: * * * The present case is analogous to the situation in Rev. Rul. 80–198. For business reasons, *P* transferred in a § 351 exchange substantially all of the assets and liabilities associated with the Manufacturing Business to *S*, in exchange for all of its stock, and *P* intends to remain in control of *S*. The costs *S* incurs to remediate the land would have been deductible in part and capitalized in part had *P* continued the Manufacturing Business and incurred those costs to remediate the land. The congressional intent to facilitate necessary business readjustments would be frustrated by not according to *S* the ability to deduct or capitalize the expenses of the ongoing business. * * * Accordingly, the contingent environmental liabilities assumed from *P* are deductible as business expenses under § 162 or are capitalized under § 263, as appropriate, by *S* under *S's* method of accounting (determined as if *S* has owned the land for the period and in the same manner as it was owned by *P).*

* * *

LIMITATIONS

The holdings described above are subject to § 482 and other applicable sections of the Code and principles of law, including the limitations discussed in Rev. Rul. 80–198, 1980–2 C.B. 113 (limiting the scope of the revenue ruling to transactions that do not have a tax avoidance purpose).

* * *

Notice that both Revenue Ruling 80–198 and Revenue Ruling 95–74 allowed the corporations to claim a deduction when the corporations paid off liabilities which would have produced such a deduction for the transferors—rather than treating the companies' payments as part of the cost of acquiring the transferred assets. *See also* Rev. Rul. 83–155, 1983–2 C.B. 38. Had these rulings not involved Section 351 exchanges, the corporations could not have claimed the deductions for such payments. *See, e.g., David R. Webb Co. v. Commissioner,* 77 T.C. 1134 (1981), *aff'd,* 708 F.2d 1254 (7th Cir.1983). This distinction creates a further disadvantage to having the corporation assume liabilities in a taxable exchange. (In addition to federal income tax consequences, assumption of liabilities can lead to state sales tax. *E.g., Beatrice Co. v. State Bd. of Equalization,* 6 Cal.4th 767, 25 Cal.Rptr.2d 438, 863 P.2d 683 (1993) (assumption of liabilities treated for sales tax purposes as consideration which did not come within the exemption for asset transfers to a new corporation in exchange solely for the first issue of stock).)

3. The reader may be excused for having a feeling of *deja vu* in going through the last two notes. In fact, similar problems of assumption of liabilities, and assignment of receivables can arise in forming a partnership (or an entity electing income tax treatment as a partnership).

Revenue Ruling 84–111

1984–2 C.B. 88.

ISSUE

Does Rev. Rul. 70–239, 1970–1 C.B. 74, still represent the Service's position with respect to the three situations described therein.

FACTS

The three situations described in Rev. Rul. 70–239 involve partnerships X, Y, and Z, respectively. Each partnership used the accrual method of accounting and had assets and liabilities consisting of cash, equipment, and accounts payable. The liabilities of each partnership did not exceed the adjusted basis of its assets. The three situations are as follows:

Situation 1

X transferred all of its assets to newly-formed corporation R in exchange for all the outstanding stock of R and the assumption by R of X's liabilities. X then terminated by distributing all the stock of R to X's partners in proportion to their partnership interests.

Situation 2

Y distributed all of its assets and liabilities to its partners in proportion to their partnership interests in a transaction that constituted a termination of Y under section 708(b)(1)(A) of the Code. The partners then transferred all the assets received from Y to newly-formed corporation S in exchange for all the outstanding stock of S and the assumption by S of Y's liabilities that had been assumed by the partners.

Situation 3

The partners of Z transferred their partnership interests in Z to a newly formed corporation T in exchange for all the outstanding stock of T. This exchange terminated Z and all of its assets and liabilities became assets and liabilities of T.

In each situation, the steps taken by X, Y and Z, and the partners of X, Y, and Z, were parts of a plan to transfer the partnership operations to a corporation organized for valid business reasons in exchange for its stock and were not devices to avoid or evade recognition of gain. Rev. Rul. 70–239 holds that because the federal income tax consequences of the three situations are the same, each partnership is considered to have transferred its assets and liabilities to a corporation in exchange for its stock under Section 351 of the Internal Revenue Code, followed by a distribution of the stock to the partners in liquidation of the partnership.

* * *

The premise in Rev. Rul. 70–239 that the federal income tax consequences of the three situations described therein would be the same, without regard to which of three transactions was entered into, is incorrect. As described below, depending on the format chosen for the transfer to a controlled corporation, the basis and holding periods of the various assets received by the corporation and the basis and holding periods of the stock received by the former partners can vary.

Additionally, Rev. Rul. 70–239 raises questions about potential adverse tax consequences to taxpayers in certain cases involving * * * personal holding companies described in Section 542, small business corporations defined in Section 1244, and electing small business corporations defined in Section 1371. Recognition of the three possible methods to incorporate a partnership will enable taxpayers to avoid the above potential pitfalls and will facilitate flexibility with respect to the basis and holding periods of the assets received in the exchange.

HOLDING

Rev. Rul. 70–239 no longer represents the Service's position. The Service's current position is set forth below, and for each situation, the methods described and the underlying assumptions and purposes must be satisfied for the conclusion of this revenue ruling to be applicable.

Situation 1

Under Section 351 of the Code, gain or loss is not recognized by X on the transfer by X of all of its assets to R in exchange for R's stock and the assumption by R of X's liabilities.

Under Section 362(a) of the Code, R's basis in the assets received from X equals their basis to X immediately before their transfer to R. Under Section 358(a), the basis to X of the stock received from R is the same as the basis to X of the assets transferred to R, reduced by the liabilities assumed by R, which assumption is treated as a payment of money to X under Section 358(d). In addition, the assumption by R of X's liabilities decreased each partner's share of the partnership liabilities, thus, decreasing the basis of each partner's partnership interest pursuant to Sections 752 and 733.

On distribution of the stock to X's partners, X terminated under Section 708(b)(1)(A) of the Code. Pursuant to Section 732(b), the basis of the stock distributed to the partners in liquidation of their partnership interests is, with respect to each partner, equal to the adjusted basis of the partner's interest in the partnership.

* * *

When X distributed the R stock to its partners, * * * such distribution will not violate the control requirement of Section 368(c) of the Code.

Situation 2

On the transfer of all of Y's assets to its partners, Y terminated under Section 708(b)(1)(A) of the Code, and, pursuant to Section 732(b), the basis of the assets (other than money) distributed to the partners in liquidation of their partnership interests in Y was, with respect to each partner, equal to the adjusted basis of the partner's interest in Y, reduced by the money distributed. Under Section 752, the decrease in Y's liabilities resulting from the transfer to Y's partners was offset by the partners' corresponding assumption of such liabilities so that the net effect on the basis of each partner's interest in Y, with respect to the liabilities transferred, was zero.

Under Section 351 of the Code, gain or loss is not recognized by Y's former partners on the transfer to S in exchange for its stock and the assumption of Y's liabilities, of the assets of Y received by Y's partners in liquidation of Y.

Under Section 358(a) of the Code, the basis to the former partners of Y in the stock received from S is the same as the Section 732(b) basis to the former partners of Y in the assets received in liquidation of Y and transferred to S, reduced by the liabilities assumed by S, which assumption is treated as a payment of money to the partners under Section 358(d).

Under Section 362(a) of the Code, S's basis in the assets received from Y's former partners equals their basis to the former partners as determined under Section 732(c) immediately before the transfer to S.

* * *

Situation 3

Under Section 351 of the Code, gain or loss is not recognized by Z's partners on the transfer of the partnership interest to T in exchange for T's stock.

On the transfer of the partnership interests to the corporation, Z terminated under Section 708(b)(1)(A) of the Code.

Under Section 358(a) of the Code, the basis to the partners of Z of the stock received from T in exchange for their partnership interests equals the basis of their partnership interests transferred to T, reduced by Z's liabilities assumed by T, the release from which is treated as a payment of money to Z's partners under Sections 752(d) and 358(d).

T's basis for the assets received in the exchange equals the basis of the partners in their partnership interests allocated in accordance with Section 732(c).

* * *

NOTE

Incorporating a partnership (or an entity electing income tax treatment as a partnership) offers the opportunity for some additional creative, albeit complex, tax planning. As the ruling illustrates, three methods traditionally have been used to transfer the partnership's assets to the corporation and the corporation's stock to the partners: (1) the partnership can transfer its assets to the corporation in exchange for stock and then distribute the stock in liquidation to its partners; (2) the partnership can dissolve and distribute its assets to the partners, who then transfer the assets to the corporation in exchange for stock; or (3) the partners can transfer their interests in the partnership to the corporation in exchange for its stock. Revenue Ruling 84–111 considers each stage in these three methods of incorporating a partnership to have independent tax significance, and, as a result, allows accomplishment of the same end to have different tax consequences.

By way of comparison, recall the similar, but more limited, choice provided in the proposed regulation dealing with partnership mergers, as discussed in Chapter III. In the merger context, the I.R.S. proposes to give partners the choice of characterizing a merger, between firms treated for tax purposes as partnerships, either as an asset transfer to the new firm, followed by a liquidation of the disappearing firm, or as a liquidation of the disappearing firm, followed by a transfer of assets to the new firm—the first two choices in Revenue Ruling 84–111—but has refused to allow characterization as a transfer of interests in the old firm to the new firm (the third choice in Revenue Ruling 84–111). Instead, the I.R.S. explained that the unique circumstances of transferring assets to a corporation justified recognition of the transfer of interests approach in Revenue Ruling 84–111. Suppose, however, parties decide to incorporate their firm by using a state statute, which allows partnerships, limited partnerships or LLCs to merge into a corporation, or, even more simply, by using a state statute that allows conversions of one form of business into another merely by filing a document with the state. In Revenue Ruling 2004–24, 2004–1 C.B. 1050, the I.R.S. found Revenue Ruling 84–111 inapplicable and treated the conversion of a partnership into a corporation through a conversion statute as if the partnership conveyed its assets to the corporation in exchange for stock and then distributed the stock to its partners on liquidation (the first option in Revenue Ruling 84–111). This suggests statutory conversions may not be the way to go if partners wish to follow one of the other routes otherwise open under Revenue Ruling 84–111.

To appreciate the consequences of the different choices available under Revenue Ruling 84–111, one must walk through each step of the transactions applying the applicable code sections. To begin the analysis, one could ask whether there is any greater possibility of recognition depending upon the route chosen. As general proposition, the steps in these transactions fall within the non-recognition provisions of Section 351 and Section 731 (which, as discussed in Chapter III, generally allows persons taxed as partners to receive distributions of property tax free from a firm treated for tax purposes as a partnership). Yet, there are exceptions in which there might be recognition depending upon the route chosen. For example, suppose partners have only a small basis in their interests in a partnership, which has a substantial sum of cash on hand. What will happen if they first liquidate the firm before transferring its assets to the corporation for stock? See I.R.C. § 731(a)(1) (can recognize gain if receive cash in excess of basis). Compare either of the other approaches: Do they entail any distribution of cash to the partners?

Next, suppose, among the partnership's assets, there is property with a built-in gain from before its contribution to the partnership—in other words, the partnership received a carryover basis in the contributed property that was less than the value of the property upon its contribution. In this event, could liquidating the partnership and then transferring the assets to the new corporation result in recognition of gain? See I.R.C. §§ 704(c)(1)(B) (contributor of appreciated property to a partnership can recognize gain if such property is distributed to other partners within seven years of its contribution); 737 (contributor of appreciated property to a partnership can recognize gain if he or she receives other property from the partnership within seven years of the contribution). Recall that the discussion of the proposed partnership merger regulations in Chapter III indicated that these provisions could trigger recognition in the case of a partnership merger characterized as a liquidation followed by a transfer of assets. Again, compare either of the other two approaches. Recall that the I.R.S. discussion of its proposed partnership merger regulations pointed out that Sections 704(c)(1)(B) and 737 would not trigger recognition if the partnership transfers its assets to the new firm and then liquidates. The same presumably would be true in a transfer of partnership interests structure.

Now, suppose the contribution of one participant in the venture consists essentially of ongoing services. What would be the impact of liquidating the partnership first, following which this individual obtains stock in exchange for his or her continuing services? In answering this question, do not forget the impact on the other participants if the service provider receives over 20 percent of the stock. *See James v. Commissioner,* reprinted earlier in this chapter. Compare the result if the partners transfer their partnership interests to the corporation in exchange for stock, since partnership interests (even of a services partner) are property. In fact, this suggests a technique of interest to someone, like the Talbots in the *James* case, who faces recognition because of shares going to a co-participant in exchange for services. What would have happened if the Talbots had first formed a joint venture with Mr. James to undertake the project, and then the parties transferred their interests in the joint venture to the corporation for shares? See *United States v. Frazell,* 335 F.2d 487 (5th Cir.1964), *cert. denied,* 380 U.S. 961 (1965) (apparently willing to treat this sort of transaction as coming within Section 351). Watch out, however, for the step transaction doctrine, as well as the caveat in Revenue Ruling 93–27 (reprinted in Chapter III), which suggests that the I.R.S. may seek to tax partnership profits interests received for services, when the interests are transferred within two years of the receipt.

Even more complex prospects for recognition come into play if the partnership transfers its assets to the corporation in exchange for stock and has the corporation assume the partnership's liabilities. Could this trigger recognition by virtue of either Section 357(c) or Section 752(b) (treating a reduction of a partner's share of partnership liabilities as the equivalent of a distribution of cash to the partner)? Would the result be any different if the partners characterize the transaction as a liquidation first or as a transfer of interests by the partners? See the analysis of the similar question in the I.R.S. discussion of its proposed partnership merger regulations in Chapter III.

One additional prospect for recognition might be of concern in view of the earlier discussion regarding the possible impact of resales on Section 351's control requirement. If one follows the route of having the partnership first transfer its assets to the corporation, and then distribute the shares it receives to the partners, the partnership is the transferor but does not end up with the shares. Nevertheless, despite the fact the subsequent distribution is an integral part of the plan, Revenue Ruling 84–111 conveniently concludes the distribution will not result in a failure to meet the control requirement.

In addition to the possibility of recognition, Revenue Ruling 84–111 states that the three methods can yield differences in the basis and holding periods for the assets received by the corporation and the stock received by the former partners. For example, assume that there is a difference between the aggregate basis of the partners in their partnership interests and the partnership's total basis in its assets. (This may have occurred because a partner sold his or her interest in a partnership owning appreciated property and no Section 754 election was in effect—which will result in the partners' aggregate basis in their interests becoming greater than the firm's basis in its assets.) If the partnership transfers its assets to the corporation and then distributes the stock, what will be the corporation's basis in the assets? See I.R.C. § 362(a) (it will keep the partnership's basis). If, however, the partnership liquidates first and the partners then exchange the assets for stock, what is the corporation's basis? Notice, in this situation, one must first apply Section 732(b) to determine the basis the partners obtained for the distributed assets before applying Section 362(a)'s substituted basis rule. This means the assets will pick the partners' basis in their partnership interests.

Revenue Ruling 84–111 also states that the choice of how to incorporate a partnership can produce consequences under a variety of other code sections. The following case provides an example of a problem created by incorporating a partnership through the method of first having the partnership transfer its assets to the corporation for stock—which means that the first shareholder of the corporation is the partnership rather than the partners.

Prizant v. Commissioner of Internal Revenue

30 T.C.M. (CCH) 817 (1971).

■ SIMPSON, JUDGE.

* * * The issues for decision are * * * and (2) whether the petitioners are entitled to treat the loss on certain stock as ordinary loss under Section

1244 of the Internal Revenue Code of 1954, relating to small business stock.

FINDINGS OF FACT

* * *

H.G. Prizant and Co. (the partnership) was a family partnership, organized on July 1, 1952. * * *

In May 1958, H.G. Prizant and Company (the corporation) was formed. * * * At such time, the partnership transferred a substantial amount of its assets and its business activity to the corporation in exchange for 100 shares of $100 par value common capital stock of the corporation. Such stock was continuously held by the partnership until June 30, 1964. The partnership, during the period prior to January 2, 1963, held cash in addition to the common stock of the corporation, and made loans to the corporation during such period in the aggregate amount of $42,000.

On January 2, 1963, at a special joint meeting of the board of directors and the shareholders, the corporation was authorized to increase its capital structure. On the same date, pursuant to a plan conforming with the requirements of Section 1244, the corporation offered for purchase 2,600 shares of common capital stock at a total subscription price of $260,000. * * * 420 shares were issued to the partnership in exchange for cancellation of debts owned the partnership in the amount of $42,000, * * *. On and after January 2, 1963, the partnership transacted no business, and its only assets were 520 shares of the corporation's common capital stock.

* * *

On June 30, 1964, the partnership transferred all of the stock it held in the corporation to [the petitioner the other two partners] * * * in accordance with their respective interests in the partnership. [The petitioner's] * * * share of such stock was 50 shares of the original issue and 105 shares of the stock issued in 1963.

The corporation became insolvent on September 9, 1965, and on their 1965 joint income tax return, the petitioners claimed an ordinary loss deduction in the amount of $10,500 with respect to the worthlessness of the stock issued in 1963.

OPINION

* * *

Section 1244(a) provides in part that "[i]n the case of an individual, a loss on Section 1244 stock issued to such individual or to a partnership" shall be treated as an ordinary loss. Section 1.1244(a)–1(b), Income Tax Regs., states, in part:

(b) Taxpayers entitled to ordinary loss. The allowance of an ordinary loss deduction for a loss on Section 1244 stock is permitted only to the following two classes of taxpayers:

(1) An individual sustaining the loss to whom such stock was issued by a small business corporation, or

(2) An individual who is a partner in a partnership at the time the partnership acquired such stock in an issuance from a small business corporation and whose distributive share of partnership items reflects the loss sustained by the partnership.

In order to claim a deduction under Section 1244 the individual, or the partnership, sustaining the loss, must have continuously held the stock from the date of issuance. * * * An individual who acquires stock from a shareholder by purchase, gift, devise, or in any other manner is not entitled to an ordinary loss under Section 1244 with respect to such stock. Thus, ordinary loss treatment is not available to a partner to whom the stock is distributed by the partnership. * * *

The regulations appear to be based upon the following statements in the conference committee report dealing with Section 1244:

It is understood that in the case of partnerships any losses from small-business stock will be passed through to the partners * * *. Also, since to qualify for the ordinary loss treatment the qualifying stock must be held by the individual or partnership to whom issued, loss on stock issued to a partnership which was distributed to a partner before the loss was sustained would not qualify. (Conf. Rept. No. 2632, 85th Cong. 2d Sess. (1958), 1958–3 C.B. 1188, 1230.)

It is agreed that the stock issued to the partnerships in 1963 qualified as Section 1244 stock. However, the respondent contends that [the petitioner] is not entitled to treat the loss with respect to the stock as an ordinary loss, because the stock was issued to the partnership but transferred to him before the loss was sustained. [The petitioner] does not challenge the validity of the regulations but contends that in substance there was no partnership in 1963 and that the stock was issued to him, his father, and his brother, as co-owners. Thus, the outcome depends upon whether the partnership was still in existence at the time of the issuance of the stock in 1963.

State law is applied in ascertaining the legal relationships between persons. * * * However, the existence of a partnership for Federal income tax purposes is a question to be decided under Federal law. * * * For the purposes of subchapter K (the provisions relating to the tax treatment of partners and partnerships), Section 708(b) provides specific tests for determining whether a partnership has terminated. Such section provides, in part:

(b) Termination—(1) General rule. * * * a partnership shall be considered as terminated only if—

(A) no part of any business, financial operation, or venture of the partnership continues to be carried on by any of its partners in a partnership, or

(B) within a 12–month period there is a sale or exchange of 50 percent or more of the total interest in partnership capital and profits.

The tests set forth in Section 708 have also been applied to determine whether a partnership has terminated under provisions outside Subchapter K. For example such section has been held to govern the question of whether a partnership exists for the purpose of applying the attribution rules of Section 318.

We have held in cases arising under Section 708 that the transfer by a partnership of all of its assets and its business activity to a corporation does not of itself terminate the existence of the partnership for Federal income tax purposes * * * Also, a partnership is not necessarily terminated within the meaning of such section although the primary purpose for which it was formed ceases to exist. * * * Thus, the transfer of its business and substantially all of its assets in 1958 did not terminate the partnership. Moreover, after that transfer, the partnership continued to hold some assets and make loans. These were not acts of individuals but of the partnership. At the time the stock was issued in 1963, the partnership still held notes and common stock of the corporation, and there is no evidence that such notes and such stock did not have income-producing potential. In addition, the evidence indicates that the partners retained their capital accounts in the partnership until dissolution in 1964. The partnership continued to file Federal partnership returns of income. Under the circumstances, it seems clear that for Federal tax purposes, the partnership had not been terminated at the time of the issuance of the stock in 1963 and that the stock was issued to the partnership, not to the individuals.

Furthermore, under Illinois law, a partnership does not cease to exist unless it is terminated. * * * Section 30 of the Illinois Uniform Partnership Act * * * provides:

Effect of dissolution—Continuance to wind up

On dissolution the partnership is not terminated, but continues until the winding up of partnership affairs is completed.

* * *

In the present case, there is no evidence of a dissolution or a winding up prior to the termination of the partnership in 1964, and hence, there has been no showing that the partnership was terminated under Illinois law prior to 1964.

* * *

NOTES

1. As indicated in Chapter I, most new businesses fail. If the participants organized the business as a partnership (or entity treated as a partnership

for income tax purposes) or an S corporation, they can at least take deductions for losses incurred by the venture on its way down. Otherwise, the owners must wait for a deduction until they either sell their shares at a loss or, ultimately, the shares become worthless. *See* I.R.C. § 165(g). Even then, they will find their deduction of limited utility. Normally, a loss on the sale or worthlessness of stock is a capital loss. *See* I.R.C. § 165(f), (g). Such losses can only offset capital gains and a small amount per year ($3,000) of ordinary income. I.R.C. § 1211(b).

Section 1244 provides an exception to this general rule. It allows the owner of "Section 1244 stock," who sells such stock at a loss, or holds it until worthless, to take an ordinary rather than a capital loss deduction. I.R.C. § 1244(a). Several limits exist on this treatment. To begin with, a taxpayer may only claim ordinary losses up to $50,000 in any one year from Section 1244 stock. I.R.C. § 1244(b). (This ceiling increases to $100,000 for married couples filing a joint return.) If the total loss for the year on disposition of Section 1244 stock exceeds this amount, the excess becomes a capital loss. (An individual owning over $50,000 of Section 1244 stock might try to spread the loss into several years by selling shares before they become worthless, but this obviously has practicality problems.)

Section 1244(c)(1)(C) creates a second limitation. For the shareholder to receive ordinary loss treatment, the corporation must not have obtained 50 percent or more of its aggregate gross receipts from various investment sources—such as royalties, rents, dividends, interest and the like—during the five years preceding the loss (or for how many years the company had existed to that point if less than five).

Additional limitations exist on whom the section benefits. Only individuals or partnerships, not trusts or corporations, can obtain the ordinary losses. I.R.C. § 1244(a), (d)(4). *See also Rath v. Commissioner,* 101 T.C. 196 (1993) (shares owned by an S corporation do not qualify for Section 1244 treatment). In addition, just the original recipient of the shares is eligible for this treatment. Treas. Reg. § 1.1244(a)–1(b). This requirement created the problem in *Prizant.* The partnership there received the shares and later distributed them to the partners, who finally claimed the loss. Since the partners were not the original recipients, they did not qualify for Section 1244 treatment. Notice the impact this has on choosing the method for incorporating a partnership. Consider, as well, the impact of the requirement on the rights of shareholders who buy from a firm commitment underwriter (in other words, an underwriter who purchases shares from the corporation to resell to investors).

The section also limits its favorable treatment to shares paid for with cash or property, not services. I.R.C. § 1244(c)(1)(B). (This, of course, creates yet another disadvantage of receiving stock for services.) Section 1244 does not cover stock exchanged for other shares or securities in the corporation. *Id.* Finally, the section only extends to stocks issued by companies which, when they issue the shares, have no more than a certain amount of capital. Specifically, the sum of the consideration the company will receive for the stock in question, plus the total amount it theretofore received in exchange for its previously outstanding stock, as a contribution to capital and as paid in surplus must not be greater than one million dollars. I.R.C. § 1244(c)(3). To the extent the issuance puts the corporation over the one million dollar mark, the company may pick which of the new shares (the total consideration for which will not exceed the maximum) will be Section 1244 stock. Treas. Reg. § 1.1244(c)–2(b)(2).

In addition to these requirements, one might recall that the *Prizant* court referred to the company adopting a "plan" to issue the stock. At the time of this opinion, Section 1244 required the corporation to adopt a formal plan to issue Section 1244 stock. Congress removed this requirement in 1978, which is probably just as well as it was a frequent source of error.

2. In 1993, Congress added another provision, Section 1202, to give favorable treatment to individuals buying stock in small corporations. Section 1202 allows individuals to exclude from their income fifty percent of their capital gains on the sale of qualifying stock. Subsequent reductions in capital gains rates, however, have deprived Section 1202 of much of its utility. The reason is that the reduction of capital gains rates does not apply if the taxpayer claims the fifty percent exclusion under Section 1202. I.R.C. § 1(h)(3)(A)(ii), (4)(A)(ii). Accordingly, Section 1202 can produce an effective tax rate of 14 percent—a 28 percent maximum on capital gains, applied to half as much gain because of Section 1202—which is not that much better than the current capital gains maximum tax rate of 15 percent. (As previously mentioned, however, the reduction in the tax rate on capital gains from twenty 20 to 15 percent will expire, barring further action by Congress, at the end of 2008—at which point Section 1202 will regain its former significance.)

To gain this favorable treatment, the section imposes a number of requirements. Several of the requirements flow from the section's goal of encouraging new long-term investment. For example, the individual must hold the stock for at least five years. I.R.C. § 1202(a). He or she normally must also acquire the stock from the issuing corporation (directly or through an underwriter) rather than buying it from an existing shareholder. I.R.C. § 1202(c)(1). (The statute, however, relaxes this later requirement in a number of circumstances to avoid problems like that in *Prizant*. Specifically, the section treats parties who receive stock by gift, at death or from a partnership in which they were a partner when the firm acquired the stock as if they, rather than their transferor, had acquired the stock originally. I.R.C. § 1202(h).) The recipient may pay for the stock with money, property (except other stock) and, unlike Section 1244, services performed for the corporation (except as an underwriter). I.R.C. § 1202(c)(1)(B). (Suppose parties try to get around these requirements by having the corporation redeem shares not entitled to Section 1202 treatment in order to reissue shares so they do qualify. See I.R.C. § 1202(c)(3) (stock purchased within two years either before or after the corporation buys stock from the purchaser (or a related party), or within one year of a redemption of over five percent of the company's stock, is not entitled to favorable treatment).)

Further restrictions exist upon the nature of the issuing corporation. It must be a C corporation (which, as discussed in Chapter II, might impact the choice of entity for a business). I.R.C. § 1202(c)(2)(A). It must meet the so-called active trade or business requirement. I.R.C. § 1202(c)(2), (e). (This excludes a variety of businesses, such as personal service firms. I.R.C. § 1202(e)(3).) It also must be a "small business," essentially having no more than $50 million in gross assets both before and immediately after the issuance. I.R.C. § 1202(d).

In addition, there is a limit on how much gain any one individual or married couple may subject to the 50 percent exclusion under this section. This limit is no more than $10 million on stock from one corporation, or no more than a ten-fold gain on the stock of any one corporation disposed of per year, whichever is greater. I.R.C. § 1202(b). There also is a limit on who can own the stock. It cannot be owned by a C Corporation. I.R.C. § 1202(a), (g). Finally, there are other limits designed to prevent various abuses. For example, suppose a party transfers appreciated property to a corporation in a Section 351 transaction in exchange for stock. Could he or she hope thereby to turn appreciation on property not subject to 1202 into gain on stock subject to the 50 percent exclusion? See I.R.C. § 1202(i) (giving stock received for property a basis for purpose of the section of no less than the exchanged property's fair market value on the date of the exchange).

In addition to the 50 percent exclusion, there is a second advantage for individuals owning stock meeting the qualifications outlined under Section 1202. Such individuals can defer recognition of income made on the sale of such stock if they held the shares more than six months before the sale and if the individuals reinvest the sale proceeds within 60 days in other stock meeting the requirements of Section 1202. I.R.C.§ 1045.

2. Alternatives to Purchasing Stock

a. *In General*

Costello v. Fazio

256 F.2d 903 (9th Cir.1958).

■ Hamley, Circuit Judge.

Creditors' claims against the bankrupt estate of Leonard Plumbing and Heating Supply, Inc., were filed by J.A. Fazio and Lawrence C. Ambrose. The trustee in bankruptcy objected to these claims, and moved for an order subordinating them to the claims of general unsecured creditors. The referee in bankruptcy denied the motion, and his action was sustained by the district court. The trustee appeals.

The following facts are not in dispute: A partnership known as "Leonard Plumbing and Heating Supply Co." was organized in October, 1948. * * * The capital contributions of the three partners, as they were recorded on the company books in September 1952, totaled $51,620.78, distributed as follows: Fazio, $43,169.61; Ambrose, $6,451.17; and Leonard, $2,000.

In the fall of that year, it was decided to incorporate the business. In contemplation of this step, Fazio and Ambrose, on September 15, 1952, withdrew all but $2,000 apiece of their capital contributions to the business. This was accomplished by the issuance to them, on that date, of partnership promissory notes in the sum of $41,169.61 and $4,451.17, respectively. These were demand notes, no interest being specified. The capital contribution to the partnership business then stood at $6,000—$2,000 for each partner.

The closing balance sheet of the partnership showed current assets to be $160,791.87, and current liabilities at $162,162.22. There were also fixed assets in the sum of $6,482.90, and other assets in the sum of $887.45. The partnership had cash on hand in the sum of $66.66, and an overdraft at the bank in the amount of $3,422.78.

* * *

The net sales of the partnership during its last year of operations were $389,543.72, as compared to net sales of $665,747.55 in the preceding year. A net loss of $22,521.34 was experienced during this last year, as compared to a net profit of $40,935.12 in the year ending September 30, 1951.

Based on the reduced capitalization of the partnership, the corporation was capitalized for six hundred shares of no par value common stock valued at ten dollars per share. Two hundred shares were issued to each of the three partners in consideration of the transfer to the corporation of their interests in the partnership. Fazio became president, and Ambrose, secretary-treasurer of the new corporation. Both were directors. The corporation assumed all liabilities of the partnership, including the notes to Fazio and Ambrose.

In June 1954, after suffering continued losses, the corporation made an assignment to the San Francisco Board of Trade for the benefit of creditors. On October 8, 1954, it filed a voluntary petition in bankruptcy. At this time, the corporation was not indebted to any creditors whose obligations were incurred by the pre-existing partnership, saving the promissory notes issued to Fazio and Ambrose.

Fazio filed a claim against the estate in the sum of $34,147.55, based on the promissory note given to him when the capital of the partnership was reduced. Ambrose filed a similar claim in the sum of $7,871.17. The discrepancy between these amounts and the amounts of the promissory notes is due to certain set-offs and transfers not here in issue.

* * *

A hearing was held before the referee in bankruptcy. In addition to eliciting the above recounted facts, three expert witnesses called by the trustee, and one expert witness called by the claimants, expressed opinions on various phases of the transaction.

Clifford V. Heimbucher, a certified public accountant and management consultant, called by the trustee, expressed the view that, at the time of incorporation, capitalization was inadequate. He further stated that, in incorporating a business already in existence, where the approximate amount of permanent capital needed has been established by experience, normal procedure called for continuing such capital in the form of common or preferred stock.

Stating that only additional capital needed temporarily is normally set up as loans, Heimbucher testified that "* * * the amount of capital employed in the business was at all times substantially more than the $6,000 employed in the opening of the corporation." He also expressed the opinion that, at the time of incorporation, there was "very little hope (of financial success) in view of the fact that for the year immediately preceding the opening of the corporation, losses were running a little less than $2,000 a month. * * *"

* * *

Robert H. Laborde, Jr., a certified public accountant, has handled the accounting problems of the partnership and corporation. He was called by the trustee as an adverse witness. * * * Laborde readily conceded that the transaction whereby Fazio and Ambrose obtained promissory notes from the partnership was for the purpose of transferring a capital account into a loan or debt account. He stated that this was done in contemplation of the formation of the corporation, and with knowledge that the partnership was losing money.

The prime reason for incorporating the business, according to Laborde, was to protect the personal interest of Fazio, who had made the greatest capital contribution to the business. In this connection, it was pointed out that the "liabilities on the business as a partnership were pretty heavy." There was apparently also a tax angle. Laborde testified that it was contemplated that the notes would be paid out of the profits of the business. He agreed that, if promissory notes had not been issued, the profits would have been distributed only as dividends, and that as such would have been taxable.

* * *

On this appeal, the trustee advances two grounds for reversal of the district court order. The first of these is that claims of controlling shareholders will be deferred or subordinated to outside creditors where a corporation in bankruptcy has not been adequately or honestly capitalized, or has been managed to the prejudice of creditors, or where to do otherwise would be unfair to creditors.

As a basis for applying this asserted rule in the case before us, the trustee challenges most of the findings of fact [that the corporation was adequately capitalized].

* * *

It does not require the confirmatory opinion of experts to determine from this data that the corporation was grossly undercapitalized. In the year immediately preceding incorporation, net sales aggregated $390,000. In order to handle such a turnover, the partners apparently found that capital in excess of $50,000 was necessary. They actually had $51,620.78 in the business at that time. Even then, the business was only "two jumps ahead of the wolf." A net loss of $22,000 was sustained in that year; there was only $66.66 in the bank; and there was an overdraft of $3,422.78.

Yet, despite this precarious financial condition, Fazio and Ambrose withdrew $45,620.78 of the partnership capital—more than eighty-eight percent of the total capital. The $6,000 capital left in the business was only one-sixty-fifth of the last annual net sales. All this is revealed by the books of the company.

But, if there is need to confirm this conclusion that the corporation was gross undercapitalized, such confirmation is provided by three of the four experts who testified. The fourth expert, called by appellees, did not express an opinion to the contrary.

We therefore hold that the factual conclusion of the referee, that the corporation was adequately capitalized at the time of its organization, is clearly erroneous.

The factual conclusion of the trial court, that the claimants, in withdrawing capital from the partnership in contemplation of incorporation, did not act for their own personal or private benefit and to the detriment of the corporation or of its stockholders and creditors, is based upon the same accounting data and expert testimony.

Laborde, testifying for the claimants, made it perfectly clear that the depletion of the capital account in favor of a debt account was for the purpose of equalizing the capital investments of the partners and to reduce tax liability when there were profits to distribute. It is therefore certain, contrary to the finding just noted, that, in withdrawing this capital, Fazio and Ambrose did act for their own personal and private benefit.

It is equally certain, from the undisputed facts, that in so doing they acted to the detriment of the corporation and its creditors. The best evidence of this is what happened to the business after incorporation, and what will happen to its creditors if the reduction in capital is allowed to stand. The likelihood that business failure would result from such undercapitalization should have been apparent to anyone who knew the company's financial and business history and who had access to its balance sheet and profit and loss statements. Three expert witnesses confirmed this view, and none expressed a contrary opinion.

Accordingly, we hold that the factual conclusion, that the claimants, in withdrawing capital, did not act for their own personal or private benefit and to the detriment of the corporation and creditors, is clearly erroneous.

Recasting the facts in the light of what is said above, the question which appellant presents is this:

Where, in connection with the incorporation of a partnership, and for their own personal and private benefit, two partners who are to become officers, directors, and controlling stockholders of the corporation, convert the bulk of their capital contributions into loans, taking promissory notes, thereby leaving the partnership and succeeding corporation grossly undercapitalized, to the detriment of the corporation and its creditors, should their claims against the estate of the subsequently bankrupted corporation be subordinated to the claims of the general unsecured creditors?

The question almost answers itself.

In allowing and disallowing claims, courts of bankruptcy apply the rules and principles of equity jurisprudence. *Pepper v. Litton,* 308 U.S. 295, 304, 60 S.Ct. 238, 84 L.Ed. 281. Where the claim is found to be inequitable, it may be set aside (*Pepper v. Litton, supra*), or subordinated to the claims of other creditors. As stated in *Taylor v. Standard Gas Co.,* * * * 306, U.S. at page 315, 59 S.Ct. at page 547, the question to be determined when the plan or transaction which gives rise to a claim is challenged as inequitable is "whether, within the bounds of reason and fairness, such a plan can be justified."

Where, as here, the claims are filed by persons standing in a fiduciary relationship to the corporation, another test which equity will apply is "whether or not under all the circumstances the transaction carries the earmarks of an arm's length bargain." *Pepper v. Litton, supra,* 308 U.S. at page 306, 60 S.Ct. at page 245.

Under either of these tests, the transaction here in question stands condemned.

Appellees argue that more must be shown than mere undercapitalization if the claims are to be subordinated. Much more than mere undercapitalization was shown here. Persons serving in a fiduciary relationship to the corporation actually withdrew capital already committed to the business, in the face of recent adverse financial experience. They stripped the business of eighty-eight percent of its stated capital at a time when it had a minus working capital and had suffered substantial business losses. This was done for personal gain, under circumstances which charge them with knowledge that the corporation and its creditors would be endangered. Taking advantage of their fiduciary position, they thus sought to gain equality of treatment with general creditors.

In *Taylor v. Standard Gas & Electric Co.,* 306 U.S. 307, 59 S.Ct. 543, 83 L.Ed. 669, and some other cases, there was fraud and mismanagement present in addition to undercapitalization. Appellees argue from this that fraud and mismanagement must always be present if claims are to be subordinated in a situation involving undercapitalization.

This is not the rule.

* * *

Nor is the fact that the business, after being stripped of necessary capital, was able to survive long enough to have a turnover of creditors a mitigating circumstance. The inequitable conduct of appellees consisted not in acting to the detriment of creditors then known, but in acting to the detriment of present or future creditors, whoever they may be.

In our opinion, it was error to affirm the order of the referee denying the motion to subordinate the claims in question. * * *

NOTES

1. Why did the three owners of the company in *Costello* cast the bulk of their contributions to the corporation in the form of loans rather than purchases of stock? Perhaps it was to gain some advantage upon the company's bankruptcy. Shareholder loans to a corporation, unlike a partner's loan to an ordinary partnership, can have a significantly different effect than a stock purchase should the business fail. One impact is between the owners themselves. Shareholders who lend money are entitled to repayment of the loan prior to the company making any liquidating distribution on stock. *But see Taylor v. Standard Gas & Electric Co.*, 306 U.S. 307 (1939) (equitable subordination of parent corporation's claim as a creditor of its subsidiary in favor of both outside creditors and preferred shareholders of the subsidiary). At the same time, shareholders lack a partner's obligation to return whatever is necessary to cover his or her share of losses. The result is to the shift a greater portion of the first losses to those owners who put more of their investment in the form of stock purchases rather than loans. Given the small total amount of stock purchases relative to loans in *Costello,* however, this effect was not significant there. The shareholders' claim in *Costello* suggests a second effect. This is to allow the corporation's owners to obtain a return of part of their investment on a par with outside creditors, rather than taking only what is left after the outside creditors get paid. (Recall, this potential exists with loans by limited partners, partners in a limited liability partnership, and members of a limited liability company as well. It is irrelevant for ordinary partners, who face unlimited personal liability for debts of the firm.) The court's holding in *Costello* shows this tactic will not always work. Still, the *Costello* result may be the exception, rather than the norm. *E.g., Obre v. Alban Tractor Co.,* 228 Md. 291, 179 A.2d 861 (1962). The more typical limit on this advantage would be the refusal of outside creditors to loan money in a situation, like *Costello,* where shareholders put in most of their investment as a loan. Instead, the outside creditors may demand the shareholders agree to subordinate the shareholders' loans, or to give the outside creditors some security for repayment of the outside creditors' loans. Either will put payment of the outside creditors ahead of the shareholders' unsecured loans should the business fail. Of course, the facts in *Costello* show there are some prospective creditors (usually trade creditors) who do not make such demands. Nevertheless, was this really the primary reason for the loans in *Costello?* After all, if the three owners expected to go bankrupt, why did they continue the business?

Examine the capital accounts the three partners in *Costello* had in their partnership before they began to recast much of their investment as loans. Consider, as well, how, under the U.P.A., they shared profits and control in their partnership, barring contrary agreement (of which there is no indication). What problem did they face if they made all their investment in the new corporation in the form of common stock purchases—assuming, as apparently the case, they wanted to keep their interests in profits, in management and upon liquidation the same vis-a-vis each other as in the partnership? Does this indicate that a second use of shareholder loans—one suggested earlier in the excerpt from Professor Herwitz' article—may have been a major motive for the loans in *Costello?* Did the court's holding defeat this purpose?

One possible motivation shareholder loans have in common with loans by partners is both ordinarily—albeit this is subject to agreement—entitle the lender to receive interest. Is there any advantage (putting aside tax treatment for the time being) to receiving interest rather than a greater profit share (or share of dividends in a corporation)? Traditionally, but again subject to agreement, interest represents a fixed obligation of the firm—payable regardless of whether the firm has earnings, and in the same amount no matter what the business earns. This gives the lender greater certainty of income (or less risk), since the company must pay the interest even if it has no earnings (subject to the practical limit of running out of money to pay). At the same time, should the company do very well, the lender gets no extra return. From the standpoint of those holding more shares, the situation looks the opposite. Should the business do poorly, they face greater risk of receiving nothing (should earnings not exceed interest), or worse, having their investment depleted to make interest payments. On the other hand, should the business do very well, those with more stock gain a greater share of the rewards. This concept is often referred to as leverage. Its utility lies in the fact that individuals do not all place the same value on certainty versus amount of income. Some persons are risk averse and much prefer a guaranteed return; others are more willing to gamble for a greater gain. Mixing loans (paying fixed interest) with stock purchases allows parties to trade a bit more certainty of income for some, in exchange for a greater share of larger earnings should the company do very well for others. The same trade exists through the use of fixed salaries and other alternatives to dividends discussed later in this chapter. In a less extreme form, it is also the underlying idea behind dividend preferences.

One final difference between loans and stock purchases is loans presumably require repayment. Hence, loans could allow for a more temporary investment. Of course, some loans are quite long-term, while the corporation is not powerless to repurchase stock.

2. Against these advantages, shareholder loans, particularly if large in amount relative to stock purchases, can create several problems. One difficulty is an outgrowth of the leverage concept just discussed. Loans normally impose fixed obligations to pay interest. Also, the company presumably must repay the principal at the agreed time(s). If the company lacks the earnings to pay the interest or principal, such payment then must come out of the shareholders' investment, or even out of borrowed money.

In either event, the result is to sap funds the firm may need to achieve profitability. Another problem also follows from the previous discussion. The larger the proportion of shareholder loans to equity investment, the more difficult it may become for the company to obtain credit from outside sources. Finally, the *Costello* opinion indicates how courts look askance at an excessive amount of shareholder debt relative to equity. If the court subordinates the loan, as done in *Costello,* the shareholders are no worse off by virtue of the court's action than they would have been had they purchased stock rather than loaned the money to begin with. (They are worse off, however, than they would be had they loaned a smaller portion of their investment and the court respected the smaller loan.) Yet, the danger exists that courts may go beyond subordinating excessive shareholder loans. A thinly capitalized corporation could provide grounds for a court to disregard the corporate entity altogether and hold the shareholders personally liable for the firm's debts. *E.g., Automotriz Del Golfo De California v. Resnick,* 47 Cal.2d 792, 306 P.2d 1 (1957). *But see Arnold v. Phillips,* 117 F.2d 497 (5th Cir.1941), *cert. denied,* 313 U.S. 583 (1941) (suggesting subordination should be a sufficient remedy when undercapitalization is due to excessive shareholder loans).

3. The terms of shareholder loans, like any loans, are a matter of contract—which normally will cover the subjects of interest, time of repayment and security for repayment. Loans to a business may contain several variations on these terms not as commonly found in a non-business setting. For example, sometimes the parties may wish to decrease the leverage effect. One way is to tie interest to earnings; for instance, making interest payments only due when the company has the earnings to cover them. Alternatively, the loan agreement may give the lender the right to convert the debt instrument into stock. In this manner, the owner of the debt instrument starts off with the advantages of a lender—including a fixed return and priority on payment if things go wrong. Should the business do very well, however, the owner of the instrument may exercise his or her option to convert; in other words, to release the corporation from its obligation to repay the debt with further interest, in exchange for receiving stock from the company at a price set by the original agreement. This stock gives its recipient a larger share in the company's growing earnings. (Some of the drafting questions raised with conversion rights are covered later in this chapter in the discussion of convertible preferred stock.) Security for repayment is closely tied in with the overall subject of priority between creditors to receive money should the company liquidate. Shareholders might obtain a mortgage on corporate assets as security for their loans—attempting to gain payment ahead of (rather than sharing pro-rata with) outside creditors. More likely, outside creditors will demand the mortgage, or else force the shareholders to subordinate the shareholders' loans (in other words, agree to take payment on liquidation only after the corporation completely pays off the outside creditor). Mortgages on the assets of a business often create added planning questions because of the need for firms to constantly turn over many of their assets in the course of business. Creditors also might seek to protect their loans by controlling actions of the

business, and even determining who runs it. (In this regard, note that Cal. Corp. Code § 204(a)(7) and Del. Gen. Corp. Law § 221 both allow the articles to grant debt holders the right to vote.) Can a shareholder, who also makes a loan, gain any advantage regarding control of the company by placing provisions regarding management in a loan contract, rather than in a shareholders agreement? Consider this question when reading the material on shareholder agreements later in this chapter. Finally, with respect to time of repayment, a corporation, like an individual, may wish the right to retire the debt early. (This could allow the company, for instance, to refinance should interest rates decline.) This is often referred to as redeeming the debt instrument.

4. Stockholders can obtain many of the advantages of shareholder loans by leasing assets to the company, rather than exchanging them (or the money to buy them) for stock. Fixed rent payments create the same leverage effect as fixed interest. The leasing shareholder is entitled to his or her property back at the end of the lease (which could include liquidation), thereby achieving both the objectives of severing rights to return of property from the allocation of profit, and allocating losses to those who make a greater investment through the purchase of stock. If the business fails, the leased property is not subject to the claims of the corporation's creditors—albeit the assets of the bankrupt estate may include the right to assume the lease notwithstanding any provision in the lease purportedly terminating the lessee's rights upon bankruptcy (11 U.S.C. § 365). Balanced against these advantages, leases create the same disadvantages as loans. In fact, there might be a somewhat greater danger of a court disregarding the corporate entity if the company leases most of its assets from its shareholders, than there is if the company acquires most of its assets through shareholder loans, since, with leases, the intermediate remedy of subordination is not available. *See Luckenbach S.S. Co. v. W.R. Grace & Co.*, 267 Fed. 676 (4th Cir.1920).

It is also useful to compare the effects of leasing property to a corporation, with those discussed earlier for leasing or loaning property to non-corporate entities. Most of the differences in practical impact between loaning and contributing property to non-corporate entities remain in broad outline applicable with a corporation. For instance, compare what happens if property belonging to the corporation appreciates in value, versus what the result is if the corporation leased the property from a shareholder.

b. *Tax Aspects*

Bradshaw v. United States

231 Ct.Cl. 144, 683 F.2d 365 (1982).

■ BENNETT, JUDGE.

* * *

Both parties agree that there are only two questions for decision. The first is whether the transfer of real property to Castlewood[, Inc. (Castlewood)], * * * in exchange for installment obligations; was a sale of the property to that corporation or, instead, was either a transfer of property to a controlled corporation solely in exchange for stock or securities of that corporation within the meaning of Section 351 or a capital contribution to that corporation.

* * *

I

On January 6, 1961, Thomas E. Swift (Thomas) purchased a tract of land, consisting of approximately 200 acres, in Dalton, Whitfield County, Georgia, for $60,000. Two dispositions of property out of this 200 acres were made by Thomas in the summer of 1968. The consolidated cases herein concern one of these dispositions, the transfer of 40.427 acres, subsequently known as Castlewood Subdivision (the subdivision), to Castlewood on July 29, 1968. The conservative fair market value of the subdivision on the date of transfer was $250,000. Thomas' adjusted basis in this portion of the property was $8,538. In exchange for the transfer, Thomas received from Castlewood five promissory notes (the Castlewood notes), each in the principal amount of $50,000 and bearing interest at the rate of 4 percent per annum. The first note matured on January 29, 1971, with each successive note maturing at 1-year intervals. Thomas received no down payment for the transfer, and no security or other collateral was taken for the purchase price. He elected to report his gain from the transaction on the installment method pursuant to Section 453(b).

* * *

Consequently, Castlewood was organized and incorporated on July 29, 1968, under the laws of the State of Georgia, to obtain, subdivide, develop and sell lots in the subdivision. On July 29, 1968 Castlewood issued its Certificate No. 1, representing 50 shares of common stock, to Thomas in exchange for the transfer to the corporation of an automobile valued at $4,500. At all times relevant herein, Thomas was the sole shareholder of Castlewood and was responsible for conducting its business affairs. * * *

The expected source of income and anticipated profit of Castlewood, and the expected source of payment of the five notes, with interest, was from the sale of the lots in the subdivision. * * *

Because of the growing character of, and need for housing in, the Dalton, Georgia area, the value of the subdivision was, at all times relevant herein, increasing. In fact, the character and location of the subdivision was such that the property could reasonably be anticipated to be readily marketable at its development. If, however, the subdivision had not been developed, or if the development process had been slowed, Castlewood could have borrowed the money against the property to pay off the notes.

Prior to the creation of Castlewood and the transfer of the property thereto, Thomas estimated that development costs for the subdivision would be approximately $50,000. He anticipated that he would have a ready source of funds from C & S Concrete Products Company © & S) to meet these development expenses. C & S was a partnership formed by Thomas, which was engaged in the manufacture of concrete products used in the building trade. At all times relevant herein, C & S was wholly owned directly or beneficially by Thomas, his wife, Frances, and their three children, Jolana, Lori and Stephen. Thomas' drawing account on C & S was, in essence, his personal bank account. Thomas had no personal bank account, and when using funds from his drawing account at C & S, he was in effect using his own personal funds.

As expected, the corporation's development expenses were primarily funded through advances from the partnership, totalling $34,116.10, at various times from August 31, 1968 through August 10, 1970. These advances were treated as interest-free loans by both parties and were charged to an open account on the books of C & S. The partnership took no collateral or other security interest. The loans were repaid in four installments over an 8–year period.

* * * From August 1970 to April 1973, Castlewood sold 16 lots in Tract I and two lots in Tract II for an aggregate sales price of $239,880. * * * The property sold had an allocated land cost (of the $250,000 purchase price) and development cost of $159,378.39, yielding a net return to the corporation of $80,501.11. Castlewood reported sales of lots on its federal income tax returns for the fiscal years ended July 31, 1971, July 31, 1972, and July 31, 1973.

* * *

By statutory notice of deficiency dated September 20, 1976, the Commissioner determined that additional income tax was due from Castlewood for its 1971 and 1972 tax years, for the reason that the transfer of the subdivision to that corporation by Thomas was not a sale, as treated by the corporation on its tax returns, but rather a transfer of property solely in exchange for stock or securities within the meaning of Section 351. Thus, he concluded that, pursuant to Section 362, Castlewood's predevelopment basis in the property was equal to that of the transferor immediately before the transfer, or $8,538. This, in turn, increased Castlewood's taxable income on sales of lots.

* * *

II

The first question concerns the proper tax treatment of Thomas' transfer of the subdivision to Castlewood in exchange for the five $50,000 promissory notes. If the transfer is treated as a sale, as plaintiff contends, then Castlewood's adjusted basis for its sales of the lots from the subdivision property would include the $250,000 purchase price (a cost basis), it would be allowed deductions of interest paid on the notes and its taxable income would be generally as shown on its returns for the years in issue. However, if, as defendant claims, the transfer was not a sale but was either a transfer under Section 351 or a contribution to the corporation's capital, then Castlewood's adjusted basis in the lots sold would be reduced to Thomas' original basis (a carryover basis) pursuant to Section 362, it would be denied deductions of the interest paid on the notes and its taxable income would be generally as shown on the notice of deficiency issued with respect to it.

The sale versus capital contribution problem arises from a situation which often confronts taxpayers with holdings in undeveloped real estate. It is not uncommon for a landowner with a large tract of land suitable for development to want to freeze as capital gains the appreciation in the value of the property that has accrued during its ownership. While an outright sale of the property achieves this result, it also deprives the landowner of any participation in the profits to be reaped from its ultimate development. On the other hand, if the landowner develops and sells the property himself, he runs the risk of being treated as a dealer of the property and any gain generated through sales, including the gain associated with the land's appreciation in value while undeveloped, is taxable to him at ordinary income rates. * * *

In the face of such a dilemma, taxpayers have devised an apparently viable solution. By selling the real property to a controlled corporation, they can realize their capital gain on the appreciation which has accrued during their ownership and, at the same time, preserve their opportunity to later participate in the developmental profits as shareholders of the development corporation. Moreover, the corporation obtains a cost basis in the real property, thereby reducing the amount of ordinary income to be received from subsequent sales.

Not unexpectedly, the Commissioner has repeatedly challenged the characterization of such a transaction as a sale, instead maintaining that the transfer is, in reality, a capital contribution and that the transferee corporation is only entitled to a carryover basis for the property. * * * The two principal reasons asserted for denying the desired tax treatment to the corporation have their origin in the dual subparts of Section 362(a).[16] While the main thesis is that Section 351 governs such a transaction and that the corporation's basis for the property is to be determined pursuant to Section 362(a)(1), it is also maintained that, regardless of the applicability of Section 351, the transfer to the corporation is, in substance, a contribution

16. Section 362(a) provides:

"If property was acquired on or after June 22, 1954, by a corporation—

"(1) in connection with a transaction to which Section 351 (relating to transfer of property to corporation controlled by transferor) applies, or

"(2) as paid-in surplus or as a contribution to capital,

"then the basis shall be the same as it would be in the hands of the transferor, increased in the amount of gain recognized to the transferor on such transfer."

to capital and that the adjusted basis for the property is to be determined under Section 362(a)(2).

* * *

The proper characterization of a transaction, as a "sale" or a "capital contribution," is a question of fact to be decided as of the time of the transfer on the basis of all of the objective evidence. * * *

In this case, the objective evidence points to a sale. First, and foremost, the price paid for the subdivision reflected its actual fair market value. Since it has been stipulated that the value of the subdivision was $250,000, the very amount for which it was sold to Castlewood, the transfer cannot be considered a "pretextuous device" to divert the earnings and profits of the corporation, otherwise taxable as ordinary income, into sales proceeds taxable as capital gain. * * *

Additionally, the various formalities of a sale were strictly observed. The five instruments involved constituted negotiable instruments in the form of "notes" under Georgia law, * * * contained an unqualified obligation to pay the principal amount, with fixed maturity dates ranging from two and one-half to six and one-half years after the date of sale and bore a reasonable rate of interest. The notes were not subordinated to general corporate creditors and contained a means for collection at maturity, which was never utilized as the principal and interest were always paid as due until the Commissioner challenged the tax treatment of those payments. On these bases, the notes contained all of the traditional elements of sales-generated debt.

Even so, defendant asks that upon consideration of the economic substance of the transfer, the transaction be recast as a capital contribution. * * *

* * * Rephrasing defendant's position, we are asked to find that the degree of risk herein was of the type normally associated with a capital contribution. Thus stated, the salient inquiry is whether the notes occupied the position of equity, the assets and prospects of the business being unable to assure payment of the debt according to its terms.

Admittedly, the stipulated facts show Castlewood to have been a "thin" corporation. Its initial capitalization consisted entirely of an automobile valued at $4,500. The corporation then issued five notes, each in the face amount of $50,000, in consideration for the subdivision property. While an additional $3,200 was contributed to Castlewood 4 months later, in practical terms it had no funds of its own with which to conduct business, instead relying on advances totalling over $34,000 from C & S to develop the property. It cannot be refuted that Castlewood has a very high ratio of debt to equity. But the mere fact that a corporation is or is not thinly capitalized does not, per se, control the character of the transaction. * * * If the corporation is adequately capitalized for its intended purpose, then we are not prevented from treating the notes as valid debt.

The facts reveal that in addition to its formal capitalization, Castlewood anticipated having access to, did have access to, and utilized funds in the form of loans from C & S, the partnership owned by Thomas and his family, which served as Thomas' personal bank account. * * * Given these resources, which were certainly adequate to finance the level of development activities undertaken, * * * there was little reason for the corporation to maintain a large surplus of liquid capital. Under the circumstances, we cannot say that undercapitalization is fatal to plaintiff's position.

Integrally related to this discussion, as defendant recognizes, is the nature or quality of the risk assumed by the transferor. However, unlike defendant, we do not find the fact that what was sold to Castlewood was unimproved real estate to be necessarily indicative of a high degree of risk. Concomitantly, nor do we view repayment of the Castlewood notes to have been dependent upon the success of the business. * * * It is of prime importance that the property was, at all times, saleable in its undeveloped condition * * * Moreover, at all times the value of the property was increasing, irrespective of its development, and, if necessary, the corporation could have borrowed the money against the property pay off the notes. * * * From the beginning, there existed a reasonable assurance of repayment of the notes regardless of the success of the business. To us, this is further indicia that the notes were debt, not equity. The facts just do not support the inference that, in holding the Castlewood notes, Thomas was assuming the risk of loss normally associated with equity participation.

* * *

NOTES

1. As *Bradshaw* illustrates, transferring property to a corporation in exchange for anything other than stock raises further questions under Section 351. Section 351(a) provides non-recognition only if a person exchanges property solely for the corporation's stock. What if the transferor receives both stock and cash or other property from the company? Despite the language of Section 351(a), receipt of money or other property along with the company's stock—this additional consideration is often referred to as "boot"—does not take the entire exchange out of Section 351. Instead, Section 351(b) requires recognition of gain (but not loss) just to the extent of the boot received. In other words, the transferor recognizes the lesser of the amount of boot (the sum of money and value of other property) received, or his or her gain on the exchange. The Internal Revenue Service calls for measuring and characterizing gain separately on each asset transferred to the corporation, disregarding any losses and any boot allocated to loss assets. Rev.Rul. 68–55, 1968–1 C.B. 140. For this purpose, the Service deems the boot to be allocated in exchange for the assets in proportion to the assets' fair market values.

2. In *Bradshaw,* the transferor received notes from the corporation rather than stock in exchange for his property. What is the effect under Section 351? Before assuming immediate recognition up to the present fair market value of the notes, consider the impact of Section 453. This section allows a

taxpayer, who sells property in exchange for payments extending for more than one tax year, to spread out reporting his or her gain on the sale so each installment carries its proportionate share of the overall gain. I.R.C. § 453(c). The result is that an individual transferring property to a corporation in exchange for the company's promise to pay normally recognizes gain, even in the absence of Section 351, only as the corporation pays off the debt. *See* Prop. Treas. Reg. § 1.453–1(f)(3)(ii).

Several caveats exist with respect to the application of Section 453. For instance, installment treatment is not available for the sale of inventory or to spread recapture income—which may be a problem when incorporating a going business. I.R.C. § 453(b)(2)(B), (i). Further, if the corporation's debt instruments are readily tradeable in established securities markets—typically not the case when forming a new corporation—then installment reporting is not available. I.R.C. § 453(f)(4), (5). At the other extreme, the payments called for may be highly contingent, rendering it difficult to determine both what gain the seller realized and how to spread the gain among the payments. In this situation, a seller may consider opting out of installment reporting—which Section 453(d) allows if affirmatively elected in the seller's tax return for the year of the sale—and, instead, arguing for open transaction treatment. On occasions in which the value of an obligation cannot be ascertained, courts have allowed the seller to recognize gain as he or she receives actual payment on the obligation, and, in marked contrast to installment reporting, only after the payments have returned all of the seller's basis. *E.g., McShain v. Commissioner,* 71 T.C. 998 (1979). *But see* I.R.C. § 453(j)(2); Temp. Treas. Reg. § 15A.453–1(d)(2)(iii) (precluding open treatment except in rare and extraordinary situations in which the value of the obligation cannot reasonably be ascertained, and instead generally requiring valuation despite the contingency by looking, for example, to the fair market value of the property sold; also precluding delay in recognition upon the receipt of contingent obligations by virtue of arguments predicated on cash or accrual method of accounting). Finally, note Section 453A may require a seller to pay the government interest on tax the seller defers by using installment reporting when the sale price exceeds $150,000, and the seller's total outstanding installment obligations during a year exceed $5 million.

3. In *Bradshaw,* the taxpayer, not the I.R.S., argued against application of Section 351. Why? One reason a taxpayer may have for wishing to avoid Section 351 is if he or she can then recognize a loss on the exchange. *But see* I.R.C. § 267(a)(1), (b)(2) (disallowing any deduction for losses incurred by a shareholder in a sale of property to a corporation in which he or she owns more than 50 percent of the outstanding stock). This was not the motivation in *Bradshaw.* Rather, the concern there lay in the effect a Section 351 transaction has on the corporation's basis in the property received.

As with Section 721, the *quid pro quo* for non-recognition under Section 351 is a substituted basis. Normally, property received in an exchange takes on a basis equal to the value of what each party gave up for it (I.R.C. § 1012), which, assuming an equal exchange, means the exchanged property will receive a basis equal to its fair market value at the time of the transfer. In a Section 351 exchange, however, the corporation retains the transferor's basis in the property the corporation receives (increased by the amount of gain the transferor recognizes if, for instance, he or she receives boot). I.R.C. § 362(a). (Needless to say, the transferor's basis may have been greater or less than the fair market value of the property at the time of the transfer.) The transferor obtains a basis in the stock he or she receives equal to his or her basis in the transferred property. I.R.C. § 358(a). If the transferor receives boot, this increases his or her basis in the stock received by the amount of gain recognized, and decreases the basis by the value of the boot—the boot picking up a basis equal to its value. I.R.C. § 358(a)(2).

As noted in the earlier discussion of incorporating a going business, often the corporation will assume the transferor's liabilities as part of the exchange of property for stock. The corporation's assumption of the transferor's liabilities in a Section 351 exchange decreases the transferor's basis in the stock received by the amount of liabilities assumed. I.R.C. § 358(d). This creates the prospect of a negative basis if the corporation assumes liabilities greater in amount than the transferor's basis in the exchanged property. By causing the transferor to recognize gain equal to any such excess, and thereby increasing his or her basis by this amount, Section 357(c) prevents such a negative basis. As noted in the earlier discussion of incorporating a going business, Section 357(c)(3) excludes liabilities producing a deduction when paid from the recognition requirement of Section 357(c). Section 358(d) matches this by not decreasing basis for the assumption of such debts.

Showing, however, that no nice deed by Congress in the tax arena goes unpunished, the fact that Section 358(d) does not reduce basis when the corporation assumes obligations covered by Section 357(c)(3) not only facilitates contributions to corporations, but also produced schemes designed to achieve immediate tax reduction. The schemes typically involved having the corporation assume obligations covered by Section 357(c)(3), which, because the corporation was stuck with the burden to pay a future claim, lowered the economic value of the stock received in the Section 351 exchange. At the same time, because of Section 358(d), the assumption did not lower the transferor's basis in the stock the transferor received. The resulting gap between the economic value of the stock received, versus the recipient's basis in the stock, produced a built-in loss for tax purposes, which the recipient could quickly recognize by selling the stock. Later, the corporation would claim a deduction upon paying off the assumed obligation. The end result was to double the tax benefit of paying claims assumed by the corporation in a Section 351 exchange. (Recall a similar strategy involving partnerships.) To prevent this abuse with corporations, Congress added Section 358(h). Section 358(h) prevents Section 358(d) from leaving the basis of the stock received in a Section 351 exchange above the stock's fair market value, except when the liability assumed is either from a trade or business transferred to the corporation, or related to assets all of which are transferred to the corporation.

In any event, these basis rules create the potential for doubling the taxable gain should the corporation sell appreciated property received in a Section 351 exchange and the shareholder sell his or her stock. Avoiding the potential doubling of future taxable gain as a result of a Section 351 exchange concerned the taxpayer in *Bradshaw* less, however, than did another reason for obtaining a higher basis. He hoped by recognizing a capital gain now on transferring the property to the company, to lower the ordinary income the corporation later faced upon sale of the property as part of its trade or business. (The company, of course, has no gain on buying property for cash or its debt.) Using recognition to increase basis might also trade immediate capital gains for a later reduction in ordinary income to the extent it raises depreciation deductions. *But see* I.R.C. § 1239 (recharacterizing gain on sale of depreciable property as ordinary income in transactions between a corporation and a majority shareholder).

One other factor might create an incentive for seeking a higher basis by avoiding Section 351. Can a transferor defer recognition by virtue of Section 453, and still obtain an immediate increase in basis for the corporation? The proposed regulations note that under Section 362(a) the company cannot receive an increased basis by virtue of giving the transferor debt instruments which constitute boot until the transferor recognizes income. Prop. Treas. Reg. § 1.453–1(f)(3)(ii). If, however, one can separate out a sale to which Section 351 (and, hence, Section 362) will not apply at all, presumably the corporation can receive a basis equal to fair market value despite the delay in the transferor's recognition. *But see* I.R.C. §§ 453(e) (requiring a person who sells to a related party—such as a corporation in which the seller owns a majority of the shares—generally to treat the amount realized by the buyer on reselling the property within two years as if received by the original seller, unless the seller can show there was no tax avoidance purpose for the transaction), and 453(g) (generally denying installment treatment for the sale of depreciable property to a related party, and denying the buyer the ability to increase its basis in the property before the seller recognizes the corresponding gain, unless the seller establishes there was no tax avoidance motive for the sale).

Suppose, instead of dealing with property whose value exceeds its basis at the time of the Section 351 exchange, the transfer involves property whose value is less than its basis at the time. Showing an uncharitable lack of symmetry, Section 362(e)(2) prevents the doubling of loss that could otherwise occur if the corporation thereafter sold the property and the transferor sold the stock. Specifically, Section 362(e)(2) limits the corporation's basis in property received in a Section 351 exchange to the fair market value of the property at the time of the exchange, when this value is less than the transferor's aggregate basis in the property transferred. By comparing the fair market value to the aggregate basis of the transferred property, Section 362(e)(2) avoids playing a "heads I win, tails you lose" game when the Section 351 exchange involves both appreciated and depreciated property. From a planning standpoint it is worth noting that Section 362(e)(2) allows the transferor to elect to limit the transferor's basis in the stock received in the exchange, instead of having the corporation limit its basis in the property—since either approach prevents doubling the loss by selling both the property and the stock. This option under Section 362(e)(2) is particularly handy if the transferor might die soon and so the stock will pick up a new basis anyway under Section 1014 (at least until repeal of Section 1014 as part of the repeal of the estate tax). By the way, even though there is no doubling of loss in the event of a Section 351 exchange with an S corporation, Section 362(e)(2) still applies

A taxpayer who wishes to avoid Section 351 cannot simply decline to apply it—the section is not elective. One obvious way to obtain recognition is to sell the property to the corporation for cash. The problem is for the company to find the money. If the seller first buys stock from the corporation for cash, which the corporation then uses to pay the seller for the property, the step transaction doctrine may collapse this into a stock for property exchange. *See, e.g., C–Lec Plastics, Inc. v. Commissioner,* 76 T.C. 601 (1981). Alternately, the seller could, as in *Bradshaw,* give the company time to pay. The *Bradshaw* opinion raises the possibility, however, that a court could, by treating the debt instrument as the equivalent of equity, recharacterize the "sale" of property for a debt instrument as either an exchange within the meaning of Section 351 or else a contribution to capital. If characterized as a contribution to capital, Section 362(a)(2) still gives the corporation a substituted basis. *See also* I.R.C. § 362(c) (giving the corporation a basis of zero when receiving a capital contribution by a non-shareholder.) (Incidentally, a contribution to capital does not constitute taxable income to the corporation. I.R.C. § 118(a). The only tax impact on a shareholder who makes a voluntary contribution to capital is to increase the basis of his or her shares by the basis of the property contributed. *Commissioner v. Fink,* 483 U.S. 89 (1987).) Yet another way to increase the transferee corporation's basis in property is by having the transferee corporation assume liabilities in excess of the transferor's basis in the property—thereby forcing the transferor to recognize gain under Section 357(c), but also increasing the corporation' basis under Section 362(a). Section 362(d) contains one limit on this approach. This provision limits any basis increase under Section 362(a) to the fair market value of the transferred property.

4. Examine the interest rate the notes bore in *Bradshaw.* Four percent per annum seems rather low even by 1968 standards. In fact, parties selling property in exchange for deferred payment often possess a significant incentive to agree to lower interest payments from the buyer, if the buyer, in turn, agrees to pay more for the property. The reason is that interest represents ordinary income, whereas a larger payment for the property generally results in more capital gains. While this strategy means less interest deductions for the buyer, the higher basis the buyer obtains can produce greater depreciation deductions (if the property is depreciable) or, as in *Bradshaw,* less ordinary income upon the sale of the property as part of the buyer's trade or business. Not surprisingly, the tax code retains

provisions designed to attack this sort of effort to hide interest in a larger purchase price. The key is to identify situations in which such hidden interest is present. Conceptually, the government could approach this task in one of two manners. It could evaluate the fair market value of the transferred property. If the principal amount of the debt exceeds this value, then there would appear to be a hidden interest component. Alternately, the government could look at the stated interest charged under the parties' agreement. If this interest is below market rates, one might presume the seller extracted additional compensation in the price. Not surprisingly, the tax code uses both approaches.

If the debt instruments are publicly traded—presumably meaning that the interest normally would reflect the market rate for debt of this risk—then the only way in which to measure whether the parties traded less interest for a larger sales price is by comparing the fair market value of the property to the principal amount of the debt. When the property exchanged for the debt is publicly traded (as, for instance, if the property in question is a publicly traded stock), then it is easy to compare the fair market value of the property to the principal amount of the debt. Accordingly, in the contexts in which either the debt instruments or the exchanged property are publicly traded—neither of which is normally the case when dealing with the issuance of debt for property upon corporate formation—Section 1273(b)(3) looks to the property's fair market value to determine the issue price of the debt. To the extent the issue price is less than the "stated redemption price at maturity"—i.e., the principal, plus the total of any called for interest payments which are not at a fixed rate (or variable based upon certain publicly available standards), unconditional and payable at least annually—then the difference constitutes original issue discount. I.R.C. § 1273(a). This, in turn, triggers application of Section 1272, which generally requires recognition of the original issue discount as taxable income spread throughout the life of the loan.

Notice, the application of Section 1272 affects not only characterization of the hidden interest, but also the timing of its recognition. To use an extreme example, if the debt instrument called for the purchasing corporation to pay nothing for several years until maturity of the entire loan, and then to pay an amount in excess of the purchased property's fair market value, the debt holders will not only recognize ordinary income based upon the difference, they must also recognize much of this income before they actually get any money. (On the other hand, the debtor can obtain an interest deduction on this original issue discount before it actually pays the sum. I.R.C. § 163(e).) This treatment flows from a second objective for the original issue discount rules—an objective which applies also to debt instruments issued for money. Companies and other borrowers often issue so-called "discount bonds"—debt instruments which pay off at maturity an amount in excess of the original loan. This amount represents deferred interest on the bond either in lieu of, or in addition to, current interest payments. United States Savings Bonds are a familiar example. The ability to defer taxable income through such investments obviously can represent a significant tax advantage. Congress enacted Section 1272 and related provisions in part to end this advantage (and one can now see why these sections refer to "original issue discount").

When neither the debt instruments nor the property exchanged for the debt are publicly traded, the tax code switches approaches. Here, Section 1274 looks to an interest rate comparison. If the debt calls for an interest rate at least equal to the Federal rate set by the Internal Revenue Service (based upon the interest paid on United States Treasury obligations), then generally there will be no original issue discount. (When the total of the principal does not exceed $2,800,000, Section 1274A imposes a nine percent ceiling on the comparison rate.) Otherwise, Section 1274 calls for computing an issue price based upon the total present value of all the payments required under the debt instrument, discounted by the Federal rate. The difference between this imputed principal, and the stated principal, becomes original issue discount taxed as discussed above. Of course, an interest rate based upon United States Treasury obligations is presumably less than what creditors will charge a private borrower. For this reason, Section 1274(b)(3) allows the I.R.S. to use a fair market value approach in certain potentially abusive situations, such as when dealing with tax shelters.

Section 1274 contains various exemptions: For example, it excludes sales in which the total payments do not exceed $250,000. I.R.C. § 1274(c)(3)(C). When neither Section 1274, nor Section 1273 apply, Section 483 might cover the transaction. Essentially, Section 483 also works through an interest rate comparison much like Section 1274—to which it cross references. The main difference is that Section 483 simply recharacterizes the unstated interest component of sums received as interest; it does not require recognition of those sums prior to their actual receipt by the holder of the debt instrument.

Bauer v. Commissioner of Internal Revenue

748 F.2d 1365 (9th Cir.1984).

This case concerns a determination of whether cash payments by two stockholders to their wholly-owned corporation were loans or contributions to capital. * * *

FACTS

* * *

Philip Bauer and his father-in-law, Philip Himmelfarb, are officers and sole stockholders of the Federal Meat Company ("Federal"). They formed Federal in 1958 with paid-in capital of $20,000. The initial and only stock issuance was 2,000 shares, of which Bauer owns 25 percent and Himmelfarb 75 percent. Federal is a custom slaughterer in the business of selling dressed meat to chain store buyers, retailers, and wholesalers. It buys live animals and has them custom slaughtered for fixed fees. Federal does not own a packing house, and it leases its premises and delivery equipment.

Since Federal's incorporation, and continuing throughout the years at issue, Bauer and Himmelfarb advanced various amounts of money to Federal. By the end of the calendar year 1958, a total of $102,650 had been advanced by Bauer and Himmelfarb. Numerous advances and repayments then occurred so that as of December 31, 1972, the net balance advanced by Bauer and Himmelfarb totaled $810,068. * * *

The parties treated all of the transactions as loans and repayments. Each advance to Federal was evidenced by a negotiable promissory note that was unsecured and was payable on demand. The notes carried a seven percent interest rate during 1972–1974 and a ten percent interest rate in 1976. The notes were not convertible into stock, nor were they subordinated to any other obligation. For each advance made to Federal, an amount representing "accrued interest payable" was entered in the corporate ledger at the end of each month as an addition to liabilities in the form of "outstanding loans payable-officers." Each year's total of accrued interest was paid within two and one-half months of the close of Federal's fiscal year. On its financial statements, Federal included the outstanding balances as a current liability labeled "loan payable-officers."

On its corporate federal income tax returns for the years at issue, Federal claimed interest expense deductions in the amounts of $79,638, $103,506, and $103,007, for its fiscal years ending April 30, of 1974, 1975, and 1976, respectively, for the amounts paid as interest to Bauer and Himmelfarb. These amounts, in turn, were reported by Bauer and Himmelfarb as interest income in the calendar year in which they were received. The amounts received from Federal characterized as loan principal repayments were not reported as income. These amounts for Bauer were: $65,000 in 1973, $25,000 in 1974, and $35,000 in 1975; for Himmelfarb, the amount was $75,000 in 1975. Bauer and Himmelfarb each received a yearly salary of $70,000 or $80,000. Federal has never paid dividends; the earnings of the corporation from its inception in 1958 were retained and reinvested to meet the continued growth of the corporation. By the end of the fiscal years in issue, the retained earnings were: 1974, $634,107; 1975, $657,973; and 1976, $486,092. (In the 1976 fiscal year, Federal suffered a net loss).

The Tax Court concluded that the advances by Bauer and Himmelfarb to Federal were capital contributions and disallowed the interest deductions claimed by Federal on the ground that no debtor-creditor relationship was established to support treatment of the payments as interest. In addition, the principal payments made by Federal to Bauer and Himmelfarb were held to be taxable dividends.

* * *

ANALYSIS

The determination of whether an advance is debt or equity depends on the distinction between a creditor who seeks a definite obligation that is payable in any event, and a shareholder who seeks to make an investment and to share in the profits and risks of loss in the venture. * * * The outward form of the transaction is not controlling; rather, characterization depends on the taxpayer's actual intent, as evidenced by the circumstances and conditions of the advance.

In 1969, Congress authorized the Secretary of the Treasury to prescribe regulations setting forth the factors to be considered in determining whether an advance is debt or equity. 26 U.S.C. § 385. The Secretary did not issue such regulations * * * [Hence] we must still be guided by the case law and by the five factors that Congress suggested, as part of the 1969 statute, might be included in the regulations. This court has identified eleven factors:

> (1) the names given to the certificates evidencing the indebtedness; (2) the presence or absence of a maturity date; (3) the source of the payments; (4) the right to enforce the payment of principal and interest; (5) participation in management; (6) a status equal to or inferior to that of regular corporate creditors; (7) the intent of the parties; (8) "thin" or adequate capitalization; (9) identity of interest between creditor and stockholder; (10) payment of interest only out of "dividend" money; and (11) the ability of the corporation to obtain loans from outside lending institutions.

* * * No one factor is controlling or decisive, and the court must look to the particular circumstances of each case. * * * "The object of the inquiry is not to count factors, but to evaluate them." * * * The burden of establishing that the advances were loans rather than capital contributions rests with the taxpayer. * * *

A. Ratio of Debt to Equity

In the present case, the Tax Court gave great weight to the eighth factor: whether Federal was adequately capitalized. The court found that Federal's debt-to-equity ratio was as high as 92 to 1 during the years in question and that Federal was seriously undercapitalized. The Tax Court found this to be a strong indication that the advances were capital contributions rather than loans. The Tax Court apparently based its finding of a debt-to-equity ratio of 92 to 1 on a paragraph of the Stipulation of Facts signed by the parties. That paragraph states:

> The ratio of stockholder debt to corporate stock was approximately 92 to 1 for the fiscal year ending April 30, 1976.

This is accurate insofar as it compares the ending debt owed to the stockholders in 1976 of $1,850,067 to their initial stock purchase in 1958 of $20,000. This is not a true or meaningful debt-to-equity ratio. First, it completely ignores the earnings that had been retained in the corporation as it grew over the 18-year period. The stockholders' equity in a corporation is composed not only of the paid-in-capital, but also of the profits that have been generated and retained in the corporation as "retained earnings." Thus, if the debt-to-equity ratio were considered to be a comparison of stockholder loans to the correct calculation of stockholder equity including retained earnings in the corporation, this "debt-to-equity" ratio would be only 1.5 to 1 in 1974–1975 and 3.6 to 1 in 1976. * * *

The more meaningful debt-to-equity ratio compares the total liabilities to the stockholders' equity. * * *

Thus, during the years in question, the total debt-to-equity ratio, as reflected on the books of the corporation, was not 92 to 1, but ranged from a little over 2 to 1 to less than 8 to 1. * * *

The purpose of examining the debt-to-equity ratio in characterizing a stockholder advance is to determine whether a corporation is so thinly capitalized that a business loss would result in an inability to repay the advance; such an advance would be indicative of venture capital rather than a loan. * * * Essentially, we are concerned with the degree of risk the loan presents to the lender and whether an independent lender, such as a bank, would be willing to make the loan. In addition to the numerical debt-to-equity ratio, other factors in the financial picture would also be important to an independent lender in analyzing the risk. Federal's history was that of a successful company whose increasing cash needs arose from growth, not a lack of profits or business reverses. Federal had virtually no fixed assets; its plant and equipment were leased. The assets were principally current assets which could be quickly turned into cash. At all times during the years in question, Federal's current assets exceeded all liabilities by at least $300,000, which presents a strong financial picture.

Federal's financial structure and these other factors indicate that Federal could readily have obtained a loan from a bank or other financial institution for the purpose for which the stockholders' loans were made, which was to finance inventory and accounts receivable. There is specific evidence in this case that one bank would have been willing to make these loans. * * *

B. Proportional Holdings of Debt and Equity

The Tax Court also gave weight to the alleged fact that Bauer and Himmelfarb had loaned Federal amounts that were roughly proportional to their respective capital investments. The court found that during the years in question Himmelfarb had advanced a total of $970,000 to Federal while Bauer had advanced $270,000, a ratio of about 3½ to 1 as compared to the 3 to 1 ratio of their stockholdings. We agree that where a stockholder owns "debt" in the same proportion to which he holds stock in a certain corporation, the characterization as "debt" may be suspect. * * * However, the Tax Court clearly miscalculated the amounts of Bauer's and Himmelfarb's advances to Federal.

The Tax Court looked only at the gross amount of Bauer and Himmelfarb's advances during the years in question. It failed to consider either the amount of the loans outstanding at the beginning of the three-year period or the effect of the repayments that Federal made during this period. At the beginning of the three-year period, Federal already owned $805,068 to Himmelfarb, but only $5,000 to Bauer. At the end of the period, the figures had grown to $1,700,068 and $150,000, a ratio of about 11 to 1. Even if the three-year period is considered in isolation—an approach that makes little sense given that the stockholders had been making loans to Federal since 1958—the net amounts advanced by Himmelfarb and Bauer during the period were $895,000 and $145,000, respectively, a ratio of about 6 to 1. These figures simply will not support a finding that Bauer and Himmelfarb made advances to Federal in proportion to their capital investments.

C. Other Factors

The Tax Court also found it significant that all of Federal's shareholder debt was evidenced by demand notes with no fixed date of maturity. Although some repayments were made during the years in question, repayments never kept up with advances. We agree that lack of a fixed date of maturity on the debt instruments, together with continual growth of the debt, may suggest that there is no intention to make full repayment. But that one factor is not enough to carry the entire weight of this case. Many other factors favor the petitioners, as the Tax Court conceded: the existence of notes; fixed and reasonable interest rates; actual timely payment of interest; corresponding treatment of the interest as income by Bauer and Himmelfarb; the cash-flow demands of the custom slaughter business; and the lack of subordination of shareholder debt to other corporate debt.

* * *

For these reasons and other reasons above specified, we hold that the Tax Court's recharacterization of Federal's debt as equity is clearly erroneous, and the decision of the Tax Court is therefore REVERSED.

NOTES

1. In *Bauer*, like *Bradshaw*, the I.R.S. argued that debt owed by the corporation to its shareholders was really equity. The tax advantage sought by the shareholders in the two cases, however, was different. In *Bradshaw*, the shareholder gained a tax advantage by structuring a transfer of property to the corporation as a sale in exchange for debt instruments instead of an exchange of property for stock. This allowed the shareholder to avoid the carryover basis that accompanies non-recognition under Section 351. In *Bauer*, by contrast, the shareholders gave money, not property, in exchange for the debt instruments. With a contribution of money, the non-recognition and carryover basis impact that flow from a Section 351 exchange are irrelevant. Instead, the advantages sought by the shareholders in *Bauer* flowed from holding debt, rather than from the characterization of the exchange.

In fact, as pointed out by the court in *Costello*, shareholders often can obtain tax advantages by loaning money to their corporation rather than buying a greater quantity of stock. *Bauer* illustrates these advantages. The corporation took a deduction for interest payments made to its two shareholders as compensation for their loans. I.R.C. § 163(a). In contrast, distribution of corporate earnings through dividends does not produce an offsetting deduction. Of course, one must consider the impact of this difference on the recipient who receives interest payments rather than dividends. At the time of the transaction in *Bauer*, this was largely a wash, since both interest or dividends (assuming the dividend comes from corporate earnings and profits) were just ordinary income. I.R.C. §§ 61(a), 301(c)(1). Now, however, dividends generally are taxed at a lower rate than ordinary income, such as from interest. I.R.C. § 1(h)(1), (11). Moreover, if the shareholder itself is a corporation, Section 243 excludes 70 (or in some instances 80 or 100) percent of the dividends received by the recipient corporation from its taxable income. Still, the extra tax paid by the recipient of interest, rather than dividends, in many, if not most, cases will not exceed the tax saved by the corporation by taking a deduction for interest payments.

Beyond the deduction available for the corporation paying interest rather than dividends, there is also the different treatment of repayment of principle. Repayment of the cash advances in *Bauer,* while not producing a deduction, was tax free to the two shareholders. Again, compare the result if, instead of retiring debt, the corporation repurchased some of its stock. To the extent the repurchase did not significantly change the relative holdings of the two shareholders—which the two presumably would not want to do—the repurchase would constitute a taxable dividend. I.R.C. § 302. (This assumes the repurchase does not exceed the corporation's earnings and profits—a concept defined later.) Moreover, retention of earnings to pay off debt generally does not create the problems with the accumulated earnings tax encountered when redeeming stock. *Compare* Treas. Reg. § 1.537–2(b)(3), *with Lamark Shipping Agency, Inc. v. Commissioner,* reprinted in Chapter VI. *But see Smoot Sand & Gravel Corp. v. Commissioner,* 241 F.2d 197 (4th Cir.1957), *cert. denied,* 354 U.S. 922. The end result is that regardless of whether the payment constitutes interest or repayment of principle, payments on shareholder loans provide a technique for avoiding the double tax phenomenon in a C corporation.

2. From the taxpayer's standpoint, the shareholders in *Bauer* reached the optimum result: They received the money they wanted from the corporation despite the fact it never declared a dividend. Blind pursuit of this goal through shareholder loans, however, will often prove counterproductive. The difficulty lies in the fact that decisions designed to maximize the amount of earnings distributed to shareholders through loan payments (thereby avoiding the need for dividends) often tend to make a loan look less like a loan and more like an equity investment in the company. This, in turn, creates the prospect of a challenge by the Internal Revenue Service along the lines encountered in *Bauer.* While the taxpayers there overcame the attack (albeit, after considerable litigation and expense), numerous other shareholders have seen courts reclassify their loans as equity. Such reclassification results in treating the "interest" payments as non-deductible dividends, and the repayment of principal as a potentially taxable redemption of stock.

To understand the problem, it is useful to consider several questions shareholders must address in loaning money to their corporation, and compare the decisions they might wish to make, against the factors mentioned in *Bauer* and other judicial opinions as indicating shareholder loans are really equity investments. The first question is how much of the funds needed by the company should the shareholders loan rather than contribute through the purchase of stock. The temptation is to assume if little is good, more is better. After all, the loan balance sets the upper limit on the amount the shareholders can receive as a tax-free repayment of principal. A bigger loan also allows larger interest payments (without exceeding reasonable interest rates) in order to funnel more earnings out of the company. As Bauer and Himmelfarb learned in the Tax Court, however, substantial debt relative to the shareholder's equity is often a damning indication that the loans really are equity. (The two shareholders were only saved by the Ninth Circuit's decision to include retained earnings as part of their equity. Notice, this suggests defining what one means by a debt-equity ratio may not always be straightforward.) Unfortunately for parties seeking clear advise on how much they can safely lend, there appears to be no firm guidelines. In the *Bradshaw* opinion above, the court saw little problem with debt fifty times larger than equity given evidence the corporation could afford to pay. Yet, in *Schnitzer v. Commissioner,* 13 T.C. 43 (1949), the court reclassified loans as equity despite a debt-equity ratio of around three to one. To confuse matters further, some courts apply an "essential assets" test under which shareholder loans providing capital for critical assets of the venture constitute equity. *E.g., Brake & Electric Sales Corp. v. United States,* 185 F.Supp. 1 (D.Mass.1960), *aff'd,* 287 F.2d 426 (1st Cir.1961). *See also Costello v. Fazio,* reprinted earlier in this chapter. (To some extent, this is a function of the loan's timing: A loan made upon incorporation is seemingly more essential than a loan made to a corporation already running without it. At any event, one cannot take this test too literally, since companies presumably borrow money because they need it.) Still another corollary to minimizing stock purchases in favor of making more shareholder loans is it leads outside lenders to demand the shareholders subordinate their loans. Such subordination, as mentioned in *Bauer,* is a factor indicating the loans are disguised equity.

A second question shareholders confront in making loans to their company is how much each should lend relative to the others. Turning loan payments into the predominant mode of distributing corporate earnings can raise concerns among the stockholders about the impact of the loans on the basic profit allocation and on the priorities between the shareholders in liquidation. At this point, shareholders may discover the useful fact that if they all make loans in the same ratio as their relative stockholdings, the loans will not alter either their share of the company's profits or their priority on liquidation vis-a-vis each other: Such loans have no economic effect *as between the stockholders.* Regrettably from the owners' standpoint, and for this very reason, shareholder loans which are proportionate to stock ownership are another red flag indicating the debt is really equity. (Again, the *Bauer* court recognized this factor, but found it inapplicable because the loan balances owed the two shareholders stood in a very different ratio from their relative shareholdings.)

Finally, the parties must consider the terms of the loans. Here, they confront a basic dilemma. The more closely they seek to match loan payments to corporate earnings (in order to leave little for dividends), the greater the danger they create if corporate earnings decline. In that event, the company may have difficulty making the loan payments. Shareholders might take a number of approaches to deal with this dilemma. Bauer and Himmelfarb made their loans payable only on demand, thereby giving themselves flexibility to recover more payments in good years and less in bad. A tempting notion is to make interest payments proportionate to earnings. Once again, however, such terms appear to courts to be earmarks of equity. *E.g., John Kelley Co. v. Commissioner,* 326 U.S. 521 (1946). (The *Bauer* court noted the lack of fixed maturity date, but concluded this was not enough by itself to justify recharacterizing the loans as equity.) Conversely, shareholders may make loans with fixed payment obligations, secure in the knowledge that if worse comes to worse they will not take their own company to court to enforce strict compliance. Yet, failure to enforce loan obligations when due also suggests the debt is really an equity investment. *E.g., Slappey Drive Industrial Park v. United States,* 561 F.2d 572 (5th Cir.1977).

This analysis suggests that "thinning" a corporation with shareholder debt is little like eating: all the things you want are fattening. Worse, there are a variety of different "diet" guides. Some courts look to "intent": In other words, based upon the factors above did the parties really intend to make loans or equity investments. *E.g., Gooding Amusement Co. v. Commissioner,* 236 F.2d 159 (6th Cir.1956), *cert. denied,* 352 U.S. 1031 (1957). Other courts look at the same factors to see if the loans are "risk" capital—dependent upon the fate of the business for their repayment—in which case they are equity. *E.g., Gilbert v. Commissioner,* 248 F.2d 399 (2d Cir.1957). Still other courts ask whether an outside creditor would make the same loans. *E.g., Scriptomatic, Inc. v. United States,* 555 F.2d 364 (3d Cir.1977). Opinions like *Bauer* simply mush all these concepts together. In 1969, Congress tried to help by enacting Section 385. It instructed the Internal Revenue Service to issue regulations based upon five criteria—largely those discussed above—to determine when shareholder "loans" constitute equity. After an abortive effort, however, it appears unlikely that the Service will ever adopt any regulations under this section. (In one area, Congress has provided a statutory safe harbor where one need not fear reclassification of debt as equity. This is for so-called "straight debt," consisting of non-convertible loans by shareholders to an S corporation. The S corporation must execute a written obligation to pay a fixed sum on demand, or on a specified due date, with fixed interest. I.R.C. § 1361(c)(5). Shareholders in an S corporation, of course, do not use debt to avoid double tax. Nevertheless, they are concerned about reclassification of loans as equity, since this could constitute a second class of stock and upset eligibility for S treatment. The safe harbor applies specifically (and only) to this concern.)

In addition to this general debt versus equity challenge, a couple of more specific limits exist on corporate interest deductions. Section 163(e)(5) and (i) denies the issuer of very high interest debt instruments—at least five percent over the federal rate at the time of issuance—which have significant original issue discount, the ability to deduct the original issue discount until actually paid (and perhaps never). Section 163(j) limits corporations taking deductions on interest paid to related persons (within the meaning of Sections 267(b) or 707(b)(1)) when the interest is not subject to tax (for instance, because the recipient is a tax-exempt organization) and the corporation pays out a sum greater than half its taxable income in interest. Finally, Section 163(*l*) prevents a corporation from recognizing a deduction for interest paid on debt when the corporation either must, or has the option to, pay the debt by giving the creditor stock in the company. Will Section 163(*l*) reach the typical convertible debt, under which the bondholder has the option to demand payment in stock? It does if the option is substantially certain to be exercised. Normally, the option price with convertible debt is higher than the stock's value at the time the debt is issued. Hence, the typical option is not substantially certain to be exercised and Section 163(*l*) does not impact the usual convertible debt instrument. The section presumably would impact, however, convertible debt if the option price was less than the market price of the stock at the time the company issued the debt. The section also denies a deduction for debt instruments which tie the amount of principal or interest payable under the instrument to the value of the corporation's stock.

3. The discussion thus far has focused on the tax advantages of shareholder loans for a profitable business. Suppose the business fails. As discussed earlier, losses on the sale or worthlessness of stock are normally capital and thus of limited utility. Section 1244 provides an important exception for smaller businesses, under which individuals can receive a limited amount of ordinary loss treatment on their stock.

Compare the treatment of debt. Losses on the sale of a debt instrument at a discount are usually capital. *See* I.R.C. § 1271(a)(1). If the creditor holds the debt instrument until the business completely fails and the debt becomes worthless, characterization depends initially upon the nature of the instrument. If it is a "security," the loss again is normally capital. *See* I.R.C. § 165(f),(g). (Section 165(g)(2)(C) specifically defines "security" for this purpose as encompassing bonds, debentures, notes, certificates or other evidences of indebtedness, with interest coupons or in registered form.) For debt instruments not fitting this definition of a security, Section 166 comes into play. It provides an ordinary loss deduction for bad debts held by corporations, and for worthless business debts held by individuals. The courts have narrowly defined the concept of a "business" debt. It does not include loans by a shareholder to his or her corporation, unless the individual can show the dominant purpose for the loan was to advance a trade or business in which he or she is personally engaged independent of the status of shareholder or investor. For example, a loan made primarily to protect one's employment is a business debt. If, as is more likely, a shareholder in a closely held corporation (even if employed by the company) makes the loan mostly to protect his or her investment in the business, or, as discussed above, to obtain earnings through interest, the loan is an investment and not a business debt. *E.g., United States v. Generes,* 405 U.S. 93 (1972).

What do these distinctions suggest regarding the choice between stock and debt? For individuals, Section 1244 stock, to the extent available, provides an advantage in a failing business over debt (except in the rare case where a shareholder can show his or her debt is a "business," rather than investment, debt). Corporations obtain an advantage with debt, other than a security, in event of loss. (Recall, Section 1244 does not benefit corporations who are shareholders. Also, parents filing a consolidated return many times cannot obtain even a capital loss deduction on the disposition of stock rather than debt in their subsidiary. Treas.Reg. § 1.1502–20.) The result is an interesting trade-off between the form of investment yielding the greatest tax advantage in a profitable business versus the one best for a failing business. Moreover, this trade-off reverses for individuals and corporate investors.

4. One alternative to shareholder loans is for the company to borrow from outside lenders. When dealing with a small corporation, such lenders are likely to demand the stockholders guarantee the loans. On occasions when a high debt-equity ratio would make loans directly by shareholders to the company suspect, the Internal Revenue Service has also challenged such guaranteed loans made by outsiders. The Service's argument is to characterize the transactions as effectively a loan by the outsider to the shareholder, followed by the shareholder's contributing the funds to the corporation. Success in this argument results in denying the company a deduction for interest it paid to the outsider, and in treating the loan payments as constructive dividends to the guaranteeing shareholder. *E.g., Plantation Patterns, Inc. v. Commissioner,* 462 F.2d 712 (5th Cir.1972), *cert. denied,* 409 U.S. 1076.

5. As noted earlier, shareholders owning assets of use to the business often lease the property to the corporation. This has tax as well as non-tax advantages (the latter having been discussed above). Lease payments, like interest, represent a tax deductible way to transfer funds from the company to its owners. I.R.C. § 162(a)(3). Even better, rental payments in many cases constitute passive income against which the recipient can deduct passive losses. I.R.C. § 469(c)(2). *But see* Treas. Reg. § 1.469–2(f)(6) (recharacterizing rental payments as non-passive if received from an activity in which the recipient materially participates). In addition, the shareholder-lessor, rather than the corporation, is entitled to the depreciation and any other deductions which go to the owner of income producing property. (Notice, however, these deductions come from a passive activity.) Finally, and perhaps most important, leasing provides significant flexibility to withdraw the property from the business without adverse tax effects. If the corporation owns the property and the property appreciates, any sale or distribution of the asset to a shareholder produces a taxable gain for the company. I.R.C. § 311(b). Along the same lines, if the company sells the asset and distributes the proceeds to a shareholder, the result is a double

tax (assuming the company is not an S corporation). One can avoid this result by the company leasing rather than owning the asset.

As with shareholder loans, however, the Internal Revenue Service may seek to thwart these advantages by characterizing the lease as something else. For instance, the Service often argues that a supposed lease of property constitutes in reality an installment or conditional sale of the property to the company leasing the property. *E.g., Transamerica Corp. v. United States,* 7 Cl.Ct. 441 (1985). Suppose, however, the lease is part of a sale and leaseback arrangement—in other words, a pair of transactions in which the owner of property sells the property to another party and then leases the property from that party. Here, it does not make sense to say what is really going on is an installment or conditional sales contract designed to transfer the property to the leasing party, since that party originally owned the property. Instead, if the leasing party effectively ends up with ownership of the property anyway, the sale and leaseback might be simply a sham. *See, e.g., Frank Lyon Co. v. United States,* 435 U.S. 561 (1978). The Service has provided the following criteria for distinguishing a sales contract from a lease.

Revenue Ruling 55–540

1955–2 C.B. 39.

> SEC. 4 DETERMINATION WHETHER AN AGREEMENT IS A LEASE OR A CONDITIONAL SALES CONTRACT
>
> 01. * * * Whether an agreement, which in form is a lease, is in substance a conditional sales contract depends upon the intent of the parties as evidenced by the provisions of the agreement, read in the light of the facts and circumstances existing at the time the agreement was executed. In ascertaining such intent no single test, or any special combination of tests, is absolutely determinative. * * * However, * * * it would appear that in the absence of compelling persuasive factors of contrary implication an intent warranting treatment of a transaction for tax purposes as a purchase and sale rather than as a lease or rental agreement may in general be said to exist if, for example, one or more of the following conditions are present:
>
> (a) Portions of the periodic payments are made specifically applicable to an equity to be acquired by the lessee. * * *
>
> (b) The lessee will acquire title upon the payment of a stated amount of "rentals" which under the contract he is required to make. * * *
>
> (c) The total amount which the lessee is required to pay for a relatively short period of use constitutes an inordinately large proportion of the total sum required to be paid to secure the transfer of the title. * * *
>
> (d) The agreed "rental" payments materially exceed the current fair rental value. This may be indicative that the payments

include an element other than compensation for the use of property. * * *

(e) The property may be acquired under a purchase option at a price which is nominal in relation to the value of the property at the time when the option may be exercised, as determined at the time of entering into the original agreement, or which is a relatively small amount when compared with the total payments which are required to be made. * * *

(f) Some portion of the periodic payments is specifically designated as interest or is otherwise readily recognizable as the equivalent of interest. * * *

02. The fact that the agreement makes no provision for the transfer of title or specifically precludes the transfer of title does not, of itself, prevent the contract from being held to be a sale of an equitable interest in the property.

03. Conditional sales of personal property are, in general, recordable under the various State recording acts if the vendor wishes to protect its lien against claims of creditors. However, the recording or failure to record such a sales contract is usually discretionary with the vendor and is not controlling insofar as the essential nature of the contract is concerned for Federal tax purposes. * * *

04. Agreements are usually indicative of an intent to rent the equipment if the rental payments are at an hourly, daily, or weekly rate, or are based on production, use, mileage, or a similar measure and are not directly related to the normal purchase price, provided, if there is an option to purchase, that the price at which the equipment may be acquired reasonably approximates the anticipated fair market value on the option date. * * *

05. In the absence of compelling factors indicating a different intent, it will be presumed that a conditional sales contract was intended if the total of the rental payments and any option price payable in addition thereto approximates the price at which the equipment could have been acquired by purchase at the time of entering into the agreement, plus interest and/or carrying charges. * * *

06. If the sum of the specified "rentals" over a relatively short part of the expected useful life of the equipment approximates the price at which the equipment could have been acquired by purchase at the time of entering into the agreement, plus interest and/or carrying charges on such amount, and the lessee may continue to use the equipment for an additional period or periods approximating its remaining estimated useful life for relatively nominal or token payments, it may be assumed that the parties have entered into a sale contract, even though a passage of title is not expressly provided in the agreement. * * *

A possible danger of holding back and leasing assets to a corporation may exist when parties incorporate a going business. Recall Revenue Ruling 80–198, reprinted earlier, allowed non-recognition upon the transfer of accounts receivable when a proprietor transferred all the assets of his business to a new corporation. Will this result still apply if one transfers less than all of the business' assets? See Priv.Letter Rul. 8139073 (not when held back significant assets to lease to corporation).

3. LATER STOCK PURCHASES

Katzowitz v. Sidler

24 N.Y.2d 512, 301 N.Y.S.2d 470, 249 N.E.2d 359 (1969).

■ KEATING, JUDGE.

Isador Katzowitz is a director and stockholder of a close corporation. Two other persons, Jacob Sidler and Max Lasker, own the remaining securities and, with Katzowitz, comprise Sulburn Holding Corp.'s board of directors. Sulburn was organized in 1955 to supply propane gas to three other corporations controlled by these men. Sulburn's certificate of incorporation authorized it to issue 1,000 shares of no par value stock for which the incorporators established a $100 selling price. Katzowitz, Sidler and Lasker each invested $500 and received five shares of the corporation's stock.

The three men had been jointly engaged in several corporate ventures for more than 25 years. In this period they had always been equal partners and received identical compensation from the corporations they controlled. Though all the corporations controlled by these three men prospered, disenchantment with their inter-personal relationship flared into the open in 1956. At this time, Sidler and Lasker joined forces to oust Katzowitz from any role in managing the corporations. * * *

Katzowitz sought a temporary injunction. * * *

Before the issue could be tried, the three men entered into a stipulation in 1959 whereby Katzowitz withdrew from active participation in the day-to-day operations of the business. The agreement provided that he would remain on the boards of all the corporations, and each board would be limited to three members composed of the three stockholders or their designees. Katzowitz was to receive the same compensation and other fringe benefits which the controlled corporations paid Lasker and Sidler. The stipulation also provided that Katzowitz, Sidler and Lasker were "equal stockholders and each of said parties now owns the same number of shares to stock in each of the defendant corporations and that such shares of stock shall continue to be in full force and effect and unaffected by this stipulation, except as hereby otherwise expressly provided." The stipulation contained no other provision affecting equal stock interests.

* * *

In December of 1961 Sulburn was indebted to each stockholder to the extent of $2,500 for fees and commissions earned up until September, 1961. Instead of paying this debt, Sidler and Lasker wanted Sulburn to loan the money to another corporation which all three men controlled. Sidler and Lasker called a meeting of the board of directors to propose that additional securities be offered at $100 per share to substitute for the money owed to the directors. * * * Katzowitz made it quite clear at the meeting that he would not invest additional funds in Sulburn in order for it to make a loan to this other corporation. The only resolution passed at the meeting was that the corporation would pay the sum of $2,500 to each director.

With full knowledge that Katzowitz expected to be paid his fees and commissions and that he did not want to participate in any new stock issuance, the other two directors called a special meeting of the board on December 1, 1961. The only item on the agenda for this special meeting was the issuance of 75 shares of the corporation's common stock at $100 per share. The offer was to be made to stockholders in "accordance with their respective preemptive rights for the purpose of acquiring additional working capital". The amount to be raised was the exact amount owed by the corporation to its shareholders. The offering price for the securities was 1/18 the book value of the stock. Only Sidler and Lasker attended the special board meeting. They approved the issuance of the 75 shares.

Notice was mailed to each stockholder that they had the right to purchase 25 shares of the corporation's stock at $100 a share. The offer was to expire on December 27, 1961. Failure to act by that date was stated to constitute a waiver. At about the same time Katzowitz received the notice, he received a check for $2,500 from the corporation for his fees and commissions. Katzowitz did not exercise his option to buy the additional shares. Sidler and Lasker purchased their full complement, 25 shares each. This purchase by Sidler and Lasker caused an immediate dilution of the book value of the outstanding securities.

On August 25, 1962 the principal asset of Sulburn, a tractor trailer truck, was destroyed. On August 31, 1962 the directors unanimously voted to dissolve the corporation. Upon dissolution, Sidler and Lasker each received $18,885.52 but Katzowitz only received $3,147.59.

The plaintiff instituted a declaratory judgment action to establish his right to the proportional interest in the assets of Sulburn in liquidation less the $5,000 which Sidler and Lasker used to purchase their shares in December, 1961.

Special Term (Westchester County) found the book value of the corporation's securities on the day the stock was offered at $100 to be worth $1,800. * * * The court reasoned that Katzowitz waived his right to purchase the stock or object to its sale to Lasker and Sidler by failing to exercise his pre-emptive right and found his protest at the time of dissolution untimely.

* * *

Directors, being fiduciaries of the corporation, must, in issuing new stock, treat existing shareholders fairly. * * * Though there is very little statutory control over the price which a corporation must receive for new shares * * * the power to determine price must be exercised for the benefit of the corporation and in the interest of all the stockholders * * *.

Issuing stock for less than fair value can injure existing shareholders by diluting their interest in the corporation's surplus, in current and future earnings and in the assets upon liquidation. Normally, a stockholder is protected from the loss of his equity from dilution, even though the stock is being offered at less than fair value, because the shareholder received rights which he may either exercise or sell. If he exercises, he has protected his interest and, if not, he can sell the rights, thereby compensating himself for the dilution of his remaining shares in the equity of the corporation. * * *

When new shares are issued, however, at prices far below fair value in a close corporation or a corporation with only a limited market for its shares, existing stockholders, who do not want to invest or do not have the capacity to invest additional funds, can have their equity interest in the corporation diluted to the vanishing point. * * *

The protection afforded by stock rights is illusory in close corporations. Even if a buyer could be found for the rights, they would have to be sold at an inadequate price because of the nature of a close corporation. Outsiders are normally discouraged from acquiring minority interests after a close corporation has been organized. Certainly a stockholder in a close corporation is at a total loss to safeguard his equity from dilution if no rights are offered and he does not want to invest additional funds.

Though it is difficult to determine fair value for a corporation's securities and courts are therefore reluctant to get into the thicket, when the issuing price is shown to be markedly below book value in a close corporation and when the remaining shareholder-directors benefit from the issuance, a case for judicial relief has been established. In that instance, the corporation's directors must show that the issuing price falls within some range which can be justified on the basis of valid business reasons. * * * If no such showing is made by the directors, there is no reason for the judiciary to abdicate its function to a majority of the board or stockholders who have not seen fit to come forward and justify the propriety of diverting property from the corporation and allow the issuance of securities to become an oppressive device permitting the dilution of the equity of dissident stockholders.

The defendant directors here make no claim that the price set was a fair one. No business justification is offered to sustain it * * *. Admittedly, the stock was sold at less than book value. The defendants simply contend that, as long as all stockholders were given equal opportunity to purchase additional shares, no stockholder can complain simply because the offering dilutes his interest in the corporation.

The defendant's argument is fallacious.

The corollary of a stockholder's right to maintain his proportionate equity in a corporation by purchasing additional shares is the right not to purchase additional shares without being confronted with dilution of his existing equity if no valid business justification exists for the dilution.

* * *

Here the obvious disparity in selling price and book value was calculated to force the dissident stockholder into investing additional sums. No valid business justification was advanced for the disparity in price, and the only beneficiaries of the disparity were the two director-stockholders who were eager to have additional capital in the business.

It is no answer to Katzowitz' action that he was also given a chance to purchase additional shares at this bargain rate. The price was not so much a bargain as it was a tactic, conscious or unconscious on the part of the directors, to place Katzowitz in a compromising situation. The price was so fixed to make the failure to invest costly. However, Katzowitz at the time might not have been aware of the dilution because no notice of the effect of the issuance of the new shares on the already outstanding shares was disclosed. * * * In addition, since the stipulation entitled Katzowitz to the same compensation as Sidler and Lasker, the disparity in equity interest caused by their purchase of additional securities in 1961 did not affect stockholder income from Sulburn and, therefore, Katzowitz possibly was not aware of the effect of the stock issuance on his interest in the corporation until dissolution.

No reason exists at this time to permit Sidler and Lasker to benefit from their course of conduct. Katzowitz' delay in commencing the action did not prejudice the defendants. By permitting the defendants to recover their additional investment in Sulburn before the remaining assets of Sulburn are distributed to the stockholders upon dissolution, all the stockholders will be treated equitably. Katzowitz, therefore, should receive his aliquot share of the assets of Sulburn less the amount invested by Sidler and Lasker for their purchase on December 27, 1961.

Accordingly, the order of the Appellate Division should be reversed, with costs, and judgment granted in favor of the plaintiff against the individual defendants.

* * *

■ FULD, C.J., dissents and votes to affirm on the opinion at the Appellate Division.

* * *

NOTE

Additional capital inputs to a business raise two broad planning concerns: (1) To what extent should participants bind themselves to make further contributions; and (2) To what extent should participants limit each other's ability to voluntarily make further contributions. In an ordinary partnership or LLP, the former concern predominated, since additional contributions (barring other agreement) yield their maker no added rights to profit or control. The first concern still exists in a corporation, and the participants should address many of the same questions considered when forming a partnership. *Katzowitz* illustrates, however, the second concern assumes major significance when forming a corporation (as it also could in forming a limited partnership or LLC under a scheme in which voting and profit rights are proportionate to contributions). This is another example of additional planning necessitated by the relationship between a contribution in the form of stock purchases and the allocation of rights in a corporation.

Future stock sales can have two adverse impacts upon existing shareholders who do not purchase further shares. The one which often first comes to mind is the potential to dilute a shareholder's percentage of voting control. (Why was this not a concern in *Katzowitz*? Note the shareholders' agreement in the case.) The problem in *Katzowitz* lay in the dilution of the economic worth of the existing shares—which came to roost in the distribution upon liquidation. With one class of stock, such dilution is a function of price. If the corporation issues new shares for less than the worth of the old, the result is to transfer wealth from the old shareholders to the new. If the new shares sell for the worth of the old, there is no such effect (the old shareholders own a smaller percentage of a larger pie—assuming the company effectively invests the new money). If the corporation sells the new shares for more than the worth of the old, the result is to enrich the old shareholders at the expense of the new. With multiple classes of stock, the effect is more complicated because of the need to consider differing rights of the shares.

What protections do shareholders have against these effects? The first possible defense lies in the fact the corporation can only issue as many shares as authorized in its articles. Cal. Corp. Code § 202(d), (e)(1); Del. Gen. Corp. Law § 102(a)(4); N.Y. Bus. Corp. Law § 402(a)(4); M.B.C.A. § 6.01(a). Perhaps the parties should draft the articles to authorize only as many shares as the company initially plans to issue. Two difficulties exist with this idea. It would lessen the flexibility of the board to issue more shares when this might be advantageous, without going through the effort of amending the articles. It also would not protect minority shareholders from the majority amending the articles to increase the number of authorized shares.

What usually protects the shareholders' interests is that the board of directors has authority over the sale of shares (unless the articles reserve this power to the shareholders). *See, e.g.,* Cal. Corp. Code § 409; Del. Gen. Corp. Law §§ 152, 161; N.Y. Bus. Corp. Law § 504; M.B.C.A. § 6.21(a), (b). Normally, the board would not wish to sell shares to outsiders at a price which dilutes the existing shareholders' economic interests. After all, the shareholders elect the board, and the directors are probably substantial shareholders themselves. This protection breaks down, however, in a situation in which, as in *Katzowitz,* the directors are also the purchasers. When the concern is dilution of voting power, rather than economic interests, the protection provided by the board's self-interest goes even further. To the extent, as a practical matter, the board represents the majority of shareholders, it would generally not desire to undermine the majority's control. Moreover, to the extent further share sales dilute the minority's voting power, one might question whether this matters given the fact of majority rule. Yet, dilution of the minority's voting power can have an impact if there is cumulative voting. (Cumulative voting is discussed later in this chapter.) Also, occasions may arise where a faction lacking a majority of shares is nevertheless able to seize a majority of the board, and may seek to purchase additional shares in order to make its dominance permanent. *Schwartz v. Marien,* 37 N.Y.2d 487, 373 N.Y.S.2d 122, 335 N.E.2d 334 (1975), provides an example. Two families each owned half the outstanding shares of a corporation, and each family occupied two of the four seats on the board. When one director died, the other family found itself in temporary control of the board. To cement this control, the family's directors voted to sell themselves several treasury shares held by the corporation. (These were shares the company had issued to the third founder of the firm, and had repurchased upon his death.)

Since the protections provided by the directors' decision-making break down when the board members sell shares to themselves, perhaps the only remaining defense needed is a claim for breach of fiduciary duty. This saved Mr. Katzowitz, as well as the plaintiffs in *Schwartz.* Still, this may not entirely cure the problem. Making a claim against the directors for breach of fiduciary duty requires undertaking the expense and uncertainty of litigation. This uncertainty is compounded by the difficulty in determining whether the price paid by the directors is less than the worth of the shares (thereby causing a dilution in the existing shareholders' economic interests). The gross disparity in *Katzowitz* made this case unusually easy. *Compare Katzowitz with Hyman v. Velsicol Corp.,* 342 Ill.App. 489, 97 N.E.2d 122 (1951). Moreover, some courts may not act to prevent sales which shift control. *E.g., Tallant v. Executive Equities, Inc.,* 232 Ga. 807, 209 S.E.2d 159 (1974).

This leaves two other planning approaches. One is to limit the majority's power to purchase additional shares without the consent of the minority. Carrying out this approach involves employing some of the techniques (such as shareholders agreements and supermajority voting requirements) for regulating the management of a corporation, which are discussed later in this chapter. Is there any problem with giving minority shareholders a veto over additional share sales? Might the answer to this question depend upon whether the majority feels the added funds are needed for expansion versus working capital? On the other hand, perhaps the majority could lend the money if the minority vetoes additional share sales. Could this provide needed funds while avoiding the problems of additional share issuances?

The second approach is to guarantee each existing stockholder the right to buy his or her pro-rata share of any newly issued stock. In this way, the corporation could raise further funds without diluting the voting or economic interests of any shareholder. Such a guarantee is referred to as a preemptive right. While at common law such rights existed as a matter of course (*e.g., Stokes v. Continental Trust Co.,* 186 N.Y. 285, 78 N.E. 1090 (1906)), statutes now generally make this subject controlled by the articles. Some statutes provide preemptive rights exist unless the articles expressly exclude them. *See, e.g.,* N.Y. Bus. Corp. Law § 622 (for corporations formed before 1997). Others exclude such rights unless the articles expressly provide them. *E.g.,* Cal. Corp. Code § 406 Del. Gen. Corp. Law § 102(b)(3); M.B.C.A. § 6.30(A). Preemptive rights have several shortcomings. The

Katzowitz opinion describes one: Such rights do not help the shareholder who lacks either the funds or the willingness to take advantage of the right. In addition, they may complicate efforts to raise money from outside sources (such as through a public offering). They also raise a number of interpretation questions, which make a challenging task for the drafter in a jurisdiction where the corporation's articles must expressly create such rights. *But see* M.B.C.A. § 6.30(b) (setting out rules to govern preemptive rights if the articles grant them without covering interpretation problems). For example, do preemptive rights encompass the purchase of treasury shares (in other words, stock the corporation once issued and repurchased)? See *Borg v. International Silver Co.,* 11 F.2d 147 (2d Cir.1925) (tradition view is no). Excluding treasury shares from preemptive rights, however, created the problem in *Schwartz.* Perhaps the articles should therefore broaden the rights to include sale of treasury shares. Next, do shares of one class possess preemptive rights to buy shares of another class? See *Thomas Branch & Co. v. Riverside & Dan River Cotton Mills,* 139 Va. 291, 123 S.E. 542 (1924) (held preferred had the right to buy common). After all, if one had non-voting, non-participating preferred shares, would the issuance of additional common dilute one's interest? What about the other way around? Suppose the corporation wishes to issue shares in exchange for property (such as the assets of a smaller firm). See *Thom v. Baltimore Trust Co.,* 158 Md. 352, 148 A. 234 (1930) (holding no rights then). If preemptive rights did apply and the shareholders exercise them, could the corporation accomplish this objective? A similar concern exists if the corporation seeks to issue shares to an employee benefit plan, or in order to discharge a debt. Finally, when does the issuance of shares become an additional sale to which the rights apply, rather than part of the original issuance that decides who has the rights? See *Yasik v. Wachtel,* 25 Del.Ch. 247, 17 A.2d 309 (Ch.1941) (later issued shares were part of one continuing planned offering). Examine how the Model Act answers these questions. Could the Model Act provide some ideas to include in articles in those states where the articles must create the rights with no statutory guidance? One final problem with preemptive rights lies in the fact they exist only by virtue of the articles (either providing them, or not excluding them, depending upon the jurisdiction). A majority could amend the articles to remove such rights. *E.g., Seattle Trust & Sav. Bank v. McCarthy,* 94 Wash.2d 605, 617 P.2d 1023 (1980). Is there any way to prevent this?

SECTION B. PROFIT AND LOSS

1. DIVIDENDS

a. *In General*

Gottfried v. Gottfried

73 N.Y.S.2d 692 (1947).

■ CORCORAN, JUSTICE.

This action was brought in the early part of 1945 by minority stockholders of Gottfried Baking Corporation (hereinafter called "Gottfried"), to compel the Board of Directors of that corporation to declare dividends on its common stock. The defendants are Gottfried itself, its directors, and Hanscom Baking Corporation (hereinafter called "Hanscom"), a wholly owned subsidiary of Gottfried. Gottfried is a closely held family corporation. All of its stockholders, with minor exceptions, are children of the founder of the business, Elias Gottfried, and their respective spouses.

Both corporations are engaged in the manufacture and sale of bakery products; Gottfried for distribution at wholesale, and Hanscom for distribution at retail in its own stores. Each corporation functions separately, in the manufacture and sale of its respective products.

At the end of 1946 the outstanding capitalization of Gottfried consisted of 4,500 shares of "A" stock, without nominal or par value, and 20,862 shares of common stock without par value. The "A" stock is entitled to dividends of $8 per share before any dividends may be paid upon the common stock, as well as a further participation in earnings. At the end of 1944, immediately before this action was commenced, Gottfried also had outstanding preferred stock in the fact amount of $79,000, and Hanscom had outstanding $86,000 face amount of preferred stock. The plaintiffs in the aggregate owned approximately 38% of each of these classes of securities. The individual defendants owned approximately 62 percent.

From 1931 until 1945 no dividends had been paid upon the common stock, although dividends had been paid regularly upon the outstanding preferred stock and intermittently upon the "A" stock. There seems to be no question with respect to the policy of the Board of Directors in not declaring dividends prior to 1944. An analysis of the financial statements of the corporation shows a net working capital deficit at the end of 1941, in which year a consolidated loss of $109,816 had been incurred. Moreover, until the end of 1943 the earned surplus was relatively small in relation to the volume of business done and the growing requirements of the business.

Although the action was brought in the early part of 1945 to compel the declaration of dividends upon the common stock, dividends actually were declared and paid upon said stock in 1945, and subsequently. The purpose of the action now, therefore, is to compel the payment of dividends upon the common stock in such amount as under all the circumstances is fair and adequate.

The action is predicated upon the claim that the policy of the Board of Directors with respect to the declaration of dividends is animated by considerations other than the best welfare of the corporations or their stockholders. The plaintiffs claim that bitter animosity on the part of the directors, who own the controlling stock, against the plaintiff minority stockholders, as well as a desire to coerce the latter into selling their stock to the majority interests at a grossly inadequate price, and the avoidance of heavy personal income taxes upon any dividends that might be declared, have been the motivating factors that have dominated the defendants. Plaintiffs, contend, moreover, that the defendants by excessive salaries, bonuses and corporate loans to themselves or some of them, have eliminated the immediate need of dividends in so far as they were concerned, while at the same time a starvation dividend policy with respect to the minority stockholders—not on the payroll—operates designedly to compel the plaintiffs to sacrifice their stock by sale to the defendants.

There is not essential dispute as to the principles of law involved. If an adequate corporate surplus is available for the purpose, directors may not withhold the declaration of dividends in bad faith. But the mere existence of an adequate corporate surplus is not sufficient to invoke court action to compel such a dividend. There must also be bad faith on the part of the directors. * * *

There are no infallible distinguishing ear-marks of bad faith. The following facts are relevant to the issue of bad faith and are admissible in evidence: Intense hostility of the controlling faction against the minority; exclusion of the minority from employment by the corporation; high salaries, or bonuses or corporate loans made to the officers in control; the fact that the majority group may be subject to high personal income taxes if substantial dividends are paid; the existence of a desire by the controlling directors to acquire the minority stock interests as cheaply as possible. But if they are not motivating causes they do not constitute "bad faith" as a matter of law.

The essential test of bad faith is to determine whether the policy of the directors is dictated by their personal interests rather than the corporate welfare. Directors are fiduciaries. Their cestui que trust are the corporation and the stockholders as a body. Circumstances such as those above mentioned and any other significant factors, appraised in the light of the financial condition and requirements of the corporation, will determine the conclusion as to whether the directors have or have not been animated by personal, as distinct from corporate, considerations.

The court is not concerned with the direction which the exercise of the judgment of the Board of Directors may take, provided only that such exercise of judgment be made in good faith. It is axiomatic that the court will not substitute its judgment for that of the Board of Directors.

It must be conceded that closely held corporations are easily subject to abuse on the part of dominant stockholders, particularly in the direction of action designed to compel minority stockholders to sell their stock at a sacrifice. But close corporation or not, the court will not tolerate directorate action designed to achieve that or any other wrongful purpose. Even in the absence of bad faith, however, the impact of dissension and hostility among stockholders falls usually with heavier force in a closely held corporation. In many such cases, a large part of a stockholder's assets may be tied up in the corporation. It is frequently contemplated by the parties, moreover, that the respective stockholders receive their major livelihood in the form of salaries resulting from employment by the corporation. If such employment be terminated, the hardship suffered by the minority stockholder or stockholders may be very heavy. Nevertheless, such situations do not in themselves form a ground for the interposition of a court of equity.

There is no doubt that in the present case bitter dissension and personal hostility have existed for a long time between the individual plaintiffs and defendants. The plaintiffs Charles Gottfried and Harold Gottfried have both been discontinued from the corporate payrolls.

It is true too that several of the defendants have in recent years received as compensation substantial sums. In the case of Maurice K. Gottfried this has taken the form of ten percent of the gross annual profits of Hansom before corporate income taxes. During the period from January 1, 1943 to December 21, 1946, he received, in addition to a fixed salary of $15,600, an aggregate sum of $220,528.91, or an average of $45,105.78 per annum. The evidence in this connection discloses, however, that he has been the chief executive officer of Hansom since its acquisition by Gottfried in 1933.

* * *

The propriety and legality of Maurice's agreement for participation in the profits of Hansom is the subject of other litigation between the parties. There is no determination in this proceeding as to such propriety or legality. The above evidence [that Hansom grew tremendously under Maurice's guidance] is discussed merely because it tends to show that the policy of Maurice and the other directors in connection with his profit participation arrangement bore no relationship to the question of whether dividends should be declared or paid, which is the only subject of the present action. Even if it had been established that such arrangement was excessive or invalid in part or in whole that question is divorced from the present issues. It should be noted in this connection that the burden of this arrangement fell equally upon the other defendant directors and not merely upon the plaintiffs.

The only other significant extra compensation to directors relates to the bonuses paid to the defendant Benjamin Gottfried of $5,000 in 1945 and $25,000 in 1946, and to the payment to defendant William Prince of $10,000 in 1946. * * * There is evidence of a long-standing bonus policy in the company which negatives any conclusion that these payments were conceived or made in lieu of dividends or in furtherance of a scheme not to pay dividends.

The evidence also discloses that substantial advances or loans have been made from time to time to several of the defendants, part of which still remain outstanding. Advances and loans of this character in varying amounts likewise had been made for many years to stockholders and directors. Without passing upon the propriety or legality of these transactions, the evidence does not sustain an inference that they were made with a view to the dividend policy of the corporation. They were incurred, in large part, long before any controversy arose with respect to dividends, nor is the aggregate amount thereof of sufficient magnitude to affect in a material way the capacity of Gottfried to pay dividends.

Plaintiff Charles Gottfried testified that Benjamin Gottfried, one of the defendants, told him that he and the other minority stockholders would never get any dividends because the majority could freeze them out and that the majority had other ways than declaring dividends of getting money out of the companies. Benjamin Gottfried denied that he had ever made such statements. There is no evidence, moreover, that such statements were made by any of the other defendants. The court does not believe that this disputed testimony carries much weight upon the question of a concerted policy on the part of the directors to refrain from declaring dividends for the purpose of "freezing out" the plaintiffs.

Nor does the evidence with respect to the financial condition of the corporation and its business requirements sustain the plaintiffs' claims. The action was started in the early part of 1945. The financial condition of Gottfried at the end of the immediately preceding year is of fundamental importance in determining the validity of plaintiffs' claim at the time that suit was brought. The consolidated balance sheet for the year ended December 30, 1944 discloses current assets of $1,055,844 against current liabilities of $468,438, or a working capital of $587,407. Of the current assets, cash represented $523,691 and inventory $357,347. The ratio of current assets to current liabilities at that time was, therefore, slightly above 2 to 1. The gross volume of business done in 1944 was $8,737,475. The net working capital, therefore, was less than 7 percent of the volume of business transacted. The net earnings for this year were $174,415.28, somewhat less than those for the two preceding war years. The earned surplus was $867,141.

The evidence discloses that at the end of 1944 expenditures in the amount of approximately $564,220 were contemplated to be made, and actually were made in 1945 in addition to ordinary operating expenses and in addition to other normal use of working capital. This sum included the retirement of the then outstanding preferred stocks of Gottfried and Hanscom in the sum of $165,000. Since all the parties held these preferred stocks in the same ratio as they held Gottfried "A" stock and common stock, each of the stockholders, including the plaintiffs, participated proportionately in the benefits of such retirement. After said retirement their respective pro rata interests in Gottfried were precisely the same as before these distributions were made. From this point of view the plaintiffs were in at least as good a position as a result of this preferred stock retirement as though dividends had been paid upon the common stock in the sum of $165,000, which is almost equivalent to the entire net earnings for the year 1944. It is noteworthy in this connection, moreover, that the retirement of the preferred stock was urged by both Charles and Harold Gottfried, two of the plaintiffs, at the annual meeting of the stockholders of Gottfried held on December 5, 1944. * * * These stockholders certainly cannot complaint because a sum almost equivalent to the prior year's entire net income was defrayed, in accordance with their own request, in the form of retirement of preferred stock rather than by payment of dividends on the common stock.

Other major items of expenditure in 1945, which appear to have been contemplated at the end of 1944, were payments of dividends on Gottfried preferred stock in the sum of $5,031, dividends on Hansom preferred stock in the sum of $5,597, and dividends on the "A" stock of $36,000. In all of these payments of dividends on stock prior to the common stock the plaintiffs were pro rata beneficiaries. In 1945 there were also payments upon outstanding mortgages in the sum of $133,626. Reduction of mortgage indebtedness seems to have been a standard policy of Gottfried when its financial condition permitted it. Payments for sites for new plants and properties deemed necessary for the corporations' operations aggregated more than $214,000.

In addition to the above-mentioned expenditures of $560,220 contemplated in 1944 and made in 1945, Gottfried in 1945 paid $31,532 in dividends on the common stock. It may be, of course, that the payment of these dividends was stimulated by the commencement of this suit. The fact remains that they were paid. Other abnormal expenditures which seem to have been contemplated at the end of 1944 were a substantial increase in inventories owing to unusual conditions in the market at the time and various post-war projects involving large sums of money which could not be effectuated during the war period.

* * *

Under these circumstances, it may not be said that the directorate policy regarding common stock dividends at the time the suit was brought was unduly conservative. It certainly does not appear to have been inspired by bad faith. * * *

The plaintiffs oppose many of these policies of expansion. There is no evidence of any weight to the effect that these policies of the Board of Directors are actuated by any motives other than their best business judgment. If they are mistaken, their own stock holdings will suffer proportionately to those of the plaintiffs. With the wisdom of that policy the court has no concern. It is this court's conclusion that these policies and the expenditures which they entail are undertaken in good faith and without relation to any conspiracy, scheme or plan to withhold dividends for the purpose of compelling the plaintiffs to sell their stock or pursuant to any other sinister design.

The plaintiffs have failed to prove that the surplus is unnecessarily large. They have also failed to prove that the defendants recognized the propriety of paying dividends but refused to do so for personal reasons. * * *

The complaint is dismissed and judgment directed for the defendants. * * *

NOTES

1. As *Gottfried* illustrates, dividends represent the traditional method by which owners of a corporation are supposed to receive the profits of the business. (The case also shows there are other ways, such as interest payments, salaries or repurchase of stock, for a company to pass funds to its owners. These often supplant dividends, especially in closely held

corporations. Consideration of these alternatives, however, will be deferred until later.) Each stockholder's proportion of any dividend is a function of both the relative amount of stock he or she owns vis-a-vis the other stockholders, and, when all shares of stock are not of the same type, the rights of the class (or classes) of stock he or she owns, relative to the other classes of stock. This means that, in contrast to partners, limited partners or members in an LLC, who can specify their division of profits directly in a partnership or LLC operating agreement, participants in a corporation must encapsulate their allocation of profits in the amount of shares issued to each stockholder, and in the rights of the various classes of stock. For the simplest case, when the parties agree to divide profits equally or in some other ratio, issuing one class of stock to them in the agreed proportion seemingly does the job. (Recall, however, a problem discussed earlier. This division of stock also governs the parties' voting rights, and their rights to distributions from the corporation even when the distribution reflects the return of invested capital rather than corporate earnings. The prior section of this chapter considered how to break the connection between allocating profit rights and the rights to return of invested capital, while the next section of this chapter will explore alternate methods to deal with voting power.) Focusing for now on achieving the agreed allocation of profit, what happens when the participants decide upon a division which does not follow simple ratios? For example, owners of a business sometimes wish the allocation to change at different levels of firm earnings. In this manner, they can accommodate differing desires as to the trade-off between risk and reward. Owners who place greater value on certainty of income can receive a higher proportion of the first earnings of the business in exchange for giving owners who are more willing to take risks for greater rewards a larger proportion of additional earnings. (This is essentially the concept of leverage discussed earlier.) Also, this can accommodate the interests of those who contribute cash or tangible property to a business and insist upon some return on their investment prior to sharing profits with those contributing services or intangibles (especially if the company pays the latter a salary).

Owners of a corporation might attempt to achieve more complicated divisions of profit (such as one which varies with differing levels of firm income) by altering their relative stock holdings at the points they wish the profit shares to change. This could entail the company, at an agreed time, issuing more shares to some owners, the company redeeming some shares from other owners, or the shareholders transferring shares between themselves (or some combination of the above). For example, suppose two owners of a corporation agree to share the first $100,000 of earnings 60 percent for one and 40 percent for the other, after which they will share all further earnings equally. They could accomplish this by the company issuing shares 60 percent to the one party and 40 percent to the other, and, after the company distributes $100,000 in dividends, it could issue more shares to the 40 percent holder, redeem shares from the 60 percent holder, or the 60 percent holder could transfer shares to the 40 percent holder, so the two parties thereafter would each own an equal amount.

While it is theoretically possible to achieve just about any desired allocation using such a scheme, several practical problems limit its utility in most situations. To begin with, changes in share ownership can create impacts beyond the desired altering of rights to future profits. These include changing voting power, and reallocating rights to return of invested capital (and even to earlier undistributed income). Moreover, unless the parties plan to make the necessary transfer of shares gratuitously, they must factor in the offsetting payment. There are also tax consequences to consider. Chapter VI will explore this. Finally, prearranging the necessary transfer may entail some complex transactional mechanics—especially if the transfer will occur more than once. (For instance, suppose the parties in the hypothetical above agreed to share the first $100,000 of each year's income 60 percent for one and 40 percent for the other, and all additional earnings equally.)

Still, corporations frequently employ several devices whose underlying purpose is to create more flexible profit divisions by changing the relative stockholdings depending upon how the company does. One such device, convertible debt, was described earlier. Convertible debt allows its holder to claim a fixed return on investment regardless of corporate earnings, but, if the company does very well, the debt holder can exchange his or her debt instrument for stock in the corporation. In this manner, the debt holder can increase his or her share in larger levels of corporate earnings (and, correspondingly, decrease the share of the other stockholders) by shifting the relative stock ownership. Along similar lines, many companies issue options (often called warrants) which grant the recipient a contractual right to buy shares from the corporation at a given price. (Many state statutes explicitly provide corporations the power to issue such options—albeit these statutes may simply express a power implicit even without them. *E.g.,* Cal. Corp. Code § 404; Del. Gen. Corp. Law § 157; N.Y. Bus. Corp. Law § 505; M.B.C.A. § 6.24; *Tribble v. J.W. Greer Co.,* 83 F.Supp. 1015 (D.Mass.1949).) While the exercise of warrants brings additional capital into the company, that is not their purpose. Rationally, the warrant's owner only exercises it when the company is doing well—making the value of the stock greater than the option price—which presumably means at a time when the corporation is least likely to need the money. What the warrant does is to give its holder the prospect of obtaining a greater share of the corporation's profits should the company prosper, without his or her needing to risk as much initial investment. (The warrant's holder, however, must give something for it, unless the company issued it as a dividend, or else the option would not bind the company.) The larger share for the warrant owner who exercises his or her rights, means a smaller relative share for the other stockholders, and so a warrant constitutes another mechanism to shift the profit allocation depending upon how the company fares.

The more typical method corporations use to achieve complex divisions of profit among their owners is to create additional classes of stock with differing rights to dividends. A very simple example of differing dividend rights would be for a corporation's articles to authorize two classes of shares, and entitle shares of one class to receive twice (or some other multiple) as much per share of any dividend as shares of the other class. (In other words, if the board declares a dividend of $1 per share for the disfavored class, it must distribute $2 per share for the favored class.) Of course, one could achieve the same effect using only one class of stock by giving some shareholders twice as many shares. Hence, creating a class of stock which is merely entitled to some greater multiple of any dividend than shares of another class is generally not particularly useful or often done. (An exception may exist when the parties are trying to achieve a different allocation of voting power from rights to profits.) Far more useful, and frequently found, is to create additional classes of stock which have the right to receive a certain amount of dividends before the company may distribute any dividend to shareholders of other classes. *Gottfried* provides an illustration. The "A" stock was entitled to receive a dividend of $8 per share before the board could declare any dividends for the other class of stock. The right to receive dividends before another class of stock is often referred to as a dividend preference, and, accordingly, shares having such a right are usually called "preferred." What makes such a dividend preference especially useful is it provides a means to achieve a profit allocation which changes at differing levels of corporate income. The distribution of the preferred controls the allocation of the lowest level of corporate earnings (that is, after payment of interest and salaries); the distribution of common and "participating" preferred (which will be described shortly) controls the allocation of greater amounts. Moreover, one can add to the number of levels at which the allocation changes by creating additional classes of preferred with some having preferences to others. (The corporation in *Gottfried* evidently had three classes before it repurchased all the shares of its "preferred" class.) On the other hand, notice the parties in *Gottfried* held the "A" and "preferred" stock in the same ratio they held the common. What purpose could the multiple classes then serve? Reconsider this question when reading Chapter VI, which deals with restructuring stock ownership. (As a hint of one possible answer, ask whether situations could arise over a period of time when members of a family might wish to restructure their stockholdings so some own common and others own preferred. If so, is there any advantage to already having the preferred outstanding?)

The articles of incorporation normally specify dividend preferences—as well as the shares' other rights when there is more than one class of stock. *E.g.*, Cal. Corp. Code §§ 203, 400, 401; Del. Gen. Corp. Law §§ 102(a)(4), 151; N.Y. Bus. Corp. Law §§ 402(a)(5), (6), 501(a); M.B.C.A. § 6.01. (An exception exists when the articles empower the board of directors to set the rights of new series of shares as part of the board's vote to issue the stock.) Drafting the dividend preference requires answering a number of questions. The most obvious is what is the amount of the preference. In *Gottfried*, the "A" stock had a preference of $8 per share. (Sometimes, the articles specify the amount as a percentage of par value. This is simply another way of giving a dollar amount.) Yet, simply specifying a dollar amount begs a fundamental question: Is this the actual sum payable each time the board declares a dividend before the other shares may receive any money? If so, the relative claims of the preferred shares to corporate earnings vis-a-vis the common would be radically different depending upon whether the board declared a dividend every quarter, yearly, or only once in several years. For this reason, articles often specify the preference as an amount accruing over a period of time (such as $8 per year). Taking this step raises three further issues for the drafter to address. Suppose the corporation has no earnings (or insufficient earnings to cover the preference amount) during the period specified. Does the sum still accrue? See *Fawkes v. Farm Lands Inv. Co.,* 112 Cal.App. 374, 297 P. 47 (1931) (holding it does if the preferred is cumulative and the articles say nothing to the contrary). The answer to this question creates two impacts. Even if a corporation had no earnings during a year, it still may be able to declare a dividend—all of which can go to the common if nothing accrued to the preferred. Also, preferred shares may have rights, as discussed below, to receive at a later time the accumulated sum of accrued dividends which the corporation skipped. Next, what happens if the corporation declares a dividend more often than the accrual period (for example, if the board declares a quarterly dividend, but the preference amount accrues every year)? Should the board pro-rate the preference amount between the dividends, or must it pay the entire preference in the first distribution? Perhaps most significant of all, what happens if the board declares a dividend less often than the accrual period—in other words, if it skips dividends? If the preferred stock is "cumulative," this means the articles require the corporation to distribute the arrearage (the accumulated skipped dividends) before paying any dividends on the junior shares. If the preferred is not cumulative, skipped dividends are lost, and the company need only pay the preference amount for the present period before declaring a dividend for the other shares. *E.g., Guttman v. Illinois Central R. Co.,* 189 F.2d 927 (2d Cir.1951), *cert. denied,* 342 U.S. 867 (1951). *But see Sanders v. Cuba Railroad Co.,* 21 N.J. 78, 120 A.2d 849 (1956) (New Jersey courts interpret non-cumulative preferred to still be entitled to skipped dividends from the years when the corporation had earnings sufficient to pay the dividend, unless the articles clearly disavow any such right). Notice the conflict of interest between the classes created by issuing non-cumulative preferred shares. The directors can increase the proportion of corporate earnings going to the junior shares by omitting dividends. The problem is compounded if the non-cumulative preferred shares lack the right to vote for directors and thereby influence the board's decision. For these reasons, most courts interpret ambiguous provisions as making the preferred cumulative. *See,* e.g., *Hazel Atlas Glass Co. v. Van Dyk & Reeves,* 8 F.2d 716 (2d Cir.1925), *cert. denied,* 269 U.S. 570.

Having specified the preference amount, one question remains regarding the preferred's rights to dividends. This is whether the preferred is entitled to any further distribution after it receives the preference amount. If the articles give the stock no right to receive dividends beyond the stated preference, it is called "non-participating". "Participating" preferred is entitled to receive additional dividends under terms specified by the articles. These provisions sometimes call for a certain amount of money to go to the common before the common and preferred stock share any additional dividends. Moreover, each share could receive an equal amount of additional dividends, or the articles may give shares of some classes a greater proportion than others. If the articles are silent, courts disagree as to whether or not preferred shares participate in further dividends. *Compare Englander v. Osborne,* 261 Pa. 366, 104 A. 614 (1918), *with St. Louis Southwestern Ry. Co. v. Loeb,* 318 S.W.2d 246 (Mo.1958).

2. When authorizing multiple classes of stock, one must consider other possible differences in their rights beyond their relative claims to dividends. These include (i) voting power, (ii) liquidation preferences, (iii) conversion rights, and (iv) redeemability. Several of these subjects are explored elsewhere in this chapter. For instance, the next section dealing with management considers differing voting rights between classes of shares. Still, there are some logical relationships between dividend preferences (as well as the more general subject of profit and loss allocation) and these other rights, which should be explored now.

Articles often deny preferred shares the right to vote; albeit there is no legal requirement that preferred be non-voting, and if the articles are silent they can vote. *E.g.,* Cal. Corp. Code § 700(a); Del. Gen. Corp. Law § 212(a); N.Y. Bus. Corp. Law § 612(a); M.B.C.A. § 7.21(a). Also, statutes may require the vote of the holders of preferred stock, even if otherwise non-voting, to approve certain fundamental changes (such as amending the articles, or mergers), particularly if the change prejudices the preferred shareholders' rights as a class. *E.g.,* Cal. Corp. Code §§ 903(a), 1201(a); Del. Gen. Corp. Law § 242(b)(2); N.Y. Bus. Corp. Law §§ 804, 903(a)(2); M.B.C.A. §§ 10.04, 11.03(f). Articles frequently draw one connection between dividend preferences and voting rights which may be logical if the preferred are otherwise non-voting. This is to provide contingent voting rights should the corporation skip a certain number of dividends. Such contingent rights require careful drafting to specify how many omissions trigger the voting power, what the extent of the voting power is (ranging from exclusive power to elect the entire board, to a right to elect just some directors, to simply a right to have one vote per share like the common), and when the power terminates (which could be upon the declaration of any dividend, upon completely curing the arrearage, or something in between).

Articles also may differentiate between classes of shares in terms of their rights upon liquidation. As discussed with dividend rights, the articles could simply entitle some shares to receive a greater proportion per share of any distribution than other shares (for instance, $2 per share for one class, for every dollar received per share by the other class). Again, however, this generally does not do much that giving some parties additional shares would not accomplish. Much more useful, and frequently found, are provisions entitling a class of shares to receive a certain amount of money from the corporation upon liquidation before the company may pay anything to other shares. This is known as a liquidation preference, and, accordingly, such shares might again be referred to as "preferred". (Keep in mind, however, that preferred shares may possess a liquidation preference and no dividend preference, or vice versa.)

Liquidation preferences can serve three purposes. One was encountered earlier. This is to disconnect rights to return of invested capital from the division of profit (and even from voting control). Hence, a party contributing cash (or tangible property) may agree to share profits equally (for instance) with a party contributing services (or highly speculative intangibles), and yet demand return of his or her investment upon liquidation before the service provider receives anything. Issuing the cash provider stock with a liquidation preference equal to its issue price can accomplish this objective.

The second goal achieved by liquidation preferences involves the allocation of losses. Suppose two parties agree to enter a business and contribute an equal amount of cash, but one party is more averse to risk than the other. In a partnership, they might agree to allocate the losses first to the less risk averse individual up to the amount of his or her investment. (This could perhaps be in exchange for a greater share of profit.) To accomplish the same objective in a corporation, the company could issue to the risk averse party all the shares of one class of stock having the right to receive back its issue price upon liquidation before the company may distribute money to the owner of the other class of stock. Moreover, just as with dividend preferences, a company may issue several classes of stock with liquidation preferences relative to each other, thereby creating a multilevel loss allocation. Keep in mind, however, what works in a corporation does not necessarily work in a partnership. Priority to distribution of assets upon liquidation of an ordinary partnership, without more, would not have the same effect of allocating losses, because partners in an ordinary partnership have the obligation, barring contrary agreement, to contribute money to the firm until they have borne their agreed share of losses. Keep in mind also, because of limited liability, shareholders do not have to worry about allocating losses in excess of their investment. This significantly reduces the importance of loss allocation in a corporation, since often in a failed business there will be little, if anything, left of the shareholders' investment to haggle over.

The third objective of a liquidation preference can be to allocate profits. Even successful corporations may eventually dissolve (perhaps after selling their assets to a bigger company). Much, if not most, of their assets will represent the accumulation of retained earnings which the directors reinvested in the business rather than distributed as dividends. At this point, it is important to recognize a relationship between dividend and liquidation rights. With only one class of stock, each share will obtain its pro-rata amount of all profits made by the corporation, whether paid as dividends or retained until liquidation. Suppose, however, the parties introduce a class of stock with a dividend preference (even one that is cumulative), but no preference on liquidation. In this event, earnings which would go to the preferred holders if paid as dividends, the common will share if the company skipped dividends and retained the earnings until its liquidation. Conversely, suppose a class of preferred is non-participating as far as dividend rights, but does participate upon liquidation. In this case, retained earnings which would have gone to the common if distributed as dividends after payment of the preference, end up shared with the preferred. *E.g., In re Clark's Will,* 131 Misc. 151, 226 N.Y.S. 141 (1928). Beyond the evident problem of fairness, one practical difficulty this shift in rights to earnings creates is it may tempt the board to liquidate the company—perhaps after selling its assets to a new corporation—in order to favor one class over the other. For these reasons, corporate articles normally try to coordinate dividend and liquidation preferences so each share's claim against earnings remains the same regardless of whether distributed as dividends or in liquidation. Hence, preferred stock with cumulative dividend rights will typically have a liquidation preference (beyond return of its issue price) for an amount equal to any dividends in arrears. Similarly, preferred which is non-participating for dividends usually is non-participating upon liquidation, and vice versa. Incidentally, it is only with respect to this third objective (profit allocation) that there is any logical necessity for stock with a liquidation preference to also possess a dividend preference.

With these goals in mind, the drafter of a liquidation preference can answer analogous questions to those raised when specifying a dividend preference. Again, the first question is what is the amount of the preference. This relates to its purpose. If the purpose is either to sever the connection between the profit division and the right to return of invested capital, or to allocate losses, then the preference amount is normally the issue price. If the purpose is to ensure the allocation of profits in conformity with a dividend preference, then an amount equal to any arrearage seems sensible. Of course, both these purposes often overlap, in which case one can simply add the two sums together. Having set the preference amount, one must consider again whether the shares can participate in any further distribution. As stated above, this may logically call for parallel treatment to that provided for dividend distributions. (First, however, one may wish to return to the common holders the issue price of the common, since only after this is done do the remaining sums represent retained earnings.) As in the case of dividends, failure to specify whether preferred participates in liquidating distributions beyond the preference amount can lead to litigation. *See Mohawk Carpet Mills, Inc. v. Delaware Rayon Co.,* 35 Del.Ch. 51, 110 A.2d 305 (1954) (denying participation when not stated).

Articles sometimes make preferred shares convertible into shares of another class (typically common). *See, e.g.,* Cal. Corp. Code § 403(a); Del. Gen. Corp. Law § 151(e); N.Y. Bus. Corp. Law § 519(a); M.B.C.A. § 6.01(c)(2) (all empowering corporations to issue convertible shares). The rationale is normally analogous to that discussed earlier for convertible debt. The holder may claim the advantage of the dividend preference to obtain a greater share of a low level of corporate earnings (and even decrease his or her risk of loss through a liquidation preference should things go badly), yet, if the corporation does very well, he or she can convert the stock into common and enjoy a share of higher levels of corporate earnings. Notice, unlike the case with debt, however, one could accomplish roughly the same objective by issuing participating (rather than convertible) preferred. (Common holders might, of course, desire a right to convert to preferred if things go poorly, and both types of shareholders might, for the same reason, wish the right to convert into debt. Some statutes, however, limit such upstream conversion. *See, e.g.,* N.Y. Bus. Corp. Law § 519(c)(3) (common cannot be subject to conversion unless another class or series of common is not subject to conversion). *But see* Cal. Corp. Code § 403(a)(1) (allowing upstream conversion into preferred); Del. Gen. Corp. Law § 151(b), (e) (same); M.B.C.A. § 6.01(c)(2).) At any event, with convertible preferred, one is allocating profits using both the techniques of multiple classes with differing rights to dividends, and altering the relative stockholdings depending upon how the company does.

Issuing convertible preferred (or convertible debt) requires addressing several planning questions. The articles (or debt agreement in the case of convertible debt) must specify when and how owners may exercise their conversion rights—in other words, when is the first and last time the owner can convert (assuming the right does not run from date of issuance until liquidation), and what type of notice must the owner give to do so. *See, e.g., Spratt v. Paramount Pictures,* 178 Misc. 682, 35 N.Y.S.2d 815 (1942) (demanding strict adherence by the shareholder seeking to exercise his or her conversion right to the requirements specified in the articles). Of critical importance, the articles must specify the conversion ratio—how many shares of common (or whatever other class the conversion is into) does the owner receive for each share of preferred (or dollar amount of debt) surrendered? In this regard, one must address what happens if the number of common increases due to stock splits, stock dividends, or other additional issuances. *See Pratt v. American Bell Tel. Co.,* 141 Mass. 225, 5 N.E. 307 (1886) (court refused to increase the number of shares which a convertible security holder would receive, in order to offset a stock split, when the conversion right did not specifically provide this protection against dilution). *See also Reiss v. Financial Performance Corp.*, 97 N.Y.2d 195, 738 N.Y.S.2d 658, 764 N.E.2d 958 (2001) (the court refused to adjust, in the absence of an agreement calling for such adjustment, the terms of warrants allowing their holder to purchase stock at a set price, in order to compensate for a reverse stock split that had made shares more valuable). Changes in conversion ratios upon these or other events can create complicated tax questions under I.R.C. Section 305(c). Chapter VI deals with this provision. Sometimes, the article provisions creating convertible preferred call for changes in conversion ratios, not only to adjust for changes in the number of outstanding common shares, but also to adjust for changes in the market price of the common. Can this create any hazard? See *Internet Law Library, Inc. v. Southridge Capital Mng't, LLC*, 223 F. Supp. 2d 474 (S.D.N.Y.2002) (the plaintiffs alleged that holders of convertible preferred sold common stock short in order to drive down the price of the common stock prior to exercising the option to convert the preferred into common at a price adjusted to reflect the market price of the common). Yet another event to consider in specifying conversion rights occurs when the corporation merges, and the common holders received shares in the surviving company or some other consideration. *See Broad v. Rockwell Intern. Corp.*, 642 F.2d 929 (5th Cir.1981), *cert. denied,* 454 U.S. 965 (common holders were cashed out in merger). Lastly, as a technical, but not trivial matter, the corporation must maintain an adequate number of authorized but unissued shares to cover any conversions.

Turning from rights of the preferred stock to rights of the corporation vis-a-vis the stock, many articles authorizing preferred give the company the option to redeem it (in other words, buy it back) at a certain price. (Articles granting a company the option to redeem common are rare, and they may not be valid under some state corporations statutes. *See, e.g., Starring v. American Hair & Felt Co.,* 21 Del.Ch. 380, 191 A. 887 (1937), *aff'd,* 21 Del.Ch. 431, 2 A.2d 249. *See also* Del. Gen. Corp. Code § 151(b) (empowering corporations to issue redeemable preferred). *But see* Cal. Corp. Code § 402 (allowing redeemable common if another class of common is not redeemable); N.Y. Bus. Corp. Law § 512(b) (same); M.B.C.A. § 6.01(c)(2) (not drawing distinction). As discussed later in this chapter, however, corporations might enter into side contracts with the purchasers of common (or preferred), giving the company the option to repurchase the stock upon certain circumstances.) There are a number of reasons why participants in a corporation might wish the company to have the option to repurchase its shares. Most of these reasons have to do with problems attendant upon share transfers in a closely held corporation, and are considered in the final section of this chapter. One motivation specifically behind redeemable preferred, however, relates to the allocation of profit and loss. Redeemable preferred provides yet another mechanism for creating a division of profit utilizing both the tools of multiple classes with differing claims against the corporation's profits, and prearranged alterations in the outstanding stock. Specifically, redeemability puts something of a cap on the profit share of those holding the redeemable stock. For example, if the stock is participating, and the corporation does very well, the company can redeem the class thereby leaving more of the increased level of profits for the remaining shareholders. *Zahn v. Transamerica Corp.,* which is reprinted in Chapter VI, provides an extreme illustration of this use of redemption. Even if the preferred is not participating, the corporation might choose to redeem it either when the company has surplus cash or when the corporation can raise money at a lesser claim against its profits. This is analogous to the reason for prepaying, or "redeeming," debt instruments discussed earlier.

Drafting a redemption provision raises several questions. Along similar lines with convertibility, one should specify when and how the corporation can exercise its right to redeem—in other words, when is the first and when is the last time the company may redeem (assuming it cannot do so anytime between issuance and liquidation). *See, e.g., Thompson v. Fairleigh,* 300 Ky. 144, 187 S.W.2d 812 (1945) (when articles specified initial but not final time, court held that the corporation must redeem, if at all, within a reasonable time after initial point). Also, what notice must the company give? See, *e.g.*, *Van Gemert v. Boeing Co.*, 520 F.2d 1373 (2d Cir.1975), *cert. denied,* 423 U.S. 947 (required compliance with New York Stock Exchange rule regarding notice). This notice is especially important if the shareholders have conversion rights which they could exercise in lieu of redemption. Of obvious importance is the redemption price. At a minimum, this will equal the issue price, plus, for reasons analogous to those discussed when dealing with liquidation preferences, any arrearage in dividends. Typically, there is some premium above this sum as well (just as with prepaying, or "redeeming," debt instruments). (A premium, however, can create a tax problem under I.R.C. Section 305(c). *See* Rev. Rul. 83–119, reprinted in Chapter VI.) If the company wishes flexibility to redeem less than the entire class, the articles should specify how it will choose (for example, by lot) which shares to redeem. *See State ex rel. Waldman v. Miller–Wohl Co.*, 42 Del. 73, 28 A.2d 148 (1942) (dispute over how to interpret a provision which called for selection of shares to redeem by lot, pro-rata or otherwise, as determined by the directors). Finally, what rights (particularly if the shares are convertible) do the stockholders have between the time the company announces it will redeem and their surrender of the shares? See, *e.g.*, M.B.C.A. § 7.21(d) (not allowing them to vote after company mails notice and deposits funds to cover redemption).

The actual redemption or repurchase of shares by the corporation raises a number of potentially difficult issues, including limitations on legally available sources of funds, fiduciary duty questions, and tax issues. Consideration of these subjects is deferred until Chapter VI. Incidently, many statutes authorize the issuance of shares redeemable at the owner's (rather than the corporation's) option. *E.g.*, Cal. Corp. Code § 402(a) (preferred holder's option); Del. Gen. Corp. Law § 151(b) (same); N.Y. Bus. Corp. Law § 512 (same); M.B.C.A. § 6.01(c)(2). What purpose might this serve? What problems might it create? One purpose could be to create a temporary investment, much like debt. Another way to accomplish this is for the corporation to agree to set aside a given amount of money to periodically buy back its outstanding preferred stock. This is known as a sinking fund.

3. The proportion of the outstanding stock which each shareholder owns, and the preferences of the various classes of stock, allocate the relative shares of corporate profit which each shareholder will receive at such time as the company distributes earnings through dividends. As noted in dealing with non-corporate forms of business, however, the owners of a firm should consider not only their relative shares of the firm's income, but also the question of when the firm will actually distribute money to them. This subject assumes even greater importance with corporations than with partnerships—witness the litigation in *Gottfried* and in numerous similar cases. For corporations, as the *Gottfried* opinion explains, the board of directors possesses discretion, within very broad limits, to decide whether or not to declare a dividend, and how much of one to declare. Why should this create any problem? After all, since the shareholders elect the directors and since the directors are likely to be substantial shareholders themselves (especially in a closely held corporation), presumably the directors have

every incentive to pay dividends when consistent with maximizing shareholder wealth.

The facts in *Gottfried* illustrate three potential difficulties with this simple reasoning. To begin with, participants in a corporation may reach different judgments as to the business wisdom of distributing earnings versus reinvesting them in the company. As in *Gottfried,* this is often a function of disagreements about whether the company will benefit through expansion. To compound this problem, owners of a business often place differing utilities upon receiving immediate income (a dollar today) versus receiving greater amounts in the future (two dollars tomorrow). In many instances, this is a function of age and other sources of income. For example, a retired individual, with limited outside income, may need distributions to live in reasonable comfort. At the same time, such a person may not be around to benefit from the long term growth in the company. Worst of all, in corporations (unlike the situation normally in partnerships), refusal to declare dividends can actually alter the relative shares of profit received by the company's various owners—instead of simply postponing enjoyment of income by all the owners. One example was confronted earlier: Skipping dividends effectively transfers a share of earnings from the holders of non-cumulative preferred to the holders of common stock. *Gottfried* illustrates the more frequent concern in closely held corporations. Directors may receive money from the company through various alternatives to dividends, such as loan payments, repurchase of stock, and, especially, salaries. Other shareholders (particularly those not employed by the company) may receive nothing but dividends. This conflict of interest between passive owners and active participants with respect to dividend policy is one of the most prevalent sources of strife in a closely held corporation.

What planning techniques are available to deal with these differences over declaring dividends? To the extent the difference reflects a broader disagreement concerning business policy (such as whether to expand), the techniques discussed in the next section of this chapter for protecting minority shareholders in the management of a closely held corporation become apropos. In fact, the declaration of dividends is itself a management decision, and hence the parties might employ the various approaches discussed in the next section (such as a shareholders contract) in an attempt to control dividend decisions. Preferred stock also might be of help—especially when the underlying problem lies in differing utilities for current versus future income. As in *Gottfried,* the declaration of dividends is typically not an all or nothing proposition. The directors are likely to distribute some earnings as dividends, and reinvest some in the business. Giving preferred shares to the stockholders who place a greater value on immediate income will provide those individuals with a larger proportion of any near-term distributions. At the same time, the stockholders who favor reinvestment can obtain a larger proportion of the common stock, thereby entitling them to a greater share of future distributions at the presumably higher levels resulting from having reinvested part of the current earnings. In this manner, dividend preferences not only allocate different levels of profit, they also can impact the timing of its receipt. Of course, even preferred stock will not help if the directors do not declare any dividends at all. A dividend preference merely means the company must pay the preference amount before it can distribute dividends for other shares—which is rather irrelevant if the directors choose not to distribute dividends for any shares. *E.g., Field v. Lamson & Goodnow Mfg. Co.,* 162 Mass. 388, 38 N.E. 1126 (1894). A company's articles can, however, not only give one class of stock a preference to dividends, when and if declared, but also could require the directors to declare for the class a certain amount of dividends at stated intervals. *E.g., Crocker v. Waltham Watch Co.,* 315 Mass. 397, 53 N.E.2d 230 (1944). (As discussed below, state statutes prevent a corporation from legally paying dividends unless a certain minimum amount of funds are available. Hence, a provision requiring the directors to pay dividends must condition the requirement upon the availability of legally adequate funds. More narrowly, the provision might only make dividends mandatory if the corporation has earnings to cover them.) Alternatively, one may note that the incentive to avoid all dividends is strongest when the directors obtain money from the company through other means (such as salaries). Participants in a closely held corporation could attempt to respond by regulating these alternate sources of distributions, rather than seeking to control dividend distributions directly. This could entail either limiting these alternate payments, or (particularly given the tax advantages of such alternate payments alluded to in *Gottfried* and discussed later in this section) ensuring that all the owners of the company partake in them.

4. In an ordinary partnership, creditors are presumably unconcerned about distributions of money from the firm to its owners, because the owners have unlimited personal liability. Once one introduces limited liability, this changes. If those with no personal liability could legally withdraw their original investment at any time, they could deprive creditors of the cushion provided by this invested capital, which the creditors may have relied upon in advancing money to the business. Worse, the unscrupulous might take advantage of such a regime by withdrawing money representing not only their investment, but also that obtained through borrowing by the firm. For this reason, as discussed in the previous chapter, the statutes governing limited partnerships, LLPs and LLCs typically restrict distributions from the firm. Based upon the same concerns, state corporations statutes impose even more elaborate restrictions upon dividends paid by corporations to their shareholders.

These dividend rules vary among the different state statutes. New York and Delaware typify the most traditional approach—often referred to as the balance sheet test. Under these statutes, dividends generally cannot exceed the amount of the corporation's "surplus." *E.g.,* Del. Gen. Corp. Law § 170(a); N.Y. Bus. Corp. Law § 510(b). "Surplus" is not any segregated stash of money; rather it is a term of art meaning the difference between the corporation's "net assets" and its "capital" or "stated capital." *E.g.,* Del. Gen. Corp. Law § 154; N.Y. Bus. Corp. Law § 102(a)(13). "Net assets" in turn, is the amount arrived at by subtracting the company's total liabilities from its total assets. *E.g.,* Del. Gen. Corp. Law § 154;

N.Y. Bus. Corp. Law § 102(a)(9). This, of course, is the amount often referred to as "equity" or "net worth" on a balance sheet, and one can now see why this approach is often referred to as the balance sheet test.

As stated before, to determine surplus, one must subtract "capital" or "stated capital"—two terms for a similar concept—from net assets. Under Delaware's statute, "capital," at least initially, represents that portion of the consideration the company received in exchange for its shares, which the directors, at the time the company sold the shares, chose to call capital. Del. Gen. Corp. Law § 154. This could be the entire purchase price, or any fraction of it, so long as the amount is no less than the aggregate par value of those shares sold which have a par value (in other words, par value multiplied by the number of such shares). (If the directors neglect to set any amount, then capital equals the aggregate par value of shares with par, and the entire sum received for shares without par.) Similarly, "stated capital" under New York law equals initially the aggregate par value of shares sold which have a par value, plus the total received for shares without par value (unless, after their sale, the board allocates some of the amount received for no-par shares to surplus rather than stated capital). N.Y. Bus. Corp. Law § 506. Under either statute, directors, by resolution, can increase capital or stated capital. Del. Gen. Corp. Law § 154; N.Y. Bus. Corp. Law § 506(c). Again, this does not involve actually transferring any funds; the company simply increases the number shown for capital or stated capital on its balance sheet, and decreases, by the same amount, the number shown for surplus (since surplus, by definition, is the difference between net assets and capital). Methods also exist to reduce capital or stated capital. These will be addressed when considering the repurchase of stock in Chapter VI. At this point, one implication for planning is evident. These statutes do not prohibit dividends which represent the return of money the shareholders paid for their stock, rather than earnings. One can maximize the directors' flexibility to declare dividends representing return of invested funds by setting a low par (or no par) in the articles, and by the directors choosing to specify little of the purchase price for the shares as capital or stated capital. (Many corporations use low par, because the franchise tax in some states is higher with no-par shares.) There are, however, two problems with this approach. For one thing, it could make prospective creditors less willing to advance money to the corporation. For another, it might undermine liquidation priorities and the more general expectations of shareholders concerning the use of their investment—a subject to be addressed more below.

New York and Delaware also illustrate a couple of common variations on the basic balance sheet test. To begin with, it is possible for a corporation to have a surplus, yet still be insolvent in the sense that it lacks sufficient liquid or current assets (cash and the like) to pay its current or soon to be due bills. New York's statute prohibits paying dividends either when the corporation is insolvent, or when paying the dividend would render the company insolvent, in this sense (N.Y. Bus. Corp. Law §§ 102(a)(8), 510(a))—albeit, such a dividend likely constitutes a fraudulent conveyance regardless of whether it violates specific provisions in the dividend statute (*e.g.*, *Wells Fargo Bank v. Desert View Bldg. Supplies, Inc.*, 475 F.Supp. 693 (D.Nev.1978), *aff'd without opinion*, 633 F.2d 221 (9th Cir. 1980)). At the other end, Delaware allows a corporation to declare a dividend, even though it has no surplus, so long as the dividend does not exceed the company's net earnings for the present or preceding year (or the combined earnings for both years). Del. Gen. Corp. Law § 170(a). This is often referred to as a "nimble" dividend, because the directors must act quickly to declare it.

California and the Revised Model Act follow new approaches, which start by abandoning the concept of stated capital as a limit on the declaration of dividends. Both statutes (like New York) prohibit dividends when the corporation is (or paying the dividend will render it) insolvent in the sense of being unable to pay its bills when due. Cal. Corp. Code § 501; M.B.C.A. § 6.40(c)(1). California then allows a dividend under either of two conditions: (1) the company may distribute a sum not in excess of the amount of the corporation's retained earnings (the accumulation of net income for each year of business, which the company neither subsequently lost nor distributed); or (2) if there are insufficient retained earnings, the company can distribute a sum which leaves it with total assets in excess of 1 1/4 times its total liabilities and current assets greater than its current liabilities (or greater than 1 1/4 times its current liabilities if the company did not manage to earn more than its interest expense the prior two years). Cal. Corp. Code § 500. The Revised Model Act is simpler: After payment of the dividend, the corporation's assets must exceed its liabilities. M.B.C.A. § 6.40(c)(2). (Both statutes also have limits to protect preferred shares, which will be addressed shortly.)

Application of these various statutes can raise a number of questions. For example, common to most of the statutory schemes is the need to put a dollar amount on the corporation's total assets. Conventional accounting practice generally uses the cost of an asset, less depreciation, as the amount placed on the books for the value of each asset. Suppose some assets have in reality declined in value since their purchase at a faster rate than reflected in the allowance for depreciation. Must the corporation revalue them in order to see if it can distribute a dividend? Alternatively, suppose some assets have in fact appreciated in value since their purchase. Can the corporation revalue them, thereby increasing the amount it may legally distribute as a dividend? *Compare Randall v. Bailey,* 288 N.Y. 280, 43 N.E.2d 43 (1942) (answering both questions in the affirmative); *Klang v. Smith's Food and Drug Centers, Inc.,* 702 A.2d 150 (Del.1997) (allowing revaluation in the context of repurchasing stock); M.B.C.A. § 6.40(d) (allowing directors to consider the "fair valuation" of the corporation's assets in determining if the corporation can legally declare a dividend), *with* Cal. Corp. Code § 114 (effectively precluding dividends based upon upward revisions in asset values, by defining the term "asset" and similar accounting terms used in the code sections dealing with dividends as meaning the item determined in accordance with generally accepted accounting principles). From a practical standpoint, it is usually safest for directors to rely on generally accepted accounting practice in deciding whether the corporation can legally declare a dividend. In fact, many statutes, if not specifically commanding this (as under Section 114 of California's corporation code), at least protect those who follow generally accepted accounting principles, and financial statements prepared by accountants, in determining the amount available for dividends. *E.g.,* M.B.C.A. § 6.40(d). *See also* N.Y. Bus. Corp. Law § 717(a)(2).

As a planning matter, these statutes may not be entirely satisfactory for the protection of all parties. Hence, creditors often impose, as a condition for their loans, further contractual restrictions upon payment of dividends. The precise restriction depends upon the particular contract negotiated. In addition, the ability to declare dividends which represent the return of invested capital, rather than earnings, may prejudice some shareholders in favor of others. For example, suppose some shareholders purchase stock with a liquidation preference in the amount of its issue price—perhaps because the parties agreed to an allocation of profit (represented by dividend rights) which does not conform to the ratio of tangible contributions. Allowing dividends which represent a return of invested capital could circumvent the purpose of this arrangement—that being to prevent the other stockholders from obtaining the capital invested by those purchasing the preferred. Some statutory schemes contain provisions designed to prevent distributions which undermine liquidation preferences. *E.g.,* Cal. Corp. Code § 502 (a corporation cannot make a distribution to junior shares which will leave its assets less than its liabilities plus the liquidation preferences of senior shares); M.B.C.A. § 6.40(c)(2) (same). More traditional statutes may only protect liquidation preferences indirectly (and incompletely) through the prohibition on dividends which invade capital or stated capital. As stated above, with shares whose selling price is above par, or with no-par shares, capital or stated capital can be considerably less than the purchase price (and, accordingly, less than the logical liquidation preference). *But see* N.Y. Bus. Corp. Law § 506(b) (preventing the allocation to surplus, rather than stated capital, of any amount received for no-par shares unless it is in excess of their liquidation preference). Alternately, corporations may be able under the traditional statutes to reduce their stated capital. *But see* N.Y. Bus. Corp. Law § 806(b)(3) (a corporation cannot, by amending its certificate, reduce its stated capital to an amount below the aggregate liquidation preferences payable upon involuntary liquidation). If statutes provide inadequate protection, participants may wish to include in the articles a provision restricting the payment of dividends when such dividends threaten the liquidation preferences of the preferred. *See, e.g.,* Del. Gen. Corp. Law § 170(a) (certificate of incorporation may restrict dividends the directors can declare); N.Y. Bus. Corp. Law § 510(a) (same). A broader question is to what extent the participants may wish to prevent payment of dividends which constitute return of invested capital, even if the dividend will not frustrate liquidation preferences. Such a dividend may still contravene the expectations of shareholders who invest money in order for it to work making money. Along similar lines, consider the impact which large dividends can have on convertible securities. If the dividends are substantial enough to cut into corporate growth, what will this do to the value of an option to convert into common stock? *See Harff v. Kerkorian*, 324 A.2d 215 (Del.Ch.1974), *aff'd in part and rev'd in part*, 347 A.2d 133 (Del.1975) (allegations that excessive dividends impaired the value of the conversion feature of plaintiffs' debentures).

b. *Tax Aspects*

(i) Taxation of Distributions

Bittker, Federal Taxation of Income, Estates and Gifts

¶¶ 92.1.2—92.3.2 (1981, and 1989 Supp.).

¶ 92.1.2 "Dividend"—A Term of Art

Under I.R.C. § 301(c), a distribution is includable in a shareholder's gross income to the extent that it is a "dividend," as defined in I.R.C. § 316; the balance of the distribution, if any, is a return of capital under I.R.C. §§ 301(c)(2) and 301(c)(3).* The term "dividend" as defined for income tax purposes by I.R.C. § 316(a) does not correspond to the term "dividend" under state law, with the result that a corporate distribution may be a "dividend" under I.R.C. § 316(a), although it impairs capital or is otherwise unlawful under state law. * * * Conversely, it is possible for a distribution to constitute a lawful "dividend" under state law without qualifying as a "dividend" under I.R.C. § 316(a). * * *

The definition of "dividend" in I.R.C. § 316 is two-edged: A distribution by a corporation to its shareholders is a "dividend" if it is made (a) out of earnings and profits accumulated after February 28, 1913 or (b) out of earnings and profits of the taxable year. "Earnings and profits" is a term of art that is examined below; but it must be pointed out here that it is not identical with "earned surplus," nor is it represented by a bank account or other specific corporate assets—a distribution is "out of" earnings and profits if the corporation operated profitably in the period under consideration, and no "tracing" or "earmarking" of funds or assets is required. * * *

Since most distributions are made by corporations that are currently profitable, I.R.C. § 316(a)(2) often makes it unnecessary to compute the corporation's post–1913 accumulated earnings and profits. This makes for simplicity, but it also means that a distribution may be a taxable "dividend" even though the corporation has a deficit * * *.

If the corporation has neither post–1913 accumulated earnings and profits nor current earnings and profits, a distribution cannot be a "dividend" and is instead subject to I.R.C. §§ 301(c)(2) and 301(c)(3). Under I.R.C. § 301(c)(2), the distribution is applied against and reduces the

* [If the shareholder is itself a corporation, Section 243 entitles it to a deduction equal to 70 percent of the dividends it receives, or 80 percent of the dividends if the corporate shareholder owns at least one-fifth of the outstanding stock of the company declaring the dividend, or 100 percent if the recipient owns four-fifths of the stock. Ed.]

adjusted basis of the shareholder's stock. If the distribution is greater than the adjusted basis of the stock, the excess is subject to I.R.C. § 301(c)(3), under which it is treated as gain from the sale or exchange of property (and thus as capital gain if the stock is a capital asset) * * *.

The second sentence of I.R.C. § 316(a) lays down an irrebuttable presumption that every distribution is out of earnings and profits to the extent thereof. Likewise, it is presumed that every distribution comes from the most recently accumulated earnings and profits. This prevents earmarking a distribution to control its tax status; for example, a corporation having current earnings and profits, post–1913 accumulated earnings and profits, and pre–1913 accumulated earnings and profits cannot make a distribution from the pre–1913 earnings and profits until the current and post–1913 earnings and profits have been exhausted.

In determining whether a distribution is out of earnings and profits of the taxable year, I.R.C. § 316(a)(2) provides that the earnings and profits for the year are to be computed as of the close of the taxable year without diminution by reason of distributions during the year. This means that a distribution will be a "dividend" if the corporation has earnings and profits at the end of the taxable year, even though it had none when the distribution occurred; contrariwise, a distribution that seemed to be a "dividend" when made may turn out to be a return of capital because the corporation has no earnings and profits at the end of the year. If the distributions for the year exceed in amount both the earnings and profits of the taxable year and the post–1913 accumulated earnings and profits, the regulations prescribe a method of allocating the two categories of earnings and profits to the various distributions in order to ascertain the "dividend" component of each one.

¶ 92.1.3 Earnings and Profits

It is a curious fact that the Internal Revenue Code, ordinarily so prodigal in the use of words, does not contain a comprehensive definition of "earnings and profits," although the term has no counterpart in the field of corporation law. The phrase entered the federal tax law in 1916, but, until 1940, it was given meaning solely by judicial and administrative construction. In 1940, the effect of a few transactions upon a corporation's earnings and profits was prescribed by statute, and Congress has intervened several times since then, but a comprehensive definition is still lacking. * * *

When we search for the meaning of "earnings and profits," then, we are in reality asking how a corporate transaction *should* affect the stockholder who receives a distribution of cash or property from the corporation after the transaction has occurred. To take a simple illustration, assume that a corporation earns $10,000 during the first year of its life, pays a federal income tax of $2,000, and distributes $9,000 to its shareholders. If other facts were ignored, it would probably be agreed that $8,000 should be taxed to the shareholders as a dividend and that the remaining $1,000 should be treated by them as a return of capital.

Not all puzzles in the computation of earnings and profits, however, are solved so easily. * * *

Although earnings and profits can be derived by adjustments to surplus, it is more common to start with taxable income, and to the extent that the Internal Revenue Code and regulations define earnings and profits, both ordinarily take taxable income as the point of departure. The regulations, state, for example that "the amount of earnings and profits in any case will be dependent upon the method of accounting properly employed in computing taxable income," so that if the corporation computes taxable income on the cash-receipts-and-disbursements basis, it may not use the accrual method for computing earnings and profits.

A full examination of the conversion of taxable income into earnings and profits is beyond the scope of this work, but the principal major adjustments and principles are summarized below.

1. *Items excluded from taxable income.* To bring earnings and profits closer to economic income, the regulations require the inclusion of "all income exempted by statute." * * *

There are, however, a number of realized income items that are "exempted" from the income only in the limited sense that income is recognized not at the outset of a transaction but at a later time (either through lower depreciation deductions or when the property is eventually sold). Section 312(f)(1) provides that such gains and losses do not enter into earnings and profits until they are recognized; thus, as to these items, the corporation's earnings and profits and its taxable income are computed in a similar manner. Nonrecognition provisions within the purview of I.R.C. § 312(f)(1) include I.R.C. §§ 1031 (like-kind exchanges), 1033 (replacements of involuntarily converted property), 351 (transfers to a controlled corporation), 361 (reorganization transfers), and 1091 (wash sale losses). In all of these transactions, unrecognized gain or loss is deferred through the operation of substituted basis rules, and it seems appropriate to apply this deferral policy to the earnings and profits account as well.

2. *Items deducted in computing taxable income.* In general, deductions allowed in computing taxable income that do not represent actual expenditures by the corporation must be restored in computing earnings and profits. Dividends received from another corporation, for example, are included in earnings and profits in full, even though they qualify for the * * * dividends-received deduction allowed by I.R.C. § 243. * * * The net operating loss deduction of I.R.C. § 172 cannot be used to reduce earnings and profits, since it is simply a carryback or carryover of losses that reduced earnings and profits in the year they occurred. The same is true of the capital loss carryback and carryover of I.R.C. § 1212.

* * *

3. *Nondeductible items.* The converse of the previous category is a class of items that deplete the income available for distributions to shareholders, but that are not allowed as deductions in computing taxable income. To prevent distributions of corporate capital from being taxed as

dividends to the shareholders, these items must be deducted in computing earnings and profits. They include dividend distributions made in prior years, federal income taxes, nondeductible expenses and interest incurred in earning tax-exempt interest, charitable contributions in excess of the deductible limit, premiums on keyman life insurance, nondeductible capital losses, and losses and expenses incurred in transactions with controlling shareholders.

4. *Financial readjustments.* The computation of earnings and profits must also take account of a great variety of financial transactions that may occur only occasionally in the life of any one corporation and that may have occurred long in the past, including (1) distributions of property and of the corporation's own stock and obligations; (2) distributions in partial liquidations or to redeem stock; * * * (4) the receipt of tax-free distributions from other corporations, such as stock dividends and non-dividend distributions of cash and property; (5) elections under Subchapter S; and (6) mergers, consolidations, liquidations, transfers of property, spin-offs, and other transactions by which one corporation succeeds to the assets and tax attributes of another corporation.

* * *

¶ 92.3 DISTRIBUTIONS IN KIND

* * *

¶ 92.3.2 Corporate Income or Loss on Distribution

* * *

Under I.R.C. § 311(b)(1), as restated in 1986, a corporation recognizes gain on a distribution of property to its shareholders in an amount computed and characterized as though the property were sold to the distributees at its fair market value. If the property is subject to liabilities or if the shareholders assume liabilities in connection with the distribution, further, I.R.C. § 311(b)(2) requires that the property's fair market value be deemed at least equal to the sum of liabilities. These rules apply to distributions of all types of property other than stock and obligations of the corporation and rights to acquire the corporation's stock. They apply to all types of distributions, except distributions in liquidations and tax-free organization and reorganization transactions.

Section 311(a), in contrast, bars the recognition of loss on any such distribution. It also frees the corporation of gain recognition on distributions to shareholders of the corporation's stock, stock rights, and obligations.

NOTE

In 2003, Congress enacted favorable treatment for dividends by taxing so-called "qualified dividends" at a maximum rate of 15 percent. Dividends paid by some foreign corporations, and payments that might be labeled "dividends," but really are more like interest (such as distributions on debt-like preferred shares or from money market funds), do not count as qualified dividends. Also, to prevent persons from taking advantage of the new preferential treatment through purchases and sales of stock around the record date that determines which shareholders are entitled to receive dividends, there is a minimum period for which the shareholder must have held the stock in order for the dividend to be qualified. I.R.C. § 1(h)(11). It should be noted, however, that the reduction in the tax rate on dividends will expire, barring further action by Congress, at the end of 2008.

(ii) Taxation of Accumulations

Given the double tax incurred upon distributing corporate earnings to the shareholders, companies have a strong incentive to delay such distributions and allow their earnings to accumulate. Even if the corporation ultimately declares a dividend, there is a savings, due to the time value of money, to deferring the second tax for as long as possible. Congress has responded to this incentive by enacting two penalty taxes.

Apelbaum, The Accumulated Earnings Tax and the Personal Holding Company Tax: Problems and Proposals

3 Boston U.J. Tax L. 53 (1985).

The Internal Revenue Code contains two provisions which impose penalty taxes on accumulations of domestic corporate earnings—the accumulated earnings tax[1] and the personal holding company tax.[2] Both are annual taxes imposed at the corporate level based on undistributed corporate income. While the taxes are not major revenue sources, they are assumed to have a deterrent effect, and are a major source of concern to closely held corporations.

* * *

A. The Accumulated Earnings Tax

* * *

* * * The two requirements for imposition [of the accumulated earnings tax] are that the corporation be "formed or availed of for the purpose of avoiding income tax with respect to its shareholders" by the accumulation of earnings, and the corporation must have "accumulated taxable income."

The first requirement, known as the "forbidden purpose" test is highly subjective. However, I.R.C. § 533 provides that if a corporation allows its earnings and profits to accumulate beyond the reasonable needs of the

1. I.R.C. §§ 531–537.

2. I.R.C. §§ 541–547.

business, a rebuttable presumption is created that the "forbidden purpose" is present.

* * *

1. The Intent to Avoid Tax—Who May Hold It

To be subject to the accumulated earnings tax, there must be an "intent" to avoid the individual income tax. In *Golconda Mining Corp.*,[33] the Tax Court held that the intent to avoid the individual tax must be held by "a single large shareholder or a small group of large shareholders who exercise effective control over the dividend policy of the company." While such "intent" clearly may exist in most closely held companies, it would seem that publicly held companies, which ordinarily have widely divergent shareholders, could not have the same intent.[†] * * *

2. Establishing "Forbidden Purpose"

a. Establishing the Rebuttable Presumption or Prima Facie Case

* * *

i. Unreasonable Accumulation of Earnings

Every accumulated earnings tax case requires a finding that the corporation has accumulated earnings beyond its reasonable needs. * * * This is not only due to the subjective nature of establishing intent, but also because in calculating the tax base (accumulated taxable income), a deduction is provided for earnings retained to meet the reasonable needs of the business.

* * *

As a general matter, the regulations state that reasonable business needs is "the amount that a prudent businessman would consider appropriate."[41] * * *

I.R.C. § 537(a)(1) states that reasonable business needs includes the "reasonably anticipated needs of the business." The regulations require that the future needs be "specific, definite, and feasible." The fact that the anticipated need does not arise due to unforeseen future events does not necessarily indicate that the prior accumulation was unreasonable, although it may be seen as evidence of earlier intent.

* * *

The regulations also state that a business expansion "to acquire a business enterprise through purchasing stock or assets," is a reasonable business accumulation. The corporation may enter "any line of business which it may undertake," although "investments in property or securities

33. *Golconda Mining Corp.*, 58 T.C. 139 (1972), *rev'd on other issue*, 507 F.2d 594 (9th Cir.1974).

† [*But see Technalysis Corp. v. Commissioner*, 101 T.C. 397 (1993). Ed.]

41. Treas. Reg. § 1.537–1(a).

which are unrelated to the activities of the business of the taxpayer corporation" are considered unreasonable. * * *

Corporations are also allowed to accumulate funds for a wide variety of business contingencies. In *Smoot Sand and Gravel,*[50] the Fourth Circuit held that "a contingency is a reasonable need for which a business may provide, if the likelihood, not merely the remote possibility, of its occurrence reasonably appears to a prudent business firm."

The regulations also permit the corporation "to provide for the retirement of bona fide indebtedness." However, courts may view the accumulations suspectedly if the corporation could meet the annual debt requirement through current earnings and profits, rather than accumulations, and where the debt is held by shareholders.

* * *

The Regulations also permit a corporation to accumulate earnings and profits to "provide necessary working capital for the business." The landmark case in this area is *Bardahl Manufacturing Corp.,*[60] which allows corporations to accumulate earnings to meet the expenses of one operating cycle, (which is mathematically derived).[61]

* * *

b. Rebutting the Presumption or Prima Facie Case

Corporations may rebut the presumption of forbidden purpose created under I.R.C. § 533 by showing the earnings were not accumulated for a tax avoidance purpose. The regulations list some non-controlling factors whose presence or non-presence is useful in determining the existence of tax avoidance purpose. The factors include: "dealings between the corporation and its shareholders [i.e. loans for the personal benefit of shareholders]," "the investment by the corporation of undistributed earnings in assets having no reasonable connection with the business of the corporation," and "the extent to which the corporation has distributed its earnings and profits."[68] The Tax Court, in *Atlantic Properties, Inc.,*[69] stated that "a corporation should not be liable for the accumulated earnings tax if it accumulates for reasons other than the forbidden purpose of Section 532(a), even though earnings may have been accumulated out of caprice, spite, miserliness, or stupidity, rather than sound business reasons." In *U.S. v. Donruss,*[71] however, the Supreme Court held that for any of these factors to rebut the Section 533 inference, it must be shown that not only is

50. *Smoot Sand and Gravel v. Commissioner,* 241 F.2d 197 (4th Cir.1957).

60. *Bardahl Manufacturing Corp.,* 24 T.C.M. 1030 (1965).

61. A corporation may accumulate an amount equal to the length of the average operating cycle times the sum of cost of goods sold and cash operating expenses. * * *

68. Treas. Reg. § 1.533–1(a)(2).

69. *Atlantic Properties, Inc.,* 62 T.C. 644 (1974), *aff'd,* 519 F.2d 1233 (1st Cir. 1975).

71. *U.S. v. Donruss,* 393 U.S. 297 (1969).

tax avoidance not a primary or dominant motive for the accumulation, but that is not one of the purposes for the accumulation.

3. Calculating the Tax

The base for the accumulated earnings tax is the corporation's accumulated taxable income, as set forth in I.R.C. § 535. The starting point for this calculation is the corporation's taxable income for the year in question. The corporation may deduct corporate taxes, and all charitable contributions. Accumulated taxable income must be increased by the amount of "special" corporate deductions allowed under I.R.C. §§ 241–250 (most notably the Section 243 dividends received deduction) except for § 248, and net operating loss deduction and carry back and carry forward deductions. The corporation also may exclude net capital gains for the year (less taxes attributable to the gains) and deduct any capital losses for the year. It is important to note that no accumulated taxable income deduction is permitted for stock redemptions paid for with current earnings and profits, * * *

I.R.C. § 562 allows the corporation a deduction for dividends paid. This includes current and consent dividends. The current dividend deduction pertains to direct dividend distributions, as well as certain stock redemptions (i.e., pro rata) which are treated as dividends at the shareholder level. * * *

The corporation is also entitled to a deduction for its "accumulated earnings credit."[75] * * * [C]orporations receive a credit equal to the greater of the amount of earnings and profits for the year retained to meet reasonable business needs (less net capital gains and related taxes), and the amount by which $250,000 exceeds the accumulated earnings and profits of the corporation at the close of the taxable year.

* * *

[Since the purpose of the accumulated earnings tax is to remove the incentive to avoid tax on dividends, Section 531 assesses the accumulative earnings tax at the highest rate that shareholders would pay on dividends. Currently, this is a rate of 15 percent; albeit, as with the rate reduction on dividends generally, barring further action from Congress, the accumulated earnings tax will return to the highest individual income tax rate in 2008. Ed.]

B. *The Personal Holding Company Tax*

* * *

Under current law a corporation will be considered a personal holding company if it meets two tests described in I.R.C. § 542:

(1) Stock ownership test—50% of the corporation's stock in value is owned directly or indirectly by five or fewer individuals; and

(2) Income test—60% of the corporation's "adjusted ordinary gross income" (gross income with various adjustments) is "personal holding

75. I.R.C. § 535(c).

company income" (passive income, personal service contract income, and compensation for the use of the corporate property by shareholders).

* * *

3. Calculating the Tax

The personal holding company penalty tax is levied on "undistributed personal holding company income" as defined in I.R.C. § 545. The starting point for this calculation is corporate taxable income. * * *

The corporation is also entitled to a deduction for dividends paid and this operates similarly to the provision for the accumulated earnings tax discussed earlier. * * * The personal holding company penalty tax is assessed on undistributed personal holding company income at a flat rate [corresponding to the highest rate on dividends. Ed.][89]

* * *

2. Alternatives to Dividends

Menard, Inc. v. Commissioner of Internal Revenue

T.C. Memo. 2004–207, 2004 WL 2066599.

FINDINGS OF FACT

* * *

I. Menards

* * *

A. Menards's Business In General

* * * Since its incorporation, Menards has been primarily engaged in the retail sale of hardware, building supplies, paint, garden equipment, and similar items. Menards has approximately 160 stores in nine Midwestern States and is one of the nation's top retail home improvement chains, third only to Home Depot and Lowe's. In * * * 1998, Menards's revenue totaled $3.42 billion.

* * *

C. Menards's Officers and Shareholders

1. Officers

During * * * 1998, Menards's corporate officers were Mr. Menard, president and chief executive officer (CEO); Mr. Prochaska, vice president of real estate; Earl Rasmussen, chief financial officer and treasurer; and

89. I.R.C. § 541.

Chris Menard (C. Menard), secretary. The officers received compensation for TYE 1998 in the following amounts:

Officer	Compensation
Mr. Menard	$20,642,485
Mr. Prochaska	121,307
Mr. Rasmussen	55,702
Mr. C. Menard	172,815

2. Shareholders

Since the incorporation of Menards, Mr. Menard has been the controlling shareholder. During the years at issue, Mr. Menard owned all of the class A voting stock and approximately 56 percent of the class B nonvoting stock. Mr. Menard's family members and trusts named after him and his family members held the remaining class B shares. In all, Mr. Menard owned approximately 89 percent of Menards's voting and nonvoting stock. Menards has never paid dividends to its shareholders.

D. Menards's Employee Compensation Plan

* * *

2. Mr. Menard's Compensation Plan

In addition to the forms of compensation available to all employees, Menards pays Mr. Menard an annual bonus. Since 1973, Mr. Menard has received an annual bonus equal to 5 percent of Menards's net income before taxes (the 5–percent bonus). The 5–percent bonus is subject to the following reimbursement agreement: In the event that the Commissioner disallows as a deduction any portion of Mr. Menard's compensation, Mr. Menard must repay to Menards the entire amount disallowed.

* * *

III. Mr. Menard

* * *

A. Mr. Menard's Duties and Responsibilities at Menards

Since he founded the company, Mr. Menard has been involved in Menards's daily business affairs. During 1998, Mr. Menard worked 6 or 7 days a week for 12 to 16 hours a day and communicated with Menards's executives on a regular basis.

As CEO of Menards, Mr. Menard was responsible for all three of Menards's major divisions.

* * *

OPINION

* * *

II. Deductibility of Compensation Paid to Mr. Menard

Section 162(a)(1) provides that a taxpayer may deduct as an ordinary and necessary business expense "a reasonable allowance for salaries or other compensation for personal services actually rendered". Thus, compensation is deductible only if (1) reasonable in amount and (2) paid or incurred for services actually rendered. * * *

Petitioners contend that Menards is entitled to deduct the full amount of Mr. Menard's compensation as an ordinary and necessary business expense under section 162. In contrast, respondent asserts that $19,261,609 of Mr. Menard's compensation is a disguised dividend.

* * *

B. Reasonableness of the Amount of Compensation

1. The Independent Investor Test

Under section 162(a)(1) the first prong of the test for the deductibility of compensation requires that the amount of compensation be reasonable. Petitioners and respondent agree that the independent investor test of *Exacto Spring Corp. v. Commissioner*, 196 F.3d 833 (7th Cir.1999), applies to our analysis of reasonableness.

In *Exacto Spring Corp.* the Court of Appeals for the Seventh Circuit rejected the multifactor test used by this Court and several Courts of Appeals to decide whether compensation is reasonable, and, in its place, adopted the independent investor test. Under the independent investor test as adopted by the Court of Appeals for the Seventh Circuit, if a hypothetical independent investor would consider the rate of return on his investment in the taxpayer corporation "a far higher return than * * * [he] had any reason to expect", the compensation paid to the corporation's CEO is presumptively reasonable. This presumption of reasonableness may be rebutted, however, if an extraordinary event was responsible for the company's profitability or if the executive's position was merely titular and his job was actually performed by someone else. On brief, respondent conceded that Mr. Menard's compensation satisfied the independent investor test.

Although we agree with respondent that Mr. Menard's compensation satisfies the independent investor test as articulated in *Exacto Spring Corp.*, our inquiry into whether the compensation was reasonable in amount does not end there. In *Exacto Spring Corp.*, the Court of Appeals for the Seventh Circuit did not address the factual situation now before us where the investors' rate of return on their investment generated by the taxpayer corporation, a closely held corporation, is sufficient to create a rebuttable presumption that the compensation paid to the corporation's CEO is reasonable, but the compensation paid by the taxpayer corporation to its CEO substantially exceeded the compensation paid by comparable publicly traded corporations to their CEOs.

* * *

To answer the question, we turn to section 1.162–7(b)(3), Income Tax Regs., which provides:

> * * * It is, in general, just to assume that reasonable and true compensation is only such amount as would ordinarily be paid for like services by like enterprises under like circumstances. * * *

The Court of Appeals for the Seventh Circuit did not discuss the above-quoted regulation in *Exacto Spring Corp. v. Commissioner, supra,* or declare it invalid. Neither party in this case has challenged the regulation or argued that it exceeds the Treasury's delegated authority to construe section 162. * * * As we read section 1.162–7, Income Tax Regs., we are required to consider evidence of compensation paid to CEOs in comparable companies when such evidence is introduced to show the reasonableness or unreasonableness of a CEO's compensation. Because each of the parties offered expert testimony on the reasonableness of Mr. Menard's compensation that relied upon data from publicly traded companies that the parties agreed are comparable, we must consider such evidence in deciding whether the presumption of reasonableness that respondent has conceded arose from Menards's rate of return on its shareholders' investment for * * *1998 has been rebutted.

* * *

5. Conclusion

After evaluating both experts' valuation methodologies in light of the record, we now compare Mr. Menard's * * * 1998 compensation to the Black–Scholes values* of compensation paid in * * * 1998 to CEOs of Home Depot, Kohl's, Lowe's, Staples, and Target. * * *

The comparison group companies compensated their CEOs for services performed in * * * 1998 in the following amounts:

Company	Compensation
Home Depot	$2,841,307
Kohl's	5,110,578
Lowe's	6,054,977
Staples	6,868,747
Target	10,479,528

Mr. Menard's compensation of $20,642,485 is nearly two times higher than Target's CEO's compensation, more than three times higher than Staples's and Lowe's CEOs' compensation, more than four times higher than Kohl's CEO's compensation, and more than seven times higher than Home De-

* [Because much of the reported compensation for the CEOs at the comparison companies came from stock options, the respondent's expert determined the total value of these CEO's compensation package by using the Black–Scholes method for valuing option contracts. Black–Scholes is a method for valuing stock options generally accepted by valuation experts. To arrive at the values of the stock options, the respondent's expert witness considered the following five Black–Scholes variables: (1) Underlying stock price, (2) exercise price, (3) volatility, (4) risk-free interest rate, and (5) time to expiration of the option. Ed.]

pot's CEO's compensation. After comparing Mr. Menard's compensation to the comparison group companies' CEOs' compensation, we conclude that (1) Mr. Menard's compensation substantially exceeded the compensation paid by comparable publicly traded companies to their CEOs, and (2) such evidence was sufficient to rebut the presumption of reasonableness created by Menards's rate of return on investment. Consequently, we examine the total record to decide what portion of Mr. Menard's compensation was reasonable.

* * *

Although comparisons to Kohl's, Staples, and Target are helpful to an extent, we can more accurately gauge a reasonable amount of compensation for Mr. Menard by focusing on how Menards compared to its direct competitors in home improvement retailing, Home Depot and Lowe's, during * * * 1998.

* * *

Ultimately, when compared to Home Depot and Lowe's, during * * * 1998, Menards was a small company that experienced less substantial revenue growth but generated a comparatively high return on equity. Considering the emphasis of the Court of Appeals for the Seventh Circuit on investors' returns in *Exacto Spring Corp. v. Commissioner*, in arriving at a reasonable amount of compensation, we attribute the most importance to Menards's comparatively high return on equity. We conclude, therefore, that as the home improvement retailer with the highest return on equity, Menards's CEO's compensation should be the highest value within the range of its direct competitors' CEOs' compensation.

* * *

C. Compensation for Services Actually Rendered

Although we have concluded that only a portion of Mr. Menard's compensation was reasonable in amount, as an alternative basis for our decision, we now consider whether Mr. Menard's compensation was payment for services actually rendered. In cases involving a closely held corporation, compensation paid to a shareholder-employee is not the product of arm's-length bargaining and deserves special scrutiny. This is particularly so in this case because the board of directors consisted of Mr. Menard; Mr. Menard's brother, L. Menard; and Mr. Rasmussen, who depended on Mr. Menard for his own annual bonus. Respondent contends that $19,261,609 of Mr. Menard's compensation was a disguised dividend.

In *Exacto Spring Corp. v. Commissioner*, 196 F.3d at 835, the Court of Appeals for the Seventh Circuit stated that the "primary purpose of section 162(a)(1)" is to prevent corporations from disguising dividends as salary. The Court of Appeals for the Seventh Circuit explained that, in addition to satisfying the independent investor test, for compensation to qualify as a deductible business expense, the compensation must be "a bona fide expense". The Court of Appeals for the Seventh Circuit described as "material" to this inquiry any evidence showing that "the company did not in fact intend to pay * * * [the CEO] that amount as salary, that * * * [the CEO's] salary really did include a concealed dividend though it need not have."

* * *

If the Commissioner introduces evidence suggesting that the compensation was a disguised dividend, even if the payment was reasonable in amount, we inquire into whether the taxpayer had a compensatory purpose for the payment. The taxpayer's failure to pay dividends since its formation, alone, is not sufficient evidence of a disguised dividend. However, the presence of the following six factors indicates that compensation was not intended for personal services rendered: (1) Bonuses paid in exact proportion to officers' shareholdings; (2) payments made in lump sums rather than as the services were rendered; (3) a complete absence of formal dividend distributions by an expanding corporation; (4) a completely unstructured bonus system, lacking relation to services performed; (5) consistently negligible taxable corporate income; and (6) bonus payments made only to the officer-shareholders.

Although not all six factors from the list, *supra*, are present with respect to Mr. Menard's compensation, other factors demonstrate that a portion of Mr. Menard's compensation was a disguised dividend. One relevant factor is that Menards has never paid a dividend, despite its tremendous growth over the years. In addition, Menards paid the 5–percent bonus in one lump sum rather than as Mr. Menard performed services. Perhaps more problematic, this lump-sum payment was "practically no different from a dividend": a profit-based, year end bonus paid to the majority shareholder-officer.

We also find significant Mr. Menard's agreement to reimburse Menards for any portion of the 5–percent bonus disallowed as a deduction. Such reimbursement clauses suggest that the taxpayer had preexisting knowledge that the compensation may not satisfy section 162(a)(1) and lead to the inference that the compensation was intended, in part, as a disguised dividend.

Petitioners assert that Menards intended Mr. Menard's salary and the 5–percent bonus as compensation purely for his services. According to petitioners, Menards's growth and performance were due to "the foresight, hard work, experience, skill, decision making ability, and energy of Mr. Menard." With the 5–percent bonus, petitioners argue, Menards intended to establish a consistent method for determining Mr. Menard's variable compensation based on his efforts and the company's resulting success.

Even though Mr. Menard's hard work contributed greatly to Menards's success and, as a result of that success, the 5–percent bonus generally increased each year, we disagree with petitioners that this arrangement evinces an intent to compensate. Although incentive compensation may encourage nonshareholder employees to put forth their best efforts, a majority shareholder invested in the company to the extent of Mr. Menard does not need the incentive. When large shareholders base their compensation on a percentage of the company's income, the arrangement may suggest an attempt to distribute profits without declaring a dividend. Contrary to petitioners' argument, the board's decision, made during the preceding fiscal year, to designate the 5–percent bonus as Mr. Menard's compensation for * * * 1998 does not insulate petitioners from the conclusion that Menards intended to distribute profits. With a corporation as successful and profitable as Menards, at the time of the board's resolution, barring some unforeseen catastrophe, the board could count on Mr. Menard's receiving a sizable bonus in * * * 1998 pursuant to the formula. Moreover, the failure of the board, whose members were Menard employees and/or family members of Mr. Menard's, to make any effort to ascertain the market value of comparable corporate executives or to periodically evaluate the formula as a gauge of reasonable compensation, reinforces the impression that it was used to enable Mr. Menard to claim an extravagant bonus unrelated to the actual market value of his services as a corporate CEO. On the basis of the evidence discussed, *supra*, we conclude that Mr. Menard's compensation was not intended entirely for personal services rendered and contained a distribution of profits. Any amount in excess of $7,066,912 is unreasonable and a disguised dividend. Accordingly, we hold that Menards is entitled to deduct $7,066,912 as an ordinary and necessary business expense pursuant to section 162(a)(1).

* * *

NOTES

1. A major tax planning objective when dealing with a C corporation is to avoid double taxation. This means minimizing distribution of earnings through dividends. Simply retaining profits in the company, however, is generally not a satisfactory solution. Not only may this run afoul of the accumulated earning tax discussed above, but it also does not put any cash in the shareholders' pockets. Hence, the owners search for alternative mechanisms to distribute profits from the corporation to themselves in such a way as to (1) generate a deduction for the company (thereby making the earnings only taxable on the owners' level), (2) be tax-free to the owners (thereby making the earnings only taxable on the corporate level), or, best of all, (3) both generate a deduction for the company and be tax-free to the owners (thereby avoiding all tax).

Menard involves a common mechanism for distributing money to the company's owner(s) in such a way as to obtain an offsetting deduction. This is to hire the owner(s) as employee(s) and pay a salary. The opinion also illustrates one limit on this technique: A corporation may deduct salaries only to the extent they are "reasonable". I.R.C. § 162(a)(1). A successful firm, like Menard's, can soon find that attempting to distribute even a fraction of its net income to the shareholder-employee(s) will bump into the ceiling of what is a reasonable salary. Moreover, this technique obviously cannot transfer earnings to owners who are not able or willing to work.

The court's opinion in *Menard* raises a second possible challenge as well. Even if reasonable, amounts labeled as salaries might really constitute disguised dividends.

The *Menard* opinion provides a discussion of both how to assess whether compensation is reasonable and of the facts that might establish a so-called salary is really a disguised dividend. Because the Tax Court's opinion in *Menard* was appealable to the Seventh Circuit, the Tax Court started by applying the "independent investor test" adopted by the law and economics oriented judges in that circuit. Under this approach, a court asks whether the return on the shareholders' investment in the corporation through dividends and through appreciation in the value of their stock was sufficient to suggest that an independent investor would have agreed to pay the challenged compensation in order to produce this return on investment. If so, the challenged compensation is presumptively reasonable and the corporation entitled to a deduction. *E.g., Exacto Spring Corp. v. Commissioner,* 196 F.3d 833 (7th Cir.1999). The Tax Court in *Menard* found, however, this presumption of reasonableness rebutted by evidence that Mr. Menard received compensation way out of line with the compensation of CEOs of other firms in the industry. This shows, not surprisingly, that a key factor in assessing reasonableness of compensation is what other folks in similar positions make.

Actually, the *Menard* opinion contains a number of ironies. The I.R.S. was fortunate that the comparison with Home Depot was for the year 1998. A little less than a decade later, Home Depot would make the news when its fired CEO received a termination package apparently worth a couple hundred million dollars. A critical fact, according to the Tax Court, showing that Mr. Menard's compensation contained a large element of disguised dividend was that it was based upon a percentage of the company's profits. Yet, Section 162(m) of the Internal Revenue Code prevents public companies from deducting even reasonable compensation, if in excess of $1 million, when paid to certain high level executives, unless the compensation is geared to performance. Finally, the Tax Court thought the agreement by Mr. Menard to reimburse the company for any compensation deemed unreasonable suggested that the compensation contained a disguised dividend. Why, in fact, did Mr. Menard's compensation agreement contain this requirement? *Compare Oswald v. Commissioner,* 49 T.C. 645 (1968) (allowing the employee who repaid the excessive compensation a deduction when a corporate by-law required the shareholder-officer to repay any salary found excessive), *with Pahl v. Commissioner,* 67 T.C. 286 (1976) (denying the deduction, and labeling the repayment a capital contribution, when the employee repaid the excessive compensation, but there was no contractual obligation to reimburse the corporation). Given these opinions, it was standard for books (including this one) to recommend reimbursement provisions. There is a lesson in this somewhere.

Incidentally, while salaries produce a deduction for the corporation, compare the result on the recipient of receiving a salary versus receiving dividends. Presently, dividends are taxed at a lower rate (albeit, this favored treatment will expire in 2008 barring further action by Congress). I.R.C. § 1(h)(1), (11). While it would not take much taxable income for the corporation before its deduction becomes worth more than the differential between the tax on dividends and on salaries, still, employment (Social Security and Medicare) taxes further complicate the picture. Salaries produce such a tax both for the corporation and the recipient. 26 U.S.C. §§ 3101, 3111. Dividends do not. *But see Joseph Radtke, S.C. v. United States,* 712 F.Supp. 143 (E.D.Wis.1989) (recharacterized dividend as a salary for purposes of employment taxes).

Earlier, in the course of discussing alternatives to the purchase of stock, this chapter explored two other common techniques for arranging corporate payments to its owners which generate a deduction for the company. These are loans by shareholders to the company, which generate interest payments, and leases of property by shareholders to the company, which produce rent payments. (Loans also produce tax-free repayment of principal.) Not surprisingly in view of the discussion thus far, the Internal Revenue Service may challenge excessive interest or rental payments as constituting disguised (and non-deductible) dividends. *E.g., Potter Electric Signal & Mfg. Co. v. Commissioner,* 286 F.2d 200 (8th Cir.1961).

Shareholders employ a variety of other techniques to obtain money from their company tax-free (albeit without generating a deduction for the firm). For example, they may borrow money from the corporation. The problem with loans is the shareholder presumably must repay them. Of course, the company will be a fairly docile creditor toward a dominant shareholder. Yet, if the shareholder-borrower does not intend to repay, courts will recharacterize the loan as a disguised dividend. *E.g., Alterman Foods, Inc. v. United States,* 505 F.2d 873 (5th Cir.1974). Moreover, an arms-length loan normally requires paying interest. Suppose the company makes an interest-free loan to a shareholder. See I.R.C. § 7872(a)(1), (c)(1)(C) (deeming the shareholder-borrower to receive a payment equal to the imputed interest and the corporation to receive the imputed interest).

In order to get money from their corporation without dividends, shareholders may sell property to it at an inflated price, or purchase property from it at a bargain price. *E.g., Honigman v. Commissioner,* 466 F.2d 69 (6th Cir.1972). They might make personal use of company assets. *E.g., Ireland v. United States,* 621 F.2d 731 (5th Cir.1980). They may have the corporation pay personal expenses. *E.g., Jack's Maintenance Contractors, Inc. v. Commissioner,* 703 F.2d 154 (5th Cir.1983). In this last event, the corporation might try to claim a deduction while the shareholder disclaims any taxable income. In all these situations, courts may find disguised dividends. Indeed, in a portion of the *Menard* opinion not reprinted above, the court dealt with expense deductions claimed by Menard's for paying expenses incurred by another company owned by Mr. Menard, which engaged in racing so-called Indy cars. The court allowed the expense deduction to the extent the sponsorship of the race cars was a reasonable expense that produced advertising benefits for Menard's stores, but denied the deduction and held the payments constituted constructive dividends to the extent the payments exceeded that amount.

2. Are there non-tax reasons for passing earnings to a corporation's owners through means other than dividends? One seemingly obvious purpose is to compensate their performing services with a salary. Yet, as pointed out when dealing with ordinary partnerships (for which there is no salary unless expressly agreed), one could just as well compensate owners through their share of the profits. (Keep in mind, however, there is an important difference between salaries and profit shares—or, in a corporation, added rights to dividends—when the business fails to earn anything.) One added factor in a corporation is that compensating for work with an added profit or dividend share may run into the problems discussed earlier created by issuing stock for services. Salaries in a partnership might also serve to provide owners with income they may need to live on. This may be even more useful in a corporation, given both the board's discretion, and statutory limitations, when it comes to declaring dividends. In partnerships, draws provide an alternate way to achieve this purpose. What about using loans from the company to its shareholders as a sort of draw; or might this create a problem with preserving limited liability?

One critical difference between a partnership and a corporation is salaries and like payments in a partnership require agreement of all the partners, whereas, in a corporation, a majority of the board of directors normally has the power to decide upon such expenditures. *See, e.g.,* Del. Gen. Corp. Law § 141(h); N.Y. Bus. Corp. Law § 713(e); M.B.C.A. § 8.11. The directors' decision can prejudice two groups. The first consists of shareholders who do not receive the salaries, interest, rent or other dividend alternative. *Gottfried* provides an example of this situation. The second group consists of the company's creditors. One limit upon the directors paying excessive salaries, interest, rent or the like (especially to themselves) lies in a possible claim against them for breaching their fiduciary duty. Recall, the plaintiffs in *Gottfried* had such a claim pending against the defendants in another proceeding. The degree of scrutiny which the court will apply in considering such a claim depends upon who approved the challenged salary. If the salary only received approval from the directors receiving the salary, then, because of the conflict of interest, it will be up to the directors to prove that the salary is fair to the corporation. *E.g., Wilderman v. Wilderman*, 315 A.2d 610 (Del.Ch.1974). By contrast, approval of the salary by disinterested directors or shareholders can shift the burden to the challenging party to show that the salaries were unfair or constituted waste. *See, e.g., Michelson v. Duncan*, 407 A.2d 211 (Del.1979). Hence, directors seeking salaries from the corporation are well advised to obtain disinterested approval. Could this occur by a seriatim approval in which the directors approve each others' compensation one at a time? See *Stoiber v. Miller Brewing Co.*, 257 Wis. 13, 42 N.W.2d 144 (1950) (no). To determine if salaries are excessive for purposes of a breach of fiduciary duty claim, courts might engage in the same sort of comparative analysis undertaken in *Menard* to assess the salary's deductibility. *E.g., Ruetz v. Topping,* 453 S.W.2d 624 (Mo.App.1970). Beyond challenges for breach of fiduciary duty, creditors might argue that excessive distribution through means other than dividends provides a basis for disregarding the corporate entity and imposing personal liability upon the shareholders for the company's debts. *E.g., DeWitt Truck Brokers, Inc. v. W. Ray Flemming Fruit Co.*, 540 F.2d 681 (4th Cir.1976). Often, however, courts tend to be fairly deferential to compensation set by the board. *E.g., Jaffe Commercial Finance Co. v. Harris,* 119 Ill.App.3d 136, 74 Ill.Dec. 722, 456 N.E.2d 224 (1983). For this reason, shareholders and creditors often seek contractual restrictions upon such payments. While creditors can impose such a restriction upon the corporation as condition of their loans, the ability of shareholders to do the same raises possible issues of impinging upon the board's power. This subject will be addressed more when dealing with management of corporations.

3. The salary in *Menard* provided the corporation with a deduction, but was immediately taxable to its recipient. Various provisions in the tax code, however, allow employees to delay recognition of certain types of compensation. The following two excerpts provide a brief introduction to three of the most important of such fringe benefits: qualified pension and profit sharing plans, deferred compensation arrangements, and stock options.

Cavitch, Tax Planning for Shareholders and Corporations

§ 5.02 (1989).

The Bonanza of Qualified Pension and Profit–Sharing Plans

Many businessmen and lawyers think of pension and profit-sharing plans as a form of fringe benefit available to employees of the giant corporations. That, of course, is true, but it is only a half-truth. More and more small and closely-held corporations are coming to realize the unique tax-saving opportunities available through a qualified pension or profit-sharing plan.*

* * *

[1]—Types of Qualified Plans

* * *

Treasury regulations categorize qualified plans as being either a pension plan, a profit-sharing plan, or a stock bonus plan. A pension plan is different from the others in that benefits under the plan must be "definitely determinable". Inasmuch as defined benefit plans, by definition, provide a determinable benefit for an employee at retirement, all defined benefit plans are considered to be pension plans.

* By "qualified" we mean a pension or profit-sharing plan which qualifies under the detailed rules set forth in IRC § 401(a) and related sections of the Code.

There are also two types of defined contribution plans which are considered to be pension plans: the "money purchase pension plan" and the "target benefit pension plan." What sets these plans apart from other defined contribution plans is that contributions to the plans by the employer are *required* in specified amounts.

* * *

A profit-sharing plan is a qualified plan which is designed to enable eligible employees to participate in the profits of the employer. The primary distinction between a profit-sharing plan and a pension plan is that under a profit-sharing plan, a fixed contribution is not required every year. The level of contribution may vary from year to year and is completely at the discretion of the employer.

* * *

A stock bonus plan may qualify for tax advantages in the same way as a pension or profit-sharing plan. The characteristics and requirements pertaining to a stock bonus plan are much the same as those pertaining to a profit-sharing plan, except that the ultimate distributions to employees are made in the corporation's own stock. Stock bonus plans may be useful in the case of rapidly growing businesses since the company may need any excess funds for reinvestment in capital rather than for contribution to a qualified plan. A stock bonus plan permits the employer to contribute stock directly to the plan for which it is entitled to a deduction. Such an approach may yield a valuable deduction to the company without an expenditure of cash.

In recent years, a specialized version of the stock bonus plan has been highly publicized as the employee stock ownership plan ("ESOP"). The ESOP is a stock bonus plan with additional restrictions applicable to it which entitle those shareholders who sell stock to the ESOP to special tax advantages. For this reason, the ESOP is often a popular alternative in situations involving a majority shareholder who wishes to dispose of all or a portion of his stock in a tax advantaged way.

[2]—Unique Tax Benefits Afforded by Qualified Plans

A qualified plan, whether a pension or a profit-sharing plan, affords a combination of tax benefits not available from any other source. The significance of these combined benefits can in appropriate cases be overwhelming.

* * *

The amount currently contributed by the corporation to the pension or profit-sharing fund is immediately deductible by it, subject to certain maximum limitations.

* * *

Although the corporation obtains an immediate deduction for its contribution, the employee beneficiary ordinarily does not currently include any part of the contribution in his taxable income.

* * *

The amount set apart and accumulated in a qualified pension or profit-sharing trust may be invested in whole or in part in income producing assets. The income received by the trust, however, will ordinarily not be taxable to it. The importance of this tax-exempt feature cannot be overemphasized. Its availability to affluent individuals is unique in the tax laws, and is the most important single reason why the qualified pension or profit-sharing plan is the best of all tax shelters. The compounding effect of earning income tax-free over a period of many years can be dramatic indeed.

Furthermore, this exemption from income tax applies not only to the portion of the trust fund which has been contributed by the employer, but also applies to earnings attributable to assets contributed by the participating employee. This can be a significant additional advantage, particularly to highly paid executives who participate in a qualified pension or profit-sharing plan.

* * *

Funds which are actually distributed or made available to a participating employee or his beneficiaries will be taxed to the recipient at that time to the extent such funds exceed the employee's own contributions to the plan. The taxable portion of the distribution will generally be taxed as ordinary income.

[4]—Requirements for Qualification

Obtaining the many tax benefits available through a qualified plan depends upon the trust being qualified within the meaning of the statute. * * *

[a]—Exclusive Benefit

The plan must be for the exclusive benefit of the employees and their beneficiaries. This does not mean that all of the employees must be eligible to participate; rather, those who do benefit must be former or present employees or their beneficiaries. The plan may not be a subterfuge for the distribution of profits to shareholders, or established primarily to provide a private bank for the corporation.

* * *

[c]—Nondiscrimination in Coverage

Perhaps the most important requirement, and the one that is likely to be the most troublesome in a closely held corporation, is the requirement respecting breadth of coverage. In order to obtain the tax benefits of qualification, a plan must satisfy any one of three alternative coverage tests. These tests are designed to insure that the plan does not unduly exclude the nonhighly compensated employees of the employer from coverage under the plan.

* * *

[e]—Nondiscrimination in Benefits or Contributions

Closely related to the nondiscrimination coverage requirement, is the requirement that contributions or benefits provided under the plan may not discriminate in favor of highly compensated employees.*

Walter, An Overview of Compensation Techniques Following TRA '86

14 J. Corp. Tax 139 (1987).

Unsecured Deferred Compensation

* * * It is well accepted under the tax law that the employer's promise to pay compensation in the future is not, without more (such as constructive receipt), taxable until the time of actual receipt.

* * *

Several interesting questions remain as to deferred compensation. The first is the timing of the employer's deduction. As a general rule, of course, the employer may not deduct compensation until the employee takes it into income. * * *

A second question concerning deferred compensation is the extent to which the employee can, prior to payment, have more than the employer's simple promise to pay, without being in constructive receipt of the payment or being deemed to have received an economic benefit. It is black-letter law that the employee will have constructive receipt if the amount is set aside irrevocably for the employee, outside the grasp of the employer's creditors. The question is how close the employee can come to that desired status without running afoul of constructive receipt. After a period during which it was unwilling to issue rulings, the Service indicated that it would resume issuing favorable rulings for certain so-called rabbi trusts. The current wisdom on the subject appears to be that such a trust can put the desired asset outside the reach of the employer corporation itself—a desirable result to the employee, in days in which changes of corporate control are possible—if the assets are subject to the claims of judgment creditors while the corporation is solvent and to general creditors in the case of insolvency. [Section 409A of the Internal Revenue Code now provides further guidelines for what is acceptable in a deferred compensation plan with respect to the question of constructive receipt. Ed.]

* * *

* [The 1996 Small Business Job Protection Act liberalized a number of requirements for qualified pension plans, especially with respect to the nondiscrimination rules. Ed.]

Incentive Stock Options

Since their creation by statute in the Economic Recovery Tax Act in 1981, incentive stock options (ISOs) have occupied a lofty place in the firmament of compensation techniques. The basic requirements for an incentive stock option plan and incentive options are familiar. The plan must be approved by stockholders and must state the maximum number of shares that may be sold under the plan, and each option must be granted at not less than fair market value at the time of grant and can have a term of no more than ten years. Special rules apply to shareholders who own more than 10 percent of the corporation's stock. Under these rules, the option price must be at least 110 percent of fair market value on the date of grant and the option can have a term of no more than five years.

* * * In addition, prior to TRA '86, an employer could not grant an employee options to acquire stock having a value of more than $100,000 in any calendar year. TRA '86 changed this rule by making the $100,000 limitation apply only to options which first become exercisable in any calendar year. * * *

The advantages of ISOs are several, particularly from the standpoint of the employee. An employee does not recognize income upon the grant of an incentive stock option. Furthermore, the exercise of the option does not result in tax under the normal tax system. Finally, assuming that the optionee satisfies the statutory holding period for the purchased shares—the greater of two years from the date of grant and one year from the date of exercise—any gain on the ultimate sale of the stock will result in long-term capital gain. Partially offsetting these advantages, however, is the fact that the difference between the option price and the fair market value at the time of exercise is an item of tax preference. Depending on the mix of the employee's income in the year of exercise, the exercise could result in the imposition of the alternative minimum tax.

The employer that grants an ISO does not fare nearly as well as the employee. Assuming that the employee receives the tax treatment outlined above, the employer will not be entitled to any deduction. Only if the employee fails to satisfy the statutory tests—such as by selling his stock before complying with the statutory holding period—and thereby disqualifying the option, will the employer be entitled to a deduction.

* * *

Nonqualified Stock Option

The definition of a nonqualified stock option is simple. It is a stock option that does not meet the special tests applicable to incentive stock options and therefore falls under the general rule of Section 83 of the Code governing compensation. Such an option is a contract between the employer and the key executive. For tax purposes, a nonqualified option may have any duration and be granted at any price, in contrast to ISOs. A nonqualified stock option does not become entangled in other technical rules that regulate incentive stock options. * * *

The tax treatment applicable to nonqualified options is easily stated. An employee is not subject to tax upon the grant of the option, even if the option price is less than the fair market value of the stock.[14] Instead, the employee will be subject to tax, at ordinary income rates, at the time the option is exercised. The amount of the income will be the difference between the fair market value of the stock acquired upon exercise and the option price that was paid. [The corporation, however, obtains a deduction at the same time, and in the same amount, as the employee recognizes income.]

NOTES

1. Another tax advantage to stock options comes from Section 162(m) of the Internal Revenue Code. This section prevents public corporations from deducting more than $1 million in compensation paid to a senior executive, unless paid as performance based compensation—such as stock options.

2. One other "fringe benefit" of note in a corporation is an agreement by the company to indemnify or provide insurance for directors and officers who may incur liability in the course of performing their duties. *E.g.,* Cal. Corp. Code § 317 (empowering corporation to indemnify and purchase insurance for officers and directors); Del. Gen. Corp. Law § 145(f), (g) (empowering corporation to agree to indemnification and furnish insurance); N.Y. Bus. Corp. Law §§ 721 (certificate or bylaws may contain or authorize an indemnity agreement), 726 (corporation may furnish insurance under certain circumstances); M.B.C.A. §§ 8.51, 8.56 (stating circumstances when corporation can indemnify directors and officers), 8.57 (corporation may furnish insurance). Along related lines, many state corporations statutes allow the articles to lessen the potential liability of a corporation's directors for breaching their duty of care. *E.g.,* Cal. Corp. Code § 204(a)(10); Del. Gen. Corp. Law § 102(b)(7); N.Y. Bus. Corp. Law § 402(b); M.B.C.A. § 2.02(b)(4).

3. Public corporations with shares listed on national stock exchanges, or with over 500 shareholders, face additional constraints on some fringe benefits. Section 402 of the Sarbanes–Oxley Act prohibits, with some exceptions, companies covered by the Act from making loans to their directors and executive officers. Also, rules by the New York Stock Exchange and the NASDAQ require shareholder approval of equity compensation plans for companies listed on these two exchanges. NYSE Listed Company Manual § 303A.08; NASD Rule 4350.

3. SUBCHAPTER S

a. *The Election*

To elect taxation under Subchapter S, a company must come within the definition of a "small business corporation" found in Section 1361.

14. This conclusion assumes that the option does not have a "readily ascertainable fair market value" within the meaning of § 83(e)(3). In view of the narrow construction of that phrase taken by the applicable regulations, Reg. § 1.83–7(b), it is a virtual certainty that a nonqualified option will not be treated as coming within § 83(e)(3).

Professor Eustice's comparison of S corporations with partnerships, excerpted in Chapter II, set out the requirements for eligibility as a "small business corporation." Briefly, these requirements include: (1) The company cannot have more than 100 unrelated shareholders; (2) Only individuals, estates and certain types of trusts (not corporations and partnerships) can be shareholders in the company; (3) Non-resident aliens cannot be shareholders in the company; (4) The company can have only one class of stock. I.R.C. § 1361(b). The mechanics of a Subchapter S election, and the termination of that election, raise several planning issues.

Newmark & Lang, The Subchapter S Revision Act of 1982

37 Tax. Law. 93 (1983).

* * *

III. ELECTING SUBCHAPTER S

A corporation is taxed as a C corporation unless it elects to be taxed as an S corporation. * * * [A]ll shareholders of a corporation on the date of election * * * must consent to the corporation's election.[60] Further, a corporation * * * may make the election within one of two alternative time periods: during the taxable year preceding the taxable year for which the election is to be effective or during the first 2–1/2 months of the taxable year for which the election is to be effective.[61] * * * Under the Revision Act, in addition to obtaining the consent of all election date shareholders, a small business corporation making a subchapter S election during the first 2–1/2 months of the taxable year is required to meet two additional requirements: (1) the corporation must qualify as a small business corporation on each day of the election year preceding the day of the election,[64] and (2) all persons who were shareholders at any time during the election year and before the day of the election must consent to the election.[65] * * *

* * * Therefore, any corporation contemplating the election of subchapter S during the first 2–1/2 months of its taxable year must begin planning for the election in the year preceding the election year. During this prior year, the corporation must ensure that on the first day of the taxable year in which its election is to be made, the corporation qualifies as a small business corporation.

* * *

60. I.R.C. § 1362(a)(2).

61. I.R.C. § 1362(b)(1).

64. I.R.C. § 1362(b)(2)(B)(i).

65. I.R.C. § 1362(b)(2)(B)(ii).

V. TERMINATION OF ELECTION

* * *

The rules relating to revocations of subchapter S elections now provide greater flexibility. New section 1362(d) allows a shareholder majority to revoke the corporation's election. * * * Nonvoting, as well as voting, shares are considered in determining whether a shareholder majority favors revocation. Notwithstanding the Revision Act's simple majority requirement, there may be instances in which shareholders will desire to enter into an agreement to require shareholders unanimity, or a percentage greater than a simple majority, to effectuate a revocation.

For planning purposes, perhaps the most important revocation changes in the Revision Act occur with respect to timing. * * * [S]ection 1362(d) allows the corporation to revoke within the first 2–1/2 months of the year * * *. This extended revocation period permits a corporation and its shareholders to proceed further into the corporation's taxable year and thus allows more opportunity to project the corporation's tax impact on its shareholders before the corporation must decide whether or not to revoke its subchapter S election for that year.

Prior law prohibited an S corporation from revoking its election in the same year in which it initially made its election. Section 1362(d) contains no such prohibition. * * *

One major planning device introduced by section 1362(d) is the provision that corporations may specify a prospective date on which a revocation is to become effective. * * *

This choice of an effective prospective revocation date, in conjunction with the 2–1/2 month revocation period, provides many planning opportunities. A corporation can utilize the 2–1/2 month period to project the effect of its current operations. With this projection, the corporation can then decide whether to revoke its S corporation election as of the beginning of the taxable year or whether it would be more beneficial to the shareholders to have the revocation become effective on some prospective date.

* * *

The section 1362(d) rule—that terminations occurring because the S corporation ceases to be a small business corporation are effective as of the date of the terminating event—does not always work against the corporation and its shareholders. Instead, it may provide some interesting planning opportunities. For example, assume calendar year Corporation X experiences large net operating losses in January through April. In April, X obtains a contract which will produce large amounts of taxable income for the remainder of the year. By intentionally terminating its S corporation election [by ceasing to be a "small business corporation"] on May 1, X can split its calendar year into two taxable years: an S short year (January 1 through April 30) and a C short year (May 1 through December 31). In conjunction with the section 1362(e) shareholder election discussed below, this method effectively passes X's January through April net operating loss to the shareholders, while preventing X's May through December income from passing through to the shareholders.

* * *

As noted above, revocations may specify a prospective revocation date other than the first day of the taxable year. Further, terminations are effective on the date that the terminating event occurs. As such, the effective date of the revocation or termination may not be necessarily the first day of the taxable year. Revocations specifying a prospective revocation date and all terminations that occur on a day other than the first day of the taxable year create an S short taxable year and a C short taxable year. As a general rule, income, losses, deductions, and credits are allocated between the S short year and the C short year on a daily pro rata basis. If all the shareholders so elect, however, then the corporation can make the allocation under the corporation's normal tax accounting rules. If the shareholders make this election, income, loss, deductions, and credit items are generally allocated between the S short year and the C short year based on when the items were realized or incurred.

This allocation election, in combination with the choice of revocation or termination date, allows an S corporation the flexibility of structuring its revocation or termination in a manner which is most beneficial to its shareholders.

* * *

In attempting to minimize a shareholder's tax liability, an S corporation and its shareholders should not be too hasty in terminating or revoking its subchapter S election. Section 1362(g) provides * * * that a corporation whose election is revoked or terminated cannot re-elect subchapter S for the following five years without the Service's consent.

* * *

b. *Operation*

(i) Generally

Bittker, Taxation of Income, Estates and Gifts

¶ 95.6.1 (1989 Supp.).

* * *

Taxable income. The taxable income of a Subchapter S corporation (with certain exceptions) is computed like that of an individual. Thus, deductions such as the deduction for intercorporate dividends allowed by I.R.C. § 243 are not available * * *. But deductions for individuals that are not allowed to partnerships because of I.R.C. § 703(a)(2) are likewise not allowed to Subchapter S corporations. * * *

If a Subchapter S corporation distributes to its shareholders property having a fair market value exceeding its adjusted basis, gain is recognized to the corporation as if the property had been sold for its fair market value. This does not mean that there is any corporate-level tax on the gain, but simply that the gain becomes part of the taxable income of the corporation, to be passed through to the shareholders.

Pass-through of items of income, loss, etc. A shareholder of a Subchapter S corporation takes into account his pro rata share of the various items of income, loss, deduction, or credit, and these items must be separately stated if their separate treatment could affect the tax liability of any shareholder. As in the case of partnerships, the character of any item, determined at the entity level, is passed through to the shareholder.* * * * [E]ach shareholder takes into account his pro rata share calculated on a day-by-day basis * * * [T]he items passed through are taken into account in the shareholder's taxable year in which the taxable year of the Subchapter S corporation ends. * * * For purposes of calculating the amount passed through to shareholders, a corporation's long-term capital gains are reduced by any corporate-level tax on capital gain, and a corporation's items of passive investment income are reduced by the portion of the corporate-level tax on excess net passive income allocable to the respective items.

Adjustments to basis of stock. The basis of a shareholder's stock is increased by items of income passed through and decreased by distributions not includable in the shareholder's income * * * and by items of loss and deduction. If the basis of stock is insufficient to cover the decrease resulting from items of loss and deduction, the basis of any corporate indebtedness to the shareholder is decreased, and in such a situation any net increase of basis for a subsequent taxable year is to be used first to restore the basis of indebtedness and increases the basis of stock only after the basis of indebtedness has been restored.

Corporate distributions. * * * Distributions to which, but for Subchapter S, I.R.C. § 301(c) would apply are treated as follows. If the Subchapter S corporation has no accumulated earnings and profits, any distribution is not to be included in the shareholder's income (but, as explained above, is to decrease the basis of the stock) to the extent that it does not exceed the basis of the stock, and, to the extent of any excess over basis, is to be treated as gain from the sale or exchange of property. If the Subchapter S corporation has accumulated earnings and profits, any distribution is to be treated as though the corporation had no accumulated earnings and profits to the extent that the distribution does not exceed the accumulated adjustments account; any portion of the distribution remaining after the exhaustion of the accumulated adjustments account is to be treated as a dividend to the extent that it does not exceed the accumulated earnings and profits; any portion of the distribution remaining after the exhaustion of the accumulated earnings and profits is treated like any other distribution by a Subchapter S corporation that has no accumulated earnings and profits.

* [The regulations contain an exception for situations in which a shareholder is using the S corporation for the principal purpose of converting ordinary income into capital gains, or capital losses into ordinary losses, on the sale of contributed property. Treas. Reg. § 1.1366–1(b). Ed.]

The statutory scheme just described rests upon two concepts, accumulated earnings and profits and accumulated adjustments account. "Accumulated earnings and profits" has its general tax-law meaning, except that there is no adjustment to the earnings and profits of a corporation for the time that it is a Subchapter S corporation under the 1982 Act (apart from adjustments necessitated by redemptions, reorganizations, liquidations, divisions, etc.), except for dividend distributions (normally, as described above, distributions by a Subchapter S corporation having accumulated earnings and profits but a zero or negative accumulated adjustments account). Thus, the earnings and profits of a Subchapter S corporation will be attributable to taxable years when it was not a Subchapter S corporation * * * and to carryovers under I.R.C. § 381. The accumulated adjustments account is, roughly speaking, the equivalent of earnings and profits for * * * Subchapter S years. It is the running total, at the corporate level, of all the items by which the shareholders' basis was increased (such as income) and decreased (such as tax-free distributions and items of loss and deduction). * * *

A Subchapter S corporation having accumulated earnings and profits may elect, with the consent of all affected shareholders, to distribute accumulated earnings and profits first, thereby waiving the protective effect of the accumulated adjustments account. A corporation might wish to do so in order to avoid the corporate-level tax and possible termination of Subchapter S status that result when a Subchapter S corporation has Subchapter C earnings and profits at the close of a taxable year in which more than 25 percent of gross receipts are passive investment income.

Miscellaneous. The 1982 Act provides that for purposes of Subchapter C (I.R.C. §§ 301 through 385) a Subchapter S corporation in its capacity as a shareholder of another corporation shall be treated as an individual. * * *

There can be no carryforward or carryback from a year in which a corporation is not a Subchapter S corporation to a year in which it is a Subchapter S corporation, but a Subchapter S year nevertheless is counted in determining the number of years to which an item may be carried back or forward. No carryforward or carryback can arise at the corporate level for a year in which a corporation is a Subchapter S corporation.

* * *

The 1982 Act provides that every Subchapter S corporation must have the calendar year as its taxable year, unless a business purpose for a different taxable year is established to the satisfaction of the IRS. * * * [*But see* I.R.C. § 444 (allowing a limited use of non-calendar years, if the corporation pays a tax for obtaining the deferral). Ed.]

* * *

(ii) Uses and Abuses

One of the major areas of tax planning for an entity treated as a partnership for income tax purposes involves allocating income and losses (including individual tax items) between partners. In an S corporation, all taxable income and losses flow through to the shareholders simply in proportion to their ownership of stock. I.R.C. § 1366(a)(1). This fact, coupled with the limitation of S corporations to only one class of stock, limits the flexibility of S corporations relative to partnerships, and, as discussed in Chapter II, can provide a reason to do business as a partnership, limited partnership LLP or LLC. The problem is exacerbated by the fact that, in a corporation, stock ownership generally controls management and liquidation rights as well as profit shares.

Nevertheless, careful planning can achieve many of the same results in an S corporation as one may have provided for in a partnership or LLC operating agreement. Easiest to obtain is a desired decoupling of management power from profit shares. For instance, suppose two individuals desire equal control over the business but agreed to an unequal division of profits. Dividing one class of voting stock to reflect the profit split creates unequal voting power. Section 1361(c)(4) provides, however, that shares differing only as to voting rights do not constitute more than one class of stock for purposes of Subchapter S eligibility. Hence, use of non-voting stock can obtain what the parties desire. (In addition, techniques discussed in the following section of this Chapter exist to assure even a minority shareholder an equal say over corporate decisions. In this regard, note that voting trusts can be shareholders of an S corporation. I.R.C. § 1361(c)(2)(iv).)

Decoupling profit shares from liquidation rights is more complicated. Take the situation in which one member puts up cash, while the other does work, and both agree to split profits equally. The cash contributor, even though willing to share profits equally, may demand return of his money prior to any proceeds upon liquidation going to the service provider. Achieving this result by issuing a class of stock with a liquidation preference would destroy eligibility for S status. The cash contributor can, however, loan money to the company, thereby obtaining a priority over any liquidating distribution on shares. Still, loaning almost all the cash in order to obtain the desired preference would leave the company with a large debt-equity ratio. If a court reclassified the debt as equity, there could be a second class of stock. (The fact that a court reclassifies so-called debt as equity would not make it a second class of stock, however, if the shareholders held it proportionately so that the "debt" had no real effect on their rights as between themselves. Treas.Reg. § 1.1361–1(*l*)(4)(ii)(B)(2). Rather, the regulations only treat reclassified debt as a second class of stock if its use was for a principal purpose of circumventing the liquidation or distribution rights established by the outstanding shares (or else to circumvent the limit on eligible shareholders). Treas.Reg. § 1.1361–1(*l*)(4)(ii)(A)(2). The problem, of course, here is that circumventing proportionate liquidation rights is precisely what the parties would be attempting to achieve.) Perhaps the debt could fit into the safe harbor provisions for "straight debt" (I.R.C. § 1361(c)(5)).

The most challenging problem occurs if the parties wish to bear losses in a different ratio from profits, or to have the allocation change at different levels of income, over time, or upon the occurrence of certain events. Can they accomplish this in an S corporation? They cannot employ the techniques described earlier to vary profit and loss allocations by using dividend and liquidation preferences. Suppose, however, the parties agree to alter their relative shareholdings upon the occurrence of events when they wish to change the profit allocation. This general approach to create varying profit divisions was explored earlier. Recall, it encountered a number of practical difficulties. There also may be some specific problems with its use in an S corporation. For example, can the change in share ownership, with its corresponding change in the allocation of taxable income and loss, take place in a timely manner? Specifically, if the allocation depends upon how the company performed during a period of time (for instance, whether it made or lost money), by the point the parties establish the relevant fact, will it be too late to effect a change in the tax allocation by transferring stock? (In this connection, see the discussion at pp. 560–61 concerning the impact of share transfers during the tax year on the allocation of income and loss from an S corporation.) Another concern exists as to whether these arrangements could create two classes of stock—those subject to transfer upon the agreed event, and those not. *See* Treas.Reg. § 1.1361–1(*l*)(2)(iii)(A) (buy-sell and redemption agreements will create a problem under the one class of stock requirement when a principal purpose of the agreement is to circumvent the one class of stock requirement and the purchase price under the contract diverges significantly from the fair market value of the stock at the time of the agreement), (4)(iii)(A) (call options equal a second class of stock if substantially certain to be exercised and have an exercise price substantially below the fair market value of the stock on the date the option was issued, modified or transferred to an ineligible shareholder). Also, might the Internal Revenue Service disregard such transfers as a sham?

One technique for minimizing tax in the partnership area involves the use of so-called family partnerships. An individual might bring close relatives into a partnership with him or her—despite their contributing little work and despite their capital being his or her gift—in order to lower net taxes by shifting income to persons paying lower marginal rates. This strategy is still available in an S corporation. *E.g., Davis v. Commissioner,* 64 T.C. 1034 (1975). The Internal Revenue Service, however, has successfully challenged such income splitting when, in reality, the family members were only nominal owners of stock in the company. *E.g., Speca v. Commissioner,* 630 F.2d 554 (7th Cir.1980). Much as under the *Culbertson* standard for family partnerships, such a challenge depends upon who really has the control and benefit of the shares. In addition, following the pattern under Section 704(e), Section 1366(e) empowers the I.R.S. to reallocate income between family members in order to insure that higher bracket members do not receive salaries or return on capital below the worth of their services or capital as a devise to shift income.

Like partners, shareholders in S corporations only can deduct losses to the extent of their basis in the firm. I.R.C. § 1366(d)(1). Unlike the rule for partners, debts owed by the company do not increase the shareholder's basis. (This is a potential disadvantage of S corporations relative to partnerships.) One exception exists. A shareholder's basis in an S corporation includes both the individual's adjusted basis in his or her stock, and his or her basis in any debt owed to the individual by the company. I.R.C. § 1366(d)(1)(B). (Contrast this with the partner's loan to a partnership. Whereas a partner's loan increases the basis of all the firm's members by their share of the partnership's liability, the S corporation shareholder's loan increases only the lending shareholder's basis by the entire amount of the loan.) Nevertheless, even this limited effect of debt creates questions.

Estate of Leavitt v. Commissioner of Internal Revenue

90 T.C. 206 (1988), *aff'd,* 875 F.2d 420 (4th Cir.1989).

■ NIMS, JUDGE.

* * *

VAFLA Corp. (hereinafter referred to as the corporation), was an electing small business corporation under subchapter S during the years in issue and was incorporated in February 1979, to acquire and operate the Six–Gun Territory Amusement Park near Tampa, Florida. The initial issue of the corporation's capital stock took place in March 1979, and consisted of 100,000 shares. Daniel Leavitt and Anthony D. Cuzzocrea each paid $10,000 cash for their shares on or before September 30, 1979.

* * *

From August 2, 1979, through August 27, 1979, Anthony D. Cuzzocrea and Daniel Leavitt, as well as other shareholders signed a guarantee agreement whereby each agreed to be jointly and severally liable for all indebtedness of the corporation to the Bank of Virginia. * * *

The corporation borrowed $300,000 from the Bank of Virginia for which it issued a promissory note to the bank dated September 12, 1979. The purpose of the loan was to fund VAFLA's existing and anticipated operating deficits.

At the time the loan was made, the corporation's liabilities exceeded its assets, and the corporation had so little available cash that it could not meet its cash-flow requirements. * * *

* * * However, * * * the corporation made the following principal payments to the Bank of Virginia:

December 26, 1979	$10,000
July 15, 1980	10,000
January 6, 1981	10,000

All interest payments were also made by the corporation. * * *

Daniel and Evelyn M. Leavitt deducted a loss of $13,808 attributable to the corporation on their 1979 joint Federal income tax return. Respondent disallowed $3,808 of this deduction. Anthony D. and Marjorie F. Cuzzocrea deducted losses of $13,808, $29,921, and $22,746 attributable to the corporation on their 1979, 1980, and 1981 joint Federal income tax returns, respectively. Respondent disallowed all of these deductions in excess of $10,000.

Respondent takes the position that shareholders Daniel Leavitt and Anthony D. Cuzzocrea may not deduct losses attributable to the corporation in excess of their initial basis in their shares in the corporation. Petitioners maintain that their guarantees of the $300,000 loan to the corporation from the Bank of Virginia increased their basis in their stock sufficiently to allow deductions for their proportionate shares of losses attributable to the corporation during the years in issue.

* * *

The corporation sustained losses for the taxable years 1979, 1980, and 1981. Before the guarantee transaction, petitioners Daniel Leavitt and Anthony D. Cuzzocrea each had an adjusted basis in their stock in the corporation of $10,000. We must determine whether petitioners' guarantee of the $300,000 loan from the Bank of Virginia to the corporation increased the basis in petitioners' stock in the corporation.

It is well settled that:

> the fact that shareholders may be primarily liable on indebtedness of a corporation to a third party does not mean that this indebtedness is "indebtedness of the corporation to the shareholder" within the meaning of Section 1374(c)(2)(B). No form of indirect borrowing, be it guaranty, surety, accommodation, comaking or otherwise, gives rise to indebtedness from the corporation to the shareholders until and unless the shareholders pay part or all of the obligation. * * * [*Raynor v. Commissioner,* 50 T.C. 762, 770–771 (1968).]

* * *

In the instant case, petitioners have never been called upon to pay any of the loan that they guaranteed. Accordingly, the guarantees that petitioners executed do not increase any indebtedness of the corporation to them.

Nevertheless, petitioners ask us to view the guarantee transactions as constructive loans from the banks to petitioners and, in turn, contributions of those same funds by petitioners to the capital of the corporation. * * * We disagree.

* * *

The Bank of Virginia loaned the money to the corporation and not to petitioners. The proceeds of the loan were to be used in the operation of the corporation's business. Petitioners submitted no evidence that they were free to dispose of the proceeds of the loan as they wished. Nor were the payments on the loan reported as constructive dividends on the corporation's Federal income tax returns or on petitioners' Federal income tax returns during the years in issue. Accordingly, we find that the transaction was in fact a loan by the bank to the corporation guaranteed by the shareholders.

Nevertheless, petitioners ask that we apply traditional debt-equity principles in determining the nature of the transaction in this case. Petitioners maintain that because the corporation was insolvent at the time the loan was made and because the bank would not have advanced the funds to the corporation without the shareholders' guarantees, the loan was in fact a loan from the bank to the shareholders who then advanced the proceeds of the loan as a contribution to the capital of the corporation. We decline to adopt traditional debt-equity principles in this case.

* * *

In *Selfe v. United States,* 778 F.2d 769 (11th Cir.1985), the 11th Circuit applied a debt-equity analysis and held that a shareholder's guarantee of a loan made to a subchapter S corporation may be treated for tax purposes as an equity investment in the corporation where the lender looks to the shareholder as the primary obligor. We respectfully disagree with the 11th Circuit and hold that a shareholder's guarantee of a loan to a subchapter S corporation may not be treated as an equity investment in the corporation absent an economic outlay by the shareholder.

The *Selfe* opinion was based primarily on *Plantation Patterns, Inc. v. Commissioner,* 462 F.2d 712 (5th Cir.1972), affg. T.C. Memo. 1970–182, in which the Fifth Circuit affirmed as not clearly erroneous a finding by this Court that a transaction structured as a loan by an independent third party to a corporation, and guaranteed by a shareholder, was in substance a loan to the shareholder followed by his contribution of the loan proceeds to the corporation, and that as a result the corporation's payments of principal and interest on the debt constituted constructive dividends to the shareholder.

However, the corporation in *Plantation Patterns* was a subchapter C corporation. We decline to apply the debt-equity analysis used in *Plantation Patterns* to the guarantee of a loan to a subchapter S corporation. Congress has promulgated a set of rules designed to limit the amount of deductions allowable to a shareholder of a subchapter S corporation to the amount he has actually invested in the corporation and the amounts of income from the corporation included in the shareholder's gross income.

* * *

To allow petitioners to increase the basis of their stock without a capital outlay or a realization of income would provide them a means of avoiding these limitations. * * *

* * * We hold that the debt-equity analysis does not apply to guaranteed loans to subchapter S corporations for which the shareholder has incurred no cost. * * *

NOTES

1. Given the consequences in *Leavitt,* should the shareholders have borrowed the money themselves and loaned it to the corporation, rather than

guaranteeing the company's loan? See *Bolding v. Commissioner*, 117 F.3d 270 (5th Cir.1997) (shareholder who borrowed money and loaned it to an S corporation was able to take losses against an increased basis). Would there be any problem then using corporate earnings to repay the loans? Keep in mind, this is an S corporation, in which there is no double tax. Would the two stockholders have faced any greater liability? Incidentally, while shareholder loans *to* the corporation increase basis, what effect does a shareholder's promise to pay the corporation (so the shareholder becomes the debtor rather than the creditor) have? See Rev.Rul. 81–187, 1981–2 C.B. 167 (does not increase basis for purposes of subchapter S).

An S corporation shareholder may carry forward losses disallowed for lack of basis until he or she obtains a sufficient basis to utilize them. I.R.C. § 1366(d)(2). Upon termination of the S election, however, the shareholder has only the post-termination transition period to use the losses, after which they can never be used. I.R.C. § 1366(d)(3). It is also important to recall that, in addition to the basis limit, the at risk limitation of Section 465 and the passive activity loss limitation of Section 469 apply to shareholders in S corporations. Indeed, borrowing money from another shareholder in order to loan the sums to the corporation may succeed in increasing the borrowing shareholder's basis, but not increase the amount at risk. *E.g., Van Wyk v. Commissioner*, 113 T.C. 440 (1999).

2. Salary, interest and rent payments to shareholders in an S corporation involve some of the same tax issues raised by such payments to parties taxed as partners. For example, Section 1372 treats S corporation shareholders, who hold over two percent of the company's outstanding stock, as if they were partners for purposes of determining their eligibility for favorable employee fringe benefit treatment. This sometimes means they cannot obtain the fringe benefit tax free and the company cannot take a deduction for providing the benefit. Similarly, the limit found in Section 267(a)(2) on a firm taking a deduction for paying a salary to an owner-employee prior to his or her recognizing income applies to S corporations, as it does to firms treated as partnerships. I.R.C. § 267(e)(1).

Some tax planning opportunities when choosing between salaries and profit distributions with firms treated as partnerships may not exist for S corporations. For example, recall the discussion of substituting an added profit share in lieu of a salary for which the partnership could not have obtained an immediate deduction. The one class of stock limitation may render this largely impractical for S corporations. On the other hand, S corporations have some opportunities not available to firms treated as partnerships. For example, lowering all the salaries to owner-employees in favor of more dividends might save on employment (Social Security and Medicare) taxes. *But see Joseph Radtke, S.C. v. United States,* 712 F.Supp. 143 (E.D.Wis.1989) (recharacterized dividend as a salary); *Joseph M. Grey Public Accountant, P.C. v. Commissioner*, 119 T.C. 121 (2002) (the court rejected the argument that the sole owner of a professional corporation taxed under Subchapter S was not an employee of the corporation for purposes of employment taxes). Notice how, in the S corporation context, it is often the I.R.S. that argues a dividend is really a salary, whereas, in C corporation cases (such as the *Menard* decision reprinted earlier), the I.R.S. tries to argue a salary is really a dividend.

There are a number of ways in which salary, interest and rent payments to shareholders in an S corporation can create different issues than involved with C corporations. For example, to the extent some shareholders, but not others, receive salaries, interest or rent payments, and to the extent the I.R.S. could argue those payments are disguised dividends, could there be a problem with the corporation effectively having two classes of stock—those whose owners get the payments and those whose owners do not? See Treas. Reg. § 1.1361–1(*l*)(2)(i), (v) Exs. 3, 4 (not unless a principal purpose of the arrangement was to avoid the single class of stock requirement). Suppose the corporation issues stock options as executive compensation; could the options constitute a second class of stock? See Treas. Reg. 1.1361–1(*l*)(4)(iii)(A), (B)(2) (not unless the option price is substantially below the fair market value of the stock on the date the option is issued, or, even if the price is at this level, not if the option contract is non-transferable and does not have a readily ascertainable fair market value). Qualified deferred compensation plans also do not create a second class of stock. Treas. Reg. § 1.1361–1(b)(4).

3. The discussion thus far has focused on planning opportunities and problems for the firm which operates as an S corporation from its inception. What added opportunities or difficulties does a C corporation face if it considers an S election? Here, a major question becomes whether a C corporation can avoid double taxation on past, rather than just future, income by converting to S status. One limitation was already noted: Distributions by a company with earnings and profits accumulated from its days as a C corporation will produce taxable dividends if they reach a point in excess of the firm's "accumulated adjustments account" (largely, its undistributed earnings since the S election). Suppose, however, the corporation retains the earnings made during its C days—perhaps putting them into various passive investments. S corporations are exempt from the accumulated earnings tax. I.R.C. § 1363(a). Hence, a company might try to use an S election to gain the advantages outlined earlier of deferring taxable distributions. To prevent this, Section 1375 creates an exception to the general rule that S corporations themselves do not pay tax. If an S corporation ends its tax year both with accumulated earnings and profits left from when it was a C corporation, and with income for the year from various passive investment sources constituting over 25 percent of that year's gross receipts, this section taxes the company's "excess net passive income" at the highest corporate tax rate. (Note, the meaning of passive income here is different from passive activity income or loss as used in Section 469's passive loss rules.) Moreover, if a company meets these two conditions for three straight years, its S status terminates. I.R.C. § 1362(d)(3)(A). Finally, suppose a C corporation has appreciated assets. Can it avoid the double tax on disposing of such assets, by first making an S election? Here, Section 1374 comes into play. Broadly speaking, Section 1374 taxes the S corporation, rather than its shareholders, on any gain

resulting from the sale or distribution of assets within 10 years after the S election, unless the corporation can establish the appreciation of the asset did not occur before its S election. (An example of such proof would be if the company bought the asset after the firm became an S corporation.)

SECTION C. MANAGEMENT

Wilkes v. Springside Nursing Home, Inc.

370 Mass. 842, 353 N.E.2d 657 (1976).

■ HENNESSEY, CHIEF JUSTICE.

On August 5, 1971, the plaintiff (Wilkes) filed a bill in equity for declaratory judgment * * * naming as defendants T. Edward Quinn (Quinn), Leon L. Riche (Riche), the First Agricultural National Bank of Berkshire County and Frank Sutherland MacShane as executors under the will of Lawrence R. Connor (Connor), and the Springside Nursing Home, Inc. (Springside or the corporation). Wilkes alleged that he, Quinn, Riche and Dr. Hubert A. Pipkin (Pipkin) entered into a partnership agreement in 1951, prior to the incorporation of Springside, which agreement was breached in 1967 when Wilkes' salary was terminated and he was voted out as an officer and director of the corporation. Wilkes sought, among other forms of relief, damages in the amount of the salary he would have received had he continued as a director and officer of Springside subsequent to March, 1967.

* * * A judgment was entered dismissing Wilkes' action on the merits. * * * On appeal, Wilkes argued in the alternative that (1) he should recover damages for breach of the alleged partnership agreement; and (2) he should recover damages because the defendants, as majority stockholders in Springside, breached their fiduciary duty to him as a minority stockholder by their action in February and March, 1967.

* * *

In 1951 Wilkes acquired an option to purchase a building and lot * * *, the building having previously housed the Hillcrest Hospital. Though Wilkes was principally engaged in the roofing and siding business, he had gained a reputation locally for profitable dealings in real estate. Riche, an acquaintance of Wilkes, learned of the option, and interested Quinn (who was known to Wilkes through membership on the draft board in Pittsfield) and Pipkin (an acquaintance of both Wilkes and Riche) in joining Wilkes in his investment. The four men met and decided to participate in the purchase of the building and lot as a real estate investment which, they believed, had good profit potential on resale or rental.

The parties later determined that the property would have its greatest potential for profit if it were operated by them as a nursing home. Wilkes consulted his attorney, who advised him that if the four men were to operate the contemplated nursing home as planned, they would be partners and would be liable for any debts incurred by the partnership and by each other. On the attorney's suggestion, and after consultation among themselves, ownership of the property was vested in Springside, a corporation organized under Massachusetts law.

Each of the four men invested $1,000 and subscribed to ten shares of $100 par value stock in Springside. At the time of incorporation it was understood by all of the parties that each would be a director of Springside and each would participate actively in the management and decision making involved in operating the corporation.[7] It was, further, the understanding and intention of all parties that, corporate resources permitting, each would receive money from the corporation in equal amounts as long as each assumed an active and ongoing responsibility for carrying a portion of the burdens necessary to operate the business.

The work involved in establishing and operating a nursing home was roughly apportioned, and each of the four men undertook his respective tasks. Initially, Riche was elected president of Springside, Wilkes was elected treasurer, and Quinn was elected clerk. Each of the four was listed in the articles of organization as a director of the corporation.

At some time in 1952, it became apparent that the operational income and cash flow from the business were sufficient to permit the four stockholders to draw money from the corporation on a regular basis. Each of the four original parties initially received $35 a week from the corporation. As time went on the weekly return to each was increased until, in 1955, it totalled $100.

In 1959, after a long illness, Pipkin sold his shares in the corporation to Connor, who was known to Wilkes, Riche and Quinn through past transactions with Springside in his capacity as president of First Agricultural National Bank of Berkshire County. Connor received a weekly stipend from the corporation equal to that received by Wilkes, Riche and Quinn. He was elected a director of the corporation but never held any other office. He was assigned no specific area of responsibility in the operation of the nursing home but did participate in business discussions and decisions as a director and served additionally as financial adviser to the corporation.

In 1965 the stockholders decided to sell a portion of the corporate property to Quinn, who in addition to being a stockholder in Springside, possessed an interest in another corporation which desired to operate a rest home on the property. Wilkes was successful in prevailing on the other stockholders of Springside to procure a higher sale price for the property than Quinn apparently anticipated paying or desired to pay. After the sale

7. Wilkes testified before the master that, when the corporate officers were elected, all four men "were * * * guaranteed directorships." Riche's understanding of the parties' intentions was that they all wanted to play a part in the management of the corporation and wanted to have some "say" in the risks involved; that, to this end, they all would be directors; and that "unless you (were) a director and officer you could not participate in the decisions of (the) enterprise."

was consummated, the relationship between Quinn and Wilkes began to deteriorate.

The bad blood between Quinn and Wilkes affected the attitudes of both Riche and Connor. As a consequence of the strained relations among the parties, Wilkes, in January of 1967, gave notice of his intention to sell his shares for an amount based on an appraisal of their value. In February of 1967 a directors' meeting was held and the board exercised its right to establish the salaries of its officers and employees. A schedule of payments was established whereby Quinn was to receive a substantial weekly increase and Riche and Connor were to continue receiving $100 a week. Wilkes, however, was left off the list of those to whom a salary was to be paid. The directors also set the annual meeting of the stockholders for March, 1967.

At the annual meeting in March, Wilkes was not reelected as a director, nor was he reelected as an officer of the corporation. He was further informed that neither his services nor his presence at the nursing home was wanted by his associates.

The meetings of the directors and stockholders in early 1967, the master found, were used as a vehicle to force Wilkes out of active participation in the management and operation of the corporation and to cut off all corporate payments to him, Though the board of directors had the power to dismiss any officers and employees for misconduct or neglect of duties, there was no indication in the minutes of the board of directors' meeting of February, 1967, that the failure to establish a salary for Wilkes was based on either ground. The severance of Wilkes from the payroll resulted not from misconduct or neglect of duties, but because of a personal desire of Quinn, Riche and Connor to prevent him from continuing to receive money from the corporation. Despite a continuing deterioration in his personal relationship with his associations, Wilkes had consistently endeavored to carry on his responsibilities to the corporation in the same satisfactory manner and with the same degree of competence he had previously shown. Wilkes was at all times willing to carry on his responsibilities and participation if permitted so to do and provided that he receive his weekly stipend.

1. We turn to Wilkes' claim for damages based on a breach of the fiduciary duty owed to him by the other participants in this venture. In light of the theory underlying this claim, we do not consider it vital to our approach to this case whether the claim is governed by partnership law or the law applicable to business corporations. This is so because, as all the parties agree, Springside was at all times relevant to this action, a close corporation as we have recently defined such an entity in *Donahue v. Rodd Electrotype Co. of New England, Inc.,* 367 Mass. 578, 328 N.E.2d 505 (1975).

In *Donahue,* we held that "stockholders in the close corporation owe one another substantially the same fiduciary duty in the operation of the enterprise that partners owe to one another." * * * As determined in previous decisions of this court, the standard of duty owed by partners to one another is one of "utmost good faith and loyalty." * * * Thus, we concluded in *Donahue,* with regard to "their actions relative to the operations of the enterprise and the affects of that operation on the rights and investments of other stockholders," "[s]tockholders in close corporations must discharge their management and stockholder responsibilities in conformity with this strict good faith standard. They may not act out of avarice, expediency or self-interest in derogation of their duty of loyalty to the other stockholders and to the corporation." * * *

In the *Donahue* case we recognized that one peculiar aspect of close corporations was the opportunity afforded to majority stockholders to oppress, disadvantage or "freeze out" minority stockholders. In *Donahue* itself, for example, the majority refused to the minority an equal opportunity to sell a ratable number of shares to the corporation at the same price available to the majority. The net result of this refusal, we said, was that the minority could be forced to "sell out at less than fair value," * * * since there is by definition no ready market for minority stock in a close corporation.

"Freeze outs," however, may be accomplished by the use of other devices. One such device which has proved to be particularly effective in accomplishing the purpose of the majority is to deprive minority stockholders of corporate offices and of employment with the corporation. * * * This "freeze-out" technique has been successful because courts fairly consistently have been disinclined to interfere in those facets of internal corporate operations, such as the selection and retention or dismissal of officers, directors and employees, which essentially involve management decisions subject to the principle of majority control. * * *

The denial of employment to the minority at the hands of the majority is especially pernicious in some instances. A guaranty of employment with the corporation may have been one of the "basic reason(s) why a minority owner has invested capital in the firm." * * * The minority stockholder typically depends on his salary as the principal return on his investment, since the "earnings of a close corporation * * * are distributed in major part in salaries, bonuses and retirement benefits." * * *[13] Other noneconomic interests of the minority stockholder are likewise injuriously affect by barring him from corporate office. * * * Such action severely restricts his participation in the management of the enterprise, and he is relegated to enjoying those benefits incident to his status as a stockholder. * * * In sum, by terminating a minority stockholder's employment or by severing him from a position as an officer or director, the majority effectively frustrate the minority stockholder's purposes in entering on the corporate venture and also deny him an equal return on his investment.

The *Donahue* decision acknowledged, as a "natural outgrowth" of the case law of this Commonwealth, a strict obligation on the part of majority

13. We note here that the master found that Springside never declared or paid a dividend to its stockholders.

stockholders in a close corporation to deal with the minority with the utmost good faith and loyalty. On its face, this strict standard is applicable in the instant case. The distinction between the majority action in *Donahue* and the majority action in this is more one of form than of substance. Nevertheless, we are concerned that untempered application of the strict good faith standard enunciated in *Donahue* to cases such as the one before us will result in the imposition of limitations on legitimate action by the controlling group of a close corporation which will unduly hamper its effectiveness in managing the corporation in the best interests of all concerned. The majority, concededly, have certain rights to what has been termed "selfish ownership" in the corporation which should be balanced against the concept of their fiduciary obligation to the minority. * * *

Therefore, when minority stockholders in a close corporation bring suit against the majority alleging a breach of the strict good faith duty owed to them by the majority, we must carefully analyze the action taken by the controlling stockholders in the individual case. It must be asked whether the controlling group can demonstrate a legitimate business purpose for its action. * * * In asking this question, we acknowledge the fact that the controlling group in a close corporation must have some room to maneuver in establishing the business policy of the corporation. It must be a large measure of discretion, for example, in declaring or withholding dividends, deciding whether to merge or consolidate, establishing the salaries of corporate officers, dismissing directors with or without cause, and hiring and firing corporate employees.

When an asserted business purpose for their action is advanced by the majority, however, we think it is open to minority stockholders to demonstrate that the same legitimate objective could have been achieved through an alternative course of action less harmful to the minority's interest. * * * If called on to settle a dispute, our courts must weigh the legitimate business purpose, if any, against the practicability of a less harmful alternative.

Applying this approach to the instant case it is apparent that the majority stockholders in Springside have not shown a legitimate business purpose for severing Wilkes from the payroll of the corporation or for refusing to reelect him as a salaried officer and director. The master's subsidiary findings relating to the purpose of the meetings of the directors and stockholders in February and March, 1967, are supported by the evidence. There was no showing of misconduct on Wilkes' part as a director, officer or employee of the corporation which would lead us to approve the majority action as a legitimate response to the disruptive nature of an undesirable individual bent on injuring or destroying the corporation. On the contrary, it appears that Wilkes had always accomplished his assigned share of the duties competently, and that he had never indicated an unwillingness to continue to do so.

It is an inescapable conclusion from all the evidence that the action of the majority stockholders here was a designed "freeze out" for which no legitimate business purpose has been suggested. Furthermore, we may infer that a design to pressure Wilkes into selling his shares to the corporation at a price below their value well may have been at the heart of the majority's plan.[14]

In the context of this case, several factors bear directly on the duty owed to Wilkes by his associates. At a minimum, the duty of utmost good faith and loyalty would demand that the majority consider that their action was in disregard of a long-standing policy of the stockholders that each would be a director of the corporation and that employment with the corporation would go hand in hand with stock ownership; that Wilkes was one of the four originators of the nursing home venture; and that Wilkes, like the others, had invested his capital and time for more than fifteen years with the expectation that they would continue to participate in corporate decisions. Most important is the plain fact that the cutting off of Wilkes' salary, together with the fact that the corporation never declared a dividend (see note 13 *supra*), assured that Wilkes would receive no return at all from the corporation.

2. The question of Wilkes' damages at the hands of the majority has not been thoroughly explored on the record before us. * * *

Therefore our order is as follows: So much of the judgment as dismisses Wilkes' complaint and awards costs to the defendants is reversed. The case is remanded to the Probate Court for Berkshire County for further proceedings concerning the issue of damages. * * *

So ordered.

NOTE

Most readers of the *Wilkes* opinion focus on the court's application of an exacting fiduciary duty between shareholders in a closely held corporation. (Since this chapter concerns the formation of a corporation, and since companies do not typically start life by issuing stock immediately to the public, this section focuses on the management of a closely held company—albeit many of the techniques explored here have uses in the public concern as well.) From the perspective of planning, however, one views *Wilkes* in a different light. This case represents a textbook example of the closely held corporation horror story referred to as a "squeeze-out". The owners of a majority of the stock used their voting power as shareholders and directors to cut a minority stockholder off from participation in management and from any income by the company. Without relief from the court, the minority shareholders' investment became worth little. Yet, such relief is the exception, not the rule. O'Neal & Thompson, *O'Neal's Oppression of Minority Shareholders* §§ 3.03, 10.04 (2d ed. 1986). Obtaining it required the court to abandon the judiciary's traditional reluctance to interfere with the business judgment of directors and majority stockholders. *See, e.g., Neidert v. Neidert,* 637 S.W.2d 296 (Mo.App.1982). It required the court to

14. This inference arises from the fact that Connor, acting on behalf of the three controlling stockholders, offered to purchase Wilkes' shares for a price Connor admittedly would not have accepted for his own shares.

resolve what are often difficult questions regarding the intent behind a majority's action in the minority shareholder's favor. *See, e.g., Zidell v. Zidell, Inc.,* 277 Or. 413, 560 P.2d 1086 (1977) (finding no squeeze-out). It also required considerable time and expense pursuing litigation to an uncertain outcome. For these reasons, minority shareholders in a closely held corporation often employ a variety of techniques to protect themselves, rather than rely exclusively on trust in the majority or on a court's willingness to find the majority breached its trust. Indeed, the Delaware Supreme Court has urged such self-reliance in rejecting the existence of any special fiduciary duty for majority shareholders in a closely held corporation. *Nixon v. Blackwell,* 626 A.2d 1366 (Del.Super.1993).

Before looking at techniques, one needs to outline the goals. *Wilkes* provides a good starting point. Notice the testimony of the participants in this venture that each wanted to sit on the board of directors because they understood this is what it took to have a say in managing the company. The participants' understanding reflects the basic rule of corporate law that (barring an exception under special statutes discussed later) the board of directors manages, or retains the ultimate responsibility to manage, the company. *E.g.,* Cal. Corp. Code § 300(a); Del. Gen. Corp. Law § 141(a); N.Y. Bus. Corp. Law § 701; M.B.C.A. § 8.01(b). (Contrast the partnership law scheme, in which all partners have the right to participate in management barring contrary agreement. U.P.A. § 18(e).) Hence, the first objective is ensuring minority shareholders a position on the board. Yet, as Mr. Wilkes discovered, being a director is no guarantee against a majority of the board making decisions prejudicial to the minority's interest, and contrary to the original understandings between the parties in undertaking the venture. For example, the board, under its power to set salaries, cut off any salary to Mr. Wilkes. Normally, the board selects officers. *E.g.,* Cal. Corp. Code § 312(b); N.Y. Bus. Corp. Law § 715(a); M.B.C.A. § 8.40(a). As seen in *Gottfried,* the board possesses discretion with respect to declaring dividends. As a result, a second objective is to control specific corporate decisions ordinarily made by the board of directors.

1. Ensuring Positions on the Board of Directors

Ringling Bros.–Barnum & Bailey Combined Shows, Inc. v. Ringling

29 Del.Ch. 610, 53 A.2d 441 (1947).

■ Pearson, Judge.

The Court of Chancery was called upon to review an attempted election of directors at the 1946 annual stockholders meeting of the corporate defendant. The pivotal questions concern an agreement between two of the three present stockholders, and particularly the effect of this agreement with relation to the exercise of voting rights by these two stockholders. At the time of the meeting, the corporation had outstanding 1000 shares of capital stock held as follows: 315 by petitioner Edith Conway

Ringling; 315 by defendant Aubrey B. Ringling Haley (individually or as executrix and legatee of a deceased husband); and 370 by defendant John Ringling North. The purpose of the meeting was to elect the entire board of seven directors. The shares could be voted cumulatively. Mrs. Ringling asserts that by virtue of the operation of an agreement between her and Mrs. Haley, the latter was bound to vote her shares for an adjournment of the meeting, or in the alternative, for a certain slate of directors. Mrs. Haley contends that she was not so bound for reason that the agreement was invalid, or at least revocable.

The two ladies entered into the agreement in 1941. It makes like provisions concerning stock of the corporate defendant and of another corporation, but in this case, we are concerned solely with the agreement as it affects the voting of stock of the corporate defendant. The agreement recites that each party was the owner * * * of 300 shares of the capital stock of the defendant corporation; that in 1938 these shares had been deposited under a voting trust agreement which would terminate in 1947, or earlier, upon the elimination of certain liability of the corporation; that each party also owned 15 shares individually; * * * that the parties desired "to continue to act jointly in all matters relating to their stock ownership or interest in" the corporate defendant (and the other corporation). The agreement then provides as follows:

"Now, Therefore, in consideration of the mutual covenants and agreements hereinafter contained the parties hereto agree as follows:

"1. Neither party will sell any shares of stock or any voting trust certificates in either of said corporations to any other person whosoever, without first making a written offer to the other party hereto of all of the shares or voting trust certificates proposed to be sold, for the same price and upon the same terms and conditions as in such proposed sale, and allowing such other party a time of not less than 180 days from the date of such written offer within which to accept same.

"2. In exercising any voting rights to which either party may be entitled by virtue of ownership of stock or voting trust certificates held by them in either of said corporations, each party will consult and confer with the other and the parties will act jointly in exercising such voting rights in accordance with such agreement as they may reach with respect to any matter calling for the exercise of such voting rights.

"3. In the event the parties fail to agree with respect to any matter covered by paragraph 2 above, the question in disagreement shall be submitted for arbitration to Karl D. Loos, of Washington, D.C. as arbitrator and his decision hereon shall be binding upon the parties hereto. Such arbitration shall be exercised to the end of assuring for the respective corporations good management and such participation therein by the members of the Ringling family as the experience, capacity and ability of each may warrant. The parties may at any time by written agreement designate any other individual to act as arbitrator in lieu of said Loos.

* * *

"5. This agreement shall be in effect from the date hereof and shall continue in effect for a period of ten years unless sooner terminated by mutual agreement in writing by the parties hereto.

* * *

"7. This agreement shall be binding upon and inure to the benefit of the heirs, executors, administrators and assigns of the parties hereto respectively."

The Mr. Loos mentioned in this agreement is an attorney and has represented both parties since 1937, and, before and after the voting trust was terminated in late 1942, advised them with respect to the exercise of their voting rights. At the annual meetings in 1943 and the two following years, the parties voted their shares in accordance with mutual understandings arrived at as a result of discussions. In each of these years, they elected five of the seven directors. Mrs. Ringling and Mrs. Haley each had sufficient votes, independently of the other, to elect two of the seven directors. By both voting for an additional candidate, they could be sure of his election regardless of how Mr. North, the remaining stockholder, might vote.[1]

Some weeks before the 1946 meeting, they discussed with Mr. Loos the matter of voting for directors. They were in accord that Mrs. Ringling should cast sufficient votes to elect herself and her son; and that Mrs. Haley should elect herself and her husband; but they did not agree upon a fifth director. The day before the meeting, the discussions were continued, Mrs. Haley being represented by her husband since she could not be present because of illness. In a conversation with Mr. Loos, Mr. Haley indicated that he would make a motion for an adjournment of the meeting for sixty days, in order the give the ladies additional time to come to an agreement about their voting. On the morning of the meeting, however, he stated that because of something Mrs. Ringling had done, he would not consent to a postponement. Mrs. Ringling then made a demand upon Mr. Loos to act under the third paragraph of the agreement "to arbitrate the disagreement" between her and Mrs. Haley in connection with the manner in which the stock of the two ladies should be voted. At the opening of the meeting, Mr. Loos read the written demand and stated that he determined and directed that the stock of both ladies be voted for an adjournment of sixty days. Mrs. Ringling then made a motion for adjournment and voted for it. Mr. Haley, as proxy for his wife, and Mr. North voted against the motion. Mrs. Ringling (herself or through her attorney, it is immaterial

1. Each lady was entitled to cast 2205 votes (since each had the cumulative voting rights of 315 shares, and there were 7 vacancies in the directorate). The sum of the votes of both is 4410, which is sufficient to allow 882 votes for each of 5 persons. Mr. North, holding 370 shares, was entitled to cast 2590 votes, which obviously cannot be divided so as to give to more than two candidates as many as 882 votes each. It will be observed that in order for Mrs. Ringling and Mrs. Haley to be sure to elect five directors (regardless of how Mr. North might vote) they must act together in the sense that their combined votes must be divided among five difference candidates and at least one of the five must be voted for by both Mrs. Ringling and Mrs. Haley.

which,) objected to the voting of Mrs. Haley's stock in any manner other than in accordance with Mr. Loos' direction. The chairman ruled that the stock could not be voted contrary to such direction, and declared the motion for adjournment had carried. Nevertheless, the meeting proceeded to the election of directors. Mrs. Ringling stated that she would continue in the meeting "but without prejudice to her position with respect to the voting of the stock and the fact that adjournment had not been taken." Mr. Loos directed Mrs. Ringling to cast her votes

882 for Mrs. Ringling,

882 for her son, Robert, and

441 for a Mr. Dunn,

who had been a member of the board for several years. She complied. Mr. Loos directed that Mrs. Haley's votes be cast

882 for Mrs. Haley,

882 for Mr. Haley, and

441 for Mr. Dunn.

Instead of complying, Mr. Haley attempted to vote his wife's shares

1103 for Mrs. Haley, and

1102 for Mr. Haley.

Mr. North voted his shares

864 for a Mr. Woods,

863 for a Mr. Griffin, and

863 for Mr. North.

The chairman ruled that the five candidates proposed by Mr. Loos, together with Messrs. Woods and North, were elected. The Haley–North group disputed this ruling insofar as it declared the election of Mr. Dunn; and insisted that Mr. Griffin, instead, had been elected. A director's meeting following in which Mrs. Ringling participated after stating that she would do so "without prejudice to her position that the stockholders' meeting had been adjourned and that the directors' meeting was not properly held." Mr. Dunn and Mr. Griffin, although each was challenged by an opposing faction, attempted to join in voting as directors for different slates of officers. Soon after the meeting, Mrs. Ringling instituted this proceeding.

The Vice Chancellor determined that the agreement to vote in accordance with the direction of Mr. Loos was valid as a "stock pooling agreement" with lawful objects and purposes, and that it was not in violation of any public policy of this state. He held that where the arbitrator acts under the agreement and one party refuses to comply with his direction, "the Agreement constitutes the willing party * * * an implied agent possessing the irrevocable proxy of the recalcitrant party for the purpose of casting the particular vote." It was ordered that a new election be held before a master, with the direction that the master should recognize and give effect to the agreement if its terms were properly invoked.

Before taking up defendants' objections to the agreement, let us analyze particularly what it attempts to provide with respect to voting, including what functions and powers it attempts to repose in Mr. Loos, the "arbitrator." * * *

Should the agreement be interpreted as attempting to empower the arbitrator to carry his directions into effect? Certainly there is no express delegation or grant of power to do so, either by authorizing him to vote the shares or to compel either party to vote them in accordance with his directions. The agreement expresses no other function of the arbitrator than that of deciding questions in disagreement which prevent the effectuation of the purpose "to act jointly". The power to enforce a decision does not seem a necessary or usual incident of such a function. Mr. Loos is not a party to the agreement. It does not contemplate the transfer of any shares or interest in shares to him, or that he should undertake any duties which the parties might compel him to perform. They provided that they might designate any other individual to act instead of Mr. Loos. The agreement does not attempt to make the arbitrator a trustee of an express trust. What the arbitrator is to do is for the benefit of the parties, not for his own benefit. Whether the parties accept or reject his decision is no concern of his, so far as the agreement or the surrounding circumstances reveal. We think the parties sought to bind each other, but to be bound only to each other, and not to empower the arbitrator to enforce decisions he might make.

From this conclusion, it follows necessarily that no decision of the arbitrator could ever be enforced if both parties to the agreement were unwilling that it be enforced, for the obvious reasons that there would be no one to enforce it. Under the agreement, something more is required after the arbitrator has given his decision in order that it should become compulsory: at least one of the parties must determine that such decision shall be carried into effect. Thus, any "control" of the voting of the shares, which is reposed in the arbitrator, is substantially limited in action under the agreement in that it is subject to the overriding power of the parties themselves.

The agreement does not describe the undertaking of each party with respect to a decision of the arbitrator other than to provide that it "shall be binding upon the parties". It seems to us that this language, considered with relation to its context and the situations to which it is applicable, means that each party promised the other to exercise her own voting rights in accordance with the arbitrator's decision. The agreement is silent about any exercise of the voting rights of one party by the other. The language with reference to situations where the parties arrive at an understanding as to voting plainly suggests "action" by each, and "exercising" voting rights by each, rather than by one for the other. There is no intimation that this method should be different where the arbitrator's decision is to be carried into effect. Assuming that a power in each party to exercise the voting rights of the other might be a relatively more effective or convenient means of enforcing a decision of the arbitrator than would be available without the power, this would not justify implying a delegation of the power in the absence of some indication that the parties bargained for that means. The method of voting actually employed by the parties tends to show that they did not construe the agreement as creating powers to vote each other's shares; for at meetings prior to 1946 each party apparently exercised her own voting rights, and at the 1946 meeting, Mrs. Ringling, who wished to enforce the agreement, did not attempt to cast a ballot in exercise of any voting rights of Mrs. Haley. We do not find enough in the agreement or in the circumstances to justify a construction that either party was empowered to exercise voting rights of the other.

Having examined what the parties sought to provide by the agreement, we come now to defendants' contention that the voting provisions are illegal and revocable. They say that the courts of this state have definitely established the doctrine "that there can be no agreement, or any device whatsoever, by which the voting power of stock of a Delaware corporation may be irrevocably separated from the ownership of the stock, except by an agreement which complies with [Delaware's statute authorizing the creation of voting trusts]," * * * and except by a proxy coupled with an interest. * * *

In our view, neither the cases nor the [voting trust] statute sustain the rule for which the defendants contend. Their sweeping formulation would impugn well-recognized means by which a shareholder may effectively confer his voting rights upon others while retaining various other rights. * * * The [voting trust] statute authorizes, among other things, the deposit or transfer of stock in trust for a specified purpose, namely, "vesting" in the transferee "the right to vote thereon" for a limited period; and prescribes numerous requirements in this connection. Accordingly, it seems reasonable to infer that to establish the relationship and accomplish the purpose which the statute authorizes, its requirements must be complied with. But the statute does not purport to deal with agreements whereby shareholders attempt to bind each other as to how they shall vote their shares. Various forms of such pooling agreements, as they are sometimes called, have been held valid and have been distinguished from voting trusts. * * * We think the particular agreement before us does not violate * * * [the voting trust statute] or constitute an attempted evasion of its requirements, and is not illegal for any other reason. Generally speaking, a shareholder may exercise wide liberality of judgment in the matter of voting, and it is not objectionable that his motives may be for personal profit, or determined by whims or caprice, so long as he violates no duty owed his fellow shareholders. * * * The ownership of voting stock imposes no legal duty to vote at all. A group of shareholders may, without impropriety, vote their respective shares so as to obtain advantages of concerted action. They may lawfully contract with each other to vote in the future in such as way as they, or a majority of their group, from time to time determine. * * * Reasonable provisions for cases of failure of the group to reach a determination because of an even division in their ranks seem unobjectionable. The provision here for submission to the arbitrator is plainly designed as a deadlock-breaking measure, and the arbitrator's decision cannot be enforced unless at least one of the parties (entitled to cast one-half of their combined votes) is willing that it be enforced. We find the provision reasonable. It does not appear that the agreement enables the parties to take any unlawful advantage of the outside shareholder, or of any other person. It offends no rule of law or public policy of this state of which we are aware.

Legal consideration for the promises of each party is supplied by the mutual promises of the other party. The undertaking to vote in accordance with the arbitrator's decision is a valid contract. * * * Accordingly, the failure of Mrs. Haley to exercise her voting rights in accordance with his decision was a breach of her contract. * * *

* * * The Court of Chancery may, in a review of an election, reject votes of a registered shareholder where his voting of them is found to be in violation of rights of another person. * * * It seems to us that upon the application of Mrs. Ringling, the injured party, the votes representing Mrs. Haley's shares should not be counted. Since no infirmity in Mr. North's voting has been demonstrated, his right to recognition of what he did at the meeting should be considered in granting any relief to Mrs. Ringling; for her rights arose under a contract to which Mr. North was not a party. With this in mind, we have concluded that the election should not be declared invalid, but that effect should be given to a rejection of the votes representing Mrs. Haley's shares. No other relief seems appropriate in this proceeding. Mr. North's vote against the motion for adjournment was sufficient to defeat it. With respect to the election of directors, the return of the inspectors should be corrected to show a rejection of Mrs. Haley's votes, and to declare the election of the six persons for whom Mr. North and Mrs. Ringling voted.

This leaves one vacancy in the directorate. The question of what to do about such a vacancy was not considered by the court below and has not been argued here. For this reason, and because an election of directors at the 1947 annual meeting (which presumably will be held in the near future) may make a determination of the question unimportant, we shall not decide it on this appeal. If a decision of the point appears important to the parties, any of them may apply to raise it in the Court of Chancery, after the mandate of this court is received there.

An order should be entered directing a modification of the order of the Court of Chancery in accordance with this opinion.

NOTES

1. *Ringling* illustrates several ways to ensure a minority stockholder obtains a position on the board of directors. (The owner of a majority of voting stock, of course, needs no such assurance.) To begin with, consider the situation of Mr. North. Prior to the falling out between Mrs. Ringling and Mrs. Haley, how could North have elected any directors when the two women together possessed a majority of the stock? The answer is cumulative voting. Cumulative voting allows stockholders to cast all their votes—

the number of their voting shares multiplied by the number of directors to be elected—for less than all the directors to be elected. Notice the impact this had in *Ringling*. Under straight voting, North would have voted his 370 shares for each of seven different candidates, while Ringling and Haley voted their combined 630 shares for each of seven candidates. This would result in the election of all Ringling and Haley's candidates as the seven individuals receiving the most votes (630 shares apiece, versus 370 shares apiece for North's candidates). Cumulative voting allowed North, however, to take his total votes (370 multiplied by seven directors, or 2590) and place them all on one candidate, or 1295 on each of two candidates, or any other distribution he wanted. If North placed 1295 votes on each of two candidates, Ringling and Haley could not divide their combined 4410 votes (630 multiplied by seven) between seven (or even six) candidates in such a way as to preclude North's two candidates from being among the seven individuals receiving the most votes, and hence elected. As evident from this example, maximizing the effectiveness of cumulative voting requires some computation. One can employ the trial and error approach. For an alternative, see Mills, *The Mathematics of Cumulative Voting,* 1968 Duke L. J. 28.

What must parties do to allow cumulative voting? In many states, they need do nothing—state statutes or constitutional provisions require cumulative voting. *E.g.*, Cal. Corp. Code § 708(a), (c) (for corporations without stock exchange listed shares). (Notice this means allowing cumulative voting even if the founders of the corporation did not want it.) Other state codes may simply allow cumulative voting if the corporation provides for it in the company's articles. *E.g.,* Del. Gen. Corp. Law § 214; N.Y. Bus. Corp. Law § 618; M.B.C.A. § 7.28(b), (c). Still other state codes provide for cumulative voting unless the articles expressly exclude it. Pa. Assoc. Code § 1758(c).

Several factors undermine the effectiveness of cumulative voting to guarantee directorships for minority shareholders. Initially, the minority shareholder still must have a substantial percentage of the voting stock before he or she can elect a director by cumulating all his or her votes on one candidate. The size of the board dictates this percentage. Specifically, to elect one board member through cumulative voting, a stockholder must control one more share than the total number of voting shares divided by the number of directors to be elected plus one (or 1 + V/(D + 1), where V is the number of voting shares, and D is the number of directors to be elected). Hence, if there are three directorships to fill, it would take one share more than one-quarter of the voting shares (1 + V/(3 + 1)) to elect a single director. Notice, reducing the number of directors elected increases the percentage of shares required to elect one director. (If only one directorship is open, nothing short of a majority of voting shares can pick the individual to fill the slot.) Two methods exist to reduce the number of directors elected at one time. Subject to statutory minima on the number of directors (*e.g.*, Cal. Corp. Code § 212(a) (three unless fewer than three shareholders); N.Y. Bus. Corp. Law § 702(a) (one); Del. Gen. Corp. Law § 141(b)(one); M.B.C.A. § 8.03(a)(one)), a majority could amend the bylaws or articles (whichever set the number) to reduce the size of the board.

Stone v. Auslander, 28 Misc.2d 384, 212 N.Y.S.2d 777 (1961). *But see* Cal. Corp. Code § 212(a) (precluding reduction of number of directors below five if 16 2/3 percent of shares vote against amendment). Alternatively, many state codes allow corporations to stagger their directors' terms in office so not all the board members stand for election at any one time. *E.g.,* Del. Gen. Law § 141(d); N.Y. Bus. Corp. Law § 704; M.B.C.A. § 8.06. *See also Humphrys v. Winous Co.,* 165 Ohio St. 45, 133 N.E.2d 780 (1956) (rejecting challenge that staggering terms contravened statute mandating cumulative voting). *But see Bohannan v. Corporation Commission,* 82 Ariz. 299, 313 P.2d 379 (1957) (completely destroying effectiveness of cumulative voting by staggering terms so only one director elected at a time would violate state constitution provision requiring cumulative voting).

Majority shareholders may employ other techniques to frustrate the minority's use of cumulative voting. They could seek to remove directors elected by the minority from the board. *But see* Cal. Corp. Code § 303(a)(1); Del. Gen. Corp. Law § 141(k)(2); N.Y. Bus. Corp. Law § 706(c)(1); M.B.C.A. § 8.08(c) (all allowing removal of directors elected through cumulative voting only if shares voted against removal would not have been sufficient to elect the director if voted cumulatively). Simplest of all, in states where cumulative voting is not mandatory, the majority could amend the articles to repeal the provision allowing cumulative voting. *Maddock v. Vorclone Corp.,* 17 Del.Ch. 39, 147 A. 255 (1929). What can one do to prevent majority shareholders from using these techniques to destroy a minority's protection of cumulative voting? Presumably, one could draft articles or bylaws to require a greater than majority vote for any amendment changing the size of the board, staggering terms, or removing a provision for cumulative voting. What vote should one require? Perhaps the statutes dealing with removal of directors provide an idea.

2. Cumulative voting allows a shareholder with less than a majority to elect a director. One might attempt to ensure a minority shareholder obtains a position on the board by taking the opposite approach. Perhaps the articles or bylaws could require more than a majority vote to elect a director. Of course, this does not, in itself, obtain a position for the minority shareholder. Rather, it can give him or her a veto on the majority's election of directors, which he or she can then use to bargain for the majority's votes in his or her favor. The practical and legal difficulties with supermajority requirements in general are explored later in this section.

3. Agreements between shareholders to vote their stock in a prescribed manner constitute another way to ensure minority stockholders receive positions on the board. They may accomplish this either by combining minority interests together into a majority, as in *Ringling,* or by obtaining a majority owner's commitment to the minority. The court in *Ringling* held such an agreement valid. This is the prevailing view—reinforced in many jurisdictions by statute. *E.g.,* Cal. Corp. Code § 706(a); Del. Gen. Corp. Law § 218(c); N.Y. Bus. Corp. Law § 620(a); M.B.C.A. § 7.31(a). Nevertheless, one cannot take the validity of such agreements completely for granted.

Selling votes for cash or some other pecuniary benefit (such as cancellation of personal debt) is contrary to public policy. *E.g.,* N.Y. Bus. Corp. Law § 609(e); *Macht v. Merchants Mortgage & Credit Co.,* 22 Del.Ch. 74, 194 A. 19 (1937). At the other extreme from selling votes for cash, stands an exchange of promises to vote the various parties' shares in accordance with the agreement. Exchanging a promise to vote in accordance with the agreement for the other party's promise to do the same should constitute, under ordinary contract law, adequate consideration to create an enforceable contract. The court in *Ringling* had no trouble seeing this (albeit the agreement there contained a mutual right of first refusal, thereby arguably giving some added consideration for the voting promises). Yet, some old opinions have refused to find such mutual promises alone constitute sufficient consideration. *E.g., Johnson v. Spartanburg County Fair Ass'n,* 210 S.C. 56, 41 S.E.2d 599 (1947). Also, if the agreement simply obligates a majority shareholder to vote in favor of a minority holder, then there is no exchange of voting promises by both sides. Finally, some old decisions take the position that voting agreements contravene public policy because they interfere with the shareholder's duty to vote shares according to his or her independent judgment, and in the best interest of the corporation. *E.g., Haldeman v. Haldeman,* 176 Ky. 635, 197 S.W. 376 (1917).

The agreement in *Ringling* raises, as well, some questions of drafting. Why did it not simply name who the parties would vote for in the future? When the purpose of a voting agreement is to ensure the contracting parties' election, specifically agreeing to vote for each other is a common approach. Parties might obtain more flexibility by agreeing to vote for each other's nominees. Agreeing to vote for each other's nominees could also help in the situation where there are more directorships than parties to the contract. Why would this not have worked in *Ringling?* (Notice the purpose behind the agreement there given cumulative voting). If Mrs. Haley and Mrs. Ringling had agreed only to agree in the future on how to vote, this presumably would not have created an enforceable contract. What, if any, problems did their agreeing to arbitration (thereby establishing a contract) create? The legal and practical aspects of arbitrating disputes between shareholders concerning the management of a closely held corporation will be explored later in this chapter. For present purposes, notice the defendant's argument that arbitrating how to vote one's shares violates public policy by separating control from the ownership of stock. While the *Ringling* opinion did not find this argument persuasive, other authorities have. *E.g., Roberts v. Whitson,* 188 S.W.2d 875 (Tex.Civ.App.1945). Yet another approach to drafting focuses less on who the parties vote for, and more on equalizing their voting power. Hence, a party with a majority of shares could agree not to vote the number of shares he or she owns which are in excess of the number owned by the other stockholders. (On the other hand, agreeing to alter the voting power of shares, rather than agreeing how the parties will vote (or not vote) their stock, may attempt to do something only valid if placed in the articles. *Compare Nickolopoulos v. Sarantis,* 102 N.J.Eq. 585, 141 A. 792 (1928), *with Sankin v. 5410 Connecticut Avenue*

Corp., *281 F.Supp. 524 (D.D.C.1968),* aff'd, *410 F.2d 1060 (D.C.Cir.1969),* cert. denied, *396 U.S. 1041 (1970).* But see *M.B.C.A. § 7.32(a)(4).)*

As in *Ringling,* not all the shareholders need be parties to (or perhaps even aware of) the voting agreement. Nevertheless, some of the opinions refusing to uphold such agreements expressed concern about their effect on non-party shareholders. *E.g., Haldeman v. Haldeman,* 176 Ky. 635, 197 S.W. 376 (1917). Hence, in a jurisdiction where the law remains unclear, having all shareholders agree to the voting contract (assuming they will) might be helpful. On a related note, what happens if one of the parties to the voting agreement dies, goes bankrupt, or sells his or her shares? If the agreement does not bind the transferee, minority stockholders relying upon the contract could lose their spots on the board. Contracts often contain clauses (such as the one in the Ringling agreement) purporting to obligate successors-in-interest, but this may not bind the transferee of stock, at least without notice of the agreement. *See, e.g., Bond v. Atlantic Terra Cotta Co.,* 137 App.Div. 671, 122 N.Y.S. 425 (1910).

Finally, a voting agreement, like any contract, may only be as useful as the remedy courts provide for its breach. In this regard, consider what happened in *Ringling.* Money damages would have provided no relief: It is unlikely Mrs. Ringling sustained any. Yet, the court did not award specific performance; rather it simply invalidated Mrs. Haley's votes. *But see* M.B.C.A. § 7.31(b) (providing specific performance to enforce voting agreements). Even had the court awarded specific performance, look at the time which elapsed: It was practically the next shareholders meeting before final judgment. What seems needed is a self-executing contract.

Perhaps the parties could have provided the arbitrator or each other with proxies to vote their shares per the agreement. Naturally, the proxies must be irrevocable, or the party refusing to comply can simply terminate his or her proxy. Merely calling the proxy irrevocable, however, does not necessarily make it so—even if the other party gave consideration for the promise not to revoke. Rather, since a proxy is a species of agency, at common law the party giving it had the power, even if not the right, to terminate the proxy unless it was "coupled with an interest." *E.g., In re Chilson,* 19 Del.Ch. 398, 168 A. 82 (1933). Narrowly interpreted, this meant having some sort of property interest (such as joint ownership) in the stock subject to the proxy. *Id.* Perhaps holding a pledge in the stock to secure a loan, or having an option to buy the stock, would also be sufficient property interests. *See, e.g., Calumet Indus., Inc. v. MacClure,* 464 F.Supp. 19 (N.D.Ill.1978). Mr. Loos, the arbitrator, certainly had no such interest, however interpreted. Nor did Mrs. Ringling have such an interest in Mrs. Haley's stock (unless by virtue of the right of first refusal under the agreement). The Delaware statute currently provides that an "interest" refers either to an interest in the stock subject to the proxy, or an interest in the corporation generally. Del. Gen. Corp. Law § 212(e). *See also* M.B.C.A. § 7.22(d); *State ex rel. Everett Trust & Savings Bank v. Pacific Waxed Paper Co.,* 22 Wash.2d 844, 157 P.2d 707 (1945). This would allow other stockholders, like Mrs. Ringling, to obtain irrevocable proxies, but still might not cover an outside arbitrator with no stock in the company. Other statutes explicitly make proxies irrevocable if so agreed as part of a voting contract between shareholders. *E.g.,* Cal. Corp. Code § 705(e)(5); N.Y. Bus. Corp. Law § 609(f)(5). *See also* M.B.C.A. § 7.22(d)(5) (irrevocable if held by a party to a voting agreement).

Placing irrevocable proxies in the hands of an arbitrator may create another problem. The arrangement starts to look a little like a voting trust, since the arbitrator can vote the shares much like a trustee. This could lead a court to conclude the contract is a voting trust, and rule it illegal because it does not comply with the specific statutory requirements governing such a trust. *Abercrombie v. Davies,* 36 Del.Ch. 371, 130 A.2d 338 (1957). *But see* Cal. Corp. Code § 706(c)(d) (otherwise legal shareholders voting agreements and proxies are not invalid as constituting a voting trust which does not comply with the statute); Del. Gen. Corp. Law § 218(d) (same); M.B.C.A. § 7.31(a)(same).

4. To avoid some of the uncertainties associated with voting agreements and irrevocable proxies, parties might use a voting trust. In a voting trust, the shareholders transfer their stock to one or more persons, who take title as trustees. Since the trustees become legal owners of the stock, their right to vote it does not depend upon a court's finding an enforceable voting agreement or a proxy coupled with an interest. Hence, a voting trust can provide a self-executing mechanism for ensuring the voting of shares in accordance with an agreed plan. Since the trustees receive their title in trust, the former shareholders give up legal title, but retain beneficial ownership. This means the trustees normally forward to the former shareholders dividends received from the corporation, and return the stock to them upon the termination of the trust. To evidence this beneficial ownership, the former shareholders often receive certificates from the trustee. One difficulty, however, with loss of legal title is that the former shareholders may lose certain protections—such as the ability to inspect books and records—accorded the legal owners of shares. *E.g., State ex rel. Crowder v. Sperry Corporation,* 41 Del. 84, 15 A.2d 661 (1940).

Voting trusts can be useful for a variety of purposes beyond securing positions on the board for minority shareholders in a closely held corporation. For example, prior to the agreement between Mrs. Haley and Mrs. Ringling, the shares in the Ringling Brothers corporation were in a voting trust. Creditors of the circus had insisted upon this arrangement in order to make sure the company had management acceptable to them until it paid their loans. Along similar lines, a dominant elderly shareholder may wish to pass the beneficial interest in his or her stock to junior members of the family, but lack confidence in their ability to run the company. Placing the stock in a voting trust with trustees in whom the elderly shareholder has confidence may be an answer. Individuals might also transfer their shares to a voting trust and then sell part of their beneficial interest. In this way, a voting trust can facilitate retention of control despite cashing out some of one's interest. (Notice, along these lines, a voting trust may avoid the problems share transfers can cause with a voting agreement.) To the extent the purpose of the trust is detrimental to the corporation, however, a court might hold it illegal. *Grogan v. Grogan,* 315 S.W.2d 34 (Tex.Civ.App.1958).

Most states have statutes which both authorize voting trusts, and regulate their creation and use. *E.g.,* Cal. Corp. Code § 706(b); Del. Gen. Corp. Law § 218(a); N.Y. Bus. Corp. Law § 621; M.B.C.A. § 7.30. Typically, to establish the trust, these statutes require transfer of shares to the trustee pursuant to a written agreement between the trustee and transferring shareholders, and the filing of the agreement with the corporation. The terms of this agreement govern the actions of the trustees, who are under a fiduciary obligation to carry out their instructions. *See, e.g., Bryson v. Bryson,* 62 Cal.App. 170, 216 P. 391 (1923). The parties confront several questions in drafting the trust agreement. The agreement could either specify who the trustees vote for as directors (particularly if its purpose is to ensure election of the shareholders setting up the trust), or leave matters to the trustees' judgment. Can trustees vote for themselves as directors? See *Taft Realty Corp. v. Yorkhaven Enterprises, Inc.,* 146 Conn. 338, 150 A.2d 597 (1959) (holding they can). Since the motivation for establishing the trust typically relates to the election of directors, the parties may forget that shareholders occasionally vote on other matters as well—for example, amendment of articles and bylaws, sale of all assets, mergers, and dissolution. Failure of trust agreements to specify whether or how trustees will vote on these matters can lead to litigation. *E.g., Clarke Memorial College v. Monaghan Land Co.,* 257 A.2d 234 (Del.Ch.1969).

Parties often name more than one trustee—especially if they want to appoint a natural person rather than a corporation—in order to avoid problems upon death or incapacity of the trustee. What happens with multiple trustees if the trustees disagree on how to vote the shares? *Compare People v. Botts,* 376 Ill. 476, 34 N.E.2d 403 (1941) (multiple trustees must act jointly or not at all), *with* Del. Gen. Corp. Law § 218(a) (majority rule). Shareholders also often appoint neutral persons, such as banks, attorneys or the like, to be trustees, but sometimes they appoint themselves. As with voting contracts, there is usually no requirement all shareholders be allowed into the trust.

Termination of the trust requires some thought. Voting trust statutes typically provide that voting trusts terminate ten years after their creation. *E.g.,* Cal. Corp. Code § 706(b); N.Y. Bus. Corp. Law § 621(a); M.B.C.A. § 7.30(b). *But see* Del. Gen. Corp. Law § 218(a). The statutes often allow, however, the parties to extend the trust for additional ten year periods by written agreement entered into prior to the trust's expiration. *E.g.,* Cal. Corp. Code § 706(b) (may extend only for the shares of the holders so agreeing, and if the agreement is made within two years of expiration); N.Y. Bus. Corp. Law § 621(d) (may extend for the shares of those so agreeing within six months of expiration); M.B.C.A. § 7.30(c) (may extend for the shares of the holders so agreeing any time before expiration, but extension only lasts ten years from the date the first shareholder signs the extension agreement). The expiration of the trust could place minority shareholders relying upon the trust in a precarious situation. (While ten years seems a long time, the relationship of the same stockholders in a closely held corporation may go on much longer than this.) Could a minority shareholder obtain a binding commitment by the majority to agree to further extensions? At the other extreme, circumstances could change before the expiration of ten years so the parties no longer desire the trust. Can all the beneficial owners terminate it early? See *H.M. Byllesby & Co. v. Doriot,* 25 Del.Ch. 46, 12 A.2d 603 (1940) (Yes, when the court found no one else had justifiably relied upon representations by the beneficial owners as to the trust's existence). The parties may wish to have a clause in the agreement allowing them to terminate the trust (thereby avoiding concern about third party reliance), but consider the problem created when a majority vote can accomplish a termination if the trust's purpose is to protect the minority.

5. Yet another way to ensure a minority shareholder receives a position on the board is by issuing two or more classes of stock with differing voting rights. For example, suppose two individuals, who form a company, agree to equal representation on its board, but also to an unequal sharing of profit and liquidation rights (perhaps reflecting unequal contributions of capital). Creating two classes of stock, equivalent in all respects except one has voting rights and the other does not, could accomplish this goal. The parties could each purchase 50 percent of the voting stock, while the individual to receive greater profit and liquidating distributions purchases additional non-voting shares. A variation on this idea would be to have classes with a different number of votes per share. This could also allow the parties to own a different number of shares, but end up with an equal number of votes. Conversely, the different classes of stock could each possess equal votes, but have unequal rights to dividends and liquidating distributions. At the extreme, the company might issue stock having votes, but no dividend or liquidation rights. A particularly effective technique is to issue classes which are each entitled to elect a number of the directors on the board. *Lehrman v. Cohen,* 43 Del.Ch. 222, 222 A.2d 800 (1966), provides a good illustration. The corporation issued shares of one class, entitled to elect two directors, to members of one family, and shares of another class, entitled to elect two directors, to members of a second family. It even issued shares of a third class—with no rights other than to elect a fifth director and to repayment upon liquidation of the rather nominal purchase price—to a neutral party.

Corporation statutes typically provide that a company's articles may authorize classes of stock with different voting and other rights. *E.g.,* Cal. Corp. Code § 400(a); Del. Gen. Corp. Law § 151(a), 212(a); M.B.C.A. § 6.01; N.Y. Bus. Corp. Law § 501(a). As a result, courts generally uphold the sort of classified stock schemes outlined above. *E.g., Lehrman v. Cohen, supra* (upheld the classified shares despite the argument that issuing shares to the neutral party constituted a voting trust which did not comply with the voting trust statute); *Diamond v. Parkersburg–Aetna Corp.,* 146 W.Va. 543, 122 S.E.2d 436 (1961) (upheld a corporate charter which granted preferred shares the right to elect one director and common shares the right to elect the other directors, against the challenge that it violated the state constitutional provision mandating cumulative voting); *Stroh v. Blackhawk Holding Corp.,* 48 Ill.2d 471, 272 N.E.2d 1 (1971) (upheld a certificate authorizing shares with voting rights but no rights to dividends or proceeds upon liquidation); *Hampton v. Tri–State Finance Corp.,* 30 Colo.App. 420, 495 P.2d 566 (1972) (upheld issuing non-voting common stock). *But see* Mo. Att'y Gen. Opin. No. 238 (1964) (creating classes of shares which vote only for some directors is contrary to state constitution provision mandating cumulative voting).

Parties providing for multiple classes of stock should be aware that the consequences can go beyond the election of directors. There are a variety of matters upon which shareholders may vote, including amendment of the articles or bylaws, merger, sale of all assets, and dissolution. Issuing multiple classes of stock raises a series of questions when such votes occur: (1) Can shares lacking voting rights in an election for directors nevertheless vote on these questions; (2) If some shares possess greater voting power in electing directors than other shares, does such weighing apply in voting on these other issues; (3) Does shareholder approval of these transactions require a majority (or whatever percentage) of the aggregate amount of stock, or of each separate class? Depending upon how one answers these questions, the impact can be quite significant and unexpected. For example, if approval of these transactions requires a majority of each class, this would give a veto to shareholders with a minority of shares overall, but a majority of one class (created perhaps to ensure representation on the board). Whether or not this would be a good idea, parties might wish to avoid surprises, and litigation producing ambiguity, by drafting articles which speak to the right of various classes of shares in voting on matters beyond just that of electing directors. (Some answers to these questions, at least in the absence of specific direction in the articles, are found in the discussions of these various transactions in Chapters VI and VII.)

2. Controlling Specific Decisions

Blount v. Taft

295 N.C. 472, 246 S.E.2d 763 (1978).

* * *

Plaintiffs and defendants are the owners of all of the outstanding 578.5 shares of the capital stock of the Eastern Lumber and Supply Company (Eastern) * * *. Plaintiffs are all members of the Blount family. Together they are the direct or beneficial owners of 41% of the outstanding shares of Eastern. The defendant, E. Hoover Taft, Jr., and the three members of his family * * * also own 41% of Eastern's capital stock, and defendant McGowan owns the remaining 18%. At the time this action was instituted McGowan held the post of Treasurer and as such was the "chief operating officer" of Eastern. * * *

In brief summary, plaintiffs' evidence, summarized except when quoted, tended to show:

In 1969 plaintiffs became concerned about "the nepotism situation which existed in Eastern." At a regular meeting of the board of directors held on 4 December 1969, plaintiff William G. Blount made a motion that in the future, unanimous approval of the stockholders be required before any relative of a stockholder could be employed by Eastern, and that unanimous approval of his continued employment be required annually. Defendant's evidence tended to show that although several other relatives of stockholders were employed by Eastern part-time during 1969, this resolution was primarily directed at the son of E.H. Taft, Jr., E. Hoover Taft III, the only relative then working full-time for the Company. E.H. Taft, Jr., opposed the Blount motion, and it was defeated when McGowan voted with the Tafts.

Thereafter, no shareholders' or directors' meeting were held until 20 August 1971. At that time, Eastern was negotiating a $250,000 business expansion loan and the directors deemed it necessary to revise and update the old bylaws, to have more frequent meetings, and to conduct the corporation's business on a more orderly and formal basis. Accordingly, E.H. Taft, Jr., and Mrs. Nelson Blount Crisp, both of whom are attorneys, drafted new bylaws to be presented to the shareholders and directors for their approval at a special joint meeting held on 20 August 1971. This meeting was called primarily to gain director and stockholder approval for the $250,000 loan. A transcript of that meeting, introduced in evidence by plaintiffs, shows that the proposed bylaws were read, article by article; that discussion frequently followed the reading of an article; and that thereafter various changes were made in the proposals.

Article III, Section 7 of the bylaws (hereinafter referred to as Section 7), which is the subject of this action, as originally drafted and presented to the stockholders, read:

"Executive Committee. The Board of Directors may, by the vote of a majority of the entire board, designate three or more directors to constitute and serve as an Executive Committee, which committee to the extent provided in such resolution, shall have and may exercise all of the authority of the Board of Directors in the management of the corporation."

Mrs. Crisp immediately proposed that the executive committee be composed of one member each from the Blount, Taft and McGowan families. E.H. Taft, Jr., expressed his approval of this proposal. * * *

Additional bylaws were read and discussed, including Article VIII, Section 4, which provided:

"Amendments. Except as otherwise provided, these bylaws may be amended or repealed and new bylaws may be adopted by the affirmative vote of a majority of the directors then holding office at any regular or special meeting of the Board of Directors." (Here it is noted that no provisions for amendments were "otherwise provided" in the bylaws adopted 20 August 1971.)

Finally, McGowan moved that the proposed bylaws be adopted as modified. Mrs. Crisp seconded the motion, but before a vote could be taken, the following exchange took place:

"M.K. BLOUNT, SR.: You haven't brought in some amendment don't you know?

"NELSON CRISP: This was as to full-time employees, the approval of full-time employees.

"MARVIN BLOUNT, JR.: Why don't you put where you have 'executive committee represented by members of each family, and Ford,' that all employees be unanimously approved. Is there any objection?

"E.H. TAFT, JR.: I have no objection.

"NELSON CRISP: He just brought out something, and this was my feeling from the beginning, that probably we do not need that in the by-laws, but rather in the meeting and in the minutes of a meeting.

"MARVIN BLOUNT, JR.: Would it hurt to put it in the by-laws?

"JOHN CAMPBELL: No."

After further discussion and an addition suggested by Mr. McGowan, Section 7 was unanimously adopted in the following words:

"Executive Committee. The Board of Directors may, by the vote of a majority of the entire board, designate three or more directors to constitute and serve as an Executive Committee, which committee to the extent provided in such resolution, shall have and may exercise all of the authority of the Board of Directors in the management of the corporation. Such committee shall consist of one member from the family of M.K. Blount, Sr., one member from the family of E.H. Taft, Jr., and one member from the family of Ford McGowan. * * *

"The Executive Committee shall have the exclusive authority to employ all persons who shall work for the corporation and that the employment of each individual shall be only after the unanimous consent of the committee and after interview."

Following this last amendment to Article III, Section 7, a motion that the bylaws be adopted as changed and read was seconded and unanimously approved by all the stockholders and directors.

At trial the testimony of plaintiffs' witnesses related mainly to their recollections of what took place at the 20 August 1971 meeting. All conceded that neither before or after the stockholders had achieved unanimity as to the terms of Section 7 did any stockholder refer to their final concurrence as "a stockholders' agreement"; that Section 7 was voted on as a part of the bylaws; and that no one had mentioned or suggested that Section 7 was not a bylaw or that it was not subject to amendment. However, Mr. Marvin K. Blount, Jr., testified that it was his "understanding" at the time that this section could not be amended except by the unanimous consent of the stockholders.

* * * Thereafter, the minutes of subsequent stockholders' and directors' meetings reveal continuous controversy between the Blounts and the Taft–McGowan group over McGowan's management of the company and the authority of the executive committee. In all controversial matter before the board of directors the Blounts were outvoted by the Tafts and McGowans.

* * *

[In a directors meeting in June 1974, the Taft–McGowan faction proposed new by-laws]. When the proposed new bylaws were distributed, the minutes show that Mr. M.K. Blount, Jr., protested they were an effort by the majority stockholders, particularly the Taft family, "to change the bylaws to the best interests of that family, particularly the Executive Committee provision." Also according to the minutes, Mr. Thomas Taft countered this charge with the assertion that the reason for the change in the Executive Committee was the Blount Family's lack of cooperation in the conduct of the affairs of the corporation "as is evidenced by their abstention on all questions brought before the Executive Committee as well as the full Board of Directors." Mr. Blount, Jr., also objected to changing the August 1971 bylaws, which had been agreed to by all the stockholders, at a directors' meeting.

Following extended discussions, the bylaws were adopted by a vote of six to three, the three votes contra being cast by M.K. Blount, Jr., Nelson B. Crisp, and W.B. Blount, Jr. The president then declared that henceforth the company would operate under the new bylaws. Whereupon, speaking in behalf of the Blount family, M.K. Blount, Jr., stated their contention that the old bylaws remained in force and that they would question and contest any actions taken under the authority of the new bylaws.

The bylaws adopted at the 20 June 1974 meeting are not in the record. However, from the statement of facts contained in the briefs of both plaintiffs and defendants we learn that "the amended bylaws did not contain the provisions of Art. III, Sec. 7 as adopted on August 20, 1971." Deleted were "the provisions of an Executive Committee composed of a representative of each of the three families, and the provision for approval of full-time employees by the Executive Committee." In lieu of the deleted provisions, "the defendants adopted over the objections of those plaintiffs who were present, a new Article III, Section 9, * * * "providing as follows:

"9. Executive Committee: The Board of Directors may, by resolution adopted by a majority of the number of directors fixed by resolution under these bylaws, designate two or more directors to constitute an Executive Committee, which Committee, to the extent provided in such resolution, shall have and may exercise all of the authority of the Board of Directors in the management of the corporation."

Pursuant to the foregoing section, the Board of Directors adopted a resolution "five for the motion and three abstentions" appointing "an

Executive Committee consisting of three members, E.H. Taft, Jr., Ford McGowan and W.G. Blount."

* * *

At the close of all the evidence the judge announced that he would hold Section 7 to be a valid stockholders' agreement which could [sic; not] be amended only [sic] by a majority vote of the directors.

* * *

The court then ordered that plaintiffs have specific enforcement of Article III, Section 7. Defendants appealed and the Court of Appeals reversed.

* * *

■ SHARP, CHIEF JUSTICE.

This appeal presents a two-part question: Was Section 7 of Eastern's bylaws, adopted 20 August 1971, a valid shareholders' agreement; and, if so, was it subject to amendment under Section 4, which authorized amendment, repeal, or re-write of the bylaws by the affirmative vote of a majority of the stockholders?

* * *

We shall here attempt no precise definition of a "shareholders' agreement." In a broad sense the term refers to any agreement among two or more shareholders regarding their conduct in relation to the corporation whose shares they own. * * * The form and substance of such an agreement will vary with the nature of the business and the objectives of the parties. * * *

By means of a shareholders' agreement a small group of investors who seek gain from direct participation in their business and not from trading its stock or securities in the open market can adopt the decision-making procedures of a partnership, avoid the consequences of majority rule (the standard operating procedure for corporations), and still enjoy the tax advantages and limited liability of a corporation. Such businesses are, with reason, often called "incorporated partnerships." * * *

In earlier years, when statutes and principles governing the law of corporations were principally concerned with corporations having publicly traded stocks, agreements among shareholders whether taking the form of voting trusts, pooling agreements, or extrinsic contracts confronted considerable judicial antipathy. Courts would invalidate such consensual arrangements on the grounds that they severed from the stock incidents of ownership, such as the rights of voting and alienation, or prevented stockholders from voting "in the best interests of the corporation," or were inconsistent with the principle of majority rule embedded in the statutory norms. * * * In connection with close corporations, agreements were also stricken if they violated the judicial doctrine, succinctly enunciated in *Jackson v. Hooper,* 76 N.J.Eq. 592, 599, 75 A. 568, 571, 27 A.L.R. (NS) 658,

663 (Ct.Err. & App. 1910), that shareholders "cannot be partners inter sese and a corporation as to the rest of the world." * * *

Over the years, however, both courts and legislatures gradually changed their thinking about the relationship which incorporation created between the state and businessman and their attitude toward shareholders' agreements. * * * As the number of closely held corporations increased, experience revealed that the problems of a corporation whose stock is not generally publicly traded are different from those of a publicly held corporation. The authorization of shareholders' agreements was a recognition of the needs of stockholders in a close corporation to be able to protect themselves from each other and from hostile invaders. * * *

In such a business, if the internal "government" of the corporations were conducted strictly by the vote of the majority of the outstanding shares, the largest shareholder(s) could dominate the policies of the corporation over the objections of other shareholders. "In a nutshell, Family A with 51% ownership of a close corporation can live in luxury off a profitable business while Family B starves with 49%." Undoubtedly, "Family B" would not have invested their money in a rarely traded stock if they had thought that they would be excluded from the decision making process and thereby the benefits of the business. * * *

To protect their investment minority shareholders frequently resort to agreements (usually, and wisely, made at the time of incorporation) between themselves and the other shareholders which guarantee to the minority such things as restrictions on the transfer of stock; a veto power over hiring and decisions concerning salaries, corporate policies or distribution of earnings; or procedures for resolving disputes or making fundamental changes in the corporate charter. * * * The agreements may also require certain affirmative actions, such as the payment of dividends. * * * It has been said that "a well-drawn stockholders' agreement entered into contemporaneously with the formation of a corporation is the most effective means of protecting the minority shareholder." * * *

North Carolina authorized shareholders' agreements in the Business Corporation Act of 1955. * * *

With respect to close corporations, the heart of the North Carolina Act is G.S. 55–73. * * * This statute labeled "Shareholders' Agreements," is divided into three sections. G.S. 55–73(a) validates and makes enforceable against its signatories for a limited period, a written "agreement between two or more shareholders" regarding the voting of their stock. * * * Section (c) of the statute provides that "an agreement between all or less than all of the shareholders" will not be invalidated as between the parties to it on the ground that it interferes with the discretion of the board of directors, but imposes upon the shareholder-parties liability for managerial acts similar to that which is imposed on directors. However, it is Section (b) of G.S. 55–73 which shareholders in a close corporation, whose stock is not generally traded in the markets maintained by securities dealers or brokers, regard as the most significant.

G.S. 55–73(b) provides, *inter alia,* that "no written agreement to which all of the shareholders have actually assented * * * which relates to any phase of the affairs of the corporation * * * shall be invalid * * * on the ground that it is an attempt by the parties thereto to treat the corporation as if it were a partnership or to arrange their relationships in a manner that would be appropriate only between partners." Such an agreement may be "embodied in the charter or bylaws or in any side agreement in writing and signed by all the parties thereto." This language has been widely borrowed for the close corporations statutes of several other jurisdictions. Cal. Corp. Code Ann. § 300(b) (West 1977); Del.Code Ann. tit. 8, § 354 (1975); Fla.St.Ann. § 607.107 (West 1977); Kan.Stat. § 17–7214 (1974); Md.Corp. & Ass'ns.Code § 104 (1973); Pa.Stat.Ann. tit. 15, § 1385 (Purdon Supp. 1978–79); S.C.Code Ann. § 33–11–220 (1977). * * *

Counsel have debated at length the question whether Section 7 of Eastern's bylaws is a bylaw or a shareholders' agreement within the meaning of G.S. 55–73(b). In our view this debate is sterile, for these terms are not mutually exclusive. Bylaws which are unanimously enacted by all the shareholders of a corporation are also shareholders' agreements. Consensual agreements coming within G.S. 55–73(b) are shareholders' agreements whether they are embodied in the bylaws or in a duly executed side agreement. No particular title, phrasing or content is necessary for a consensual arrangement among all shareholders to constitute a "shareholders' agreement." Consequently, we hold that section 7 of the bylaws adopted on 20 August 1971 is a shareholders' agreement within the meaning of G.S. 55–73(b). * * *

However, contrary to the arguments of counsel, this holding does not determine this case. Since consensual arrangements among shareholders are *agreements*—the products of negotiation—they should be construed and enforced like any other contract so as to give effect to the intent of the parties as expressed in their agreements * * *.

The trial judge ruled that Section 7, as a shareholders' agreement, was incapable of amendment or repeal for ten years except by unanimous assent of all the stockholders. Section 7, however, was only *one* of a complete set of bylaws, all of which after a section-by-section consideration which involved several revisions of Section 7 were unanimously adopted as a whole by a vote of all of Eastern's shareholders. Thus, the entire bylaws constituted an agreement among the shareholders. Article VIII, Section 4 of those bylaws (hereinafter "Section 4") authorized the repeal of "these bylaws" by a majority vote of the directors, except as otherwise provided therein. As we noted in the preliminary statement of facts, neither in Section 7 nor elsewhere in the bylaws was there any other provision regarding amendment or repeal of "these bylaws." Nothing else appearing, therefore, the presumption is that the parties intended Section 4 to apply to every section of the bylaws.

Plaintiffs argue, however, that because Section 7 is the only bylaw which "arranges (the shareholders') relationships in a manner that would be appropriate only between partners," it alone should be treated as a shareholders' agreement and thus be the only bylaws not subject to amendment or repeal under Section 4. This contention misunderstands the significance of G.S. 55–73(b).

That section creates no distinctions between a shareholders' agreement in which the parties seek to deal with the corporation as a partnership and any other stockholders' agreement "which relates to any phase of the affairs of the corporation." It adds nothing, either expressly or impliedly, to the words of the agreement; nor does it suspend the rules of contract law relating to its construction, modification or rescission. G.S. 55–73(b) merely provides that a shareholders' agreement in which the parties seek to deal with affairs of the corporation in a manner "which would be appropriate only between partners" *is not invalid for that reason.* Section (b), like the other two sections of G.S. 58–73, simply abrogates, as to agreements within its purview, certain judicial doctrines which had formerly invalidated particular shareholders' agreements on those grounds which the statute now disallows. A shareholders' agreement is not valid and enforceable merely because it fits the specifications of G.S. 55–73. It can be invalidated under the law of contracts upon any grounds which would entitle a party to such relief. * * *

* * * The statute was not intended to, and it does not, define "shareholders' agreements" to mean only those arrangements which "are an attempt * * * to treat the corporation as if it were a partnership" or which "arrange * * * relationships in a manner that would be appropriate only between partners."

G.S. 55–73(b) permits shareholders to embody their agreement "in the charter or the bylaws or in any side agreement in writing signed by all the parties thereto." Had Section 7 been a "side agreement" signed by all the stockholders, and not been made a part of the bylaws, it is plausible to argue that absent an internal provision governing its amendment it could be amended only by unanimous consent of all the stockholders. * * *

* * * Here Section 7 and Section 4 were unanimously incorporated into the bylaws at the same time. There being no internal provision in Section 7 or elsewhere in the bylaws prohibiting its amendment except by unanimous consent of the shareholders, we conclude that the parties intended Section 7 to be subject to amendment by the directors or shareholders according to the procedures applicable to the other bylaws. In any event, that is the agreement they made. We hold, therefore, that if a shareholders' agreement is made a part of the charter of bylaws it will be subject to amendment as provided therein or, in the absence of an internal provision governing amendments, as provided by the statutory norms.

* * * Since the purpose of these arrangements is to deviate from the structures which are generally regarded as the incidents of a corporation, it is not unreasonable to require that the degree of deviation intended be explicitly set out. * * *

Having concluded that the shareholders made Section 7 subject to the amendment power conferred upon the directors by Section 4, it will be enforced unless enforcement would contravene some principle of equity or public policy. Plaintiffs have not alleged that the acts of defendant constituted oppression or a breach of fiduciary duty imposed by G.S. 55–32, G.S. 55–73(c), or the common law. * * * Further the record before us discloses no violation of public policy. * * *

This decision, of course, will expose plaintiffs as minority shareholders in a close corporation to a risk from which Section 7 for a while protected them. However, minority shareholders who would have protection greater than that afforded by Chapter 55 of the General Statutes and the judicial doctrines prohibiting breach of fiduciary relationship must secure it themselves in the form of "a well drawn" shareholders' agreement.

For the reasons stated in this opinion the action of the Court of Appeals in reversing the judgment of the trial court is

Affirmed.

NOTES

1. *Blount* illustrates an observation made before: Merely obtaining a position on the board does not, in itself, give a minority shareholder protection against a majority of directors making specific decisions for the company (on such matters as jobs, salaries, dividends and other business policy) which are contrary to the minority stockholder's interest and expectation. As the court discusses, one common way parties may attempt to gain such protection is through an agreement among shareholders dictating what these specific corporate decisions will be. This idea should strike a familiar chord: It is what individuals can do in drafting a partnership or LLC operating agreement. Nevertheless, as the opinion also explains, the validity of such agreements in the corporate context may be uncertain.

The problem becomes clear when one asks in what capacity should the parties make a contract controlling corporate decisions ordinarily made by the board of directors. Suppose the parties cast the agreement as a promise of how they will vote as directors. In this event, they confront judicial authority holding that agreements under which directors bargain away their discretion to exercise independent judgment are contrary to public policy. *E.g., Burnett v. Word, Inc.,* 412 S.W.2d 792 (Tex.Civ.App.1967). Alternately, the parties may make the agreement in their role as shareholders. This creates the challenge that the agreement infringes upon the board's statutory power to manage the company. *E.g., McQuade v. Stoneham,* 263 N.Y. 323, 189 N.E. 234 (1934). Finally, the parties might argue they are binding each other as partners who are conducting their business through a corporation. This approach too faces hostile authority. *E.g., Jackson v. Hooper,* 76 N.J.Eq. 592, 75 A. 568 (1910) (persons engaged in business "cannot be partners inter sese and a corporation to the rest of the world.")

Most courts, however, find these somewhat abstract objections to agreements controlling specific corporate decisions less important than the practicalities of the situation. Accordingly, some decisions have upheld agreements dictating matters normally within the board's discretion when the agreement protected shareholders in a closely held corporation, and did not prejudice individuals who were not a party to the agreement. *E.g., Galler v. Galler,* 32 Ill.2d 16, 203 N.E.2d 577 (1964). Still, this may not create entirely satisfactory conditions from a planning perspective to recommend using these sort of agreements, since in many jurisdictions the state of judicial authority might not be sufficient to allow an attorney to give a firm opinion that the agreement is valid. From this perspective, it is fortunate that many state corporations statutes contain sections, like those of North Carolina discussed in *Blount,* which can remove the objections to the legality of agreements controlling decisions normally made by the board. *E.g.,* Cal. Corp. Code § 300(b); Del. Gen. Corp. Law §§ 350, 354; N.Y. Bus. Corp. Law § 620(b); M.B.C.A. § 7.32. These sections fall into two broad types. One type, found in Delaware and California, applies only if the company elects classification as a statutory close corporation. The question of whether and how to elect such status will be addressed shortly. A second type of provision, found in New York and the Model Act, does not require such a special election. Instead, it can apply to any corporation without publicly traded stock.

Assuming the validity of agreements controlling matters ordinarily decided by the board, there remain questions concerning the drafting of such a contract. Examine again the situation in *Wilkes.* What matters does it suggest minority shareholders address in an agreement controlling certain decisions of the board? Another issue to consider in drafting the agreement is how long it will last. See M.B.C.A. § 732(b)(3) (shareholders agreement valid for 10 years unless contract provides otherwise). In addition to the terms of the agreement, consider who should be parties to it. The presence or absence of non-consenting shareholders, who the agreement might injure, has been an important factor to a number of courts in ruling upon the validity of such agreements. *Compare Odman v. Oleson,* 319 Mass. 24, 64 N.E.2d 439 (1946), *with Clark v. Dodge,* 269 N.Y. 410, 199 N.E. 641 (1936). Consistent with these cases, many of the statutes which validate shareholders agreements despite impinging upon the board's authority only apply if all shareholders are a party to the contract. *E.g.,* Cal. Corp. Code §§ 186, 300; N.Y. Bus. Corp. Law § 620(b)(1); M.B.C.A. § 7.32(b)(1). *But see* Del. Gen. Corp. Law § 350 (agreement among shareholders holding a majority of the outstanding voting stock is not invalid "as between the parties to the agreement").

Closely related is the question of what happens if a party to the contract transfers his or her shares to an individual who has not consented to the agreement. In this event, is the transferee bound to comply with the contract? If not, can he or she also challenge continued adherence by the remaining parties? Can one of the remaining parties use the transfer as an excuse to attack the agreement's continuing validity? The answers provided by the statutes vary. *See, e.g.,* Cal. Corp. Code § 300(b) (transferee is bound by agreement if a copy of it is filed with the secretary of the corporation and notice of it is placed on the share certificates; otherwise section only renders the agreement valid as between the parties to it); Del. Gen. Corp. Law § 350 (agreement rendered valid only as between parties to it); N.Y. Bus. Corp. Law § 620(b)(2) (provision impinging upon board's power is valid only so long as any transferee had knowledge or notice of it); M.B.C.A. § 732(c) (agreement valid despite transfer, but transferee without notice has the right to rescind purchase). In a jurisdiction, like Delaware, where providing notice might not bind a transferee to the agreement, restricting the transfer of shares could be an answer. Share transfer restrictions are considered later in this chapter.

Finally, in what document should parties place agreements seeking to control specific corporate decisions? To validate such an agreement under New York's statute, it must be in the certificate of incorporation. N.Y. Bus. Corp. Law § 620(b). In *Blount,* the parties placed their agreement in the bylaws. What problem did this create? What can be done to prevent a majority shareholder from amending articles or bylaws in order to remove a provision designed to protect minority shareholders? Notice this problem would not occur if the parties make their agreements in a separate contract between themselves.

2. As noted above, many state corporation statutes provide special treatment for companies electing the status of "close corporation." (Recall the court in *Wilkes* used the term close corporation as a generic label for companies with few shareholders—who are typically involved in managing the company and have no market for their shares. *See also Donahue v. Rodd Electrotype Co.,* reprinted in Chapter VI. This is not the same meaning given the term in these statutes, nor is the impact the same. To avoid confusion, it is useful to refer to companies qualifying for "close corporation" treatment under these special provisions as statutory close corporations, and distinguish that from companies which courts might treat differently simply because they are closely held (in other words, have few shareholders).)

To elect statutory close corporation status under these sections, typically the company must limit the number of shareholders it will have. *E.g.,* Cal. Corp. Code § 158(a) (no more than 35); Del. Gen. Corp. Law § 342(a)(1) (no more than 30). Some states also require limitations on transfer (Del. Gen. Corp. Law § 342(a)(2)), or, at least, notice on the shares to transferees that the company is a statutory close corporation. *E.g.,* Cal. Corp. Code § 418(c). The Delaware act, in addition, precludes the company from making a "public offering" within the meaning of the 1933 Securities Act if it wishes to be a statutory close corporation. Del. Gen. Corp. Law § 342(a)(3). Assuming the corporation meets these requirements, it elects to be a statutory close corporation by stating as much in its articles. *E.g.,* Cal. Corp. Code § 158(a); Del. Gen. Corp. Law § 343(a).

Becoming a statutory close corporation is elective. (This is an important difference from, and reason to distinguish, judicial use of the term in cases like *Wilkes.*) Because this status is elective, it is important to consider all the consequences before making the choice. The primary advantage of this election is to trigger application of the sections discussed above which validate shareholders agreements concerning matters normally within the board's authority. There may, however, be other advantages as well. For example, some statutes allow shareholders in a statutory close corporation to place a provision in its articles allowing a minority of shareholders to dissolve at will or upon agreed events. *E.g.,* Del. Gen. Corp. Law § 355. (The utility of such a provision will be considered later in this chapter.) Other results of becoming a statutory close corporation may or may not be what the parties desire. For instance, statutes may allow increased availability of involuntary dissolution or other judicial intervention with a statutory close corporation. *E.g.,* Cal. Corp. Code § 1800(a)(2) (extending standing to any shareholder in a statutory close corporation to petition for involuntary dissolution in situations when the code otherwise requires one-third of the shares to petition); Del. Gen. Corp. Law § 353 (allowing the court to appoint a provisional director in case of deadlock among the board of a statutory close corporation under a lesser showing of harm from the deadlock than required for the court to act in case of deadlocks in other corporations).

3. Several statutes contain additional provisions which shareholders might use to subject specific corporate decisions to binding agreements. Many codes allow a corporation—whether or not a statutory close corporation—to provide in its articles for the shareholders to elect its officers (instead of the board appointing them). *E.g.,* N.Y. Bus. Corp. Law § 715(b). *See also* Cal. Corp. Code § 312(b) (board selects officers, unless otherwise stated in articles or bylaws); Del. Gen. Corp. Law § 142(b) (bylaws specify manner for selection of officers). If the shareholders elect officers, then presumably they could agree who to elect as part of a shareholders voting contract—the validity of which is fairly clear—rather than as part of a contract seeking to control actions of the board. Some statutes provide an even more radical approach for shareholders in a statutory close corporation—or, under the Model Act, for any company if provided in a shareholders agreement (M.B.C.A. § 7.32(a)(1)). Such a corporation may place in its articles a provision eliminating the board of directors and allowing the shareholders to manage the company. *E.g.,* Del. Gen. Corp. Law § 351. How desirable would this be? Keep in mind, agreements controlling actions of the board are valid in a statutory close corporation anyway. Moreover, consider the administrative inconvenience a corporation without a board might face when dealing with banks or agencies whose custom and forms call for any company contracting with them to supply a copy of a resolution by its board of directors approving the contract.

4. Supermajority voting requirements provide another way to protect minority shareholders. *Blount* gives an example of such a requirement: The corporation's bylaws demanded a unanimous vote of the board's executive committee to hire any employee. Many statutes explicitly empower corporations to include supermajority voting requirements in their articles (or sometimes bylaws). *E.g.,* Cal. Corp. Code §§ 204(a)(5); Del. Gen. Corp. Law §§ 141(b), 216; N.Y. Bus. Corp. Law §§ 616, 709; M.B.C.A. §§ 7.27, 8.24(c). *But see* Cal. Corp. Code § 710 (limiting amendments to add a supermajority requirement once a corporation has 100 shareholders). In the absence of

such legislation, the danger exists that a court might invalidate a supermajority requirement on the grounds it conflicts with code provisions requiring a majority vote for specified actions (or even in cases where the statute is silent, that it conflicts with the implied corporate norm of majority rule). *E.g., Benintendi v. Kenton Hotel,* 294 N.Y. 112, 60 N.E.2d 829 (1945). *But see Katcher v. Ohsman,* 26 N.J.Super. 28, 97 A.2d 180 (1953). Also, where the statute mandates the supermajority provision be in the articles (as in California and New York), placing it in the bylaws makes it invalid. *E.g., Model, Roland & Co. v. Industrial Acoustics Co.,* 16 N.Y.2d 703, 261 N.Y.S.2d 896, 209 N.E.2d 553 (1965). (What would happen if the parties made a shareholders agreement to vote in a certain manner as shareholders or directors only when all concur? Can this be invalid as constituting a supermajority provision which is not in the articles? *Compare Gazda v. Kolinski,* 91 A.D.2d 860, 458 N.Y.S.2d 387 (1982), *aff'd,* 64 N.Y.2d 1100, 489 N.Y.S.2d 907, 479 N.E.2d 252 (1985), *with Adler v. Svingos,* 80 A.D.2d 764, 436 N.Y.S.2d 719 (1981).)

Supermajority requirements often apply to shareholder votes. For example, earlier it was suggested that parties could use a supermajority requirement for election of directors as an indirect means of ensuring minority stockholders get a position on the board. Parties also can use this technique for matters subject to director vote (as in *Blount*). This can provide a mechanism to protect minority shareholders from adverse board action—assuming the parties couple it with one of the techniques discussed earlier to ensure minority shareholders have a position on the board—without the legal challenges a shareholders agreement controlling board actions might face. It also may allow greater flexibility than attempting to specify future board actions. Supermajority requirements usually apply only to specific matters. For example, notice how one could use the technique to prevent circumvention of cumulative voting, or the problem in *Blount,* by requiring more than a majority shareholder (or director) vote to amend the articles and bylaws. What matters could the parties have subjected to this technique to avoid the squeeze-out in *Wilkes*? Shareholders might, however, make all decisions subject to such a requirement. What problems could this create? (On the other hand, is this any different from the situation in a two-man partnership, or in a corporation with an equal division of voting stock between two shareholders and an even-numbered board?) Determining the required supermajority vote to approve a resolution is a function of to whom the parties wish to give a veto. Requiring a unanimous shareholder vote, for example, gives a veto to even a token shareholder. Also, the parties need to be clear as to whether the required vote is a percentage of all outstanding shares (or of all the directors)—which normally is what they intend—or just the percentage of those shares voted (or of those directors voting).

One difficulty with a supermajority requirement is it does not allow a minority shareholder to force action—for example, the distribution of dividends—when inaction may be contrary to his or her interest and expectations. He or she could attempt to use the requirement as leverage to bargain for such action, especially when many or all corporate decisions require his or her vote. Such tactics, however, create the danger of deadlock or abuse. *See, e.g., Smith v. Atlantic Properties, Inc.,* 12 Mass.App.Ct. 201, 422 N.E.2d 798 (1981).

Sometimes parties may attempt to use high quorum requirements to accomplish the same goals as a supermajority voting requirement. This is less efficient, since minority shareholders or directors must absent themselves from the meeting to block unfavorable action. Deliberately staying away from a meeting for such a purpose may provoke an unfavorable response from a court. *Compare Gearing v. Kelly,* 11 N.Y.2d 201, 227 N.Y.S.2d 897, 182 N.E.2d 391 (1962) (shareholder who encouraged a director to deliberately stay away from a board meeting in order to prevent a quorum cannot challenge the action taken at the meeting), *with Hall v. Hall,* 506 S.W.2d 42 (Mo.App.1974) (a shareholder is legally entitled to stay away from a shareholders meeting to prevent any action).

5. As evident from *Wilkes,* one of the most critical board decisions a minority shareholder often wishes to guarantee is his or her continued employment by the company. The typical pattern of closely held corporations distributing much of their earnings to their owners through salaries renders continued employment important to provide a source of income from the company. Being an officer in the corporation can also provide authority over specific aspects of the company's operations about which the shareholder may have a particular concern.

One additional method exists for ensuring continued employment beyond those techniques described above. This is to make a contract between the corporation and the shareholder, in which the company agrees to employ the shareholder for a specified period of time in a particular position and at a given salary, and the shareholder agrees to work for the company under these terms. While some older opinions question the authority of a board of directors to approve an employment contract extending beyond its term in office (*e.g., Borland v. John F. Sass Printing Co.,* 95 Colo. 53, 32 P.2d 827 (1934)), most courts recognize that the board, under its power to manage the company, can bind the corporation to a long term employment contract, just as the board can bind the firm to all kinds of contracts. *E.g., In re Paramount Publix Corp.,* 90 F.2d 441 (2d Cir.1937). A number of corporations statutes reinforce this view. *E.g.,* Cal. Corp. Code § 312(b); M.B.C.A. § 8.44(b). Still, such contracts may occasionally run into a problem if a court interprets a particular corporation's articles or bylaws to limit the term of the office which is the subject of the contract, and to override any contractual right to continue in office past that term. *E.g., Pioneer Specialties, Inc. v. Nelson,* 161 Tex. 244, 339 S.W.2d 199 (1960).

Long term employment contracts are more useful in securing sustained income, than they are as a tool to obtain continued power over the running of the business. Their inability to realize the latter goal stems from two problems. To begin with, an officer's authority is subject to commands from higher corporate officers (*e.g., Lydia E. Pinkham Medicine Co. v. Gove,* 305 Mass. 213, 25 N.E.2d 332 (1940)), and, ultimately, to the overriding power of the board of directors. *E.g., Sterling Industries v. Ball Bearing Pen*

Corp., 298 N.Y. 483, 84 N.E.2d 790 (1949). Indeed, a contract whereby the board granted unchecked power to an officer to manage the company could be contrary to the statutes giving this responsibility to the board. *E.g., Kennerson v. Burbank Amusement Co.*, 120 Cal.App.2d 157, 260 P.2d 823 (1953). *But see* Cal. Corp. Code § 300(a) (may delegate management of day-to-day business so long as under the ultimate direction of the board). In addition, should the board terminate an officer in breach of an employment contract, most courts limit relief to money damages, and will not require the board to reinstate the officer. *E.g., Zannis v. Lake Shore Radiologists, Ltd.*, 73 Ill.App.3d 901, 29 Ill.Dec. 569, 392 N.E.2d 126 (1979) (despite the contract containing an advance agreement to specific performance). Still, in drafting the employment contract, it is useful for the shareholder-employee to obtain a commitment to a minimum level of responsibility rather than just a promise of compensation and benefits. Otherwise, a majority seeking to squeeze him or her out could try to avoid breaching the employment contract by making the job so demeaning, the shareholder-employee ultimately resigns. On the other hand, specifying responsibilities cuts both ways. The corporation should be able to discharge the individual who cannot or will not perform. Who can make such a determination in a closely held corporation?

SECTION D. DISSOLUTION AND CHANGES IN OWNERSHIP

1. SHARE TRANSFER RESTRICTIONS

Zidell v. Zidell, Inc.

277 Or. 423, 560 P.2d 1091 (1977).

■ HOWELL, JUSTICE.

* * * [P]laintiff Arnold Zidell, suing derivatively on behalf of four of the Zidell corporations, sought a decree directing Jay Zidell, one of the individual defendants, to transfer at cost to the corporations the shares in each that he had purchased from defendant Jack Rosenfeld. Plaintiff's theory was that the opportunity to purchase the Rosenfeld shares belonged to the corporations, and that the directors breached their duties to the corporations by arranging for a private, rather than a corporate, purchase.

The trial court found that plaintiff had failed to establish any right to relief and entered a decree dismissing the complaint, from which plaintiff appeals. We affirm.

* * *

Prior to the sale in question, plaintiff and defendant Emery Zidell [plaintiff's brother] each controlled 37 ½ percent of the shares in these corporations. Jack Rosenfeld's 25 percent interest was, therefore, the key to ultimate control by either plaintiff or Emery Zidell. During 1971 plaintiff asked Rosenfeld whether he would be interested in selling his stock in the

Zidell corporations. Rosenfeld replied: "I would be interested in selling my stock. Everything I have is for sale." Nothing further was done or said at that time, but plaintiff later reported this conversation to Emery Zidell. Without informing plaintiff of his intentions, Emery then went to Rosenfeld and began negotiations for the purchase of some of Rosenfeld's shares. The purchase was consummated in May, 1972.

Under the terms of the purchase agreement, Rosenfeld agreed to sell to Jay Zidell, Emery's son, all of his stock in Tube Forgings of America, and slightly more than half of his 25 percent interest in each of the other three corporations. * * * It is undisputed that plaintiff did not learn of the purchase until after it was an accomplished fact.

Plaintiff contends that this transaction was, in effect, a purchase of control by Emery, and we will so consider it. Clearly, Jay Zidell would have been unable to make the purchase without his father's financial backing. The terms of the agreement were apparently negotiated by Emery Zidell and Jack Rosenfeld. Rosenfeld testified that it was Emery who suggested the exact number of shares in Zidell, Inc., Zidell Dismantling, and Zidell Explorations which would be transferred, and the transferred shares were just enough to give Emery and Jay Zidell together a majority of the outstanding shares. We consider this case, therefore, as though the purchase of a controlling interest was made by Emery who, at the time of these transactions, was a member of the board of all of the corporations. Viewed in this manner, the central issue in this case is whether Emery Zidell violated any duty to the corporations involved by purchasing a controlling interest in each without offering to the corporations an opportunity to negotiate for the purchase of the Rosenfeld shares.

As a general rule, a director violates no duty to his corporation by dealing in its stock on his own account. Plaintiff, however, contends that the rule should be otherwise when the stock is that of a closely-held corporation and the purchase is made at a favorable price and for the purpose of affecting control of the corporation. He argues that Rosenfeld's stock was sold at a bargain price and that the corporations had an interest in insuring that all the shareholders benefited equally from such a purchase.

We will accept, for purposes of this opinion, plaintiff's contention that the price paid Rosenfeld for the stock was low in comparison to the stock's actual value and that this purchase, therefore, was a bargain. Nevertheless, we disagree with plaintiff's contention that the bargain was one which rightfully belonged to the corporations.

Plaintiff presented no evidence that the corporations have made a practice of purchasing their own stock or that they ever contemplated doing so in order to maintain proportionate control, and there is no basis for inferring an agreement to that effect. Absent such a corporate policy, there is normally no special corporate interest in the opportunity to purchase its own shares. * * *

Only a few cases have held that the purchase of shares by the director of a corporation amounts to the usurpation of a corporate opportunity. Those cases that we have examined all turn on special factual situations, and each is distinguishable from this case.

Thus, in *Sladen v. Rowse,* 347 A.2d 409 (R.I.1975), the court imposed a constructive trust for the benefit of the corporation on shares purchased by a director of a family corporation. Prior to the purchase, the shares were owned by the only substantial shareholder who was not a family member. The board of directors had considered purchasing these shares to protect the family's controlling interests but had taken no action because the price was too high. Nevertheless, the defendant director did not report to the board that he had been approached about the possibility of a sale of the shares to the corporation at a reduced price. Instead, he secretly appropriated the opportunity for himself and used corporate funds (which he later repaid) to finance part of the transaction.

* * *

In *Faraclas v. City Vending Company,* [232 Md. 457, 194 A.2d 298 (1963)] the corporation had attempted to redeem certain shares, but the purported redemption was invalid because the corporation was insolvent at the time. Learning of the defect in the attempted redemption, one of the directors purchased the shares for himself. The court held that this was a violation of his fiduciary duty. In distinguishing the case before it from the general rule that a corporation normally has no interest in dealings in its stock, the court stated:

> "The line is drawn at the point where a purchase for the director's own account has the effect of thwarting a declared corporate policy." 194 A.2d at 301.

In our opinion this is a reasonable place to draw the line, particularly in a case like this one. At all relevant times, the individual defendants in this case, who were the parties to the stock transaction, held a majority of the corporate stock and controlled the boards of directors. So far as the record shows, they still do. Were we to hold that this stock purchase constituted a corporate opportunity, a decree that the stock be offered to the corporations would be meaningless. The boards of directors would, undoubtedly, vote to reject the offer. There are no disinterested board members to whom the decision could be referred. Therefore, to be effective the decree would have to mandate the purchase of these shares by the corporations. Certainly where there is no guidance in the form of a "declared corporate policy," such a decree would be an unwarranted intrusion into corporate affairs. It would affect not only the proportionate ownership in the corporations but also their capital structure.

Plaintiff urges us to adopt the standards employed by the Massachusetts court in *Donahue v. Rodd Electrotype Co. of New England, Inc.,* 328 N.E.2d 505 (Mass.1975). * * *

The opinion in *Donahue* evidences a concern to provide greater protection for the minority shareholder in a close corporation than had previously been available in the courts. That court eloquently demonstrates that such a shareholder, because there is rarely any market for his shares, is especially vulnerable to oppressive or unfair treatment by the majority. We do not believe, however, that the protective approach taken in that case would require the corporation to tailor its policies to favor a minority shareholder at the expense of the majority. * * * That, however, is apparently what plaintiff is seeking in the present case. He is asking that the court require these corporations to purchase Rosenfeld's shares in order to prevent, for plaintiff's benefit, a consolidation of control in the hands of Emery Zidell.

We recognize that this consolidation has placed plaintiff at a disadvantage. Plaintiff, in his capacity as minority shareholder, had a personal interest in maintaining the balance of power which existed prior to the consolidation. Such an interest on the part of the shareholders in closely-held corporations is frequently protected by special provisions in the corporate articles or bylaws or in shareholder agreements, requiring that before any shares are sold they must first be offered to the corporation or pro rata to all other shareholders. These parties, however, had no such agreement.

Like any minority shareholder who has not obtained by agreement a larger voice in corporate affairs than his stock ownership alone gives him, plaintiff is without an effective voice in corporate policy. He has not, however, shown that the welfare of the corporations requires that they redeem the Rosenfeld stock to prevent its coming under the control of Emery Zidell.

We agree with the trial court that plaintiff has failed to prove that the defendants have usurped a corporate opportunity.

Affirmed.

Rafe v. Hindin

29 A.D.2d 481, 288 N.Y.S.2d 662 (1968).

■ BELDOCK, PRESIDING JUSTICE.

On November 1, 1963 the plaintiff and the individual defendant organized the corporate defendant for the purpose of purchasing and developing a parcel of real property in Port Jefferson Station, New York. Each owned one certificate for 50% of the outstanding stock. There was a legend on each certificate, signed by the parties, which made it non-transferable except to the other stockholder; and written permission from the other stockholder was required to transfer the stock to a third party on the books of the corporation.

In April, 1967, being in financial difficulties, the plaintiff found a prospective purchaser for his stock for $44,000. The plaintiff offered to sell his stock to the individual defendant at that price. The latter refused to buy the stock and also refused to consent to the sale thereof to the plaintiff's prospective purchaser.

The plaintiff then instituted this action for a judgment declaring void the legend on the certificate, declaring the stock transferable to a third party without the consent of the individual defendant, and granting other incidental relief.

* * *

The plaintiff moved for summary judgment. Special Term denied the motion on the grounds that (1) the restriction on the sale of stock is not unreasonable on its face and (2) whether the individual defendant's refusal to consent to the transfer is reasonable is a question of fact. This is an appeal by the plaintiff from the order denying his motion for summary judgment.

The legend on the stock certificate was not contained either in the certificate of incorporation or in the by-laws of the corporation, but was the result of agreement between the parties. That fact is not a sufficient ground for invalidating the restriction. A restriction on the alienation of stock made between all the stockholders of a corporation may be enforced, if reasonable, even though it is not contained in the certificate of incorporation or the by-laws. * * *

The legend contained two separate restrictions: (a) each stockholder is required to sell to the other stockholder, but no price is stated at which the offeror is required to sell or the offeree to purchase, and no time limit is set for the offeree to exercise his option to purchase; and (b) each stockholder is required to obtain the consent of the other stockholder to a proposed transfer of the stock to a third party, but there is no provision that the second stockholder may not unreasonably withhold his consent. We are concerned on this appeal solely with the validity of the second restriction.

There is a conflict of authority in other States on the subject of the validity of a restriction on the transfer of stock in a close corporation without the consent of either all or a stated percentage of the other stockholders or the board of directors of the corporation.

In *Longyear v. Hardman,* 219 Mass. 405, 106 N.E. 1012, it was held that a provision in a certificate of incorporation that none of the shares of stock shall be sold without the consent of the holders of three-quarters of the stock was not palpably unreasonable or unconscionable because in a small business corporation there is a personal relation analogous to a partnership and there should be retained the right to choose one's associates; harmony of purpose and of business methods and ideals among stockholders may be a significant element in success.

* * *

In *Tracey v. Franklin,* 31 Del.Ch. 477, 67 A.2d 56, 11 A.L.R.2d 990, affg. 30 Del.Ch. 407, 61 A.2d 780, it was held that a provision whereby two stockholders in a close corporation agreed not to sell their shares, except on the consent of both, was invalid because a restraint on alienation of property is against public policy; and that the fact that two stockholders wish to solidify ownership in themselves is not a legally sufficient purpose to justify the restraint on alienation. * * *

In New York, certificates of stock are regarded as personal property and are subject to the rule that there be no unreasonable restraint on alienation.

* * *

The legend on the stock certificate at bar contains no provision that the individual defendant's consent may not be unreasonably withheld. Since the individual defendant is thus given the arbitrary power to forbid a transfer of the shares of stock by the plaintiff, the restriction amounts to annihilation of property. The restriction is not only not reasonable, but it is against public policy and, therefore, illegal. It is an unwarrantable and unlawful restraint on the sale of personal property, the sale and interchange of which the law favors, and in restraint of trade.

The individual defendant argues that there was an oral agreement between the parties that his consent would not be unreasonably withheld and that, in fact, the withholding of his consent to the transfer to the plaintiff's prospective purchaser was reasonable. Assuming that there was such an oral agreement prior to the issuance of the shares of stock and assuming further that the inclusion of such a provision in the written legend on the stock certificate would make reasonable what we hold to be an unreasonable restraint on alienation, it is our opinion that proof of such an oral agreement would be inadmissible at the trial as in violation of the parol evidence rule. * * *

It is further noted that, because the individual defendant is given by the legend on the stock certificate the arbitrary right to refuse for any reason or for no reason to consent to the transfer of the plaintiff's stock to a prospective purchaser, and since no price is stated at which the plaintiff must sell to the individual defendant and which the latter is required to pay to the plaintiff for the plaintiff's stock, the legend may be construed as rendering the sale of the plaintiff's stock impossible to anyone except to the individual defendant at whatever price he wishes to pay. This construction makes the restriction illegal.

* * *

The order denying the plaintiff's motion for summary judgment should be reversed, on the law, with $10 costs and disbursements; the motion should be granted; and judgment should be directed to be entered (1) declaring void the legend on the certificate requiring the consent of the individual defendant to the transfer of the plaintiff's stock to a third-party and (2) directing the corporate defendant, upon submission to it of a properly endorsed assignment of the stock and appropriate payment to it on account of any taxes on the transfer, to record the transfer in its stock transfer book, to cancel the plaintiff's stock certificate, to issue a new stock certificate to the plaintiff's transferee, and to record the plaintiff's transferee in its stock book as the present holder of the stock.

* * *

NOTES

1. *Zidell* illustrates one problem which may occur in a closely held corporation when the stockholders can freely transfer their shares: The transfer could upset the balance of power. Suppose, however, Rosenfeld sold his shares to an outsider. What concerns might either or both of the Zidells have about entry of a business associate whom they did not choose (and may not even know)? So long as the two Zidells act together, the new shareholder would seem largely powerless to set corporate policy. (Unlike a partner, a stockholder lacks even apparent authority to act for the firm. *E.g., Mease v. Warm Mineral Springs, Inc.,* 128 So.2d 174 (Fla.App.1961).) Yet, if the two brothers have a falling out—which they in fact did—the outsider can play a dominant role. Moreover, in a situation like *Rafe,* in which a holder of 50 percent or more of the voting stock wants to sell out, the remaining shareholders face the prospect of an outsider with control equal to or greater than theirs.

Beyond these broad managerial concerns, share transfers raise several legal problems for the non-selling stockholders. Courts and legislatures have shown increasing solicitude for the minority shareholder in a closely held corporation. *E.g., Wilkes v. Springside Nursing Home, Inc.,* reprinted earlier in this chapter; Cal. Corp. Code § 1800(b)(5) (allowing involuntary dissolution to protect the interest of a minority shareholder). Hence, entry of a new and possibly less deferential shareholder can constrain the non-selling stockholders' freedom of action even if they retain a majority of voting shares. On the other hand, as noted earlier, shareholders agreements might not bind an individual obtaining stock from one of the parties to the contract. As a result, a non-selling minority shareholder may no longer be able to count on the protection of such agreements should the transferee and any other non-signatories to the contract together possess a controlling interest. Further along these lines, a non-consenting new stockholder might challenge the validity of agreements impinging upon the board's power to manage the corporation. *See, e.g.,* Del. Gen. Corp. Law § 350 (validating shareholder agreements in a statutory close corporation, despite impinging upon the board's power, "as between the parties to the agreement"). Moreover, some statutes require restrictions upon transfer in order to elect statutory closed corporation treatment (*e.g.,* Del. Gen. Corp. Law § 342(a)(2)), and transfers could endanger continued close corporation status by increasing the number of shareholders over the allowed maximum. *But see* Cal. Corp. Code § 418(d) (voiding a voluntary transfer which would place the company over the limit if shares contain notice). As discussed later in this chapter, transfer of shares can sometimes create a problem with continued eligibility for taxation under subchapter S. Another tax problem with the sale of a majority of the company's outstanding shares is that this could trigger application of Section 382 of the Internal

Revenue Code, thereby limiting the firm's ability to utilize net operating loss carryovers under Section 172. (Chapter VII will explore this topic.) Finally, resales of stock can endanger compliance with state and federal securities laws. (The next chapter will address this subject in some detail.)

2. One way to deal with these concerns is to prohibit the transfer of shares without the consent of the corporation or other stockholders. *Rafe* involved such a consent restriction. The court's holding indicates the initial problem with this type of agreement: Courts may find it constitutes an impermissible restraint upon alienation. As the opinion explains, attitudes among the states toward these agreements vary, making this a hazardous area for planning purposes in a jurisdiction where there is no binding authority on point. Obtaining a favorable outcome may depend in some states upon convincing the court that special needs exist for the restraint in this particular corporation. *E.g., Fayard v. Fayard,* 293 So.2d 421 (Miss. 1974). At the other end of the scale, courts examine the degree to which the provision completely blocks transfer. For example, the *Rafe* opinion suggested the restraint there may have stood if Hinden could not unreasonably have withheld consent to a sale. Some opinions also look at the length of time the restriction prevents sale without consent. *E.g., Gray v. Harris Land & Cattle Co.,* 227 Mont. 51, 737 P.2d 475 (1987). In a number of states, statutes expressly permit consent restraints. *E.g.,* Del. Gen. Corp. Law § 202(c)(3). *See also* M.B.C.A. § 6.27(d)(3) (consent restraint allowed if not unreasonable).

Even if enforceable, to what extent do consent restraints provide a practical solution to the problems created by unrestricted share transfers? Consider the impact of the restriction upon Rafe, who was in financial difficulties and needed to sell his shares. Consider, as well, what would happen if, as a result of his financial difficulties, Rafe filed bankruptcy. Alternately, what happens under a consent restraint if a stockholder dies? Can a consent restriction prevent a transfer by operation of law due to death or bankruptcy? (If it somehow could, what would become of the shares, particularly in the case of a stockholder's death?) If it cannot prevent the transfer, does the restriction fulfill its purpose? Moreover, instead of focusing simply on the transfer of stock, one might ask what underlies the concern with choosing one's business associates. To the extent the concern rests upon the need for owners in a closely held business to get along, consider what the relations between Rafe and Hinden would have been like had the court upheld the restriction.

3. Contrast what happens in a partnership under the U.P.A. if a member dies, goes bankrupt or wants out. As discussed in the previous chapter, there is no need for an agreement restricting a partner's right to transfer his or her entire ownership (including management rights) in the firm without consent: The U.P.A. provides this (barring contrary agreement), allowing only assignment of the limited right to receive a share in the firm's profits. Instead of allowing transfer, the U.P.A. dissolves the partnership upon these events and gives each partner (or perhaps his or her

estate) the right to cash out by demanding liquidation. Could such a scheme provide a viable solution in a closely held corporation?

Corporations codes typically allow voluntary dissolution of a company upon a vote of a majority of the directors and a majority of the shareholders. *E.g.,* Del. Gen. Corp. Law § 275; N.Y. Bus. Corp. Law § 1001; M.B.C.A. § 14.02. *But see* Cal. Corp. Code § 1900(a) (allowing voluntary dissolution upon a vote of only 50 percent of the shareholders and without the requirement of director approval). This, in itself, does not provide dissolution at the will (or upon the death or bankruptcy) of a minority shareholder. Perhaps the parties could agree to vote as stockholders and directors to dissolve the company upon these occasions. Presumably, an agreement obligating stockholders to vote to dissolve should be valid under the general principles discussed in the *Ringling* decision. The validity of an agreement binding directors to vote for dissolution is far less clear. *Compare Flanagan v. Flanagan,* 273 App.Div. 918, 77 N.Y.S.2d 682 (1948), *aff'd,* 298 N.Y. 787, 83 N.E.2d 473 (1948), *with Application of Hega Knitting Mills, Inc.,* 124 N.Y.S.2d 115 (1953). Some state codes, however, enable articles of a statutory close corporation to give any shareholder or percentage of shareholders the option to dissolve the company at will or upon the occurrence of specified conditions. *E.g.,* Del. Gen. Corp. Law § 355. *See also* M.B.C.A. § 7.32(a)(7) (validating a shareholders agreement in any non-publicly traded corporation which gives one or more shareholders the right to force dissolution).

Assuming one could provide for dissolution in lieu of transfer upon a shareholder's death, bankruptcy, or desire to cash out, is this a practical solution? Recall the problems presented by dissolution and liquidation of a partnership. Will the same problems exist with dissolving and liquidating a corporation?

4. The analogy to the partnership setting nevertheless may suggest a useful idea. In order to cope with the problems of dissolution, partners often agree to a buy-out of one's interest by the others upon death, bankruptcy or the like. Could the same solution avoid the problems attendant upon a transfer of shares in a corporation? Courts generally reject the challenge that advance buy-out agreements covering stock constitute an impermissible restraint upon alienation. *E.g., Allen v. Biltmore Tissue Corp.,* 2 N.Y.2d 534, 161 N.Y.S.2d 418, 141 N.E.2d 812 (1957). A buy-out agreement seemingly provides a way to meet the continuing stockholders' concerns about transfers without freezing in any shareholder. It can apply to prevent an involuntary conveyance to an undesired party upon such events as death. *E.g., Ward v. City Drug Co.,* 235 Ark. 767, 362 S.W.2d 27 (1962). (Whether a buy-out would prevent a transfer upon bankruptcy depends upon the application of the Bankruptcy Code provisions discussed in the *Broyhill* opinion in the previous chapter.) Such agreements can serve other purposes as well. For example, while Rafe found a buyer for his shares—no doubt aided by the fact he owned 50 percent and the fact the company was developing valuable real estate—typically not much market exists for shares in a closely held corporation

(especially if the shares represent only a minority position). Without a prospective purchaser, a consent restraint becomes irrelevant. A buy-out agreement, however, could provide shareholders with some liquidity.

Writers often refer to several types of stock buy-out agreements made in advance of the actual purchase: (1) rights of first refusal (which allow the company or other shareholders to buy the stock at the price offered by a third party before the third party may buy); (2) first options (which give the company or other shareholders the right to buy at a price set by the agreement before the owner may sell to a third party); (3) repurchase agreements (which allow the corporation to buy the stock from a holder upon a triggering event including something other than an impending sale); or (4) buy-sell agreements (which may obligate the corporation or other shareholders to buy, as well the holder to sell, upon a triggering event). These labels, however, are simply shorthand (and not always consistently applied) ways to describe several possible answers to questions faced by all advance buy-out agreements: who buys, upon what events, at whose option, and at what price. Effective drafting requires an exploration of these issues beyond simple labels.

a. *Drafting Problems*

Earthman's Inc. v. Earthman

526 S.W.2d 192 (Tex.Civ.App.1975).

■ EVANS, JUSTICE.

This case with all its facets is essentially a suit to recover damages for conversion of corporate stock. After a jury trial, Mrs. Earthman, the plaintiff, recovered judgment on the verdict against her former husband, J.B. Earthman, III, his brother, * * *, his father * * *, and three Earthman family corporations: Earthman's Inc., Mission Life Insurance Company, and Resthaven Memorial Gardens, Inc.

* * *

Mrs. Earthman was divorced from her husband, J.B. Earthman, III, in March 1971. Under the divorce decree, Mrs. Earthman was awarded:

"65% of the total stock owned by the parties, or either of them, with James Bradshaw Earthman, III, ordered to forthwith transfer to Dorothy Monroe Earthman the following shares:

"(1) 1300 shares of Earthman's Inc.;

"(2) 10,833 shares of Resthaven Memorial Gardens, Inc.;

"(3) 325 shares of Mission Life Insurance Company,"

The shares so awarded to Mrs. Earthman represented 21% ownership in Earthman's Inc., 21% in Resthaven, and 13% in Mission. There seems to be no question but that the three corporations were closely held and were owned and controlled by J.B. Earthman and his sons, J.B. Earthman, III, Robert Earthman, and Michael Earthman.

* * *

Mrs. Earthman filed this suit on August 21, 1971. In her original petition, Mrs. Earthman alleged that the three corporations had refused to transfer to her name the stock which had been awarded to her under the decree, * * * and asked that the court declare her rights and order the proper stock certificates delivered to her.

* * *

By letter dated April 5, 1972 the Earthmans' attorney advised Mrs. Earthman's attorney that Earthman's Inc. was exercising an option to purchase the Earthman's stock under Article V of its articles of incorporation and that it therefore refused her request to transfer such stock to her. * * *

On August 28, 1973, Mrs. Earthman filed her second amended petition, in this suit, alleging that * * * the defendants had acted in a conspiracy to defraud her of her shares of stock and sought damages for the conversion as well as exemplary damages.

* * *

The Earthman defendants next contend that there was no conversion on April 5, 1972 because they had reasonable excuse or probable cause for their actions. They point out the general rule that a corporation is not liable for damages for conversion where it refuses to issue or transfer stock, unless its refusal is without legal justification or excuse.

The legal justification for the refusal to effectuate transfer of the 1300 shares of capital stock of Earthman's, Inc. was based upon a provision of Article V of the articles of incorporation of that company which provides as follows:

> "The shares of stock of the corporation are to be held by each shareholder upon the condition that he will not sell, assign, transfer, pledge or in any way dispose of or encumber any of such shares without first offering (in writing, mailed to the Corporation's office) the same for sale to the Corporation which shall have the right to purchase all or any portion of such shares within sixty (60) days from the date of the offer. * * * If for any reason the Corporation does not purchase any shares of stock which it has the right to purchase under any provision of this Article, remaining shareholders of the Corporation so electing shall have the right to purchase all or any portion of such shares (pro rata, according to their stock ownership, or as they may otherwise agree) within ten (10) days following the end of the time during which the Corporation had the right to purchase such shares under this Article. The price for purchase of shares of stock under any provision of this Article shall be the book value of such shares as at the close of the month preceding the date of the offer * * * such book

value to be determined by the certified public accountants serving the Corporation at such time, in accordance with the accounting practices followed in preparing the most recent annual financial statement to the corporation. Such purchase price shall be paid in cash forthwith after notification of the election to purchase or, at the option of the purchaser, 20% of the purchase price may be so paid in cash and the balance may be paid in no more than four equal annual installments with interest at the rate of 6% per annum."

In the letter of April 5, 1972 counsel for Earthman's, Inc. stated that Earthman's, Inc. construed the delivery of the two certificates representing 1300 shares of the company stock as an attempt by J.B. Earthman, III to transfer stock to Mrs. Earthman in derogation of Article V, that the company was therefore entitled to purchase such stock at book value and that it exercised its right and option to purchase such stock on terms as stated in the article.

A provision which restricts a stockholder's right to sell or transfer his stock, particularly one which affords a prior right of purchase to the corporation or to another stockholder, is not looked upon with favor in the law and is strictly construed. * * * It has generally been held that such a restriction is inapplicable to a transfer occurring as a result of an involuntary sale or by operation of law unless by specific provision in the restriction it is made applicable. * * *

In *Messersmith v. Messersmith,* 229 La. 495, 86 So.2d 169 (1956), it was contended that certain community owned stock should not be divided in kind, as decreed by the divorce court, and that the husband should be permitted to retain the stock and to pay his wife one-half its book value in accordance with a restrictive clause in the corporate charter requiring a stockholder, who wished to sell his stock, to first offer it to the other stockholders or officers of the corporation. The Louisiana Supreme Court determined that the restrictive provision of the charter could not prevent the recognition of the wife's share of the ownership in the corporation and held that she was entitled to have delivered to her in kind the interest awarded to her under the divorce decree. In so holding that court stated:

> "* * * The restriction in the charter cannot affect the status of the stock purchased during the existence of the community or the rights the wife may assert thereunder. Such a restriction cannot negative the wife's present interest as co-owner, and as a co-owner in community she is clearly entitled to be recognized as such and obtain the exclusive management and control of her vested interest. (citing cases)." (86 S.2d p. 173).

We are of the opinion that the restrictive provision in question should not be construed so as to preclude Mrs. Earthman's right to have her shares of ownership reflected on the books of the corporation and to have the stock certificates evidencing her ownership issued to her. We hold that the trial court properly determined that this provision did not afford to the corporation the right or option to purchase the shares of Earthman's Inc. so awarded to Mrs. Earthman.

* * *

[The judgment was reversed on other grounds.]

NOTES

1. Buy-out agreements covering stock must address the same basic issues confronted in drafting buy-outs of partnership, limited partnership, LLP and LLC interests. To begin with, the agreement must specify what events trigger the buy-out. This was the problem area in *Earthman.* Listing triggering events flows logically from carefully identifying the purposes behind the agreement. With ordinary partnerships, the purpose of the buy-out—at least on an initial level—is to control the consequences of dissolution. Hence, one can look to the statutory causes of dissolution in order to find a basic set of potential conditions for exercising the agreement. Buy-outs for shares focus, at first glance, on different concerns.

As discussed above, a primary motivation for the buy-out often is to prevent shares going beyond the original owners, without creating the legal and practical problems of a restraint on transfer without consent. This leads to agreements, such as in *Earthman,* triggering the buy-out upon a sale or transfer. The problem in *Earthman* (and numerous similar cases) is that the parties forgot to consider involuntary transfers which occur upon death, bankruptcy and divorce. (Similar ambiguity sometimes occurs over whether the agreement applies to sales between existing shareholders, rather than to outsiders (*e.g., Remillong v. Schneider,* 185 N.W.2d 493 (N.D.1971)), whether it applies to gifts (*e.g., Louisiana Weekly Publ. Co. v. First Nat. Bank of Commerce,* 483 So.2d 929 (La.1986)) and whether it applies to offers to sell the entire company (*e.g., Frandsen v. Jensen–Sundquist Agency, Inc.*, 802 F.2d 941 (7th Cir.1986).)

Moreover, one could go beyond focusing simply on the transfer of shares, and view the underlying factors which make stockholders in closely held companies concerned about changes in share ownership. To the extent they are worried about individuals in whom they lack confidence gaining a voice in management, consider what will happen if a shareholder becomes mentally incompetent. Even without a transfer, will the other owners have confidence in this person, or in whoever the court may appoint as conservator of his or her estate? Perhaps a motive lies in problems created by the transfer of shares to individuals—such as spouses and children—who will not actively work in the business. As discussed earlier, the clash of interests between active participants and passive owners is a common problem in closely held corporations. Yet, can the same problem arise, even without a share transfer, upon the disability or retirement of an owner-employee? Ultimately, perhaps the underlying theme behind all these reasons for restricting transfer is the perceived need for owners in a closely held business to be able to get along with each other. Seen in this light, is a buy-out agreement needed, even without the precipitating threat of a share transfer, whenever the parties reach a point of irreconcilable dissension?

As stated above, another motivation for buy-out agreements lies in the liquidity concerns of shareholders in closely held corporations. Even if stockholders in closely held companies face no legal restrictions on transfer, few persons may be interested in buying their shares. What circumstances does this suggest as triggering events: Anytime a shareholder wants to cash out; or are there some occasions where stockholders may present a particularly sympathetic need for money? (For example, what tax burden faces the estate of a deceased shareholder whose primary asset was his or her stock in a closely held corporation?)

Compare the list of triggering events suggested by the foregoing discussion, with the causes of partnership dissolution and any other occurrences commonly triggering the buy-out of a partner, limited partner, or member in an LLC. The similarly of the two lists is not coincidental. The same basic events will occur in the lives of the owners of any type of business. Also, as with a buy-out agreement for a partnership, limited partnership, or LLC interest, the contract must specify who has the option to force the sale—the buyer, the seller or both. The answer to this question too logically flows from considering the purposes for the buy-out.

Finally, as in the non-corporate context, the more unbalanced a buy-out agreement is in terms such as price, the more prescient and unambiguous the triggering events term must be. For example, suppose a buy-out agreement, which gives the corporation the right to repurchase shares upon termination of the shareholder's employment with the company, contains a price term (such as book value) which becomes highly favorable to the corporation. Might this tempt those in charge of the corporation to terminate the shareholder's employment in order to trigger the buy-out? If the shareholders' employment is at will, is there anything to protect the shareholder from this tactic? *Compare Gallagher v. Lambert*, 74 N.Y.2d 562, 549 N.Y.S.2d 945, 549 N.E.2d 136 (1989), *with Chaplin v. Magic Woods, Inc.*, 794 P.2d 1176 (Kan.App.1990). How might one draft buy-out terms to avoid such problems?

2. The next term the parties must consider is the price. One difference here from buy-outs in the non-corporate setting stems from the refusal of courts to enforce unreasonable restraints on alienating shares. Could parties set a buy-out price so low that its practical effect is to preclude transfer of the shares? (For example, the corporation could have the first right to purchase shares of any stockholder desiring to sell at $.01 per share or some other token amount.) Generally, courts have not been sympathetic to challenges against buy-out contracts on the ground the price is less than fair market value; yet there may be some point at which a court could find the disparity is so great that the buy-out unreasonably restrains alienation. *Compare In re Mather's Estate,* 410 Pa. 361, 189 A.2d 586 (1963), *with Systematics, Inc. v. Mitchell,* 253 Ark. 848, 491 S.W.2d 40 (1973).

3. As in the non-corporate setting, the agreement must specify who purchases the departing owner's interest: the firm or the other owners. Tax considerations largely dictated this choice for ordinary partnerships, since the decision otherwise lacked much real economic significance. Tax factors remain important in the corporate setting as well. For example, assume, as is common, the parties plan to pay for a buy-out with corporate earnings. If the remaining owners buy the departing participant's stock, what tax problem occurs when a C corporation distributes earnings to them in order to pay for the purchase? Perhaps the company can make these distributions through increased salary, interest, loan payments, or the like. Otherwise, if it increases dividends, the parties will pay for the stock with what remains after the government takes two tax bites. (Of course, the parties might fund a buy-out triggered by death through insurance. If, however, the company pays the premiums, but the proceeds go to pay for a purchase by the other shareholders rather than by the firm, or simply to benefit the heirs, then the company's payment becomes a constructive dividend. *E.g., Johnson v. Commissioner,* 74 T.C. 1316 (1980).) Moreover, to the extent the purchase price exceeds the selling shareholder's basis, a third tax becomes due. (Basis effects may somewhat offset this disadvantage. If the shareholders buy the departing owner's stock, they obtain a cost basis in the stock. I.R.C. § 1012.) What is the result if the company makes the purchase? In general, this should result in removing one layer of tax. The problem is complicated, however, by a series of Interval Revenue Code provisions designed to prevent the use of share repurchases as a means to bail out corporate earnings without paying taxable dividends. I.R.C. §§ 302–306. Repurchases by the corporation may also create problems with the accumulated earning tax. *E.g., Lamark Shipping Agency, Inc. v. Commissioner* reprinted in Chapter VI. As discussed in Chapter III, life insurance proceeds are often used to fund a buy-out following a shareholder's death. The proceeds normally will not be taxable income (I.R.C. § 101(a)(1)); albeit, the Internal Revenue Code imposes a number of notice and consent requirements in order for an employer to enjoy tax free receipt of the policy proceeds (I.R.C. § 101j), and the proceeds can produce alternate minimum tax. *See* I.R.C. § 56(g)(4)(B); Rev. Rul. 54–230, 1954–1 C.B. 114.

In addition to these tax factors, non-tax concerns assume a much greater role in determining whether the corporation or the other shareholders should make the purchase. To begin with, as true with non-corporate forms providing limited liability, corporation statutes typically limit the amount of funds a company can use to repurchase its shares. *E.g.,* Cal. Corp. Code §§ 166, 500–503; Del. Gen. Corp. Law § 160(a)(1); N.Y. Bus. Corp. Law § 513; M.B.C.A. §§ 1.40(6), 6.40. Moreover, the corporation's decision whether to buy the stock may create more complicated fiduciary duty problems than usually encountered in the partnership setting. For example, to what extent must directors or shareholders put aside their own interests in deciding if the company should exercise an option to buy shares which the directors or shareholders might wish to own themselves? *Compare Lash v. Lash Furniture Co. of Barre, Inc.,* 130 Vt. 517, 296 A.2d 207

(1972), *with Boss v. Boss,* 98 R.I. 146, 200 A.2d 231 (1964). (This could occur either because the director or shareholder wishes to buy shares subject to a repurchase agreement, or because the director or shareholder owns the shares subject to such an agreement.) Is there a way to mitigate this problem through drafting? For example, could the agreement preclude the interested director or shareholder from voting? One factor sometimes favoring purchases by the other stockholders stems from the tie-in between share holdings and voting rights. For example, suppose members of two families each own half the shares. Purchase of a deceased shareholder's stock by the company would upset the balance of power between the two families. Purchase of the shares by other members of the decedent's family would not.

The tax and non-tax issues raised by buy-outs of stock are sufficiently complex (especially when the corporation acts as purchaser) to justify treatment beyond that minimally necessary for planning at corporate formation. Chapter VI considers these issues in detail when it explores buy-outs and other techniques useful for restructuring the ownership of a corporation.

Rainwater v. Milfeld

485 S.W.2d 831 (Tex.Civ.App.1972).

■ SHARPE, JUSTICE.

This appeal is from a judgment rendered after non-jury trial in favor of appellees that appellant take nothing by his suit for specific performance of an alleged contract involving the transfer of certain shares of stock in M & D Enterprises, Inc., a Texas Corporation.

R.S. Rainwater brought this suit against Dana Milfeld and Laurella Milfeld for specific performance of an alleged agreement under which the Milfelds were to transfer certain of stock to him. * * *

The record reflects that M & D Enterprises, Inc., is a Texas Corporation whose principal business is the operation of the Holiday Inn Motel in Victoria, Texas. Originally, fifty percent of the corporation stock was owned by the Milfelds (Laurella J. and Dana) and the other fifty percent by some people named Dodson. The Dodsons, with the consent of the Milfelds, sold their said fifty percent stock ownership to appellant R.S. Rainwater, to the extent of 5%, and to his son, William I. Rainwater to the extent of 45%. The motel was constructed in 1966 and apparently never performed as any of its stockholders thought it should. The record reflects considerable controversy and differences of opinion between the Milfelds and the Rainwaters concerning the operation of the motel. There were four directors of the corporation, the two Milfelds and the two Rainwaters.

* * *

The bylaws of the corporation, relating to sale and transfer of shares of stock therein are as follows:

"ARTICLE FIVE—TRANSFER OF SHARES

* * *

SECTION 2. NO SHARES OF THIS CORPORATION SHALL BE SOLD OR TRANSFERRED at anytime by any shareholder unless and until such shares shall have been first offered to the corporation and other shareholders as hereinafter provided.

(a) Any shareholder desiring to sell his shares or any part thereof to any person, firm or corporation other than this corporation, shall first obtain a bona fide offer in writing from the proposed purchaser thereof stating the value or price in money at which such share or shares are proposed to be bought by such purchaser.

(b) Such shareholder shall then offer such shares proposed to be sold to the corporation at the price or value offered by the prospective purchaser as above provided and the corporation shall thereupon within five (5) days from the date such shares are offered to it, either accept or reject the offer in writing. Failure to accept in writing within such time shall be conclusively presumed and taken as a refusal of the offer.

(c) In the event the corporation refuses such offer, the shareholder desiring to sell shall offer such shares to the other shareholders of the corporation who shall each have the right and option to purchase such proportionate part of the shares offered for sale as the shares owned by each such purchasing shareholder bears to the total number of shares of the corporation issued and outstanding excluding therefrom the number of shares held by the shareholder offering to sell. Provided, further, that in the event any shareholder declines to purchase his proportionate part of the shares offered, each of the remaining shareholders shall have the right and option to purchase declining shareholders' proportionate part of the shares offered for sale in the proportion that the number of shares held by each such remaining shareholder bears to the total number of shares held by such remaining holders. The option to purchase hereby given to the remaining shareholders shall be at the price or value offered by the prospective purchaser as hereinabove provided, and such shareholders shall, within ten (10) days from the date any such shares are offered to them, either accept or reject the offer in writing. Failure of any shareholder to accept such offer in writing within such time shall be conclusively presumed and taken as a refusal of the offer.

(d) No shares of this corporation shall ever be sold to anyone other than the corporation or other shareholders of the corporation at a price of value less than at which they have been offered to the corporation and the other shareholders as hereinabove provided."

On September 3, 1970 the attorneys for the Milfelds wrote a letter reading in part as follows:

* * *

"Dear Mr. Rainwater:

This office represents Dana Milfeld and his brother L.J. Milfeld.

The Milfelds have received an offer from Mr. Abe Nosser to purchase their stock in M & D Corporation for $402,500.00 as per the enclosed offer dated August 12, 1970. The terms are self-explanatory.

In accordance with the By–Laws of the corporation, the Milfelds are at this time offering their stock to the corporation on the same basis as Mr. Nosser's offer to purchase. * * *

In accordance with Section 2, Subsection (c), if the corporation refuses to purchase, then we tender the stock to R.S. Rainwater and William I. Rainwater individually upon the same terms. * * * "

* * *

The attorneys for the Rainwaters and for M & D Corporation replied to the Milfeld letter of September 3, 1970 by letter of September 11, 1970 reading as follows:

* * *

"(b) On behalf of M & D Corporation the offer to purchase these shares at the $402,500.00 figure is rejected.

(c) On behalf of William I. Rainwater, who currently owns 45% of the outstanding shares of the stock of the corporation, and pursuant to Section 2(c), Article Five of the Bylaws of the Corporation, such offer is rejected.

(d) Pursuant to said Article Five, Section 2(c) of the Bylaws of the Corporation, R.S. Rainwater, who currently owns 5% of the outstanding shares of the Corporation exercises his option to purchase an equal proportionate part of the shares offered for sale and hereby tenders the sum of $40,250.00 to your client in exchange for 5,000 shares of outstanding capital stock of the Corporation, which funds will be delivered to you or to your clients upon delivery to him of stock certificate properly endorsed and ready for transfer on the books of the corporation into Mr. Rainwater's name. Mr. Rainwater further elects not to exercise his option to purchase the remaining shares offered for sale by your clients."

* * *

It is apparent from the foregoing that the offer of the Milfelds to sell their fifty percent stock ownership in M & D Enterprises, Inc. for $402,500.00 was rejected by the corporation and by William I. Rainwater who owned 45% of the stock of the corporation; and that R.S. Rainwater, who owned 5% of the corporation stock, gave the Milfelds notice that he intended to exercise an option pursuant to Art. 5. Sec. 2(c) of the bylaws of the corporation to purchase an equal proportionate amount of the shares offered for sale, and tendered the sum of $40,250,00 to the Milfelds in exchange for 5,000 shares of the corporation stock, and that R.S. Rainwater further elected not to exercise an option to purchase the remaining shares offered for sale by the Milfelds.

The position taken by appellant is that when any given amount of corporate stock is offered to the stockholders pursuant to Article 5 of the bylaws, any stockholder has the absolute right to buy his proportionate part of the offer without regard to whether the balance of the stock offered is purchased by the other stockholder(s) or himself. We do not agree.

* * *

The unambiguous meaning of Article Five of the bylaws is that when an offer to sell stock is made to the corporation and alternatively to the stockholders, that if the corporation rejects the offer the accepting stockholder may buy the entire amount offered in proportion to their ownership. It is not reasonable to interpret the provision so that one stockholder may buy his proportionate share of the total and leave the balance of the offer unaccepted either by the stockholders or himself.

The following sentence extracted from Article 5, Sec. 2(c) of the bylaws, when read in context with the preceding language of that section, demonstrates that the construction contended for by appellant is untenable.

> "* * * Provided, further, that in the event any shareholder declines to purchase his proportionate part of the shares offered, each of the remaining shareholders shall have the right and option to purchase declining shareholders' proportionate part of the shares offered for sale in the proportion that the number of shares held by each such remaining shareholder bears to the total number of shares held by such remaining holders. * * * "

It is clear in this case that the offer of the Milfelds was to sell their entire 50% of the stock in the M & D Enterprises, Inc. The Milfeld offer was based upon that of Mr. Abe Nosser to purchase the entire 50% of the stock owned by the Milfelds; and Mr. Nosser's offer expressly stated that "I would not be interested in a position of less than the 50%." The Milfelds' offer to sell their 50% of the stock was not accepted by the Rainwaters. The proposal made by appellant R.S. Rainwater amounts to no more than a counter-offer which was not accepted by the Milfelds.

It is obvious, from the testimony adduced at trial, that neither the Rainwaters nor the Milfelds wanted to place themselves in a minority position as far as their interests in the corporation were concerned. The previous relationship between the families, regarding the ownership of the stock indicates that none of the parties would jeopardize their fellow family member's standing in the control of the corporation by selling a portion of their stock and leaving the other in a minority position.

It is therefore apparent, and we so hold, that under a proper construction of the by-laws of the corporation, and in view of the offer of sale made by the Milfelds and its non-acceptance by the Rainwaters, the trial court properly denied specific performance of the alleged agreement relied upon by appellant.

* * *

The judgment of the trial court is affirmed.

NOTE

Buy-out agreements covering stock raise several questions less likely to occur in the non-corporate context. *Rainwater* illustrates one concern flowing from the divisible nature of stock: Must the purchase include all the shares, or can the buyer exercise an option just for some? Why did the attempted purchase of only some of the shares (so-called block-busting) upset their holder in *Rainwater*? On the other hand, what problem can an all or nothing approach create, particularly in a situation in which several remaining stockholders have the option to purchase their pro-rata share of the departing owner's stock only if all exercise the option? Did the agreement in *Rainwater* contain a viable alternative? (By the way, was the agreement in *Rainwater* really unambiguous?)

Was there another circumstance where the agreement in *Rainwater* used successive options—that is, if one party did not buy, another party had the option? Notice the agreement gave the first option to the corporation. What if the company could not exercise the option because the firm lacked legally adequate funds? (Successive obligations to purchase, however, may create a tax problem considered in Chapter VI.)

Another question is in what document to include the buy-out agreement. There is no partnership or LLC operating contract, but a shareholders agreement or a separate contract are possible locations. (Keep in mind, if the corporation is to be the purchaser, it must be a party to the contract.) Sometimes, as in *Rainwater*, parties place the restrictions in bylaws or articles. Recall the problem encountered in *Blount* created by placing items of a contractual nature in a document, like bylaws or articles, susceptible to amendment by majority vote. A majority shareholder wishing to be relieved of a buy-out obligation found in a bylaw or article could attempt to amend it out of existence. *See Silva v. Coastal Plywood & Timber Co.*, 124 Cal.App.2d 276, 268 P.2d 510 (1954). Alternately, stockholders might amend the bylaws or articles containing a buy-out agreement to change key terms, such as the price. *Lambert v. Fishermen's Dock Co-op., Inc.*, 61 N.J. 596, 297 A.2d 566 (1972). While some courts apply a "vested rights" concept to preclude these amendments from changing the rules for existing shareholders, one cannot count on this. Compare the *Lambert* and *Silva* decisions. Beyond the problem of alteration, can the placement of the agreement in the articles, bylaws or as a separate instrument affect its validity? Compare the discussion on this point in *Rafe,* reprinted earlier, *with Carlson v. Ringgold County Mut. Tel. Co.*, 252 Iowa 748, 108 N.W.2d 478 (1961) (suggesting restriction must be in the articles, or at least authorized by the articles).

Related to the problem of where to put the buy-out agreement, is the need for notice to prospective purchasers. The problem of bona fide purchasers arises with stock, unlike partnership interests, because shares are normally freely tradeable. Where should notice go?

One other question which the buy-out agreement might address is when does the selling shareholder's status as a shareholder terminate—upon the triggering event or upon the actual transfer of the shares. *See Stephenson v. Drever*, 16 Cal.4th 1167, 69 Cal.Rptr.2d 764 (1997) (issue of whether a shareholder, who was obligated under a buy-out agreement to sell his shares upon the termination of his employment, but who had not sold the shares after his employment terminated because of an inability to agree on the shares' valuation, was still a shareholder for purposes of bringing a suit claiming that the majority shareholder breached the majority shareholder's fiduciary duty). Of course, one might ask why a shareholder, who has contracted to sell out, would want to retain the status of shareholder. For example, if, as in *Stephenson*, the selling shareholder wants to retain the status for purposes of bringing a lawsuit claiming breach of fiduciary duty, why does a selling shareholder want to bring such a suit? Presumably, the reason for the suit is that the selling shareholder believes that the conduct purportedly breaching the defendant's fiduciary duty has resulted in the selling shareholder receiving a lower price for the shares. Is this something that the pricing term of the buy-out agreement can address, thereby rendering the termination of status question moot?

b. *Tax Aspects*

Robinson v. Commissioner of Internal Revenue

805 F.2d 38 (1st Cir.1986).

■ TORRUELLA, CIRCUIT JUDGE.

This appeal concerns the meaning of the timing provisions of Section 83 of the Internal Revenue Code, * * * which governs the taxation of property transferred in connection with a performance of services.

I. *The Stock Option Agreement*

Appellant Prentice Robinson held an option to purchase stock, at a below market price, in Centronics Data Computer Corp. * * * Robinson received the option as part of his employment package when he became a Centronics employee during the spring of 1969.

The distinguishing feature of the stock option agreement that leads to this dispute is a provision that required Robinson to sell his shares back to Centronics, at his original cost, if he wished to dispose of them in less than one year from the day he exercised the stock option. * * *

The option agreement also required that the stock certificate issued to Robinson carry the following legend:

> The shares represented by this certificate have not been registered under the Securities Act of 1933 and may not be sold, offered for sale or otherwise transferred or disposed unless a registration statement under such Act is in effect with respect thereto or unless the company

has received an opinion of counsel satisfactory to it, that an exemption from such registration is applicable to said shares.

To further protect its interests, Centronics placed a "stop transfer order" with the corporation's transfer agent. The stop transfer order required the agent to notify Centronics of any request to transfer Robinson's stock to a new owner and prohibited the agent from transferring the shares without Centronics approval and without an opinion of Centronics' counsel that the transfer did not violate securities laws.

On March 4, 1974, Robinson exercised the option. The present appeal requires us to determine when Robinson realized a benefit from the option agreement and when, not whether, he should have paid Federal income taxes on it.

II. *Section 83*

Section 83 of the Internal Revenue Code * * * states that the value of property transferred in connection with the performance of services shall be taxable income "in the first taxable year in which the rights of the person having the beneficial interest in such property *are transferable or are not subject to a substantial risk of forfeiture,* whichever is applicable." I.R.C. § 83(a) (emphasis added). Appellant contends that the sellback provision of the option agreement, combined with the legend on the stock certificate and the stop transfer order, (1) subjected his stock to a substantial risk of forfeiture and (2) rendered it non-transferable until 1975. We agree and therefore reverse the opinion of the Tax Court below.

III. *"Substantial Risk of Forfeiture"*

While not defining the term "substantial risk of forfeiture," Congress offered some guidance as to its meaning in § 83(c)(1) and in the legislative history of that section. I.R.C. § 83(c)(1) is a "special rule" that states "[t]he rights of a person in property are subject to a substantial risk of forfeiture if such person's rights to full enjoyment of such property are conditioned upon the future performance of substantial services by any individual." The Committee Reports on the Bill enacting § 83 explain that "[i]n other cases the question of whether there is a substantial risk of forfeiture depends upon the facts and circumstances." H.R.Rep. No. 91–413 (Pt. 1), 91st Cong., 1st Sess. 62, 88 * * *; S.Rep No. 91–552, 91st Cong. 1st Sess. 119, 121 * * *. Congress thus left further definition of the term to the Treasury Department and the courts.

The Treasury Regulations pursuant to § 83, like § 83 itself, do not define what constitutes a substantial risk of forfeiture. They recapitulate the "special rule" and the facts and circumstances test and then add an additional rule: "A substantial risk of forfeiture exists where rights in property that are transferred are conditioned, directly or indirectly, ... upon the occurrence of a condition *related to a purpose of the transfer,* and the possibility of forfeiture is substantial if such condition is not satisfied." 26 C.F.R. 1.83–3(c)(1) (emphasis added). Satisfaction of either the § 83(c)(1) special rule or the Treasury regulation additional rule indicates a substantial risk. In other cases the "facts and circumstances" may still be such that there is a substantial risk of forfeiture.[2]

Neither the statutory nor the regulatory rule fit appellant's situation. We, therefore, must resort to logic and common sense. The sellback provision of the stock option agreement contemplates a forfeiture of Robinson's beneficial interest in the stock transfer if he sells the stock in less than a year. But the forfeiture is not conditioned on his future performance of any services. And the Tax Court found that the sellback provision was not related to the purpose of the transfer.

Accordingly, we are left with the question of whether, in the facts and circumstances of Robinson's case, the risk of forfeiture was "substantial." The Tax Court found that the risk was insubstantial, because the sellback provision would expire in one year. We cannot agree with this logic.

Whether a condition creates a substantial risk of forfeiture is not a function of time, nor, as the Commissioner urges in this appeal, is it a function of the likelihood of triggering the event that will require the forfeiture to take place. To the extent that the substantiality of the risk depends on probability, the probability should be measured by the likelihood of the forfeiture taking place once the triggering event occurs. *See* 26 C.F.R. 1.83–3(c)(1). Here, the likelihood of the triggering event (sale of the stock in less than a year) was very low; Robinson would not be so foolish as to risk the forfeiture. But, if he had sold the stock in less than a year, the probability of Centronics enforcing the sellback provision was very high. The company had a fiduciary duty to its shareholders to do so.

This probability alone, however, does not satisfy § 83(a). Otherwise, a clever draftsman could evade the purpose of § 83 by adding a formula forfeiture provision to transfers of property in exchange for services. Congress enacted § 83 to curb the use of sales restrictions to defer taxes on property given in exchange for services. * * * Congress drafted a broad rule that declares property to be vested and taxable as soon as it can be transferred or is not subject to a "*substantial* risk of forfeiture." The use of the modifier *substantial* indicates that the risk must be real; it must serve a significant business purpose apart from the tax laws.

The § 83(c)(1) special rule providing that conditions based on future performance of services create a substantial risk illustrates this requirement. Conditioning the right to property on future performance of services serves an important business purpose: ensuring continued performance and loyalty. The Treasury regulation additional rule, that conditions related to the purpose of the transfer of the property create a substantial risk, is consistent with this principle as well. Section 83 property is transferred for some reason that has an existence apart from the tax laws: for example, the transferee invented a new device, performed some essential task, or

2. Accordingly, the Tax Court erred when it treated the § 83(c)(1) special rule and the Treasury Regulation additional rule as defining the only conditions that create a substantial risk under IRC § 83.

brought some needed expertise to the organization. If the risk of forfeiture relates to this reason, it is substantial.

Applying the same principle to this case we find that Robinson's stock was subject to a substantial risk of forfeiture until the sellback provision elapsed. The tax court found as fact that Centronics imposed the sellback provision to prevent Robinson from engaging in insider trading. The officers of the corporation wanted to prevent Robinson from using his knowledge of the company to make a profit on a short term change in the corporation's position.[4] The Sellback condition thus served a significant business purpose.[5]

IV. *"Transferable"*

We now turn to the analysis of whether Robinson's stock was transferable according to § 83(a) prior to the expiration of the sellback provision. Under § 83, rights in property are transferable "only if the rights in such property of any transferee are not subject to a substantial risk of forfeiture." § 83(c)(2).[6] We have already held that the sellback provision subjected Robinson's interest in the stock to a substantial risk of forfeiture. The transferability question hinges on whether Robinson can transfer the stock free of this risk.

Under Delaware law a purchaser of stock who has knowledge of a sale restriction on the stock is bound by the restriction. * * * Accordingly, only a purchaser who was unaware of the sell-back provision would not be bound by it. In order to sell the stock to an unknowing purchaser, the Tax Court found that Robinson would have faced several hurdles which he could have surmounted in only extraordinarily unusual circumstances.

First, he would have had to violate the option agreement forbidding him to sell the shares to anyone without offering them first to Centronics at his original cost. Robinson testified, and the Commission does not dispute, that such a breach would have threatened his continued employ-

4. In enacting Rule 16b, Congress determined that insider trading with a period between purchase and sale of six months or less was of sufficient concern that it should be prohibited. Recognizing that the harm caused by such short swing insider trading accrues to the corporation, Congress provided that any profit made on the prohibited trade should be disgorged to the corporation. The likelihood of harm to the corporation from insider trading diminishes as the length of time between purchase and sale increases. Centronics extended the statutory six month forfeiture to a contractual one year forfeiture. We express strong reservations on whether contractual insider trading forfeitures extending longer than one year would create a substantial risk of forfeiture.

5. The 1981 amendment to § 83 that declares that the risk of forfeiture from the Rule 16b insider trading forfeiture provision is "substantial" supports our conclusion. *See* 95 Stat. 260, 26 U.S.C. § 83(c)(3). The 16b insider trading forfeiture provision has the same effect as Robinson's sellback condition. While the amendment was not explicitly retroactive (and we make no determination that it should or should not be given retroactive effect), it suggests that a similar contractual risk of forfeiture should be considered substantial as well.

6. We agree with appellant that this § 83(1)(2) "special rule" does not define "transferable." But because we find that this special rule covers appellant's case we have no need to go into the exact definition of "transferable" within § 83.

ment with Centronics. Second, the stock certificate carried a legend that the Tax Court concluded limited "lawful transfer of the restricted securities ... [to] an exempt private resale unless the Option Stock were registered." As the Tax Court found, "a purchaser in a private resale must be an informed person, frequently represented by counsel." Finally, the stop transfer order prohibited the transfer of the official stock certificate without Centronics' approval.

These hurdles rendered the stock nontransferable until the sellback provision lapsed. The Tax Court's contrary finding was not based upon evidence of the practical workings of the securities markets, but rather upon a hypothetical, back-door transfer in breach of the option agreement. This was error. Transferability under § 83(a) depends on standard practices and assumes observance of contracts, not hypothetical *sub rosa* violations.

Accordingly, the order of the Tax Court is reversed.

NOTES

1. Earlier, this chapter considered issuing restricted shares in order to delay the tax faced by individuals receiving stock in exchange for services. To achieve this effect, the restraint must both render the shares non-transferable, and subject them to a substantial risk of forfeiture—in which case the recipient need recognize no income until the shares become free of either condition. I.R.C. § 83(a). These two, conditions, however, are not completely independent. Section 83(c)(2) deems property not transferable if it remains subject to a substantial risk of forfeiture in the hands of any transferee. This means that the pivotal question governing whether a restriction will postpone recognition under Section 83(a) normally is whether the restraint creates a substantial risk of forfeiture. As *Robinson* illustrates, determining this fact is not always easy.

Section 83(c)(1) specifies that a substantial risk of forfeiture exists when an individual's right to full enjoyment of property rests upon future performance by him or her of substantial services. Thus, a performance incentive provision which requires surrender of shares if their recipient does not do a significant task creates such a risk. *See* Treas.Reg. § 1.83-3(c)(4) Ex.(3). Suppose, however, the parties condition retention of the shares upon some factor other than performing future work—for example, upon not competing with the issuer after retirement. This raises the question of whether Section 83(c)(1) is the exclusive definition of conditions which create a substantial risk of forfeiture. The statute itself is not entirely clear. The legislative history and the regulations, however, indicate Section 83(c)(1) is not exclusive. S. Rep. No. 91-552, 91st Cong., 1st Sess. 121 (1969); Treas.Reg. § 1.83-3(c)(1). Rather, they state the question of whether such a risk exists turns upon the facts and circumstances.

How then can one determine if a risk is substantial? At first glance, this would seem to require evaluating how likely the loss of the shares is to occur—if improbable, then the risk is minimal rather than substantial.

Notice, however, the court in *Robinson* only looked to the probability of the corporation enforcing its rights. (For example, had Mr. Robinson possessed sufficient control of the company to prevent it exercising its option to reclaim the shares, the risk would not have been substantial. *See* Treas. Reg. § 1.83–3(c)(3).) The court rejected the Internal Revenue Service's position, and refused to look at the probability of the event occurring which triggered the company's right. (In the case, this event—Mr. Robinson's attempt to sell the stock despite the restriction within the period of only one year—was very unlikely.) In lieu of examining the triggering event's chances of occurring, the court equated substantiality with having a business purpose for the restriction. In fact, the regulations suggest a similar approach when they state a risk is substantial if the condition relates to the purpose for which the corporation transferred the restricted shares. Treas. Reg. § 1.83–3(c)(1). (While the purpose for the restriction in *Robinson* did not relate to the reason why Mr. Robinson received his shares, the court held this portion of the regulations was not exclusive.)

Beyond the question of whether a risk is substantial, one must also ask whether its consequence equals a forfeiture. Surrendering the stock without compensation clearly qualifies. *See* Treas.Reg. § 1.83–3(c)(4) Ex.(3). Suppose, however, the restriction requires payment in exchange for returning the shares. The regulations state that a restraint requiring payment of fair market value for returning the property does not constitute a risk of forfeiture. Treas.Reg. § 1.83–3(c)(1). This implies paying less than fair market value can be a forfeiture. *See* Treas.Reg. § 1.83–3(c)(4) Ex.(1),(4). If payment does not preclude a surrender from constituting a forfeiture, even a buy-out agreement can constitute a restriction postponing recognition under Section 83(a). (This assumes a business purpose for the contract, and the price formula, such as a fixed price or book value, will diverge significantly from fair market value.) In fact, *Robinson* involved one type of buy-out agreement—a first option.

In *Robinson,* the restriction ran only one year. Suppose, at the other extreme, the buy-out provision runs until the shareholder's death or retirement, at which point the shareholder, or his or her estate, must sell the shares back to the corporation. As discussed later, this would be an example of a restriction which by its terms can never lapse. *See* Treas.Reg. § 1.83–5(c) Ex.(1). Both the legislative history and the regulations suggest non-lapse restrictions may not constitute a substantial risk of forfeiture. *See* S. Rep. No. 91–552, 91st Cong. 1st Sess. 121 (1969); Treas.Reg. § 1.83–3(c)(1). Instead, such restraints lower the value of the property, and thus the amount of income immediately recognized. I.R.C. § 83(a).

Finally, instead of a transfer restriction consisting essentially of a buy-out agreement, consider the effect of a prohibition on transfer without consent. As explained above, risks of forfeiture may render shares "non-transferable" within the meaning of Section 83. Is the converse true: Can prevention of transfer expose shares to a substantial risk of forfeiture? While there is no risk with a consent restraint that the recipient must give up the stock, one might argue the shares could decline in value during the period the restriction precludes their sale (and this decline would be a "forfeiture"). The regulations apparently reject this line of reasoning. Treas.Reg. § 1.83–3(c)(1). *See also Merlo v. Commissioner*, T.C. Memo 2005–178 (restriction on sale because of corporate policy against insider trading did not equal a risk of forfeiture).

2. The court in *Robinson* also discussed the shares' transferability. There is an important non-tax lesson here for parties imposing share transfer restrictions. Such a restraint does little good without ensuring prospective purchasers receive notice of it. This means putting a warning on the share certificates.

3. In *Robinson,* the recipient wanted the court to find the shares subject to a substantial risk of forfeiture in order to delay recognition of taxable income. Recall, however, the trade-offs this delay entails. It postpones the corporation's deduction. I.R.C. § 83(h). (Although, it increases the amount of the deduction if the property appreciates.) It may deny the recipient the tax incidents going to an owner of stock (for example, under subchapter S). *See* Treas.Reg. § 1.83–1(a). Most significantly, it increases the amount of ordinary income the recipient must recognize if the shares appreciate before the restriction expires. *See* I.R.C. § 83(a). If individuals are contemplating restraints primarily to delay taxable income, these disadvantages may lead them to reconsider. Often, however, parties impose share transfer restrictions for a variety of business and legal reasons discussed above having nothing to do with Section 83. (In fact, without a business purpose, the restriction will not delay recognition under the test applied in *Robinson.*) If parties imposed the restriction for business reasons and do not desire to delay recognition, what can they do to avoid the disadvantages Section 83 may impose upon the recipient of restricted shares?

Section 83(b) allows one who receives restricted property in connection with performing services to elect immediate recognition of the difference between the property's present value (disregarding the restriction) and what the recipient paid for it. One problem with a Section 83(b) election lies in what happens if the recipient thereafter forfeits the shares. He or she will have paid tax on the property's excess of value (without considering the risk of loss) over its purchase price, but cannot obtain a deduction for suffering this loss. I.R.C. § 83(b)(1). (The regulations allow the recipient to obtain a capital loss limited to the amount he or she paid for the property. Treas. Reg. § 1.83–2(a).) This prospect may lead the parties to prefer to draft restrictions which do not create a substantial risk of forfeiture—assuming they can otherwise accomplish their objectives. As the following case illustrates, in one situation persons should automatically choose to make a Section 83(b) election.

Alves v. Commissioner of Internal Revenue

734 F.2d 478 (9th Cir.1984).

■ SCHROEDER, CIRCUIT JUDGE.

Lawrence J. Alves appeals a Tax Court decision sustaining the Commissioner's finding of deficiency for 1974 and 1975. * * * The appeal raises an unusual question under Section 83 of the Internal Revenue Code * * *. Section 83 requires that an employee who has purchased restricted stock in connection with his "performance of services" must include as ordinary income the stock's appreciation in value between the time of purchase and the time the restrictions lapse, unless at the time he purchased the stock he elected to include as income the difference between the purchase price and the fair market value at that time. The issue here is whether Section 83 applies to an employee's purchase of restricted stock when, according to the stipulation of the parties, the amount paid for the stock equaled its full fair market value, without regard to any restrictions. The Tax Court, with two dissenting opinions, held that Section 83 applies to all restricted stock that is transferred "in connection with the performance of services," regardless of the amount paid for it. * * * We affirm.

FACTS

General Digital Corporation (the company) was formed in April, 1970, to manufacture and market micro-electronic circuits. At its first meeting, the company's board of directors * * * voted to sell an additional 264,000 shares of common stock to seven named individuals, including Alves. All seven became company employees.

Alves joined the company as vice-president for finance and administration. As part of an employment and stock purchase agreement dated May 22, 1970, the company agreed to sell Alves 40,000 shares of common stock at ten cents per share "in order to raise capital for the Company's initial operations while at the same time providing the Employee with an additional interest in the Company * * *." * * * The six other named individuals signed similar agreements on the same day. The agreement divided Alves' shares into three categories: one-third were subject to repurchase by the company at ten cents per share if Alves left within four years; one-third were subject to repurchase if he left the company within five years; and one-third were unrestricted.

* * *

On July 1, 1974, when the restrictions on the four-year shares lapsed, Alves still owned 4,667 four-year shares that had a fair market value at that time of $6 per share. On March 24, 1975, the restrictions on the 7,093 remaining five-year shares lapsed with the fair market value at $3.43 per share.

* * * Alves * * * did not report the difference between the fair market value of the four and five-year shares when the restrictions ended, and the purchase price paid for the shares. The Commissioner treated the difference as ordinary income in 1974 and 1975, pursuant to Section 83(a).

In proceedings before the Tax Court, the parties stipulated that: (1) General Digital's common stock had a fair market value of 10 cents per share on the date Alves entered into the employment and stock purchase agreement; (2) the stock restrictions were imposed to "provide some assurance that key personal would remain with the company for a number of years;" (3) Alves did not make an election under Section 83(b) when the restricted stock was received; (4) the free shares were not includable in gross income under Section 83; and (5) the four and five-year restricted shares were subject to a substantial risk of forfeiture until July 1, 1974, and March 24, 1975, respectively.

* * *

DISCUSSION

* * *

The Tax Court concluded that Alves obtained the stock "in connection with the performance of services" as company vice-president. To the extent that this conclusion is a finding of fact, it is not clearly erroneous. * * * Although payment of full fair market value may be one indication that stock was not transferred in connection with the performance of services, the record shows that until the company sold stock to TVI, it issued stock only to its officers, directors, and employees, with the exception of the shares sold to the underwriter. Alves purchased the stock when he signed his employment agreement and the stock restrictions were linked explicitly to his tenure with the company. In addition, the parties stipulated that the restricted stock's purpose was to ensure that key personnel would remain with the company. Nothing in the record suggests that Alves could have purchased the stock had he not agreed to join the company.

Alves maintains that, as a matter of law, Section 83(a) should not extend to purchases for full fair market value. He argues that "in connection with" means that the employee is receiving compensation for his performance of services. In the unusual situation where the employee pays the same amount for restricted and unrestricted stock, the restriction has no effect on value, and hence, Alves contends, there is no compensation.

The plain language of Section 83(a) belies Alves' argument. The statute applies to all property transferred in connection with the performance of services. No reference is made to the term "compensation." Nor is there any statutory requirement that property have a fair market value in excess of the amount paid at the time of transfer. Indeed, if Congress intended Section 83(a) to apply solely to restricted stock used to compensate employees, it could have used much narrower language. Instead, Congress made section 83(a) applicable to all restricted "property," not just stock; to property transferred to "any person," not just to employees; and to property transferred "in connection with * * * services" not just compensation for employment.

* * *

Alves suggests that the language of Section 83(b) indicates that Congress meant for that section to apply only to bargain purchases and that Section 83(a) should be interpreted in the same way. Section 83(b) allows taxpayers to elect to include as income in the year of transfer "the excess" of the full fair market value over the purchase price. Alves contends that a taxpayer who pays full fair market value would have "zero excess," and would fall outside the terms of Section 83(b).

Section 83(b), however, is not a limitation upon Section 83(a). Congress designed Section 83(b) merely to add "flexibility," not to condition Section 83(a) on the presence or absence of an "excess." * * *

Moreover, nothing in Section 83(b) precludes a taxpayer who has paid full market value for restricted stock from making an 83(b) election. Treasury Regulations promulgated in 1978 and made retroactive to 1969 specifically provide that Section 83(b) is available in situations of zero excess:

> If property is transferred * * * in connection with the performance of services, the person performing such services may elect to include in gross income under Section 83(b) the excess (if any) of the fair market value of the property at the time of transfer * * * over the amount (if any) paid for such property * * * *The fact that the transferee has paid full value for the property transferred, realizing no bargain element in the transaction, does not preclude the use of the election as provided for in this section.* 26 C.F.R. § 1.83.2(a) (1983) (emphasis added). * * *

Alves last contends that since every taxpayer who pays full fair market value for restricted stock would, if well informed, choose the Section 83(b) election to hedge against any appreciation, applying Section 83(a) to the unfortunate taxpayer who made no election is simply a trap for the unwary. The tax laws often make an affirmative election necessary. Section 83(b) is but one example of a provision requiring taxpayers to act or suffer less attractive tax consequences. A taxpayer wishing to avoid treatment of appreciation as ordinary income must make an affirmative election under 83(b) in the year the stock was acquired.

* * * The decision of the Tax Court is affirmed.

NOTES

1. Unfortunately, a Section 83(b) election may not always be available. For example, in *Cramer v. Commissioner*, 101 T.C. 225 (1993), *aff'd.*, 64 F.3d 1406 (9th Cir.1995), the court held that the recipient of a stock option lacking a readily ascertainable fair market value cannot make a Section 83(b) election. On the other hand, in *Theophilos v. Commissioner,* 85 F.3d 440 (9th Cir.1996), the Ninth Circuit held that a contract by an employee to buy stock was itself property for purposes of Section 83, and, hence, the employee could pay tax under Section 83(a) based upon the value of the contract, rather than the higher value of the stock the employee later purchased under the contract. Consider the tax planning impact of the apparent distinction between *Cramer* and *Theophilos* in a situation in which stock is expected to increase in value prior to a service provider's actual purchase of the shares under rights granted at the time the service provider starts work. Under *Cramer*, if the employee receives an option to

purchase stock, then valuation cannot occur until exercise of the options; under *Theophilos*, if the employee enters a contract binding the employee to purchase the shares, then valuation can occur upon entry of the contract. Of course, the recipient must weigh the tax advantage of the contract to purchase, against the freedom from economic risk (if the stock declines before the purchase date) under the option.

2. Only a share transfer restriction which creates a substantial risk of forfeiture postpones recognition under Section 83(a). What effect can other restrictions have on the tax obligations of an individual who receives stock in connection with performing services? Typically, a buyer will not pay as much for stock subject to a transfer restraint as he or she would pay without the limit on resale. Nevertheless, Section 83 does not allow the recipient to take the restraint into account in valuing his or her shares. I.R.C. § 83(a). An exception exists if the restriction by its terms will never lapse. In fact, Section 83(d)(1) makes a non–lapse restriction, which sets the only price the recipient can sell his or her shares for, prima facie evidence that the value of the shares is the price set by the agreement. Hence, as suggested earlier, the parties might use such an agreement to lower the tax faced by an individual receiving stock for services. The regulations take some of the potential away from this approach. They indicate the Service might seek to prove that a self–evidently low price formula does not equal the fair market value of the shares, even as so restricted. See Treas.Reg. § 1.83–5(a), (c) Ex. (4). (On the other hand, the regulations view an agreement which specifies the price simply as fair market value, as not constituting a non–lapse restriction. Treas.Reg. § 1.83–3(h).)

According to the regulations, a non-lapse restriction is a transfer restraint which permanently binds the recipient to offer or sell the property at a price determined by formula (in essence, a permanent buy-out agreement). Treas. Reg. § 1.83–3(h). To say the restriction is permanent, however, does not mean it never ends. The requirement that a recipient (or his or her estate) return shares upon retirement, death, or a desire to sell means the restriction ultimately must come to an end upon the reconveyance. Nevertheless, this is a non-lapse restriction, because the recipient (or his or her transferee, other than the issuer) cannot hold the shares free of the restraint. *See* Treas.Reg. §§ 1.83–3(h), 1.83–5.

Moreover, despite the fact the terms of a restriction may state it will never lapse, it is always possible for the company to cancel the restraint. For instance, if the restraint gives the corporation a right of first refusal, the company may decline to exercise its right. *See* Treas.Reg. § 1.83–5(b)(1). In this event, Section 83(d)(2) requires the recipient to recognize as ordinary income the amount by which the stock increased in value due to canceling the restraint (less anything he or she paid to get the company to cancel). This requirement, however, does not apply if the recipient can show the cancellation was not compensatory (for example, if the company did not exercise the right of first refusal because it lacked the funds). Also, for the recipient to avoid tax, the company must agree not to claim a deduction for the cancellation.

3. Share transfers and transfer restrictions raise further concerns when dealing with S corporations. Transfer of stock could upset in a couple of ways eligibility as a "Small Business Corporation," thereby causing a termination of the S election. *But see* I.R.C. § 1362(f) (allowing S corporations to avoid inadvertent terminations by taking corrective steps within a reasonable time after discovering the event which upset eligibility). If the conveyance breaks up blocks of stock (as occurs when the transferor sells some and keeps some) the result can be, in an extreme case, to exceed the limit of 100 unrelated shareholders. Alternately, the transferor may convey to a corporation, partnership or trust ineligible to be a shareholder in an S corporation. (A probate or bankruptcy estate can be a stockholder in an S corporation, however. I.R.C. § 1361(b)(1)(B), (c)(3). Hence, the transfer to an estate upon a shareholder's death or bankruptcy does not end the S election.) The 1982 amendments to subchapter S eliminated one former concern with transfers. Conveying shares to an individual who refuses to consent to continued S status does not end an S election already in effect—albeit the code requires unanimous consent to elect S treatment initially, and a majority shareholder vote can terminate the election. I.R.C. § 1362(a)(2),(d)(1)(B). Because of the problems transfers can create with S eligibility, S corporations often restrict transfer of their shares. Keep in mind, however, unlike the situation under some state corporation codes which mandate transfer restrictions in order to be a statutory close corporation (*e.g.,* Del. Gen. Corp. Law § 342(a)(2)), nothing in Subchapter S requires restraining alienation of stock.

Beyond the question of whether transfer restraints can help preserve eligibility for S treatment, one might ask can they ever threaten this eligibility. Specifically, suppose the parties restrict only some of the shares issued by the corporation. Does this create two classes of stock? See Treas. Reg. § 1.1361–1(*l*)(2)(iii)(A), (B) (bona fide agreements to purchase stock at time of death, divorce, disability or termination of employment, or any buy-sell or redemption agreement which is not for a principal purpose of avoiding the one class of stock requirement, will not create a problem under the one class requirement).

Finally, recall the tax issues raised by transfers of interests in a firm treated as a partnership for income tax purposes. Do transfers of shares in an S corporation raise any of the same concerns? Subchapter S has no equivalent to a Section 754 election to adjust the firm's basis in its assets in order to maintain parity with its owners' basis in their interests. As pointed out in Chapter II, this creates something of a disadvantage for an S corporation vis-a-vis a partnership—at least from the standpoint of an individual buying from a prior owner at a price greater than the prior owner's basis. On the other hand, Subchapter S has no equivalent to Section 708(b)(1)(B), which terminates a partnership for tax purposes upon sale or exchange within one year of over half the interests in the firm. Instead, an S corporation can survive even a 100 percent turnover in its ownership. Also, an S corporation shareholder selling out need not worry about Section 751(a), which removes from capital gains treatment the portion of a partner's sale representing certain ordinary income items. He or she need not worry about recognition due to relief from liabilities, as would a selling partner. *See* I.R.C. § 752(d). One area does raise similar concerns. How do the parties allocate income and loss items between buyer and seller when the transfer occurs during the middle of a tax year? Section 1377(a)(1) gives specific guidance for S corporations: Each day of the year receives an equal portion of each tax item (no matter when in the year the transaction producing the item actually occurred), which the parties then allocate pro-rata among the owners of the shares on that day. Notice, this creates the potential for events controlled by the buyer of an S corporation to impact the tax paid by the seller. As an extreme example, the corporation may have lost money before the sale, but made money after the sale sufficient to yield a net profit for the year. The seller then will recognize taxable income without having obtained the economic benefit of the later profit. Section 1377(a)(2) provides an option. The affected parties may agree, in the case of a complete termination of a shareholder's interest, to have two short tax years for the company—one up to, and one after, the termination. The regulations also allow the stockholders to elect this option whenever a shareholder disposes of over 20 percent of the corporation's outstanding stock—even if this does not amount to a complete termination of the shareholder's interest. Treas. Reg. § 1.1368–1(g). There will also be no pro-rata allocation, and two short tax years, if the buyer terminates the S election. I.R.C. § 1362(e)(3). Incidentally, following the transfer of all of a shareholder's stock in an S corporation, neither the transferor (who is no longer a shareholder), nor the transferee (who cannot succeed to the transferor's right to take suspended losses), can thereafter take advantage of any carried forward losses from before the transfer, which had been unused for lack of basis in the transferred shares. Treas. Reg. § 1.1366–2(a)(5).

2. DISSOLUTION FOR DEADLOCK OR OPPRESSION: A POSTSCRIPT RE FAILED PLANNING

Gidwitz v. Lanzit Corrugated Box Co.

20 Ill.2d 208, 170 N.E.2d 131 (1960).

■ HERSHEY, JUSTICE.

This action was brought by certain shareholders of Lanzit Corrugated Box Co., an Illinois corporation, under subparagraphs (1), (2), and (3) of paragraph (a) of Section 86 of the Business Corporation Act of this State * * * on the theory that both the directors and shareholders of this corporation are deadlocked and that the original defendants had committed illegal, oppressive or fraudulent acts.

* * *

The [trial] court * * * decreed that the assets and business of the corporation be liquidated * * *

From this voluminous record the undisputed facts appear to be that this is a family corporation, all shares being owned or controlled by the Gidwitz family, so that fifty percent of the shares are owned by the defendants and the other fifty percent owned or claimed to be under the control of plaintiffs.

Subparagraphs (1),(2), and (3) of paragraph (a) of section 86 of the Business Corporation Act * * * invoked here, read as follows:

"Courts of equity shall have full power to liquidate the assets and business of a corporation:

"(a) In an action by a shareholder when it is made to appear:

"(1) That the directors are deadlocked in the management of the corporate affairs and the shareholders are unable to break the deadlock, and that irreparable injury to the corporation is being suffered or is threatened by reason thereof; or

"(2) That the shareholders are deadlocked in voting power, and have failed, for a period which includes at least two consecutive annual meeting dates, to elect successors to directors whose term has expired or would have expired upon the election of their successors; or

"(3) That the acts of the directors or those in control of the corporation are illegal, oppressive, or fraudulent, * * *."

We turn at once to subparagraph (3) of paragraph (a) of Section 86, which applies when "the acts of the directors or those in control of the corporation are illegal, oppressive, or fraudulent." There appears to be no claim that the acts of the directors or officers in this case are "illegal" or "fraudulent," but only that the "deadlock" is "oppressive" to the plaintiffs as shareholders because they, as directors, are precluded thereby from participating at the policy level in the direction and supervision of Joseph Gidwitz's activities as president of the corporation.

* * *

In the situation at hand we have neither majority nor minority stockholders—the shares are split between the dissident factions and families. By virtue of his assumption of the prime office of president at a time of mutual agreement between the owners of all of the shares, and the support of his family with one half of the shares, Joseph Gidwitz is able to manage, operate, and control Lanzit almost as a sole proprietorship, while paying technical respect to the existing corporate structure and the laws relating to corporations. * * *

It appears from the record that for ten years no annual meeting of shareholders has been held at which the shareholders were called upon or permitted to vote for directors of the corporations. This indicates a deprivation of shareholders' rights. * * * A special meeting of shareholders was held on February 16, 1959, pursuant to the call of Victor and Carrie

Gidwitz at which they proposed that the number of directors be increased to five. The proposal was ruled out of order by Joseph Gidwitz.

Prior to this special shareholders' meeting, the plaintiffs also called a directors' meeting on February 13, 1959. At the directors' meeting seven resolutions were presented, including an amendment to the bylaws to increase the board of directors from four to five directors. On each resolution the vote was evenly split between the directors from the two families.

* * *

From these actions it is readily apparent that the two families, each owning and voting one half of the stock, are irreconcilably split in all matters relating to the management of the corporation—and that the family of Joseph Gidwitz is determined to completely control the operation and management of the corporation by virtue of his corporate office as president, regardless of the views of the other one-half of the corporate shareholders or directors.

While during the past ten years there were a few meetings of directors called and held, it appears that at none of them were matters of business or corporate policy presented to the board for action, discussion or approval.

* * *

The bylaws of the corporation require that the president shall submit to the board of directors and to the shareholders, when so requested, a full report of the operations of the corporation, and shall from time to time report to the board of directors all matters within his knowledge which the best interests of the corporation require to be brought to their notice. This Joseph avoided by either not having shareholders' or board-of-directors' meetings, or choosing to find nothing, that could affect his control or management, which the best interests of the corporation required be called to the attention of the directors or shareholders.

* * *

Section 10(g) of Article III of the bylaws of this corporation provided that the powers of the directors were "To appoint or employ and remove, suspend or discharge the registered agent, such subordinate officers, agents, factors and employees of the corporation as the Board may deem necessary from time to time, and to determine and fix their duties; and to fix, increase and decrease their remuneration as when so deemed advisable by the Board." Other provisions in the by-laws only permitted the president to appoint, discharge and fix the compensation of "employees and agents" of the corporation.

In 1954, Joseph, as president of Lanzit, gave salary increases to two assistant secretaries of the company without authorization from or approval by the board of directors. Assistant secretaries of the corporation are corporate officers as provided by Section 1 of Article IV of the bylaws.

Joseph likewise provided for charges against Victor's salary as secretary and treasurer, and made deductions from Victor's salary without authority or approval from the board of directors.

* * * Joseph Gidwitz was president of Rockwell Realty in which all of the shareholders of Lanzit were also owners, and, with his two brothers, was a partner in Tribros Investment Company. Joseph negotiated five interest-bearing loans with these two companies without consulting the board of directors. * * * Joseph, in effect, borrowed from himself and realized a profit thereon.

It further appears that in no one of said loans, nor in the loan from the American National Bank, did Joseph seek the advice of, consult with or inform the board of directors.

Joseph executed to himself a proxy to vote the Chippewa stock owned by Lanzit without consulting the board of directors, and without knowing the Lanzit bylaw provisions in respect to the execution of proxies.

Again without consultation with or authorization from the board of directors, Joseph, as president of Lanzit, organized one of Lanzit's departments into a separate corporation which, in the course of five years, sustained losses alleged to be as much as $290,000. Joseph testified that he never consulted the directors of Lanzit at any time as to how the separate corporation's stock, known as "Custom Made Container Company," should be voted, or who its directors or officers should be.

The record in addition supports numerous acts of hostility toward and deprivation of the rights of Victor Gidwitz and Carrie Gidwitz as stockholders.

It is clear that Joseph Gidwitz has used his position as president of a closely held corporation, split fifty-fifty in stock ownership between his family and the family of plaintiffs, to completely control and manage the corporation without majority stock support. The plaintiffs, as stockholders, have been effectively deprived of their rights and privileges. The record indicates a continuing course of conduct on the part of Joseph Gidwitz and the defendants to seize and hold the corporate entity to the complete exclusion of plaintiffs from their lawful right to participate in the management of Lanzit. Moreover, plaintiffs, have even been deprived of their effective power as directors and officers of Lanzit.

Since 1948 the shareholders of the corporation have received no dividends, and Joseph, as president, has not seen fit to present the matter of payment of dividends to the board of directors.

The record exhibits a continuing course of oppressive conduct for which the future holds little or no hope of abatement. A continuing course of refusal of the controlling group to agree with the plaintiffs on any issue is evidenced. Moreover, Joseph has acted in an arbitrary and highhanded manner as president of the corporation—refusing to follow the dictates or direction of the corporate bylaws, or to subordinate his actions to the advice or control of the board of directors. The rights to which plaintiffs as officers, directors and shareholders of Lanzit are entitled have been abused and denied. It is not necessary that fraud, illegality or even loss be shown to exhibit oppression of plaintiffs and their interest in the corporation. Corporate dissolution is a drastic remedy that must not be lightly invoked. * * * Nevertheless, when oppression is positively shown, the oppressed are entitled to the protection of the law.

* * *

The cumulative effects of these many acts and incidents, and their indicated continuing nature, combine to constitute that oppression which entitles plaintiffs to the only remedy provided by law—dissolution.

In view of these conclusions it is unnecessary to discuss the applicability of subparagraphs (1) and (2) of paragraph (a) of Section 86.

The decree of the superior court of Cook County is, therefore, affirmed.

NOTE

Gidwitz is typical of numerous cases brought to dissolve a closely held corporation beset with factional strife. The question for the court was whether the statutory grounds for dissolution existed. (In this regard, compare the Illinois statute involved in *Gidwitz,* with Cal. Corp. Code § 1800, N.Y. Bus. Corp. Law §§ 1104, 1104–a, and M.B.C.A. § 14.30. *See also* Del. Gen. Corp. Law § 226 (authorizing appointment of a custodian in case of deadlock).) From a planning prospective, however, the case presents a different issue. Was it possible at the formation stage to have avoided, or at least better planned for, the problems which befell the corporation in *Gidwitz*? One can view the problems in *Gidwitz* on two levels: the symptomatic and the causal. Looking at the symptoms, which statutory ground for dissolution existed? While the court did not reach the issue, could it have been deadlock among the directors and shareholders? If so, is the lesson to avoid equal divisions of power? Alternately, was the problem "oppression" by the faction in effective control of the corporation of those out of power? (Indeed, *Gidwitz* illustrates that given the usual powers of a corporation's president, equal ownership of voting stock and an equal division of directorships may not insure an equal division of power. Should the parties curb the powers of the president to prevent this phenomenon?) Does this result suggest that a solution to deadlock is likely to increase the risk of "oppression"? If one cannot avoid either deadlock or oppression, are cures available through planning?

Arbitration may provide one possible approach to shareholder dissension. While courts traditionally allowed individuals to revoke, at any time prior to the award, their promise to arbitrate (*E.g., Jefferson County v. Barton—Douglas Contractors, Inc.,* 282 N.W.2d 155 (Iowa 1979)), most states now have statutes making agreements to arbitrate future disputes enforceable. *E.g.,* Cal. Civ. Proc. Code § 1281; N.Y. Civ. Prac. Law § 7501. Moreover, the Federal Arbitration Act makes agreements to arbitrate disputes arising out of transactions in commerce as valid and enforceable as any other contract. 9 U.S.C. § 2. This preempts state laws singling out arbitration agreements for unfavorable treatment. *E.g., Securities Indus.*

Ass'n v. Connolly, *883 F.2d 1114 (1st Cir.1989). Still, there may be legal problems with agreeing to arbitrate disputes concerning the management of a corporation, since arbitrating day-to-day issues of business judgement could conflict with the board's statutory power.* See Application of Vogel, *268 N.Y.S.2d 237, 25 A.D.2d 212 (1966),* aff'd, *19 N.Y.2d 589, 278 N.Y.S.2d 236, 224 N.E.2d 738 (1967). Some states, however, have statutes specifically allowing arbitration of management disputes.* E.g., *Ariz. Gen. Corp. Law § 10–206. Also, the Federal Arbitration Act may preempt state laws preventing arbitration of management disputes if the management of the corporation constitutes an activity in commerce.* See, e.g., Goodwin v. Elkins & Co., *730 F.2d 99 (3d Cir.1984) (involving an arbitration provision in a partnership agreement).*

Even if enforceable, how practical is an arbitration agreement as a solution for shareholder conflict? Arbitration is generally cheaper and faster than litigation. (Still, arbitrators usually charge something, and the agreement should specify who pays.) Parties can select an arbitrator with business expertise (often lacking in a judge or jury), and even use someone already familiar with the company. (Albeit, they should guard against bias. Along these lines, the agreement must specify how the parties pick the arbitrator.) Also, an arbitrator can mold more flexible relief than a court. *See, e.g., Staklinski v. Pyramid Electric Co.,* 6 N.Y.2d 159, 188 N.Y.S.2d 541, 160 N.E.2d 78 (1959) (arbitrator reinstated a manager to his position). Yet, if the shareholders' dispute does not relate to one discrete transaction, but instead pervades their entire relationship, the parties could be constantly embroiled in arbitration. This is an awkward way to run a business. Keep in mind, as well, if the parties wish arbitration to be an alternative to involuntary dissolution, perhaps they should agree not to seek such dissolution before arbitrating their dispute. *See Application of Cohen,* 183 Misc. 1034, 52 N.Y.S.2d 671 (1944) (refusal to enjoin dissolution pending arbitration). *But see In re Validation Review Assocs., Inc.,* 223 A.D.2d 134, 646 N.Y.S.2d 149 (1996) (agreement waiving rights to seek judicial dissolution might be unenforceable as contrary to public policy).

If arbitration does not work, and the shareholders cannot otherwise resolve their disputes, the only solution left may be for one to buy out the other. Hence, shareholder dissension could an appropriate triggering event for a buy-out agreement. In fact, some corporations codes give the corporation or shareholders opposing an involuntary dissolution the option to buy out the stockholder seeking dissolution at fair value. *E.g.,* Cal. Corp. Code § 2000; N.Y. Bus. Corp. Law § 1118. As in the partnership context, a buy-out agreement triggered by dissension must provide a means (especially when dealing with equal owners) of determining which party buys out the other. *Cf. Hendley v. Lee,* 676 F.Supp. 1317 (D.S.C.1987) (court ordered a buy-out as a remedy for deadlock, and selected wealthier shareholder as the buyer).

Perhaps one must go beyond dealing with symptoms. Is it possible to identify and cut off the sources of strife before they lead to deadlock or oppression. The opinion does not disclose what led to the fight among the

Gidwitz family. However, disputes in closely held businesses often find their origins in a limited number of classic sources.

O'Neal & Thompson, O'Neal's Oppression of Minority Shareholders

(2d ed. 1985).

§ 2:01. Scope of chapter

This chapter examines the business situations out of which squeeze plays typically arise, with a view to determining what are the underlying causes of squeeze-outs. Particular attention is given to the part played in squeeze-outs by the failure of businessmen and women to obtain legal advice and the failure of lawyers, when consulted, to foresee squeeze-out problems which might arise and to use in the solution of those problems timely and effective planning, drafting and other preventive law techniques.

The squeeze-out settings discussed in this chapter probably are not exhaustive. They are based, however, on hundreds of fact patterns drawn from judicial opinions or supplied by lawyers and other business advisers. Undoubtedly they are the most frequently occurring of the situations productive of squeeze plays.

* * *

Lawyers who organize a corporation or prepare buy-sell agreements or other shareholder agreements may become liable for malpractice if they fail to take appropriate steps to protect minority shareholders. * * *

§ 2:02. Greed and desire for power; personality clashes, marital discord, and family quarrels; basic conflicts of interest and disagreements over policy

As might be expected, many squeeze-outs are attributable largely to the avarice of individuals who see and seize opportunities to enlarge their power and influence and increase their wealth. Trusting or less able associates are common targets of squeeze-outs. An opportunity for a squeeze-out also often arises when a business associate is absent for a considerable time due to military service or other reasons.

* * *

Of course, dissension in a close corporation often results from "personality clashes" among shareholders. As shareholders in a close corporation usually are also directors, officers, and key employees, they come in frequent and close contact, and any dissension among them tends to escalate until a squeeze play develops. Before buying into a close corporation, a prospective shareholder should consider carefully whether the personalities of the participants and prospective participants are such that he likely can work with them harmoniously. Many persons, however, receive their interest in a close corporation by inheritance or gift and do not have an opportunity to choose their associates.

In a family company or other close corporation, a person who marries a shareholder or a relative of other shareholders may soon thereafter acquire a substantial amount of stock. * * * If the marriage is later dissolved, the stage is set for an attempt to squeeze out the ex-husband. In other situations, the wife may be subjected to a squeeze play when matrimonial discord develops. Similarly, quarrels among members of a family arising out of intrafamily jealousies or disputes may carry over into the business relations of shareholder-participants in a family company.

Nevertheless, squeeze-outs result far less often than might be supposed from sheer grabs for power or profits or from personality clashes or family quarrels. The majority of squeeze-outs cases are characterized by basic conflicts of interest among the participants in the enterprise, protracted policy disagreements, prolonged and bitter dissension prior to the squeeze play, or demonstrated inability of one or more of the participants (because of habitual drinking or lack of business skills, for example) to carry a fair share of the responsibility and work involved in operating the business. These major causes of squeeze-outs are discussed in some detail in the remaining sections of this chapter.

§ 2:03. The inactive shareholder

Whenever all the shareholders in an enterprise are actively working full time to build its business, dissension is relatively rare. Often trouble develops only after one of the original participants becomes inactive or his interest is acquired by an inactive shareholder.

A shareholder of course may withdraw from active participation in the business for many reasons. He may make a felicitous marriage and no longer be willing to remain active in the business; he may reach retirement age; he may become insane; he may sell his interest; or he may die, passing the stock to his widow or other heirs.

A great potential exists for friction between active and inactive participants. Differences are especially likely to occur over the respective amounts to allocate to salaries and dividends. Whenever all shareholders of a closely held corporation devote full time to its affairs, they ordinarily take a substantial part of the earnings of the corporation in salaries rather than in dividends to minimize "double taxation." This practice, however, is obviously not satisfactory to a shareholder who is not on the payroll.

An incapacitated shareholder or the widow of a deceased shareholder may well expect to receive the same return from the corporation that the shareholder received when he was active. The persons still active in the business, however, in all probability will not be willing to place or keep on the payroll a shareholder who is not working. They may even be opposed to paying substantial dividends to a shareholder not actively contributing to the corporation's success. The active participants, having been forced to take on additional duties, understandably may feel that the returns of the business are largely due to their efforts. Therefore, they may raise their own salaries, decrease or stop dividends, and perhaps take other steps to squeeze-out the inactive shareholder. These conflicts between the interests of active and inactive shareholders may well lead to bitter disputes and expensive litigation.

In a family company, the following pattern typically emerges (although this pattern has become less typical in recent years with more women entering the family business). The founder of the business has both male and female offspring, and these children in turn marry and have children. Male descendants are brought into the business, and eventually they become key executives. The women in the family often marry men who are active in some other business or profession. The founder, in an effort to treat all of his children the same, gives each of them the same number of shares of voting common stock.

This division of corporate interests creates a situation rife with potential conflict. * * *

The women descendants naturally begin to look upon their inheritance as simply a "piece of paper," as it is bringing them no benefits. The males, on the other hand, take the position that their sisters' livelihood is the primary responsibility of their husbands and feel no obligation to supplement their sisters' incomes by paying dividends which would be disadvantageous to the males and might adversely affect the business itself. Ordinarily, the men can attain their objectives without drawing from the corporation salaries which the courts will declare to be unreasonably high. They continue in complete control of the corporation, expand the business, and at the same time maintain a standard of living perhaps considerably higher than that enjoyed by their sisters.

* * *

§ 2:04. Death of founder or other key shareholder

The previous section shows how the death of an active shareholder can bring an inactive shareholder into the business and set up a squeeze-play situation because of the sharp conflict of interest between active and inactive shareholders. The death of a founder of a business or of a principal shareholder may also produce other circumstances conducive to dissension. For example, the successor shareholder may want to participate actively in the business; but the other participants may not be willing for him to do so because they feel that he does not have sufficient training and experience. Or personality clashes may prevent the new shareholder and the other participants from working together harmoniously. * * *

§ 2:05. The problem of the aged founder who "hangs on"

Not uncommonly the founder of an enterprise, accustomed to running it as a "one-man show," regards the company and its assets as his own absolute property. He often becomes more tyrannical as he grows older. He may insist on retaining complete control long after he should retire, imposing on the business superannuated methods and practices, ignoring wishes of his codirectors and advice of associates, and disregarding corporate procedures.

* * *

The age of a participant who retains control of an enterprise after his mental facilities have begun to fail may contribute to squeeze-outs in another way. His weakness and gullibility may be seized upon by an associate and utilized to squeeze-out a third participant.

* * *

§ 2:06. Drive of superior talent to rise

Even where all the shareholders actively participate in the management and operation of the business, dissension and eventually an attempt at squeeze-out may develop if some of the participants are obviously more competent than others. * * *

The relationship among individuals in a business enterprise is in some respects similar to that of persons in a marriage. Frequently one participant in an enterprise starts out with a status equal to that of another who over a period of time "outgrows" him. * * *

The more able participants often feel that the others are holding back the growth of the enterprise or are getting an unduly large portion of the returns of the business. Perhaps in the beginning the money, assets, or business contacts of the less able participants were needed to launch the business; but when the success of the enterprise has been assured, the more able may decide to eliminate what by then seems to them to be a parasitic group. At the same time, the less competent often develop great jealousy for the obvious talents of the gifted.

* * *

Serious dissension is likely to develop in a family company unless the family produces each generation one, and only one, strong leader capable of unifying the various factions in the family. The failure of the family to produce a strong leader leaves a vacuum which may encourage incompetent or inexperienced members of the family, hired managers, or banker-creditors to try to take over the company. On the other hand, two or more strong executives in a generation almost invariably give rise to a bitter contest for leadership.

* * *

§ 2:07. The autocratic controlling shareholder; acquiescence by some shareholders in assumption of special privileges by others

In many instances a shareholder who also holds a directorship and the chief executive position in a corporation runs the business in a one-person, autocratic manner that is not appropriate in an incorporated enterprise that has other shareholders. He disregards the views of his codirectors and completely ignores customary corporate procedures and paraphernalia. Such high-handed practices lead to conflicts with other strong-minded personalities among the shareholders and set the stage for a squeeze play.

* * *

§ 2:08. Disregard of corporate ritual and failure to keep proper records

Failure to observe the formalities of corporate operation and neglect of paper work often lead to dissension which eventuates in a squeeze-out. In many small business corporations, especially in family corporations and in businesses which were originally conducted in the partnership form, meetings of shareholders and directors are not held and traditional corporate ritual is disregarded. * * *

Informal corporate conduct and haphazard recordkeeping can produce serious trouble whenever a controversy arises among shareholders. There may be no way to establish unequivocally what corporate action has been taken on the matter in question or when and by whose authority the action was performed, particularly if some of the supposed participants are now dead or no longer employed. Without proof, each faction naturally becomes suspicious of the other and "plugs" for its own version of the facts. * * *

§ 2:10. Viewing incorporated enterprise as a "partnership" or "family business"

Many shareholders in small, incorporated businesses apparently do not understand fully the consequences which flow from incorporation, and in particular they do not realize that in the absence of special arrangement, ultimate, and near-absolute control of a corporation rests in holders of a majority of its voting shares. The participants in a small business usually think of themselves as partners and they often refer to themselves as such. In fact, a business sometimes operates originally as a partnership, perhaps for many years, before it is incorporated. The only reason for incorporation is often to obtain limited liability or some tax advantage. After incorporation, the participants assume that no change in their relationship has occurred and that partnership rules continue to apply.

* * *

This tendency of shareholders in a small incorporated enterprise to regard themselves as partners quite often leads to strife. In the first place, minority participants, thinking of themselves as partners, are surprised and hurt when majority shareholders exercise the power they have under the principle of majority rule, assume complete control of the enterprise and ignore the views and wishes of the minority.

* * *

§ 2:11. The obstreperous or uncooperative shareholder; the deteriorating shareholder-employee; majority shareholders' view that they are justified in eliminating a minority shareholder when personal relationships deteriorate

Time and again, when questioned about squeeze-out problems, lawyers and other business advisers comment on the problem of the minority shareholder who "throws his weight around" and makes life miserable for management. An unreasonable and obstreperous shareholder may voice frequent objections and criticisms of management, harass employees, demand information on corporate affairs at unreasonable times, bring shareholder's derivative actions, and in general give company managers a "rough time."

* * *

A similar problem arises whenever a shareholder who was once a capable corporate officer or key employee begins to deteriorate physically or mentally and is unable to perform his duties properly. A shareholder-employee may decline in vigor and usefulness long before he reaches retirement age, perhaps because of excessive use of alcohol, poor health, or simply loss of interest in the business. He may become generally incompetent or untrustworthy, failing to report to work during regular working hours, missing important meetings, making costly errors, and leaving company offices unlocked or company property unprotected. Whenever such deterioration occurs in the work of a business associate, relations between him and the other shareholders are likely to become strained; and they may decide not only to remove them as a corporate employee but also to try to eliminate him as a shareholder.

* * *

§ 2:12. Entry of minority shareholders into a competing business

A squeeze-play is often triggered when minority shareholders withdraw from employment with the company and enter a competing business while they continue to own stock in the old company. * * *

§ 2:13. Failure to provide properly for new inventions by inventor-shareholder

* * *

In many instances dissension eventually develops between the inventor and the other participants because no provision has been made for the possibility—indeed, in many instances, the probability—that the inventor will continue to work on the machine he has invented or the process he has evolved, will improve his original invention, or perhaps even make a new discovery which will render the old invention obsolete and the patents based on it valueless.

* * *

§ 2:14. Issuance of small number of shares as qualifying shares or as incentive to employees; gifts of shares to children

For various reasons, close corporations sometimes issue or individual shareholders sometimes transfer a few shares to a person with the intent that he will be a "nominal" shareholder and not participate in control or exercise in any substantial way the rights of a shareholder. This practice is dangerous, for not only does the recipient have inspection rights and other shareholder rights which he may decide to use, but also in a surprising number of cases he will at one time or another find himself holding the balance of power between opposing groups of shareholders. Furthermore, should corporate decisions later displease him, he may succeed, as a disgruntled holder of a few shares often does, in stirring up trouble among the other shareholders.

* * *

Whenever qualifying shares or any other small block of shares represent the balance of power in a corporation beset with dissension, the value of those shares to the competing factions increases considerably. Accordingly, the holder of such shares, out of sheer self-interest, may actively try to stir up trouble between the other shareholders. * * *

§ 2:15. Difficulty of disposing of a minority interest in a close corporation

The difficulty a holder of a minority interest in a close corporation has in disposing of his interest without serious financial loss undoubtedly prolongs dissension in many instances and encourages squeeze plays.

* * *

A minority shareholder who cannot dispose of his shares may manifest his dissatisfaction by refusing to cooperate or even by actively obstructing company operations. Realizing the minority owner's weak position, the majority may be tempted to apply a squeeze.

* * *

§ 2:16. Difficulty of valuing a business interest

Whenever some or all of the shareholders in a close corporation must agree on a precise dollar value of an interest in the business, the difficulty of valuing such an interest can initiate or contribute to dissension. Because valuation of a business is not an exact science but involves many subjective and complex determinations, shareholders may sharply disagree on their individual estimates of the value of a business interest. If they cannot reach a compromise, dissension culminating in a squeeze-out attempt may follow.

The situation which perhaps most commonly requires shareholders to place a value on a business interest occurs when a minority shareholder decides to withdraw from the business and sell his stock. * * *

The difficulty of valuing a business interest may produce a squeeze-out when majority shareholders want to sell all the corporation's assets or to merge or consolidate the corporation with another company. * * *

§ 2:17. Failure to consider all ramifications of business bargain and reduce entire bargain to writing

* * *

Wherever the participants' business bargain is not fully and accurately reflected in written documents, the potentiality for a squeeze play increases. Misunderstanding of the terms of the original agreement or of subsequent agreements modifying it can lead to bitter disputes producing a squeeze-out attempt. Oral assurances by the majority shareholder provide unreliable protection to the minority shareholder against squeeze-outs, because they may later be opportunely forgotten by the majority, or because persons who subsequently acquire control of the corporation may refuse to honor them.

* * *

§ 2:18. Undercapitalization of business

The failure of the organizers of a new business to provide it with adequate resources can lay a foundation for later dissension among the owners and an ultimate squeeze play. In a typical situation, the participants cause the corporation to issue only a small amount of stock, for example, 100 shares with a par value of one dollar each. The bulk of the money and other assets necessary to launch the enterprise is then loaned by one, some, or all of the shareholders, often on a short-term basis or at least without clearly articulated long-term arrangements to leave the assets with the company and without definite commitments to provide additional future financing if needed. Later, one of the participants may withdraw funds he had advanced the corporation, even though the corporation badly needs to retain them; or he may refuse to lend the corporation his proportionate part of additional funds then believed by his associates to be necessary for the company's success. The other shareholders are likely to conclude that he is shirking his fair share of the risks of the business and that he should not stand to gain his original share of the corporation's earnings if it should ultimately succeed. They are tempted to solve the corporation's financing problem and to reduce simultaneously the dissenting shareholder's proportionate interest in the corporation by issuing additional shares of stock to themselves or by first advancing additional sums to the corporation in the form of loans and later causing the corporation to pay off the loans by issuing stock to the lenders. * * *

§ 2:19. Failure to appreciate problems that might arise out of change in ownership and control

A person buying an interest in an existing corporation or joining with four or five other people in organizing a corporation often fails to foresee that a single individual might eventually acquire a majority of the voting stock. * * * Yet time and again in a corporation with shares more or less evenly distributed among a number of holders one of the original shareholders or even an outsider gradually buys up stock in the corporation until he gains absolute or near-absolute control.

* * *

Sometimes a person purchasing a minority interest in a corporation controlled by a majority shareholder he trusts and believes he can work with congenially does not foresee that the majority stock may eventually be sold to a purchaser with less exacting standards of business ethics who will take full advantage of the power his majority position carries. In all likelihood, when the time comes for the transfer of the majority interest, the minority shareholder is not in a financial position to purchase it. The majority shares then are sold to an outsider, and the minority shareholder finds himself at the mercy of an unknown purchaser. Similarly, a person taking a minority interest in a close corporation often fails to look forward to the time when the controlling shareholder in whom he has confidence will die or retire and some younger member of the family will take over control and operation of the business. Furthermore, he sometimes does not anticipate that years later the controlling shareholder may become less active in the business, place his son or daughter in an executive position, and turn management over to that person. Dissension then is likely to occur, because the mature and experienced minority shareholder who has been active in the business for a considerable time may resent taking orders from the son or daughter.

§ 2:20. Business participants' failure to obtain preventive legal services and inability of many lawyers to supply adequate preventive services

Other sections of this chapter point out underlying causes of squeeze-outs and set forth typical situations in which squeeze plays occur. Acting on this information, skilled lawyers, if consulted in time, can decrease substantially the number of squeeze plays by removing some of the causes of squeeze-outs and taking suitable precautionary steps to protect holders of minority interests. Unfortunately the atmosphere of optimism and goodwill which prevails during the initial stages of a business undertaking usually obscures the possibility of future disagreements and conflicts among the participants. Furthermore, even if the participants foresee the possibility of future dissension, they are reluctant to call in legal counsel to provide against the contingency.

* * *

Perhaps one further comment should be made, to give balance to what has already been said in this chapter. Thomas P. Murphy, a scholar and author who has devoted considerable time to the study of problems of small businesses, comments as follows:

> "One further thought, in my own observation of new enterprise I have always been impressed with the delicate mental climate that surrounds its birth. The entrepreneur needs good legal advice. But, in my judgment, it is more important to get the business started even if it is on a less than perfect basis. Legal counsel which dwells too strongly on the hazards can only cause apprehension in a human situation which calls for the best of good will and mutual trust.

NOTE

Professor O'Neal's study illustrates that problems of shareholder dissension and oppression often arise out of common patterns. This fact has several implications. To begin with, while the study concerned closely held corporations, many of the same sources of strife exist in the non-corporate setting. In addition, this fact suggests at least a partial answer to the question raised in Chapter I as to the attorney's appropriate role in so-called business decisions. Can the attorney forming a closely held corporation (or any closely held firm) be effective if he or she does not consider the sort of personal problems which may lead to dispute between the parties? Finally, this fact raises a particular concern for the young attorney. How can he or she anticipate problems without years of experience dealing with business clients? Professor O'Neal's study provides a start. In addition, notice that it relied largely on reported judicial decisions involving strife in closely held companies. Reading cases can provide an attorney years' worth of vicarious experience.

CHAPTER V

FINANCING

Chapters III and IV explored various contributions to a new business including, of course, money. The discussion there assumed the parties contributing cash would be among a small number of original participants establishing and operating the business. This chapter addresses what happens when the business reaches the stage where its needs exceed the resources of its original members and it must start looking for outside sources of financing. The discussion of outside financing requires resolving three questions: (1) how much money should the business obtain; (2) what will the business offer in order to obtain it; and (3) who will provide it. This three part approach provides the outline for the three sections of this chapter.

SECTION A. ASSESSING FINANCIAL NEEDS

Answering the question of how much money to seek requires a business judgment based upon a (hopefully realistic) projection of cash needs. The Schollhammer & Kuriloff excerpt on evaluating new business ventures in Chapter I discussed how to construct such a projection. In addition to estimating overall cash needs, those running the business must consider how much of future requirements the firm should meet with present financing.

Deloitte & Touche, Raising Venture Capital

52–53 (1982).

Another factor to consider in structuring the deal is the timing of the financing. One method is to try to raise enough money in the initial round to finance the company through the research and product development phase into production and achievement of a certain sales goal. This strategy requires more initial funding and presents a higher risk to the investors. To compensate for this higher risk, the investors require a higher rate of return and, therefore, a larger percentage ownership of the company. The result would be a lower price per share for the stock you sell to the investors.

This strategy, however, reduces the risk of running out of money at a critical time in the company's development if the spending at various stages exceeds expectations. It also reduces the amount of time top management needs to spend seeking financing. Each round of venture capital financing requires a considerable amount of management time in preparing and updating the business plan and the financial forecasts, meeting with various capital investor groups, and negotiating the deals.

The more popular strategy is staged financing, a process of timing each stage of the financing to coincide with the achievement of a significant milestone. This strategy has many benefits to both you and the investors. For the investors, each milestone represents a "step-down in risk". That is, as the company demonstrates its ability to achieve various goals, its probability of succeeding increases and its danger of failing decreases.

Typically, a company will have three phases:

- The start-up phase is used to prove its technological principles and build prototypes. At the completion of this phase the technological risk is reduced.
- The execution phase is used to build up production and begin marketing. At the completion of this phase, the marketing risk is reduced.
- The expansion phase is used to solidify your market share.

A round of financing occurs at the beginning of each stage. In exchange for the reduction in risk, you can negotiate higher prices per share in each successive round.

* * *

The risk in using this approach is that the money raised in any given round of financing may not be sufficient to achieve the specified milestone if unexpected complications or delays occur. If additional financing becomes necessary before the next milestone is achieved, the price per share may be much lower than otherwise anticipated, or the company may be forced to seek other sources for interim financing, such as bank loans, which may be very expensive and not readily available.

NOTE

To what extent can the attorney contribute to evaluating how much money the company should seek? For example, this chapter will later explore exemptions from registration under the securities laws. Some of these exemptions involve a maximum dollar limit. Is meeting such limits a factor the attorney should encourage his or her clients to consider when determining how much money they should attempt to raise? Is there any danger to doing so?

SECTION B. DETERMINING THE NATURE AND WORTH OF THE INVESTMENTS OFFERED

1. SOME FURTHER DETAILS ON INTERESTS IN A BUSINESS

The next question is what type of interests to offer. The preceding chapters outlined several categories of investments parties may receive in exchange for contributing money to a venture. These include general and limited partnership interests (if the business is a partnership, limited partnership or LLP), limited liability company membership interests (if the business is an LLC), common and preferred stock (if the business is a corporation), and debt (for any type of business). What new considerations arise with these investments as the business seeks money from persons beyond a small number of original founders?

To begin with, whatever interests the firm offers must be acceptable to the investors the firm seeks. Achieving acceptance by prospective investors in later stages of financing raises several additional concerns beyond those explored in dealing with formation of the venture. For example, consider the expectations of a person asked to infuse new capital into a business whose principal assets consist of intangibles or other property of speculative value. In many respects, this investor may feel the same as an initial cash contributor who goes into business with a person that contributes only services or other intangibles. Recall how an initial cash contributor might demand return of his or her investment prior to sharing distributions in liquidation with the service or intangible provider, and the mechanisms available to achieve this goal in either a corporation or non-corporate form of business. Significantly, when dealing with later investors, it may not matter that earlier participants also put in cash, if, as is commonly the case, the business already has expended the earlier cash contributions.

The normal progression of additional financing to involve larger numbers of investors can have an impact on the acceptability of the offered investments. For example, recall the discussion in Chapter II of how the various attributes of a corporation—specifically, limited liability, representative governance, freely tradeable interests, and fungible units of ownership—work well together with a publicly owned business, and how it may be difficult to duplicate this using a non-corporate form. Another factor resulting from larger numbers of investors is that it becomes less practical individually to negotiate and tailor an agreement acceptable to all the parties, as done at the inception of the venture. Instead, the firm must offer investments designed to be acceptable on a take it or leave it basis. This may favor offering investments which are more familiar, as well as being aware that when offering investments, like selling clothes, there often are fashions. (This does not mean creativity is dead. Quite the contrary, sellers of securities are constantly coming up with new investment packages.) Ultimately, if the business seeks to raise money through an offering to the general public, the firm should be prepared to issue securities of a type, in a quantity and with a price to be marketable in such an offering:

> "Once a company has decided to make a public offering, it must determine, in consultation with its managing underwriter, what class of securities should be offered. Most first offerings include common stock. Some first offerings consist of a package including other securities such as debentures, which may or may not be convertible into common stock, or warrants to purchase common stock. It is normally

not practicable to have a publicly-traded security convertible into common stock or a publicly-traded warrant to purchase common stock unless a public market exists for the underlying common stock.

"There are two other interrelated variables to consider, the number of shares offered and the offering price for the shares. It is generally felt that a minimum of 300,000 to 350,000 shares, and preferably 400,000 shares or even slightly more, is desirable in the public 'float' to constitute a broad national distribution and to support an active trading market thereafter. As to price level, many of the larger investment banking firms and many investors are not particularly interested in dealing with securities offered at less than $10. The $5 level is often another psychological break-point below which many investment bankers and investors lose interest. Any offering with an initial price of $20 or more is likely to import a prestige image. During some periods of interest in new issues, however, many high risk issues have been marketed at or below $1 per share.

"For an offering of $5,000,000, 500,000 shares at $10 per share would be considered in the optimum range. If the offering is below $4,000,000, a decrease in the offering price per share is recommended, rather than a reduction in the number of shares offered below 400,000. These are matters of judgment, however, which should be reviewed carefully with the underwriters in each situation. In determining the amount of public investment which can be profitably employed in the business, the underwriters will normally evaluate the company's needs for funds and the dilution in earnings per share to result from the issuance of additional stock. If the optimum level of proceeds to the company would constitute too small an offering, it may be desirable for existing shareholders to sell some of their own shares as part of the offering in order to increase its size. Sometimes the underwriters will suggest, or even insist on, a partial secondary offering with some shares to be sold by existing shareholders even though the shareholders would prefer to retain all their shares."

Schneider, Manko & Kant, *Going Public—Practice, Procedure & Consequences,* 27 Vill. L. Rev. 1 (1981) (as updated by the authors).

Larger numbers of investors introduce the need for other adjustments to the type of investment offered. For example, suppose the company wishes to offer debt instruments to a significant number of persons. It becomes less practical for a multitude of long-term creditors to protect their rights under their contracts than it is for one lender, such as a bank, to enforce its rights. The common solution is to issue bonds or debentures (the difference traditionally being that debentures are unsecured, whereas bonds are secured, albeit many persons use the term bonds to cover both secured and unsecured instruments) under a trust indenture. The trust indenture not only provides one document to specify uniform terms for a number of bonds, but also empowers a single administrator (the trustee) to take action if necessary to enforce the bondholders' rights. *See* Committee on Developments in Business Financing, ABA Section on Corporation,

Banking and Business Law, *Model Simplified Indenture,* 38 Bus. Law. 741 (1983).

As the firm seeks larger numbers of investors, it may encounter legal or quasi-legal restrictions on the type of interests it can offer, which the firm did not face as a closely held venture. For one thing, as the business seeks money from a wider circle of individuals, it may need to first obtain approval from state officials pursuant to state securities laws. (A further exploration of these laws will occur later in this chapter.) State securities law administrators will often deny approval for selling certain types of securities to the general public on the ground such an offering is not fair or equitable. For example, the North American Securities Administrators Association (NASAA) suggests that its members—the state officials who administer the individual state securities laws—adhere to the following policies with respect to approving the sale to the general public of shares having lesser voting rights, preferred stock and debt:

> "The offer and sale of securities that have less than equal voting rights may be deemed to be inconsistent with public investor protection and against public policy by the Administrator unless:
>
> A. The securities are given preferential treatment as to dividends and liquidation or the less than equal voting rights are justified to the satisfaction of the Administrator; and
>
> B. The terms of the voting rights are prominently disclosed on the cover page of the issuer's offering circular or prospectus."

NASAA, Statement of Policy Regarding Unequal Voting Rights (October 24, 1991).

> "III. A public offering of preferred stock may be disallowed by the Administrator if the Issuer's ADJUSTED NET EARNINGS for the last fiscal year or its average ADJUSTED NET EARNINGS for the last three (3) fiscal years prior to the public offering were insufficient to pay its fixed charges and preferred stock dividends, whether or not accrued, and to meet the redemption requirements, if applicable, of the preferred stock being offered.
>
> IV. As an alternative to III. above, the Administrator may choose to apply a CASH ANALYSIS. The Administrator may consider the Statement of Cash Flows if the statement demonstrates that the issuer has had positive 'Net Cash Provided by Operating Activities' for its last fiscal year. The Administrator may request that the issuer submit a financial statement demonstrating an average positive 'Net Cash Provided by Operating Activities' for the last three (3) fiscal years prior to the public offering. In either instance there must be sufficient cash to cover the preferred stock dividend whether or not declared.
>
> V. Section III. and IV. above shall not apply to public offerings of convertible preferred stock that are superior in right to payment of dividends, interest and liquidation proceeds to any convertible debt and preferred stock that are or may be legally or beneficially, directly or indirectly, owned by PROMOTERS. The risks of failure to declare or

pay dividends and the equity characteristics of the convertible preferred stock must be disclosed in the offering prospectus. An offering of such securities may be reviewed using guidelines for equity offerings.

VI. If the Issuer's NET EARNINGS are subject to cyclical fluctuations or if the Administrator deems it necessary for investor protection, the Administrator may require that the Issuer establish redemption requirements.

VII. A public offering of EQUITY SECURITIES may be dissallowed by the Administrator if the Issuer's articles of incorporation authorize its board of directors to issue preferred stock in the future without a vote of the common shareholders unless:

A. The issuer represents in its prospectus or offering document that it will not offer preferred stock to PROMOTERS except on the same terms as it is offered to all other existing shareholders or to new shareholders; or

B. The issuance of preferred stock is approved by a majority of the Issuer's INDEPENDENT DIRECTORS who do not have an interest in the transaction and who have access, at the issuer's expense, to issuer's or independent legal counsel."

NASAA, Statement of Policy Regarding Preferred Stock (April 22, 1997) (definitions omitted).

"III. A public offering of debt securities may be disallowed by the Administrator if the Issuer's ADJUSTED CASH FLOW for the last fiscal year or its average ADJUSTED CASH FLOW for the last three (3) fiscal years prior to the public offering was insufficient to cover its fixed charges, meet its debt obligations as they became due, and service the debt securities being offered.

* * *

VI. Unless the Administrator permits otherwise, public offerings of debt securities shall be offered and sold pursuant to a Trust Indenture ('Indenture') which adequately protects the rights of the purchasers. * * * "

NASAA, Statement of Policy Regarding Debt Securities (April 25, 1993) (definitions omitted, as are provisions regarding convertible debt, and redemption or sinking fund requirements).

Another source of restriction stems from the common desire of a company with numerous investors to list its securities for trading on a stock exchange. The major exchanges will not list certain types of securities, such as preferred shares which do not at least have contingent voting rights in case of failure to declare dividends. *E.g.,* N.Y. Stock Exchange Listed Company Manual § 313.00.

Finally, there can be additional tax factors to consider. For instance, a larger number of investors undermines the ability of the firm to obtain flow-through tax treatment. An S corporation cannot have more than 100 unrelated shareholders. I.R.C. § 1361(b)(1)(A). Along somewhat similar lines, Section 7704 of the Internal Revenue Code taxes so-called publicly traded partnerships (unless 90 percent of their income is from passive sources, including rents and oil and gas royalties) as corporations. A partnership (including any entity, such as a limited partnership, LLP or LLC, which elects to be treated as a partnership for income tax purposes) is publicly traded under Section 7704(b) if interests in the firm either are traded through an established securities market, or are readily tradeable on a secondary market or the substantial equivalent. It is pretty obvious when interests are actually traded on an established securities market; but when are partnership interests readily tradeable on a secondary market or the substantial equivalent? The Internal Revenue Service provides the following guidance:

> * * * [I]nterests in a partnership are readily tradeable on a secondary market or the substantial equivalent thereof if—
>
> (i) Interests in the partnership are regularly quoted by a person, such as a broker or dealer, making a market in the interests;
>
> (ii) Any person regularly makes available to the public (including customers or subscribers) bid or offer quotes with respect to interests in the partnership and stands ready to effect buy or sell transactions at the quoted prices for itself or on behalf of others;
>
> (iii) The holder of an interest in the partnership has a readily available, regular, and ongoing opportunity to sell or exchange such interest through a public means of obtaining or providing information of offers to buy, sell, or exchange interests in the partnership; or
>
> (iv) Prospective buyers and sellers have the opportunity to buy, sell, or exchange interests in the partnership in a time frame and with the regularity and continuity that is comparable to that described in the other provisions of this paragraph. * * *

Treas. Reg. § 1.7704–1. In addition to this general criteria, the regulation sets forth a series of "private transfers" which do not count in determining if interests are readily traded on a secondary market or the substantial equivalent to a secondary market. These include, among others, transfers between family members, transfers upon death or buy-outs by the partnership upon death or retirement, issuances of interests by the partnership, block transfers of over 2 percent of the total interests in partnership capital and profits, and transfers which the partnership refuses to recognize. Of practical significance, the regulation also establishes a safe harbor within which partnership interests are not considered readily tradeable in a secondary market. This safe harbor exists when the firm never registered the sale of partnership interests under the 1933 Securities Act and has less than 100 partners.

Section 382 creates another tax factor to consider when deciding what types of interests to offer later investors. This section, which Chapter VII will discuss in detail, limits the ability of a corporation to utilize net operating loss carryovers following an "ownership change." (A net operating loss carryover arises by virtue of Section 172, which allows taxpayers to deduct prior years' losses against later years' income.) Issuing stock to new investors in an amount sufficient to result in their owning over 50 percent of the firm's outstanding shares could constitute such an ownership change. Temp. Treas. Reg. § 1.382–2T(e)(1)(iii) Ex. (5). Issuing non-convertible debt securities will not. Consider the impact of this fact for a start-up company which has been operating at a loss as a "C" corporation, and needs to raise more money.

2. VALUATION REVISITED

In addition to deciding what type of interest to sell investors, those in charge of the firm must decide how much of an interest the firm should offer the investors in order to obtain the needed cash. This returns one to the subject of valuing a business and interests in a business. Before reading the following excerpt, which explores the manner in which securities analysts evaluate investments, the reader may find it useful to review the Schollhammer & Kuriloff excerpt in Chapter I, which discussed how to determine the prospects for a new venture, and the material on valuation contained in the last section of Chapter I.

W. Bauman & J. Komarynsky, Chapter 16: Security Analysis, Handbook of Modern Finance

(Logue 1984).

COMPANY ANALYSIS

After the outlook for the economy and the prospects for various industries have been examined, the next step in the top-down approach is to * * * understand the nature and operating characteristics of a company so judgments can be formed regarding the returns and risks expected from an investment in that company's securities. The company analysis usually focuses on the following variables: (1) market characteristics of the company's products and/or services, (2) quality of management, (3) evaluation of the soundness of the company's assets and financial structure, (4) analysis of operating results, and (5) per share statistics.

MARKET POSITION FOR PRODUCTS AND SERVICES

In an analysis of market characteristics of a company, the nature and potential demand for the company's products and/or services must be examined thoroughly. * * * Major consideration should be given to factors such as (1) product or service substitutes; (2) luxuries as opposed to necessities; (3) elasticity of demand; (4) geographic markets (local, regional, national, and international); (5) quality of product or services; and (6) product line diversification.

* * *

QUALITY OF MANAGEMENT

Another very important influence on the returns and risks from investment in securities is the quality of the company's management. * * *

In appraising the management of a company, an analyst is concerned with the results achieved by management in the past and whether management has specific objectives, plans, and a timetable for achieving those objectives in the future. Next, the analyst should try to ascertain whether management is improvement oriented, has an innovative spirit, has a strong desire to make its company grow, and is people oriented with respect to employees, customers, and the general community. Finally, the analyst should try to determine whether management is profit oriented or oriented toward its own personal welfare.

* * *

FINANCIAL ANALYSIS OF A COMPANY

Different parties conducting financial analyses of companies have different concerns. Short-term creditors are primarily concerned with the ability of a company to repay its maturing short-term obligations. Investors in intermediate notes and long-term bonds are interested in the company's ability to generate adequate earnings in order to meet all contractual obligations, that is, to pay predetermined interest and to repay principal at maturity. Investors in equity securities are primarily interested in the stability and growth of the company's profits. Insiders, who are the company's managers, usually are concerned with all aspects of financial analysis.

Reliable information is needed to perform financial analysis. The primary sources of information are published by the company: (1) balance sheet statements, (2) income statements, (3) statement of changes in shareholders' equity, and (4) funds flow statements.

* * *

RATIO ANALYSIS

The main purpose of financial statement analysis for the investment analyst is to evaluate past performance of a company in terms of the soundness of its financial position, operating performance, and risk. The most common method of analysis uses financial ratios. The commonly used ratios for security analysis are (1) liquidity ratios, (2) activities ratios, (3) leverage ratios, and (4) profitability ratios.

Liquidity Ratios. Liquidity ratios are designed to measure whether or not a company has the ability to meet its short-term obligations. Bondholders are concerned with the liquidity of a company because low liquidity has a negative impact on the investment value of a company's bonds; that is, the company may find it difficult to meet interest payments and to repay principal. Stockholders, both common and preferred, are also concerned with the liquidity position of the company, because there is the risk that dividends, like interest payments, may be negatively affected. Two common liquidity ratios are the current ratio and the quick ratio.

* * *

Activity Ratios. Activity ratios, also known as asset management ratios, indicate how effectively the company is utilizing its resources. Analysis of these ratios involves the comparison between the level of sales and the investment in various assets or capital categories. The four activities ratios most widely used by investment analysts are (1) inventory turnover, (2) accounts receivable turnover, (3) assets turnover, and (4) equity turnover.

* * *

Leverage Ratios. Leverage deals with different methods of financing business enterprise. It measures the relationship between ownership (equity) financing and creditorship (debt) financing. The extent to which a company utilizes creditor capital in financing business operations has a number of implications to investors. For example, the bondholders prefer a larger equity base to provide a margin of safety for their invested capital, that is, to minimize financial risk. The owners of common stocks, on the other hand, may favor larger financial leverage for two reasons: First, by raising funds through creditor capital, the holders of common stock gain the benefits of maintaining control in the company; second, the financial leverage may enhance the return on their invested capital. Note, however, that financial leverage may also magnify losses. A number of ratios are used to measure the impact of leverage on the financial position of a company.

* * *

Profitability Ratios. The analysis of profitability is a very important task of the investment analyst. This analysis is designed to relate a company's returns (earnings) to sales and to invested capital. The most commonly used profitability ratios are (1) gross profit margin, (2) net profit margin, (3) rate of return on equity, and (4) rate of return on total operating assets.

* * *

After all necessary financial ratios have been calculated for a particular company, the next important task is to make comparisons. First, the trend and stability of those ratios over long time periods should be examined because ratios for only one period may be misleading. Trend comparisons add depth to the analysis because they look at several years, thus helping to determine the degree of stability in the operating performance of the company. Next, the ratios of the company under study should be compared with the ratios of similar companies in the same industry. Finally, the overall performance of the studied company should be compared with the performance of the industry and, where appropriate, with the performance of the economy.

PER SHARE STATISTICS—ANALYSIS AND FORECASTING

Once the financial condition and operating efficiency of a company have been analyzed, the next tasks are to analyze the trends and stability of the per share statistics and to forecast future trends. The major per share statistics for analyzing common stocks are (1) earnings per share, (2) cash flow per share, (3) dividends per share, (4) dividend payout ratio, (5) P/E ratio, (6) book value per share, and (7) the ratio of market price to book value per share. * * *

* * *

The trend and stability of the earnings per share must be determined. If the earnings per share fluctuates very widely, this may have a negative impact on the trend in the market price and, therefore on the returns for the investor. The higher the volatility in earnings per share, the higher the risk. In the case of cash flow per share, a more complete picture of the company's profitability is desirable. Cash flow per share includes not only earnings per share, but also such arbitrary items as depreciation, depletion, and other noncash expenses.

The trends, stability, and growth in dividend payments, as well as the payout ratio, must be considered. Some investors prefer a high payout ratio and great stability in dividend payment because of their need for income. On the other hand, some investors prefer smaller dividends, with the company reinvesting more earnings for future growth.

The P/E ratio, sometimes called the earnings multiplier, is a function of the quality and expected future growth in earnings. Usually, investors pay more for a common stock if earnings are expected to increase substantially.

The final important per share statistic is the book value per share and particularly its relationship to the market price. * * * In some cases, book value per share may be misleading because of different accounting methods used to value inventory and compute depreciation. * * *

A very important task in stock analysis is estimating or forecasting the future benefits of owning a security. The choice of any security for an investment portfolio is influenced largely by expectations about the company's potential. Several methods used to determine the outlook for a company's future sales, earnings, and investment return are discussed briefly here.

The forecasting of the future potential for a company usually starts with forecasting its sales. The sales forecast generally relies on the relationship of a company's sales to various external and internal variables. Major external factors are: (1) general economic condition; (2) disposable personal income; (3) level of interest rates, particularly if the company sells durable goods; (4) competitive position of the company in its industry; (5) product or services substitution; and (6) other economic and industry factors that influence demand for a company's products and/or services. The following internal factors are usually important: (1) the nature and quality of product and/or services; (2) innovation and improvements of products; (3) activities in promotion of sales; (4) services provided to customers, in the case of durable goods; (5) productive capacity and efficiency; and (6) availability of the product at the right time and the right place.

The next step is forecasting earnings and dividends of a company. Estimating earnings requires thorough examination of such factors as (1) rate of change of the company's sales; (2) cost of raw material and energy; (3) cost of labor, including fringe benefits; (4) other operating and administrative expenses; (5) extraordinary income and expenses; (6) depreciation; (7) interest payments; and (8) income taxes. In addition, future capital investment, financing methods, and their impact on the company's operating performance should be considered. Finally, the kind of accounting policies and practices being followed by the company should be examined, because different accounting practices may significantly affect the quality of reported earnings.

In estimating dividends, the following factors should be examined: (1) outlook for and stability of the company's earnings; (2) outlook for liquidity; (3) need for future financing; (4) legal restrictions on a company's dividend policies, such as capital impairment rules and maintenance of retained earnings and working capital; and (5) attitude of management with regard to dividend policies.

Methods of forecasting the future potential of a company vary from a simple, naive projection type to sophisticated econometric models. For example, some analysts perform their forecasts by calculating the annual percentage changes for each year over some past time period (such as 5 to 10 years), then making a forecast on the expectation that the future trend will be similar to the past one. * * *

Regression and correlation analysis also may be used to forecast a company's sales and earnings. In performing a regression analysis, the analyst uses a company's sales or earnings as a dependent variable and selects external or internal variables (listed previously) as independent or explanatory variables. This method is used to estimate a regression equation showing the structural relationship that existed in the past between explanatory variables and a dependent variable. For example, disposable personal income and the level of interest rate can be used as the explanatory variables for a company's sales of durable goods, the dependent variable. Once the regression model has been estimated with past data and the level of statistical significance has been determined, the model can then be used to estimate future sales or earnings for the company.

* * *

In utilizing these forecasting techniques, it is assumed that past relationships will be similar in the future. Frequently, however, the past may not be a good predictor of the future. Therefore, in making any prediction of a company's sales, earnings, and investment return the process of forecasting just described (which is based on historical information) should be modified by subjective forecasting based on seasoned judgment.

Several methods that can be used to forecast the future performance of companies are described here. Other analytical forecasting techniques, such as time series analysis and probabilistic forecasting, are discussed in books on business forecasting and econometric statistics.

VALUATION OF COMMON STOCKS

The purpose of owning common stocks as investments is to receive a return in the form of cash dividend payments and market price appreciation. To enjoy the opportunity of a return, investment risks must be assumed by the investor. Therefore, the objectives of investors are to seek a return from stocks and to limit risk of loss. At the very heart of the investment selection process is the task of estimating the rate of return expected from individual investments within some planning time horizon and estimating the level of risks or probabilities of receiving this return. The two parameters—expected return and risk—are vitally linked to determine the value of a stock. * * * Within the context of security analysis, this value is variously referred to as the estimated investment value, intrinsic value, true value, or present value.

The position of the traditional or fundamental analytical school of thought is that the market fluctuates widely around the true value, so that the price is sometimes above and at other times below its value. According to this view, the task of the security analyst is to estimate the value of a security through an independent analysis of the corporate issuer, its industry, and the external environment. The results of this analysis enable the analyst to recommend the possible purchase of a stock that is undervalued (i.e., the market price is below the estimated value), because the security offers a high expected return, or to recommend the possible sale of a stock that is overvalued, because the security offers a low or negative expected return.

The position of the efficient market hypothesis (EMH) school is that the current market price is the best available estimate of a stock's true value. The argument used to support this position is that many investors and analysts analyze all relevant information regarding investments as soon as it becomes available and act promptly on the information, so stock prices adjust quickly to the value estimated by these intelligent and fully informed market participants.

* * *

ESTIMATED INVESTMENT VALUE

The most widely recognized theory explaining investment value is the present value theory. This theory is used routinely by bond investors through the application of bond value tables, by lenders through present value tables, and by insurers through annuity tables. Professional investors in common stocks are increasingly recognizing the relevance of this theory and are applying it by the use of dividend discount models. Accordingly, the value placed on a stock is determined by the expected size and timing of future cash payments, and by the level of risk or uncertainty associated with such payments. At the fulcrum of each fundamental investment decision to buy, hold, or sell are three parameters: the present value (estimated investment value), the estimated future cash payments, and the expected rate of return or discount rate. Using a dividend discount model, the estimated worth of a stock to an investor is equal to the sum of the discounted future cash payments expected. Mathematically, this may be expressed as:

$$V_0 = \frac{D_1}{(1+r)^1} + \frac{D_2}{(1+r)^2} + \ldots + \frac{D_n}{(1+r)^n} + \frac{V_n}{(1+r)^n} \qquad (16.1)$$

where: V_0 = estimated present value *or* current market price
D = expected future dividend payments in years 1, 2, and so on through year n
r = expected or assumed rate of return or discount rate in years 1, 2, and so on through year n, which is determined by the degree of uncertainty of future cash payments
n = final year of the investment holding period or of the planning time horizon
V_n = expected present value or stock price at the end of year n

This equation may be illustrated by a simple example. Assume that the Husky Company paid an annual divided of $1.00 last year; that the company and its dividends are growing at 8 percent per year; and that the investor expects a rate of return of 13 percent and plans to hold the stock for two years then sell it at a price level to provide a dividend yield [(in other words, the next year's dividend divided by the price)] of 5 percent. Therefore, the dividend rate is expected to be $1.08 in the first year ($1.00 x 1.08) and $1.17 in the second year ($1.08 x 1.08) [and $1.26 in the third year ($1.08 × 1.08 × 1.08)]. The stock price at the end of the second year is expected to be $25.20. [($1.26 ÷ 0.05)]. (Values are rounded to the nearest cent to simplify the example.)

* * *

The estimated investment value or present value of Husky Company is:

$$V_0 = \frac{\$1.08}{(1.13)^1} + \frac{\$1.17}{(1.13)^2} + \frac{\$25.20}{(1.13)^2}$$

$$V_0 = \$0.96 + \$0.92 + \$19.74$$

$$V_0 = \$21.62$$

If the investor purchases the stock at $21.62, receives dividends of $1.08 and $1.17 in each of the next two years, and sells the stock at the end of that time at $25.20, he will earn an average annual rate of return of 13 percent.

This discount rate of 13 percent is equal to the expected rate of return only if the stock is purchased at \$21.62. Investors who believe that market prices tend to be efficient accept the current market price of a stock as being a correct reflection of the market consensus and assume that it is equal to the estimated present value. The discount rate r then becomes the unknown variable in the equation. If the Husky Company stock sells at \$21.92, the investor finds through trial and error, that the discount rate is 12 percent.

* * *

On the other hand, fundamental analysts, who believe that the market is not efficient and that market prices fluctuate above and below the true values, seek to purchase undervalued stocks. Under these circumstances, the analyst selects a discount rate for a stock that is considered to be appropriate. The appropriate discount rate is frequently considered to be composed of three components:

i = real or riskless interest rate, which is adjusted for and free from inflation and other investment risks.

f = inflation premium, which is the inflation rate in the general price level for goods and services.

k = risk premium, which is the additional return required by investors for assuming the risks inherent in the particular investment.

Therefore, the discount rate r for a stock is:

$$r = i + f + k$$

The analyst estimates the three components to find r. There are different ways to find r; the following simple illustration demonstrates one method. Assume that the current short-term U.S. Treasury bill interest rate reflects the real interest rate plus the expected inflation rate. The Treasury bill rate is 8 percent, but is expected to drop to 7 percent and stay around that level over the next several years. The expected inflation rate is 4 percent. Therefore, the real rate of interest is assumed to be 3 percent. An analysis of the risks of the Husky Company and its stock leads to the conclusion that it requires a risk premium of 6 percent. Therefore, the stock's discount rate should be 13 percent:

$$r = 0.03 + 0.04 + 0.06$$

$$r = 0.013 \text{ or } 13\%$$

Under these circumstances, Husky Company stock should be purchased at a price of \$21.62, or less, so as to provide a discount rate of 13 percent or more. If the price of the stock is \$21.24, the stock is considered undervalued and the expected return is 14 percent:

$$\$21.24 = \frac{\$1.08}{(1 + r)^1} + \frac{\$1.17}{(1 + r)^2} = \frac{\$25.20}{(1 + r)^2}$$

$$r = 0.14 \text{ or } 14\%$$

$$r = i + f + k + a$$
$$r = 0.03 + 0.04 + 0.06 + 0.01$$
$$r = 0.14 \text{ or } 14\%$$

In the case of Husky Company, the alpha of 1 percent is an additional return expected to occur when the stock price rises to the estimated sale price of $25.20 during the investor's planning time horizon of two years.

The estimated sale price or terminal value of $25.20 for Husky Company stock is an important figure in determining investment values. This terminal value is nothing more than the present value of the stock two years from now based on the discounted level of dividends that are expected to be paid in the third and subsequent years.

Constant Growth Model. Equation 16.1 can be greatly simplified for companies whose cash dividend rates are expected to grow at a constant rate, which tends to be true for stable or mature companies. The estimated investment value or present value of such a stock is:

$$V_0 = \frac{D_1}{r - g} \qquad (16.2)$$

where: g = expected average annual rate of growth in dividends per share

D_1 = dividends per share expected during the next four quarters

If the dividends of Husky Company are expected to grow at a stable rate of 8 percent, its estimated present value is $21.60.

$$V_0 = \frac{\$1.08}{0.13 - 0.08}$$

$$V_0 = \$21.60$$

* * *

Earnings Multiplier Model. Because corporate earnings are the primary source of funds with which a going concern pays dividends over the long run, many analysts estimate the investment value of stocks by relating earnings per share to stock prices in the form of P/E ratios. The P/E ratio (*PER*) as calculated for a stock is equal to the current market price (P_0) divided by the expected earnings per share (E_1):

$$PER = \frac{P_0}{E_1}$$

If the market price of Husky Company stock is $19 3/4 and its expected earnings are $1.80, then its P/E ratio is 11.0:

$$PER = \frac{\$19.75}{\$\ 1.80}$$

$$\text{PER} = 11.0$$

Closely related to the P/E ratio is the earnings multiplier that is used to estimate a stock's true value. The investment value for a stock is equal to the *normalized* annual earnings per share expected in the next four quarters (*E1*) multiplied by a selected earnings multiplier (*M*):

$$V_o = (E^1)(M) \tag{16.4}$$

The normalized earnings per share is the expected reported earnings corrected for nonrecurring accounting type distortions and abnormal business cycle aberrations. A multiplier is selected based on two variables: (i) the expected future growth rate of earnings per share and (2) the riskiness of earnings per share. The relations of both these variables in the valuation process may be seen by a derivation of the equation for the constant growth model (Equation 16.2):

$$V_o = \frac{D_1}{r - g}$$

If both sides of this equation are divided by E_1, the result is the earnings multiplier *M*.

$$\frac{V_0}{E_1} = \frac{D_1/E_1}{r - g}$$

It was noted in equation 16.4 that

$$V_0 = (E_1)(M)$$

So,

$$\frac{V_0}{E_1} = M$$

Therefore,

$$M = \frac{D_1/E_1}{r - g} = \frac{P}{r - g}$$

Consequently, the earnings multiplier (within the simplified context of constant growth) is equal to the dividend payout ratio (*p*) divided by the discount factor (*r*—*g*). The multiplier is, therefore, positively correlated to both the earnings growth rate and the payout ratio; that is, the higher the payout ratio or the higher the growth, then the higher the multiplier should be. Likewise, the multiplier is negatively correlated with the discount rate; that is, the greater the riskiness of the stock or the higher the rate of return required, then the lower the multiplier should be.

If, for example, Husky Company stock has a dividend rate of \$1.08, normalized earnings per share of \$1.80, a discount rate of 13 percent, and a growth rate of 8 percent, then its multiplier is 12.0:

$$M = \frac{\$1.08/\$1.80}{0.13 - 0.08} = \frac{0.60}{0.05}$$

$$M = 12.0$$

The estimated value of Husky Company stock is \$21.60:

$$V_o = (\$1.80)(12.0)$$

$$V_o = \$21.60$$

If the price of Husky Company stock is \$19 3/4 and sells at a P/E ratio of 11 times earnings, the stock is undervalued because its earnings multiplier (the expected P/E ratio) is 12 times earnings.

INVESTMENT RISK

An important task of security analysis is the classification of stocks on the basis of risk measures. The expected rate of return and the probability distribution of returns for a stock are subject to several different risks. These risks need to be identified so investors may select stocks to diversify their portfolios and protect against excessive risks. Modern portfolio theory has contributed a methodology by which the various risks of common stocks may be controlled within the context of constructing portfolios. To construct a suitably diversified portfolio, the investor needs to rely on several inputs that are generated from the security analysis process. Within the context of modern portfolio theory, risk is measured as the volatility, variability, or standard deviation of expected rates of returns of stocks over a relevant time period. The standard deviation (S) is a convenient statistic used to measure the dispersion or deviations of individual values from the average or mean of their values. For example, the average annual (geometric) mean return on common stocks, as measured by the Standard & Poor's Composite Stock Index, during 1926–1981, was 9.1 percent with a market risk (S_m) of 21.9 percent. Because the distribution of these returns approximates a normal distribution, about two-thirds of the annual returns fell within a range of 9.1 percent ± 21.9 percent, or between 31.0 percent and minus 12.8 percent. This risk measure of approximately 22 percent for the stock market has remained surprisingly constant over the years, so this figure is often used in projecting the risk of the stock market into the future.

Total Risk of a Stock. In like fashion, the total risk of an individual stock (designated as stock i) can be measured as the standard deviation (S_i) of its (monthly, quarterly, or annual) expected rate of return over a particular time period, such as five years. It has been observed that some stocks have higher total risks (higher S_i) than others for a variety of reasons, such as greater volatility of corporate sales, product prices, and earnings or greater operating leverage or financial leverage. Based on modern portfolio theory, stocks with higher risk are expected to have higher expected returns because investors have an aversion to risk and therefore require a higher return or risk premium.

* * *

NOTE

Professors Bauman and Komarynsky provide an overview of how analysts evaluate the worth of securities. This is important for those structuring the offering of securities, since they must make the offering attractive to investors, and yet they do not want to dilute the interests of the business' current owners any more than necessary. What is the attorney's role in all of this? Presumably, he or she is not the expert to advise the business on the value of the offered investments; indeed, admittedly many law students and attorneys might find the excerpt reprinted above to be rather intimidating. (Many finance texts contain much more difficult descriptions than this, however.) Still, without some basic familiarity with these concepts, it may be difficult for an attorney to carry out his or her role in advising, drafting or negotiating for a business raising money.

In fitting together the pieces on valuation reprinted thus far in this book, keep in mind several things. To begin with, there are two valuation questions: the worth of the overall business (on which the Small Business Administration bulletin, reprinted at the end of Chapter I, largely focused), and the worth of the individual interests in the business (with which Professors Bauman and Komarynsky are primarily concerned). These obviously are mathematically related; although the relationship requires more than simple division to establish if the capital structure of the firm consists of anything more than one class of undifferentiated shares or percentage rights. Next, note that what might initially appear to be different approaches to valuation often are just more simplified versus more sophisticated ways of performing the same measurement. For example, one can estimate future earnings of a going business by assuming the firm will make the same as the average or typical year's earnings during the past several years, or one can construct a regression analysis working from sales and those factors which affect sales, as described in the except above. Similarly, one could capitalize earnings to present value by dividing by the rate of return which investors demand for this amount of risk and with this expected rate of growth; or one can take each future year's expected earnings (or dividend or interest payment if looking at specific securities) and obtain the present value through Formula 16.1 in the excerpt above. In terms of determining the rate of return, the SBA bulletin simply states that this is subjective and points to a variety of qualitative factors, while Professors Bauman and Komarynsky break this down into factors representing the risk free rate of return and an added compensation for the riskiness of this investment. Later, this book (particularly when discussing the price at which to sell a business in Chapter VII) will have occasion to explore the computation of the rate of return for a business of a given level of risk. Finally, both the Small Business Administration and the Bauman and Komarynsky pieces focus largely upon mature businesses with an established earnings record. How can one capitalize earnings for the developing venture which has yet to turn a significant profit? The answer is that investors are always capitalizing future earnings; past earnings are only relevant insofar as they provide a guide to what the future holds. Without the benefit of prior earnings history, one must look to the techniques discussed in the Schollhammer and Kuriloff excerpt in Chapter I for projecting future earnings based upon assumptions about sales and expenses, noting always that such projections carry more risk than estimates based upon past earnings, and that the projection should hopefully reflect a sophisticated market study and a well thought out business plan, rather than just wishful thinking.

Incidentally, those structuring an offering of investments must also remember one concept which is not mentioned in the excerpts. This is the question of whether one is dealing with valuation "before" or "after the money"; in other words, the value of the business with or without the sought after financing. For example, suppose one projects the business will achieve certain future earnings, but only if it raises a certain amount of funds. The discounted value of these earnings is the value of the business after it receives the investor's money. This represents an appropriate basis for pricing the interests sold to the new investors. It does not represent, however, the value of what the original owners contribute; rather that figure is the value of the business "before the money" (which presumably equals the value "after the money," less the added funds).

3. THE DEFINITION OF A SECURITY: ENTERING THE REALM OF SECURITIES REGULATION

The question of what type of investment to offer provides an opportune time to begin considering federal and state securities laws. As the title of these acts suggests, their requirements and prohibitions became applicable when dealing with "securities". What precisely is a "security"?

Robinson v. Glynn

349 F.3d 166 (4th Cir.2003).

■ WILKINSON, J.

Plaintiff James Robinson filed suit against Thomas Glynn, Glynn Scientific, Inc., and GeoPhone Company, LLC, alleging that Glynn committed federal securities fraud when he sold Robinson a partial interest in GeoPhone Company. The district court found that Robinson's membership interest in GeoPhone was not a security within the meaning of the federal securities laws, and it dismissed Robinson's securities fraud claim. Because Robinson was an active and knowledgeable executive at GeoPhone, rather than a mere passive investor in the company, we affirm. To do otherwise would unjustifiably expand the scope of the federal securities laws by treating an ordinary commercial venture as an investment contract.

I.

* * * In 1995, Glynn organized GeoPhone Corporation to develop and commercially market the GeoPhone telecommunications system. The GeoPhone system was designed around a signal processing technology, Convolutional Ambiguity Multiple Access (CAMA), that Glynn purportedly designed. Glynn was GeoPhone Corporation's majority shareholder and chairman. In September 1995, GeoPhone Corporation became a limited liability company, GeoPhone Company, LLC. * * *

In March 1995, Glynn and his associates contacted James Robinson, a businessman with no prior telecommunications experience, in an effort to raise capital for GeoPhone. Over the next several months, Glynn met and corresponded with Robinson, attempting to convince Robinson to invest in GeoPhone. Glynn described to Robinson the CAMA technology, its centrality to the GeoPhone system, and GeoPhone's business plan. In July 1995, Robinson agreed to loan Glynn $1 million so that Glynn could perform a field test of the GeoPhone system and the CAMA technology.

In addition to Robinson's loan, in August 1995 Robinson and Glynn executed a "Letter of Intent," in which Robinson pledged to invest up to $25 million in GeoPhone, LLC if the field test indicated that CAMA worked in the GeoPhone system. Robinson's $25 million investment was to be comprised of his initial $1 million loan, an immediate $14 million investment upon successful completion of the field test, and a later $10 million investment. In October 1995, engineers hired by Glynn performed the field test, but, apparently with Glynn's knowledge, they did not use CAMA in the test. Nevertheless, Glynn allegedly told Robinson that the field test had been a success.

Consistent with the Letter of Intent, in December 1995 Robinson and Glynn executed an "Agreement to Purchase Membership Interests in GeoPhone" (APMIG). Under the APMIG, Robinson agreed to convert his $1 million loan and his $14 million investment into equity and subsequently to invest the additional $10 million. Robinson and Glynn also entered into an "Amended and Restated GeoPhone Operating Agreement" (ARGOA), which detailed the capital contribution, share ownership, and management structure of GeoPhone.

Pursuant to the ARGOA, Robinson received 33,333 of GeoPhone's 133,333 shares. On the back of the share certificates that Robinson received, the restrictive legend referred to the certificates as "shares" and "securities." It also specified that the certificates were exempt from registration under the Securities Act of 1933, and stated that the certificates could not be transferred without proper registration under the federal and state securities laws.

In addition, the ARGOA established a seven-person board of managers that was authorized to manage GeoPhone's affairs. Two of the managers were to be appointed by Robinson with the remaining five appointed by Glynn and his brother. Finally, the ARGOA vested management of GeoPhone in Robinson and Glynn based on each member's ownership share. Robinson was named GeoPhone's treasurer, and he was appointed to the board of managers and the company's executive committee. Glynn served as GeoPhone's chairman and was intimately involved in the company's operations and technical development.

* * *

[I]n 1998 Robinson allegedly learned for the first time that the CAMA technology had never been implemented in the GeoPhone system—not even in the field test that had provided the basis for Robinson's investment. Robinson then filed suit in federal court, claiming violation of the federal securities laws, specifically §§ 10(b) of the Securities Exchange Act of 1934 and Rule 10b–5. The district court, however, granted summary judgment to Glynn, because it found that Robinson's membership interest in GeoPhone, LLC did not constitute a security under the federal securities laws. Robinson now challenges the district court's dismissal of his federal securities law claim.

II.

In order to establish a claim under Rule 10b–5, Robinson must prove fraud in connection with the purchase of securities. The Securities Act of 1933, 15 U.S.C. §§ 77b(a)(1), and the Securities Exchange Act of 1934, 15 U.S.C. §§ 78c(a)(10), define a "security" broadly as "any note, stock, treasury stock, security future, bond, debenture, . . . , investment contract, . . . , or, in general, any interest or instrument commonly known as a 'security.' "In this case, Robinson claims that his membership interest in GeoPhone, a limited liability company (LLC), qualifies as either an "investment contract" or "stock" under the Securities Acts.

A.

* * * The Supreme Court has defined an investment contract as "a contract, transaction or scheme whereby a person invests his money in a common enterprise and is led to expect profits solely from the efforts of the promoter or a third party." *S.E.C. v. W.J. Howey, Co.,* 328 U.S. 293, 298–99, 66 S.Ct. 1100, 90 L.Ed. 1244 (1946). The parties agree that Robinson invested his money in a common enterprise with an expectation of profits. Their disagreement concerns whether Robinson expected profits "solely from the efforts" of others, most notably Glynn.

Since *Howey,* however, the Supreme Court has endorsed relaxation of the requirement that an investor rely only on others' efforts, by omitting the word "solely" from its restatements of the *Howey* test. And neither our court nor our sister circuits have required that an investor like Robinson expect profits "solely" from the efforts of others. Requiring investors to rely wholly on the efforts of others would exclude from the protection of the securities laws any agreement that involved even slight efforts from investors themselves. It would also exclude any agreement that offered investors control in theory, but denied it to them in fact. Agreements do not annul the securities laws by retaining nominal powers for investors unable to exercise them.

What matters more than the form of an investment scheme is the "economic reality" that it represents. The question is whether an investor, as a result of the investment agreement itself or the factual circumstances that surround it, is left unable to exercise meaningful control over his investment. * * * *see also Williamson v. Tucker,* 645 F.2d 404, 424 (5th Cir.1981). * * *

B.

In looking at the powers accorded Robinson under GeoPhone's operating agreement, as well as Robinson's activity as an executive at GeoPhone, it is clear that Robinson was no passive investor heavily dependent on the efforts of others like Glynn. Under the ARGOA, management authority for GeoPhone resided in a board of managers. Robinson not only had the power to appoint two of the board members, but he himself assumed one of the board seats and was named as the board's vice-chairman. The board, in turn, delegated extensive responsibility to a four-person executive committee of which Robinson was also a member.

In addition, Robinson served as GeoPhone's Treasurer. Among his powers were the ability to select external financial and legal consultants; to consult with GeoPhone's Chief Financial Officer on all financial matters relating to the company; to review status reports from the President and other officers; and to assemble the executive committee in order to discuss variations from GeoPhone's operating plan. Beyond even these fairly extensive powers, the ARGOA forbade GeoPhone from either incurring any indebtedness outside the normal course of business without Robinson's approval or diluting his interest in GeoPhone without first consulting him. In short, Robinson carefully negotiated for a level of control "antithetical to the notion of member passivity" required to find an investment contract under the federal securities laws.

None of this, of course, establishes that Robinson could entirely direct the affairs of GeoPhone. He controlled neither the board nor the executive committee, and he lacked the technological expertise of Glynn and others at the company. But Robinson was not interested in sole managerial control of GeoPhone; he was interested instead in sufficient managerial control to ensure that other managers like Glynn could neither harm nor dilute his investment. Through his positions as Treasurer, Vice–Chairman of the Board, and member of GeoPhone's executive committee, Robinson may have lacked "decisive control over major decisions," but he preserved "the sort of influence which generally provide[d][him] with access to important information and protection against a dependence on others."

Robinson argues, however, that his lack of technological expertise relative to Glynn prevented him from meaningfully exercising his rights. * * * To the extent that Robinson needed assistance in understanding any particular aspect of the CAMA technology, nothing prevented him from seeking it from outside parties or others at GeoPhone. In fact, prior to purchasing all of Glynn's shares in GeoPhone, Robinson asked his accountant to scrutinize the company's financial records, and he hired an outside engineer to study the company's technology and market potential.

Indeed, the record amply supports the district court's conclusion that Robinson exercised his management rights despite his lack of technical expertise. For instance, Robinson reviewed GeoPhone's technology and financial records, as well as weekly status reports from GeoPhone's President, Chief Operating Officer, and Chief Financial Officer covering numerous aspects of GeoPhone's operation. He disapproved disbursements and proposed licenses of the GeoPhone technology. Robinson even expressed to the board of managers problems he perceived with GeoPhone, including the company's technological development, its management, and marketability. In the end, Robinson generally asserts that he lacked technical sophistication, without explaining in any detail what was beyond his ken or why it left him powerless to exercise his management rights.

Moreover, Robinson's argument would work a fundamental and unjustifiable expansion in the securities laws by bringing innumerable commercial ventures within their purview. Business ventures often find their genesis in the different contributions of diverse individuals—for instance, as here, where one contributes his technical expertise and another his capital and business acumen. Yet the securities laws do not extend to every person who lacks the specialized knowledge of his partners or colleagues, without a showing that this lack of knowledge prevents him from meaningfully controlling his investment. Here, Robinson concedes that "nothing of consequence that would affect [his] position adversely could be done without [his] prior expressed approval," thus undermining his claim that his lack of technical expertise left him powerless over his investment. In essence, Robinson was a savvy and experienced businessman who negotiated for formal management rights and actively exercised those rights, only now relying on his lack of technical sophistication to claim the cover of the federal securities laws.

* * *

Finally, Robinson argues that he and Glynn considered his interest in GeoPhone a security, based on language in the APMIG, in the ARGOA, and on the back of Robinson's GeoPhone certificates. For instance, the restrictive legend on the back of Robinson's certificates refers to the certificates as "shares" and "securities." While this may be persuasive evidence that Robinson and Glynn believed the securities laws to apply, it does not indicate that their understanding was well-founded. * * * It is the "economic reality" of a particular instrument, rather than the label attached to it, that ultimately determines whether it falls within the reach of the securities laws. * * *

III.

Robinson further claims that his membership interest in GeoPhone was not only an "investment contract" within the meaning of the federal securities laws, but "stock" as well. Congress intended catch-all terms like "investment contract" to encompass the range of novel and unusual instruments whose economic realities invite application of the securities laws; but the term "stock" refers to a narrower set of instruments with a common name and characteristics. *See Landreth Timber Co. v. Landreth,* 471 U.S. 681, 686, 105 S.Ct. 2297, 85 L.Ed.2d 692 (1985). Thus the securities laws apply "when an instrument is both called 'stock' and bears stock's usual characteristics." Yet Robinson's membership interest was neither denominated stock by the parties, nor did it possess all the usual characteristics of stock.

The characteristics typically associated with common stock are (i) the right to receive dividends contingent upon an apportionment of profits; (ii) negotiability; (iii) the ability to be pledged or hypothecated; (iv) the conferring of voting rights in proportion to the number of shares owned; and (v) the capacity to appreciate in value. Robinson's membership interest in GeoPhone lacked several of these characteristics.

First, as is common with interests in LLCs, GeoPhone's members did not share in the profits in proportion to the number of their shares. Pursuant to the ARGOA, Robinson was to receive 100 percent of GeoPhone's net profits up to a certain amount, only after which were funds to be distributed pro rata to the members in proportion to their relative shares.

Second, like interests in LLCs more generally, Robinson's membership interests were not freely negotiable. According to the ARGOA, Robinson could only transfer his interests if he first offered other members the opportunity to purchase his interests on similar terms. Moreover, unlike with stock (except some stock in close corporations), anyone to whom Robinson or other members transferred their interests would not have thereby acquired any of the control or management rights that normally attend a stock transfer. Rather, the ARGOA requires that transferees satisfy several conditions to become members, in addition to receiving the approval of a majority of GeoPhone's managers.

* * *

Similarly, Robinson could pledge his interest, but the pledgee would acquire only distribution rights and not control rights. As for the apportionment of voting rights, the parties dispute whether voting rights were conferred in proportion to members' interests in GeoPhone. Even resolving this dispute in Robinson's favor, it remains clear that Robinson's membership interest lacked the ordinary attributes of stock.

Finally, from the very beginning Robinson and Glynn consistently viewed Robinson's investment as a "membership interest," and never as "stock." The purchase and operating agreements that Robinson and Glynn executed, as well as the agreement in which Robinson bought out Glynn's interest in GeoPhone, all termed Robinson's investment as a "membership interest" rather than "stock." Even the shares that Robinson received as a result of his investments declared Robinson the holder of "membership interests in GeoPhone Company, L.L.C., within the meaning of the Delaware Limited Liability Company Act." Robinson thus cannot argue that he was misled into believing that his membership interests were stock whose purchases were governed by the securities laws. And it would do violence to the statutory language of the securities laws to include within the term "stock" an instrument that was neither labeled stock nor like stock.

IV.

The parties have vigorously urged us to rule broadly in this case, asking that we generally classify interests in limited liability companies, or LLCs, as investment contracts (Robinson's view) or non-securities (Glynn's view). LLCs are particularly difficult to categorize under the securities laws, however, because they are hybrid business entities that combine features of corporations, general partnerships, and limited partnerships. * * * Precisely because LLCs lack standardized membership rights or organizational structures, they can assume an almost unlimited variety of forms. It becomes, then, exceedingly difficult to declare that LLCs, whatever their form, either possess or lack the economic characteristics associated with investment contracts. Even drawing firm lines between member-managed and manager-managed LLCs threatens impermissibly to elevate form over substance. Certainly the members in a member-managed LLC will often have powers too significant to be considered passive investors under the securities laws. And yet even members in a member-managed LLC may be unable as a practical matter to exercise any meaningful control, perhaps because they are too numerous, inexperienced, or geographically disparate. By the same token, while interests in manager-managed LLCs may often be securities, their members need not necessarily be reliant on the efforts of their managers.

We decline, therefore, the parties' invitation for a broader holding. On the facts of this case, it is clear that Robinson did not lack the ability to meaningfully exercise the rights granted him under GeoPhone's operating agreement. To the contrary, Robinson had a significant say in GeoPhone's management.

* * *

Reves v. Ernst & Young

494 U.S. 56 (1990).

■ JUSTICE MARSHALL delivered the opinion of the Court.

This case presents the question whether certain demand notes issued by the Farmer's Cooperative of Arkansas and Oklahoma are "securities" within the meaning of § 3(a)(10) of the Securities Exchange Act of 1934. We conclude that they are.

I

The Co–Op is an agricultural cooperative that, at the time relevant here, had approximately 23,000 members. In order to raise money to support its general business operations, the Co–Op sold promissory notes payable on demand by the holder. Although the notes were uncollateralized and uninsured, they paid a variable rate of interest that was adjusted monthly to keep it higher than the rate paid by local financial institutions. The Co–Op offered the notes to both members and nonmembers, marketing the scheme as an "Investment Program." Advertisements for the notes, which appeared in each Co–Op newsletter, read in part: "YOUR CO–OP has more than $11,000,000 in assets to stand behind your investments. The Investment is not Federal [sic] insured but it is ... Safe ... Secure ... and available when you need it." App. 5 (ellipses in original). Despite these assurances, the Co–Op filed for bankruptcy in 1984. At the time of the filing, over 1,600 people held notes worth a total of $10 million.

After the Co–Op filed for bankruptcy, petitioners, a class of holders of the notes, filed suit against Arthur Young & Co., the firm that had audited the Co–Op's financial statements (and the predecessor to respondent Ernst & Young). Petitioners alleged, *inter alia,* that Arthur Young had intentionally failed to follow generally accepted accounting principles in its audit, specifically with respect to the valuation of one of the Co–Op's major assets, a gasohol plant. Petitioners claimed that Arthur Young violated these principles in an effort to inflate the assets and net worth of the Co–Op. Petitioners maintained that, had Arthur Young properly treated the plant in its audits, they would not have purchased demand notes because the Co–Op's insolvency would have been apparent. On the basis of these allegations, petitioners claimed that Arthur Young had violated the antifraud provisions of the 1934 Act as well as Arkansas' securities laws.

Petitioners prevailed at trial on both their federal and state claims, receiving a $6.1 million judgment. Arthur Young appealed, claiming that the demand notes were not "securities" under either the 1934 Act or Arkansas law, and that the statutes' antifraud provisions therefore did not apply. A panel of the Eighth Circuit, agreeing with Arthur Young on both the state and federal issues, reversed. * * *

II

A

This case requires us to decide whether the note issued by the Co–Op is a "security" within the meaning of the 1934 Act. * * *

* * * In defining the scope of the market that it wished to regulate, Congress painted with a broad brush. It recognized the virtually limitless scope of human ingenuity, especially in the creation of "countless and variable schemes devised by those who seek the use of the money of others on the promise of profits," *SEC v. W.J. Howey Co.,* 328 U.S. 293, 299, 66 S.Ct. 1100, 1103, 90 L.Ed. 1244 (1946) * * *. Congress therefore did not attempt precisely to cabin the scope of the Securities Acts.[1] Rather, it

1. We have consistently held that "[t]he definition of a security in § 3(a)(10) of the 1934 Act, is virtually identical [to the 1933 Act's definition] and, for present purposes, the coverage of the two Acts may be considered the same." *United Housing Foun-*

enacted a definition of "security" sufficiently broad to encompass virtually any instrument that might be sold as an investment.

* * *

A commitment to an examination of the economic realities of a transaction does not necessarily entail a case-by-case analysis of every instrument, however. Some instruments are obviously within the class Congress intended to regulate because they are by their nature investments. In *Landreth Timber Co. v. Landreth,* 471 U.S. 681 * * * (1985), we held that an instrument bearing the name "stock" that, among other things, is negotiable, offers the possibility of capital appreciation, and carries the right to dividends contingent on the profits of a business enterprise is plainly within the class of instruments Congress intended the securities laws to cover. *Landreth Timber* does not signify a lack of concern with economic reality; rather, it signals a recognition that stock is, as a practical matter, always an investment if it has the economic characteristics traditionally associated with stock. Even if sparse exceptions to this generalization can be found, the public perception of common stock as the paradigm of a security suggests that stock, in whatever context it is sold, should be treated as within the ambit of the Acts. * * *

We made clear in *Landreth Timber* that stock was a special case, explicitly limiting our holding to that sort of instrument. * * * Although we refused finally to rule out a similar *per se* rule for notes, we intimated that such a rule would be unjustified. Unlike "stock," we said, " 'note' may now be viewed as a relatively broad term that encompasses instruments with widely varying characteristics, depending on whether issued in a consumer context, as commercial paper, or in some other investment context." * * * While common stock is the quintessence of a security, * * * and investors therefore justifiably assume that a sale of stock is covered by the Securities Acts, the same simply cannot be said of notes, which are used in a variety of settings, not all of which involve investments. Thus, the phrase "any note" should not be interpreted to mean literally "any note," but must be understood against the backdrop of what Congress was attempting to accomplish in enacting the Securities Acts.

Because the *Landreth Timber* formula cannot sensibly be applied to notes, some other principle must be developed to define the term "note." A majority of the Courts of Appeals that have considered the issue have adopted, in varying forms, "investment versus commercial" approaches that distinguish, on the basis of all of the circumstances surrounding the transactions, notes issued in an investment context (which are "securities") from notes issued in a commercial or consumer context (which are not). * * *

The Second Circuit's "family resemblance" approach begins with a presumption that *any* note with a term of more than nine months is a "security." * * * Recognizing that not all notes are securities, however, the

dation, Inc. v. Forman, 421 U.S. 837, 847, n. 12 95 S.Ct. 2051, 2058 n. 12, 44 L.Ed. 621 (1975)(citations omitted). We reaffirm that principle here.

Second Circuit has also devised a list of notes that it has decided are obviously not securities. Accordingly, the "family resemblance" test permits an issuer to rebut the presumption that a note is a security if it can show that the note in question "bear[s] a strong family resemblance" to an item on the judicially crafted list of exceptions, * * *, or convinces the court to add a new instrument to the list. * * *

In contrast, the Eighth and District of Columbia Circuits apply the test we created in *SEC v. W.J. Howey Co.,* * * * to determine whether an instrument is an "investment contract" to the determination whether an instrument is a "note." Under this test, a note is a security only if it evidences "(1) an investment; (2) in a common enterprise; (3) with a reasonable expectation of profits; (4) to be derived from the entrepreneurial or managerial efforts of others." * * *

We reject the approaches of those courts that have applied the *Howey* test to notes; *Howey* provides a mechanism for determining whether an instrument is an "investment contract." The demand notes here may well not be "investment contracts," but that does not mean they are not "notes." To hold that a "note" is not a "security" unless it meets a test designed for an entirely different variety of instrument "would make the Acts' enumeration of many types of instruments superfluous," *Landreth Timber,* 471 U.S., at 692, and would be inconsistent with Congress' intent to regulate the entire body of instruments sold as investments * * *.

The other two contenders—the "family resemblance" and "investment versus commercial" tests—are really two ways of formulating the same general approach. Because we think the "family resemblance" test provides a more promising framework for analysis, however, we adopt it. The test begins with the language of the statute; because the Securities Acts define "security" to include "any note," we begin with a presumption that every note is a security. We nonetheless recognize that this presumption cannot be irrebuttable. As we have said * * * Congress was concerned with regulating the investment market, not with creating a general federal cause of action for fraud. In an attempt to give more content to that dividing line, the Second Circuit has identified a list of instruments commonly denominated "notes" that nonetheless fall without the "security" category. [Under Second Circuit opinions,] * * * types of notes that are not "securities" include "the note delivered in consumer financing, the note secured by a mortgage on a home, the short-term note secured by a lien on a small business or some of its assets, the note evidencing a 'character' loan to a bank customer, short-term notes secured by an assignment of accounts receivable, or a note which simply formalizes an open-account debt incurred in the ordinary course of business (particularly if, as in the case of the customer of a broker, it is collateralized)" * * * [and] "notes evidencing loans by commercial banks for current operations" * * *.

We agree that the items identified by the Second Circuit are not properly viewed as "securities." More guidance, though, is needed. It is impossible to make any meaningful inquiry into whether an instrument bears a "resemblance" to one of the instruments identified by the Second

Circuit without specifying what it is about *those* instruments that makes *them* non-"securities." Moreover, as the Second Circuit itself has noted, its list is "not graven in stone," and is therefore capable of expansion. Thus, some standards must be developed for determining when an item should be added to the list.

An examination of the list itself makes clear what those standards should be. In creating its list, the Second Circuit was applying the same factors that this Court has held apply in deciding whether a transaction involves a "security." First, we examine the transaction to assess the motivations that would prompt a reasonable seller and buyer to enter into it. If the seller's purpose is to raise money for the general use of a business enterprise or to finance substantial investments and the buyer is interested primarily in the profit the note is expected to generate, the instrument is likely to be a "security." If the note is exchanged to facilitate the purchase and sale of a minor asset or consumer good, to correct for the seller's cash-flow difficulties, or to advance some other commercial or consumer purpose, on the other hand, the note is less sensibly described as a "security." * * * Second, we examine the "plan of distribution" of the instrument, * * * to determine whether it is an instrument in which there is "common trading for speculation or investment." Third, we examine the reasonable expectations of the investing public: The Court will consider instruments to be "securities" on the basis of such public expectations, even where an economic analysis of the circumstances of the particular transaction might suggest that the instruments are not "securities" as used in that transaction. * * * Finally, we examine whether some factor such as the existence of another regulatory scheme significantly reduces the risk of the instrument, thereby rendering application of the Securities Act unnecessary. * * *

We conclude, then, that in determining whether an instrument denominated a "note" is a "security," courts are to apply the version of the "family resemblance" test that we have articulated here: a note is presumed to be a "security," and that presumption may be rebutted only by a showing that the note bears a strong resemblance (in terms of the four factors we have identified) to one of the enumerated categories of instrument. If an instrument is not sufficiently similar to an item on the list, the decision whether another category should be added is to be made by examining the same factors.

B

Applying the family resemblance approach to this case, we have little difficulty in concluding that the notes at issue here are "securities." Ernst & Young admits that "a demand note does not closely resemble any of the Second Circuit's family resemblance examples." * * * Nor does an examination of the four factors we have identified as being relevant to our inquiry suggest that the demand notes here are not "securities" despite their lack of similarity to any of the enumerated categories. The Co–Op sold the notes in an effort to raise capital for its general business operations, and purchasers bought them in order to earn a profit in the form of interest.[4] Indeed, one of the primary inducements offered purchasers was an interest rate constantly revised to keep it slightly above the rate paid by local banks and savings and loans. From both sides, then, the transaction is most naturally conceived as an investment in a business enterprise rather than as a purely commercial or consumer transaction.

As to the plan of distribution, The Co–Op offered the notes over an extended period to its 23,000 members, as well as to nonmembers, and more than 1,600 people held notes when the Co–Op filed for bankruptcy. To be sure, the notes were not traded on an exchange. They were, however, offered and sold to a broad segment of the public, and that is all we have held to be necessary to establish the requisite "common trading" in an instrument. See, e.g. *Landreth Timber, supra* (stock of closely held corporations not traded on any exchange held to be a "security"); * * *.

The third factor—the public's reasonable perceptions—also supports a finding that the notes in this case are "securities". We have consistently identified the fundamental essence of a "security" to be its character as an "investment." * * * The advertisements for the notes here characterized them as "investments," * * * and there were no countervailing factors that would have led a reasonable person to question this characterization. In these circumstances, it would be reasonable for a prospective purchaser to take the Co–Op at its word.

Finally, we find no risk-reducing factor to suggest that these instruments are not in fact securities. * * *

We therefore hold that the notes of issue here are within the term "note" in § 3(a)(10).

* * *

NOTES

1. This book has dealt with essentially five types of interests in a business: partnership interests (including interests in an LLP), limited partnership interests, limited liability company membership interests, stock and debt. The *Williamson* decision cited in *Robinson* addressed whether a partnership interest can constitute an investment contract, and, hence, a security:

> All of this indicates that an investor who claims his general partnership or joint venture interest is an investment contract has a difficult burden to overcome. On the face of a partnership agreement, the investor retains substantial control over his investment and an ability

4. We emphasize that by "profit" in the context of notes, we mean "a valuable return on an investment," which undoubtedly includes interest. We have, of course, defined "profit" more restrictively in applying the *Howey* test to what are claimed to be "investment contracts." See, e.g., *Forman,* 421 U.S., at 852 ("[P]rofit" under the *Howey* test means either "capital appreciation" or "a participation in earnings"). * * * Because the *Howey* test is irrelevant to the issue before us today * * * we decline to extend its definition of "profit" beyond the realm in which that definition applies.

> to protect himself from the managing partner or hired manager. Such an investor must demonstrate that, in spite of the partnership form which the investment took, he was so dependent on the promoter or on a third party that he was in fact unable to exercise meaningful partnership powers.[14] A general partnership or joint venture interest can be designated a security if the investor can establish, for example, that (1) an agreement among the parties leaves so little power in the hands of the partner or venturer that the arrangement in fact distributes power as would a limited partnership; or (2) the partner or venturer is so inexperienced and unknowledgeable in business affairs that he is incapable of intelligently exercising his partnership or venture powers; or (3) the partner or venturer is so dependent on some unique entrepreneurial or managerial ability of the promoter or manager that he cannot replace the manager of the enterprise or otherwise exercise meaningful partnership or venture powers.

645 F.2d at 424. *But see Banghart v. Hollywood General Partnership*, 902 F.2d 805 (10th Cir.1990) (will only look at the partnership agreement to see if a general partnership interest is a security). While the court in *Robinson* evaluated whether the LLC interest was either an "investment contract" or "stock" in order to determine if the interest was a security, a number of state securities laws contain provisions specifically addressing whether interests in a limited liability company are "securities" under the states' securities laws. *E.g.,* Cal. Corp. Code § 25019. In the *Landreth Timber* decision discussed in *Reves,* the Supreme Court held that stock in a corporation (even if closely held) is, by express definition, one type of security—at least so long as the stock possesses those features normally associated with corporate stock, rather than representing a right to a cooperative apartment, for example. *See United Housing Foundation, Inc. v. Forman,* 421 U.S. 837 (1975). By contrast, *Robinson* shows that courts will be reluctant to label interests in non-corporate forms to be stock for purposes of the securities laws. *Reves* discusses the test for determining when debt instruments (notes) constitute a security. How would the test apply to the use of corporate debt discussed in Chapter IV?

Beyond these categories, as both the laundry lists contained in the statutory definitions, and the discussions in the courts' opinions show, numerous other items can constitute a security. Indeed, anytime a business seeks to raise money, the parties must at least consider the possibility that the transaction, no matter what it appears to be on its face, might involve the sale of a security. Suppose, however, the business seeks to acquire property or services, rather than cash, in exchange for stock, debt or another interest; could this involve the sale of a security? Stock, as just stated, is a security by definition regardless of the consideration paid for it; while the fact that a firm issues debt in exchange for property should be a factor against finding the debt instrument equals a "note" under the family resemblance test outlined in *Reves*. Yet, what about an "investment contract," for which the *Howey* test speaks of "an investment of money?"

14. We emphasize that this dependence does not by itself establish that a partnership interest satisfies the third prong of the *Howey* test. * * * [O]ne would have to show that the reliance on the manager which forms the basis of the partner's expectations was an understanding in the original transaction, and not some subsequent decision to delegate partnership duties.

See *International Brotherhood of Teamsters v. Daniel*, 439 U.S. 551, 560 n.12 (1979) (not absolutely necessary that investment be in cash rather than goods or services). Also, with respect to the elements of the *Howey* test, can a fixed return constitute "profits"? See *SEC v. Edwards*, 540 U.S. 389 (2004) (yes).

2. What is the impact of finding that a transaction involves the sale of securities? In *Reves* and *Williamson*, the plaintiffs sought to turn their allegations of misrepresentation by the defendants into a federal cause of action, instead of simply a state common law tort, by arguing they purchased securities. Yet, this has limited relevance from a planning, rather than a litigation strategy, standpoint. Instead, from a planning standpoint, one must ask whether the securities laws require any special action by persons selling securities. If so, given the fact that limited and some ordinary partnership interests, some limited liability company interests, stock, even in a closely held corporation, and much corporate debt, are securities, have Chapters III and IV overlooked an important consideration? The answer to the question of whether the securities laws require some special action by persons selling securities, it turns out, depends upon to whom the venture sells the security. This is the subject of the next section of this chapter.

SECTION C. TARGETING THE APPROPRIATE INVESTORS

1. GOING PUBLIC

At first blush, the most tempting source of financing for a growing business may be to sell securities to the public at large. Businessmen who follow the stock market often tell stories about companies in their field whose shares sell at many times per-share earnings. Doing some arithmetic, they might figure their company could sell a million dollars worth of shares and still leave them with a comfortable majority. They might even plan to sell off a few of their own shares and start living in a more comfortable style. Determining whether this is a viable option requires addressing both the business practicalities and the legal requirements involved with taking a company public.

a. *Business Considerations*

Deloitte & Touche, Strategies For Going Public

(1983).

SECTION 2
SHOULD YOU GO PUBLIC?

* * *

The decision to go public is a major one in any company's life and is not one to be reached lightly. You must carefully weigh the advantages, disadvantages, and alternatives before proceeding.

THE ADVANTAGES

Going public may provide possible benefits to both a company and its stockholders. The major benefits include:

Less dilution. If your company is at the stage where it is ready to go public, you may command a higher price for your securities through a public offering than through a private placement or other form of equity financing. This means you give up less of your company to receive the same amount of funding.

* * *

Enhanced ability to raise equity. If your company continues to grow, you will eventually need additional permanent financing. If your stock performs well in the stock market, you will be able to sell additional stock on favorable terms.

Liquidity and valuation. Once your company goes public, a market will be established for your stock and you will have an effective way of valuing that stock. You and your co-founders may have invested everything you own into the company. A public market makes it easier for you to dispose of a portion of your interest, should you want to diversify your investment portfolio or should you merely want some spending money. * * *

Major stockholders, such as venture capital firms, may require this liquidity. Venture capital firms generally organize funds with a fixed life of five years or so. At the end of that period they need to liquidate the fund. By going public, you provide the venture capitalists with the ability to sell their holdings or to have publicly-tradeable stock which can be distributed to their fund participants.

Stock options offered by emerging public companies have much appeal and can help you to recruit or retain well-qualified executives and to motivate your employee-shareholders. * * * Unlike options offered by a nonpublic company, yours will have an easily determinable value and your stock can be sold over the counter.

Prestige. You and your co-founders gain an enormous amount of personal prestige from being associated with a company that goes public. It is one measure of success, and many of today's entrepreneurs start companies with the goal of eventually taking those companies public.

A public market for your stock will also enhance your corporate image and generate more interest in the company from your customers, suppliers, and business associates.

* * *

THE DISADVANTAGES

There are also some very significant disadvantages to going public that should be weighed against the many advantages.

Expense. The cost of going public is substantial, both initially and on an ongoing basis. As for the initial costs, the underwriters' commission can run as high as 10% or more of the total offering. Additionally, you can incur out-of-pocket expenses of $200,000 to $300,000 for even a small offering. * * *

On an ongoing basis, regulatory reporting requirements will increase paperwork. You will have to hold formal board and stockholder meetings and devote a significant amount of time to investor relations.

Disclosure of information. As a publicly-held corporation, your company's operations and financial situation are open to public scrutiny. Information concerning the company, officers, directors, and certain shareholders—information not ordinarily disclosed by privately held companies—will now be available to competitors, customers, employees, and others. Such information as your company's sales, profits, your competitive edge, and the salaries and perquisites of your officers and directors must be disclosed not only when you initially go public, but also on a continuing basis thereafter.

Pressure to maintain growth pattern. You will be subject to considerable internal and external pressure to maintain the growth rate you have established. If your sales or earnings deviate from the established trend, stockholders may become apprehensive and sell their stock, driving down its price. Additionally, you will have to begin reporting operating results quarterly. People will evaluate the company on a quarterly, rather than an annual, basis. This will intensify the pressure and shorten your planning and operating horizons significantly. The pressure may tempt you to make short-term decisions that could have harmful long-term impact on the company.

Loss of control. If a sufficiently large proportion of your shares is sold to the public, you may be threatened with the loss of control of the company. And once your company is publicly-held, the potential exists for further dilution of your control through subsequent public offerings and acquisitions.

* * *

SECTION 3
ARE YOU READY TO GO PUBLIC?

The majority of companies that have recently gone public have reached certain levels of size, profitability, and growth. The public market most readily accepts companies that have achieved:

- Sales of $15–20 million;
- Net income of $1 million or more in the current fiscal year; and

- An annual growth rate of 30–50%, with the prospect of continuing growth at that rate for the next few years. To draw financial and institutional investors, the company must have the near-term potential to generate revenues of $50–100 million.

This is not to say that you must wait until you reach those levels to go public. There have been many early-stage companies—companies that had yet to show a profit—that have gone public. * * *

But such companies are unproven and lack sufficient operating history. These are not unsubstantial risks, and underwriters look for some key compensating factors, factors which create "glamour" or "sizzle" in a company:

- *Management team.* Underwriters view the quality of the management team as the most critical factor. Top management personnel must have the capability to deal with the anticipated growth and to maintain the company's leadership position. One or two executives who have successfully built other public companies and have established credibility in the financial community may be all that is necessary to alleviate the anxiety that underwriters and investors have about an unproven company.

- *Leadership position in the industry.* In order to attract investors, an unproven company needs a product that indicates it is on the leading edge in its field. Whether it be new technology or enhancement of an old idea, the investing public needs to perceive the company's potential as unlimited, with exciting new product development in a growth industry and the probability of being more than just a one-product company.

- *Market opportunity.* Your product must have a market that will support growth of 30–50% a year.

There are, however, some hazards to an early offering. You must be confident that your business and your product are sufficiently developed and that your key people are in place. A company that flounders after going public will lose credibility in the public market, and the investors' confidence in it will be difficult, if not impossible, to regain. If you have any doubts at all, you should seek other forms of financing. When your company strengthens, you can proceed with the public offering.

Public offerings are not limited to these growth companies. Many offerings are underwritten for companies with a long and continuous record of good sales and earnings. These companies may not be spectacular, but they offer the public a good long-term investment at a reasonable price-earnings ratio.

There are many companies, too, that have no operating history nor all the characteristics discussed above. High-risk investments, such as the so-called "penny stocks", can attract that segment of the market comprising speculators rather than long-term investors. These types of offerings, however, are generally not done by the major underwriting firms.

The timing of your offering will be a major consideration. If your stock is attractive, you can sell it at any time. To obtain the best price for your stock, however, market conditions must be favorable and the investing public must be in the mood to buy a new issue. Your investment bankers are in the best position to advise you whether now is an opportune time or, in their words, whether the "window" for new issues is open.

* * *

SECTION 5
THE UNDERWRITERS

Most initial public offerings are arranged through an investment banking firm. One of an investment banker's many functions is to underwrite securities. * * *

* * * While nothing prevents you from conducting your own public offering, the use of underwriters can help assure that it will be successful.

If you conduct your own offering, you may find it very difficult to find a sufficient number of buyers for your stock. The key reason for using underwriters is that they can develop a marketing structure (the underwriting syndicate) to sell the stock. The syndicate has access to buyers, as those buyers are their clients. Underwriters are also familiar with market conditions; they know the mood of institutional and individual investors regarding new stock issues; and they are familiar with the prices of stock of similar companies. They are in the best position to advise you as to what price to ask for your stock as well as when to sell it. Their sponsorship also extends well past the initial offering—their continuing sponsorship will affect how your stock performs in that "after-market".

Selecting an Underwriter

Public offerings are normally conducted by a group, or syndicate, of underwriters. Your company only needs to select the lead, or managing, underwriters. The managing underwriters will form the syndicate for you.

Ideally, you will have already developed a relationship with an investment banker by the time you decide to go public. Most companies approach an investment banker (or vice versa) a year or two in advance. Many start-up companies make this connection during early-stage private placements. * * *

If you do not already have an investment banker, there are many things to consider. * * *

Investment bankers, unlike other professionals, do not charge hourly rates for their services. You compensate them only through commissions on any successful deals they package for you. These commissions do not vary significantly from firm to firm, so pick from the best firms available.

The best way to approach an investment banker is through a mutual contact (your accountants or attorneys may be able to assist you). Investment bankers are not very responsive to unsolicited letters, particularly if they suspect they are form letters sent to every investment banker in the area.

This is not to say you shouldn't shop around. You should, by all means, explore at least a few possibilities. * * *

Selecting the right investment banker will be a major factor in the success of your offering. In selecting one, you should know the characteristics of a good investment banker:

- *Reputation.* In an initial offering the reputation of the underwriter is of great importance. Institutional and individual investors will have greater confidence in your stock if a highly regarded investment banking firm is named in your prospectus as the managing underwriter. * * * The professional reputation of the investment banking firm will also affect its ability to form a strong syndicate of firms to effectively sell and distribute the stock.

- *Distribution capability.* You will want the underwriters to distribute your stock to a client base that is sufficiently strong and varied to generate continuing market interest in the stock after the initial offering. Each investment banking firm has a different client base. You should find out how diversified that base is. Some firms have access to many institutional investors while others emphasize individual investors. Some have an international emphasis while others are domestically-oriented. Evaluate the quality of their clients, whether they are long-term investors or speculators. Only when the underwriters, through their own clients and a strong syndicate, effectively distribute your stock, will your stock perform well in the after-market.

- *Experience.* The investment banking firm should have experience in underwriting issues of companies in the same or similar industries. This will influence its ability to price the issue accurately and will give it credibility when explaining and selling the company to the public.

Once the stock has been issued to the public, managing underwriters assume responsibility for continued sponsorship of your company to the financial community. * * * Before you select an investment banking firm, you should evaluate the after-market performance of other initial public offerings which the firm has underwritten, and evaluate the following characteristics:

- *Market-making capability.* When a company first goes public, shares are traded on the over-the-counter market. A number of investment banking firms will become the market makers in this new stock, that is they will deal in your stock, offering firm prices to buy shares from or sell shares to the general public. The managing underwriters generally serve as the principal market-makers. In order to maintain a market, they will need to devote a sufficient amount of capital to take large positions (*i.e.,* be "short" or "long") in your stock. Without this, large shareholders will not have much liquidity, interest will wane, and the market price of your stock will suffer.

• *Research capability.* The financial community will look to the managing underwriter as a primary source of information about the newly public company. Therefore, the selected investment banking firm should have experienced analysts—analysts who are respected by the financial community—closely following the industry in which your company does its business.

• *Ability to provide financial advice.* During and after your offering you will look to your investment bankers for financial advice. You may need help to obtain additional financing in the future, advice on potential mergers and acquisitions, or insight into the investing public's attitude toward your company.

* * * You should also take the time to be sure you are comfortable not only with the people whom you will be directly involved with initially, but also with those who will have ongoing responsibility for market-making, research, and sales sponsorship. The personal chemistry between your investment bankers and you, your management team, and your board of directors is of utmost importance.

You may also consider using more than one managing underwriter. A company often uses two or more underwriting firms to co-manage its offerings if the company has a good relationship with more than one firm or if the company sees advantages to combining the client bases, research capabilities, geographic strengths, etc. of the underwriting firms.

* * *

Types of Underwritings

There are generally two types of underwritings. Under a *firm commitment* the underwriters agree to buy, at a fixed price, all the stock being offered. They then resell it to the public. If they are unable to resell all of the stock, they must keep it until they can sell later.

Under a *best efforts commitment,* the underwriters agree to use their "best efforts" to sell the new issue on the issuer's behalf. If they don't sell the entire amount to the public they have no obligation to purchase the balance. As such, they are acting merely as your agent.

There are many variations of the best efforts commitment. Under "all or none" agreements, the underwriters will either sell the entire issue, or cancel the whole offering and return the purchase price of investors who purchased part of the issue. Other agreements call for a minimum number of shares to be sold, i.e., the underwriters and the issuer may agree that 66–2/3 percent of the shares must be sold for the offering to be effective, and the remaining 33–1/3 percent would then be sold on a strictly best efforts basis.

From your viewpoint, the firm commitment would be the best arrangement, as it assures you that you will receive a certain sum of money by a certain date. The next most desirable arrangement would be the best efforts, all or none. This puts the risk of sale on you, but at least assures you that you won't go public unless all of the stock is sold. With a strictly best efforts arrangement, the amount of money you receive may fall significantly short of your needs, and you will also be strapped with all the requirements of a public company.

The type of underwriting that is offered to you will depend on the underwriting firm that you are using and the nature of your stock offering. If one of the major firms agrees to underwrite you, it will almost always agree to a firm commitment. The smaller firms that will handle the highly speculative offerings will only do so on a best efforts basis.

* * *

SECTION 9
CLOSING THE DEAL

Signing the Underwriting Agreement

As a rule, you will not enter into a written underwriting agreement until the morning of the date the registration statement is to be declared effective by the SEC.

Prior to that time you have an oral agreement with the underwriters or, in some cases, a letter of intent. The purpose of a letter of intent is to outline the basic method of financing acceptable to both parties, the price range at which the underwriters believe the shares can be sold to the public, and the approximate underwriting compensation. The letter of intent is not a legal commitment by either side to proceed with any predetermined transaction.

After the close of business on the day before the effective date, the managing underwriters and the company agree on the selling price to the public. The morning of the effective date, the managing underwriters and the other underwriters participating in the syndicate sign an "agreement among underwriters". This agreement authorizes the managing underwriters to sign the underwriting agreement, specifies the terms on which the participating underwriters will participate in the syndicate, and spells out the powers of the managing underwriters to manage the offering.

Immediately thereafter, the underwriting agreement is signed by the company, the managing underwriters, and the selling shareholders (if any). The underwriting agreement will include the offering price of the stock; commissions, discounts, and expense allowances; the method of underwriting; and an indemnification agreement.

* * * Until [the underwriting agreement is signed], the company has no legal right to compel the underwriters to proceed with the offering.

As a practical matter, once preparation of the registration statement begins, reputable underwriters rarely refuse to complete the offering unless there are significant adverse changes in market conditions or the registration process reveals serious problems of the company of which the underwriters were not previously aware. The managing underwriters have a vested interest in completing the offering, since they have invested considerable time and expense in investigating the company's business and affairs, helping to prepare the registration statement, and organizing a selling syndicate.

However, if the market drops significantly during the waiting period, it is not unusual for an offering to be postponed or cancelled after the registration process starts. If the market is not willing to accept the originally anticipated price range or is unwilling to absorb an offering as big as the one contemplated, the company may be faced with accepting an offering of unsatisfactory size or price, postponing the offering until the market improves, or even abandoning the offering completely.

* * *

NOTES

1. The advice reprinted above reflects the traditional wisdom that companies generally are not ready for a public offering until they have reached a certain level of profitability; albeit there are some offerings by companies that have yet to earn a profit. One famous example of a successful public offering despite the company having not reached profitability is the initial public offering by Yahoo!, Inc. Yahoo went public nine months after the founding of the company (during which nine months Yahoo had a net loss of $634,000 from revenues of $1.4 million).

As explained in the reprint, the ability of a company to have a successful public offering prior to profitability depends upon the prospects of the company. It also depends upon the overall stock market. For example, during the bull market of 1999, there were almost 500 initial public offerings of stock, of which almost three-quarters were from companies that were unprofitable at the time of the offering. After the market bubble burst, in 2002, there were under 100 initial public offerings of stock, of which only around 15 percent were from unprofitable companies. In 2006, there were around 200 initial public offerings of stock, of which around one-third were from unprofitable companies. McKay, *In the Red Selling Stock*, Wall Street J. C1, C2 (June 4, 2007).

2. One alternative to offering stock through an underwriter, which some companies have recently begun to explore, is to offer stock through the Internet. So far, these efforts have met with limited success, perhaps because the Internet cannot substitute for two values that an underwriter provides beyond simply finding buyers for a company's securities. As mentioned in the excerpt above, underwriters provide knowledge of market conditions to help a company price the securities the company proposes to sell. In addition, a well-known underwriter adds credibility to the initial public offering. In other words, investors may be wary of purchasing stock in a company they know little about other than through a flashy site on the Internet. Indeed, the investor might well worry that the whole offering is nothing more than an elaborate fraud. Purchasing stock through a well-known underwriter arguably gives the investor assurance that there is

some merit to the offering. After all, well-established underwriters have their reputations to worry about, and so, presumably, are not going to peddle completely worthless investments.

b. *Federal Registration*

Schneider, Manko & Kant, Going Public—Practice Procedures & Consequences

27 Vill. L. Rev. 1 (1981)*.

INTRODUCTION

When a company wishes to "GO PUBLIC" it faces a complex and challenging process. It is the purpose of this article to focus on the sections of the Securities Act of 1933 (the '33 Act) dealing with registration as it applies to companies selling securities to the public for the first time—"going public." * * * In a nutshell, the '33 Act is designed to prohibit the public distribution of securities without disclosure of relevant information to the investor. * * *

THE REGISTRATION STATEMENT

The registration statement is the disclosure document required to be filed with the SEC in connection with a registered offering. It consists physically of two principal parts. Part I of the registration statement is the prospectus, which is the only part that normally goes to the public offerees of the securities. * * * Part II of the registration statement contains supplemental information which is available for public inspection at the office of the SEC.

The registration forms[4], Regulation S–K[5], Regulation S–X[6] and the Industry Guides[7] (when applicable) specify the information to be contained in the registration statement. Regulation S–K sets forth detailed disclosure requirements which are applicable in various contexts under the securities laws; Regulation S–X similarly sets forth financial statement requirements; and the Industry Guides require specific disclosure applicable to certain prescribed businesses such as oil and gas and banking. In addition, Regula-

* [This excerpt reflects revisions made by Messrs Schneider, Manko and Kant through May 1988. Ed.]

4. On March 3, 1982, the Commission announced the adoption of comprehensive revisions to the various disclosure forms and rules governing the registration of securities under the '33 Act. * * * The adoption culminated several years of effort to integrate the disclosure requirements of the '33 and '34 Acts and to improve and simplify the disclosure requirements of those Acts. * * * Although the new integrated disclosure system provides for abbreviated registration forms for various types of issuers, a full disclosure document such as the text describes will be required for an initial public offering.

5. *See* SEC Regulation S–K, 17 C.F.R. §§ 229.1–229.800 (1988).

6. *See* SEC Regulation S–X, 17 C.F.R. §§ 210.1–01–210.12–29 (1988).

7. *See* SEC Securities Act Release No. 6384 (March 3, 1982).

tion C[8] sets forth certain general requirements as to the registration of securities including filing fees * * * and other mechanical aspects of registration.

The registration forms contain a series of "items" and instructions (generally referring to the disclosure requirements contained in Regulation S–K), in response to which disclosures must be made. But they are not forms in the sense that they have blanks to be completed like a tax return. Traditionally, the prospectus describes the company's business and responds to all the disclosures required in narrative rather than item-and-answer form. It is prepared as a brochure describing the company and the securities to be offered. The usual prospectus is a fairly stylized document, and there is a customary sequence for organizing the material.

Form S–1 traditionally has been the most common registration form used. * * * [In 1992, however, the SEC introduced a new form, SB–2, designed for smaller issuers—generally, companies with less than $25 million in revenues and in publicly held shares. The SEC also introduced a new disclosure regulation, S–B (17 C.F.R. §§ 228.10–228.202). Regulation S–B is a small business parallel to Regulation S–K. Ed.]

* * *

In the typical first public offering, the items to which it is most difficult to respond, and which require the most creative effort in preparation, deal with the description of the company's business, properties, material transactions with insiders, and use of proceeds. Other matters to be disclosed in the prospectus deal with the details of the underwriting, the plan for distributing the securities, capitalization, pending legal proceedings, competition, description of securities being registered, identification of directors and officers and their remuneration, options to purchase securities, and principal holders of securities. There are also detailed requirements concerning financial statements and financial information concerning the company's business segments.

In Part II of the registration statement is supplemental information of a more formal type which is not required to be given to each investor. Unlike the prospectus, Part II is prepared in item-and-answer form. One requirement which is sometimes troublesome calls for disclosure of recent sales of unregistered securities and a statement of the exemption relied upon. Counsel may discover the past issuances of securities violated the '33 Act. In some such cases, the result may be that the company's financial statements must reflect a very large contingent liability under the '33 Act. * * * Part II also contains supplemental financial schedules, as well as a list of exhibits which are filed with the registration statement. Although the information in Part II normally is not seen by individual investors, sophisticated analysts and financial services may make extensive use of it, particularly the supplemental financial schedules.

8. *See* SEC Regulation C, 17 C.F.R. §§ 230.400–230.499T (1988).

In preparing a prospectus, the applicable form is merely the beginning. The forms are quite general and apply to all types of businesses, securities, and offerings except for a few industries or limited situations for which special forms have been prepared. In the course of administration over the years, the Commission has given specific content to the general disclosure requirements. It often requires disclosures on a number of points within the scope of the form but not explicitly covered by the form itself. Furthermore, in addition to the information that the form expressly requires, the company must add any information necessary to make the statements made not misleading. * * *

The Commission's views on many matters change from time to time. SEC practitioners, both lawyers and accountants, constantly exchange news of what the Commission is currently requiring as reflected in its letters of comments.

The Commission has also evolved certain principles of emphasis in highlighting disclosures of adverse facts. It cannot prohibit an offering from being made if disclosure is adequate, but its policies on disclosure can make the offering look highly unattractive. In particular, if there are sufficient adverse factors in an offering, these are required to be set forth in detail in the very beginning of the prospectus under a caption such as "Introductory Statement," "Certain Considerations" or "Risk Factors of the Offerings." However, many new issues of going businesses do not require this treatment and counsel must make a judgment in each case. Some of the adverse factors which may be collected under such a heading include lack of business history; adverse business experience; operating losses; dependence upon particular customers, suppliers and key personnel; lack of a market for the security offered; competitive factors; certain types of transactions with insiders; a low book value for the stock compared to the offering price; potential dilution which may result from the exercise of convertible securities, options, or warrants; and a small investment by the promoters compared with the public investment.

To the same end, the SEC has required that boldface reference be made to certain adverse factors on the prospectus cover page. * * * To add to the brew, the Commission sometimes insists that certain factors be emphasized beyond what the attorneys working on the matter consider to be their true importance. A usual example is that prominent attention must be called to transactions between the company and its management. * * *

The SEC, which reviews the registration statement, has no authority to pass on the merits of a particular offering. * * * The sole thrust of the Federal statute is disclosure of relevant information. No matter how speculative the investment, no matter how poor the risk, the offering will comply with Federal law if all the required facts are disclosed.

* * *

The prospectus is a somewhat schizophrenic document, having two purposes which often present conflicting pulls. On the one hand, it is a selling document. It is used by the principal underwriters to form the underwriting syndicate and a dealer group, and by the underwriters and dealers to sell the securities to the public. From this point of view, it is desirable to present the best possible image. On the other hand, the prospectus is a disclosure document, an insurance policy against liability. With the view toward protection against liability, there is a tendency to resolve all doubts against the company and to make things look as bleak as possible. In balancing the purposes, established underwriters and experienced counsel, guided at least in part by their knowledge of SEC staff attitudes, traditionally lean to a very conservative presentation, avoiding glowing adjectives and predictions. The layman frequently complains that all the glamor [sic] and romance have been lost. "Why can't you tell them," he says, "that we have the most aggressive and imaginative management in the industry?" It takes considerable client education before an attorney can answer this question to the client's satisfaction.

Until relatively recently, it was traditional to confine prospectuses principally to objectively verifiable statements of historic fact. It is now considered proper, and in some instances essential, to include some information in a prospectus, either favorable or adverse to the company, which is predictive or based upon opinions or subjective evaluations. However, no such "soft information" should be included in the prospectus unless it has a reasonable basis in fact and represents management's good faith judgment.[14]

PREPARING THE REGISTRATION STATEMENT

The "quarterback" in preparing the registration statement is normally the attorney for the company.[15] * * *

14. *See* SEC Securities Act Rule 175, 17 C.F.R. § 230.175 (1988); Regulation S–K. Item 10(b), 17 C.F.R. § 229.1(b) (1988). * * *

15. On the lawyer's role in assisting in the preparation of registration statements, *see* Association of the Bar of the City of New York, *Report by Special Committee on Lawyers Role in Securities Transactions,* 38 Bus. Law. 1879, 1891–96 (1977), which proposes, *inter alia,* the following guidelines for practitioners:

Guideline Four:

The lawyer should assist the issuer, on the basis of information furnished to the lawyer, in reaching its decisions as to what information should be included in the registration statement, how it should be included, and to what extent its omission would raise the questions under the 1933 Act—i.e., he should assist the issuer in making judgments as to materiality and compliance with the requirements of the registration form and instructions.

Comment

(a) Within the confines of the agreed assignment of responsibilities and of a realistic evaluation of the extent to which a lawyer's consideration of essentially non-legal matters is useful to the client and warranted by the circumstances, the lawyer should study documents or otherwise inquire into other matters, not primarily legal in nature and not within counsel's expertise as such, in order to provide himself with a background from which better to assist the issuer in making its decisions.

(b) The determination of "materiality" of a fact or its omission, or of whether there is a material inaccuracy in a statement, involves many questions of fact and judgment. Usually any legal judgment will be based on a factual analysis peculiarly within the knowledge and capability of the management of the issuer. Although a lawyer can be helpful in bringing his experience, interrogation techniques and judgment to bear on questions of materiality, he cannot—and should not—take over from the issuer or other more qualified parties the responsibility for decisions in these gray areas. There will, of course, be matters where the subject involved is primarily a legal issue, or where the facts are so clear that a positive judgment can be made based on administrative regulations or administrative or judicial precedent.

More frequently, however, the lawyer can only give the client the benefit of an experienced judgment which he will often (as a practical matter) have to make without having knowledge of all relevant facts and which must be combined with the business judgment of the client, the underwriters, the auditors and perhaps other experts to enable the client to arrive at a final decision. * * *

(c) The lawyer should not allow the impression to be created that he will normally "investigate" factual matters covered in a registration statement, personally examining into primary sources or data, or that he can verify the reliability of other persons providing this information. * * * Except in the case of investigations into certain legal matters (such as due incorporation or valid issuance of securities) which the lawyer undertakes to perform personally rather than to rely on others, the lawyer rarely will go to primary records or other sources but will rely on interrogations of, and reports or compilations prepared by, others including other professionals such as auditors, engineers and other lawyers. Such reliance on others is entirely appropriate. By questioning the issuer's officers and the other persons providing the information, the lawyer can secure an understanding of the material provided, the means by which it was prepared, and its relevance and importance, and he can, if appropriate, suggest that further investigation or inquiry be undertaken. He can also attempt to cross-check information which seems subject to doubt for some reason, or otherwise warrants such inquiry, by questioning persons who appear familiar with it. Where, because of suspicious or other unusual circumstances, the lawyer believes special investigation of a particular matter is required, he should take this up with the issuer, and a procedure for such investigation should be decided upon. * * *

Guideline Five:

The lawyer should assist in the drafting of the registration statement or portions thereof with the goal that, to the extent feasible, the registration statement says what the lawyer understands the issuer intends it to say, is unambiguous, and is written in a way that is designed to protect the issuer from later claims of overstatement, misleading implications, omissions or other deficiencies due to the manner in which the statements in question have been written. The lawyer should be careful, however, to dispel any impression that his assistance in drafting the registration statements can ensure it will be free from all misleading, unclear or ambiguous statements.

Comment:

The lawyer's assistance in drafting the registration statement may entail preparation of initial drafts or portions thereof, and discussion and revision of drafts prepared by himself and by others. Such assistance should not be misunderstood as indicating that the lawyer has sufficient knowledge concerning the substantive content of the document that he can or does take responsibility for its accuracy or completeness. * * *

Guideline Six:

The lawyer should avoid statements in the prospectus which could give a mistaken impression that he has passed upon matters which he has not, or that he takes responsibility for the accuracy and completeness of the prospectus.

Comment:

Normally, except for references to specific opinions given by the lawyer on particular matters which are referred to with the lawyer's consent, the only mention of the lawyer in a prospectus should be to his specific opinion as to the validity of the securities being issued. The lawyer should take care that the use of his name for express purposes is not taken as authorization to rely on it for any other purposes, expressly or impliedly. In this connection, the lawyer should consider the advisability of including the following legend whenever his name appears:

[The lawyer/law firm] has passed on the validity of the securities being issued [or other specific matters, *e.g.*, status of litigation] but purchasers of the securities offered by this Prospectus should not rely on [the lawyer/law firm] with respect to any other matters.

* * * In no event should the lawyer permit his name to be used in connection with a

* * * Counsel normally assists the company and its management in preparing the document and in performing their "due diligence" investigation to verify all disclosures for accuracy and completeness. Counsel often serves as the principal draftsman of the registration statement. Counsel typically solicits information both orally and in writing from a great many people, and exercises his best judgment in evaluating the information received for accuracy and consistency. Experience indicates that executives often overestimate their ability to give accurate information from their recollections without verification. It shows no disrespect, but merely the professionally required degree of healthy skepticism, when the lawyer insists on backup documentation and asks for essentially the same information in different ways and from different sources.

A lawyer would be derelict in the discharge of his or her professional obligations if the lawyer allowed the client's registration statement to include information which the lawyer knew or believed to be inaccurate, or if the lawyer failed to pursue an investigation further in the face of factors arousing suspicions about the accuracy of the information received. On the other hand, it should be understood that a lawyer generally is not an expert in the business or financial aspects of a company's affairs. The normal scope of a professional engagement does not contemplate that the lawyer will act as the ultimate source to investigate or verify all disclosures in the registration statement or to assure that the document is accurate and complete in all respects. Indeed, in many cases the lawyer would lack the expertise to assume that responsibility. In some instances, the lawyer may lack the technical background even to frame the proper questions and must depend upon the client for education about the nature of the business. Counsel does not routinely check information received against books of original entry or source documents, as auditors do, nor does counsel generally undertake to consult sources external to the client to obtain or verify information supplied by the client.

In the last analysis, the company and its management must assume the final responsibility to determine that the information in the registration statement is accurate and complete. Management cannot properly take a passive role and rely entirely upon counsel to identify the information to be assembled, verify the information and prepare the registration statement properly.

Clients may have, quite appropriately, a different expectation of the lawyer's role relating to those parts of the prospectus which deal with primarily "legal" matters such as descriptions of litigation, legal proceedings, tax consequences of various transactions, interpretation of contracts and descriptions of governmental requirements. * * * In addition, company counsel normally renders a formal opinion on the legality of the securities being registered, which is filed as an exhibit to the registration statement.

registration statement if he believes the client engaged him in order to make use of his name and reputation rather than for legal advice and assistance.

In connection with a common stock offering, the opinion would state that the shares being offered are legally issued, fully paid and non-assessable.

* * *

REVIEW BY THE SEC

[When dealing with an issuer's first public offering, a]fter the registration statement is filed initially, the Commission's Division of Corporation Finance reviews it to see that it responds appropriately to the applicable form. The Division's staff almost always finds some deficiencies, which are communicated either by telephone, usually to company counsel or through the "letter of comments" or "deficiency letter." Amendments to the registration statement are then filed in response to the comments. When the comments are reflected to the satisfaction of the SEC staff, the SEC issues an order allowing the registration statement to become effective. Only after the registration statement is effective may sales to the public take place.

* * *

If counsel, or the accountants with respect to financial comments, believe that the staff's comments are inappropriate or should not be met for some other reason, the comments will be discussed with the examiner, usually by telephone but in person if the matter is sufficiently serious. If a point cannot be resolved to counsel's satisfaction through discussions with the examiner, it is considered appropriate to request that the matter be submitted to the Branch Chief who supervises the examiner. When a significant issue is involved, higher levels of staff review may be requested if counsel remains unsatisfied. * * * As a practical matter, an offering cannot usually come to market unless an accommodation has been reached on all comments. Therefore, the staff usually has the last word on whether the company has adequately responded to the comments, even if the comments are not legally binding in the formal sense.

* * *

When the comment letter is received, there is a natural tendency to focus attention solely on the points raised by the Commission. However, it is most important to remember that the registration statement must be accurate as of the time it becomes effective. Accordingly, it must be reviewed carefully in its entirety just before the effective date to be sure that all statements are updated to reflect significant intervening developments, whether or not they relate to sections covered by the Commission's comments. The Commission also has a rule relating to the updating of financial statements. Generally speaking, the rule requires the most recent financial statements to be as of a date within 135 days of the date the filing is expected to become effective.

* * *

PRE-EFFECTIVE AND POST-EFFECTIVE OFFERS

Prior to the initial filing of the registration statement, no public offering, either orally or in writing, is permitted. For this purpose, the concept of offering has been given an expansive interpretation. Publicity about the company or its products may be considered an illegal offering, in the sense that it is designed to stimulate an interest in the securities, even if the securities themselves are not mentioned. A violation of this prohibition is often referred to as "gun jumping." Under a specific rule, limited announcements concerning the proposal to make a public offering through a registration statement are permitted.[21]

In the interval between the first filing with the Commission and the effective date, the so-called "waiting period," the company and the underwriters may distribute preliminary or "red herring" prospectuses. The term "red herring" derives from the legend required to be printed in red ink on the cover of any prospectus which is distributed before the effective date of the registration statement. The legend is to the effect that a registration statement has been filed but has not become effective, and the securities may not be sold nor may offers to buy be accepted prior to the effective date.

During the waiting period between the filing of the registration statement and its effective date, the lead underwriter may escort company executives on a tour around the country—often called a "road show" or "dog and pony show." The purpose of this tour is to attend meetings with prospective underwriters, who will be invited into the underwriting syndicate, and possibly also analysts and potential institutional investors.

During the waiting period, oral selling efforts are permitted but no written sales literature—that is, "free writing"—is permitted other than the red herring prospectus. Tombstone advertisements, so-called because the very limited notice of the offering which is permitted is often presented in a form resembling a tombstone, are not considered selling literature and may be published during the waiting period, although it is much more common for them to be published after the effective date. * * * Through the use of a red herring prospectus and by making oral offers by telephone or otherwise, the underwriters may offer the security and may accept "indications of interest" from purchasers prior to the effective date. However, as indicated, no sales can be made during the waiting period.

* * *

[T]he public offering price, the underwriting compensation and the composition of the underwriting syndicate usually are not known at the time the registration statement initially is filed. Therefore, the information is omitted from the red herring, leaving appropriate blanks. Normally, the information is not available until immediately before the registration statement's effective date. Although it was once necessary to file a last minute pre-effective amendment for the purpose of completing this data,

21. SEC Securities Act Rule 135, 17 C.F.R. § 230.135 (1988).

the current rules now permit the registration statement to become effective with the underwriting information not yet filed. The information can be supplied by filing the final prospectus containing all of the previously omitted data within five business days after the effective date.

* * *

TIMETABLE

Although laymen find it difficult to believe, the average first public offering normally requires two to three months of intensive work before the registration statement can be filed. * * *

The overall time lapse between the beginning of preparation of a company's first registration statement and the final effective date may well exceed six months. Rarely will it be less than three months.

* * *

EXPENSES

* * *

Legal fees for a first offering can vary over a wide range depending on the complexity of the offering, the ease with which information can be assembled and verified, the extent of risk factors or other difficult disclosures and other factors. Fees in the range of $125,000 to $150,000 would be typical. This amount includes not only the preparation of the registration statement itself, but also all of the corporate work, house cleaning and other detail which is occasioned by the public offering process. Fees for smaller offerings tend to be somewhat lower. In part, this may reflect the fact that offerings for start-up companies, which tend to be smaller in size, typically require less legal work in investigating business operations, since there are none. However, start-up offerings can be more difficult in other respects—for example, risk factors are more prevalent and minor matters may require disclosure on points which would be immaterial to an established company with a history of operations. Therefore, start-up offerings occasionally are even more demanding than offerings of larger seasoned companies.

Accounting fees can vary significantly depending on the complexity of the business, whether the financial statements to be included in the registration statement have been audited in the normal course, and the extent to which the independent accountants may be involved in the development of financial and other information to be included in the registration statement. Other factors which will cause accounting fees to vary from one registration statement to another are the extent to which the independent accountants are required to participate in meetings with counsel and underwriters' representatives and the nature and extent of procedures performed at the request of the underwriters for purposes of the "comfort letter." If there have been no prior audits and new accountants are engaged at the time of the offering, fees ranging up to $100,000 and even higher would not be unusual. If the company's financial statements have been audited regularly for several years in the past, the added accounting expense for a public offering, in addition to the normal audit expense, could be much less * * *. Obviously, accounting expenses for start-up companies with limited past transactions can be substantially lower.

* * *

For each registration statement, there is a filing fee at the rate of 1/40 of one percent of the maximum aggregate offering price of the securities (or $250 per $1 million of offering price), with a minimum fee of $100, which fee is non-refundable.

* * *

The company normally pays the underwriters' counsel a special fee for compliance with applicable state securities laws (so-called "blue sky" work), which can range up to many thousands of dollars, depending on the number and identity of the jurisdictions involved. Blue sky work is not included in the estimate for legal fees given above.*

* * *

For a normal first public stock offering of several million dollars, total expenses in the $225,000 to $500,000 range would be typical, exclusive of the underwriting discount or commission but inclusive of any expense allowance (whether or not accountable) payable to the underwriters. However, it should be emphasized that there are wide variations among offerings. The estimates for aggregate as well as individual expenses given above can be too low if unusual problems or complications develop in a particular offering.[36]

* * *

Another cost of going public arises out of the heavy burden and time demand it may impose on the company's administrative and executive personnel. Throughout the period of selecting the underwriters and preparing the registration statement, these activities can, and often do, absorb a significant amount of executive time.

* * *

'34 ACT CONSEQUENCES OF GOING PUBLIC

Note: For a more extensive and technical summary of the consequences of a company becoming publicly owned, see Schneider & Shargel, "Now That You are Publicly Owned . . . ," 36 BUS. LAW. 1631 (1981).

* [Blue sky requirements are addressed later in this chapter. Ed.]

36. * * * Periodically since our 1981 review, the authors have conducted informal surveys among experienced professionals to update the information. The ranges of estimates for categories were quite wide. We believe the ranges stated herein reasonably reflect typical offerings in the mid-range. * * *

There are certain continuing consequences arising under the Securities Exchange Act of 1934 once a company goes public. If any company has total assets of more than $5,000,000 [(now $10,000,000. Ed.)] and a class of equity securities held by more than 500 persons at any fiscal year end, such class of equity securities must be registered under section 12(g) within 120 days after the first fiscal year end on which the company meets these tests. Likewise, any company which has a class of securities listed on a stock exchange must register those securities under section 12(b). These registrations under section 12 of the '34 Act are one time registrations which apply to that entire class of securities and should be distinguished from registration under the '33 Act which relate only to specific securities involved in a particular offering.

* * *

The company must file certain periodic reports with the Commission. Companies with exchange listed securities also file copies with the exchange. The required reports include a Form 10–K report which is filed with the SEC on an annual basis. The Form 10–K report requires a description of the company's business, property and financial condition. The working of the disclosure items is substantially similar to the corresponding disclosure items in Form S–1. The general philosophy of the current Form 10–K is to keep the full range of '33 Act registration statement disclosures current on an annual basis. However, many companies have a more condensed disclosure in their Form 10–K's than in their '33 Act prospectuses.

In addition, the company must file interim quarterly reports on Form 10–Q. The principal content of Form 10–Q is unaudited quarterly financial information, but there are also other items which call for disclosures only if specific reportable events have occurred during the period covered by the report. Furthermore, for certain significant events, a report must be filed on Form 8–K, which is normally due within 15 days after the reportable event.

[In 1992, the SEC introduced new 1934 Act registration and disclosure forms for small business issuers. Ed.]

Companies which have filed a registration statement under the '33 Act are required under section 15(d) of the '34 Act to file periodic reports for the balance of the year in which the registration statement becomes effective, and for each subsequent year if they have 300 or more holders of the registered security at the start of the fiscal year. Additionally, companies having their first public offering are required by the '33 Act to file reports with the Commission on Form SR. These reports, which are filed following the offering on a semi-annual basis until the offering has terminated and the proceeds have been applied, cover the status of the offering (in the case of a best efforts underwriting) and the application of the proceeds. The periodic reporting requirements discussed above are applicable even if the company does not meet the section 12(g) registration requirements.

* * *

NOTES

1. The article above mentions the prohibition on so-called "gun jumping"—in other words, communications, prior to filing the registration statement, when those communications might, under a very broad definition, constitute an offer to sell securities. The article also mentions the limitation on so-called "free writing"—in other words, written offers (broadly defined) to sell securities, when the writing does not contain all of the information required under the Securities Act to be included in a prospectus. In 2005, the Securities Exchange Commission promulgated complex new rules creating safe harbors in both areas.

Under the new rules dealing with gun jumping, communications more than 30 days before filing a registration statement do not constitute a prohibited offer, at least so long as they do not refer to the expected public offering, and the issuer takes reasonable steps to prevent further dissemination of the communication during the 30 days prior to the offer. Sec. Act Rule 163A. Also, the regular release of factual business information, which is not intended for use by persons in their capacity as investors, is not an offer. Sec. Act Rule 169. Issuers already registered under the 1934 Securities Exchange Act (particularly if the issuer is a so-called well known seasoned issuer) have even more latitude to make pre-filing communications. Sec. Act Rules 163, 168. The new rules also replace the former prohibition on written communication after filing the registration statement, when the writing does not meet the requirements for a statutory prospectus or tombstone advertisement, by now allowing issuers to use writings that meeting the definition of a so-called free writing prospectus. Sec. Act Rules 164, 433.

2. To get some further prospective on why a registration statement should be prepared with painstaking (and expensive) care, contrast the results in the following two decisions:

Escott v. BarChris Construction Corporation

283 F.Supp. 643 (S.D.N.Y.1968).

■ McLEAN, DISTRICT JUDGE.

This is an action by purchasers of 5 ½ percent convertible subordinated fifteen year debentures of BarChris Construction Corporation (BarChris).

* * *

The action is brought under Section 11 of the Securities Act of 1933 (15 U.S.C. 77k). Plaintiffs allege that the registration statement with respect to these debentures * * * contained material false statements and material omissions.

Defendants fall into three categories: (1) the persons who signed the registration statement; (2) the underwriters, consisting of eight investment banking firms, led by Drexel & Co. (Drexel); and (3) BarChris's auditors, Peat, Marwick, Mitchell & Co. (Peat, Marwick).

The signers, in addition to BarChris itself, were the nine directors of BarChris, plus its controller, defendant Trilling, who was not a director. Of the nine directors, five were officers of BarChris, i.e., defendants Vitolo, president; Russo, executive vice president; Pugliese, vice president; Kircher, treasurer; and Birnbaum, secretary. Of the remaining four, defendant Grant was a member of the firm of Perkins, Daniels, McCormack & Collins, BarChris's attorneys. He became a director in October 1960. Defendant Coleman, a partner in Drexel, became a director on April 17, 1961, as did the other two, Auslander and Rose, who were not otherwise connected with BarChris.

Defendants, in addition to denying that the registration statement was false, have pleaded the defenses open to them under Section 11 of the Act.

* * *

Before discussing these questions, some background facts should be mentioned. At the time relevant here, BarChris was engaged primarily in the construction of bowling alleys, somewhat euphemistically referred to as "bowling centers." * * *

BarChris was an outgrowth of a business started as a partnership by Vitolo and Pugliese in 1946. The business was incorporated in New York in 1955. * * *

The introduction of automatic pin setting machines in 1952 gave a marked stimulus to bowling. It rapidly became a popular sport, with the result that "bowling centers" began to appear throughout the country in rapidly increasing numbers. BarChris benefited from this increased interest in bowling. Its construction operations expanded rapidly.

* * *

For some years the business had exceeded the managerial capacity of its founders. Vitolo and Pugliese are each men of limited education. * * *

Rather early in their career they enlisted the aid of Russo, who was trained as an accountant. * * * He eventually became executive vice president of BarChris. In that capacity he handled many of the transactions which figure in this case.

In 1959 BarChris hired Kircher, a certified public accountant who had been employed by Peat, Marwick. He started as controller and became treasurer in 1960. In October of that year, another ex-Peat, Marwick employee, Trilling, succeeded Kircher as controller. At approximately the same time Birnbaum, a young attorney, was hired as house counsel. He became secretary on April 17, 1961.

In general, BarChris's method of operation was to enter into a contract with a customer, receive from him at that time a comparatively small down payment on the purchase price, and proceed to construct and equip the bowling alley. When the work was finished and the building delivered, the customer paid the balance of the contract price in notes, payable in installments over a period of years. BarChris discounted these notes with a factor and received part of their face amount in cash. The factor held back part as a reserve.

In 1960 BarChris began a practice which has been referred to throughout this case as the "alternative method of financing." In substance this was a sale and leaseback arrangement. * * * Actually this amounted to constructing and installing the equipment in a building. When it was completed, it would sell the interior to a factor, James Talcott Inc. (Talcott), who would pay BarChris the full contract price therefor. The factor then proceeded to lease the interior either directly to BarChris's customer or back to a subsidiary of BarChris. In the latter case, the subsidiary in turn would lease it to the customer.

Under either financing method, BarChris was compelled to expend considerable sums in defraying the cost of construction before it received reimbursement. As a consequence, BarChris was in constant need of cash to finance its operations, a need which grew more pressing as operations expanded.

In December 1959, BarChris sold 560,000 shares of common stock to the public at $3.00 per share. This issue was underwritten by Peter Morgan & Company, one of the present defendants.

By early 1961, BarChris needed additional working capital. The proceeds of the sale of the debentures involved in this action were to be devoted, in part at least, to fill that need.

The registration statement of the debentures, in preliminary form, was filed with the Securities and Exchange Commission on March 30, 1961. * * * The registration statement became effective on May 16. The closing of the financing took place on May 24. On that day BarChris received the net proceeds of the financing.

By that time BarChris was experiencing difficulties in collecting amounts due from some of its customers. Some of them were in arrears in payments due to factors on their discounted notes. As time went on those difficulties increased. Although BarChris continued to build alleys in 1961 and 1962, it became increasingly apparent that the industry was overbuilt. Operators of alleys, often inadequately financed, began to fail. Precisely when the tide turned is a matter of dispute, but at any rate, it was painfully apparent in 1962.

In May of that year BarChris made an abortive attempt to raise more money by the sale of common stock. It filed with the Securities and Exchange Commission a registration statement for the stock issue which it later withdrew. In October 1962 BarChris came to the end of the road. On October 29, 1962, it filed in this court a petition for an arrangement under Chapter XI of the Bankruptcy Act. BarChris defaulted in the payment of the interest due on November 1, 1962 on the debentures.

The Debenture Registration Statement

In preparing the registration statement for the debentures, Grant acted for BarChris. He had previously represented BarChris in preparing the registration statement for the common stock issue. In connection with the sale of common stock, BarChris had issued purchase warrants. In January 1961 a second registration statement was filed in order to update the information pertaining to these warrants. Grant had prepared that statement as well.

Some of the basic information needed for the debenture registration statement was contained in the registration statements previously filed with respect to the common stock and warrants. Grant used these old registration statements as a model in preparing the new one, making the changes which he considered necessary in order to meet the new situation.

The underwriters were represented by the Philadelphia law firm of Drinker, Biddle & Reath. John A. Ballard, a member of that firm, was in charge of that work, assisted by a young associate named Stanton.

Peat, Marwick, BarChris's auditors, who had previously audited BarChris's annual balance sheet and earnings figures for 1958 and 1959, did the same for 1960. These figures were set forth in the registration statement. * * *

The registration statement in its final form contained a prospectus as well as other information. Plaintiffs' claims of falsities and omissions pertain solely to the prospectus, not to the additional data.

The prospectus contained, among other things, a description of BarChris's business, a description of its real property, some material pertaining to certain of its subsidiaries, and remarks about various other aspects of its affairs. It also contained financial information. It included a consolidated balance sheet as of December 31, 1960, with elaborate explanatory notes. These figures had been audited by Peat, Marwick. It also contained unaudited figures as to net sales, gross profit and net earnings for the first quarter ended March 31, 1961, as compared with the similar quarter for 1960. In addition, it set forth figures as to the company's backlog of unfilled orders as of March 31, 1961, as compared with March 31, 1960, and figures as to BarChris's contingent liability, as of April 30, 1961, on customers' notes discounted and its contingent liability under the so-called alternative method of financing.

Plaintiffs challenge the accuracy of a number of these figures. They also charge that the text of the prospectus, apart from the figures, was false in a number of respects, and that material information was omitted.

* * *

The "Due Diligence" Defenses

Section 11(b) of the Act provides that:

"* * * no person, other than the issuer, shall be liable * * * who shall sustain the burden of proof—

* * *

(3) that (A) as regards any part of the registration statement not purporting to be made on the authority of an expert * * * he had, after reasonable investigation, reasonable ground to believe and did believe, at the time such part of the registration statement became effective, that the statements therein were true and that there was no omission to state a material fact required to be stated therein or necessary to make the statements therein not misleading; * * * and (C) as regards any part of the registration statement purporting to be made on the authority of an expert (other than himself) * * * he had no reasonable ground to believe and did not believe, at the time such part of the registration statement became effective, that the statements therein were untrue or that there was an omission to state a material fact required to be stated therein or necessary to make the statements therein not misleading * * *."

Section 11(c) defines "reasonable investigation" as follows:

"In determining, for the purpose of paragraph (3) of subsection (b) of this section, what constitutes reasonable investigation and reasonable ground for belief, the standard of reasonableness shall be that required of a prudent man in the management of his own property."

Every defendant, except BarChris itself, to whom, as the issuer, these defenses are not available, and except Peat, Marwick, whose position rests on a different statutory provision, has pleaded these affirmative defenses.

* * *

I turn now to the question of whether defendants have proved their due diligence defenses. The position of each defendant will be separately considered.

* * *

Birnbaum

Birnbaum was a young lawyer, admitted to the bar in 1957, who, after brief periods of employment by two different law firms and an equally brief period of practicing in his own firm, was employed by BarChris as house counsel and assistant secretary in October 1960. Unfortunately for him, he became secretary and a director of BarChris on April 17, 1961, after the first version of the registration statement had been filed with the Securities and Exchange Commission. He signed the later amendments, thereby becoming responsible for the accuracy of the prospectus in its final form.

Although the prospectus, in its description of "management," lists Birnbaum among the "executive officers" and devotes several sentences to a recital of his career, the fact seems to be that he was not an executive officer in any real sense. He did not participate in the management of the company. As house counsel, he attended to legal matters of a routine nature. Among other things, he incorporated subsidiaries, with which BarChris was plentifully supplied.

* * *

It seems probable that Birnbaum did not know of many of the inaccuracies in the prospectus. He must, however, have appreciated some of them. In any case, he made no investigation and relied on the others to get it right. * * * [H]e was entitled to rely upon Peat, Marwick for the 1960 figures, for books of account or financial transactions. But he was not entitled to rely upon Kircher, Grant and Ballard for the other portions of the prospectus. As a lawyer, he should have known his obligations under the statute. He should have known that he was required to make a reasonable investigation of the truth of all the statements in the unexpertised portion of the document which he signed. Having failed to make such an investigation, he did not have reasonable ground to believe that all these statements were true. Birnbaum has not established his due diligence defenses except as to the audited 1960 figures.

* * *

Grant

Grant became a director of BarChris in October 1960. His law firm was counsel to BarChris in matters pertaining to the registration of securities. Grant drafted the registration statement for the stock issue in 1959 and for the warrants in January 1961. He also drafted the registration statement for the debentures. In the preliminary division of work between him and Ballard, the underwriters' counsel, Grant took initial responsibility for preparing the registration statement, while Ballard devoted his efforts in the first instance to preparing the indenture.

Grant is sued as a director and as a signer of the registration statement. This is not an action against him for malpractice in his capacity as a lawyer. Nevertheless, in considering Grant's due diligence defenses, the unique position which he occupied cannot be disregarded. As the director most directly concerned with writing the registration statement and assuring its accuracy, more was required of him in the way of reasonable investigation than could fairly be expected of a director who had no connection with this work.

There is no valid basis for plaintiffs' accusation that Grant knew that the prospectus was false in some respects and incomplete and misleading in others. Having seen him testify at length, I am satisfied as to his integrity. I find that Grant honestly believed that the registration statement was true and that no material facts had been omitted from it.

* * *

Much of this registration statement is a scissors and paste-pot job. Grant lifted large portions from the earlier prospectuses, modifying them in some instances to the extent that he considered necessary. But BarChris's affairs had changed for the worse by May 1961. Statements that were accurate in January were no longer accurate in May. Grant never discovered this. He accepted the assurances of Kircher and Russo that any change which might have occurred had been for the better, rather than the contrary.

It is claimed that a lawyer is entitled to rely on the statements of his client and that to require him to verify their accuracy would set an unreasonably high standard. This is too broad a generalization. It is a matter of degree. To require an audit would obviously be unreasonable. On the other hand, to require a check of matters easily verifiable is not unreasonable. Even honest clients can make mistakes. The statute imposes liability for untrue statements regardless of whether they are intentionally untrue. The way to prevent mistakes is to test oral information by examining the original written record.

There were things which Grant could readily have checked which he did not check. For example, he was unaware of the provisions of the agreements between BarChris and Talcott. * * * [H]e readily could have ascertained that BarChris's contingent liability on Type B leaseback arrangements was 100 percent, not 25 percent as stated in the prospectus. He did not appreciate that if BarChris defaulted in repurchasing delinquent customers' notes upon Talcott's demand, Talcott could accelerate all the customer paper in its hands, which amounted to over $3,000,000.

As to the backlog figure, Grant appreciated that scheduled unfilled orders on the company's books meant firm commitments, but he never asked to see the contracts which, according to the prospectus, added up to $6,905,000. Thus, he did not know that this figure was overstated by some $4,490,000.

* * * On the subject of minutes, Grant knew that minutes of certain meetings of the BarChris executive committee held in 1961 had not been written up. Kircher, who had acted as secretary at those meetings, had complete notes of them. Kircher told Grant that there was no point in writing up the minutes because the matters discussed at those meetings were purely routine. Grant did not insist that the minutes be written up, nor did he look at Kircher's notes. If he had, he would have learned that on February 27, 1961 there was an extended discussion in the executive committee meeting about customers' delinquencies, * * * that on March 18, 1961 the committee was informed that BarChris was constructing or about to begin constructing twelve alleys for which it had no contracts, and that on May 13, 1961 Dreyfuss, one of the worst delinquents, had filed a petition in Chapter X.

* * *

There is more to the subject of due diligence than this, particularly with respect to the application of proceeds and customers' delinquencies.

The application of proceeds language in the prospectus was drafted by Kircher back in January. It may well have expressed his intent at that time, but his intent, and that of the other principal officers of BarChris, was very different in May. Grant did not appreciate that the earlier language was no longer appropriate. He never learned of the situation which the company faced in May. He knew that BarChris was short of cash, but he had no idea how short. He did not know that BarChris was withholding delivery of checks already drawn and signed because there was not enough money in the bank to pay them. He did not know that the officers of the company intended to use immediately approximately one-third of the financing proceeds in a manner not disclosed in the prospectus, including approximately $1,000,000 in paying old debts.

In this connection, mention should be made of a fact which has previously been referred to only in passing. The "negative cash balance" in BarChris's Lafayette National Bank account in May 1961 included a check dated April 10, 1961 to the order of Grant's firm, Perkins, Daniels, McCormack & Collins, in the amount of $8,711. This check was not deposited by Perkins, Daniels until June 1, after the financing proceeds had been received by BarChris. Of course, if Grant had knowingly withheld deposit of this check until that time, he would be in a position similar to Russo, Vitolo and Pugliese. I do not believe, however, that that was the case. I find that the check was not delivered by BarChris to Perkins, Daniels until shortly before June 1.

This incident is worthy of mention, however, for another reason. The prospectus stated on page 10 that Perkins, Daniels had "received fees aggregating $13,000" from BarChris. This check for $8,711 was one of those fees. It had not been received by Perkins, Daniels prior to May 16. Grant was unaware of this. In approving this erroneous statement in the prospectus, he did not consult his own bookkeeper to ascertain whether it was correct. Kircher told him that the bill had been paid and Grant took his word for it. If he had inquired and had found that this representation was untrue, this discovery might well have led him to a realization of the true state of BarChris's finances in May 1961.

As far as customers' delinquencies is concerned, although Grant discussed this with Kircher, he again accepted the assurances of Kircher and Russo that no serious problem existed. He did not examine the records as to delinquencies, although BarChris maintained such a record. Any inquiry on his part of Talcott or an examination of BarChris's correspondence with Talcott in April and May 1961 would have apprised him of the true facts. It would have led him to appreciate that the statement in this prospectus, carried over from earlier prospectuses, to the effect that since 1955 BarChris had been required to repurchase less than one-half of one per cent of discounted customers' notes could no longer properly be made without further explanation.

Grant was entitled to rely on Peat, Marwick for the 1960 figures. He had no reasonable ground to believe them to be inaccurate. But the matters which I have mentioned were not within the expertised portion of the prospectus. As to this, Grant, was obliged to make a reasonable investigation. I am forced to find that he did not make one. After making all due allowances for the fact that BarChris's officers misled him, there are too many instances in which Grant failed to make an inquiry which he could easily have made which, if pursued, would have put him on his guard. In my opinion, this finding on the evidence in this case does not establish an unreasonably high standard in other cases for company counsel who are also directors. Each case must rest on its own facts. I conclude that Grant has not established his due diligence defenses except as to the audited 1960 figures.

The Underwriters and Coleman

The underwriters other than Drexel made no investigation of the accuracy of the prospectus. * * * They all relied upon Drexel as the "lead" underwriter.

Drexel did make an investigation. The work was in charge of Coleman, a partner of the firm, assisted by Casperson, an associate. Drexel's attorneys acted as attorneys for the entire group of underwriters. Ballard did the work, assisted by Stanton.

* * *

In April 1961 Ballard instructed Stanton to examine BarChris's minutes for the past five years and also to look at "the major contracts of the company."[23] Stanton went to BarChris's office for that purpose on April 24. He asked Birnbaum for the minute books. He read the minutes of the board of directors and discovered interleaved in them a few minutes of executive committee meetings in 1960. He asked Kircher if there were any others. Kircher said that there had been other executive committee meetings but that the minutes had not been written up.

Stanton read the minutes of a few BarChris subsidiaries. His testimony was vague as to which ones. * * *

As to the "major contracts," all that Stanton could remember seeing was an insurance policy. Birnbaum told him that there was no file of major contracts. Stanton did not examine the agreements with Talcott. He did not examine the contracts with customers. He did not look to see what contracts comprised the backlog figure. Stanton examined no accounting records of BarChris. His visit, which lasted one day, was devoted primarily to reading the directors' minutes.

On April 25 Ballard wrote to Grant about certain matters which Stanton had noted on his visit to BarChris the day before, none of which Ballard considered "very earth shaking." As far as relevant here, these were (1) Russo's remark as recorded in the executive committee minutes of November 3, 1960 to the effect that because of customers' defaults, BarChris might find itself in the business of operating alleys; (2) the fact that the minutes of Sanpark Realty Corporation were incomplete; and (3) the fact that minutes of the executive committee were missing.

23. Stanton was a very junior associate. He had been admitted to the bar in January 1961, some three months before. This was the first registration statement he had ever worked on.

On May 9, 1961, Ballard came to New York and conferred with Grant and Kircher. They discussed the Securities and Exchange Commission's deficiency letter of May 4, 1961 which required the inclusion in the prospectus of certain additional information, notably net sales, gross profits and net earnings figures for the first quarter of 1961. They also discussed the points raised in Ballard's letter to Grant of April 25. As to the latter, most of the conversation related to what Russo had meant by his remark on November 3, 1960. Kircher said that the delinquency problem was less severe now than it had been back in November 1960, that no alleys had been repossessed, and that although he was "worried about one alley in Harlem", * * * that was a "special situation." Grant reported that Russo had told him that his statement on November 3, 1960 was "merely hypothetical." On the strength of this conversation, Ballard was satisfied that the one-half of one per cent figure in the prospectus did not need qualification or elaboration.

As to the missing minutes, Kircher said that those of Sanpark were not significant and that the executive committee meetings for which there were no written minutes were concerned only with "routine matters."

It must be remembered that this conference took place only one week before the registration statement became effective. Ballard did nothing else in the way of checking during that intervening week.

Ballard did not insist that the executive committee minutes be written up so that he could inspect them, although he testified that he knew from experience that executive committee minutes may be extremely important. If he had insisted, he would have found the minutes highly informative, as has previously been pointed out. * * * Ballard did not ask to see BarChris's schedule of delinquencies or Talcott's notices of delinquencies, or BarChris's correspondence with Talcott.

Ballard did not examine BarChris's contracts with Talcott. He did not appreciate what Talcott's rights were under those financing agreements or how serious the effect would be upon BarChris of any exercise of those rights.

Ballard did not investigate the composition of the backlog figure to be sure that it was not "puffy." He made no inquiry after March about any new officers' loans, although he knew that Kircher had insisted on a provision in the indenture which gave loans from individuals priority over the debentures. He was unaware of the seriousness of BarChris's cash position and of how BarChris's officers intended to use a large part of the proceeds.

* * *

Like Grant, Ballard, without checking, relied on the information which he got from Kircher. He also relied on Grant who, as company counsel, presumably was familiar with its affairs.

The formal opinion which Ballard's firm rendered to the underwriters at the closing on May 24, 1961 made clear that this is what he had done. The opinion stated (italics supplied):

> "In the course of the preparation of the Registration Statement and Prospectus by the Company, we have had numerous conferences with representatives of and counsel for the Company and with its auditors and we have raised many questions regarding the business of the Company. Satisfactory answers to such questions were in each case given us, and all other information and documents we requested have been supplied. We are of the opinion that the *data presented* to us are accurately reflected in the Registration Statement and Prospectus and that there has been omitted from the Registration Statement no material facts *included in such data.* Although *we have not otherwise verified* the completeness or accuracy of the information furnished to us, on the basis of the foregoing and with the exception of the financial statements and schedules (which this opinion does not pass upon), we have no reason to believe that the Registration Statement or Prospectus contains any untrue statement of any material fact or omits to state a material fact required to be stated therein or necessary in order to make the statements therein not misleading."

Coleman testified that Drexel had an understanding with its attorneys that "we expect them to inspect on our behalf the corporate records of the company including, but not limited to, the minutes of the corporation, the stockholders and the committees of the board authorized to act for the board." Ballard manifested his awareness of this understanding by sending Stanton to read the minutes and the major contracts. It is difficult to square this understanding with the formal opinion of Ballard's firm which expressly disclaimed any attempt to verify information supplied by the company and its counsel.

In any event, it is clear that no effectual attempt at verification was made. The question is whether due diligence required that it be made. Stated another way, is it sufficient to ask questions, to obtain answers which, if true, would be thought satisfactory, and to let it go at that, without seeking to ascertain from the records whether the answers in fact are true and complete?

I have already held that this procedure is not sufficient in Grant's case. Are underwriters in a different position, as far as due diligence is concerned?

The underwriters say that the prospectus is the company's prospectus, not theirs. Doubtless this is the way they customarily regard it. But the Securities Act makes no such distinction. The underwriters are just as responsible as the company if the prospectus is false. And prospective investors rely upon the reputation of the underwriters in deciding whether to purchase the securities.

* * *

The purpose of Section 11 is to protect investors. To that end the underwriters are made responsible for the truth of the prospectus. If they may escape that responsibility by taking at face value representations made to them by the company's management, then the inclusion of underwriters among those liable under Section 11 affords the investors no additional protection. To effectuate the statute's purpose, the phrase "reasonable investigation" must be construed to require more effort on the part of the underwriters than the mere accurate reporting in the prospectus of "data presented" to them by the company. It should make no difference that this data is elicited by questions addressed to the company officers by the underwriters, or that the underwriters at the time believe that the company's officers are truthful and reliable. In order to make the underwriters' participation in this enterprise of any value to the investors, the underwriters must make some reasonable attempt to verify the data submitted to them. They may not rely solely on the company's officers or on the company's counsel. A prudent man in the management of his own property would not rely on them.

It is impossible to lay down a rigid rule suitable for every case defining the extent to which such verification must go. It is a question of degree, a matter of judgment in each case. In the present case, the underwriters' counsel made almost no attempt to verify management's representations. I hold that that was insufficient.

On the evidence in this case, I find that the underwriters' counsel did not make a reasonable investigation of the truth of those portions of the prospectus which were not made on the authority of Peat, Marwick as an expert. Drexel is bound by their failure. It is not a matter of relying upon counsel for legal advice. Here the attorneys were dealing with matters of fact. Drexel delegated to them, as its agent, the business of examining the corporate minutes and contracts. It must bear the consequences of their failure to make an adequate examination.

The other underwriters, who did nothing and relied solely on Drexel and on the lawyers, are also bound by it. It follows that although Drexel and the other underwriters believed that those portions of the prospectus were true, they had no reasonable ground for that belief, within the meaning of the statute. Hence, they have not established their due diligence defence, except as to the 1960 audited figures.

* * *

In re Donald J. Trump Casino Securities Litigation—Taj Mahal Litigation

7 F.3d 357 (3d Cir.1993).

■ BECKER, CIRCUIT JUDGE.

This is an appeal from orders of the district court for the District of New Jersey dismissing a number of complaints brought under various provisions of the Securities Act of 1933 and the Securities Exchange Act of

1934 by a class of investors who purchased bonds to provide financing for the acquisition and completion of the Taj Mahal, a lavish casino/hotel on the boardwalk in Atlantic City, New Jersey. The defendants are Donald J. Trump ("Trump"), Robert S. Trump, Harvey S. Freeman, the Trump Organization Inc., Trump Taj Mahal Inc., Taj Mahal Funding Inc. and Trump Taj Mahal Associates Limited Partnership (the "Partnership") (collectively the "Trump defendants") and Merrill Lynch, Pierce, Fenner and Smith Inc. ("Merrill Lynch"). The complaints allege that the prospectus accompanying the issuance of the bonds contained affirmatively misleading statements and materially misleading omissions in contravention of the federal securities laws.

The district court dismissed the securities law claims under Fed. R. Civ. P. 12(b)(6) for failure to state a claim upon which relief can be granted. The linchpin of the district court's decision was what has been described as the "bespeaks caution" doctrine, according to which a court may determine that the inclusion of sufficient cautionary statements in a prospectus renders misrepresentations and omissions contained therein nonactionable. While the viability of the bespeaks caution doctrine is an issue of first impression for this court, we believe that it primarily represents new nomenclature rather than substantive change in the law. As we see it, "bespeaks caution" is essentially shorthand for the well-established principle that a statement or omission must be considered in context, so that accompanying statements may render it immaterial as a matter of law.

* * *

I. Facts and Procedural History

In November, 1988 the Trump defendants offered to the public $675 million in first mortgage investment bonds (the "bonds") with Merrill Lynch acting as the sole underwriter. The interest rate on the bonds was 14%, a high rate in comparison to the 9% yield offered on quality corporate bonds at the time. The Trump defendants issued the bonds to raise capital to: (1) purchase the Taj Mahal, a partially-completed casino/hotel located on the boardwalk, from Resorts International, Inc. (which had already invested substantial amounts in its construction); (2) complete construction of the Taj Mahal; and (3) open the Taj Mahal for business.

As is well-known, the Taj Mahal was widely touted as Atlantic City's largest and most lavish casino resort.

* * *

Plaintiffs ground their lawsuits in the text of the prospectus. Their strongest attack focuses on the "Management Discussion and Analysis" ("MD & A") section of the prospectus, which stated: "The Partnership believes that funds generated from the operation of the Taj Mahal will be sufficient to cover all of its debt service (interest and principal)." * * * The plaintiffs' primary contention is that this statement was materially misleading because the defendants possessed neither a genuine nor a reasonable belief in its truth. * * *

After learning that the Trump defendants planned to file Chapter 11 bankruptcy proceedings and establish a reorganization plan, various bondholders filed separate complaints in the United States District Courts for the Southern District of New York, the Eastern District of New York and the District of New Jersey.

* * *

IV. The Alleged Affirmative Material Misrepresentations in the Prospectus

* * *

A. *General Legal Principles*

At a minimum, each of the securities fraud provisions which the bondholders allege the Trump defendants violated requires proof that the defendants made untrue or misleading statements or omissions of material fact. * * * We have squarely held that opinions, predictions and other forward-looking statements are not per se inactionable under the securities laws. Rather, such statements of "soft information" may be actionable misrepresentations if the speaker does not genuinely and reasonably believe them. * * * Therefore, the plaintiffs' complaint does not falter just because it alleges that the defendants made a misrepresentation with their statement that they *believed* they would be able to repay the principal and interest on the bonds. Rather, the complaint cannot survive a motion to dismiss because ultimately it does not sufficiently allege that the defendants made a *material* misrepresentation.

* * *

[M]ateriality is a relative concept, so that a court must appraise a misrepresentation or omission in the complete context in which the author conveys it. * * * In other words, a particular misrepresentation or omission significant to a reasonable investor in one document or circumstance may not influence a reasonable investor in another. We accordingly take into account not only the assertion that the Partnership believed the Taj Mahal could meet the obligations of the bonds, but also other relevant statements contained in the prospectus.

B. *The Text of the Prospectus*

The prospectus at issue contained an abundance of warnings and cautionary language which bore directly on the prospective financial success of the Taj Mahal and on the Partnership's ability to repay the bonds. We believe that given this extensive yet specific cautionary language, a reasonable factfinder could not conclude that the inclusion of the statement "the Partnership believes that funds generated from the operation of the Taj Mahal will be sufficient to cover all of its debt service (interest and principal)" would influence a reasonable investor's investment decision. More specifically, we believe that due to the disclaimers and warnings the prospectus contains, no reasonable investor could believe anything but that the Taj Mahal bonds represented a rather risky, speculative investment which might yield a high rate of return, but which alternatively might result in no return or even a loss. We hold that under this set of facts, the bondholders cannot prove that the alleged misrepresentation was material.

The statement the plaintiffs assail as misleading is contained in the MD & A section of the prospectus, which follows the sizable "Special Considerations" section, a section notable for its extensive and detailed disclaimers and cautionary statements. More precisely, the prospectus explained that, because of its status as a new venture of unprecedented size and scale, a variety of risks inhered in the Taj Mahal which could affect the Partnership's ability to repay the bondholders. For example, it stated:

> The casino business in Atlantic City, New Jersey has a seasonal nature of which summer is the peak season.... Since the third interest payment date on the Bonds [(which constitutes the first interest payment not paid out of the initial financing)] occurs before the summer season, the Partnership will not have the benefit of receiving peak season cash flow prior to the third interest payment date, which could adversely affect its ability to pay interest on the Bonds.
>
> ... The Taj Mahal has not been completed and, accordingly, has no operating history. The Partnership, therefore, has no history of earnings and its operations will be subject to all of the risks inherent in the establishment of a new business enterprise. Accordingly, the ability of the Partnership to service its debt to [Taj Mahal Funding Inc., which issued the bonds,] is completely dependent upon the success of that operation and such success will depend upon financial, business, competitive, regulatory and other factors affecting the Taj Mahal and the casino industry in general as well as prevailing economic conditions....
>
> The Taj Mahal will be the largest casino/hotel complex in Atlantic City, with approximately twice the room capacity and casino space of many of the existing casino/hotels in Atlantic City. [No] other casino/hotel operator has had experience operating a complex the size of the Taj Mahal in Atlantic City. Consequently, no assurance can be given that, once opened, the Taj Mahal will be profitable or that it will generate cash flow sufficient to provide for the payment of the debt service....

* * *

The prospectus went on to relate, as part of its "Security for the Bonds" subsection, the potential effect of the Partnership's default on its mortgage payments. For example, this subsection unreservedly explained that if a default occurred prior to completion of the Taj Mahal, "there would not be sufficient proceeds [from a foreclosure sale of the Taj Mahal] to pay the principal of, and accrued interest on, the Bonds." * * *

The "Special Considerations" section also detailed the high level of competition for customers the completed Taj Mahal would face once opened to the public:

> Competition in the Atlantic City casino/hotel market is intense. At present, there are twelve casino/hotels in Atlantic City.... Some Atlantic City casino/hotels recently have completed renovations or are in the process of expanding and improving their facilities.... *The Partnership believes* that, based upon historical trends, *casino win per square foot of casino space will decline in 1990* as a result of a projected increase in casino floor space, including the opening of the Taj Mahal.

* * * ([E]mphasis added). In a section following the MD & A section, the prospectus reiterated its reference to the intense competition in the Atlantic City casino industry:

> Growth in Atlantic City casino win is expected to be restrained until further improvements to the City's transportation system and infrastructure are undertaken and completed and the number of non-casino hotel rooms and existing convention space are increased. No assurance can be given with respect to either the future growth of the Atlantic City gaming market or the ability of the Taj Mahal to attract a representative share of that market.

* * * The prospectus additionally reported that there were risks of delay in the construction of the Taj Mahal and a risk that the casino might not receive the numerous essential licenses and permits from the state regulatory authorities. * * *

In this case the Partnership did not bury the warnings about risks amidst the bulk of the prospectus. Indeed, it was the allegedly misleading statement which was buried amidst the cautionary language. At all events, in addition to reading the allegedly misleading statement setting forth the Partnership's belief that it could repay the principal and interest on the bonds, a prospective investor would have also read the dire warnings and cautionary statements a sampling of which we have just outlined. Moreover, an investor would have read the sentence immediately following the challenged statement, which cautioned: "[n]o assurance can be given, however, that actual operating results will meet the Partnership's expectations."

* * *

C. The Bespeaks Caution Doctrine

The district court applied what has come to be known as the "bespeaks caution" doctrine. In so doing it followed the lead of a number of courts of appeals which have dismissed securities fraud claims under Rule 12(b)(6) because cautionary language in the offering document negated the materiality of an alleged misrepresentation or omission. * * * We are persuaded by the *ratio decidendi* of these cases and will apply bespeaks caution to the facts before us.

The application of bespeaks caution depends on the specific text of the offering document or other communication at issue, i.e., courts must assess the communication on a case-by-case basis. * * * Nevertheless, we can state as a general matter that, when an offering document's forecasts, opinions or projections are accompanied by meaningful cautionary statements, the forward-looking statements will not form the basis for a securities fraud claim if those statements did not affect the "total mix" of information the document provided investors. In other words, cautionary language, if sufficient, renders the alleged omissions or misrepresentations immaterial as a matter of law.

The bespeaks caution doctrine is, as an analytical matter, equally applicable to allegations of both affirmative misrepresentations and omissions concerning soft information. Whether the plaintiffs allege a document contains an affirmative prediction/opinion which is misleading or fails to include a forecast or prediction which failure is misleading, the cautionary statements included in the document may render the challenged predictive statements or opinions immaterial as a matter of law. Of course, a vague or blanket (boilerplate) disclaimer which merely warns the reader that the investment has risks will ordinarily be inadequate to prevent misinformation. To suffice, the cautionary statements must be substantive and tailored to the specific future projections, estimates or opinions in the prospectus which the plaintiffs challenge.

Because of the abundant and meaningful cautionary language contained in the prospectus, we hold that the plaintiffs have failed to state an actionable claim regarding the statement that the Partnership believed it could repay the bonds. We can say that the prospectus here truly bespeaks caution because, not only does the prospectus generally convey the riskiness of the investment, but its warnings and cautionary language directly address the substance of the statement the plaintiffs challenge. That is to say, the cautionary statements were tailored precisely to address the uncertainty concerning the Partnership's prospective ability to repay the bondholders.

* * *

D. Conclusion

* * * Given this context, we believe that no reasonable jury could conclude that the subject projection materially influenced a reasonable investor.[17]

* * *

17. The plaintiffs have also alleged that the prospectus was materially misleading in its estimation that as of its opening date the Taj Mahal would be worth approximately $1.1 billion. An independent appraisal conducted by the Appraisal Group International ("AGI") had arrived at that estimate. The plaintiffs submit that this estimate lacked an adequate basis in fact because AGI based it on " 'the capitalization of income approach,' even though at the time of the Prospectus it was impossible to make any reasonable estimate of the Taj Mahal's future income." * * *

We conclude that, given the text of the prospectus, the plaintiffs have failed to state a claim under the securities laws through this allegation. As we discussed more fully above, * * * the prospectus explicitly disclosed that the Taj Mahal, as a new enterprise, lacked any operating history, including any history of earnings. Moreover, the prospectus clearly and precisely set forth the speculative nature

NOTES

1. The BarChris offering, as is typical of a public offering, involved corporate counsel (Birnbaum), outside counsel for securities work (Grant), and the underwriters' counsel (Ballard and Stanton). Birnbaum and Grant became liable under Section 11 by virtue of their being directors and in that capacity signing the registration statement. (Does this say anything about the desirability of the company's attorney also sitting on its board?) What, if any, liability could the underwriters' counsel face? Suppose Grant had become aware of the false representations in the BarChris registration statement he helped prepare, but had not signed the statement or been a director. In *Central Bank of Denver, N.A. v. First Interstate Bank of Denver, N.A.*, 511 U.S. 164 (1994), the Supreme Court ruled out civil liability under Rule 10b–5 for aiding and abetting a securities fraud, but noted that attorneys, accountants and other professionals might sufficiently participate in the fraud to make their own conduct directly violate the securities law. If an attorney prepares a registration statement, which he or she knows to be false, is this participating in the fraud so as to make the attorney liable under Rule 10b–5 to the defrauded investors, or is it "just" aiding and abetting the "company's fraud"? See *In re Enron Corp. Securities, Derivative & ERISA Litigation*, 235 F. Supp. 2d 549 (S.D.Tex. 2002)(holding that such conduct is participating in the fraud). Equally important, what are the attorney's ethical obligations in this situation? See American Bar Association, Model Rules of Professional Conduct, Rules 1.2 (a lawyer shall not assist a client in conduct the lawyer knows is fraudulent), 1.6 (lawyer's duty to preserve client confidences), 4.1 (a lawyer shall not knowingly make a false statement of material fact to a third person in the course of representing a client).

2. As part of its efforts in the 1980s to ease registration requirements, the Securities Exchange Commission promulgated Rule 176. This rule lists certain circumstances as bearing upon whether a person undertook a reasonable investigation for purposes of Section 11 liability. One factor listed is reasonable reliance upon officers, employees and others. Whether this would have changed the result in *BarChris* is not at all clear, since the rule simply lists such reliance as a circumstance to consider and qualifies the relevance of such reliance by the responsibilities of the relying party with respect to the filing.

3. While *BarChris* illustrates the need for thorough investigation, *Trump* shows the utility of thoughtful and complete drafting. *Trump* also raises the issue of how to deal with so-called soft information, such as the prediction that the casino would earn enough to pay the bonds, or the $1.1 billion valuation of the casino discussed in footnote 17 of the court's opinion. The court states that such statements can be false if the speaker

of this estimate and the consequent uncertainty that the Taj Mahal would actually be worth $1.1 billion by its opening date. This cautionary discussion, in combination with the more general warnings which alerted investors to the variety of highly uncertain circumstances the Taj Mahal confronted, rendered the estimate of the Taj Mahal's worth on its opening date immaterial.

does not genuinely and reasonably believe them. *See also* Sec. Act Rule 175 (forward looking statements are not fraudulent so long as made in good faith and with a reasonable basis). The subjective part of this test—whether the speaker really believes the statement—hopefully should not create a problem; but what does it take for the belief to be reasonable (or to have a reasonable basis)? Perhaps the ultra-cautious might suggest avoiding all statements of soft information in the prospectus. Are there any practical or legal problems with this idea? Recall the material on valuation earlier in this chapter. Will investors put money in a business without information as to its expected earnings? Can hard data—such as historic earnings figures for the company—always be adequate for this purpose (especially when dealing with a fledgling firm)? If investors do not get soft information from the prospectus—where it can be surrounded with suitable cautions—is there any other way they may receive such information (perhaps without written caveats)? Finally, is there any legal requirement to put soft information into the prospectus? See Sec. Act Reg. S–K, Item 303(a), Instruction 7 (encouraged but not required). Could such information, however, be necessary to render statements of hard data not misleading (as, for example, when the company's internal projections show an earnings decline)? See *Craftmatic Sec. Litig. v. Kraftsow*, 890 F.2d 628 (3d Cir.1989)(finding the omitted information there too speculative to be material). Notice, the court in *Trump* took into account claims based upon misleading omissions of soft information in its discussion of the "bespeaks caution doctrine."

4. In 1995, Congress built upon the "bespeaks caution" doctrine by adding Section 27A to the Securities Act. Section 27A creates a safe harbor which prevents liability for making a forward-looking statement (a prediction) that does not pan out so long as the statement identifies the prediction as a forward-looking statement and accompanies the forward-looking statement with "meaningful cautionary statements identifying important factors that could cause actual results to differ materially from those in the forward-looking statement." In a significant change from Section 11, Section 27A also cuts off liability unless the speaker made the forward-looking statement knowing that it was false or misleading. Compare this scienter requirement under Section 27A with Rule 175's suggestion that predictions made without a reasonable basis may be misleading. Can one reconcile the two provisions? Suppose the speaker knows that he or she lacks a reasonable basis for the prediction, even though he or she believes, based on blind faith, that the prediction will come to pass. Interestingly, Section 27A protects oral as well as written forward-looking statements, so long as the speaker also tells the person who hears the oral prediction where the listener can readily obtain written material which contains adequate cautionary information. Significantly, Congress excluded a number of situations from the reach of Section 27A. Most important to the present discussion, Section 27A does not apply to forward-looking statements made in connection with an initial public offering. In other words, only corporations which have already gone public (and, for example, are making additional offerings) benefit from Section 27A.

5. It is also useful to examine first hand what a prospectus contains in order to get some idea of the disclosure (and work) required. If one has not already seen a prospectus, a local stockbroker will undoubtedly be happy to oblige. Registration statements are also available through the Securities Exchange Commission's site on the Internet (http://www.sec.gov).

6. After going public, if a company ends up with over 500 shareholders or with shares listed on a national securities exchange, it must comply with the requirements of the 1934 Securities Exchange Act. Messrs Schneider, Manko and Kant discussed the periodic reporting requirements imposed by the 1934 Act toward the end of their article. In the Sarbanes–Oxley Act, Congress increased the requirements imposed on companies registered under the 1934 Act to a degree that might impact the decision to go public. Some of these requirements simply increase what the company must disclose in its periodic reports; for example, requiring disclosure concerning off-balance sheet transactions. Sarbanes–Oxley Act § 401. Potentially more burdensome requirements impact the timing of disclosure; for example requiring real time disclosure of material changes in financial condition. *Id.* at § 409. In a provision sometimes argued to impose significant expense, the Act requires an issuer's chief executive and chief financial officers to certify both that the company's filed financial statements fairly present the company's condition and that these officers have designed, and evaluated the effectiveness of, internal controls to make sure these officers know material information concerning the company. *Id.* at § 302. There are also provisions impacting the governance of the issuer; most notably requiring national securities exchanges to adopt listing standards requiring that audit committees of the board of directors be composed entirely of independent directors (one of whom must be a financial expert), and that the audit committees must be responsible for appointment and oversight of the company's outside auditors. *Id.* at § 301. As discussed earlier, the Act can impact a public company's relationship with its attorneys (*Id.* at § 307), as well as with its outside accountants. *Id.* at § 201 (precluding auditors from performing other work for the company).

c. *State Securities Laws*

Benjamin v. Cablevision Programming Investments

114 Ill.2d 150, 102 Ill.Dec. 296, 499 N.E.2d 1309 (1986).

■ JUSTICE RYAN delivered the opinion of the court.

The plaintiff, Samuel Benjamin, M.D., brought this action under the Illinois Securities Law of 1953, as amended (the Illinois Securities Act or the Act) * * * to void the sale of one limited partnership unit in Cablevision Programming Investments (Cablevision) and to recover the purchase price, plus interest and attorney fees. * * *

Cablevision, established as a limited partnership under the laws of the State of Illinois, with its principal place of business in Chicago, invests in and/or loans monies to companies engaged in the business of acquiring, owning, producing and distributing television programming to cable-television systems. In August of 1980, the plaintiff, a resident of Torrence, California, purchased one limited partnership unit in California for $200,000. The relevant facts surrounding this transaction are not in dispute. The plaintiff was never physically present in Illinois in connection with this sale. The plaintiff was solicited in California for the purchase of a limited partnership interest. The plaintiff received, in California, an investment letter, a selling circular, and a subscription agreement. These documents were sent by the defendants from Chicago. The plaintiff signed the subscription agreement in California and returned it to Cablevision's Chicago office with a check for $40,000. Upon receipt of the check and the subscription agreement, Charles F. Dolan, and Linda Kreer Witt, president of Communications Management Corporation, executed the agreement on behalf of Cablevision. Confirmation of the sale and evidence of ownership of his interest in Cablevision were prepared by the defendants in Chicago and mailed to the plaintiff in California.

In September of 1982, the Securities Division of the Illinois Secretary of State's Office, in response to the plaintiff's inquiry, advised the plaintiff that a registration statement had not been filed in connection with the sale of limited-partnership interests in Cablevision and that the defendants had failed to file the prescribed "report of sale" necessary to preserve a limited-offering exemption. * * *

On March 2, 1983, the plaintiff filed a two-count complaint in the circuit court of Cook County seeking to void the sale of his interest in Cablevision and to recover the purchase price, together with interest and attorney fees. Count I alleged that the defendants violated section 5 of the Illinois Securities Act by selling limited partnership interests to more than 35 persons in Illinois without filing a formal registration statement with the Secretary of State. As an alternative grounds for rescission, count II alleged that if the defendants sold limited partnership units to less than 35 persons in Illinois, then the defendants failed to properly qualify the sale to the plaintiff under the limited-offering exemption of section 4(G) due to their neglect to file the requisite post-sale report. The complaint contained no allegations of fraud, material misrepresentation, material omission, or other deceptive practices in connection with the plaintiff's purchase.

* * * [T]he defendants moved to dismiss the complaint for failure to state a cause of action. The defendants alleged that neither count of the plaintiff's complaint contained sufficient allegations of fact establishing that the sale of the limited-partnership unit to the plaintiff was a "*sale in this State*" (count I) or a sale made to "*a person in this State*" (count II). The circuit court agreed and granted the motion to dismiss for failure to state a cause of action for rescission.

Section 5 of the Illinois Securities Act * * * requires, in pertinent part, that all securities except those exempt under section 3 or those sold in transactions exempt under Section 4 shall be registered with the Secretary of State *prior to sale in this State.* * * *

Section 2.5 [in effect at the time of the transaction] had the following definition of "sale" or "sell":

> " 'Sale' or 'sell' shall have the full meaning of that term as applied by or accepted in courts of law or equity, and shall include every disposition, or attempt to dispose, of a security for value. 'Sale' or 'sell' shall also include a contract to sell, or exchange, an attempt or an offer to sell, an option of sale or a solicitation of an offer to buy, directly or indirectly; * * *." * * *

Thus, it is clear from the statutory definition that the term "sale," as used in the Act, encompasses not only transactions that fall within the common legal understanding of that term, but also is much broader and includes other activities which in law are recognized only as preliminary steps in the consummation of a sale, such as an offer or a solicitation of an offer.

* * *

Both parties rely on *Green v. Weis, Voisin, Cannon, Inc.* (7th Cir.1973), 479 F.2d 462, to support their positions. In *Green,* the plaintiffs were residents of Chicago. All except one of the plaintiffs were solicited in Illinois for the sale of common stock of London Ben, Inc., by Weis, Voisin, Cannon, Inc., the underwriter and agent for the sale of London Ben stock. Each of the plaintiffs accepted the offer to sell by signing an investment letter and sending it with a payment to the Weis, Voisin offices in Chicago. After the plaintiffs' checks and investment letters were received in Chicago, the checks were forwarded by Weis, Voisin to its New York offices and deposited in its New York bank account, from which State the confirmations and stock certificates had also issued. The plaintiffs thereafter attempted to rescind these sales on the grounds that the securities were neither registered nor exempt from registration * * *. In reversing the district court, the seventh circuit held that the defendants' solicitations of Illinois residents in Illinois resulted in a sale of securities in Illinois. Reasoning that the scope of the term "sale" as defined in section 2.5 is not limited to general contract principles or to the Uniform Commercial Code, the court concluded that the defendants' solicitation of Illinois residents and other contacts with this State pursuant to such solicitations were sufficient to bring the various transactions within the statutory definition of "sale" and thus the purview of the Illinois Securities Act. Because the statutory definition of "sale" controlled, the court pointed out that "[w]hether or not a common law definition of sale would therefore place the consummation of the sale in New York is therefore irrelevant." 479 F.2d 462, 465.

* * * *Green* does not stand for the narrow principle that because the Illinois Securities Act is primarily intended to protect Illinois residents and those within Illinois' boundaries, the purchaser's location and actions in connection with the sale, not the seller's, determines whether a sale of a security is a "sale in this State." In *Green,* the court was concerned that the Illinois Securities Act and its protections for Illinois residents would be thwarted if solicitations could be made in Illinois to Illinois residents while

the consummation of the transaction occurred in another State. The court thus reasoned that the term "sale," as defined in section 2.5 of the Act, must be strictly applied to achieve the broad paternalistic purpose of the Act.

* * *

Just as this State has an interest in protecting those within its borders from unscrupulous conduct, it also must be concerned with and seek to prevent those within its borders from engaging in such conduct. * * * The liberal application of the statutory definition of the term "sale" will fulfill this purpose of the Act and will prevent this State from being a haven for unscrupulous dealers in securities.

On the basis of the above record, we find that the factual allegations of count I sufficiently allege a sale of security "in the State." Under section 2.5, the term "sale" includes within its scope the full meaning of a sale applied by or accepted in courts of law or equity, a solicitation of an offer to purchase, a subscription or an offer to sell and any act by which a sale is made. The activities of the defendants in preparing and mailing the investment letter, the offering circular, and the subscription agreement may be found to be an "offer to sell" or "a solicitation of an offer to buy" a limited partnership interest in Cablevision as those terms are used in the Act. The conduct of the plaintiff in signing the subscription agreement, and placing it in the mail with a check addressed to the defendants in Chicago, may be found to be an "offer to buy." The defendants, in executing the subscription agreement and cashing the check may be found to have accepted the plaintiff's offer to purchase, thus consummating the transaction in this State. Because the defendants' activities which fell within the statutory definition of "sale" took place within this State, the factual allegations of count I sufficiently allege a sale of a security "in this State." The fact that a portion of the transaction took place in California is not sufficient to place this transaction outside the provisions of the Illinois Securities Act.

* * *

The defendants also contend that a literal application of the term "sale" to the Act's registration provisions would result in a single sale occurring simultaneously in a number of States, each State having some insignificant and fleeting connection with the transaction. The defendants assert that a securities transaction with extremely tenuous connections with Illinois might therefore constitute a "sale in this State" or raise substantial doubts on that issue, leaving sellers uncertain whether the Illinois registration requirements apply to such transaction. We note that it is quite possible that the securities laws of two or more States may apply to a single transaction. In order for the Illinois Securities Act to apply, however, the transaction must have some physical nexus with Illinois. There must be either a "disposition or an attempt to dispose, of a security for value," a "contract to sell" a security, an "offer" to sell a security, or an "application of an offer" to buy a security * * *. Furthermore, these activities must take place within Illinois. Contrary to the defendants' assertion, a securities transaction with extremely insignificant, fleeting, or tenuous connections with Illinois will not constitute a "sale in this State." Because the term "sale" is broadly and unambiguously defined, the literal application of the expansive statutory definition will eliminate uncertainty regarding whether Illinois registration and reporting requirements apply to interstate securities transactions.

For the reasons stated above, we hold that the circuit court erred in granting the defendant's motion to dismiss count I of the complaint.

* * *

NOTES

1. State securities laws, often called blue sky laws, can impose an additional significant burden on a public offering. Every state (albeit not the District of Columbia) requires, to some extent, registration of securities sold in the state. Loss & Seligman, *Securities Regulation* 92 (3d ed. 1989). As *Benjamin* illustrates, which state an issuer is selling securities in, and hence which state's (or states') registration laws the issuer must comply with, is not always obvious. In *Benjamin,* the court held the issuer sold securities in Illinois, despite the fact the buyers were in California. What about California's securities law; would it also apply to this transaction? See Cal. Corp. Code § 25008 (which adopts language from the 1956 version of the Uniform Securities Act):

> § 25008. Offer or sale of security; offer to sell or to buy
>
> (a) An offer or sale of a security is made in this state when an offer to sell is made in this state, or an offer to buy is accepted in this state, or (if both the seller and the purchaser are domiciled in this state) the security is delivered to the purchaser in this state. * * *
>
> (b) An offer to sell or to buy is made in this state when the offer either originates from this state or is directed by the offeror to this state and received at the place to which it is directed. An offer to buy or to sell is accepted in this state when acceptance is communicated to the offeror in this state; and acceptance is communicated to the offeror in this state when the offeree directs it to the offeror in this state reasonably believing the offeror to be in this state and it is received at the place to which it is directed. A security is delivered to the purchaser in this state when the certificate or other evidence of the security is directed to the purchaser in this state and received at the place to which it is directed.
>
> (c) An offer to sell or to buy is not made in this state merely because (1) the publisher circulates or there is circulated on his behalf in this state any bona fide newspaper or other publication of general, regular and paid circulation which has had more than two-thirds of its circulation outside this state during the past 12 months, or (2) a radio or television program originating outside this state is received in this state.

Offerings over the Internet would seem to present a particular challenge in terms of figuring out what states' laws govern. Almost all states, however, have exempted Internet offerings from their blue sky laws unless the securities are actually sold (as opposed just to offered for sale) in the state. *E.g.*, Fisch, *Can Internet Offerings Bridge the Small Business Capital Barrier?*, 2 J. Small & Emerging Bus. L.57, 74–75 (1998).

2. What exactly does registration under state blue sky laws entail? It is impossible to give a definitive answer to this question—at least short of writing a treatise. The problem is that these laws can vary substantially from state to state; indeed, the very necessity of researching all the applicable requirements for a multistate offering (sometimes referred to as making blue sky survey) is one of the costs these laws impose upon going public. To alleviate some of this problem, the National Conference of Commissioners on Uniform State Laws and the American Bar Association promulgated the Uniform Securities Act, originally in 1956, with a revised version in 1985, and yet another revised version in 2002. Most states have adopted either one or another version of the Uniform Securities Act—albeit with a degree of modifications which makes reliance solely upon the Uniform Act itself hazardous. Worse, key commercial jurisdictions provide some of the more substantial divergences. New York, for example, has not adopted the Uniform Securities Act. Instead, it has a statute which has grown by a process of accretion over the years. N.Y. Gen. Bus. Law §§ 352–359–h. Fortunately from an issuer's standpoint, New York's registration requirement (at least with the exception of real estate and theatrical financings) is modest both with respect to what offerings it reaches and what it entails. *See* N.Y. Gen. Bus. Law § 359–ff. California, on the other hand, has modeled its securities law on the Uniform Act, yet with a degree of modifications which make both the coverage and the demands of California's statute generally greater than many Uniform Act states.

With those caveats in mind, it is useful to briefly explore the registration process established by the Uniform Securities Act. The 1956 version of the Act established three methods of registering the sale of securities in a state: notification, coordination and qualification. Notification refers to the procedure established by Section 302 of the 1956 version of the Act, under which seasoned companies meeting certain financial tests can file a shortened registration statement. (By way of contrast, California's version of notification applies to companies with securities registered under the 1934 Securities Exchange Act or the Investment Company Act of 1940. Cal. Corp. Code § 25112.) Issuers have made little use of the notification procedure, however, and the 1985 revision of the Uniform Securities Act dropped it. (Section 302 of the 2002 version of the Act provides for filing notice of securities offerings, when state registration is preempted by federal law.) Far more useful is the coordination procedure. This allows a company registering under the 1933 Securities Act to file copies of its federal materials, instead of preparing entirely new disclosure documents for the state. Uniform Securities Act § 303; Cal. Corp. Code § 25111. Otherwise, the issuer must register by qualification. Uniform Securities Act

§ 304. *See also* Cal. Corp. Code § 25113. This requires preparation and filing of a disclosure document.

Disclosure, however, often is not the critical burden imposed by blue sky laws. After all, a company going public will need to prepare federal disclosure materials anyway. Moreover, a number of states have enacted provisions that allow issuers of securities meeting certain limitations—for example, the sale involves less than $1 million—to use a so-called Small Corporation Offering Registration document, which is simpler than the disclosure document otherwise required. *E.g.*, Cal. Corp. Code § 25113(b). If disclosure is not the significant requirement added by state securities laws, then what is? The answer in many states is something often referred to as merit review. As mentioned in the Schneider, Manko & Kant article, under the Federal scheme an issuer may attempt to sell any security, no matter how unsound the investment, so long as the issuer fully discloses all the material facts concerning the security. *But see* Sec. Act § 7(b) (the SEC may limit the sale of securities, or the use of the proceeds of such sale, by "blank check" companies—i.e. development stage companies with no business plan or purpose other than perhaps to merge with an unidentified company—until the company states a specific use for the proceeds, and also may give the purchasers of such securities a right of rescission). Indeed, occasionally there have been filings in which the issuer frankly admitted the securities offered were worthless, and any purchasers could expect to lose all their money. (Why did the issuers register these presumably hopeless offerings? While at least one instance involved a joke, a serious reason could exist when the issuer is under a contractual obligation to register a secondary offering, in other words, an offering of shares owned by certain of its stockholders.) Many state securities laws, on the other hand, either require the seller to receive a state official's approval of the merits of the proposed offering, or else allow the state official to stop an offering which the official finds to be unsatisfactory on its merits. For example, Section 25140 of the California Corporations Code empowers the California Corporations Commissioner to refuse to qualify the sale of securities in California (or to stop the sale of an offering through coordination or notification) unless the offering is "fair, just and equitable." While the "fair, just and equitable" language is quite common among the states, the Uniform Securities Act contains a somewhat narrower standard, which states can choose to have either supplement or supplant the "fair, just and equitable" standard:

> "The administrator may issue a stop order denying effectiveness to, or suspending or revoking the effectiveness of, a registration statement if the administrator finds that the order is in the public interest and that:
>
> * * *
>
> (7) the offering:
>
> (A) will work or tend to work a fraud upon purchasers or would so operate; [or]

(B) has been or would be made with unreasonable amounts of underwriters' and sellers' discounts, commissions, or other compensation, or promoters' profits or participations, or unreasonable amounts or kinds of options[; or

(C) is being made on terms that are unfair, unjust, or inequitable]."

Uniform Securities Act (2002 rev.) § 306(a).

Probably more important than the statutory standard for merit review, which in any case is quite vague, are the policies of the particular state's administrator. These can vary substantially from state to state (and even over time within the same state as personnel in government change). Ad Hoc Subcommittee on Merit Regulation of the State Regulation of Securities Committee of the American Bar Association, *Report on State Regulation of Securities Offerings,* 41 Bus. Law. 785 (1986). Indeed, the need to keep on top of current administrative attitudes, and to reconcile sometimes inconsistent requirements, adds to the burden for those undertaking a multistate offering. Nevertheless, despite the variation, certain common themes exist.

Brandi, Securities Practitioners and Blue Sky Laws: A Survey of Comments and a Ranking of States By Stringency of Regulation

10 J.Corp.L. 689 (1985).

* * *

V. Merit Standards

Under the registration by qualification provision, the most common areas of merit regulation are offering price and dilution, cheap stock, promoters' investment, escrow of promoter stock, options and warrants to promoters and insiders, voting rights, and offering expenses and commissions to underwriters.

A. Offering Price and Dilution

* * *

As a means of providing the new investor with some measure of protection, many merit states provide guidelines for determination of the initial offering price.

Setting the price per share equal to that of a comparable firm with a public market is one technique utilized by merit states when the filing entity can provide adequate verification as to why such a firm's price is applicable to its own securities. A second method of price determination is based on the limitation of allowable dilution to new investors. Under this method some minimum level of acceptable dilution is set and is then used in combination with the price paid by promoters and insiders to determine the maximum offering price to the public.

* * *

For the firm able to show that an adequate public market already exists for its securities, the price may be set in accordance with that market price. * * *

Another technique utilized by firms that have a history of earnings prior to the offering is a price-earnings ratio technique. These firms are usually required to limit the initial public price to some standard multiple of earnings per share.

* * *

B. Cheap Stock

The amount of cheap stock sold to insiders at prices below the public price is often restricted by substantive regulation. These restrictions pertain either to the amount of allowable dilution or the amount of cheap stock allowed.

* * *

C. Promoters' Investment

The promoters' investment test is based on the theory that requiring the promoters of firms at the development stage to invest a minimum proportion of the total equity capital desired instills a sense of good faith in such promoters. * * *

D. Escrow of Promoter Stock

Promotional or cheap stock may be subject to escrow in some states. * * *

Escrow provisions do not generally require escrow of all promoter stock but rather only that portion representing the difference between publicly contributed funds and promoter funds. * * *

E. Options and Warrants to Promoters and Insiders

Often promoters and insiders are granted options or warrants as incentives to purchase shares or in lieu of compensation for services. Options or warrants may also be attached to offerings as "sweeteners" intended to enhance the marketability of the issue.

Merit restrictions on the issuance of such options and warrants usually concern the restriction of unreasonable amounts of such attachments. The restrictions set a maximum percentage of shares to which such "sweeteners" may be attached.

* * *

F. Voting Rights

Firms often desire to issue different classes of stock with varying rights. One area of variation is that of the right to vote on matters concerning firm options, directors, business combinations, or termination. Restrictions in this area are aimed at preventing promoters from obtaining public financing without relinquishing some control to that public.

G. Offering Expenses and Commissions to Underwriters

These regulations are intended to prevent excessive or unreasonable payment of offering expenses or underwriter commissions. * * *

The assumption underlying this restriction is based on the fact that underwriter fees and commissions are in part based on an assessment of the risks inherent in an issue. Since merit laws are in part designed to reduce risk to investors, such restrictions serve as one method of removing high risk issues from the state market.

In an attempt to coordinate standards among the states, the North American Securities Administrators Association (NASAA) has promulgated various policy statements which it recommends the individual state administrators follow.* Three of these policy statements were quoted previously when dealing with the question of what type of interest to offer investors. As further examples, consider the following policies with respect to promoter's investment, shares issued to promoters, and offering expenses and warrants:

Statement of Policy Regarding Promoter's Equity Investment

Adopted on April 27, 1997.

* * *

II. DEFINITIONS. The terms used in this Statement of Policy are defined pursuant to the NASAA Statement of Policy Regarding Corporate Securities Definitions.

III. A public securities offering by a PROMOTIONAL OR DEVELOPMENT STAGE COMPANY may be disallowed by the Administrator if the PROMOTERS' EQUITY INVESTMENT is less than:

A. Ten percent (10%) of the first $1,000,000 of the aggregate public offering; and

B. Seven percent (7%) of the next $500,000 of the aggregate public offering; and

* Naturally, individuals dealing with this area in practice will wish to read these policy statements in full, rather than as edited here. For further information on the policy statements, one may contact the North American Securities Administrators Association at One Massachusetts Avenue, N.W., Suite 310, Washington, D.C. 20001.

C. Five percent (5%) of the next $500,000 of the aggregate public offering; and

D. Two and one-half percent (2 ½ %) of the balance over $2,000,000, which may include items submitted by the PROMOTER to meet this requirement whose value has been accepted by the Administrator.

Statement of Policy Regarding Promotional Shares

as amended through September 28, 1999.

* * *

Terms used in this Statement of Policy are defined pursuant to the NASAA Statement of Policy Regarding Corporate Securities Definitions.

* * *

II. ESCROW OF PROMOTIONAL SHARES. The Administrator may require that some or all of the PROMOTERS deposit some or all of their PROMOTIONAL SHARES into an Escrow Account ("Escrow") with an ESCROW AGENT, according to the terms of an Escrow Agreement ("Agreement"), as a condition to registering a public offering of EQUITY SECURITIES.

* * *

Statement of Policy Regarding Underwriting Expenses, Underwriter's Warrants, Selling Expenses and Selling Security Holders

as amended through September 28, 1999.

* * *

II. An offer or sale of securities may be disallowed by the Administrator if the underwriting expenses to be incurred exceed seventeen percent (17%) of the gross proceeds from the public offering.

III. Underwriting expenses may include but are not limited to:

A. Commissions to underwriters or broker-dealers;

B. Non-accountable fees or expenses to be paid to the underwriter or broker-dealer;

C. Underwriter's warrants, which shall be valued using the following formula:

$$\frac{[165\,\%\ \text{x Aggregate Offering Price}] - (\text{Exercise Price x \# of shares offered to public})}{2} \text{ x } \frac{\text{\# shares underlying warrants}}{\text{\# shares offered to the public}}$$

The value may be reduced by 20% if the exercise period of the warrants is extended from one year after the public offering to two years after the public offering and by 40% if the exercise period of the warrants is extended from one year after the public offering to three years after the public offering. Warrants granted to underwriters are subject to the following restrictions:

1. The underwriter is a managing underwriter;
2. The public offering is either a firmly underwritten offering or a "minimummaximum" offering. Options or warrants may be issued in a "minimummaximum" public offering only if:
   (i) The options or warrants are issued on a pro rata basis; and
   (ii) The "minimum" amount of securities has been sold;
3. The exercise price of the warrants must be at least equal to the public offering price;
4. The number of shares covered by underwriter's options or warrants does not exceed ten percent (10%) of the shares of common stock actually sold in the public offering;
5. The life of the options or warrants does not exceed a period of five (5) years from the completion date of the public offering;
6. The options or warrants are not exercisable for the first year after the completion date of the public offering; and
7. Options or warrants may not be transferred, except:
   (i) To partners of the underwriter, if the underwriter is a partnership;
   (ii) To officers and employees of the underwriter, who are also shareholders of the underwriter, if the underwriter is a corporation; or
   (iii) By will, pursuant to the laws of descent and distribution, or by the operation of law.
8. The warrant agreement may not allow for a reduction in the exercise price of the options or warrants resulting from the subsequent issuance of shares by the issuer except where such issuances are pursuant to a:
   (i) Stock dividend or stock split; or
   (ii) merger, consolidation, reclassification, reorganization, recapitalization, or sale of assets.

D. Right of first refusal, which shall be valued at 1% of the public offering or the amount payable to the underwriter if the issuer terminates the right of first refusal;

E. Solicitation fees payable to the underwriter, which shall be valued at the lesser of actual cost or 1% of the public offering if the fees are payable within one year of the offering;

F. Financial consulting or financial advisory agreements with an underwriter or any other similar type of agreement or fees, however designated, which shall be valued at actual cost;

G. Underwriter's due diligence expenses;

H. Payments made either six months prior to or required to be made six months following the public offering to investor relations firms designated by the underwriter; and

I. Other underwriting expenses incurred in connection with the public offering of securities as determined by the Administrator.

IV. Underwriting expenses shall not include financial consulting or financial advisory agreements with the underwriter payable at the time the services are rendered provided that such agreement was entered into at least twelve months before the registration is filed with the Securities and Exchange Commission.

V. An offer or sale of securities may be disallowed by the Administrator if the direct and indirect selling expenses of the offering exceed twenty percent (20%) of the gross proceeds from the public offering.

VI. Selling expenses may include but are not limited to:

A. Commissions to underwriters or broker-dealers;

B. Non-accountable fees or expenses to be paid to the underwriters or broker-dealers;

C. Auditors' and accountants' fees;

D. Legal fees;

E. The cost of printing prospectuses, circulars and other documents required to comply with securities laws and regulations;

F. Charges of transfer agents, registrars, indenture trustees, escrow holders, depositories, engineers, appraisers, and other experts;

G. The cost of authorizing and preparing the securities, including issue taxes and stamps;

H. Financial consulting or financial advisory agreements with an underwriter or any similar type agreement or fees, however designated, which shall be valued at actual cost, excluding financial and consulting agreements which is entered into at least twelve months before the registration is filed with the Securities and Exchange Commission;

I. Payments made either six months prior to or required to be made six months following the public offering to investor relations firms designated by the underwriter;

J. Other cash expenses incurred in connection with the public offering of securities as determined by the Administrator; and

K. Expenses incurred in connection with bridge financing in the twelve month period preceding a public offering of securities including, but not limited to:

1. Direct expenses attributable to the financing including interest charges and those expenses set forth in Section III and elsewhere in Section VI of this Policy Statement;

2. Warrants and options valued as set forth in Section III.C. of this Policy Statement; and
3. Expenses attributable to the issuance of securities that are not options, warrants, or convertible securities, to be valued using the following formula:

$$\frac{[(\text{Public Offering Price per share} - \text{Cost per share}) \times \text{Number of Securities Issued} \times 100]}{\text{Aggregate Public Offering Proceeds}}$$

VII. A public offering or sale of securities, that includes selling security holders offering more than ten percent (10%) of the securities to be sold in the public offering, may be disallowed by the Administrator unless:

A. Selling security holders offering or selling more than ten percent (10%) but less than fifty percent (50%) of the securities to be sold in the public offering pay a pro rata share of all selling expenses of the public offering, excluding the legal and accounting expenses of the public offering; or

B. Selling security holders offering more than fifty percent (50%) of the securities to be sold in the offering pay a pro rata share of all selling expenses of the public offering; and

C. The prospectus or offering document discloses the amount of selling expenses that the selling security holders will pay.

VIII. With the exception of underwriter's or broker-dealer's compensation, the provisions of VII.A., B., and C. above, shall not apply if the selling security holders have a written agreement with the Issuer, that was entered into in an arm's-length transaction, whereby the Issuer has agreed to pay all of the selling security holders' selling expenses.

3. As these materials indicate, compliance with state securities law merit standards can undermine the plans of a company seeking to go public. Is there a way to avoid these laws? Perhaps the company can avoid selling its securities in a particular state which is especially restrictive. More recently, companies have been able to avoid state merit review by listing their shares on the stock exchanges—specifically, the New York or American Stock Exchange or on the Nasdaq computerized market. A number of state securities laws have exempted from their registration requirements securities listed on such national exchanges. *E.g.*, Uniform Securities Act (1985 rev.) § 401(b)(7); Cal. Corp. Code § 25100(*o*). An amendment to Section 18 of the 1933 Securities Act essentially makes such an exemption from state blue sky laws a federal requirement. Specifically, Section 18(a) of the Securities Act, as amended, preempts any state attempt to require registration or qualification, or subject to merit review, the sale of so-called covered securities. Section 18(b) defines covered securities to include securities listed for trading on the New York or American Stock exchanges or on the National Market System of the Nasdaq Stock Market. Significantly, when dealing with an initial public offering, this preemption extends to securities which will be covered securities at the close of the transaction.

Listing one's shares on the stock exchange, however, itself imposes some merit requirements on the company. Specifically, in order to list the company's securities, the company must agree to abide by the rules of the exchange. These rules require, as mentioned earlier, companies grant their securities holders certain rights. Moreover, the company must meet certain guidelines as to size, which might pose a problem for some firms seeking to go public. For example, the following chart sets out requirements for listing on the Nasdaq national market:

NASDAQ GLOBAL SELECT MARKET

INITIAL LISTING

Companies must meet all of the criteria under at least one of the three financial standards and the applicable liquidity requirements below.

FINANCIAL AND QUALITATIVE REQUIREMENTS

NASDAQ Global Select Market Initial Listing Requirements[1]

Requirements	Standard 1	Standard 2	Standard 3	Marketplace Rules
Pre-tax earnings[2] (income from continuing operations before income taxes)	Aggregate in prior three fiscal years ≥ $11 million and Each of the two most recent fiscal years ≥ $2.2 million and Each of the prior three fiscal years ≥ $0	N/A	N/A	4426(c)(1)
Cash flows[3]	N/A	Aggregate in prior three fiscal years ≥ $27.5 million and Each of the prior three fiscal years ≥ $0	N/A	4426(c)(2)
Market capitalization[4]	N/A	Average ≥ $550 million over prior 12 months	Average ≥ $850 million over prior 12 months	4426(c)(2)(C) 4426(c)(3)(A)
Revenue	N/A	Previous fiscal year ≥ $110 million	Previous fiscal year ≥ $90 million	4426(c)(2)(C) 4426(c)(3)(B)
Bid price[5]	$5.00	$5.00	$5.00	4426(d)
Market makers[6]	3	3	3	4310(c)(1)
Corporate governance	Yes	Yes	Yes	4350, 4351 and 4460

[1] These requirements apply to all companies, other than closed-end management investment companies. A closed end management investment company, including a business development company, is not required to meet the financial requirements of Marketplace Rule 4426(c). If the common stock of an issuer is included in The NASDAQ Global Select Market, any other security of that same issuer, such as other classes of common or preferred stock that qualifies for listing on The NASDAQ Global Market shall also be included in The NASDAQ Global Select Market.

[2] In calculating income from continuing operations before income taxes for purposes of Rule 4426(c)(1), NASDAQ will rely on an issuer's annual financial information as filed with the Securities and Exchange Commission (SEC) in the issuer's most recent periodic report and/or registration statement. If an issuer does not have three years of publicly reported financial data, it may qualify under Rule 4426(c)(1) if it has: (i) reported aggregate income from continuing operations before income taxes of at least $11 million and (ii) positive income from continuing operations before income taxes in each of the reported fiscal years. A period of less than three months shall not be considered a fiscal year, even if reported as a stub period in the issuer's publicly reported financial statements.

[3] In calculating cash flows for purposes of Rule 4426(c)(2), NASDAQ will rely on the net cash provided by operating activities reported in the statements of cash flows, as filed with the SEC in the issuer's most recent periodic report and/or registration statement, excluding changes in working capital or in operating assets and liabilities.

If an issuer does not have three years of publicly reported financial data, it may qualify under Rule 4426(c)(2) if it has: (i) reported aggregate cash flows of at least $27.5 million and (ii) positive cash flows in each of the reported fiscal years. A period of less than three months shall not be considered a fiscal year, even if reported as a stub period in the issuer's publicly reported financial statements.

[4] In the case of an issuer listing in connection with its initial public offering, compliance with the market capitalization requirements of Rules 4426(c)(2) and (c)(3) will be based on the company's market capitalization at the time of listing.

[5] The bid price requirement is not applicable to a company listed on The NASDAQ Global Market that transfers its listing to The NASDAQ Global Select Market.

[6] An electronic communications network (ECN) is not considered a market maker for the purpose of these rules. Note that the company must also have sufficient market makers to satisfy Rule 4450(a) or (b), which may require four (4) market makers.

LIQUIDITY REQUIREMENTS

Companies must meet all of the criteria in their specific category. The charts below are presented in two separate groups: (i) new company listings and (ii) closed-end management investment companies.

NASDAQ Global Select Market Initial Listing Requirements

New Company Listings				
Requirements	**Initial Public Offerings and Spin-Off Companies**	**Seasoned Companies: Currently Trading Common Stock or Equivalents**	**Affiliated Companies[1]**	**Marketplace\ Rules**
Beneficial shareholders (round lot) **or** Beneficial shareholders **or** Beneficial shareholders and Average monthly trading volume over past twelve months	450 **or** 2,200	450 **or** 2,200 **or** 550 and 1.1 million	450 **or** 2,200 **or** 550 and 1.1 million	4426(b)(1)
Publicly held shares[2]	1,250,000	1,250,000	1,250,000	4426(b)(2)
Market value of publicly held shares **or** Market value of publicly held shares and Shareholders' equity	$70 million	$110 million **or** $100 million and $110 million	$70 million	4426(b)(3)

[1] Companies affiliated with another company listed on The NASDAQ Global Select Market. For purposes of Rule 4426, an issuer is affiliated with another company if that other company, directly or indirectly though one or more intermediaries, controls, is controlled by, or is under common control of the issuer. For purposes of these rules, control means having the ability to exercise significant influence. Ability to exercise significant influence will be presumed to exist where the parent or affiliated company directly or indirectly owns 20% or more of the other company's voting securities, and also can be indicated by representation on the board of directors, participation in policy making processes, material intercompany transactions, interchange of managerial personnel, or technological dependency.

[2] In computing the number of publicly held shares for purposes of Rule 4426(b), NASDAQ will not consider shares held by an officer, director or 10% shareholder of the issuer.

NASDAQ GLOBAL MARKET

INITIAL LISTING

Companies must meet all of the criteria under at least one of the three standards below.

NASDAQ Global Market Initial Listing Requirements

Requirements	Standard 1 Marketplace Rule 4420(a)	Standard 2 Marketplace Rule 4420(b)	Standard 3 Marketplace Rule 4420(c)[1, 2]
Stockholders' equity	$15 million	$30 million	N/A
Market value of listed securities **or** Total assets and Total revenue	N/A	N/A	$75 million **or** $75 million and $75 million
Income from continuing operations before income taxes (in latest fiscal year **or** in 2 of last 3 fiscal years)	$1 million	N/A	N/A

Requirements	Standard 1 Marketplace Rule 4420(a)	Standard 2 Marketplace Rule 4420(b)	Standard 3 Marketplace Rule 4420(c) [1, 2]
Publicly held shares[3]	1.1 million	1.1 million	1.1 million
Market value of publicly held shares	$8 million	$18 million	$20 million
Bid price	$5	$5	$5[2]
Shareholders (round lot holders)[4]	400	400	400
Market makers[5]	3	3	4
Operating history	N/A	2 years	N/A
Corporate governance[6]	Yes	Yes	Yes

[1] For initial listing under Standard 3, a company must satisfy one of the following: the market value of listed securities requirement **or** the total assets and the total revenue requirement. Under Marketplace Rule 4200(a)(20), listed securities is defined as "securities listed on NASDAQ or another national securities exchange".

[2] Seasoned companies (those companies already listed or quoted on another marketplace) qualifying only under the market value of listed securities requirement of Standard 3 must meet the market value of listed securities and the bid price requirements for 90 consecutive trading days prior to applying for listing.

[3] Publicly held shares is defined as total shares outstanding, less any shares held by officers, directors or beneficial owners of 10% or more.

[4] Round lot holders are shareholders of 100 shares or more.

[5] An electronic communications network (ECN) is not considered a market maker for the purpose of these rules.

[6] Marketplace Rules 4350, 4351 and 4360

NASDAQ CAPITAL MARKET

INITIAL LISTING

NASDAQ Capital Market Initial Listing Requirements

Requirements	Standard 1	Standard 2[1]	Standard 3	Marketplace Rules[2]
Stockholders' equity	$5 million	$4 million	$4 million	4310(c)(2) 4320(e)(2)
Market value of publicly held shares	$15 million	$15 million	$5 million	4310(c)(2) 4320(e)(2)
Operating history	2 years	N/A	N/A	4310(c)(2) 4320(e)(2)
Market value of listed securities[3]	N/A	$50 million	N/A	4310(c)(2) 4320(e)(2)
Net income from continuing operations (in the latest fiscal year or in 2 of the last 3 fiscal years)	N/A	N/A	$750,000	4310(c)(2) 4320(e)(2)
Publicly held shares[4]	1 million	1 million	1 million	4310(c)(7) 4320(e)(5)
Bid price	$4	$4	$4	4310(c)(4) 4320(e)(2)
Shareholders (round lot holders)[5]	300	300	300	4310(c)(6) 4320(e)(4)
Market makers[6]	3	3	3	4310(c)(1) 4320(e)(1)
Corporate governance	Yes	Yes	Yes	4350, 4351 and 4360

[1] Seasoned companies (those companies already listed or quoted on another marketplace) qualifying only under the market value of listed securities requirement must meet the market value of listed securities and the bid price requirements for 90 consecutive trading days prior to applying for listing.

[2] Marketplace Rule 4310 is applicable to domestic (U.S.) and Canadian securities. Marketplace Rule 4320 is applicable to non-U.S. securities other than Canadian securities.

[3] Under Marketplace Rule 4200(a)(20), listed securities is defined as "securities listed on NASDAQ or another national securities exchange".

[4] Publicly held shares is defined as total shares outstanding, less any shares held by officers, directors or beneficial owners of 10% or more. In the case of ADRs, for initial inclusion only, at least 400,000 shall be issued.

[5] Round lot holders are shareholders of 100 shares or more.

[6] An electronic communications network (ECN) is not considered a market maker for the purpose of these rules.

2. ALTERNATIVES TO GOING PUBLIC

Many businesses would rather avoid the expense and burden of a public offering. How might they obtain additional financing? To answer this question, one must explore two more specific inquiries: (1) What alternative sources of money are available, and (2) Can those sources be tapped without triggering the registration requirements of Federal and state securities laws?

a. *Availability of Venture Capital*

Bartlett, Venture Capital, Law, Business Strategies, and Investment Planning

(1988).

§ 6.1 SOURCES OF FINANCE

* * * The sources of investment capital are numerous, ranging from commercial banks making fixed-rate, secured loans to individual investors willing to provide risk equity capital in hopes of a spectacular return down the road. A number of guidebooks list the types of capital sources a founder may use and others specify the name, address, and telephone number of particular firms. * * *[1]

§ 6.2 "BACKDOOR" FINANCE—TAX DEDUCTIONS

One of the most attractive sources of financing in recent years is, post–1986, no longer promising; that is, federal assistance in the form of tax benefits accruing to investors, buying into the enterprise as limited partners and using early-stage losses to offset income from other sources. So-called "backdoor" financing has been substantially curtailed by the 1986 amendments to the Internal Revenue Code. Under the Tax Reform Act of 1986, losses from "passive" activity (subject to limited transition rules) may only be set against income from "passive" activity or utilized when the investment is sold.

* * *

§ 6.4 "SOFT" AND "HARD" STATE AND LOCAL AID

The states are trying a number of devices to incubate technologically oriented industry. The bottom line is a multitude of programs offering "hard" inducements, for example, loans and investments from a state-affiliated fund, plus "soft" dollars in the form of low-cost facilities and services and "backdoor" financing in the form of state tax deductions and credits.

* * *

[H]owever, the financial impact of the programs is not of the make-or-break variety. Moreover, once having accepted government assistance, a firm is subject to conditions both special (i.e., locate in a given location, hire local residents) and general (e.g., affirmative action, union wages).

* * *

1. Pratt's Guide has become widely accepted as the semi-official source for identifying specific venture capital firms. * * *

§ 6.5 SBA LOANS

The most significant program of federal government assistance to small business is the loan, and loan guarantee, program run since 1953 by the Small Business Administration (SBA), coupled in 1958 with the creation of privately owned concerns called Small Business Investment Companies (SBICs), which utilize funds borrowed from the federal government at soft rates to finance small business. Both programs are administered by the SBA but have different impacts on early-stage financings.

An SBA loan (whether in the person of a direct loan from the SBA or, more commonly, a bank loan guaranteed by the SBA) is, despite the favorable terms, the equivalent of bank financing. Although interest rates can be soft, a loan entails a promise of repayment within a finite period of time and an interest cost from the date the loan is made. Further, it introduces a partner to the enterprise with a lender's mentality. In the typical case—a guaranteed bank loan[12]—the fact that the SBA guarantees 90% [now reduced to 80%; Ed.] (or less) of the loan should give no encouragement that the bank is likely to relax its attitude toward repayment. * * * Moreover, the SBA ordinarily requires the founder(s) to guarantee loans personally and, on occasion, its collection efforts are rigorous. * * * The principal advantage of an SBA-guaranteed loan is that the bank is likely to go higher in the loan-to-value ratio on tangible assets and to extend maturities. * * *

Size standards for eligible recipients of SBA loans—"small business concerns"—vary according to the classification of the firm. For manufacturing concerns, for example, the limit is generally from 500 to 1,000 employees, while retail firms are classified according to annual receipts.

§ 6.6 SBICs

SBICs are privately organized corporations (or partnerships) licensed and regulated by the SBA. They are entitled to borrow money from the SBA.

* * *

SBICs are typical late-round investors, advancing loans coupled with equity options, often subordinated convertible debt.

* * *

12. There are several threshold requirements for SBA financial assistance. For example, the applicant must attempt to obtain financing from other nonfederal sources, including the owner's resources and private lenders. 13 C.F.R. § 122.5–1 (1987). The maturity of each loan is to be the shortest feasible term commensurate with the ability of the borrower to repay and the maximum maturity for a loan is 10 years (with some exceptions). 13 C.F.R. § 122.6–1 (1987). The limit on direct loan amounts is $350,000 by statute, $150,000 by SBA administrative ruling. 13 C.F.R. § 122.7–1 (1987). For immediate participation loans (loans the SBA purchases from financial institutions), the statutory limit is the lesser of 90% of the loan or $350,000; administratively, it is the lesser of 75% of the loan or $150,000. 13 C.F.R. § 122.7–2 (1987). * * *

An SBIC's investment program is limited to firms that qualify as small business concerns, including those that qualify under the SBA standards and firms meeting net worth and income tests applicable only to SBICs. This was not an onerous requirement in the world of venture finance in the 1950s and 1960s, since the test is applied when the investment is made and few unseasoned companies enjoy 2 years of average net after-tax profit exceeding $2 million annually.

* * *

§ 6.7 BANK–AFFILIATED SBICs

One of the more significant impelling forces in the current period behind the formation of new SBICs has not been cheap debt but the election of many banks and bank holding companies to organize SBICs so as to participate legally in a nonbank investment activity * * *.

[A]n SBIC * * * enables the bank to hold up to 50% of the vote in a small business concern.

* * * To those in search of financing, a bank-affiliated SBIC is little different from a free-standing venture pool. With certain major exceptions, the tendency of the bank-affiliated pools, however, has been to focus on later-state financings, LBOs, and investments in other venture pools (the "fund of funds" concept), versus early-round investing in emerging companies.

§ 6.8 BANK FINANCING

The question whether a start-up should rely on commercial bank financing (if the same is obtainable) is to be approached quite cautiously. A commercial bank can make a very poor partner for a fledgling enterprise; the lenders tend to want their money back at just the wrong moment. Often the only type of bank financing available to a start-up is a demand note secured by a floating lien on all the assets of the operation and the personal signature of the founder, a dangerous weapon in the hands of a nervous bank. * * * Some banks, particularly those located in the classic high tech areas, have become experienced in lending to early-stage companies and are less likely to panic. Indeed, some banks are willing to negotiate compensation for their added risk by accepting equity in the borrower—an equity "kicker"—or an interest rate tied to a fixed base or index plus increases depending on the fortunes of the borrower.

§ 6.9 CAPITAL FROM OPERATIONS

The most frequent source of capital for unseasoned companies is the most obvious, right under the founder's nose; that is, saving cash by cutting the burn rate.

* * *

Raising cash internally involves, in turn, two methods: increase cash flow and/or cut costs; and, of these, the fastest, surest, most feasible method is to cut costs—fire people, give up space, cut R & D, reconfigure the product. Of course, it is risky to "cut out the fat." Without R & D, new product opportunities collapse; perhaps a quick death is being traded for a slow death. * * *

§ 6.10 PLACEMENT AGENTS

Founders desperate for financing debate whether the faucet will turn on if they engage a placement agent, a question to be addressed in a real world context. In the first place, the great majority of first-round financings are not economically interesting to an investment banking firm. The fee for a placement is usually in the range of 2 to 5% of the amount raised.

* * *

If an agent is engaged to place securities privately, he will surely act only on a "best efforts" basis. * * * Moreover, the founder should understand that the agent is not obligated to sell an untried security; that remains the responsibility of the founder. The agent is engaged to help prepare a private placement memorandum and to expose the opportunity to a list of prospects, to screen buyers, and to schedule meetings for the founder to do his stuff. Purchasers in early rounds are not interested in discussing the merits of the investment with a salesman. The founder, and only the founder, has that reservoir of knowledge about the technology and its potential application which potential buyers are interested to hear. Moreover, the agent will look to the founder for a so-called "friends" list, that is, potential investors already known to the founder.

* * *

§ 6.11 "HIGH NET WORTH" INDIVIDUALS

Sometimes, if the forecast returns are not attractive to professionally managed venture funds, the founder can search for those rich individuals who: (i) are anxious to invest in start-ups; (ii) are not jaded, like the "vulture capitalists"; and (iii) will accept situations the professionals are unlikely to favor. This individuals [sic] indubitably exist. * * * The trick, of course, is to find him.

* * *

§ 6.12 USE YOUR PROFESSIONALS

Circulation of business plans among venture capital firms picked randomly out of a book is not likely to be particularly productive. So-called "over-the-transom" submissions to venture firms number in the hundreds each month and very few are favored. Most venture firms make their investment decision on the basis of plans they have helped develop on their own or which have been forwarded to them by sources they know and respect. The trick, therefore, is to obtain an introduction. If a placement agent is not available, one technique is to employ a law or accounting firm enjoying cordial relationships with a number of venture firms. * * *

§ 6.13 VENTURE CAPITAL CLUBS AND OTHER VENUES

One often-tried gambit for raising cash is to make a presentation at a forum organized by a "venture capital club." * * * Venture capital clubs consist of an organizer and a mailing list of individuals and/or entities in a given region that have demonstrated some interest in venture capital. * * * The most important part of a typical meeting is the "Five Minute Forum," in which anyone can speak about his venture for a limit of one to five minutes. * * *

At this point, some words of caution are in order. First, there are hidden legal difficulties in the venture capital club. * * * Availability of an exemption from registration of an offering under the 1933 Act can be lost because attendees at a luncheon are publicly solicited to buy securities in the companies making presentations. * * * Secondly, it is not clear how effective such symposiums have been in raising money, except for the commercial sponsor of the event.

* * *

NOTES

1. Mr. Bartlett suggests using the business' lawyers and accountants to contact venture capital firms. This raises the question of what role an attorney should play in helping his or her clients find venture capital. Mr. Bartlett implicitly recommends an active role. For example, the attorney might build a "war chest" of venture capital sources to which he or she can refer clients whose area of business and stage of financing fits the investment profile sought by a specific venture capital firm. Attorneys also might develop personal contacts with several venture capitalists. In acting as matchmaker, however, to what extent is the attorney putting his or her own credibility on the line? For instance, suppose the client is forever late in paying legal bills, or suppose the attorney feels the client is a hopeless dreamer. What obligations does the attorney owe to this one client?

2. Mr. Bartlett largely dismisses tax shelter investors as a source of financing after 1986. This may be too broad a generalization. Recall from the discussions in Chapters II and III how some investors—such as those with passive income, or C corporations—can still utilize passive losses.

A variety of other funding sources also exist beyond those outlined by Mr. Bartlett. For example, companies with which the firm does business (its vendors) may provide financing (such as by supplying goods or services in exchange for stock, and, of course, by allowing installment payments for goods and services). Sometimes, a firm may seek investments from other companies in its field. For example, some biotechnology companies have been able to enter licensing agreements with established pharmaceutical companies where the contract provides that the pharmaceutical company will make pre-development royalty payments in exchange for rights to use the intellectual property developed by the biotechnology company. For a discussion of a couple possible problems with such contracts, see Gevurtz, *Biotechnology: Business Organization Issues*, 32 McGeorge L. Rev. 237

(2000). Of course, the problem of protecting trade secrets becomes important when one approaches a company in the same field.

The following provides another view of private sources of capital, in this instance written from the vantage point of one who is a principal in a venture capital firm, and with the perspective of seeing the high-tech stock bubble of the late 1990s.

Mcilwraith,[1] The Outlook for the Private Equity Market

51 Case Western Reserve L. Rev. 423 (2001).

* * *

I. Historical Overview of Private Equity

* * *

In a venture capital transaction, the company is usually early-stage, meaning pre-revenue or with initial revenues but still twelve months or more away from profitability. The venture investors generally back an existing management team, which usually includes one or more of the company's founders. Venture investors, whether angels or institutional investors, typically own less than 50% of the company and do not control it. They do not want to have control of the company, except when the company falls well short of its projections and a change in management is necessary to keep the company afloat. Venture investors generally seek a * * * five to ten times return on their investment. * * *

There are five sources of private equity capital: angels, incubators, private equity firms, strategic partners, and government programs. Angels include wealthy individuals—doctors, successful entrepreneurs, retired executives, and relatives. * * *

In the last five years, angel investment activity has increased substantially as we experienced a seemingly never-ending series of successes in the public and private equity markets. There has also been a significant increase in the number of strategic investments made by large corporations, such as Intel, in early-stage private companies. A number of high profile incubators, such as CMGI, have been formed to take advantage of the attractive market for growing companies.

The amount of venture capital available for investment in private companies has grown dramatically * * *. [T]he amount invested in funds has grown from $5 billion in 1990 to more than $60 billion in 1999, and the number of venture capital firms receiving funding has grown from approximately 100 to over 500.

* * *

1. Managing Director, Blue Chip Venture Company, Cincinnati, Ohio. This Article is an edited version of the presentation given by Mr. McIlwraith on November 10, 2000, at the George A. Leet Business Law Symposium at Case Western Reserve University School of Law.

The increase in the amount of venture capital available increased the amount of venture capital invested in companies * * *. [T]he scale of the increase resulted in a much larger number of companies being funded, an approximately three-fold increase since 1990. It also resulted in a significant increase in the average amount invested per company from approximately $3.9 million in 1990 to $17.1 million in the first half of 2000. * * *

The amount of investment capital available from venture funds, combined with a large increase in competition for investments from angel and strategic investors and incubators, has driven the valuations of early-stage companies seeking growth capital to extraordinary levels. * * *

At these valuations, a company will need to be worth several hundred million dollars at the time the venture fund achieves "liquidity" on its investment, through an IPO or sale of the company, in order for the venture fund to earn an attractive rate of return. Considering that many of these companies have little if any revenues and no earnings at the time of investment, achieving such a return is no easy matter.

* * *

II. Current Private Equity Trends

* * *

From 1997 through 1999, the free flow of private equity capital from multiple sources and the apparent ease of going from start-up stage to IPO, even before proving the business model, caused entrepreneurs to change their approach to raising equity capital. Instead of seeking out investors who would add value to the process of building the entrepreneur's business beyond the capital, entrepreneurs sought one thing—a high valuation for their companies regardless of the source of the capital. As a result, companies often received funding from: angel investors who offered only capital and a high valuation; strategic investors who offered capital and a high valuation, but often attached strings relating to business relationships and rights; and newly-formed venture capital firms whose partners had little experience in helping build young, high-risk enterprises.

In many cases the companies being funded had a questionable, or at least unproven, business model. Many "pure play" dot-com companies were in this category. Business strategies tied to "monetizing eyeballs" and business-to-business exchanges that would "disrupt" the natural order of business relationships were the rage. Traditional business rules were ignored, and companies pursued their strategies with incredible rates of spending or "cash burn," fueled by a seemingly unending supply of private, and sometimes public, capital. An IPO was a foregone conclusion in the eyes of many entrepreneurs and their investors.

* * *

Recently, companies and investors are learning how fast things change. Angel investors are pulling back from "committed" investments as the value of their public stock portfolios shrinks. At the same time strategic investors, such as Intel and MarchFIRST, have slowed the flow of investments into private companies as the period of time required to achieve liquidity increases substantially and their core businesses are adversely impacted by the market downturn. The pace of IPOs has slowed, and early-stage companies with little or no proof of a sustainable business strategy are finding no interest from the public markets. Private companies are struggling to grow, or even stay in business, as planned later round financings take much longer to consummate and angel and strategic investors refuse to provide the "bridge" financing necessary to allow continued growth until the next round closes. * * *

At the same time, venture funds appear to be paralyzed and confused as they consider new investment opportunities while trying to save companies in their current portfolio that are running out of money pursuing a questionable business model. * * * Venture funds are returning to basics, seeking to invest in businesses with early proof of a viable business model and customers and to co-invest with one or more firms in a financing round.

III. The Lawyer's Role in the Investment Process

In a typical venture capital investment transaction the lawyers have three basic roles: (1) assisting their respective clients (the company and the investors) with the outline of the key terms of the investment, usually through the negotiation of a term sheet; (2) drafting or reviewing and commenting on the investment agreements containing the agreed-upon terms; and (3) conducting legal due diligence on matters such as the company's capitalization, governance documents, and material contracts. Although the length of the documents and the "side" they favor ebbs and flows with the market, there are almost always four basic agreements: a stock purchase agreement, which sets forth the terms of the purchase of shares and contains representations, warranties, and covenants of the company and the investors; a shareholders agreement, which contains provisions providing for board of directors representation and share transfer restrictions; an amendment to the company's articles or certificate of incorporation, which contains the terms of the preferred stock being purchased; and a registration rights agreement, which contains provisions with respect to the future public offering and sale of the shares purchased by the investor.

In most cases these documents, while heavily negotiated by the lawyers, will never be looked at again after the closing unless the management team and the venture capitalists become adversaries over the progress or direction of the business or over how the value created should be shared at the time of an IPO or sale of the company. That being said, they require special attention by the lawyers up front. Counsel for the investors needs to not only make sure the agreements contain the agreed upon terms, but must also tailor his or her "form" agreements to the company and its business. For example, if it's a technology company, the representations and warranties should include a focus on intellectual propriety rights and ownership. Too often the agreements remain in their "form" state failing to cover the matters most important to the investor, but including provisions that are irrelevant (e.g., an extensive environmental representation when the company is a technology consulting firm located on the twentieth floor of a downtown office building).

* * *

A good lawyer can make a big difference in how efficiently and smoothly a venture capital investment transaction is consummated. Rather than competing with the other side's lawyer regarding a finer point in the standard two to three page employee benefits plan representation, the lawyer should spend time with his client to determine what matters are really important and negotiate with these matters in mind. If the lawyer is representing the investor, he or she might determine what aspects of the company's business creates the value that has the investor excited (e.g., proprietary software) and then make sure the agreements contain relevant provisions. If the lawyer is representing the company, the focus might be on the investor's ability to control the company or dictate the terms of future financings through covenants.

* * *

IV. Possible Impact of Current Trends and Recommendations for Companies

The correction in the public markets and apparent trends in the private equity markets will likely lead to a slowdown in the number and pace of venture financings. Marginal companies—very early-stage with little proof of concept for their business strategies—will have trouble finding private equity capital. Companies that have completed first round financings may find it difficult to close "planned" second round financings on schedule, making bridge financing from current investors a necessity.

As private company valuations decline, sometimes more than fifty percent below the last financing round level, companies will face serious difficulties in consummating subsequent financing rounds as earlier investors seek to protect their positions through anti-dilution provisions or threats of legal action. Capital structure difficulties may scare away future investors who do not want to get entangled in a dispute between the company and earlier round investors.

* * *

What should companies do to minimize the adverse impact of these private equity market trends? I have a few recommendations that are appropriate for today and have been proven over time:

Accept more money than the budget requires. Markets change rapidly, as do sales projections. Companies should always consider taking more money that [sic] the budget suggests is required. We have rarely seen companies hit sales projections, and the expenses of growing a young company always seem to be higher than planned. Although taking more money results in greater dilution to founders and management, that dilution will matter little if the company is successful, and will definitely not matter if the company fails. And you never know when we will experience a market like the one we are facing now, where even good companies are struggling to raise more capital.

Choose equity partners wisely. * * * Companies need to choose their equity partners wisely, considering the depth of the investors' resources and whether the assistance that a venture fund can provide in the process of building a company is important. Companies also need to consider the chemistry between management and the investors and among the co-investors, if applicable. During tough times, which virtually always occur over the five years it takes to build a company, these relationships will be critical to keeping the company on track with minimal distractions.

Build a real company. During the past few years many companies focused almost exclusively on the exit, such as an IPO or strategic sale, or on the next financing round, rather than focusing on near-term business-building matters and proving the business strategy is viable. Management teams and investors were focused on getting rich quick. They forgot that, absent the assistance of blind luck, the way to create value is to build a high-growth, profitable enterprise.

b. *Exemptions from the Registration Requirement*

Having located possible sources of venture capital, the question becomes whether the firm can tap these sources without the expense and burden of registration under Federal and state securities laws. It is a mistake to assume simply because one does not make an offering of stock through an underwriter to the public at large, these laws do not apply. Rather, the attorney must look at precisely when the securities acts require registration. Section 5 of the Securities Act of 1933 creates a blanket prohibition on offering or selling a security by using any means of transportation or communication in interstate commerce unless a registration statement is filed (for making offers) or in effect (for selling). This means, unless the business can raise funds without selling a "security" (recall the discussion earlier), it must find an exemption from registration, or it must register. The same is generally true under state blue sky laws. *E.g.,* Uniform Securities Act (1985 rev.) § 301; Cal. Corp. Code § 25110. Section 3 of the 1933 Securities Act exempts certain securities and Section 4 exempts certain transactions from registration. State blue sky laws often employ a similar pattern of exempting types of securities and types of transactions. *E.g.,* Uniform Securities Act (1985 rev.) §§ 401, 402; Cal. Corp. Code §§ 25100, 25102, 25105. The following materials explore several of the more widely used exemptions, first under the federal, and then under the state, acts.

(i) Private Offerings

Doran v. Petroleum Management Corp.

545 F.2d 893 (5th Cir.1977).

■ GOLDBERG, CIRCUIT JUDGE:

In this case a sophisticated investor who purchased a limited partnership interest in an oil drilling venture seeks to rescind. The question raised is whether the sale was part of a private offering exempted by § 4(2) of the Securities Act of 1933, * * * from the registration requirements of that Act * * *. We hold that in the absence of findings of fact that each offeree had been furnished information about the issuer that a registration statement would have disclosed or that each offeree had effective access to such information, the district court erred in concluding that the offering was a private placement. Accordingly, we reverse and remand.

I. Facts

Prior to July 1970, Petroleum Management Corporation (PMC) organized a California limited partnership for the purpose of drilling and operating four wells in Wyoming. The limited partnership agreement provided for both "participants," * * * and "special participants."

PMC and Inter–Tech Resources, Inc., were initially the only "special participants" in the limited partnership. They were joined by four "participants." As found by the district court, PMC contacted only four other persons with respect to possible participation in the partnership. All but the plaintiff declined.

During the late summer of 1970, plaintiff William H. Doran, Jr., received a telephone call from a California securities broker previously known to him. The broker, Phillip Kendrick, advised Doran of the opportunity to become a "special participant" in the partnership. PMC then sent Doran the drilling logs and technical maps of the proposed drilling area. PMC informed Doran that two of the proposed four wells had already been completed. Doran agreed to become "special participant" in the Wyoming drilling program. In consideration for his partnership share, Doran agreed to contribute $125,000 toward the partnership. Doran was to discharge this obligation by paying PMC $25,000 down and in addition assuming responsibility for the payment of a $113,643 note owed by PMC to Mid–Continent Supply Co. Doran's share in the production payments from the wells was to be used to make the installment payments on the Mid–Continent note.

* * *

Following the cessation of production payments between November 1971 and August 1972 and the decreased yields thereafter, the Mid–Continent note upon which Doran was primarily liable went into default. * * *

On October 16, 1972, Doran filed this suit in federal district court seeking * * *, rescission of the contract based on violations of the Securities Acts of 1933 and 1934, and a judgment declaring the defendants liable for payment of the state judgment obtained by Mid–Continent.

The court below found that the offer and sale of the "special participant" interest was a private offering because Doran was a sophisticated investor who did not need the protection of the Securities Acts. The court also found that there was no evidence that PMC, its officers, or Kendrick made any misrepresentation or omissions of material facts to Doran. * * * Doran filed this appeal.

II. The Private Offering Exemption

No registration statement was filed with any federal or state regulatory body in connection with the defendants' offering of securities. Along with two other factors that we may take as established—that the defendants sold or offered to sell these securities, and that the defendants used interstate transportation or communication in connection with the sale or offer of sale—the plaintiff thus states a prima facie case for a violation of the federal securities laws. * * *

The defendants do not contest the existence of the elements of plaintiff's prima facie case but raise an affirmative defense that the relevant transactions came within the exemption from registration found in § 4(2). * * * Specifically, they contend that the offering of securities was not a public offering. The defendants, who of course bear the burden of proving this affirmative defense, must therefore show that the offering was private. * * *

This court has in the past identified four factors relevant to whether an offering qualifies for the exemption. The consideration of these factors, along with the policies embodied in the 1933 Act, structure the inquiry. * * * The relevant factors include the number of offerees and their relationship to each other and the issuer, the number of units offered, the size of the offering, and the manner of the offering. Consideration of these factors need not exhaust the inquiry, nor is one factor's weighing heavily in favor of the private status of the offering sufficient to ensure the availability of the exemption. Rather, these factors serve as guideposts to the court in attempting to determine whether subjecting the offering to registration requirements would further the purposes of the 1933 Act.

The term, "private offering," is not defined in the Securities Act of 1933. The scope of the § 4(2) private offering exemption must therefore be determined by reference to the legislative purposes of the Act. In *SEC v. Ralston Purina Co.,* [346 U.S. 119], the SEC had sought to enjoin a corporation's offer of unregistered stock to its employees, and the Court grappled with the corporation's defense that the offering came within the private placement exemption. The Court began by looking to the statutory purpose:

> Since exempt transactions are those as to which "there is no practical need for * * *[the bill's] application," the applicability of [§ 4(2)] should turn on whether the particular class of persons affected need the protection of the Act. An offering to those who are shown to be able to fend for themselves is a transaction "not involving any public offering."

346 U.S. at 124, 73 S.Ct. 984. According to the Court, the purpose of the Act was "to protect investors by promoting full disclosure of information thought necessary to informed investment decisions." *Id.* at 124, 73 S.Ct.

984. It therefore followed that "the exemption question turns on the knowledge of the offeree." *Id.* at 126–27, 73 S.Ct. at 985. That formulation remains the touchstone of the inquiry into the scope of the private offering exemption. It is most nearly reflected in the first of the four factors: the number of offerees and their relationship to each other and to the issuer.

In the case at bar, the defendants may have demonstrated the presence of the latter three factors. A small number of units offered, relatively modest financial stakes, and an offering characterized by personal contact between the issuer and offeree free of public advertising or intermediaries such as investment bankers or securities exchanges—these aspects of the instant transaction aid the defendants' search for a § 4(2) exemption.

Nevertheless, with respect to the first, most critical, and conceptually most problematic factor, the record does not permit us to agree that the defendants have proved that they are entitled to the limited sanctuary afforded by § 4(2). We must examine more closely the importance of demonstrating both the number of offerees and their relationship to the issuer in order to see why the defendants have not yet gained the § 4(2) exemption.

A. *The Number of Offerees*

Establishing the number of persons involved in an offering is important both in order to ascertain the magnitude of the offering and in order to determine the characteristics and knowledge of the persons thus identified.

The number of offerees, not the number of purchasers, is the relevant figure in considering the number of persons involved in an offering. * * * A private placement claimant's failure to adduce any evidence regarding the number of offerees will be fatal to the claim. * * * The number of offerees is not itself a decisive factor in determining the availability of the private offering exemption. Just as an offering to few may be public, so an offering to many may be private. * * * Nevertheless, "the more offerees, the more likelihood that the offering is public." *Hill York Corp. v. American International Franchises, Inc.,* * * *, 448 F.2d at 688. In the case at bar, the record indicates that eight investors were offered limited partnership shares in the drilling program—a total that would be entirely consistent with a finding that the offering was private.

The defendants attempt to limit the number of offerees even further, however. They argue that Doran was the sole offeree because all others contacted by PMC were offered "participant" rather than "special participant" interests. * * *

The argument is, in any event, unsupported by the record. * * *

In considering the number of offerees solely as indicative of the magnitude or scope of an offering, the difference between one and eight offerees is relatively unimportant. Rejecting the argument that Doran was the sole offeree is significant, however, because it means that in considering the need of the offerees for the protection that registration would have afforded we must look beyond Doran's interests to those of all his fellow offerees. Even the offeree-plaintiff's 20–20 vision with respect to the facts underlying the security would not save the exemption if any one of his fellow offerees was in a blind.

B. *The Offerees' Relationship to the Issuer*

Since *SEC v. Ralston, supra,* courts have sought to determine the need of offerees for the protections afforded by registration by focusing on the relationship between offerees and issuer and more particularly on the information available to the offerees by virtue of that relationship. * * * Once the offerees have been identified, it is possible to investigate their relationship to the issuer.

The district court concluded that the offer of a "special participant" interest to Doran was a private offering because Doran was a sophisticated investor who did not need the protections afforded by registration. It is important, in light of our rejection of the argument that Doran was the sole offeree, that the district court also found that all four "participants" and all three declining offerees were sophisticated investors with regard to oil ventures.

* * *

1. The role of investment sophistication

The lower court's finding that Doran was a sophisticated investor is amply supported by the record, as is the sophistication of the other offerees. Doran holds a petroleum engineering degree from Texas A & M University. His net worth is in excess of $1,000,000. His holdings of approximately twenty-six oil and gas properties are valued at $850,000.

Nevertheless, evidence of a high degree of business or legal sophistication on the part of all offerees does not suffice to bring the offering within the private placement exemption. We clearly established that proposition in *Hill York Corp. v. American International Franchises, Inc.,* * * * 448 F.2d at 690. We reasoned that "if the plaintiffs did not possess the information requisite for a registration statement, they could not bring their sophisticated knowledge of business affairs to bear in deciding whether or not to invest * * *." Sophistication is not a substitute for access to the information that registration would disclose. * * * As we said in *Hill York,* although the evidence of the offerees' expertise "is certainly favorable to the defendants, the level of sophistication will not carry the point. In this context, the relationship between the promoters and the purchasers and the 'access to the kind of information which registration would disclose' become highly relevant factors." 448 F.2d at 690.[10]

In short, there must be sufficient basis of accurate information upon which the sophisticated investor may exercise his skills. Just as a scientist cannot be without his specimens, so the shrewdest investor's acuity will be

10. We do not intimate that evidence of the offerees' sophistication is required in all cases to establish a private offering exemption under § 4(2). * * *

blunted without specifications about the issuer. For an investor to be invested with exemptive status he must have the required data for judgment.

2. The requirement of available information

The interplay between two factors, the relationship between offerees and issuer and the offerees' access to information that registration would disclose, has been a matter of some conceptual and terminological difficulty. For purposes of this discussion, we shall adopt the following conventions: We shall refer to offerees who have not been furnished registration information directly, but who are in a position relative to the issuer to obtain the information registration would provide, as having "access" to such information. By a position of access we mean a relationship based on factors such as employment, family, or economic bargaining power that enables the offerees effectively to obtain such information. * * * When offerees, regardless of whether they occupy a position of access, have been furnished with the information a registration statement would provide, we shall say merely that such information has been disclosed. When the offerees have access to or there has been disclosure of the information registration would provide, we shall say that such information was available.

The requirement that all offerees have available the information registration would provide has been firmly established by this court as a necessary condition of gaining the private offering exemption. Our decisions have been predicated upon *Ralston Purina, supra,* where the Supreme Court held that in the absence of a showing that the "key employees" to whom a corporation offered its common stock had knowledge obviating the need for registration, the offering did not qualify for the private offering exemption. The Court said that an employee offering would come within the exemption if it were shown that the employees were "executive personnel who because of their position have access to the same kind of information that the act would make available in the form of a registration statement." * * *

* * * Because the district court failed to apply this test to the case at bar, but rather inferred from evidence of Doran's sophistication that his purchase of a partnership share was incident to a private offering, we must remand so that the lower court may determine the extent of the information available to each offeree.

More specifically, we shall require on remand that the defendants demonstrate that all offerees, whatever their expertise, had available the information a registration statement would have afforded a prospective investor in a public offering. Such a showing is not independently sufficient to establish that the offering qualified for the private placement exemption, but it is necessary to gain the exemption and is to be weighed along with the sophistication and number of the offerees, the number of units offered, and the size and manner of the offering. * * * Because in this case these latter factors weigh heavily in favor of the private offering exemption, satisfaction of the necessary condition regarding the availability of relevant information to the offerees would compel the conclusion that this offering fell within the exemption.

* * *

C. *On Remand: The Issuer–Offeree Relationship*

In determining on remand the extent of the information available to the offerees, the district court must keep in mind that the "availability" of information means either disclosure of or effective access to the relevant information. The relationship between issuer and offerees is most critical when the issuer relies on the latter route.

To begin with, if the defendants could prove that all offerees were actually furnished the information a registration statement would have provided, whether the offerees occupied a position of access pre-existing such disclosure would not be dispositive of the status of the offering. If disclosure were proved and if, as here, the remaining factors such as the manner of the offering and the investment sophistication of the offerees weigh heavily in favor of the private status of the offering, the absence of a privileged relationship between offerees and issuer would not preclude a finding that the offering was private. Any other conclusion would tear out of context this court's earlier discussions of the § 4(2) exemption and would conflict with the policies of the exemption.

Alternatively it might be shown that the offeree had access to the files and record of the company that contained the relevant information. Such access might be afforded merely by the position of the offeree or by the issuer's promise to open appropriate files and records to the offeree as well as to answer inquiries regarding material information. In either case, the relationship between offeree and issuer now becomes critical, for it must be shown that the offeree could realistically have been expected to take advantage of his access to ascertain the relevant information.[12] Similarly the investment sophistication of the offeree assumes added importance, for it is important that he could have been expected to ask the right questions and seek out the relevant information.

In sum, both the relationship between issuer and offeree and the latter's investment sophistication are critical when the issuer or another relies on the offeree's "access" rather than the issuer's "disclosure" to come within the exemption. * * *

1. Disclosure or access: a disjunctive requirement

That our cases sometimes fail clearly to differentiate between "access" and "disclosure" as alternative means of coming within the private offering exemption is, perhaps, not surprising. Although the *Ralston Purina* decision focused on whether the offeree had "access" to the required information, * * * the holding that "the exemption question turns on the knowl-

12. For example, this offeree's ability to compel the issuer to make good his promise may depend on the offeree's bargaining power or on his family or employment relationship to the issuer.

edge of the offeree," * * * could be construed to include possession as well as access. Such an interpretation would require disclosure as a necessary condition of obtaining a private offering notwithstanding the offerees' access to the information that registration would have provided.

Both the Second and the Fourth Circuits, however, have interpreted *Ralston Purina* as embodying a disjunctive requirement. * * *

The cases in this circuit are not inconsistent with this view. * * *

2. The role of insider status

Once the alternative means of coming within the private placement exemption are clearly separated, we can appreciate the proper role to be accorded the requirement that the offerees occupy a privileged or "insider" status relative to the issuer. That is to say, when the issuer relies on "access" absent actual disclosure, he must show that the offerees occupied a privileged position relative to the issuer that afforded them an opportunity for effective access to the information registration would otherwise provide.[15] When the issuer relies on actual disclosure to come within the exemption, he need not demonstrate that the offeree held such a privileged position. Although mere disclosure is not a sufficient condition for establishing the availability of the private offering exemption, and a court will weigh other factors such as the manner of the offering and the investment sophistication of the offerees, the "insider" status of the offerees is not a necessary condition of obtaining the exemption.

* * *

IV. Conclusion

An examination of the record and the district court's opinion in this case leaves unanswered the central question in all cases that turn on the availability of the § 4(2) exemption. Did the offerees know or have a realistic opportunity to learn facts essential to an investment judgment? We remand so that the trial court can answer that question.

* * *

NOTES

1. How is Mr. Doran—a sophisticated investor who did not prove the defendants mislead him—able to sue in order to rescind and get his money back? See Sec. Act § 12(1). Would he have done so had the venture gone

15. That all offerees are in certain respects "insiders" does not ensure that the issuer will gain the private placement exemption. An insider may be an insider with respect to fiscal matters of the company, but an outsider with respect to a particular issue of securities. He may know much about the financial structure of the company but his position may nonetheless not allow him access to a few vital facts pertaining to the transaction at issue. If Doran had effective access to all information that registration would provide, he would be a transactional insider. That is all we require regarding the availability of information. If, on the other hand, his inside knowledge was incomplete or his access ineffective, he would be a transactional outsider despite the fact that we might consider him an "insider" for other purposes.

well? Is there any way for an issuer—which realizes too late it violated Section 5 through the sale of an unregistered security—to avoid acting as an insurer of its success until the statute of limitations expires? Suppose, upon realizing its error, the issuer immediately offers to rescind the sale? See SEC No Action Letter, Steiger Tractor, Inc. (July 21, 1975) (SEC view that a rescission offer does not preclude potential liability under Section 12). What other sanctions may be imposed if there is an unregistered sale of securities and no exemption? See Sec. Act § 24 (criminal liability). By the way, is it only the issuer who is liable for the sale of unregistered securities? See *Pinter v. Dahl,* 486 U.S. 622 (1988) (parties, who solicit investors, at least in part motivated by the solicitor's own financial interest, can also be liable for selling unregistered securities).

Doran involved the sale of limited partnership interests. *Benjamin v. Cablevision Programming Investments,* reprinted earlier, also involved an attempt to rescind the purchase of unregistered limited partnership interests—in that instance for violating the Illinois Securities law. Does this suggest a potentially serious omission in the discussion of forming various non-corporate entities in Chapter III? Recall, as well, that stock, even in a closely held corporation, is a security, and that debt instruments issued by a business also can be a security. Does this suggest an equally serious omission in Chapter IV? The moral is to provide a warning against the temptation to assume that the formation of non-corporate entities and closely held corporations does not require dealing with securities laws generally, and with the registration requirement of those laws particularly.

2. What exactly are the criteria for the private offering exemption? The court points to two seemingly disparate tests. The first is a list of four factors (which stem from a 1935 SEC General Counsel Opinion). How significant is this list? After all, the defendants established three and one-half of the factors, but the court still remanded for determination of an issue which, on its face, did not even seem to make the list. Indeed, two of the four factors appear largely spurious. The number of units (such as shares of stock) offered is a function of the price per unit. Even a one-person corporation could issue its sole owner thousands upon thousands of shares if the price per share is low enough. Yet, this would certainly not be a public offering. On the other hand, a limited partnership might issue only several hundred units (limited partnership interests); yet this would probably entail a public offering. Similarly, the size of the offering (in terms of dollars raised) generally does not lead to different results in decided cases. In fact, private placements to institutional investors can run into the tens or hundreds of millions of dollars. Schneider, *The Statutory Law of Private Placements,* 14 Rev. Sec. Reg. 869 (1981). The manner of offering—more specifically the lack of general solicitations or advertising—is a very relevant factor; albeit one which is probably a necessary, but not a sufficient, condition for a private offering. This brings one to the number of offerees and their relationship with issuer. Yet, the small number of offerees, in itself, could not save the defendants in *Doran.* Indeed, some courts have held that even an offer to one person could be a public offering. *E.g., G. Eugene England Foundation v. First Federal Corp.,* 663 F.2d 988 (10th

Cir.1973). At the other end, there is no maximum number which, in itself, constitutes an offering public versus private. *SEC v. Ralston Purina Co.,* 346 U.S. 119 (1953).

Perhaps the key lies in the other source looked to by the court: the Supreme Court's test in *Ralston Purina.* This approach—which the *Doran* court cubbyholed into the factor of the relationship of offerees to the issuer—examines whether the offerees could fend for themselves, rather than needing the protection of registration. Who exactly does this encompass? To begin with, the typical issuer (a corporation or non-corporate entity) cannot provide information itself; it takes people to do this. Suppose a corporation or non-corporate entity proposes to sell securities to the persons establishing or running the company: do the promoters or top managers of a company need the protection of reading a registration statement for which they themselves would have provided the information (either from their own knowledge or by tracking the information down from others in the company)? Of course, especially as the organization grows, not all insiders may have either knowledge of, or access to, the necessary facts—thus raising the court's caveat in footnote 18 that not all insiders are really insiders for this purpose. The general point remains, however, if one can say of an individual, "if he or she does not know about this company, who does?" then that individual hardly needs the protection of registration. Moving beyond insiders, suppose the firm's representatives negotiate a loan with a bank, or an investment from a venture capital firm. Do such institutions need the protection of reading a registration statement? Why not? This brings one to the court's discussion of sophistication and availability of information.

Looking first at sophistication, how does one know if an offeree is "sophisticated"? Suppose, instead of having a petroleum engineering degree, Doran was a medical doctor worth over $1,000,000, and with oil and gas holdings valued at $850,000. Would he still be sophisticated? Suppose his net worth resulted from a lucrative medical practice, and he lost money on his oil and gas investments: Any different result? The court in *Doran* indicates sophistication without available information is not enough. What about the converse? Is it sufficient to provide all the information which a registration statement would disclose in order to solicit friends, neighbors or relatives? See *SEC v. Continental Tobacco Co.,* 463 F.2d 137 (5th Cir.1972) (no). What if the offeree is involved in the formation of the business and expected to play an active role thereafter? Must that person be sophisticated about investments in general? What if the court disagrees with the seller's judgment as to the sophistication of a particular offeree? Alternately, suppose an offeree misleads the issuer as to his or her background and sophistication. Is good faith adequate to establish the exemption? See *SEC v. Holschuh,* 694 F.2d 130 (7th Cir.1982) (no, although it may be relevant to what sanction is imposed).

Next, consider the requirement of available information. As the court explains, one possibility here is for the issuer actually to furnish the offerees with the information a registration statement would have provided. To the extent the issuer accomplishes this by preparing and distributing a memorandum or circular, then what has it saved by avoiding registration? Is there any difference in potential liability for misstatements? *Compare* Sec. Act § 11 (which the court applied in *BarChris*), *with Ernst & Ernst v. Hochfelder*, 425 U.S. 185 (1976) (no liability for misstatements under Section 10(b) and Rule 10B–5 unless there was scienter). Beyond this, does such an offering circular or memorandum need to contain precisely the same information a registration statement would provide? See *Livens v. William D. Witter, Inc.,* 374 F.Supp. 1104 (D.Mass.1974) (no). Also, an offering document for a private placement does not require SEC review.

Finally, keep in mind the court looked at the number, sophistication and access to information of offerees, not just purchasers. What, if anything, is the practical significance of this?

3. On remand in *Doran,* who has the burden of proof on the question raised by the Court of Appeals? Suppose the issuer is unable to determine what information all the offerees received or had access to? Suppose an issuer does not know how sophisticated each offeree was, or worse, to whom and to how many individuals offers were made? See *Western Federal Corp. v. Erickson,* 739 F.2d 1439 (9th Cir.1984) (exemption denied). What steps can the issuer take before litigation to prevent a fatal failure of proof on these questions?

4. What if one of the initial buyers who is informed and sophisticated resells to someone who is not? This is precisely what happens in a firm commitment underwriting. Does this mean resales could destroy the private offering exemption? If so, what can the issuer do? See Sec. Act Rel. No. 5121 (December 30, 1970):

> An important factor to be considered is whether the securities offered have come to rest in the hands of the initially informed group or whether the purchasers are merely conduits for a wider distribution. It is essential that the issuer of the securities take careful precautions to assure that a public offering does not result through resales of securities purchased in transactions meeting the tests set forth in the *Ralston Purina* case, for, if in fact the purchasers do acquire the securities with a view to distribution, the seller assumes the risk of possible violation of the registration requirements of the Act and consequent civil and criminal liabilities.
>
> These possibilities have led to the practice whereby issuers procure from the initial purchasers representations that they have acquired the securities for investment. A statement from an initial purchaser that he is purchasing for investment is not conclusive as to his actual intent. However, since the terms of an exemption are to be strictly construed against a claimant who has the burden of proving its availability, in many cases the issuer has placed a legend on such securities and stop-transfer instructions have been issued to the transfer agent. These precautions—placing the legend on the securities and issuing the stop-transfer orders—are not to be regarded as a basis for

exemption, but they have proved in many cases to be an effective means of preventing illegal distributions. The use of the legend also alerts the buyer to the restricted character of the securities he has acquired and thus calls attention to material facts which assist in the protection of public investors.

* * *

The Division will regard the presence or absence of an appropriate legend and stop-transfer instructions as a factor in considering whether the circumstances surrounding the offering are consistent with the exemption under Section 4(2) of the Act. Consequently, issuers are urged to stamp or print on the face of certificates or other instruments evidencing restricted securities a conspicuous legend referring to the fact that the securities have not been registered under the Securities Act of 1933 and may be offered and sold only if registered pursuant to the provisions of that Act or if an exemption from registration is available. Issuers are also urged to issue stop-transfer instructions to prevent the transfer of the securities in such cases.

Later, this chapter will explore when and how owners can resell unregistered securities.

5. Suppose, after starting a private offering, the issuer changes its mind and decides to go public (or, after an abortive effort at going public, the issuer decides to undertake a private offering). If a court were to treat the effort to sell shares in a private offering, and the effort to go public, as all part of one offering—in other words, to integrate the two offerings—the result could be that the later public sales would turn the earlier private offers (even if there were no private sales) into a violation of Section 5 (or that the earlier public offers would turn the later private sales into a violation of Section 5). Fortunately, in Rule 155, the Securities Exchange Commission created a safe harbor under which abortive private offerings in which no securities were sold will not be integrated with a subsequent public offering (or an abortive public offering in which no securities were sold will not be integrated with subsequent private sales).

(ii) Regulation D

Section 3(b) of the Securities Act of 1933 empowers the Securities Exchange Commission to create exemptions for so-called small offerings (under $5 million) where the Commission finds regulation is not necessary to protect the public interest. (This does not mean the Commission grants ad hoc exemptions to individual offerings; rather the Commission has the power to enact rules exempting categories of transactions.) In addition, as the administrative agency charged with enforcing the 1933 Act, the SEC may promulgate regulations interpreting various provisions of the statute, including Section 4(2). In 1982, the SEC carried out both tasks by adopting an integrated set of exemptions grouped together under the title Regulation D.

Securities Act Release No. 33–6455

Interpretive Release on Regulation D, March 3, 1983.

* * * This release is intended to assist those persons who wish to make offerings in reliance on the exemptions in Regulation D by presenting the staff's views on frequently raised questions. * * *

Regulation D is composed of six rules, Rules 501–506. [It now also contains Rules 507 and 508. Ed.] The first three rules [501–503] set forth general terms and conditions that apply in whole or in part to the exemptions. * * * The exemptions of Regulation D are set forth in Rules 504–506.

* * *

I. *Definitions—Rule 501*

A. Accredited Investor—Rule 501(a)

Defined in Rule 501(a), the term "accredited investor" is significant to the operation of Regulation D. * * * [F]or instance, accredited investors are not included in computing the number of purchasers in offerings conducted in reliance on Rules 505 and 506. Also, if accredited investors are the only purchasers in offerings under Rules 505 and 506, Regulation D does not require delivery of specific disclosure as a condition of the exemptions. Finally, in an offering under Rule 506, the issuer's obligation to ensure the sophistication of purchasers applies to investors that are not accredited. * * *

The definition sets forth eight categories of investor that may be accredited. The following questions and answers cover certain issues under various of those categories. * * *

1. General

The definition of "accredited investor" includes any person who comes within or "who the issuer reasonably believes" comes within one of the enumerated categories "at the time of the sale of the securities to that person." What constitutes "reasonable" belief will depend on the facts of each particular case. For this reason, the staff generally will not be in a position to express views or otherwise endorse any one method for ascertaining whether an investor is accredited.

(1) *Question:* A director of a corporate issuer purchases securities offered under Rule 505. Two weeks after the purchase, and prior to completion of the offering, the director resigns due to a sudden illness. Is the former director an accredited investor?

Answer: Yes. The preliminary language to Rule 501(a) provides that an investor is accredited if he falls into one of the enumerated categories "at the time of the sale of securities to that person." One such category includes directors of the issuer. *See* Rule 501(a)(4). The investor in this case had that status at the time of the sale to him.

* * *

5. Natural Persons—Rules 501(a)[(5)–(6)]

Rules 501(a)[(5)] and [(6)] apply only to natural persons. Paragraph [(5)] accredits any natural person with a net worth at the time of purchase in excess of $1,000,000. If the investor is married, the rule permits the use of joint net worth of the couple. Paragraph [(6)] accredits any natural person whose income has exceeded $200,000 in each of the two most recent years and is reasonably expected to exceed $200,000 in the year of the investment.

(20) *Question:* A corporation with a net worth of $2,000,000 purchases securities in a Regulation D offering. Is the corporation an accredited investor under Rule 501(a)[(5)]?

Answer: No. Rule 501(a)[(5)] is limited to "natural" persons.*

(21) *Question:* In calculating net worth for purposes of Rule 501(a)[(5)], may the investor include the estimated fair market value of his principal residence as an asset?

Answer: Yes. Rule 501(a)[(5)] does not exclude any of the purchaser's assets from the net worth needed to qualify as an accredited investor.

(22) *Question:* May a purchaser take into account income of a spouse in determining possible accreditation under Rule 501(a)[(6)]?

Answer: No. Rule 501(a)[(6)] requires "individual income" over $200,000 in order to qualify as an accredited investor. [As amended in 1987, the rule accredits spouses having a combined income over $300,000. Ed.]

* * *

B. Aggregate Offering Price—Rule 501(c)

The "aggregate offering price," defined in Rule 501(c), is the sum of all proceeds received by the issuer for issuance of its securities. The term is important to the operation of Rules 504 and 505, both of which impose a limitation on the aggregate offering price as a specific condition to the availability of the exemption.

(31) *Question:* The sole general partner of a real estate limited partnership contributes property to the program. Must that property be valued and included in the overall proceeds of the offering as part of the aggregate offering price?

Answer: No, assuming the property is contributed in exchange for a general partnership interest.

* * *

(34) *Question:* An offering of interests in an oil and gas limited partnership provides for additional voluntary assessments. These assess-

* [Rule 501(a)(3), however, now accredits corporations or other for profit entities if they have over $5 million in assets. Ed.]

ments, undetermined at the time of the offering, may be called at the general partner's discretion for developmental drilling activities. Must the assessments be included in the aggregate offering price, and if so, in what amount?

Answer: Because it is unclear that the assessments will ever be called, and because if they are called, it is unclear at what level, the issuer is not required to include the assessments in the aggregate offering price. In fact, the assessments will be consideration received for the issuance of additional securities in the limited partnership. This issuance will need to be considered along with the original issuance for possible integration, or, if not integrated, must find its own exemption from registration.

(35) *Question:* In purchasing interests in an oil and gas partnership, investors agree to pay mandatory assessments. The assessments, essentially installment payments, are non-contingent and investors will be personally liable for their payment. Must the issuer include the assessments in the aggregate offering price?

Answer: Yes.

* * *

D. Purchaser Representative—Rule 501(h)

A purchaser representative is any person who satisfies, or who the issuer reasonably believes satisfies, four conditions enumerated in Rule 501(h). Beyond the obligations imposed by that rule, any person acting as a purchaser representative must consider whether or not he is required to register as a broker-dealer under section 15 of the Securities Exchange Act of 1934 (the "Exchange Act") * * * or as an investment adviser under section 203 of the Investment Advisers Act of 1940.

* * *

(39) *Question:* May the issuer in a Regulation D offering pay the fees of the purchaser representative?

Answer: Yes. Nothing in Regulation D prohibits the payment by the issuer of the purchaser representative's fees. Rule 501(h)(4), however, requires disclosure of this fact.[25]

* * *

II. *Disclosure Requirements—Rule 502(b)*

A. When Required

Rule 502(b)(1) sets forth the circumstances when disclosure of the kind specified in the regulation must be delivered to investors. The regulation requires the delivery of certain information ["a reasonable time"] prior to

25. Note 3 to Rule 501(h) points out that disclosure of a material relationship between the purchaser representative and the issuer will not relieve the purchaser representative of the obligation to act in the interest of the purchaser.

sale if the offering is conducted in reliance on Rule 505 or 506 and if there are unaccredited investors. If the offering is conducted in compliance with Rule 504 or if securities are sold only to accredited investors, Regulation D does not specify the information that must be disclosed to investors.[26]

* * *

B. What Required

Regulation D divides disclosure into two categories; that to be furnished by non-reporting companies and that required for reporting companies. In either case, the specified disclosure is required to the extent material to an understanding of the issuer, its business and the securities being offered.

* * *

(42) *Question:* When an issuer is required to deliver specific disclosure, must that disclosure be in written form?

Answer: Yes.

(43) *Question:* * * * With a limited partnership that has been formed with minimal capitalization immediately prior to a Regulation D offering, must the Regulation D disclosure document contain an audited balance sheet for the issuer?

Answer: In analyzing this or any other disclosure question under Regulation D, the issuer starts with the general rule that it is obligated to furnish the specified information "to the extent material to an understanding of the issuer, its business, and the securities being offered." Thus, in this particular case, if an audited balance sheet is not material to the investor's understanding, then the issuer may elect to present an alternative to its audited balance sheet.

* * *

C. General

Rule 502(b)(2) also contains four general provisions applicable to all classes of issuer in all offerings where specified disclosure is required.

These provisions govern exhibits, disclosure of additional information to non-accredited investors, the opportunity for further investor inquiries, and disclosure of certain additional information in business combinations.

(52) *Question:* In a Rule 505 or 506 offering of interests in a limited partnership where certain purchasers are not accredited investors, must the issuer obtain an opinion of counsel regarding the legality of the

26. As noted in Preliminary Note 1. Regulation D transactions are exempt from the registration requirements of the Securities Act, not the antifraud provisions. Thus, nothing in Regulation D states that an issuer need not give disclosure to an investor. Rather, the regulation provides that in certain instances the exemptions from the registration will not be conditioned on a particular content, format or method of disclosure.

securities being issued or an opinion regarding the tax consequences of an investment in the offering?

Answer: Rule 502(b)(2)(iii) provides that the issuer is not required to furnish the exhibits that would accompany the form of registration or report governing the issuer's disclosure document if the issuer identifies the contents of those exhibits and makes them available to purchasers upon written request prior to purchase. Any form of registration to which the issuer refers in preparing its disclosure document under Regulation D requires that the issuer furnish the exhibits required by Item 601 of Regulation S–K. Item 601 requires that the issuer furnish, among other exhibits, an opinion of counsel as to the legality of the securities being issued. Thus, under Rule 502(b)(2)(iii), the issuer should identify the contents of this opinion of counsel and make it available to purchasers upon written request. Item 601 also sets forth certain requirements for an opinion as to tax matters. Such an opinion is required to support any representations in a prospectus as to material tax consequences. Thus, assuming the Regulation D issuer will make representations in the disclosure document as to material tax consequences of investing in a limited partnership, the issuer should identify the contents of and make available upon request an opinion supporting that discussion.

III. *Operational Conditions*

A. Integration—Rule 502(a)

Rule 502(a) achieves two purposes. First, it explicitly incorporates the doctrine of integration into Regulation D. Second, it establishes an exception to the operation of that doctrine.

Integration operates to identify the scope of a particular offering by considering the relationship between multiple transactions. It is premised on the concept that the Securities Act addresses discrete offerings and on the recognition that not every offering is in fact a discrete transaction. The integration doctrine prevents an issuer from circumventing the registration requirements of the Securities Act by claiming a separate exemption for each part of a series of transactions that comprises a single offering. Because the determination of whether transactions should be integrated into one offering is so dependent on particular facts and circumstances, the staff does not issue interpretations in this area. The Note to Rule 502(a), however, does set forth a number of factors that should be considered in making an integration determination.

Rule 502(a) also sets forth an exception to the integration doctrine. It provides that a Regulation D offering will not be integrated with offers or sales that occur more than six months before or after the Regulation D offering. This six month safe harbor rule only applies, however, where there have been no offers or sales (except under an employee benefit plan) of securities similar to those in the Regulation D offering within the applicable six months.

* * *

B. Calculation of the Number of Purchasers—Rule 501(e)

Rule 501(e) governs the calculation of the number of purchasers in offerings that rely either on Rule 505 or 506. Both of these rules limit the number of non-accredited investors to 35. Rule 501(e) has two parts. The first excludes certain purchasers from the calculation. The second establishes basic principles for counting of corporations, partnerships, or other entities.

* * *

(55) *Question:* An accredited investor in a Rule 506 offering will have the securities she acquires placed in her name and that of her spouse. The spouse will not make an investment decision with respect to the acquisition. How many purchasers will be involved?

Answer: The accredited investor may be excluded from the count under Rule 501(e)(1)(iv) and the spouse may be excluded under Rule 501(e)(1)(i). The issuer may also take the position, however, that the spouse should not be deemed a purchaser at all because he did not make any investment decision, and because the placement of the securities in joint name may simply be a tax or estate planning technique.

* * *

(57) *Question:* An investor in a Rule 506 offering is a general partnership that was not organized for the specific purpose of acquiring the securities offered. The partnership has ten partners, five of whom do not qualify as accredited investors. The partnership will make an investment of $100,000. How is the partnership counted and must the issuer make any findings as to the sophistication of the individual partners?

Answer: Rule 501(e)(2) provides that the partnership shall be counted as one purchaser. The issuer is not obligated to consider the sophistication of each individual partner.

* * *

(59) *Question:* An investor in a Rule 506 offering is an investment partnership that is not accredited under Rule 501(a)(8). Although the partnership was organized two years earlier and has made investments in a number of offerings, not all the partners have participated in each investment. With each proposed investment by the partnership, individual partners have received a copy of the disclosure document and have made a decision whether or not to participate. How do the provisions of Regulation D apply to the partnership as an investor?

Answer: The partnership may not be treated as a single purchaser. Rule 501(e)(2) provides that if the partnership is organized for the specific purpose of acquiring the securities offered, then each beneficial owner of equity interests should be counted as a separate purchaser. Because the individual partners elect whether or not to participate in each investment, the partnership is deemed to be reorganized for the specific purpose of acquiring the securities in each investment. Thus, the issuer must look through the partnership to the partners participating in the investment. The issuer must satisfy the conditions of Rule 506 as to each partner.

C. Manner of Offering—Rule 502(c)

Rule 502(c) prohibits the issuer or any person acting on the issuer's behalf from offering or selling securities by any form of general solicitation or general advertising. The analysis of facts under Rule 502(c) can be divided into two separate inquiries. First, is the communication in question a general solicitation or general advertisement? Second, if it is, is it being used by the issuer or by someone on the issuer's behalf to offer or sell the securities? If either question can be answered in the negative, then the issuer will not be in violation of Rule 502(c).

* * *

In analyzing what constitutes a general solicitation, the staff considered a solicitation by the general partner of a limited partnership to limited partners in other active programs sponsored by the same general partner. In determining that this did not constitute a general solicitation the Division underscored the existence and substance of the pre-existing business relationship between the general partner and those being solicited.

* * *

(60) *Question:* If a solicitation were limited to accredited investors, would it be deemed in compliance with Rule 502(c)?

Answer: The mere fact that a solicitation is directed only to accredited investors will not mean that the solicitation is in compliance with Rule 502(c). Rule 502(c) relates to the nature of the offering not the nature of the offerees.

D. Limitations on Resale—Rule 502(d)

Rule 502(d) makes it clear that Regulation D securities have limitations on transferability and [lists] certain precautions [the issuer can take] to restrict the transferability of the securities.

(61) *Question:* An investor in a Regulation D offering wishes to resell his securities within a year after the offering. The issuer has agreed to register the securities for resale. Will the proposed resale under the registration statement violate Rule 502(d)?

Answer: No. The function of Rule 502(d) is to restrict the unregistered resale of securities. Where the resale will be registered, however, such restrictions are unnecessary.

IV. *Exemptions*

A. Rule 504

Rule 504 is an exemption under section 3(b) of the Securities Act available to non-reporting and non-investment companies for offerings not in excess of $[1,0]00,000.

* * *

B. Rule 505

Rule 505 provides an exemption under section 3(b) of the Securities Act for non-investment companies for offerings not in excess of $5,000,000.

* * *

C. Questions Relating to Rules 504 and 505

Both Rules 504(b)(2)(i) and 505(b)(2)(i) require that the offering not exceed a specified aggregate offering price. The allowed aggregate offering price, however, is reduced by the aggregate offering price for all securities sold within the last twelve months in reliance on section 3(b) or in violation of section 5(a) of the Securities Act.

(67) *Question:* An issuer preparing to conduct an offering of equity securities under Rule 505 raised $2,000,000 from the sale of debt instruments under Rule 505 eight months earlier. How much may the issuer raise in the proposed equity offering?

Answer: $3,000,000. A specific condition to the availability of Rule 505 for the proposed offering is that its aggregate offering price not exceed $5,000,000 less the proceeds for *all* securities sold under section 3(b) within the last 12 months.

(68) *Question:* An issuer is planning a Rule 505 offering. Ten months earlier the issuer conducted a Rule 506 offering. Must the issuer consider the previous Rule 506 offering when calculating the allowable aggregate offering price for the proposed Rule 505 offering?

Answer: No. The Commission issued Rule 506 under section 4(2), and Rule 505(b)(2)(i) requires that the aggregate offering price be reduced by previous sales under section 3(b).

* * *

(71) *Question:* Note 2 to Rule 504 is not restated in Rule 505. Does the principle of the note apply to Rule 505?

Answer: Yes. Note 2 to Rule 504 sets forth a general principle to the operation of the rule on limiting the aggregate offering price which is the same for both Rules 504 and 505. It provides that if, as a result of one offering, an issuer exceeds the allowed aggregate offering price in a subsequent unintegrated offering, the exemption for the first offering will not be affected.

D. Rule 506

(72) *Question:* May an issuer of securities with a projected aggregate offering price of $3,000,000 rely on Rule 506?

Answer: Yes, the availability of Rule 506 is not dependent on the dollar size of an offering.

* * *

E. Questions Relating to Rules 504–506

(74) *Question:* If an issuer relies on one exemption, but later realizes that exemption may not have been made available, may it rely on another exemption after the fact?

Answer: Yes, assuming the offering met the conditions of the new exemption. No one exemption is exclusive of another.

* * *

(76) *Question:* Is Regulation D available to an underwriter for the sale of securities acquired in a firm commitment offering?

Answer: No. As Preliminary Note 4 indicates, Regulation D is available only to the issuer of the securities and not to any affiliate of that issuer or to any other person for resales of the issuer's securities.

* * *

V. *Notice of Sale—Form D*

Rule 503 requires the issuer to file a notice of sale on Form D. The notice must be filed not later than 15 days after the first sale, every six months thereafter and no later than 30 days after the last sale.

(81) *Question:* Where can an issuer obtain copies of Form D and where must the form be filed?

Answer: Form D is available through the Public Reference Branch of the Commission's main office, 450 5th Street, N.W., Washington, D.C. 20549, (202) 272–7460, or any of its regional or branch offices. The form should be filed at the Commission's main office. There is no filing fee.

* * *

NOTE

As the Release points out, Regulation D contains three specific exemptions. Rule 504 provides an exemption for offerings of no more than $1 million. Significantly, this exemption does not concern itself with the number of buyers, their qualifications, or the information they receive. After some vacillation, however, Rule 504 currently contains a nuanced limit on resales and general solicitations. Specifically, an issuer can avoid limits on resales, and can engage in general solicitations, only if (i) the issuer registers the offering pursuant to a state blue sky law which requires delivery of a disclosure document to investors, or (ii) the issuer sells the securities pursuant to a state blue sky law exemption which allows general solicitations of an offering open only to accredited investors.

Rule 505 allows an exemption for selling up to $5 million worth of securities. This rule, too, generally does not concern itself with the nature of the buyers. Unlike Rule 504, however, Rule 505 limits their number (up to 35 plus any number of accredited investors) and requires their receipt (unless they are accredited investors) of specified information. Also, the issuer cannot engage in a general solicitation, and must be concerned about resales, regardless of compliance with state blue sky laws.

Both Rules 504 and 505 contain dollar limits. This is because both exemptions stem from the Securities Exchange Commission's authority under Section 3(b) of the Securities Act to create exemptions when the Commission concludes registration is not needed "by reason of the small amount involved or the limited character of the public offering." Note carefully the precise definition of the dollar limit as set out in Regulation D and discussed in the interpretive release above. For instance, the definition limits not only the amount which the issuer can raise in the offering at hand (which can create a problem in trying to figure out if several sales are part of the same offering), but also limits the amount the issuer can raise within twelve months if it makes multiple offerings exempt under Section 3(b) (for instance, other offerings exempt under Rules 504 or 505). Keep in mind here the need to consider separately the question of what size is the present offering, and what is the total of all Section 3(b) offerings within the 12 month period. For example, suppose a firm issues securities first to several insiders, and then to several outside investors, so that the total price exceeds the relevant dollar limit under Rules 504 or 505. If this is one offering, then the exemption is unavailable. If, however, these are two separate offerings, the exemption could be available—even though the sales occur within 12 months—because the sale to the insiders can be exempt under Section 4(2) and so does not count for the 12 month limit. *See* the Answer to Question 68 in the Interpretive Release above. (Incidentally, why, in Question 31 of the Release, did the general partner's contribution not count as part of the aggregate offering price? Recall, the aggregate offering price equals the total received from the sale of "securities". Is a general partnership interest normally a security?)

Rule 506 provides an exemption without any dollar limit. Essentially, it differs from Rule 505 in two ways. Conceptually, it differs from Rule 505 (and 504) because the authority for Rule 506 does not come from Section 3(b) (which extends only to offerings up to $5 million). Instead, this is an "interpretation" of the private offering exemption found in Section 4(2). Moreover, it is not an interpretation of what Section 4(2) requires for every private placement. Rather, it is a "safe harbor," within which the Securities Exchange Commission deems a private offering to occur, but outside of which issuers take their chances with cases like *Doran*. Practically speaking, Rule 506 differs from Rule 505 by imposing a trade-off: no dollar limit, but now the up to 35 unaccredited purchasers must all be sophisticated (or, more precisely, the purchaser, or his or her "purchaser representative," must have knowledge and experience in financial and business matters making him or her capable of evaluating the merits and risks of the prospective investment). Notice here how Regulation D has divided investors into three groups: accredited, sophisticated but not accredited, and everybody else. Review the questions raised in the Notes following *Doran* about acceptable offerees for a private placement. How does Regulation D address these questions?

This discussion of Rule 506, in turn, raises the issue of how Regulation D overall compares to the private offering exemption as interpreted by cases like *Doran*. Regulation D provides many more specific rules to follow. Is this good or bad from a planning standpoint? Regulation D looks to the character and number of purchasers, rather than offerees. Can this matter? Suppose the issuer is mistaken about the qualifications of an offeree, or makes some other inadvertent mistake. What is the result under Regulation D, as opposed to when dealing with the private offering exemption generally? Examine carefully the specific language of Rules 501–506, and see Rule 508. Also, in terms of technical errors, what is the result of failing to file a Regulation D notice as required under Rule 503—specifically, does this preclude the exemption? See Rule 507.

In any event, it turns out that the specific limits on the amount raised, or requirements as to the number and qualification of purchasers, have not been the source of the most difficulty under Regulation D. Rather, the greatest difficulty probably has come from the prohibition on general solicitations. (Recall that the absence of a general solicitation was also part of the test for a private offering under cases like *Doran*.) One difficulty with the general solicitation limitation is the lack of precise guidelines in the regulation as to what is a general solicitation. Fortunately, the Interpretive Release provides some guidance when it suggests that a general solicitation might exist unless there is a preexisting relationship between the business, or persons already involved in the business, and the purchaser. Yet, limiting one's search for investors to persons already connected to the business or connected to those involved in the business severely cuts down on the prospects for raising money. Is there a way to deal with this problem?

Langevoort, Angels on the Internet: The Elusive Promise of "Technological Disintermediation" for Unregistered Offerings of Securities

2 J. Small & Emerging Bus. L. 1, 7–9 (1998).

* * *

The Securities Act of 1933 is hopelessly vague on the circumstances under which issuers may seek out investors without making a public offering of securities requiring registration.

* * *

For nearly all of the history of small business capital policy, the SEC has adhered to a subtextual principle: any "general solicitation" of investors is necessarily inconsistent with the notion of a nonpublic offering. In other words, one cannot advertise or otherwise cast one's net broadly in the hopes of finding qualified investors, but instead must solicit only those whom, based on some pre-existing relationship, one has good reason to believe do not need the protection of the registration requirement.

* * *

Most notably, the prominence of the ban was underscored by the fact that in the same rulemaking the Commission created protection from private liability for "immaterial and inadvertent" slips in compliance with the highly technical requirements of Regulation D, but pointedly excepted the general solicitation ban from this good faith defense. More recently, the Commission has issued a statement that the posting of notices of exempt offerings on an issuer's Web site would involve a general solicitation.

More interesting than the ban itself, however, is the way in which it has been interpreted. There are no authoritative judicial rulings here; until recently, nearly everything we knew about the ban came from a long series of no-action letters issued by the SEC staff. While trying to derive precise guidance from these letters is futile, there has consistently been a dominant message: the "pre-existing relationship" test is the key. Print or broadcast advertising that might somehow whet the appetite of investors for the stock in question is almost certainly impermissible, even if directed solely to accredited investors. Rather, there has to be a two-step process. First, someone must go prospecting for permissible investors and determine that they are qualified without hinting at a specific investment possibility. Then, after some decent interval, such pre-qualified investors may be contacted with the investment proposal.

Until recently, this pre-qualification task was a cumbersome and fairly expensive one, conducted through mailings, telephone solicitations and examining records of previous investments. As a practical matter, the only entity with the natural interest and expertise to undertake this pre-qualification task was a registered broker-dealer, which would then earn a fee or commission by assisting the issuer in selling the securities to individuals on its prospect list. The no-action letters effectively channeled Regulation D financings in this direction. In this sense, the general solicitation requirement encouraged, if not insisted on, the intermediation of small business capital raising of any form that went much beyond friends, family members and employees of the issuer or its principals. This created a significant added expense.

Beginning in the mid–1980s, however, communications technology brought an alternate promise. Databases could be developed that matched small businesses looking for capital with lists of qualified investors. The breakthroughs in this area came from a series of quasi-public entities (often associated with universities and state government offices) that aggressively pushed computer-based systems that invited potential investors to subscribe to the system and then immediately be qualified as accredited investors; simultaneously, small issuers looking for capital could register their interests as well. The computer would match promising businesses and investors, and let them proceed from there on their own. At first, the legal question confronted was simply whether these systems were exchanges, broker-dealers or investment advisers. By the late 1980s, the SEC staff was consistently taking a no-action position on these questions when the systems were truly non-profit in nature and made no representations as to the quality of the underlying investments.

Soon, of course, the question whether issuers who participated in such systems ran afoul of the general solicitation ban had to be answered. By the early 1990s, the Commission staff said "No," so long as the advertising seeking accredited investor subscribers was carefully controlled and did not identify particular investments and no investment advice was offered. * * * This guidance encouraged the further development of these systems, and in late 1996, a Small Business Administration-sponsored system, ACE–Net, linked many of the existing matching systems into a comprehensive investor search system.

* * *

With ACE–Net, contacts with potential subscribers can be made over the Internet. Once investors are pre-qualified, they receive a password allowing access to investment opportunities, with a search engine that allows browsing.

* * *

So far, this kind of disintermediation has been permitted when the matching system is nonprofit in nature and completely independent of the issuer. This leads naturally to the question of how or why that factor is significant. The answer would seem to be that it is not very significant; at least so far as the general solicitation, rather than registration, standard is concerned. This was made clear in the no-action letter regarding IPOnet, no doubt the most important step in the development of SEC policy along these lines. IPOnet is a business enterprise developed to aid issuers in directly marketing securities over the Internet, both in public and private offerings. It is associated with W.J. Gallagher, a registered securities dealer. So far as private offerings are concerned, Gallagher will survey electronically those investors who become members of the system to determine if they wish to register as accredited or sophisticated investors, and if so, determine whether they meet the requirements for such status. Once that happens, investors receive a password allowing them access to information about exempt offerings. In some cases, Gallagher will act as a broker-dealer to facilitate subsequent transactions; in others, the issuer will proceed to complete sales on its own, in which case IPOnet will simply charge a listing fee. The Commission staff indicated that such a procedure is permissible, though (perhaps retrogressively) it limited access by qualified investors to offerings posted after they have been qualified.

Thus far, then, the two-step procedure remains in place. It can simply be done much more efficiently in an Internet-based environment. As computer usage by investors becomes more widespread, we will not be far from the point at which regularly updated databases of all willing accredited investors are widely available and can be marketed to issuers with a variety of additional services.

* * *

NOTES

1. Regulation A (Sec. Act Rules 251–269) is another exemption created by the SEC pursuant to Section 3(b). Regulation A, however, does not provide so much of an exemption, as it does a simplified form of registration. For instance, in contrast to the information requirements under Regulation D—which, depending on the size of the offering, may not be that dissimilar in terms of content from Regulation A—Regulation A requires the issuer to file its offering statement with the SEC for review prior to any sales. Nevertheless, the documentation is shorter than with full registration (especially the financial statements, which need not be audited) and so some cost savings are possible under Regulation A. The preference of many underwriters for audited financials and full registration, however, may offset this advantage. Moreover, use of Regulation A might preclude registration by coordination under state blue sky laws (since this is not technically a registration) thereby undercutting the cost savings. Looking beyond cost savings, Regulation A allows a company without an established market for its securities to communicate certain factual information about the firm and its business to prospective investors in order to "test the water" before committing itself to the expense of preparing a Regulation A offering document. At any event, use of Regulation A is subject to a number of limits, most especially the maximum of $5 million worth of securities which the issuer may offer in any one year under the Regulation.

2. Two years before the Securities Exchange Commission adopted Regulation D, Congress amended the 1933 Act to add Section 4(6), an exemption for small offerings to accredited investors. Does it do anything Regulation D does not? In 1996, Congress added Section 28 to the Securities Act. Section 28 allows the Securities Exchange Commission to establish exemptions under a general public interest standard without any dollar limit. Hence, the $5 million benchmark of Section 3(b) is no longer a cap on the Commission's authority to establish exemptions along the lines of Rules 504 and 505. So far, however, the Commission has not exploited its new authority by changing Regulation D.

(iii) Intrastate Offerings

Section 3(a)(11) of the 1933 Act exempts securities which are part of an issue offered and sold exclusively to residents of the state where the issuer is doing business and incorporated (or, for a non-corporation, is a resident). Examination of this provision raises several immediate questions: (i) when is a person a resident of a state for purposes of the section; (ii) what does the section mean by "doing business" in the state; (iii) when can the issuer sell securities out of the state (in other words, when are securities part of a different "issue"); and (iv) what happens if a resident purchaser resells to one who is a resident of another state?

Securities Act Release No. 5450

January 7, 1974.

NOTICE OF ADOPTION OF RULE 147 UNDER THE SECURITIES ACT OF 1933

* * *

The Securities and Exchange Commission today adopted Rule 147 which defines certain terms in, and clarifies certain conditions of Section 3(a)(11) of the Securities Act of 1933 ("the Act").

* * *

Section 3(a)(11) was intended to allow issuers with localized operations to sell securities as part of a plan of local financing. Congress apparently believed that a company whose operations are restricted to one area should be able to raise money from investors in the immediate vicinity without having to register the securities with a federal agency. In theory, the investors would be protected both by their proximity to the issuer and by state regulation. Rule 147 reflects this Congressional intent and is limited in its application to transactions where state regulation will be most effective. The Commission has consistently taken the position that the exemption applies only to local financing provided by local investors for local companies. To satisfy the exemption, the entire issue must be offered and sold exclusively to residents of the state in which the issuer is resident and doing business. An offer or sale of part of the issue to a single non-resident will destroy the exemption for the entire issue.

Certain basic questions have arisen in connection with interpreting Section 3(a)(11). They are:

* * *

The Transaction Concept

Although the intrastate offering exemption is contained in Section 3 of the Act, which Section is phrased in terms of exempt "securities" rather than "transactions," the legislative history and Commission and judicial interpretations indicate that the exemption covers only specific transactions and not the securities themselves. Rule 147 reflects this interpretation.

The "Part of an Issue" Concept

The determination of what constitutes "part of an issue" for purposes of the exemption, i.e. what should be "integrated", has traditionally been dependent on the facts involved in each case. The Commission noted in Securities Act Release 4434 that "any one or more of the following factors may be determinative of the question of integration:

"1. are the offerings part of a single plan of financing;

"2. do the offerings involve issuance of the same class of security;

"3 are the offerings made at or about the same time;

"4. is the same type of consideration to be received; and

"5. are the offerings made for the same general purpose."

In this connection, the Commission generally has deemed intrastate offerings to be "integrated" with those registered or private offerings of the same class of securities made by the issuer at or about the same time.

* * *

[Rule 147] provides in Subparagraph (b)(2) that, for purposes of the rule only, certain offers and sales of securities, discussed below, will be deemed not to be part of an issue and therefore not be integrated, but the rule does not otherwise define "part of an issue." Accordingly, as to offers and sales not within (b)(2), issuers who want to rely on Rule 147 will have to determine whether their offers and sales are part of an issue by applying the five factors cited above.

The "Person Resident Within" Concept

The object of the Section 3(a)(11) exemption, i.e., to restrict the offering to persons within the same locality as the issuer who are, by reason of their proximity, likely to be familiar with the issuer and protected by the state law governing the issuer, is best served by interpreting the residence requirement narrowly. In addition, the determination of whether all parts of the issue have been sold only to residents can be made only after the securities have "come to rest" within the state or territory. Rule 147 retains these concepts, but provides more objective standards for determining when a person is considered a resident within a state for purposes of the rule and when securities have come to rest within a state.

The "Doing Business Within" Requirement

Because the primary purpose of the intrastate exemption was to allow an essentially local business to raise money within the state where the investors would be likely to be familiar with the business and with the management, the doing business requirement has traditionally been viewed strictly. First, not only should the business be located within the state, but the principal or predominant business must be carried on there. Second, substantially all of the proceeds of the offering must be put to use within the local area.

Rule 147 reinforces these requirements by providing specific percentage amounts of business that must be conducted within the state, and of proceeds from the offering that must be spent in connection with such business. In addition, the rule requires that the principal office of the issuer be within the state.

Synopsis of Rule 147

1. *Preliminary Notes*

The first preliminary note to the rule indicates that the rule does not raise any presumption that the Section 3(a)(11) exemption would not be available for transactions which do not satisfy all of the provisions of the rule.

* * *

The fourth preliminary note indicates that the rule is available only for transactions by an issuer and that the rule is not available for secondary transactions.

* * *

2. *Transactions Covered—Rule 147(a)*

Paragraph (a) of the rule provides that offers, offers to sell, offers for sale and sales of securities that meet all the conditions of the rule will be deemed to come within the exemption provided by Section 3(a)(11). Those conditions are: (1) the issuer must be resident and doing business within the state or territory in which the securities are offered and sold (Rule 147(c)); (2) the *offerees* and purchasers must be resident within such state or territory (Rule 147(d)); (3) resales for a period of 9 months after the last sale which is part of an issue must be limited as provided (Rule 147(e) and (f)). In addition, the revised rule provides that certain offers and sales of securities by or for the issuers will be deemed not "part of an issue" for purposes of the rule only (Rule 147(b)).

3. *"Part of an Issue"—Rule 147(b)*

* * * For the purpose of the rule only, subparagraph (b)(2) provides that all securities of the issuer offered, offered for sale or sold * * * prior to or subsequent to the six month period immediately preceding or subsequent to any offer, offer to sell, offer for sale or sale pursuant to Rule 147 will be deemed not part of an issue provided that there are no offers, offers to sell or sales of securities of the same or similar class by or for the issuer during either of these six month periods. If there have been offers or sales during the six months, then in order to determine what constitutes part of an issue, reference should be made to the five traditional integration factors discussed above. * * *

Paragraph (b), as revised, is intended to create greater certainty and to obviate in certain situations the need for a case-by-case determination of when certain intrastate offerings should be integrated with other offerings, such as those registered under the Act or made pursuant to the exemption provided by Section 3 or 4(2) of the Act.

4. *Nature of the Issuer—Rule 147(c)—"Person Resident Within"—Rule 147(c)(1)*

Subparagraph (c)(1) of the rule defines the situations in which issuers would be deemed to be "resident within" a state or territory. A corporation, limited partnership or business trust must be incorporated or organized pursuant to the laws of such state or territory. Section 3(a)(11) provides specifically that a corporate issuer must be incorporated in the state. A general partnership or other form of business entity that is not formed under a specific state or territorial law must have its principal office within the state or territory. * * *

5. *Nature of the Issuer—Rule 147(c)—Doing Business Within—Rule 147(c)(2)*

Subparagraph (c)(2) of the rule provides that the issuer will be deemed to be "doing business within" a state or territory in which the offers and sales are to be made if: (1) at least 80 percent of its gross revenues and those of its subsidiaries on a consolidated basis (a) for its most recent fiscal year (if the first offer of any part of the issue is made during the first six months of the issuer's current fiscal year) or (b) for the subsequent six month period, or for the twelve months ended with that period (if the first offer of any part of the issue is made during the last six months of the issuer's current fiscal year) were derived from the operation of a business or property located in or rendering of services within the state or territory; (2) at least 80 percent of the issuer's assets and those of its subsidiaries on a consolidated basis at the end of the most recent fiscal semi-annual period prior to the first offer of any part of the issue are located within such state or territory; (3) at least 80 percent of the net proceeds to the issuer from the sales made pursuant to the rule are intended to be and are used in connection with the operation of a business or property or the rendering of services within such state or territory; and (4) the issuer's principal office is located in the state or territory.

* * *

Finally, subparagraph (c)(2) of the rule provides that an issuer which has not had gross revenues from the operation of its business in excess of $5,000 during its most recent twelve month period need not satisfy the revenue test of subsection (c)(2)(i).

The provisions of paragraph (c) are intended to assure that the issuer is primarily a local business. * * * The following examples demonstrate the manner in which these standards would be interpreted:

Example 1. X corporation is incorporated in State A and has its only warehouse, only manufacturing plant and only office in that state. X's only business is selling products throughout the United States and Canada through mail order catalogs. X annually mails catalogs and order forms from its office to residents of most states and several provinces of Canada. All orders are filled at and products shipped from X's warehouse to customers throughout the United States and Canada. All the products shipped are manufactured by X at its plant in State A. These activities are X's sole source of revenues.

Question. Is X deriving more than 80 percent of its gross revenues from the "operation of a business or * * * rendering of services" within State A?

Interpretive Response. Yes, this aspect of the "doing business within" standard is satisfied.

Example 2. Assume the same facts as Example 1, except that X has no manufacturing plant and purchases the product it sells from corporations located in other states.

Question. Is X deriving more than 80 percent of its gross revenues from the "operation of a business or * * * rendering of services" within State A?

Interpretive Response. Yes, this aspect of the "doing business within" standard is satisfied.

Example 3. Y Corporation is incorporated in State B and has its only office in that state. Y's only business is selling undeveloped land located in State C and State D by means of brochures mailed from its office throughout the United States.

Question. Is Y deriving more than 80 percent of its gross revenues from the "operation of a business or of property or rendering of services" within State B?

Interpretive Response. There are not sufficient facts to respond. If Y owns an interest in the developed land, it might not satisfy the "80 percent of assets" standard as well as the "80 percent of gross revenues" standard. Moreover, Y could not use more than 20 percent of the proceeds of any offerings made pursuant to the rule in connection with the acquisition of the undeveloped land.

Example 4. Z company is a firm of engineering consultants organized under the laws of State E with its only office in that state. During any year, Z will provide consulting services for projects in other states. 75 percent of Z's work in terms of man hours will be performed at Z's offices where it employs some 50 professional and clerical personnel. Z has no employees located outside of State E. However, professional personnel visit project sites and clients' offices in other states. Approximately 50 percent of Z's revenue is derived from clients located in states other than State E.

Question. Is Z deriving more than 80 percent of its gross revenues from "rendering services" within State E?

Interpretive Response. Yes, this aspect of the "doing business within" standard is satisfied.

Example 5. The facts are the same as in Example 4. In addition, at the end of Z's most recent fiscal quarter 25 percent of its assets are represented by accounts receivable from clients in other states.

Question. Does Z satisfy the "assets" standard?

Interpretive Response. Yes, Z satisfies the "assets" standard. For purposes of the rule, accounts receivable arising from a business conducted in the state would generally be considered to be located at the principal office of the issuer.

6. *Offerees and Purchasers: Persons Resident—Rule 147(d)*

Paragraph (d) of the rule provides that offers and sales may be made only to persons resident within the state or territory. An individual offeree or purchaser of any part of an issue would be deemed to be a person resident within the state or territory if such person has his principal residence in the state or territory. Temporary residence, such as that of many persons in the military service, would not satisfy the provisions of paragraph (d). In addition, if a person purchases securities on behalf of other persons, the residence of those persons must satisfy paragraph (d). If the offeree or purchaser is a business organization its residence will be deemed the state or territory in which it has its principal office, unless it is an entity organized for the specific purpose of acquiring securities in the offering, in which case it will be deemed to be a resident of a state only if all of the beneficial owners of interests in such entity are residents of the state.

* * *

7. *Limitations on Resales—Rule 147(e)*

Paragraph (e) of the rule provides that during the period in which securities that are part of an issue are being offered and sold and for a period of nine months from the date of the last sale by the issuer of any part of the issue, resales of any part of the issue by any person shall be made only to persons resident within the same state or territory. This provides objective standards for determining when an issue "comes to rest." * * *

Persons who acquire securities from issuers or affiliates in transactions complying with the rule would acquire unregistered securities that could only be reoffered and resold pursuant to an exemption from the registration provisions of the Act.

* * *

8. *Precautions Against Interstate Offers and Sales—Rule 147(f)*

Paragraph (f) of the rule requires issuers to take steps to preserve the exemption provided by the rule, since any resale of any part of the issue before it comes to rest within the state to persons resident in another state or territory will, under the Act, be in violation of Section 5. The required steps are: (i) placing a legend on the certificate or other document evidencing the security stating that the securities have not been registered under the Act and setting forth the limitations on resale contained in paragraph (e); (ii) issuing stop transfer instructions to the issuer's transfer agent, if any, with respect to the securities, or, if the issuer transfers its own securities, making a notation in the appropriate records of the issuer; and (iii) obtaining a written representation from each purchaser as to his residence.

* * *

NOTES

1. Rule 147 is roughly analogous to Rule 506. Both are "safe harbor" provisions. If an issuer follows them, the Securities Exchange Commission deems the issuer in compliance with a statutory exemption (Sections 3(a)(11) and 4(2) respectively) whose general phraseology otherwise can leave the issuer subject to considerable uncertainty in planning the sale. Failure to follow either rule, however, does not prevent the issuer from arguing it still met the statutory exemption as interpreted by the courts. On the other hand, there are some seeming differences in philosophy reflected in the two rules, which impact upon the desirability of planning transactions around them. Rule 506 reflects an apparent desire to liberalize standards, as compared with decisions like *Doran*. This is illustrated, for instance, in Rule 506's use of reasonable belief and good faith tests, and in its examination of purchasers rather than offerees. Compare, however, the approach under Rule 147. One mistaken offer (not even a sale) to a non-resident dooms the exemption (just as presumably true without the rule). Moreover, the three-part, 80 percent doing business test may be more conservative than the cases. *See, e.g., SEC v. McDonald Investment Co.*, 343 F.Supp. 343 (D.Minn.1972) (exemption denied when the issuer used the proceeds of the offering primarily, if not entirely, to make loans to land developers outside of the issuer's state).

2. Each exemption discussed thus far can require the issuer to establish facts about the parties to which the issuer offers or sells securities—the parties' residence, their wealth or income, their sophistication. Often, by virtue of the close relationship between the prospective buyer and those conducting the offering, the issuer may know these facts. Otherwise, how do issuers go about finding these items out prior to making an offer or a sale? If the issuer presents a prospective buyer with a questionnaire, must it verify the answers?

(iv) Exemptions From State Blue Sky Laws

Finding an exemption from registration under the 1933 Securities Act still leaves the issuer facing the requirements imposed by the state or states in which it plans to sell securities. State securities laws, however, also provide various exemptions. These often vary from the Federal categories and from state to state. Therefore, it is necessary to carefully research the statutes and regulations of each state in which an issuer plans to make an offering.

Looking at the three federal exemptions considered above, are there state parallels? Needless to say, blue sky laws do not contain an intrastate exemption. A few go the other way and only require registration of intrastate offerings. *E.g.*, N.Y. Gen. Bus. Law § 359–ff. More broadly, state securities laws often exempt securities listed on a national exchange from their provisions. *E.g.*, Cal. Corp. Code § 25100(*o*). Indeed, even if the state statute does not contain such an exemption, recall, as mentioned earlier in this Chapter, that federal law preempts states from requiring registration of securities that will be listed on the New York or American stock exchange, or the Nasdaq, at the completion of the offering. Sec. Act § 18(a), (b). Of course, this is not much help to a firm seeking to avoid going public, albeit, as discussed earlier, it may be extremely useful to a firm going public but seeking to avoid the burdens of state registration.

What about private offerings? A few states mimic the general language of Section 4(2) of the Federal Securities Act. *See, e.g.,* N.Y. Gen. Bus. Law § 359–ff(5) (incorporating all Federal exemptions, except Section 3(a)(11), by reference). Several provide an even more narrow exemption for isolated transactions, which might only cover one or two sales to separate parties. *See, e.g., Marshall v. Harris,* 276 Or. 447, 555 P.2d 756 (1976). The more common approach is to codify fairly specific criteria, typically involving some maximum number of offerees or purchasers, for a private offering type of exemption. For example, the Uniform Securities Act (2002 revision) provides the following exemptions:

> **SECTION 202 EXEMPT TRANSACTIONS** The following transactions are exempt from Sections 301 through 306 and 504.
>
> * * *
>
> (13) a sale or offer to sell to:
>
> (A) an institutional investor;
>
> (B) a federal covered investment adviser; or
>
> (C) any other person exempted by rule adopted or order issued under this [Act];
>
> (14) a sale or an offer to sell securities of an issuer, if part of a single issue in which:
>
> (A) not more than 25 purchasers are present in this State during any 12 consecutive months, other than those designated in paragraph (13);
>
> (B) a general solicitation or general advertising is not made in connection with the offer to sell or sale of the securities;
>
> (C) a commission or other remuneration is not paid or given, directly or indirectly, to a person other than a broker-dealer registered under this [Act] or an agent registered under this [Act] for soliciting a prospective purchaser in this State; and
>
> (D) the issuer reasonably believes that all the purchasers in this State, other than those designated in paragraph (13), are purchasing for investment;
>
> * * *

Notice that Section 202(14) limits the number of purchasers in the state. Some state exemptions place a limit on the total number of purchasers or offerees anywhere. *See, e.g.,* Cal. Corp. Code § 25102(f). In a portion of the opinion not reprinted in this book, the *Benjamin* court held that purchasers in the state does not have the same meaning as sales in the state.

While Section 202(14) employs a few concepts seen before in Regulation D, it is nowhere near the equivalent to Regulation D. This seems strange insofar as one of the purposes of Regulation D is to serve as a model for a uniform federal-state limited offering exemption. In fact, a state equivalent to Regulation D (at least in part) is found in the Uniform Limited Offering Exemption (ULOE) drafted by the North American Securities Administrators Association. Rather than include the ULOE in the Uniform Securities Act, the drafters of the 2002 version of the Act encourage the administrator of the securities law in each Uniform Act state to adopt the ULOE under the rulemaking authority granted in Section 203 of the Uniform Securities Act. The ULOE reads as follows:

Uniform Limited Offering Exemption

Adopted September 21, 1983.

With Amendments Adopted Through April 29, 1989.

PRELIMINARY NOTES

* * *

1. Nothing in this exemption is intended to or should be construed as in any way relieving issuers or persons acting on behalf of issuers from providing disclosure to prospective investors adequate to satisfy the anti-fraud provisions of this state's securities law.

2. In view of the object of this rule and the purposes and policies underlying this act, the exemption is not available to any issuer with respect to any transaction which, although in technical compliance with this rule, is part of a plan or scheme to evade registration or the conditions or limitations explicitly stated in this rule.

3. Nothing in this rule is intended to relieve registered broker/dealers or agents from the due diligence, suitability, or know your customer standards or any other requirements of law otherwise applicable to such registered persons.

RULE

By authority delegated the administrator in Section ___ of this act to promulgate rules, the following transaction is determined to be exempt from the registration provisions of this act:

1. Any offer or sale of securities offered or sold in compliance with Securities Act of 1933, Regulation D, Rules 230.505 and/or 230.506,[1]

1. In those states where facts and circumstances permit, it would not be inconsistent with the regulatory objectives of this exemption for a state to elect to accept Rule 506 offerings within the ambit of their exemption. In doing so, however, the state disqualification provisions of this rule and the federal disqualification provisions of Rule 505 should be made applicable.

With inclusion of Rule 506, the major objective of the exemption is not limited to facilitating the capital-raising ability of small business. The removal of the dollar limit makes the exemption available to private placements of all sizes. In large private offerings, including any offer or sale made exempt by application of Rule 508(a), * * * and which satisfies the following further conditions and limitations:

A. No commission, fee or other remuneration shall be paid or given, directly or indirectly, to any person for soliciting any prospective purchaser in this state unless such person is appropriately registered in this state.[2 & 3]

It is a defense to a violation of this subsection if the issuer sustains the burden of proof to establish that he or she did not know and in the exercise of reasonable care could not have known that the person who received a commission, fee or other remuneration was not appropriately registered in this state.

B. No exemption under this rule shall be available for the securities of any issuer if any of the parties described in Securities Act of 1933, Regulation A, Rule 230.252 section (c), (d), (e) or (f):

1. Has filed a registration statement which is subject of a currently effective registration stop order entered pursuant to any state's securities law within five years prior to the filing of the notice required under this exemption.

the problems associated with determining that all the investors are experienced enough to fully understand the risks of the offering and controlling the manner and scope of the offering so that it does not become a public offering are magnified. Also, and largely because of the removal of the dollar limit, the exemption becomes more attractive to tax shelter investments.

Tax shelter offerings that would be permitted by Rule 506, particularly those with abusively high write-off-ratios, involve special facts and circumstances, and enforcement experience shows that they have greater potential for regulatory concerns and many lack economic substance and fail to contribute to job creation. In recognition of these concerns, Rule 506 is not adopted as part of the basic ULOE.

In those states where facts and circumstances permit, it would not be inconsistent with the regulatory objective of this exemption to further condition the exemption with the following provision:

"In the case of offerings of direct participation programs as defined in Section 34 or Article III of the National Association of Securities Dealers, Inc., Rules of Fair Practice, delivery of a disclosure document containing the information required by Rule 502(b) of Regulation D to individuals covered by subsections (5) and (6) of Rule 501(a) of Regulation D is required."

2. In those states where facts and circumstances permit, it would not be inconsistent with the regulatory objectives of this exemption for a state to substitute the following for section 1.A.

a. All persons who offer or sell securities in this state to nonaccredited and/or accredited investors as defined in Securities Act of 1933, Regulation D, Rule 230.501(a)(5)—(6) shall be appropriately registered in accordance with this state's securities law.

It is a defense to a violation of this subsection if the issuer sustains the burden of proof to establish that he or she did not know and in the exercise of reasonable care could not have known that the person who received a commission fee or other remuneration was not appropriately registered in this state.

3. In those states where facts and circumstances permit, it would not be inconsistent with the regulatory objective of this exemption for a state to provide for a system or process to simplify and facilitate the registration of broker/dealers and agents which would not otherwise be required to be registered except for this exemption. Such a system or process should at a minimum, grant jurisdiction as well as the ability to effectively limit and control persons offering and selling securities within the state.

2. Has been convicted within five years prior to the filing of the notice required under this exemption of any felony or misdemeanor in connection with the offer, purchase or sale of any security or any felony involving fraud or deceit, including but not limited to forgery, embezzlement, obtaining money under false pretenses, larceny or conspiracy to defraud.

3. Is currently subject to any state administrative enforcement order or judgment entered by that state's securities administrator within five years prior to the filing of the notice required under this exemption or is subject to any state's administrative enforcement order or judgment in which fraud or deceit, including but not limited to making untrue statements of material facts and omitting to state material facts, was found and the order or judgment was entered within five years prior to the filing of the notice required under this exemption.

4. Is subject to any state's administrative enforcement order or judgment which prohibits, denies or revokes the use of any exemption from registration in connection with the offer, purchase or sale of securities.

5. Is currently subject to any order, judgment, or decree of any court of competent jurisdiction temporarily or preliminarily restraining or enjoining, or is subject to any order, judgment or decree of any court of competent jurisdiction, permanently restraining or enjoining, such party from engaging in or continuing any conduct or practice in connection with the purchase or sale of any security or involving the making of any false filing with the state entered within five years prior to the filing of the notice required under this exemption.

6. The prohibitions of paragraphs 1–3 and 5 above shall not apply if the person subject to the disqualification is duly licensed or registered to conduct securities related business in the state in which the administrative order or judgment was entered against such person or if the broker/dealer employing such party is licensed or registered in this state and the Form B–D filed with this state discloses the order, conviction, judgment or decree relating to such person. No person disqualified under this subsection may act in a capacity other than that for which the person is licensed or registered.

7. Any disqualification caused by this section is automatically waived if the state securities administrator or agency or the state which created the basis for disqualification determines upon a showing of good cause that it is not necessary under the circumstances that the exemption be denied.

It is a defense to a violation of this subsection if issuer sustains the burden of proof to establish that he or she did not know and in the exercise of reasonable care could not have known that a disqualification under this subsection existed.

C. The issuer shall file with the state administrator a notice on Form D (17 CFR 239.500):

1. No later than (10 days prior)[4] to the receipt of consideration or the delivery of a subscription agreement by an investor in this state which results from an offer being made in reliance upon this exemption and at such other times and in the form required under Regulation D, Rule 230.503 to be filed with the Securities and Exchange Commission.

2. The notice shall contain an undertaking by the issuer to furnish to the state securities administrator, upon written request, the information furnished by the issuer to offerees, except where the state administrator pursuant to regulation requires that the information be filed at the same time with the filing of the notice.[5]

3. Unless otherwise available, included with or in the initial notice shall be a consent to service of process.

4. Every person filing the initial notice provided for in 1 above shall pay a filing fee of....

D. In all sales to nonaccredited investors in this state one of the following conditions must be satisfied or the issuer and any person acting on its behalf shall have reasonable grounds to believe and after making reasonable inquiry shall believe that one of the following conditions is satisfied:

1. The investment is suitable for the purchaser upon the basis of the facts, if any, disclosed by the purchaser as to the purchaser's other security holdings, financial situation and needs. For the purpose of this condition only, it may be presumed that if the investment does not exceed 10% of the investor's net worth, it is suitable.

2. The purchaser either alone or with his/her purchaser representative(s) has such knowledge and experience in financial and business matters that he/she is or they are capable of evaluating the merits and risks of the prospective investment.

2. A failure to comply with a term, condition or requirement of sections 1.A, [C[6]], and D of this rule will not result in loss of the exemption from the requirements of section [301] of this act for any offer or sale to a particular individual or entity if the person relying on the exemption shows:

A. the failure to comply did not pertain to a term, condition or requirement directly intended to protect that particular individual or entity; and

B. the failure to comply was insignificant with respect to the offering as a whole; and

C. a good faith and reasonable attempt was made to comply with all applicable terms, conditions and requirements of Sections 1.A, [C[6]], and D.

4. In those state where facts and circumstances permit, it would not be inconsistent with the Regulatory objectives of this exemption for a state to consider a post-sale notice patterned after the notice provisions of Regulation D (Rule 230.503).

5. This latter filing requirement is not intended to provide the basis for a fairness type of review of the offering.

6. In those states which have adopted a post-sale notice patterned after the notice provisions of Regulation D (Rule 230.503) it would not be inconsistent with the regulatory

3. Where an exemption is established only through reliance upon Section 2 of this rule, the failure to comply shall nonetheless be actionable by the [administrator] under Section [408] of the Act.[7]

4. Transactions which are exempt under this rule may not be combined with offers and sales exempt under any other rule or section of this Act; However, nothing in this limitation shall act as an election. Should for any reason the offer and sale fail to comply with all of the conditions for this exemption, the issuer may claim the availability of any other applicable exemption.

5. The administrator may, by rule or order, increase the number of purchasers or waive any other conditions of this exemption.

6. The exemption authorized by this rule shall be known and may be cited as the "Uniform Limited Offering Exemption."

NOTE

The ULOE did not succeed in creating a uniform Regulation D type of exemption among the states. *E.g.*, Fein, Makins & Cahalan, *ULOE: Comprehending the Confusion*, 43 Bus. Law. 737 (1988). Dissatisfied with the burden which the lack of uniformity among the states imposed upon those selling securities, Congress amended Section 18 of the Securities Act in 1996. As mentioned earlier, one aspect of the 1996 amendment is to preempt of state registration requirements for securities listed on national exchanges. A second aspect of this amendment is important for those seeking to use Regulation D in order to avoid both state and federal registration. Paragraphs (a) and (b)(4)(D) of Section 18 preempt the states from requiring registration of any security, the sale of which is exempt from federal registration by virtue of Rule 506. Hence, a critical advantage of the Rule 506 exemption under Regulation D is that it avoids registration under both federal and state securities laws. The states, however, still can require issuers to file with the state a notice of the sale of securities fitting within this exemption, so long as the notice requirement is substantially the same as Regulation D's notice requirement. Since the preemption only extends to sales meeting the Rule 506 exemption, issuers who cannot meet the sophisticated buyer requirement of Rule 506 might still look to the ULOE in those states which adopted the ULOE parallel to Rule 505.

Interestingly enough, in one situation, the federal government has taken its lead from a state exemption. California Corporations Code Section 25102(n) contains a special exemption for offerings by California companies

objectives of this exemption to include the notice filing requirements of section 1.C within the substantial compliance provisions of section 2 or to eliminate the filing as a condition and adopt a rule similar to Rule 230.507.

7. The cited reference is to the section of the Uniform Securities Act which authorizes the state administrator to bring a civil action to enjoin rule violations. Those states which have authority to bring an administrative enforcement action for rule violations may wish to include a reference to that statutory authority. If the administrator lacks authority to bring enforcement actions based solely on rule violations, he/she may wish to consider a statutory amendment.

to a limited class of qualified investors. Unlike Regulation D, Section 25102(n) contains no ban on general solicitations—albeit, Section 25102(n) limits general announcements and cold calls—thereby removing what has turned out to be, as noted earlier, perhaps the most difficult requirement in the Regulation D exemptions. In Rule 1001, the Securities Exchange Commission used the Commission's authority under Section 3(b) by creating a special exemption from Federal registration for offerings up to $5 million when the offering is exempt from California registration under Section 25102(n). In adopting Rule 1001, the Securities Exchange Commission invited other states to follow California's lead in creating exemptions similar to Section 25102(n).

(v) The Resale Problem

Resale by the initial buyer to unqualified purchasers can endanger each of the exemptions explored above. As a result, the issuer often restricts the rights of investors to transfer their securities. Moreover, Section 5 of the 1933 Act, by its terms, proscribes all non-exempt sales of securities without registration, not just sales by the issuer. Similarly, state securities laws also may proscribe non-exempt resales. E.g., Uniform Securities Act § 301; Cal. Corp. Code § 25130. Few investors, however, would be interested in a security which is permanently unsalable. Therefore, it is useful to explore when buyers can resell unregistered securities.

One approach, of course, is to register the shares at the time the initial purchaser wishes to resell them. A problem here, beyond the cost and burdens of registration generally, is that the registration process calls for the issuer to furnish information about itself. Hence, it would be necessary for the reselling shareholder to secure the cooperation of the issuer to register the secondary offering. For this reason, investors planning ultimately to cash out in a public offering sometimes insist upon a contractual commitment by the issuer to later register their shares. Needless to say, drafting this sort of commitment requires addressing questions such as what events trigger the duty to register—for example, this could be upon the demand of the shareholder, after a certain period of time, or when the issuer goes public—who pays, and whether the right to demand registration is transferable in a private resale. Alternately, notice both the small offering exemption (Section 3(b) and Rules 504 and 505) and the intrastate offering exemption (Section 3(a)(11)) come under Section 3, which exempts securities rather than just transactions. Taken literally, this would appear to make any resales of securities issued pursuant to these exemptions equally exempt from registration. Nevertheless, as explained in the release introducing Rule 147, the Securities Exchange Commission, with the support of the courts, views these provisions as providing only an exemption for the original issuance of securities, and not for any resales. This means securities holders must look elsewhere to exempt their resales.

Section 4(1) of the 1933 Act exempts transactions by one who is not an "issuer, underwriter, or dealer." Since a resale by definition does not involve the issuer, and since the security holder is usually not a dealer in securities, whether this section exempts a particular resale from registration depends for the most part on whether the seller is an underwriter. Section 2(11) of the Act defines an underwriter to include "*any person* who has purchased from an issuer with a view to ... *the distribution* of any security, *or participates* ... in any *such undertaking*...." Thus, whether a reseller of unregistered securities is an underwriter generally depends on whether the resale is part of a "distribution".

When a party who is in control of the issuer sells some of his or her securities, an additional complication arises by virtue of the last sentence in Section 2(11). If that person sells through a broker (or to another party who distributes the securities through further resales), when can the broker or other party be considered an underwriter (as one who "offers or sells for an issuer [defined under the last sentence of Section 2(11) to include, for this purpose, a person controlling the issuer] in connection with the distribution")? This again generally depends on whether the sale constitutes part of a "distribution". To provide guidelines on when a resale is part of a "distribution", the SEC promulgated Rule 144.

Securities Act Release No. 5223

January 11, 1972.

NOTICE OF ADOPTION OF RULE 144 RELATING TO THE DEFINITION OF THE TERMS "UNDERWRITER" IN SECTIONS 4(1) AND 2(11) AND "BROKERS' TRANSACTIONS" IN SECTION 4(4) OF THE SECURITIES ACT OF 1933, ADOPTION OF FORM 144, AND RESCISSION OF RULES 154 AND 155 UNDER THAT ACT

The Securities and Exchange Commission today announced the adoption of Rule 144 under the Securities Act of 1933 ("Act"). The new rule relates to the application of the registration provisions of the Act to the resale of securities acquired directly or indirectly from issuers or from affiliates of such issuers in transactions not involving any public offerings ("restricted securities") and securities held by affiliates.

* * *

In brief, the rule provides that any affiliate or other person who sells restricted securities of an issuer for his own account, or any person who sells restricted or any other securities for the account of an affiliate of the issuer, is not deemed to be engaged in a distribution of the securities, and therefore is not an underwriter as defined in Section 2(11) of the Act, if the securities are sold in accordance with all the terms and conditions of the rule. The rule requires, among other things, that the restricted securities must have been beneficially owned for a period of at least two years by the person for whose account they are sold; that the amount sold shall not exceed one percent of the class outstanding, or if traded on an exchange, the lesser of that amount or the average weekly volume on all such exchanges during the four weeks preceding the sale; and that the securities must be sold in brokers' transactions. In addition, there must be adequate information available to the public in regard to the issuer of the securities and notice of the sale (Form 144) must be filed with the Commission concurrently with the sale.

A number of persons have commented that it is not clear whether the rule, as proposed, was intended to be the exclusive means for selling restricted securities without registration under the Securities Act. * * * [T]he rule as adopted is not exclusive. However, persons who offer or sell restricted securities without complying with Rule 144 are hereby put on notice by the Commission that in view of the broad remedial purposes of the Act and of public policy which strongly supports registration, they will have a substantial burden of proof in establishing that an exemption from registration is available for such offers or sales and that such persons and the brokers and other persons who participate in the transactions do so at their risk.

* * *

Background and Purpose

* * *

Resales of securities acquired in private placements are frequently made under claims of an exemption pursuant to Section 4(1) of the Act, that is, a transaction by a person other than an issuer, underwriter, or dealer. This Section was intended to exempt only trading transactions between individual investors with respect to securities already issued and not to exempt distributions by issuers or acts of other individuals who engage in steps necessary to such distribution.

Generally, the majority of questions arising under this Section have dealt with whether the seller is an "underwriter." The term underwriter is broadly defined in Section 2(11) of the Act to mean any person who has purchased from an issuer with a view to, or offers or sells for an issuer in connection with, the distribution of any security, or participates or has a direct or indirect participation in any such undertaking or participates or has a participation in the direct or indirect underwriting of any such undertaking. The interpretation of this definition has traditionally focused on the words "with a view to" in the phrase "purchased from an issuer with a view to ... distribution." Thus, an investment banking firm which arranges with an issuer for the public sale of its securities is clearly an "underwriter" under that Section. Not so well understood is the fact that individual investors who are not professionals in the securities business may be "underwriters" within the meaning of that term as used in the Act if they act as links in a chain of transactions through which securities move from an issuer to the public. It is difficult to ascertain the mental state of the purchaser at the time of his acquisition, and the staff has looked to subsequent acts and circumstances to determine whether such person took with a view to distribution at the time of his acquisition. Emphasis has been placed on factors such as the length of time the person has held the securities ("holding period") and whether there has been an unforeseeable change in circumstances of the holder. Experience has shown, however, that reliance upon such factors as the above has not assured adequate protection of investors through the maintenance of informed trading markets and has led to uncertainty in the application of the registration provisions of the Act.

Moreover, the Commission hereby emphasizes and draws attention to the fact that the statutory language of Section 2(11) is in the disjunctive. Thus, it is insufficient to conclude that a person is not an underwriter solely because he did not purchase securities from an issuer with a view to their distribution. It must also be established that the person is not offering or selling for an issuer in connection with the distribution of the securities and that the person does not participate or have a participation in any such undertaking, and does not participate or have a participation in any such underwriting of such an undertaking.

* * *

Explanation and Analysis of the Rule

* * * [T]he Commission is of the view that "distribution" is the significant concept in interpreting the statutory term "underwriter." In determining when a person is deemed not to be engaged in a distribution several factors must be considered.

First, the purpose and underlying policy of the Act to protect investors requires, in the Commission's opinion, that there be adequate current information concerning the issuer, whether the resales of securities by persons result in a distribution or are effected in trading transactions. Accordingly, the availability of the rule is conditioned on the existence of adequate current public information.

Secondly, a holding period prior to resale is essential, among other reasons, to assure that those persons who buy under a claim of a Section 4(2) exemption have assumed the economic risks of investment, and therefore, are not acting as conduits for sale to the public of unregistered securities, directly or indirectly, on behalf of an issuer. * * *

A third factor, which must be considered in determining what is deemed not to constitute a "distribution," is the impact of the particular transaction or transactions on the trading markets. It is consistent with the rationale of the Act that Section 4(1) be interpreted to permit only routine trading transactions as distinguished from distributions. Therefore, a person reselling securities under Section 4(1) of the Act must sell the securities in such limited quantities and in such a manner so as not to disrupt the trading markets. The larger the amount of securities involved, the more likely it is that such resales may involve methods of offering and amounts of compensation usually associated with a distribution rather than routine trading transactions. Thus, solicitation of buy orders or the payment of extra compensation are not permitted by the rule.

In summary, if the sale in question is made in accordance with all the provisions of the rule, as outlined below, any person who sells restricted securities shall be deemed not to be engaged in a distribution of such securities and therefore not an underwriter thereof. The rule also provides that any person who sells restricted or other securities on behalf of a person in a control relationship with the issuer shall be deemed not to be engaged in a distribution of such securities and therefore not to be an underwriter thereof, if the sale is made in accordance with all the conditions of the rule.

* * *

NOTES

1. Over the years, the Securities Exchange Commission has made several amendments to Rule 144. One of the more significant is the addition of paragraph 144(k). This provision allows persons, who were not, at the time of the resale, or for the previous three months, an affiliate of the issuer (in other words, not persons who controlled, were controlled by, or under common control with, the issuer), and who held their securities for two years, to resell without any other restrictions or requirements. A later amendment to the rule has lowered the holding period for affiliates, or for non-affiliates who comply with the notice, manner of sale, quantity and available information requirements, to one year. Other, more narrow, changes involve sales volume (now allowing volume equal to the greater, rather than the lesser, of the alternatives listed in the Release above) and the manner of sale (now allowing direct transactions with a market maker).

Note under Rule 144, as with registration, the information requirement looks to the issuer. This generally is no problem if the issuer is a 1934 Securities Exchange Act reporting company, since 1934 Act filings meet the requirement under Rule 144(c). Otherwise, it may be important for a purchaser to obtain the issuer's promise to undertake actions necessary to allow resales.

Incidentally, what exactly does "control" mean for purposes of Section 2(11) and Rule 144? Unlike various provisions in the Internal Revenue Code (such as Section 368(c)), there is no numerical test. Instead, perhaps a good pragmatic rule of thumb is to see what individual or group would have the power as a realistic matter—rather than as technical matter, which would be a majority of the board of directors for a corporation—to have a particular issuer file a registration statement. *See* Sommer *Who's "in Control"?—S.E.C.,* 21 Bus. Law. 559 (1966).

2. Rule 144, like Rules 506 and 147, is a safe harbor provision. What sort of transactions might Section 4(1) exempt despite their falling outside of Rule 144? There are two significant examples. The first is a resale of registered shares by a non-affiliate of the issuer. (Rule 144 only covers the sale of "restricted securities"—that is securities never sold through a public offering—or else sales involving an affiliate of the issuer.) Hence, it is Section 4(1), unqualified by Rule 144, which allows the ordinary stockholder to sell his or her General Motors shares without registering. *See also* Sec. Act § 4(4) (exempting the broker's execution of the customer's order).

At the other extreme, suppose the initial buyer of an unregistered security resells to an insider or to a sophisticated and fully informed purchaser. While this might seem to fit the private offering exemption, Section 4(2) applies only to transactions "by the issuer." (The same is true for Regulation D and generally for Section 3(a)(11). *See* Sec. Act Rule 147 Preliminary Note 4 (although Section 3(a)(11), but not Rule 147, can also apply to sales by persons controlling the issuer).) On the other hand, such a private transaction would not seem to be part of a "distribution," and so Section 4(1) should apply even without Rule 144. This is sometimes referred to as the "Section 4(1½) exemption," since it represents something of a cross between Sections 4(1) and 4(2), although it falls under the former section. *See generally The Section "4(1½)" Phenomenon, Private Resales of Restricted Securities, a Report to the [ABA] Committee on Federal Regulation of Securities from the Study Group on Section "4(1½)" of the Subcommittee on 1933 Act,* 34 Bus. Law. 1961 (1979). Once one accepts the notion that resales through private placements can be exempt under Section 4(1), the same type of questions faced with private offerings under Section 4(2) arise. For example, what sort of purchasers can the security holder safely sell to, and what are the consequences of further resales by those purchasers? The safe harbor of Rule 506 does not apply. The Securities Exchange Commission promulgated Rule 144A, however, which creates a safe harbor for private placement resales to certain categories of institutional investors.

3. What about resales under state securities laws? See Uniform Securities Act (2002 revision) §§ 201(1) (exempting from registration "an isolated nonissuer transaction, whether effected by or through a broker-dealer or not"), (2) (exempting non-issuer sales of securities of a class that has been in the hands of the public at least 90 days, subject to a number of requirements); Cal. Corp. Code § 25104(a) (exempting any offer or sale of a security by the bona fide owner thereof for his or her own account if the sale (1) is not accompanied by the publication of any advertisement and (2) is not effected by or through a broker-dealer in a public offering); Sec. Act § 18(a), (b)(4)(A) (preempting state registration requirements for resales which are exempt from federal registration by virtue of Section 4(1) of the Securities Act, if the issuing company is registered under the 1934 Securities Exchange Act).

(vi) The Attorney's Role

Opinions of the Committee on Professional Ethics of the American Bar Association, Formal Opinion 335

60 A.B.A.J. 488 (February 2, 1974).

Release #5168 of the Securities and Exchange Commission * * * set forth certain basic standards of conduct required of broker-dealers to meet their responsibilities in connection with sales of unregistered securities. In a footnote to the next-to-last paragraph of the release, dealing with the obligation of broker-dealers to review the surrounding facts and obtain the opinion of competent disinterested counsel concerning the legality of sales, it referred to Securities Act Release #4445 * * * in the following manner:

"In this regard, the commission has stated that 'if an attorney furnishes an opinion based solely on hypothetical facts which he has made no effort to verify, and if he knows that his opinion will be relied upon as the basis for a substantial distribution of unregistered securities a serious question arises as [sic] the propriety of his professional conduct.' "

The commission's repetition of this language led to inquiries of this committee as to the circumstances under which and the extent to which the Code of Professional Responsibility might require that a lawyer make some effort to verify or supplement the facts submitted to him as the basis for an opinion that certain sales of securities need not be registered under the Securities Act of 1933.

* * *

The lawyer should, in the first instance, make inquiry of his client as to the relevant facts and receive answers. If any of the alleged facts, or the alleged facts taken as a whole, are incomplete in a material respect, or are suspect, or are inconsistent, or either on their face or on the basis of other known facts are open to question, the lawyer should make further inquiry. The extent of this inquiry will depend in each case upon the circumstances. For example, it would be less where the lawyer's past relationship with the client is sufficient to give him a basis for trusting the client's probity than where the client has recently engaged the lawyer, and less where the lawyer's inquiries are answered fully than when there appears a reluctance to disclose information.

Where the lawyer concludes that further inquiry of a reasonable nature would not give him sufficient confidence as to all the relevant facts, or for any other reason he does not make the appropriate further inquiries, he should refuse to give an opinion. However, assuming that the alleged facts are not incomplete in a material respect, or suspect, or in any way inherently inconsistent, or on their face or on the basis of other known facts open to question, the lawyer may properly assume that the facts as related to him by his client, and checked by him by reviewing such appropriate documents as are available, are accurate.

Preliminarily, we state two examples as a means of defining the extremes of the problem in giving an opinion to a security holder who wishes to sell securities to the public without registration. On the one extreme, if a lawyer is asked to issue an opinion concerning a modest amount of a widely traded security by a responsible client, whose lack of relationship to the issuer is well known to the lawyer, he may ordinarily proceed to issue the opinion with considerable confidence. On the other extreme, if he is asked to prepare an opinion letter covering a substantial block of a little-known security, where the client (be it selling shareholder or broker) appears reluctant to disclose exactly where the securities came from or where the surrounding circumstances raise a question as to whether or not the ostensible sellers may be merely intermediaries for controlling persons or statutory underwriters, then searching inquiry is called for.

* * *

It is difficult to state a formula for determining how far a lawyer must go to satisfy the requirement that he make a reasonable effort to verify particular facts in such a case. However, it would seem that, for example, the verification from the issuer or its counsel of the number of shares of the class outstanding and the verification (perhaps through financial journals) of the relevant trading volume, an attempt (by checking through a quotation service and/or the relevant "pink" quotation sheets) to determine whether or not the broker is making solicitations of offers to buy the securities, and the inspection of a written statement from the issuer of the securities that it has complied with the reporting requirements mentioned in Rule 144 should normally be sufficient where verification is indicated.

Another example would be where a corporate client requests an opinion as to whether a proposed transaction would be within the private offering exemption furnished by Section 4(2) of the Securities Act of 1933. In this situation, the lawyer should obtain from the client information, preferably in writing, from which the lawyer may reach the legal conclusion that the exemption is (or is not) available. Here again, the lawyer may properly rely upon the information furnished by a client well known to him assuming that it is not inconsistent, suspect, otherwise open to question, or incomplete in a material respect.

If the lawyer has some reason to believe that one or more of the statements of fact furnished him as a basis for the opinion may not be correct, he should make a determination as to whether to refuse to give an opinion or whether to attempt to verify one or more of the relevant facts. * * * If he does determine that he will proceed, he should decide on the extent of verification in the light of the particular situation. If, for example, the lawyer has any reason to doubt the reliability of the information relevant to whether the offerees have the requisite sophistication to meet the standard applicable to the Section 4(2) exemption, he should reasonably satisfy himself that the client correctly understands the concept of "sophistication," and he might appropriately obtain from his client further information on each offeree and his background in order to determine that each was sufficiently "sophisticated" to be able to fend for himself and did not need the protection of a registration statement.

Where information which may be relevant to a determination of whether or not the exemption provided by Section 4(2) is available may be quite difficult, if not impossible, to verify, it might in fact be necessary to rely completely on the client, but this necessity does not decrease the lawyer's ultimate responsibility to exercise his independent judgment in determining whether the client had a reasonable basis for its determination that each client was sufficiently "sophisticated" and whether, in view of all the facts developed, the Section 4(2) exemption is available. If the lawyer considers that there is any material deficiency in that information, he should simply refuse to give an opinion on the subject.

A properly drafted opinion will recite clearly the sources of the attorney's knowledge of the facts. Where verification is otherwise called for, an attorney should make appropriate verification and should not rely on the use of such phrases as "based upon the facts as you have given them to me" or "apart from what you have told me, I have not inquired as to the facts."

The essence of this opinion, * * * is that, while a lawyer should make adequate preparation, including inquiry into the relevant facts, that is consistent with the above guidelines, and while he should not accept as true that which he should not reasonably believe to be true, he does not have the responsibility to "audit" the affairs of his client or to assume, without reasonable cause, that a client's statement of the facts cannot be relied upon.

The steps reasonably required of the lawyer in making his investigation must be commensurate with the circumstances under which he is called upon to render the opinion, but he must bear in mind that his responsibility is to render to the client his considered, independent opinion whether, having made at least inquiries such as those suggested by the above guidelines, the claimed exemption is or is not available under the law. While the responsibility of the lawyer is to his client, he must not be oblivious of the extent to which others may be affected if he is derelict in fulfilling that responsibility. * * *

NOTE

Errors and omissions insurance for attorneys typically excludes securities practice from the standard coverage. Instead, the attorney must purchase a special rider to cover securities work. This coverage not only costs extra, the insurer will not issue it unless satisfied as to the competence of the lawyer to handle the subject matter. Does advising on the availability of exemptions require special coverage?

CHAPTER VI

Corporate Restructuring Transactions

Even with the most careful planning at formation, changing circumstances involving a business or its principals often precipitate a major restructuring. For example, Chapters III and IV suggested a number of events which might trigger a change in ownership through the buy-out of one or more partners, limited partners, LLC members or shareholders. As discussed in those earlier chapters, many times parties plan for such a buy-out at the inception of the enterprise. Still, on other occasions, they may need to negotiate the purchase at the time it is to occur. In either event, the problems entailed in buying out a stockholder—particularly when the corporation, rather than the other shareholders, acts as purchaser—justify a further examination beyond that provided in Chapter IV. This is the subject of Section A of this chapter, which explores both purchases by other stockholders (cross purchases) and redemptions by the corporation. Often, the impetus for restructuring may consist, not of the need to change ownership by buying some owners out, but rather of a desire to alter the nature of the interests of the various participants in the enterprise. In a partnership, limited partnership, LLP or LLC, this involves simply amending the partnership or LLC operating agreement. In a corporation, however, this could entail a more complicated transaction to change the firm's capital structure. Section B will explore the use of stock dividends and recapitalizations to accomplish this goal. Finally, change may occur within the business itself. It may become necessary or desirable to scale back operations, or to divide operations into separate firms. This, too, involves special problems in the corporate setting. Section C of this chapter considers both corporate contractions and divisions.

SECTION A. RESTRUCTURING THROUGH BUY-OUTS

1. CROSS-PURCHASES

a. *Corporate and Securities Law Aspects*

Rochez Bros., Inc. v. Rhoades

491 F.2d 402 (3d Cir.1973).

■ VAN DUSEN, CIRCUIT JUDGE.

* * *

The case arises from the sale of 50% of the issued and outstanding stock of MS & R, Inc. by Rochez Bros., Inc. to Charles R. Rhoades on November 13, 1967, in accordance with an agreement of sale dated September 16, 1967, * * *. The interest of Rochez Bros. in MS & R began on July 1, 1964, when Rochez Bros. bought 50% of the stock of MS & R for $272,500. At the same time Rhoades, who already owned 33 1/3% of the MS & R stock, brought his stock ownership up to 50%. This evenly divided stock ownership continued until November 13, 1967, when Rhoades bought out Rochez Bros., thus becoming the sole owner of the stock of MS & R. During this time, Rhoades was full-time Chairman of the Board, Chief Executive Officer, and President of MS & R. Joseph Rochez, the President of Rochez Bros., was a part-time Vice President of MS & R and a member of its three-man Board of Directors. Rhoades ran the business activities of MS & R on a day-to-day basis, while Rochez was primarily concerned with general policy matters in relation to finance and growth of the company.

As a result of increasing dissension between the two men, founded both in personality differences and business disagreements, both Rochez and Rhoades were authorized by the Board in the spring of 1967 to contact prospective purchasers of the company, but these efforts produced no results. At this time, they also began discussing a buy-sell agreement whereby one of them would buy out the other's interest. Finally, on September 11, 1967, Rochez Bros. named the price for which it was willing to sell its stock in MS & R to Rhoades, subject to the condition that the sale should be concluded by noon on September 15 and that Rhoades should put $50,000 in escrow, to be forfeited if no closing occurred. On September 16, 1967, an agreement of sale was executed, under which Rhoades bought the stock of Rochez Bros. in MS & R for $598,000. The closing and delivery of the stock certificates to Rhoades took place on November 13, 1967.

Prior to the September 16 agreement, Rhoades answered a newspaper advertisement placed by one Wingate Royce, of New York City, in January or February of 1967. Royce phoned Rhoades, who told Royce that he was interested in discussing financing for MS & R. Rhoades then sent Royce MS & R financial information and made an appointment for Royce to come to

Pittsburgh on April 21, 1967. Royce did visit the MS & R plant on that date and was introduced by Rhoades to Rochez, who declined to hire him to find a purchaser of MS & R. Rhoades, however, did agree to retain Royce to find leads and make introductions to bring about the sale of MS & R. Rhoades never informed Rochez Bros. of the employment of Royce or the negotiations for the sale of MS & R that followed.

Thereafter, in May 1967, Royce brought MS & R as a potential acquisition to the attention of J. Walter English, of Simmonds Precision Products Co. In May 1967, English visited MS & R after Royce had informed Rhoades that Simmonds was a potential purchaser. * * *

Royce also informed Rhoades of the interest of Carus Chemical Company in acquiring MS & R stock. In the latter part of August 1967, the Carus brothers visited the MS & R plant and told Rhoades that Carus would be interested in purchasing MS & R stock.

Upon conclusion of the agreement of September 16, 1967, for the purchase of the Rochez stock, Rhoades increased his efforts to sell MS & R. On September 18, 1967, he telephoned both Simmonds and Carus and began negotiations that led to offers from both. However, the Carus offer was unattractive to Rhoades since it in effect required him, continuing as director, to earn the purchase price out of future profits of MS & R. The Simmonds offer also fell through, both because Rhoades found it unattractive taxwise and because Simmonds did not wish to become involved in a possible lawsuit with Rochez Bros. Finally, in April 1968, Rhoades began negotiations with Esterline Corporation, through the initiative of Western Pennsylvania National Bank, which resulted in a formal agreement on July 16, 1968, in which Esterline agreed to pay $4,250,000 in cash and 50,000 shares of Esterline restricted stock for the 100% of MS & R stock then held by Rhoades and two other persons to whom he had sold some shares.

Rochez Bros. brought this action under section 10(b) of the Securities Exchange Act, 15 U.S.C. 78j(b) and Rule 10b–5 of the Securities and Exchange Commission with pendent jurisdiction fraud counts under Pennsylvania law. The case was tried to the court, which entered judgment of January 22, 1973, in favor of Rochez and against Rhoades in the amount of $402,000, with interest from September 16, 1967. The district court on the same day also entered a separate order dismissing the action as to MS & R, the corporate defendant.

I. LIABILITY OF RHOADES

Defendant Rhoades contests the district court's decision on the ground that plaintiff failed to demonstrate the following elements necessary to establish liability under section 10(b) of the Securities Exchange Act and Rule 10b–5 of the Securities and Exchange Commission.

A. Scienter

* * * Defendant was under a duty to disclose all material facts to plaintiff, and his failure to do so when he had actual knowledge of those facts satisfies any scienter requirement.

B. Materiality

The test of the materiality of undisclosed or misrepresented facts is basically an objective one—i.e., whether "a reasonable man would attach importance [to them] in determining his choice of action in the transaction in question." * * * Under this test there is little doubt that information concerning negotiations by one owner of 50% of the stock of a business with potential purchasers is material, for a reasonable man who owned the other 50% of the stock would surely attach importance to that information in deciding whether to sell out to his co-owner. Defendant's arguments on this point do not directly dispute this reasoning, but rather contest the district court's finding of those facts held to be material. We must, therefore, review the record to determine if the district court's finding that defendant was engaged in negotiations with Simmonds and Carus for the sale of MS & R, and that these negotiations had reached a stage where their existence and contents were material, is clearly erroneous. * * *

There is ample evidence that Rhoades hired Royce to find a purchaser of MS & R and that this fact was concealed from Rochez.[9] There was equally adequate proof that Royce helped to arrange the visit of English to MS & R, that Simmonds was interested in the prospect of acquiring MS & R and that Rhoades knew it. * * * Finally, even if we were to accept defendant's protestations that he rejected all advances made by Simmonds and Carus concerning the purchase of MS & R, it is undisputed that they displayed a strong interest in such an acquisition, and that interest would certainly be a factor affecting the decision of a reasonable man in Rochez's position with respect to the transaction between him and Rhoades. We therefore hold that the district court's findings supporting its conclusion that there were material facts that defendant failed to disclose are not clearly erroneous.

C. Due Care

The cases generally hold that before an insider may claim reliance on a material misrepresentation or nondisclosure, he must fulfill a duty of due care in seeking to ascertain for himself the facts relevant to a transaction. * * * However, the cases also hold that a plaintiff cannot fail in his duty of due care if he lacked any opportunity to detect the fraud. * * * The nondisclosed facts here were in Rhoades' personal knowledge or private files and were not available to Rochez. There is no evidence that any

9. Defendant argues that his hiring of Royce cannot be characterized as a concealment from or a surprise to Rochez since the latter specifically turned down Royce's services after having been introduced to him by Rhoades. This argument overlooks several important facts. Royce testified that "[w]hen he (Rhoades) took me by to meet Rochez, he asked me not to tell them what we were talking about" * * *. In a memorandum the day before Royce's visit, Rhoades directed that MS & R mail would thenceforth be opened only by MS & R employees and not by Rochez Bros. employees (who shared that same office) * * *. Furthermore, Rhoades admitted that he never told anyone from Rochez Bros. about the letter employment agreement with Royce * * *. Thus, even if Rochez declined to hire Royce as a finder (as Rhoades testified), it does not relieve Rhoades from the duty of revealing that he had in fact hired Royce in opposition to Rochez' wishes, as found by the district court. * * *

corporate books, records, or minutes available to Rochez contained information with respect to the employment of Royce or the negotiations with Simmonds or Carus. Thus, Rochez's status as an insider, his financial expertise, and his business acumen are all irrelevant, for he had no access to the critical information or any opportunity to discover the non-disclosed facts. We therefore conclude from the record that Rochez adequately fulfilled his duty of due care.

D. Reliance

* * *

Defendant stresses a number of facts which he claims show that Rochez would have proceeded to reach the same buy-sell agreement with defendant as he did on September 16, 1967, even if he had known of the negotiations with Simmonds and Carus. First, from earlier negotiations to sell MS & R authorized by the Board of Directors, Rochez knew that Rhoades had valued a 50% interest in MS & R to a possible outside purchaser at $1.75 million. * * * Rochez considered that valuation ludicrously high. Second, Rochez initiated the deal on September 11, 1967, and gave Rhoades only until September 15, 1967, to agree to it and to put up $50,000, which would be forfeited if the closing did not take place. Third, when Rochez set the price at which Rochez Bros. would sell its MS & R stock to Rhoades, he stated that he did not care where Rhoades got the money and that he assumed that Rhoades had outside investors waiting in the wings. These facts demonstrate that Rochez did not share Rhoades' sanguine estimation of the worth of MS & R stock, was most anxious to press forward with the deal, and was unconcerned with the source of the money that was to pay for the shares of MS & R stock held by Rochez Bros. However, they do not compel the conclusion that Rochez would have been indifferent to the amount of money that Simmonds or Carus was willing to pay. Even if it is true, as Rhoades contends, that as of September 16, when the firm commitment was signed, he had not yet received any specific offer from either Simmonds or Carus, the record indicates that negotiations had progressed far enough that an offer of a price by one of the prospective purchasers was to be expected shortly. On the basis of the evidence before it, the district court could properly have concluded that if Rochez had been apprised of the undisclosed facts, he would not have plunged ahead with the buy-sell agreement with Rhoades on the same terms without first finding out how much Simmonds or Carus was prepared to pay, and that these estimates would have influenced his willingness to sell to Rhoades at the price he had originally asked.

E. Conclusion

On the basis of the foregoing analysis, we affirm the decision of the district court as to the liability of defendant Rhoades under Rule 10b–5.

* * *

NOTE

The purchase of stock by some shareholders from others represents a relatively straight-forward purchase and sale transaction, which stands in marked contrast to the complexity introduced with corporate redemptions. Still, as *Rochez Bros.* illustrates, even this transaction is not without the potential for legal difficulties. The situation in which a shareholder sells out, only to watch the business then take off (or, as in *Rochez Bros.,* be sold at a higher price) occurs with appalling frequency. This often generates a certain amount of ill will, as well as contributing to family lore. Occasionally, it also produces a lawsuit in which the seller claims the buying stockholder failed to disclose material facts. This suggests the need for complete candor in all buy-out negotiations. The cautious might also wish to document their candor.

Can a cross-purchase involve any other duties for the buyer? Recall the claim made in *Zidell v. Zidell Inc.,* reprinted in Chapter IV, that the purchase of shares breached a duty owed to the corporation or its minority shareholders. While the court in *Zidell* rejected the claim, note the cases it distinguished under which such a duty could exist.

b. *Tax Aspects*

Garber Industries v. Commissioner of Internal Revenue

435 F.3d 555 (5th Cir.2006).

Petitioner Garber Industries Holding Co., Inc. appeals the order of the Tax Court limiting the company's deduction of net operating loss carryforwards and assessing a deficiency. Because we agree that the 1998 stock sale from Kenneth Garber to his brother Charles Garber resulted in an "ownership change" to Garber Industries under § 382 of the Internal Revenue Code, the deduction of the loss carryforwards was properly limited and the judgment of the Tax Court is affirmed.

I.

Garber Industries Holding Co., Inc. ("Garber Industries") was incorporated in December 1982. * * * Garber Industries suffered operating losses from 1983 to 1989 and again in 1992. Under I.R.C. § 172, net operating losses ("NOLs") could be carried forward and deducted. At the end of 1997, the balance of NOL carryforwards was over twenty million dollars.

* * *

The critical transfer with respect to this case occurred in April 1998 when Kenneth Garber and his wife sold all of their shares of Garber Industries stock (65% [of the outstanding stock]) to Charles Garber. Charles Garber's ownership interest increased from 19% [which he held before the sale] to 84%. No other Garber Industries' stock changed ownership in that year.

On its 1998 return, Garber Industries deducted a net operating loss carryover of $808,935. The IRS audited the taxpayer's 1997 and 1998 returns and determined that the company had undergone an ownership change under section 382 as a result of Kenneth's stock sale to Charles in 1998. Under the Internal Revenue Code, an ownership change limits the amount of NOL carryover that can be deducted. As applied to Garber Industries, an ownership change would limit the NOL deduction to $121,258. In June 2001, the Commissioner issued a Notice of Deficiency resulting from the reduction in the amount of allowable deduction of net operating loss.

Garber Industries challenged the deficiency in the Tax Court. * * * The Tax Court ruled in favor of the Commissioner and held that sale between the brothers did constitute an ownership change thus limiting the deductibility of the NOL carryforwards and creating a larger tax deficiency for Garber Industries. Garber Industries appeals.

II.

The sole issue in this case is whether an ownership change occurred in relation to Garber Industries, as a result of the 1998 stock sale from Kenneth to Charles Garber, which triggers a limitation in the deduction of NOL carryforwards by the corporation under § 382 of the Internal Revenue Code. Whether an ownership change occurred depends on whether ownership of Kenneth's and Charles' Garber Industries stock can be aggregated or attributed to each other under the ownership rules set forth in §§ 382 and 318. If the brothers' stock can be aggregated or its ownership attributed to each other, then a sale between them does not cause an ownership change.

The purpose of section 382 is to prevent trafficking in net operating loss carryovers, which in the absence of a limitation may ordinarily be carried forward for 20 years. The statute limits the use of NOL carryovers by the "new loss corporation"—the corporation possessing the losses after an ownership change. 26 U.S.C. § 382(a). An ownership change occurs if, immediately after an "owner shift" or "equity structure shift," the percentage of stock owned by one or more shareholders owning 5% or more of the corporation ("5% shareholder") has increased by more than 50 percentage points over the lowest percentage of stock owned by such persons during the testing period. 26 U.S.C. § 382(g)(1), (k)(7). The testing period is the three year period ending on the date of the owner shift or equity structure shift. 26 U.S.C. § 382(i). An owner shift is any change in corporate ownership affecting the percentage of stock owned by a 5% shareholder. 26 U.S.C. § 382(g)(2).

Both Kenneth and Charles Garber were 5% shareholders. In the absence of an exception or modification to the above rules, the 1998 stock sale from Kenneth to Charles clearly caused an owner shift or ownership change because the sale caused the ownership of Charles Garber to increase by more than 50 percentage points (from 19% to 84%).

In some circumstances, § 382 allows stock owned by family members to be grouped together for purposes of determining whether an ownership change occurred.

* * *

The plain language of these statutes supports the Tax Court's decision that the Garber Industries stock owned by Kenneth can not be attributed his brother Charles, or vice versa. Section 382(*l*)(3)(A) states that "an individual and all members of his family described in paragraph (1) of section 318(a) shall be treated as 1 individual for purposes of applying this section." The family members listed in paragraph (1) of section 318(a) are a person's "spouse", "his children, grandchildren, and parents." This list does not include siblings, which is the relationship between Charles and Kenneth Garber. Accordingly, the stock owned by each brother is not treated as owned by the other and the transaction between them as 5% shareholders triggers an ownership change in the company. We see nothing in the statute or argument of Garber Industries that persuades us that this simple reading of section 382 is not the correct one.

Garber Industries puts forward an alternative analysis that requires some background about the application of § 318. The parties agree that if the attribution rules of § 318 are applied to the facts of this case without the modifications in § 382, the stock of each brother would not be considered constructively owned by the other for two reasons. First, section 318(a)(1)(A) does not include siblings in the list of family members whose stock is considered owned by other family members and, second, because § 318(a)(5)(B) bars double attribution—that is attribution from child to parent and then from parent to a sibling as would be required for the Garber brothers' stock to be aggregated together. Garber Industries argues that when § 382(*l*)(3)(A) removed the application of § 318(a)(5)(B), double attribution is allowed. Under this interpretation, the stock of Kenneth could be attributed to his parent and then to Charles so that the 1998 sale between them would not cause an ownership change. We disagree.

We read subsection (*l*) of § 382 as having two parts that must be considered together in determining the operating rules for constructive ownership in the context of NOL carryforwards. First, the section states that "paragraphs (1) and (5)(B) of section 318(a) shall not apply." * * * Critically, it removes both subsection (1), which establishes the attribution scheme, and subsection (5)(B), which limits attribution between individuals to one step (no double attribution). The second clause of § 382(*l*)(3)(A)(i) replaces the attribution rules of § 318(a)(1) and (a)(5)(B) with a different method of grouping ownership among family members, "an individual and all members of his family described in paragraph (1) of section 318(a) shall be treated as 1 individual for purposes of applying this section." * * * [W]e read § 382 as totally replacing the attribution rules of § 318 with the family grouping model of § 382. Under this interpretation, when determining whether stock of family members can be aggregated under section 382, the only question is whether they are members of the same "family" as described by section 318—an individual, his spouse, children and grandchildren. * * *

Garber Industries also suggests that § 382 can be read to allow ownership to be attributed to and from a parent without regard to whether the parent is also a shareholder of the loss corporation. If this were allowed, a family group could be formed to aggregate the stock of Kenneth and Charles Garber around their common parent[, despite their parents not having been stockholders in Garber Industries]. We agree with the Tax Court that the individual or individuals who form the basis for the ownership analysis must be shareholders of the loss corporation. The whole point of section 382 is to identify ownership changes relative to 5% shareholders; a change of ownership by such a shareholder is the only change the statute addresses. 26 U.S.C. § 382(g)(1), (g)(2) and (k)(7). An ownership change is defined in terms of owner shifts affecting 5% shareholders. 26 U.S.C. § 382(g). All stock owners who are less than 5% shareholders of the corporation are grouped and their stock is treated as owned by one 5% shareholder. *Id.* Accordingly, it follows that the "individual" referred to in the constructive ownership analysis provisions of § 382(*l*)(3)(A) must be a shareholder and that individual is the starting point for the formation of a family group consisting of that individual's spouse, parents, children and grandchildren.

III.

In summary, the Tax Court properly interpreted § 382 as applied to a sale of stock between two shareholder brothers, when no parent or grandparent was a shareholder of the loss corporation.

NOTES

1. In contrast to a redemption of stock by the corporation, a purchase of one stockholder's shares by another stockholder is normally a very straightforward transaction from a tax standpoint. The seller recognizes gain or loss, and the buyer receives a basis equal to the purchase price, just as with any other purchase and sale.

Garber Industries illustrates, however, that sometimes the tax impact is not so simple. Garber Industries, like many new firms, had losses, rather than taxable income, during its early years in existence. Section 172 of the Internal Revenue Code allows the corporation to carry these losses forward to offset against taxable income in later years—thereby creating the concept of "net operating loss carryovers" (NOLs). When Kenneth Garber agreed to sell his interest to his brother Charles, neither probably gave any thought to the impact of the transaction on the company's future ability to utilize the NOLs. Nevertheless, the transaction triggered a provision in the Internal Revenue Code (Section 382) designed to prevent persons from buying corporations in order to use the corporations' accumulated NOLs. Since the traditional focus of Section 382 is on the acquisition of a corporation by an outsider, Chapter VII of this book, dealing with the purchase and sale of a corporation, will look at Section 382. In a nutshell, Section 382 limits the ability of a corporation, following an ownership change, to utilize NOLs. The limit is determined by the corporation's value at the time of the ownership change. The lesson from *Garber Industries* is that provisions in the tax code sometimes create consequences far from the situations in which one normally assumes they will apply.

2. One tax-advantaged cross-purchase occurs if an employee stock ownership plan (an ESOP) is the buyer. Recall that Chapter IV outlined how a corporation can obtain a deduction for contributions made to a qualified profit sharing plan, such as an ESOP. This means that a cross-purchase undertaken through an ESOP essentially produces an immediate deduction for the corporation—something not normally the case for either a normal cross purchase by other shareholders or a redemption by the corporation. There also can be favorable tax treatment for a party selling shares to the ESOP in a C corporation and reinvesting in other shares—assuming the ESOP owns at least 30 percent of the employer corporation's outstanding stock. I.R.C. § 1042. Of course, there is a cost for all this. The purchase is for benefit of the corporation's employees—who will ultimately have the right to the stock or to its appraised value. I.R.C. § 409(h).

2. REDEMPTIONS

The alternative to structuring a buy-out as a cross-purchase is to have the corporation acquire the stock. Corporations statutes typically contain express authorization for companies to repurchase or redeem their own shares. *E.g.*, Cal. Corp. Code § 510; Del. Gen. Corp. Law § 160(a); N.Y. Bus. Corp. Law § 513; M.B.C.A. § 6.31(a). (Some writers use the term redemption to refer to acquisitions pursuant to an option in the articles, and the term repurchase to refer to an acquisition pursuant to a side contract. The tax code, however, generally refers to all purchases by a company of its own shares as a redemption. I.R.C. § 317(b). These materials will use the terms repurchase and redemption interchangeably.) Repurchases can serve other purposes beyond buying out a stockholder. For example, the corporation may need shares to meet its obligations under an employee stock option plan, or to cover outstanding convertible securities or warrants. Of course, the company could always issue new shares for these objectives—albeit, this may require amending the articles if the amount of outstanding stock bumps up against the number of shares authorized. Issuing new stock, however, can dilute earnings per share, which the company might avoid by repurchasing the necessary stock. Repurchasing shares also serves as a method to get money from the company to its stockholders. Can those managing the company take advantage of this fact to bail money out of the corporation without taxable dividends, or in disregard of the financial limits which corporations statutes impose upon the declaration of dividends? Can they use this as a technique to get money to favored shareholders and leave out others? Publicly held corporations sometimes justify their repurchases by saying the stock was at a bargain price. Is propping up the price of shares a legitimate purpose for repurchases? If the market underrates the company's stock, might this suggest some failure of the company to disseminate all material information? These other purposes for redemptions make this a much more complicated transaction than a cross-purchase. (Later, Chapter VII will explore use of redemptions to facilitate or foil the purchase of a corporation.)

a. *Corporate and Securities Law Aspects*

(i) Funds Available

Neimark v. Mel Kramer Sales, Inc.

102 Wis.2d 282, 306 N.W.2d 278 (App.1981).

■ DECKER, CHIEF JUDGE.

This appeal questions whether the trial court erred in this shareholder's derivative action by ordering specific performance of a stock redemption agreement upon death of the principal shareholder of defendant corporation. We vacate the judgment and remand with directions.

Plaintiff seeks specific performance of an agreement for the redemption of stock owned by the late Mel Kramer (Kramer), founder and majority shareholder of Mel Kramer Sales, Inc. (MKS). MKS is a closely-held Wisconsin corporation engaged in the business of selling automotive parts and accessories. The interests of the shareholders are:

Shareholder	Number of Shares	Percentage
Mel Kramer/Estate of Mel Kramer	1,020	51
Delores Kramer	200	10
Jack Neimark	580	29
Jerome Sadowsky	200	10

* * *

On June 22, 1976, a stock redemption agreement was executed by MKS and its stockholders. The agreement requires MKS to purchase, and a deceased shareholder's estate to sell, all of the deceased shareholder's stock in MKS at $400 per share, less a specified credit. The agreement also provided Delores Kramer with the option to sell her shares to MKS in the event of Kramer's death.

Under the agreement, Kramer's 1,020 shares were to be redeemed by MKS within thirty days after the appointment of his estate's personal representative, Delores Kramer, in the following manner. The redemption price of $408,000, less a specifically provided $50,000 credit, constituting a net price of $358,000, was to be paid in installments of $100,000 at the closing, and the balance in five consecutive annual installments. The first installment after the closing was to be $43,200, with four remaining installments of $53,700, plus interest at 6%. If Delores Kramer elected to redeem her shares, her stock was to be purchased at the same per-share price payable in two installments of $40,000, on the sixth and seventh anniversaries of the closing, plus interest at 6% after five years.

The agreement provided that the $100,000 payment for Kramer's shares was to be funded by a life insurance policy on Kramer's life. Upon Kramer's death, MKS received the $100,000 proceeds from the life insurance policy, and it was reflected in MKS's retained earnings as of December 31, 1976.

* * *

After Kramer's death [which occurred on December 5, 1976], Delores Kramer indicated a reluctance to have MKS redeem the shares owned by her husband's estate. Neimark insisted that MKS redeem the estate's shares, and on May 23, 1977, the board of directors met to consider Neimark's demand. The MKS attorney who was the author of the stock redemption agreement was present at this meeting and explained to the board that redemption of the stock by MKS would violate Sec. 180.385(1), Stats.[2] The board voted 3–1 not to purchase the Kramer estate's shares. Neimark, of course, cast the losing vote.

On November 30, 1978, Neimark commenced an action for specific performance of the 1976 agreement and alternatively, sought monetary damages. * * *

Subsequently, a third party offered to purchase the business for $1,000,000. Neimark conditioned his approval of the sale on the requirement that Delores Kramer and the Kramer estate receive proceeds equal only to the redemption price of the shares which was substantially less than the tendered per-share price. * * *

II. LAWFULNESS OF REDEMPTION

* * *

Section 180.385(1), Stats., prohibits, *inter alia,* acquisition by a corporation of its own stock if the corporation would thereby be rendered insolvent. "Insolvent" is defined in Sec. 180.02(14) as the "inability of a

2. Section 180.385(1), Stats., provides:

180.385 Right of corporation to acquire and dispose of its own shares.

(1) Unless otherwise provided in the articles of incorporation, a corporation shall have the right to purchase, take, receive, or otherwise acquire, hold, own, pledge, transfer, or otherwise dispose of its own shares; provided that no such acquisition, directly or indirectly, of its own shares for consideration other than its own shares of equal or subordinate rank shall be made unless all of the following conditions are met:

(a) At the time of such acquisition the corporation is not and would not thereby be rendered insolvent;

(b) The net assets of the corporation remaining after such acquisition would be not less than the aggregate preferential amount payable in the event of voluntary liquidation to the holders of shares having preferential liquidation; and

(c) 1. Such acquisition is authorized by the articles of incorporation or by the affirmative vote or the written consent of the holders of at least a majority of the outstanding shares of the same class and of each class entitled to equal or prior rank in the distribution of assets in the event of voluntary liquidation; or

2. Such acquisition is authorized by the board of directors and the corporation has unreserved and unrestricted earned surplus equal to the cost of such shares. * * *

corporation to pay its debts as they become due in the usual course of its business." The purpose of prohibiting own stock acquisition by a corporation if it would thereby be rendered insolvent is to protect the creditors, preferred security holders, and in some cases, common stockholders whose stock is not acquired, from director action which would strip funds from the corporation and create a distributive preference to the stockholder whose stock is acquired.

* * *

The trial court's finding of fact, that performance of the stock redemption agreement would not render the corporation insolvent, is supported by ample evidence, and is not contrary to the great weight and clear preponderance of the evidence. The evidence establishes the fact that the corporation had the ability to pay its debts as they became due. In arriving at that conclusion, the trial court is not restricted to analyzing the cash and cash-equivalent assets of the corporation. The flow of cash to maintain solvency can be generated by a multitude of means other than cash generated solely from sales.

In this case, MKS had a $275,000 line of credit with a local bank. Its annual financial statements for 1976, 1977, and 1978, and the May 31, 1979, financial statement, disclose no inability of MKS to pay its debts as they became due if the redemption agreement had been performed.

* * *

Contrary to the English rule, American courts at common law generally permit a corporation to acquire its own shares. The American rule has undergone harsh criticism because of the opportunity it affords to prefer selected stockholder/sellers and strip funds from the corporation to the disadvantage of preferred security interest holders, other common stockholders, and creditors. The rule sought protection for those persons by vaguely requiring that the purchase be "without prejudice" to their interests. * * * Additional statutory restrictions resulted and culminated in the two major restraints (for the purposes of this case): the purchase must be made out of earned surplus and cannot be made if insolvency, in the equity sense, is present or would result. "[I]nsolvency in the equity sense has always meant an inability of the debtor to pay his debts as they mature." * * *

The self-evident applicability of the insolvency test at the time of acquisition of the stock is not equally self-evident in the case of an installment purchase. Considerations of "corporate flexibility" in the acquisition of its stock for legitimate purposes, balanced by "protection for creditors," led the majority of American courts to apply the insolvency test contemporaneously with each installment payment. * * * [W]e agree with the reasoning of the majority of American courts that the protection of the corporation's creditors requires that the insolvency limitation be applied both at the time of purchase and when each installment payment is made pursuant to the purchase agreement. When the payment is actually made, the assets leave the corporation and concomitantly the loss of financial protection occurs. If insolvency results or would result, the purchase may constitute a fraudulent conveyance. In any event, the hazard of fraud to creditors is too great to permit the insolvency test to be applied at times remote to payment for the share repurchase.

Section 180.385(1)(a), Stats., recognized the problem inherent in the single application of the insolvency test and achieved flexibility by prohibiting a purchase resulting in a corporation that "is" insolvent or "would * * * be" rendered insolvent. Thus, flexibility is achieved by the statute in its application of the insolvency test to each purchase payment.

When applying the insolvency test at the stage of each payment for a stock repurchase to achieve creditor protection, consistency suggests that the amount of each payment, not the total purchase price, should be component of the determination of solvency. The weight of authority has so applied the tests and we adopt that method of application. That method is in accord with the equity sense insolvency test expressly prescribed by Sec. 180.02(11) and 180.385(1)(a), Stats.

Defendants have not demonstrated insolvency in the equity sense to the trial court or to us. Our review of the corporate financial statements in evidence discloses no arguable claim of insolvency in the equity sense. The only claim of MKS's insolvency made by defendants is premised upon a deduction of the total stock redemption purchase price from the corporate assets, thereby creating a balance sheet negative net worth, although the installment payments of the purchase price are spread over five years. We reject the argument because it applies a bankruptcy rather than equity insolvency test and is contrary to secs. 180.02(11) and 180.385(1)(a), Stats.

The second limitation upon the corporate repurchase of its stock pertinent to this case is the restriction that "the corporation has unreserved and unrestricted earned surplus equal to the cost of such shares." Sec. 180.385(1)(c)2., Stats. * * * Earned surplus is defined in sec. 180.02(11).[8] In this case, the parties do not dispute the amount of earned surplus.

Our review of the record again establishes the following undisputed evidence with respect to paid-up capital stock, retained earnings, and total stockholders' equity.

	12/31 1976	12/31 1977	12/31 1978	5/31 1979
Paid-up Capital Stock	69,400	69,400	69,400	69,400
Retained Earnings	246,409	276,073	317,586	317,584
Current Earnings				31,575
Stockholders' Equity	315,809	345,473	386,986	418,559

We subtract projected payments pursuant to the stock redemption agreement.

8. For the purpose of this case, earned surplus can be considered to be the retained earnings of the corporation.

Retained and Current Earnings Adjusted to Reflect Deducted Installment Payments	276,073	217,586	205,961
Installment Payments Without Interest	100,000	43,200	53,700
Net Retained Earnings	176,073	174,386	152,261

* * *

The same problem arose with the application of the surplus cutoff test that developed in applying the insolvency cutoff test: in the case of an installment purchase, should the surplus test be applied at the time of purchase or at the time cash payment is made? Most cases demonstrate little effort to distinguish between the methods of applying both tests and resolve the question by the easier and more convenient method of applying both tests in the same fashion.

For example, the effect of the Fourth Circuit Court of Appeals' holding in *Mountain State Steel Foundries, Inc. v. Commissioner,* 284 F.2d 737 (1960), was to treat an installment repurchase transaction as if each successive installment constituted an independent purchase transaction by applying the surplus test at the time of each payment. *In re Matthews Construction Co.,* 120 F.Supp. 818 (S.D.Cal.1954), also involved application of the surplus cutoff test and like *Mountain State,* indiscriminately applied the reasoning found in *Robinson v. Wangemann,* 75 F.2d 756 (1935), that a contract of sale was executory until each payment was made in cash, and therefore applied the surplus cutoff test to each installment payment.

Professor Herwitz discusses a number of reasons for applying the surplus to the time of purchase rather than at each installment payment.[10] We agree with his view that the statutory surplus cutoff rule should be applied only once, and at the time of purchase, for the following reasons:

(1) unlike the equity insolvency test, a surplus test does not center upon current liabilities;

(2) unlike the application of the insolvency tests, the surplus test is analogous to a purchase for cash and a loan of the unpaid cash price back to the corporation;

(3) installment application of the surplus test could bar performance of a valid obligation of the corporation to the selling stockholder but permit the corporation to disburse funds to current stockholders;

(4) the statutory requirement that surplus be restricted by such a purchase agreement could be frustrated by a construction that would require restriction only on an installment-by-installment basis and permit

10. [Herwitz, Installment Purchase of Stock: Surplus Limitations, 79 Harv.L.Rev. 303 (1965).]

distributions to shareholders even though the surplus was insufficient to consummate the purchase agreement;

(5) in the manner described in (4), a limited amount of surplus could be used to justify the purchase of an unlimited amount of stock;

(6) when applied to installment payments, the surplus test could be continued indefinitely with current stockholders receiving distributions, putting the selling stockholder in limbo without the status of either creditor or stockholder;

(7) if a default in an installment is compelled by the surplus test, the selling stockholder could possibly obtain a windfall return of all of stock, including the part for which payment had already been made;

(8) a creditor with knowledge of the purchase agreement could be unprotected by installment application of the statutory surplus test limitation, * * *;

(9) if interest has been deducted in computing corporate net income, application of the surplus test upon an installment basis to the interest on the purchase price is unsupportable because it would take interest into account twice;

(10) the unpaid selling stockholder is given no consideration, at least to the extent of undistributed surplus, over the other stockholders who are the beneficiaries of the stock purchase; and

(11) the application of the surplus cutoff test at the outset of an installment purchase would in no way hamper or alter the installment application of the equity insolvency test.

We consider it a futile exercise to attempt to ground our decision upon the subtleties and nuances of semantic lexicography in defining "purchase," "acquisition," and the other acquisitory words of transfer used in the statute. The above reasons persuade us that the application of the surplus cutoff test is required to be timed to the purchase rather than the payment of cash. Such a construction comports with the need for corporate flexibility in acquiring its own stock for legitimate purposes and the protection of creditors and holders of other securities of the corporation.

The Minnesota and Texas Supreme Courts, and the Ninth Circuit Court of Appeals, have taken similar views in *Tracy v. Perkins–Tracy Printing Co.,* 278 Minn. 159, 153 N.W.2d 241 (1967); *Williams v. Nevelow,* 513 S.W.2d 535 (Tex.1974); and *Walsh v. Paterna,* 537 F.2d 329 (9th Cir.1976). Although differing state statutory formulations were involved, like Wisconsin's, the statutes do not specifically resolve the issues presented there or here.

Although it is apparent from the MKS financial statements that application of the surplus cutoff test upon an installment basis would not have precluded specific performance as ordered by the trial court, application of the test at the outset will preclude specific performance upon the basis of the facts as presented to us. However, we note that the stock redemption agreement provides:

(f) *Insufficient Corporate Surplus.* If the Corporation does not have sufficient surplus or retained earnings to permit it to lawfully purchase all of such shares, each of the parties shall promptly take such measures as are required to reduce the capital of the Corporation or to take such other steps as may be necessary in order to enable the Corporation to lawfully purchase and pay for the Decedent's shares.

We vacate the judgment of the circuit court and remand for further proceedings consistent with this opinion. The circuit court is directed to apply the surplus cutoff test to the time of specific performance of the stock redemption agreement if it concludes that the evidence justifies specific performance. Because we adopt an application of the statute which has not heretofore been explicated, we think it is fair to permit the parties to offer current financial data with respect to MKS and the ability of the parties to the redemption agreement to take the necessary steps to enable the corporation to lawfully purchase and pay for the redeemed stock. Such evidence will enable a current evaluation of the propriety of specific performance. In the event the trial court deems specific performance appropriate, it shall make the necessary findings and requirements with regard to providing sufficient earned surplus and assuring solvency as a condition to specific performance.

* * *

Judgment vacated and cause remanded for further proceedings consistent with this opinion.

NOTES

1. From the standpoint of creditors and holders of senior stock, corporate distributions to repurchase shares present the same hazard as dividends. Accordingly, state corporations statutes impose limitations on stock repurchases analogous (but not necessarily identical) to those they place upon dividends. (Recall, the limits on dividends were discussed in Chapter IV.) California and the Revised Model Act take the simplest approach. These statutes place limitations upon "distributions", which the acts define to include cash or property paid to shareholders either as a dividend or in exchange for selling back their stock. Cal. Corp. Code §§ 166, 500–503; M.B.C.A. §§ 1.40(6), 6.40(c). (California, however, relaxes the rules for the redemption of a deceased or disabled stockholder's shares, if the company uses insurance proceeds. Cal. Corp. Code §§ 503.1, 503.2.) More traditional statutes, such as those in Delaware, New York, and the Wisconsin statute dealt with in *Neimark,* contain separate provisions governing repurchases. At first glance, these sections seem to track the respective states' dividend restrictions. For example, Delaware's law generally precludes repurchases when the company's capital is impaired, or when the repurchase will cause the capital to become impaired; put another way, when the amount paid in the repurchase exceeds the amount of the corporation's surplus. Del. Gen. Corp. Law § 160(a)(1). (Recall, Delaware follows this same balance sheet test as a limit on dividends. Del. Gen. Corp. Law § 170(a).) New York adds

to the surplus test, the limit that the company not be or become insolvent when making the repurchase. N.Y. Bus. Corp. Law § 513(a). (This parallels New York's surplus and solvency limits on dividends. N.Y. Bus. Corp. Law § 510.)

It turns out, however, that the traditional statutes allow repurchases to indirectly come out of capital in such a way as to do a complete end run around any protection against shareholders withdrawing their investment before the company pays its debts. This phenomenon stems from the question of how to treat the repurchased shares. Such shares, if not "canceled", are referred to as treasury stock. If the company treats treasury stock just as any other asset, then the repurchase will have no effect upon the corporation's surplus. (The acquisition of a new asset, treasury stock, offsets the decrease of an existing asset, cash, so nothing else on the balance sheet changes.) Since the company still has its surplus under such an approach, it can continue to buy back its shares until it dissipates all its other assets. This result illustrates that treasury stock is really not an asset at all. (The company whose only "asset" consists of stock in itself is worth nothing.) Statutes like Delaware's and New York's implicitly recognize treasury stock is not an asset; otherwise it would make no sense to talk about the purchase impairing capital (purchase of an asset can never impair capital) or coming out of surplus. Hence, the repurchase of stock lowers the firm's net assets by the amount paid out. The real question lies in whether the effect of this decrease in net assets shows up in a reduction of surplus, of capital, or of both. If one were to parallel dividend treatment, the repurchase should leave capital unchanged, and, accordingly, reduce surplus (which is, by definition, the difference between net assets and capital). This would give creditors and senior stockholders an equivalent protection in either type of distribution. From the company's standpoint, such a rule would limit total repurchases to the extent of its surplus. On the other hand, with share repurchases, less stock remains in the hands of the shareholders, and, if capital represents money the company received for outstanding stock, perhaps the repurchase should correspondingly reduce capital as it reduces outstanding stock. Statutes like Delaware's and New York's leave this question substantially to the discretion of the directors. New York's law provides that repurchases do not decrease capital—and hence must reduce surplus—if the company retains the shares as treasury stock. N.Y. Bus. Corp. Law § 515(c). However, the directors may choose to treat the purchase price as coming out of stated capital—in other words, decrease the company's total stated capital by the aggregate par value of the repurchased shares (or whatever greater amount the board fixed as stated capital when the company issued those shares). N.Y. Bus. Corp. Law § 516(a)(4). In this event, the directors must cancel the stock (meaning that the stock reverts to the status of unissued shares). N.Y. Bus. Corp. Law § 515(a), (d). Delaware's statute is similar. It allows the directors to reduce the corporation's capital by retiring (canceling) the shares, or by applying the capital represented by shares toward their repurchase. Del. Gen. Corp. Law § 244(a). Notice, reducing capital by canceling repurchased shares increases or at least preserves the corporation's surplus (since surplus equals the difference between net assets and capital). The company, in turn, can use the surplus to repurchase more shares, and repeat the procedure until it has no more capital or surplus (in other words, its remaining assets equal its debts). Indeed, the New York and Delaware statutes allow the board to short-circuit the process of using the corporation's surplus to repurchase stock, and then replenishing the surplus by canceling the shares, by allowing the board to treat the purchase price as coming directly out of capital. Del. Gen. Corp. Law § 160(a)(1); N.Y. Bus. Corp. Law § 515(a). By way of comparison, California and the Revised Model Act avoid the whole problem, since they do not base their distribution limits on any notion of capital. Moreover, California and the Revised Model Act abolish the concept of treasury shares and, instead, provide that repurchased shares return to the status of unissued stock. Cal. Corp. Code § 510(a); M.B.C.A. § 6.31(a).

2. As *Neimark* illustrates, the problem grows more complicated when the corporation plans to pay for the repurchased shares in installments. The question is when to measure the repurchase against the statutory financial limits—at the time the corporation obtains the shares back in exchange for its promise to pay; at the time it actually makes each installment payment; or at both times. Many statutes (such as the one in *Neimark*) further compound the question by imposing two limits—an equitable solvency and a surplus test. *E.g.,* N.Y. Bus. Corp. Law § 513(a). California and the Revised Model Act also impose both an insolvency and a more general, albeit not a surplus, test. Cal. Corp. Code §§ 500, 501; M.B.C.A. § 6.40(c). While some statutes, such as that in Delaware, do not impose a solvency limit, a repurchase by an insolvent corporation might constitute, as the court in *Neimark* points out, a fraudulent conveyance. The time of measurement, the court held in *Neimark,* need not be the same for these two tests. The end result is that the courts stand divided—with many of the principal cases cited in *Neimark*—both on when to measure solvency and when to measure surplus.

A number of statutes attempt to address the question. California, for example, specifies measurement of both of its tests at the time of the actual payment. Cal. Corp. Code § 166. Moreover, in determining the company's retained earnings or liabilities in order to measure the permissibility of each payment, the California code disregards the company's remaining liability from repurchasing the shares. Cal. Corp. Code §§ 500(b), 502, 503. One exception exists to this rule. The California code applies the tests at the time of purchase if the company issues a negotiable instrument (within the meaning of U.C.C. § 8–102) as evidence of its promise to pay. Cal. Corp. Code § 166. Delaware goes in the other direction. It's statute indicates that corporate obligations exchanged for stock, which do not invade capital when issued, are valid regardless of the situation when paid. Del. Gen. Corp. Law § 160.

From a planning standpoint, both times of measurement present advantages and problems. Measuring all at once the impact of a substantial purchase created the potential failure to meet the surplus limit in *Neimark.*

(To see why, compare the amount of the corporation's retained earnings in December 1976—which the court took to equal the company's earned surplus—against the total amount of the purchase.) Such a result is not unexpected; after all, the reason for installment payments is presumably because an immediate disbursement poses too great a burden on the company. Is there any way for a company to get around this result in a jurisdiction which follows the approach of testing at the time of acquisition? Suppose the parties agree to an installment acquisition, in which the seller surrenders the shares only as the company pays. On the other hand, does this idea create any problems? (Reconsider this question after exploring the tax treatment of share repurchases.) The Revised Model Act, much like the Delaware law, generally measures the effect of the repurchase at the outset. M.B.C.A. § 6.40(e)(1). It allows the parties, however, to avoid the problem of an immediate test by providing that the debt issued for the stock is not payable unless a distribution at the time of each payment would be legal. M.B.C.A. § 6.40(g). While the approach of testing at the time of each payment may save the repurchase initially, it also raises problems for the seller. The opinion in *Neimark* listed some of these in deciding to test surplus at the outset. For example, if the company defaults in mid-stream because it lacks surplus, in what position does this put the seller? The parties may wish to provide for return of the redeemed shares to the seller in this event. (Mechanically, this could entail a pledge of the redeemed shares if held as treasury stock, or, in a jurisdiction like California in which redeemed shares revert to the status of unissued, it could entail an agreement by the company to issue new shares to the seller upon default.) In either event, one problem is that if the corporation returns all the shares, this may be unfair to the company, since it already paid something; if it returns only part, this may be unfair to the seller, who now owns a less powerful block. Moreover, a corporation which wants out of the repurchase could deliberately flunk the surplus test by issuing dividends or by increasing its capital. Is there any way to have the transaction tested only at the outset in a jurisdiction following the time of payment approach? Suppose the company pays for the stock immediately with cash (or property), which the recipient then loans the company (or sells back to it in exchange for installment payments). Alternately, could the seller avoid the hazards of the time of payment test by demanding a security interest in corporate assets? *Compare Matter of National Tile & Terrazzo Co.,* 537 F.2d 329 (9th Cir.1976) (held that the mortgage survives if the corporation had an adequate surplus when it created the debt, even though the debt became unenforceable because of insolvency at the time of payment), *with Reiner v. Washington Plate Glass Co.,* 711 F.2d 414 (D.C.Cir.1983) (held that the security interest fails with the underlying obligation). Still another approach might be to ask the non-selling shareholders to guarantee the corporation's payment.

3. The agreement in *Neimark* called upon the parties to take whatever steps were necessary in order to obtain sufficient surplus for the corporation to legally carry out the repurchase. How could they accomplish this? The contract itself contained one idea; reducing the corporation's capital.

(Since surplus is the difference between net assets and capital, reducing capital increases surplus.) As noted above, canceling repurchased shares provides one mechanism to reduce capital. Corporations statutes often provide other mechanisms as well. For example, many statutes give the board the power to decrease capital until the capital equals the aggregate par value of the outstanding stock. *E.g.*, Del. Gen. Corp. Law § 244(a); N.Y. Bus. Corp. Law § 516(a). Moreover, even the aggregate par value of the outstanding stock is not an immutable barrier below which the company cannot reduce its capital. The directors and shareholders can vote to amend the corporation's articles to lower par value (or change the stock into no-par shares). *E.g.*, Del. Gen. Corp. Law § 242(a)(3); N.Y. Bus. Corp. Law § 801(b)(10), (11). (The amendment might not, in itself, lower capital; but it clears the way for a resolution which does.)

Reducing capital removes this supposed cushion for creditors and senior shareholders. Statutes sometimes contain restrictions upon reductions in capital in order to mitigate this danger. Delaware's law provides that no capital reduction can occur unless the assets remaining are sufficient to pay the corporation's debts. Del. Gen. Corp. Law § 244(b). (This may be rather superfluous, since a reduction in capital cannot create a surplus—thereby allowing a distribution of assets—if assets are less than liabilities; and, in and of itself, reducing capital does not reduce assets.) New York's statute forbids reductions in capital by board resolution below the aggregate liquidation preferences of the outstanding shares. N.Y. Bus. Corp. Law § 516(b). This same limitation does not exist, however, on a reduction in capital through canceling repurchased shares. *See* N.Y. Bus. Corp. Law § 515.

4. Beyond reducing capital, are there any other ways to increase the amount legally available to repurchase stock? The court in *Neimark* stated that on remand the parties could produce current financial data. Does this mean the plaintiff could introduce evidence to show the corporation's assets are worth more than shown on the balance sheet? Recall the conflicting authority cited in Chapter IV regarding the ability to revalue assets for purposes of declaring dividends. See p. 457 *supra*. Alternately, is it possible to combine a cross purchase (which, of course, is not subject to the statutory limits on corporate share repurchases) with a follow-up transaction (say a merger) under which the corporation will become responsible to pay for the purchased shares (or, more precisely, to pay off loans incurred to buy the shares)? Chapter VII will explore this in considering leveraged buy-outs. See pp. 938–951 *infra*.

(ii) Fiduciary Obligations and Securities Law Concerns

Kaplan v. Goldsamt

380 A.2d 556 (Del.Ch.1977).

■ BROWN, VICE CHANCELLOR.

Plaintiff Kaplan, as a shareholder of the defendant American Medicorp, Inc. ("Medicorp") has sued derivatively on behalf of the corporation seeking judgment in the form of money damages or, alternatively, rescission of an agreement and transaction whereby Medicorp, during the spring of 1976, purchased 550,000 shares of its own common stock from the defendant Robert S. Goldsamt for the sum of $5,225,000. * * *

Plaintiff originally based his suit upon the theory that Goldsamt, as a dominant shareholder of Medicorp, was guilty of fraudulent self-dealing in that he used his position to coerce the other members of the Board of approve the purchase of his shares at a price unfair to the corporation. Shortly before trial, however, plaintiff amended his complaint to charge that the defendant directors, while not subservient to Goldsamt, had improperly caused the corporation to buy his shares at an excessive price so as to prevent him from ousting them through a proxy fight and to thereby preserve their respective positions and business relationships with Medicorp. In particular, plaintiff contends that the proxy statement to shareholders which preceded shareholder approval of the purchase was materially false and misleading. Secondly, he contends that the per share price paid to Goldsamt for his stock was sufficiently excessive and unnecessary as to constitute a waste of corporate assets. It is on these latter two contentions that the decision on liability must turn.

* * *

I.

Turning to the facts of the matter, Medicorp was founded by Goldsamt and came into being through his efforts. Although only 38 years of age Goldsamt has already started three companies, one of which (Medicorp) went on the New York Stock Exchange. * * *

Medicorp is in the proprietary hospital business. In other words, it owns and operates hospitals. * * * During the 1960's Goldsamt was one of those who foresaw the business potential in hospital operations engendered through the Medicare program and related federal legislation. * * * Because federal regulations originally allowed a return on goodwill created by the difference between the purchase price and the book, or hard asset value of the hospital acquired, Medicorp was able to grow rapidly during the latter 1960's, and, although revisions in applicable regulations eventually made it less desirable to acquire existing hospitals as a means of expansion, Medicorp has nonetheless risen to its present position wherein it employs some 13,000 persons and ranks among the top three or four proprietary hospital companies in the country. At the pinnacle of its rise, its stock was traded in excess of $40 per share on the New York Stock Exchange.

The change in the law which removed the goodwill advantage theretofore accompanying the acquisition of existing facilities eventually brought about a change in Medicorp's fortunes and dictated a change in its policy. * * * Management decided that Medicorp's future course would be best served if it turned to a policy which centered on the efficient operation of its facilities through the hiring of the best available personnel and the reduction of costs and overhead through a sharing of equipment among its hospitals and the large-lot purchase of supplies and materials. * * *

This change in Medicorp's business approach paralleled a lessening of interest on the part of Goldsamt. He admittedly is not one who is interested in the day-to-day operation of a business—particularly that of Medicorp. Rather Goldsamt's main enthusiasm was directed toward the location and acquisition of properties on behalf of the corporation. With the end of the "acquisition game" brought about by the change in government policy, Goldsamt's interest in Medicorp waned and he began to look about for new ventures. Although he remained a director of Medicorp, he went to Europe for some two years. * * *

On returning from Europe in late 1974, Goldsamt, as well as the other directors, found that Medicorp's fortunes were turning around. To those in management, at least, the corporation's future outlook appeared to be brightening. At the same time its stock was trading at a comparatively low price having reached a low at one point of less than $2 per share. It was felt by all that the stock was trading below its true value. Accordingly, a plan was adopted setting aside a fund to permit the corporation to purchase shares of its own stock on the open market so as to shrink its capital structure. It is within the area of this decision that Goldsamt developed a complete difference of opinion with his fellow members of the board. This difference of opinion is at the core of the present suit.

It was Goldsamt's view that the market price of Medicorp's stock was so low when compared to its actual worth that the corporation should use all possible cash and surplus to buy as much of it as legally possible, at least until such time as the trading price approached true intrinsic value. He considered any other use of available corporate assets to border on business madness. The remaining directors * * *, however, felt differently. They felt that the continued success of the enterprise depended upon the ability to retain key personnel. They believed that to devote all available assets to the acquisition of the corporation's own stock would produce economic stagnation and would conceivably indicate a future corporate policy leaning toward liquidation or sale of assets. It was felt that this type of atmosphere would be likely to cause many able employees to leave and seek positions elsewhere with growing and progressive organizations, thus undermining the very basis on which the existing turnaround in fortune was being accomplished. * * *

This conflict between Goldsamt and the remainder of the Board became irreconcilable. During late 1974 through 1975, the issue was raised by Goldsamt in virtually all board meetings that he attended. As a personal trait, Goldsamt apparently has a penchant for unreserved self-expression that is on a par with his considerable business abilities. He was not above telling the other board members in unflattering terms precisely what he thought of their judgments on the point. During a December 1974 meeting he characterized them as "idiots" because of their proposal to build a new hospital in Louisville, Kentucky rather than to purchase Medicorp stock. As a result the plan was tabled and not approved until several months thereafter. His verbal remonstrations with the Board sometimes carried over to company personnel. As a precautionary measure, the Board eventually decided to change its alternate meeting site from Philadelphia, the home office of the corporation, to New York so as to avoid any adverse consequences on management's morale that Goldsamt's unrestrained airing of his views might have.

* * *

[A] significant meeting of the Board occurred on January 28, 1976. Again there was a discussion as to the cash forecast of the company and as to what to do with it. The subject again generated a fair amount of feeling. On this occasion Goldsamt specifically urged that consideration be given to making a tender offer for a large block of Medicorp stock. The other board members present were opposed to this, primarily because they felt, first, that the stock was worth more than its current selling price and, second, that it was also worth more than the price that would then be required to attract a substantial number of shares through a tender offer. Because they all agreed that they would not tender their own shares under such circumstances, they felt that it would be improper to ask public shareholders to sell their shares for a price considered to be unrealistically low by the Board itself. Goldsamt again made reference to the ultimate possibility of a proxy fight to resolve the impasse.

At the time, Medicorp shares were trading at 6 7/8–7 on the market. During the debate about the advisability of a tender offer, Goldsamt was asked to identify a price at which he thought his recommended tender should be made. His response was $10.00 per share. Later, as the meeting was about to close, someone casually asked Goldsamt if he would be willing to sell his Medicorp holdings for $10.00 per share. He replied that he would. Prior to this time there had been no discussion by anyone concerning the possibility of Goldsamt selling his shares. In fact Goldsamt considered $10.00 to be a woefully inadequate price. His explanation of his impromptu decision is that he was fed up with the thinking of his fellow directors and the he wished no longer to be associated with the Board. In his words,

> "* * * while I thought, frankly, that it was a miserable price, I thought at least I would have control of my own funds, and my history has been rather good with that."

Since Goldsamt was known to change his mind quickly, the Board immediately went into action. On the following day an executive committee of Kemper, Miller and Leiman met with Goldsamt and confirmed that he was indeed willing to sell. Effort was made to have him lower his price (both then and, later, by Leiman individually), but he would not budge on this point. He was then asked if he would be willing to act as a consultant to the corporation and not compete with it for a period of time. Goldsamt was receptive to this. It was then agreed between Miller, Kemper and Leiman that Leiman would research the various questions of law that might be involved and that Kemper would have [the investment banking firm of] Loeb, Rhoades consider the price factor.

On February 3 Leiman and an associate of his firm met with Kemper and one of his partners from Loeb, Rhoades. It was reported that it was the feeling of Loeb, Rhoades that to acquire 550,000 shares other than through the purchase of Goldsamt's block would require a tender offer at a price of about $9.00 per share. To this would have to be added a soliciting dealer fee of $.40 per share, plus expenses of approximately $.10 per share.

On February 5, 1976 a quorum of Medicorp's Board (excluding Goldsamt who thereafter did not participate in discussions concerning the transactions) was convened and, based on reports given by Miller, Kemper and Leiman, and the discussion that followed it was agreed that the purchase of Goldsamt's shares at a price of $5,225,000 along with a five-year noncompetition and consultation agreement at $275,000 was a good opportunity for Medicorp which it could then afford and which would be of benefit to it.

* * *

During the foregoing process the Board was made aware that the New York Stock Exchange felt that the matter should also be submitted to Medicorp's stockholders for approval. The Board did not feel that legally this was necessary, but it understandably agreed to do so. At a Board meeting on March 25 it was further agreed that an opinion in addition to that of Loeb, Rhoades should be obtained. The investment firm of Bache Halsey Stuart, Inc. ("Bache") was contacted and its subsequent opinion concurred with that of Loeb, Rhoades, namely that "it is reasonable to conclude that a tender offer price of $9.00 per share together with estimated fees and expenses of $.50 per share * * * would be required to effectuate a successful tender offer for the purchase of 550,000 shares."

On April 9, 1976 Medicorp's Notice of Annual Meeting and attached Proxy Statement were mailed to its shareholders. The Proxy Statement described the terms of the agreements and in an appendix the agreements themselves were set forth. On May 20 the annual meeting was held and the agreements with Goldsamt were approved by a vote of 81 percent of the shares voting on the proposal. The agreements were consummated on May 21, 1976 whereupon Goldsamt resigned from Medicorp's Board of Directors.

* * *

II.

Plaintiff takes the position that the determination of the price to be paid to Goldsamt for his shares was not based upon any independent opinion as to value. He says that on the contrary, the defendant Board simply paid Goldsamt his asking price because he refused to accept anything less. He suggests that the noncompetition and consultation agreement was something concocted by the Board to make the deal look better, but that actually Goldsamt was paid $10.00 per share because that was his price for removal as a director and influential shareholder. Plaintiff further suggests that the real motivation for this decision was the Board's desire to insure its continuing control of Medicorp rather than to serve the best interests of the corporation and its stockholders. He says that because of these realities of the situation, the proxy statement sent to the shareholders was materially false and misleading in several ways.

To begin with, plaintiff contends that the proxy statement was defective in that it failed to specifically disclose that at the time the corporation was proposing to purchase 550,000 shares from Goldsamt at the stated price of $9.50 per share it was also actively engaged in a program of buying shares on the market from its "little" shareholders at a much lower price. In particular, plaintiff asserts that it was misleading to fail to disclose that on February 5, 1976, the day the Board approved the agreements with Goldsamt, the corporation had purchased 6,000 shares on the market at quotations ranging from 6 7/8 to 7. He likewise feels it improper not to have disclosed that during the week preceding February 5, 1976 the corporation had purchased 64,200 shares on the market at quotations ranging 6 5/8 to 7 1/4. He suggests that such disclosure was required because of the fact that the Board had inside information available to it indicating that the stock was worth more than its trading price, and, relying on *Brophy v. Cities Service Co.,* 31 Del.Ch. 241, 70 A.2d 5 (1949); *S.E.C. v. Texas Gulf Sulphur,* 401 F.2d 833 (2d Cir.1968); and *Gould v. American Hawaiian Steamship Co.,* 351 F.Supp. 853 (D.Del.1972), he contends that it is improper to engage in a purchase of stock based on inside information, the result of which is to treat public shareholders differently than insider shareholders.

This, however, is not persuasive. In the authorities cited the undisclosed information was utilized by insiders to acquire stock for their individual accounts or to obtain a personal gain. That was not the situation here since it was the corporation buying its own stock from an insider based on information which to the Board made it beneficial to the corporation to do so. Moreover, the proxy statement did disclose that between January 1, 1975 and March 30, 1976 Medicorp had purchased on the open market 268,760 shares of its own common stock for an aggregate price of $1,809,163 at per share prices ranging from $1.75 to $8.88. * * * It would seem that any discerning reader could perceive from this that Medicorp was proposing to pay Goldsamt more than the market price and more than it had previously paid for the stock of other shareholders.

Secondly, plaintiff says that the proxy statement artfully misrepresented the roles of Loeb, Rhoades and Bache in arriving at the contract price. He relies on the following language of the proxy statement (with his emphasis supplied):

> "The Company asked Loeb, Rhoades & Co., * * * *to express its judgment* * * * as to the cost of conducting a tender offer for the purchase of 550,000 shares. On February 3, 1976, * * * Loeb Rhoades & Co. advised the Company that *in its judgment,* it would cost the

Company approximately $9.50 per share, or an aggregate of $5,250,000, to conduct a successful public tender offer for the purchase of 550,000 shares of its Common Stock * * * *This judgment* was confirmed by Loeb, Rhoades & Co. on and as of February 5, 1976, when the Board of Directors considered the proposed transactions with Mr. Goldsamt.

"The Board of Directors determined that it was advisable to obtain *an additional opinion* from a second investment banking firm with respect to the cost to the Company of conducting a successful public tender offer for the purchase of 550,000 of its shares. Consequently, the Company requested Bache Halsey Stuart Inc. ('Bache') for *its opinion* in this regard. Bache has advised the Company that, based solely on the market prices at the time *Loeb Rhoades & Co. expressed its judgment* and on *Bache's appraisal* of the market activity of the Company's Common Stock, it is reasonable to conclude that a tender offer price of $9.00 per share, together with estimated fees and expenses of $.50 per share as set forth above, would be required to effectuate a successful public tender offer for the purchase of 550,000 shares. *This opinion* was *confirmed* by Bache on and as of April 7, 1976."

He suggests that the natural inference from this is that the Board arrived at the $9.50 figure based on the independent "judgment" of Loeb, Rhoades and the additional "opinion" of Bache as to the price that would be necessary on February 5, 1976 to acquire 550,000 Medicorp shares through a tender offer, an inference which was false since the Board had already decided to meet the price demanded by Goldsamt regardless of the opinions of the investment banking firms. * * * He relies on the recent decision of *Royal Industries, Inc. v. Monogram Industries, Inc.*, 1976–77 CCH Fed.Sec.L.Rep. ¶ 95,863 (C.D.Ca.1976) as being on all fours in condemning a similar misrepresentation of an investment house evaluation.

Again, however, I feel that in his zeal to establish fraud, plaintiff has elected to read only what suits his purpose. And, if the Court is asked to brand language misleading then as a starting point a plaintiff must be charged with accepting that which it actually says. In this light, a portion of the proxy statement not mentioned by plaintiff discloses the following:

"In reaching its decision concerning the *price proposed to be paid* by the Company to Mr. Goldsamt for the shares, the Board of Directors concluded that it would be desirable *to compare this proposed price with an estimate of the cost to the Company of conducting a successful public tender offer for the purchase of 550,000 shares of its Common Stock,* * * * "(Emphasis added.)

The import of this is that before reaching its final decision on the $9.50 price it proposed to pay Goldsamt, the board deemed it advisable to "compare this proposed price" with an estimate of the cost of conducting a public tender offer for the same amount of shares. In other words, the proxy statement concedes that the board first determined to pay Goldsamt $9.50 before comparing this figure with tender offer estimates from either

Loeb, Rhoades or Bache. Thus, fairly read, it does not represent that the price was reached only as a result of the Bache and Loeb, Rhoades estimates as to a tender offer figure. Since the proxy statement says the contrary to what plaintiff would infer, I cannot conclude it to be misleading in this respect.

In *Royal Industries, Inc. v. Monogram Industries, Inc.* a press release to shareholders indicated that Royal's Board of Directors was "guided" in its decision to oppose Monogram's tender offer by an "evaluation prepared by Dean Witter & Co., Inc., regarding the adequacy of the offer." This was held to be misleading because the evaluation had been prepared "virtually overnight" and without the necessary time and deliberation for a fair evaluation of Monogram's proposed cash offer. More importantly, however, it was factually determined that Royal's Board was not guided by the evaluation, but rather by the defensive and self-serving reactions of the directors and management. Here the challenged message to shareholders was not sent out immediately following an "overnight" evaluation by Loeb, Rhoades. It went to shareholders some two months later. Moreover, as noted previously, the proxy statement here does not indicate that the Board was "guided" by Loeb, Rhoades in reaching its decision in the sense that the judgment of Loeb, Rhoades was the determining factor. Thus, the situations are distinguishable.

Plaintiff also charges that the reasons given in support of the Board's decision to purchase Goldsamt's shares were false and without foundation. In the words of the proxy statement:

> "A further consideration in the Board's determination to purchase the Shares was the continuing differences between Mr. Goldsamt and officers and other directors of the Company over the management policies of the Company. These differences have absorbed valuable time and effort of the Board and management of the company. Accordingly, the Board believes it to be in the best interest of the Company to remove this dissidence and thereby eliminate possible disruption of the Company's activities, unnecessary expense, and damage to its employee relations."

Plaintiff says that the reference to damage to employee relations was misleading since there was no proof that any person had either left Medicorp because of Goldsamt or refused to come with the corporation because of him. He further relies on the failure of the Board to establish any expense caused the corporation by Goldsamt, unnecessary or otherwise. Finally, he points out that the defendants did not show disruption of any business program approved by the majority of the Board. * * *

I find this argument also to be unpersuasive. The evidence clearly indicated a long-festering disagreement between Goldsamt and the other directors as to the business direction Medicorp should take. He was against growth and expansion under the existing circumstances while the others were for it. He was unwilling to accept their majority view. He was outspoken, in his objections and scornful of their decisions. Because of his protestations, approval of the Louisville project was delayed several months. Because of his boardroom and related actions, the site of the directors' meetings was changed to another city for the protection of employee morale. As a stockholder of some magnitude, he represented a force with which to be reckoned so long as he maintained his dissident views. In short, his potential for disruption was there and his past conduct had indicated that he was quite capable of putting it into effect. From the evidence I am convinced that it was because of the immediate past conduct of Goldsamt together with his sometimes abrasive personality and his outspoken minority views as to Medicorp's business goals that prompted the Board to act quickly in accepting his offer to sell his stock and resign as a director. Viewed in light of the existing facts, I cannot find the reasons listed by the Board in the proxy statement to be misleading. Plaintiff's view seems to be that you must permit at least one horse to escape the corral before the expense of fixing the fence to retain the others can be justified.

Finally, plaintiff charges that the proxy statement was misleading in that it failed to disclose that the Board's decision was also prompted by the fact that Goldsamt had "threatened" a proxy fight at both the September 1975 and January 29, 1976 Board meetings. I see no merit in this argument either. * * *

While the potential for a proxy fight exists in any dissident shareholder having considerable stock ownership, this differs from an immediate threat to do battle. I am not convinced from the evidence that a desire to avoid an impending proxy fight as opposed to a desire, among other things, to eliminate the potential expense and disruption of a proxy fight in the future was a critical factor in the Board's decision. Consequently, I cannot conclude that it was a material omission to fail to mention it in the proxy statement.

To summarize this point, while a corporation must adequately inform shareholders as to matters under consideration, the requirement of full disclosure does not mean that a proxy statement must satisfy unreasonable or absolute standards. Many people may disagree as to what should or should not be in such a statement to shareholders, and as to alleged omissions the simple test (sometimes difficult of application) is whether the omitted fact is material.

This long standing view of the Delaware courts comports with the recent expression of the United States Supreme Court in *TSC Industries, Inc. v. Northway, Inc.*, 426 U.S. 438, 96 S.Ct. 2126, 48 L.Ed.2d 757 (1976) wherein it was stated that in order for an omission to be material,

> "* * * there must be a substantial likelihood that the disclosure of the fact would have been viewed by the reasonable investor as having significantly altered the 'total mix' of information made available." Id., 96 S.Ct. at 2133.

Measured against this standard, I view plaintiff's several accusations that the proxy statement was materially false and misleading to be unfounded.

III.

Plaintiff's second point of contention is that even if the proxy statement is not held to have been misleading, the price paid to Goldsamt was far too high and for this reason the corporation is entitled to relief against the individual defendants for having wasted corporate assets. Plaintiff's approach to this is threefold. Through his financial analyst, Carol Goldman, he has offered expert testimony to show, in the opinion of Goldman, first that 550,000 shares of Medicorp stock could have been acquired through a public tender offer at a cost no greater than $8.25 per share; second, that the intrinsic value of Medicorp stock on February 5, 1976 was approximately $7.25 per share; and, third, that through purchases on the market over a period of six to nine months, and while adhering to Securities and Exchange Commission regulations, the corporation could have acquired 550,000 shares of its common stock at an average price of $8.25 per share, even allowing for the gradual increase in price that such a purchase program by the corporation might have occasioned.

In arriving at his tender offer figure, Goldman compared and analyzed tender offers of comparable size and stock price ranges made by other companies over a period extending from April 1974 through mid–1976. He calculated the average premium paid in these comparable tender offers to be 23 percent. Because 550,000 shares of Medicorp would have then represented only 6 percent of its stock float, and because he felt that the lower the percentage of the float sought the lower the premium required to get it, Goldman deemed it appropriate to reduce the 23 percent average to 15 percent in the case of Medicorp. Applying this 15 percent premium to Medicorp's closing price of $6.75 on February 5, 1976 and adding to the product the estimated per share figure of $.50 for expenses involved in making a tender offer, Goldman reasoned that an offered price of $8.25 would have easily attracted 550,000 shares from the public investors. * * *

As to the intrinsic value analysis, plaintiff relies upon *Gibbons v. Schenley Industries, Inc.*, Del.Ch., 339 A.2d 460 (1975) and *In re Olivetti Underwood Corporation*, Del.Ch., 246 A.2d 800 (1968) for the proposition that market price should be given at least a 50 percent weight factor. Starting from this Goldman then discounted Medicorp's net asset book value from $16.79 to $5.88 by eliminating an included goodwill figure of $10.91. He did so based on the knowledge that both the federal government and the State of California (where 25 percent of Medicorp's beds are located) were challenging the amount of goodwill claimed by Medicorp for the purpose of receiving payment under medicare and medicaid programs. Goldman further concluded that Medicorp's price/earning ratio should be 5.9x7 based on a 25 percent discount from the industry average. This price/earnings multiple of 5.9 he applied against earnings of $1.24 realized for a trailing twelve-month period. From all this he concluded that the intrinsic value of Medicorp stock on February 5, 1976 was not more than $7.25 per share.

The open market purchase figure was derived by an examination of the actual trading price for Medicorp stock over the six-to-nine-month period subsequent to February 5, 1976.

* * *

In opposition to the foregoing, defendants offered the testimony of their own expert, Frederick Frank, a partner in the New York investment banking firm of Lehman Brothers. * * *

As to intrinsic value, Frank considered it unrealistic to entirely discount the goodwill element so as to ascribe to Medicorp a net asset book value of $5.88 per share. In the area of price earnings evaluation, Frank chose to work with "normalized earnings" and, relying upon elements particular to the proprietary hospital industry, he concluded that based on factors existing in early 1976 it would have been appropriate to anticipate annual earnings for Medicorp of between $1.49 and $1.66 per share. (Medicorp's Board chose to base its future plans on anticipated earnings for 1976 of $1.61 per share, a figure which proved to be low in view of actual 1976 earnings of $1.71 per share.) Frank questioned Goldman's basis for arriving at his price/earnings multiple since Goldman included companies not strictly in the proprietary hospital business in deriving his average industry multiple. Using the multiple of the composite price/earnings ratio of the three leading companies which were in the same business as Medicorp (which companies were also utilized by Goldman in his comparisons), and discounting it 10 percent because of a comparison of Medicorp to them, Frank concluded that a proper price/earnings multiple for Medicorp would have been 8.8x7 which, applied against his earnings estimates of $1.49 to $1.66, would have indicated value of $13.11 to $14.61 per share in February 1976 as opposed to Goldman's calculation of $7.25. * * *

Without further belaboring detail, Frank was also of the opinion that Loeb, Rhoades' estimated tender offer price was reasonable under the circumstances, as was the Board's assumption that on February 5, 1976, 550,000 shares could not have been purchased on the market within a reasonable time at ascertainable prices.

No doubt the foregoing appears complicated, particularly to those not trained in the area of financial and market analysis. At the same time it illustrates that all such opinions depend upon the subjective approach taken by those rendering them. This, of course, highlights the issue here. The question for determination is not whether the stock actually could have been acquired less expensively on the market or through a tender offer. The issue is whether on February 5, 1976 the individual defendants exercised honest and reasonable judgment in agreeing upon the $9.50 per share figure in view of all the circumstances.

Defendants, relying on *Schiff v. RKO Pictures Corp., supra,* take the position that in view of the approval of the transaction by the shareholders of Medicorp, the burden is on the plaintiff to demonstrate improper conduct on their part. At the same time it has been held that a waste of corporate assets cannot be ratified by stockholders, except by unanimous vote. * * * As summarized as *Folk, The Delaware General Corporation Law,* § 144 at 84–85 (1972):

> "* * * the validating effect of (stockholder) ratification would be overturned only by the objectors' demonstrating that the transaction amounted to waste, which, as previously indicated, could not be effectively ratified. But if in fact waste of assets is alleged, the court will examine a transaction, notwithstanding independent stockholder ratification, but it will limit its scrutiny to determining whether the consideration is so inadequate that no person of sound, ordinary business judgment would deem it worth what the corporation paid; on this test the court will uphold the transaction if ordinary businessmen might differ on the sufficiency of its terms."
>
> * * * Applying this test, the transaction here must be upheld.

In the area of valuation, wide discretion is allowed to directors, and as long as they appear to act in good faith, with honest motives, and for honest ends, the exercise of their discretion will not be interfered with by the courts. * * *

By statute a director is fully protected in relying in good faith on reports to the corporation made by an appraiser selected with reasonable case. 8 *Del.C.* § 141(e). While it was admittedly predisposed to do so, the Board here did not enter into the agreement with Goldsamt until it first obtained a comparison from Loeb, Rhoades as to the likely cost of a tender offer. Before it finally submitted the matter to the shareholders it obtained a similar opinion from Bache. * * * To the extent that the Board relied upon these reports in confirming its decision to go through with the Goldsamt transaction, I fail to see how the individual members can be held accountable for improper conduct.

Furthermore, in making his arguments as to the waste of assets, plaintiff seems to take financial matters out of context and attempts to limit the issue to one of value alone. In so doing, he ignores the other considerations which motivated the Board as discussed previously herein. He ignores also the fact that the Board did not pay Goldsamt his precise asking price of $10.00 per share, but rather that it exacted from him an agreement not to compete with the corporation he founded and to be available for consultation purposes for a period of five years. * * *

While plaintiff would have the cases distinguished for factual reasons, I am of the opinion that the decision here is controlled by the principal set forth in *Cheff v. Mathes,* Del.Supr., 41 Del.Ch. 494, 199 A.2d 548 (1964) and *Kors v. Carey,* 39 Del.Ch. 47, 158 A.2d 136 (1960). These cases stand for the proposition that the use of corporate funds to acquire the shares of a dissident stockholder faction is a proper exercise of business judgment where it is done to eliminate what appears to be a clear threat to the future business or the existing, successful business policy of a company and is not accomplished for the sole or primary purpose of perpetuating the control of management. In so doing, the fact that a price paid is in excess of market does not necessarily make the transaction improper.

* * *

In final analysis, I am satisfied that the defendant members of the Board of Directors acted in good faith and based upon reasonable investigation and advice under the circumstances. Viewed overall, I do not find that the price paid to Goldsamt for his 550,000 shares and the five-year noncompetition and consultation agreement to have been a waste of corporate assets.

Accordingly, for the reasons herein given, I conclude that the allegations of the amended complaint have not been established. Judgment will be entered in favor of the defendants. * * *

Donahue v. Rodd Electrotype Company of New England, Inc.

367 Mass. 578, 328 N.E.2d 505 (1975).

■ TAURO, CHIEF JUSTICE.

The plaintiff, Euphemia Donahue, a minority stockholder in the Rodd Electrotype Company of New England, Inc. (Rodd Electrotype), a Massachusetts corporation, brings this suit against the directors of Rodd Electrotype, Charles H. Rodd, Frederick I. Rodd and Mr. Harold E. Magnuson, against Harry C. Rodd, a former director, officer, and controlling stockholder of Rodd Electrotype and against Rodd Electrotype (hereinafter called defendants). The plaintiff seeks to rescind Rodd Electrotype's purchase of Harry Rodd's shares in Rodd Electrotype and to compel Harry Rodd "to repay to the corporation the purchase price of said shares, $36,000, together with interest from the date of purchase." The plaintiff alleges that the defendants caused the corporation to purchase the shares in violation of their fiduciary duty to her, a minority stockholder of Rodd Electrotype.

The trial judge, after hearing oral testimony, dismissed the plaintiff's bill on the merits. * * *

The case is before us on the plaintiff's application for further appellate review.

* * *

The evidence may be summarized as follows: In 1935, the defendant, Harry C. Rodd, began his employment with Rodd Electrotype, then styled the Royal Electrotype Company of New England, Inc. (Royal of New England). At that time, the company was a wholly-owned subsidiary of a Pennsylvania corporation, the Royal Electrotype Company (Royal Electrotype). Mr. Rodd's advancement within the company was rapid. The following year he was elected a director, and, in 1946, he succeeded to the position of general manager and treasurer.

In 1936, the plaintiff's husband, Joseph Donahue (now deceased), was hired by Royal of New England as a "finisher" of electrotype plates. His duties were confined to operational matters within the plant. Although he ultimately achieved the positions of plant superintendent (1946) and corporate vice president (1955), Donahue never participated in the "management" aspect of the business.

In the years preceding 1955, the parent company, Royal Electrotype, made available to Harry Rodd and Joseph Donahue shares of the common stock in its subsidiary, Royal of New England. Harry Rodd took advantage of the opportunities offered to him and acquired 200 shares for $20 a share. Joseph Donahue, at the suggestion of Harry Rodd, who hoped to interest Donahue in the business, eventually obtained fifty shares in two twenty-five share lots priced at $20 a share. The parent company at all times retained 725 of the 1,000 outstanding shares. One Lawrence W. Kelley owned the remaining twenty-five shares.

In June of 1955, Royal of New England purchased all 725 of its shares owned by its parent company. * * * Lawrence W. Kelley's twenty-five shares were also purchased at this time * * *. A substantial portion of Royal of New England's cash expenditures was loaned to the company by Harry Rodd, who mortgaged his house to obtain some of the necessary funds.

The stock purchases left Harry Rodd in control of Royal of New England. Early in 1955, before the purchases, he had assumed the presidency of the company. His 200 shares gave him a dominant eighty percent interest. Joseph Donahue, at this time, was the only minority stockholder.

Subsequent events reflected Harry Rodd's dominant influence. In June, 1960, more than a year after the last obligation to Royal Electrotype had been discharged, the company was renamed the Rodd Electrotype Company of New England, Inc. In 1962, Charles H. Rodd, Harry Rodd's son (a defendant here), who had long been a company employee working in the plant, became corporate vice president. In 1963, he joined his father on the board of directors. In 1964, another son, Frederick I. Rodd (also a defendant), replaced Joseph Donahue as plant superintendent. By 1965, Harry Rodd had evidently decided to reduce his participation in corporate management. That year Charles Rodd succeeded him as president and general manager of Rodd Electrotype.

From 1959 to 1967, Harry Rodd pursued what may fairly be termed a gift program by which he distributed the majority of his shares equally among his two sons and his daughter, Phyllis E. Mason. Each child received thirty-nine shares. Two shares were returned to the corporate treasury in 1966.

We come now to the events of 1970 which form the grounds for the plaintiff's complaint. In May of 1970, Harry Rodd was seventy-seven years old. The record indicates that for some time he had not enjoyed the best of health and that he had undergone a number of operations. His sons wished him to retire. Mr. Rodd was not averse to this suggestion. However, he insisted that some financial arrangements be made with respect to his remaining eighty-one shares of stock. A number of conferences ensued. Harry Rodd and Charles Rodd (representing the company) negotiated terms of purchase for forty-five shares which, Charles Rodd testified, would reflect the book value and liquidating value of the shares.

A special board meeting convened on July 13, 1970. As the first order of business, Harry Rodd resigned his directorship of Rodd Electrotype. The remaining incumbent directors, Charles Rodd and Mr. Harold E. Magnuson (clerk of the company and a defendant and defense attorney in the instant suit), elected Frederick Rodd to replace his father. The three directors then authorized Rodd Electrotype's president (Charles Rodd) to execute an agreement between Harry Rodd and the company in which the company would purchase forty-five shares for $800 a share ($36,000).

* * *

Harry Rodd completed divestiture of his Rodd Electrotype stock in the following year. As was true of his previous gifts, his later divestments gave equal representation to his children. Two shares were sold to each child on July 15, 1970, for $800 a share. Each was given ten shares in March, 1971. Thus, in March, 1971, the shareholdings in Rodd Electrotype were apportioned as follows: Charles Rodd, Frederick Rodd and Phyllis Mason each held fifty-one shares; the Donahues held fifty shares.

A special meeting of the stockholders of the company was held on March 30, 1971. At the meeting, Charles Rodd, company president and general manager, reported the tentative results of an audit conducted by the company auditors and reported generally on the company events of the year. For the first time, the Donahues learned that the corporation had purchased Harry Rodd's shares. According to the minutes of the meeting, following Charles Rodd's report, the Donahues raised questions about the purchase. They then voted against a resolution, ultimately adopted by the remaining stockholders, to approve Charles Rodd's report. * * *

A few weeks after the meeting, the Donahues, acting through their attorney, offered their shares to the corporation on the same terms given to Harry Rodd. Mr. Harold E. Magnuson replied by letter that the corporation would not purchase the shares and was not in a financial position to do so.[10] This suit followed.

In her argument before this court, the plaintiff has characterized the corporate purchase of Harry Rodd's shares as an unlawful distribution of corporate assets to controlling stockholders. She urges that the distribution constitutes a breach of the fiduciary duty owed by the Rodds, as controlling stockholders, to her, a minority stockholder in the enterprise, because the Rodds failed to accord her an equal opportunity to sell her shares to the corporation. The defendants reply that the stock purchase was within the

10. Between 1965 and 1969, the company offered to purchase the Donahue shares for amounts between $2,000 and $10,000 ($40 to $200 a share). The Donahues rejected these offers.

powers of the corporation and met the requirements of good faith and inherent fairness imposed on a fiduciary in his dealings with the corporation. They assert that there is no right to equal opportunity in corporate stock purchases for the corporate treasury. For the reasons hereinafter noted, we agree with the plaintiff and reverse the decree of the Superior Court. However, we limit the applicability of our holding to "close corporations," as hereinafter defined. Whether the holding should apply to other corporations is left for decision in another case, on a proper record.

A. *Close Corporations.* * * * We deem a close corporation to the typified by: (1) a small number of stockholders; (2) no ready market for the corporate stock; and (3) substantial majority stockholder participation in the management, direction and operations of the corporation.

* * *

Because of the fundamental resemblance of the close corporation to the partnership, the trust and confidence which are essential to this scale and manner of enterprise, and the inherent danger to minority interests in the close corporation, we hold that stockholders in the close corporation owe one another substantially the same fiduciary duty in the operation of the enterprise that partners owe to one another.

* * *

B. *Equal Opportunity in a Close Corporation.* Under settled Massachusetts law, a domestic corporation, unless forbidden by statute, has the power to purchase its own shares. * * * When the corporation reacquiring its own stock is a close corporation, the purchase is subject to the additional requirement, in the light of our holding in this opinion, that the stockholders, who, as directors or controlling stockholders, caused the corporation to enter into the stock purchase agreement, must have acted with the utmost good faith and loyalty to the other stockholders.

To meet this test, if the stockholder whose shares were purchased was a member of the controlling group, the controlling stockholders must cause the corporation to offer each stockholder an equal opportunity to sell a ratable number of his shares to the corporation at an identical price.[24] Purchase by the corporation confers substantial benefits on the members of the controlling group whose shares were purchased. These benefits are not available to the minority stockholders if the corporation does not also offer them an opportunity to sell their shares. The controlling group may not, consistent with its strict duty to the minority, utilize its control of the corporation to obtain special advantages and disproportionate benefit from its share ownership. * * *

The benefits conferred by the purchase are twofold: (1) provision of a market for shares; (2) access to corporate assets for personal use. By

24. Of course, a close corporation may purchase shares from one stockholder without offering the others an equal opportunity if all other stockholders give advance consent to the stock purchase arrangements through acceptance of an appropriate provision in the articles of organization, the corporate by-laws * * * or a stockholder's agreement. * * *

definition, there is no ready market for shares of a close corporation. The purchase creates a market for shares which previously had been unmarketable. It transforms a previously illiquid investment into a liquid one. If the close corporation purchases shares only from a member of the controlling group, the controlling stockholder can convert his shares into cash at a time when none of the other stockholders can. Consistent with its strict fiduciary duty, the controlling group may not utilize its control of the corporation to establish an exclusive market in previously unmarketable shares from which the minority stockholders are excluded. * * *

The purchase also distributes corporate assets to the stockholder whose shares were purchased. Unless an equal opportunity is given to all stockholders, the purchase of shares from a member of the controlling group operates as a *preferential* distribution of assets. In exchange for his shares, he receives a percentage of the contributed capital and accumulated profits of the enterprise. The funds he so receives are available for his personal use. The other stockholders benefit from no such access to corporate property and cannot withdraw their shares of the corporate profits and capital in this manner unless the controlling group acquiesces. Although the purchase price for the controlling stockholder's shares may seem fair to the corporation and other stockholders under the tests established in the prior case law * * *, the controlling stockholder whose stock has been purchased has still received a relative advantage over his fellow stockholders, inconsistent with his strict fiduciary duty—an opportunity to turn corporate funds to personal use.

The rule of equal opportunity in stock purchases by close corporations provides equal access to these benefits for all stockholders. We hold that, in any case in which the controlling stockholders have exercised their power over the corporation to deny the minority such equal opportunity, the minority shall be entitled to appropriate relief.

C. *Application of the Law to this Case.* We turn now to the application of the learning set forth above to the facts of the instant case.

The strict standard of duty is plainly applicable to the stockholders in Rodd Electrotype. Rodd Electrotype is a close corporation. Members of the Rodd and Donahue families are the sole owners of the corporation's stock. * * * The shares have not been traded, and no market for them seems to exist. Harry Rodd, Charles Rodd, Frederick Rodd, William G. Mason (Phyllis Mason's husband), and the plaintiff's husband all worked for the corporation. The Rodds have retained the paramount management positions.

Through their control of these management positions and of the majority of the Rodd Electrotype stock, the Rodds effectively controlled the corporation. In testing the stock purchase from Harry Rodd against the applicable strict fiduciary standard, we treat the Rodd family as a single controlling group. We reject the defendants' contention that the Rodd family cannot be treated as a unit for this purpose. From the evidence, it is clear that the Rodd family was a close-knit one with strong community of interest. * * * Harry Rodd had hired his sons to work in the family business, Rodd Electrotype. As he aged, he transferred portions of his stock holdings to his children. Charles Rodd and Frederick Rodd were given positions of responsibility in the business as he withdrew from active management. In these circumstances, it is realistic to assume that appreciation, gratitude, and filial devotion would prevent the younger Rodds from opposing a plan which would provide funds for their father's retirement.

Moreover, a strong motive of interest requires that the Rodds be considered a controlling group. When Charles Rodd and Frederick Rodd were called on to represent the corporation in its dealings with their father, they must have known that further advancement within the corporation and benefits would follow their father's retirement and the purchase of his stock. The corporate purchase would take only forty-five of Harry Rodd's eighty-one shares. The remaining thirty-six shares were to be divided among Harry Rodd's children in equal amounts by gift and sale. Receipt of their portion of the thirty-six shares and purchase by the corporation of forty-five shares would effectively transfer full control of the corporation to Frederick Rodd and Charles Rodd, if they chose to act in concert with each other or if one of them chose to ally with his sister. Moreover, Frederick Rodd was the obvious successor to his father as director and corporate treasurer when those posts became vacant after his father's retirement. Failure to complete the corporate purchase (in other words, impeding their father's retirement plan) would have delayed, and perhaps have suspended indefinitely, the transfer of these benefits to the younger Rodds. They could not be expect to oppose their father's wishes in this matter.

On its face, then, the purchase of Harry Rodd's shares by the corporation is a breach of the duty which the controlling stockholders, the Rodds, owed to the minority stockholders, the plaintiff and her son. The purchase distributed a portion of the corporate assets to Harry Rodd, a member of the controlling group, in exchange for his shares. The plaintiff and her son were not offered an equal opportunity to sell their shares to the corporation. In fact, their efforts to obtain an equal opportunity were rebuffed by the corporate representative. * * *

Because of the foregoing, we hold that the plaintiff is entitled to relief. Two forms of suitable relief are set out hereinafter. The judge below is to enter an appropriate judgment. The judgment may require Harry Rodd to remit $36,000 with interest at the legal rate from July 15, 1970, to Rodd Electrotype in exchange for forty-five shares of Rodd Electrotype treasury stock. This, in substance, is the specific relief requested in the plaintiff's bill of complaint. * * * In the alternative, the judgment may require Rodd Electrotype to purchase all of the plaintiff's shares for $36,000 without interest. In the circumstances of this case, we view this as the equal opportunity which the plaintiff should have received. Harry Rodd's retention of thirty-six shares, which were to be sold and given to his children within a year of the Rodd Electrotype purchase, cannot disguise the fact that the corporation acquired one hundred percent of that portion of his holdings (forty-five shares) which he did not intend his children to own.

The plaintiff was entitled to have one hundred percent of her forty-five shares similarly purchased.

The final decree, in so far as it dismissed the bill as to Harry C. Rodd, Frederick I. Rodd, Charles J. Rodd, Mr. Harold E. Magnuson and Rodd Electrotype Company of New England, Inc., and awarded costs, is reversed. The case is remanded to the Superior Court for entry of judgment in conformity with this opinion.

* * *

Zahn v. Transamerica Corporation

162 F.2d 36 (3d Cir.1947).

■ BIGGS, CIRCUIT JUDGE.

Zahn, a holder of a Class A common stock of Axton–Fisher Tobacco Company, a corporation of Kentucky, sued Transamerica Corporation, a Delaware company, on his own behalf and on behalf of all stockholders similarly situated, in the District Court of the United States for the District of Delaware. His complaint as amended asserts that Transamerica caused Axton–Fisher to redeem its Class A stock at $80.80 per share on July 1, 1943, instead of permitting the Class A stockholders to participate in the assets on the liquidation of their company in June, 1944. He alleges in brief that if the Class A stockholders had been allowed to participate in the assets on liquidation of Axton–Fisher and had received their respective shares of the assets, he and the other Class A stockholders would have received $240 per share instead of $80.80. * * * Transamerica filed a motion to dismiss. The court below granted the motion holding that Zahn had failed to state a cause of action. * * * He appealed.

The facts follow as appear from the pleadings, which recite provisions of Axton–Fisher's charter. Prior to April 30, 1943, Axton–Fisher had authorized and outstanding three classes of stock, designated respectively as preferred stock, Class A stock and Class B stock. * * * Upon liquidation of the company and the payment of the sums required by the preferred stock, the Class A stock was entitled to share with the Class B stock in the distribution of the remaining assets, but the Class A stock was entitled to receive twice as much per share as the Class B stock.

Each share of Class A stock was convertible at the option of the shareholder into one share of Class B stock. All or any of the shares of Class A stock were callable by the corporation at any quarterly dividend date upon sixty days' notice to the shareholders, at $60 per share with accrued dividends. * * *

[Starting in 1941, Transamerica began purchasing Axton–Fisher stock. By] the end of May, 1944 Transamerica owned virtually all of the outstanding Class B stock of Axton–Fisher. Since May 16, 1941, Transamerica had control of and had dominated the management, directorate, financial policies, business and affairs of Axton–Fisher. Since the date last stated

Transamerica had elected a majority of the board of directors of Axton–Fisher. These individuals are in large part officers or agents of Transamerica.

In the fall of 1942 and in the spring of 1943 Axton–Fisher possessed as its principal asset leaf tobacco which had cost it about $6,361,981. This asset was carried on Axton–Fisher's books in that amount. The value of leaf tobacco had risen sharply and, to quote the words of the complaint, "unbeknown to the public holders of * * * Class A common stock of Axton–Fisher, but known to Transamerica, the market value of * * * [the] tobacco had, in March and April of 1943, attained the huge sum of about $20,000,000."

The complaint then alleges the gist of the plaintiff's grievance, viz., that Transamerica, knowing of the great value of the tobacco which Axton–Fisher possessed, conceived a plan to appropriate the value of the tobacco to itself by redeeming the Class A stock at the price of $60 a share plus accrued dividends, the redemption being made to appear as if "incident to the continuance of the business of Axton–Fisher as a going concern," and thereafter, the redemption of the Class A stock being completed, to liquidate Axton–Fisher; that this would result, after the disbursal of the sum required to be paid to the preferred stock, in Transamerica gaining for itself most of the value of the warehouse tobacco. The complaint further alleges that in pursuit of this plan Transamerica, by a resolution of the Board of Directors of Axton–Fisher on April 30, 1943, called the Class A stock at $60 and, selling a large part of the tobacco to Phillip–Morris Company, Ltd., Inc., together with substantially all of the other assets of Axton–Fisher, thereafter liquidated Axton–Fisher, paid off the preferred stock and pocketed the balance of the proceeds of the sale. * * *

Assuming as we must that the allegations of the complaint are true, it will be observed that agents or representatives of Transamerica constituted Axton–Fisher's board of directors at the times of the happening of the events complained of, and that Transamerica was Axton–Fisher's principal and controlling stockholder at such times. It will be observed also that jurisdiction in the suit at bar is based upon diversity of citizenship and jurisdictional amount. * * *

* * * The law of Kentucky determines the existence of fiduciary duty, or the lack of it, between Transamerica (as the board of directors of Axton–Fisher, as its officership or as its controlling stockholder) and Axton–Fisher's minority Class A stockholders.

* * *

The circumstances of the case at bar are *sui generis* and we can find no Kentucky decision squarely in point. In our opinion, however, the law of Kentucky imposes upon the directors of a corporation or upon those who are in charge of its affairs by virtue of majority stock ownership or otherwise the same fiduciary relationship in respect to the corporation and to its stockholders as is imposed generally by the laws of Kentucky's sister States.

* * *

It is clear that under the law of Kentucky the fiduciary relationship of directors is such that a court of equity will not permit them to make a profit of their trust and that directors of a corporation are required to manage and conduct their trust so as to realize whatever profit may accrue in the course of the business for the benefit of their cestuis que trust.

It is appropriate to emphasize at this point that the right to call the Class A stock for redemption was confided by the charter of Axton–Fisher to the directors and not to the stockholders of that corporation. We must also re-emphasize the statement of the court in *Haldeman v. Haldeman,* [176 Ky. 635, 197 S.W. 376], * * * that there is a radical difference when a stockholder is voting strictly as a stockholder and when voting as a director; that when voting as stockholder he may have the legal right to vote with a view of his own benefits and to represent himself only; but that when he votes as a director he represents all the stockholders in the capacity of a trustee for them and cannot use his office as a director for his personal benefit at the expense of the stockholders.

Two theories are presented on one of which the case at bar must be decided: One, vigorously asserted by Transamerica * * * is that the board of directors of Axton–Fisher, whether or not dominated by Transamerica, the principal Class B stockholder, at any time and for any purpose, might call the Class A stock for redemption; the other, asserted with equal vigor by Zahn, is that the board of directors of Axton–Fisher as fiduciaries were not entitled to favor Transamerica, the Class B stockholder, by employing the redemption provisions of the charter for its benefit.

* * *

The difficulty in accepting Transamerica's contentions in the case at bar is that the directors of Axton–Fisher, if the allegations of the complaint be accepted as true, were the instruments of Transamerica, were directors voting in favor of their special interest, that of Transamerica, could not and did not exercise an independent judgment in calling the Class A stock, but made the call for the purpose of profiting their true principal, Transamerica. In short a puppet-puppeteer relationship existed between the directors of Axton–Fisher and Transamerica.

The act of the board of directors in calling the Class A stock, an act which could have been legally consummated by a disinterested board of directors, was here effected at the direction of the principal Class B stockholder in order to profit it. Such a call is voidable in equity at the instance of a stockholder injured thereby. It must be pointed out that under the allegations of the complaint there was no reason for the redemption of the Class A stock to be followed by the liquidation of Axton–Fisher except to enable the Class B stock to profit at the expense of the Class A stock. As has been hereinbefore stated the function of the call was confided to the board of directors by the charter and was not vested by the charter in the stockholders of any class. It was the intention of the framers of Axton–Fisher's charter to require the board of directors to act disinterestedly if that body called the Class A stock, and to make the call with a due regard for its fiduciary obligations. If the allegations of the complaint be proved, it follows that the directors of Axton–Fisher, the instruments of Transamerica, have been derelict in that duty. Liability which flows from the dereliction must be imposed upon Transamerica which, under the allegations of the complaint, constituted the board of Axton–Fisher and controlled it.[14]

* * *

The judgment will be reversed.

NOTES

1. Two groups of stockholders might complain about a corporation's acquisition of its own shares. *Kaplan* and *Donahue* involve objections by those left out of the purchase. Their claims generally pursue any of three legal theories. The most straightforward occurs when the directors cause the company to purchase shares from themselves. This constitutes an interested director transaction, and the directors must validate it by meeting the applicable common law or statutory guidelines. Generally, this entails either approval, after full disclosure, by a vote of the disinterested members of the board, approval, after full disclosure, by a shareholder vote, or proof by the directors that the transaction was fair to the corporation. *E.g.,* Cal. Corp. Code § 310; Del. Gen. Corp. Law § 144; N.Y. Bus. Corp. Law § 713; M.B.C.A. §§ 8.60–8.63. Note, these statutes vary as to precisely what disclosure they require, how many of the disinterested directors must vote to approve, whether the votes of interested shareholders count, and whether fairness remains at issue even with disinterested approval. More-

14. The circumstances alleged in the case at bar are suggestive of those which were before the Court of Appeals for the Seventh Circuit in *Lebold v. Inland Steel Co.,* [125 F.2d 369 (7th Cir.1941)]. In the *Lebold* case the majority stockholders forced the dissolution of the corporation and thereafter themselves continued the highly profitable business which had belonged to the corporation. This conduct of the majority stockholders resulted in their acquiring the share of the profits of the corporate business to which the minority would have been entitled had the corporation continued in existence. The dissolution of the company was carried out precisely in the manner required by the law of West Virginia.

District Judge Lindley, speaking for the court, stated in part, 125 F.2d at pages 373, 374, "What defendant might have accomplished under color of the West Virginia statute was discontinuance of the business. What it did, was to take, through form of a sale, the physical assets and the entire business of the Steamship Company. Whether we stamp the happenings as dissolution or with some other name, equity looks to the essential character and result to determine whether there has been faithlessness and fraud upon the part of the fiduciary. However proper a plan may be legally, a majority stockholder can not, under its color, appropriate a business belonging to a corporation to the detriment of the minority stockholder. The so-called dissolution was a mere device by means of which defendant appropriated for itself the transportation business of the Steamship Company to the detriment of plaintiffs. * * *"

over, as the *Kaplan* opinion states, even with disinterested approval, a grossly excessive price remains subject to a challenge as "waste". From a planning standpoint, examine the steps taken in *Kaplan* which helped validate the purchase from a director there. Along these lines, notice the care which must go into disclosure before a shareholder vote, in order to preclude claims, like Kaplan's, that the disclosure was misleading.

Kaplan illustrates a second claim often made when the corporation purchases shares of an obstreperous minority stockholder. It should go almost without saying that directors cannot have the corporation repurchase shares for no business purpose, but simply to keep themselves in power. *E.g., Bennett v. Propp,* 41 Del.Ch. 14, 187 A.2d 405 (1962). On the other hand, as the court in *Kaplan* states, Delaware and other jurisdictions have allowed purchases when the dissident shareholder posed some threat to the future business or successful practices of the company. *But see* N.Y. Bus. Corp. Law § 513(c) (limiting "greenmail" payments without shareholder vote). Application of the Delaware approach entails difficult questions of proof, and the wisdom of such a rule has provoked considerable controversy. The problem before the corporate counsel asked to advise on this transaction, however, is different, albeit no less troubling. To the directors he or she must deal with, the threat to corporate welfare posed by the dissident shareholder may be obvious. What is the obligation, however, of the company's attorney to his or her client (which is the corporation) in this instance? On the other hand, does this obligation necessarily conflict with giving advice which may be in the individual directors' long range best interest—even if not what they may immediately wish to hear? Incidentally, in *Kaplan,* what danger to corporate welfare precisely did Goldsamt pose? Along these lines, can the business need for harmonious relations among the stockholders vary with the size of the corporation? Chapter VII will further explore the use of corporate stock repurchases as a defensive response to attempts to acquire control of a corporation.

The third and most far reaching challenge is to insist the corporation must give all its stockholders an equal opportunity to sell back their shares whenever the company repurchases from any of them. *Donahue* accepted this sort of approach in cases when a closely-held corporation repurchases stock from a controlling shareholder. *But see Nixon v. Blackwell,* 626 A.2d 1366 (Del.1993) (rejecting an equal opportunity rule for repurchases by closely held corporations). Will this apply to repurchases from a *minority* shareholder in a closely-held firm? What is the impact of this approach upon the company's exercise of its option (or fulfillment of its obligation) under a buy-out agreement? See footnote 24 of the *Donahue* opinion. Courts generally have been unwilling to find any obligation for a widely-held company to give all its stockholders an equal opportunity to sell back their shares. *E.g., Karfunkel v. USLIFE Corp.,* 116 Misc.2d 841, 455 N.Y.S.2d 937 (1982).

2. The second group of stockholders who might challenge a corporate repurchase are those who sell back their shares. *Zahn* raises both of their two possible grounds for complaint. The selling stockholders may claim the

corporation (or its managers or controlling shareholders) misled them into selling their shares, either through misstatements or non-disclosure. Recall *Rochez Bros. Inc. v. Rhoades,* reprinted earlier in this chapter. (In *Zahn,* the failure to disclose the increased liquidation value of the company presumably lulled the "A" stockholders into not converting to "B" shares.)

The more difficult claim occurs when (as in *Zahn*) the nature of the transaction precludes the selling stockholders from having an individual choice as to whether to give up their shares. This is often referred to as a "freeze-out." In addition to exercising a corporate option to redeem (as in *Zahn*), other techniques to force out minority shareholders include: (i) liquidating the corporation pursuant to a plan to sell its assets to a new firm owned only by the majority shareholders (*e.g., Lebold v. Inland Steel Co.,* discussed in footnote 14 of the *Zahn* opinion); (ii) merging the corporation with a new company owned only by the majority under a plan which calls for giving the minority cash in exchange for their shares (*e.g., Alpert v. 28 Williams Street Corp.,* reprinted in Chapter VII); and (iii) reverse stock splits in a ratio in which the minority would not get a whole share and under a plan which gives cash in lieu of fractional shares (*e.g., Teschner v. Chicago Title & Trust Co.,* 59 Ill.2d 452, 322 N.E.2d 54 (1974)). Language in the *Zahn* opinion suggests that directors subservient to the majority of shareholders may have a fiduciary duty not to force out the minority in order to financially benefit the majority. (Recall similar language in the partnership context in *Page v. Page.*) One problem with this under the facts in *Zahn* is that the very purpose for giving the company an option to redeem a class of shares is to benefit the other class(es). Indeed, in a subsequent opinion dealing with the measure of damages against Transamerica, the court backed away from the broad reading of the prior opinion, and, instead, concluded the only sin lay in nondisclosure rather than in exercising the option. *Speed v. Transamerica,* 235 F.2d 369 (3d Cir.1956). Still, the broader implications in *Zahn* may be relevant to freeze-outs through liquidation, merger or reverse stock splits, when one cannot say the minority bought shares explicitly giving the company the right to force them out for the benefit of the majority. Chapter VII will return to this subject in considering freeze-outs as the final step in a corporate acquisition.

3. Can securities laws impact a corporation's repurchase of its stock? In this situation, the stockholder sells shares to the issuing company, rather than vice versa. Hence, Section 4(1) of the 1933 Securities Act—covering transactions by one who is not an issuer, underwriter or dealer—should exempt the sale from registration. (Selling back to the corporation hardly constitutes participating in a distribution so as to make the selling stockholder a statutory underwriter—even without meeting the safe harbor guidelines of Rule 144.) Nevertheless, the sale of a security still occurs, which brings into play provisions of the 1934 Securities Exchange Act. Broadly speaking, share repurchases raise three concerns under the 1934 Act. The first is that the company (acting through its insiders) might, if not actually mislead the stockholders into selling their shares back to it, at least take advantage of superior knowledge relative to the outside stock-

holders from whom it buys back shares. A second concern is that a company might make a repurchase offer in such a manner as to place unfair pressure upon stockholders to sell. The third concern focuses, not upon the stockholders selling to the company, but upon other individuals who may buy shares at about the same time. The worry here is that the repurchases may artificially inflate the price of the stock.

As seen earlier in *Rochez,* making misleading statements or failing to disclose material facts to a seller of stock can violate Rule 10b–5. While mere non-disclosure by a purchaser generally violates the rule only if a fiduciary relationship exists between the buyer and seller, such a relationship exists between the company repurchasing its own shares and its stockholders. *See, e.g., Staffin v. Greenberg,* 672 F.2d 1196 (3d Cir.1982). *But see American General Ins. Co. v. Equitable General Corp.,* 493 F.Supp. 721 (E.D.Va.1980). What sort of facts must the company disclose as material? Must it disclose the fact that if it buys back its shares with surplus cash, earnings per share will rise (since there are less shares outstanding to divide into the same earnings)? See *Vaughn v. Teledyne, Inc.,* 628 F.2d 1214 (9th Cir.1980) (holding this fact was too obvious to require disclosure). What about disclosure of projections for future earnings? See Sec. Act Rule 175 (communicating a projection which lacks a reasonable basis can be a fraudulent statement). Must it disclose its intention to make further purchases at a higher price? (The court skirted around this question in *Kaplan.*) Note, Rule 10b–5 applies, as in *Rochez,* to repurchases of shares by a closely-held as well as by a public corporation.

Concerns about unfair pressures to sell lie at the heart of the Williams Act, which amended the 1934 Securities Exchange Act to add provisions regulating tender offers and substantial acquisitions of shares. The Williams Act, however, exempts repurchases by the issuer from most of its general provisions regulating tender offers and purchases creating over five percent ownership. Sec. Exch. Act §§ 13(d)(6)(C), 14(d)(8)(B). *But see* Sec. Exch. Act § 14(e) (prohibiting false, deceptive or manipulative practices in connection with any tender offer by any person). Instead, Section 13(e)(1) of the Securities Exchange Act, as amended by the Williams Act, grants the Securities Exchange Commission authority to make rules governing issuer repurchases. This authority extends only to corporations with securities registered pursuant to Section 12 of the 1934 Act (and to registered investment companies). Pursuant to this authority, the SEC has regulated three types of repurchases which have the potential for undue pressure. Rule 13e–1 requires specified disclosures by the issuer who seeks to repurchase its shares during a tender offer by another person. Rule 13e–4 regulates tender offers by the issuer. The rule imposes disclosure requirements, and substantive regulations on the manner and terms of the offer, along the lines imposed by the Williams Act on tender offers by non-issuers. (Chapter VII will explore the Williams Act requirements for tender offers generally.) One substantive requirement of note, in view of the earlier discussion regarding selective repurchases under state law, is that Rule 13e–4(f)(8)(i) requires an issuer tender offer to be open to all holders of the sought after class of shares. Finally, Rule 13e–3—there is no Rule 13e–2—

regulates going private transactions. This encompasses purchases or tender offers by the issuer (or an affiliate of the issuer), or mergers, recapitalizations, sales of assets, or the like, which result in a company ceasing to be registered under the 1934 Act, or ceasing to be listed on an exchange or traded on the NASD interdealer quotation system. The issuer (or its affiliate) making the purchase must provide specified disclosures to its stockholders. Most significantly, these disclosures call for a discussion of whether and why the issuer or its affiliate considers the purchase fair to its shareholders—which, of course, sets up a possible securities fraud claim by disgruntled stockholders who can argue the company did not really believe the transaction was fair, or left out material facts in its discussion of fairness.

Several provisions in the 1934 Act, and in the rules promulgated pursuant to the Act, are relevant to issuer repurchases designed to prop up the price of stock. Section 9(a)(2) prohibits a series of transactions in securities registered on a national exchange if those transactions (among other things) raise the price of the shares for the purpose of inducing their purchase. Section 9(a)(6) gives the SEC authority to promulgate rules limiting transactions in shares registered on a national exchange made for the purpose of stabilizing the price of the stock. Section 10(b) gives the SEC broad authority to make rules against manipulative or deceptive conduct in connection with the purchase or sale of securities (whether registered or not). In addition to Rule 10b–5, the Commission has created several rules under the mandate of Section 10(b) which can impact repurchases. These include: Rule 10b–6 (prohibiting issuers and others involved in the distribution of a security from bidding for or buying, subject to certain exceptions, shares of the same class as they are distributing); Rules 10b–7 and 10b–8 (allowing certain purchases for the purpose of stabilizing at market levels (but not higher) the price of shares undergoing a distribution); and Rule 10b–18 (creating a safe harbor, under which the Commission will not deem issuer repurchases to be manipulative, if they meet certain guidelines as to their timing during the day, their price, and their volume). Notice these prohibitions generally come into play for issuer repurchases only when the corporation is buying its shares at the same time as it, or others on its behalf, are trying to sell its stock. (One hidden danger here, however, is that convertible securities or outstanding warrants could constitute a continuing offer by the corporation to sell to the convertible security or warrant holders the stock they have the option to buy. *See* Sec. Act § 2(3) (conversion right or warrant which is not exercisable until *some future date* does not constitute an offer to sell a security). Hence, a corporation with warrants or convertible stock or bonds outstanding may need to worry about these rules in making repurchases. *But see* Sec. Exch. Act Rule 10b–6(a)(vii) (exempting the exercise of conversion rights from constituting a distribution for purposes of this rule).) Also, these rules normally should not impact the non-public corporation. For example, Rule 10b–6's prohibition on buying at the same time one is distributing stock seemingly contemplates at least a distribution which would not be exempt from registration under the 1933 Act. *See* Sec. Exch. Act Rule 10b–6(c)(5).

Finally, what about state securities laws? Generally, the sale by a stockholder back to the corporation, at least if an isolated transaction, should fit into various exemptions allowing non-issuer transactions without qualification. *E.g.*, Uniform Securities Act (2002 rev.) § 202(1); Cal. Corp. Code § 25104(a).

b. *Tax Aspects*

(i) Treatment of the Selling Shareholder

David Metzger Trust v. Commissioner of Internal Revenue

693 F.2d 459 (5th Cir.1982), *cert. denied,* 463 U.S. 1207 (1983).

■ HIGGINBOTHAM, CIRCUIT JUDGE:

We decide today a story driven by tensions as old as Genesis but told in the modern lexicon of the tax law. It is the story of David who built a business and left it in the charge of his eldest son Jacob to be shared with Jacob's two sisters Catherine and Cecelia, of their alienation and resulting quarrel with the tax collectors. In reviewing this decision of the Tax Court we are asked to determine the tax consequences of a reallocation of ownership of this family-owned business operated as a closely held corporation. In doing so we face three questions: (1) whether the attribution rules of I.R.C. § 318(a) must be applied despite family discord in determining whether a redemption meets the "not essentially equivalent to a dividend test" of § 302(b)(1); (2) whether a trust may waive the attribution rules of § 318(a) by filing a waiver agreement pursuant to § 302(c)(2)(A)(iii); (3) whether the attribution rules of § 267(c) must be applied to interest payments between family members in discord. * * *

FACTS

The relevant facts are not in dispute * * *. Appellant David Metzger Trust was created by David Metzger in 1942 to benefit his wife as life income beneficiary and his three children, Jacob, Catherine, and Cecelia, as one-third remaindermen each. Jacob, the eldest son, was named trustee of the Trust. Four years later, David incorporated the family business as Metzger Dairies, Inc., the other appellant. The Trust became a shareholder of Metzger Dairies.

On David's death in 1953 Jacob Metzger assumed control of Metzger Dairies. Catherine and Cecelia were directors. In the years following the father's death the sibling quarrel grew in intensity. By the 1960's, open animosity developed among Jacob, Catherine, and Cecelia. Whatever the source of their alienation, a downturn in the success of the dairy only exacerbated the problem. Catherine and Cecelia became angry when the corporation stopped paying dividends. Catherine resented what she considered to be Jacob's interference in the management of Metzger Dairy of San Antonio, a corporation of which her son was president but whose stock was owned of the most part by the same parties who owned the stock of Metzger Dairies. Cecelia was annoyed at both Jacob and Catherine because both corporations failed to pay dividends. The argument among Jacob, Catherine, and Cecelia over these and other issues unrelated to the business of the corporations continued until 1972, when the acrimony reached the point that Jacob, Catherine and Cecelia concluded it was necessary to terminate their joint ownership of the corporations.

After lengthy negotiations all agreed that Jacob and his family would own Metzger Dairies, Catherine and her family would own Metzger Dairy of San Antonio, and Cecelia and her family would be cashed out. The plan was for Metzger Dairies to redeem all shares owned by Catherine, Cecelia, the trusts for Catherine and Cecelia, and the David Metzger Trust. It was necessary to include the David Metzger Trust in the redemption because Catherine and Cecelia were due to receive one-third of the Trust corpus on the death of David Metzger's widow.

Immediately before the redemption, the stock of Metzger Dairies was held as follows:

Stockholder	Shares
David Metzger Trust	420
Nora Metzger (David Metzger's widow)	420
Jacob Metzger	600
Trust for Jacob Metzger	120
Catherine	600
Trust for Catherine	120
Cecelia	600
Trust for Cecelia	120

The redemption occurred on January 22, 1973, leaving Metzger Dairies' stock as follows:

Stockholder	Shares
Jacob Metzger	600
Trust for Jacob Metzger	120
Trust for David Metzger, II (son of Jacob)	294
Trusts for Nan Metzger (daughter of Jacob)	207

The Commissioner concedes that the principal motivation for the redemption was not to receive undistributed earnings, but to end a business relationship that was characterized by hatred and discord among Jacob, Catherine, and Cecelia. On February 10, 1976, Jacob, as trustee of the David Metzger Trust, delivered to the IRS a waiver agreement, executed pursuant to 26 C.F.R. § 1.302–4 and purporting to waive any future interest the trust might have in the corporation.

The deferred obligation of Metzger Dairies to pay for Cecelia's 600 shares was evidenced by a promissory note executed by the corporation and payable to Cecelia in three annual installments of principal, plus interest, beginning January 22, 1974. Interest payments were actually made on

January 21, 1974, January 7, 1975, and January 5, 1976. As a cash basis taxpayer, Cecelia reported interest income in 1974, 1975 and 1976, the respective years of receipt. Metzger Dairies was an accrual basis taxpayer and claimed deductions in the fiscal years ending September 30, 1973, September 30, 1974, and September 30, 1975, for the liability for interest as it accrued.

In May 1977 the Commissioner of Internal Revenue assessed deficiencies against David Metzger Trust for the calendar year 1973 and against Metzger Dairies for the fiscal years ending September 30, 1973, and September 30, 1974.[2] On August 17, 1977, Metzger Dairies and the Trust petitioned the Tax Court for a redetermination of these deficiencies. * * * The Tax Court upheld the deficiencies. * * *

THE TRUST'S APPEAL

(a) *The Statutory Framework*

While ordinary income treatment for dividends and capital gains treatment for sales of stock are primer categories of the Internal Revenue Code, their line of separation with stock redemptions is less than bright. Stock redemptions may resemble both sales of stock and dividends, since they involve corporate payment to a shareholder for stock but may also distribute corporate earnings. The desire for tax advantage insures recurring disputes over when a stock redemption is a dividend and when it is a purchase of stock. * * * [A] workable decision mechanism must be capable of looking through innovative form to the economic realty beneath. It is not surprising then that the categorization process is heavily indexed by actual changes in corporate ownership. That is, when a redemption significantly reduces a stockholder's voting interest in a corporation, it resembles a sale of stock more than a dividend and is to be accorded capital gains treatment. On the other hand, if the redemption is basically a pro rata distribution, it is treated as a dividend. * * *

Our specific analysis is channelled by the Code's structure: payments to shareholders from accumulated earnings will be treated as dividends unless the payment can be brought under an exception. * * * Section 302 provides the exceptions. If the redemption is "not essentially equivalent to a dividend," § 302(b)(1), a "substantially disproportionate redemption of stock," § 302(b)(2), or a "termination of (the) shareholder's interest," § 302(b)(3), it will be treated as a distribution in exchange for the stock. At first glance, all three of these provisions are applicable to the Metzger transaction since the corporation purchased all the stock of Catherine, Cecelia, their trusts, and the David Metzger Trust, while at the same time

2. The Commissioner assessed a deficiency of $292,977.47 against the Trust on the grounds that the $585,303.25 it received in redemption of the Metzger Dairies stock should have been reported as dividend income. The Commissioner assessed deficiencies against Metzger Dairies of $2,106.86 (FY 1973) and $24,856.38 (FY 1974) mainly after disallowing interest deductions of $32,167.28 (FY 1973) and $31,533.07 (FY 1974) for interest accrued but not paid to Cecelia until more than 2½ months after the close of the fiscal year.

made no payments to the other stockholders, namely Jacob Metzger and his trust. Yet the attribution rules of the Code pose immediate problems.

Attribution

If a father sells some of his shares back to a corporation, yet after the transactions he and his ten year old son end up owning the same combined percentage of voting shares, the transaction cast as a stock purchase might be an extraction of corporate earnings in nondividend form. The Code responds to this risk, with fixed attribution rules. An individual is considered to own the stock owned by his spouse, children, grandchildren, and parents. § 318(a)(1). An estate or trust is considered to own the stock owned by a beneficiary of the estate or trust. § 318(a)(3). A beneficiary is considered to own proportionately the stock owned by the estate or trust of which he is a beneficiary. § 318(a)(2). By these rules the Trust is the owner of the entire stock of Metzger Dairies both before and after the redemption.[6]

The Code provides that, with one exception, these attribution rules "shall apply in determining the ownership of stock for purposes of" § 302. § 302(c)(1). The one exception is that § 318(a)(1), the rules governing attribution of ownership from individuals to individuals, shall not apply in the case of a distribution described in § 302(b)(3), that is, a complete termination of a shareholder's interest, if:

1. "immediately after the distribution the distributee has no interest in the corporation (including an interest as officer, director, or employee), other than an interest as a creditor" (§ 302(c)(2)(A)(i));

2. "the distributee does not acquire any such interest (other than stock acquired by bequest or inheritance) within 10 years * * * "(§ 302(c)(2)(A)(ii));

3. the distributee files an agreement (a "waiver agreement") as prescribed by Treasury regulations (§ 302(c)(2)(A)(iii)).

In other words, § 302(c)(2)(a) by its terms permits an *individual* to avoid attribution of ownership if he gets out of the corporation and agrees to stay out.

The commands of §§ 302 and 318 are unambiguous. * * * The Trust argues however (1) that family discord should "mitigate" against the applicability of the attribution rules, and (2) that the Trust's filing of a waiver agreement and complete termination of its actual interest in the

6. Before redemption the Trust was the constructive owner of Nora, Jacob, Catherine, and Cecelia's shares, because they were its beneficiaries. § 318(a)(3)(B). Jacob, Catherine and Cecelia were the constructive owners of the shares held by their individual trusts. § 318(a)(2)(B). Thus, the Trust constructively owned all of Metzger Dairies' stock.

After redemption the Trust remained constructive owner of all the stock because the shares held by the trusts for Jacob's children were attributable to the children, § 318(a)(2)(B), thence to Jacob, § 318(a)(1)(A), and finally to the Trust, § 318(a)(3)(B).

corporation * * * effectively waived the attribution rules. We turn to the first contention.

(b) A Family Discord Exception to Attribution?

The Trust argues that family discord may "mitigate" the application of the attribution rules in determining dividend equivalency, especially given the undisputed fact that the purpose of the redemption was not to distribute corporate earnings. From the stipulated fact that the purpose of redemption was to bring peace to a family quarrel, the Trust launches two attacks upon the attribution rules. First, it argues that because it is undisputed here that the family cannot function as an economic unit, the attribution rules, built as they are upon that premise, are inapplicable. Second, the Trust argues that even if the Trust by virtue of attribution is virtually the sole shareholder before and after, the redemption was nonetheless not essentially equivalent to a dividend. The argument continues that this follows from the undisputed purpose of the redemption. That is, the purpose not being to bail out corporate earnings, the central base for application of nonequivalency has been touched.

As will be seen the first argument fails because it is built upon the erroneous assumption that attribution is treated by the Code as a rebuttable presumption rather than a mandated view of familial relationships. The second argument fails because it denies full sway to the decision of the Supreme Court in *United States v. Davis,* 397 U.S. 301, 90 S.Ct. 1041, 25 L.Ed.2d 323 (1970). Indeed, *Davis* provides much of the answer to the first argument as well. For this reason we will address the arguments together, separating them only when necessary to context.

Davis

* * * In *Davis,* the taxpayer had purchased the preferred stock of a corporation in 1945 in order to increase the corporation's working capital so that it might qualify for an RFC loan. As originally planned, the loan was fully repaid and the corporation redeemed the taxpayer's preferred stock. By this time, however, the corporation's common stock was held entirely by the taxpayer, his wife, his son, and his daughter. The Commissioner viewed the redemption as essentially equivalent to a dividend because after application of the attribution rules the taxpayer "owned" 100% of the corporation's common stock. Any distribution to him, therefore, was a pro rata distribution to all the corporation's stockholders, or the essential equivalent of a dividend.

The Supreme Court agreed with the Commissioner's analysis. In its first step it held that the attribution rules had to be applied in determining dividend equivalency under § 302(b)(1). * * *

Second, the Court held that the presence or absence of a tax-avoidance motive could not be considered in determining dividend equivalency under § 302(b)(1). * * *

In *Davis* the Court reasoned:

> After application of the stock ownership attribution rules, this case viewed most simply involved a sole stockholder who causes part of his shares to be redeemed by the corporation. We conclude that such a redemption is always 'essentially equivalent to a dividend' within the meaning of that phrase in § 302(b)(1) * * *

Id. 397 U.S. at 307, 90 S.Ct. at 1045. *Davis* teaches that in applying the "essentially equivalent to a dividend" test after the attribution rules are applied, if the resulting structure has virtually the same incidents of ownership the corporate payments distribute earnings despite an indisputable contrary business purpose.

Treas. Reg. § 1.302–2(b)

Confronted by the Supreme Court's holding in *Davis,* the Trust argues that its position nevertheless is supported by Treas.Reg. § 1.302–2(b), language in *Davis* interpreting § 302(b)(1) as applying whenever there is a "meaningful reduction in the shareholder's proportionate interest," and the legislative history of § 302(b)(1).

Treas.Reg. § 1.302–2(b) provides:

> The question whether a distribution in redemption of stock of a shareholder is not essentially equivalent to a dividend under Section 302(b)(1) depends upon the facts and circumstances of each case. One of the facts to be considered in making this determination is the constructive stock ownership of such shareholder under Section 318(a).

* * *

* * * The regulation is ambiguous. It can be interpreted as the Trust would have it, namely that attribution is only a presumption. On the other hand, it can be interpreted as saying that attribution rules must be given full effect, but are not necessarily decisive on the ultimate issue of dividend equivalency.

"Meaningful Reduction"

It is true, as the Trust points out, that some commentators and courts have indicated that *Davis* does not foreclose arguments for capital gains treatment based on family discord. * * * In *Robin Haft Trust v. Commissioner,* 510 F.2d 43 (1st Cir.1975), the First Circuit held that family discord might "negate the presumption" of the attribution rules that the taxpayer trusts exercised continuing control over the corporation after their actual holdings had been redeemed. *Id.* at 48. The trusts had been set up to benefit four children and were funded by shares of the corporation. The father of the children also owned a large percentage of the corporation's stock. While the father was going through divorce proceedings and was not even in contact with the children, the trusts' shares were redeemed as part of the program to terminate the involvement of the wife's family in the corporation. The IRS applied the attribution rules. Since the percentage of shares constructively owned by each of the trusts increased after the redemption, the IRS determined that the payment to the trusts was ordinary income. The Tax Court upheld the Commissioner. The First Circuit, however, directed the Tax Court "to reconsider taxpayers' claims in the light of the facts and circumstances of the case, including the existence of family discord tending to negate the presumption that taxpayers would exert continuing control over the corporation despite the redemption." *Id.* at 48.

For the most part, courts and commentators who urge that *Davis* leaves open the family discord question have emphasized that the *Davis* Court, despite its preference for objective tests, defined the "essentially equivalent to dividend" test in open-ended terms. "[T]o qualify for preferred treatment under (§ 302(b)(1)), a redemption must result in a meaningful reduction of the shareholder's proportionate interest in the corporation." 397 U.S. at 313, 90 S.Ct. at 1048. In *Robin Haft Trust,* the First Circuit concluded that "[t]his language certainly seems to permit, if it does not mandate, an examination of the facts and circumstances to determine the effect of the transaction transcending a mere mechanical application of the attribution rules." 510 F.2d at 48. * * *

These interpretations are not persuasive. The *Davis* Court was referring to a meaningful reduction in the shareholder's interest *after* application of the attribution rules. It would be strange indeed if what the Court really meant was that the attribution rules are to be applied before determining dividend equivalency, but then in the course of determining dividend equivalency their applicability could be reconsidered. If that were so, the attribution rules would hardly "provide a clear answer to what would otherwise be a difficult tax question * * *." 397 U.S. at 306, 90 S.Ct. at 1044.

Legislative History of § 302(b)(1)

The Trust also points to the legislative history of §§ 302 and 318. It is not necessary to traverse a long and complicated history here. Section 302's predecessor was a single dividend equivalency test. It had been interpreted flexibly, so that a redemption with a legitimate business purpose was treated as not "essentially equivalent to a dividend." In 1954 the House version of § 302 contained only the safe harbors of § 302(b)(2) ("substantially disproportionate redemption") and § 302(b)(3) ("termination of shareholder's interest"). The Senate added § 302(b)(1), the old essential equivalency test, because the House rules "appeared unnecessarily restrictive." S.Rep. No. 1622, 83d Cong., 2d Sess. 44, *reprinted in* 1954 U.S. Code Cong. & Ad. News 4621, 4675. Thus, several commentators have argued that Congress meant to reinstate subjective inquiry. In *Davis,* however, while conceding that "[t]he intended scope of § 302(b)(1) as revealed by this legislative history is certainly not free from doubt," 397 U.S. at 311, 90 S.Ct. at 1047, the Court concluded that Congress was rejecting past decisions that looked to motive. Section 302(b)(1) was not intended to be a mechanical test, but it was not intended to be a subjective test, either. Rather, Congress intended "a factual inquiry," "devoted solely to the question of whether or not the transaction by its nature may properly be characterized as a sale of stock by the redeeming shareholder to the corporation." S.Rep. No. 1622, 83d Cong., 2d Sess., *reprinted in* 1954 U.S.Cong. & Ad.News 4621, 4870–4871. The Senate Report adds that "the presence or absence of earnings and profits of the corporation is not material" to dividend equivalency. *Id.* at 4871. If so, motive could hardly be material since in the absence of earnings there would be no motive to seek capital gain treatment. The issue, as the *Davis* Court said, was not the taxpayer's motive but whether there was "a meaningful reduction of the shareholder's proportionate interest in the corporation." 397 U.S. at 313, 90 S.Ct. at 1048.

We return to the first level of the Trust argument—that attribution bottomed as it is on assumed family unity ought not to be applied when the assumption is contrary to stipulated fact. Nothing in the legislative history suggests that the attribution rules are to be "mitigated" in special cases. On the contrary, the Senate Report states that "the rules for constructive ownership of stock section 318(a) shall apply for purposes of this section generally." S.Rep.No. 1622, 83d Cong., 2d Sess., *reprinted in* 1954 U.S.Cong. & Ad.News 4621, 4872. Neither the language of the statute, the Supreme Court's opinion in *Davis,* nor the legislative history supports treating the attribution rules as rebuttable presumptions as the Trust is seeking.

Under the Trust's approach the Commissioner and the courts would be forced to highly case specific inquiries into elusive fact patterns. The pattern, intensity, and predicted duration of a family fight are difficult enough for the Solomonic justice of our domestic relations courts. It is hardly the basis for a soundly administered tax policy. The fixity of the attribution rules then in this sense is not their weakness but their strength.

In summary, we believe that the Commissioner and Tax Court were correct in refusing to take family discord into account in applying the attribution rules.[16] When a question is raised as to the dividend equivalency of a redemption, under § 302(b)(1) the correct approach is to apply the attribution rules *first,* then to determine whether there has been "a meaningful reduction of the shareholder's proportionate interest," without regard to whether the interest is actually or constructively held. What is "meaningful" then, to borrow a word, is essentially an inquiry into structure, a structure that applies statutorily dictated rules of economic unity.

(c) Waiver of Attribution by Trusts?

The Trust's second contention is that it executed a waiver agreement that met the requirements of § 302(c)(2)(A)(iii) and hence qualified for the

16. The Tax Court in its opinion below did suggest that in cases of non-pro rata distribution family hostility "can be a relevant fact to be considered in determining whether the reduction in the shareholder's interest is meaningful so as to qualify the distribution as not essentially equivalent to a dividend under Section 302(b)(1)." 76 T.C. 42, 62–63 (1981). That notion is inconsistent with our approach. Regardless, such a case was not presented below or here.

statutory exception to the attribution rules. This contention presents the question whether a trust may "waive" attribution of ownership even though § 302(c)(2)(A)(iii), by its terms, permits only attribution of ownership to *individuals* to be waived.[17] Our resolution of this issue will not have a lasting effect on the law of this circuit, because section 228 of the Tax Equity and Fiscal Responsibility Act of 1982, Pub.L. No. 97–248, 96 Stat. 324, has amended § 302(c)(2) prospectively so as to expressly prohibit waivers of attribution to and from entities (including trusts).[18]

* * *

Having concluded that family hostility does not mitigate the application of the attribution rules in determining dividend equivalency, and that a trust may not waive those rules, we therefore reach the conclusion that the deficiency was properly assessed against the Trust. The second issue raised by this appeal is the appropriateness of interest deductions claims by Metzger Dairies.

THE CORPORATION'S APPEAL

Section 267 of the Code disallows deductions for certain transactions between related taxpayers. The underlying philosophy of § 267(a)(2), the subsection at issue here, is that related taxpayers should not be able to generate tax deductions in a given year without corresponding income. Metzger Dairies as an accrual basis taxpayer claimed deductions for amounts that were not actually paid to Cecelia until more than 2 ½ months after the close of its fiscal year. Cecelia, as a cash basis taxpayer, did not report those amounts as income until the following taxable year. Therefore, if Metzger Dairies and Cecelia were related taxpayers within the meaning of § 267, Metzger Dairies was not entitled to certain interest deductions.

Section 267(b) defines relationships covered by § 267(a). These include "[a]n individual and a corporation more than 50 percent in value of the outstanding stock of which is owned, directly or indirectly, by or for such individual." § 267(b)(2). Section 267(c), however, provides that "[f]or purposes of determining, in applying subsection (b), the ownership of stock * * * (2) [a]n individual shall be considered as owning the stock owned, directly or indirectly, by or for his family." Section 267(c)(4) defines the family of an individual as including his brothers and sisters. Therefore, putting § 267(b), § 267(c)(2), and § 267(c)(4) together, Cecelia and Metzger Dairies (since Jacob owned a controlling interest in the corporation after the redemption) were related persons with the meaning of § 267. If

17. Section 302(c)(2) states that the attribution rules of *Section 318(a)(1)* shall not apply if certain conditions are met. The attribution rules relating to trusts are contained in 318(a)(2) and 318(a)(3).

18. Section 228(a) outlines procedures by which entities may waive attribution from *individuals* to *individuals.* The conference committee report states, "Under the bill, only family attribution under Section 318(a)(1) may be waived by an entity and its beneficiaries. The waiver rules would not be extended to waivers of attribution to and from entities and their beneficiaries (Secs. 318(a)(2) and 318(a)(3))." H.R.Rep. No. 760, 97th Cong., 2d Sess. 545 (1982). * * *

the literal language of § 267 is followed, the Commissioner was correct in disallowing the deductions.

Appellant Metzger Dairies, however, argues that the attribution rules of § 267 should not apply because of family hostility. Metzger Dairies seeks an exception to § 267(c) similar to the family discord exception to § 318(a) sought by the David Metzger Trust.

Metzger Dairies cites no case in support of such an exception.

* * *

In sum, § 267(c) provides constructive ownership rules which "shall" be applied in determining the relatedness of taxpayers. We see no reason to deviate from this express statutory command. Indeed, by our reading, the Fifth Circuit and Supreme Court precedents forbid it. Accordingly, we hold that Metzger Dairies was not entitled to the interest deductions claimed because it and Cecelia were related with the meaning of § 267.

* * *

NOTES

1. When a stockholder sells shares back to the corporation, two treatments are possible. The tax law could treat this just as any other sale of property—meaning no recognition to the extent the price does not exceed the stockholder's basis in the shares, and, normally, capital gain for the excess (or, unless Section 267 of the Internal Revenue Code applies, capital loss for any deficiency). Alternately, the law could treat this simply as a distribution from the company to the stockholder; taxable as a dividend to the extent it does not exceed the corporation's earnings and profits (and return of capital and capital gain to the extent it does).

Traditionally, as in *Metzger*, the primary impact of this distinction lay in the more favorable tax rates for capital gains versus ordinary income. However, the 2003 reduction of the tax on dividends to match the tax rate on capital gains has, at least for the time being, substantially removed this advantage. What difference does this now leave between the two treatments? If the redeemed stock is covered by Section 1202 (in other words, stock issued up to a certain level of capital by a small business corporation), then the effective tax rate for a redemption treated as a sale can be a percentage point less than the rate applied to taxation of dividends. Looking to the future, the equivalent income tax rates for dividends and capital gains will expire, barring further action by Congress, in 2008—at which point, the desirability of the capital gains tax rates, versus the ordinary income tax rates applied to dividends, will reappear. If the shareholder has capital losses from other sources, capital gains become desirable in that capital losses can only offset $3000 per year of ordinary income, but there is no limit to offsetting such losses against long term capital gains. Beyond the ordinary income versus capital gains impact, sale treatment results in no recognition of income for an amount equal to the stockholder's basis in the surrendered shares, whereas distribution treatment means recognizing the entire amount received (assuming it does not exceed earnings and profits). (What happens with dividend treatment to the basis of the surrendered shares? See Treas. Reg. 1.302–2(c) (indicating it goes to the stockholder's remaining shares).) Also, if the redemption occurs in exchange for debt instruments, sale treatment could allow installment reporting, whereas dividend treatment would not. Wile, *Dividend Redemptions and the Installment Method,* 66 Taxes 507 (1988). On the other hand, if the stockholder is itself a corporation, distribution treatment becomes more advantageous because of the dividend received deduction of Section 243. *But see* I.R.C. § 1059 (when a corporation receives an "extraordinary dividend" from stock not held more than two years, the corporation must decrease its basis in the stock by the amount of the dividend which is nontaxable by virtue of Section 243, and must recognize gain if this amount exceeds the corporation's basis in the stock). Finally, distribution treatment in an S corporation, much as with distributions from a partnership, normally are tax-free up to the amount of the shareholder's basis in his or her shares, after which they produce capital gains—which normally leaves only subtle impacts (such as the amount of basis to be offset) between distribution and sale treatment of a redemption of stock in an S corporation. *See* I.R.C. § 1368; Rev. Rul. 95–14, 1995–1 C.B. 169 (applying Section 1368 to a redemption by an S corporation when the redemption received distribution treatment under Section 302).

2. Section 302 governs which redemptions the law will tax as a sale of shares, and which as a distribution from the corporation. Section 302(b)(1) provides the basic guideline: It treats redemptions which are "not essentially equivalent to a dividend," as a sale. One can examine whether a repurchase is economically different from a dividend by considering its impact on either of two levels. On the corporate level, one can ask whether the redemption corresponds to a major contraction of the company. Section 302(b)(4) and (e) does this, as explored in the final section of this chapter. Section 302(b)(1) looks, instead, at the effect of the repurchase on the shareholder level. To understand this effect, consider three extreme examples. If an individual owns all the stock in a corporation and sells some back, he or she still owns all the stock. Hence, this repurchase is economically indistinguishable from a dividend. The same would be true if there is more than one common shareholder, but all sell back precisely the same fraction of their shares—the sale would have no effect other than to take money out of the company. (It is true the shareholders all have less shares, but absolute numbers of common shares have no economic significance; only the relative holdings do. Moreover, the corporation could always replenish the number of shares each party has through tax-free stock splits or stock dividends.) Compare these two examples with a situation in which one of two or more stockholders sells back to the corporation all of his or her shares. Here, something more has occurred than taking money out of the company: There has been a change in the ownership of the firm. The Supreme Court in the *Davis* decision—discussed in *Metzger*—focused on this comparison. It held a redemption must result in a "meaningful

reduction in the [selling] shareholder's proportionate interest'' for it not to be essentially equivalent to a dividend.

How much of a proportionate reduction must occur to be meaningful? In Revenue Ruling 78–401, 1978–2 C.B. 127, the Internal Revenue Service concluded that a reduction in the stockholder's proportionate holding from 90 percent of the outstanding common shares to 60 percent did not qualify. Yet, in Revenue Ruling 75–502, 1975–2 C.B. 111, a reduction from 57 percent to 50 percent did. How can 7 percent be a meaningful reduction, when 30 percent is not? Compare the impact upon the selling stockholder's control over the corporation in the two cases: In the latter, the 7 percent reduction meant going from a majority shareholder to a co-equal status; in the former, the 30 percent reduction still left the selling stockholder in control. *But see Wright v. United States,* 482 F.2d 600 (8th Cir.1973) (held a reduction from 85 to 61.7 percent had a meaningful impact upon control because the stockholder no longer owned the two-thirds votes required under the state's corporation law to approve certain fundamental actions). What happens, however, if the selling stockholder owned only a minority of voting shares even before the sale? In this event, the redemption will typically not cause any meaningful reduction in the selling stockholder's ability to control the company, since he or she had none to start with. *But see* Rev. Rul. 76–364, 1976–2 C.B. 91 (reduction from 27 to 22 percent found meaningful because the stockholder thereby lost the ability to exercise control by acting in concert with any one of the three other stockholders in the company). In the situation when the stockholder lacked control to start with, the Service has shifted attention to a disproportionate reduction in the stockholder's share of earnings and of assets upon liquidation (the two other interests which go to the owner of stock). In fact, the Service has been fairly liberal in this regard. *E.g.,* Rev. Rul. 75–512, 1975–2 C.B. 112 (reduction from owning 30 percent of outstanding common stock to 24.3 percent adequate); Rev. Rul. 76–385, 1976–2 C.B. 92 (reduction from .0001118 percent of common stock to .0001081 percent adequate); Rev. Rul. 77–426, 1977–2 C.B. 87 (redemption of 5 percent of non-voting, non-participating, preferred stock held entirely by a stockholder who owned no common was adequate). *But see Johnson Trust v. Commissioner,* 71 T.C. 941 (1979) (reduction from 43.6 percent to 40.8 percent held not meaningful). Note the asymmetry here. For the non-controlling stockholder, a moderate reduction in his or her relative share of earnings and assets is meaningful. For the stockholder who remains in control after the redemption, however, the Service will ignore even large reductions in his or her share of earnings and assets, and focus instead only upon the impact of the redemption upon his or her control. *But see Henry T. Patterson Trust v. United States,* 729 F.2d 1089 (6th Cir.1984) (alternate holding: reduction in ownership from 97 percent to 93 percent was meaningful under unique facts of case).

3. From a planning perspective, the problem with Section 302(b)(1)'s essential equivalence test lies in its lack of clear-cut benchmarks. For this reason, Section 302(b)(2) is useful. It provides a ''safe harbor,'' giving sale treatment to substantially disproportionate redemptions as measured un-

der three precise numerical tests: (1) After the redemption, the selling stockholder must own less than 50 percent of the total combined voting power of all classes of stock entitled to vote; (2) The redemption must reduce the selling shareholder's percentage of voting stock to less than 80 percent of what it was before the redemption (for example, if the selling stockholder owned 25 percent of the voting shares before the redemption, he or she must own less than 20 percent after); and (3) the redemption must also reduce the selling shareholder's combined percentage ownership of all common, voting and non-voting, to less than 80 percent of what it was before the redemption. (Keep in mind, the reduction measured is a decrease in the percentage holding. Hence, a 20 percent decrease in the selling stockholder's total number of shares is not adequate. This is because the redemption also decreases the total number of outstanding shares, thereby making a smaller total number owned, a larger fraction of what is left.) If there is more than one class entitled to vote, measuring combined voting power involves the same questions faced when dealing with Section 351's control requirement in Chapter IV. *See also* Treas. Reg. § 1.302–3(a) (contingent voting rights do not count unless the contingency occurred). When there are multiple classes of common, the statute calls for measuring total ownership by fair market value. I.R.C. § 302(b)(2)(C). *See also* Rev. Rul. 87–88, 1987–2 C.B. 81 (measure fair market value for purposes of Section 302(b)(2)(C) on an aggregate rather than a class-by-class basis). One gap in Section 302(b)(2)'s coverage occurs when the selling stockholder owns no voting or common shares to start with, and hence cannot meet the 80 percent tests. *But see* Rev. Rul. 81–41, 1981–1 C.B. 121 (applied Section 302(b)(2) when selling shareholder only owned voting preferred, but not common). The stockholder without voting shares, however, generally receives sympathetic treatment under the general test of Section 302(b)(1).

4. Suppose the corporation undertakes a series of redemptions. For example, the company might first redeem a substantial fraction of one stockholder's shares (perhaps enough to meet the numerical tests of Section 302(b)(2)), and then redeem shares from another stockholder, and so on until the end effect is the relative holdings did not significantly change. Alternately, the company may redeem a small fraction of one stockholder's shares (such that the effect would be insufficient under either Section 302(b)(1) or (b)(2)), but then continue to redeem shares from this party in small bites so the end result is a significant reduction in this person's percentage holding. (Why might the company structure the redemption in the latter manner? Recall the earlier discussion of financial limits on share repurchases. Also, suppose the shareholder is itself a corporation, for which dividend treatment is superior to sale treatment.) Section 302(b)(2)(D) expressly excludes from the category of a substantially disproportionate redemption, one made pursuant to a planned series of purchases which as a group lack a disproportionate effect. In applying Section 302(b)(1), the courts will also look to the end result of a planned series of redemptions in which the latter purchases undercut the effect of the former. *E.g., Blount v. Commissioner,* 425 F.2d 921 (2d Cir.1969). Similarly, some cases have looked to the end result of a planned series of redemptions from the same

stockholder in order to accord sale treatment, even though individually the repurchases were not meaningful. *E.g., Bleily & Collishaw, Inc. v. Commissioner,* 72 T.C. 751 (1979), *aff'd,* 647 F.2d 169 (9th Cir.1981). *But see Benjamin v. Commissioner,* 592 F.2d 1259 (5th Cir.1979) (refused to consider the combined effect of a series of redemptions from a shareholder who had wide discretion as to when the corporation would complete the plan).

5. The facts in *Metzger* illustrate one of the major sources of difficulty encountered in applying Section 302. Not only must one consider shares actually owned by the selling stockholder, one must also take into account shares constructively owned by that person under the attribution rules of Section 318. The purpose of the attribution rules becomes clear when one examines a corporation in which a husband owns half the shares, and a wife the other half. If the company redeems the husband's shares, is it fair to say the ownership has really changed (even aside from factors such as community property)? To resolve such questions, Section 318 provides a set of rules to determine when certain provisions of the tax code, such as Section 302, will treat one person's shares as if also owned by another person. (Other provisions, however, such as Section 267 discussed in the court's opinion, may have their own attributions rules which differ from those in Section 318. Yet other provisions, such as Section 368(c) encountered earlier, have no attribution at all.)

Section 318(a) establishes several categories in which attribution occurs. Between family members, it attributes to an individual, stock owned by his or her spouse, children, grandchildren and parents. I.R.C. § 318(a)(1). From entities to individuals, it attributes to a person, his or her proportionate share of stock owned by any partnership of which he or she is a member, by any estate or trust (other than either a qualified employees' trust, or a grantor trust) of which he or she is a beneficiary, by any S corporation in which he or she is a shareholder, or, by any other corporation in which he or she owns, actually or constructively, at least 50 percent of the stock. I.R.C. § 318(a)(2), (a)(5)(E). (The section considers the individual taxable on the trust's income to constructively own all the stock owned by a grantor trust.) Conversely, from individuals to entities, the section considers a partnership to constructively own all shares owned by any of its partners; an estate or trust (other than either a qualified employees' trust or a grantor trust) to constructively own all shares owned by any of its beneficiaries (unless the beneficiary has only a remote contingency interest in the trust); a grantor trust to constructively own all shares owned by the person who is taxable on its income; an S corporation to constructively own all shares owned by any of its stockholders, and any other corporations to constructively own all shares owned by a stockholder with at least 50 percent of its stock. I.R.C. § 318(a)(3), (a)(5)(E). Finally, the section considers any person who has an option to acquire stock to own the shares. I.R.C. § 318(a)(4).

These rules can work in combination to make chains of attribution. I.R.C. § 318(a)(5)(A). *Metzger* provides an example. The trust constructively owned all shares actually or constructively owned by its beneficiaries. The beneficiaries, in turn, constructively owned their proportionate share of stock held by other trusts in which they were also beneficiaries. (See footnote 6 in the court's opinion.) In two circumstances, however, the code refuses to attribute shares only constructively owned. It will not do so for attribution based upon family relation. I.R.C. § 318(a)(5)(B). (As a result, there is no automatic attribution between brothers and sisters, for example.) It also refuses to attribute to a partner, beneficiary or shareholder, stock constructively owned by the partnership, estate, trust or corporation by virtue of attribution from another partner, beneficiary or shareholder. I.R.C. § 318(a)(5)(C). (Hence, there is no automatic attribution between partners, beneficiaries or shareholders. The chain of attribution in *Metzger* was the reverse of the disallowed one: first from trust to beneficiary, then from beneficiary to trust.)

The question before the court in *Metzger* was whether it could find a meaningful reduction in the trust's proportionate holding based upon the fact the attributions were not realistic given the hostility between the family members. As the court discusses, there is considerable disagreement on this point. What about the converse situation: Can a court refuse to find a meaningful reduction because shares held by parties friendly to the selling stockholder (but not within the attribution rules) still leave him or her in effective control? See footnote 16 in the court's opinion.

6. Section 302(b)(3) provides another safe harbor—this being a redemption of all of a shareholder's stock in the company. At first glance, this provision seems both obvious and of limited utility: Obvious, because a complete termination of interest is the prototype of a redemption which differs in impact from a dividend; and of limited utility, because a complete redemption would meet the substantially disproportionate test (unless the stockholder lacked voting shares to start with), and would fit without question the definition of a meaningful reduction in proportionate holdings under the general test. What makes this provision very useful, however, is a complementary provision in Section 302(c)(2), under which a stockholder who completely sells out may obtain a waiver from attribution based upon family relation when such attribution would otherwise preclude sale treatment.

The first thing to notice about this waiver is it applies only to attribution based upon family relations (in other words, the constructive ownership of shares owned by a spouse, child, grandchild, or parent). I.R.C. § 302(c)(2)(A). This, in turn, was the genesis of the issue facing the court in *Metzger* as to whether a trust can take advantage of the attribution waiver. At this point, one might ask why a trust (or an estate, partnership, or corporation for that matter) would benefit by waiving attribution based upon family relations: After all, an entity cannot have a spouse, children, grandchildren or parents (at least within the meaning of Section 318). The answer lies in the possibility of chains of attribution. Hence, while the trust may have no family, its beneficiaries can, and any shares they constructively own through family attribution will be constructively owned by the trust.

As the court states, Congress, in 1982, amended Section 302(c)(2) to resolve this question. Entities may obtain a waiver of attribution, but only if the beneficiary, partner or shareholder whose family relation produced the constructive ownership problem also undertakes a complete termination of his or her interest, and agrees, as well, to be liable for any tax deficiency in case of a reacquisition (including by the entity, rather than the individual). I.R.C. § 302(c)(2)(C). (In addition, as the *Metzger* opinion notes, Congress intended the 1982 amendment to overrule legislatively the decision in *Rickey v. United States,* 592 F.2d 1251 (5th Cir.1979). The court there, despite clear statutory language, allowed waiver of all attribution from the beneficiary to the trust, rather than just allowing waiver of the attribution from relative to beneficiary, which had impacted the trust.)

A second problem with the attribution waiver is that transactions which took place long before the redemption may preclude the waiver's use. Specifically, the waiver does not apply if the selling stockholder acquired any of his or her shares within the preceding 10 years from a person whose stock the selling shareholder would now constructively own under Section 318. I.R.C. § 302(c)(2)(B). It also does not apply if the selling stockholder conveyed within the last 10 years any shares to a person whose stock the selling shareholder now constructively owns, unless that person no longer has the shares or else the corporation now redeems them. I.R.C. § 302(c)(2)(B)(ii). Mitigating the need for prescience, these restrictions do not apply if the earlier transfers did not have a tax avoidance purpose. I.R.C. § 302(c)(2)(B). (Moreover, such a purpose does not exist simply because a stockholder, who wishes to transfer control over the corporation to relatives, gives the relatives some shares before the redemption, with the objective of lowering the amount of capital gains he or she would recognize upon a redemption of the remaining shares. Rev. Rul. 77–293, 1977–2 C.B. 91.)

Most significantly, the selling shareholder who wishes to take advantage of the attribution waiver must give up for ten years all interest in the corporation other than as a creditor. I.R.C. § 302(c)(2)(A)(i), (ii) (The Code excepts, however, reacquisition through bequest or inheritance.) To police this, the selling stockholder must agree to notify the I.R.S. of any reacquisition, and there is an extended statute of limitations for any tax deficiency assessed because the reacquisition destroyed the waiver. I.R.C. § 302(c)(2)(A)(iii). What sort of connections can the selling shareholder maintain with the corporation? Section 302(c)(2)(A)(i) speaks specifically to two types of interests. It prohibits retention of an interest as an officer, director or employee, if the selling stockholder wants the attribution waiver. Suppose, however, the corporation hires the selling shareholder to provide consulting or professional services as an independent contractor? *Compare Lynch v. Commissioner*, 801 F.2d 1176 (9th Cir.1986) (performing any services for the corporation in any capacity voids the waiver), *with Cerone v. Commissioner*, 87 T.C. 1 (1986) (depends upon whether the employment allows the selling shareholder to exercise control over the corporation or produces a sufficient salary to give the selling shareholder a continued financial stake in the corporation). On the other hand, the section allows retention of an interest as a creditor. What this entails is an open question. The regulations suggest subordinating the loan, or agreeing that payments will be contingent upon earnings, are hazardous for the waiver. Treas. Reg. § 1.302–4(d). *But see Dunn v. Commissioner,* 615 F.2d 578 (2d Cir.1980) (court held there was a complete termination of interest despite the fact that the redemption agreement postponed payments if they would be contrary to working capital and profit retention clauses in the corporation's franchise agreement). What about a pledge of the purchased shares as security for payment? See *Lynch v. Commissioner,* 83 T.C. 597, 610 (1984), *rev'd on other grounds,* 801 F.2d 1176 (9th Cir.1986):

> "[T]he Commissioner argues that the pledge agreement entered into between the petitioner and Gilbert demonstrates that the note was more in the nature of a retained equity interest than an interest as a creditor. In support of his contention, the Commissioner relies upon section 1.302–4(e), Income Tax Regs., which provides:
>
> > (e) In the case of the distributee to whom section 302(b)(3) is applicable, who is a creditor after such transaction, the acquisition of the assets of the corporation in the enforcement of the rights of such creditor shall not be considered an acquisition of an interest in the corporation for purposes of section 302(c)(2) unless stock of the corporation, its parent corporation, or, in the case of a redemption of stock of a parent corporation, of a subsidiary of such corporation is acquired.
>
> In our view, such regulations have no applicability in the present case. By its own terms, section 1.302–4(e) Income Tax Regs., pertains to the enforcement of a creditor's rights. Such regulations provide that if, in the enforcement of his claim as a creditor, a stockholder acquires the assets of the corporation, the acquisition of such assets will not be considered an acquisition of an interest in the corporation for purposes of the applicability of the attribution rules under section 302(c)(2), but the regulations imply that if the stockholder acquires stock, the acquisition of such stock will constitute a prohibited interest * * *. However, the petitioner did not in fact acquire either the assets or the stock of the corporation. He had merely a right to acquire such stock in the event of a default by the corporation, and the regulations do not deal with that security interest. The holding of such a security interest is common in sales agreements, and in our judgment, it is not inconsistent with the interest of a creditor."

As the tax court's opinion indicates, while holding a security interest in pledged shares does not preclude the waiver, reacquiring the pledged shares upon default does. This suggests that other security may be better. Incidentally, acquiring legal title to shares as a custodian or voting trustee may void the waiver even though one did not obtain any beneficial interest. Rev. Rul. 81–233, 1981–2 C.B. 83; Rev. Rul. 71–426, 1971–2 C.B. 173. *But see* Rev. Rul. 72–380, 1972–2 C.B. 201 (becoming executor of an estate with shares does not produce a prohibited reacquisition since reacquiring shares through inheritance or bequest is an exception and this is less extreme);

Rev. Rul. 79–334, 1979–2 C.B. 127 (applying same reasoning to appointment by will as trustee of trust containing shares). What about relationships other than employee, creditor or shareholder? The Service has ruled leasing property at fixed rent to the company is not a prohibited interest (Rev. Rul. 77–467, 1977–2 C.B. 92), and retaining rights in a pension plan may be acceptable under some conditions. Rev. Rul. 84–135, 1984–2 C.B. 80. Finally, suppose that the seller retains a number of interests, none of which, in itself, constitutes a prohibited interest. Can the combination yield a prohibited interest? See *Hurst v. Commissioner*, 124 T.C. 16 (2005) (no).

In any event, keep in mind the seller must meet the termination of all interests test of Section 302(c)(2)(A) only if he or she needs to obtain a waiver of family attribution. If he or she qualifies for sale treatment even with constructively owned shares, there is no need to bother with such a complete cut-off. Suppose, however, the selling stockholder remains an officer or director of the company, and receives long-term subordinated notes in exchange for his or her shares, with interest dependent upon earnings. Can this impact compliance with the tests under Section 302(b)(1), (2) or (3), even if there is no constructively owned shares problem? See *Lisle v. Commissioner,* 35 T.C.M. (CCH) 627 (1976) (considering such factors to determine if there was in fact a redemption, and, if so, whether it constituted a complete termination within the meaning of Section 302(b)(3) rather than Section 302(c)(2)(A)).

7. Death is often the occasion for a repurchase of shares in a closely held corporation. As discussed in Chapter IV, the surviving shareholders many times would like to avoid the problems which may result from having to deal with the decedent's heirs as co-owners. At the same time, the estate may face a need for money to pay, among other things, estate taxes (at least until and unless there is a permanent repeal of the estate tax). From an income tax standpoint, death may provide a particularly desirable opportunity to sell shares back to the corporation. Because of the stepped-up basis property obtains under Section 1014 upon death—at least until and unless Section 1014 is permanently repealed as part of a repeal of the estate tax—a redemption after death can bail money out of the corporation with no tax. Obtaining this advantage, however, requires treating the redemption as a sale rather than as a dividend. In this regard, Section 303 provides a useful additional safe harbor (beyond those found in Section 302) under which to claim sale treatment for stock redeemed after a shareholder's death.

Several requirements exist to take advantage of Section 303. To begin with, the deceased shareholder's estate must have included the redeemed stock for federal estate tax purposes. I.R.C. § 303(a). Nevertheless, it is possible the corporation will redeem the shares from someone other than the estate, such as a beneficiary. In this case, the selling shareholder may only take advantage of Section 303 to the extent that the payment of estate taxes and deductible administrative estate expenses either directly reduced his or her interest in property received from the estate, or else he or she is under a binding obligation to contribute to such taxes and expenses. I.R.C.

§ 303(b)(3). A highly significant requirement is that the value of all the stock of the redeeming corporation included in the estate (whether or not redeemed) must exceed 35 percent of the estate's total value in excess of certain deductible expenses. I.R.C. § 303(b)(2)(A). (One can combine, however, stocks in two or more different companies to meet this 35 percent test if the estate includes 20 percent or more of the entire value of each corporation's outstanding stock. I.R.C. § 303(b)(2)(B).) This may provide something of a counterpoint to the common strategy of the elderly stockholder in a closely held corporation who transfers shares before death in order to avoid paying estate tax on them. In addition, Section 303 only covers the amount realized on redemption up to the sum of estate taxes and certain deductible estate expenses (albeit, there is no requirement the money actually go toward such uses). I.R.C. § 303(a). This, of course, means that Section 303 treatment largely goes by the boards if there is a permanent repeal of the estate tax. Finally, the redemption and payment must take place within a limited period of time. I.R.C. § 303(b)(1), (4). (Issuing a promissory note, however, can equal payment. Rev. Rul. 65–289, 1965–2 C.B. 86.)

8. Can a stockholder avoid the prospect of dividend treatment by selling his or her shares to a party other than the issuing corporation? The answer, of course, is yes; but if the stockholder's real objectives are to bail earnings out of the issuing corporation without taxable dividends, and at the same time leave his or her ownership essentially unchanged, selling stock to a third party normally accomplishes neither goal. Perhaps, however, the stockholder can sell shares to an outside party with the understanding that this person will resell them back to the corporation. One obvious danger with such an arrangement is the Internal Revenue Service disregarding the middle steps and treating this as a redemption from the original stockholder. *See, e.g., Estate of Schneider v. Commissioner*, 855 F.2d 435 (7th Cir.1988). *But see* Rev. Rul. 78–197, 1978–1 C.B. 83. A less obvious danger is that the third party just might decide to keep the shares, which could pose quite a problem if the shares have voting rights. Sale of non-voting preferred shares, however, may encounter problems under Section 306, discussed later in this chapter.

What about selling the shares to another company controlled by the stockholder? This solves the loss of control problem. While it does not immediately bail money out of the issuing corporation, it gets money out of another company without that firm declaring a dividend, and the acquiring corporation can later receive dividends with less cost because of the deduction provided by Section 243. Selling to a subsidiary of the issuing corporation can achieve similar effects. Not surprisingly, Congress acted to stop such efforts. Its tool is Section 304. Under this section, if a stockholder sells shares to a corporation he or she controls (defined as owning, actually or constructively, 50 percent or more of either the total voting power or the total value of all shares), or if the stockholder sells shares to a subsidiary of the issuing corporation (defined under the same 50 percent criteria), then the stockholder must meet one of the tests under Section 302 (or 303) for sale treatment, almost as if he or she had sold the shares back to the issuing corporation. One important difference, however, is the shares remain outstanding, and the stockholder can still constructively own a portion of them through attribution from a controlled corporation. I.R.C. § 318(a)(2)(C). Hence, it is more difficult to qualify a sale to a controlled corporation for sale rather than distribution treatment. (What is the result in this respect if the stockholder sells to a subsidiary: Can there be a chain of attribution back through the parent to the selling stockholder? See Treas. Reg. § 1.318–1(b)(1) (refusing to attribute to a corporation stock in itself owned by a subsidiary).) Moreover, if the sale receives distribution treatment, it will be a dividend to the extent of the combined earnings and profits of both the acquiring and issuing companies. I.R.C. § 304(b)(2). (Of course, one type of shareholder might like the impact of Section 304 creating dividend rather than sale treatment; this being a shareholder which itself is a corporation. Section 1059(e)(1) responds to this possibility by treating such a redemption as an extraordinary dividend triggering Section 1059's basis reduction and gain recognition requirements.)

Suppose an individual transfers shares to a corporation in exchange for this company's stock and boot, and immediately thereafter owns over 80 percent of the acquiring company. Does Section 351 or 304 apply? Section 351 governs the receipt of stock. *See* I.R.C. §§ 304(a)(1)(B), (2)(A) (covering exchange of stock in return for *property*); 317(a) (excluding stock in the company making the distribution from the definition of property for purposes of sections including 304). (Notice, this means Section 304 does not cover the sale of stock in exchange for the purchasing corporation's shares, even if Section 351 does not apply. *Bhada v. Commissioner,* 89 T.C. 959 (1987).) Anything else, Section 304 controls. I.R.C. § 304(b)(3)(A). This includes assumption of liabilities, with one exception. I.R.C. § 304(b)(3)(B). The exception is when the transferring stockholder incurred the liability to acquire the stock.

9. Whether or not the redemption yields sale or dividend treatment, the selling shareholder may also find him or herself subject to a special 50 percent excise tax on "greenmail gain." I.R.C. § 5881. This tax applies if a selling stockholder held the shares less than two years before the redemption, he or she made or threatened a public tender offer, and the corporation's reacquisition offer was not open to all its shareholders.

10. Divorce (of the marital kind) can also lead to a "divorce" of the business kind, that is a buy-out of the shares owned (for example, as a result of community property laws) by one of the divorcing spouses (typically the one who is not as active in the business). A transfer of the shares between the spouses in connection with the divorce is tax-free under Section 1041. What if the corporation redeems one spouse's shares? See Treas. Reg. § 1.1041–2 (treating the redemption of stock incident to a divorce the same as any other redemption, unless, under general tax principles discussed later, or a written agreement between the divorcing spouses, the redemption constitutes a constructive distribution to the other spouse, in which event the Service will deem the stock constructively transferred between spouses in a transaction covered by Section 1041 and

then redeemed from the spouse who must recognize the constructive distribution).

(ii) Treatment of the Corporation

Lamark Shipping Agency, Inc. v. Commissioner of Internal Revenue

42 T.C.M. (CCH) 38 (1981).

■ DAWSON, JUDGE:

Respondent determined deficiencies in petitioner's Federal income tax for * * * accumulated earnings tax. * * * [T]he * * * issue presented for decision is whether petitioner's accumulation of earnings during the taxable year in issue was beyond the reasonable needs of its business and for the purpose of avoiding income taxes with respect to its shareholders under Section 532(a).

FINDINGS OF FACT

* * *

The business of petitioner was originally established as a sole proprietorship by Victor A. Lamark (Victor) in 1925, and was operated under the name Lamark Shipping Agency. Albert A. Lamark (Albert), Victor's brother, has been an employee of the business since 1930. The business was incorporated on October 13, 1966. Initially all the outstanding stock (2,000 shares) of the Corporation was held by Victor. Subsequently he transferred 100 shares to Albert, 100 shares to his nephew, Joseph J. Lamark, Jr. (Jay), and 30 shares to his sister, Rose Kozak. * * *

* * * From October 14, 1966 through December 3, 1976, the board of directors of the Corporation consisted of Victor, Albert, and Jay. During this period the officers of the Corporation were Victor, President and Treasurer; Albert, Vice President; Jay, Secretary; * * *.

At all times the business of the Corporation has been the solicitation of contracts for the transport of cargo and passengers in the international shipping trade. The Corporation's principal source of income is commissions paid by various international carriers.

* * *

During the early 1970's the Corporation's major account was the Prudential–Grace line, which the Corporation and its predecessor had served since 1932. The line was originally known as the Grace line until it was sold to the Prudential line in 1970. Soon after the sale the new management informed the Corporation that it intended to phase out the line's agencies and establish its own offices in the United States and abroad to solicit business. In accordance with this plan the Prudential–Grace line terminated its agency relationship with the Corporation on March 31, 1975.

* * *

Sometime in the fall of 1975, approximately five or six months after the loss of the Prudential–Grace line, petitioner heard rumors to the effect that another major account, the Moller line, was about to open its own sales office in Pittsburgh and cancel its agency contract. Victor attempted to dissuade the Moller officials from doing so. Yet, despite his efforts, the Corporation received word on March 23, 1976, that the Moller line was cancelling its agency contract effective September 1, 1976.

* * *

Despite the loss of the Prudential–Grace and Moller lines, the Corporation's commission income remained fairly stable during the 1976 fiscal year and surpassed the amounts received in fiscal 1974, a year which the corporate minutes has characterized as a "banner year" for the Corporation. This was attributable to several factors, including increased commission rates negotiated by petitioner with some of the lines, the expansion of export services by some of the lines, and a general boom in the export and passenger shipping business.

* * *

In the course of attempting to secure new lines to offset the loss of the Moller and Prudential–Grace lines, a conflict developed between Victor and Jay over whether to take on a Russian line which had recently commenced service between the United States and the Far East. * * * Jay was in favor of taking on the Russian representation. Victor, on the other, was staunchly opposed to such action because the line was a nonconference line and used what he felt were unfair trade practices to snatch business from competing conference lines. * * *

Although he was 72 when he divested his stock ownership in the Corporation, Victor was in good health and would have preferred to continue working with the company. However, he felt that this was not feasible for two reasons. First, he and Jay were at loggerheads over the Russian line issue and also had other disagreements concerning plans for the long-range future of the Corporation. These disagreements were serious enough that at one point Jay had considered leaving the company. Second, Victor became convinced, following the loss of two of its biggest accounts, that the Corporation would soon go under, and in any event could not continue to pay the large salaries which the officers had been receiving. He felt it was too risky, from a personal investment standpoint, to retire and remain a passive stockholder. Therefore, he decided to get out of the business altogether. He considered and rejected the alternative of liquidating the Corporation, partly because of his reluctance to terminate a 50–year old family business, and partly out of a sense of loyalty to the company's employees, some of whom had been with the company for many years. Eventually he settled on a plan where all but one share of his stock would be redeemed by the Corporation, with the remaining share to be purchased individually by Jay. It was further decided that the stock of Albert and Rose Kozak would also be redeemed, thereby vesting complete ownership of the Corporation in Jay.

The stock ownership of the Corporation prior to the implementation of this plan was as follows:

	Number of Shares Owned	Percent of Total Shares Outstanding
Victor Lamark	1,770	92.43%
Albert Lamark	25	1.31
Jay Lamark	100	5.22
Rose Kozak	20	1.04
Total	1,915	$100.00%

On May 25, 1976, Albert was paid $5,000 in the complete redemption of his 25 shares of stock of the Corporation. On June 1, 1976, Rose Kozak was paid $4,000 in the complete redemption of the 20 shares owned by her. To redeem 1,769 of the 1,770 shares owned by Victor, the Corporation paid him $283,271.91 in cash on July 16, 1976, * * *. The redemption proceeds were reported by Victor on his 1976 Federal income tax return as a distribution qualifying for long-term capital gain treatment. The income tax savings to Victor as a consequence of reporting the $283,271.91 cash payment * * * as a capital gain distribution versus an ordinary income dividend amounted to $63,059.18.

The remaining share of stock owned by him was sold to Jay for $60,000 pursuant to an agreement executed on February 28, 1976 contemporaneously with the stock redemption agreement between Victor and the Corporation. The purpose of this arrangement was to require Jay to pay a premium out of his personal assets for the transfer of control of the business brought about by the redemption of Victor's stock. The gain on this sale was reported on his 1976 Federal income tax return as long-term capital gain.

* * *

In February 1976 the petitioner borrowed $80,000 from the Pittsburgh National Bank and Jay personally guaranteed the loan. Petitioner loaned $60,000 of the proceeds to Jay to enable him to finance the purchase of the single share of stock from Victor. Since the redemptions had exhausted nearly all of the Corporation's working capital, it was necessary to retain $20,000 of the loan proceeds in the business to meet operating expenses.

* * *

Petitioner paid only one dividend from the date of incorporation through September 30, 1977. That dividend totaled $8,000 and was paid during the taxable year ended September 30, 1974.

On April 6, 1979, respondent informed petitioner of a proposed statutory notice of deficiency for accumulated earnings taxes under Section 531 for the taxable years ended September 30, 1975 and 1976. On May 14, 1979, petitioner submitted to respondent a statement pursuant to Section 534(c) which alleged that the earnings in question were accumulated "to protect the corporation from the drastic financial consequences attendant upon the loss of major accounts, not to redeem stock." In the alternative, the statement alleged that "even if the surplus had been accumulated to redeem V.A. Lamark's stock, this would have been an accumulation to meet reasonable needs under the applicable cases." On May 24, 1979, respondent mailed a statutory notice of deficiency to petitioner wherein respondent determined that petitioner was liable for accumulated earnings taxes for the taxable year ended September 30, 1976 in the amount of $31,811.[5] * * *

OPINION

The accumulated earnings tax is designed to foster the payment of dividends to the shareholders of a corporation by imposing a penalty tax on accumulated earnings and profits in excess of the reasonable needs of the business. * * * The tax is imposed by Section 531 and applies to any corporation "formed or availed of for the purpose of avoiding the income tax with respect to its shareholders * * * by permitting earnings and profits to accumulate instead of being divided or distributed." Section 532(a). In *United States v. Donruss Co.,* 393 U.S. 297 (1969), the Supreme Court held that tax avoidance need only be one of the purposes which contributed to the decision to accumulate, rather than the dominant or controlling purpose.

Section 533(a) provides that the accumulation of earnings beyond the reasonable needs of the business is determinative of the existence of a tax avoidance purpose unless the corporation proves otherwise by a preponderance of the evidence. The concept of "reasonable needs of the business" is also important in the computation of the tax, since section 535(c)(1) allows a credit against the accumulated taxable income subject to the tax for the amount of any current earnings and profits which are retained by the corporation for its reasonable business needs. Thus, even if tax avoidance is found to have played a role in the decision to accumulate, the taxpayer can still escape the tax to the extent that it can prove its accumulation of current earnings was necessary to meet reasonable business needs, thereby reducing or eliminating its accumulated taxable income by way of the accumulated earnings credit.[6]

* * *

5. The accumulated taxable income on which this tax was determined was calculated as follows:

1976 taxable income	$187,279.35
Less: 1976 Federal income taxes	(76,082.18)
Accumulated taxable income	$111,197.17

Petitioner was not entitled to any portion of the minimum accumulated earnings credit under Section 535(c)(2) since its accumulated earnings and profits at the close of the prior year exceeded $150,000.

6. The taxpayer is also entitled to a minimum $150,000 credit against accumulated taxable income under Section 535(c)(2)

Once the reasonable needs of the corporation have been ascertained, the next step is to determine whether its earnings and profits were permitted to accumulate beyond those needs. Normally this requires more than a simple comparison of the corporation's total accumulated earnings and profits with its business needs. Because some of these earnings may be held in the form of illiquid assets such as land, plant and equipment, and thus may not be available for current distribution to shareholders, the focus generally is on the net liquid assets of the business and whether they exceed the immediate or reasonably anticipated needs of the business. * * * It should be emphasized that the accumulated earnings tax applies only to current year's accumulated taxable income as that term is defined in section 535; previously accumulated earnings are not subject to the penalty. However, prior year's accumulations are relevant in the computation to the extent they are available in the form of liquid assets to meet the taxpayer's current needs and render the accumulation of current earnings unnecessary.

* * *

The parties in this case have confined their arguments to the familiar issues of whether the accumulation of earnings during the year was for the reasonable needs of the business and not for the purpose of avoiding income taxes. Nevertheless, the facts fairly present another, more fundamental, legal issue which neither party has addressed: whether the distribution of all of petitioner's current earnings and profits in the redemption of its stock during the year bars the imposition of the penalty on the ground that no earnings were actually permitted to accumulate within the corporation.

The facts herein indicate that the portion of the redemption distribution's allocable to earnings and profits greatly exceeded petitioner's earnings and profits for its fiscal year ended September 30, 1976. * * * Section 312(a) provides that amounts paid in connection with a redemption of stock are treated as distributions of earnings and profits to the extent they are not properly chargeable to the capital account under Section 312(e). * * * Thus, * * * it can be argued that petitioner did not actually accumulate any earnings during the year and that the imposition of the accumulated earnings tax under such circumstances is inappropriate.

In *GPD, Inc. v. Commissioner,* 60 T.C. 480 (1973) (Court—reviewed), revd. and remanded 508 F.2d 1076 (6th Cir.1974), this Court decided this issue in favor of the taxpayer on similar facts and was reversed on appeal by the Sixth Circuit. Inasmuch as this case is appealable to the Third Circuit, we are not constrained to follow the Sixth Circuit's reversal * * *. Therefore, the matter is open for our reconsideration. However, because neither party has raised or briefed the merits of what has proved to be a fairly nettlesome legal issue, we think it inappropriate to undertake a

regardless of its business needs. This amount, however, is subject to reduction by the amount of any accumulated earnings and profits on hand at the beginning of the taxable year.

reassessment of our position in *GPD* at this time.[15] Accordingly, we will decide this case solely on the basis of the arguments raised at trial and briefed by the parties.

We are confronted, then, with the question of whether the hypothetical accumulation of current earnings (resulting from a failure to distribute such amounts in the form of taxable dividends) exceeded petitioner's reasonable business needs during the year in issue. Normally this determination requires a comparison of the corporation's net liquid assets at year-end (generally current assets minus current liabilities) to its aggregate business needs. If net liquid assets are found to exceed business needs, a presumption is created that current earnings were accumulated with a tax avoidance motive. Section 533. * * *

In the present case, however, a substantial portion of petitioner's current and accumulated earnings and profits were distributed during the year, nearly all of it in the form of cash, in order to redeem the stock of several of its shareholders. Because the use of funds to redeem stock does not necessarily qualify as a reasonable business need, particularly where the facts suggest that the redemption is primarily a device to bail out earnings and profits at capital gain rates, the Corporation's net liquid assets at year-end ($28,231.41) paint a completely misleading picture of its ability pay dividends during the taxable year. By contrast, had the Corporation elected to invest its idle cash in the acquisition of additional plant and equipment during the year, the year-end net liquid assets figure would be an appropriate measure of its dividend-paying capacity because the use to which the excess funds were directed would unquestionably constitute a

15. The resolution of this issue depends on how one interprets the relationship between several different Code provisions. Section 532(a) provides that the accumulated earnings tax applies to any corporation formed or availed of for the purpose of avoiding income taxes with respect to its shareholders "*by permitting earnings and profits to accumulate* instead of being divided or distributed." (Emphasis added). Once this statutory requirement is satisfied, section 531 imposes the penalty on the corporation's accumulated taxable income as computed under section 535. Accumulated taxable income is essentially a measure of the corporation's current earnings and profits and is generally equal to taxable income after certain adjustments, less the dividends paid deduction and the accumulated earnings credit. The dividends paid deduction is defined in sections 561 through 565. The key provision insofar as the present issue is concerned is section 562(c), which provides that no distribution shall be eligible for the dividends paid deduction unless the distribution is pro rata. Under this rule a non-pro rata stock redemption does not qualify for the dividends paid deduction, and consequently does not reduce accumulated taxable income (assuming, of course, that the redemption does not otherwise qualify as a reasonable business need eligible for the accumulated earnings credit provided under section 535(c)).

However, sections 312(a) and 316(a) provide that amounts paid in connection with a redemption of stock are treated as distributions out of current earnings and profits to the extent they are not properly chargeable to the capital account under section 312(e). Thus, under the statutory framework it is possible to have a stock redemption which consumes all of the current year's earnings and profits without effecting a corresponding reduction in the corporation's accumulated taxable income. Since section 532(a) arguably requires an *accumulation* of earnings and profits during the taxable year, the imposition of the accumulated earnings tax under these circumstances is subject to serious question.

* * *

reasonable business need. Thus, it becomes necessary to examine the circumstances surrounding the redemptions to determine whether they served a reasonable business purpose. If this question is answered in the negative, the assets distributed must be considered in the same light as unrelated business investments or shareholder loans; i.e., the amounts must be added back to the corporation's net liquid assets and deemed available for the payment of dividends. * * *

* * * [P]etitioner contends that it did not form an intention to redeem its stock until just before the distributions took place. Until that time, it alleges, its sole purpose in accumulating earnings was to protect against the loss of accounts. Thus, petitioner insists that at no time did it actually *accumulate* earnings, on a day-to-day basis, with the purpose of avoiding income taxes by distributing earnings in a stock redemption. Petitioner's argument ignores the fact that all the events of the taxable year are relevant in determining whether earnings were accumulated with the proscribed purpose.

* * *

Petitioner maintains that this redemption and the transfer in ownership which accompanied it were essential if the business was to continue to operate as a going concern. In support thereof petitioner contends the following:

(1) Victor and Jay anticipated serious financial difficulty in the face of the loss or impending loss of two of its major accounts, the Prudential–Grace and Moller lines, and thus they felt the Corporation could not afford to continue to pay the large salaries which the officers had been receiving.

(2) Dissension had arisen between Jay and Victor over whether to take on representation of a nonconference Russian line. The two also had disagreements over other policy matters, and at one point Jay gave serious consideration to leaving the Corporation.

(3) Because of his problems with Jay and his belief that the business was headed downhill, Victor decided it was time to cash in his investment, even though he was in good health and would have preferred to continue working with the company.

(4) Rather than liquidate the 50–year old family business and dismiss loyal employees, Victor chose to transfer control of the Corporation to Jay by selling one share of stock to him directly and causing the Corporation to redeem the remainder.

In short, petitioner argues that, because of the business reversals and the disagreements with Jay, Victor decided it was necessary to leave the company and allow Jay the opportunity to make a fresh start unencumbered by the burdensome salaries which Victor and Albert had been drawing. Since the only other alternative was liquidation, or so petitioner contends, the redemption necessarily satisfied a reasonable business purpose.

* * *

The cases dealing with the reasonable needs issue in a redemption context are difficult to reconcile and can hardly be said to constitute a uniform body of law on the subject. No doubt this is due in large measure to the difficulties inherent in attempting to distinguish between corporate and shareholder purposes in a closely held corporate setting. In most cases the presence of a shareholder benefit is readily discernible because the redemption proceeds are invariably taxed to the departing shareholders at favorable capital gain rates. Since capital gain distributions are not the kind of distributions which the accumulated earnings tax was designed to promote, the courts have been understandably reluctant to accord "reasonable need" characterization to earnings accumulated for the purpose of a redemption.

Nevertheless, the redemption of a dissenting minority or 50 percent shareholder has been found to serve a reasonable business purpose where the action appeared necessary to promote the harmonious transaction of corporate business or to prevent the sale of the minority stock to a hostile outsider. The case frequently cited for this proposition is *Mountain State Steel Foundries, Inc. v. Commissioner,* 284 F.2d 737 (4th Cir.1960). * * * In that case the stock of Mountain State Steel was owned equally by two families. The Stratton family was aggressive and wanted to plough corporate profits back into the business in order to expand and modernize. The Miller family, consisting of the widow and daughters of one of the original founders of the business, was more conservative and preferred greater financial security than the uncertain flow of dividends from the corporation would provide. Eventually the widow demanded that the business be sold, but no purchasers were found who were willing to pay the desired price. An agreement was finally reached whereby the corporation agreed to redeem the Miller stock for $450,000, payable $50,000 in cash with the balance to be paid in installments over a period of years.

The Commissioner asserted an accumulated earnings tax deficiency in the year of redemption and the three subsequent years. The Fourth Circuit disagreed, concluding that on the facts presented the accumulations in the year of redemption and in later years to discharge the resulting indebtedness served a legitimate corporate purpose, as follows (284 F.2d at 745):

> When the stockholders have such conflicting interests, the corporation and its future are necessarily affected. When the situation results in demands that the business be sold or liquidated, as it did here, the impact of the conflict upon the corporation is direct and immediate. * * * The resolution of such a conflict, so that the need of the corporation may govern managerial decision, is plainly a corporate purpose.

* * *

The leading case concerning the redemption of a majority stock interest is *Pelton Steel Casting Co. v. Commissioner,* 28 T.C. 153 (1957), affd. 251 F.2d 278 (7th Cir.1958), cert. denied 356 U.S. 958 (1958). There two shareholders, one owning 60 percent of the corporation and the other owning 20 percent, decided to sell their stock but were unable to find a purchaser who could meet their price. A third shareholder, who owned the remaining 20 percent of the stock, had devoted most of his life to the business and was concerned that a sale of the majority interest to another corporation would interfere with his management of the business and possibly cause the loss of some key employees. Accordingly, he devised a plan whereby the corporation would redeem the shares for approximately $800,000, with $300,000 payable out of the corporation's liquid assets and the balance to be paid from the proceeds of a $500,000 loan. To insure the availability of the necessary cash the corporation declared no dividends for 1946. The redemption took place the following year. Subsequently the Commissioner determined an accumulated earnings tax deficiency for 1946 on the ground that the accumulation for the proposed redemption did not serve a reasonable business need, but instead indicated a purpose to avoid income taxes.

This Court sustained the Commissioner's determination and cited several factors as the basis for its decision. First, we observed that a dividend distribution would not necessarily have made it impossible for the proposed redemption to occur, since the distribution presumably would have resulted in a corresponding reduction in the redemption price to be paid by the corporation. Second, we were unable to identify any reasonable corporate purpose served by the redemption. There was no evidence that the company was threatened with a sale of stock to an undesirable outsider. In fact, from a corporate standpoint the redemption may well have been counter-productive, since it caused a significant drain on the taxpayer's financial resources at a time when the taxpayer was alleging a need to accumulate earnings for additional working capital and plant improvements. Finally, in our view the fact that a majority stock interest was redeemed made it unlikely that the redemptions were motivated by anything other than a desire on the part of the redeeming shareholders to liquidate their interest at capital gain rates. Thus, we concluded that the redemption served no reasonable business purpose, but instead provided proof of the existence of the proscribed purpose.

We think the rationale of *Pelton Steel* applies with even greater force in the present case. Here nearly 95 percent of the outstanding stock of the Corporation, all of it belonging to a single shareholder, was redeemed in a transaction which consumed most of the Corporation's current and accumulated earnings and profits. The redemption proceeds were reported by Victor as long-term capital gain on his 1976 Federal income tax return. This personal tax benefit, coupled with Victor's undisputed control over corporate affairs before the redemption, raises, at the very least, a presumption that his personal objectives outweighed any alleged corporate purpose for the redemption.

The circumstances under which the redemption plan was conceived also suggest that personal considerations predominated in Victor's decision to leave the company. Victor was clearly worried about the future of the company in light of the loss of two major accounts, which collectively had accounted for 44 percent of the Corporation's gross revenues for the taxable year ended September 30, 1974. When asked at trial whether he considered simply retiring and assuming the role of a passive stockholder, he stated that it would have been unwise "to retain stock in a company if you know that their business is slipping." * * * Although we accept Victor's testimony that he left the business with great reluctance and would have preferred to continue on as an owner-employee, even though he was 72 years old, we nevertheless think his departure was spurred principally by a belief that the redemption and sale to Jay was the best financial avenue open to him. * * *

Petitioner concedes that, to a certain extent, Victor's decision to leave the company was in fact motivated by personal considerations. But at the same time petitioner contends that the redemption served a vital corporate purpose because the only other alternative was liquidation. Granted, it is entirely possible that this was the only other option Victor was willing to consider under the circumstances, and, indeed, we have found as a fact that at one point he considered and rejected this alternative. Nevertheless, this does not necessarily call for the conclusion that the distribution in redemption was essential from the standpoint of the Corporation. We note that petitioner has offered no rebuttal to respondent's contention that a dividend could have been declared during the year without frustrating the planned redemption. We found this to be a telling argument in *Pelton Steel,* and it is even more persuasive on these facts. Since Victor owned nearly 95 percent of the outstanding stock of the Corporation immediately preceding the redemption, the benefit of any dividend distribution declared on the common shares would have inured almost entirely to him, with the hold-over shareholder (Jay) deriving only a minor benefit. Likewise, the additional cash drain on the Corporation (relative to that caused by the redemption) would have been negligible. Furthermore, the distribution of earnings via a dividend would have reduced the book value of the Corporation and facilitated the forthcoming transfer of ownership to Jay in much the same manner as did the redemption. Thus, we are not convinced that the wholesale bail-out of earnings and profits which accompanied the redemption was an unavoidable result of the desired shift in ownership.

Moreover, our doubts as to the validity of the alleged corporate purpose are compounded by the seemingly inconsistent positions which petitioner has taken during this litigation. The bulk of petitioner's argument on brief was aimed at establishing that the Corporation was near the brink of economic collapse during the taxable year in issue. * * * Yet, despite the grim financial outlook portrayed by petitioner, the Corporation ultimately distributed virtually all of its liquid assets during the taxable year in the redemption of Victor Lamark's stock. As a result, the company found itself bereft of working capital and was forced to borrow $20,000 from the Pittsburgh National Bank to meet operating expenses immediately following the distribution. * * *

It is not our intention to suggest that the redemption of the stock of a majority shareholder can never be beneficial to a corporation. With regard to the present case, we are not prepared to say that the shift in ownership and control to Jay could not, in the long run, have a positive impact on the Corporation. By relieving the company of the salaries which Victor and Albert had been drawing, and by allowing Jay to exercise his unfettered judgment in the management of corporate affairs, the shift in ownership could conceivably have lifted the Corporation out of its alleged financial difficulties. The fact remains, however, that where a majority interest is redeemed in a capital gain distribution the personal shareholder benefit inevitably permeates the entire transaction, and absent evidence of a bona fide and predominant corporate purpose, the distribution cannot qualify as a business need for purposes of the accumulated earnings tax. In this case petitioner has failed to rebut the unfavorable inferences which may be drawn from the evidence before us.

Accordingly, we find that respondent has met his burden of proof on this issue and hold that the redemption of Victor Lamark's stock did not serve a reasonable business need. Because the assets distributed in that redemption exceeded the Corporation's current earnings and profits, we conclude that all of the latter were accumulated beyond the reasonable needs of the business, thereby creating a presumption of a tax avoidance motive under Section 533(a). That presumption stands unless petitioner proves otherwise by a preponderance of the evidence.

On this ultimate issue we find petitioner has failed to meet its burden of proof. Although throughout these proceedings Victor and Jay have vehemently denied that the Corporation ever accumulated earnings with the proscribed purpose, their testimony is unpersuasive. * * * We refuse to believe that the redemption of Victor's stock was made in blissful ignorance of the favorable tax consequences which ensued. * * * Moreover we note that from the date of its incorporation in 1966 until the end of the taxable year in issue the Corporation has paid only one dividend. That dividend totaled $8,000 and was paid during the taxable year ended September 30, 1974. * * * The failure to pay dividends in this case allowed Victor and the other redeeming shareholders to drain the Corporation of $288,478.40 in retained earnings, reducing its once-substantial cash hoard to almost nothing, while suffering only a capital gains tax in the process. Under these circumstances we find that the testimony elicited at trial is insufficient to overcome the presumption of tax avoidance created by Section 533(a).

Accordingly, we hold that petitioner was availed of during the taxable year for the purpose of avoiding income taxes with respect to its shareholders by permitting earnings to accumulate instead of distributing them in the form of taxable dividends. Since petitioner has failed to prove that it was necessary to accumulate current year's earnings to meet its reasonable business needs, no accumulated earnings credit will be allowed to offset its accumulated taxable income.

* * *

NOTES

1. If a corporation repurchases its shares for cash (or its promise to pay cash), it faces no recognition of income. Suppose, however, the company

exchanges some property it owns for the shares. If the fair market value of the property exceeds the corporation's basis in the asset, the company must recognize the difference as taxable gain. I.R.C. § 311(b)(1). The reverse is not true: If the fair market is less than the firm's basis, the company cannot recognize the loss. I.R.C. § 311(a). Assuming the redemption is a necessary expenditure of corporate funds, can the company claim a deduction? See I.R.C. § 162(k)(no). Suppose, however, in addition to repurchasing its shares, the corporation obtains a covenant not to compete from selling stockholders. See I.R.C. § 197 (providing a deduction based upon a fifteen year amortization for certain intangible assets, including covenants not to compete agreed to in connection with the acquisition of an interest in a trade or business). *Frontier Chevrolet Co. v. Commissioner*, 329 F.3d 1131 (9th Cir.2003) (applying Section 197 to a covenant not to compete entered into in connection with the redemption of stock).

2. As the court notes in *Lamark Shipping,* redemptions affect a corporation's earnings and profits. Exchange of appreciated assets for the redeemed stock increases earnings and profits by the amount of gain the company recognizes. I.R.C. § 312(b). If the redemption receives characterization as a distribution rather than a sale, then it reduces earnings and profits just as any distribution. *See* I.R.C. § 312(a). What happens if the redemption qualifies for sale treatment? In this event, some of the payment presumably constitutes a distribution of accumulated profits (which ought to reduce earnings and profits), while some of it presumably represents the return of invested capital (and should not reduce earnings and profits). The trick is to figure out how much belongs in each category. The opinion in *Lamark Shipping* cited Section 312(e) as governing this question. In 1984, Congress repealed Section 312(e), and enacted Section 312(n)(7) in its place. The legislative history explains the effect of this change as follows:

> "In any case of a distribution by a corporation in redemption of its own stock, earnings and profits are to be reduced in proportion to the amount of the corporation's outstanding stock that is redeemed. For example, assume that X corporation has 1,000 shares of $10 par value stock outstanding, and that A and B each acquired 500 of original issue shares at a price of $20 per share. Assume further that X corporation, which has operated a profitable services oriented business since its inception, holds net assets worth $100,000 consisting of cash ($50,000) and appreciated improved real property ($50,000), and has current and accumulated earnings and profits of $50,000. If X corporation distributes $50,000 in cash to A in redemption of A's share in X corporation, earnings, profits and capital account would each be reduced by $25,000. After the transaction, X corporation would have $25,000 of earnings and profits. However, the committee does not intend that earnings and profits be reduced by more than the amount of redemption." S. Rep. No. 98–169, 98th Cong., 2d Sess. 202.

Besides earnings and profits, a redemption can affect one other corporate tax attribute: this being the firm's ability to use net operating loss carryovers under Section 172. For example, if the company redeems all the shares of a majority stockholder, there would occur an "ownership change" triggering Section 382 (assuming there was no family attribution between the selling and remaining stockholders). I.R.C. § 382(g). As seen in *Garber Indus.* earlier, Section 382 imposes a limit upon how much a corporation may use existing net operating loss carryovers following an ownership change. I.R.C. § 382(a), (b). Chapter VII will explore the workings of Section 382 in some depth.

3. As explained earlier, the primary advantage of structuring a buy-out as a redemption rather than a cross-purchase is to allow corporate earnings to fund the purchase without paying a double tax. The counterpoint, illustrated by *Lamark Shipping,* is the corporation might pay an accumulated earnings tax on the income it used to redeem the stock. This depends upon a number of factors. The primary issue considered in *Lamark Shipping* is whether the redemption itself constituted a reasonable need of the business, instead of serving primarily the interests of the shareholders. If it did, funds reasonably retained for the redemption do not contribute to the company's accumulated taxable income, nor demonstrate the purpose of accumulating income for tax avoidance rather than legitimate reasons. I.R.C. §§ 533(a), 535(a), (c)(1). The court's opinion notes the difficulty of making such a determination, and discusses some of the key cases and factors. The clearest business need would probably be a redemption to resolve a deadlock between equal shareholders. *Cf. Emeloid Co. v. Commissioner,* 189 F.2d 230 (3d Cir.1951). A number of favorable decisions also exist for repurchases of dissident minority interests (albeit, one might question the ability of a minority to disrupt corporate affairs). *E.g., Gazette Publishing Co. v. Self,* 103 F.Supp. 779 (E.D.Ark.1952). Purchases of majority stockholder interests, as in *Lamark Shipping,* have not fared as well. In one instance, the code specifically indicates that redemption constitutes a reasonable business need. This is a redemption covered by Section 303. I.R.C. § 537(a)(2), (b)(1).

Even if a redemption serves a corporate purpose, there is still the question of whether the accumulation of earnings is really necessary for the redemption. After all, if the corporation accumulates its earnings in order to buy back its stock, the redemption price goes up—particularly if the purchase is from a substantial majority stockholder. See the discussion of the *Pelton Steel* decision in *Lamark Shipping.* The reverse of this may also be true: Even though the redemption might not have a business purpose, the corporation may have accumulated the funds for another legitimate reason. This was the alternate argument Lamark Shipping Agency made. Why did it fail? Pursuing this reasoning further, suppose the corporation borrows to fund the buy-out (either from an outside source, or by issuing notes to the selling shareholder), and then uses its earnings to pay off the debt. Can it argue the repayment of debt is a legitimate corporate purpose, even if the redemption was not? See Treas. Reg. § 1.537–2(b)(3) (permitting accumulation of earnings for retirement of bona fide indebtedness created in connection with the trade or business.) Similarly, in terms of timing, notice Section 537 only explicitly protects accumulations to make a

Section 303 redemption to the extent the accumulation occurs during or after the year the stockholder died, not before. I.R.C. § 537(b)(1).

Finally, consider the court's discussion of the fact that Lamark Shipping Agency did not really retain earnings during the course of the year, as it paid the money out in the redemption. Nevertheless, the court, following the Third Circuit's view, held there to be an accumulation of earnings to avoid tax. From a practical standpoint, what impact can this have on a corporation's ability to redeem its stock without serious tax penalty? After all, money the company pays out in a redemption is not available for dividends. Mitigating this problem, remember corporations can accumulate without penalty up to $250,000 (or $150,000 for certain service firms) in earnings and profits. I.R.C. § 535(c)(2).

(iii) Treatment of the Remaining Shareholders

Revenue Ruling 69–608

1969–2 C.B. 42.

Advice has been requested as to the treatment for Federal income tax purposes of the redemption by a corporation of a retiring shareholder's stock where the remaining shareholder of the corporation has entered into a contract to purchase such stock.

Where the stock of a corporation is held by a small group of people, it is often considered necessary to the continuity of the corporation to have the individuals enter into agreements among themselves to provide for the disposition of the stock of the corporation in the event of the resignation, death, or incapacity of one of them. Such agreements are generally reciprocal among the shareholders and usually provide that on the resignation, death, or incapacity of one of the principal shareholders, the remaining shareholders will purchase his stock. Frequently such agreements are assigned to the corporation by the remaining shareholder and the corporation actually redeems its stock from the retiring shareholder.

Where a corporation redeems stock from a retiring shareholder, the fact that the corporation in purchasing the shares satisfies the continuing shareholder's executory contractual obligation to purchase the redeemed shares does not result in a distribution to the continuing shareholder provided that the continuing shareholder is not subject to an existing primary and unconditional obligation to perform the contract and that the corporation pays no more than fair market value for the stock redeemed.

On the other hand, if the continuing shareholder, at the time of the assignment to the corporation of his contract to purchase the retiring shareholder's stock, is subject to an unconditional obligation to purchase the retiring shareholder's stock, the satisfaction by the corporation of his obligation results in a constructive distribution to him. The constructive distribution is taxable as a distribution under Section 301 of the Internal Revenue Code of 1954.

If the continuing shareholder assigns his stock purchase contract to the redeeming corporation prior to the time when he incurs a primary and unconditional obligation to pay for the shares of stock, no distribution to him will result. If, on the other hand, the assignment takes place after the time when the continuing shareholder is so obligated, a distribution to him will result. While a pre-existing obligation to perform in the future is a necessary element in establishing a distribution in this type of case, it is not until the obligor's duty to perform becomes unconditional that it can be said a primary and unconditional obligation arises.

The application of the above principles may be illustrated by the situations described below.

* * *

Situation 2

A and *B* are unrelated individuals who own all of the outstanding stock of corporation *X*. An agreement between them provides unconditionally that within ninety days of the death of either *A* or *B*, the survivor will purchase the decedent's stock of *X* from his estate. Following the death of *B*, *A* causes *X* to assume the contract and redeem the stock from *B*'s estate.

The assignment of the contract to *X* followed by the redemption by *X* of the stock owned by *B*'s estate will result in a constructive distribution to *A* because immediately on the death of *B, A* had a primary and unconditional obligation to perform the contract.

* * *

Situation 4

A and *B* owned all of the outstanding stock of *X* corporation. *A* and *B* entered into a contract under which, if *B* desired to sell his *X* stock, *A* agreed to purchase the stock or to cause such stock to be purchased. If *B* chose to sell his *X* stock to any person other than *A*, he could do so at any time. In accordance with the terms of the contract, *A* caused *X* to redeem all of *B*'s stock in *X*.

At the time of the redemption, *B* was free to sell his stock to *A* or to any other person, and *A* had no unconditional obligation to purchase the stock and no fixed liability to pay for the stock. Accordingly, the redemption by *X* did not result in a constructive distribution to *A*.

Situation 5

A and *B* owned all of the outstanding stock of *X* corporation. An agreement between *A* and *B* provided that upon the death of either, *X* will redeem all of the *X* stock owned by the decedent at the time of his death. In the event that *X* does not redeem the shares from the estate, the agreement provided that the surviving shareholders would purchase the unredeemed shares from the decedent's estate. *B* dies and, in accordance with the agreement, *X* redeemed all of the shares owned by his estate.

In this case *A* was only secondarily liable under the agreement between *A* and *B*. Since *A* was not primarily obligated to purchase the *X* stock from the estate of *B*, he received no constructive distribution when *X* redeemed the stock.

* * *

Situation 7

A and *B* owned all of the outstanding stock of *X* corporation. An agreement between the shareholders provided that upon the death of either, the survivor would purchase the decedent's shares from his estate at a price provided in the agreement. Subsequently, the agreement was rescinded and a new agreement entered into which provided that upon the death of either *A* or *B*, *X* would redeem all of the decedent's shares of *X* stock from his estate.

The cancellation of the original contract between the parties in favor of the new contract did not result in a constructive distribution to either *A* or *B*. At the time *X* agreed to purchase the stock pursuant to the terms of the new agreement, neither *A* nor *B* had an unconditional obligation to purchase shares of *X* stock. The subsequent redemption of the stock from the estate of either pursuant to the terms of the new agreement will not constitute a constructive distribution to the surviving shareholder.

Revenue Ruling 78–60

1978–1 C.B. 81.

Advice has been requested whether under section 302(a) of the Internal Revenue Code of 1954 the stock redemptions described below qualified for exchange treatment, and whether under Section 305(b)(2) and (c) the shareholders who experienced increases in their proportionate interests in the redeeming corporation as a result of the stock redemptions will be treated as having received distributions of property to which Section 301 applies.

Corporation *Z* has only one class of stock outstanding. The *Z* common stock is held by 24 shareholders, all of whom are descendants, or spouses of descendants, of the founder of *Z*.

In 1975, when *Z* had 6,000 shares of common stock outstanding, the board of directors of *Z* adopted a plan of annual redemption to provide a means for its shareholders to sell their stock. The plan provides that *Z* will annually redeem up to 40 shares of its outstanding stock at a price established annually by the *Z* board of directors. Each shareholder of *Z* is entitled to cause *Z* to redeem two-thirds of one percent of the shareholder's stock each year. If some shareholders choose not to participate fully in the plan during any year, the other shareholders can cause *Z* to redeem more than two-thirds of one percent of their stock, up to the maximum of 40 shares.

Pursuant to the plan of annual redemption, *Z* redeemed 40 shares of its stock in 1976. Eight shareholders participated in the redemptions.

Issue 1

Section 302(a) of the Code provides that if a corporation redeems its stock, and if section 302(b)(1), (2) or (3) applies, the redemption will be treated as a distribution in part or full payment in exchange for the stock.

* * *

None of the redemptions here qualified under section 302(b)(3) of the Code because all of the shareholders who participated in the redemptions continue to own stock of Z. Moreover, none of the redemptions qualified under section 302(b)(2) because none of the shareholders who participated in the redemptions experienced a reduction in interest of more than 20 percent, as section 302(b)(2)(C) requires. Therefore, the first question is whether the redemptions were "not essentially equivalent to a dividend" within the meaning of section 302(b)(1).

* * *

In this case, an important fact is that the 1976 redemptions were not isolated occurrences but were undertaken pursuant to an ongoing plan for *Z* to redeem 40 shares of its stock each year. None of the reductions in proportionate interest experienced by *Z* shareholders as a result of the 1976 redemptions was "meaningful" because the reductions were small and each shareholder has the power to recover the lost interest by electing not to participate in the redemption plan in later years.

Accordingly, none of the 1976 redemptions qualified for exchange treatment under section 302(a) of the Code. All of the redemptions are to be treated as distributions of property to which section 301 applies.

Issue 2

Section 305(b)(2) of the Code provides that section 301 will apply to a distribution by a corporation of its stock if the distribution, or a series of distributions that includes the distribution, has the result of the receipt of property by some shareholders, and increases in the proportionate interests of other shareholders in the assets or earnings and profits of the corporation.

Section 305(c) of the Code authorizes regulations under which a redemption treated as a section 301 distribution will be treated as a section 301 distribution to any shareholder whose proportionate interest in the earnings and profits or assets of the corporation is increased by the redemption.

Section 1.305–7(a) of the Income Tax Regulations provides that a redemption treated as a section 301 distribution will generally be treated as a distribution to which sections 305(b)(2) and 301 of the Code apply if the proportionate interest of any shareholder in the earnings and profits or assets of the corporation deemed to have made the stock distribution is increased by the redemption, and distribution has the result described in section 305(b)(2). The distribution is to be deemed made to any shareholder whose interest in the earnings and profits or assets of the distributing corporation is increased by the redemption.

* * * A distribution of property incident to an isolated redemption will not cause section 305(b)(2) to apply even though the redemption distribution is treated as a section 301 distribution.

Section 305 of the Code does not make the constructive stock ownership rules of section 318(a) applicable to its provisions.

The 16 shareholders of *Z* who did not tender any stock for redemption in 1976 experienced increases in their proportionate interest of the earnings and profits and assets of *Z* (without taking into account constructive stock ownership under section 318 of the Code) as a result of the redemptions. Shareholders *B* and *X*, who surrendered small amounts of their stock for redemption in 1976, also experienced increases in their proportionate interests. The 1976 redemptions were not isolated but were undertaken pursuant to an ongoing plan of annual stock redemptions. Finally, the 1976 redemptions are to be treated as distributions of property to which section 301 of the Code applies.

Accordingly, *B*, *X* and the 16 shareholders of *Z* who did not participate in the 1976 redemptions are deemed to have received stock distributions to which sections 305(b)(2) and 301 of the Code apply. See examples (8) and (9) of section 1.305–3(e) of the regulations for a method of computing the amounts of the deemed distributions.

NOTES

1. The two rulings above indicate the two ways in which redemptions can constitute a constructive dividend to the non-selling stockholders. Revenue Ruling 69–608 shows the danger when the remaining stockholders have a primary and unconditional contractual obligation to buy the selling shareholder's stock, which the corporation carries out. What is the impact of this as far as drafting buy-out agreements in advance of the triggering event—the utility of which was discussed in Chapter IV? For example, suppose the drafter wishes to provide for successive options, under which, if the remaining shareholders do not wish to buy the stock, then the corporation has the next option to do so. On the other hand, is there any problem if the drafter desires a mandatory buy-sell agreement with successive obligations? To be safe, whose obligation should be first? Does the ruling have any significance for parties agreeing upon an immediate buy-out of one shareholder? Presumably, they should be sure of what they want before committing to a cross-purchase. *See, e.g., Jacobs v. Commissioner,* 41 T.C.M. (CCH) 951 (1981). Also, joint obligations by the corporation and remaining shareholders are hazardous. *E.g., Yelencsics v. Commissioner,* 74 T.C. 1513 (1980). Keep in mind, as well, participants in a corporation may have entered mandatory buy-sell contracts years earlier, and forgotten they ever did so as they now agree upon a redemption without first canceling the old

contract. Yet another situation creating a potential problem in this regard occurs when a state court divides property between divorcing spouses. If the state court directs one spouse to buy the other's marital interest in stock, what will happen if the spouse has the corporation make the purchase instead? See Treas. Reg. § 1.1041–2 (treating the redemption of stock incident to a divorce as a constructive distribution to the other spouse, if such treatment is called for by principles applicable to redemptions generally (in other words, if the corporation's redemption satisfies the non-selling spouse's obligation), but allowing the divorcing spouses to avoid uncertainty in the application of such principles by specifying in a written agreement which spouse must recognize the income from the redemption).

Revenue Ruling 78–60 illustrates a second danger, that created by Section 305(b)(2) and (c). These provisions will receive more careful explanation later in this chapter. For present purposes, it is sufficient to realize this danger is not usually present in a buy-out. To begin with, for Section 305(c) to apply, the redemption must receive distribution rather than sale treatment. (Note this gives the remaining shareholders a stake in the selling stockholder's obtaining sale treatment.) Moreover, the regulations do not apply Section 305(c) to isolated redemptions, but only to repurchases which are part of a periodic redemption plan (as is the ruling). Treas. Reg. § 1.305–3(e) Ex. (10), (11). (Recall, however, that the idea of periodic redemptions was raised earlier as a means to deal with the financial limitations on corporate stock repurchases in those states following the *Neimark* approach under which the court compares the total obligation incurred by the corporation in order to repurchase the stock against the amount of the corporation's surplus at the time of the acquisition.)

Beyond these two situations, is there any more general danger that a redemption may constitute a constructive dividend for the remaining stockholders? After all, the repurchase benefits them by increasing their percentage of ownership in the company. The response, of course, is that the decreased worth of the corporation because of the pay-out offsets the increased proportionate holding. Would this response still apply, however, if the corporation managed to purchase the shares at less than fair market value? *See Holsey v. Commissioner,* 258 F.2d 865 (3d Cir.1958) (holding no constructive dividend even then).

2. One other possible effect of redemptions upon the remaining shareholders is potentially to curb their ability to take advantage of Section 1202's exclusion of 50 percent of the gain on the sale of qualifying stock. I.R.C. § 1202(c)(3) (redemptions from a shareholder (or a related party) within two years, either before or after, the shareholder acquires stock, or redemptions of over five percent of the corporation's outstanding stock within one year of the purchase, prevents the purchased stock from qualifying for favorable treatment). Still, the reduction in capital gains rates (at least through 2008) has marginalized the advantage of Section 1202 stock in any event.

SECTION B. RESTRUCTURING THROUGH STOCK DIVIDENDS AND RECAPITALIZATIONS

1. STOCK DIVIDENDS AND STOCK SPLITS

a. *Corporate and Securities Law Aspects*

A corporation can issue additional shares to its stockholders, without receiving consideration in return, in transactions commonly referred to as a stock dividend and a stock split. *E.g.*, Cal. Corp. Code § 409(a)(2); Del. Gen. Corp. Law § 173; N.Y. Bus. Corp. Law § 511; M.B.C.A. § 6.23(a). (The difference between these two transactions will be described shortly.) Such share distributions can achieve a number of objectives. To begin with, consider the simplest situation: A corporation, which has only one class of stock outstanding, distributes additional shares of this class pro-rata among its stockholders. Fundamentally, this transaction seems meaningless. Each stockholder may have more certificates, or a larger number printed on his or her certificate, but his or her entitlement to dividends, to liquidating distributions, or to voting power remains unchanged. Nevertheless, there can be some utility for such a distribution. It lowers the value of each individual share, and thus can facilitate their trading. In addition, some empirical studies have suggested a further effect in companies with widely held shares. The price per share may not decline proportionately to the increased outstanding stock (thus actually enriching the recipient shareholders). *E.g.*, Lewellen, The Cost of Capital 113 (1969). *But see* E. Brigham, Financial Management Theory and Practice 481–85 (5th ed. 1988). In part, this may be a function of increased marketability at lower prices. It may also reflect assumptions about the prospects for the corporation, as often companies distribute stock dividends or make stock splits when they expect increased earnings. (To prevent investors, however, from misconstruing the significance of stock dividends and stock splits, the accounting profession, the New York Stock Exchange, and the Securities Exchange Commission have proposed or adopted standards—discussed below—for both terminology and accounting treatment of these transactions.)

A stock dividend with more potential uses occurs when a corporation with one class outstanding distributes a new class of preferred shares among its common holders. This often occurs in a closely held corporation as one or more shareholders grow less active in the business (typically because of advancing age). At this point, dividend preferences become useful as a potential substitute for lost salary (albeit, the preference only has an effect if the stockholders do not retain the preferred and common shares in the same ratio). The preferred stock, if non-voting, can also smooth the transition of control to the remaining active owners. In part, this occurs because the distribution lowers the value of the outstanding common, since those shares no longer represent the entire ownership in the company. (Indeed, if the parties set the liquidation preference of the preferred shares near the present value of the business assets, and the dividend preference near the current earnings, they might reduce the immediate value of the common stock to fairly little, depending upon the prospects for future earnings growth.) Lowering the value of the common, in turn, makes it easier to fund a buy-out of the inactive participant's remaining voting shares. It also lessens the burdens upon the parties increasing their participation in running the venture to purchase additional voting common from the corporation. In addition, distributing non-voting stock allows an elderly shareholder to give or bequeath voting shares to individuals he or she wishes to assume a role in running the business, and non-voting shares to other individuals whom he or she simply wants to benefit economically. Of course, distributing debt instruments or even cash may achieve these same effects. Compare, however, the tax and corporate law impacts of such a distribution.

Pro-rata distributions of additional shares, when the corporation has only one class outstanding, cannot, in themselves, serve to shift interests between stockholders. This is no longer necessarily true once the company has common and preferred shares outstanding. For example, distributions on preferred of either common or more preferred can increase the preferred's claim to future cash dividends vis-a-vis the common if either the stock distribution occurs only for the preferred, or if the preferred was originally non-participating. Alternately, a stock split increasing only the number of common shares raises the common's claim to cash dividends vis-a-vis participating preferred. Such stock distributions may be useful to achieve shifts in profit interests agreeable to all. They could also, however, lead to abuse of one class by another.

Turning to the mechanics of the transaction, the traditional theory behind a stock dividend is that it constitutes a dividend like any other, except paid in shares of the corporation's own stock. This means complying with a mix of the statutory requirements for both stock issuances and dividends. As with all issuances of stock, the articles must authorize the shares the company proposes to distribute. The authority of directors to declare dividends of cash or property—such as the corporation's own shares—substitutes for the normal requirement that the company receive consideration in exchange for issuing its stock. *See, e.g.,* Del. Gen. Corp. Law § 173. In states adhering to traditional concepts of stated capital, the corporation must increase the capital shown on its books to reflect the issuance of additional shares as a dividend (just as it must increase capital if it sold further shares). Del. Gen. Corp. Law § 173, N.Y. Bus. Corp. Law § 511(a). *But see* N.Y. Bus. Corp. Law § 511(d) (allowing distribution of treasury shares without the need to increase capital). How much should this increase be? Consistent with the latitude given the directors to set the capital from shares sold at any amount equal to or greater than the aggregate par value of those shares, the Delaware statute allows the board in the case of a stock dividend to increase capital by any amount the board desires so long as the amount is not less than the aggregate par value of the shares distributed as a dividend. Del. Gen. Corp. Law § 173. New York also follows a pattern paralleling its treatment of sales: The company must capitalize dividends of par value shares at their aggregate par, and dividends of no-par shares at whatever amount the board fixes. N.Y. Bus. Corp. Law § 511(a)(1), (2). On the other hand, the accounting profession, the New York Stock Exchange and the Securities Exchange Commission have urged companies to capitalize an amount equal to the fair market value of the shares issued in a stock dividend. Accounting Research Bulletin No. 43 Ch. 7b (1953); N.Y.S.E. Listed Company Manual pp. 7–13—7–16 (1983); Sec. Exch. Act. Rel. No. 8268. Of course, if the company increases its capital, it must decrease its surplus by an equivalent amount. *E.g.,* N.Y. Bus. Corp. Law § 511(a)(1), (2). This places the same limit on stock dividends as exists on dividends generally; that is, the amount of the dividend (as presumably measured by the amount capital increases) cannot exceed the amount of a corporation's surplus. *E.g., Northern Bank & Trust Co. v. Day,* 83 Wash. 296, 145 P. 182 (1915).

The traditional view of a stock split, in contrast, is it constitutes a form of recapitalization. (A later portion of this chapter explores recapitalizations generally.) Carrying out a stock split may require amendment of the articles to increase the number of authorized shares and to lower the par value of the shares. Then, through article amendment (or possibly just an exchange offer), the corporation gives each shareholder of the class affected the right to obtain a greater number of shares for each share owned. *See, e.g.,* Cal. Corp. Code § 188 (stock split effected by article amendment); Del. Gen. Corp. Law § 242(a) ("subdivision" of stock into a greater number of shares can be effected by article amendment). (Alternately, in a reverse stock split, the directors and shareholders amend the articles to reduce the number of authorized shares and thereby force each stockholder to exchange his or her stock for a lower number of shares. *See, e.g.,* Del. Gen. Corp. Law § 242(a) ("combination" of shares into a lesser number of shares can be effected by article amendment); *Lerner v. Lerner,* 306 Md. 771, 511 A.2d 501 (1986).) Under traditional stated capital statutes, the central difference between a stock split and a stock dividend is that the split need not increase capital. *E.g.,* Del. Gen. Corp. Law § 173; N.Y. Bus. Corp. Law § 511(a), (d). (This is why the corporation may need to amend its articles to decrease par value if it undertakes a stock split.) Hence, a company can engage in a stock split even if it does not have any surplus.

As pointed out above, a number of agencies have been concerned with investors possibly misunderstanding stock dividends and stock splits. This could be particularly the case in situations when the company makes only a small increase in the number of shares outstanding, and, therefore, the price may not change to fully reflect the dilution. One response has been to require dividend characterization of distributions equal to less than 25 percent of the number of already outstanding shares, with capitalization of the fair market value of the distributed stock. Accounting Research Bulletin No. 43 Ch. 7b (1953); N.Y.S.E. Listed Company Manual pp. 7–13—7–16 (1983); Sec. Exch. Act Rel. No. 8268. At the same time, these authorities have sought to discourage companies from referring to any distribution in which the firm does not capitalize fair market value as a dividend, rather than a split. Moving in opposite direction are those statutes which have done away with the concept of stated capital. Under such statutes, no real distinction may remain between share distributions through a stock split or stock dividend. Also, with these statutes, the limitations applicable to distributions of cash or other property do not apply to distributions of the company's own shares regardless of how characterized. *See* Cal. Corp. Code §§ 166, 409(a)(2); M.B.C.A. §§ 1.40(6); 6.23. One problem with giving directors too much discretion to declare share dividends is the possibility for prejudice between outstanding classes as outlined above. To some extent, the dividend rights of various shares may limit this danger. For example, if a dividend preference specified payment in cash, this should preclude stock dividends to the preferred which prejudice the common. In addition, some statutes attempt to deal with the problem by limiting stock dividends which consist of a different class of shares than held by the recipients. *E.g.,* M.B.C.A. § 6.23(b); N.Y. Bus. Corp. Law § 511(a)(3). Also, perhaps preemptive rights might apply to the stock dividend. *Id.* at § 511(a)(4). Otherwise, the only protection lies in an uncertain claim for breach of fiduciary duty.

Since stock dividends and stock splits involve issuing additional shares, application of federal and state securities laws becomes a possible concern. One approach is to say these laws do not apply because such transactions do not constitute a "sale" of securities—that is a disposition "for value". *E.g.,* H.R. Rep. No. 152, 73d Cong., 1st Sess. 25 (1933) (Conference Committee report indicating Congress assumed that stock dividends did not constitute a sale under the 1933 Securities Act); Sec. Act. Rule 145(a)(1) (excepting stock splits and reverse stock splits from reclassifications deemed to constitute a sale under the 1933 Securities Act); Uniform Securities Act (1985 revision) § 101(13)(vi) (expressly excluding stock dividends from the definition of a sale). Suppose, however, the corporation gives stockholders a choice of receiving a dividend of further shares or of cash: Is there now a "sale" when stockholders waive the cash and take shares? See Sec. Act Rel. No. 929 (1936)(still no sale); Uniform Securities Act (1985 revision) § 101(13)(vi)(same). (A possible exception exists if the company had already declared a cash dividend—making it a debt owed—and then asked its stockholders to waive the cash in exchange for further shares.)

Some state securities laws, by contrast, treat stock dividends and stock splits as a sale, but then may create an exemption when the dividend is not in exchange for anything of value from the shareholders (other than giving up an option for a cash dividend). *E.g.*, Uniform Securities Act (2002 revision) §§ 102(26), 202(22)(A). As yet another approach, California's securities law only excludes stock dividends from the definition of a sale when the dividend consists of a distribution of voting common stock to holders of voting common, in a corporation having no other class of voting shares, and when there is no option to receive cash or other property. Cal. Corp. Code § 25017(f). California exempts stock splits and reverse stock splits from qualification only so long as they do *not* fall into any of the following three broad categories:

> "* * * (1) any stock split or reverse stock split if the corporation has more than one class of shares outstanding and the split would have a material effect on the proportionate interests of the respective classes as to voting, dividends or distributions; (2) any stock split of a stock which is traded in the market and its market price as of the date of directors' approval of the stock split adjusted to give effect to the split was less than two dollars ($2) per share; [this is designed to stop creation of cheap or 'penny' stocks] and (3) any reverse stock split if the corporation has the option of paying cash for any fractional shares created by such reverse split and as a result of such action proportionate interests of the shareholders would be substantially altered." Cal. Corp. Code § 25103(f).

A major impact of California's approach is to give its corporation's commissioner authority to review the fairness of stock dividends or stock splits which may prejudice one class of shares to favor another. *See* 10 Cal. Code Reg. § 260.140.70.

b. *Tax Aspects*

(i) Treatment Upon Receipt

Revenue Ruling 76–258

1976–2 C.B. 95.

Advice has been requested whether a distribution of preferred stock that is immediately redeemable at the option of a shareholder is an election within the meaning of section 305(b)(1) of the Internal Revenue Code of 1954 and, thus, a distribution of property to which section 301 applies.

X corporation distributed pro rata shares of its preferred stock to the holders of its common stock. The preferred stock is redeemable at any time after the distribution at the option of a shareholder. The preferred stock is redeemable at its par value for money.

Section 305(a) of the Code provides, generally, that gross income does not include the amount of any distribution of the stock of a corporation made by such corporation to its shareholders with respect to its stock, except as otherwise provided in section 305(b).

Section 305(b)(1) of the Code provides, in part, that section 305(a) shall not apply to a distribution by a corporation of its stock and the distribution shall be treated as a distribution of property to which section 301 applies, if the distribution is, at the election of any of the shareholders (whether exercised before or after the declaration thereof), payable either (A) in its stock, or (B) in property.

Since the preferred stock is redeemable immediately after the distribution at the option of a shareholder, a shareholder may either hold the preferred stock or have it redeemed for money. Thus, the effect of the immediate redeemability feature of the preferred stock is to give a shareholder an election to receive either stock or property within the meaning of section 305(b)(1)(A) and (B) of the Code.

Accordingly, in the instant case, the distribution is treated as a distribution of property to which section 301 of the Code applies.

NOTE

Suppose a corporation has one class of stock outstanding. If it issues additional shares pro-rata to its stockholders, either as a dividend or as a stock split, have the shareholders received any income? The stockholders now have more share certificates (or a larger number printed on their certificates), but their real interest as measured by their entitlement to dividends or to distributions upon liquidation remains unchanged. Reflecting this fact, Section 305(a) states, as a general rule, that distributions by a corporation of its own stock to its shareholders with respect to their shares do not constitute income. (Keep in mind, this only covers distributions of stock in the corporation itself, not stock it owns in another company. Also, the distribution must be with respect to stock; i.e. not compensation for services or in exchange for property, even though paid to shareholders.)

As the ruling above shows, to every general rule there are exceptions—in this instance, set out in Section 305(b). The first exception (and the one involved in the ruling) is a distribution in which shareholders can elect to receive either stock or property (such as cash). I.R.C. § 305(b)(1). The notion is that those electing to receive stock have, in effect, taken the money or other property and reinvested it by purchasing stock. The above ruling holds that the corporation cannot slip around this exception by issuing stock immediately redeemable at the shareholder's option. Moreover, if even one shareholder receives the option to get other property, every shareholder receiving stock (including those who had no choice to take property) must recognize income. Rev. Rul. 83–68, 1983–1 C.B. 75. What fiduciary duty problem might this fact create?

Suppose the corporation does not provide its shareholders an election, but rather just gives property to some and stock to others. (Because all shares of the same class are ordinarily entitled to the same dividend, this is usually possible only if the company has more than one class outstanding.) Such an action brings into play the exception found in Section 305(b)(2). This exception covers a distribution, or series of distributions, which result in some shareholders receiving property, while others enjoy an increase in their proportionate share of the corporation's profits or assets. The legislative history provides a simple example of stock dividends falling within this exception:

> "[I]f a corporation has two classes of common stock, one paying regular cash dividends and the other paying corresponding stock dividends (whether in common or preferred stock), the stock dividends are to be taxable." S. Rep. No. 91–552, 91st Cong., 1st Sess., at 153.

On the other hand, not every stock dividend which corresponds to another class receiving money or other property comes within the exception. Consider the following example from the Senate Report:

> "[I]f a corporation has a single class of common stock and a class of preferred stock which pays cash dividends and is not convertible, and it distributes a pro rata common stock dividend with respect to its common stock, the stock distribution is not taxable because the distribution does not have the result of increasing the proportionate interests of any of the stockholders."

To understand why there is no increase in the proportionate interest of the common holders receiving the dividend of common, ask whether this dividend either changed their interests vis–a–vis the other common holders, or gave them any additional dividend or liquidation rights as against non–participating, non–convertible preferred. Suppose, however, the stock dividend in the prior example consisted of preferred shares: Would this increase the recipients' interests in profits or upon liquidation? See Treas. Reg. § 1.305–3(e) Ex. (3). (To answer this question, consider the impact of the additional issuance not only if the company makes enough money to cover the dividend preference of all the shares, and has enough assets upon liquidation to cover the entire liquidation preference, but also what happens if it does not.) As these examples indicate, stock dividends in the multiple class situation can have a real economic effect. They also indicate that determining if such an effect is present in a given case requires careful evaluation of the rights of the various classes. Keep in mind, however, not every stock dividend increasing the proportionate interests of its recipients comes within the exception. There must be a corresponding distribution of property for the other shares. Such a distribution may not always take the form of a dividend—as illustrated by a third example in the legislative history:

> "In determining whether there is a disproportionate distribution, any security convertible into stock or any right to acquire stock is to be treated as outstanding stock. For example, if a corporation has common stock and convertible debentures outstanding, and it pays interest on the convertible debentures and stock dividends on the common stock, there is a disproportionate distribution, and the stock dividends are to be taxable."

(This example ignores the possibility that the debt instrument might contain an antidilution feature applicable to stock dividends. Such a provision can prevent the stock dividend from yielding any increased interest to its recipients. Treas. Reg. § 1.305–3(d)(4).) Finally, how close in time must the property distribution occur to the stock distribution to be related? See Treas. Reg. § 1.305–3(b)(4) (presuming distributions occurring more than three years apart are unrelated unless pursuant to a common plan).

Section 305(b)(3) pursues this line of thought one step further in creating a third exception to tax-free treatment. It covers a distribution, or series of distributions, which result in some common shareholders receiving preferred stock, while other common stockholders receive more common.

The notion is that receiving preferred is not too dissimilar from receiving cash or other property (perhaps because the recipient can sell it without giving up any stake in the corporation's growth), and, hence, the result is fairly similar to the exception provided by Section 305(b)(2).

Section 305(b)(4) makes any distribution of stock with respect to preferred shares taxable. Why do stock dividends going to holders of preferred shares always increase their recipient's proportionate interest in the company's earnings or assets? It is easy to see why this effect occurs if the dividend goes only to the preferred holders, but the exception also applies if the dividend goes equally to all classes. To understand the answer, as well as the scope of the exception, look at how the regulations define preferred stock for purposes of this section. Treas. Reg. § 1.305–5(a). The definition focuses, not on the preference, but on the limited participation rights of the shares in corporate growth. (Hence, participating preferred are not preferred for purposes of this section.) If shares are non-participating, what is the impact of any stock dividend upon them?

The final exception is for distributions of convertible preferred, unless the recipients can convince the Internal Revenue Service the distribution will not have the same result as one coming within Section 305(b)(2). I.R.C. § 305(b)(5). The Senate Report provides a pair of examples which explain how a distribution of convertible preferred may or may not have the effect of some recipients getting cash, while others get common stock:

> "[I]f a corporation makes a pro rata distribution on its common stock of preferred stock convertible into common stock at a price slightly higher than the market price of the common stock on the date of distribution, and the period during which the stock must be converted is 4 months, it is likely that a distribution would have the result of a disproportionate distribution. Those stockholders who wish to increase their interests in the corporation would convert their stock into common stock at the end of the 4–month period, and those stockholders who wish to receive cash would sell their stock or have it redeemed. On the other hand, if the stock were convertible for a period of 20 years from the date of issuance, there would be a likelihood that substantially all of the stock would be converted into common stock, and there would be no change in the proportionate interest of the common shareholders."

If the stock dividend falls within any of the exceptions under Section 305(b), the recipient treats it just as any other distribution under Section 301, measured by the fair market value of the stock received. Treas. Reg. §§ 1.305–1(b)(1). The company reduces earnings and profits accordingly. *See* I.R.C. § 312(d)(1)(B). A corporation recognizes no gain or loss on distribution of its own shares. I.R.C. § 311(a)(1). Note, finally, Section 305 treats a distribution of warrants the same as a distribution of stock. I.R.C. § 305(d)(1).

(ii) Treatment Upon Disposition

Even though the recipient of shares in a tax-free stock dividend pays nothing for them, he or she obtains a basis in the shares, courtesy of

Section 307(a). Under this section, and regulations issued pursuant to it, the recipient allocates to the new shares a part of the basis in the shares he or she initially owned proportionate to the relative fair market values of the two groups of stock. Treas. Reg. § 1.307–1(a). Suppose the recipient later sells the shares acquired (either to a third party, or back to the corporation in a redemption which qualifies for sale treatment). Ordinarily, he or she might not expect to recognize income except for the amount received in excess of this basis, which would be capital gain. As the following case illustrates, Section 306 severely complicates this conclusion.

Fireoved v. United States

462 F.2d 1281 (3d Cir.1972).

■ ADAMS, CIRCUIT JUDGE.

* * *

I. *Factual Background.*

On November 24, 1948, Fireoved and Company, Inc. was incorporated for the purpose of printing and selling business forms. * * * The corporation had authorized capital stock of 500 shares of $100 par value non-voting, non-cumulative preferred stock and 100 shares of $1 par value voting common stock. On December 31, 1948, in consideration for $100 cash, the corporation issued Eugene Fireoved 100 shares of common stock, for $500 cash, it issued him five shares of preferred stock; and in payment for automotive equipment and furniture and fixtures, valued at $6,000, it issued him an additional 60 shares of preferred stock.

In 1954, when Mr. Fireoved learned that his nephew, Robert, was planning to leave the business, he began discussions with Karl Edelmayer and Kenneth Craver concerning the possibility of combining his business with their partnership, Girard Business Forms, that had been printing and selling business forms for some time prior to 1954. Messrs. Fireoved, Edelmayer and Craver agreed that voting control of the new enterprise should be divided equally among the three of them. Because Mr. Fireoved's contribution to capital would be approximately $60,000 whereas the partnership could contribute only $30,000, it was decided that preferred stock should be issued to Mr. Fireoved to compensate for the disparity. In furtherance of this plan, the directors and shareholders of Fireoved and Company, in late 1954 and early 1955, held several meetings at which the following corporate changes were accomplished: The name of the company was changed to Girard Business Forms; the authorized common stock was increased from 100 to 300 shares and the authorized preferred stock was increased to 1000 shares; Mr. Fireoved exchanged his 100 shares of common and 65 shares of preferred stock for equal amounts of the new stock; an agreement of purchase was authorized by which the company would buy all the assets of the Edelmayer–Craver partnership in return for 200 shares of common and 298 shares of preferred stock; and Mr. Fireoved was issued 535 shares of the new preferred stock as a dividend on his 100 shares of common stock, thereby bringing his total holding of preferred stock to 600 shares to indicate his $60,000 capital contribution compared to the $29,800 contributed by the former partnership.

As the business progressed, Mr. Edelmayer demanded more control of the company. In response, Mr. Fireoved and Mr. Craver each sold 24 shares of common stock in the corporation to him on February 28, 1958.

On April 30, 1959, the company redeemed 451 of Mr. Fireoved's 600 shares of preferred stock at $105 per share, resulting in net proceeds to him of $47,355. The gain from this transaction was reported by Mr. and Mrs. Fireoved on their joint return for the year 1959 as a long-term capital gain. Subsequently, the Commissioner of Internal Revenue (Commissioner) assessed a deficiency against the Fireoveds of $15,337.13 based on the Commissioner's view that the proceeds from the redemption of the 451 shares of preferred stock should have been reported as ordinary income and tax paid at that rate based on Section 306. Mr. and Mrs. Fireoved paid the assessment on March 14, 1963, but on March 10, 1965, filed a claim for a refund with the Commissioner.

After the Commissioner disallowed the refund claim on March 8, 1966, the Fireoveds instituted the present action against the United States on August 4, 1967 seeking a refund on the $15,337.13 plus interest on the ground that the transaction came within an exception to Section 306, and that they were therefore entitled to report the income as a long-term capital gain. The case was tried to the court without a jury on stipulated facts. It is from the district court's determination * * * that $8,885.50 should be refunded to the taxpayers that both parties appeal.

II. *Background of Section 306.*

Because we are the first court of appeals asked to decide questions of law pursuant to Section 306, it is appropriate that we first examine the circumstances that led to the inclusion in 1954 of this section of the Code.

Generally, a taxpayer will benefit monetarily if he is able to report income as a long term capital gain rather than as ordinary income. Under normal circumstances a cash dividend from a corporation constitutes ordinary income to the shareholder receiving such money. Therefore, it would be to the advantage of a shareholder if a method could be devised by which the money could be distributed to him, that would otherwise be paid out as cash dividends, in a form that would permit the shareholder to report such income as a long term capital gain.

A temporarily successful plan for converting ordinary income to long term capital gain is described by the facts of *Chamberlin v. Commissioner,* 207 F.2d 462 (6th Cir.1953). There a close corporation had assets of $2.5 million, approximately half of which were in the form of cash and government securities. To have distributed the cash not required in the operation of the business to the shareholders as a dividend would have subjected them to taxation at ordinary income rates. The corporation therefore amended its charter to authorize 8,020 shares of preferred stock to be issued to the shareholders as a dividend on their common stock. * * * While these corporate changes were taking place, negotiations occurred between the shareholders and two insurance companies for the purchase of the newly issued preferred stock. In addition, the corporation constructed a timetable for retirement of the preferred stock, which proved satisfactory to the purchasing companies. When the transaction was completed, the selling shareholders reported the gain they realized from the sale of the preferred stock to the insurance companies as a long-term gain from the disposition of a capital asset. The Commissioner contended that the gain should have been reported as ordinary income and accordingly assessed a deficiency against the selling shareholders. The Tax Court agreed with the Commissioner. On review, the Sixth Circuit reversed, holding for the taxpayer thus giving the approval of a federal court to what has been termed "a preferred stock bail-out."

The legislative reaction to the *Chamberlin* decision was almost immediate, resulting in the addition of Section 306 to the 1954 Code, in order to prevent shareholders from obtaining the tax advantage of such bail-outs when such shareholders retain their ownership interests in the company.

Section 306 * * * may be briefly summarized as it relates to this case: for tax purposes, Congress created a new type of stock known as Section 306 stock. When a corporation having accumulated or retained earnings and profits issues a stock dividend which is not otherwise subject to taxation at the time of issuance (other than common on common), the stock received is Section 306 stock. The effect of owning such stock is that on its redemption, if the corporation has sufficient retained earnings at that time, the gain is taxed at ordinary income rates while any loss resulting may not be recognized for federal tax purposes. Section 306(b) sets forth several exceptions to the general rule which serve to remove the Section 306 taint from stock disposed of under those circumstances.

Based on the history of Section 306 and its plain meaning evidenced by the provisions, it is not disputed that the 535 shares of preferred stock issued to Mr. Fireoved as a stock dividend in 1954 were Section 306 stock.[9] Additionally, it is clear that in 1959, when the company redeemed 451 shares of Mr. Fireoved's preferred stock, the general provisions of Section 306—aside from the exceptions—would require that any amount realized by Mr. Fireoved be taxed at ordinary income rates rather than long term capital gain rates, because the company had earnings at that time of $48,235—more than the $47,355 required to redeem the stock at $105 per share.

Thus, the questions to be decided on this appeal are (1) whether certain of the exceptions to Section 306 apply to permit the Fireoveds' reporting their gain as a long term capital gain, and (2) whether 65 of the

9. The company had accumulated earnings and profits of more than $50,000 in 1954, the dividend was not common on common, and the receipt of the dividend was not a taxable event when it occurred in 1954. * * *

451 shares redeemed are not Section 306 stock because of the first in-first out rule of Treasury Regulation 1.1012–1(c).

III. *Was the distribution of the stock dividend "in pursuance of a plan having as one of its principal purposes avoidance of Federal income tax?"*

Mr. Fireoved asserts that the entire transaction should fall within the exception established by section 306(b)(4)(A), which provides: "if it is established to the satisfaction of the Secretary or his delegate * * * that the distribution, and the disposition or redemption * * * was not in pursuance of a plan having as one of its principal purposes the avoidance of Federal income tax," then the general rule of section 306(a) will not apply.

As a threshold point on this issue, the Government maintains that because Mr. Fireoved never attempted to obtain a ruling from the "Secretary or his delegate" the redemption should be covered by section 306(a), and the district court should not have reached the question whether the exception applied to Mr. Fireoved. Mr. Fireoved urges that the district court had that power to consider the matter *de novo,* even without a request by the taxpayer to the Secretary or his delegate. Because the ultimate result we reach would not be altered by whichever of these two courses we choose we do not resolve this potentially complex procedural problem.

The district court, based on the assumption that it had the power to decide the question, found that although one of the purposes involved in the issuance of the preferred stock dividend may have been business related, another principal purpose was the avoidance of Federal income tax.

Mr. Fireoved's analysis of the facts presented in the stipulations would reach the conclusion that the *sole* purpose of the stock dividend was business related. He relies heavily on that portion of the stipulation which describes why the decision was made to combine his business with the Edelmayer–Craver partnership: " 'The partnership could provide the additional manpower which the expected departure of Robert L. Fireoved from the corporation would require. Additionally, the partnership needed additional working capital which the corporation had and could provide.' " * * *

* * * The stipulation demonstrates no more than that the reorganized company required more capital than could be supplied by the partnership alone. The stipulation is completely in harmony with the following fact situation: After the partnership was combined with the corporation, the business required the $30,000 contributed by the partnership and all of the $60,000 Mr. Fireoved had in the corporation. Mr. Fireoved decided to take the stock dividend rather than to distribute the cash to himself as a dividend, and then to make a loan to the corporation of the necessary money because if he took the cash, he would subject himself to taxation at ordinary income rates. Therefore "one of the principal purposes" of the stock dividend would be for "the avoidance of Federal income tax."

In a situation such as the one presented in this case, where the facts necessary to determine the motives for the issuance of a stock dividend are peculiarly within the control of the taxpayer, it is reasonable to require the taxpayer to come forward with the facts that would relieve him of his liability. Here the stipulation was equivocal in determining the purpose of the dividend and is quite compatible with the thought that "one of the principal purposes" was motivated by "tax avoidance." We hold then that the district court did not err in refusing to apply the exception created by section 306(b)(4)(A).

IV. *Did the prior sale by Mr. Fireoved of 24% of his underlying common stock immunize such portion of the section 306 stock he redeemed in 1959?*

The district court construed section 306(b)(4)(B) to mean that any time a taxpayer in Mr. Fireoved's position sells any portion of his underlying common stock and later sells or redeems his section 306 stock, an equivalent proportion of the section 306 stock redeemed will not be subject to the provisions of section 306(a). The Government has appealed from this portion of the district court's order and urges that we reverse it, based on the history and purpose of section 306 and the particular facts here.

The stipulations indicate that, "On February 28, 1958, Fireoved and Craver each sold 24 shares of common stock in the corporation to Edelmayer," and that appropriate stock certificates were issued. From this fact, Mr. Fireoved reasons that his sale of 24 of his 100 shares of common stock was undertaken solely for the business purpose of satisfying Mr. Edelmayer's desire for more control of the corporation, and therefore he should be given the benefit of section 306(b)(4)(B). In addition, Mr. Fireoved contends that the disposition of his section 306 stock was related to a business purpose because he used part of the proceeds to pay off a $20,000 loan that the company had made to him.

Mr. Fireoved has the same burden here of showing a lack of a tax avoidance purpose that he had in Section III *supra.* It is clear from the limited facts set forth in the stipulations that he has not established that the disposition of 24% of the 535 shares of the section 306 preferred stock he owned "was not in pursuance of a plan having as one of its principal purposes the avoidance of federal income tax."[12] More important, however,

12. Consistent with Mr. Fireoved's sale of 24 shares of common stock in 1958 could have been his knowledge that one year later he would be selling his Section 306 stock and a desire on his part to avoid taxation at ordinary income rates. As noted later in the opinion, the sale of just 24 shares was enough so that he retained effective control—in the form of veto power—over the corporation. Moreover, the fact that Mr. Fireoved needed $20,000 of the proceeds to pay off a loan to the corporation would not meet his burden. The proceeds of the redemption totaled $47,355. Thus, although $20,000 of the redemption may not have been to avoid taxes, we can ascribe no purpose other than tax avoidance to the receipt of the additional $27,355. Therefore, since one of the principal purposes of the redemption of 451 shares of preferred stock was "the avoidance of Federal income tax," Mr. Fireoved may not take advantage of § 306(b)(4)(B) for any part of the redemption.

is that an examination of the relevant legislative history indicates that Congress did not intend to give capital gains treatment to a portion of the preferred stock redeemed on the facts presented here.

It is apparent from the reaction evinced by Congress to the *Chamberlin* case, *supra,* that by enacting section 306 Congress was particularly concerned with the tax advantages available to persons who controlled corporations and who could, without sacrificing their control, convert ordinary income to long term capital gains by the device of the preferred stock bail-out. The illustration given in the Senate Report which accompanied section 306(b)(4)(B) is helpful in determining the sort of transactions meant to be exempted by section 306(a):

> Thus if a shareholder received a distribution of 100 shares of section 306 stock on his holdings of 100 shares of voting common stock in a corporation and sells his voting common stock before he disposes of his section 306 stock, the subsequent disposition of his section 306 stock would not ordinarily be considered a tax avoidance disposition *since he has previously parted with the stock which allows him to participate in the ownership of the business.* However, variations of the above example may give rise to tax avoidance possibilities which are not within the exception of subparagraph (B). Thus if a corporation has only one class of common stock outstanding and it issues stock under circumstances that characterize it as section 306 stock, a subsequent issue of a different class of common having greater voting rights than the original common will not permit a simultaneous disposition of the section 306 stock together with the original common to escape the rules of subsection (a) of section 306.

S.Rep.No. 1622, 83d Cong., 2d Sess., 1985 U.S.C.C.A. News, pp. 4621, 4881 (emphasis added).

Thus, it is reasonable to assume that Congress realized the general lack of a tax avoidance purpose when a person sells *all* of his control in a corporation and then either simultaneously or subsequently disposes of his section 306 stock. However, when *only a portion* of the underlying common stock is sold, and the taxpayer retained essentially all the control he had previously, it would be unrealistic to conclude that Congress meant to give that taxpayer the advantage of section 306(b)(4)(B) when he ultimately sells his section 306 stock. * * *

Shortly after Mr. Fireoved's corporation had been combined with the Edelmayer–Craver partnership, significant changes to the by-laws were made. The by-laws provided that corporate action could be taken only with the unanimous consent of all the directors. In addition, the by-laws provided that they could be amended either by a vote of 76% of the outstanding common shares or a unanimous vote of the directors. When the businesses were combined in late 1954, each of the directors held 1/3 of the voting stock, thereby necessitating a unanimous vote for amendment to the by-laws. After Messrs. Fireoved and Craver each sold 24 shares of common stock to Mr. Edelmayer, Mr. Fireoved held 25 1/3% of the common (voting) stock, Mr. Craver 25 1/3% and Mr. Edelmayer 49 1/3%. It is crucial to note that the by-laws provided for a unanimous vote for corporate action, and after the common stock transfer, the by-laws were capable of amendment only by a unanimous vote because no two shareholders could vote more than 74 2/3% of the common stock and 76% of the common stock was necessary for amendment. Thus, although Mr. Fireoved did sell a portion of his voting stock prior to his disposition of the section 306 stock, he retained as much control in the corporation following the sale of his common stock as he had prior to the sale. Under these circumstances it is not consonant with the history of the legislation to conclude that Congress intended such a sale of underlying common stock to exempt the proceeds of the disposition of section 306 stock from treatment as ordinary income. Accordingly, the district court erred when it held that any of the preferred shares Mr. Fireoved redeemed were not subject to section 306(a) by virtue of section 306(b)(4)(B).

V. *Does the rule of first in-first out mean that 65 of the 451 redeemed shares were those which Mr. Fireoved acquired when he incorporated his business in 1948 and thus should not be treated as section 306 stock?*

The district court held that 65 of 451 shares of preferred stock that Mr. Fireoved redeemed in 1959 represented the original shares issued to him in 1948 and were not, therefore, section 306 stock, and that the proceeds from their sales should be treated as a long term capital gain. The court reached this conclusion by applying Treas.Reg. § 1.1012–1(c). This regulation provides that when an individual acquires shares of the same class of stock in the same corporation on different dates and for different prices, sells a portion of those shares, and cannot adequately identify which lots were sold, for the purpose of determining the basis and the holding period, the first shares acquired are deemed to be the first shares sold.

Both the district court and Mr. Fireoved reason that the 65 preferred shares he received in 1948 were the first such shares owned by him. In 1954, when the corporation was recapitalized, Mr. Fireoved surrendered his certificate for 65 shares, received a 535 share stock dividend and was issued a certificate representing 600 shares of preferred stock. When he disposed of 451 shares in 1959, it was impossible to identify which shares of the 600 share certificate were being sold. By applying the convenient tool of section 1.1012–1(c), one might conclude that the 65 original shares were sold first because they were received first.

Superficially, this analysis appears to be correct. However, it overlooks the existence of section 1223(5) of the Code and the regulations issued pursuant thereto. * * * These provisions broadly state that the holding period for stock received as a stock dividend is equal to the period for which the underlying stock was held. Applying this test we discover that the preferred stock dividend of 535 shares was issued with respect to the original 100 shares of common received by Mr. Fireoved. Therefore, the holding period for the 535 shares dividend relates back to the date on which the underlying common was issued. Coincidentally, the original 65 shares of preferred stock were issued on the same date as the common. Because the constructive date of issuance for all of the 600 shares of preferred stock owned by Mr. Fireoved is identical, neither the 65 shares nor the 535 shares are first in, but rather are in at the same time.

Since it is impossible adequately to identify which shares were sold when Mr. Fireoved redeemed 451 shares of preferred stock, we hold that a pro rata portion of the 65 shares were redeemed in 1959. In other words, the percentage of the 600 shares of preferred which were not section 306 stock may be represented by the fraction 65/600. That percentage of the 451 shares redeemed in 1959, therefore, would not be section 306 stock.

IV. *Conclusion.*

Because we affirm in part and reverse in part the judgment of the district court, the cause will be remanded for proceedings consistent with this opinion.

NOTES

1. Shares received in a tax-free stock dividend (other than a distribution of common on common) come within the definition of "section 306 stock." I.R.C. § 306(c)(1)(A). (The full parameters of this term will be outlined later in this chapter.) As the court explains in *Fireoved,* Congress provided special rules for taxing the disposition of such stock in order to prevent efforts to bail money out of a corporation at capital gains, rather than ordinary income, rates.

The precise treatment of section 306 stock depends upon whether its owner sells it back to the company or sells it to a third party. If sold back to the company, the selling shareholder treats the entire amount received in exchange as a distribution from the corporation (which means a dividend to the extent of earnings and profits, and return of capital and normally capital gains for anything in excess). I.R.C. § 306(a)(2). Recall, as discussed earlier when dealing with sale versus distribution treatment for redemptions generally, that the reduction of the tax rate on dividends to match the rate on capital gains has removed what had been traditionally the primary disadvantage of distribution, versus sale, treatment. Accordingly, at least until the favorable treatment of dividends expires (barring further action by Congress) at the end of 2008, the negative impact of distribution treatment focuses on items such as the inability of the seller to offset his or her basis in the redeemed stock or to use installment reporting of any extended payout. Recall also that some shareholders, such as one which itself is a corporation, generally might prefer distribution, rather than sale, treatment.

If a third party purchases the section 306 stock, the result is more complicated. The seller treats the consideration received as ordinary income (albeit subject to the same maximum rate as a dividend) up to an amount measured by a hypothetical distribution of cash rather than the section 306 stock to begin with. I.R.C. § 306(a)(1)(A), (D). (In other words, the section asks how much would have been a dividend had the corporation originally given the selling stockholder cash equal to what he or she received from the buyer.) If there is any excess, the selling stockholder treats it just as if it was the entire amount received in a sale of the stock, except he or she may recognize no loss on the transaction. I.R.C. § 306(a)(1)(B), (C). Note several differences between redemptions of Section 306 stock and the sale of such stock to third parties. For redemptions, the section looks to earnings and profits at the point of disposition; for other sales, it looks to the time the stockholder originally received the stock. In addition, in a sale to third parties, the Code simply slaps an ordinary income designation on an amount measured by what the dividend would have been; but it is not really a dividend for purposes such as the Section 243 deduction or for reducing the corporation's earnings and profits (albeit, the tax on this income is limited to the favorable dividend rate). On the other hand, sales to third parties and redemptions of section 306 stock retain key similarities. In both, there is the loss of capital gains treatment, and the inability to offset basis. What happens to the unused basis from the section 306 shares? See Treas. Reg. § 1.306–1(b)(2) Ex. (2) (it goes back to the remaining shares—which simply returns the stockholder to where he or she was before receiving the Section 306 stock, at least as far as the basis goes).

Section 306(b) contains four exceptions to the unfavorable treatment accorded sales of section 306 stock. The first is for a sale which completely terminates the seller's actual and constructive (under Section 318) ownership of stock in the corporation. I.R.C. § 306(b)(1). A second exception exists for redemptions in complete or partial liquidations of the corporation. I.R.C. § 306(b)(1)(B), (2). The third occurs when the disposition involves a nontaxable transaction (such as a reorganization). I.R.C. § 306(b)(3). However, the stock the shareholder receives in such a transaction in return for his or her section 306 stock usually will be section 306 stock as well. I.R.C. § 306(c)(1)(B), (C). *Fireoved* involved the fourth exception, one for transactions which lack any tax avoidance motive. I.R.C. § 306(b)(4). What action does one have to prove lacked tax avoidance motive: The acquisition of the section 306 stock, its disposition, or both? Notice the difference in the answer to this question when the stockholder also disposes of the shares he or she had before the section 306 stock (which the court held to mean at least disposing of enough of these shares to affect control). While the statute says one must convince the Internal Revenue Service of one's pure motives—albeit the *Fireoved* court seemed willing to review the matter when the taxpayer did not do this—the shareholder usually cannot undertake such persuasion in advance of the disposition. This is because the Service will not ordinarily give an advance ruling on the issue. Rev. Proc. 2000–3, 2000–1 C.B. 103. In any event, at least so long as capital gains and dividends are taxed at the same rate, how difficult should it now be to show a lack of tax avoidance motive to the use of Section 306 shares?

2. As pointed out previously, a stock dividend of preferred shares upon common often occurs in a closely-held corporation as a major shareholder approaches retirement. This transaction can facilitate the transfer of con-

trol, and possibly provide a source of income to substitute for lost salary. It also forms the basis of an estate planning technique known as a freeze. The elderly shareholder could keep the preferred, and give away his or her common stock to junior members of the family. As the business grows, so would the value of the common. The value of the preferred, however, (if it is non-participating) would remain stable. The result would be to avoid estate tax on the continued appreciation of the firm. Since, however, the common stock might not be worth much when transferred, there could be relatively little gift tax liability.

Needless to say, this technique raises substantial questions as to the value of the common and preferred stock. Specifically, taxpayers may be tempted to whipsaw the treasury by claiming a low value upon the common stock at the time of transfer (to minimize gift tax liability), but only a low value upon the retained preferred at the time of death (to minimize estate tax liability). To facilitate such valuation claims, the preferred might possess a non-cumulative dividend preference or other rights which lapse over time, thereby gradually transferring their value to the common. Congress has responded by enacting a series of provisions (Sections 2701–2704) specifically addressing the valuation issue. Generally speaking, these sections minimize the value assignable to various discretionary rights (such as conversion or redemption rights or non-cumulative dividend preferences) possessed by the retained shares, and thereby increase the gift tax liability on transfer of the common. These provisions also establish a minimum value of 10 percent for the residual right to future appreciation held by the common.

In any event, should a permanent repeal of the estate tax actually take place, then the utility of the freeze technique will melt.

2. RECAPITALIZATIONS

a. *Corporate and Securities Law Aspects*

Honigman v. Green Giant Company

208 F.Supp. 754 (D.Minn.1961), aff'd, 309 F.2d 667 (8th Cir.1962), *cert. denied,* 372 U.S. 941 (1963).

■ NORDBYE, DISTRICT JUDGE.

This cause came before the Court for trial without a jury. Jurisdiction is based upon diversity of citizenship.

The plaintiff, Edith Honigman, * * * is the owner of 1,570 shares of Class B non-voting stock in the defendant company, a Minnesota corporation. She allegedly brings this action in behalf of herself and all other Class B stockholders, and derivatively in behalf of the corporation against the company and its Directors, to set aside the issuance of so-called premium shares to Class A stockholders in a plan of recapitalization of the company, or in the alternative to set aside the entire plan.

* * *

The Green Giant Company is engaged in the growing, processing, and selling of vegetables and food products. As of 1914 in the early history of the company, it had a handful of employees, including one Edward B. Cosgrove, with annual sales of some $7,000. In about 1918, Mr. Cosgrove became General Manager; in 1929, President; and in 1954, Chairman of the Board. At the end of its fiscal year on March 31, 1960, the company and a wholly owned subsidiary had sales in excess of $64,000,000 for that year and a net worth of $23,462,544. It had outstanding 21,233 shares of 5 percent cumulative preferred stock, with a par value of $100 per share; 44 shares of Class A common stock; and 428,998 shares of Class B stock; the Class A stock had all the voting rights and a majority of these shares, 26 in number, were owned by Edward B. Cosgrove. The capital stock of the company never had been listed on any exchange, and the dealings in its stock were * * * in over-the-counter transactions.

In 1959 the Board of Directors of the company, by resolution, authorized the employment of Glore, Forgan & Co., investment bankers of Chicago, Illinois, to make a study of the capital structure of the company and prepare a report and recommendation to the Board. Although the company had made marked success in its business enterprises, there had been a growing feeling that a recapitalization of the company whereby the voting rights would be held by all the common shareholders would not only benefit the shareholders, but advantages of considerable magnitude would likewise inure to the company. * * * Under [the plan proposed by the investment bankers], Class A and Class B shares were to be exchanged for a new class of voting common stock. Each Class B shareholder was to receive one share of the new common stock for each share of the Class B stock. Each Class A shareholder was to receive ten shares of what is termed convertible common stock, each of which would be converted annually into one hundred new voting shares, and in this manner, after the confirmation of the plan and at the end of a ten-year period, the holders of 44 shares of Class A stock would receive 44,000 shares of the new common stock. Under the plan, the present Class B stockholders would have 49.37 percent of the voting power upon its adoption, and over the ten-year period, the percentage in voting power yearly would increase until by the tenth year it would be 90.70 percent. The participation of the Class A shareholders in the assets of the company under the plan would be increased from about .01 percent to 9.3 percent.

On July 15, 1960, the plan was submitted to the Class A and Class B shareholders and was approved by all of the Class A shareholders and by the holders of 395,982 shares or 92.3 percent of all the outstanding Class B stock. 4,799 of Class B shares were voted against it. Upon the approval of the plan, steps were taken to change the shares on the basis thereof. The necessary amendments to the Articles of Incorporation have been completed under Minnesota law and put into effect, and convertible common stock and the common stock have been issued as provided by the plan. * * * It appears that all of the Class B shareholders who voted against the plan, except the plaintiff, have exchanged their shares for certificates representing the new common shares.

After the plan was adopted * * * the value of the share interest represented by the old Class B shareholders increased on the market by more than 33 1/3 percent. On November 1, 1960, a merger of the Michigan Mushroom Company and the Green Giant Company was consummated under the terms of which the Green Giant Company issued to the former stockholders of the Michigan Company 3,000 shares of Green Giant preferred stock and 35,200 shares of the new common stock.

Plaintiff contends that the issuance of the premium stock under the plan to the Class A shareholders is unfair, illegal and void. * * *

It seems wholly unrealistic to suggest, as plaintiff does, that the Class A shareholders should be relegated to the same number of shares in the recapitalization of the company when they forego the exclusive voting control which they maintained as Class A shareholders. That the market of the Class A shares far exceeded the market value of the same number of Class B shares is uncontradicted. It appears from the evidence that, before there was any consideration of any recapitalization of the company, Mr. Edward B. Cosgrove received an offer for his controlling interest in the Class A stock of some $2,000,000. * * * One may theorize on the principles of so-called corporate democracy and urge that no premium should be paid for its extension, and further contend that because the book value of the Class A shares does not exceed the book value of the Class B shares, these two classes of stock would have the basis of equality in any recapitalization; however, in doing so, one ignores the undeniable disparity in the market value of the two classes of common stock. No Class A shareholder could be expected to forego the power of control of a company of this size without receiving in return a consideration commensurate with the value of the control which he forgoes. It seems evident, therefore, that in light of the evidence in considering the fairness of the plan, we must commence with the premise that the A shareholders in surrendering their exclusive voting rights were entitled to a premium in exchanging their stock for the new voting common stock. It would be wholly unreasonable to expect that any recapitalization of the company could be effected in affording equal voting to all of the common stock which did not result in some dilution of the equity of the B stockholders. * * *

It may well be that in any recapitalization if changes in the stock structure are made, with stock premiums being issued to those who share their exclusive voting rights with other shareholders, there must be a showing of fairness and validity, not only to the class of stockholders who hold no voting rights, but the corporation as well. And here, where the proposers of the plan are Directors who were elected by the A stockholders, it seems entirely fair to place the burden of proof upon the defendants to sustain the plan's fairness. * * * True, it would appear that, in the absence of fraud or violation of any fiduciary relationship, the wisdom and fairness of any plan of recapitalization formulated according to state law primarily would be a matter for the stockholders to determine in effecting such recapitalization, particularly when it must be recognized that material benefits flow to the B stockholders from the recapitalization and to the corporation as well. At least, under these circumstances the judgment of the vast majority of the stockholders affected should be accorded great weight.

A corporation which lodges its voting plan in a small group of stockholders does not produce a healthy corporate situation, and this is true with reference to the Green Giant Company, although under the management of the A stockholders, the company achieved outstanding business success. However, the death of Edward B. Cosgrove, or the sale of his stock to others who then would have control of the company, might produce a situation which would be extremely detrimental to the future of the company. The fact that the apparent sagacity and business acumen of Mr. Cosgrove and his associates has resulted in such outstanding success of the company does not mean that others in control would produce the same result or that they would not attempt to mulct the company to the aggrandizement of themselves and to the detriment of the B stockholders. Moreover, the unique and abnormal corporate structure of this company would naturally deter desirable personnel from throwing in their lot with such a company by reason of the power that was lodged in a small minority group of stockholders. Consequently, it must be recognized that any dilution of the interest in the corporate equity of the B stockholders in this recapitalization is not without its counterpart of benefit to them. Certainly, the holders of 92.3 percent of the Class B stock who voted for the plan must have recognized the benefits which would inure to them with voting rights in a soundly reorganized company. And although the increase in the value of the Class B shares of some 33 1/3 percent immediately after the recapitalization may have been due in part to the two for one split in the new stock, and possibly to some extent due to the general market advance in food stock companies generally in 1960, there can be little doubt that the reorganization itself was the major factor in the market increase of the new voting stock.

Although the ratio of 1,000 to 1 for the A stock in exchange for the new voting stock which will be the ultimate result at the end of the ten-year period may seem liberal, it must be borne in mind that there were only 44 shares of Class A stock outstanding, and that these new shares had an abnormal market value. In these 44 shares was lodged the entire destiny of the company. It was the power of control which was lodged in these few shares which created their value, and if the power of control had been vested in a larger number of shares, the ratio would have been proportionately less. But regardless of the ratio and return to the A stockholders—whether they were 44 shares in number or 44,000 shares in number—the increased equity of the Class A stockholders in the company did not exceed 9.3 percent.

Plaintiff questions the reasonableness of the allocation of the same premium to each of the A shares in that it was Edward B. Cosgrove who controlled the voting stock by reason of his ownership of 26 shares of Class A stock. Therefore, she urges that the Class A shareholders, other than Edward B. Cosgrove, were not entitled to any premium even though the premium shares to him could be sustained. However, it would seem that any attempt to differentiate as among the A shareholders in any recapitalization would be indefensible. None of the A shareholders challenge the fairness of the equal treatment accorded the minority A shareholders, and there is convincing evidence that the value of all the A stock exceeded the value of the convertible common stock issued to the A shareholders.

Plaintiff refers to Subdivision 1 of Section 301.15, Minnesota Statutes Annotated, which provides,

> "Consideration. No shares shall be allotted except in consideration of cash, or other property, tangible or intangible, received or to be received by the corporation, or services rendered or to be rendered to the corporation, or of an amount transferred from surplus to stated capital upon a share dividend."

And also to Subdivision 1 of Section 301.16, Minnesota Statutes Annotated, which provides,

> "Unfair allotment. Shares with or without par value shall not be allotted for a cash consideration which is unfair to the then shareholders nor for a consideration other than cash upon a valuation thereof which is unfair to such shareholders."

* * *

Plaintiff contends that under the showing herein no consideration was received by the corporation for the issuance of the premium shares. At least, she urges that the premium shares were grossly excessive as compared to the intangible considerations which the company received, and hence that the Minnesota statutes referred to afford a basis for equity to step in and either limit the A shareholders to 44 shares of new holding stock, or return to the company any premium above a fair consideration, or in the alternative that the entire recapitalization should be set aside. * * * Obviously, to determine the value of this recapitalization to the corporation and to attempt to spell out in dollars and cents that which the corporation received as a so-called consideration for the premium stock presents practical difficulties. However, it seems undeniable that the corporation received benefits by reason of the plan. On account of the unique corporate structure, this corporation was saddled with definite limitations in any attempt to expand, to develop, to obtain equity financing, or to merge with other companies, and the progress made by the present management was no assurance that such development would continue in the future. These facts must have been the motivating considerations in the near unanimous vote of the Class B shareholders who favored the plan. The Class B stock, with no voting rights, was not listed on any of the country's exchanges. Any mergers or consolidations by Green Giant with other companies upon which the entire future of the defendant company might depend were closed to it. This fact was adequately demonstrated when immediately after the recapitalization the company was able to effect a merger with the Michigan Mushroom Company, which merger would have been quite impossible before the recapitalization. Of course, it is true that the Class B shareholders are clothed with the privilege to maintain their preemptive right in the corporate equity. But no recapitalization could be effected without some dilution of their interest in the corporate equity. Consequently, if it is fair and reasonable under the plan, that because of the benefits the Class B stockholders would receive, they should release some of their share in the corporate equity to the Class A shareholders, such benefits to the Class B stockholders obviously enter into the consideration which the Class A stockholders gave for their stock premium.

After due consideration, the Court is satisfied that a fair analysis of all the circumstances justifies a finding that defendants have sustained the burden of proof in establishing that the premium shares issued to the Class A stockholders is commensurate with the benefit received by the corporation and that the plan is fair and reasonable to the Class B stockholders. The Court concludes that the consideration flowing to the corporation fairly satisfies any demands of the Minnesota statutes relied upon, as well as the basic principles of fair dealing required by equity. No doubt persons may differ as to the best way to capitalize this company. But no one can deny that some plan was imperative. Here, we have no plan or scheme or artifice by the Class A shareholders or the Directors to persuade unfairly the Class B stockholders into approval of the plan. * * * And the Court cannot ignore the persuasive fact that the holders of 92.3 percent of all outstanding Class B stock concluded that the plan was fair to them and likewise to the corporation. That fact speaks more persuasively than the arguments of those who attempt to theorize on unrealistic principles of so-called corporate democracy. No one contends that the Class B stockholders were not fully informed of the Class A stock control when they invested in the company stock, and so far as the charge of immoral and reprehensible conduct directed at the Class A stockholders is concerned, suffice it to say that their position in this proceeding must be judged by that which businessmen of ordinary prudence would have done under similar circumstances. The integrity of the Class A stock is not challenged here.

* * *

NOTES

1. The parties and the court in *Honigman* refer to the transaction there as a "recapitalization". What exactly is a recapitalization? In fact, this is not a term which possesses any precise meaning under state corporations statutes or common law. (Later, it will be seen that this term is used, but not defined, in the Internal Revenue Code.) Broadly, when people speak of a recapitalization they mean a change in a corporation's capital structure; in other words, in the mix or relative rights of its outstanding stock and securities. Of course, two transactions already considered—redemption of

outstanding shares and issuance of further shares (as in a stock dividend)—change a company's capital structure. As seen in *Honigman,* however, a recapitalization can involve the exchange of outstanding stock for new stock issued by the company. Moreover, as discussed below, a recapitalization can entail altering the relative rights of shares, even without an actual exchange, by amendment to the articles. Recapitalizations can also involve exchanges of debt securities as well as stock.

Recapitalizations serve a variety of purposes. In *Honigman,* the purpose was to shift voting control from a class of common shares held by a few individuals to the common stock held by the public. Recapitalizations geared toward altering voting rights occur in a number of other situations as well. For example, many times, closely held corporations employ the classified voting schemes discussed in Chapter IV, under which different classes of shares each may elect a portion of the board. If such a firm decides to go public, it may be useful or necessary to recapitalize in order to have a single class of voting common. *Dean v. Commissioner,* reprinted below, provides another example. There, inactive shareholders in a closely held corporation exchanged voting common for non-voting preferred in order to concentrate control in the hands of the active participants. The same type of transaction regularly occurs when an active participant in a closely held company approaches retirement. The exchange of some or all of his or her voting shares for non-voting stock can facilitate the transfer of control to the next generation. (Not only does the exchange, if it is not pro-rata among all stockholders, immediately decrease the exchanging party's voting control, but, whether or not it is pro-rata, the exchange can also accomplish the same transfer of control objectives discussed earlier for stock dividends. These include: (i) decreasing the value of any remaining voting shares held by the exchanging party in order to ease the eventual buy-out of this stock; (ii) decreasing the price of newly issued voting shares in order to facilitate their purchase from the company by the next generation; and (iii) allowing an elderly shareholder to pass on voting shares to those he or she wishes to actively run the business, and give non-voting stock to other individuals who will not actively participate.)

Recapitalizations are also useful to alter financial rights of shareholders. For instance, as discussed earlier when dealing with stock dividends, some shareholders may reach the point at which they desire preferred rather than common shares. (This is particularly likely as a major shareholder in a closely held corporation reaches retirement and thus becomes concerned with insuring a steady source of income to substitute for lost salary.) Issuing preferred shares as a stock dividend may give such shares to those who really do not want them. It also undermines the effect of the dividend preference, since the preference is meaningless if all stockholders own preferred in the same proportion as they own common. An exchange of common for preferred just by those shareholders who so desire could be better. Alternately, suppose a closely held corporation, with preferred stock outstanding, wishes to go public. It may be useful or necessary to exchange newly issued common for the outstanding preferred in order to create the single class structure often most conducive to a successful initial public offering. Corporations which are substantially behind in paying dividends on their cumulative preferred shares have been a source of frequently litigated recapitalizations. Such companies might attempt to wipe out the arrearage—thereby clearing the way for earlier payment of dividends to the common holders—by exchanging newly issued shares for the outstanding preferred. *E.g., Johnson v. Fuller,* 121 F.2d 618 (3d Cir.1941), *cert. denied,* 314 U.S. 681.

Recapitalizations can also involve restructuring debt. For example, a company overly burdened by debt payments may be able to convince some of its creditors—for instance, if they are also shareholders—to swap their debt for stock, or for another debt with easier payments. (The same sort of restructuring of debt occurs in a more extreme form in a bankruptcy reorganization.)

2. Mechanically, a recapitalization might consist of nothing more than the corporation offering to trade newly issued stock or securities for the outstanding stock or securities held by those who wish to engage in the exchange. *Dean v. Commissioner,* reprinted later in this chapter, provides an example of this. If the articles do not authorize the stock the corporation wishes to issue in the trade, then the directors and shareholders must vote to amend the articles; otherwise such a transaction is presumably within the board's power to undertake. Can anyone object to such a voluntary exchange? If the trade is not equally available to all (as can be the case when the corporation has multiple classes of stock outstanding), then those individuals left out of any portion of the exchange might challenge the transaction as a breach of fiduciary duty. In this regard, recall the discussion earlier of challenges made against redemptions from some, but not all, stockholders, and notice, as well, the plaintiff's complaint in *Honigman* that the plan gave too much to the holders of the "A" common. What about those able to participate in the exchange: Can they ever object? Presumably not (so long as the company does not mislead them), since they have a choice. *E.g., Shanik v. White Sewing Machine Corp.,* 25 Del.Ch. 371, 19 A.2d 831 (Sup.Ct.1941). *But see Patterson v. Durham Hosiery Mills,* 214 N.C. 806, 200 S.E. 906 (1939) (The corporation offered to holders of its outstanding preferred—whose dividends were in arrears—the option to exchange their stock for a new class of shares with a dividend preference superior to those they held. The court ruled this constituted an invalid attempt to coerce the preferred holders to give up their rights to accumulated dividends or else find themselves in an inferior position).

One difficulty with a totally voluntary exchange is that enough individuals may decline to participate to prevent it from achieving its goal. Is there a way for a majority of shareholders to force everyone to go along? Since the articles specify the relative rights of various classes of stock, perhaps the majority could amend the articles to change the rights of the shares. For example, in *Honigman,* one could have given the "B" shares voting rights simply by amending the articles to do so. Alternately, the majority might seek to alter the financial rights of shares by amending the articles. *E.g., Western Foundry Co. v. Wicker,* 403 Ill. 260, 85 N.E.2d 722

(1949) (amendment eliminating dividend arrearage and making preferred stock non-cumulative); *Goldman v. Postal Telegraph,* 52 F.Supp. 763 (D.Del.1943) (amendment lessening liquidation preference); *Cowan v. Salt Lake Hardware Co.,* 118 Utah 300, 221 P.2d 625 (1950) (amendment giving the company the option to redeem the outstanding preferred).

What protection does the minority possess against such a "cram-down" recapitalization (or, viewed from the other side, what impediments does the majority face in carrying out such a transaction)? The first challenge exists if the applicable corporations statute does not explicitly allow for the amendment in question. Historically, many courts have refused to interpret ambiguous statutory provisions as authorizing amendments which take away financial rights from an objecting minority. *E.g., Consolidated Film Indus. v. Johnson,* 22 Del.Ch. 407, 197 A. 489 (1937). Modern statutes, however, tend to explicitly provide broad authority for amendments to the articles changing financial and other rights of shares. *E.g.,* Cal. Corp. Code § 900(a); Del. Gen. Corp. Law § 242(a)(3), (4); N.Y. Bus. Corp. Law § 801(b)(11), (12); M.B.C.A. § 10.01. Some courts have held shares issued prior to the enactment of a statute authorizing article amendments changing their rights have "vested rights" which the state cannot constitutionally authorize the corporation to amend away. *Compare Keller v. Wilson & Co.,* 21 Del.Ch. 391, 190 A. 115 (1936), *with O'Brien v. Socony Mobil Oil Co.,* 207 Va. 707, 152 S.E.2d 278 (1967), *cert. denied,* 389 U.S. 825. This becomes less relevant over the years as fewer such shares remain extant.

The next line of defense is the one the court found most important in *Honigman*; the requirement of shareholder approval for the amendment. Corporations statutes typically require approval by a vote of each separate class adversely affected by the amendment—even if the class is otherwise non-voting. *E.g.,* Cal. Corp. Code § 903(a), Del. Gen. Corp. Law § 242(b)(2); N.Y. Bus. Corp. Law § 804; M.B.C.A. § 10.04. Moreover, as illustrated by the *Kaplan* opinion earlier in this chapter, the management must be careful not to mislead the stockholders in soliciting the shareholders' approval of any transactions. The protection of a stockholder vote may break down, however, if the holders of a majority of the adversely affected shares also hold shares in classes potentially favored by the change. In addition, sometimes the shareholders may feel coerced into voting for the amendment. *See Lacos Land Co. v. Arden Group, Inc.,* 517 A.2d 271 (Del.Ch.1986).

This brings one to the possibility of a challenge, such as in *Honigman,* that the transaction is unfair. Courts differ as to the vigor with which they will review a recapitalization for fairness. *Compare Kamena v. Janssen Dairy Corp.,* 133 N.J.Eq. 214, 31 A.2d 200 (Ch.1943), *aff'd,* 134 N.J.Eq. 359, 35 A.2d 894 (Err. & App.1944) (enjoined plan as objectively unfair); *with Barrett v. Denver Tramway Corp.,* 53 F.Supp. 198 (D.Del.1943), *aff'd,* 146 F.2d 701 (3d Cir.1944) (refused to enjoin plan which the court regarded as unfair because, under Delaware law, unfairness must reach the level of constructive fraud or bad faith before a court will act). Moreover, as stated in *Honigman,* the degree of review depends upon the extent to which the shareholders who the plan arguably disfavors (and presumably who have no offsetting conflict of interest) voted to approve it. *See also Davis v. Louisville Gas & Electric Co.*, 16 Del.Ch. 157, 142 A. 654 (1928).

What factors (other than disinterested approval) go into evaluating a recapitalization's fairness? The existence of a legitimate corporate purpose for the plan influenced the court in *Honigman,* and is possibly a *sine quo non* for a finding of fairness. *Cf. Tanzer Economic Associates, Inc. v. Universal Food Specialties, Inc.*, 87 Misc.2d 167, 383 N.Y.S.2d 472 (1976). The Court in *Honigman* also compared the value of what the various shareholders surrendered and what they received. *See also Kamena v. Janssen Dairy Corp.,* 133 N.J.Eq. 214, 31 A.2d 200 (Ch.1943), *aff'd,* 134 N.J.Eq. 359, 35 A.2d 894 (Err. & App.1944). Of course, comparing the values of voting control versus an increased equity interest, as in *Honigman,* or even the values of very different types of securities exchanged, can be a daunting task. Recall the material in Chapter V explored the conventional methodology of valuing stocks based upon dividend yield. As *Honigman* illustrates, one may need to add a premium for controlling interests, or subtract a discount for minority interests. Some additional guidelines suggested by the Internal Revenue Service for valuing different types of shares in a closely held company are reproduced below. Many recapitalizations involve a sacrifice by holders of preferred shares—such as giving up the right to dividends in arrears or lowering a liquidation preference. Proponents of such a plan typically justify the sacrifice as necessary for the corporate welfare. Even if true, the question arises as to what extent it is fair to impose this sacrifice upon preferred shares rather than upon the common. For example, should the preferred be entitled to insist upon receipt of stock or securities in the recapitalization with a value at least equal to the preferred's liquidation preference plus any dividend arrearage, before the common holders get any stock or securities? (This is the traditional approach in a bankruptcy reorganization. *E.g., In re Childs Company,* 69 F.Supp. 856 (S.D.N.Y.1946).) See *Bove v. Community Hotel Corp.,* 105 R.I. 36, 249 A.2d 89 (1969) (rejecting the absolute priority approach as a test of fairness in a recapitalization). If not, how can one evaluate the worth of a liquidation preference or claim to dividends in arrears in order to compare against the value of stock or securities received in exchange? For one idea, see *SEC v. Central–Illinois Sec. Corp.,* 338 U.S. 96, 140 (1949) ("investment value" approach used for recapitalizations ordered under the Public Utility Holding Company Act, which ignores the liquidation preference and discounts the arrearage claim to the present value of a pay-off with expected future earnings).

Returning to mechanics, notice the plan of recapitalization in *Honigman* went beyond simply amending the articles. It also required the shareholders to exchange their stock for newly issued shares. Where is the authority for this? In many instances, the question is rather academic. For example, as pointed out above, the trade of the "B" shares for the newly issued common in *Honigman* did nothing more than amending the articles to give the "B" shares the vote would have done. Hence, the mandatory exchange of certificates in this instance seems gratuitous and unobjectionable. Perhaps the same could be said about the exchange of the "A" shares for the new convertible common—albeit, here the amendment would not entail a simple alteration of the rights of the stock, but rather a complete redescription. What about more complicated exchanges; for example, an exchange of outstanding preferred for a package of other stock including common and preferred? In fact, many statutes expressly or implicitly authorize "amendments" to the articles which require shareholders to exchange their stock for other stock. *E.g.*, Cal. Corp. Code § 900(a) (allowing amendments to include provisions to exchange, reclassify or cancel shares); Del. Gen. Corp. Law § 242(a) (allowing amendments to reclassify shares and to include provisions to carry out an exchange of shares); N.Y. Bus. Corp. Law § 801(b)(11) (allowing amendments to change shares of one class into shares of one or more other classes); M.B.C.A. § 10.04(a)(2) (implicitly allowing amendments to effect an exchange of shares). How far can this go? For example, can one amend the articles to force the exchange of shares not only for other shares, but for debt securities as well?

A second method exists to accomplish a mandatory or "cram-down" recapitalization. This is to form a wholly-owned subsidiary and merge this company with the parent. *E.g., Bove v. Community Hotel Corp.*, 105 R.I. 36, 249 A.2d 89 (1969). Corporations statutes typically allow merging companies to force their stockholders to exchange outstanding shares for whatever stock, securities or other consideration the plan of merger provides. *E.g.*, Cal. Corp. Code § 1101(d); Del. Gen. Corp. Law § 251(b); N.Y. Bus. Corp. Law § 902(a)(3); M.B.C.A. § 11.07(a)(8). Hence, a company merging with its wholly-owned subsidiary could adopt a plan which cancels all the shares in the subsidiary that the parent owns, and forces its shareholders to trade their stock for whatever the plan requires; beyond which the merger will have no practical impact. Procedurally, the merger must receive approval by a shareholder (as well as director) vote. Cal. Corp. Code § 1201(a); Del. Gen. Corp. Law § 251(c); N.Y. Bus. Corp. Law § 903; M.B.C.A. § 11.04(b). Some statutes, however, do not require approval by individual classes of stock, nor allow shares without voting rights generally to vote on the merger, even though the merger plan may adversely impact such stock. *E.g.*, Del. Gen. Corp. Law § 251(c). Compensating somewhat, merger provisions typically extend to dissenting stockholders the right to demand the company cash them out at a fair price set by appraisal. Cal. Corp. Code § 1300; Del. Gen. Corp. Law § 262; N.Y. Bus. Corp. Law § 910(a)(1)(A); M.B.C.A. § 13.02(a)(1). (Some acts also extend such appraisal rights to article amendments adversely impacting various rights of stock. *E.g.*, N.Y. Bus. Corp. Law § 806(b)(6).)

3. Does a recapitalization involve the "sale" of securities, thereby triggering application of federal and state securities laws? Section 2(3) of the 1933 Securities Act defines sales to include every contract of sale or disposition of a security "for value." Value encompasses receipt of items beyond money, including return of the issuer's outstanding stocks or bonds. *E.g., United States v. Riedel,* 126 F.2d 81 (7th Cir.1942). Hence, if a recapitalization consists of a voluntary exchange of stocks or debt instruments between the company and those of its securities holders who so desire, there is a

sale. What about involuntary recapitalizations accomplished through an amendment to the company's articles (or through a merger with a subsidiary)? Conceptually, two problems exist with calling this a sale. It lacks the individual voluntary consent—at least of those not voting for the plan—normally associated with the notion of a sale. It also, in the case of an article amendment, may not even involve the actual exchange of securities.

For some time, the Securities Exchange Commission took the position in its Rule 133 that involuntary transactions, such as "cram-down" recapitalizations, involved no sale. The Commission's position changed in 1972, when it rescinded Rule 133, and adopted Rule 145. Rule 145(a)(1) directly impacts recapitalizations through article amendments. It deems a reclassification of a corporation's securities, which involves the substitution of one security for another, to constitute a sale whenever the company submits the reclassification to a vote of the shareholders. (The Rule excepts, however, stock splits and reverse stock splits.) The Rule removes any further argument that the involuntary nature of a recapitalization through article amendment means it is not a sale. This still leaves the question, however, of when amendments without the exchange of securities constitute a sale. In the language of the Rule, can there be a substitution of one security for another if certificates do not actually change hands? The answer is yes, depending upon how significantly the amendment alters the rights of the outstanding shares. L. Loss, *Fundamentals of Securities Regulation* 264 (1983):

> "[A] change in interest or dividend rate or liquidation preference or underlying security, or a change in the identity of the issuer, would seem quite clearly to result in a new security. On the other hand, there is likely to be an agreement that a mere change in the name of the security (perhaps from common to Class B stock), or a change in the name of the issuer without a change of identity, or certain types of charter amendment affecting the powers of the directors, do not make a new security. In between come a great variety of other changes—for example, from par to no par or vice versa, changes in par or stated value, changes in redemption or cumulative or conversion features, various changes in voting rights. There the answer must depend on the context. * * *"

Assuming the recapitalization constitutes a sale, then the corporation must register under the 1933 Securities Act unless it can find an exemption. The various exemptions outlined in Chapter V—private offerings, offerings meeting the terms of Regulation D, and intrastate offerings—can apply to recapitalizations which otherwise come within their terms. Sec. Act Rule 145, Preliminary Note. In addition, two other exemptions may be relevant here. Section 3(a)(9) exempts,

> "Except with respect to a security exchanged in a case under title 11, any security exchanged by the issuer with its existing security holders exclusively where no commission or other remuneration is paid or given directly or indirectly for soliciting such exchange."

Notice, at first glance, Section 3(a)(9) seems to fit recapitalizations perfectly. Yet, problems can arise. For example, suppose a company uses the technique of merging with its subsidiary to accomplish a recapitalization. Section 3(a)(9) circumscribes the parties to the exchange: The transaction can only occur between the issuer of the securities exchanged and the holders of its outstanding securities. Is the corporation resulting from a merger still the same issuer of the shares surrendered? Might this depend on which firm merges into the other? As another potential problem, suppose at about the time of the recapitalization, the company sells securities to non-shareholders for cash (either in a registered offering or pursuant to another exemption). Will this destroy the 3(a)(9) exemption for the recapitalization, as the exchange is no longer exclusively with the corporation's existing securities holders? The answer is yes if the two transactions are part of the same "issue". *E.g.,* Sec. Act Rel. No. 2029. This, in turn, depends upon the criteria—discussed in Chapter V—for the integration of offerings. Another problem exists if the exchange involves consideration other than securities; for example, the company either gives or receives cash in order to equalize values. The Securities Exchange Commission interprets the word "exclusively" in Section 3(a)(9) to refer not only to who the issuer can deal with—just its securities holders—but also to what it can receive from them: The exchange must involve exclusively the surrender of securities. III L. Loss & J. Seligman, *Securities Regulation* 1232 (3d ed. 1989). There is one exception to this. Rule 149 allows securities holders to pay cash to the issuer to the extent necessary to make an equitable adjustment for differences between members of the same class in dividends or interest payments paid or payable. On the other hand, there is no limit on the flow of consideration from issuer to securities holders. The corporation may provide its holders cash as well as securities in the exchange. *See* Sec. Act Rule 150. One other potential problem created by the limitation on what the corporation can receive occurs when the recapitalization involves preferred shares with dividends in arrears. Does surrender of the right to the arrearage constitute consideration independent of the surrender of the preferred shares? See Diverse Graphics, Inc., No Action Letter (June 20, 1972) (indicating it does not). Finally, suppose the company employs a proxy solicitation firm to encourage votes in favor of the recapitalization. Note, the exemption does not apply if the corporation paid (directly or indirectly) any compensation for soliciting the exchange.

Section 3(a)(10) provides a second exemption for securities issued in exchange for the surrender of outstanding securities. This exemption lacks the limitations found in Section 3(a)(9). The transaction can involve parties other than the issuer of the surrendered securities and its securities holders (thereby making it useful for mergers). The exchange can involve partial payment for the newly issued securities in cash as well as in surrendered securities (or other surrendered claims or property interests). Also, there is no limit on paid solicitation of the exchange. The offsetting requirement is that the exchange must receive approval by a court, or other governmental agency authorized to give such approval, after a hearing upon the fairness of the exchange. The Securities Exchange Commission answered some questions about this requirement in a letter from the Commission's general counsel:

> "1. Is adequate notice to all persons to whom it is proposed to issue securities of the hearing on the fairness of their issuance necessary for an exemption under Section 3(a)(10)?

"Although the wording of Section 3(a)(10) does not demand such notice, in my opinion this requirement is to be implied from the necessity for a 'hearing * * * at which all persons to whom it is proposed to issue securities * * * shall have the right to appear.' * * *

> "2. Is a grant of 'express authorization of law' to a state governmental authority to approve the fairness of the terms and conditions of the issuance and exchange of securities necessary for an exemption under Section 3(a)(10), or is express authorization merely to approve the terms and conditions sufficient?

"The punctuation and grammatical construction of the last clause of Section 3(a)(10) indicate that the words 'expressly authorized * * * by law' were not intended to modify 'courts or officials or agencies of the United States'. In my opinion a State governmental authority (with the possible exception of a banking or insurance commission) must possess express authority of law to approve the *fairness* of the terms and conditions of the issuance and exchange of the securities in question. This interpretation seems necessary to give meaning to the express requirement of a hearing upon the fairness of such terms and conditions, which must subsume authority in the supervisory body to pass upon the fairness from the standpoint of the investor, as well as the issuer and consumer, and to disapprove terms and conditions because unfair either to those who are to receive the securities or to other security holders of the issuer, or to the public. This requirement seems the more essential in that the whole justification for the exemption afforded by Section 3(a)(10) is that the examination and approval by the body in question of the fairness of the issue in question is a substitute for the protection afforded to the investor by the information which would otherwise be made available to him through registration. The requisite express authorization of law to approve the fairness of such terms and conditions, however, probably need not necessarily be *in haec verba,* but to give effect to the words 'express' and 'by law', must be granted clearly and explicitly.

> "3. Does a hearing by an authority expressly authorized by law to hold such a hearing satisfy the requirement of a hearing in Section 3(a)(10), if the state law does not require a hearing?

"I believe that, as a corollary to the view expressed in my answer to the second question, supra, and in order that a hearing have legal sanction, the approving authority must be expressly authorized by law to hold the hearing; but in my opinion it is unnecessary that the hearing be mandatory under applicable state law. Therefore, if state law expressly authorizes the approving authority to hold a hearing on the fairness of the terms and conditions of the issuance and exchange of securities, and such a hearing is in fact held, this requirement of Section 3(a)(10) is satisfied. * * * "Sec. Act Rel. No. 312 (1935).

One area in which courts approve the exchange of securities is in a bankruptcy reorganization. Section 3(a)(10), however, excludes from its coverage securities exchanged in Title 11 reorganizations. (Instead, provisions in the bankruptcy law provide certain exemptions from registration. 11 U.S.C. §§ 364, 1125, 1145.) On the other hand, a number of states, including prominently California, provide under their securities laws for fairness hearings on exchanges. *E.g.*, Cal. Corp. Code § 25142. Indeed, these state provisions may allow issuers to request such a hearing even if the transaction would be exempt from qualification. Sometimes, it may be easier to go through such a hearing than to register under the 1933 Securities Act.

There is one other point to note about both Sections 3(a)(9) and 3(a)(10). While they come under the category of exempt securities, the Securities Exchange Commission treats them both (like the intrastate and small offering exemptions) as a transaction exemption. *See, e.g.*, Sec. Act Rel. No. 646. Hence, resales face the same statutory underwriter questions discussed in Chapter V. *See also* Rule 145(c), (d) (providing further guidelines for who is an underwriter in transactions deemed to be sales under this Rule).

Registration of a recapitalization can be on a Form S–4. To the extent the transaction requires a shareholder vote in a 1934 Act reporting company, the proxy solicitations rules promulgated pursuant to Section 14 of the Securities Exchange Act come into play. Form S–4, however, can satisfy the proxy statement requirements, thus avoiding the need to prepare two separate documents. Moreover, Form S–4 allows a 1934 Act reporting company to provide much of the called-for information by incorporating its 1934 Act filings by reference. This may suggest a public company might not gain much by avoiding registration under Sections 3(a)(9) or 3(a)(10). Also, Rule 145(b)(1) allows the corporation to send basic notice of the meeting to vote on the transaction to its stockholders without the notice coming within the rules governing a prospectus. Of course, these requirements focus on the sale of securities by the company. A recapitalization involves securities flowing in two directions: The company is both issuing and receiving them. While the company's acquisition of its own shares should be exempt from registration under Section 4(1), recall the discussion earlier concerning possible disclosure obligations applicable to repurchases by a 1934 Act reporting company of its own shares.

State blue sky laws also may cover recapitalizations whether carried out through exchange offers or by article amendment. *Compare* Uniform Securities Act (1956) § 401(j)(6)(C) (exempting reclassification of securities through shareholder vote from the definition of a "sale"), *with* Uniform Securities Act (1985 revision) § 101(13)(vi) (removing this part of the 1956 Act from the definition of a "sale"); Uniform Securities Act (2002 revision)

§ 102(26) (same). *See also* Cal. Corp. Code §§ 25017(a) (expressly including any exchange of securities, or any change in the rights of outstanding securities, in the definition of a "sale"), 25103(b), (c), (e), (g) (exemptions applicable to recapitalizations which have too little contact with California, or too slight an effect on the securities holders' rights, to require registration), 25120 (requiring qualification for securities issued in a recapitalization). The state law exemptions applicable to limited offerings (which were discussed in Chapter V) may be applicable to recapitalizations. *See, e.g.,* Uniform Securities Law (2002 revision) § 402(14); 10 Cal. Code Reg. § 260.103. There also might be parallel exemptions to Sections 3(a)(9) of the Federal Act. *E.g.,* Uniform Securities Act (1985 revision) § 402(14). Otherwise, corporations must qualify under the applicable state securities law(s), which can entail merit review.

b. *Tax Aspects*

(i) Treatment Upon the Exchange

Dean v. Commissioner of Internal Revenue

10 T.C. 19 (1948).

* * *

The question presented is as to whether or not the petitioners realized a capital gain when, in the recapitalization of the North Star Woolen Mills Co., they exchanged stock having a $50 par value for no par value preferred stock with a cumulative return of $5 per share, at a ratio of one share of $50 par value stock for 1 1/4 shares of preferred stock.

FINDINGS OF FACT

* * *

North Star Woolen Mills Co. (hereinafter called North Star) for many years prior and subsequent to 1941 manufactured blankets and other textile articles.

Prior to December 1941 its capital stock consisted of 8,000 shares of one class having a par value of $50. The issued stock was held as follows:

	Shares
William G. Northup	705
William G. Northup and his sister, Marjorie N. Dean, as trustee under testamentary trust created by their father's last will and testament	800
J.N. Lindeke	200
Ethel X. Northup, petitioner Docket No. 10020	1,000
William G. Northup, as executor of the estate of his deceased mother, Leila T. Northup	475

	Shares
Marjorie N. Dean, petitioner Docket No. 10018	845
Virginia Dean Grant–Lawson, petitioner in Docket No. 10019, daughter of Marjorie N. Dean	105
Marjorie Dean, daughter of Marjorie N. Dean	105
Estate of Leila Lewin–Harris, deceased, daughter of Marjorie N. Dean	105
Directors' qualifying shares	2
Total	4,342

For many years prior to 1941 North Star had become increasingly a one-man company, with William G. Northup having the entire executive responsibility. In 1939 Northup's chief assistant urged upon him the necessity of developing executive employees having a financial interest in the company who would be secure in their positions in event of the death of William G. Northup, when the stock control of the company would fall into the hands of women having no experience with the company, much of said stock being held by nonresidents of this country.

Shortly thereafter this manager resigned and the same proposition was urged upon Northup by one of his directors and subsequently by his banker at a time when North Star was obtaining large amounts of its needed capital from bank borrowings and when it was contemplating the purchase of a new mill at Lima, Ohio. Northup then, complying with this advice and with the triple purpose of preventing the company from falling under the voting control of inexperienced women, of inducing new executive talent to take a financial interest in the company in addition to the salary received, and of placing the stock of the company in a position so that it would be attractive to investors, devised a plan the more pertinent features of which were:

The capital of the corporation was to consist of 14,000 shares, of which 8,000 would be common stock of the par value of $50 and 6,000 would be preferred shares without par value. * * * [T]he preferred shares were to have no voting power unless one year's dividend was passed.

On December 17, 1941, the stockholders, at a special meeting, approved this plan as an amendment to the articles of incorporation and adopted a resolution that each holder of an outstanding share should be given the privilege of exchanging one of said shares for 1 1/4 of the preferred shares; that the cumulative dividends on the preferred shares would be $5 and the redemption amount, in the event of dissolution of the company, would be $100. All stock other than the preferred was reclassified as common shares.

* * *

The list of the stockholders exchanging old shares for preferred shares is as follows:

Stockholder	Shares Exchanged	New Preferred Shares Received
Marjorie N. Dean, the petitioner in Docket No. 10018	845	1,056 ¼
Virginia Dean Grant–Lawson, the petitioner in Docket No. 10019	105	131 ¼
Marjorie Dean	105	131 ¼
Ethel X. Northup, the petitioner in Docket No. 10020	1,000	1,250
William G. Northup, as executor of the estate of Leila T. Northup, deceased	200	250
Total	2,255	2,818 ¾

* * *

OPINION

■ HARLAN, JUDGE; Petitioner contends that by virtue of the provisions of [the predecessors to Sections 354(a) and 368(a)(1)(E)] North Star, in December 1941, accomplished a reorganization for which no gain or loss is recognized to the stockholders.

Respondent argues that the reorganization, consisting of a recapitalization, was but a subterfuge whereby a part of North Star's surplus was channeled to the preferred stockholders and that the taxpayers thereby received taxable capital gain in the year when the preferred stock was received.

When this recapitalization occurred it would seem to be established that petitioners' contention had been approved by the Board of Tax Appeals in *Elmer W. Hartzell,* 40 B.T.A. 492. In that case the taxpayer had received preferred stock in exchange for his common stock in pursuance of a plan of the stockholders so designed that the older stockholders of the corporation would turn the corporate management over to a group of younger stockholders and that the latter would acquire all of the voting common stock, while the older stockholders would receive the nonvoting preferred stock. The Board approved this recapitalization as a tax-free reorganization. This decision was later acquiesced in by the Commissioner. * * *

However, in the case at bar the Commissioner contends that the present case is controlled by the recent decisions of the United States Supreme Court and the Court of Appeals for the Seventh Circuit in the recent cases of *Adams v. Commissioner,* 331 U.S. 737; *Bazley v. Commissioner,* 331 U.S. 737; and *Heady v. Commissioner,* 162 Fed.(2d) 699.

In the *Bazley* case the taxpayer and his wife owned all of the capital stock except one qualifying share. There were 1,000 shares with a par value of $100 each. Under the recapitalization plan each old share was exchanged for 5 new shares having no par value and a stated value of $60. In addition debenture bonds of a face value of $400,000, payable in 10 years but callable at any time, were distributed pro rata among the stockholders. The corporation had an earned surplus of $855,783.82. The Supreme Court, in sustaining the decision of the Tax Court, held that for a recapitalization to constitute a tax-free reorganization it must not "exempt from payment of a tax what is a practical matter of realized gain." More particularly, the Court said:

> In the case of a corporation which has undistributed earnings the creation of new corporate obligations which are transferred to stockholders in relation to their former holdings so as to produce for all practical purposes the same result as the distribution of cash earnings of equivalent value cannot obtain tax immunity because cast in the form of a recapitalization-reorganization.

The Court held that the debentures issued were virtually cash because they were callable by a corporation controlled by those holding debentures.

The *Adams* case in its legal aspects was similar to the *Bazley* case.

In *Heady v. Commissioner, supra,* the two stockholders owning all of the stock in a corporation, which consisted of 1,000 shares of no par value, desired to sell the stock. Realizing no success, a plan was devised to employ a practical manager having special ability and background to operate the corporation and ultimately purchase the stock. The corporation was recapitalized by substituting 1,000 shares of $1 par value stock for the old issue and issuing debenture bonds in the amount of $135,000. * * * The debenture bonds were issued pro rata to the old stockholders. The contract of employment with the new manager permitted him to buy the capital stock of the corporation as rapidly as he was able to retire the debenture bonds, so that when the bonds were retired he would own the corporate assets. The Court held that the purpose of this recapitalization was not a corporate business purpose, but merely a business purpose of the stockholders * * *.

A number of distinctions between the case at bar and the three cases relied upon by the Commissioner would seem to be apparent. In the case before us, no debenture obligations were issued. The preferred stock was not distributed in proportion to the common stockholdings, but in exchange therefor; the petitioners retained no control when they surrendered their common shares. The purpose behind the distribution of preferred shares in the case at bar was admitted to be to transfer voting control from one group of stockholders to another, and an issue of debenture bonds or preferred stock in proportion to the stockholdings would have been useless for this purpose.

* * *

The respondent also complains that the recapitalization lacked sincerity because nothing was accomplished by the recapitalization. * * *

It is to be noted, however, that after the 1941 recapitalization a new manager was employed, who testified that, if the possibility of the corporation devolving upon inexperienced women upon the death of William G. Northup had continued and if he had not been promised the right to purchase into the corporate stock, he would not have been interested in remaining with the company. This promise made to this manager was carried out in September 1945, by the authorized sale of stock to him and other employees.

* * *

It is therefore our conclusion that the law of the *Elmer W. Hartzel* case, *supra,* is controlling under the facts in the case at bar.

* * *

NOTES

1. Ordinarily, exchanging some shares of stock for others—just like any other exchange of property—produces taxable income or loss measured by the difference between the taxpayer's basis in the stock surrendered, and the fair market value of the shares received. I.R.C. § 1001. (Recall, however, corporations do not face tax when they issue their own shares in exchange for property, including other shares. I.R.C. § 1032.) Section 1036 provides one exception to this rule, as it precludes recognition of gain or loss when a stockholder exchanges common shares for other common in the same corporation, or preferred shares for other preferred in the same company. (This exchange can either occur with the corporation, or between individual shareholders. Treas. Reg. § 1.1036–1(a).) What about a shareholder exchanging with the company its outstanding common for newly issued preferred (as in *Dean*), or outstanding preferred for newly issued common? For such transactions, one must look to Sections 354 and 368, if the shareholder is to avoid recognition.

Section 354(a)(1) precludes a taxpayer from recognizing gain or loss when he or she exchanges, pursuant to a plan of "reorganization," stock or securities in a corporation which is a party to this reorganization, for other stock or securities either in the same company or in another firm which is also a party to the reorganization. Section 368(a) defines the term reorganization to include seven different types of transactions. Three of these transactions (Section 368(a)(1)(A), (B) and (C)) involve methods of buying and selling businesses in corporate form, and will be addressed in Chapter VII. One (Section 368(a)(1)(D)), this chapter will address later when dealing with dividing a corporate business, and also may play a role in corporate acquisitions. Section 368(a)(1)(F) covers transactions such as changing the state of incorporation. Section 368(a)(1)(G) involves reorganizations in a bankruptcy proceeding. The reorganization of present interest is Section 368(a)(1)(E): "a recapitalization."

The Code does not define the term "recapitalization," and the regulations only tangentially do so by way of examples. Treas. Reg. § 1.368–2(e). As stated earlier, the term lacks any precise meaning under state corporate law. A broad judicial definition for tax purposes refers to a reshuffling of an existing company's capital structure. *Helvering v. Southwest Consolidated Corp.,* 315 U.S. 194, 202 (1942). In *Dean,* it simply consisted of the company's offer to exchange new shares for the outstanding shares of those holders who wished. One significant point to observe about the recapitalization in *Dean* is it accomplished tax-free the same result as a pro-rata stock dividend followed by a taxable exchange of shares among the stockholders. Moreover, a recapitalization need not even involve the actual exchange of shares—an amendment to the articles substantially changing the interests of shares (for instance, by increasing the liquidation preference of preferred) can constitute a recapitalization. Rev. Rul. 56–654, 1956–2 C.B. 216. Hence, a tax-free recapitalization can encompass either the voluntary or involuntary share exchanges discussed earlier.

In dealing with reorganizations in general, courts and the regulations have imposed several requirements not expressly stated in Section 368. Two of these—that there be some degree of continuity of the business enterprise before and after the reorganization, and that there be some degree of continuity in those holding equity interests in the corporation before and after the reorganization—do not apply to recapitalizations. Treas. Reg. § 1.368–1(b). The requirement that the transaction serve a business purpose, however, does apply. *See, e.g., Wolf Envelope Co. v. Commissioner,* 17 T.C. 471 (1951). In a closely held company, in which estate planning and similar shareholder concerns often motivate a recapitalization, this requirement could pose a problem. *See* Rev. Proc. 81–60, 1981–2 C.B. 680 (for purposes of obtaining a favorable advance ruling on a recapitalization, the Internal Revenue Service requires a statement of a *corporate* purpose). Nevertheless, courts often recognize that these shareholder interests, if not sufficient business purposes in themselves, frequently coincide with the interest of a closely held corporation in, for example, transferring voting control to a younger generation more actively involved in running the company. *See, e.g., Wolf Envelope Co. v. Commissioner,* 17 T.C. 471 (1951). (In this regard, how (other than a suggestion of sexism) can one distinguish the court's finding a legitimate corporate purpose in *Dean*, with the holding that there was no corporate purpose in the *Heady* case discussed in *Dean*?)

Needless to say, there is some trade-off involved in avoiding recognition by virtue of the reorganization provisions. As with most non-recognition provisions, the *quid pro quo* is a substituted basis. I.R.C. § 358(a)(1). (The reader may recall the discussion of Section 358's basis rules in connection with Section 351 transactions.) Incidentally, there is no need to consider the corporation's resulting basis when dealing with a recapitalization, since the company simply receives back its own stock or securities in which it can have no basis. *E.g.,* Rev. Rul. 74–503, 1974–2 C.B. 117.

2. In *Dean,* the five women exchanged all their common shares for the new preferred. Suppose, instead, they had exchanged only a portion of their common. In this event, the end result would be economically indistinguishable from a stock dividend of preferred to the five women, and common to the others (who saw their percentage holdings of the common increase due to the exchange). Yet, Section 305(b)(3) makes such a stock dividend taxable. Does this mean parties can use recapitalizations to accomplish tax-free the equivalent result to a taxable stock dividend? The answer lies in Section 305(c) and the regulations issued thereunder.

Section 305(c) empowers the Internal Revenue Service to issue regulations under which various transactions, including recapitalizations, constitute a stock distribution governed by Sections 301 and 305(b) for any shareholder whose proportionate interest in the corporation's earnings or assets increases. (The reader may recall having already encountered Section 305(c) in dealing with the potential tax effects of redemptions upon the non-selling shareholders. In addition to redemptions and recapitalizations, changes in conversion ratio (the number of shares the holder of convertible stock or debt instruments can obtain in exchange for surrendering the convertible security), a change in redemption price (for redeemable shares), and a difference between the redemption and issue price (for redeemable shares) can bring Section 305(c) into play.) The regulations issued pursuant to Section 305(c) indicate generally that they will treat any transaction as a stock distribution for purposes of Sections 301 and 305(b) if the transaction has the effect of increasing the proportionate interest of a shareholder in the corporation's earnings or assets, and also has the same result as a stock distribution made taxable by Section 305(b)(2), (3), (4) or (5). Treas. Reg. § 1.305–7(a). When specifically addressing recapitalizations, however, the regulations identify only two types which the Service deems to constitute a stock distribution covered by Sections 301 and 305(b). Treas. Reg. § 1.305–7(c)(1). The first is a recapitalization which is part of a plan to increase periodically a shareholder's proportionate interest in the company's earnings or assets. The second is a recapitalization designed to wipe out a dividend arrearage by exchanging the preferred for new shares worth more (or with a greater liquidation preference) than the old.

Where does this leave a recapitalization which is equivalent in effect to a distribution of common shares to some common stockholders and preferred shares to other holders of common? In fact, the regulations give such a recapitalization as an example of one which Section 305 does not make taxable. Treas. Reg. § 1.305–3(e)(12). The explanation is that the recapitalization involved in this example was not part of any continuing transaction, and the legislative history of Section 305(c) suggests the section was not to apply to isolated recapitalizations for legitimate business purposes. 115 Cong. Rec. 37902 (1969) (remarks of Senator Long). (Recall, the regulations make this same distinction for redemptions coming within Section 305(c).) Hence, isolated recapitalizations, not part of a plan to periodically increase a shareholder's interest or made to wipe out a dividend arrearage (the two specifically mentioned categories of deemed distributions), can obtain tax-free the same result as taxable stock dividends. *See also* Treas. Reg. § 1.305–5(d) Exs. (2), (6) (allowing isolated recapitalizations to accomplish results which might otherwise equal a taxable stock dividend on preferred).

On the other hand, even if the recapitalization, in itself, does not create a problem under Section 305(c), the shares issued may do so. For example, suppose, as part of a plan to pass ownership to the next generation, a corporation engages in a recapitalization in which a parent exchanges common shares for preferred stock redeemable upon the parent's death. Further, suppose, whether intentionally or inadvertently, the redemption price is greater than the issue price of the preferred shares. Here, one confronts regulations issued pursuant to the command in Section 305(c) that address redemption premiums—in other words, the amount by which the redemption price exceeds the stock's issue price—when the premium exceeds the original issue discount de minimis level. The regulations promulgated pursuant to this authority call for constructive distribution treatment following original issue discount principles (which are discussed in Chapter IV) in cases in which either the redemption is mandatory or the shareholder had the right to force redemption, except if the redemption option is subject to a contingency that is beyond the legal or practical control of the shareholders holding the option and the contingency renders the likelihood of redemption remote. Treas. Reg. § 1.305–5.

3. If a company has only one class of stock outstanding, and all the shareholders make precisely the same exchange, the recapitalization can produce no transfer of wealth between them. In a situation, like *Dean,* however, when all shareholders do not make the same trade, the potential exists for some to gain at the expense of others. Not only may this create fairness questions, but it also can create tax consequences. For example, the failure to realistically value preferred stock issued in a recapitalization could lead to setting a redemption price that is enough in excess of the share's issue price so as to trigger application of Section 305(c). *See* Revenue Ruling 83–119, 1983 C.B. 57 (involving an earlier version of Section 305(c)). More broadly, the enrichment of some shareholders at the expense of others in an unequally valued exchange might create a gift tax liability or constitute taxable compensation, depending upon the motivation for the disparity in value. Rev. Rul. 74–269, 1974–1 C.B. 87.

This discussion indicates the importance of valuing the stock exchanged in a recapitalization. When parties deal at arms length, and with no other obligation between them, presumably negotiations will yield an equivalence in value between the surrendered and received shares. *See, e.g., United States v. Davis,* 370 U.S. 65 (1962). Often, however, recapitalizations do not involve parties dealing completely at arms length, and with no other concerns. In this event, they may face the need to establish an equivalence in value between surrendered and received shares. The basics of such valuation questions have been explored earlier in this book. The following ruling provides some additional guidelines focusing on valuing preferred and common shares in a closely held corporation.

Revenue Ruling 83–120

1983–2 C.B. 170.

SEC. 1. PURPOSE

The purpose of this Revenue Ruling is to amplify Rev.Rul. 59–60, 1959–1 C.B. 237, by specifying additional factors to be considered in valuing common and preferred stock of a closely held corporation for gift tax and other purposes in a recapitalization of closely held businesses. This type of valuation problem frequently arises with respect to estate planning transactions wherein an individual receives preferred stock with a stated par value equal to all or a large portion of the fair market value of the individual's former stock interest in a corporation. The individual also receives common stock which is then transferred, usually as a gift, to a relative.

* * *

SEC. 3. GENERAL APPROACH TO VALUATION

Under Section 25.2512–2(f)(2) of the Gift Tax Regulations, the fair market value of stock in a closely held corporation depends upon numerous factors, including the corporation's net worth, its prospective earning power, and its capacity to pay dividends. In addition, other relevant factors must be taken into account. *See* Rev.Rul. 59–60. The weight to be accorded any evidentiary factor depends on the circumstances of each case. *See* Section 25.2512–2(f) of the Gift Tax Regulations.

SEC. 4. APPROACH TO VALUATION—PREFERRED STOCK

.01 In general the most important factors to be considered in determining the value of preferred stock are its yield, dividend coverage and protection of its liquidation preference.

.02 Whether the yield of the preferred stock supports a valuation of the stock at par value depends in part on the adequacy of the dividend rate. The adequacy of the dividend rate should be determined by comparing its dividend rate with the dividend rate of high-grade publicly traded preferred stock. A lower yield than that of high-grade preferred stock indicates a preferred stock value of less than par. If the rate of interest charged by independent creditors to the corporation on loans is higher than the rate such independent creditors charge their most credit worthy borrowers, then the yield on the preferred stock should be correspondingly higher than the yield on high quality preferred stock. A yield which is not correspondingly higher reduces the value of the preferred stock. In addition, whether the preferred stock has a fixed dividend rate and is non-participating influences the value of the preferred stock. A publicly traded preferred stock for a company having a similar business and similar assets with similar liquidation preferences, voting rights and other similar terms would be the ideal comparable for determining yield required in arms length transactions for closely held stock. Such ideal comparables will frequently not exist. In such circumstances, the most comparable publicly-traded issues should be selected for comparison and appropriate adjustments made for differing factors.

.03 The actual dividend rate on a preferred stock can be assumed to be its stated rate if the issuing corporation will be able to pay its dividends in a timely manner and will, in fact, pay such dividends. The risk that the corporation may be unable to timely pay the stated dividends on the preferred stock can be measured by the coverage of such stated dividends by the corporation's earnings. Coverage of the dividend is measured by the ratio of the sum of pre-tax and pre-interest earnings to the sum of the total interest to be paid and the pre-tax earnings needed to pay the after-tax dividends. *Standard & Poor's Ratings Guide,* 58 (1979). Inadequate coverage exists where a decline in corporate profits would be likely to jeopardize the corporation's ability to pay dividends on the preferred stock. The ratio for the preferred stock in question should be compared with the ratios for high quality preferred stock to determine whether the preferred stock has adequate coverage. Prior earnings history is important in this determination. Inadequate coverage indicates that the value of preferred stock is lower than its par value. Moreover, the absence of a provision that preferred dividends are cumulative raises substantial questions concerning whether the stated dividend rate will, in fact, be paid. Accordingly, preferred stock with noncumulative dividend features will normally have a value substantially lower than a cumulative preferred stock with the same yield, liquidation preference and dividend coverage.

.04 Whether the issuing corporation will be able to pay the full liquidation preference at liquidation must be taken into account in determining fair market value. This risk can be measured by the protection afforded by the corporation's net assets. Such protection can be measured by the ratio of the excess of the current market value of the corporation's assets over its liabilities to the aggregate liquidation preference. The protection ratio should be compared with the ratios for high quality preferred stock to determine adequacy of coverage. Inadequate asset protection exists where any unforeseen business reverses would be likely to jeopardize the corporation's ability to pay the full liquidation preference to the holders of the preferred stock.

.05 Another factor to be considered in valuing the preferred stock is whether it has voting rights and, if so, whether the preferred stock has voting control. See, however, Section 5.02 below.

.06. Peculiar covenants or provisions of the preferred stock of a type not ordinarily found in publicly traded preferred stock should be carefully evaluated to determine the effects of such covenants on the value of the preferred stock. In general, if covenants would inhibit the marketability of the stock or the power of the holder to enforce dividend or liquidation rights, such provisions will reduce the value of the preferred stock by comparison to the value of preferred stock not containing such covenants or provisions.

.07 Whether the preferred stock contains a redemption privilege is another factor to be considered in determining the value of the preferred stock. The value of a redemption privilege triggered by death of the preferred shareholder will not exceed the present value of the redemption premium payable at the preferred shareholder's death (i.e., the present value of the excess of the redemption price over the fair market value of the preferred stock upon its issuance). The value of the redemption privilege should be reduced to reflect any risk that the corporation may not possess sufficient assets to redeem its preferred stock at the stated redemption price. See .03 above.

SEC. 5. APPROACH TO VALUATION—COMMON STOCK

.01 If the preferred stock has a fixed rate of dividend and is nonparticipating, the common stock has the exclusive right to the benefits of future appreciation of the value of the corporation. This right is valuable and usually warrants a determination that the common stock has substantial value. The actual value of this right depends upon the corporation's past growth experience, the economic condition of the industry in which the corporation operates, and general economic conditions. The factor to be used in capitalizing the corporation's prospective earnings must be determined after an analysis of numerous factors concerning the corporation and the economy as a whole. *See* Rev.Rul. 59–60, at page 243. In addition, after-tax earnings of the corporation at the time the preferred stock is issued in excess of the stated dividends on the preferred stock will increase the value of the common stock. Furthermore, a corporate policy of reinvesting earnings will also increase the value of the common stock.

.02 A factor to be considered in determining the value of the common stock is whether the preferred stock also has voting rights. Voting rights of the preferred stock, especially if the preferred stock has voting control, could under certain circumstances increase the value of the preferred stock and reduce the value of the common stock. This factor may be reduced in significance where the rights of common stockholders as a class are protected under state law from actions by another class of shareholders, * * * particularly where the common shareholders, as a class, are given the power to disapprove a proposal to allow preferred stock to be converted into common stock. * * *

Often, particularly in the estate and gift tax context, it is in the taxpayer's interest to argue for a low valuation on stock. In this regard, consider the utility of the reference in Revenue Ruling 83–120 to discounting the value of preferred stock based upon covenants which might inhibit the marketability of the stock or the enforcement of the preferred's dividend or liquidation rights. Not surprisingly, there has been considerable litigation between the I.R.S. and taxpayers involving the appropriate valuation for estate and gift tax purposes of stock subject to disadvantageous terms which taxpayers argue justify a valuation discount. *See, e.g.,* Manigault & Hodges, *Valuation Discounts—An Analysis of the Service's Position Compared With Litigated Cases*, 91 J. Tax. 26 (1999). In this regard, one must also keep in mind the special valuation rules established for estate and gift tax purposes by Sections 2701–2704, as discussed earlier in describing estate freezes.

4. Non-pro-rata exchanges of common for preferred in a recapitalization can produce other unexpected consequences. For example, suppose an elderly stockholder owning a majority of the common agrees to exchange his or her stock for non-voting, non-participating preferred in order to pass

control to younger participants. (Assume also the younger participants are not family members within Section 318's attribution rules.) This would constitute an "ownership change" triggering Section 382. I.R.C. § 382(g). The result would be to limit the corporation's ability to utilize any net operating loss carryovers it may have based upon losses incurred before the recapitalization. I.R.C. § 382(a), (b). (Chapter VII will explore the operation of Section 382 in some detail.)

5. Section 354(a)(1) applies by its terms to exchanges in which the taxpayer receives only stock or securities in a corporation which is a party to the reorganization. Yet, much like Section 351, receipt of other consideration along with the allowed stock or securities (again called boot) does not automatically mean recognition for the entire exchange. Instead, Section 356(a)(1) requires the recognition of gain, but not loss (I.R.C. § 356(c)), just up to the amount of boot received. (Also, the corporation must recognize any gain if the boot consists of an appreciated asset. I.R.C. § 361(c)(2).) One difference from dealing with boot in a Section 351 transaction is how to categorize the gain to the boot's recipient: Should it constitute simply gain on the sale of an asset (stock), or, because the transaction bails money or other property out of a corporation in exchange for its own stock, is dividend treatment appropriate? Section 356(a)(2) addresses this question. It requires categorization of the gain as a dividend if the exchange has the effect of a distribution of a dividend—limited, however, to the recipient's ratable share of the corporation's earnings and profits. How can one determine if the receipt of boot in a recapitalization has the effect of a distribution of a dividend?

Revenue Ruling 84–114

1984–2 C.B. 90.

ISSUE

When nonvoting preferred stock and cash are received in an integrated transaction by a shareholder in exchange for voting common stock in a recapitalization described in section 368(a)(1)(E) of the Internal Revenue Code, does the receipt of cash have the effect of the distribution of a dividend within the meaning of section 356(a)(2)?

FACTS

Corporation *X* had outstanding 420 shares of voting common stock of which *A* owned 120 shares and *B, C* and *D* each owned 100 shares. *A, B, C* and *D* were not related within the meaning of section 318(a) of the Code. *X* adopted a plan of recapitalization that permitted a shareholder to exchange each of 30 shares of voting common stock for either one share of nonvoting preferred stock or cash. Pursuant to the plan, *A* first exchanged 15 shares of voting common stock for cash and then exchanged 15 shares of voting common stock for 15 shares of nonvoting preferred stock. The facts and circumstances surrounding these exchanges were such that the exchanges constituted two steps in a single integrated transaction for purposes of section 368(a)(1)(E) and 356(a)(2). The nonvoting preferred stock had no conversion features. In addition, the dividend and liquidation rights payable to *A* on 15 shares of nonvoting preferred stock were substantially less than the dividend and liquidation rights payable to *A* on 30 shares of voting common stock. *B, C,* and *D* did not participate in the exchange and will retain all their voting common stock in *X*. *X* had a substantial amount of post–1913 earnings and profits.

The exchange by *A* of voting common stock for nonvoting preferred stock and cash qualified as a recapitalization within the meaning of section 368(a)(1)(E) of the Code.

LAW AND ANALYSIS

* * *

Section 356(a)(1) of the Code provides that if section 354 would apply to an exchange but for the fact that the property received in the exchange consists not only of property permitted by section 354 to be received without the recognition of gain but also of other property or money, then the gain, if any, will be recognized, but in an amount not in excess of the sum of the money and fair market value of the other property. Section 356(a)(2) provides that if such exchange has the effect of the distribution of a dividend (determined with the application of section 318(a)), then there will be treated as a dividend to each distributee such an amount of the gain recognized under section 356(a)(1) as is not in excess of each distributee's ratable share of the undistributed earnings and profits of the corporation accumulated after February 28, 1913.

* * *

Rev.Rul. 74–515, 1974–2 C.B. 118, and Rev.Rul. 74–516, 1974–2 C.B. 121, state that whether a reorganization distribution to which section 356 of the Code applies has the effect of a dividend must be determined by examining the facts and circumstances surrounding the distribution and looking to the principles for determining dividend equivalency developed under section 356(a)(2) and other provisions of the Code. * * * Rev.Rul. 74–516 indicates that in making a dividend equivalency determination under section 356(a)(2), it is proper to analogize to section 302 in appropriate cases.

In *United States v. Davis,* 397 U.S. 301 (1970), rehearing denied, 397 U.S. 1071 (1970), 1970–1 C.B. 62, the Supreme Court of the United States held that a redemption must result in a meaningful reduction of the shareholder's proportionate interest in the corporation in order not to be essentially equivalent to a dividend under section 302(b)(1) of the Code.

* * *

The specific issue is whether, in determining dividend equivalency under section 356(a)(2) of the Code, it is proper to look solely at the change in *A*'s proportionate interest in *X* that resulted from *A*'s exchange of voting common stock for cash, or instead, whether consideration should be given to the total change in *A*'s proportionate interest in *X* that resulted from the exchange of voting common stock for both cash and nonvoting preferred stock.

* * *

Since the exchange of voting common stock for cash and the exchange for voting common stock for nonvoting preferred stock constitute an integrated transaction, in this situation involving a single corporation it is proper * * * that both exchanges are taken into consideration in determining whether there has been a meaningful reduction of *A*'s proportionate interest in *X* within the meaning of *Davis*. * * *

If the exchange of voting common stock for preferred stock and cash in this situation had been tested under section 302 of the Code as a redemption, it would not have qualified under section 302(b)(2) or (3) because there was neither an adequate reduction in *A*'s voting stock interest nor a complete termination of that interest. In determining whether this situation is analogous to a redemption meeting the requirements of section 302(b)(1), it is significant that *A*'s interest in the voting common stock of *X* was reduced from 28.57 percent (120/420) to 23.08 percent (90/390) so that *A* went from a position of holding a number of shares of voting common stock that afforded *A* control of *X* if *A* acted in concert with only one other shareholder, to a position where such action was not possible. Moreover, it is significant that *A* no longer holds the largest voting stock interest in *X*. In addition, although *A* received dividend and liquidation rights from the 15 shares of nonvoting preferred stock, these were substantially less than the dividend and liquidation rights of the 30 shares of voting common stock *A* surrendered. Accordingly, the requirements of section 302(b)(1) would have been met if the transaction had been tested under section 302, and, therefore, the cash received by *A* did not have the effect of the distribution of a dividend within the meaning of section 356(a)(2).

HOLDING

When *A* received cash and nonvoting preferred stock of *X* in an integrated transaction in exchange for voting common stock of *X* in a recapitalization described in section 368(a)(1)(E) of the Code, the receipt of cash did not have the effect of the distribution of a dividend within the meaning of section 356(a)(2).

While the test for dividend treatment under Section 356(a)(2) looks to the standard developed in dealing with redemptions, the impact is not precisely the same. Unlike redemptions, loss of sale treatment in the reorganization context will not preclude the taxpayer from offsetting his or her basis from the amount received. This is because Section 356(a)(2) only extends dividend treatment up to the amount of gain (rather than for the entire amount realized). As a result, with the recent action by Congress to make dividends and capital gains generally taxable at the same rate, there usually will be little practical significance to dividend treatment under Section 356(a)(2), except, as discussed shortly, in the event the boot consists of debt instruments, or if the recipient of the boot has capital losses from other sources that the recipient could offset if the boot constitutes capital gains. (As previously mentioned, however, the reduction in the tax rate on dividends will expire, barring further action by Congress, at the end of 2008—at which point the significance of Section 356(a)(2) on the rate of taxation will reappear.) Incidentally, while the ruling does not address this issue, look at how the recapitalization there contained elements equivalent to stock dividends taxable under Section 305(b)(1) and (2)—once again illustrating how a recapitalization can accomplish, tax free, the same end result as a taxable exchange.

6. In 1997, Congress amended Section 354 to treat certain types of preferred stock as boot rather than stock. Specifically, Section 354(a)(2)(c) removes "nonqualified preferred stock" from the category of "stock or securities" for purposes of Section 354. Section 351(g) defines "nonqualified preferred stock" as stock which has a dividend preference, but does not participate in corporate growth to any significant extent (in other words, non-participating, non-convertible preferred). In addition, to constitute nonqualified preferred, either the corporation must have the right to redeem the shares within 20 years of their issuance (and be likely to exercise the right), or the owners must have the right to force the corporation to redeem the shares within 20 years of the shares' issuance, and the redemption right must not be subject to a contingency which makes the likelihood of redemption remote. The right or obligation to redeem in case of death, disability or termination of employment generally does not count toward making the preferred nonqualified, however, for corporations which are not publicly traded. Alternately, non-participating, non-convertible preferred will constitute nonqualified preferred stock if the dividend rate on the stock varies with interest rates, commodity prices or the like. Section 354(a)(2)(C)(ii) contains a potentially useful exception to the treatment of nonqualified preferred stock as boot. This exception covers recapitalization of a "family-owned corporation." A family-owned corporation for this purpose refers to a corporation in which members of the same family own at least 50 percent of the voting stock and 50 percent of each class of stock for an eight year period which starts five years before the recapitalization.

7. The discussion thus far has focused upon the tax impact of recapitalizations involving the exchange of stock. Exchanges with the corporation can also, as outlined earlier, involve its debt instruments. If the debt instrument constitutes a "security," then the exchange can be a "recapitalization" within the meaning of Section 368. *E.g.,* Treas. Reg. § 1.368–2(e)(1). (This regulation gives the discharge of corporate debt instruments by

issuing stock to their holders as one example of a recapitalization. Why, since repayment of principal is tax-free to the recipient, would this transaction produce any tax result even if not a reorganization? The answer is that the repayment may be less than the amount of principal (producing a loss), or may be greater than the amount of principal (producing a gain).) The term "security" in this context generally means a long-term debt instrument. *See, e.g., Neville Coke & Chemical Co. v. Commissioner,* 148 F.2d 599 (3d Cir.1945), *cert. denied,* 326 U.S. 726. Note, this is a very different meaning than the definition of a security under the securities laws.

The introduction of debt instruments into the picture creates several possibilities for recognition. Two of these possibilities occur when an individual surrenders back to the corporation its own debt securities in a recapitalization. Section 354(a)(2)(B) calls for recognition by the individual surrendering the debt instrument to the extent the consideration he or she receives in exchange is attributable to accrued interest on the debt. In addition, the corporation may recognize income if it discharges its indebtedness at less than the principal amount. Rev. Rul. 77–437, 1977–2 C.B. 28. For this purpose, the Code treats a corporation which discharges its debt by issuing its stock as if it paid off the debt with an amount of money equal to the fair market value of the stock. I.R.C. § 108(e)(8). This is an exception to the general rule that a corporation recognizes no income upon issuing its own shares. Similarly, the Code treats the corporation which discharges its debts by issuing new debt instruments, as if it paid all the old debt with an amount of money equal to the issue price of the new debt instruments (as computed in accordance with the original issue discount provisions). I.R.C. § 108(e)(10).

Further possibilities for recognition exist when the debt instruments move in the other direction, that is when the corporation issues its debt as part of the transaction. To begin with, recall the discussion of the *Bazley* decision in *Dean.* In *Bazley,* the Supreme Court held that the exchange of outstanding stock for corporate debt, when the exchange had no different effect than a dividend, did not constitute a recapitalization at all. Even if the transaction qualifies as a recapitalization—as can a non-pro-rata exchange of stock for debt (*Seide v. Commissioner,* 18 T.C. 502 (1952)), or a trade of debt for debt (*Commissioner v. Neustadt's Trust,* 131 F.2d 528 (2d Cir.1942)—Section 354(a)(2)(A) comes into play. This provision excludes securities received in a reorganization from non-recognition when their principal amount is greater than the principal amount of the securities surrendered in the exchange. Further along the same line, if the exchange involves the surrender of no debt, but only stock, the provision excludes from non-recognition all of the debt securities received. In either event, the excess of the principal amount of securities received over those surrendered constitutes boot. I.R.C. § 356(d)(2)(B).

Receipt of debt instruments constituting boot (either because of Section 354(a)(2)(A), or because the instrument does not constitute a security) raises the stakes under the dividend equivalence test of Section 356(a)(2). Sale treatment allows the recipient of the debt instrument to report his or her gain proportionately as the company pays off the debt. I.R.C. § 453(c). (This assumes the debt instruments are not payable on demand, or readily tradeable. I.R.C. § 453(f)(4), (5).) Installment reporting is not available for any debt instruments treated as a dividend. I.R.C. § 453(f)(6).

Finally, what significance remains to the question of whether an exchange of stock for debt can constitute a recapitalization, given the treatment of all the securities received in such an exchange as boot? To answer this question, consider the relative ability of the exchanging shareholder to offset his or her basis in the surrendered shares from the amount of income he or she must recognize. In a redemption failing the tests for sale treatment (which is what one would have with the pro-rata exchange of debt for stock that does not equal a recapitalization), he or she must recognize the entire amount realized (assuming it is less than earnings and profits). In a recapitalization, as stated above, he or she need recognize only the lesser of the amount of boot or amount of gain. There is one important caveat to this distinction. If the transferring shareholder receives only securities in return (rather than securities and stock), Section 356(a) does not apply at all. *See* Treas. Reg. § 1.354–1(d) Ex. (3). (A careful reading of Section 356(a) shows it only applies by its terms when a party receives *both* property allowed by Section 354 and boot.) In this regard, it is useful to note that the Internal Revenue Service may seek to characterize an exchange of stock for both other stock and securities, as in reality an exchange of stock for stock, and a separate exchange of stock for securities—thereby bringing this caveat into play. Treas. Reg. § 1.301–1(*l*).

(ii) Treatment Upon Disposition

Revenue Ruling 82–191

1982–2 C.B. 78.

ISSUE

Is the voting preferred stock received by *A* "Section 306 stock" within the meaning of section 306(c) of the Internal Revenue Code?

FACTS

X corporation had outstanding 100 shares of no par value voting common stock. Shareholder *A* owned 20 of these shares. *X* had accumulated earnings and profits. For valid business reasons *X* entered into a plan of recapitalization under which all the *X* shareholders surrendered their outstanding shares of voting common stock (old common) to *X* in exchange for shares of a class of newly created voting preferred stock. *A* received 15 of these shares, while the remaining shareholders received 80. The preferred stock was nonredeemable, limited and preferred as to dividends, and had a fixed liquidation preference. A holder thereof was not entitled to any further participation in *X* beyond these payments. The transaction was claimed to qualify as a reorganization (recapitalization) under section 368(a)(1)(E) of the Code and no gain or loss was claimed to be recognized to the exchanging shareholders under section 354. Shortly thereafter, and as an integral part of the overall transaction, *A* purchased from *X* for an amount equal to approximately one-half its value all the outstanding shares (10) of a newly created class of nonvoting common stock (new common) of *X*. This gave *A* an unrestricted interest in the future equity growth of *X* and an unrestricted right, after liquidation of the preferred stock, to share in the assets or earnings and profits of *X* upon its liquidation.

LAW AND ANALYSIS

Section 306(c)(1)(B) of the Code provides that "section 306 stock" is any stock, except common stock, that is received by a shareholder pursuant to a plan of reorganization under section 368 with respect to the receipt of which gain or loss to the shareholder was to any extent not recognized by reason of section 354, but only to the extent that the effect of the transaction is substantially the same as the receipt of a stock dividend.

Section 306 of the Code was enacted in 1954 to prevent what is known as a "preferred stock bailout." *S.Rep. No. 1622,* 83rd Cong., 2d Sess. 46 (1954). The object of such a bailout is to allow the shareholder to receive corporate earnings and profits, which otherwise might be taxed as ordinary income, at favorable capital gains rates by way of the sale of other than common stock received as a distribution on their common stock. The shareholders would then retain their unrestricted right to share in the equity growth of the corporation through the ownership of their common stock. This bailout can be achieved by the shareholders of the common stock through the disposition of any stock which is other than common stock and which is received in a transaction described in section 306(c). In Rev.Rul. 76–387, 1976–2 C.B. 96, the factors used to determine whether the stock in question was other than common stock were whether it could be disposed of without a loss in voting control and without a loss in an interest in the unrestricted equitable growth of the corporation. In other words, if a stock in question is nonvoting and is limited in either the right to dividends or the right to assets upon liquidation then it is considered to be other than common stock, and the disposition of such stock may result in the bailout abuse that Congress intended to preclude. Subsequently, in Rev.Rul. 79–163, 1979–1 C.B. 131, the definition of other than common stock was refined so that only the restrictions on the right to dividends or the right to assets upon liquidation were considered critical, even though the stock in question was the only stock outstanding entitled to vote.

Taking into consideration the definition of other than common stock as set forth above, the preferred stock issued by *X* in the instant case is considered to be other than common stock within the meaning of section 306(c) of the Code because it was both limited and preferred as to dividends and had a fixed liquidation preference. Thus, the question presented is whether the disposition of any of the preferred stock by *A* will allow *A* to bail out the earnings and profits of *X* without the loss of *A*'s interest in the unrestricted equitable growth of *X* through the continued ownership of the *X* new common purchased by *A*.

The classic bailout situation generally involves the issuance of preferred stock to those shareholders who already own the common stock of the corporation or who receive the common stock as part of a plan. The instant case differs in form from the classic bailout situation since the former shareholders of *X* old common apparently own no *X* common stock, old or new, immediately after the recapitalization exchange. The substance of the transaction, however, is that the right to share in the future unrestricted equitable growth of *X* is represented by the new common (which *A* purchased pursuant to the plan of reorganization) and much of the earnings and profits up to the date of the recapitalization are represented by the *X* preferred stock. If the form of the transaction was followed in this case, *A* could later dispose of his or her preferred stock without the loss of his or her right to participate in the future equity growth of *X* and section 306 of the Code apparently would not be applicable because no shareholder owned any common stock of *X* immediately after the exchange.

In the instant transaction, it is not reasonable to assume that at the time of the exchange it was intended that no old shareholder be entitled to participate in *X* beyond the preferred stock preferences. Therefore, the transaction in the instance case will be treated, for federal income tax purposes, as though *A* exchanged 15 shares of his or her *X* old common for 15 shares of the *X* preferred stock. *A* also exchanged 5 shares of his or her *X* old common plus cash for the *X* new common, and the new common will be treated as the old common for purposes of making the section 306 determination.

HOLDING

The *X* preferred stock received by *A* is "section 306 stock" within the meaning of section 306(c)(1)(B) of the Code.

NOTES

1. Earlier, in discussing the further disposition of shares received in stock splits and stock dividends, this chapter explained the impact of selling "section 306 stock." As the ruling above shows, recapitalizations can also produce such stock. In fact, the definition of section 306 stock encompasses four categories. The first—that encountered before—is stock received as a distribution on outstanding shares (other than a distribution of common on common), which is tax-free under Section 305(a). I.R.C. § 306(c)(1)(A). The second—in which recapitalizations fit—is stock (other than common) received tax-free in a reorganization (as defined under Section 368(a)), or a corporate division (as outlined in Section 355); but only if the receipt was either in exchange for other section 306 stock or else substantially equivalent to a stock dividend. I.R.C. § 306(c)(1)(B). To determine whether the receipt of stock is substantially the same as a stock dividend, the regulations ask how Section 356 would have categorized the receipt of cash instead of the stock in question. If Section 356(a)(2) or (b) would have branded such cash as a dividend, then the stock received is substantially equivalent to a stock dividend. Treas. Reg. § 1.306–3(d). *But see* Rev. Rul.

88–100, 1988–2 C.B. 46 (will not apply the "cash in lieu of" test if non-section 306 preferred stock is exchanged for substantially similar preferred stock in a reorganization; rather, the new shares will not be section 306 stock). As discussed earlier, whether cash would have been a dividend may largely depend upon the extent to which the recipient surrendered a meaningful portion of his or her equity position in the exchange. *E.g.*, Rev. Rul. 70–199, 1970–1 C.B. 68. (Why would "A" not have suffered a meaningful reduction in his or her equity if he or she received cash instead of the preferred shares in the exchange described in the ruling reprinted above?)

Both categories exclude common stock. In fact, one can remove the section 306 taint from shares by exchanging them in a tax-free transaction for common. I.R.C. § 306(c)(1)(B), (e)(1). As the ruling reprinted above explains, defining common for purposes of Section 306 is not simply a matter of looking at labels. Instead, the question is whether the shares possess an interest in growth of the corporation's equity; more specifically, is there a maximum upon the amount the shares may receive either as a dividend or in a liquidating distribution? If there is no limit upon either, the shares are common, even if non-voting, and even if they possess some dividend or liquidation preference. (Hence, fully participating preferred can constitute common for purposes of Section 306.) *See also* Rev. Rul. § 81–91, 1981–1 C.B. 123. Under this rationale, shares redeemable at the company's option are not common. Rev. Rul. 57–132, 1957–1 C.B. 115. (Recall such redemption rights put a cap on the share's ability to enjoy growth in profits.) Common shares convertible into senior securities are also not common for purposes of Section 306. I.R.C. § 306(e)(2).

Suppose a shareholder manages to dispose of section 306 stock in a tax-free transaction other than a reorganization or corporate division. For example, he or she might transfer the stock to another corporation in a transaction covered by Section 351, or he or she might simply give the shares away. To the extent, as normally the case, the transferred shares (as well as any shares received in exchange) have a substituted basis, they become section 306 stock. I.R.C. § 306(c)(1)(C). This is the third category of section 306 stock. One tax-free disposition where (at least until repeal of the estate tax) there is no substituted basis is the passing of property upon death. I.R.C. § 1014. Hence, death (for now) removes the section 306 taint.

One common exception to all three of these categories of section 306 stock is they do not apply to shares issued at a time when the issuing corporation had no earnings and profits (which would have meant if the recipient had received money rather than the shares to start with, he or she would not have recognized any dividend). I.R.C. § 306(c)(2). This exception has important planning implications. Recall in the *Gottfried* case in Chapter IV, the parties had owned preferred stock in the same ratio as common (and hence the preferred had no economic impact). Why did they do this? Suppose one anticipates that preferred stock might be desirable at some point in a company's life—perhaps, for reasons discussed before, as some owners approach retirement. Issuing the shares at a latter point through stock dividends and recapitalizations can create section 306 stock.

Issuing the shares at the formation of the corporation, when there are no earnings and profits, will not. Suppose a shareholder already has section 306 stock. Can he or she take advantage of this exception to remove the taint? For example, why not form a new company (having no earnings and profits) and exchange the section 306 stock for new preferred in a section 351 transaction? The answer is section 306(c)(3) would make the preferred shares into section 306 stock. This provision imports the dividend measurement of Section 304(b)(2) (for redemptions by a company under common control with the issuer) so that not only the new corporation's but also the original issuer's earnings and profits count. This is the fourth category of section 306 stock.

2. What happens if stock entitled to a 50 percent exclusion of capital gains under Section 1202 is exchanged in a recapitalization? See I.R.C. § 1202(h)(4) (the stock received for the qualified shares will also be entitled to favorable treatment and picks up the surrendered shares' holding period; however, if the received stock would not qualify under Section 1202 but for this provision, then only the gain up to the point of the exchange qualifies for the 50 percent exclusion).

SECTION C. RESTRUCTURING THROUGH DIVISIONS AND CONTRACTIONS

1. DIVIDING THE BUSINESS

Coady v. Commissioner of Internal Revenue

33 T.C. 771 (1960), *aff'd*, 289 F.2d 490 (6th Cir.1961).

■ TIETJENS, JUDGE:

* * *

The issue for decision is whether the transfer by the Christopher Construction Company of a portion of its assets to E.P. Coady and Co. in exchange for all of the Coady Company's stock, and the subsequent distribution by the Christopher Company of such Coady stock to petitioner in exchange for his Christopher stock, constituted a distribution of stock qualifying for tax-free treatment on the shareholder level under the provisions of Section 355 of the 1954 Internal Revenue Code.

* * *

Christopher Construction Co., an Ohio corporation, is now engaged, and for more than 5 years prior to November 15, 1954, was engaged, in the active conduct of a construction business primarily in and around Columbus, Ohio. * * *

At all times material hereto, the stock of the Christopher Company was owned by M. Christopher and the petitioner [Edmund P. Coady]. * * * [E]ach owned 50 percent of the company's stock.

Sometime prior to November 15, 1954, differences arose between the petitioner and Christopher. As a result, they entered into an agreement for the division of the Christopher Company into two separate enterprises. Pursuant to that agreement, the Christopher Company, on November 14, 1954, organized E.P. Coady and Co., to which it transferred the following assets, approximating one-half the Christopher Company's total assets:

A contract for the construction of a sewage disposal plant at Columbus, Ohio, dated June 1, 1954.

A part of its equipment.

A part of its cash, and certain other items.

In consideration for the receipt of these assets, E.P. Coady and Co. transferred all of its stock to the Christopher Company. The Christopher Company retained the following assets, which were of the same type as those transferred to E.P. Coady and Co.:

A contract for a sewage treatment plant in Charleston, West Virginia.

A part of its equipment.

A part of its cash.

Immediately thereafter, the Christopher Company distributed to the petitioner all of the stock of E.P. Coady and Co. held by it in exchange for all of the stock of the Christopher Company held by petitioner. The fair market value of the stock of E.P. Coady and Co. received by petitioner was $140,000. His basis in the Christopher Company stock surrendered was $72,500.

Since the distribution, both E.P. Coady and Co. and the Christopher Company have been actively engaged in the construction business.

On their 1954 Federal income tax return, petitioner and his wife reported no gain or loss on the exchange of the Christopher Company stock for the stock of E.P. Coady and Co.

Respondent determined that petitioner realized a capital gain on that exchange in the amount of $67,500. * * *

Petitioner contends that the distribution to him of the E.P. Coady and Co. stock qualified for tax-free treatment under the provisions of section 355 of the 1954 Code, arguing that it was received pursuant to a distribution of a controlled corporation's stock within the meaning of that section.

Respondent on the other hand maintains petitioner's receipt of the Coady stock did not fall within those distributions favored by section 355, inasmuch as the 5-year active business requirements of 355(b) were not met. More particularly he argues that section 355 does not apply to the separation of a "single business"; and, inasmuch as the Christopher Company was engaged in only one trade or business (construction contracting), the gain realized by petitioner upon receipt of the Coady stock was taxable. As authority for his position respondent points to that portion of his regulations which expressly provides that section 355 does not apply to the division of a single business.

Conceding that the Christopher Company was engaged in a "single business" immediately prior to the instant transaction, petitioner contends that the regulations, insofar as they limit the applicability of section 355 to divisions of only those corporations which have conducted two or more separate and distinct businesses for a 5-year period, are without support in the law, are without justification, are unreasonable and arbitrary, and therefore are invalid.

Thus, the issue is narrowed to the question of whether the challenged portion of the regulations constitutes a valid construction of the statute, or whether it is unreasonable and plainly inconsistent therewith. * * *

Section 355 of the 1954 Code represents the latest of a series of legislative enactments designed to deal with the tax effect upon shareholders of various corporate separations. * * * [P]resent law groups the statutory requirements into two sections, 355 and 368(c). A careful reading of section 355, as well as the Finance Committee report which accompanied its enactment, reveals no language, express or implied, denying tax-free treatment at the shareholder level to a transaction, otherwise qualifying under section 355, on the grounds that it represents the division or separation of a "single" trade or business.

In general, section 355(a) prescribes the form in which a qualifying transaction must be cast, providing that a divisive distribution will not give rise to taxable gain or loss if: (1) The distributing corporation distributes stock or securities of a corporation of which it has, immediately prior to the distribution, 80 percent control as defined in section 368(c); (2) the distribution is not principally a device for distributing earnings and profits of either the distributing or controlled corporations; (3) the 5-year active business requirements of 355(b) are satisfied; and (4) the distributing corporation distributes either all its stock and securities in the controlled corporation, or so much thereof as constitutes control, as defined in 368(c), and retention of the balance is shown not to be in pursuance of a plan having as one of its principal purposes tax avoidance. The distribution itself must be either to a shareholder with respect to its stock, or a security holder with respect to securities. With respect to a distribution of stock, the distribution need not be on a pro rata basis; the shareholder need not surrender stock in the distributing corporation; and the distribution need not have been made in pursuance of a plan of reorganization. However, subsection (a) contains no language which would require that the distributing corporation be engaged in more than one trade or business prior to the distribution.

The active business requirements of 355(b)(1) prohibit the tax-free separation of a corporation into active and inactive entities. Section 355(b)(1)(A) extends the provisions of 355(a) only to those divisive distributions where the distributing corporation and the controlled corporation are engaged immediately after the distribution in the active conduct of a trade or business. In the case of those distributions which involve liquidation of the transferor, 355(b)(1)(B) requires that immediately before the distribution the transferor have no assets other than stock or securities in the controlled corporations, and that immediately thereafter each of the controlled corporations is engaged in the active conduct of a trade or business. Neither 355(b)(1)(A) nor (B) concerns itself with the existence of a plurality of businesses per se; rather both speak in terms of a plurality of corporate entities engaged in the active conduct of a trade or business, a distinction we believe to be vital in light of provisions of 355(b)(2).

Section 355(b)(2) details the rules for determining whether a corporation is engaged in the active conduct of a trade or business, and provides that a corporation shall be treated as so engaged, if, and only if: (1) It is engaged in the active conduct of a trade or business, or substantially all its assets consist of stock and securities of a corporation controlled by it immediately after the distribution which is so engaged; (2) such trade or business has been actively conducted throughout the 5-year period ending on the date of the distribution; (3) such trade or business was not acquired within that 5-year period in a transaction in which gain or loss was recognized; and (4) control of a corporation, which at the time of acquisition of control was conducting such trade or business, was not acquired within that 5-year period, or, if acquired within that period, was acquired by reason of a transaction in which no gain or loss was recognized, or by reason of such transactions combined with acquisitions made before the beginning of that 5-year period. Again we note the statute avoids the use of the plural when referring to "trade or business," but rather provides that: "[A] corporation shall be treated as engaged in the active conduct of *a* trade or business if only and if * * * it is engaged in the active conduct of *a* trade or business * * * (and) such trade or business has been actively conducted through the 5-year period ending on the date of the distribution." (Emphasis supplied.)

Respondent maintains that a reading of 355(b)(2)(B) in conjunction with the requirement of 355(b)(1) that both "the distributing corporation, *and* the controlled corporation * * *, (be) engaged immediately after the distribution in the active conduct of a trade or business" (emphasis supplied) indicates Congress intended the provisions of the statute to apply only where, immediately after the distribution, there exist two separate and distinct businesses, one operated by the distributing corporation, and one operated by the controlled corporation, both of which were actively conducted for the 5-year period immediately preceding the distribution. In our judgment the statute does not support this construction.

* * *

[F]rom the fact that the statute requires, immediately after the distribution, that the surviving corporations each be engaged in the conduct of a trade or business with an active 5-year history, we do not think it inevitably follows that each such trade or business necessarily must have been conducted on an individual basis throughout that 5-year period. As long as the trade or business which has been divided has been actively conducted for 5 years preceding the distribution, and the resulting businesses (each of which in this case, happens to be half of the original whole) are actively conducted after the division, we are of the opinion that the active business requirements of the statute have been complied with.

* * *

There being no language, either in the statute or committee report, which denies tax-free treatment under Section 355 to a transaction solely on the ground that it represents an attempt to divide a single trade or business, the Commissioner's regulations which impose such a restriction are invalid, and cannot be sustained.

* * *

NOTES

CORPORATE AND SECURITIES LAW ASPECTS OF CORPORATE DIVISIONS

1. *Coady* illustrates an alternative to a buy-out as a means to separate warring shareholders. Perhaps the business is susceptible to division between the factions so each can carry on one venture without the other. This is not an uncommon way to handle a partnership dissolution triggered by dissension, and it can also work in a corporation.

A corporate division can serve other purposes as well. Recall, Chapter II discussed a number of reasons why parties may wish to operate businesses in multiple corporations. For instance, parties many times desire to operate different businesses in different corporations in order to insulate the assets of one venture from liabilities incurred in another. If the parties did not start each new line of business in its own separate company, this goal may call for a corporate division. Still other purposes for corporate divisions include compliance with antitrust or other regulatory directives against continuing to operate certain businesses together. Also, some shareholders may be more interested in continuing a particular line of business (which perhaps is not presently doing very well) than others, and, therefore, all the owners might desire to split this venture off to those who want it.

Finally, corporations sometimes spin off stock in subsidiaries to the parent's shareholders for abusive ends. For example, a company might use this as a technique to bail out earnings without paying taxable dividends. Specifically, a corporation could distribute stock in a subsidiary to the corporation's shareholders, who then plan to sell the subsidiary. If, as in *Coady,* the initial distribution is tax-free, the shareholders could use this technique to get corporate earnings while recognizing only capital gains upon the sale. (Alternately, the corporation might use its earnings to stuff its subsidiary with cash and with marketable securities whose basis equaled their fair market value. The shareholders could then liquidate the subsidiary after the spin-off and obtain the cash and securities.) Another potential abuse occurs when companies use spin-offs to create a public market in stock without registration under the 1933 Securities Act. Here, a public corporation may acquire the shares of a privately held company (or have a subsidiary acquire the assets of such a company). The public company might then distribute the stock to its own shareholders, claiming there was no sale, and hence no requirement of registration under the 1933 Securities Act. *E.g., SEC v. Datronics Engineers, Inc.*, 490 F.2d 250 (4th Cir.1973), *cert. denied,* 416 U.S. 937 (1974). Attempts by the government to prevent these two abuses have created much of the complexity involved in corporate divisions.

2. Achieving the objectives outlined above, as well as other possible goals for a corporate division, entails undertaking either or both of two steps. The first is to get the businesses operating in separate corporations (unless they already are). Mechanically, this means forming a new corporation, and having the existing company transfer one of its businesses to the new company in exchange for all the new firm's stock. Alternately, one could form two new corporations, and have the existing company transfer different businesses to the new firms in exchange for all their stock. In the first instance, the result is to split the businesses between two companies in a parent-subsidiary relation. In the second, the businesses end up in two corporations with a common holding company. In either case, the transaction involves the state corporate law and general planning issues addressed when dealing with forming a corporation in Chapter IV. In addition, several other concerns exist here, particularly when the original firm transfers all its businesses, and becomes a holding company. To begin with, does this transaction require shareholder approval under statutes demanding such a vote in order for a corporation to sell substantially all its assets? See *Katz v. Bregman,* reprinted later in this chapter. *But see* Cal. Corp. Code §§ 181, 1001(a), 1201(b) (effectively excluding a sale to a wholly-owned subsidiary in exchange for the subsidiary's stock from the requirement of shareholder approval); Del. Gen. Corp. Law § 271(c) (excluding a sale to a wholly-owned subsidiary from any requirement of shareholder approval); (M.B.C.A. § 12.01(3) (same). Further, the corporation may need to comply with the bulk transfer acts (Article 6 of the Uniform Commercial Code). These might require public notice before transferring inventory and equipment to the subsidiary. *See* U.C.C. §§ 6–102, 6–103(7).

Simply having the businesses operate in separate corporations, when one company owns the stock in another, may or may not, in itself, achieve the parties' goals. For example, it would not accomplish the objective in *Coady* of allowing the shareholders to go their different ways with each owning his or her own business. On the other hand, this would seem, at first glance, sufficient to accomplish the objective of insulating one business from the risks of another. Further reflection leads one, however, to question whether even for this purpose merely separating the businesses into different corporations is enough. It is true that, so long as the court respects the separate entities, the parent corporation is not at risk from the liabilities of the subsidiary. Yet, what happens if it is the parent which goes under? In this event, the parent's creditors end up owning the stock in the subsidiary, with the result that the parent's shareholders lose their investment in both firms. To avoid this danger—particularly when one cannot predict which business might fail—the shareholders of the initial company might prefer to hold the stock in any new corporations themselves.

For these reasons, it may be necessary to distribute the stock in a subsidiary corporation to the parent's shareholders. In fact, parties might do this to accomplish some of the objectives outlined above even when the subsidiary had long existed as a separate corporation. Three methods exist to carry out this second step in a corporate division. One is simply to distribute the shares as a dividend to the parent's stockholders. This is commonly referred to as a spin-off. From a state corporations law standpoint, this requires complying with all the applicable limits on the declaration of dividends. In this regard, suppose the spin-off encompasses a substantial part of the parent company's assets. Could this fact pose a problem under state statutes limiting dividends? Note that while the spin-off removes assets from the distributing corporation, neither the spin-off nor the creation of the subsidiary, in themselves, lessen the distributing company's debts or reduce its capital. (Keep in mind, even though a spun-off corporation may agree to assume some of the parent firm's debts as part of taking over one of its businesses, this does not relieve the parent company from any liability unless the creditors agree to a novation. *See, e.g., Darcy v. Brooklyn & N.Y. Ferry Co.*, 127 App.Div. 167, 111 N.Y.S. 514 (1908).) Hence, spinning off stock representing a large portion of a distributing corporation's assets may leave the company with liabilities in excess of its remaining assets, or, at least, with impaired capital. To deal with this problem, the distributing corporation might attempt to convince some of its securities holders to exchange their debt instruments for debt securities issued by the spun-off corporation, and also might take some of the steps outlined earlier to reduce its capital. Another problem with a spin-off may occur when the distributing corporation has outstanding preferred stock, whose holders' rights the company must respect in making any dividend. For example, could a spin-off of shares constituting a significant portion of the corporation's assets constitute a liquidation, thereby triggering a liquidation preference? See *Schenker v. E. I. du Pont de Nemours & Co.*, 329 F.2d 77 (2d Cir.1964), *cert. denied,* 377 U.S. 998 (held it did not). Along similar lines, a spin-off could involve the rights of convertible security holders. *Pittsburgh Terminal Corp. v. Baltimore & Ohio RR. Co.*, 680 F.2d 933 (3d Cir.) *cert. denied*, 459 U.S. 1056 (1982) (convertible debenture holders entitled to notice of spin-off).

The second method of distributing stock in the subsidiary is the one employed in *Coady*. This is to have some or all of the parent's shareholders exchange all or a portion of their stock in the parent for the parent's stock in the subsidiary. This is known as a split-off. Notice several advantages of a split-off over a spin-off. Distributing stock in the subsidiary through such redemptions need not be pro-rata among the shareholders of the parent, as would be a dividend distribution. Moreover, it can reduce or eliminate some shareholders' stake in the parent. Hence, a split-off can accomplish the objective of dividing feuding shareholders, as it did in *Coady*. In addition, a redemption by the parent of some of its shares in exchange for stock in the subsidiary may set up a reduction in capital or otherwise avoid some (albeit not all) of the limits on distributions faced by dividends. In any event, a split-off faces the same corporate law issues confronted by redemptions generally, as discussed earlier in this chapter. Also, could a split-off which involves stock constituting a large percent of the parent's assets trigger the need for shareholder approval as a sale of substantially all assets? See M.B.C.A. § 12.01 Official Comment (yes, if parent is left without a significant continuing business activity).

Both methods discussed thus far of distributing the shares in a subsidiary involve operating companies in a parent-subsidiary relationship. Suppose the operating companies are both subsidiaries of a parent, which is merely a holding company. (This was the alternate way to put businesses into separate corporations discussed above.) This opens up a third method of distribution, that being to dissolve the parent and pass out the shares in a liquidating distribution to the parent's stockholders. This is know as a split-up. Dissolution usually requires a vote of the parent's shareholders as well as directors. *E.g.,* Del. Gen. Corp. Law § 275; M.B.C.A. § 14.02. *But see* Cal. Corp. Code § 1900(a) (allowing voluntary dissolution upon a vote of only 50 percent of the shareholders and without the requirement of director approval); N.Y. Bus. Corp. Law § 1001 (requiring approval by a two thirds or a majority shareholder vote—depending upon the year of incorporation—but not requiring approval by the directors). Moreover, the parent would need to discharge or make adequate provision for the payment of its debts before it could distribute the stock in the subsidiaries to its shareholders. *E.g.,* Cal. Corp. Code § 2004; Del. Gen. Corp. Law § 281(a); N.Y. Bus. Corp. Law § 1005(a)(3); M.B.C.A. § 14.05(a)(3), (4). Would having the subsidiaries assume the debts constitute making adequate provision for their payment? See Cal. Corp. Code § 2005(a) (yes, if the assuming company is financially responsible). Also, the corporation must respect any liquidation preferences among its outstanding stock. Chapter VII will provide a more detailed consideration of liquidating a company.

Finally, suppose the parent wishes to enter into contracts with the subsidiary it plans to spin off. Does the parent owe any fiduciary obligations to the subsidiary or its prospective shareholders if the two entities enter these contracts prior to the parent distributing the shares? See *Anadarko Petroleum Corp. v. Panhandle Eastern Corp.,* 545 A.2d 1171 (Del.1988) (holding it does not).

3. While the issuance of stock to the parent in step one of a corporate division involves the sale of a security, if the transaction stopped here, Section 4(2) presumably would exempt it from registration under the 1933 Securities Act. After all, the parent hardly needs the protection of registration. Distributing stock in the subsidiary to the parent's shareholders in step two of a corporate division, however, raises considerable complications. To begin with, under the Securities Exchange Commission's Rule 145, the subsequent distribution of stock may result in recharacterizing the first step in the corporate division. Rule 145(a)(3) provides that a sale of a company's assets in exchange for another corporation's stock (or other

securities) constitutes a purchase of securities by the asset selling company's shareholders (rather than by the company itself) in transactions meeting two conditions: The shareholders must vote upon the sale of assets (as, for instance, in a sale of substantially all assets), and the company must distribute the stock or securities to its shareholders. The practical impact of treating the initial exchange of assets for stock as a purchase of stock by individual shareholders (rather than by the company) is to make it more difficult to exempt the transaction from registration. One must now measure each stockholder against the requirements of the various exemptions.

Rule 145 will not apply if the shareholders do not vote on the initial acquisition of the subsidiary's stock, or if the acquisition occurred some time earlier and only later does the parent decide to spin the shares off to its own stockholders. In this event, one must focus upon whether the distribution, in itself, is a transaction requiring registration. In a spin-off, this distribution occurs as a dividend with no consideration flowing in exchange for the shares. Given this fact, is there any "sale" to trigger the registration requirements of the 1933 Act? In *SEC v. Datronics Engineers, Inc.,* 490 F.2d 250 (4th Cir.1973), *cert. denied,* 416 U.S. 937 (1974), the Fourth Circuit indicated at least under some circumstances there is:

> "The pattern of the spin-offs in each instance was this: Without any business purpose of its own, Datronics would enter into an agreement with the principals of a private company. The agreement provided for the organization by Datronics of a new corporation, or the utilization of one of Datronics' subsidiaries, and the merger of the private company into the new or subsidiary corporation. It stipulated that the principals of the private company would receive the majority interest in the merger-corporation. The remainder of the stock of the corporation would be delivered to, or retained by, Datronics for a nominal sum per share. Part of it would be applied to the payment of the services of Datronics in the organization and administration of the proposed spin-off, and to Datronics' counsel for legal services in the transaction. Datronics was bound by each of the nine agreements to distribute among its shareholders the rest of the stock.
>
> * * *
>
> "Datronics and the other appellees contend, and the District Court concluded, that this type of transaction was not a sale. The argument was that it was no more than a dividend parceled out to stockholders from its portfolio of investments. A noteworthy difference here, however, is that each distribution was an obligation. Their contention also loses sight of the definition of 'sale' contained in § 2 of the 1933 Act, 15 U.S.C. § 77b. As pertinent here, that definition is as follows:
>
> > " 'When used in this subchapter, unless the context otherwise requires—
>
> * * *

" '(3) The term "sale" or "sell" shall include every contract of sale or *disposition* of a security or interest in a security, *for value.* The term "offer to sell," "offer for sale," or "offer" shall include every attempt or offer to dispose of, or solicitation of an offer to buy, a security or interest in a security, *for value.* * * * ' (Accent added.)

"As the term 'sale' includes a 'disposition of a security', the dissemination of a new stock among Datronics' stockholders was a sale. However, the appellees urged, and the District Court held, that this disposition was not a statutory sale because it was not "for value", as demanded by the definition. Here, again, we find error. Cf. Securities and Exchange Commission v. Harwyn Industries Corp., 326 F.Supp. 943, 954 (S.D.N.Y.1971). Value accrued to Datronics in several ways. First, a market for the stock was created by its transfer to so many new assignees—at least 1000, some of whom were stockbroker-dealers, residing in various states. Sales by them followed at once—the District Judge noting that "[i]n each instance dealing promptly began in the spun-off shares". This result redounded to the benefit not only of Datronics but, as well, to its officers and agents who had received some of the spun-off stock as compensation for legal or other services to the spin-off corporations. Likewise, the stock retained by Datronics was thereby given an added increment of value. The record discloses that in fact the stock, both that disseminated and that kept by Datronics, did appreciate substantially after the distributions."

In *Datronics,* the spin-offs involved transactions whose sole purpose was to create a public market in unregistered shares. What about spin-offs by public corporations for legitimate business purposes? In this instance, will the distributing company receive the "value" which the court identified in *Datronics*? Will it receive some other "value"? The Securities Exchange Commission takes the position that there still is a "sale." *See, e.g.,* Comment, *Registration of Stock Spin-offs Under the Securities Act of 1933,* 1980 Duke L. J. 965, 982. (Incidentally, why was Datronics' spin-off—even if a sale—not exempt under Section 4(1), as a transaction by one who is not an issuer, underwriter or dealer? Was Datronics an underwriter, since it participated in a distribution? See Sec. Act Rel. No. 4982 (1969) (taking the position that the distributing corporation is acting as a statutory underwriter). If Datronics was an underwriter, what is the effect of this fact on whether its initial acquisition of shares constituted an exempt transaction?) What about spin-offs by a closely held corporation? Here, of course, one might find an exemption. Further, one court has held in this context there is no sale (because the "value" identified in *Datronics* flowed from the public dispersal of the stock). *Rathborne v. Rathborne,* 508 F.Supp. 515 (E.D.La.1980), *aff'd,* 683 F.2d 914 (5th Cir.1982).

Of course, this analysis of whether a sale occurred would not apply to a split-off; in other words, an exchange of shares in the parent for shares in the subsidiary. What exemptions from registration might be available for this transaction? Section 3(a)(9), discussed above for recapitalizations, will not apply, because this is not an exchange between the issuer (which is the subsidiary, not the parent whose stockholders will receive the shares) and its securities holders. This brings one to the split-up; in other words, a liquidating distribution of shares in the subsidiary. Is there any disposition for value here? See Bromberg, *Corporate Liquidation and Securities Law—Problems in the Distribution of Portfolio Securities,* 3 B.C. Ind. & Com. L. Rev. 1 (1961) (arguing there is not).

Finally, what about application of state blue sky laws? Compare Uniform Securities Act (1985 revision) § 101(13)(vii) (excluding dividends of stock, whether or not of stock in the company making the dividend, from the definition of a "sale"), *with* Uniform Securities Act (2002 revision) §§ 102(26) (no longer excluding dividends from the definition of sale), 202 (22) (exemption for distributions of stock to corporation's stockholders); California Corporation Commissioner's Opinion Nos. 71/132C, 74/25C (spin-offs not a sale).

TAX ASPECTS OF CORPORATE DIVISIONS

1. As stated above, a corporate division may involve two steps, the first being to separate the operating assets for the two businesses into two different corporate entities (unless, of course, the parties are already operating the businesses in separate corporations). Normally, the transfer of assets to a corporation in exchange for stock, when immediately after the exchange the transferor will own a controlling amount of stock (within the meaning of Section 368(c)), constitutes a transaction covered by Section 351. As discussed in Chapter IV, this generally means nonrecognition of gain or loss, and a substituted basis for both the assets transferred to the corporation and the stock received by the transferor. I.R.C. §§ 358(a), 362(a). The transferor corporation also may divide its liabilities with the controlled corporation pursuant to Section 357. *But see Beatrice Co. v. State Bd. of Equalization*, 6 Cal.4th 767, 25 Cal.Rptr.2d 438, 863 P.2d 683 (1993) (assumption of transferor's liabilities by the new corporation triggered state sales tax). Hence, if the division stops with simply forming a parent and subsidiary, it involves nothing new.

In the second step of a corporate division (if desired), the transferor company distributes to its shareholders the stock it received in exchange for its assets. Does this have any impact upon taxation of the first step? Recall, under Section 351(c), the subsequent distribution by a transferor, which is itself a corporation, of the shares it received to its own stockholders will not upset the control requirement. Nevertheless, this second step can affect the tax treatment of the first. This is because the second step may (as in *Coady*) receive tax-free treatment under Section 355. If so, Section 351 no longer governs the first step. Instead, the first step now constitutes part of a reorganization within the meaning of Section 368(a)(1)(D). What difference does this make? After all, the transferor corporation still receives tax-free treatment upon exchanging assets for stock in the new corporation—this time provided by Section 361(a) instead of Section 351. One difference lies in the allocation of earnings and profits between the new and old corporations. In a simple Section 351 transaction in which one company transfers part of its assets to another, no such allocation ordinarily occurs. Treas. Reg. § 1.312–11(a). In a Section 368(a)(1)(D) reorganization, however, the old corporation allocates part of its accumulated earnings and profits to the new company (usually in proportion to the values of the transferred and retained businesses). Treas. Reg. § 1.312–10(a). (No other tax attributes, however, flow from the old to the new corporation in this reorganization. I.R.C. § 381(a) (last sentence). Incidentally, should the division involve a preexisting subsidiary, rather than one just created in a Section 368(a)(1)(D) reorganization, the regulations specify how to allocate earnings and profits between the distributing company and its former subsidiary. I.R.C. § 312(h)(1); Treas. Reg. § 1.312–10(b).) Another difference is that Section 361(a) allows tax-free receipt of "securities," which Section 351 does not.

2. If the only objective of the transaction is for two corporations to operate businesses conducted before by just one, the parties can stop with one company held as a subsidiary of the other. As explained above, however, many times (such as in *Coady*) the parties' goal requires distributing the stock in the subsidiary to the parent's shareholders. Indeed, this could also become desirable in cases when the subsidiary had existed for some time as a separate corporation. Ordinarily, the rules governing distributions to shareholders, redemptions and liquidations would dictate the tax impact of this step in the division, depending upon whether it was a spin-off, split-off or split-up. If the participants cast the distribution as a spin-off (in other words, a dividend to the parent's shareholders consisting of stock in the subsidiary), then Section 301 normally would dictate the consequences to the shareholders. (Recall, Section 305, which potentially provides tax-free treatment of stock dividends, only applies to distributions of stock in the distributing company itself.) This means dividend treatment for an amount equal to the lesser of the parent's earnings and profits or the fair market value of the distributed stock, and return of capital and capital gains for any excess of the value of the distributed stock over earnings and profits. If structured as a split-off (in other words, a redemption of stock in the parent in exchange for stock in the subsidiary) the redemption rules of Section 302 normally would dictate whether the exchanging stockholders receive sale or distribution treatment. Finally, if structured as a split-up (in other words, a liquidating distribution of stock in the two subsidiaries), Section 331 normally should govern. This Section generally treats amounts received in a complete liquidation of a corporation as if received in exchange for selling the stockholder's shares in the company. (Note this avoids the dangers of dividend treatment found with a spin-off or split-off.) Of major significance for all three types of transactions is the tax impact on the parent. If, as one would usually expect, the fair market value of the shares in the subsidiary exceeds the parent's basis in them, the parent in any taxable distribution or exchange must recognize gain. I.R.C. §§ 311(b), 336(a). This means the second step in a corporate division could entail paying a costly double tax.

Fortunately, as indicated in *Coady,* Section 355 allows under certain conditions a spin-off, split-off or split-up to proceed tax-free. (The section expressly makes the transaction tax-free to the recipient shareholder. Tax-free treatment for the distributing corporation is less explicit. *See* I.R.C. §§ 355(c)(2) (excluding distribution of stock or securities in a spun-off or split-off corporation from the recognition rule of Section 311(b)), 361(c) (excluding from recognition the distribution of stock or securities of a corporation which is a party to a reorganization—such as a reorganization under Section 368(a)(1)(D)). This leaves a gap, however, for a split-up which is not part of a Section 368(a)(1)(D) reorganization.) To obtain this favorable treatment, the transaction must meet four requirements:

(i) The distribution must consist solely of stock or securities in a corporation (or corporations) controlled by the distributing company (within the meaning of Section 368(c)) immediately prior to the exchange. I.R.C. § 355(a)(1)(A).

(ii) The reason for the distribution must not be as a device to distribute earnings and profits, but must be for a business purpose. I.R.C. § 355(a)(1)(B); Treas. Reg. § 1.355–2(b).

(iii) The activities of the corporations surviving the division (in other words, the former parent and subsidiary in a spin-off or split-off, or the two former subsidiaries in a split-up) must satisfy the active business requirement. I.R.C. § 355(a)(1)(C), (b).

(iv) The corporation must either distribute all the stock and securities it owns in the controlled company, or else distribute at least a controlling interest and establish to the Internal Revenue Service a lack of any tax avoidance motive for retaining the rest. I.R.C. § 355(a)(1)(D).

In addition, the regulations state that the continuity of interest test—a judicially imposed limitation upon reorganizations, which requires those who owned the corporation before the reorganization to substantially continue their ownership thereafter—applies to a Section 355 division. Treas. Reg. § 1.355–2(c). As *Coady* illustrates, the continuity of interest requirement does not preclude a corporate division which separates the ownership of former co-shareholders. Moreover, those types of transactions which create continuity of interest problems in the acquisition context (i.e. receipt of consideration other than stock, or subsequent sale of one's interest) often preclude a tax-free division regardless of the continuity of interest test. Hence, this test rarely comes into play in a Section 355 division.

Needless to say, tax-free treatment comes with the trade-off of a substituted basis. Just as with Sections 351 and 354 encountered before, Section 358(a) specifies that the basis the shareholder obtains in the shares he or she receives in a split-off or split-up equals the basis he or she had in the shares surrendered in exchange (with adjustments for recognition of gain and receipt of boot). In a spin-off, there is no exchange. Section 358(c), however, pretends there is for purposes of shifting some of the basis to the newly acquired shares.

Finally, note the *Coady* opinion's rejection of the interpretation of Section 355 contained in the initial regulations dealing with this section. The Service subsequently conceded the invalidity of the regulation involved in *Coady.* Rev. Rul. 64–147, 1964–1 C.B. 136. After meeting similar judicial reactions to the other parts of the existing Section 355 regulations, the I.R.S. introduced new regulations which became final in 1989.

3. Inspection under Section 355 of the purposes behind a corporate division has both a negative and a positive component. The statute itself denies tax-free treatment to transactions used principally as a device for the distribution of a corporation's earnings and profits. I.R.C. § 355(a)(1)(B). Yet, the absence of such a tax avoidance motive is not enough. Under the regulations and judicial decisions, the parties still must establish a business purpose for the division. *E.g.,* Treas. Reg. § 1.355–2(b)(1); *Commissioner v. Wilson,* 353 F.2d 184 (9th Cir.1965).

What sort of evidence does the Internal Revenue Service look to in order to establish that a corporate division was a device to bail out earnings and profits? A subsequent sale of the distributed stock by its recipients would seem suspicious. Section 355, however, indicates such a sale, *in itself,* is not enough to establish the forbidden purpose—unless the parties arranged it prior to the division. I.R.C. § 355(a)(1)(B). How far can parties go before they have arranged a sale prior to the division? Clearly, a binding agreement is too much; but what about negotiations or discussions which did not yet reach the point of agreement? See Treas. Reg. § 1.355–2(d)(2)(iii)(D) (if the buyer and seller discussed the sale, and both could reasonably anticipate it, then ordinarily it is prearranged). Also, what if the recipients sold only a portion of the distributed stock? See Treas. Reg. § 1.355–2(d)(2)(iii)(A) (the greater the percentage sold, the stronger the evidence of devise). Other evidence of a motive to use the transaction as a bail-out device includes the nature and use of the assets placed in the spun-off corporation. For example, concentrating liquid assets in one corporation beyond the amount reasonably needed by its business looks questionable. Treas. Reg. § 1.355–2(d)(2)(iv)(B). (In this case, it is possible the shareholders are putting together the type of assets they may plan to sell out.) The Service takes the same position when the principal business of one company after the division is to supply goods or services to the other firm. Treas. Reg. § 1.355–2(d)(2)(iv)(C). On the other hand, several factors tend to disprove any intent to bail out earnings. For example, if the companies involved had no current or accumulated earnings and profits, the distribution would hardly seem a plan to avoid dividend treatment. Treas. Reg. § 1.355–2(d)(5)(ii). Similarly, if the exchange (as in *Coady*) is not pro-rata, so that it could have qualified for sale treatment under Section 302, it would not seem to be a device to bail out earnings without dividends. Treas. Reg. § 1.355–2(d)(5)(iv). *See also* Treas. Reg. § 1.355–2(d)(2)(ii) (pro-rata distribution is evidence of a device to avoid taxes). Less conclusive, but still indicative of the lack of a tax avoidance motive, are the existence of a business purpose, the fact the distributing company is widely held, or the fact the distributees are corporations eligible for the dividends received deduction. Treas. Reg. § 1.355–2(d)(3). While not mentioned by the regulations, the reduction, at least for the time being, in the tax rate on dividends to match the tax rate on capital gains, would seem to undercut an inference that a corporate division was a device to bail out earnings without dividends.

Normally, one might assume if a transaction was not a device to bail out earnings, it must have a business purpose (and vice versa). Regrettably, from the standpoint of simplicity, this assumption is in error. Transactions which are not a device to bail out earnings may still fail the business purpose test. For instance, it is possible for a court to be unable to discern either a tax avoidance or a business purpose for the division. *Commissioner v. Wilson,* 353 F.2d 184 (9th Cir.1965). (This could occur because the parties acted senselessly, or because their motive remains hidden in a fog.) Alternately, the purpose behind the division, while not tax avoidance, may not be an acceptable "business" purpose. The problem here is one encountered before when discussing recapitalizations. The impetus for the division, especially when dealing with closely held corporations, may be a shareholder purpose (for example, to facilitate an estate plan) rather than a corporate purpose. The Service takes the position that the division must serve a corporate purpose in order to be tax-free. Treas. Reg. 1.355–2(b)(2). Judicial opinions are in conflict on this question. *Compare Rafferty v. Commissioner,* 452 F.2d 767 (1st Cir.1971), *cert. denied,* 408 U.S. 922 (1972), *with Parshelsky's Estate v. Commissioner,* 303 F.2d 14 (2d Cir. 1962). Suppose, however, as is often the case with family businesses and personal disagreements between owners, shareholder and corporate purposes overlap: Will the transaction in such a case meet the business purpose requirement?

Revenue Ruling 2003–52

2003–1 C.B. 960.

* * *

FACTS

Corporation X is a domestic corporation that has been engaged in the farming business for more than five years. The stock of X is owned 25 percent each by Father, age 68, Mother, age 67, Son, and Daughter. Although Father and Mother participate in some major management decisions, most of the management and all of the operational activities are performed by Son, Daughter, and several farmhands. The farm operation consists of breeding and raising livestock and growing grain.

Son and Daughter disagree over the appropriate future direction of X's farming business. Son wishes to expand the livestock business, but Daughter is opposed because this would require substantial borrowing by X. Daughter would prefer to sell the livestock business and concentrate on the grain business. Despite the disagreement, the two siblings have cooperated on the operation of the farm in its historical manner without disruption. Nevertheless, it has prevented each sibling from developing, as he or she sees fit, the business in which he or she is most interested.

Having transferred most of the responsibility for running the farm to the children, Father and Mother remain neutral on the disagreement between their children. However, because of the disagreement, Father and Mother would prefer to bequeath separate interests in the farm business to their children.

For reasons unrelated to X's farm business, Son and Daughter's husband dislike each other. Although this has not impaired the farm's operation to date, Father and Mother believe that requiring Son and Daughter to run a single business together is likely to cause family discord over the long run.

To enable Son and Daughter each to devote his or her undivided attention to, and apply a consistent business strategy to, the farming business in which he or she is most interested, to further the estate planning goals of Father and Mother, and to promote family harmony, X transfers the livestock business to newly formed, wholly owned domestic corporation Y and distributes 50 percent of the Y stock to Son in exchange for all of his stock in X. X distributes the remaining Y stock equally to Father and Mother in exchange for half of their X stock. Going forward, Daughter will manage and operate X and have no stock interest in Y, and Son will manage and operate Y and have no stock interest in X. Father and Mother will also amend their wills to provide that Son and Daughter will inherit stock only in Y and X, respectively. After the distribution, Father and Mother will still each own 25 percent of the outstanding stock of X and Y and will continue to participate in some major management decisions related to the business of each corporation.

Apart from the issue of whether the business purpose requirement of § 1.355–2(b) is satisfied, the distribution meets all of the requirements of §§ 368(a)(1)(D) and 355 of the Internal Revenue Code.

LAW

* * *

To qualify as a distribution described in § 355, a distribution must, in addition to satisfying the statutory requirements of § 355, satisfy certain requirements in the regulations, including the business purpose requirement. * * * A shareholder purpose (for example, the personal planning purposes of a shareholder) is not a corporate business purpose. Depending upon the facts of a particular case, however, a shareholder purpose for a transaction may be so nearly coextensive with a corporate business purpose as to preclude any distinction between them. In such a case, the transaction is carried out for one or more corporate business purposes. A transaction motivated in substantial part by a corporate business purpose does not fail the business purpose requirement merely because it is motivated in part by non-federal tax shareholder purposes.

* * *

ANALYSIS

The disagreement of Son and Daughter over the farm's future direction has prevented each sibling from developing, as he or she sees fit, the business in which he or she is most interested. The distribution will eliminate this disagreement and allow each sibling to devote his or her undivided attention to, and apply a consistent business strategy to, the farming business in which he or she is most interested, with the expectation that each business will benefit. Therefore, although the distribution is intended, in part, to further the personal estate planning of Father and Mother and to promote family harmony, it is motivated in substantial part by a real and substantial non-federal tax purpose that is germane to the business of X. Hence, the business purpose requirement of § 1.355–2(b) is satisfied.

* * *

Incidently, it is nice that the Internal Revenue Service provided guidance in Revenue Ruling 2003–52, since the Service has announced a policy of not giving rulings on whether corporate divisions have a business purpose or constitute a device to avoid taxes. Rev. Proc. 2003–48, 2003–29 I.R.B. 86.

The fact that a corporate division may involve two transactions—the formation of a subsidiary, and the distribution of the subsidiary's stock to the parent's shareholders—creates an additional problem with respect to the business purpose requirement. The parties may have a legitimate reason for the former transaction, but not for the latter. The regulations give the example of a company which conducts two lines of business, and wishes to insulate one from the risks of the other. Treas. Reg. § 1.355–2(b)(5) Ex.(3). This goal justifies forming a subsidiary to which the company transfers the risky business, but not the subsequent distribution of the subsidiary's stock. (Recall, however, that the discussion of this objective earlier pointed out a reason for the subsequent distribution, which the Service may have overlooked.)

4. Not satisfied with the government's ability to always distill the motives behind a transaction, Section 355 buttresses its effort to distinguish between legitimate corporate divisions, and attempts to bail out corporate earnings, by imposing an active business requirement. This requirement also has two components. The first looks to the situation immediately after the distribution. Each surviving corporation must then be engaged in the active conduct of a trade or business. I.R.C. § 355(b)(1). In this way, the statute seeks to prevent a company from spinning off the type of investment assets which shareholders would most desire to subsequently cash out through selling or liquidating one of the companies.

What exactly does the active conduct of a trade or business entail? The regulations give the following criteria:

> "(ii) *Trade or business.* A corporation shall be treated as engaged in a trade or business immediately after the distribution if a specific group of activities are being carried on by the corporation for the purpose of earning income or profit, from such group of activities, and the activities included in such group include every operation which forms a part of, or a step in, the process of earning income or profit from such group. Such group of activities ordinarily must include the collection of income and the payment of expenses.
>
> (iii) *Active conduct.* For purposes of section 355, the determination of whether a trade or business is actively conducted is a question of fact to be determined under all the facts and circumstances. In general, the corporation must perform active and substantial management and operational functions. * * * "Treas. Reg. § 1.355–3(b)(2).

Several types of activities present recurring difficulty in this area. One involves the situation in which the activities of the surviving corporations have a vertical relationship; in other words, one company supplies goods or services to the other company. In its initial regulations interpreting Section 355, the Internal Revenue Service took the position that the supplying firm in such cases did not actively conduct a separate trade or business, because it did not independently produce income. Yet, many firms exist, not the result of any corporate division, whose source of income consists of selling goods or services to another venture. Reflecting this reality, and judicial opinions hostile to its initial regulation on this point (*e.g., King v. Commissioner,* 458 F.2d 245 (6th Cir.1972)), the Service's current regulations recognize that such activity can constitute a separate trade or business. For example, a coal mine supplying all its output to a steel mill would be a separate trade or business. Treas. Reg. § 1.355–3(c) Ex. (11). Even research and development or sales operations can be separate businesses from a production operation they support. *Id.* at Exs. (9), (10). Presumably, at some point, however, the spun-off activity will have so little viability on its own that no one could call it a trade or business. Recall also that such a vertical relationship may be evidence of a purpose to bail out earnings, even if there are two active businesses.

Leasing real estate or other property constitutes a second trouble spot. When the lessee is the other company surviving the division, this raises the vertical relationship problem just discussed. Beyond this, leasing property, either to the other corporation or to a third party, may constitute the type of inactive undertaking Section 355 meant to exclude. *E.g., Rafferty v. Commissioner,* 452 F.2d 767 (1st Cir.1971), *cert. denied,* 408 U.S. 922 (1972). Essentially, this depends upon the extent to which the lessor provides significant services in managing and operating the property. *E.g.,* Treas. Reg. § 1.355–3(b)(2)(iii); Rev. Rul. 80–101, 1980–1 C.B. 121.

An exception exists to the requirement that each surviving corporation must actively conduct a trade or business. This is for parent companies. Essentially, Section 355(b)(3) provides that the active business test will be applied on a group basis for companies that qualify (even if not electing) to be the common parent of an affiliated group. Along somewhat similar lines, acting as a managing partner in a partnership or a managing member in an LLC, that itself conducts an active business, can be an active business. Rev. Rul. 2002–49, 2002–2 C.B. 288. Suppose the corporation simply owns a large stake in an LLC or partnership that conducts an active business: can this constitute the active conduct of a trade or business? See Rev. Rul. 2007–42, 2007–28 I.R.B. 44 (a one-third interest did, but a 20 percent interest did not).

The second component of the active trade or business requirement is the one involved in *Coady.* This deals with the history of the business activity prior to the division. The concern here is with efforts to bail out earnings by buying or establishing a line of business which the stockholders can sell after receiving it in a tax-free spin-off. To deter this, the statute requires the trade or business undertaken by each surviving corporation to be one that has been actively conducted throughout the five years preceding the distribution. I.R.C. § 355(b)(2)(B). This does not say the corporation conducting the business after the division must have been the party conducting the business throughout the prior five years. In fact, as discussed above, the spun-off corporation often comes into existence and receives its assets in a Section 368(a)(1)(D) reorganization immediately preceding the Section 355 distribution. However, neither the business, nor control of the corporation conducting the business, can have changed hands during the prior five years in a taxable event (as opposed to a non-recognition transaction, such as a reorganization). I.R.C. § 355(b)(2)(C), (D).

When the division involves two distinct lines of business, this five year rule is fairly straight-forward. One simply needs to check if each endeavor has been going on for five years, and how, if at all, each enterprise changed hands during this time. In this regard, it is useful to note that normal evolution of the venture (as in adding or dropping related product lines) does not interrupt the five year period. Treas. Reg. § 1.355–3(b)(3)(ii). In *Coady,* only a single line of business existed prior to a division which cut the enterprise in half. In this event, one can no longer find a separate five year history for each business operating after the division. Nevertheless, the court held the five year requirement satisfied, as each venture assumed the history of the single enterprise of which it had been a part. The result in *Coady,* however, creates a problem when a firm has expanded its operations over the prior five years and now wishes to spin off the expansion. For instance, a company may have built or purchased a plant in a new geographic area, or introduced new products. If viewed as a separate line of business before the division, the spun-off expansion will not have required five year history. *E.g., Nielsen v. Commissioner,* 61 T.C. 311 (1973). If, however, viewed as part of only one line of business existing before the division, the spun-off expansion satisfies the five year rule under the *Coady* approach if the overall business did. *E.g., Lockwood's Estate v. Commissioner,* 350 F.2d 712 (8th Cir.1965). How can one tell in which camp the expansion belongs?

Revenue Ruling 2003–38

2003–1 C.B. 811.

* * *

FACTS

Corporation D has operated a retail shoe store business, under the name "D," since Year 1 in a manner that meets the requirements of § 355(b) of the Internal Revenue Code. D's sales are made exclusively to customers who frequent its retail stores in shopping malls and other locations. D's business enjoys favorable name recognition, customer loyalty, and other elements of goodwill in the retail shoe market. In Year 8, D creates an Internet web site and begins selling shoes at retail on the web site. To a significant extent, the operation of the web site draws upon D's experience and know-how. The web site is named "D.com" to take advantage of the name recognition, customer loyalty, and other elements of goodwill associated with D and the D name and to enhance the web site's chances for success in its initial stages. In Year 10, D transfers all of the web site's assets and liabilities to corporation C, a newly formed, wholly owned subsidiary of D, and distributes the stock of C pro rata to D's shareholders. Apart from the issue of whether the web site is considered an expansion of D's business and therefore entitled to share the business's five-year history at the time of the distribution in Year 10, the distribution meets all the requirements of § 355.

LAW

* * *

In determining whether an active trade or business has been conducted by a corporation throughout the five-year period preceding the distribution, the fact that a trade or business underwent change during the five-year period (for example, by the addition of new or the dropping of old products, changes in production capacity, and the like) shall be disregarded, provided that the changes are not of such a character as to constitute the acquisition of a new or different business. In particular, if a corporation engaged in the active conduct of one trade or business during that five-year period purchased, created, or otherwise acquired another trade or business in the same line of business, then the acquisition of that other business is ordinarily treated as an expansion of the original business, all of which is treated as having been actively conducted during that five-year period, unless that purchase, creation, or other acquisition effects a change of such character as to constitute the acquisition of a new or different business.

* * *

In Example (8) of [Treas. Reg.] § 1.355–3(c), corporation X had owned and operated hardware stores in several states for four years before purchasing the assets of a hardware store in State M where X had not previously conducted business. Two years after the purchase, X transferred the State M store and related business assets to new subsidiary Y and distributed the Y stock to X's shareholders. * * * [T]he example concludes that X and Y both satisfy the requirements of § 355(b).

Rev. Rul. 2003–18, 2003–7 I.R.B. 467, concludes that the acquisition by a dealer engaged in the sale and service of brand X automobiles of a franchise (and the assets needed) to sell and service brand Y automobiles is an expansion of the brand X business and does not constitute the acquisition of a new or different business * * * because (i) the product of the brand X automobile dealership is similar to the product of the brand Y automobile dealership, (ii) the business activities associated with the operation of the brand X automobile dealership (i.e., sales and service) are the same as the business activities associated with the operation of the brand Y automobile dealership, and (iii) the operation of the brand Y automobile dealership involves the use of the experience and know-how that the dealer developed in the operation of the brand X automobile dealership.

ANALYSIS

The product of the retail shoe store business and the product of the web site are the same (shoes), and the principal business activities of the retail shoe store business are the same as those of the web site (purchasing shoes at wholesale and reselling them at retail). Selling shoes on a web site requires some know-how not associated with operating a retail store, such as familiarity with different marketing approaches, distribution chains, and technical operations issues. Nevertheless, the web site's operation does draw to a significant extent on D's existing experience and know-how, and the web site's success will depend in large measure on the goodwill associated with D and the D name. Accordingly, the creation by D of the Internet web site does not constitute the acquisition of a new or different business * * *. Instead, it is an expansion of D's retail shoe store business. Therefore, each of D and C is engaged in the active conduct of a five-year active trade or business immediately after the distribution.

* * *

5. Normally, the split-off of a corporation, most of the assets of which are cash or investments, should fail either (or both) the devise or the active business tests. It is possible, however, for such a transaction to pass both tests. As mentioned above, non-pro-rata distribution of the corporation's stock could defeat the inference that the transaction is a devise to bail out earnings without taxable dividends (since a non-pro-rata distribution could avoid dividend treatment under Section 302 anyway). Also, the active business test could be satisfied even if the corporation has considerable cash and investment assets in addition to its active business. To preclude tax-free treatment for such a transaction, Section 355(g) prevents distribu-

tions from qualifying for tax-free treatment under Section 355 if either of the two corporations emerging from the transaction is a "disqualified investment corporation," and any person, who did not own at least half of the stock of the disqualified investment corporation before the transaction, emerges as the owner of at least half of the stock of that corporation.

6. Section 355 allows both tax-free distributions on stock (spin-offs) and distributions in exchange for stock (split-offs and split-ups). I.R.C. § 355(a)(1)(A)(i) and (ii), (2)(B). In either case, Section 355(a)(1)(A) specifies that the only item which the shareholders may receive tax-free is stock or securities in a corporation which the distributing company controlled immediately prior to the distribution. (This could either be a subsidiary in existence for some time, or one just created in Section 368(a)(1)(D) reorganization. I.R.C. § 355(a)(2)(C).) Section 368(c) (encountered earlier when dealing with Section 351 transactions) gives the definition of control as ownership of 80 percent of the total combined voting power of all voting shares, and 80 percent of the total number of shares of all non-voting classes. Suppose a parent corporation contemplating a tax-free spin-off of shares in a subsidiary presently fails to meet this test. If it acquires the necessary shares in a taxable transaction, the five year active business test will preclude use of Section 355. I.R.C. § 355(b)(2)(D). Is it possible, however, to acquire the necessary shares in a non-recognition transaction? What if their former owner will receive them back in the division? See Rev. Rul. 63–260, 1963–2 C.B. 147 (ignoring transitory acquisition of stock made in order to satisfy requirements for a tax-free division under Section 355). Returning to the discussion at the start of this chapter, recall that a redemption by the corporation can achieve the same end result as a cross purchase. In this light, can a parent corporation avoid the problem with a taxable acquisition of control by having the subsidiary redeem the shares of the other stockholder(s), instead of the parent corporation, itself, acquiring enough shares to give it control of the subsidiary? See *McLaulin v. Commissioner*, 276 F.3d 1269 (11th Cir.2001) (no). On the other hand, suppose a corporation, which is a member of an LLC, buys out the interests of the other members, places some of the assets of the LLC in a newly formed subsidiary, and then spins off the newly formed subsidiary to the parent's shareholders. Notice here that the corporation did not acquire control of the subsidiary—as opposed to the LLC (which is not a corporation)—in a taxable transaction. On the other hand, did the corporation in this situation acquire a new business in a taxable transaction, thereby running afoul of the five-year active business requirement? See Rev. Rul. 2002–49, 2002–2 C.B. 288 (no).

As under Sections 351 and 354, the receipt of something other than the allowed stock or securities of a controlled corporation (as always, called boot) does not make the entire transaction taxable. Instead, Section 356 forces recognition of income, but not loss (I.R.C. § 356(c)), just to the extent of the boot received. (If the distribution is in exchange for stock (a split-off or a split-up), Section 356(a)(1) makes the lesser of the amount of gain or of boot taxable. Section 356(a)(2) requires dividend treatment of this amount (up to the recipient's ratable share of accumulated earnings and profits) if the distribution has the effect of a dividend. Recall, this is the treatment accorded boot in a recapitalization, or, indeed, in any reorganization. Not surprisingly, the test for dividend equivalence involves the same sort of search for a disproportionate reduction of interest as undertaken when dealing with boot in a recapitalization. *E.g.,* Rev. Rul. 93–62, 1993–2 C.B. 118. Should the distribution not be in exchange for stock (a spin-off), then Section 356(b) treats the entire amount of boot received as if it is a Section 301 distribution.) If the boot consists of appreciated assets, the corporation must also recognize income. I.R.C. § 355(c).

Also as under Sections 351 and 354, debt instruments create added complications in a Section 355 transaction. To begin with, unless they constitute "securities", the debt instruments are boot. Even if they constitutes securities, exchange of debt instruments in a corporate division creates prospects for recognition along the lines discussed earlier when dealing with recapitalizations. For instance, the excess of the principal amount of securities received over the principal amount of securities surrendered constitutes boot. I.R.C. §§ 355(a)(3)(A), 356(d)(2)(C). Moreover, anything received in exchange for accrued but unpaid interest on surrendered securities constitutes interest income. I.R.C. § 355(a)(3)(C).

Even if a transaction generally qualifies under Section 355, shareholders may not be able to receive some shares in the controlled corporation tax-free. Section 355(a)(3)(B) treats shares the distributing corporation purchased in a taxable transaction within the preceding five years as boot. (If the distributing company bought a controlling interest in a taxable transaction within this period, then the active business requirement precludes tax-free treatment altogether. I.R.C. § 355(b)(2)(D).) Moreover, stock rights and warrants do not count as stock for purposes of Section 355. *E.g., Redding v. Commissioner,* 630 F.2d 1169 (7th Cir.1980), *cert. denied,* 450 U.S. 913 (1981). The regulations, however, treat stock rights issued in a Section 355 division as securities with a principle amount of zero, thereby avoiding treatment of such rights as boot. Treas. Reg. § 1.355–1(c). The treatment of nonqualified preferred stock as boot under Sections 351 and 354 does not apply to Section 355. Still, preferred stock received in a tax-free transaction may be section 306 stock. *E.g.,* Rev. Rul. 77–335, 1977–2 C.B. 95.

A tax-free distribution under Section 355 may either be pro-rata among the shareholders or not pro-rata. I.R.C. § 355(a)(2)(A). This allows use of corporate divisions, as done in *Coady,* as a tax-free method to divorce feuding shareholders. How far can one take this? Suppose the parties in *Coady* had equally owned two corporations (instead of starting with just one corporation, as in *Coady*, or with equal ownership in a parent corporation, which, in turn, already owns a subsidiary). Could they use Section 355 to create a tax-free transaction in which one shareholder ends up owning all of one corporation and the other shareholder ends up owning all of the other? See Treas. Reg. § 1.355–4 (stating that Section 355 will not apply to a transaction, like this, which is really an exchange of stock between shareholders). *But see Badanes v. Commissioner,* 39 T.C. 410 (1962). One problem in a non-pro-rata exchange, particularly if used to separate hostile shareholders, is that the size of the two businesses may not be equal (or otherwise correspond to the size of the stockholders' interests). Can the parties have the parent add assets to the subsidiary (or vice versa), which are unrelated to the subsidiary's business, in order to equalize values? See Treas. Reg. § 1.355–2(d)(2)(iv)(B) (allowing such an action if for a legitimate business purpose rather than to bail out earnings). Alternately, can they equalize values by having one group pay cash, as well as surrender stock, in the exchange? (Notice the statute speaks of a distribution of stock, which might exclude a purchase for cash.) If they do not equalize values, the result could be a gift or compensation, much as discussed when dealing with recapitalizations. *E.g.,* Rev. Rul. 77–20, 1977–1 C.B. 92. Another problem in a non pro-rata distribution is that it could constitute an "ownership change" triggering Section 382's limitation on the use of net operating loss carryovers. This will be discussed in Chapter VII.

Finally, not only does the statute limit the consideration which shareholders may receive tax-free to stock and securities in a controlled corporation, but it also commands the parent either to distribute to its stockholders all the stock or securities the parent owns in the controlled company, or at least distribute to them a controlling interest (within the meaning of Section 368(c)) and establish to the Internal Revenue Service the lack of any tax avoidance motive for keeping the rest. I.R.C. § 355(a)(1)(D).

7. In recent years, Congress has become concerned with the use of tax-free divisions as part of an acquisition of a corporation by a party who does not want all of the corporation's properties. Specifically, Congress felt that the corporation, even if not the recipients, should recognize the gain inherent in the distribution of stock or securities when the spin-off, split-off or split-up is part of transaction in which control passes to an outsider. Congress accomplished this goal in two stages. First, it enacted Section 355(d). This provision forces the distributing corporation to recognize gain (to the extent the fair market value of the distributed stock or securities exceeds the distributing company's basis in the stock or securities) on a distribution to a party who purchased his or her shares in the distributing corporation, or in the controlled subsidiary, within five years of the Section 355 distribution, and who, based on those purchases, ends up after the distribution with at least 50 percent of either of the two companies' stock. (Why will such a purchase not have caused the transaction to flunk the active business requirement? Notice that with an unequal division of assets, a relatively small ownership interest could justify receipt of a controlling interest in one of the two split up corporations.) A few years later, Congress added Section 355(e). Broadly speaking, Section 355(e) forces the distributing company to recognize gain on the distribution (much as under Section 355(d)) anytime the corporate division is part of a plan under which outsiders acquire 50 percent or more of the distributing company's or former subsidiary's stock. Unlike Section 355(d), Section 355(e) can reach divisions in which the acquisition of the controlling stock occurred after (as well as before) the corporate division or in a tax-free

transaction (as opposed to a purchase). Chapter VII, dealing with the sale of a business in the corporate form, will explore this subject in more detail.

2. SHRINKING THE BUSINESS

a. *Corporate Law Aspects*

Katz v. Bregman

431 A.2d 1274 (Del.Ch.1981).

■ MARVEL, CHANCELLOR.

The complaint herein seeks the entry of an order preliminarily enjoining the proposed sale of the Canadian assets of Plant Industries, Inc. to Vulcan Industrial Packaging, Ltd., the plaintiff Hyman Katz allegedly being the owner of approximately 170,000 shares of common stock of the defendant Plant Industries, Inc., on whose behalf he has brought this action, suing not only for his own benefit as a stockholder but for the alleged benefit of all other record owners of common stock of the defendant Plant Industries, Inc. * * *

The complaint alleges that during the last six months of 1980, the board of directors of Plant Industries, Inc., under the guidance of the individual defendant Robert B. Bregman, the present chief executive officer of such corporation, embarked on a course of action which resulted in the disposal of several unprofitable subsidiaries of the corporate defendant located in the United States, namely Louisiana Foliage Inc., a horticultural business, Sunaid Food Products, Inc., a Florida packaging business, and Plant Industries (Texas), Inc., a business concerned with the manufacture of woven synthetic cloth. As a result of these sales Plant Industries, Inc. by the end of 1980 had disposed of a significant part of its unprofitable assets.

According to the complaint, Mr. Bregman thereupon proceeded on a course of action designed to dispose of a subsidiary of the corporate defendant known as Plant National (Quebec) Ltd., a business which constitutes Plant Industries, Inc.'s entire business operation in Canada and has allegedly constituted Plant's only income producing facility during the past four years. The professed principal purpose of such proposed sale is to raise needed cash and thus improve Plant's balance sheets. And while interest in purchasing the corporate defendant's Canadian plant was thereafter evinced not only by Vulcan Industrial Packaging, Ltd. but also by Universal Drum Reconditioning Co., which latter corporation originally undertook to match or approximate and recently to top Vulcan's bid, a formal contract was entered into between Plant Industries, Inc. and Vulcan on April 2, 1981 for the purchase and sale of Plant National (Quebec) despite the constantly increasing bids for the same property being made by Universal. One reason advanced by Plant's management for declining to negotiate with Universal is that a firm undertaking having been entered into with Vulcan that the board of directors of Plant may not legally or ethically negotiate with Universal. * * *

In seeking injunctive relief, as prayed for, plaintiff relies on two principles, one that found in 8 Del.C. § 271 to the effect that a decision of a Delaware corporation to sell "* * * all or substantially all of its property and assets * * *"requires not only the approval of such corporation's board of directors but also a resolution adopted by a majority of the outstanding stockholders of the corporation entitled to vote thereon at a meeting duly called upon at least twenty days' notice.

* * *

Turning to the possible application of 8 Del.C. § 271 to the proposed sale of substantial corporate assets of National to Vulcan, it is stated in *Gimbel v. Signal Companies, Inc.*, Del.Ch., 316 A.2d 599 (1974) as follows:

> "If the sale is of assets quantitatively vital to the operation of the corporation and is out of the ordinary and substantially affects the existence and purpose of the corporation then it is beyond the power of the Board of Directors."

According to Plant's 1980 10K form, it appears that at the end of 1980, Plant's Canadian operations represented 51% of Plant's remaining assets. Defendants also concede that National represents 44.9% of Plant's sales' revenues and 52.4% of its pre-tax net operating income. Furthermore, such report by Plant discloses, in rough figures that while National made a profit in 1978 of $2,900,000, the profit from the United States businesses in that year was only $770,000. In 1979, the Canadian business profit was $3,500,000 while the loss of the United States businesses was $344,000. Furthermore, in 1980, while the Canadian business profit was $5,300,000, the corporate loss in the United States was $4,500,000. And while these figures may be somewhat distorted by the allocation of overhead expenses and taxes, they are significant. In any event, defendants concede that "* * * National accounted for 34.9% of Plant's pre-tax income in 1976, 36.9% in 1977, 42% in 1978, 51% in 1979 and 52.4% in 1980."

While in the case of *Philadelphia National Bank v. B.S.F. Co.*, Del.Ch., 199 A.2d 557 (1969), rev'd on other grounds, Del.Supr., 204 A.2d 746 (1964), the question of whether or not there had been a proposed sale of substantially all corporate assets was tested by provisions of an indenture agreement covering subordinated debentures, the result was the same as if the provisions of 8 Del.C. § 271 had been applicable, the trial Court stating:

> "While no pertinent Pennsylvania case is cited, the critical factor in determining the character of a sale of assets is generally considered not the amount of property sold but whether the sale is in fact an unusual transaction or one made in the regular course of business of the seller * * *."

* * *

In the case at bar, I am first of all satisfied that historically the principal business of Plant Industries, Inc. has not been to buy and sell industrial facilities but rather to manufacture steel drums for use in bulk shipping as well as for the storage of petroleum products, chemicals, food, paint, adhesives and cleaning agents, a business which has been profitably performed by National of Quebec. Furthermore, the proposal, after the sale of National, to embark on the manufacture of plastic drums represents a radical departure from Plant's historically successful line of business, namely steel drums. I therefore conclude that the proposed sale of Plant's Canadian operations, which constitute over 51% of Plant's total assets and in which are generated approximately 45% of Plant's 1980 net sales, would, if consummated, constitute a sale of substantially all of Plant's assets. By way of contrast, the proposed sale of Signal Oil in *Gimbel v. Signal Companies, Inc., supra,* represented only about 26% of the total assets of Signal Companies, Inc. And while Signal Oil represented 41% of Signal Companies, Inc. total net worth, it generated only about 15% of Signal Companies, Inc. revenue and earnings.

I conclude that because the proposed sale of Plant National (Quebec) Ltd. would, if consummated, constitute a sale of substantially all of the assets of Plant Industries, Inc., as presently constituted, that an injunction should issue preventing the consummation of such sale at least until it has been approved by a majority of the outstanding stockholders of Plant Industries, Inc., entitled to vote at a meeting duly called on at least twenty days' notice. * * *

NOTES

1. Corporations statutes typically require shareholder approval for a company to sell substantially all of its assets—except in cases when such a sale occurs in the ordinary course of the company's business. *E.g.,* Cal. Corp. Code § 1001(a); Del. Gen. Corp. Law § 271(a); N.Y. Bus. Corp. Law § 909. *Katz* indicates how a significant enough sale of assets—whether pursuant to a retrenchment or just to a redirection of the business—may bring these provisions into play even though the sale excluded a large portion of the corporation's properties. *But see* M.B.C.A. § 12.02(1) (only requiring shareholder approval when the sale leaves the corporation without significant continuing business activity). What if, instead of selling assets no longer needed because the corporation decides to cut back its operation, the company distributes the assets to its shareholders? Assuming the sale would have required a shareholder vote, will the distribution? See M.B.C.A. § 12.01(4) (not requiring stockholder approval for a pro-rata distribution to the holders of one or more classes of shares). If a sale requires shareholder approval, some statutes also give dissenting stockholders the right to demand the company purchase their shares at a fair value set by appraisal. *E.g.,* N.Y. Bus. Corp. Laws § 910(a)(1)(B); M.B.C.A. § 13.02(a)(3). In addition, sale of substantial assets may trigger the bulk transfer acts (Article 6 of the Uniform Commercial Code). These acts cover transfers by a business which primarily sells goods from inventory, or manufactures and sells from inventory. U.C.C. § 6–102(3). Such a business must give to its creditors ten days advance notice, in person or by mail, before it makes a bulk transfer of inventory or inventory plus equipment, or else the creditors may follow the goods into the hands of the buyer. U.C.C. §§ 6–102, 6–105, 6–107. (In a

corporate division, however, in which the transfer is to a new company formed to carry on the business, public notice is adequate. U.C.C. § 6–103.) Note, finally, the sale of substantially all assets, in itself, does not constitute a liquidation so as to trigger liquidation preferences—it depends upon what the company does with the proceeds. *E.g., Maffia v. American Woolen Co.,* 125 F.Supp. 465 (S.D.N.Y.1954).

2. When a corporation decides to cut back operations, it can either divert the proceeds from selling the unneeded assets (or the assets themselves) to other lines of endeavor, use the freed resources to pay creditors (the need for which sometimes motivates the cutback), or make a distribution to its shareholders. Such a distribution could either occur as a dividend or through a redemption. In either event, the corporate law issues raised are those involved in making dividends or redemptions generally, as discussed in Chapter IV and earlier in this chapter. As noted when dealing with spin-offs and split-offs, statutory limits on dividends and payments in redemptions can become a more significant concern as the corporation starts thinking about distributing a large portion of its assets. Taking the steps outlined earlier to reduce capital might help. Such distributions could also raise questions as to the rights of any preferred shares outstanding: Specifically, which if any, preference—dividend or liquidation—will such a distribution trigger? See *Roberts v. Roberts–Wicks Co.,* 184 N.Y. 257, 77 N.E. 13 (1906) (payment from capital reduction surplus constituted a return of capital, not a dividend, and so dividend preference did not apply).

3. If a corporation accomplishes a cutback by selling its assets in exchange for stock or other securities in another company, and then distributes the stock or securities to its own shareholders, the securities laws issues discussed when dealing with spin-offs come back into play.

b. *Tax Aspects*

If the company decides not to redeploy to other activities the resources freed by its cutback, but instead to distribute either the assets or the proceeds of their sale to its shareholders, the result is also to create the prospect of additional tax for the firm and its stockholders. The tax impacts on the shareholders and the corporation of disbursements from the firm, either directly through dividends, or indirectly through share repurchases, generally have been explored earlier. Section 302(b)(4) and (e), however, adds a major wrinkle in this situation. Section 302(b)(4) creates a fourth category of redemptions which qualify for sale rather than distribution treatment as far as taxation of the selling shareholder. This is for redemptions made in "partial liquidation" of the redeeming firm. Section 302(e)(1) defines redemptions in partial liquidation as those in which the effect of the distribution is not essentially equivalent to a dividend, as measured on the corporate level.

Recall, the not essentially equivalent test for redemptions was discussed earlier as the general standard set by Section 302(b)(1) for obtaining sale treatment. Section 302(b)(1), however, focuses on the effect of the redemption on the shareholder level: Specifically has there been a meaningful reduction in the selling shareholder's proportionate interest. *United States v. Davis,* 397 U.S. 301 (1970). Now, the test is on the corporate level. What can happen to the corporation to make a repurchase economically different from a dividend? If the disbursement to the shareholders represents the funds from a significant contraction of the company, then it starts to look more like a partial return of their capital, and less like a distribution of earnings as in a traditional dividend. This, of course, explains the term partial liquidation, but still leaves the question of how much of a contraction must occur.

Revenue Ruling 74–296

1974–1 C.B. 80.

Advice has been requested whether a distribution, under the circumstances described below, qualifies as a distribution in partial liquidation under section 346(a)(2) of the Internal Revenue Code of 1954.

X corporation operated a full line department store, which offered a comprehensive selection of brand merchandise and a number of services, and also offered a variety of credit arrangements. In 1971 two new shopping center complexes opened in the vicinity of *X*'s store which adversely affected sales. Pursuant to a plan adopted in 1972 *X* changed its operation from that of a large department store to a small discount apparel store operation by eliminating 33 of the 40 departments, changing the type of merchandise sold, and eliminating most forms of credit. As a result of the change, leased floor space was reduced by 85 percent; accounts receivable dropped from 570x dollars to 10x dollars; inventory related to the discontinued departments was disposed of through a series of sales; the number of employees was reduced from approximately 275 persons to about 20 persons; sales declined from about 4,000x dollars to about 600x dollars per year; and fixed assets (display counters and cash registers) related to the discontinued departments were disposed of for their salvage value which totaled less than 1x dollars.

The disposition of the inventory and the collection of the accounts receivable related to the discontinued departments resulted in the realization of approximately 800x dollars in cash after the payment of all liabilities related to the discontinued departments. Early in 1973 *X* distributed 600x dollars in cash to its shareholders, pro rata, in redemption of a part of its outstanding common stock. *X* had paid regular dividends on its stock for many years prior to the distribution. There was no intention to expand the business of *X* except through internal growth of the discount operations.

Section 346(a)(2) of the Code provides, in part, that a distribution shall be treated as in partial liquidation of a corporation if it is not essentially equivalent to a dividend, is in redemption of a part of the stock of the corporation pursuant to a plan, and occurs within the taxable year in which the plan is adopted or within the succeeding taxable year.

Section 1.346–1(a) of the Income Tax Regulations provides that a distribution which will qualify as a distribution in partial liquidation of a corporation under section 346(a)(2) of the Code is one which results from a genuine contraction of the corporate business.

Rev.Rul. 60–232, 1960–2 C.B. 115, holds that, in a contraction qualifying pursuant to section 346(a)(2) of the Code, the qualifying amounts distributed will include not only the net proceeds derived from the sale of operating assets, or the operating assets themselves, but also includes that portion of the working capital (including cash) reasonably attributable to the business activity terminated.

Rev.Rul. 60–322, 1960–2, C.B. 118, holds that a distribution did not result from a genuine contraction where a corporation, due to a steady decline in demand for its products, distributed cash to its shareholders, in redemption for part of their stock, that was realized from the sale of portfolio bonds and excess inventories, which it had decided to gradually sell off because of a decline in the demand for the inventory. The corporation did not change the activities or operation of its business, but simply reduced its inventory to reflect the decline in the demand for that inventory.

The instant case is distinguishable from Rev.Rul. 60–322 in that *X* discontinued most of the activities and operation of its business, and then changed the nature of its remaining business. Furthermore, there was no sale of investment property.

Accordingly, the distribution of 600x dollars to *X*'s shareholders in exchange for a portion of their shares in *X* resulted from a genuine contraction of *X*'s business and, therefore, qualifies as a partial liquidation under section 346(a)(2) of the Code.

* * *

NOTES

1. The ruling refers to a partial liquidation under Section 346. In the 1982 amendments to the tax code, Congress added Section 302(d)(4), and moved the definition of partial liquidation (with only minor changes) from Section 346 to Section 302(e). The practical result of the move on the selling shareholder is nil: Now he or she obtains sale rather than distribution treatment by virtue of Section 302's redemption rules rather than through Section 331's liquidation provision. Congress' objective was to change the treatment of the corporation in a partial liquidation, albeit this became obsolete when in 1986 Congress repealed the favorable treatment accorded corporations distributing appreciated assets in liquidation. At any event, authorities, such as this ruling, interpreting the meaning of a partial liquidation as used in Section 346, presumably remain equally valid for interpreting Section 302(e).

2. As the ruling suggests, there are no fixed standards for how much contraction is enough. Hence, from the planning perspective, the not equivalent to a dividend test on the corporate level suffers from the same

problem as its twin on the shareholder level: It is too vague for parties often to structure a transaction around with confidence of the tax impact. From this perspective, it is again useful that Section 302 thoughtfully comes through with another safe harbor.

Section 302(e)(2) specifies that a distribution attributable to the company ceasing to conduct a trade or business qualifies as one which is not equivalent to a dividend on the corporate level. In addition, to come within this safe harbor, the company must still be engaged after the distribution in the conduct of another trade or business. Does this mean a corporation can stop one business, start another, and call it a partial liquidation within the meaning of the safe harbor (rather than relying on the general standard as did the firm in the ruling)? Also, what is to prevent a firm with surplus profits it wishes to distribute from starting a business activity for a short period of time in order to turn around and liquidate this business? Section 302(e)(3) answers both questions. For the safe harbor to apply, Section 302(e)(3)(A) requires both the disposed of and retained businesses to have been actively conducted for the prior five years. Further, if the corporation was not the party who conducted either or both of the businesses during the prior five year period, the company must have acquired the business during this period in a non-recognition transaction (such as a reorganization). I.R.C. § 302(e)(3)(B). The requirements of this safe harbor should strike a familiar chord. They are similar to the requirements imposed for a tax-free distribution of stock under Section 355. In fact, the regulations issued by the Service under old Section 346 cross reference Section 355 in order to define what is entailed by the active conduct of a trade or business. Treas. Reg. § 1.346–1(c).

3. The distribution in a partial liquidation might consist of either the proceeds from selling the assets no longer needed, or the assets themselves. *See* I.R.C. § 302(e)(2)(A). Distributing the assets could allow a spin-off sort of transaction in which the owners can now operate one of the businesses as a partnership, limited partnership, LLP or LLC. Unlike a Section 355 transaction, however, the recipients must recognize taxable gain, and the corporation must also recognize gain if it distributes assets having a greater value than the company's basis in them. I.R.C. § 311(b). (In other words, Section 302(b)(4) only affects the sale versus dividend question; it does not prevent recognition of gain.) The corporation may distribute not only the operating assets of the curtailed business (or the proceeds from their sale), but it may also pass out an amount equal to the working capital which it would have used in this activity and now no longer needs. Rev. Rul. 60–232, 1960–2 C.B. 115. (On the other hand, simply distributing unneeded working capital is not a contraction of the business. Rev. Rul. 60–322, 1960–2 C.B. 118.)

What happens if the company uses the proceeds from the curtailed activity, and later decides to make a distribution to its shareholders? This endangers partial liquidation treatment, since the use of the proceeds may offset the contraction. The result then is the subsequent distribution reflects disbursement of earnings rather than funds from a corporate cutback. *E.g.*, Rev. Rul. 67–299, 1967–2 C.B. 138. *But see* Rev. Rul. 71–250, 1971–1 C.B. 112 (a corporation may temporarily invest the funds in order to preserve them while it figures out what it wants to do). In this regard, note that abandoning plans for expansion does not equal a contraction. Treas. Reg. 1.346–1(a). Further limiting delay, Section 305(e)(1)(B) requires that the distribution occur within the same tax year as the company adopts the plan for a partial liquidation, or the year after. Note also it is unclear whether the corporation may distribute only part of the proceeds of the cutback and retain some for other uses. *Compare Gordon v. Commissioner*, 424 F.2d 378 (2d Cir.1970), *cert. denied*, 400 U.S. 848 (1970), *with* Rev.Rul. 74–296, reprinted above.

By its terms, Sections 302(b)(4) provides sale treatment for redemptions of stock. Nevertheless, distributions to shareholders pursuant to a cutback meeting the standard for a partial liquidation may qualify for sale treatment even though the stockholders do not surrender any of their shares in exchange. The Service deems the stockholders receiving the property to have surrendered shares having a fair market value equal to the distribution. Rev. Rul. 90–13, 1990–1 C.B. 65; Rev. Rul. 77–245, 1977–2 C.B. 105. This constructive redemption approach also might thwart any efforts by the stockholders to set the number of shares they will surrender in a pro-rata redemption with an eye toward how much basis they wish to offset.

4. Section 302(b)(4) does not apply for shareholders who themselves are corporations. I.R.C. § 302(b)(4)(A). Given the dividends received deduction of Section 243, this should not bother them too much. *But see* I.R.C. § 1059(e)(1)(A) (a corporation owning shares must treat the amount it receives in a partial liquidation as an extraordinary dividend, meaning it will reduce the basis of its remaining stock by the non-taxed portion of the amount received, and recognize gain to the extent the non-taxed amount is in excess of the basis of the remaining stock).

CHAPTER VII

PURCHASE AND SALE OF A BUSINESS

The purchase and sale of a business—or, more specifically, the purchase and sale of a business conducted in the corporate form—provides a fitting climax to a course on business planning. It is potentially the most challenging and complex transaction a business attorney will encounter. Indeed, he or she may feel like a circus conductor trying to get a number of elephants—represented, in the attorney's case, by the corporate, securities, tax, antitrust, labor, financial and other issues potentially raised in a corporate acquisition—to all form a pyramid upon a small ball. This chapter seeks to walk through the transaction in chronological sequence; dealing first with preliminary events (Section A), then with structuring the acquisition (Section B) and finally with follow-up transactions (Section C).

SECTION A. PRELIMINARY CONSIDERATIONS

1. TO SELL OR NOT TO SELL

Paramount Communications, Inc. v. Time Incorporated

571 A.2d 1140 (Del.1989).

■ HORSEY, JUSTICE:

Paramount Communications, Inc. ("Paramount") and two other groups of plaintiffs * * *, shareholders of Time Incorporated ("Time"), a Delaware corporation, separately filed suits in the Delaware Court of Chancery seeking a preliminary injunction to halt Time's tender offer for 51% of Warner Communication, Inc.'s ("Warner") outstanding shares at $70 cash per share. The court below * * * denied plaintiff's motion. * * *

On the same day, plaintiffs filed in this Court an interlocutory appeal, which we accepted on an expedited basis. * * * This is the written opinion articulating the reasons for our July 24 bench ruling [affirming the lower court decision]. * * *

The principal ground for reversal, asserted by all plaintiffs, is that Paramount's June 7, 1989 uninvited all-cash, all-shares, "fully negotiable" (though conditional) tender offer for Time triggered duties under *Unocal Corp. v. Mesa Petroleum Co.*, Del.Supr., 493 A.2d 946 (1985), and that Time's board of directors, in responding to Paramount's offer, breached those duties. * * *

Shareholder Plaintiffs also assert a claim based on *Revlon v. MacAndres & Forbes Holdings, Inc.*, Del.Supr., 506 A.2d 173 (1986). They argue that the original Time–Warner merger agreement of March 4, 1989 resulted in a change of control which effectively put Time up for sale, thereby triggering *Revlon* duties. Those plaintiffs argue that Time's board breached its *Revlon* duties by failing, in the face of the change of control, to maximize shareholder value in the immediate term.

* * *

I

* * * Time's traditional business is publication of magazines and books; however, Time also provides pay television programming through its Home Box Office, Inc. and Cinemax subsidiaries. In addition, Time owns and operates cable television franchises through its subsidiary, American Television and Communication Corporation. During the relevant time period, Time's board consisted of sixteen directors. Twelve of the directors were "outside," nonemployee directors. Four of the directors were also officers of the company. * * *

As early as 1983 and 1984, Time's executive board began considering expanding Time's operations into the entertainment industry. In 1987, Time established a special committee of executives to consider and propose corporate strategies for the 1990s. The consensus of the committee was that Time should move ahead in the area of ownership and creation of video programming. This expansion, as the Chancellor noted, was predicated upon two considerations: first, Time's desire to have greater control, in terms of quality and price, over the film products delivered by way of its cable network and franchise; and second, Time's concern over the increasing globalization of the world economy. Some of Time's outside directors * * * had opposed this move as a threat to the editorial integrity and journalistic focus of Time.[4] Despite this concern, the board recognized that a vertically integrated video enterprise to complement Time's existing HBO and cable networks would better enable it to compete on a global basis.

* * *

On July 21, 1988, Time's board met, with all outside directors present. The meeting's purpose was to consider Time's expansion into the entertainment industry on a global scale. Management presented the board with a profile of various entertainment companies in addition to Warner, including Disney, 20th Century Fox, Universal, and Paramount. Without any definitive decision on choice of a company, the board approved in principle a strategic plan for Time's expansion. The board gave management the

4. The primary concern of Time's outside directors was the preservation of the "Time Culture." They believed that Time had become recognized in this country as an institution built upon a foundation of journalistic integrity. Time's management made a studious effort to refrain from involvement in Time's editorial policy. Several of Time's outside directors feared that a merger with an entertainment company would divert Time's focus from news journalism and threaten the Time Culture.

"go-ahead" to continue discussions with Warner concerning the possibility of a merger. * * *

The board's consensus was that a merger of Time and Warner was feasible, but only if Time controlled the board of the resulting corporation and thereby preserved a management committed to Time's journalistic integrity. To accomplish this goal, the board stressed the importance of carefully defining in advance the corporate governance provisions that would control the resulting entity. Some board members expressed concern over whether such a business combination would place Time "*in play.*" The board discussed the wisdom of adopting further defensive measures to lessen such a possibility.[5]

Of a wide range of companies considered by Time's board as possible merger candidates, * * *, the board, in July 1988, concluded that Warner was the superior candidate for a consolidation. Warner stood out on a number of counts. Warner had just acquired Lorimar and its film studios. Time–Warner could make movies and television shows for use on HBO. Warner had an international distribution system, which Time could use to sell films, videos, books and magazines. Warner was a giant in the music and recording business, an area into which Time wanted to expand. None of the other companies considered had the musical clout of Warner. Time and Warner's cable systems were compatible and could be easily integrated; none of the other companies considered presented such a compatible cable partner. Together, Time and Warner would control half of New York City's cable system; Warner had cable systems in Brooklyn and Queens; and Time controlled cable systems in Manhattan and Queens. Warner's publishing company would integrate well with Time's established published company. Time sells hardcover books and magazines, and Warner sells softcover books and comics. Time–Warner could sell all of these publications and Warner's videos by using Time's direct mailing network and Warner's international distribution system. Time's network could be used to promote and merchandise Warner's movies.

* * *

[After earlier negotiations reached an impasse,] Warner and Time resumed negotiations in January 1989. * * * Time insider directors Levin and Nicholas met with Warner's financial advisors to decide upon a stock exchange ratio [in other words, how many shares in the combined business the former Warner stockholders would receive]. Time's board had recognized the potential need to pay a premium in the stock ratio in exchange for dictating the governing arrangement of the new Time–Warner. * * * The parties ultimately agreed upon an exchange rate * * * [under which] Warner stockholders would have owned approximately 62% of the common stock of Time–Warner.

5. Time had in place a panoply of defensive devices, including a staggered board, a "poison pill" preferred stock rights plan triggered by an acquisition of 15% of the company, a fifty-day notice period for shareholder motions, and restrictions on shareholders' ability to call a meeting or act by consent.

On March 3, 1989, Time's board, with all but one director in attendance, met and unanimously approved the stock-for-stock merger with Warner.

* * *

At its March 3, 1989 meeting, Time's board adopted several defensive tactics. Time entered an automatic share exchange agreement with Warner. Time would receive 17,292,747 shares of Warner's outstanding common stock (9.4%) and Warner would receive 7,080,016 shares of Time's outstanding common stock (11.1%). Either party could trigger the exchange. Time sought out and paid for "confidence" letters from various banks with which it did business. In these letters, the banks promised not to finance any third-party attempt to acquire Time. Time argues these agreements served only to preserve the confidential relationship between itself and the banks. The Chancellor found these agreements to be inconsequential and futile attempts to "dry up" money for a hostile takeover. Time also agreed to a "no-shop" clause, preventing Time from considering any other consolidation proposal, thus relinquishing its power to consider other proposals, regardless of their merits. Time did so at Warner's insistence. Warner did not want to be left "on the auction block" for an unfriendly suitor, if Time were to withdraw from the deal.

* * *

The board scheduled the stockholder vote [to approve the merger] for June 23 * * *.

On June 7, 1989, these wishful assumptions were shattered by Paramount's surprising announcement of its all-cash offer to purchase all outstanding shares of Time for $175 per share. The following day, June 8, the trading price of Time's stock rose from $126 to $170 per share. Paramount's offer was said to be "fully negotiable."

Time found Paramount's "fully negotiable" offer to be in fact subject to at least three conditions. First, Time had to terminate its merger agreement and stock exchange agreement with Warner, and remove certain other of its defensive devices, including the redemption of Time's shareholder rights. Second, Paramount had to obtain the required cable franchise transfers from Time in a fashion acceptable to Paramount in its sole discretion. Finally, the offer depended upon a judicial determination that section 203 of the General Corporate Law of Delaware (The Delaware Anti–Takeover Statute) was inapplicable to any Time–Paramount merger. While Paramount's board had been privately advised that it could take months, perhaps over a year, to forge and consummate the deal, Paramount's board publicly proclaimed its ability to close the offer by July 5, 1989. Paramount executives later conceded that none of its directors believed that July 5th was a realistic date to close the transaction. On June 8, 1989, Time formally responded to Paramount's offer. Time's chairman and CEO, J. Richard Munro, sent an aggressively worded letter to Paramount's CEO, Martin Davis. Munro's letter attacked Davis' personal integrity and called Paramount's offer "smoke and mirrors." Time's nonmanagement directors were not shown the letter before it was sent. However, at a board meeting that same day, all members endorsed management's response as well as the letter's content. Over the following eight days, Time's board met three times to discuss Paramount's $175 offer. The board viewed Paramount's offer as inadequate and concluded that its proposed merger with Warner was the better course of action. Therefore, the board declined to open any negotiations with Paramount and held steady its course toward a merger with Warner.

In June, Time's board of directors met several times. During the course of their June meetings, Time's outside directors met frequently without management officers or directors being present. At the request of the outside directors, corporate counsel was present during the board meetings and, from time to time, the management directors were asked to leave the board sessions. During the course of these meetings, Time's financial advisors informed the board that, on an auction basis, Time's per share value was materially higher than Warner's [sic] $175 per share offer. After this advice, the board concluded that Paramount's $175 offer was inadequate.

At these June meetings, certain Time directors expressed their concern that Time stockholders would not comprehend the long-term benefits of the Warner merger. Large quantities of Time shares were held by institutional investors. The board feared that even though there appeared to be wide support for the Warner transaction, Paramount's cash premium would be a tempting prospect to these investors. * * *

The following day, June 16, Time's board met to take up Paramount's offer. The board's prevailing belief was that Paramount's bid posed a threat to Time's control of its own destiny and retention of the "Time Culture." Even after Time's financial advisors made another presentation of Paramount and its business attributes, Time's board maintained its position that a combination with Warner offered greater potential for Time. * * * Time's advisors suggested various options, including defensive measures. The board considered and rejected the idea of purchasing Paramount in a "Pac Man" defense.[10] The board considered other defenses, including a recapitalization, the acquisition of another company, and a material change in the present capitalization structure or dividend policy. * * * Finally, Time's board formally rejected Paramount's offer.[11]

At the same meeting, Time's board decided to recast its consolidation with Warner into an outright cash and securities acquisition of Warner by Time; and Time so informed Warner. Time accordingly restructured its proposal to acquire Warner as follows: Time would make an immediate all-cash offer for 51% of Warner's outstanding stock at $70 per share. The remaining 49% would be purchased at some later date for a mixture of cash

10. In a "Pac Man" defense, Time would launch a tender offer for the stock of Paramount, thus consuming its rival.

11. Meanwhile, Time had already begun erecting impediments to Paramount's offer. Time encouraged local cable franchises to sue Paramount to prevent it from easily obtaining the franchises.

and securities worth $70 per share. To provide the funds required for its outright acquisition of Warner, Time would assume 7–10 billion dollars worth of debt.

* * *

On June 23, 1989, Paramount raised its all-cash offer to buy Time's outstanding stock to $200 per share. Paramount still professed that all aspects of the offer were negotiable. Time's board met on June 26, 1989 and formally rejected Paramount's $200 per share second offer. The board reiterated its belief that, despite the $25 increase, the offer was still inadequate. The Time board maintained that the Warner transaction offered a greater long-term value for the stockholders and, unlike Paramount's offer, did not pose a threat to Time's survival and its "culture." Paramount then filed this action in the Court of Chancery.

II

The Shareholder Plaintiffs first assert a *Revlon* claim. They contend that the March 4 Time–Warner agreement effectively put Time up for sale, triggering *Revlon* duties, requiring Time's board to enhance short-term shareholder value and to treat all other interested acquirers on an equal basis. The Shareholder Plaintiffs base this argument on two facts: (i) the ultimate Time–Warner exchange ratio * * * resulting in Warner shareholders' receipt of 62% of the combined company; and (ii) the subjective intent of Time's directors as evidenced in their statements that the market might perceive the Time–Warner merger as putting Time up "for sale" and their adoption of various defensive measures.

* * *

A.

We first take up plaintiffs' principal *Revlon* argument, summarized above. In rejecting this argument, the Chancellor found the original Time–Warner merger agreement not to constitute a "change of control" and concluded that the transaction did not trigger *Revlon* duties. The Chancellor's conclusion is premised on a finding that "(b)efore the merger agreement was signed, control of the corporation existed in a fluid aggregation of unaffiliated shareholders representing a voting majority—in other words, in the market." The Chancellor's findings of fact are supported by the record and his conclusion is correct as a matter of law. However, we premise our rejection of plaintiffs' *Revlon* claim on different grounds, namely, the absence of any substantial evidence to conclude that Time's board, in negotiating with Warner, made the dissolution or break-up of the corporate entity inevitable, as was the case in *Revlon*.

Under Delaware law there are, generally speaking and without excluding other possibilities, two circumstances which may implicate *Revlon* duties. The first, and clearer one, is when a corporation initiates an active bidding process seeking to sell itself or to effect a business reorganization involving a clear break-up of the company. See, e.g., *Mills Acquisition Co. v.*

Macmillan, Inc., Del.Supr., 559 A.2d 1261 (1988). However, *Revlon* duties may also be triggered where, in response to a bidder's offer, a target abandons its long-term strategy and seeks an alternative transaction involving the break-up of the company. Thus, in *Revlon,* when the board responded to Pantry Pride's offer by contemplating a "bust-up" sale of assets in a leveraged acquisition, we imposed upon the board a duty to maximize immediate shareholder value and an obligation to auction the company fairly. If, however, the board's reaction to a hostile tender offer is found to constitute only a defensive response and not an abandonment of the corporation's continued existence, *Revlon* duties are not triggered, though *Unocal* duties attached.[14] * * *

The plaintiffs insist that even though the original Time–Warner agreement may not have worked "an objective change of control," the transaction made a "sale" of Time inevitable. Plaintiffs rely on the subjective intent of Time's board of directors and principally upon certain board members' expression of concern that the Warner transaction might be viewed as effectively putting Time up for sale. * * *

We agree with the Chancellor that such evidence is entirely insufficient to invoke *Revlon* duties; and we decline to extend *Revlon's* application to corporate transactions simply because they might be construed as putting a corporation either "in play" or "up for sale." * * *

Finally, we do not find in Time's recasting of its merger agreement with Warner from a share exchange to a share purchase a basis to conclude that Time had either abandoned its strategic plan or made a sale of Time inevitable. * * * The legal consequence is that *Unocal* alone applies to determine whether the business judgment rule attached to the revised agreement. * * *

B.

We turn now to plaintiff's *Unocal* claim. * * *

In *Unocal,* we held that before the business judgment rule is applied to a board's adoption of a defensive measure, the burden will lie with the board to prove (a) reasonable grounds for believing that a danger to corporate policy and effectiveness existed; and (b) that the defensive measure adopted was reasonable in relation to the threat posed. * * *

Unocal involved a two-tier, highly coercive tender offer. In such a case, the threat is obvious: shareholders may be compelled to tender to avoid being treated adversely in the second stage of the transaction. * * * In subsequent cases, the court of Chancery has suggested that an all-cash, all-shares offer, falling within a range of values that a shareholder might

14. * * *
Since *Revlon,* we have stated that differing treatment of various bidders is not actionable when such action reasonably relates to achieving the best price available for the stockholders. *Macmillan,* 559 A.2d at 1286–87.

reasonably prefer, cannot constitute a legally recognized "threat" to shareholder interests sufficient to withstand a *Unocal* analysis.

* * *

Thus, Paramount would have us hold that only if the value of Paramount's offer were determined to be clearly inferior to the value created by management's plan to merge with Warner could the offer be viewed—objectively—as a threat.

* * * We disapprove of such a narrow and rigid construction of *Unocal,* for the reasons which follow.

Plaintiffs' position represents a fundamental misconception of our standard of review under *Unocal* principally because it would involve the court in substituting its judgment as to what is a "better" deal for that of a corporation's board of directors. To the extent that the Court of Chancery has recently done so in certain of its opinions, we hereby reject such approach as not in keeping with a proper *Unocal* analysis. * * *

Thus, we have said that directors may consider, when evaluating the threat posed by a takeover bid, the "inadequacy of the price offered, nature and timing of the offer, questions of illegality, the impact on 'constituencies' other than shareholders ... the risk of nonconsummation, and the quality of securities being offered in the exchange." 493 A.2d at 955. The open-ended analysis mandated by *Unocal* is not intended to lead to a simple mathematical exercise: that is, of comparing the discounted value of Time-Warner's expected trading price at some future date with Paramount's offer and determining which is the higher. Indeed, in our view, precepts underlying the business judgment rule militate against a court's engaging in the process of attempting to appraise and evaluate the relative merits of a long-term versus a short-term investment goal for shareholders. * * *

In this case, the Time board reasonably determined that inadequate value was not the only legally cognizable threat that Paramount's all-cash, all shares offer could present. Time's board concluded that Paramount's eleventh hour offer posed other threats. One concern was that Time shareholders might elect to tender into Paramount's cash offer in ignorance or a mistaken belief of the strategic benefit which a business combination with Warner might produce. Moreover, Time viewed the conditions attached to Paramount's offer as introducing a degree of uncertainty that skewed a comparative analysis. Further, the timing of Paramount's offer to follow issuance of Time's proxy notice was viewed as arguably designed to upset, if not confuse, the Time stockholders' vote. Given this record evidence, we cannot conclude that the Time board's decision of June 6 that Paramount's offer posed a threat to corporate policy and effectiveness was lacking in good faith or dominated by motives of either entrenchment or self-interest.

* * *

Paramount argues that, assuming its tender offer posed a threat, Time's response was unreasonable in precluding Time's shareholders from accepting the tender offer or receiving a control premium in the immediately foreseeable future. * * *

Here, on the record facts, the Chancellor found that Time's responsive action to Paramount's tender offer was not aimed at "cramming down" on its shareholders a management-sponsored alternative, but rather had as its goal the carrying forward of a pre-existing transaction in an altered form.[19] Thus, the response was reasonably related to the threat. The Chancellor noted that the revised agreement and its accompanying safety devices did not preclude Paramount from making an offer for the combined Time–Warner company or from changing the conditions of its offer so as not to make the offer dependent upon the nullification of the Time–Warner agreement. Thus, the response was proportionate. We affirm the Chancellor's rulings as clearly supported by the record. Finally, we note that although Time was required, as a result of Paramount's hostile offer, to incur a heavy debt to finance its acquisition of Warner, that fact alone does not render the board's decision unreasonable so long as the directors could reasonably perceive the debt load not to be so injurious to the corporation as to jeopardize its well being.

C.

Conclusion

Applying the test for grant or denial of preliminary injunctive relief, we find plaintiffs failed to establish a reasonable likelihood of ultimate success on the merits. Therefore, we affirm.

NOTES

1. In considering whether or not to sell a business, it is useful to break down the discussion by asking in what role does the decision-maker act. Most litigation, like *Time*, involves individuals acting in a representative capacity—in other words, decisions by the board of directors of the target company. Attorneys, however, can find themselves asked to advise persons who act in a proprietary capacity—in other words, sole proprietors, partners, or significant shareholders of the target firm, who must decide whether to sell their own interest.

Generally, there are few legal restrictions on the decision of whether or not to sell by those acting in a proprietary capacity. *But see Brown v. Halbert,* reprinted later in this chapter. The issue then becomes a mix of economics and emotions. The economic analysis involves a comparison of the price against the discounted future profits of the business (as well as weighing the prospects of obtaining more money from another buyer). Of

19. The Chancellor cited *Shamrock Holdings, Inc. v. Polaroid Corp.,* Del.Ch., 559 A.2d 257 (1989), as a closely analogous case. In that case, the Court of Chancery upheld, in the face of a takeover bid, the establishment of an employee stock ownership plan that had a significant antitakeover effect. The Court of Chancery upheld the board's action largely because the ESOP had been adopted *prior* to any contest for control and was reasonably determined to increase productivity and enhance profits. The ESOP did not appear to be primarily a device to affect or secure corporate control.

course, the comparison is hardly that simple. The future profits of the business are an unknown, and often equally unknown is whether a particular price represents the best the seller can do from this or another buyer. In addition, the buyer may not offer to pay the purchase price immediately in cash, but rather might propose giving its stock or debt. Receipt of such consideration, if not immediately marketable, requires comparing two streams of future income. The seller also needs to consider not just the gross price, but what its after-tax receipt will be. Moreover, when the business employs the seller, he or she might consider whether he or she can obtain another job at equivalent salary and benefits.

Many times, of greater importance than the economics of the sale (at least when dealing with a closely held business) are emotional or intangible factors. Owner-operators of a business, regardless of whether they plan to go to work for someone else (often the buyer), or to "start enjoying life" by living on the proceeds of the sale, will find they miss being the boss of their former business kingdom. Moreover, even when the dominant owner is at retirement age, he or she might feel an obligation to children or long time employees to keep the business in the family. (Recall the *Lamark Shipping Agency* case in Chapter VI. Unfortunately, such a goal of a dominant older shareholder frequently fails to take into account the real desires of the next generation in the family.) On the other hand, many times the impetus for sale comes from similar factors: The dominant owner reaches an age when he or she can no longer run the business and he or she lacks a successor interested in taking over; or the ownership is divided into several factions which cannot get along.

2. When the board of directors is considering the sale of the company, the analysis is different. While the attorney may encourage the proprietor to consider emotional and intangible factors, as well as the personal employment provided by the business, the law forbids the directors to base their decision upon any financial or emotional attachments to their jobs. *E.g., Bennett v. Propp,* 41 Del.Ch. 14, 187 A.2d 405 (1962). (On the other hand, how can one explain the legitimacy with which the court in *Time* treats the insistence by Time's board on Time's management controlling a combined Time–Warner corporation?) Instead, the directors' obligation lies in maximizing the shareholders' welfare (which presumably means the stockholders' economic welfare). *E.g., Unocal Corp. v. Mesa Petroleum Co.,* 493 A.2d 946 (Del.1985) (albeit, also stating that directors can consider other constituencies of the corporation, such as creditors, customers and employees).

Yet, even in looking just to the economic interests of the shareholders, the directors' role is not the same as the proprietor's. The difference lies in the fact that the board faces two questions: the economic one, and a "jurisdiction" one; this being whether the directors or the stockholders should make the economic decision. Complicating things further, the law at first glance seems to suggest a different answer to the jurisdictional question depending upon the structure of the acquisition. If the acquisition occurs through a sale by the target corporation of its assets to the purchaser (throughout this chapter referred to as a "sale of assets transaction"), or through a statutory merger, then state corporations statutes typically require approval of the transaction by *both* the target's directors and its shareholders. See pp. 1010–1012 *infra.* Can the directors simply approve any merger or sale of all assets, regardless of what they think of its economic wisdom, on the ground the stockholders should have the opportunity to make the decision? See *Smith v. Van Gorkom,* 488 A.2d 858 (Del.1985) (holding such an action breaches the directors' duty of care). On the other hand, if the acquirer buys the target's outstanding shares directly from the target's stockholders (which will be referred to throughout this chapter as a "sale of stock transaction"), then state corporations statutes traditionally have provided no explicit role for the board. Nevertheless, as *Time* illustrates, various techniques exist whereby the board might seek to exercise an effective veto over the acquisition of the target even though a sale of stock transaction.

3. Precisely what tactics are available for the board to block a sale of stock transaction which it opposes? Time, Inc. either considered or used a variety of the most common takeover defenses. Prior to the events described in the opinion, Time had article and bylaw provisions in place giving it a staggered board of directors, long advance notice provisions for shareholder motions, and limits on the powers of stockholders to call a meeting or to act by consent. (See footnote 5 of the court's opinion.) What is the specific purpose of these? Staggering the directors' terms in office means it takes several elections before a purchaser of a majority of the corporation's stock can replace all (or even most) of its directors. Of course, this will not do much good if the shareholders have the power to remove directors with or without cause. *But see* Del. Gen. Corp. Law § 141(k) (allowing removal only with cause when directors have staggered terms, unless the certificate of incorporation provides to the contrary). Perhaps more important, even if the buyer cannot remove the incumbent directors, the directors may feel pressure to resign rather than oppose a majority shareholder. Also, the corporations statutes of some states (such as California) do not authorize a company to have staggered terms. *See* Cal. Corp. Code § 301(a). *But see* Cal. Corp. Code § 301.5 (creating an exception for companies with listed shares). Presumably, Time's shareholder action limitations seek to complement the staggered terms provisions by crimping an acquirer's ability to put its plans into play without working through the board. Yet, such limitations cannot prevent all shareholder action, and some doubt may exist as to their legality under state corporations statutes which give the stockholders the right to act through unanimous consent and the like. *See Datapoint Corp. v. Plaza Securities Co.,* 496 A.2d 1031 (Del.1985).

Other anti-takeover article provisions (apparently not used by Time) include supermajority requirements for a merger with a related person (typically defined as someone holding over a certain percentage of the company's outstanding stock). (Chapter IV discussed the legality of supermajority provisions.) This is sometimes coupled with a so-called fair price amendment. The fair price amendment waives the supermajority requirement if shares cashed out in the merger receive a price at least equal to a formula specified in the provision. (Needless to say, the price formula tends to be quite generous, often looking to the highest price the buyer paid for shares, or at which the stock traded over several prior years, or looking to earnings or premium computations which can even go higher.) Notice, these supermajority and fair price provisions only come into play if the buyer seeks to acquire some shares by purchases directly from their owners, and then to complete its acquisition of the target through a statutory merger. A significant variation gives the non-selling shareholders the right to demand the corporation redeem their stock under a fair price formula following the acquisition of a certain percentage of shares, even if the buyer does not propose a merger. (Recall, however, Chapter IV indicated there might be statutory limits on giving common shareholders the option to redeem their shares. See page 451 *supra.*) Why exactly do these provisions deter takeovers? Consider the incentive a "fair price" provision can create for shareholders faced with an offer to buy their shares, if the price formula is very generous. Yet other anti-takeover article provisions go back to the idea of altering the voting rights of shares along the lines discussed in Chapter IV. For example, a corporation might issue a class of stock having a greater number of votes per share to parties unlikely to sell out to a hostile acquirer. One problem with this sort of approach for public companies is that amending the articles and issuing such supervoting stock can result in delisting the company's shares from the stock exchanges and a ban on quoting its stock through the NASDAQ system. *E.g.,* N.Y. Stock Exchange Listed Company Manual § 313.00. The same difficulty applies to article amendments limiting the right of stockholders to vote more than so many shares, or requiring new stockholders to undertake a waiting period after the purchase before they obtain voting rights.

Time, Inc. also had a "poison pill" preferred stock rights plan. What exactly is this? While there are a number of variations, in its original form this consists of a series of convertible preferred stock which the corporation issues to its common shareholders as a stock dividend. These preferred shares may or may not have voting or much dividend rights; since this is a stock-dividend on common there will not be any change in the common shareholders' relative rights regardless. What makes the shares a "poison pill" lies, in part, in their conversion rights, and specifically in the so-called flip-over provision. Under this provision, if an acquirer purchases more than a certain percentage of the target's stock and then merges with the target, the holders of the preferred can convert it into the *acquirer's* common stock at a highly favorable ratio (such as the equivalent of paying half the current market price for the acquirer's common). In addition, the preferred typically has one or two important redemption features. The board can redeem them at a modest price for a short period of time following the start of a takeover attempt. The preferred holder often has a redemption option (variously referred to as a "back end" or "flip in" provision) which triggers after an acquirer buys a certain percentage of stock. This serves as a poison pill by giving the holder the right to force the company to repurchase the preferred at a very generous price. (Alternatively, some flip-in provisions allow the preferred holders to buy more common stock in the target at a highly favorable price after the acquirer reaches a certain percentage.) The designation of the rights of the preferred, however, denies this flip-in option to any preferred shares purchased by the acquirer. Recognizing there is no necessity for the flip-over or flip-in rights to attach to preferred shares, many companies have simply distributed, as a dividend to their shareholders, warrants containing these features, or convertible debt securities with the same options.

Even a cursory examination of the poison pill plan raises a series of legal questions (putting aside, for now, the question common to all the defensive steps of whether the board has a legitimate reason for engaging in the activity). To begin with, will the plan require amending the articles to create a new class of stock (at least if the plan calls for using convertible preferred)? Perhaps not, if the articles give the board the power to set the specific rights of a series of shares at the time the corporation issues the stock. *Moran v. Household Intern., Inc.*, 500 A.2d 1346 (Del.1985). Turning to the flip-over provision, how can one company create an obligation for another corporation to sell stock at a favorable price? Notice the feature comes into play if there is a merger of the two firms, when, as discussed later in this chapter, the surviving entity becomes liable for the debts of the merging firms. (In fact, however, no buyer has yet put this issue to a direct legal test.) Looking at the flip-in provision, note it does not allow the acquirer to force redemption or exercise the favorable purchase rights of any poison pill shares it buys. Can a corporation discriminate between shareholders owning the same class of stock in this manner? *Compare Amalgamated Sugar Co. v. NL Industries, Inc.*, 644 F.Supp. 1229 (S.D.N.Y. 1986), *with Harvard Industries v. Tyson,* 1986–87 Fed. Sec. L. Rep. (CCH), ¶ 93,064 (E.D. Mich. 1986). *See also* N.Y. Bus. Corp. Law § 505(a)(2) (allowing such discrimination). As a last legal question, what are the tax impacts of issuing or exercising poison pill stock or warrants? See Rev. Rul. 90–11, 1990–1 C.B. 10 (issuance of rights did not constitute a distribution of stock or property).

What exactly does a poison pill plan accomplish? Keep in mind, the flip-over provision only comes into play if the acquirer seeks a follow-up merger (much like the usual fair price amendment). On the other hand, the flip-in provision can apply to make the takeover much more expensive even if the acquirer does not seek such a merger. Also, why do the plans often give the board the option to redeem the shares for a short period of time after the acquirer launches its bid? In fact, this redemption option is something of the Achilles' heel of a poison pill. Before purchasing enough stock to trigger the pill, determined bidders might engage in a proxy contest to elect directors sympathetic to redeeming the pill. Fearful that shareholders might succumb to the promise of a premium price tender offer if they vote the right way, some corporations have adopted so-called "dead hand" or "no-hand" poison pills. Such plans limit the ability of newly elected directors to redeem the pill. These limitations, however, have met a cool reception from the courts. *E.g.*, *Quickturn Design Systems, Inc. v. Shapiro*, 721 A.2d 1281 (Del.1998). On the other hand, consider the utility of combining staggered board terms with the poison pill. If the chink in the poison pill is the prospect for a pre-tender proxy contest, and the chink in the staggered terms defense is the unwillingness of directors to remain in place after an acquirer has purchased controlling shares, notice how the combination works to cover both weak spots.

The defenses outlined thus far are typically in place (as they were for Time) prior to any hostile offer. If the target has not adopted such plans, or if its defenses appear inadequate (which the existence of a hostile bid might indicate to the extent these tactics are designed to deter any attempt at an unfriendly takeover), then other defenses exist which the target can adopt while under siege. Time's board considered a number of such tactics. One strategy is to sue the buyer. Perhaps the buyer's tender offer solicitations contain misrepresentations or omissions which make the solicitation misleading. *See, e.g., Gulf & Western Industries, Inc. v. Great Atlantic & Pacific Tea Co.,* 476 F.2d 687 (2d Cir.1973). This, however, may only produce delay until the bidder corrects the misstatement or omission. *See, e.g., Dan River, Inc. v. Icahn,* 701 F.2d 278 (4th Cir.1983). A suit based upon antitrust or regulatory barriers might provide, if successful, a more permanent solution. *See, e.g., Gulf & Western Industries, Inc. v. Great Atlantic & Pacific Tea Co., supra.* Notice how Time stirred up a number of local cable franchisees to sue Paramount. (See footnote 11 of the court's opinion.) A variation of this approach is to launch a public relations campaign in the hope that opposition by employees, customers, members of the business community and the community generally might cause the buyer to reconsider. (Time made a futile attempt to persuade banks not to loan a buyer any money for a takeover.)

Time's board also considered a "Pac Man" defense—in other words, attempting to buy a majority of the acquiring corporation's shares before the acquirer can purchase a majority of the target. If both corporations end up owning a majority of each others' shares, who controls? See, *e.g.,* Cal. Corp. Code § 703(b); Del. Gen. Corp. Law § 160(c); N.Y. Bus. Corp. Law § 612(b); M.B.C.A. § 7.21(b) (all apparently denying the shares held by both corporations the right to vote in this situation).

Time's board also considered a recapitalization. Recall, Chapter VI explored recapitalizations. How can a recapitalization serve as a takeover defense? It can do so in two ways, which are part of two broader sets of anti-takeover strategies. The "recapitalization" considered by Time's board may have entailed the corporation's repurchase of a substantial amount of the company's outstanding common stock. This is one of a constellation of techniques seeking to use transactions in the target company's shares to prevent a takeover. Essentially, the company's repurchase of its shares (the directors hope) will create competition for the hostile buyer and raise the price of the target's stock. Of course, while the repurchase may raise the price per share paid by the hostile bidder, there are less shares left for it to buy. (This assumes management or its allies do not hold a large block of stock which could become the majority after a corporate repurchase.) For this reason, it might appear better to find a friendly outside buyer for the target's outstanding shares. The board may encourage another firm to enter the bidding for the corporation. Such a company is often referred to as a "white knight." Yet, this just means selling the target to a different buyer; what advantage can this provide? Perhaps better yet might be to find a purchaser who will buy enough to stop the hostile bidder, but not enough to take control (presumably because managers or other non-selling stockholders own the balance). Such a party is often referred to as a "white squire". Could an Employee Stock Ownership Plan (an ESOP) set up by the target for the benefit of its employees—and with friendly individuals acting as trustees—play such a role? See *Donovan v. Bierwirth,* 680 F.2d 263 (2d Cir.1982), *cert. denied,* 459 U.S. 1069 (court held trustees breached their fiduciary duty under ERISA by their actions siding with management during a tender offer.) (Could one avoid the trustee fiduciary duty problem by having the trustees vote the shares in the plan which are not yet allotted to specific employees (which normally means the vast majority of shares in the plan) in the same percentage as the employees—who presumably oppose a takeover—vote under their statutory right the allotted shares (so-called "mirrored voting")? *Compare Shamrock Holdings, Inc. v. Polaroid Corp.*, 559 A.2d 257 (Del.Ch.1989), *with NCR Corp. v. AT & T*, 761 F.Supp. 475 (S.D.Ohio 1991).) Still another bidder could be a corporation organized by management (often with outside investors and with considerable borrowed money) to buy the shares. This is often referred to as a management buyout or MBO. Also, because of the usually large use of borrowed money, it is one type of leveraged buyout, or LBO. An MBO—regardless of whether management undertakes it in response to a hostile offer or without such provocation—creates a conflict of interest situation in which actions of the target's board to favor the MBO may be subject to judicial review for fairness (at least in the absence of disinterested director or shareholder approval). *See, e.g., Mills Acquisition Co. v. Macmillan, Inc.*, 559 A.2d 1261 (Del.1989). *See also* Cal.Corp.Code § 1203 (requiring an outside fairness opinion of an MBO).

Chapter VI explored the legal issues raised by a corporation repurchasing its own shares. Particularly relevant for present purposes is the question of whether the corporation can selectively purchase only some stockholders' shares. For example, if the company repurchases shares to provide competition for the hostile bidder and raise the price, it presumably would not wish to buy from the hostile buyer. Can the target discriminate in this manner? *Compare Unocal Corp. v. Mesa Petroleum Co.,* 493 A.2d 946 (Del.1985), *with* Sec. Exch. Act Rule 13e–4(f)(8). The converse strategy may be to buy just the prospective acquirer's shares. Since this essentially means paying off the buyer to go away, it is often referred to as "greenmail." The *Kaplan* opinion in Chapter VI gives the Delaware court's view of the acceptability of these payments. Some state corporation statutes can require such payments to receive shareholder approval. N.Y. Bus. Corp. Law § 513(e).

The opposite approach to buying the target's shares is for the target to issue more. The notion is to keep supplying more stock which the hostile bidder will need to buy. The result, however, can be to lower the price of the target's shares and make the bidder's offer look all the more attractive.

Again, issuing the new shares to a friendly party—a white knight, a white squire or an ESOP—might appear to hold more promise.

The other effect of a recapitalization stems from the question of how the target is going to pay to repurchase its stock. Perhaps it possesses a large amount of cash on hand. Otherwise, it might borrow. Consider the effect of either of these two actions on the desirability of the target as a takeover candidate. After all, the buyer may have planned to use the target's cash to help finance the purchase, and a debt laden company might not seem such a good buy—especially if the acquirer planned to borrow heavily itself to make the purchase. If this is the goal of the recapitalization, then the directors could have the company repurchase shares or they could just declare an extraordinarily large dividend. Here too, the recapitalization is simply one of a constellation of transactions involving the target, whose unifying objective is to make the underlying company—as opposed to its management structure or outstanding shares—less attractive to a buyer. Such tactics often go under the rubric of scorched earth; albeit, in some cases, the transaction might involve a profitable restructuring, the untapped opportunity for which being what tempted the prospective buyer. As another example of this sort of tactic, the target could sell a line of business it suspects the buyer is really after (a "crown jewel"). In Time's case, the corporation pushed through the purchase of Warner (a defensive acquisition). Examine why this made Time unattractive as a takeover candidate for Paramount.

4. Beyond the question of tactics, there is the more important subject of strategy: What exactly is it the directors of a company faced with an uninvited buyer should seek to accomplish, and how do these defenses fit into achieving such goals? Some boards of directors, and even their attorneys, may be tempted to view these takeover defenses as simply an arsenal of weaponry to be deployed against any acquisition or acquirer the board does not like. Note, however, the general standard set out in *Time* under which the Delaware courts judge the legality of the board's action: The directors must prove they possessed reasonable grounds for believing a threat to corporate policy and effectiveness existed and the defensive measure used was reasonable in relation to the threat posed. (If the directors, however, decide to sell the company, then the more narrow *Revlon* test, of getting the most money for the stockholders from the sale, can apply. As to precisely what constitutes a sale triggering *Revlon*, compare the discussion of this issue in *Time* with another decision involving Paramount: *Paramount Communications Inc. v. QVC Network Inc.*, 637 A.2d 34 (Del.1994) (sale of a majority interest to a single person or cohesive group triggers *Revlon*).) Other jurisdictions have been more or less rigorous than Delaware in the degree to which they demand the board (rather than an objecting stockholder) bear the burden of proof on the issue of whether a legitimate purpose existed for the defensive action, but all agree the directors must have some rational business purpose for the action, other than just maintaining themselves in power. *Compare Heckmann v. Ahmanson,* 168 Cal.App.3d 119, 214 Cal.Rptr. 177 (1985), *with Treadway Companies, Inc. v. Care Corp.,* 638 F.2d 357 (2d Cir.1980). Moreover, in addition

to legal limits, there are practical concerns. How effective are these defenses in preventing any and all takeovers, no matter how determined the buyer, or how high a price the buyer is willing to pay? In fact, looking at the arsenal carefully suggests the efficacy of most of these strategies may extend only to achieving more specific objectives.

To find appropriate goals from both a legal and practical standpoint, it might be helpful to return one's focus to the basic jurisdictional question: Why should directors rather than just shareholders make the decision of whether to sell the company? One inherent advantage of the board lies in its ability to take coordinated action, in contrast to the atomistic response of individual stockholders. This potential advantage has both a defensive and an offensive aspect. Defensively, the directors might seek to prevent the buyer from forcing the stockholders to sell when the stockholders really did not want to sell. Here, one confronts the phenomenon of coercive two-tier or partial tender offers. Suppose the buyer offers to purchase a majority, but not all, of the target's outstanding shares at a price which is greater than the current trading market, but perhaps not sufficiently high to move the holders of a majority of the stock to wish to sell. (Keep in mind, the current trading level represents the price at which enough shareholders are willing to sell to satisfy the demand at this price. By definition, the stockholders who are not selling in the current market find the price less (perhaps substantially) than they think the stock is worth to retain.) What happens then if the buyer discloses it might seek to force those with shares it does not purchase in the first tier of its offer to sell in a second phase? (The techniques for forcing out minority stockholders will be explored toward the end of this chapter.) Moreover, implicit, if not explicit, in this disclosure might be that those forced to sell in the second phase will not receive as much as those who accept the initial offer (perhaps because the later sellers will receive a package of debt securities rather than cash). How will shareholders react to this offer? If a majority reject it, then it comes to nothing. But, lacking the practical ability to organize a concerted response, each stockholder must worry about how the other shareholders will react (knowing that the other stockholders are also worrying about his or her response). This could lead shareholders who do not find the price adequate, if all other things were equal, to nevertheless tender their shares in order to make sure they are not stuck in the non-tendering minority who will get a worse deal. At any event, this is the theory. Can some of the defenses outlined above help here? Consider why many defenses, such as supermajority requirements for mergers with a large shareholder, fair price amendments, or flip-over provisions in a poison pill, seek to limit the acquirer's ability to complete a follow on merger which might force out non-selling stockholders.

A more ambitious goal is to try to force the buyer to pay a higher price, even if the buyer presented a non-coercive offer for all the target's shares. The notion here is that while the buyer may offer a price the stockholders would willingly accept, the shareholders would not object to more, and using the board offensively to orchestrate a concerted stand can obtain a higher price than an uncoordinated acceptance or rejection of an offer by individual shareholders. In this light, ask again what is the utility of the feature in a poison pill plan which allows the board to redeem the rights if it agrees to the acquisition. Does this objective suggest a benign explanation for the board's seeking out an alternative buyer—be it a white knight, white squire, an MBO, or the target itself undertaking a recapitalization—which, after all, might serve to create a little price-raising competition on the buyer's side? (Some commentators have argued that efforts to jack up the price the buyer must ultimately pay for the target in this manner, while possibly raising the return for the shareholders of the individual target company, are counterproductive for the overall body of shareholders of all companies. By raising the price of takeovers, the argument goes, there will be less of them. *E.g.*, Easterbrook & Fischel, *The Proper Role of a Target's Management in Responding to a Tender Offer,* 94 Harv. L. Rev. 1161 (1981). While this is an interesting notion, as a practical matter the duty of directors under present law runs to the shareholders of their company and not to the entire universe of shareholders. *See, e.g., Revlon, Inc. v. MacAndrews & Forbes Holdings, Inc.,* 506 A.2d 173 (Del.1985). Moreover, without a ban on efforts to force bidders to pay more by all prospective targets, it would appear futile for any one board to remain passive in the hope of increasing takeovers economy wide.)

This brings one to the objective upheld by the court in *Time.* What exactly was it? Bluntly, taking things at face value, it appears the board decided Time (and, hence, its shareholders) would be economically better off through the combination with Warner than the acquisition by Paramount, and the shareholders would be too ignorant, mistaken or confused to figure this out. Putting aside any policy question and just focusing on the planning impact, how far can directors safely go in relying on this opinion? After all, a board might always take a patronizing (and self-interested) attitude that it knows what is in the company's best interest, that shareholders are often ignorant or confused, and that no uninvited outsider could possibly do a better job than it. Perhaps a more prudent reading might limit acting on the "board knows best" justification to occasions when the takeover would threaten a specific and apparently sensible strategic plan started before any threat of a hostile takeover. Moreover, keep in mind the practical limitations of the defenses outlined above as far as allowing the board to completely substitute its judgment for the shareholders'.

Finally, can the directors act for objectives other than the shareholders' economic benefit (and, of course, other than for the directors' own economic benefit)? What about opposing a takeover, based upon concerns regarding its impact upon the corporation's creditors, employees, customers or even the community in general? Judicial opinions have not always supplied consistent standards. *Compare Unocal Corp. v. Mesa Petroleum Co.,* 493 A.2d 946 (Del.1985), *with Revlon, Inc. v. MacAndrews & Forbes Holdings, Inc.,* 506 A.2d 173 (Del.1985). A number of states, however, have added provisions to their corporations statutes explicitly allowing directors to consider these other constituencies in responding to a takeover bid. *E.g.,* N.Y. Bus. Corp. Law § 717(b). At any event, in at least two instances it would appear directors can oppose an acquisition based upon concerns other than shareholder welfare. One would be if the buyer plans to loot the corporation—in other words, to misappropriate its assets. *See, e.g., Gerdes v. Reynolds,* 28 N.Y.S.2d 622 (Sup. Ct. 1941). (While looting would harm any non-selling shareholders, presumably the directors right, if not duty, to oppose the acquisition would extend even if the looter offered to buy every share and therefore only act to the detriment of the corporation's creditors. *Cf. Francis v. United Jersey Bank,* 87 N.J. 15, 432 A.2d 814 (1981).) A second instance occurs if the acquisition would be illegal under the antitrust laws. *See, e.g., Panter v. Marshall Field & Co.,* 646 F.2d 271 (7th Cir.1981), *cert. denied,* 454 U.S. 1092. When exactly does a business combination run afoul of the antitrust laws?

1992 Department of Justice and Federal Trade Commission Horizontal Merger Guidelines

0. Purpose, Underlying Policy Assumptions and Overview

These Guidelines outline the present enforcement policy of the Department of Justice and the Federal Trade Commission (the "Agency") concerning horizontal acquisitions and mergers ("mergers") subject to § 7 of the Clayton Act,[1] to § 1 of the Sherman Act,[2] or to § 5 of the FTC Act.[3] * * *

Although the Guidelines should improve the predictability of the Agency's merger enforcement policy, it is not possible to remove the exercise of judgment from the evaluation of mergers under the antitrust laws. Because the specific standards set forth in the Guidelines must be applied to a broad range of possible factual circumstances, mechanical application of those standards may provide misleading answers to the economic questions raised under the antitrust laws. * * *

0.1 Purpose and Underlying Policy Assumptions of the Guidelines

* * *

The unifying theme of the Guidelines is that mergers should not be permitted to create or enhance market power or to facilitate its exercise. Market power to a seller is the ability profitably to maintain prices above competitive levels for a significant period of time. In some circumstances, a sole seller (a "monopolist") of a product with no good substitutes can maintain a selling price that is above the level that would prevail if the market were competitive. Similarly, in some circumstances, where only a few firms account for most of the sales of a product, those firms can

1. 15 U.S.C. § 18 (1988).

2. 15 U.S.C. § 1 (1988). Mergers subject to § 1 are prohibited if they constitute a "contract, combination . . . , or conspiracy in restraint of trade."

3. 15 U.S.C. § 45 (1988). Mergers subject to § 5 are prohibited if they constitute an "unfair method of competition."

exercise market power, perhaps even approximating the performance of a monopolist, by either explicitly or implicitly coordinating their actions. Circumstances also may permit a single firm, not a monopolist, to exercise market power through unilateral or non-coordinated conduct—conduct the success of which does not rely on the concurrence of other firms in the market or on coordinated responses by those firms. In any case, the result of the exercise of market power is a transfer of wealth from buyers to sellers or a misallocation of resources.

* * *

0.2 Overview

The Guidelines describe the analytical process that the Agency will employ in determining whether to challenge a horizontal merger. First, the Agency assesses whether the merger would significantly increase concentration and result in a concentrated market, properly defined and measured. Second, the Agency assesses whether the merger, in light of market concentration and other factors that characterize the market, raises concern about potential adverse competitive effects. Third, the Agency assesses whether entry would be timely, likely and sufficient either to deter or to counteract the competitive effects of concern. Fourth, the Agency assesses any efficiency gains that reasonably cannot be achieved by the parties through other means. Finally the Agency assesses whether, but for the merger, either party to the transaction would be likely to fail, causing its assets to exit the market. The process of assessing market concentration, potential adverse competitive effects, entry, efficiency and failure is a tool that allows the Agency to answer the ultimate inquiry in merger analysis: whether the merger is likely to create or enhance market power or to facilitate its exercise.

1. Market Definition, Measurement and Concentration

1.0 Overview

* * *

A market is defined as a product or group of products and a geographic area in which it is produced or sold such that a hypothetical profit-maximizing firm, not subject to price regulation, that was the only present and future producer or seller of those products in that area likely would impose at least a "small but significant and nontransitory" increase in price, assuming the terms of sale of all other products are held constant. A relevant market is a group of products and a geographic area that is no bigger than necessary to satisfy this test. * * *

Absent price discrimination, a relevant market is described by a product or group of products and a geographic area. In determining whether a hypothetical monopolist would be in a position to exercise market power, it is necessary to evaluate the likely demand responses of consumers to a price increase. A price increase could be made unprofitable by consumers either switching to other products or switching to the same product produced by firms at other locations. The nature and magnitude of these two types of demand responses respectively determine the scope of the product market and the geographic market.

In contrast, where a hypothetical monopolist likely would discriminate in prices charged to different groups of buyers, distinguished, for example, by their uses or locations, the Agency may delineate different relevant markets corresponding to each such buyer group. Competition for sales to each such group may be affected differently by a particular merger and markets are delineated by evaluating the demand response of each such buyer group. A relevant market of this kind is described by a collection of products for sale to a given group of buyers.

Once defined, a relevant market must be measured in terms of its participants and concentration. Participants include firms currently producing or selling the market's products in the market's geographic area. In addition, participants may include other firms depending on their likely supply responses to a "small but significant nontransitory" price increase. A firm is viewed as a participant if, in response to a "small but significant and nontransitory" price increase, it likely would enter rapidly into production or sale of a market product in the market's area, without incurring significant sunk costs of entry and exit. Firms likely to make any of these supply responses are considered to be "uncommitted" entrants because their supply response would create new production or sale in the relevant market and because that production or sale could be quickly terminated without significant loss.[7] Uncommitted entrants are capable of making such quick and uncommitted supply responses that they likely influenced the market premerger, would influence it post-merger, and accordingly are considered as market participants at both times. This analysis of market definition and market measurement applies equally to foreign and domestic firms.

If the process of market definition and market measurement identifies one or more relevant markets in which the merging firms are both participants, then the merger is considered to be horizontal. * * *

1.1 Product Market Definition

The Agency will first define the relevant product market with respect to each of the products of each of the merging firms.

1.11 General Standards

Absent price discrimination, * * * the Agency will begin with each product (narrowly defined) produced or sold by each merging firm and ask what would happen if a hypothetical monopolist of that product imposed at

7. Probable supply responses that require the entrant to incur significant sunk costs of entry and exit are not part of market measurement, but are included in the analysis of the significance of entry. See Section 3. Entrants that must commit substantial sunk costs are regarded as "committed" entrants because those sunk costs make entry irreversible in the short term without foregoing that investment; thus the likelihood of their entry must be evaluated with regard to their long-term profitability.

least a "small but significant and nontransitory" increase in price, but the terms of sale of all other products remained constant. If, in response to the price increase, the reduction in sales of the product would be large enough that a hypothetical monopolist would not find it profitable to impose such an increase in price, then the Agency will add to the product group the product that is the next-best substitute for the merging firm's product.

In considering the likely reaction of buyers to a price increase, the Agency will take into account all relevant evidence, including, but not limited to, the following:

(1) evidence that buyers have shifted or have considered shifting purchases between products in response to relative changes in price or other competitive variables;

(2) evidence that sellers base business decisions on the prospect of buyer substitution between products in response to relative changes in price or other competitive variables;

(3) the influence of downstream competition faced by buyers in their output markets; and

(4) the timing and costs of switching products.

* * *

In attempting to determine objectively the effect of a "small but significant and nontransitory" increase in price, the Agency, in most contexts, will use a price increase of five percent lasting for the foreseeable future.

* * *

1.2 Geographic Market Definition

* * *

1.2.1 General Standards

* * *

The "smallest market" principle will be applied as it is in product market definition.

* * *

1.4 Calculating Market Shares

1.41 General Approach

The Agency normally will calculate market shares for all firms (or plants) identified as market participants in Section 1.3 based on the total sales or capacity currently devoted to the relevant market together with that which likely would be devoted to the relevant market in response to a "small but significant and nontransitory" price increase. Market shares can be expressed either in dollar terms through measurement of sales, shipments, or production, or in physical terms through measurement of sales, shipments, production, capacity, or reserves.

* * *

1.5 Concentration and Market Shares

Market concentration is a function of the number of firms in a market and their respective market shares. As an aid to the interpretation of market data, the Agency will use the Herfindahl–Hirschman Index ("HHI") of market concentration. The HHI is calculated by summing the squares of the individual market shares of all the participants.[17] * * *

1.51 General Standards

In evaluating horizontal mergers, the Agency will consider both the post-merger market concentration and the increase in concentration resulting from the merger.[18] Market concentration is a useful indicator of the likely potential competitive effect of a merger. The general standards for horizontal mergers are as follows:

a) Post–Merger HHI Below 1000. The Agency regards markets in this region to be unconcentrated. Mergers resulting in unconcentrated markets are unlikely to have adverse competitive effects and ordinarily require no further analysis.

b) Post–Merger HHI Between 1000 and 1800. The Agency regards markets in this region to be moderately concentrated. Mergers producing an increase in the HHI of less than 100 points in moderately concentrated markets post-merger are unlikely to have adverse competitive consequences and ordinarily require no further analysis. Mergers producing an increase in the HHI of more than 100 points in moderately concentrated markets post-merger potentially raise significant competitive concerns depending on the facts set forth in Sections 2–5 of the Guidelines.

c) Post–Merger HHI Above 1800. The Agency regards markets in this region to be highly concentrated. Mergers producing an increase in the HHI of less than 50 points, even in highly concentrated markets post-merger, are unlikely to have adverse competitive consequences and ordi-

17. For example, a market consisting of four firms with market shares of 30 percent, 30 percent, 20 percent and 20 percent has an HHI of 2600 ($30^2 + 30^2 + 20^2 + 2\ 0^{20} = 2600$). The HHI ranges from 10,000 (in the case of a pure monopoly) to a number approaching zero (in the case of an atomistic market). Although it is desirable to include all firms in the calculation, lack of information about small firms is not critical because such firms do not affect the HHI significantly.

18. The increase in concentration as measured by the HHI can be calculated independently of the overall market concentration by doubling the product of the market shares of the merging firms. For example, the merger of firms with shares of 5 percent and 10 percent of the market would increase the HHI by 100 (5 x 10 x 2 = 100). The explanation for this technique is as follows: In calculating the HHI before the merger, the market shares of the merging firms are squared individually: $(a)^2 + (b)^2$. After the merger, the sum of those shares would be squared: $(a + b)^2$, which equals $a^2 + 2ab + b^2$. The increase in the HHI therefore is represented by 2ab.

narily require no further analysis. Mergers producing an increase in the HHI of more than 50 points in highly concentrated markets post-merger potentially raise significant competitive concerns, depending on the factors set forth in Sections 2–5 of the Guidelines. Where the post-merger HHI exceeds 1800, it will be presumed that mergers producing an increase in the HHI of more than 100 points are likely to create or enhance market power or facilitate its exercise. The presumption may be overcome by a showing that factors set forth in Section 2–5 of the Guidelines make it unlikely that the merger will create or enhance market power or facilitate its exercise, in light of market concentration and market shares.

1.52 Factors Affecting the Significance of Market Shares and Concentration

* * *

1.521 Changing Market Conditions

Market concentration and market share data of necessity are based on historical evidence. However, recent or ongoing changes in the market may indicate that the current market share of a particular firm either understates or overstates the firm's future competitive significance. * * *

1.522 Degree of Difference Between the Products and Locations in the Market and Substitutes Outside the Market

All else equal, the magnitude of potential competitive harm from a merger is greater if a hypothetical monopolist would raise price within the relevant market by substantially more than a "small but significant and nontransitory" amount. This may occur when the demand substitutes outside the relevant market, as a group, are not close substitutes for the products and locations within the relevant market. * * *

2. The Potential Adverse Competitive Effects of Mergers

2.0 Overview

Other things being equal, market concentration affects the likelihood that one firm, or a small group of firms, could successfully exercise market power. The smaller the percentage of total supply that a firm controls, the more severely it must restrict its own output in order to produce a given price increase, and the less likely it is that an output restriction will be profitable. If collective action is necessary for the exercise of market power, as the number of firms necessary to control a given percentage of total supply decreases, the difficulties and costs of reaching and enforcing an understanding with respect to the control of that supply might be reduced. However, market share and concentration data provide only the starting point for analyzing the competitive impact of a merger. * * *

2.1 Lessening of Competition Through Coordinated Interaction

* * *

In this phase of the analysis, the Agency will examine the extent to which post-merger market conditions are conducive to reaching terms of coordination, detecting deviations from those terms, and punishing such deviations. Depending upon the circumstances, the following market factors among others, may be relevant: the availability of key information concerning market conditions, transactions and individual competitors; the extent of firm and product heterogeneity; pricing or marketing practices typically employed by firms in the market; the characteristics of buyers and sellers; and the characteristics of typical transactions. * * *

It is likely that market conditions are conducive to coordinated interaction when the firms in the market previously have engaged in express collusion and when the salient characteristics of the market have not changed appreciably since the most recent such incident.

* * *

2.12 Conditions Conducive to Detecting and Punishing Deviations

* * *

In some circumstances, coordinated interaction can be effectively prevented or limited by maverick firms—firms that have a greater economic incentive to deviate from the terms of coordination than do most of their rivals (e.g., firms that are usually disruptive and competitive influences in the market). Consequently, acquisition of a maverick firm is one way in which a merger may make coordinated interaction more likely, more successful, or more complete. * * *

2.2 Lessening of Competition Through Unilateral Effects

* * *

2.21 Firms Distinguished Primarily by Differentiated Products

* * *

A merger between firms in a market for differentiated products may diminish competition by enabling the merged firm to profit by unilaterally raising the price of one or both products above the premerger level. Some of the sales loss due to the price rise merely will be diverted to the product of the merger partner and, depending on relative margins, capturing such sales loss through merger may make the price increase profitable even though it would not have been profitable premerger. Substantial unilateral price elevation in a market for differentiated products requires that there be a significant share of sales in the market accounted for by consumers who regard the products of the merging firms as their first and second choices, and that repositioning of the non-parties' product lines to replace the localized competition lost through the merger be unlikely.

* * *

2.22 Firms Distinguished Primarily by Their Capacities

Where products are relatively undifferentiated and capacity primarily distinguishes firms and shapes the nature of their competition, the merged firm may find it profitable unilaterally to raise price and suppress output. The merger provides the merged firm a larger base of sales on which to enjoy the resulting price rise and also eliminates a competitor to which customers otherwise would have diverted their sales. Where the merging firms have a combined market share of at least thirty-five percent, merged firms may find it profitable to raise price and reduce joint output below the sum of their premerger outputs because the lost markups on the foregone sales may be outweighed by the resulting price increase on the merged base of sales.

This unilateral effect is unlikely unless a sufficiently large number of the merged firm's customers would not be able to find economical alternative sources of supply, i.e., competitors of the merged firm likely would not respond to the price increase and output reduction by the merged firm with increases in their own outputs sufficient in the aggregate to make the unilateral action of the merged firm unprofitable. Such non-party expansion is unlikely if those firms face binding capacity constraints that could not be economically relaxed within two years or if existing excess capacity is significantly more costly to operate than capacity currently in use.

* * *

3. Entry Analysis

3.0 Overview

A merger is not likely to create or enhance market power or to facilitate its exercise, if entry into the market is so easy that market participants, after the merger, either collectively or unilaterally could not profitably maintain a price increase above premerger levels. Such entry likely will deter an anti-competitive merger in its incipiency, or deter or counteract the competitive effects of concern.

* * *

4. Efficiencies

* * *

Some mergers that the Agency otherwise might challenge may be reasonably necessary to achieve significant net efficiencies. Cognizable efficiencies include, but are not limited to, achieving economies of scale, better integration of production facilities, plant specialization, lower transportation costs, and similar efficiencies relating to specific manufacturing, servicing, or distribution operations of the merging firms. * * * [T]he Agency will reject claims of efficiencies if equivalent or comparable savings can reasonably be achieved by the parties through other means. The expected net efficiencies must be greater the more significant are the competitive risks identified in Sections 1–3.

5. Failure and Exiting Assets

5.0 Overview

Notwithstanding the analysis of Sections 1–4 of the Guidelines, a merger is not likely to create or enhance market power or to facilitate its exercise, if imminent failure, as defined below, of one of the merging firms would cause the assets of that firm to exit the relevant market. In such circumstances, post-merger performance in the relevant market may be no worse than market performance had the merger been blocked and the assets left the market.

5.1 Failing Firm

A merger is not likely to create or enhance market power or facilitate its exercise if the following circumstances are met: 1) the allegedly failing firm would be unable to meet its financial obligations in the near future; 2) it would not be able to reorganize successfully under Chapter 11 of the Bankruptcy Act; 3) it has made unsuccessful good-faith efforts to elicit reasonable alternative offers of acquisition of the assets of the failing firm that would both keep its tangible and intangible assets in the relevant market and pose a less severe danger to competition than does the proposed merger; and 4) absent the acquisition, the assets of the failing firm would exit the relevant market.

* * *

NOTE

The Justice Department's guidelines provide only an introduction to a complex subject whose details are beyond the scope of this course. In fact, the general business attorney will often feel this is an appropriate point to bring in an expert. Nevertheless, the guidelines should give one enough of the concepts involved to assess whether a particular acquisition at least raises a serious antitrust issue. In this regard, how might one assess the Time–Warner merger: Was there any place where these firms were competitors (in other words, the merger was horizontal)? What additional facts would one need to know in order to evaluate the competitive significance of this merger?

Notice that Time and Warner had a vertical relationship in some of their activities. Warner supplied movies to Time's HBO and Cinemax subsidiaries. Does this fact have any relevance in weighing the competitive impact of a merger? While the 1992 Merger Guidelines only speak to the potential anticompetitive effects of horizontal mergers, earlier Supreme Court opinions have held that vertical integration could create an anticompetitive effect (based upon the notion of foreclosing sources of supply or outlets to competitors). *E.g., Brown Shoe Co. v. United States*, 370 U.S. 294 (1962). In guidelines issued in 1984, the Department of Justice expressed its policy with respect to attacking vertical mergers:

> In certain circumstances, the vertical integration resulting from vertical mergers could create competitively objectionable barriers to

entry. Stated generally, three conditions are necessary (but not sufficient) for this problem to exist. First, the degree of vertical integration between the two markets must be so extensive that entrants to one market (the "primary market") also would have to enter the other market (the "secondary market") simultaneously. Second, the requirement of entry at the secondary level must make entry at the primary level significantly more difficult and less likely to occur. Finally, the structure and other characteristics of the primary market must be otherwise so conducive to non-competitive performance that the increased difficulty of entry is likely to affect its performance.

* * *

The Department is unlikely to challenge a merger on this ground unless overall concentration of the primary market is above 1800 HHI.

* * *

A high level of vertical integration by upstream firms into the associated retail market may facilitate collusion in the upstream market by making it easier to monitor price. * * *

The Department is unlikely to challenge a merger on this ground unless (1) overall concentration of the upstream market is above 1800 HHI.

* * *

Non-horizontal mergers may be used by monopoly public utilities subject to rate regulation as a tool for circumventing that regulation. The clearest example is the acquisition by a regulated utility of a supplier of its fixed or variable inputs. After the merger, the utility would be selling to itself and might be able arbitrarily to inflate the prices of internal transactions.

1984 Department of Justice Merger Guidelines ¶ 4.2 et seq.

One other type of anticompetitive effect from a non-horizontal merger involves the loss of potential competitors. *E.g. United States v. Falstaff Brewing Corp.*, 410 U.S. 526 (1973). When a firm enters a concentrated market by merging with a major company already in the market, this cuts off the opportunity for increased competition which could have occurred had the merging outsider entered the market on its own. Moreover, the threat of *de novo* entry might have disciplined the existing firms in the market; which threat is now gone because of the merger. The Department of Justice is unlikely to challenge a merger on these grounds, however, unless the market involved has a concentration above 1800 HHI and no more than a few firms have the same or comparable advantage in entering the market as does the merging outsider. 1984 Department of Justice Merger Guidelines, ¶ ¶ 4.131, 4.133.

Later, this chapter will discuss a procedural requirement involving acquisitions and the antitrust laws; this being the notification required by the Hart–Scott–Rodino Antitrust Improvements Act. Finally, on a related subject, acquisitions in certain highly regulated industries may require advance approval by the government agency charged with regulating the field. *E.g.*, 12 U.S.C. §§ 1828, 1842 (Federally insured banks); 49 U.S.C. § 1378 (airlines); Cal. Ins. Code § 1215.2 (insurance companies). Obtaining such approval will often raise the same competitive issues as involved under the antitrust laws.

2. NEGOTIATING THE BASIC DEAL

a. *Price*

Piemonte v. New Boston Garden Corporation

377 Mass. 719, 387 N.E.2d 1145 (1979).

■ WILKINS, JUSTICE.

The plaintiffs were stockholders in Boston Garden Arena Corporation (Garden Arena), a Massachusetts corporation whose stockholders voted on July 19, 1973, to merge with the defendant corporation in circumstances which entitled each plaintiff to "demand payment for his stock from the resulting or surviving corporation and an appraisal in accordance with the provisions of * * * [the Massachusetts corporations statute]." * * * Each party has appealed from a judgment determining the fair value of the plaintiffs' stock. * * *

On July 18, 1973, Garden Arena owned all the stock in a subsidiary corporation that owned both a franchise in the National Hockey League (NHL), known as the Boston Bruins, and a corporation that held a franchise in the American Hockey League (AHL), known as the Boston Braves. Garden Arena also owned and operated Boston Garden Sports Arena (Boston Garden), an indoor auditorium with facilities for the exhibition of sporting and other entertainment events, and a corporation that operated the food and beverage concession at the Boston Garden. A considerable volume of documentary material was introduced in evidence concerning the value of the stock of Garden Arena on July 18, 1973, the day before Garden Arena's stockholders approved the merger. Each side presented expert testimony. The judge gave consideration to the market value of the Garden Arena stock, to the value of its stock based on its earnings, and to the net asset value of Garden Arena's assets. Weighing these factors, the judge arrived at a total, per share value of $75.27.[3]

* * *

3. The judge determined the market value, earnings value, and net asset value of the stock and then weighted these values as follows:

Market Value:	$ 26.50	× 10%	=	$ 2.65
Earnings Value:	$ 52.60	× 40%	=	$21.04
Net Asset Value:	$103.16	× 50%	=	$51.58
Total Value Per Share:				$75.27

The Delaware courts have adopted a general approach to the appraisal of stock which a Massachusetts judge might appropriately follow, as did the judge in this case. The Delaware procedure, known as the "Delaware block approach," calls for a determination of the market value, the earnings value, and the net asset value of the stock, followed by the assignment of a percentage weight to each of the elements of value.

* * *

Market Value

The judge was acting within reasonable limits when he determined that the market value of Garden Arena stock on July 18, 1973, was $26.50 a share. Each party challenges this determination. The plaintiffs' contention is that market value should be disregarded because it was not ascertainable due to the limited trading in Garden Arena stock. The defendant argues that the judge was obliged to reconstruct market value based on comparable companies, and, in doing so, should have arrived at a market value of $22 a share.

Market value may be a significant factor, even the dominant factor, in determining the "fair value" of shares of a particular corporation * * *. Shares regularly traded on a recognized stock exchange are particularly susceptible to valuation on the basis of their market price, although even in such cases the market value may well not be conclusive. * * * On the other hand, where there is no established market for a particular stock, actual market value cannot be used. In such cases, a judge might undertake to "reconstruct" market value, but he is not obliged to do so. Indeed, the process of the reconstruction of market value may actually be no more than a variation on the valuation of corporate assets and corporate earnings.

In this case, Garden Arena stock was traded on the Boston Stock Exchange, but rarely. Approximately ninety percent of the company's stock was held by the controlling interests and not traded. * * * In 1972, 4,372 shares were traded at prices ranging from $20.50 a share to $29 a share. * * * The last prior sale of 200 shares on December 4, 1972, was made at $26.50 a share. The judge accepted that sale price as the market price to be used in his determination of value.

The judge concluded that the volume of trading was sufficient to permit a determination of market value and expressed a preference for the actual sale price over any reconstruction of a market value, which he concluded would place "undue reliance on corporations, factors, and circumstances not applicable to Garden Arena stock." The decision to consider market value and the market value selected were within the judge's discretion.

Valuation Based on Earnings

The judge determined that the average per share earnings of Garden Arena for the five-fiscal-year period which ended June 30, 1973, was $5.26.

To this amount he applied a factor, or multiplier, of 10 to arrive at $52.60 as the per share value based on earnings.

Each party objects to certain aspects of this process. * * *

Delaware case law, which, as we have said, we regard as instructive but not binding, has established a method of computing value based on corporate earnings. The appraiser generally starts by computing the average earnings of the corporation for the past five years. * * * Extraordinary gains and losses are excluded from the average earnings calculation. * * * The appraiser then selects a multiplier (to be applied to the average earnings) which reflects the prospective financial condition of the corporation and the risk factor inherent in the corporation and the industry. * * * In selecting a multiplier, the appraiser generally looks to other comparable corporations.[9] * * *

The judge chose not to place "singular reliance on comparative data preferring to choose a multiplier based on the specific situation and prospects of the Garden Arena." He weighed the favorable financial prospects of the Bruins: the popularity and success of the team, the relatively low average age of its players, the popularity of Bobby Orr and Phil Esposito, the high attendance record at home games (each home team retained all gate receipts), and the advantageous radio and television contracts. On the other hand, he recognized certain risks, the negative prospects: the existence of the World Hockey Association with its potential, favorable impact on players' bargaining positions, and legal threats to the players' reserve clause. He concluded that a multiplier of 10 was appropriate. There was ample evidentiary support for his conclusion. He might have looked to and relied on price-earnings ratios of other corporations, but he was not obliged to.

The judge did not have to consider the dividend record of Garden Arena, as the defendant urges. Dividends tend to reflect the same factors as earnings and, therefore, need not be valued separately. * * * And since dividend policy is usually reflected in market value, the use of market value as a factor in the valuation process permitted the low and sporadic dividend rate to be given some weight in the process. Beyond that, the value of the plaintiffs' stock should not be depreciated because the controlling interests often chose to declare low dividends or none at all.

The judge did not abuse his discretion in including expansion income (payments from teams newly admitted to the NHL) received during two of the five recent fiscal years. * * * Expansion income did not have to be treated as extraordinary income. The judge concluded that it did not distort "an accurate projection of the earnings value of Garden Arena" and noted, as of July 18, 1973, an NHL expansion plan for the admission of two more teams in 1974–1975 and for expansion thereafter.

9. Although Delaware courts have relied on, and continue to rely on, Professor Dewing's capitalization chart (see 1 A.S. Dewing, The Financial Policy of Corporations 390–391 (5th ed. 1953)), they have recognized that it is somewhat outdated and no longer the "be-all and end-all" on the subject of earnings value. * * *

Valuation Based on Net Asset Value

The judge determined total net asset value by first valuing the net assets of Garden Arena apart from the Bruins franchise and the concession operations at Boston Gardens. He selected $9,400,000 (the June 30, 1973, book value of Garden Arena) as representing that net asset value. Then he added his valuations of the Bruins franchise ($9,600,000) and the concession operation ($4,200,000) to arrive at a total asset value of $23,200,000, or $103.16 a share.

The parties raise various objections to these determinations.

* * *

The plaintiffs object that the judge did not explicitly determine the value of the Boston Garden and implicitly undervalued it. Garden Arena had purchased the Boston Garden on May 25, 1973, for $4,000,000, and accounted for it on the June 30, 1973, balance sheet as a $4,000,000 asset with a corresponding mortgage liability of $3,437,065. Prior to the purchase, Garden Arena had held a long-term lease which was unfavorable to the owner of the Boston Garden. The existence of the lease would tend to depress the purchase price.

The judge stated that the $9,400,000 book value "*includes* a reasonable value for Boston Garden" (emphasis supplied). He did not indicate whether, if he had meant to value the Boston Garden at its purchase price (with an adjustment for the mortgage liabilities), he had considered the effect the lease would have had on that price. While we recognize that the fact-finding role of the judge permits him to reject the opinions of the various experts, we conclude, in the absence of an explanation of his reasons, that it is possible that the judge did not give adequate consideration to the value of the Garden property. The judge should consider this subject further on remand.

A major area of dispute was the value of the Bruins franchise. The judge rejected the value advanced by the plaintiffs' expert ($18,000,000), stating that "(a)lthough the defendant's figure of ($9,600,000) seems somewhat low in comparison with the cost of expansion team franchises, *the Court is constrained* to accept defendant's value as it is the more creditable and legally appropriate expert opinion in the record" (emphasis supplied). Although the choice of the word "constrained" may have been inadvertent, it connotes a sense of obligation. As the trier of fact, the judge was not bound to accept the valuation of either one expert or the other. He was entitled to reach his own conclusion as to value. * * *

Because the judge may have felt bound to accept the value placed on the Bruins franchise by the defendant's expert, we shall remand this case for him to arrive at his own determination of the value of the Bruins franchise. * * *

The defendant argues that, in arriving at the value of the assets of Garden Arena, the judge improperly placed a separate value on the right to operate concessions at the Boston Garden. We agree with the judge. The fact that earnings from concessions were included in the computation of earnings value, one component in the formula, does not mean that the value of the concessions should have been excluded from the computation of net asset value, another such component.

The value of the concession operation was not reflected in the value of the real estate. Real estate may be valued on the basis of rental income, but it is not valued on the basis of the profitability of business operations within the premises. * * *

We do conclude, however, that the judge may have felt unnecessarily bound to accept the plaintiffs' evidence of the value of the concession operation. He stated that "since the defendant did not submit evidence on this issue, the Court will accept plaintiffs' expert appraisal of the value of the concession operation." * * * The judge was not obliged to accept the plaintiffs' evidence at face value merely because no other evidence was offered.

* * *

Weighing of Valuations

* * *

Any determination of the weight to be given the various elements involved in the valuation of a stock must be based on the circumstances. * * * The decision to weight market value at only 10% was appropriate, considering the thin trading in the stock of Garden Arena. The decision to attribute 50% weight to net asset value was reasonably founded. The judge concluded that, because of tax reasons, the value of a sports franchise, unlike many corporate activities, depends more on its assets than on its earnings; that Garden Arena had been largely a family corporation in which earnings were of little significance; that Garden Arena had approximately $5,000,000 in excess liquid assets; and that the Garden property was a substantial real estate holding in an excellent location.

* * *

Although we would have found no fault with a determination to give even greater weight to the price per share based on the net asset value of Garden Arena, the judge was acting within an acceptable range of discretion in selecting the weights he gave to the various factors.

* * *

Conclusion

We have concluded that the judge's method of valuing the Garden Arena stock was essentially correct. In this opinion, we have indicated, however, that the case should be remanded to him for clarification and further consideration on the record of three matters: his valuation of the Boston Garden, the Bruins franchise, and the concession operation.

So ordered.

Gilbert v. MPM Enterprises, Inc.

709 A.2d 663 (Del.Ch.1997).

Shareholder in closely held corporation dissented from approval of merger agreement and arguably perfected his statutory right to appraisal of the fair value of his shares pursuant to 8 Del. C. § 262. * * *

I. BACKGROUND

MPM Enterprises ("MPM") manufactures screen printers for the surface mount technology ("SMT") industry. Broadly speaking, the SMT industry transforms bare circuit boards into completed products with electronic components soldered directly onto the surface of printed circuit boards. The equipment used in the industry includes screen printers, which "squeegee" solder paste through screens (stencils) onto bare boards * * *.

The SMT industry and MPM grew significantly during the 1980s and dramatically in the early 1990s. In fiscal years 1991–1994, MPM's sales increased from $13.5 million to $55.5 million and MPM's net income rose from $8,300 to $6.5 million. In March 1995, MPM and Cookson Group PLC ("Cookson"), a London-based multinational manufacturer and marketer of industrial materials, signed an Agreement of Merger providing for immediate cash payment to MPM's stockholders of $62.698 million with potential earn-out payments up to an additional $73.635 million. MPM merged into a Cookson subsidiary on 2 May 1995.

Petitioner Jeffrey D. Gilbert ("Gilbert"), a former MPM director, owns 600 shares of MPM's common stock and 200 shares of MPM's preferred stock. These shares provided Gilbert with an eight percent ownership of MPM * * *. If he had accepted the terms of the merger, Gilbert would have received approximately $4.56 million and had the opportunity to receive as much as an additional $5.36 million, if MPM achieved the terms of the earn-out. Despite these prospective payments, Gilbert pursued his statutory right to an appraisal of his shares. * * *

Typically both sides in an appraisal proceeding present expert opinions on the fair value of the petitioner's shares. In theory, these opinions facilitate judicial fact finding and conclusions by wrapping the experts' factual assumptions in complicated financial models with which they, and usually not the court, are conversant. One might expect the experts' desire to convince the Court of the reasonableness and validity of their assumptions and financial models would produce a somewhat narrow range of values, clearly and concisely supported, despite the individual parties' obvious conflicting incentives. Unfortunately, as this case and other cases most decidedly illustrate, one should not put much faith in that expectation, at least when faced with appraisal experts in this Court.

* * *

Petitioner's expert values MPM at $357.1 million with Gilbert's shares worth approximately $26 million. Respondent's expert concluded that the merger yielded MPM's shareholders a fair value of only $81.7 million, with Gilbert entitled to approximately $5.942 million. * * *

II. ANALYSIS

Petitioner's expert, Patricof & Co. Capital Corp. ("Patricof"), determined the fair value of petitioner's shares by performing a comparative company analysis and a discounted cash flow (DCF) analysis. Patricof relied equally on these approaches and averaged the results to reach the conclusion that the fair value of MPM's equity is $357.1 million. Respondent's expert, Advest, Inc. ("Advest"), also relied on the comparative company ("guideline company") and DCF models. Its overall approach to determining the fair value of petitioner's shares, however, is quite different. First, Advest determined the "fair market value" of MPM. This was determined by constructing a DCF that represented the transaction from the seller's point of view (the sell-side DCF) and a DCF that represented the transaction from the buyer's point of view (the buy-side DCF).[11] * * * Advest also determined MPM's fair market value by comparing MPM's EBITDA, EBIT and P/E ratios to those ratios of its comparable companies. * * *

A. The Appropriate Valuation Method

I conclude that the only appropriate way to determine the fair value of petitioner's shares is to compare petitioner's DCF with respondent's sell-side DCF. As described above, Advest's buy-side analysis was constructed in a such a way as to produce a figure representing the value of MPM to Cookson. If Advest had been hired by Cookson to analyze the transaction, this analysis would assist Cookson in its determination of an appropriate offering price. The analysis thus includes consideration of the price at which purchase of MPM would dilute, rather than support, Cookson's earnings and concludes with determination of the "maximum prices at which 100% of the value of the synergies brought to the transaction by the buyer are given to the seller and at which no value is created for the buyer." Our law neither contemplates nor allows this valuation method, and I give it no further consideration.

I find the comparable company (or guideline company) analyses relatively weak compared with the experts' DCF valuations. As explained below, I find that petitioner's selection of companies fails to provide a comparable data set. And, since Advest concludes that its own guideline company analysis (which itself is not free of concern)[13] does not provide as

11. It is not clear why Advest took the time to construct a buy-side analysis as its report recognizes that under our law, petitioner is entitled to his pro rata share of the corporation valued as a going concern without consideration of "any element of value arising from the accomplishment or expectation of merger". * * *

13. I note, for example, that Advest's guideline company analysis claims that public companies trade on multiples of their P/E ratio and that valuations of mergers and acquisitions transactions are based on multiples of the total enterprise value. Even if true, however, Advest fails to explain why the latter, if either, is more appropriate for use in an appraisal valuation under 8 Del. C. § 262, which specifically excludes any benefits arising from a merger or acquisition. * * *

much of an appropriate measure of MPM's value as its sell-side DCF, I conclude that by far the best way to proceed is to compare and contrast petitioner's DCF with respondent's sell-side DCF.

B. Similarities in Both DCF Approaches

A discounted cash flow approach requires the creation of a financial forecast that projects the corporation's future revenues and expenses, typically for the next five years. The cash flows used by the experts in this proceeding were similar in structure and both were based on a financial forecast prepared by MPM management in April 1995 (the "April forecast"). This forecast was the last forecast prepared by management prior to the merger date. It includes estimates of MPM's revenues and expenses for fiscal years 1996 through 1998. * * *

I conclude that management was in the best position to forecast MPM's future before the merger, and finding no evidence that the April forecast included benefits to be obtained via the merger or that the April forecast represented a deliberate attempt to falsify MPM's projected revenues and expenses, I accept management's projections with minor changes to reflect MPM's actual financial results and other financial information obtained after the preparation of the projections, but before the merger.

Since the April forecast extended out only three years, each expert needed to establish appropriate assumptions for MPM's growth and expenses for the remaining two years of the five-year discounted cash flow. These assumptions naturally rest upon each expert's preferred view of MPM's future opportunities. For example, petitioner envisions that revenues will grow at 23.5% for the last two years while respondent concludes that revenues will grow at only 10%.

* * *

1. Financial Forecast: Revenue Growth

* * *

The next step in the cash flow forecast is to determine if there are necessary revenue growth adjustments to the April forecast. The April forecast projected revenue growth of 38.9%, 20%, and 22.2% for 1996 through 1998. Respondent's expert urges me to reduce the growth rates to 33.89%, 15%, and 10%. Petitioner urges growth rates of 66%, 23.5%, and 23.5%. Each side points to numerous factors in support of its proposed changes. For example, in just one area of dispute, petitioner notes that MPM had developed a new printer, the Ultraprint 3000 series, which was described by industry surveys (and even respondent) as a top-of-the-line printer, featuring significant improvements in automation and processing speed. Management expected the Ultraprint 3000 series to increase MPM's domestic and international market share. Respondent notes that although the series was introduced at a trade show in February 1995 and although MPM had approximately 55 orders scheduled for shipment before the end of the fiscal year, at the time of the merger, the series still had design and software problems, and six or fewer machines had actually been produced. Respondent further notes that the initial shipments of the Ultraprint 2000, another printer introduced at the February trade show, revealed a design flaw, which led MPM to offer replacement printers, or loaners, to its customers pending the resolution of the problem. Other disputes involved issues such as the growth rate of the industry—both domestically and internationally—and the degree to which a model produced by one of MPM's main competitors would compete with the Ultraprint 3000 series. The arguments presented by both sides appear to have merit with one exception: I decline to consider the validity of the 1997 and 1998 growth rates selected by petitioner's expert as his report admits the rates were selected to ensure that petitioner received the full amount of the earn-out payments. Petitioner argues that it is only reasonable to assume that MPM, as the seller, would not have agreed to sell MPM if it did not expect to receive the full amount of the earn-out payments. If this is reasonable, I fail to see why it would not also be reasonable to assume that Cookson, as the buyer, would not have agreed to purchase MPM if it expected that it would have to pay the full amount. Yet, obviously, both parties cannot be correct. This ability of both parties to view the same transaction and conclude that they stand in a winning position is one of the main advantages of an earn-out. The seller, convinced of the value of what he is selling, feels sure to receive the full amount of additional contingent payments. The buyer, less sure of the value, but willing to pay for value that is not yet apparent, agrees to a structure that requires him (or allows him) to pay now for value he perceives now and pay later for additional value, but only if that additional value materializes. Both parties bear the risk of their own error in judgment. Basing growth rates on the expectation of the receipt of the full earn-out payments is nothing more than basing growth on a wish. If the parties were forced to close the transaction with one lump-sum payment, the value would be somewhere between the up-front payment and the sum of the up-front payment and the earn-out. Such a value would provide immediate payment, but would reduce the seller's potential upside in exchange for reducing the buyer's potential downside. * * *

Remaining still is the question whether and if so, how, adjustments should be made to the April forecast's projection of revenue growth. None of the factors cited by either side appear to be factors that were not known and able to be considered by MPM at the time it prepared the April forecast. Accordingly, even if I were to determine that the arguments on one side appear to be stronger than those on the other, I fail to find any way in which I could conclude that the same conclusion had not been reached by, and that the implications of that decision had not been reflected by, management in its preparation of the April forecast. Therefore, I decline to adjust the revenue growth figures as projected in the April forecast.

The final issue relating to the revenue forecast is the determination of appropriate growth rates for 1999 and 2000, the last two years of the experts' cash flow forecasts and two years beyond the time covered by the April forecast. Both experts, apparently having no reason to justify departing from their previous assumptions, continued growth in 1999 and 2000 at the same level as 1998. I adopt their method and continue growth at the same rate (22.2%) as projected in the April forecast.

* * *

3. Terminal Value

With the above guidance, the experts should be able to construct a single cash flow projection for MPM through the year 2000. At this point they will need to determine MPM's terminal value—the value representative of MPM at the end of fiscal year 2000. In their computations of terminal value, both experts compiled a list of companies comparable to MPM. The value of each company's equity was then expressed as a multiple of either its net income or earnings before interest, taxes, depreciation, and amortization ("EBITDA"). The experts then applied the median of the comparable multiples to MPM's net income or EBITDA to predict the value of MPM's equity.

Petitioner's comparable companies consisted of seven companies "whose business is manufacturing and marketing electronic production equipment." Respondent contends that petitioner's comparables are not, in fact, comparable because five of the seven are engaged in the manufacture of equipment used in the production of integrated circuits and semiconductors, and only two manufacture screen printers like MPM.

* * *

Advest's list of selected comparables consists of only three companies, all of which are significantly less successful than MPM by every financial measure provided. Two of the three (the two with the best performance) were also included in Patricof's comparables. All three companies manufacture equipment for the SMT industry. Although Advest's selection of comparable companies is low in number, it has convincingly demonstrated the appropriateness of the selection, especially in comparison to Patricof's selection, which included non-SMT industry companies.

Rather than employ a multiple of net income (Patricof's selected multiple), Advest based its calculation of MPM's terminal value on a multiple of EBITDA. According to respondent, use of EBITDA, rather than net income, more accurately reflects MPM's equity value by removing any distortions caused by MPM's increased capital expenditures and increased depreciation over the time horizon of the cash flows. Both net income and EBITDA are acceptable multiples with which to determine terminal value, but petitioner has provided no explanation of why, in this case, net income, rather than EBITDA, should be used. Accordingly, I accept respondent's use of EBITDA to determine MPM's terminal value.

Apparently noting that MPM's performance was superior to that of the comparable companies, respondent added 12% premium to the multiple resulting in an EBITDA multiple of 7.5. Petitioner also added a premium

(10%) to its multiple (apparently for similar reasons), and I accept Advest's premium as a reasonable way to account for MPM's superior performance.

4. Discount Rate

Advest's suggested discount rate is based, in part, on a survey of venture capitalist firms, all of which indicated they required returns of up to 50% for similar investments in companies like MPM. * * * To support its suggested cost of capital, Patricof employed the capital asset pricing model ("CAPM") to calculate a 20.6% cost of equity and a 19.9% WACC.[30]

Respondent argues that CAPM is used primarily for companies with publicly traded shares and is not appropriate for use in this instance. * * * I conclude that Patricof has sufficiently supported its use of the CAPM but not each assumption it has employed in the model. Therefore, I accept Patricof's overall approach to the determination of MPM's discount rate except to the extent it is based on information obtained from Patricof's selection of comparable companies. Accordingly, MPM's discount rate shall be that rate determined through use of Patricof's CAPM model except that the comparable beta employed shall be based on the average beta of respondent's comparable companies.

* * *

The parties shall confer and submit an appropriate form of order consistent with the substantive findings above.

NOTES

1. Valuing a business, or interests in a business, has been a constant area of concern throughout this book. Chapter I laid the groundwork by considering both how to evaluate a new venture, and the basics of valuing a going business. Chapter V provided a more sophisticated exploration of how securities analysts often measure the worth of stocks. Chapters III and VI utilized these concepts in dealing with buy-out agreements and recapitalizations. Now, in negotiating the price at which to sell a business, one is again dealing with the subject valuing a firm. *Piemonte* and *Gilbert* provide samples of the use of valuation techniques in the context of selling a business, and, more specifically, in the course of appraisal proceedings under which shareholders dissenting from the transaction can receive the appraised worth of their stock paid to them in cash.

Notice the court in *Piemonte* employed the weighted average of several approaches to valuation. Is this a sensible basis upon which to negotiate the price? After all, presumably the buyer intends to put the business to that purpose which gives the highest value; continuing it for earnings, or liquidating it for asset value. In this event, what relevance does a lower valuation figure, reflecting an unintended use, have to the negotiations?

30. * * * The capital asset pricing model is a commonly used method that seeks to determine a subject company's cost of equity by determining the hypothetical risk premium that the market would demand to make the investment. * * *

Gilbert illustrates how Delaware courts, ironically enough, have abandoned the "Delaware block" approach to valuation used in *Piemonte*. In its place, the court in *Gilbert* used a discounted cash flow method of valuation. In fact, the difference between *Piemonte* and *Gilbert* provides a good opportunity to compare and contrast the various valuation approaches discussed throughout this book.

Piemonte should remind one of the valuation methods discussed by the Small Business Administration Bulletin in Chapter I. By contrast, *Gilbert* is much more attuned to the valuation methods discussed in the piece by Bauman and Komarynsky in Chapter V. Consider the points of convergence and distinction between the two approaches. To begin with, *Piemonte* gave little weight to market value, while *Gilbert* ignored this altogether. This reflects the fact that there is no active market to set the price for shares in a closely held corporation, as in *Gilbert*, while thin trading, as in *Piemonte*, does not establish a very reliable price. Suppose, however, that there is a deep trading market in a corporation's shares: Can one simply rely on the market to set the price? From the standpoint of those negotiating to sell the company, the answer is no. Instead, as the Delaware Supreme Court pointed out in *Smith v. Van Gorkom*, 488 A.2d 858 (Del.1985), the market price of a widely held stock reflects the value of a minority interest. For reasons which are subject to some debate (*compare* Romano, *A Guide to Takeovers: Theory, Evidence, and Regulation*, 9 Yale J. Reg. 119 (1992), *with* Stout, *Are Takeover Premiums Really Premiums? Market Price, Fair Value, and Corporate Law*, 99 Yale L.J. 1235 (1990)), buyers typically pay a premium over the market price in order to purchase a controlling interest in the corporation. Next, consider the use of asset based valuation. *Gilbert* ignored this, while *Piemonte* gave this factor considerable importance. Yet, look at some of the assets valued in *Piemonte*, such as the franchise and the concession rights. These assets only have value insofar as they generate earnings for the business of running a hockey team. Hence, how can one value these assets independent of their earnings potential?

Most interesting is to compare the capitalized earnings valuation in *Piemonte* with the discounted cash flow valuation in *Gilbert*. To begin with, note two differences in the way the cases measured future earnings. *Piemonte* based the prediction of future earnings on an average of past years' earnings. What result would this lead to in a situation, such as in *Gilbert,* in which earnings have increased from year to year? In fact, using an average in *Gilbert* apparently would have predicted future earnings of only half the most recent year's $6.5 million income. Would this be realistic? How does one suppose MPM's management prepared its future earnings forecast? Also, *Piemonte* apparently looked at earnings per share computed in accordance with accepted accounting principles. By contrast, *Gilbert* looked to cash flow and to earnings before interest, depreciation, amortization and taxes. The acceptance of alternatives to accounting based earnings in more recent cases, such as *Gilbert*, reflects the recognition that accounting items, such as depreciation, can distort the real economic impact of earnings. To see why, assume a corporation purchased for $1 million a manufacturing plant with an expected life of 20 years. Straight line depreciation would lower the corporation's earnings for accounting purposes by $50,000 each year. Yet, to treat the corporation's earnings as $50,000 less because in 20 years the company will no longer have the plant ignores the fact that until that time the corporation (or its owners) have the extra money to invest. Keep in mind that because of the time value of money, $50,000 per year for 20 years is worth more than $1 million 20 years in the future. Next, compare the method used in the two cases for determining the present value of the future stream of earnings. *Gilbert* followed the formula set out on page 589 (albeit, looking at corporate cash flow instead of dividends on individual shares). By contrast, *Piemonte* simply multiplied earnings by a so-called multiplier (albeit, *Gilbert* did this too in order to obtain a terminal value for the earnings stream after five years). As discussed in Chapter V, the simple multiplier approach to capitalizing earnings is only mathematically justified if one assumes there will be a perpetual stream of earnings at the same level (in which case, the multiplier equals the reciprocal of the rate of return demanded for an investment of this risk), or if one assumes a stream of earnings perpetually growing at a constant rate (in which case, the multiplier equals the reciprocal of the demanded rate of return minus the growth rate). This means that to the extent one obtains the multiplier by examining the price-earnings ratio of the stocks of other corporations, this only makes sense if one assumes that the other corporations not only present similar risks to the company one is valuing, but also that both the company one is valuing and the corporations one uses as a comparison are all expected to have earnings grow at the same constant rate. *Gilbert*'s use of the more sophisticated formula avoids these problems, but creates another: How does one determine the rate of return investors will demand for an earnings stream with this amount of risk? The court decided to apply the Capital Asset Pricing Model (CAPM), but did not explain how this method works. In *In re Pullman Construction Indus. Inc.,* 107 B.R. 909 (Bkrtcy.N.D.Ill.1989), a Federal bankruptcy court provided the following explanation:

> The CAPM method measures the risk associated with a specific investment relative to the risk of a portfolio of investments, and prices or values that investment relative to the return on the portfolio. The general CAPM cost of capital equation is summarized as follows:
>
> $$R(c) = R(f) + B(a) \times [R(m) - R(f)]$$
>
> where
>
> R(c) = the CAPM cost of capital
> R(f) = the after-tax risk-free rate of return
> B(a) = the beta, or risk, of the asset
> R(m) = the return on the market portfolio
> R(m) − R(f) = the market risk premium
>
> The derivation of each of the components of the CAPM equation used in calculating Pullman's cost of capital is as follows:
>
> The after-tax risk-free rate of return is first calculated. This is the rate of return an investor could expect to receive by investing in a risk-free asset, after paying taxes on the investor's return.

One year Treasury Bills, backed by the full faith and credit of the United States Government, are generally considered to be the best proxy for the risk-free rate. * * *

The "beta" coefficient measures the risk of an investment in Pullman's business relative to the risk of the market as a whole. * * * Since Pullman is not publicly traded, it is impossible to measure changes in the return on Pullman's common stock over time against a portfolio of market securities. Accordingly, a group of publicly-traded companies in the construction industry was selected in order to measure the risk of the special trade contracting industry against the risk of the entire market. This group of companies was used as Pullman's "Peer Group." These comparable publicly-traded companies were selected through an analysis of publicly-traded companies in the special trade contracting and non-residential general contracting businesses.

* * *

Beta statistics for each company in the Peer Group were calculated by * * * utilizing a linear regression technique. The linear regression methodology calculates the relationship between monthly returns on the peer company stock and monthly returns on a weighted New York Stock Exchange portfolio of stocks during the period January, 1983 through December, 1987. * * * A calculated beta of 1.0 generally indicates that the volatility or risk of an investment in a stock is equal to the volatility or risk of the market as a whole; that is, a one percent change in the value of the market portfolio is accompanied by a one percent change in the value of the stock. Betas above 1.0 indicate stocks that are more volatile (risky) than the market, while betas less than 1.0 indicate stocks that are less volatile (risky).

The betas calculated by this linear regression method for all Peer Group companies are equity or stock betas, which measure the risk of an investment in the equity of a company. Such equity returns are affected by the level of debt, or leverage, that the company carries. In order to estimate the risk of the *business* rather than the risk of an investment in the *equity* of the business, an asset beta is calculated which adjusts to eliminate the financial risk of leverage. The asset beta for each Peer Group company was calculated from its equity beta, using the following formula (referred to as "unlevering the beta") * * *:

beta(a) = [beta(d) x (1—Tc) x (D/V)] [+] [beta(e) x (E/V)]

where

beta(a)	=	asset beta
beta(e)	=	beta of the company's equity, as calculated
beta(d)	=	beta of the company's debt, assumed to be .195
E	=	Market value of equity
D	=	Market value of debt
V	=	Market value of capital (i.e., D + E)
[Tc	=	Marginal tax rate]

* * *

Once the asset betas were calculated for each Peer Group company, the Peer Group asset beta was calculated as the average of the asset betas for each company in the Peer Group. * * *

Next, the market risk premium was calculated. This is defined as the premium which investors demand over the risk-free rate in order to compensate them for investments in common stock.

* * *

—The market risk premium between the equal weighted NYSE portfolio and the after-tax risk-free rate was calculated by Ernst & Whinney for each year from 1926 to 1987. The average of these annual premiums, 14.98% was used as the market risk premium in the CAPM equation.

The CAPM cost of capital * * * was calculated using the risk-free rate (5.83%), the market risk-premium (14.98%) and the applicable asset betas * * *.

2. Beyond simply providing another opportunity to look at techniques to value businesses and interests in businesses, is there anything else to consider in the context of negotiating the price for a corporate acquisition? In fact, such a negotiation can introduce several additional considerations. To begin with, if the buyer proposes to pay with its stock rather than cash, the need exists to compare interests in two businesses. (In this regard, note the temptation a buyer paying with its shares faces to take actions which might increase the market price of the buyer's stock. Is there any legal restriction on the buyer repurchasing some of its shares in order to get the price up in advance of an acquisition? See *SEC v. Georgia–Pacific Corp.*, Fed.Sec.L.Rep. (CCH) ¶ 91,680 (1966) (complaint brought by SEC alleging that such repurchases violated Section 10(b) and Rules 10b–5 and 10b–6). Recall also the discussion in Chapter VI of the securities laws which impact redemptions for the purpose of increasing the price of stock.) More significantly, when dealing with the acquisition of the entire firm, it is important to keep in mind the potential differences in the values attached to the firm by the prospective purchaser and by its current owners.

By definition, unless there is a forced liquidation or some element of coercion, a sale takes place because the buyer offers a price greater than what the seller thinks the business is worth to retain. It is useful in negotiating the price to try to ascertain why the buyer sees extra value in target above what the current owners recognize. (If the seller can figure out what extra value the buyer perceives, the seller may be able to guess at how much the buyer thinks the business is worth and so how high the negotiations can push the buyer.) This difference could reflect any number of factors. The buyer may know something about the target corporation which the target's current owners do not, or visa versa. Alternately, the buyer may conclude it can run the business (or otherwise exploit the assets) more profitably than the current management. There may also be "synergistic effects"—in other words, mechanisms such as economies of scale, or efficiency from vertical integration, which result in the combination of the buyer's and seller's businesses operating more profitably than would the two firms separately. One potential synergistic effect—increased profits due to the removal of competition between the buyer and seller—was encountered before as something which can render the acquisition illegal under the antitrust laws. Tax laws can also produce synergistic (at least from the companies' standpoint) effects, in which the combination results in a reduction in the net taxes owned. This shall be addressed later in this chapter. Market factors, too, may motivate the buyer to pay a higher price. For example, suppose the buyer's stock sells at a larger price-earnings ratio than does the target's stock. Assume, as well, the buyer can acquire the target without lowering the price-earnings ratio which the buyer's stock thereafter commands on the stock market. In this event, the buyer can afford to pay more than the current market price for the target, and still have the price of the buyer's stock increase by virtue of the increased earnings it obtains by acquiring the target, now multiplied by the higher price-earnings ratio associated with the buyer's stock. Somewhat overlapping effects relate to diversification and liquidity. A buyer may desire the target in order to diversify its businesses and thereby decrease the risk associated with holding its stock (albeit, the buyer's stockholders might accomplish this for themselves by holding diversified portfolios of stock). At the same time, the target's shareholders, if the company is closely held or has only a thin market for its stock, might discount the worth of their shares because of their lack of liquidity and greater risk.

On the other hand, the difference between the buyer's and seller's evaluations of the worth of the target can go in the other direction: the seller may conclude the target is worth more than the buyer is willing to pay. If this difference in perceptions is real (rather than representing negotiating positions), then there will generally be no sale (assuming the seller is not under any compulsion to liquidate). Nevertheless, sometimes the parties can still reach a mutually desired agreement. This is because often the reason for the difference in valuations results from different expectations about the future of the target's business. Specifically, buyers discount the price they are willing to pay, in order to compensate for uncertainties they face. For example, the target might not have the profit making potential the buyer thought. Perhaps, a critical contract right is non-assignable (*see PPG Industries, Inc. v. Guardian Indus. Corp.*, reprinted later in this chapter), or key employees will refuse to stay with the firm after the sale. Alternately, the target might face more liabilities than expected. *See Ramirez v. Amsted Industries, Inc.*, reprinted later in this chapter. At the same time, sellers may be more optimistic that these problems will not come to pass. Is there a way to bridge the gap? Suppose the parties structure a deal which will give the seller a price exceeding its perception of what the business is worth, assuming the seller is justified in its optimism concerning future prospects, but will lower the price to protect the buyer, should the purchaser's fears come to pass. This could take several forms. The sellers could warrant the existence of certain facts and agree to indemnify the buyer if the facts do not turn out as warranted. Several problems, however, may exist with this scheme, all stemming from the question of who exactly is providing the warranty or indemnity agreement. To the extent the target corporation provides the warranty, what use will this be for the acquirer if the acquirer merges with the target or purchases all the target's outstanding stock, or even if, after selling its assets to the acquirer, the target company dissolves? On the other hand, if the warranty comes from the target's shareholders, how realistic is the acquirer's remedy if the target's shares were widely held? Moreover, what might be the individual shareholders' reaction to assuming a potential liability to the buyer; at least if the liability could exceed what they will obtain from the transaction? An alternative could be to structure the transaction so that the buyer pays something immediately, but more when (and if) things turn out in accordance with the seller's optimistic assumptions. This is an earn-out provision as discussed in *Gilbert.* Note here, however, the enforcement problem falls on the seller's side: Widely scattered shareholders might be concerned about their practical ability to seek a remedy against a buyer who defaults upon its obligation under the earn-out, not to mention the seller's lack of security in event of default. This suggests a third possible approach—escrowing a portion of the purchase price with a third party, to go to the sellers if all goes well after the sale, and back to the buyer if all does not (or some to the sellers and some back to the buyer depending upon what assumptions concerning the business prove unfounded). Naturally, with earn-out or escrow provisions, it is important to consider both the business and accounting choices the buyer can make in running the business, which might affect what the seller receives.

One final set of considerations exists by virtue of the fact that the transaction involves both the sale of the overall business and the sale of individual interests in the business. This fact initially creates a minor technical complication when the buyer pays with its stock rather than cash. The purchase price often will not break down into a whole number of the buyer's shares for each share of the target. The buyer may respond by issuing fractional shares having voting and dividend rights equal to a portion of a share, by issuing scrip generally having no right except to be accumulated and turned in for whole shares once an individual puts together enough, or by paying cash. *E.g.,* Cal. Corp. Code § 407; Del. Gen. Corp. Code § 155; N.Y. Bus. Corp. Law § 509; M.B.C.A. § 6.04.

A more significant question concerns what proportion of the whole price each shareholder receives, particularly if there are different classes of shares, or if there exists a controlling block of stock. This would appear to depend upon the structure of the acquisition. If the target sells its assets to the buyer and then liquidates, the stockholder's liquidation rights should control their relative receipts. See p. 1130–1131 *infra.* On the other hand, if the acquirer purchases the target's outstanding stock directly from the shareholders, it would seem each gets whatever price the shareholder and the acquirer can reach agreement upon. Is there any legal limit upon this conclusion? See pp. 972–995 *infra.* Finally, as discussed later in this chapter, if the acquirer and the target merge, the merger agreement or plan dictates what each stockholder receives. What protection does this leave for a shareholder who is not satisfied with what the plan provides for the shares of the class he or she holds? See pp. 1011–1013 *infra*.

b. *Type and Source of Payment*

In addition to how much the buyer will pay, it is also necessary to agree upon what the purchaser will use for payment. At the outset, the parties confront a basic choice as to whether the medium will consist of stock in the acquirer (assuming the purchaser is a corporation), or of something else (presumably cash or the promise to pay cash). The impacts of this decision permeate the entire transaction. The more technical effects of using stock include:

(i) Potentially differing corporate law requirements regarding shareholder approval of the transaction and concerning appraisal rights for dissenting stockholders;

(ii) Less ability of the purchaser to avoid the assumption of all the selling firm's debts;

(iii) Compliance with registration requirements under federal and state securities laws, unless the buyer can find an exemption covering the issuance of its stock; and

(iv) The prospect of structuring a tax-free transaction for the seller, and of the buyer inheriting various tax attributes from the target.

The middle section of this chapter, dealing with structuring the acquisition, will explore these factors. It is important, however, not to lose sight of the less technical concerns involved in this choice. From the acquirer's side, the use of stock involves the same practical factors considered when discussing the issuance of additional shares in Chapter IV. For example, giving the target's shareholders voting stock will dilute the voting control of the acquirer's current stockholders. The impact on the economic interests of the acquirer's existing stockholders is a function of the price—they suffer dilution if the value of the target is not equal to the value of the shares paid for it, which is often viewed more simply as whether earnings per share will decline. It is also a function of the cost and availability of other sources of payment (in other words, can the acquirer fund the purchase from its current resources, and, if not, what will be the interest charge if the acquirer borrows to pay for the acquisition). Dilution of voting and economic interests, in turn, raise the subject of preemptive rights. While such rights, as noted in Chapter IV, do not usually apply to shares issued for property (as in a merger or other acquisition), the purchaser must check its articles or state law to ensure the applicable article or state law is not inconsistent with this general rule.

What about from the seller's side? Here, one must ask why the target's stockholders would sell their business for stock in the buyer, since this means they simply are exchanging one type of stock for another. Perhaps they think the buyer is overpaying, in which case they can increase their worth at the expense of diluting the interests of the buyer's current stockholders. More positively, both sides might expect the acquisition to produce synergistic effects which will make shares in the combined entity worth more than all the stock in the two firms separately. Many times, the motivation lies in the greater marketability of the buyer's shares: For example, if a public corporation acquires a closely held firm, the seller's stockholders can trade an illiquid investment for one they might easily cash out.

If the buyer does not issue stock, it faces the problem of coming up with the payment.

Wieboldt Stores, Inc. v. Schottenstein

94 B.R. 488 (N.D.Ill.1988).

■ HOLDERMAN, DISTRICT JUDGE:

Wieboldt Stores, Inc. ("Wieboldt") filed this action on September 18, 1987 under the federal bankruptcy laws, * * *, the state fraudulent conveyance laws, * * *, and the Illinois Business Corporation Act, * * *. Pending before the court are numerous motions to dismiss this action * * *.

I. INTRODUCTION

Wieboldt's complaint against the defendants concerns the events and transactions surrounding a leveraged buyout ("LBO") of Wieboldt by WSI Acquisition Corporation ("WSI"). WSI, a corporation formed solely for the purpose of acquiring Wieboldt, borrowed funds from third-party lenders and delivered the proceeds to the shareholders in return for their shares. Wieboldt thereafter pledged certain of its assets to the LBO lenders to secure repayment of the loan.

* * *

II. FACTS

A. PARTIES

* * *

2. *Defendants*

Wieboldt brings this action against 119 defendants. These defendants can be grouped into three non-exclusive categories: (1) controlling shareholders, officers and directors; (2) other shareholders of Wieboldt's common stock who owned and tendered more than 1,000 shares in response to the tender offer ("Schedule A shareholders"); and (3) entities which loaned money to fund the tender offer.

a. *Controlling Shareholders, Officers and Directors*

* * * [After 1982,] Jerome Schottenstein and * * * certain persons and entities affiliated with * * * [him, and Julius and Edmond Trump,] each owned approximately 15% of Wieboldt's then outstanding shares and became Wieboldt's controlling shareholders.

* * *

c. *The LBO Lenders and Related Entities*

* * *

Wieboldt has included as defendants in this action four of the entities which were involved in these financial transactions: One North State Street Limited Partnership ("ONSSLP"), * * * BA Mortgage and International Realty Corporation ("BAMIRCO"), and General Electric Credit Corporation ("GECC").[6] The roles these entities played in the tender offer and subsequent buyout are described below.

B. THE TENDER OFFER AND RELATED TRANSACTIONS

By January, 1985 Wieboldt's financial health had declined to the point at which the company was no longer able to meet its obligations as they came due. On January 23, 1985 WSI sent a letter to Mr. Schottenstein in which WSI proposed a possible tender offer for Wieboldt common stock at $13.50 per share. The following day, Mr. Schottenstein informed Wieboldt's Board of Directors of the WSI proposal and the Board agreed to cooperate with WSI in evaluating the financial and operating records of the company. WSI proceeded to seek financing from several lenders, including Household Commercial Financial Services ("HCFS").

During 1985 it became apparent to Wieboldt's Board that WSI would accomplish its tender offer by means of an LBO through which WSI would pledge substantially all of Wieboldt's assets, including the company's fee and leasehold real estate assets, as collateral. Many of these real estate assets already served as collateral for $35 million in secured loan obligations from Continental Illinois National Bank ("CINB") and other bank creditors. Wieboldt was at least partially in default on these obligations at the time of the LBO.

In order to free these assets for use as collateral in obtaining tender offer financing, WSI intended to sell the One North State Street property [which housed Wieboldt's main store and executive offices] and pay off the CINB loan obligations. [ONSSLP purchased the property using a mortgage loan from BAMIRCO.]

The sale of the One North State Street property did not generate sufficient funds to pay off the CINB loan obligations. Consequently, WSI sought additional funds from GECC through the sale of Wieboldt's custom-

6. These entities are collectively referred to in this opinion as "State Street defendants."

er charge card accounts. GECC agreed to enter into an accounts purchase agreement after WSI acquired Wieboldt through the tender offer. One term of the accounts purchase agreement required Wieboldt to pledge all of its accounts receivable to GECC as additional security for Wieboldt's obligations under the agreement. Thus, by October 1985, HCFS, BAMIRCO, and GECC had each agreed to fund WSI's tender offer, and each knew of the other's loan or credit commitments. These lenders were aware that WSI intended to use the proceeds of the financing commitments to (1) purchase tendered shares of Wieboldt stock; (2) pay surrender prices for Wieboldt stock options; or (3) eliminate CINB loan obligations.

The Board of Directors was fully aware of the progress of WSI's negotiations. The Board understood that WSI intended to finance the tender offer by pledging a substantial portion of Wieboldt's assets to its lenders, and that WSI did not intend to use any of its own funds or the funds of its shareholders to finance the acquisition. Moreover, * * * the members knew that the proceeds from the LBO lenders would not result in * * * [any] working capital [for Wieboldt].

Nevertheless, in October, 1985 the Board directed Mr. Darrow and Wieboldt's lawyers to work with WSI to effect the acquisition. During these negotiations, the Board learned that HCFS would provide financing for the tender offer only if Wieboldt would provide a statement from a nationally recognized accounting firm stating that Wieboldt was solvent and a going concern prior to the planned acquisition and would be solvent and a going concern after the acquisition. Mr. Darrow informed WSI that Wieboldt would only continue cooperating in the LBO if HCFS agreed not to require this solvency certificate. HCFS acceded to Wieboldt's demand and no solvency certificate was ever provided to HCFS on Wieboldt's behalf.

On November 18, 1985 Wieboldt's Board of Directors voted to approve WSI's tender offer, and on November 20, 1985 WSI announced its offer to purchase Wieboldt stock for $13.50 per share. By December 20, 1985 the tender offer was complete and WSI had acquired ownership of Wieboldt through its purchase of 99% of Wieboldt's stock at a total price of $38,462,164.00. All of the funds WSI used to purchase the tendered shares were provided by HCFS and were secured by the assets which BAMIRCO and GECC loan proceeds had freed from CINB obligations. After the LBO,

1. Wieboldt's One North State Street property was conveyed to ONSSLP * * *;

2. Substantially all of Wieboldt's remaining real estate holdings were subject to first or second mortgages to secure the HCFS loans; and

3. Wieboldt's customer credit card accounts were conveyed to GECC and Wieboldt's accounts receivable were pledged to GECC as security under the GECC accounts purchase agreement.

In addition, Wieboldt became liable to HCFS on an amended note in the amount of approximately $32.5 million.[9] Wieboldt did not receive any amount of working capital as a direct result of the LBO.

9. The amount of WSI's note to HCFS represents the $38 million that WSI paid to Wieboldt shareholders less an immediate payment on that amount from the proceeds of the One North State sale.

On September 24, 1986 certain of Wieboldt's creditors commenced an involuntary liquidation proceeding against Wieboldt under Chapter 7 of the United States Bankruptcy Code ("the Code").

* * *

III. DISCUSSION

* * *

C. RULE 12(b)(6) MOTIONS TO DISMISS

The controlling shareholders, insider shareholders, Schedule A shareholders, and the State Street defendants move to dismiss the complaint on the grounds that Wieboldt has failed to state a claim under either the federal or the state fraudulent conveyance laws. In addition, the board of directors seek dismissal of the counts against them because Wieboldt has failed to state a claim for breach of fiduciary duty.

* * *

1. *Applicability of Fraudulent Conveyance Law*

Both the federal Bankruptcy Code and Illinois law protect creditors from transfers of property that are intended to impair a creditor's ability to enforce its rights to payment or that deplete a debtor's assets at a time when its financial condition is precarious. * * *

The controlling shareholders, insider shareholders, and some of the Schedule A shareholders argue that fraudulent conveyance laws do not apply to leveraged buyouts. * * *

Although some support exists for defendants' arguments,[13] this court cannot hold at this stage in this litigation that the LBO in question here is entirely exempt from fraudulent conveyance laws. Neither Section 548 of the Code nor the Illinois statute exempt such transactions from their statutory coverage. Section 548 invalidates fraudulent "transfers" of a debtor's property. Section 101(4) defines such a transfer very broadly to include "every mode, direct or indirect, absolute or conditional, voluntary or involuntary, of disposing of or parting with property or with an interest in property, including retention of title as a security interest." 11 U.S.C. § 101(4). Likewise, the Illinois statute applies to gifts, grants, conveyances, assignments and transfers. Ill.Rev.Stat. ch. 59, § 4. The language of these statutes in no way limits their application so as to exclude LBOs.

In addition, those courts which have addressed this issue have concluded that LBOs in some circumstances may constitute a fraudulent convey-

13. See, e.g., Baird & Jackson, "Fraudulent Conveyance Law and Its Proper Domain," 38 Vand.L.Rev. 829 (1985).

ance. * * * Defendants have presented no case law which holds to the contrary.

* * *

2. *The Structure of the Transaction*

Although the court finds that the fraudulent conveyance laws generally are applicable to LBO transactions, a debtor cannot use these laws to avoid any and all LBO transfers. In this case, certain defendants argue that they are entitled to dismissal because the LBO transfers at issue do not fall within the parameters of the laws. These defendants argue that they are protected by the literal language of Section 548 of the Code and the "good faith transferee for value" rule in Section 550.[15] They contend, initially, that they did not receive Wieboldt property during the tender offer and, secondarily, that, even if they received Wieboldt property, they tendered their shares in good faith, for value, and without the requisite knowledge and therefore cannot be held liable under Section 550.

The merit of this assertion turns on the court's interpretation of the tender offer and LBO transactions. Defendants contend that the tender offer and LBO were composed of a series of interrelated but independent transactions. They assert, for example, that the transfer of property from HCFS to WSI and ultimately to the shareholders constituted one series of several transactions while the pledge of Wieboldt assets to HCFS to secure the financing constituted a second series of transactions. Under this view, defendants did not receive the *debtor's* property during the tender offer but rather received WSI's property in exchange for their shares.

Wieboldt, on the other hand, urges the court to "collapse" the interrelated transactions into one aggregate transaction which had the overall effect of conveying Wieboldt property to the tendering shareholders and LBO lenders. This approach requires the court to find that the persons and entities receiving the conveyance were direct transferees who received "an interest of the debtor in property" during the tender offer/buyout, and that WSI and any other parties to the transactions were "mere conduits" of Wieboldt's property. If the court finds that all the transfers constituted one

15. While Section 548 defines the nature of the transactions that are avoidable by the debtor, Section 550 places limits on Section 548 by defining the kind of transferee from whom a debtor may recover transferred property. Section 550(a) permits a trustee to recover fraudulently transferred property from

1. the initial transferee;

2. the entity for whose benefit such transfer was made; or

3. an immediate or mediate transferee of such initial transferee (a "subsequent transferee").

11 U.S.C. § 550(a). Section 550(b) states that a trustee may not recover from

1. a subsequent transferee who takes the property for value, in good faith, and without knowledge of the voidability of the transfer; or

2. an immediate or mediate good faith transferee of such a transferee. 11 U.S.C. § 550(b).

transaction, then defendants received property from Wieboldt and Wieboldt has stated a claim against them.

Few courts have considered whether complicated LBO transfers should be evaluated separately or collapsed into one integrated transaction. However, two United States Courts of Appeals opinions provide some illumination on this issue. See *Kupetz v. Wolf,* 845 F.2d 842 (9th Cir.1988); *United States v. Tabor Court Realty,* 803 F.2d 1288 (3d Cir.1986), *cert. denied, McClellan Realty Co. v. United States,* 107 S.Ct. 3229, 97 L.Ed.2d 735 (1987).

In *Kupetz,* the debtor corporation (Wolf & Vine) was owned in equal shares by an individual, Morris Wolf, and the Marmon Group. When Mr. Wolf retired, Marmon decided to sell the company and concluded that David Adashek was a suitable buyer. Mr. Adashek subsequently obtained control of the company through a series of transactions which constituted an LBO.[16] Thereafter, Wolf & Vine could not service the additional debt that resulted from the buyout. The company eventually filed for bankruptcy under Chapter 11 of the Code.

The dispute before the district court resulted when the trustee in bankruptcy sought to avoid the LBO transfers on the grounds that the manner in which the sale was financed constituted a fraudulent conveyance to Mr. Wolf and the Marmon Group. After the case proceeded to a jury trial, the district court directed a verdict in favor of the selling shareholders on the fraudulent conveyance claims. * * * The trustees appealed.

The Ninth Circuit affirmed the district court's decision and declined to strike down the LBO on fraudulent conveyance grounds. The court concluded that the trustee could not avoid the transfer to the shareholders because (1) they did not sell their shares in order to defraud Wolf & Vine's creditors; (2) they did not know that Mr. Adashek intended to leverage the company's assets to finance the purchase of shares; and (3) the LBO had the indicia of a straight sale of shares and was not Wolf & Vine's attempt to redeem its own shares. * * * However, the Ninth Circuit in its opinion in *Kupetz* stated:

> In an LBO, the lender, by taking a security interest in the company's assets, reduces the assets available to creditors in the event of failure of the business. The form of the LBO, while not unimportant, does not alter this reality. Thus, where the parties in an LBO fully intend to hinder the general creditors and benefit the selling shareholders the

16. These transactions were:

1. Mr. Adashek formed Little Red Riding Hood (Riding Hood) with $100.00 in capital;

2. Riding Hood purchased all of the shares of Wolf & Vine for $3 million;

3. Riding Hood financed the transaction with a $1.1 million loan from CINB and the Bank issued letters of credit in favor of the sellers for the remaining amount;

4. Riding Hood merged into Wolf & Vine and Wolf & Vine assumed Riding Hood's obligation to the sellers;

5. Wolf & Vine pledged its assets to the bank to secure the loan and the letters of credit. * * *

conveyance is fraudulent under (the fraudulent conveyance laws). 845 F.2d at 846.

In *Kupetz* the Ninth Circuit discussed shareholder liability under the fraudulent conveyance laws. The Third Circuit in *United States v. Tabor Court,* 803 F.2d 1288 (3d Cir.1986), *cert. denied McClellan Realty Co. v. United States,* 107 S.Ct. 3229, 97 L.Ed.2d 735 (1987), addressed the liability of an LBO lender. In *Tabor Court,* the controlling shareholders of the debtor corporation (Raymond Group) solicited a purchaser for the company. The purchaser formed a holding company (Great American) to purchase Raymond Group's outstanding shares. Great American acquired Raymond Group by borrowing funds from a third party lender (IIT) and securing the loan with both first and second mortgages on Raymond Group's assets.[19] After the company failed and many of its assets had been sold to various investment groups, the United States government sought to reduce to judgment certain tax liens on Raymond Group's property and satisfy the judgments out of assets which the company owned before it mortgaged those assets to secure the LBO funds. * * *

The Third Circuit affirmed the district court's conclusion that the mortgages that the Raymond Group gave to IIT were fraudulent conveyances within the meaning of the constructive and intentional fraud sections of the Pennsylvania UFCA. * * * In affirming the district court, the Third Circuit noted that all three parties—the lender, the debtor, and the purchaser—participated in the loan negotiations, and that IIT therefore knew of the purpose to which Great American intended to put the loan proceeds. * * * The court held that the district court, in interpreting the LBO, correctly integrated the series of transactions because the Raymond Group merely served as a conduit for the transfer between IIT and Great American (and ultimately to the shareholders), and did not receive the funds as any form of consideration. * * *

Neither of these cases involved transactions which were identical to the WSI–Wieboldt buyout. However, the *Kupetz* and *Tabor Court* opinions are nonetheless significant because the courts in both cases expressed the view that an LBO transfer—in whatever form—was a fraudulent conveyance if the circumstances of the transfer were not "above board." * * * These cases indicate that a court should focus not on the formal structure of the transaction but rather on the knowledge or intent of the parties involved in the transaction.

Applying this principle to defendants' assertions, it is clear that, at least as regards the liability of the controlling shareholders, the LBO lenders, and the insider shareholders, the LBO transfers must be collapsed into one transaction. The complaint alleges clearly that these participants in the LBO negotiations attempted to structure the LBO with the requisite knowledge and contemplation that the full transaction, tender offer and

19. The loan proceeds went from the lender to the debtor corporation, who turned them over immediately to the holding company, which used the funds to purchase shares. * * *

LBO, be completed. The Board and the insider shareholders knew that WSI intended to finance its acquisition of Wieboldt through an LBO * * * and not with any of its own funds * * *. They knew that Wieboldt was insolvent before the LBO and that the LBO would result in further encumbrance of Wieboldt's already encumbered assets. * * *. Attorneys for Schottenstein Stores apprised the Board of the fraudulent conveyance laws and suggested that they structure the LBO so as to avoid liability. * * * Nonetheless, these shareholders recommended that Wieboldt accept the tender offer and themselves tendered their shares to WSI. * * *

Wieboldt's complaint also alleges sufficient facts to implicate LBO lenders in the scheme. HCFS, BAMIRCO and GECC were well aware of each other's loan or credit commitments to WSI and knew that WSI intended to use the proceeds of their financing commitments to purchase Wieboldt shares or options and to release certain Wieboldt assets from prior encumbrances. * * * Representatives of the lenders received the same information concerning the fraudulent conveyance laws as did the Board of Directors. * * * These LBO lenders agreed with WSI and the Board of Directors to structure the LBO so as to avoid fraudulent conveyance liability. * * *

The court, however, is not willing to "collapse" the transaction order to find that the Schedule A shareholders also received the debtor's property in the transfer. While Wieboldt directs specific allegations of fraud against the controlling and insider shareholders and LBO lenders, Wieboldt does not allege that the Schedule A shareholders were aware that WSI's acquisition encumbered virtually all of Wieboldt's assets. Nor is there an allegation that these shareholders were aware that the consideration they received for their tendered shares was Wieboldt property. In fact, the complaint does not suggest that the Schedule A shareholders had any part in the LBO except as innocent pawns in the scheme. They were aware only that WSI made a public tender offer for shares of Wieboldt stock. * * * Viewing the transactions from the perspective of the Schedule A shareholders and considering their knowledge and intent, therefore, the asset transfers to the LBO lenders were indeed independent of the tender offer to the Schedule A shareholders.

This conclusion is in accord with the purpose of the fraudulent conveyance laws. The drafters of the Code, while attempting to protect parties harmed by fraudulent conveyances, also intended to shield innocent recipients of fraudulently conveyed property from liability.

* * *

3. *The Elements of a Fraudulent Conveyance*

As discussed above, the transfers to and between the debtor and the LBO lenders, controlling shareholders, and insider shareholders are subject to the provisions in Section 548(a) of the Code and Section 4 of the Illinois statute. The court now must determine whether Wieboldt's complaint states sufficient facts to allege the elements of these causes of action.

a. *Section 548(a)(1)*

In order to state a claim for relief under Section 548(a)(1) of the Code, a debtor or trustee must allege (1) that the transfer was made within one year before the debtor filed a petition in bankruptcy, and (2) that the transfer was made with the actual intent to hinder, delay or defraud the debtor's creditors. 11 U.S.C. § 548(a)(1). * * *Although defendants do not dispute that the LBO transfers occurred within a year of the date on which Wieboldt filed for bankruptcy, they vigorously assert that Wieboldt has failed to properly allege "intent to defraud" as required by Section 548(a)(1).

"Actual intent" in the context of fraudulent transfers of property is rarely susceptible to proof and "must be gleaned from inferences drawn from a course of conduct." * * * A general scheme or plan to strip the debtor of its assets without regard to the needs of its creditors can support a finding of actual intent. * * *

* * * Count I, which Wieboldt brings against the controlling and insider shareholders, states that these defendants exchanged their shares with the actual intent to hinder, delay or defraud Wieboldt's unsecured creditors. * * * The complaint also states generally that the LBO Lenders and the controlling and insider shareholders structured the LBO transfers in such a way as to attempt to evade fraudulent conveyance liability. * * * These allegations are a sufficient assertion of actual fraud. * * *

b. *Section 548(a)(2)*

Unlike Section 548(a)(1), which requires a plaintiff to allege "actual fraud," Section 548(a)(2) requires a plaintiff to allege only constructive fraud. A plaintiff states a claim under Section 548(a)(2) by alleging that the debtor (1) transferred property within a year of filing a petition in bankruptcy; (2) received less than the reasonably equivalent value for the property transferred; and (3) either (a) was insolvent or became insolvent as a result of the transfer, (b) retained unreasonably small capital after the transfer, or (c) made the transfer with the intent to incur debts beyond its ability to pay. 11 U.S.C. § 548(a)(2).

Defendants argue that Wieboldt's allegation of insolvency is insufficient as a matter of law to satisfy the insolvency requirements in Section 548(a)(2)(B)(i). Section 101(31)(A) of the Code defines "insolvency" as a condition which occurs when the sum of an entity's debts exceeds the sum of its property "at a fair valuation." 11 U.S.C. § 101(31)(A). Wieboldt's complaint alleges that the corporation was insolvent in November, 1985 "in that the fair saleable value of its assets was exceeded by its liabilities when the illiquidity of those assets is taken into account." (Complaint, ¶¶ 112, 121).

Wieboldt's allegations satisfy the "insolvency" requirement of Section 548(a)(2)(B)(i). * * *

Finally, defendants claim that Wieboldt cannot state a claim under Section 548(a)(2) because it received "reasonably equivalent value" * * *.

Wieboldt granted a security interest in substantially all of its real estate assets to HCFS and received from the shareholders in return 99% of its outstanding shares of stock.[25] * * * This stock was virtually worthless to Wieboldt. * * * Wieboldt received less than a reasonably equivalent value in exchange for an encumbrance on virtually all of its non-inventory assets, and therefore has stated a claim against the controlling and insider shareholders.

Likewise, the court need not dismiss Wieboldt's Section 548(a)(2) claim against the State Street defendants on the grounds that Wieboldt received reasonably equivalent value in exchange for its One North State Street property. The effect and intention of the parties to the One North State Street conveyance was to generate funds to purchase outstanding shares of Wieboldt stock. Although Wieboldt sold the property to ONSSLP for $30 million, and used the proceeds to pay off part of the $35 million it owed CINB, Wieboldt did not receive a benefit from this transfer. * * * Defendants knew that the conveyance would neither increase Wieboldt's assets nor result in a net reduction of its liabilities. In fact, all parties to the conveyance were aware that the newly unencumbered assets would be immediately remortgaged to HCFS to finance the acquisition. * * * According to the complaint, therefore, Wieboldt received less than reasonably equivalent value for the conveyance of the One North State Street property and has stated a claim against the State Street defendants under Section 548(a)(2).

In sum, Counts II and IV of Wieboldt's complaint state a claim under Section 548(a)(2). Defendants' motions to dismiss these counts are denied.

* * *

4. *Breach of Fiduciary Duty*

Counts IX and X of Wieboldt's complaint purport to state a claim for relief against Wieboldt's former Board of Directors for breach of fiduciary duty. The complaint alleges that the directors owed Wieboldt a fiduciary duty of "utmost good faith, care, and loyalty" when dealing with the corporation and was required to investigate thoroughly corporate transactions such as the LBO. * * * The complaint also alleges that the directors owed a duty to Wieboldt's unsecured creditors to preserve the corporation's assets. * * * Wieboldt alleges that the Board of Directors breached these duties "by assisting in the formulation and completion of the LBO" despite Wieboldt's insolvency and knowing that the LBO would injure Wieboldt's unsecured creditors.

* * *

25. Defendants argue that WSI (and not Wieboldt) received the outstanding shares of Wieboldt stock. However, a court analyzing an allegedly fraudulent transfer must direct its attention to "what the Debtor surrendered and what the Debtor received, irrespective of what any third party may have gained or lost." * * * As discussed in Section C.2. of this opinion, the court considers the tender offer and buyout transfers as one transaction for the purposes of this motion.

The directors' assertion that they did not owe a duty to the corporation during the formulation and execution of the LBO is incorrect.

* * *

Applying these principles to Wieboldt's complaint, it appears that Wieboldt has stated a claim against the directors for breach of fiduciary duty. Although the directors may have adequately investigated the terms of the LBO and had anticipated the effect the LBO would have on the corporation * * *, the court can reasonably infer from the complaint that the directors did not act in good faith and in furtherance of the corporation's best interests. Four of the nine directors owned shares of Wieboldt stock before the tender offer and therefore would have personally received a direct benefit by approving the tender offer. * * * The remaining directors were affiliated with one of Wieboldt's two controlling shareholders, Mr. Schottenstein and his affiliates or MBT Corporation and the Trump brothers. * * * In addition, the directors approved the tender offer notwithstanding their concurrent knowledge the Wieboldt was insolvent. * * * The court can reasonably infer from these facts that the directors acted in their own interests in approving the tender offer notwithstanding the fact that the LBO would result in harm to the corporation.

The complaint alleges sufficient facts to support a cause of action against the directors for breach of their fiduciary duty to the corporation. The directors' motions to dismiss Counts IX and X are denied.

5. *Illinois Business Corporation Act*

In Count XI, Wieboldt attempts to state a claim under Sections 8.65(a)(1) and 9.10(c)(1) of the Illinois Business Corporations Act * * *. Section 9.10(c)(1) prohibits a board of directors from authorizing a distribution to shareholders that would have the effect of rendering the corporation insolvent. Section 8.65(a)(1) provides that directors who assent to a distribution prohibited by Section 9.10 are jointly and severally liable to the corporation for the amount of the distribution.

* * *

The directors' primary contention is that the exchange between HCFS and the shareholders was not an improper distribution. Both Wieboldt and the directors contend that legislative history controls the meaning of the term "distribution" as it is used in Section 9.10. Wieboldt maintains that the court must "collapse" this transaction and find that the Board made an illegal distribution because the effect of the payment of cash from HCFS to the shareholders was to transfer Wieboldt assets to Wieboldt shareholders. Wieboldt maintains that the Illinois statute encompasses such an indirect transfer. The directors assert that the Illinois statute does not contemplate a transfer whereby no corporate assets pass directly from the corporation to its shareholders.

Neither Section 9.10 nor any other section of the IBCA defines the term "distribution" as it is used in the Act. However, the Revised Model

Business Corporations Act ("MBCA"), from which the IBCA derives, defines "distribution" very broadly. Section 1.40(6) provides that the term "distribution" encompasses:

> a direct or indirect transfer of money or other property (except [a corporation's] own shares) or incurrence of indebtedness by a corporation to or for the benefit of its shareholders in respect to any of its shares. A distribution may be in the form of a declaration or payment of a dividend; a purchase, redemption, or other acquisition of shares; a distribution of indebtedness; or otherwise.

* * * In the absence of contrary authority, it appears likely that the Illinois Legislature contemplated a broad range of transfers, including indirect transfers such as the exchange of cash and shares between HCFS and the shareholders. The directors' motions to dismiss Count XI therefore are denied.

* * *

NOTES

1. If the buyer does not issue stock, then it either must have the money available to pay the seller, or it must borrow. The fancy term for the purchase of a business through borrowing (at least if the lender counts on the assets or earnings of the business for repayment) is a leveraged buy-out (or LBO). The buyer can look essentially to two sources from whom to borrow. In *Wieboldt Stores,* the purchaser looked to third party lenders. These lenders can be financial institutions who provide individually negotiated loans (as in *Wieboldt Stores*), or a number of investors to whom the purchaser issues bonds (often called junk bonds because of their high risk). The alternative to borrowing from third parties is to borrow from the selling stockholders; in other words, give the selling stockholders debt instruments which allow the buyer to pay them off over time.

In either case, typically the acquirer plans to pay off the loans out of the earnings or assets of the target. This can create both practical and legal problems. The practical problem is that the target is expected to service greater debt, without the proceeds of those loans going toward the production of greater income producing capability for the corporation. The result is more risk of bankruptcy. (This admittedly ignores the often touted beneficial incentives created by an LBO—in other words, the notion that pressure to meet greater debt payments on the one hand, and the greater rewards for doing so for the leveraging buyer of the company on the other, will produce more efficient decisions.)

With or without reaching bankruptcy, a number of legal questions arise. To begin with, how exactly does the target come to pay loans made to enable the buyer to purchase the company? There are a number of possibilities depending upon the structure of the acquisition. In *Wieboldt Stores,* the purchaser bought the target's outstanding stock. Such a purchaser could simply attempt to service the loans through periodic dividends from the target, which is now its subsidiary. This might not be an acceptable solution, however, even if one avoids the tax problem by virtue of the buyer being a corporation and so entitled to the dividends-received deduction under Section 243. The primary problem exists from the lender's standpoint, and specifically lies in the security for its loan. If the buyer but not the target is liable, then the lender's collateral (assuming the buyer does not have significant other assets) will consist at most of a pledge of the acquired stock. This will put the lender in an inferior position to the target's creditors should the target fail to generate enough earnings to cover the payments. What lenders seek, as in *Wieboldt Stores,* is a security interest in the target's assets. Can the acquired corporation, however, just agree to assume gratuitously the obligation of its new controlling shareholder? See, *e.g., Real Estate Capital Corp. v. Thunder Corp.,* 31 Ohio Misc. 169, 287 N.E.2d 838 (1972) (corporation's mortgage of its property, in order to secure a loan to another company owned by its 80 percent shareholder, held ultra vires and invalid); *Roxbury State Bank v. The Clarendon,* 129 N.J.Super. 358, 324 A.2d 24 (1974) (corporation's mortgage of its property to finance an outside buyer's purchase of its stock could be invalid as a fraudulent conveyance, since it constituted an obligation incurred without fair consideration). *But see Telefest, Inc. v. VU–TV, Inc.,* 591 F.Supp. 1368 (D.N.J.1984).

On the other hand, suppose the acquiring corporation merges with the target. As discussed later in this chapter, the combined entity resulting from a merger assumes both of the merging companies' debts by operation of law. This was the technique used in the *Kupetz* case (discussed in the *Wieboldt Stores* opinion) for putting the target corporation on the line for the acquirer's debt. Other possibilities include the buyer's purchasing the target corporation's assets, instead of its outstanding stock, which could then allow the buyer to pledge the assets to secure the loan. Notice, however, where the sales proceeds go in this transaction. Finally, perhaps the target itself could borrow the money. It might then redeem most of its outstanding stock (thereby leaving little left for the buyer to acquire with the buyer's own funds). This last bootstrap approach will be considered in some detail later in this chapter. As a variation, the target could borrow after the buyer (using temporary unsecured loans) purchases the outstanding stock. The target then can transfer the proceeds of its loans—through a dividend, a redemption, or even a loan—to the purchaser in order for the purchaser to pay off the bridge financing. This appears to be, more or less, what the parties did in the *Tabor* case discussed in *Wieboldt Stores.*

Needless to say, the target's assumption of the debt incurred to purchase the firm can prejudice the target's other creditors. This is obvious in a case like *Wieboldt Stores* in which the target went bankrupt. Yet, prejudice can also occur even when the target remains afloat. The increased risk facing the target's existing bondholders can lower the price they will receive if they try to sell their bonds. The court's opinion in *Wieboldt Stores* provides a good run-through of both the various challenges creditors might assert against an LBO, at least if the target fails, and who—directors of the target, the selling shareholders, or the lenders in the LBO—will suffer the consequences if these challenges are successful. In this regard, one should note that some courts have disagreed with *Wieboldt Stores* as to whether state corporate law dividend limits apply to a leveraged buy-out. *E.g., In re C–T of Virginia, Inc.,* 958 F.2d 606 (4th Cir.1992). What lessons does the prospect of such challenges create from a planning standpoint? Initially, one might ask whether the structure by which the target comes to pay the loan will impact the prospects of a challenge. Compare the gratuitous assumption of the buyer's obligations by the target, with the other alternatives described above. Can both the lender and the selling shareholders show their individual transactions involved an exchange for fair consideration in these other structures, and, hence, cannot be a fraudulent conveyance? Notice how the court in *Wieboldt Stores* responded to this approach of looking at each transaction separately. In fact, the court used the parties' attempt at structuring the transaction to avoid the fraudulent conveyance law, as evidence against them. If legal structure does not provide an answer, perhaps fiscal prudence does. Examine the tests contained in the fraudulent conveyance laws, which separate the invalid from the permissible when it comes to transfers or obligations made without fair consideration. What investigation might lenders, directors and controlling shareholders make to ensure not only the solvency of the target upon completion of the transaction, but also that the target does not have unreasonably small capital and does not thereafter plan to incur debts beyond its ability to pay? See Kirby, McGuinness & Kandel, *Fraudulent Conveyance Concerns in Leveraged Buyout Lending,* 43 Bus. Law. 27 (1987). The AICPA, however, has barred accountants from issuing solvency opinions for leveraged buy-outs—thereby ruling out the approach started but not followed through by the lenders in *Wieboldt.* At the other extreme, can anything be said for ignorance under the court's opinion? Compare how the former public shareholders of Wieboldt fared, as against the results for the controlling stockholders. Note also how the court explained the *Kupetz* and *Tabor* decisions.

2. Financing an acquisition through borrowing also raises the possible application of margin rules. Acting pursuant to Section 7 of the 1934 Securities Exchange Act, the Federal Reserve Board has promulgated a series of regulations which limit lending activities by stock brokers (Regulation T), banks (Regulation U) and others (Regulation G), as well as borrowing (Regulation X), for the purpose of purchasing or carrying securities. 12 C.F.R. §§ 207.1 *et seq.,* 220.1 *et seq.,* 221.1 *et seq.,* 224.1 *et seq.* While Section 7 and these regulations appear primarily directed against excessive lending for investment or speculative purchases of stock (particularly at the retail level), the Federal Reserve Board, the Securities Exchange Commission and the courts have held the regulations can apply to loans made for the purpose of purchasing a controlling amount of stock. *E.g.,* 12 C.F.R. § 221.110(b)(2); *Pargas, Inc. v. Empire Gas Corp.,* 423 F.Supp. 199 (D.Md.), *aff'd,* 546 F.2d 25 (4th Cir.1976).

What planning implications flow from the potential application of these regulations? Consider first the situation in which the acquirer approaches a bank or other lending institution seeking a loan. For Regulations U or G to apply, the loan must be for the purpose of buying or carrying margin stocks. 12 C.F.R. §§ 207.1(b), 221.1(b). This can cover, as stated above, the acquisition of the target's stock, but presumably would not cover the purchases of the target corporation's assets. What about a merger in which the acquiring corporation borrows to cash out the target's shareholders? See Federal Reserve Board ruling dated November 29, 1979, reprinted in 35 Bus. Law. 559 (1980) (implicitly considering a reverse triangular cash-out merger to constitute a purchase of stock). Note, as well, not all shares are "margin" stock. This is a term of art in each regulation, encompassing (depending upon the regulation) shares listed or otherwise traded on a national exchange, and some, but not all, stock traded over the counter (OTC). 12 C.F.R. §§ 207.2(i), 221.2(h). Hence, the regulations do not cover bank or other loans for the purchase of a privately held firm's outstanding shares.

In addition, for Regulations U or G to apply, margin stocks must directly or indirectly secure the loan. 12 C.F.R. §§ 207.1(b), 221.1(b). In this light, consider again the importance lenders often attach to having the target's assets, rather than its stock, provide security for their loans. On the other hand, suppose the lender makes an unsecured loan. While this would seem to preclude application of the regulations, there are a couple caveats. If the loan agreement restricts the borrower's ability to dispose or pledge margin stocks (unless not more than 25 percent of the assets so restricted are margin stocks), than the regulations consider the stocks to indirectly secure the loan. 12 C.F.R. §§ 207.2(f), 221.2(g). Moreover, if the borrower is a shell corporation set up to acquire the target, the regulations again deem the acquired stock under some circumstances to indirectly secure the loan. 12 C.F.R. § 207.112(h). This depends upon (i) whether the borrowing entity has other substantial assets or cash flow to service the debt, (ii) whether another company with such assets or cash flow guarantees the loan, or (iii) whether the acquisition is friendly or the loan is contingent on the acquirer obtaining enough shares for a short form merger (typically 90%) so that the acquirer can count on getting access to the target's assets—in any of which cases it is credible to accept that the purchased stock is not indirectly securing the loan.

Of course, if the regulations apply, this does not prevent the lender from making a loan. Rather, the impact is to limit the amount of the loan to a percentage set by the Federal Reserve Board (currently 50 percent) of the value of the margin stock (excluding options) used as collateral, plus (except for credit from or arranged by securities broker-dealers) the full value of whatever other non-stock collateral the borrower puts up. 12 C.F.R. §§ 207.3(c), 207.7, 221.3, 221.8.

Suppose a securities broker-dealer becomes involved in arranging the financing for the acquisition. Such arranging can bring Regulation T into play. The regulation generally prohibits broker-dealers from arranging for any credit, except if the broker-dealer itself could have provided the credit legally under the regulation. 12 C.F.R. § 220.13. Significantly, however, the regulation creates an exception from this general restriction for investment banking services in connection with exchange offers, mergers or acquisitions. (Investment banking services for this purpose can include such things as most underwritings, private placements, and giving advise.) One source of financing an underwriter might help arrange is a public or private placement of bonds (such as junk bonds) to a number of investors. The exception in Section 220.13 for underwriting activities involving acquisitions extends only to loans permissible under the other margin regulations; which brings one back to Regulations U and G. Do the purchasers of junk bonds constitute lenders within the meaning of Regulation G? See 12 C.F.R. § 207.112(c) (yes, if purchase large denominations). *But see* Fed. Res. Bd. Release 25 (Jan. 10, 1986) (public offering of debt securities not covered by margin rules).

3. Borrowing to finance the purchase of a business can entail certain tax advantages both for the acquirer and the selling stockholders. The benefits to the purchaser's side follow from the same principles discussed when considering the choice between issuing stock or debt in forming a corporation. The key advantage of debt is that interest is normally deductible by the payor, whereas dividends are not. In fact, the impact of this deduction is to have the government subsidize leveraged buy-outs.

Several restrictions exist, however, upon an acquirer's ability to deduct such interest. To begin with, Section 279 of the Internal Revenue Code disallows a deduction in excess of 5 million dollars for interest paid on so-called corporate acquisition indebtedness. Fortunately from the buyer's standpoint, the section's definition of corporate acquisition indebtedness is narrow and not difficult to avoid. To fall within the Section, not only must the acquirer issue the debt in consideration for purchasing stock or assets of another corporation, but the debt must be subordinated to unsecured or trade creditors, must be convertible into the issuer's stock (or accompanied by a warrant to purchase such stock), and the issuer must have either a debt-equity ratio of over 2 to 1 or annual interest obligations of one-third or more of its projected earnings. I.R.C. § 279(b). Note, however, that one cannot slip around the section by issuing up to $5 million worth of corporate acquisition indebtedness, and the rest of the price in other debt instruments, since Section 279(a)(2) reduces the $5 million ceiling by all debt issued to acquire stock or assets of another company.

A second limitation exists by virtue of Section 163(e)(5) and (i). These provisions are designed to deny the issuer of junk bonds the ability to deduct original issue discount. Specifically, if the debt instrument has a maturity of over 5 years, yields an interest rate of at least 5 percent more than the Federal rate at the time of issuance, and has significant original issue discount (in other words, much of the interest is not received in fixed annual or more frequent payments, but rather deferred, for instance, until maturity) then the issuer cannot take the deduction to which it is normally entitled for original issue discount—at least until it actually pays the sum, and perhaps never.

Section 172(b)(1)(E) and (h) imposes a third limitation. This comes into play when the interest deduction from a leveraged buy-out produces (or adds to) a net operating loss (NOL) that the corporation wishes to carry back and use against earlier income. Specifically, the provision bars a corporation from carrying back the portion of the firm's NOLs resulting from an interest deduction "allocable" (as specified in the section) either to the acquisition of 50 percent or more of another corporation's stock or to extraordinarily large dividends or redemptions (as determined under certain percentage tests).

Finally, if the acquirer purchases less than half the target's stock, then the use of debt to finance the purchase can result in denying the buyer the dividends-received deduction of section 243. I.R.C. § 246A.

What are the tax advantages of debt from the seller's side? The interest subsidy also helps the seller by allowing the buyer to finance a higher purchase price from the same cash flow. Moreover, if the buyer pays the seller with debt instruments (instead of borrowing from third parties), the selling shareholders may be able to spread out their recognition of gain by virtue of installment reporting. *But see* I.R.C. § 453(k)(2)(A) (precluding installment reporting for the sale of stock or securities which are traded on an established securities market).

c. *The Negotiation Process*

Jewel Companies, Inc. v. Pay Less Drug Stores Northwest, Inc.

741 F.2d 1555 (9th Cir.1984).

■ REINHARDT, CIRCUIT JUDGE:

This case arises out of a takeover battle for the acquisition of a publicly traded company, the Pay Less Drug Stores ("Pay Less"). Plaintiff, the Jewel Companies, Inc. ("Jewel") appeals an order granting summary judgment for the defendant, Pay Less Drug Stores Northwest, Inc., ("Northwest").[1] Jewel alleges that Northwest's actions constitute tortious interference with a merger agreement between Pay Less and Jewel. * * *

Most of the facts material to this appeal are not in dispute. In September 1979, Pay Less retained the investment banking firm of Goldman, Sachs & Co. to locate a merger partner. Jewel, a Chicago-based company engaged primarily in the retail grocery business, was among the companies contacted. On November 9, 1979, Jewel and Pay Less agreed to a tax-free merger in which each outstanding share of Pay Less stock would be exchanged for .652 shares of Jewel stock. The merger agreement was executed in writing, formally approved by both boards of directors, signed on behalf of each corporation by its respective president, and made public in a press release on November 9, 1979.[2]

1. Although they bear similar corporate names because of a common corporate ancestor, Pay Less and Northwest were entirely unrelated companies prior to the events at issue here.

2. At this time Jewel also agreed to purchase the 297,010 shares of Pay Less stock that were held by a foundation that the founder of Pay Less had established. Jewel

The merger agreement included several covenants the meaning of which is in dispute and is central to the issues before us on appeal. Articles 9.9 and 10.5 of the Jewel–Pay Less merger agreement obligated the board of directors of each firm to "use its best efforts to fulfill those conditions . . . over which it has control or influence and to consummate the Merger." Pay Less was further obligated under article 9 of the agreement to forbear from the sale or transfer of any of its properties or assets, and from entering into or terminating any contract other than in the ordinary course of business. The merger agreement further provided that Pay Less could not "agree to, or make any commitment to" effect any sale, transfer, or extraordinary action prohibited in Article 9. Article 7 of the Jewel–Pay Less merger agreement incorporated several prerequisites to closing the transaction. The obligations of both firms to consummate the merger were conditioned upon Pay Less obtaining the affirmative vote of a majority of the outstanding shares of Pay Less stock. The obligation of each firm to close the transaction was also contingent upon Jewel obtaining the required governmental consents.

Northwest had discussed the possibility of a merger with Pay Less several times in the 1970s. When the Jewel–Pay Less merger agreement was publicly announced, Northwest's management considered making a competing bid to acquire Pay Less. * * * Northwest made public its intention to make a competing bid in a press release issued December 31, 1979. At that time Northwest offered $22.50 per share for Pay Less stock. * * *

Two days later Jewel filed this action in state court, seeking a temporary restraining order against Northwest's tender offer and alleging tortious interference with contract * * *.

The Northwest tender offer was formally commenced on January 17. * * * On January 29, as a 10% shareholder of Pay Less, Jewel called a shareholders' meeting to take place on March 4 for the purpose of voting on the Jewel–Pay Less merger agreement, thereby hoping to conclude the balloting before Northwest became record owner of the shares tendered.

Northwest increased its tender offer price to $24 per share on February 1 and Pay Less' Board of Directors unanimously recommended that its shareholders accept the Northwest offer. On this date Northwest and Pay Less, through its Board of Directors, entered into an Indemnity and Record Date Agreement which provided in relevant part that:

(1) Northwest would indemnify Pay Less and its directors for any alleged breach of the Jewel Agreement;

also entered into a written agreement for an option to purchase an additional 421,486 shares. The option agreement provided that Mrs. Mary C. Skaggs, the widow of Pay Less's founder and the owner of the 421,486 shares, would vote her shares in favor of the Jewel merger, but if the merger were terminated or cancelled, Jewel would nevertheless have the option to purchase her shares for the same .652 exchange ratio offered to other Pay Less shareholders.

(2) February 23, 1980 would be the record date for determining the shareholders eligible to vote on the Jewel proposal. March 1, 1980, or not less than ten New York Stock Exchange trading days following the expiration date of the tender offer in the event that the tender offer were extended, would be the record date for determining the shareholders entitled to notice of and to vote on the Northwest merger agreement;

(3) if for some reason a majority of the record owners of Pay Less stock did approve the Jewel merger (a theoretical possibility if the mechanics of recording the transfer of shares on the corporate records were not completed by the Jewel record date, set for February 23, 1980), then the Pay Less Board of Directors would nevertheless abandon the Jewel merger pursuant to Cal. Corp. Code § 1105; and,

(4) Northwest and Pay Less would issue a joint press release in which Pay Less would make a recommendation to its shareholders in favor of acceptance of the tender offer, including a statement to the effect that the price offered under the tender offer is significantly more favorable to its shareholders generally than the terms offered under the Jewel Merger Agreement.

Finally, on February 1, the Pay Less Board signed a merger agreement with Northwest. The board sent all of its shareholders a 29–page letter comparing the two merger offers and setting forth the history of the two proposals. Although it unanimously recommended the Northwest offer, Pay Less advised its shareholders that the March 4 meeting to consider the Jewel merger agreement would go forward as scheduled.

By February 25, a majority of Pay Less's shares had been tendered to Northwest and Jewel withdrew its request for a shareholders' meeting. The meeting nevertheless took place as scheduled on March 4. Northwest, by then the majority shareholder, passed a shareholder resolution rejecting the Jewel merger agreement. The Pay Less Board, which had been reconstituted to include a majority of Northwest representatives, terminated the Jewel agreement. On March 7, Jewel tendered the 297,010 shares of Pay Less stock that it had purchased on November 9, 1979 for $15 a share to Northwest for $24 per share.

Northwest removed Jewel's initial suit for a preliminary injunction against Northwest's interference with the Jewel Agreement to federal district court shortly after it was filed. * * *

Jewel has dropped all of its claims in this suit except for its claim of tortious interference with contract and prospective commercial advantage for which it now requests damages as its sole relief.

* * *

II. *The Role of the Board of Directors in a Negotiated Merger Transaction Under the California Corporate Code*

The district court rejected plaintiff's claim that defendant Northwest tortiously induced Pay Less to breach its merger agreement with Jewel on the ground, *inter alia,* that the Jewel–Pay Less agreement was not a valid contract. The district court ruled that under California law, a merger agreement entered into by the boards of directors of two corporations has no legal effect prior to shareholder approval.

The view of negotiated merger transactions expressed by the district court is at odds with the provisions of the California Corporate Code. According to the district court's ruling, the board of directors of a corporation may never bind itself in a merger agreement to exert its best efforts to obtain the requisite shareholders' approval or to forbear from entering into a competing arrangement with another firm pending approval or rejection by the shareholders. In so ruling, the district court has circumscribed the role of corporate boards of directors in a manner which contravenes their traditional management function and which is contrary to the law of California.

The California Corporate Code provides in the broadest terms that "the business and affairs of the corporation shall be managed and all corporate powers shall be exercised by or under the direction of the board." Cal. Corp. Code § 300(a). Accordingly, directors routinely exercise their business judgment to determine whether or not to enter into contracts or to embark on new business ventures.

* * *

Far from diminishing the role of the board in negotiated merger transactions, the California Corporate Code confers considerable latitude on the directors. The Code explicitly provides that the board has broad authority to determine whether to merge its firm, to select a merger partner, and to negotiate the terms on which such a transaction is to take place. To this end, section 1101 of the Code specifically states that a merger agreement embodying these decisions must be negotiated and signed by the two boards prior to consummation of the transaction.

Other provisions of California's Corporate Code strongly indicate that merger agreements contemplated by section 1101 are considered binding contracts between the two boards. Section 1200 of the California Corporate Code requires that all "corporate reorganizations," a definition which includes negotiated merger transactions pursuant to Chapter 11 of the Code, must be approved by the board of each corporation which will either acquire or divest itself of property or assets in a non-cash merger. But where consummation of such a transaction requires shareholder approval, the shareholders need only approve "the principal terms of a reorganization." Cal. Corp. Code § 1201(a). Moreover, section 1201(f) further provides that "(A)ny (shareholder) approval required by this section may be given before or after the approval by the board."

We therefore conclude that the California Corporate Code contemplates that the boards of two corporations seeking merger or reorganization under Chapters 11 and 12 of the California Corporate Code may enter into a binding merger agreement governing the conduct of the parties pending submission of the agreement to the shareholders for approval. The critical issue in the appeal before us then becomes whether such a merger agreement can be exclusive, i.e., whether the board may lawfully agree in such a merger agreement to forbear from entering into competing and inconsistent agreements until the shareholders' vote occurs.

* * *

In light of California's statutory scheme preserving the board's traditional management function in the case of corporate control transactions, we see no reason to conclude that the drafters of the Corporate Code intended to deprive a corporate board of the authority to agree to refrain from negotiating or accepting competing offers until the shareholders have considered an initial offer. That there is no statutory intent to prohibit a board from entering an exclusive merger contract can be readily inferred from the provisions of the California Corporate Code relating to merger agreements that we have previously discussed. These provisions reinforce, and in some circumstances serve to augment the board's basic discretion as authorized in section 300 of that Code. They seem to us to provide for a proper devolution of responsibility in a negotiated merger transaction: Full initial discretion regarding the terms of the agreement lies with the board, the ultimate determination with the shareholders.

The Code's provision for abandonment of a merger by the board is an example of the broad discretion conferred on boards of directors. That section provides that "(t)he board may, in its discretion, abandon a merger, subject to the contractual rights, if any, of third parties, including other constituent corporations, without further approval by the outstanding shares (Section 152), at any time before the merger is effective." California Corporate Code § 1105.[10] * * *

We do, of course, recognize that a board may not lawfully divest itself of its fiduciary obligations in a contract. * * * However, to permit a board of directors to decide that a proposed merger transaction is in the best interests of its shareholders at a given point in time, and to agree to refrain from entering into competing contracts until the shareholders consider the proposal, does not conflict in any way with the board's fiduciary obligation. * * *

An exclusive board-negotiated merger agreement may confer considerable benefits upon the shareholders of a firm. A potential merger partner may be reluctant to agree to a merger unless it is confident that its offer will not be used by the board simply to trigger an auction for the firm's assets. Therefore, an exclusive merger agreement may be necessary to secure the best offer for the shareholders of a firm. * * * An exclusive merger agreement may also be the least costly means of merging the firm.

10. The Code's abandonment provision further supports the legality of an exclusive merger agreement between two boards because it recognizes that the acquiring party possesses significant legal rights prior to the time the agreement becomes final. The Code does not expressly state whether the term "third parties" is intended to refer to the other party to a merger agreement. However, leading authorities on California Corporate law have interpreted the section as referring particularly to the acquiring party.

It increases the likelihood that the firm can be merged without expensive litigation or proxy battles.

It is true that in certain situations the shareholders may suffer a lost opportunity as a result of the board's entering into an exclusive merger agreement. As the district court took great pains to point out, subsequent to a contractual commitment unanticipated business opportunities and exigencies of the marketplace may render a proposed merger less desirable than when originally bargained for. But all contracts are formed at a single point in time and are based on the information available at that moment. The pursuit of competitive advantage has never been recognized at law as a sufficient reason to render void, or voidable, an otherwise valid contract, and in our view, it was not the intention of the drafters of California's Corporate Code to make this any less true of negotiated merger agreements. * * *

Moreover, in many ways shareholders have more safeguards from market losses in board negotiated transactions than in others. Even after the merger agreement is signed a board may not, consistent with its fiduciary obligations to its shareholders, withhold information regarding a potentially more attractive competing offer. * * * While the board can bind itself to exert its best efforts to consummate the merger under California law, it can only bind the corporation temporarily, and in limited areas,[12] pending shareholder approval. The shareholders retain the ultimate control over the corporation's assets. They remain free to accept or reject the merger proposal presented by the board, to respond to a merger proposal or tender offer made by another firm subsequent to the board's execution of exclusive merger agreement, or to hold out for a better offer. Given the benefits that may accrue to shareholders from an exclusive merger agreement, we fail to see how such an agreement would compromise their legal rights.

There are, no doubt, advantages to both exclusive and nonexclusive merger agreements. Determination of the best contract for a given transaction will depend on the particular corporations involved, the intentions of their respective boards, and the preferences for risk and return of both the board and the shareholders. Our role is not to pronounce on general matters of corporate strategic planning. It is, however, our duty to point out that the fears expressed by the district court that exclusive merger agreements are anticompetitive and contrary to public policy because they subvert the welfare of shareholders are without merit.

We therefore hold that the district court erred in ruling that a merger agreement between boards of directors is of no legal effect prior to shareholder approval. To the contrary, we hold that under California law a corporate board of directors may lawfully bind itself in a merger agreement

12. The board can bind the corporation temporarily with provisions like those included in the Jewel–Pay Less agreement, which essentially require the board of the target firm to refrain from entering any contract outside the ordinary course of business or from altering the corporation's capital structure. Such provisions are intended, essentially, to preserve the status quo until the shareholders consider the offer.

to forbear from negotiating or accepting competing offers until the shareholders have had an opportunity to consider the initial proposal.[13]

III. *Interpretation of the Jewel–Pay Less Merger Agreement*

* * *

Disposition of plaintiff's claims on a motion for summary judgment is inappropriate here. While we have held that under California law the Pay Less board may lawfully commit itself to submit the Jewel proposal to its shareholders on an exclusive basis, the record on appeal does not make it clear whether such an exclusive arrangement was intended by the parties to the transaction at issue. In particular, the record does not demonstrate conclusively whether the parties intended that the Jewel–Pay Less agreement would obligate the Pay Less board to abstain from negotiating or executing a competing merger agreement with the board of another firm.

While the specific provisions of the Jewel–Pay Less contract, if taken literally, would appear to preclude the board's entering into a competing arrangement, their effect here is not entirely clear.[14] The history of the particular negotiations and the custom and practice in the field of corporate acquisitions may well determine in large part the purpose and effect of these provisions.

* * *

IV. *Justifiable Interference With Contract*

The district court made a further ruling that even if the Jewel–Pay Less agreement were binding and valid, Northwest's interference with that agreement would have been justified.

* * *

[T]he ruling might be understood to mean that in the view of the district judge, society's interest in promoting competition justifies, as a matter of law, a competitor's interference with an otherwise valid merger agreement. We find no support in California law for such a view. To the contrary, the district court's assertion that the policy of promoting free and competitive markets can legally justify interference with an otherwise valid contract has been specifically rejected by the California Supreme Court.

* * *

13. We do not decide the question whether upon the unsolicited receipt of a more favorable offer after signing a merger agreement the board still must recommend to its shareholders that they approve the initial proposal.

14. * * * We should also point out that while the Jewel–Pay Less agreement does not set forth an exclusivity provision in so many words, it is equally true that if the parties had desired to execute an agreement that was *not* exclusive and did *not* require them to abstain from entering into competing contracts, they could have included an express provision to that effect. * * * Freund & Easton, *The Three Piece Suitor: An Alternative Approach to Negotiated Corporate Acquisitions,* 34 Bus.Law. 1679, 1689 (1979) ("a cautious target may want to provide specifically in the merger agreement that its board is free to accept—if not solicit—a better offer").

NOTES

1. Beyond the terms of the sale, the process of negotiation itself raises a series of questions for the parties and their attorneys. To begin with, there is the elementary contracts issue of when exactly do the parties reach a stage at which they have any contractual obligations toward each other. Problems in this regard typically arise at two points. The first occurs when representatives of the buyer and seller execute a document, often referred to as a letter of intent or an agreement in principle, setting out a preliminary agreement. Since this document typically only covers the basic terms of the deal, leaving the details for further negotiation and drafting, the question exists as to whether there is yet any contract at all. *E.g., Itek Corp. v. Chicago Aerial Industries, Inc.*, 248 A.2d 625 (Del.1968) (depends upon whether the parties presently intend to be bound). *See also Mid–Continent Telephone Corp. v. Home Telephone Co.,* 319 F.Supp. 1176 (N.D.Miss.1970) (failure to settle all the details does not prevent a binding contract). This question is not only important to the obligations of buyer and seller, but also to whether another buyer can make a better deal with the target without facing tort liability for interfering with a contract. *E.g., Texaco, Inc. v. Pennzoil, Co.,* 729 S.W.2d 768 (Tex.App.1987). Given the stakes involved, prudence may dictate letters of intent or agreements in principle state clearly whether or not they constitute a contract. Further, prospective buyers may wish to investigate whether the seller has reached such an understanding with another party.

Once the negotiators have worked out all the terms, a second issue arises. As discussed in *Jewel,* state corporations statutes require mergers or sales of substantially all of a company's assets to receive approval by the directors and by the shareholders. This, of course, means the target is not bound to enter the merger or to sell its assets if the shareholders vote down the transaction. *Jewel* indicates, however, a binding contract can exist before shareholder approval takes place. Exactly who does this contract bind to do what? The answer to these questions gets into the broader subject of the contest which often takes place between buyer and seller regarding the solicitation or acceptance of other bids.

2. The conflicting interests between buyer and seller as far as the desirability of competing bids influences much of what occurs in the process of negotiating the sale of a business. (This phenomenon is hardly unique to the sale of a business, witness the reluctance of car dealers, for example, to quote a price which remains effective once the customer leaves the lot.) What the buyer of a business wants to avoid is a bidding war with other prospective purchasers. The best way to close off the bidding is to enter a contract to purchase the target—in other words, to merge, to purchase the target's assets or to purchase the target's stock—thereby providing a cause of action against the target if it reneges (or against its shareholders if they renege), and against another bidder if the other bidder interferes with the contract. One difficulty is that it may take some time both to complete the negotiations and the drafting of a highly involved contract and to gain the necessary shareholder approval. (The parties also may need time to under-

take investigations of each other and to obtain regulatory approvals; albeit they could still enter the contract, but subject performance under the contract to conditions. For example, a buyer might wish to condition its obligation to close the transaction on the absence of any material change in the selling company's business or financial condition.)

Jewel Companies attempted a second best solution. Its merger agreement with Pay Less Drug Stores called upon the boards of both companies to do what they could to consummate the merger, and prohibited Pay Less from selling its assets or entering any other contract outside the ordinary course of business (thereby precluding a merger with, or sale of all assets to, anyone other than Jewel before the Pay Less shareholders voted). As a variation on this approach, some agreements contain clauses prohibiting the target's board from soliciting other offers. Recall, Time's agreement with Warner in *Time* contained a term prohibiting consideration of other offers. (Conversely, some agreements expressly reserve the right of the target to look for a better deal and to refuse to complete the transaction if it finds one.)

The *Jewel* court held the "no-shop" provision there to be a presently binding and valid contract. Contrast the Delaware Supreme Court's decision in *Omnicare, Inc. v. NCS Healthcare, Inc.*, 818 A.2d 914 (Del.2003). In *Omnicare*, a company's board agreed to submit the merger for a shareholder vote, without allowing itself an out should a better deal come along. At the same time, a few shareholders, who owned a majority of the company's outstanding stock, agreed to vote for the merger no matter what. The Delaware Supreme Court found this to be invalid:

> Although the minority stockholders were not forced to vote for the Genesis merger, they were required to accept it because it was *a fait accompli*. * * * In this case, despite the fact that the NCS board has withdrawn its recommendation for the Genesis transaction and recommended its rejection by the stockholders, the deal protection devices approved by the NCS board operated in concert to have a preclusive and coercive effect. Those tripartite defensive measures—the Section 251(c) provision [requiring the board to submit the merger for a shareholder vote], the voting agreements [irrevocably pledging controlling shareholders to vote for the merger], and the absence of an effective fiduciary out clause [which would have enabled the board to cancel the deal if a better offer came along]—made it "mathematically impossible" and "realistically unattainable" for the Omnicare transaction [a competing offer to the Genesis merger] or any other proposal to succeed, no matter how superior the proposal.
>
> The deal protection devices adopted by the NCS board were designed to coerce the consummation of the Genesis merger and preclude the consideration of any superior transaction. The NCS directors' defensive devices are not within a reasonable range of responses to the perceived threat of losing the Genesis offer because they are preclusive and coercive. Accordingly, we hold that those deal protection devices are unenforceable. 818 A.2d at 936.

See also ACE Ltd. v. Capital Re Corp., 747 A.2d 95 (Del.Ch.1999) (refused to enforce a provision barring discussions with, or even providing information to, third parties). *But see* Del. Gen. Corp. Law § 146 (allowing agreements under which the corporation binds itself to submit a matter to a shareholder vote even if the board later changes its mind).

Even if enforceable, no-shop agreements have their limitations. Jewel's failure to obtain summary judgment illustrates the difficulty of avoiding ambiguities in drafting these sort of clauses. Moreover (barring an agreement by the majority shareholders to vote for the merger no matter what) the target's shareholders can always vote down the transaction if they learn a better deal is waiting in the wings, since, as the court explained, the clause cannot go so far as to prevent disclosure of a better offer to the stockholders. (Incidentally, an agreement, as in *Jewel,* limiting the target's ability to sell its assets or to enter into other transactions outside the ordinary course of business, serves a purpose even after the shareholders approve the merger. The term can prevent the target from taking any action before the closing which undermines the buyer's getting everything it bargained for.)

A possibly superior alternative for the buyer is to enter a contract purchasing or giving it the option to purchase some of the target's assets or stock. (Time's agreement with Warner in *Time* did this by giving each company an option to buy a considerable block of the other's stock.) These are often referred to as lock-up or leg-up agreements. Since the target does not need its shareholders to approve the sale of only some property (assuming the amount involved is not sufficient to come within the statutes governing the sale of substantially all assets), or the sale of authorized but unissued shares, a binding lock-up or leg-up contract does not take long to enter. (The buyer could also purchase shares relatively quickly directly from some of the target's shareholders. Notice, Jewel purchased shares held by a foundation. Such toehold share purchases will be considered a little later in this chapter.) Lock-up or leg-up contracts give the buyer several advantages. They can deter other bidders from entering the scene (for example, if the buyer has an option to purchase the target's most desirable division or "crown jewel"). The agreement can make it costly for the target not to complete the merger (thereby encouraging shareholder approval). If all else fails, the agreement can give the prospective buyer a consolation prize—the low cost acquisition of assets or stock—should the overall sale fall through. (Jewel made $9 a share on its toehold purchase.) Another way to provide a consolation prize is simply to agree to a termination fee payable to the disappointed party if the merger does not go through. Could such a fee, however, constitute an unenforceable penalty under contract law? See *Brazen v. Bell Atlantic Corp.*, 695 A.2d 43 (Del. 1997) (upheld a $550 million termination fee as a reasonable effort to estimate liquidated damages).

If it is easy to see why the buyer wants to enter agreements cutting off competing bids, why does the target's board go along? After all, it would seem in the target's interest to encourage a bidding war. One answer is this may serve as the necessary enticement to get any offer for the company. If prospective purchasers refuse to put forward their best offer only to serve as a "stalking-horse" for the seller to shop for other bids, then it might make sense for the board to agree to no-shop or lock-up provisions. (Along the same lines, if the target already has one offer, it might use a lock-up or leg-up as an enticement to get another higher bid.) At the other extreme, the target's board might agree to the lock-up or no-shop clauses because the board wants to force its own shareholders into accepting the deal the board prefers—either because the directors have some personal financial advantage in one buyer prevailing (as, for instance, in a management buyout, or when one bidder (a "white knight") will continue the current managers in their positions, while the other will not), or just because the board does not want its judgment second guessed by the stockholders. Given these conflicting motives and impacts, it is not surprising that courts generally have refused to hold lock-ups and no-shop clauses either per se legal or per se illegal. *E.g., Revlon, Inc. v. MacAndrews & Forbes Holdings, Inc.,* 506 A.2d 173 (Del.1985).

3. A difficult pair of questions arising during the course of the negotiations is when and what to tell the shareholders. One answer is easy: Do not lie. *See, e.g., Basic Inc. v. Levinson,* 485 U.S. 224 (1988) (falsely denying that merger negotiations were underway led to liability under Rule 10b–5). Why not just announce to the shareholders any discussions regarding the sale of the company? There are a couple of problems with this solution. One occurs if the negotiations ultimately fail. Disappointed stockholders might claim the announcement was misleading. *Cf. In re Gulf Oil/Cities Service Tender Offer Litigation,* 725 F.Supp. 712 (S.D.N.Y.1989). Accordingly, the corporation's management must carefully draft the statement not to be too optimistic (or too pessimistic, *see SEC v. Texas Gulf Sulphur Co.,* 401 F.2d 833 (2d Cir.1968), *cert. denied,* 394 U.S. 976 (1969)), which might make it easier simply to say nothing. Moreover, the seller may feel the news of negotiations can be upsetting to its employees or customers, and, if the transaction does not go through after disclosure, the result could be to make the seller look like "spoiled goods" to other prospective buyers. In addition, the prospective buyer may insist upon silence. An announcement of merger negotiations could trigger other bids by showing the target is for sale. The disclosure will also typically cause the price of the target's shares to rise. Such a price rise can make the purchaser's offer look less desirable even though the purchaser's offer caused the price to increase. (Shareholders often have short memories.)

This, in turn, raises the question of whether the target has any legal obligation to disclose the negotiations until, of course, it presents the agreement to the stockholders for approval. Generally, no obligation exists under Rule 10b–5—assuming (i) the target is not repurchasing its shares, (ii) it has not previously made (nor are those in close association with it continuing to make) statements which have become misleading by virtue of the failure to disclose, and (iii) the information has not leaked out to selected traders. *See, e.g., Staffin v. Greenberg,* 672 F.2d 1196 (3d Cir.1982). *See also Basic Inc. v. Levinson, supra,* 485 U.S. at 238 n. 17. On the other hand, if the target has shares listed on the stock exchange, or is otherwise a 1934 Securities Exchange Act reporting company, it faces obligations to disclose at the time it makes its 1934 Act filings, or possibly earlier under the rules of the exchange. *E.g.,* N.Y.S.E. Listed Company Manual §§ 205.01, 205.05 (allowing delay in disclosure only if for a legitimate business reason and if the information does not leak out).

4. Negotiating the sale of a business involves more than haggling and drafting. A critical part of the process is investigation. The purchaser of a business is concerned that the target's assets might turn out to be less than the purchaser thought, or the liabilities greater, or, because of some other fact unknown to the buyer, it has misjudged the target's prospects. Similar concerns exist from the seller's side if the acquirer plans to pay with its stock, or even with its debt instruments. Escrows, earn-out arrangements, indemnity agreements and warranties, as discussed earlier, can provide some means to cope with these uncertainties. So can a careful investigation of the seller's business (or of the buyer's, if the buyer is paying with stock or debt).

In this regard, note that warranties can be as much or more useful for their ability to smoke out potential problems, as for any contractual protection they provide. (This presumes the seller will be reluctant to warrant the existence of conditions about which it has substantial doubt.) The alternative to the seller representing or warranting various facts about its business can be for it to invite the buyer to inspect the facilities and books. While the purchaser may wish to do so, this can entail both greater expense and less satisfaction than warranties, because of the buyer's lesser familiarity with the seller's operations. Opening up the seller's operations for inspection also often requires preparation of confidentiality agreements in order to preserve trade secrets. *But see Smith v. Dravo Corp.*, 203 F.2d 369 (7th Cir.1953) (extending trade secret protection even when prospective buyer did not enter a confidentiality agreement). Seen in this light, it might be useful to reconsider the common instinct of sellers and their attorneys to spend time and energy fighting to minimize the seller's representations and warranties. After all, the greater the buyer's uncertainty, or the more energy it must spend to gather facts about the target, the lower the price it will be willing to pay. *See* Gilson, *Value Creation by Business Lawyers: Legal Skills and Asset Pricing*, 94 Yale L.J. 239 (1984). Common areas for representations and warranties by the seller include: due incorporation and continued good standing of the target company, the accuracy of its financial statements, its ownership and the condition of its important assets (including rights to intellectual property and collectability of accounts receivable), the lack of any liabilities or contingent liabilities other than those shown in its financial statements (including the lack of any threatened litigation, its compliance with government regulations affecting its business, and its payment of all taxes due), and the state of its employee relations. One problem here is that even the target's management may not know every fact related to these warranties. Hence, the agreement often phrases the warranties in language such as "to the best of the seller's knowledge." Needless to say, in evaluating the utility of warranties as an investigation device, the buyer must consider what disincentives exist (both legal and practical) to prevent the seller from misrepresenting the facts.

Part of the investigation often involves the employment of outsiders; for example, accountants to audit the seller's (or buyer's) financial statements. The buyer may demand an opinion letter from counsel addressing the seller's proper organization and continued good standing under state corporation law, as well as covering a variety of legal questions concerning the seller's assets or liabilities, such as the validity of patents, the assignability of contracts, the extent of possible liabilities under pension plans, whether there is any known threat of future litigation, and whether the seller is in compliance with all government regulations applicable to its business. (Recall the discussion concerning legal opinion letters in Chapter I. Incidentally, beyond potential liabilities for an inaccurate formal opinion, attorneys involved in negotiations can be liable for intentional or even negligent misrepresentations of fact. *Cicone v. URS Corp.,* 183 Cal.App.3d 194, 227 Cal.Rptr. 887 (1986).) Recent concern with environmental liabilities has led many potential buyers to hire consultants who can check on the history of the seller's property and operations to determine if the property might contain any hazardous waste.

This investigation takes time, and is probably more efficiently done with the selling company's cooperation. Hence, a hurried or hostile takeover exposes the buyer to somewhat greater risk than a friendly acquisition. What makes a hurried or hostile takeover feasible is the information which securities laws require public companies to make generally available. If the buyer is a 1934 Act reporting company, the existence of such publicly available information also limits the seller's need to investigate, despite the buyer paying with its stock or securities. Not only does investigation take time, but it also costs money (for accountants and the like). Hence, the buyer must ultimately make a judgment as to when the expense of further investigation outweighs the risk that it overlooked something important.

In the end, however, investigations and warranties cannot avoid all unpleasant surprises. In this event, rather then fearing the warranty as a sword for the buyer, the seller may seek to use the warranty as a shield from the buyer.

AES Corp. v. The Dow Chemical Company

325 F.3d 174 (3d Cir.2003).

I. Introduction

The AES Corporation ("AES") operates power facilities. AES alleges that Dow Chemical Company ("Dow") and its subsidiary, Destec Energy, Inc. ("Destec"), violated Sections 10(b) and 20(a) of the Securities Exchange Act of 1934 (the "Exchange Act") in connection with a transaction in which AES purchased the stock of one of Destec's subsidiaries, Destec Engineering, Inc. ("DEI"). DEI's sole asset was a contract to design and construct a power plant in The Netherlands (the "Elsta Plant"). According to AES, Dow and Destec conspired to sell DEI at an artificially inflated price by making misrepresentations material to an evaluation of DEI.

During the pendency of this case in the District Court, AES and Destec entered into a settlement agreement. Thus, only the claims against Dow remain. There has been no discovery. Dow moved for summary judgment, relying solely on documents relating to the transactions in which AES acquired DEI's stock. * * * The District Court * * * granted Dow's summary judgment motion. The District Court held that certain clauses in the transaction documents rendered AES's reliance on the alleged misrepresentations unreasonable as a matter of law.

II. Background

Dow formed Destec to build and run power plants that would supply power to Dow Chemical facilities and third-party users. In 1996, after determining that it could not profitably run Destec as its subsidiary, Dow retained Morgan Stanley to perform a valuation of Destec in order to initiate a public sale.

Morgan Stanley issued a Confidential Offering Memorandum on behalf of Destec. As a precondition to receiving the Offering Memorandum, AES signed a Confidentiality Agreement that provided in part:

> We [AES] acknowledge that neither you [Destec], nor Morgan Stanley [Destec's Investment Banker] or its affiliates, nor your other Representatives, nor any of your or their respective officers, directors, employees, agents or controlling persons within the meaning of section 20 of the Securities Exchange Act of 1934, as amended, make any express or implied representation or warranty as to the accuracy or completeness of the Information, and we agree that no such person will have any liability relating to the Information or for any errors therein or omissions therefrom. We further agree that we are not entitled to rely on the accuracy or completeness of the Information and that we will be entitled to rely solely on any representations and warranties as may be made to us in any definitive agreement with respect to the Transaction, subject to such limitations and restrictions as may be contained therein.

Dow was not a party to the Confidentiality Agreement but is alleged to have been a "controlling person" of Destec within the meaning of § 20(a) of the Exchange Act.

The Offering Memorandum included projections and estimates about the future performance of Destec's businesses, including DEI and the Elsta Plant. Like the Confidentiality Agreement, the Offering Memorandum warned readers that they were not to rely on the accuracy or completeness of information contained therein. It further stated:

> [o]nly those particular representations and warranties which may be made to a purchaser in a definitive agreement, when, as, and if

> executed, and subject to such limitations and restrictions as may be specified in such definitive agreement, shall have any legal effect.

Dow and Destec provided information about Destec to potential bidders in several other ways. First, Destec officers gave a presentation to potential bidders, which AES representatives attended. Dow and Destec also sent certain documents to potential bidders and made others available in a room at a Destec facility in Houston, Texas. Further, Dow and Destec gave potential bidders a computer model to value the Destec assets. This model included assumptions about the expenses and revenues of the Elsta Plant. Lastly, Dow and Destec allowed AES, as part of its due diligence, to visit the Elsta Plant.

AES contacted Dow about the possibility of purchasing the international assets of Destec. Dow responded that it would prefer to sell all of Destec, rather than dispose of it piecemeal. As a result, AES approached NGC Corporation ("NGC") to propose submitting a joint bid for all of Destec, and a joint bid was subsequently made.

The AES/NGC joint bid was accepted by Dow. The transaction took place in two steps. First, NGC acquired all of the stock of Destec pursuant to an Agreement and Plan of Merger (the "Merger Agreement") entered into by Dow, Destec, and NGC. Second, AES purchased all of the international assets of Destec, including all of DEI's outstanding stock, pursuant to an Asset Purchase Agreement between AES and NGC.

Section 4.6 of the Merger Agreement, to which AES was not a party, provided as follows:

> Except for the representations and warranties contained in this Article IV, neither Dow nor any other person makes any other express or implied representation or warranty on behalf of Dow.

Article IV of the Merger Agreement contained two pages of representations and warranties of Dow. It warranted that it was duly organized as a corporation; that it was authorized to enter the agreement; that the execution and consummation of the agreement would not violate the terms of any court order or Dow contract; that no government approval was necessary; and that no broker was entitled to a fee in connection with the transaction. Article IV contained no representation or warranty with respect to the Elsta Plant.

Similarly, Section 3.4 of the Asset Purchase Agreement, signed by NGC and AES, states that "except for the representations and warranties contained in this Article III, neither NGC nor any other person * * * makes any other express or implied representation or warranty on behalf of NGC." * * * Article III of the Asset Purchase Agreement contains limited representations and warranties by NGC very similar to those made by Dow in the Merger Agreement.

* * *

According to AES, shortly after purchasing DEI and Destec's other international assets, it realized that the Elsta Plant would cost far more to complete than its due diligence investigation had indicated and would open for operation much later than Dow and Destec had represented it would. Instead of providing the predicted $31 million in profit, the project ultimately occasioned a $70 million loss. AES contends that Dow knew specific facts about the Elsta Plant that contradicted the representations it had made prior to and during due diligence. Its complaint alleges fourteen affirmative misrepresentations and eight material omissions upon which it relied. Some involved profit and cost projections, but others involved currently existing facts. Further, AES contends that, as part of the scheme to defraud, Dow concealed the true state of the Elsta Plant and frustrated its due diligence efforts by causing Destec and its employees to provide false and misleading information to AES.

III. Analysis

A. The Federal Law

* * *

The "reasonable reliance" element of a Rule 10b–5 claim requires a showing of a causal nexus between the misrepresentation and the plaintiff's injury, as well as a demonstration that the plaintiff exercised the diligence that a reasonable person under all of the circumstances would have exercised to protect his own interests. * * *

The District Court held that as a result of AES's contractual commitment not to rely on any representations other than those incorporated in the final agreements, its alleged reliance was unreasonable as a matter of law. AES insists that this holding is incorrect in light of Section 29(a) of the Exchange Act. Section 29(a) provides: "Any condition, stipulation, or provision binding any person to waive compliance with any provision of this title or of any rule or regulation thereunder, or of any rule of an exchange required thereby shall be void."

* * *

C. The Role of the Non–Reliance Clause

* * *

As we have noted, reliance is an essential element of a Rule 10b–5 claim. It necessarily follows that, if a party commits itself never to claim that it relied on representations of the other party to its contract, it purports anticipatorily to waive any future claim based on the fraudulent misrepresentations of that party. The same is true if the commitment is more limited, e.g., a promise not to claim reliance on any representation not set forth in the agreement. The scope of the anticipatory waiver is more limited, but it is nevertheless an anticipatory waiver of potential future claims under Rule 10b–5.

* * *

[T]his is not to say that a plaintiff's declaration in a contract of an intent not to rely may not be evidence that he or she did not rely on representations of the defendants. That declaration, alone or in conjunction with other evidence of non-reliance, may establish an absence of reliance and, when unrebutted, may even provide a basis for summary judgment in the defendant's favor. Thus, in this case, the non-reliance clauses are some evidence of an absence of reliance. However, the District Court did not find that the evidence of non-reliance was unrebutted. Indeed, Dow does not contend that the information provided by it and its associates played no material role in AES's decision to enter the agreement.

Dow does contend, and we understand the District Court to have held, that the non-reliance clauses establish as a matter of law that any reliance of AES was unreasonable reliance. We find the same tension between Section 29(a) and this argument, however, as we have found between Section 29(a) and the argument that the non-reliance clauses foreclose an assertion by AES that it relied. If all of the evidence bearing on the reasonableness of AES's reliance does not entitle Dow to summary judgment under traditional summary judgment principles, it would offend Section 29(a) to bar its claim based solely on a contractual commitment not to claim reliance.

IV. The Issue for Decision on Remand

This leaves for resolution the issue of whether, viewing all of the relevant circumstances and applying the reasonable reliance standard * * *, a reasonable trier of fact could only conclude that AES failed to exercise ordinary care in protecting its own interest. We decline to address that issue, however, because we conclude that it is premature to do so.

* * *

The non-reliance clauses are, of course, among the circumstances to be considered in determining the reasonableness of any reliance here. Importantly, they reflect the fact that the seller was unwilling to vouch for the accuracy of the information it was providing and the fact that the buyer was willing to undertake to verify the accuracy of that data for itself. Clearly, in such circumstances, a buyer who relies on seller-provided information without seeking to verify it has not acted reasonably. Clearly, a buyer in a non-reliance clause case will have to show more to justify its reliance than would a buyer in the absence of such a contractual provision. For this reason, cases involving a non-reliance clause in a negotiated contract between sophisticated parties will often be appropriate candidates for resolution at the summary judgment stage. We are unwilling, however, to hold that the extraction of a non-reliance clause, even from a sophisticated buyer, will always provide immunity from Rule 10b–5 fraud liability.

AES's complaint alleges that Dow and its subsidiaries were in exclusive control of the information necessary to accurately evaluate the Elsta Plant. It further alleges that, as a part of its fraudulent scheme to sell DEI to someone at a price far above its worth, Dow controlled release of the relevant information to AES both initially as well as during the period that it was conducting its investigation to determine the accuracy of the information initially disclosed. Much of that information involved projections and other "soft" data that a seller dealing in good faith would understandably be unwilling to guarantee. According to AES, it conducted a diligent investigation that was reasonably calculated to determine the reliability of Dow's representations but revealed no reason to suspect that Dow was intentionally misleading it. Dow allegedly saw to it that all information received by AES would reassure it of the reliability of the earlier supplied data; Dow allegedly also prevented AES from securing the data in Dow's and Destec's files that would have disclosed the fraud.

* * *

While AES may have an uphill battle here and summary judgment for the defendants may be appropriate at some point, we decline to give controlling significance to the existence of a non-reliance clause in a vacuum. We fully appreciate that the avoidance of costly discovery is one of the objectives of negotiating such clauses. Nevertheless, to hold that a buyer is barred from relief under Rule 10b–5 solely by virtue of his contractual commitment not to rely would be fundamentally inconsistent with Section 29(a).

In reaching this conclusion, we have not been unmindful of the decision of the Court of Appeals for the Second Circuit in *Harsco Corp. v. Segui,* 91 F.3d 337 (2d Cir.1996). The court there affirmed the dismissal of a Rule 10b–5 security fraud claim based on a stipulation in the stock purchase agreement that the sellers were "not [to] be deemed to have made . . . any representation or warranty other than as expressly made by" the sellers in the agreement. * * *

We find *Harsco'* s reasoning unpersuasive.

* * *

The judgment of the District Court will be reversed and this matter will be remanded for further proceedings consistent with this opinion.

NOTES

1. Could either party be happy about the situation in which it finds itself after this opinion? If not, what could the attorneys for AES or Dow have done differently in putting the sale together? Would the solution lie in different language for the contractual documents, or would it lie in the what transpired during the due diligence investigation? Incidentally, while *AES* involved the impact of warranties and waivers on claims of securities fraud under federal law, similar issues arise under state common law. *E.g., Abry Partners V, L.P. v. F & W Acquisition LLC*, 891 A.2d 1032 (Del.Ch. 2006).

2. Changes in accounting rules governing acquisitions have increased the impact of unpleasant surprises such as in *AES*. For years, acquirers often sought to avoid treating, in their financial statements, an acquisition as if

they purchased the acquired company's assets, rather than pooled the assets of the two companies together. The problem with such purchase accounting when the acquirer paid a total price that was greater than the fair market value of the acquired company's individual assets—which would be typical in buying a successful business—was that the difference showed up on the acquirer's balance sheet as goodwill. When the acquirer later amortized the goodwill, based upon the notion that the goodwill was gradually "used up," this lowered the acquirer's post-acquisition reported earnings. In 2001, the Financial Accounting Standards Board eliminated the ability to record an acquisition as a pooling of interests, rather than a purchase. Statement of Financial Accounting Standards No. 141. At the same time, however, the FASB replaced the requirement of a gradual write-off for goodwill with an annual impairment test that requires the acquirer to review regularly whether a lack of performance requires writing off any goodwill (which otherwise remains on the books without diminution). Financial Accounting Standards No. 142. The end result can be to flag the failure of the acquired business to perform as advertised.

3. The directors, in approving the purchase or sale of a business, must act with due care. This fact, too, affects the negotiating process. While courts are generally reluctant to second guess the business judgment of a disinterested board, hasty decisions, without consulting financial experts, can lead to trouble. *See, e.g., Smith v. Van Gorkom,* 488 A.2d 858 (Del.1985).

3. Preacquisition Transactions

a. *Toehold Share Purchases*

Often, a party seeking to buy a corporation will start by acquiring a minority of its shares either in open market purchases or in negotiated transactions with one or more major stockholders. This can give the buyer several advantages. To the extent the buyer makes open market purchases, it may be able to acquire some stock at a lower price than it will later need to pay once the news of the prospective takeover gets out. Moreover, the leg up a buyer obtains through already holding a substantial stake in the target can deter other prospective bidders. It might also put pressure on management to agree to sell the firm. The buyer, however, confronts a number of legal constraints in making toehold share purchases. In addition, transactions between it and the controlling shareholders or management of the target can face judicial scrutiny.

Brown v. Halbert

271 Cal.App.2d 252, 76 Cal.Rptr. 781 (1969).

■ Harold C. Brown, Associate Justice.

This action was instituted by four minority stockholders in the Tulare Savings & Loan Association (hereafter Association), individually and on behalf of all other minority stockholders similarly situated. The purpose of the first cause of action was to impose a trust on a portion of the funds the defendants realized as a result of a sale of their majority stock interest allegedly in violation of their fiduciary obligations to the minority stockholders. * * *

The principal defendant was Edward F. Halbert, who was the dominant stockholder (Mr. Halbert and his wife owned 53% of the 1,000 shares issued) and also was the president, chairman of the board of directors and manager of the Association.

The facts presented to the trial court posed the problems: (1) whether the defendant Halbert, as dominant stockholder, president of the Association and chairman of the board of directors, occupied a fiduciary relationship to the stockholders; and (2) whether he violated such relationship by the manner of selling a controlling block of stock to outside purchasers at a price not made available to the minority group of shareholders.

* * *

In November of 1962 a Mr. Douglas McDonald, president of Lincoln Savings & Loan Association of Los Angeles, and his assistant, David Prince, called on Mr. Halbert at the Association's business office in Tulare. *Mr. McDonald asked Mr. Halbert if the Association was for sale. Halbert stated, "No, the Association is not for sale. However my wife and I would entertain selling our stock," and stated a price of two and one-half times book value. There was no evidence produced that the board of directors or stockholders had been consulted as to whether the company was for sale.* Other meetings were had between McDonald and Halbert and on January 14, 1963, McDonald by phone offered to purchase the Halberts' stock for his asking price of two and one-half times book value. That evening the Halberts received a $20,000 deposit and signed a contract for the sale of their stock. This agreement provided that the Association had issued 1,000 shares of guaranty stock and the Halberts owned a majority (53%). The agreed purchase price was $1,548.05 per share. *The right was given to purchasers to inspect the books.* An escrow was to be opened and the closing date was May 15, 1963. The sellers (Halberts) agreed "That upon the close of this escrow they will submit such resignations as officers and directors * * * as may be requested *by the Buyer and will hold such director and/or stockholders' meetings as may be requested by buyer for the purpose of electing new officers and directors of said Association.*" (Emphasis added.) It was agreed *that no dividends were to be paid.* The minority stockholders were not informed of the terms of the sale until after it had been negotiated, although it was generally rumored that Halbert wanted to sell his stock.

* * *

Buyers thereafter, through their attorneys and accountants, made a thorough examination of the company's books and records. The authorization for this investigation was obtained from Mr. Halbert who also gave them copies of the examination by the Federal Home Loan Bank and the one by the State Savings and Loan Commissioner. Halbert adhered to the agreement and no dividends were paid. No request was made of the board of directors to obtain approval to permit buyers to inspect the Association's books and records. Likewise no authorization was obtained from the board to refrain from the payment of dividends.

* * *

Upon completion of the purchase of the Halberts' stock, the purchasers evidenced their desire to buy the stock of the minority stockholders.

They offered $300 per share. Mr. Halbert made no effort to encourage the buyers to pay the minority stockholders for their shares, a price equivalent to the price he received. The evidence indicates that Mr. Halbert assisted the buyers in purchasing the minority stock.

* * *

Stockholder William Willeford, who had been director and stockholder for approximately 20 years, was told by Mr. Halbert that the new owners would not be paying dividends and the stock would not be worth much. * * *

Halbert introduced the buyers to other stockholders who also were offered $300 per share for their stock. *To stockholder Christensen, Halbert advised that she should take the $300 as she might get nothing.*

* * *

On May 31, 1963, the new stockholders met at the Association office with employees and proceeded to prepare the necessary notice for a stockholders meeting for the election of new directors and officers and to effectuate new policies. Stockholders Brown, Christensen and Willeford, learning of the meeting, appeared at the office and accepted a new offer of $611 per share for their stock and resigned as directors. Thereafter all but a few shares of stock of the minority stockholders was purchased for $611 to $650 per share.

* * *

There is but little dispute between the parties as to the facts. It is the application of the facts to existing legal principles that gives rise to the respective contentions of the parties.

* * *

The evidence here does not establish fraud or concealment on the fiduciary, nor is it the ordinary case of the fiduciary withholding information in the purchase of the minority shares. Also, the facts do not involve a sale of the majority block of stock to looters or incompetents for which the fiduciary might be held chargeable. * * *

The facts do disclose that Halbert sold his stock to purchasers who after acquiring the stock announced that their policy of operation radically changed previous policies of the Association, i.e., there would be no distribution of profits by payment of dividends for a period of ten to twenty years. The obvious effect of such policy on minority stockholders would be to create a feeling of uncertainty as to the value of their stock, resulting in a susceptibility to pressure to sell.

Every sale of a block of control stock should not per se be subject to attack, but where the amount received by the majority-director seller is so disproportionate to the price available to the minority stockholders, then such fiduciary-seller must show that no advantage was taken if the sale is questioned. This is especially true in the instant case where Halbert in his triple fiduciary capacity was completely indifferent to his obligations to the minority stockholders. He did not advise the directors or stockholders that he had been approached by persons who desired to acquire the Association. After obtaining an agreement for the price he desired for his own stock and while still an officer-director, he failed to make any effort to obtain for the minority substantially the same price that he received and, in fact, worked actively for the buyers in assisting them to acquire all the stock at a low figure by voicing his recommendation to the minority holders that they sell at below book value. Halbert's other actions in permitting the buyers access to the books, records and reports of the Association, and his agreement to refrain from the payment of dividends only serve to fortify the conclusion that he worked to obtain an advantage for himself and effectively placed the buyers of his stock in a position to dictate terms to the detriment of the minority holders. Further, in advising the minority stockholders to sell their stock for $300 or they might get nothing, he was using his office, experience and reputation gained in the conduct of their affairs to prevent the minority an opportunity to obtain a higher price for their stock.

The evidence clearly indicates that respondent Halbert had no accurate knowledge or clear conception of his fiduciary duties in his triple capacity as president, chairman of the board and dominant stockholder, and that his complete indifference and affirmative actions took the form of rationalization on his part that such success as attended the Association was due to his efforts alone and that he and a favored few should reap the rewards to the exclusion of the other stockholders.

Because of the errors in the instructions and the clear violation by Halbert of his fiduciary obligations to the minority stockholders, the judgment of the trial court must be reversed.

* * *

In the determination that there was a violation of fiduciary obligation which was actionable by minority stockholders, we have not adopted specific rules of procedure for fiduciaries but have determined that each case must be decided on its merits. In this area it seems that no hard and fast rule is workable. * * *

* * * The rule we have adopted here simply is that it is the duty of the majority stockholder-director, when contemplating the sale of the majority stock at a price not available to other stockholders and which sale may prejudice the minority stockholders, is to act affirmatively and openly with full disclosure so that every opportunity is given to obtain substantially the

same advantages that such fiduciary secured and for the full protection of the minority. This duty was violated here.

It is concluded that a review of the record clearly establishes that Halbert failed to perform his obligations as a fiduciary in the protection of the interests of the minority stockholders. The respondents therefore may not retain the advantage realized from Halbert's actions in the sale of the majority stock at 2½ times book value while the minority interests received but book value, and that difference when ascertained must be equitably distributed to all stockholders who sold their stock to the buyers.

* * *

NOTE

Brown raises the question of what dealings are appropriate between the buyer and the target's controlling shareholder(s) or management. Naturally, it would smooth the acquisition if the buyer could secure the cooperation of the target's directors or significant stockholder(s)—indeed, it is impossible to make the purchase over the opposition of a majority shareholder. Even without holding a majority of shares, a person may own enough stock to provide working control of a corporation whose other shares are widely dispersed. Obtaining this block in a toehold acquisition can give the buyer a powerful leg up toward acquiring the whole company (or might be all the buyer wants if the buyer then has control), while trying to make a tender offer for enough of the scattered shares to give control when opposed by a dominant stockholder can be an uphill battle. Management's cooperation can avoid the need to combat the various defensive measures outlined earlier in this chapter, as well as providing advantages under some state takeover laws (which will be discussed shortly). Under these circumstances, it might make economic sense from the buyer's standpoint to pay something extra to the controlling shareholder(s) (or even managers) above what the buyer will pay the small shareholders. Conversely, one might expect controlling shareholders (or even managers), as in *Brown,* to seek to exploit their position by demanding such a premium.

The general rule is that stockholders can sell their shares at whatever price the buyer will pay, and, if the buyer will pay more for a controlling block, the seller is not obligated to share the premium with the other stockholders. *E.g., Zetlin v. Hanson Holdings, Inc.,* 48 N.Y.2d 684, 421 N.Y.S.2d 877, 397 N.E.2d 387 (1979). As *Brown* illustrates, there are exceptions. One exception exists if the buyer loots the corporation. *E.g., DeBaun v. First Western Bank & Trust Co.,* 46 Cal.App.3d 686, 120 Cal.Rptr. 354 (1975). The difficulty with this rule from a planning perspective is that buyers do not often inform the seller of their plans to loot the firm (or, to be more precise, to appropriate the firm's assets other than through a legal dividend). The question therefore becomes what obligation does the seller have to check out the buyer? More specifically, must the seller automatically investigate a buyer even in the absence of any reason for suspicion. *Compare Levy v. American Beverage Corp.,* 265 App.Div. 208,

38 N.Y.S.2d 517 (1942), *with Northway, Inc. v. TSC Industries, Inc.*, 512 F.2d 324 (7th Cir.1975), *rev'd on other grounds,* 426 U.S. 438 (1976). If not, what facts should raise a suspicion? Suppose the premium offered for the shares is extremely high? *Compare Clagett v. Hutchison,* 583 F.2d 1259 (4th Cir.1978), *with Gerdes v. Reynolds,* 28 N.Y.S.2d 622 (Sup.Ct.1941). The buyer's prior history (*see, e.g., DeBaun v. First Western Bank & Trust Co.,* 46 Cal.App.3d 686, 120 Cal.Rptr. 354 (1975)), or lack of funds (*see, e.g., Insuranshares Corp. v. Northern Fiscal Corp.*, 35 F.Supp. 22 (E.D.Pa.1940)) might raise suspicions. Keep in mind as well, the risk of looting varies with the nature of a corporation's properties—a firm with a large amount of liquid assets presents more opportunity for conversion than a company with most of its worth tied up in fixed assets. One variation on the looting problem occurs if the buyer intends to exploit its control of the corporation through transactions between it and the target, which may not be optimally beneficial to the target, even if not rising to the level of outright misappropriation of assets. *See Perlman v. Feldmann,* 219 F.2d 173 (2d Cir.1955) (holding the controlling shareholder liable for the premium received from such a buyer).

A second exception involves the "sale of directorships." Often, the target's directors will resign seriatim following the sale of a controlling block of stock and appoint the buyer's nominees to fill the vacancies as they do so. Indeed, many times, the contract purchasing the shares expressly requires this to occur. (The agreement in *Brown* stopped just short of this.) The difficulty is this looks like the sale of a corporate office by its current holder—something the current directors have no right to do. *E.g., Petition of Caplan,* 20 A.D.2d 301, 246 N.Y.S.2d 913 (1964). On the other hand, it might appear an empty formality to require the buyer to call a shareholders meeting to replace the directors, or, worse, in a corporation in which the shareholders lack the power to remove directors without cause, it might seem poor policy to tell the existing directors they cannot resign when they sold their stock in the company, and thereby clear the way for the new stockholder to put his or her ideas into play. For these reasons, some courts have allowed the seriatim replacement of directors when the purchaser buys enough stock to give working control (raising, of course, the factual question of how many shares, if less than a majority, give working control of a particular corporation). *E.g., Carter v. Muscat,* 21 A.D.2d 543, 251 N.Y.S.2d 378 (1964). (Incidentally, Federal law requires 1934 Securities Exchange Act reporting companies to file a disclosure document in the event of such a seriatim replacement of directors. Sec. Exch. Act § 14(f).)

At the other end from selling offices, lies the fact that many times the buyer would like to retain the services of the target's key personnel, or, at the very least, ensure they remain available for consulting and do not go into competition with the firm. Employment or non-competition agreements directed toward achieving such ends are permissible. *E.g., Smith v. Good Music Station, Inc.,* 36 Del.Ch. 262, 129 A.2d 242 (1957). An agreement which really represents a bribe for selling out the shareholders' interests obviously is not. *See, e.g., Barr v. Wackman,* 36 N.Y.2d 371, 368 N.Y.S.2d 497, 329 N.E.2d 180 (1975). The more subtle problem here is that the parallel negotiation of both the individual employment contracts and the sale of the business puts the board in something of a conflict of interest. For this reason, the court might subject the sale of a business, when accompanied by simultaneous negotiation of employment contracts, to a greater degree of scrutiny for fairness than normally applied to an arms length deal. *See Smith v. Good Music Station, Inc., supra.*

Brown involves a fourth problem area. The purchaser initially inquired into a transaction (sale of the Association) equally beneficial to all stockholders of the target, but the controlling shareholder (who was also a director and officer) restructured the deal so as to obtain a premium for selling his shares. He then aided the purchaser in buying the minority shares for less than he received. Not all courts accept the *Brown* opinion's condemnation of such a transaction. *E.g., Tryon v. Smith,* 191 Or. 172, 229 P.2d 251 (1951). Moreover, there is authority for the proposition that whether a controlling shareholder breaches his or her duty in acting as did the defendant in *Brown* might depend upon the role in which the controlling shareholder acts. Specifically, in *Thorpe v. CERBCO, Inc.*, 676 A.2d 436 (Del.1996), the Delaware Supreme Court held that two brothers, who owned a majority of the voting stock in CERBCO, breached their fiduciary duty as directors when they failed to inform the other board members of an offer they received to buy CERBCO's only profitable subsidiary, and, instead, made a counteroffer to sell their CERBCO stock. Nevertheless, the court refused to award significant damages for this breach. The reason was that the defendant brothers possessed the votes as shareholders to block the sale of the subsidiary (which would have required shareholder approval as a sale of substantially all assets). Explicit in this rationale was that the majority shareholders had the right to vote selfishly *as shareholders* to block a transaction in order to restructure the transaction more toward their own benefit.

Finally, both the Williams Act and some state takeover statutes may impact the ability to pay a control premium just to some shareholders.

Wellman v. Dickinson

475 F.Supp. 783 (S.D.N.Y.1979), *aff'd,* 682 F.2d 355 (2d Cir.1982), *cert. denied,* 460 U.S. 1069 (1983).

■ ROBERT L. CARTER, DISTRICT JUDGE.

I

Status of the Proceedings

This litigation stems from the acquisition by Sun Company, Inc. ("Sun"), a Pennsylvania corporation whose principal business is oil and gas, of roughly 34% of the stock of Becton, Dickinson & Company ("BD"), a New Jersey corporation which manufactures health care products and medical testing and research equipment. Sun's brilliantly designed, lightning strike took place in January, 1978, and gave rise to seven separate actions which were consolidated for trial. In 78 Civ. 1055, the Securities and Exchange Commission ("Commission") brings an enforcement action against Sun, L.H.I.W., Inc. (an acronym for Lets Hope It Works), the corporation Sun formed to receive the BD shares; Salomon Brothers ("Salomon"), a New York limited partnership engaged in the investment banking and brokerage business; F. Eberstadt & Co., Inc., ("Eberstadt"), a Delaware corporation engaged in investment banking, institutional stock brokerage and the management of pension funds and advisory accounts and which, along with Salomon, handled the Sun acquisition; F. Eberstadt & Co. Managers & Distributors, Inc. ("M & D"), a Delaware company 75% owned by Eberstadt and 25% owned by the estate of Ferdinand Eberstadt, which manages the two Eberstadt mutual funds involved in this proceeding; Robert Zeller, chief executive officer of Eberstadt and vice chairman of M & D; Fairleigh S. Dickinson, Jr., former chairman of BD and one of its principal stockholders; J.H. Fitzgerald Dunning, a former director and large stockholder in BD; and Kenneth Lipper, a partner in Salomon. The Commission charges the defendants with violating or aiding and abetting the violation of Sections 10(b), 13(d), 14(d) and 14(e) of the Securities Exchange Act of 1934 * * *.

In 78 Civ. 539, BD, its officers and several of its shareholders individually and derivatively sue Sun, L.H.I.W., Dickinson, Dunning, Salomon, Eberstadt, Chemical Fund, Inc., and Surveyor Fund, Inc., alleging violations of the Exchange Act similar to those charged in the Commission's case, and in addition, charging Dickinson and Dunning with violations of their fiduciary obligation to BD and its shareholders. The Chemical and Surveyor Funds are open end investment companies managed by M & D.

* * *

II

Findings of Fact

The background and governing facts in this complex drama embrace personality conflicts, animosity, distrust, and corporate politics, as well as a display of ingenuity and sophistication by brokers, investment bankers and corporate counsel.

Fairleigh S. Dickinson, Jr. was the son of one of the founders of BD. He held the reins of the company from 1948 until 1973. When he became BD chief in 1948, BD was a private family enterprise with gross sales of 10 million dollars annually. When he released the reins of the company in 1973, it was a public company with gross sales of $300 million annually. Dickinson loosened his hold on the helm but did not entirely let go. In 1974, he stepped upstairs to become Chairman of the Board, while Wesley Howe became Chief Executive and Marvin Asnes became Chief Operating Officer. Differences between the management team and the chairman became evident in late 1976 when Dickinson threatened to fire Asnes.

* * *

In early April [1977], Dickinson, Howe, and Asnes met, presumably to bring their differences into the open and to resolve them. The meeting settled nothing. Howe and Asnes then decided on a show of strength. They canvassed the board, found enough votes to get rid of Dickinson, and on April 18 sent out notices for an April 20 meeting. * * * Dickinson was deposed as chairman and nudged out the back door with the title of Honorary Chairman.

Obviously this must have been a terrible personal blow. Dickinson was now stripped of all power within what he must still have regarded as a family enterprise. On April 21, Dickinson had a meeting at Salomon to secure advice on how to proceed. Richard Rosenthal, John Gutfreund, and Kenneth Lipper of Salomon, two BD directors, Kane and Thompkins, Jerome Lipper and Salomon Brothers counsel, Martin Lipton were in attendance. The meeting centered on BD's trouble and the possibility of restoring Dickinson to power. A lawsuit based on procedural irregularities at the board meeting was ruled out. Nor was a proxy fight considered a viable option when the small percentage of total BD shares Dickinson held was revealed. Although Dickinson and members of his family still held the largest segment of stock in the company, acquisitions, public offerings and the sale of some of their holdings had caused their aggregate portion to be reduced to approximately 5% of BD's outstanding shares. Discussion then turned to more practical solutions, e. g., for Dickinson to sell his shares on the open market to BD or to a third party, or to bring pressure on management through the outside directors. Dickinson vetoed the idea of selling his stock on the open market since he felt that that course would leave the shareholders of BD saddled with bad management. He accepted two remaining options to vote with outside directors to bring pressure on management and to sell his stock to a company interested in a takeover of BD and engaged Salomon for the latter purpose.

A few days later, on or about April 25, Dickinson advised Zeller [Eberstadt's chief executive] that he was asking Salomon to involve Eberstadt in the effort to interest a company in acquiring his stock. Zeller confirmed these arrangements with Gutfreund.

* * *

From the spring of 1977 forward, Salomon and Eberstadt, particularly Lipper and Zeller, worked zealously to interest a company in acquiring a minority interest or in buying 100% of BD.

* * *

Harry Sharbaugh, Sun's chief executive, had determined in 1977 that Sun needed to diversify by investing in institutions outside the energy field. Sun sought the acquisition of no less than a 20% interest and not more than a 50% interest in 3 or 4 companies over the succeeding two or three years by investing some 300–400 million dollars in each organization. Sun's corporate development committee was given responsibility for developing major acquisition opportunities for Sun. In August, Salomon was engaged to undertake some studies in connection with Sun's diversification program and Horace Kephart, a senior vice president concerned with corporate development and diversification, was given responsibility for dealing with Salomon. Kenneth Lipper was one of the Salomon partners in charge of the Sun account. Thus, the stage was now set for the main event.

Kephart discussed Sun's diversification program with Lipper, and in late November the two met at Salomon. Kephart was given a copy of BD's annual report, and Lipper suggested that Sun might consider BD as an acquisition possibility in its corporate development program.

* * *

On December 22, Kephart assembled a study team of Sun executives to carry the analysis of the potential BD acquisition to "the next stage of sophistication."

* * *

On January 5, Kephart presented the study team's findings to the corporate development committee at a meeting to which members of the board were invited to attend in informal session. * * * The consensus was that the matter should go forward. On the next day Wachtell, Lipton was employed as Sun's counsel and thereafter, Cleary, Gottlieb, Steen & Hamilton ("Cleary, Gottlieb") was employed by Salomon.

* * *

Between December 22 and January 13 (when the executive committee authorized the acquisition and the expenditure of up to 350 million dollars), the study group was engaged in the examination of a myriad of alternatives. The study team knew that 10–13% of BD shares were held by non-management individuals who were willing to sell and that a large percentage of BD stock was in the hands of institutions. The study team concluded that the optimum percentage level for Sun to reach was over 33 1/3%. At that level, Sun could utilize equity accounting and would have sufficient holdings to have a significant voice in BD's future direction. Even if BD increased the number of authorized shares, Sun's strength could not be diluted enough to frustrate these two objectives. The study team considered it acceptable for Sun to hold 20–30% of the stock for a short time, but a percentage in excess of 33 1/3% was the basic objective.

On January 10 and 11, Kephart and the study team, augmented by Salomon (Rosenthal, Lipper, Gutfreund), Eberstadt (Zeller), Fogelson [of Wachtell, Lipton], Howard Blum, Sun's staff counsel, and Nathan [an attorney with Cleary, Gottlieb] met in Sun's headquarters to devise final recommendations to present to the Sun Board. There was an extended discussion of strategy. Kephart led the discussion, considering (1) open market purchases, (2) a conventional tender offer, and (3) private purchases. In the face of a hostile target, a conventional tender offer was not considered attractive. It was felt that it would lead to competitive bidding which would make the desired acquisition more expensive, and there was certain to be time consuming legal maneuvering to try to thwart the acquisition effort. What was needed was a procedure that would enable the acquisition to be effectuated quickly and put Sun in physical possession of the shares in the shortest possible time. There was a discussion of legal risk, but this was not a concern about the risk of litigation itself since everyone accepted that as inevitable. Rather, the participants were concerned with the chance that Sun's objective would be thwarted in mid-stream by legal maneuvers.

Four possible strategies were listed by Kephart on a blackboard and rated in terms of legal risk, quick control and price: (1) to seek shares sequentially, first from individuals, then from institutions; (2) to seek shares simultaneously from these two groups; (3) to tender immediately; and (4) to contact management.

Simultaneous acquisition was considered the most desirable in terms of quick control and price, although there was a measurable legal risk that the effort would be aborted. Sun was advised by its lawyers that the exact boundary line between a private purchase and a tender offer had not been defined in the law. Nonetheless, the lawyers believed simultaneous purchases from large individual and institutional shareholders, carried out off the market after the New York Stock Exchange had closed and with as much secrecy as possible, constituted the strategy best suited to meet Sun's needs. The tender offer approach was rated best in terms of legal risk, but disadvantageous in terms of price. It would also give BD a wide opportunity to make counter moves. The lawyers felt it necessary to keep the solicitees limited in number in order for the acquisition to be considered a private transaction. There were discussions of the possibility of attaining the objective with purchases from 4 individuals and 6 institutions, but approaching as many as 40 solicitees was discussed. * * *

On January 11, these recommendations were presented to Sun senior officials. On January 13, the executive committee approved the "private transaction" proposal and authorized a $350 million expenditure for a 34% acquisition. * * *

On January 11, Fogelson, Nathan and Blum carefully considered the approach to be made to solicitees. * * * [T]he lawyers decided on preparing two scripts: one for those soliciting individuals and a second one for those soliciting institutions. The instructions stressed confidentiality and it was agreed that a lawyer would be at the side of each solicitor to monitor the latter's side of the conversation.

* * *

[A] two-tiered price offer with a most favored nation clause was agreed upon. * * * [S]olicitees were to be offered a top price of $45 per share with no recourse or $40 per share with the right to receive the highest price subsequently paid to any other solicitee. It was the understanding of Salomon, Sun and Eberstadt that all solicitees would get the benefit of the highest price paid.

Blum advised Rosenthal [of Salomon] that the price should be negotiated, not fixed, and that if another price were suggested by solicitees, it should not be rejected but referred back to Sun. He told Rosenthal that there should be no specified time to respond, but Rosenthal said time deadlines would be set within the time frame normally allowable in block trading. * * *

Kephart advised Lipper on January 13 that the executive committee had given the go ahead sign. He authorized the making of an offer to Dickinson and Dunning prior to January 16. * * * Lipper, Zeller and Jerome Lipper arranged to see Dickinson in his hospital room the next day, January 14. * * * After the price options were outlined, Dickinson indicated that he was ready to accept but only if the proposal was presented to Dunning as well. Dickinson chose the $45 price and asked that his shares be paid for with a cash down payment and the remainder in installments. He was told that the propriety of the installment payments would have to be referred to the lawyers.

* * * Mrs. Turner (Dickinson's daughter) then arrived in Dickinson's hospital room, and Zeller and Lipper offered her the same proposition offered to her father. Zeller and Lipper kept their appointment the next day with Dunning and made the proposal to him. Dunning liked the proposition and promised to advise them as soon as he talked to his brothers and to his co-trustee.

* * *

Nilsen of Chemical Fund was called at 3:45, and was offered the proposal before the offer was made to any other institution. Nilsen accepted the $45 price for the two Eberstadt funds, Chemical and Surveyor, and for Eberstadt's discretionary accounts.

At 4:00 P.M. all the persons assigned to do the solicitation met in the trading room of Salomon. Each solicitor had a script from which to read, and a lawyer was teamed up with each caller. Shortly after 4:00 P.M. the telephoning began. Some 30 institutions were contacted.

* * *

The callers followed the script. There were slight variations, but each solicitee was told that a non-disclosed purchaser, sometimes identified as in the top fifty of Fortune Magazine's 500, was looking for 20% of BD stock; that no transaction would be final unless 20% of the shares were acquired; that the $45 option was a top final price and the $40 option could be accepted with protection in the event shares were later bought at a higher figure; and that the desired 20% goal was within reach or that the order was filling up fast and a hurried response was essential. Each solicitee was asked to respond within one hour or less, although some were given until the next day. Sun was identified to a few institutions, but to most the purchaser's specific identity was not revealed.

The institutions solicited had to consult with their in-house officials hurriedly. By 4:45 Kephart advised Burtis that verbal commitments for 3.1 million shares had been obtained. At 5:35 P.M. the total had reached 20%, and Kephart was given authorization to seal the bargain with these institutions that had committed their shares. Those institutions were called again, and Kephart was put on the phone. He identified himself, and after confirming that the solicitees were interested in selling at $45 a share, he accepted on behalf of Sun's subsidiary L.H.I.W. * * *

On January 17 and 18, couriers were dispatched all over the country with Sun's checks to pay for the stock, to obtain signatures or collect prepared purchase agreements, to take physical possession of the stock certificates and to have the solicitees sign powers of attorney to allow Sun to vote their proxies.

* * *

Sun's Williams Act filing did not take place until January 19 when its 13(d) was filed.

* * *

III

Determination

Threshold Considerations

* * *

The next threshold inquiry concerns whether this was a privately negotiated transaction or series of such transactions or a public offering. There can be no disagreement that a purely private transaction is not subject to the pre-filing strictures under Section 14. * * * These activities are covered by Section 13(d) when 5% of a company's shares are acquired.

Although the difference between a privately negotiated transaction and a tender offer was alluded to on several occasions in the course of the debate on the Williams Act, * * * the distinction was never articulated. * * * Our first responsibility is therefore to distinguish a privately negotiated transaction, which is outside the scope of Section 14 of the Williams Act, from a public transaction, which may not be. While no differentiation between private and public has been spelled out in the Williams Act or the debates leading to its enactment, we have not been cast totally adrift. Some guidelines developed in defining a private offering exemption under Section 4(1) of the Securities Act of 1933, * * * should be of aid in determining whether this transaction may properly be classified as one privately negotiated or publicly offered.

Arms-length negotiations between two persons epitomize a private transaction. As the number of actors increases, the identifiable characteristics of a private activity become blurred.

* * *

It must be conceded, of course, that *Ralston Purina* was concerned with the meaning of a private offering exemption under the 1933 Act, and we are faced with an entirely different statutory provision in the case at hand. Yet logic does make its demands. If statutory purpose gives proper definitional aid in distinguishing a public from a private offering under the

1933 Act, it would seem to follow that the purposes of the Williams Act would help define the contours of privately negotiated transactions exempted from the reach of Section 14.

* * *

Here, there were face to face transactions with four persons—Dickinson, Dunning, Turner and Lufkin. A total of 39 individuals and institutions were solicited with holdings involving a variety of discretionary accounts. There was no common characteristic binding the solicitees together except that they were uniformly shareholders with substantial BD holdings. Among those approached were highly knowledgeable individuals like Lufkin as well as unsophisticated investors like Smith, Willock and Drake. There were insurance companies, mutual funds, banks, a state entity, partnerships and corporations. The solicitation was nationwide.

* * *

It should be noted that Senator Williams proposed exempting privately negotiated transactions from Section 14(d)'s pre-acquisition filing requirements to avoid requiring prematurely the disclosure of the terms of such transactions which the parties involved might prefer be kept secret. None of the solicitees involved here had any concern about any premature disclosure. That was solely Sun's anxiety.

Since these were undoubtedly not "privately negotiated" transactions in which there was a mutual desire to avoid premature disclosure, the "access to information standard" derived from *Ralston Purina* and its cognate cases becomes even more relevant. The cases indicate that the supposed sophistication of the solicitees will not suffice to render the transaction private if they are given no information on which to exercise their skills. The procedure employed in this case required a hurried response on the basis of little information other than the price offered. The solicitors had no authorization to engage in negotiations with those they called. Their job was to obtain quick, oral commitments.

* * *

Based on the decided case law distinguishing "public" from "private" transactions, defendants have failed to carry their burden of showing that Sun's acquisition was "privately negotiated." * * *

This is not the end but merely the beginning of the inquiry. The conclusion that this was a public solicitation does not necessarily mean that the pre-acquisition filing requirements of the Williams Act apply. We now proceed to consider that issue.

Section 14(d) Claims

The Senate subcommittee introduced its report on the proposed Williams Act with a brief description of a typical tender offer:

> The offer normally consists of a bid by an individual or group to buy shares of a company usually at a price above the market price. Those

accepting the offer are said to tender their stock for purchase. The person making the offer obligates himself to purchase all or a specified portion of the tendered shares if certain specified conditions are met. S.Rep.No. 550, 90th Cong., 1st Sess. 2 (1967).

* * *

The buyer need not seek one hundred percent or even a majority of the stock of a company in order for its bid to qualify as a tender offer. The Williams Act was drafted to cover only those tender offers resulting in ownership of more than 10% (now 5%) of the stock of a corporation. Thus, the Act recognizes the possibility that a purchase of even less than 5% might be a tender offer, although exempted from regulation.

* * *

All of these elements bid, premium price, obligation to purchase all or a specified portion of the tendered shares if certain specified conditions are met (in this instance, if 20% of the outstanding shares are acquired) are present here. * * *

What is probably more important than the fact that this transaction has all the characteristics of a tender offer that were identified by Congress in the debates on consideration of the Williams Act is that Sun's acquisition is infected with the basic evil which Congress sought to cure by enacting the law. This purchase was designed in intent, purpose and effect to effectuate a transfer of at least a 20% controlling interest in BD to Sun in a swift, masked maneuver. It would surely undermine the remedial purposes of the Act to hold that this secret operation, which in all germane respects meets the accepted definition of a tender offer, is not covered by Section 14(d)'s pre-acquisition filing requirements because Sun's coup was not heralded by widespread publicity and because no shares were placed in a depository. Sun wanted no publicity. It deliberately chose to keep its moves hidden because as Kephart stated, Sun executives were fearful that they might have large sums of corporate funds committed before having in hand shares and proxies representing a 33 1/3% controlling interest in BD. Nor did Sun put trust in a depository. It wanted to have physical possession of the stock certificates purchased as quickly as possible.

The argument that the solicitees were sophisticated investors and therefore did not need Section 14 disclosure is no more convincing in this connection than it was in relation to the issue of whether this was merely a private transaction.

* * *

Even if this transaction were not seen as a *conventional* tender offer, it would not necessarily fall outside the ambit of Section 14(d). As discussed above, the concept of a tender offer has never been precisely defined either in the Williams Act itself or by the Commission. Congress left to the Commission the task of providing through its experience concrete meaning to the term. The Commission has not yet created an exact definition, but in this case and in others, it suggests some seven elements as being characteristic of a tender offer: (1) active and widespread solicitation of public shareholders for the shares of an issuer; (2) solicitation made for a substantial percentage of the issuer's stock; (3) offer to purchase made at a premium over the prevailing market price; (4) terms of the offer are firm rather than negotiable; (5) offer contingent on the tender of a fixed number of shares, often subject to a fixed maximum number to be purchased; (6) offer open only a limited period of time; (7) offeree subjected to pressure to sell his stock. These characteristics were recently accepted as appropriately describing the nature of a tender offer. See *Hoover v. Fuqua Industries, Inc.*, C. 79–1062A (N.D.Ohio June 11, 1979). In that case, the Commission also had listed an 8th characteristic not included here—whether the public announcements of a purchasing program concerning the target company precede or accompany rapid accumulation of large amounts of the target company's securities. The reason this last characteristic was left out undoubtedly was because publicity was not a feature of this transaction.

At any rate, it seems to me that the list of characteristics stressed by the Commission are the qualities that set a tender offer apart from open market purchases, privately negotiated transactions or other kinds of public solicitations. With the exception of publicity, all the characteristics of a tender offer, as that term is understood, are present in this transaction. The absence of one particular factor, however, is not necessarily fatal to the Commission's argument because depending upon the circumstances involved in the particular case, one or more of the above features may be more compelling and determinative than the others.

There was certainly "active and widespread solicitation" involved. Defendants contend that there was no widespread public solicitation of the general body of shareholders. But institutional holdings accounted for roughly 40% of all BD's outstanding shares as of January 16, and there was surely widespread solicitation of this class of shareholders. In addition, there was solicitation of individual shareholders holding a considerable percentage of BD shares. Measured by the size of the holdings solicited (34%), the geographic dimensions of the effort (from New York to California and from Massachusetts to North Carolina) and by the number of solicitees approached (30 institutions and 9 individuals * * *), there was widespread solicitation of BD's shareholders. * * *

The second characteristic, substantial percentage, does not move us very far, for unless the solicitation embraces at least 5% of the issuer's stock, the Act would not be called into play. The third element, premium over market, is regarded as one of the typical indicia of a conventional tender offer and was certainly present here.

The fourth element—the firm terms of the offer and the absence of opportunity for negotiation is stressed by the Commission. Defendants argue that the solicitees were not told that negotiations were barred, but the price was so attractive that none sought to negotiate. No negotiation took place and indeed if any had occurred, the whole project would have been derailed. It is undisputed that the solicitors could not barter about the terms of the offer. Any desire by a solicitee to deviate from the proffered terms had to be referred to Kephart. He, in turn, had to call * * * to obtain permission to accept such a variation. That time-consuming process would have slowed the project and increased the legal risk of BD's being able to abort the acquisition. This project was structured so that there would be no individualized negotiations. The hope and expectation were that the price would be so attractive that negotiation would be unnecessary.

The fifth, sixth, and seventh elements were also present. The offer was contingent on Sun's achieving a stated percentage of BD shares—another characteristic of a typical tender offer. * * * Time constraints were placed on each solicitee, and although some were given additional time to respond, most felt that they had to reply within the time constraints imposed. * * * The solicitors tried to exert a maximum amount of pressure on the solicitees they contacted. The latter were told that favorable responses were coming in fast, and it was implied that either they had better make a hurried acceptance of this attractive offer or their chance would be gone.

The one element missing is publicity. Lack of publicity, however, should be no deterrent to classifying this transaction as a tender offer since, as has been stated, a principal objective of the Williams Act was to prevent secret corporate takeovers.

* * *

Accordingly, in acquiring 34% of BD stock in the transaction at issue here, Sun made a tender offer for BD stock without a pre-acquisition filing in violation of Section 14(d) of the Williams Act.

Section 13(d) Group

The Williams Act requires the filing of a 13(d) statement with the issuer, the exchange on which the securities are traded and the Commission ten days after a direct or indirect acquisition of beneficial ownership of more than 5% of the issuer's registered securities. Plaintiffs allege that Dickinson and others (who, in combination, were directly or indirectly the beneficial owners of more than 5% of BD) failed to meet Section 13(d)'s requirements despite agreeing to act together regarding the disposition of the securities they held. Defendants contend that no such agreement was made, that no group had been formed and that in any event, the filing of a 13(d) statement is mandated only when an agreement is made to acquire securities. They argue that even if Dickinson and others did act in concert pursuant to pre-arrangements, there is no violation because the group disposed of, rather than acquired, BD securities.

This last argument has surface appeal * * *. However, the statutory language clearly and unambiguously covers the disposition of securities, as well as their acquisition.

* * *

The formation of a group beneficially owning more than 5% of a class of a security triggers the filing requirements of Section 13(d). *GAF Corp. v. Milstein,* * * *, 453 F.2d at 716–18. Proof of the existence of a group requires a showing of an agreement to act together for a common purpose. * * *

The existence of the group may be established by "direct or circumstantial evidence to support the inference of a formal or informal agreement or understanding." * * * Both the direct and circumstantial evidence in this case compel the conclusion that as early as April, 1977 Dickinson, Eberstadt and M & D (then holding beneficial ownership of more than 5% of BD stock) had reached a common understanding to take concerted action to find a purchaser for their shares as a part of an effort to effectuate a shift in corporate control of BD. * * * Lufkin and Dunning committed themselves to this endeavor sometime later. When the common understanding was arrived at by those who in combination held more than 5% of B.D. stock, the 13(d) requirements came into play.

* * *

Sun's 13(d) Statement

Sun's 13(d) statement was filed on January 19. In the "purpose of the transaction" section, Sun's statement indicates that it purchased its interest in BD to acquire a "significant equity interest" while it evaluates the company and that it is considering seeking additional shares, proposing a merger, or seeking representation on the Board. The statement goes on to state that Sun's current interest constitutes approximately 34.1%; that as such it may account for its interest by the "equity method;" that under New Jersey law and BD's certificate of incorporation, "mergers and certain other business combinations" and amendments to the company's charter of incorporation require a 2/3 affirmative vote of outstanding shares; and that under BD by-laws, a holder of more than 25% may call a special meeting.[23]

23. In pertinent part, Sun's 13(d) reads as follows:

Purpose of Transaction.

Sun desires to diversify its business interests and activities. Based on a review of publicly available information, Sun believes that an equity interest in the Company is consistent with Sun's diversification objectives. The shares specified in Item 5 hereof were purchased to provide Sun with a significant equity interest in the Company while Sun continues its evaluation of the Company and its industry.

Sun intends to continue to study the Company and its industry and to take such action as Sun considers desirable in the light of its evaluation and circumstances then prevailing. Sun is considering, among possible courses of action: (i) seeking to purchase additional Shares in brokerage transactions, in private transactions, in a tender offer or exchange offer, or otherwise; (ii) proposing a merger or other form of combination between Sun or the Subsidiary and the Company; or (iii) seeking representation on the Company's Board of Directors. Sun has not formed an intention with respect to pursuing any of such courses of action. Depending upon the results of Sun's evaluation and circumstances then prevailing, Sun may determine to hold its Shares as an investment or to dispose of all or a portion of such Shares.

Except to the extent indicated above, Sun has no present plans or proposals with respect to a merger or liquidation of the Company, the sale or transfer of a material amount of the assets of the Company, any change in the Company's Board of Directors or management or any other material change in the Company's business or corporate structure. The Shares referred to in Item 5 hereof constitute approximately 34.1% of the Shares reported by the Company to be outstanding at September 30, 1977. As the owners of

Sun was concerned about getting 33 1/3% to secure a significant voice in the future course BD would take. Sun depicts itself as only concerned with equity accounting, but its real purpose was to obtain a sufficient foothold in various companies outside the energy field to be able to block attempts by other offerors to establish large positions in the same securities. On February 9, Kephart sent a memorandum to two members of [Sun's] BD study team assigning them the task of finding how 500–700 million dollars could be marshalled by February 17. Kephart testified that that was the sum it would cost for a 100% takeover of BD. * * *

It is settled that the filing requirements of Section 13(d) mandate completely truthful statements. * * * While the issue is a close one, the omissions here seem more technical than substantive. Although the statement does not say that Sun was planning a 100% takeover, it does indicate that that was one of the options under consideration. Also it sets forth the power that Sun's holding affords to block mergers or amendments to BD's articles of incorporation. Sun's statement thus sufficiently complied with Section 13(d) requirements.

Sun's Sale from Dickinson and Turner

Plaintiffs urge that Sun's purchase from Dickinson and Turner on terms different from those agreed upon with other solicitees violated Section 10(b) of the Exchange Act and Rule 10b–13 * * * promulgated thereunder. Among other things, Rule 10b–13 is designed to prevent large shareholders from using their power to exact advantages which other shareholders could not obtain and to prevent tender offerors from changing the terms of the offer and giving late tenderers a higher price. The Commission's purpose in promulgating Rule 10b–13 was " 'to safeguard the interests of the persons who have tendered their securities pursuant to the stated terms of a tender offer' by prohibiting the offeror from making any 'outside' purchases on different terms during the offer's duration." * * * Turner and Dickinson were allowed to take a part of the payment for their shares in cash and in installments over an 8 year period at 8% interest. No other solicitee was given the same opportunity. The deferred payment to Dickinson and Turner was a tax benefit to them which was not offered to Willock, Smith and Drake for example. This arrangement appears to be a definite infraction of Section 10(b) of the Exchange Act, Rule 10b–13 promulgated thereunder.

* * *

approximately 34.1% of the outstanding Shares, Sun and the Subsidiary may account for their interest in the Company [sic] the "equity method." Under New Jersey law and the Company's Restated Certificate of Incorporation, mergers and certain other business combinations by the Company, as well as amendments to the Company's Restated Certificate of Incorporation, require the affirmative vote of the holders of 66 2/3% of the outstanding Shares. In addition, under the Company's By-laws, any holder of more than 25% of the outstanding Shares may call a special meeting of the Company's stockholders, although a majority of the outstanding Shares entitled to vote is required to constitute a quorum at a meeting of the Company's stockholders.

Plaintiffs' Remaining Contentions

Plaintiffs assert that Dickinson violated Section 10(b) of the Exchange Act, Section 14(e) of the Williams Act, Rule 10b–5, and his fiduciary obligations to BD shareholders. The argument appears to be that Dickinson transgressed those provisions * * * by failing to advise BD management that he was shopping around for a purchaser for his holdings, and by accepting a premium for his shares from Sun without allowing the other BD shareholders to participate. * * * Dickinson, however, had been stripped of all effectiveness within the organization by the time he sold his stock to Sun, had been terminated as an employee of the company and had not been placed on the company slate for reelection as a director. * * *

Even though still a director, he was under no duty to * * * reveal his plans to management. * * *

Although Dickinson did not advise other shareholders that he was receiving a premium for his shares, no Section 10(b) liability is created by that omission. * * * A stockholder has no duty to other stockholders to refuse a premium or to advise them that he is receiving a premium. The fact that Dickinson participated in a transaction which favored only himself, some of his shareholder friends, and various institutional shareholders does not constitute a breach of any statutory or common law obligation Dickinson owed BD shareholders.

* * *

NOTES

1. *Wellman* illustrates how toehold share purchases by a prospective acquirer (or even purchases just for investment) can trigger application of the Williams Act. The Act imposes formal disclosure requirements in two situations. One occurs after a person acquires shares giving him or her beneficial ownership of over 5 percent of any class of equity securities registered under Section 12 of the Securities Exchange Act (or of certain other specialized types of shares, such as those issued by a registered closed-end investment company). In this event, Section 13(d) of the Securities Exchange Act (which the Williams Act added) requires the purchaser to send to the issuer of the purchased securities, and file with the Securities Exchange Commission, a statement containing certain specified disclosures (a Schedule 13D).

In *Wellman,* the buyer did not dispute that it needed to file (and, indeed, it did file) a Schedule 13D after it made its purchases. Sometimes, however, application of Section 13(d) is not so straightforward—as the court's consideration of whether several of the target's shareholders had to file a Schedule 13D shows. To begin with, Section 13(d)(3) deems two or more parties who act as a group for the purpose of acquiring, holding or disposing of securities, to be one person under Section 13(d). This is necessary, otherwise parties could avoid Section 13(d) filings by having a number of individuals each purchase less than five percent of the target's shares. Still, Section 13(d)(3) raises some questions. To begin with, how much of an agreement must exist between the members before they constitute a group? For instance, how much agreement existed among the group members in *Wellman*? Moreover, what exactly is it the group must exist to do? The statute refers to groups acting for the purpose of acquiring, disposing (as in *Wellman*), or even holding securities. Hence, if several shareholders gather together to gain control of a corporation, Section 13(d) could apply, even though the shareholders do not plan to buy any more stock. *E.g., GAF Corp. v. Milstein,* 453 F.2d 709 (2d Cir.1971), *cert. denied,* 406 U.S. 910 (1972). *But see Bath Industries, Inc. v. Blot,* 427 F.2d 97 (7th Cir.1970). This interpretation, in turn, raises the question of when was the acquisition of shares by the group, which triggered the 13D filing? (Keep in mind that even if the purpose of the group need not be to acquire shares, the statute only requires filing after an acquisition.) The answer is upon the formation of the group (assuming its members' total ownership exceeds five percent), since at this point the group (treating it as something of an entity) acquired the shares theretofore owned separately by its members. *E.g.,* Sec. Exch. Act Rule 13d–5(b). A somewhat related problem involves determining when a person has acquired beneficial ownership of shares. Here, one confronts schemes (which have landed some people in jail) to "park" stock—in other words, to have friendly parties hold legal title to shares they will later transfer to the acquirer, in order to delay the acquirer's need to make a 13D filing. Rule 13d–3 specifies a number of criteria for determining who is the beneficial owner of shares. Finally, several exceptions exist to the requirement for a 13D filing. For example, Section 13(d)(6)(B) excludes acquisitions of no more than two percent of the class of shares in one year.

Disclosure under Section 13(d) requires giving information about the acquirer, the source of its funds, the number of shares it owns or has a right to acquire, any arrangements it has with respect to the issuer's securities, and its purpose for acquiring the shares (such as to obtain control, to liquidate or merge the issuer, or to make any other major change in the target's business or structure). How can a purchaser respond to this last item if it is not entirely sure what it will do? Consider how Sun handled this in its 13D filing unsuccessfully challenged in *Wellman.* Overall, the disclosure is not particularly burdensome to prepare (in comparison, for instance, with a public offering). Why then do acquirers seek to delay it for as long as possible? Consider what the filing of a Schedule 13D can do to the price of stock the acquirer seeks to buy.

2. Section 14(d) of the 1934 Securities Exchange Act, as amended by the Williams Act, contains the second trigger for formal disclosure under the Williams Act. This section applies to anyone making a tender offer (using the mails or means of interstate commerce) for shares of an equity security registered under Section 12 of the Securities Exchange Act (or for certain other specialized types of shares), if, after the transaction (assuming it is successful), the person will own over five percent of the sought after class of stock. The section requires the filing of a statement (a Schedule TO) with the Securities Exchange Commission prior to the tender offer.

Why was there such a fuss in *Wellman* over whether the buyer made a tender offer requiring a filing under Section 14(d), rather than just an acquisition triggering a Section 13(d) statement? Schedule TO does require disclosing a bit more information than does Schedule 13D; for example, it demands financial information about the acquirer, if the acquirer is not a natural person, and if the information would be material to the target's shareholders in deciding what to do with their shares. This, however, was probably not the major concern. Rather, a critical difference exists in the timing of the two filings: Section 14(d) requires filing before the tender offer, whereas Section 13(d) allows a filing up to 10 days after the acquisition. As suggested above, timing is important, because the acquirer would like to buy as many shares as it can before the price rises in response to its announcement. (Incidentally, an outside buyer has no duty to the target's shareholders under Rule 10b–5 to divulge its intent to later make a higher priced tender offer. *E.g., General Time Corp. v. Talley Industries, Inc.,* 403 F.2d 159 (2d Cir.1968), *cert. denied,* 393 U.S. 1026 (1969).) One other potentially important factor hinges on the existence of a tender offer triggering application of Section 14(d), rather than just an acquisition triggering Section 13(d). Section 14(d) not only requires disclosure, but also imposes substantive rules upon the terms of a tender offer. These rules will be addressed later in the chapter. For now, however, one substantive regulation, Rule 14d–10, is worth noting. This provision demands a tender offer generally be open to all members of the sought after class of shares. Hence, if toehold acquisitions from a control group constitute a tender offer, the offer must be equally available to all the target's shareholders—albeit, the acquirer does not have to buy all the shares of the class; it can buy a portion on a pro-rata basis. Sec. Exch. Act § 14(d)(6). Moreover, recall the discussion in the court's opinion concerning the violation of Rule 10b–13. This rule, which is now labeled Rule 14e–5, generally prohibits a party, while making a tender offer, from purchasing shares other than through the offer. Consider the impact of these rules on the buyer's ability to pay a premium just to individuals holding a controlling block of shares, at least once the buyer commences a tender offer. Nor can one assume that the acquirer can avoid any problem with these rules by refusing to pay any control premium directly for stock. *See, e.g., Katt v. Titan Acquisitions Ltd.*, 244 F.Supp.2d 841 (M.D.Tenn.2003) (plaintiff claimed that golden parachute payments to senior executives constituted a disguised extra payment for the executives to tender their stock).

These differences indicate the importance of knowing what is a tender offer. No provision in the statute or the rules defines the term. Traditionally, one thinks of a tender offer as a general invitation (typically through a newspaper advertisement) to the shareholders of a company proposing to buy some or all of their shares. As *Wellman* shows, the meaning of the term for purposes of Section 14 goes beyond this. The eight factor test suggested by the S.E.C. and used in *Wellman* has become a standard in the area. *See, e.g., SEC v. Carter Hawley Hale Stores, Inc.,* 760 F.2d 945 (9th Cir.1985). *But see Hanson Trust PLC v. SCM Corp.,* 774 F.2d 47 (2d Cir.1985). Of course, as *Wellman* illustrates, these factors do not always produce an easy answer (especially when the court does not say how many factors must be present). Looking at the eight factors, how many of them would be applicable to open market purchases—in other words, purchases of shares through the exchanges at prevailing market prices? See, *e.g., Brascan Ltd. v. Edper Equities Ltd.,* 477 F.Supp. 773 (S.D.N.Y.1979) (finding no tender offer). Incidentally, the court's opinion in *Wellman* is probably both unnecessarily confusing and confused on the question of whether there is a tender offer, because it attacks the same question twice. Specifically, the preliminary discussion of whether there was a private transaction is simply another way of trying to determine whether there was a tender offer. Unlike the 1933 Act, there is no statutory exemption from Section 14(d) of the Williams Act for private transactions. The statutory issue is whether there is a tender offer, and the notion of private transactions is relevant only insofar as a private negotiated sale is presumably not a tender offer.

3. In addition to triggering application of the Williams Act, toehold share purchases can bring various state takeover laws into play. These acts (or at least those relevant to toehold purchases) fall into three broad categories. The first group, in which Delaware and New York fit, place limits upon the ability of large shareholders to enter into mergers or other business combinations with the corporation. Specifically, Delaware and New York establish a moratorium period (of three years or five years respectively) after the acquisition of a certain level of voting stock (15 percent in Delaware and 20 percent in New York) during which the buyer cannot complete a merger or other business combination with the target unless the board of the target approved either the share acquisition or the combination prior to the share purchase taking place. Del. Gen. Corp. Law § 203; N.Y. Bus. Corp. Law § 912. (Delaware also allows the combination without delay if the buyer acquired 85 percent of the target's shares, or if two-thirds of the other stockholders approve the transaction.) A number of other states have statutes which do not contain a moratorium period, but require either a supermajority vote by the target's shareholders (or possibly by disinterested directors), or the shareholders' receipt of at least a certain minimum price, in any follow-on merger. *E.g.,* Ill. Bus. Corp. Act. § 7.85. (New York does this as well for combinations after the five year waiting period.) Consider the planning impact of these statutes. As discussed earlier, a principal objective of toehold share purchases is often to gain clout for negotiating the subsequent acquisition. The effect of these statutes, especially New York's, is to undermine the bargaining position of any buyer who acquires the threshold percentage of stock without prior board agreement. Moreover, the result of the minimum price formulas found in some of these acts can be to deprive the buyer of the option to pay just some stockholders a control premium. *See, e.g.,* N.Y. Bus. Corp. Law § 912(c)(3)(A)(i), (B)(i), (E)(iii).

The second type of takeover statute requires a disinterested shareholder vote either before a party can acquire a so-called controlling amount of voting stock or to allow the buyer to vote such a controlling block. *E.g.,* Ohio Gen. Corp. Law § 1701.831; Ind. Bus. Corp. Law § 23–1–42–1, *et seq.* (The Supreme Court upheld the constitutionality of the Indiana statute in

CTS Corp. v. Dynamics Corp. of America, 481 U.S. 69 (1987).) Since a controlling amount of stock under these acts can be as little as 20 percent, they too can undermine the use of toehold share purchases as a strategy of gaining a leg up before actually going through with the entire transaction.

Pennsylvania has pioneered a third category of act, which gives the stockholders of the target the right to demand the acquirer cash them out at fair value—set at not less than the highest price the buyer paid to acquire shares in the previous 90 days—once the buyer has obtained 20 percent of a corporation's stock. Pa. Assoc. Code §§ 2542–47. The impact on toehold purchases is to undermine the buyer's ability to selectively pay a control premium. (Pennsylvania's statute also contains provisions fitting within the first (limiting business combinations with a major shareholder) and second (requiring a disinterested shareholder vote to enfranchise and retain a control block) categories of takeover statutes; as well as various other provisions impacting takeovers which are noted elsewhere in this chapter. Pa. Assoc. Code §§ 2555–56, 2561–68.)

Many of these statutes contain provisions which render them inapplicable to various firms incorporated in the jurisdiction. For example, they may exclude companies whose shares are not widely traded. *E.g.,* Del. Gen. Corp. Law § 203(b)(4); N.Y. Bus. Corp. Law § 912(d)(1). Most allow companies to opt out of the regulation by article provision. *E.g.,* Del. Gen. Corp. Law § 203(b)(1), (2), (3); N.Y. Bus. Corp. Law § 912(d)(3).

4. A variety of other laws and rules may impact upon toehold purchases. For example, an acquisition can trigger the need to notify the Justice Department and the Federal Trade Commission under the Hart–Scott–Rodino Antitrust Improvements Act of 1976, 15 U.S.C. § 18a. This depends upon the size of the acquisition. Either the acquisition must result in the acquirer holding assets or stock of the target worth at least $200 million (to be adjusted for inflation after 2004), or, if the acquirer ends up with assets or stock worth between $50 million and $200 million, then either the target or the acquirer must have assets or sales (or just assets if dealing with a manufacturing corporation as target) of at least $100 million, while the other party to the acquisition must have assets or sales of at least $10 million.

For planning purposes, a critical aspect of the Hart–Scott–Rodino Act is the delay it imposes before the parties can carry out the acquisition: 30 days (15 for cash tender offers) after filing, subject to extension if the agencies ask for more information. (Providing the government time to prevent an anticompetitive acquisition before it occurs is, of course, the whole purpose of the Act; albeit the filing requirement extends well beyond the range of mergers which violate the substantive antitrust laws.) In fact, the purchases in *Wellman* could not have closed in a day had the transaction there not occurred before the Hart–Scott–Rodino Act took effect. Can parties in a situation like *Wellman* immediately enter a binding contract of sale with the transfer of the shares delayed and contingent, or would the contract itself constitute an acquisition?

Toehold share purchases also can create difficulties if the parties thereafter wish to carry out a tax-free reorganization. *E.g, Chapman v. Commissioner,* reprinted later in this chapter.

5. Suppose the buyer encounters overwhelming resistance after making toehold purchases or announcing a tender offer. In this event, the buyer may decide to sell out the shares it acquired, or withdraw its tender offer. If the buyer made its purchases in stages, so that it acquired some shares after becoming a 10 percent stockholder, the buyer should keep in mind Section 16(b) of the 1934 Securities Exchange Act in deciding when to sell following a failed bid for control. *See Foremost–McKesson, Inc. v. Provident Securities Co.,* 423 U.S. 232 (1976). Specifically, if the purchaser resells within six months the shares acquired when it was a 10 percent stockholder, it must disgorge its profits to the issuing corporation (assuming the corporation has shares registered under Section 12 of the Act). Pennsylvania's takeover statute goes even further—requiring a party who buys shares giving it over 20 percent of a company's stock, to disgorge its profits to the corporation if it resells within a year and a half. Penn. Assoc. Code §§ 2571–76. Of course, an even worse danger with a toehold purchase when the buyer does not succeed in acquiring the target is the buyer might be able to sell only at a loss.

Typically, the tender offeror makes its bid subject to conditions (such as a certain number of shares tendered) which allow it to withdraw the offer without contractual liability in the event the offer is undersubscribed or if other problems occur. (The tender offeror must carefully outline the conditions which allow it to withdraw the offer. *See, e.g., Lowenschuss v. Kane,* 520 F.2d 255 (2d Cir.1975) (a tender offeror, who did not condition its offer on a lack of litigation, can be liable to the tendering stockholders for breach of contract damages, when the offer was enjoined because of antitrust violations).) Needless to say, the withdrawal of the offer may cause the price of the stock to fall, and leave large blocks of the target's shares in the hands of parties (arbitrageurs) who bought it to make a quick profit in the contest for control. Can the tender offeror now go back and make open market purchases on the cheap? *Compare Hanson Trust PLC v. SCM Corp.,* 774 F.2d 47 (2d Cir.1985), *with Field v. Trump,* 850 F.2d 938 (2d Cir.1988).

b. *Bootstrap Transactions and Disposing of Unwanted Assets*

Commissioner of Internal Revenue v. Morris Trust

367 F.2d 794 (4th Cir.1966).

* * *

In 1960, a merger agreement was negotiated by the directors of American Commercial Bank, a North Carolina corporation * * *, and Security National Bank of Greensboro, a national bank. * * *

For many years, American had operated an insurance department. This was a substantial impediment to the accomplishment of the merger, for a national bank is prohibited from operating an insurance department except in towns having a population of not more than 5000 inhabitants. To avoid a violation of the national banking laws, therefore, and to accomplish the merger under Security's national charter, it was prerequisite that American rid itself of its insurance business.

The required step to make it nubile was accomplished by American's organization of a new corporation, American Commercial Agency, Inc., to which American transferred its insurance business assets in exchange for Agency's stock which was immediately distributed to American's stockholders. * * * The merger of the two banks was then accomplished.

Though American's spin-off of its insurance business was a "D" reorganization, as defined in § 368(a)(1), provided the distribution of Agency's stock qualified for non-recognition of gain under § 355, the Commissioner contended that the active business requirements of § 355(b)(1)(A) were not met, since American's banking business was not continued in unaltered corporate form. He also finds an inherent incompatibility in substantially simultaneous divisive and amalgamating reorganizations.

Section 355(b)(1)(A) requires that both the distributing corporation and the controlled corporation be "engaged immediately after the distribution in the active conduct of a trade or business." There was literal compliance with that requirement, for the spin-off, including the distribution of Agency's stock to American's stockholders, preceded the merger. The Commissioner asks that we look at both steps together, contending that North Carolina National Bank was not the distributing corporation and that its subsequent conduct of American's banking business does not satisfy the requirement.

* * *

Section 355(b) requires that the distributing corporation be engaged in the active conduct of a trade or business "immediately after the distribution." * * * It is in marked contrast to 355(b)'s highly particularized requirements respecting the duration of the active business prior to the reorganization and the methods by which it was acquired. Th[is] * * * suggest[s] a literal reading of the post-reorganization requirement and a holding that the Congress intended to restrict it to the situation existing "immediately after the distribution."

* * *

Applied, to this case, there is no violation of any of the underlying limiting principles. There was no empty formalism, no utilization of empty corporate structures, no attempt to recast a taxable transaction in nontaxable form and no withdrawal of liquid assets. There is no question but that American's insurance and banking businesses met all of the active business requirements of § 355(b)(2). It was intended that both businesses be continued indefinitely, and each has been. American's merger with Security, in no sense, was a discontinuance of American's banking business, which opened the day after the merger with the same employees, the same depositors and customers. There was clearly the requisite continuity of stockholder interest, for American's former stockholders remained in 100% control of the insurance company, while, in the merger, they received 54.385% of the common stock of North Carolina National Bank, the remainder going to Security's former stockholders. There was a strong business purpose for both the spin-off and the merger, and tax avoidance by American's stockholders was neither a predominant nor a subordinate purpose. In short, though both of the transactions be viewed together, there were none of the evils or misuses which the limiting principles and the statutory limitations were designed to exclude.

We are thus led to the conclusion that this carefully drawn statute should not be read more broadly than it was written to deny nonrecognition of gain to reorganizations of real businesses of the type which Congress clearly intended to facilitate by according to them nonrecognition of present gain.

* * * Insofar as it is contended that § 355(b)(1)(A) requires the distributing corporation to continue the conduct of an active business, recognition of gain to American's stockholders on their receipt of Agency's stock would depend upon the economically irrelevant technicality of the identity of the surviving corporation in the merger. Had American been the survivor, it would in every literal and substantive sense have continued the conduct of its banking business.

Surely, the Congress which drafted these comprehensive provisions did not intend the incidence of taxation to turn upon so insubstantial a technicality.

* * *

The requirement of § 368(a)(1)(D) that the transferor or its stockholders be in control of the spun-off corporation immediately after the transfer is of no assistance to the Commissioner. It is directed solely to control of the transferee, and was fully met here. It contains no requirement of continuing control of the transferor. Though a subsequent sale of the transferor's stock, under some circumstances, might form the basis of a contention that the transaction was the equivalent of a dividend within the meaning of § 355(a)(1)(B) and the underlying principles, the control requirements imply no limitation upon subsequent reorganizations of the transferor.

* * *

Nor can we find elsewhere in the Code any support for the Commissioner's suggestion of incompatibility between substantially contemporaneous divisive and amalgamating reorganizations. The 1954 Code contains no inkling of it; nor does its immediate legislative history. * * *

The Congress intended to encourage six types of reorganizations. They are defined in 368 and designated by the letters "A" through "F." The "A" merger, the "B" exchange of stock for stock and the "C" exchange of stock for substantially all of the properties of another are all amalgamating reorganizations. The "D" reorganization is the divisive spin-off, while the "E" and "F" reorganizations, recapitalizations and reincorporations, are neither amalgamating nor divisive. All are sanctioned equally, however. Recognition of gain is withheld from each and successively so. Merger may follow merger, and an "A" reorganization by which Y is merged into X corporation may proceed substantially simultaneously with a "C" reorganization by which X acquires substantially all of the properties of Z and with an "F" reorganization by which X is reincorporated in another state. The "D" reorganization has no lesser standing. It is on the same plane as the others and, provided all of the "D" requirements are met, is as available as the others in successive reorganizations.

* * *

To the extent that our own decision in *Elkhorn*[18] is relevant, it tends to support our conclusion, not to militate against it.

Elkhorn was one of the interesting cases which contributed to the development of the judicial principles which served, as best they could, to confine pretensive arrangements in the early days long before adopting of the 1954 Code. Mill Creek Coal Company wanted to acquire for Mill Creek stock one of the mining properties of Elkhorn. Had the bargain been effectuated, directly, it would have been clearly a taxable transaction, for Elkhorn had other mining properties. In an attempt to avoid the tax, Elkhorn's other properties were spun-off to a new Elkhorn; old Elkhorn conveyed its remaining properties to Mill Creek for stock and by successive transactions, Elkhorn stockholders wound up owning stock in new Elkhorn which owned all of old Elkhorn's mining properties, except the ones transferred to Mill Creek, and the Mill Creek stock received by old Elkhorn. They were in precisely the same position as they would have been in if old Elkhorn had transferred the Mill Creek properties to Mill Creek for stock. It was an obviously transparent attempt to circumvent the requirement that substantially all of the properties must be transferred to qualify for nonrecognition in what would now be classified as a "C" reorganization.

The contention in *Elkhorn* was not that its stockholders realized gain on the spin-off. The opinion [instead required] * * * the recognition of gain as a result of the subsequent "C" reorganization.

It is difficult now to envision any other result in *Elkhorn,* since the stockholders' purpose of formalistic transformation of a clearly taxable transaction into the form of a series of untaxable transactions was so blatant. Nothing of the sort is present here. Interestingly, however, *Elkhorn* would question the recognition of gain in the merger exchange here, as to which the Commissioner wisely makes no contention under the 1954

18. Helvering v. Elkhorn Coal Co., 4 Cir., 95 F.2d 732.

Code, not recognition of gain at the earlier spin-off step. As to the first step, the *Elkhorn* opinion appears to oppose the Commissioner's present position.

For the reasons which we have canvassed, we think the Tax Court * * * correctly decided that American's stockholders realized no recognizable taxable gain upon their receipt in the "D" reorganization of the stock of Agency.

Affirmed.

NOTES

1. Prospective buyers of a corporation often do not desire to obtain all of the company's assets. This could reflect simply a judgment as to what activities or properties of the seller will complement the purchaser's business. Alternately, as in *Morris Trust,* it could stem from state or federal regulations which prevent the purchaser's acquisition of one of the target's lines of business. In the *Morris Trust,* the problem involved the permissible activities for a national bank. Sometimes, the difficulty exists because the acquirer engages in an activity directly competing with one of the selling firm's ventures. As discussed earlier, if this competition occurs in a concentrated market, the acquisition could violate the antitrust laws. To avoid the violation, the purchaser may propose not to buy the directly competing operation. Overlapping to some extent with the problem of unwanted properties, purchasers often desire to finance at least a portion of the purchase out of the assets of the selling company.

Several techniques exist to deal with unwanted assets. The simplest occurs if the parties structure the acquisition as a sale by the target corporation of its assets to the purchasing company. With an asset transaction, the sale could exclude the undesired properties—in exchange, of course, for a lower purchase price. For reasons set out in the next section of this chapter, however, the parties may not wish to engage in a sale of assets type of transaction, or, even if they do, there may be undesirable tax consequences to the selling corporation holding back substantial unwanted properties.

Alternately, the buyer could purchase the entire target corporation (either as an entity, or all of its assets), and afterwards sell off the undesired properties. Several difficulties, however, may exist with this seemingly straight-forward approach. To begin with, the buyer may not be willing to pay a price commensurate with what the seller thinks the items are worth for properties which the buyer really does not want. This becomes a greater problem if the seller's shareholders harbor any thoughts of continuing the line of business in which the buyer lacks interest. The parties can avoid this side issue snagging the negotiations by not making the unwanted assets part of the transaction. Moreover, if the problem with the properties lies in regulatory barriers, the buyer would need to check on whether it could have even temporary ownership. The buyer also might require larger bridge financing (short term loans) to cover the acquisition until it could dispose of the unwanted assets.

Consider, as well, the tax impact of the buyer acquiring and then disposing of undesired properties. As discussed later in this chapter, if the parties structure the acquisition as a sale by the target company of its assets in a fully taxable transaction, then the buyer could resell the unwanted property at the same price it paid, without taxable gain. Otherwise, if the buyer purchases the stock in the target company, or obtains the target's assets in a tax-free transaction, generally there will be no increase in the basis of the assets to reflect their fair market value at the time of the acquisition. In this event, the resale of the unwanted properties can produce a taxable gain, borne directly or indirectly (through ownership of the target corporation) by the buyer, even though the buyer paid fair market value for the unwanted property. (Of course, the buyer could attempt to discount the price it pays for these assets to reflect any built-in taxable gain. However, this again further complicates the negotiations.) Moreover, if the buyer purchases stock in the target company, then a distribution by the target to the buyer of the proceeds of selling any unwanted assets will involve a taxable dividend (or redemption). *E.g., Television Industries, Inc. v. Commissioner,* 284 F.2d 322 (2d Cir.1960). This is especially important when the party who bought the target is not a corporation entitled to the dividends-received deduction of Section 243.

This shows why a purchaser often may request the target company engage in cooperative transactions to dispose of unwanted assets. The target might accomplish this by declaring an in-kind dividend with the unwanted property—or, if this is impractical, selling the assets and declaring a cash dividend—prior to the buyer acquiring the target. Alternately, the target company might redeem some of the former stockholders' shares. (This is often referred to as a bootstrap redemption, because it uses the target's funds to lessen the amount of stock for the purchaser to acquire. Note, however, a dividend has the same effect, even though it does not reduce the number of outstanding shares, since it lessens the per-share value.) Finally, if the unwanted property consists of a going business, the target can engage in a corporate division or spin-off (as in *Morris Trust*). From a state corporate law or Federal securities law standpoint, these transactions involve the issues explored by the discussions in Chapters IV and VI of dividends, redemptions and corporate divisions. In addition, keep in mind the possibility that bootstrap redemptions may involve a fraudulent conveyance, as in the *Wieboldt Stores* decision earlier in this chapter. Beyond corporate law concerns, *Morris Trust* shows that undertaking these transactions in the context of a sale of business raises some new tax questions.

2. Disposing of unwanted assets through a pre-sale dividend to the target's outgoing shareholders produces taxable gain to the target company if its basis in the distributed assets is less than the property's fair market value. I.R.C. § 311(b). The recipient shareholders, in turn, recognize income upon receipt of the dividend, following principles familiar from

Chapter IV. Rev. Rul. 75–493, 1975–2 C.B. 109. For many years, sellers sought a somewhat superior tax result by having the corporation redeem some of their shares, rather than having the corporation give them a pre-sale dividend. If the redemption qualified for sale, rather than distribution, treatment, then the selling shareholders could qualify for capital gains rather than dividend tax rates on the money they received from the corporation. Indeed, a bootstrap redemption typically has a significant leg-up (as compared with redemptions generally) in terms of obtaining sale, rather than distribution, treatment. This is because even a pro-rata redemption from all the selling shareholders would qualify for sale treatment if it occurred after the sale of stock to the acquirer and thus terminated the selling shareholders' interests in the target corporation. Suppose, however, the redemption occurs before the acquirer buys the remaining shares held by the selling shareholders. Even here, the redemption can receive sale, rather than distribution, treatment, if the court decides that the redemption is part of the same transaction as the sale of the remaining stock, which terminates the selling shareholders' interests. *E.g., Monson v. Commissioner*, 79 T.C. 827 (1982). In any event, with the reduction of the tax rate on dividends to match the rate on capital gains, bootstrap redemptions no longer have much advantage over pre-sale dividends. On the other hand, suppose another corporation owns most or all of the stock in the target, and wishes to sell its subsidiary. In this case, Section 243 substantially reduces the burden on the parent receiving a pre-sale dividend. In fact, stripping the subsidiary through such a dividend, and lowering the selling price accordingly, can result in trading higher dividends (shielded from full taxation by Section 243) for lower gain on the sale of shares; not a bad deal. *But see Waterman Steamship Corp. v. Commissioner,* 430 F.2d 1185 (5th Cir.1970), *cert. denied,* 401 U.S. 939 (1971) (court recharacterized the pre-sale dividend as part of the purchase price—thereby treating it as gain on the sale—when the buyer furnished the target the funds to pay the dividend); I.R.C. § 1059 (lowering a corporate shareholder's basis in its stock by the amount of any dividend it receives which escapes tax because of Section 243, if the corporation held the shares for two years or less before announcement of the dividend, and the dividend is larger than ten percent of the shareholder's basis in its shares (five percent for preferred stock)); Treas. Reg. § 1.61–9(c) (taxing a dividend to the purchaser rather than the seller of stock, if the seller holds legal title to the shares after the sale effectively took place solely to secure receipt of the dividend, which the parties credit against the payment of the purchase price).

What, if any, tax impact does a bootstrap redemption have on the outside buyer? Chapter VI noted that redemptions could constitute constructive dividends to the non-selling shareholders if either the redemption relieved them of a primary and unconditional contractual obligation to buy the redeemed shares themselves, or if Section 305(c) and the regulations issued thereunder applied (as they would if the redemption was part of a plan to periodically increase the interest of the non-selling shareholders, and constituted a Section 301 distribution to the selling stockholders). This can apply as well to create constructive dividends for the outside buyer, if the redemption relieves it of a primary and unconditional obligation to buy the redeemed shares, or if the redemption fits within Section 305(c). *E.g., Skyline Memorial Gardens, Inc. v. Commissioner,* 50 T.C.M. (CCH) 360 (1985), *aff'd,* 831 F.2d 856 (9th Cir.1987).

Morris Trust illustrates the potential for a disposition of unwanted assets to be completely tax-free for both the target corporation and the recipient shareholders. This is by making the disposition through a corporate division. The court in *Morris Trust* rejected the Internal Revenue Service's argument that a tax-free corporate division under Section 355 could not precede a tax-free reorganization under Section 368. The I.R.S. has accepted the *Morris Trust* holding. Rev. Rul. 68–603, 1968–2 C.B. 148. Nevertheless, there remain limitations on this approach. Some constraints are obvious. For example, the active business requirement of Section 355(b) limits this approach to situations in which the unwanted assets constitute an active business with the requisite five year history.

More dramatically, the 1997 Taxpayer Relief Act limited the ability to have a tax-free spin-off of unwanted assets in a *Morris Trust* type of transaction. The Act added a new paragraph, Section 355(e), to Section 355. Under this paragraph, if the corporate division is part of a plan under which at least 50 percent of the stock in either the distributing or distributed corporation thereafter changes hands, then the distributing corporation must recognize gain in the corporate division. To illustrate, suppose in *Morris Trust* the pre-merger shareholders of the distributing corporation (American) ended up with less than 50 percent of the stock (measured either by value or by voting power) of the corporation (North Carolina National Bank), into which the distributing corporation merged. In this event, Section 355(e) would apply and the distributing corporation will recognize gain equal to the amount the distributing corporation would have recognized had it sold the distributed stock at fair market value in the spin-off. Notice, incidentally, as illustrated by this example, Section 355(e) ignores the fact that the distributing or distributed corporation might not be the surviving company in a post division merger; the question is simply how much stock in the surviving firm did the shareholders of the pre-acquisition distributing or distributed corporation end up with after the merger.

Does this mean that spin-offs have lost all their utility as a pre-acquisition transaction? The answer is no. To begin with, notice that the transaction in *Morris Trust* itself would have remained tax free even with Section 355(e). This is because the shareholders of the distributing corporation received 54 percent of the stock in the corporation which survived the merger. Moreover, Section 355(e) only imposes one level of tax, this being on the distributing corporation. If the division comes within Section 355, it still remains tax-free to the shareholders—thereby avoiding the double tax which otherwise could occur. Incidentally, lest parties deny that the distribution was part of a plan to sell the corporation, Section 355(e) states that divisions within two years of a change in share holdings are presumed, in the absence of contrary evidence, to be pursuant to such a plan. Displaying an interesting disregard of statutory language, however, regulations promulgated by the Internal Revenue Service (Treas. Reg. § 1.355–7) effectively turn the two year statutory presumption of a plan into a two year outer boundary for when one even asks the question. Specifically, the regulations announce a facts and circumstances test; but only if there was "an agreement, understanding, arrangement or substantial negotiations for the acquisition" during the two years prior to the distribution will there be a further examination of the facts and circumstances to see if the distribution was part of the acquisition plan. The regulations then provide a series of factors and safe harbors to deal with situations in which there was such an agreement, etc. within two years of the distribution.

There has been one good (from the taxpayers' standpoint) outcome from Congress' reexamination of tax-free spin-offs in advance of mergers. This has to do with the question of whether it matters which company—the spun-off subsidiary or the distributing parent—subsequently undergoes a merger or other acquisition. In *Morris Trust,* the court upheld the transaction when the parent, rather than the spun-off corporation, subsequently merged. In this event, the parent's former shareholders continued, after the merger of the parent, to hold a controlling interest in the spun-off subsidiary. Hence, the corporate division qualified as a reorganization under Section 368(a)(1)(D). Suppose, however, the merger involved the spun-off subsidiary. If the spun-off subsidiary merges, the parent's shareholders presumably no longer will have at least eighty percent ownership of the spun-off company after the entire transaction. Accordingly, the I.R.S. for years had taken the position that the transaction failed to qualify as a reorganization under Section 368(a)(1)(D)—which requires the parent or its shareholders control the spun-off subsidiary immediately after the reorganization—and, therefore, was not tax-free under Section 355. Rev. Rul. 70–225, 1970–1 C.B. 80. Congress, however, did not like the artificiality of distinguishing tax treatment depending on which company subsequently merges. (Recall, in a corporate division, which business goes into the parent, and which into the subsidiary, is somewhat arbitrary.) Accordingly, in 1998, Congress amended Section 368 to legislatively overrule Revenue Ruling 70–225. I.R.C. § 368(a)(2)(H)(ii). *See also* Rev. Rul. 98–27 1998–1 C.B. 1159 (not applying the step transaction doctrine to hold that the subsidiary did not meet the pre-division control requirement of Section 355(a) simply because the parties planned a post-division merger of the subsidiary).

Suppose, following the corporate division, the parent's shareholders sell all their stock in the parent in a taxable transaction, or the parent sells all its assets in a taxable transaction. (By contrast, in *Morris Trust,* the acquisition of the parent occurred in a tax-free merger.) In this event, the pre-arranged taxable sale would presumably show that the corporate division was a device to bail earnings out of the corporation, and, hence, disqualified from tax-free treatment by Section 355(a)(1)(B). *See* Treas. Reg. § 1.355–2(d)(2)(iii). Could the buyer get around this result by purchasing stock in the target corporation first, and then have the target corporation conduct a split-off which leaves the buyer in control of one company with the desired assets and the target's former shareholders owning another corporation having the undesired properties? See I.R.C. § 355(d) (making the target recognize gain in such a transaction).

Incidentally, it is important to keep in mind that the trade-off for obtaining a tax-free disposition of unwanted assets though a corporate division is the assets remain in a corporation. Accordingly, the potential double taxation of any appreciation of the assets remains.

Revenue Ruling 75–360

1975–2 C.B. 110.

The purpose of this Revenue Ruling is to explain the position of the Internal Revenue Service with respect to the decision of the Tax Court of the United States in *Arthur D. McDonald,* 52 T.C. 82 (1969). * * *

In that decision, the Tax Court held that a redemption of the petitioner's stock pursuant to a plan for acquisition of the redeeming corporation by another corporation was not essentially equivalent to a dividend within the meaning of section 302(b)(1) of the Internal Revenue Code of 1954, and therefore qualified for exchange treatment under section 302(a).

As more fully stated in the Tax Court's opinion, the petitioner owned all the outstanding preferred stock of E & M Enterprises, Inc. ("E & M") and ten of the eleven shares of its outstanding common stock. Borden Company ("Borden") made an initial verbal offer to exchange 5,500 shares of its common stock for all the preferred and common shares of E & M. In the next month Borden submitted a substitute offer in the form of a proposed "Plan of Reorganization." This plan, which was executed, provided that E & M would redeem all of the petitioner's preferred stock for $43,500 in cash and that Borden would acquire all of the common stock of E & M in exchange for 4,839 shares of Borden voting common stock. The difference between the 5,500 shares of Borden common stock originally offered for the business and the 4,839 shares agreed on in the plan represented the amount of $43,500 to be paid to the petitioner by E & M in redemption of his preferred stock. Upon the recommendation of Borden, E & M acquired the cash to carry out the redemption by obtaining a short-term bank loan. A week later E & M common stock was exchanged for Borden stock, and Borden, on the same day, paid E & M $96,000, a portion of which was used by E & M to pay off the bank loan.

Before the Tax Court the Commissioner incorrectly treated the redemption of the petitioner's stock and exchange of E & M stock for Borden stock as separate transactions, and therefore conceded that the exchange constituted a tax-free reorganization within the meaning of section 368(a)(1)(B) of the Code. Thus, there was presented for determination by the Tax Court only the issue of whether the redemption, when viewed as a separate transaction, was substantially pro rata and should be treated as a distribution subject to section 301 of the Code. The Tax Court correctly found a single integrated transaction, stating, "The record in this case establishes clearly that the redemption was merely a step in the plan of Borden for the acquisition of E & M, so that it is the results of the plan that are significant to us."

Viewing the redemption and reorganization together, the court concluded that the petitioner's interest in E & M had been substantially changed, so that the redemption was not essentially equivalent to a dividend. In reaching this conclusion, the court refrained from comment concerning the propriety of treating the exchange as tax-free because that issue was not before it.

The Service recognizes it was in error in arguing the various steps were separate transactions thereby affording tax-free treatment on the stock exchange. Accordingly, since the acquisition was not solely for voting stock of the acquiring corporation but partly for cash, it is the position of the Service that the acquisition of stock of E & M did not constitute a reorganization. Therefore, under the factual situation presented in *McDonald,* the entire transaction is considered a taxable sale or exchange. In view of this conclusion, the redemption issue dealt with by the Tax Court in *McDonald* was not the correct issue for decision. Therefore, the Service does not consider *McDonald* to be an appropriate precedent. * * *

NOTE

The ruling above shows how easy it is to so focus upon the immediate tax impact of a pre-sale redemption (or other pre-sale disposition of unwanted assets), that one loses sight of the disposition's possible impact upon the taxation of the ultimate sale of the business. As outlined later in this chapter, the transfer of a business can take the form of a sale by the target corporation of its assets in either a taxable or tax-free exchange, a sale by the target's shareholders of their stock in either a taxable or tax-free exchange, or a statutory merger or consolidation. One requirement for a tax-free sale of assets type of transaction is that the purchaser buy substantially all of the selling company's assets. I.R.C. § 368(a)(1)(C). Suppose the selling company possesses enough assets, which the purchaser does not want, to threaten the parties' ability to meet the substantially all assets test. Can a pre-sale disposition of the unwanted property through a dividend, redemption or corporate division, improve matters? This was the selling corporation's strategy in the *Elkhorn* decision discussed in *Morris Trust.* The *Elkhorn* court rejected tax-free treatment for the subsequent sale of assets. Along the same line, the Internal Revenue Service traditionally has measured the substantially all assets test against the amount of properties possessed by the corporation before any dividends, redemptions or spin-offs made as part of the plan of reorganization. *See* Rev.Proc. 77–37, 1977–2 C.B. 568. *But see* Rev.Rul. 88–48, 1988–1, C.B. 117 (when the target corporation sold half its assets to a third party for cash, and then transferred both the remaining assets and the cash to the acquirer for voting stock, the substantially all assets test was met); Rev. Rul. 2001–25, 2001–2 C.B. 1291 (same result in a situation in which the sale took place after the acquisition of the target in a reverse triangular merger and the target held the sale proceeds).

Interestingly, however, in Revenue Ruling 2003–79, 2003–29 I.R.B. 80, the Internal Revenue Service created a major exception to measuring the substantially all assets test based upon assets possessed before any spin-offs that are part of the acquisition plan. In this ruling, the Service concluded that *Elkhorn* only applies if it is the spun-off corporation that subsequently sells its assets in what the spun-off corporation claims is a tax-free sale of assets transaction—in which event, the assets sold by the spun-off corporation must constitute substantially all of the assets of the both the spun-off subsidiary and its pre-spin-off parent in order to qualify as a tax-free sale of assets transaction. By contrast, if the company, which plans to sell its assets, transfers unwanted assets to a newly formed subsidiary and spins off the subsidiary in a tax-free corporate division, then, according to Revenue Ruling 2003–79, Congressional intent precludes counting the unwanted assets in determining whether the subsequent sale of the remaining assets by the pre-spin-off parent corporation meets the substantially all assets requirement for a tax-free sale of assets transaction. Notice the premium this distinction places upon which company undertakes the subsequent attempt to have a tax-free sale of assets transaction following a tax-free corporate division.

Turning from the substantially all assets issue, Revenue Ruling 75–360 (reprinted above) concerned a requirement for a tax-free sale of stock type of transaction: The selling shareholders may receive only voting stock in the buyer in exchange for their stock in the target. I.R.C. § 368(a)(1)(B). Will every pre-sale disposition of assets to the target's shareholders violate this requirement? In fact, the Internal Revenue Service has repeatedly ruled that pre-sale dividends to the target's shareholders did not violate the solely for voting stock limit. *E.g.*, Rev.Rul. 68–435, 1968–2 C.B. 155. Is the difference that a dividend does not involve an exchange for shares? A less formalistic and more probable distinction might be the source of funds for the pre-sale transaction. Notice where the money used to redeem the shares came from in the *McDonald* case discussed in the ruling. If the funds do not come even indirectly from the buyer, then one can argue the redemption or dividend is irrelevant to the requirement that the buyer obtain the acquired shares solely in exchange for its voting stock. *See* Treas. Reg. § 1.368–1(e)(6)Ex. 9 (adopting this approach in the context of determining whether to count pre-acquisition redemptions in assessing compliance with the continuity-of-interest requirement for reorganizations).

Assuming a redemption does not prevent compliance with the solely for voting stock requirement, what effect might it have on the other prerequisite for a tax-free sale of stock transaction—that the purchaser own at least 80 percent of the target's outstanding stock immediately after the exchange? Clearly, with the redeemed shares out of the way, the purchaser need acquire less to end up holding 80 percent of what is left. Some provisions of the tax code related to other types of acquisitions, however, demand the acquirer obtain at least 80 percent of the target's shares in the transaction (rather than simply owning that much of whatever is outstanding after the dust settles). I.R.C. §§ 338(d) (purchaser must acquire within one year, shares giving it control, in order to make an election to step up the basis of the target's assets under Section 338), 368(a)(2)(E) (parent must acquire at least 80 percent of the target's shares solely in exchange for the parent's voting stock for a tax-free reverse triangular merger). Can one subtract the redeemed shares before calculating this 80 percent? *See* Treas.Reg. §§ 1.338–3(b)(5), 1.368–2(j)(6) Ex. (2), (3) (giving generally an affirmative response).

Finally, what might be the impact of pre-acquisition dispositions of assets on the requirements for a tax-free statutory merger? The regulations require that the surviving corporation end up with substantially all of the assets of target corporation in order for a statutory merger to be tax-free. However, conveniently enough, assets disposed of by the target prior to the merger—whether or not the disposition is part of an overall plan for the acquisition—do not count in applying this test. Temp. Treas. Reg. §§ 1.368–2T(b)(1)(ii)(A), (iv) Ex. 8 . Also, the regulations disregard pre-acquisition redemptions in applying the continuity-of-interest test for tax-free mergers (and other reorganizations), so long as the consideration does not come from the acquiring corporation. Treas. Reg. § 1.368–1(e)(6)Ex. 9.

SECTION B. STRUCTURING THE ACQUISITION

Already, in discussing various preliminary considerations for a corporate acquisition—including the role of the target's board in deciding whether to sell, what share of the purchase price the various stockholders of the target receive, the mechanics and rules governing a leveraged buy-out, problems in the negotiating process, and the disposition of unwanted assets—this chapter has indicated the potential importance of the manner in which the parties structure the ultimate acquisition. Now is the time to explore the mechanics of the various alternatives, and the impacts of the choice, in greater detail.

1. CORPORATE MECHANICS

Hariton v. Arco Electronics, Inc.

41 Del.Ch. 74, 188 A.2d 123 (1963).

■ SOUTHERLAND, CHIEF JUSTICE.

This case involves a sale of assets under § 271 of the corporation law, * * *. It presents for decision the [following] question * * *:

A sale of assets is effected under § 271 in consideration of shares of stock of the purchasing corporation. The agreement of sale embodies also a plan to dissolve the selling corporation and distribute the shares so received to the stockholders of the seller, so as to accomplish the same result as would be accomplished by a merger of the seller into the purchaser. Is the sale legal?

The facts are these:

The defendant Arco and Loral Electronics Corporation, a New York corporation, are both engaged, in somewhat different forms, in the electronic equipment business. In the summer of 1961 they negotiated for an amalgamation of the companies. As of October 27, 1961, they entered into a "Reorganization Agreement and Plan." The provisions of this Plan pertinent here are in substance as follows:

1. Arco agrees to sell all its assets to Loral in consideration (inter alia) of the issuance to it of 283,000 shares of Loral.

2. Arco agrees to call a stockholders meeting for the purpose of approving the Plan and the voluntary dissolution.

3. Arco agrees to distribute to its stockholders all the Loral shares received by it as a part of the complete liquidation of Arco.

At the Arco meeting all the stockholders voting (about 80%) approved the Plan. It was thereafter consummated.

Plaintiff, a stockholder who did not vote at the meeting, sued to enjoin the consummation of the Plan on the grounds (1) that it was illegal, and (2) that it was unfair. The second ground was abandoned. Affidavits and documentary evidence were filed, and defendant moved for summary judgment and dismissal of the complaint. The Vice Chancellor granted the motion and plaintiff appeals.

The question before us we have stated above. Plaintiff's argument that the sale is illegal runs as follows:

The several steps taken here accomplish the same result as a merger of Arco into Loral. In a "true" sale of assets, the stockholder of the seller retains the right to elect whether the selling company shall continue as a holding company. Moreover, the stockholder of the selling company is forced to accept an investment in a new enterprise without the right of appraisal granted under the merger statute. § 271 cannot therefore be legally combined with a dissolution proceeding under § 275 and a consequent distribution of the purchaser's stock. Such a proceeding is a misuse of the power granted under § 271, and a de facto merger results.

The foregoing is a brief summary of plaintiff's contention.

* * *

We now hold that the reorganization here accomplished through § 271 and a mandatory plan of dissolution and distribution is legal. This is so because the sale-of-assets statute and the merger statute are independent of each other. They are, so to speak, of equal dignity, and the framers of a reorganization plan may resort to either type of corporate mechanics to achieve the desired end. This is not an anomalous result in our corporation law. * * *

Plaintiff concedes, as we read his brief, that if the several steps taken in this case had been taken separately they would have been legal. That is, he concedes that a sale of assets, followed by a separate proceeding to dissolve and distribute, would be legal, even though the same result would follow. This concession exposes the weakness of his contention. To attempt to make any such distinction between sales under § 271 would be to create uncertainty in the law and invite litigation.

We are in accord with the Vice Chancellor's ruling, and the judgment below is affirmed.

NOTES

1. Perhaps few other transactions in business planning present the parties with as many options to achieve the same basic result, and, accordingly, place such a premium upon form, as does the acquisition of one business conducted through a corporation by another. To begin with, the participants might choose to undertake a statutory merger or consolidation. (This is the form the plaintiff in *Hariton* unsuccessfully argued the transaction must take.) Every state's corporations statute contains a provision allowing two or more corporations to merge into one entity. *E.g.,* Cal. Corp. Code § 1100; Del. Gen. Corp. Law § 251(a); N.Y. Bus. Corp. Law § 901; M.B.C.A. § 11.02(a). This entity could be either one of the corporations which existed before the combination, or a new corporation created by the transaction—in which case, some statutes refer to the transaction as a consolidation. *E.g.,* Del. Gen. Corp. Law § 251(a); N.Y. Bus. Corp. Law § 901(a)(2).

Procedurally, the statutory merger provisions call upon the boards of the merging companies to agree upon a plan of merger. *E.g.,* Cal. Corp. Code § 1101; Del. Gen. Corp. Law § 251(b); N.Y. Bus. Corp. Law § 902; M.B.C.A. §§ 11.02, 11.04(a). This "marriage" contract sets forth the various terms and conditions of the transaction, including such items as which corporation will survive the merger, any changes in the articles of the surviving corporation (for instance, changing the name or authorized stock; or else providing new articles in the case of a consolidation), provisions for the management of the surviving company (such as roles for the former officials of the merging firms), and various representations, warranties, and contingencies terminating the transaction (to deal with some of the risks discussed earlier in this chapter). Most important, the plan of merger specifies what the shareholders of each of the constituent companies get. (Needless to say, the shareholders of the disappearing corporation must exchange their stock in that company for something else; while the stockholders of the surviving firm may, or may not, simply keep their shares.) In this regard, it is useful to note that most state corporation statutes do not restrict the consideration stockholders can receive as part of a plan of merger to shares in the surviving company. Rather, the plan might call for the shareholders to receive debt securities, cash or other property in whole or in part payment for their stock (or the plan might even cancel some shares without consideration). *E.g.,* Cal. Corp. Code § 1101(d); Del. Gen.

Corp. Law § 251(b); N.Y. Bus. Corp. Law § 902(a)(3); M.B.C.A. § 11.02(c)(3). (One impact of this is to create a possible mechanism for involuntarily cashing out minority shareholders; a subject explored later in this chapter.)

Inevitably, not all the stockholders may be pleased with the terms of the merger agreement. The shareholders possess three legal protections against a merger contrary to their wishes; or, viewed from the other perspective, the proponents of the merger face three potential hurdles from the stockholders of the constituent companies. The first is the requirement of a vote by the shareholders of each of the merging companies to approve the transaction. *E.g.,* Cal. Corp. Code §§ 1200(a), 1201, 1202; Del. Gen. Corp. Law § 251(c); N.Y. Bus. Corp. Law § 903; M.B.C.A. § 11.04(b). Statutes vary as to how they handle several particulars of this requirement. For example, they differ in the level of approval needed (at least in the absence of a valid supermajority provision in the articles). *Compare* Cal. Corp. Code §§ 152, 1201(a); Del. Gen. Corp. Law § 251(c); M.B.C.A. § 11.04(e) (all generally requiring a majority vote), *with* N.Y. Bus. Corp. Law § 903(a)(2) (requiring a two-thirds vote for corporations in existence prior to 1998 unless the corporation's articles expressly calls for only a simple majority vote). (Note, these four statutes measure the applicable percentage against the number of outstanding shares, rather than against the number of shares actually voted. Note also that a number of states have adopted takeover statutes—discussed when dealing with toehold share purchases—some of which can effectively raise the vote needed for a merger if an acquirer has already obtained a substantial percentage of the target's stock. *E.g.,* Del. Gen. Corp. Law § 203; N.Y. Bus. Corp. Law § 912.) A second area of difference exists with respect the overlapping questions of whether otherwise non-voting stock can vote on the merger, and the necessity of approval by separate classes of shares (at least in the absence of governing provisions in the articles). *Compare* Del. Gen. Corp. Law § 251(c) (only requiring approval by the shares entitled to vote, and not requiring separate approval by each class), *with* Cal. Corp. Code § 1201(a) (requiring separate approval by each class of shares, except for preferred shares whose rights remain unchanged in the merger); N.Y. Bus. Corp. Law § 903(a)(2) (requiring approval by the shares entitled to vote, but also separate approval by a majority of each class of shares (whether or not voting shares) if the plan of merger contains any provision which would require approval by that class if undertaken as an amendment to the certificate of incorporation); M.B.C.A. § 11.04(e), (f)(1) (requiring approval by the shares entitled to vote, but also separate approval by a majority of each class of shares if the merger converts the shares into other securities or cash or property, or if the plan of merger contains any provision which would require approval by that class if undertaken as an amendment to the articles of incorporation). The requirement of a shareholder vote may not only impede the merger because of the prospect of disapproval, but also because of the administrative burden and cost of obtaining the vote (including compliance with the Federal proxy regulations for 1934 Securities Exchange Act reporting companies). In this regard, it is useful to note the varying exceptions to the requirement of stockholder approval found in some of the state corporations statutes. For example, when the parent company owns an overwhelming percentage (typically 90 percent) of the shares in its subsidiary, state corporations acts commonly allow the subsidiary to merge into the parent without the approval of either company's stockholders (and often without the approval of the subsidiary's board of directors). *E.g.,* Cal. Corp. Code §§ 181, 1110, 1201(a); Del. Gen. Corp. Law § 253; N.Y. Bus. Corp. Law § 905; M.B.C.A. § 11.05. (This is often referred to as a short-form merger.) Some statutes also allow the surviving company in a merger to forego a vote of its shareholders if its articles will not change, its shareholders will not exchange their stock for different shares, and it will issue a relatively small amount of its common stock, or rights to acquire its common stock (typically no more than 20 percent of the number already outstanding) as part of the plan of merger (thus meaning little dilution of its shareholders' interests). *E.g.,* Del. Gen. Corp. Law § 251(f); M.B.C.A. § 11.04(g). *See also* Cal. Corp. Code § 1201(b), (c), (d) (not requiring approval by shareholders of a merging corporation, whether or not the survivor, if they end up owning five-sixths of the voting stock of the company surviving the merger (or its parent), unless their company amends its articles, or else they exchange their stock in the merger for shares with different rights).

A second protection accorded to shareholders opposing a plan of merger is the right to demand the corporation cash them out at a fair price set by appraisal. *E.g.,* Cal. Corp. Code §§ 1300 *et. seq.;* Del. Gen. Corp. Law § 262; N.Y. Bus. Corp. Law §§ 623, 910; M.B.C.A. § 13.01 *et. seq.* (Recall also the *Piemonte* and *Gilbert* cases reprinted earlier in this chapter.) From the standpoint of the objecting shareholders, the problems with the appraisal procedure include the necessity of complying with fairly exacting statutory guidelines for preserving and asserting this right (*see, e.g.,* Cal. Corp. Code §§ 1300(b)(2), 1301, 1302, 1304; Del. Gen. Corp. Law § 262(a), (d), (e); N.Y. Bus. Corp. Law §§ 623(a), (b), (h)(2), 910(a)(1); M.B.C.A. §§ 13.21, 13.23, 13.26), the expense of litigating over the value of the shares (*but see* Cal. Corp. Code § 1305(e); Del. Gen. Corp. Law § 262(j); M.B.C.A. § 13.31 (all empowering the court to allocate the costs of the appraisal proceeding, including, in some cases, attorney's fees)), and the sometimes highly conservative valuation standards employed in these proceedings. *See, e.g., Francis I. duPont & Co. v. Universal City Studios, Inc.,* 312 A.2d 344 (Del.Ch.1973), *aff'd,* 334 A.2d 216 (1975). *But see* N.Y. Bus. Corp. Law § 623(h)(4); M.B.C.A. § 13.01(4); *Weinberger v. UOP, Inc.,* 457 A.2d 701 (Del.1983). From the standpoint of the proponents of the merger, the primary problems with this procedure are the risks of the court setting a value so high as to dilute the interests of the remaining stockholders, and of so many stockholders exercising the right that the surviving corporation will have difficulty funding the repurchases. *Cf.* Cal. Corp. Code § 1306 (dissenting shareholders become creditors if the corporation cannot legally pay them because of limits on payments to shareholders). For this reason, merger agreements sometimes condition completion of the transaction upon no more than a certain number of shareholders perfecting their appraisal rights. State statutes often contain exceptions excluding shares from possessing appraisal rights. For example, many states limit the rights to holders of shares entitled to vote on the merger (or to minority shareholders of the subsidiary in a short-form merger). *E.g.,* Cal. Corp. Code § 1300(a); N.Y. Bus. Corp. Law § 910(a)(1); M.B.C.A. § 13.02(a)(1). Some curtail the rights for shares traded on securities markets. *E.g.,* Cal. Corp. Code § 1300(b)(1); Del. Gen. Corp. Law § 262(b); N.Y. Bus. Corp. Law § 910(a)(1)(A)(iii); M.B.C.A. § 13.02(b)(1). Some preclude appraisal for shareholders of the surviving corporation, regardless of their power to vote, when the merger does not effect a change in their basic rights. *E.g.*, N.Y. Bus. Corp. Law § 910(a)(1)(A)(ii).

Finally, dissident shareholders might initiate a court challenge to the merger. The requirement of shareholder approval sets the stage for disgruntled stockholders to pick apart solicitations in support of the merger looking for misrepresentations upon which to base a claim of fraud. *See, e.g., Mills v. Electric Auto–Lite Co.,* 396 U.S. 375 (1970) (misleading statement in violation of federal proxy rules). (For an illustration in the context of a share repurchase of the type of challenges stockholders might assert when the solicitation refers to the opinions of investment bankers, see the *Kaplan* opinion reprinted in Chapter VI.) In addition or as an alternative to a claim for fraud, shareholders might challenge the merger as a breach of the directors' or controlling stockholders' fiduciary duty. The subject of fiduciary duty in parent-subsidiary and freeze-out mergers will be considered at a later point in this chapter. When dealing with mergers between two companies in an arm-length relationship, the directors' and stockholders' approval enjoys the presumptions of the business judgment rule. *E.g., Cole v. National Cash Credit Ass'n,* 18 Del.Ch. 47, 156 A. 183 (1931) ("The inadequacy [in the value of what the stockholders received in the merger, relative to what they gave up] must be so gross as to lead the court to conclude that it was due not to an honest error in judgment but rather to bad faith, or to a reckless indifference. . . ."). Even the relaxed standard of the business judgment review, however, will not protect directors who approve a merger in an ill-informed manner. *Smith v. Van Gorkom,* 488 A.2d 858 (Del.1985). In any event, the appraisal statutes in some jurisdictions (either explicitly, or by judicial interpretation) may preclude shareholders from challenging the merger based upon breach of fiduciary duty. *E.g., Steinberg v. Amplica, Inc.,* 42 Cal.3d 1198, 233 Cal. Rptr. 249, 729 P.2d 683 (1986).

Given the differences in state laws concerning the rights of shareholders in a merger, what happens when the proposed merger is between companies incorporated in different states? State statutes generally contain separate provisions dealing with mergers between domestic and foreign corporations in an effort to answer such questions (typically providing each corporation follows its own state's procedures governing shareholder rights). *E.g.,* Cal. Corp. Code § 1108; Del. Gen. Corp. Law § 252; N.Y. Bus. Corp. Law § 907; M.B.C.A. § 11.02(b).

2. *Hariton* illustrates a second mode for structuring the acquisition of a business: The target corporation could sell its assets to the purchasing company. Often, the purchaser will assume some or all of the target's liabilities, and the target will dissolve following the sale. (Later, this chapter will address what happens to the unassumed liabilities of the target, and the mechanics of the target's liquidation.) If the parties undertake these two additional steps, the result of a sale of assets transaction largely parallels a statutory merger; yet the mechanics, particularly as they impact upon the rights of the shareholders, can be radically different.

Again, the boards of the two companies must reach an agreement; in this case a contract of sale rather than a plan of merger. This agreement will cover much the same ground as a merger plan—for instance, specifying the price (albeit not necessarily the distribution to the target's stockholders), and any representations, warranties and contingencies. Because a sale of assets transaction often entails the conveyance of a considerable number of individual properties, however, the drafting of this contract and related documentation can be significantly more complex than drafting a merger agreement.

Hariton arose out of the differences with respect to shareholder rights in a sale of assets transaction versus a statutory merger. Several dissimilarities exist with respect to the rights of the stockholders of the selling company. State corporations statutes require a corporation to obtain the approval of its shareholders in order to sell substantially all of its assets outside the ordinary course of business. *E.g.,* Cal. Corp. Code §§ 1001(a), 1200(c), 1201, 1202; Del. Gen. Corp. Law § 271(a); N.Y. Bus. Corp. Law § 909(a)(3); M.B.C.A. § 12.02. (As to what constitutes a sale of substantially all assets, see *Katz v. Bregman,* reprinted in Chapter VI.) Some states, however, differentiate between the precise vote required for a merger, and that required to sell a company's assets. *E.g.,* Cal. Corp. Code §§ 1001(a)(2), 1201(a) (requiring a class vote to approve a merger in certain circumstances in which approval by voting shares (without a class vote) would be sufficient for a sale of assets producing an economically equivalent end result). More significantly, some states do not provide appraisal rights for the target's shareholders in a sale of assets transaction. *See, e.g.,* Del. Gen. Corp. Law § 262(b). (This is what led to the plaintiff's complaint in *Hariton.*) Of course, if the target sells its assets for cash, and soon liquidates, there is little point to an appraisal and cash-out—a fact reflected in many statutes that otherwise provide appraisal rights upon a sale of substantially all assets. *E.g.,* N.Y. Bus. Corp. Law § 910(a)(1)(B). *See also* Cal. Corp. Code §§ 181(c), 1300(a) (no appraisal rights unless the target sells its assets in exchange for the buyer's stock or long-term unsecured debt securities). Failure to provide appraisal rights, however, is a two-edged sword: No longer can the proponents of the transaction argue the appraisal statute preempts any claim for breach of fiduciary duty. Still, in an arms-length transaction with no misrepresentations, the business judgment rule substantially limits judicial review of the sale anyway. *E.g., Cottrell v. Pawcatuck Co.,* 36 Del.Ch. 169, 128 A.2d 225 (1956), *cert. denied,* 355 U.S. 12 (1957).

The more significant distinction between a merger and a sale of assets transaction lies, not in the rights of the selling company's shareholders, but in the rights of the stockholders of the buyer. Under most statutes, they possess neither the right to vote, nor appraisal rights. *See, e.g.,* Del. Gen. Corp. Law § 271(a); N.Y. Bus. Corp. Law §§ 909(a)(3), 910(a)(1)(B); M.B.C.A. §§ 12.02, 13.02(a)(3) (all providing rights only to the seller's stockholders). Several developments have eroded this distinction. To begin with, as noted earlier, many statutes do not require approval of a merger by (or grant appraisal rights to) the shareholders of the surviving corporation, if their rights do not change, and if they do not suffer significant dilution through the issuance of new stock in the transaction. This corresponds to the situation from the buyer's perspective in many, if not most, sale of assets transactions. Often, however, the purchaser's stockholders will suffer significant dilution through the issuance of additional common shares in exchange for the target's properties. Of course, if the corporation has insufficient authorized but unissued shares for the transaction, the board will need to go to the stockholders to approve an amendment of the articles increasing the number of authorized shares. *E.g.,* Cal.Corp.Code § 902(a); Del.Gen.Corp.Law § 242(b); N.Y.Bus.Corp.Law § 803; M.B.C.A. § 10.03(b). More commonly, the rules of the major stock exchanges could require the corporation, if it has shares listed on the exchange, to put a transaction which involves substantial dilution (regardless of how structured) to a shareholder vote. *E.g.,* N.Y.S.E. Listed Company Manual § 312.03(c) (requiring such a vote if the transaction involves issuing common stock equal to 20 percent or more of the common shares already outstanding). The Model Business Corporation Act has borrowed this approach. Section 6.21(f) of the Model Act requires the directors to obtain the approval of the shareholders in order to issue shares for consideration other than cash if the newly issued shares will have a voting power in excess of 20 percent of the voting power of the shares outstanding before the issuance.

More broadly, consider the legal issue in *Hariton.* The plaintiff argued that a sale of assets transaction which creates an outcome equivalent to a merger must adhere to the statutory merger procedures. The Delaware Supreme Court rejected the idea (thereby showing the rewards often available for the creative use of various provisions of the corporations statutes). Courts in some other jurisdictions, however, have accepted this de facto merger doctrine. *E.g., Farris v. Glen Alden Corp.,* 393 Pa. 427, 143 A.2d 25 (1958). (This shows why planners must exercise caution against being too clever in relying upon formalistic distinctions. The balancing of creativity and caution lies at the heart of an attorney's judgment.)

California (joined to a greater or lesser extent by several other states) has taken the equivalence concept underlying the de facto merger doctrine one step further. California's statute creates a set of requirements for stockholder approval, and rights of shareholder appraisal, which apply for all reorganizations. Cal.Corp.Code §§ 1200 *et seq.,* 1300 *et seq.* The California Code, in turn, defines the term reorganization to include statutory mergers (other than short-form mergers), acquisitions of stock in exchange for the acquirer's (or its parent's) stock, and, of relevance here, acquisitions of substantially all of a corporation's assets in exchange for the acquirer's (or its parent's) stock or long-term (over 5–years) unsecured debt securities. Cal.Corp.Code § 181. What this means in a sale of assets in exchange for the purchaser's stock is that both the seller's and the buyer's shareholders possess voting and appraisal rights, unless the exception for shareholders who end up with five-sixths of the buyer's stock (and without change of their rights) applies.

3. A third possible mode for an acquisition is to structure the transaction as a sale and purchase of the target corporation's outstanding stock. Simply, this means the target corporation's stockholders individually sell their shares to the purchasing company. The purchaser can then either run the target as a subsidiary, or liquidate it, thereby achieving the same end result as a merger. (Indeed, this final step could be a parent-subsidiary merger. The subject of dealing with the target following an acquisition of its stock is explored toward the end of this chapter.) Again, however, despite the similarity of outcome between a sale of stock transaction, and a merger, the mechanics are very different.

To begin with, there is a critical difference between a sale of stock transaction, and both a merger and a sale of assets transaction, with respect to the role of the boards of directors. The sale of stock transaction does not require any agreement between the boards of the acquirer and target companies. Rather, the contract is between the purchasing company (normally requiring approval by its board of directors) and the target's individual shareholders. This means the acquisition can go forward even if the target's board does not agree—making the stock acquisition the vehicle of choice for a "hostile take-over." (Of course, parties can use a sale of stock transaction in a "friendly acquisition," and such a transaction can involve agreement between the respective boards of directors—essentially, setting out the terms of the acquirer's offer to the target's shareholders, and the target board's agreement to recommend (or at least not oppose) this offer. Recall the advantages such board agreement can provide when the target has various takeover defenses (such as a poison pill) in place or under many states' takeover statutes. *See, e.g.,* Del.Gen.Corp.Law § 203(a)(1); N.Y.Bus.Corp.Law § 912(b), (c)(1).)

There are also significant differences with respect to shareholder voting and appraisal rights. As with the sale of assets transaction, most statutes accord neither voting nor appraisal rights to the stockholders of the purchasing corporation. Again, the stock exchange rules or M.B.C.A. Section 6.21(f) may require a purchaser to put the transaction to a vote of its shareholders if the acquisition entails issuing a substantial amount of the purchaser's common or voting stock. Moreover, when the acquirer liquidates the target following a sale of stock transaction, a court might deem the whole acquisition to constitute a de facto merger which must follow the state's merger statute. *Applestein v. United Bd. & Carton Corp.,* 60 N.J.Super. 333, 159 A.2d 146 (Ch.1960), *aff'd,* 33 N.J. 72, 161 A.2d 474. *But see Orzeck v. Englehart,* 41 Del.Ch. 361, 195 A.2d 375 (1963). California's statute, as noted above, attempts to create largely equivalent protections in all "reorganizations." In the context of sale of stock transactions, this means requiring a vote of the acquirer's stockholders (and granting them appraisal rights) unless the exception for shareholders who end up owning five-sixths of the purchasing company applies. Cal.Corp.Code §§ 1200(b), 1201(a), (b), 1300.

What about the shareholders of the target? Traditionally, they vote "with their feet;" individually accepting or rejecting the purchaser's offer. (For this reason, even California's statute does not require a formal vote by the target's (as opposed to the acquirer's) stockholders in a sale of stock type of reorganization. Cal.Corp.Code §§ 1200(b), 1201(a).) Some state takeover statutes, however, require the purchase of a controlling percentage of stock to receive approval by a vote of target's shareholders. *E.g.,* Ohio Gen.Corp.Law § 1701.831. *See also* Ind.Bus.Corp.Law § 23–1–42–1, *et seq.* (requiring a vote of disinterested stockholders to give the acquirer the right to vote its shares). Mechanically, arranging for individual shareholder sales can be as burdensome as arranging a shareholder vote on a merger; including the need to comply with Federal requirements for tender offers if the target corporation is a 1934 Securities Exchange Act reporting company. Moreover, shareholders who later decide they received a bad deal (or even those who opposed the transaction from the start) might allege fraud occurred in soliciting the sale of their shares. *See, e.g., Flynn v. Bass Bros. Enterprises, Inc.,* 744 F.2d 978 (3d Cir.1984). They might also complain of breaches of fiduciary duty (as in *Brown v. Halbert,* reprinted earlier in this chapter) if some stockholders receive more for their shares than others.

Shareholders in the target who refuse to go along with the majority present a very different challenge in the sale of stock transaction than in a merger or in a sale of assets transaction. On the positive side (at least vis-a-vis the proponents of the merger), such shareholders traditionally lack appraisal rights. *See, e.g.,* Del.Gen.Corp.Law § 262(b); N.Y.Bus.Corp.Law § 910; M.B.C.A. § 13.02(a). (This is true even in California. *See* Cal.Corp. Code §§ 1200(b), 1201(a), 1300(a).) Indeed, a buyer short on funds, and not wishing to overly dilute its own stockholders' interests, might seek to exploit this fact by undertaking a stock purchase in which it does not acquire all the target's outstanding stock. As mentioned earlier, however, certain types of "poison pill" plans and "fair price amendments" give the target's stockholders, other than the acquirer, the right to cash out. Moreover, several states have enacted takeover statutes which essentially give appraisal rights in a sale of stock transaction. *E.g.,* Pa. Assoc. Code §§ 2542–47. On the other hand, if the buyer does not wish to leave minority interests in the target outstanding, the lack of compulsion in a sale of stock transaction poses a problem. Later, this chapter will deal with techniques to remove an objecting minority. For now, it is useful to note that some statutes create a procedure for a mandatory (rather than a voluntary) sale of shares transaction (typically referred to as a share exchange). *E.g.,* N.Y.Bus.Corp. § 913; M.B.C.A. § 11.03. The trade-off these statutes impose in order to gain the compulsion of the minority is to require adherence to procedures—including approval by both boards of directors, an affirmative vote by the exchanging stockholders, and appraisal rights for the exchanging shareholders—which largely parallel the requirements for a sale of assets transaction. N.Y.Bus.Corp.Law §§ 910(a)(1)(C), 913; M.B.C.A. §§ 11.03, 11.04.

Kirschner Brothers Oil, Inc. v. Natomas Company

185 Cal.App.3d 784, 229 Cal.Rptr. 899 (1986).

■ SCOTT, ASSOCIATE JUSTICE.

Plaintiffs, all holders of Natomas Company (Natomas) preferred stock, filed similar actions against Natomas, one of its directors, and Diamond Shamrock Corporation. Plaintiffs sought to enjoin a proposed merger, as well as damages for breach of fiduciary duty. After a preliminary injunction was denied, the merger or reorganization was effected. According to its terms, each share of Natomas preferred was exchanged for a share of the preferred stock of another corporation, New Diamond. Subsequently summary judgment was entered in favor of defendants. Plaintiffs, now all former Natomas preferred shareholders, have appealed. * * *

I

Natomas is a California corporation. In 1980, 2.5 million Natomas $4 "Series C" cumulative convertible preferred shares were issued. The rights of the preferred shareholders were specified in a certificate of determination issued by the Natomas board of directors.

In May 1983, Diamond Shamrock Corporation, through a wholly owned subsidiary, commenced a hostile tender offer for Natomas common stock and stated its intention to propose a merger between Natomas and the subsidiary. Shortly thereafter, the boards of Diamond Shamrock and Natomas approved a plan and agreement of reorganization between the two companies, and the tender offer was terminated.

According to the plan, a new holding company, New Diamond, was to be formed, which in turn would form two wholly owned subsidiaries, D Sub, Inc., and N Sub, Inc. In two reverse triangular "phantom" mergers, D Sub, Inc., would merge into Diamond Shamrock, and N Sub, Inc., into Natomas; New Diamond would issue New Diamond common shares to common shareholders of Natomas and Diamond Shamrock in exchange for their shares. New Diamond would thus become the sole shareholder of Natomas' common shares.

Before the merger of N Sub, Inc., into Natomas, the latter was to spin off or distribute to its common shareholders the common shares of American President Companies, Ltd. (APC), which held the shares of Natomas' real estate and transportation subsidiaries.

The agreement was to be submitted to Natomas' common and preferred shareholders, voting as separate classes. Upon the approval of each class, the Natomas common shares would be converted into New Diamond common shares and the Natomas preferred into New Diamond preferred, convertible into New Diamond common. Failure to obtain the approval of the Natomas preferred shareholders would not prevent consummation of the merger, however, and it is that feature of the reorganization plan which is at the heart of this litigation. If a majority of Natomas common shareholders approved the agreement but its preferred shareholders did not, the reorganization would still take place. The Natomas common shares would be converted into New Diamond common, but the Natomas preferred would remain outstanding and continue to be convertible into Natomas common.

* * *

II

* * *

a.

We consider plaintiffs' first contention that defendants breached their fiduciary duties by abridging the preferred shareholders' statutory right under section 1201, subdivision (a), to vote on the Natomas merger.

The Corporations Code recognizes several methods of reorganization whereby two or more corporations are combined into a single business enterprise. * * * Section 1201 spells out when a vote by the shareholders of any corporation involved in a reorganization is required. Subdivision (a) of section 1201 provides in pertinent part: "The principal terms of a reorganization shall be approved by the outstanding shares ... of each class of each corporation the approval of whose board is required under Section 1200 ... except that (unless otherwise provided in the articles) *no approval of any class of outstanding preferred shares of the surviving or acquiring corporation or parent party shall be required if the rights, preferences, privileges and restrictions granted to or imposed upon such class of shares remain unchanged....* " (Emphasis added.)

Plaintiffs contend that despite the appearance of the transaction at issue, in reality Natomas was acquired by Diamond Shamrock. Therefore, plaintiffs reason, Natomas was not a "surviving corporation" under either reorganization alternative and the preferred shareholders' approval was required by section 1201, subdivision (a), for either to become effective.

Ignoring for the moment the fact that a majority of the preferred shareholders did approve the reorganization, we consider the argument unpersuasive. The reorganization at issue here was structured as a "reverse triangular 'phantom' merger," well-recognized as a method of reorganization which preserves the existing corporate entity of the target corporation. * * * Notwithstanding the fact that the parent holding company, New Diamond, would wholly own Natomas, it is still undisputed that N Sub, Inc., corporation merged into Natomas, leaving the latter intact as a legal entity. Similarly, D Sub, Inc., merged into Diamond Shamrock, which also remained a legal entity. The Corporations Code defines a "surviving corporation" simply as "a corporation into which one or more other corporations are merged." (§ 190.) * * *

In a related argument, plaintiffs contend the reorganization violated their voting rights under the certificate of determination. In particular, plaintiffs focus on the tenth paragraph of the certificate, which provides in pertinent part: "(E)xcept as otherwise expressly required by law, the Series C Preferred Shares shall have voting rights except as set forth below:

> "(a) So long as any of the Series C Preferred Shares are outstanding, the consent of the holders of at least a majority of the then outstanding Preferred Shares ... shall be necessary to permit, effect or validate any one or more of the following:
>
> "(i) ...
>
> "(ii) ... the consolidation or merger of the Company into any other corporation, ... unless each holder of Preferred Shares immediately preceding such consolidation or merger shall receive the same number of shares, with substantially the same rights and preferences, of the resulting corporations...."

Plaintiffs argue that this provision gave them the right to vote on either reorganization plan, but the provision is inapplicable. It applies on its face to a merger of Natomas into another company. As has been discussed, that did not occur here.

b.

Plaintiffs also contend that even if Natomas was a surviving corporation, their vote was required under section 1201, subdivision (a), because their rights were being changed. * * * As we understand this contention, it is * * * that the second alternative proposal, which would have permitted merger without their vote and left them with Natomas preferred, would have adversely affected their right to a public market for Natomas common and preferred shares. * * *

The trial court rejected the argument that the preferred had a right to a public market for their shares and denied the injunction. Thereafter, as already discussed, a majority of both the common and preferred shareholders voted to approve the plan which gave them New Diamond shares for their shares. On appeal, if this "right to a public market" argument survives even though the preferred shareholders voted to approve the reorganization, it does so because plaintiffs now argue that their affirmative vote was unlawfully coerced. Plaintiffs insist that the preferred had no real choice but to approve the merger. Plaintiffs reason that the reorganization plan made it economically unfeasible for the preferred shareholders to remain as shareholders of Natomas because as a practical matter the conversion value and marketability of their Natomas shares would vanish with the merger. The preferred shareholders were thus forced to approve the reorganization and accept the alternative which granted them preferred shares in New Diamond.

Plaintiffs' rights and privileges argument before the trial court rested on the premise that as preferred shareholders, they had a right to the continued existence of a public market for their shares, but no authority cited then or now supports that proposition.

* * *

c.

Plaintiffs argue for the first time on appeal that their vote on the reorganization plan was also required by section 1201, subdivision (d). In pertinent part, that subdivision mandates approval of a merger by shareholders who will receive shares having "different rights" than those surrendered. Shares in a foreign corporation received in exchange for shares in a domestic corporation have "different rights" within the meaning of that subdivision.

What plaintiffs' argument ignores, of course, is that whether or not subdivision (d) of section 1201 was applicable to the reorganization at issue, the preferred shareholders did approve the plan which gave them foreign (i.e., New Diamond) preferred in exchange for their shares. The alternative plan, under which merger would have taken place without their affirmative vote, did not violate subdivision (d), as under that plan the preferred would have kept their shares of the California corporation.

III

Plaintiffs contend that there is a triable issue of fact as to whether defendants breached their fiduciary duty to the preferred shareholders by structuring the merger to the detriment of those shareholders and by "negotiating for themselves" while failing to protect or enhance the interests of those shareholders.

In support of this contention, plaintiffs focus primarily on Jones v. H.F. Ahmanson & Co., supra, 1 Cal.3d 93.

* * *

In light of the foregoing authority, we conclude that in this case, the fiduciary duty of the directors of Natomas did not include the obligation to negotiate or structure the reorganization such that the preferred shareholders would receive rights and privileges in excess of their entitlement under the certificate of determination.

* * *

IV

When the trial court in this case ruled on the motion for summary judgment, it acknowledged the "fairness doctrine," but concluded that its application did not require defendants to obtain something more for the preferred shareholders than they were entitled to by statute or by the "governing corporate documents." The court concluded that plaintiffs were provided with the voting rights to which they were entitled under section

1201 and the certificate of determination. It also concluded that defendants' fiduciary duty to plaintiffs did not encompass the duty to negotiate for some unspecified financial benefits to which plaintiffs were not entitled by statute or the certificate of determination. We agree. Summary judgment was proper.

Judgment is affirmed.

NOTES

1. The statutory merger or consolidation, the sale of assets transaction, and the sale of stock transaction constitute the three basic modes of structuring a corporate acquisition. *Kirschner Brothers Oil* shows there exist a range of variations on these approaches. To begin with, the case introduces the triangular merger. A triangular merger simply means that the merger takes place between the target and a subsidiary of the acquirer, rather than between the target and the acquiring corporation itself. This subsidiary might be either an existing corporation which is actually conducting some business before the merger, or, as in *Kirschner Brothers Oil,* and as is often the case, a new company set up for purposes of the transaction. (In *Kirschner Brothers Oil,* the acquisition involved a new parent and two new subsidiaries in order to undertake a double triangular merger.) The survivor of the merger can be either the subsidiary, in which case the transaction is referred to as a forward triangular (or subsidiary) merger, or the target, a so-called reverse triangular (or subsidiary) merger. (The target was the survivor in *Kirschner Brothers Oil.* The court referred to this as a "reverse triangular 'phantom' merger" because the merging subsidiary came into existence only for a fleeting moment before merging into the target.)

As with any merger, the shareholders of the merging companies receive in exchange for their shares the type of consideration provided by the plan of merger. For the acquiring parent, the plan will provide it with stock in the corporation surviving the merger, since this is the point of the whole transaction. In a forward triangular merger, the parent can simply keep its shares in the subsidiary; in a reverse triangular merger, the parent exchanges its shares in the subsidiary for shares in the target. In principle, the target's existing shareholders could also receive shares in the surviving company; in other words, keep their shares in the target in a reverse triangular merger, or exchange for stock in the subsidiary in a forward triangular merger. (The merger plan in *Kirschner Brothers Oil* let the target's preferred stockholders retain their stock in the target unless they voted to approve the merger. It was this aspect of the plan which triggered the litigation.) Ordinarily, however, this is unsatisfactory from both the buyer's and seller's standpoints. This chapter will explore in a later section the problems the buyer might face if it acquires less than total ownership of a business it intends to run as a subsidiary. The plaintiff's argument in *Kirschner Brothers Oil* explains why the target's shareholders commonly reject such an exchange: fear of detrimental actions by the parent company will make it more difficult to sell minority shares in a controlled subsidiary without a discount. An alternative is to provide the target's shareholders cash or other property in exchange for their shares. In *Kirschner Brothers Oil,* the target's common shareholders (and its preferred shareholders if they approved the transaction) received stock in the acquiring parent. In fact, stock in the parent represents a common way to compensate the target's existing shareholders in a triangular merger. (While shares in the parent might fit within the ambit of property under those statutes allowing the plan of merger to call for the exchange of shares for cash or other property, many statutes explicitly list shares in another corporation as acceptable for exchange. *E.g.,* Cal. Corp. Code § 1101(d); Del. Gen. Corp. Law § 251(b); M.B.C.A. § 11.02(c)(3).) Technically, to make this exchange, the parent issues its shares to its subsidiary in return for stock in the subsidiary. Then, the surviving firm exchanges, as part of the merger, the stock in the parent for the shares in the target owned by the target's existing stockholders. The surrendered shares in the target are canceled in a forward triangular merger, or can be reissued (or canceled and new shares issued) to the parent in a reverse triangular merger.

Mechanically, undertaking a triangular merger means going through the same procedures as for any merger, since most state statutes do not provide any special provisions for such transactions. *See, e.g.,* Del. Gen. Code § 251; N.Y. Bus. Corp. Law §§ 901–903; M.B.C.A. §§ 11.02, 11.04. Notice, however, a critical distinction as far as obtaining shareholder approval (or granting appraisal rights) on the buyer's side. The merging corporation—whose stockholder must approve the transaction, and whose stockholder possesses appraisal rights—is the subsidiary of the acquiring parent. This means it is the parent (acting through its board of directors) who must vote to approve the merger, and it is the parent which possesses appraisal rights (which, needless to say, it will not exercise). The shareholders of the acquiring parent have neither a vote nor appraisal rights—despite the fact the target's existing shareholders may receive stock in the parent. (Keep in mind, in theory, the parent exchanged its stock in return for stock in its subsidiary, a transaction which does not require shareholder approval unless the parent needed to amend its articles to increase the amount of authorized shares.) Once again, there are exceptions. If the parent has shares listed on a major stock exchange, the exchange rules might require it to put the acquisition to a vote of its stockholders (depending upon how many shares it will issue in the transaction). *E.g.,* N.Y.S.E. Listed Company Manual § 312.00 (referring to direct or indirect acquisitions). Similarly, Section 6.21 of the Model Act will require approval by the parent's shareholders if the parent will issue enough stock to the subsidiary in exchange for stock in the subsidiary so that the newly issued stock in the parent possesses more than 20 percent of the voting power of the already outstanding stock in the parent. The parent's shareholders might argue the transaction constitutes a de facto merger with the parent. *In re Penn Central Securities Litigation,* 367 F.Supp. 1158 (E.D.Pa.1973). *But see Terry v. Penn Central Corp.,* 668 F.2d 188 (3d Cir.1981) (rejecting the argument as a matter of Pennsylvania law). California's statute (joined by a few other states), not surprisingly, grants the parent's shareholders voting and appraisal rights when the parent issues enough shares in the transaction to avoid the five-sixths ownership exception. Cal. Corp. Code §§ 1200(d), 1201(a), (b). (This was irrelevant to the plaintiffs' claim in *Kirschner Brothers Oil,* since the plaintiffs there were shareholders of the target.) To complete the picture, California's statute covers, in the same manner, a sale of assets or a sale of stock transaction in which a subsidiary acquires assets or stock using shares in its parent rather than in itself.

2. Notice, in a reverse triangular merger, the shareholder of the disappearing corporation (that being the acquiring parent) ends up owning most or all of the surviving corporation's stock. (This was the genesis of the plaintiffs' contention in *Kirschner Brothers Oil* that in reality Diamond Shamrock acquired Natomas.) As one might suspect, this idea has uses beyond triangular mergers. There is no reason that the acquiring corporation (in the sense that its shareholders will end up owning most of the combined enterprise) must be the survivor if it merges directly with the target. The target could be the surviving firm, but with its former shareholders holding only a minority interest (or cashed out altogether). This is often referred to as an upside-down merger. The upside-down concept extends to sale of assets and sale of stock transactions as well. The acquirer could sell its assets to the target in exchange for enough stock issued by the target to become the target's majority stockholder. Alternately, the acquirer's stockholders could sell their shares to the target in exchange for enough newly issued stock to obtain a majority interest in the target. One potential use of an upside-down sale of assets or sale of stock transaction is to deprive the target's stockholders of voting and appraisal rights normally accorded to the selling shareholders. Such an upside-down sale of assets or sale of stock transaction, however, if followed by a liquidation, may be more likely to provoke a de facto merger label. *E.g., Farris v. Glen Alden Corp.,* 393 Pa. 427, 143 A.2d 25 (1958).

3. Yet another variation involves forming a new business entity. For example, the parties could create a new corporation to which the two combining corporations sell their assets in exchange for the new company's stock, or to which the stockholders of the two combining corporations sell their shares in exchange for the new firm's stock. Mechanically, this simply entails a dual sale of assets or dual sale of stock transaction. Still, it can provide some differences in the rights of the shareholders involved. For example, under a statute, like California's, which extends appraisal rights to the acquirer's but not the target's shareholders in a sale of stock transaction, the dual transfer of shares to a new corporation seemingly precludes appraisal rights for the stockholders on both sides of the transaction.

A more extreme idea would be to have the two corporations involved enter into a partnership or joint venture. This creates the prospect of combining two businesses without the approval of (or appraisal rights for) either company's shareholders. The only statutory provision which might on its face apply to create such rights would be the sections governing sale of substantially all assets. Assuming these sections would cover an outright contribution by the corporations of their assets to the partnership—a proposition by no means clear—would they apply if the corporations only contributed the use of their assets? (Recall the distinction discussed in Chapter III.) Alternately, the corporations could operate their own properties, but for the benefit of the partnership. Finally, in this context too, disgruntled stockholders might argue the partnership constitutes a de facto merger. *E.g., Pratt v. Ballman-Cummings Furniture Co.,* 254 Ark. 570, 495 S.W.2d 509 (1973) (accepting the argument).

4. Beyond the subject of corporate mechanics, *Kirschner Brothers Oil* raises the question of what obligations directors of the selling corporation have toward owners of different classes of stock. For example, if a merger agreement calls for all classes to surrender their shares, stockholders of one class might challenge the fairness of the division of consideration between the classes. *E.g., Jedwab v. MGM Grand Hotels, Inc.*, 509 A.2d 584 (Del.Ch.1986) (finding the division fair). Alternatively, if, as somewhat the case in *Kirschner Brothers Oil*, directors approve a transaction which leaves some classes out of the exchange, the stockholders left out might challenge their exclusion. The court in *Kirschner Brothers Oil* seemed unsympathetic to this type of challenge. *See also Dalton v. American Investment Co.*, 490 A.2d 574 (Del.Ch.), *aff'd*, 501 A.2d 1238 (Del.1985) (board did not breach its duty in accepting a deal for the common only when the impetus for this structure came from the buyer). Does either *Brown v. Halbert*, reprinted earlier in this Chapter, or *Zahn v. Transamerica Corp.*, reprinted in Chapter VI, suggest a contrary conclusion?

2. Acquirer's Rights and Liabilities

PPG Industries, Inc. v. Guardian Industries Corporation

597 F.2d 1090 (6th Cir.), *cert. denied,* 444 U.S. 930 (1979).

■ Lively, Circuit Judge.

The question in this case is whether the surviving or resultant corporation in a statutory merger acquires patent license rights of the constituent corporations. The plaintiff, PPG Industries, Inc. (PPG), appeals from a judgment of the district court dismissing its patent infringement action on the ground that the defendant, Guardian Industries, Corp. (Guardian), as licensee of the patents in suit, was not an infringer. * * *

I

Prior to 1964 both PPG and Permaglass, Inc., were engaged in fabrication of glass products which required that sheets of glass be shaped for particular uses. Independently of each other the two fabricators developed similar processes which involved "floating glass on a bed of gas, while it was being heated and bent." This process is known in the industry as "gas hearth technology" and "air float technology"; the two terms are interchangeable. After a period of negotiations PPG and Permaglass entered into an agreement on January 1, 1964 whereby each granted rights to the other under "gas hearth system" patents already issued and in the process of prosecution.

* * *

Assignability of the agreement and of the license granted to Permaglass and termination of the license granted to Permaglass were covered in the following language:

> SECTION 9. ASSIGNABILITY
>
> * * *
>
> 9.2 This Agreement and the license granted by PPG to PERMAGLASS hereunder shall be personal to PERMAGLASS and non-assignable except with the consent of PPG first obtained in writing.
>
> SECTION 11. TERMINATION
>
> * * *
>
> 11.2 In the event that a majority of the voting stock of PERMAGLASS shall at any time become owned or controlled directly or indirectly by a manufacturer of automobiles or a manufacturer or fabricator of glass other than the present owners, the license granted to PERMAGLASS under Subsection 4.1 shall terminate forthwith.
>
> * * *

As of December 1969 Permaglass was merged into Guardian pursuant to applicable statutes of Ohio and Delaware. Guardian was engaged primarily in the business of fabricating and distributing windshields for automobiles and trucks. It had decided to construct a facility to manufacture raw glass and the capacity of that facility would be greater than its own requirements. Permaglass had no glass manufacturing capability and it was contemplated that its operations would utilize a large part of the excess output of the proposed Guardian facility.

The "Agreement of Merger" between Permaglass and Guardian did not refer specifically to the 1964 agreement between PPG and Permaglass. However, among Permaglass' representations in the agreement was the following:

> (g) Permaglass is the owner, assignee or licensee of such patents, trademarks, trade names and copyrights as are listed and described in Exhibit "C" attached hereto. None of such patents, trademarks, trade names or copyrights is in litigation and Permaglass has not received any notice of conflict with the asserted rights of third parties relative to the use thereof.

Listed on Exhibit "C" to the merger agreement are the nine patents originally developed by Permaglass and licensed to PPG under the 1964 agreement which are involved in this infringement action.

Shortly after the merger was consummated PPG filed the present action, claiming infringement by Guardian. * * *

One of the defenses pled by Guardian in its answer was that it was a licensee of the patents in suit. It described the merger with Permaglass and claimed it "had succeeded to all rights, powers, ownerships, etc., of Permaglass, and as Permaglass' successor, defendant is legally entitled to operate in place of Permaglass under the January 1, 1964 agreement between Permaglass and plaintiff, free of any claim of infringement of the patents...."

* * *

II

Questions with respect to the assignability of a patent license are controlled by federal law. It has long been held by federal courts that agreements granting patent licenses are personal and not assignable unless expressly made so. * * * The district court recognized this rule in the present case, but concluded that where patent licenses are claimed to pass by operation of law to the resultant or surviving corporation in a statutory merger there has been no assignment or transfer.

There appear to be no reported cases where the precise issue in this case has been decided. At least two treatises contain the statement that rights under a patent license owned by a constituent corporation pass to the consolidated corporation in the case of a consolidation, W. Fletcher, Cyclopedia of the Law of Corporations § 7089 (revised ed. 1973); and to the new or resultant corporation in the case of a merger, A. Deller, Walker on Patents § 409 (2d ed. 1965). However, the cases cited in support of these statements by the commentators do not actually provide such support because their facts take them outside the general rule of non-assignability.

* * *

We conclude that the district court misconceived the intent of the parties to the 1964 agreement. * * * The agreement provides with respect to the license which Permaglass granted to PPG that Permaglass reserved "a non-exclusive, non-transferable, royalty-free, world-wide right and license *for the benefit and use of Permaglass.*" (emphasis added). Similarly, with respect to its own two patents, PPG granted to Permaglass "a non-exclusive, non-transferable, royalty-free right and license...." Further, the agreement provides that both it and the license granted to Permaglass "shall be personal to PERMAGLASS and non-assignable except with the consent of PPG first obtained in writing."

The quoted language from Sections 3, 4 and 9 of the 1964 agreement evinces an intent that only Permaglass was to enjoy the privileges of licensee. If the parties had intended an exception in the event of a merger, it would have been a simple matter to have so provided in the agreement. * * *

The district court also held that the patent licenses in the present case were not transferred because they passed by operation of law from Permaglass to Guardian. This conclusion is based on the theory of continuity which underlies a true merger. However, the theory of continuity relates to the fact that there is no dissolution of the constituent corporations and, even though they cease to exist, their essential corporate attributes are vested by operation of law in the surviving or resultant corporation. * * * It does not mean that there is no transfer of particular assets from a constituent corporation to the surviving or resultant one.

The Ohio merger statute provides that following a merger all property of a constituent corporation shall be "deemed to be *transferred* to and vested in the surviving or new corporation without further act or deed, ..." (emphasis added). Ohio Revised Code, (former) § 1701.81(A)(4). This indicates that the transfer is by operation of law, not that there is no transfer of assets in a merger situation. The Delaware statute, which was also involved in the Permaglass–Guardian merger, provides that the property of the constituent corporations "shall be vested in the corporation surviving or resulting from such merger or consolidation, ..." 8 Del.C. § 259(a). The Third Circuit has construed the "shall be vested" language of the Delaware statute as follows:

> In short, the underlying property of the constituent corporations is *transferred* to the resultant corporation upon the carrying out of the consolidation or merger. . . . Koppers Coal & Transportation Co. v. United States, 107 F.2d 706, 708 (3d Cir.1939) (emphasis added).

* * * A transfer is no less a transfer because it takes place by operation of law rather than by a particular act of the parties. The merger was effected by the parties and the transfer was a result of their act of merging.

* * *

NOTE

Consider the impact of the court's decision in *PPG Industries.* Assuming the patents were critical to Permaglass' operations, the end result was to frustrate the purposes behind the merger. (It is unclear whether PPG was willing to sell Guardian a license; even if so, this meant Guardian would need to pay more for something it thought it already bought.) The moral is that above all else in structuring the acquisition of a business, one must make sure the purchaser obtains everything it thought it was buying.

Achieving this result is easiest in a purchase of stock transaction. Here, if the acquirer does not liquidate the target after buying the outstanding stock, then the acquirer will own a subsidiary corporation which simply retains all its former properties. Several caveats exist, however, with respect to this conclusion. Sometimes, the target possesses contractual rights (particularly franchises) which expire even if there is a change in the target's stock ownership. (In fact, the contract involved in *PPG Industries* provided for such termination.) A more common problem is that the target might not own all the properties which the buyer (and even the target) assume it does. For example, if Permaglass had simply been infringing upon PPG's patents from the start, Guardian would have found itself again without the business it thought it acquired. For this reason, buyers typically undertake careful investigation, as well as demand representations and warranties, concerning the target corporation's ownership of all critical properties. A further problem along this line involves the target's "human capital": Are key personnel going to stay with the company following an ownership change, or will they depart and, worse yet, enter into competition with the firm? To deal with this, the negotiations may involve employment, or at least non-competition, agreements. Non-competition agreements are enforceable so long as they are reasonable. *E.g., Haynes v. Monson,* 301 Minn. 327, 224 N.W.2d 482 (1974). Recall, however, as noted earlier in this chapter, such contracts must not, in reality, constitute a bribe to the target's directors for selling out the shareholders' interests. Moreover, as discussed below, continuing the target's personnel may create successor liability problems under the de facto merger doctrine and with respect to labor contracts.

At the other extreme from a purchase of stock, as far as ease in obtaining all the desired properties, lies a purchase of assets transaction. One advantage of this structure from the standpoint of what the acquirer obtains has been noted before: With a sale of assets, the buyer can purchase just the properties it wants, whereas with a stock transaction or a statutory merger, the parties must use various techniques outlined previously to deal with the undesired items. The reverse side to this flexibility is the increased drafting burden of specifying exactly what the buyer gets and what the seller keeps. For example, without clarity in the sale contract, the buyer and seller can end up in a dispute over whether the company's working capital (cash, receivables and the like) go to the purchaser, or whether this is simply a final period profit to be kept by the seller. Moreover, the transfer of individual assets raises the burdens and costs of the transaction in other ways. The parties must ensure they take the steps necessary to record—for example, under state statutes dealing with real property conveyances—the transfer of title for the specific properties involved. In some states, sales or transfer taxes might apply to the conveyance of individual assets, whereas they generally would not apply to a sale of stock or a statutory merger. *See, e.g.,* Sato, *The Sales Tax and Capital Transactions,* 45 Calif. L. Rev. 450 (1957). Beyond these transaction costs, *PPG Industries* introduces the fact that the target may lack the right to convey all its properties. Many contracts, such as the license agreement in *PPG Industries,* contain provisions restricting their assignment. (Of course, the buyer may negotiate with the other party to the contract about waiving the restriction. This adds to the complexity of the transaction, and, even if successful, would probably require the buyer to pay something for the waiver.)

Between the sale of stock and the sale of assets, as far as ease of obtaining all the target's properties, lies the statutory merger. Following the shareholders' approval of the merger, state corporation statutes normally require the surviving company to file the merger agreement or plan (plus related documentation) with the appropriate state official. *E.g.,* Cal. Corp. Code §§ 1103, 1109; Del. Gen. Corp. Law § 251(c); N.Y. Bus. Corp. Law § 904; M.B.C.A. § 11.06. As the court states in *PPG Industries,* the result is to transfer by operation of law all the disappearing corporation's properties to the surviving company. *See also* Cal. Corp. Code § 1107(a); N.Y. Bus. Corp. Law § 906(b)(1), (2); M.B.C.A. § 11.07(a)(3). The problem illustrated by the holding in *PPG Industries* is that courts might interpret some anti-assignment clauses to preclude even transfer by operation of law in a merger. *But see* M.B.C.A. § 11.07 Official Comment (stating that succession to assets and rights upon a merger is not a transfer and does not come within prohibitions upon assignment unless specifically stated in the agreement). Is there a way to deal with this problem in the context of a statutory merger? Suppose Permaglass rather than Guardian had been the surviving corporation. In fact, avoiding problems with non-assignable franchises, licenses or other contract rights is often the motivation for the so-called upside-down transactions discussed earlier, such as upside-down mergers, reverse triangular mergers, or even upside-down sale of assets transactions. (Incidentally, notice the representation contained in the Guardian–Permaglass merger agreement concerning Permaglass' patent rights. What, if anything, is wrong with this provision? An interesting question is whether Guardian was aware of the PPG–Permaglass cross-licensing agreement, and, if so, whether it received an opinion from attorneys as to the merger's effect on the ability to use the patents.)

Ramirez v. Amsted Industries, Inc.

86 N.J. 332, 431 A.2d 811 (1981).

■ CLIFFORD, J.

This products liability case implicates principles of successor corporation liability. We are called upon to formulate a general rule governing the strict tort liability of a successor corporation for damages caused by defects in products manufactured and distributed by its predecessor. * * *

I

On August 18, 1975 plaintiff Efrain Ramirez was injured while operating an allegedly defective power press on the premises of his employer, * * *. The machine involved, known as a Johnson Model 5, sixty-ton punch press, was manufactured by Johnson Machine and Press Company (Johnson) in 1948 or 1949. As a result of the injuries sustained plaintiffs filed suit against Amsted Industries, Inc. (Amsted) as a successor corporation to Johnson, seeking to recover damages on theories of negligence, breach of warranty and strict liability in tort for defective design and manufacturing. After discovery had been completed, Amsted moved for summary judgment on the ground that the mere purchase of Johnson's assets for cash in 1962 did not carry with it tort liability for damages arising out of defects in products manufactured by Johnson. The trial court granted summary judgment for Amsted, holding that there is no assumption of liability when the successor purchases the predecessor's assets for cash and when the provisions of the purchase agreement between the selling and purchasing corporations indicate an intention to limit the purchaser's assumption of liability. That holding was consistent with the traditional rule governing the liability of successor corporations. See McKee v. Harris–Seybold Co., 109 N.J.Super. 555, 264 A.2d 98 (Law Div.1970), aff'd 118 N.J.Super. 480, 288 A.2d 585 (App.Div.1972).

On their appeal to the Appellate Division plaintiffs argued that a corporation that purchases the assets of a manufacturer and continues the business of the selling corporation in an essentially unchanged manner should not be allowed to use exculpatory contractual language to avoid liability for contingent personal injury claims arising out of defects in the predecessor's product. The Appellate Division agreed and reversed the trial court. * * *

II

* * *

As indicated above, the machine that caused the injury was manufactured in 1948 or 1949 by Johnson Machine and Press Company of Elkhart, Indiana. In 1956 Johnson transferred all of its assets and liabilities to Bontrager Construction Company (Bontrager), another Indiana corporation. Johnson transacted no business as a manufacturing entity following its acquisition by Bontrager, but Bontrager did retain a single share of Johnson common stock in order to continue the Johnson name in corporate form. Bontrager's primary activity then became the manufacture of the Johnson press line.

By purchase agreement dated August 29, 1962, Amsted acquired all of the assets of Bontrager, including all the Johnson assets that Bontrager had acquired in 1956, plus the one share of Johnson stock. The purchase price was $1,200,406 in cash.[2] The assets purchased by Amsted in the 1962 transaction included the manufacturing plant in Elkhart, which had been operated by Johnson prior to its transfer to Bontrager in 1956. Amsted also acquired all of Bontrager's inventory, machinery and equipment, patents and trademarks, pending contracts, books and records, and the exclusive right to adopt and use the trade name "Johnson Machine and Press Corporation." Bontrager further agreed to "use its best efforts to make available" to Amsted the services of all of its present employees except its three principals, who covenanted not to compete with Amsted for a period of five years.

In addition, the August 1962 agreement provided that Amsted would assume responsibility for certain specified debts and liabilities necessary to an uninterrupted continuation of the business. Included, however, was the following reservation:

2. * * * Bontrager distributed the cash proceeds of the transaction to its shareholders and dissolved its inert corporate existence not long thereafter. * * *

> It is understood and agreed that Purchaser shall not assume or be liable for any liability or obligations other than those herein expressly assumed by Purchaser; all other liabilities and obligations of Seller shall be paid, performed and discharged by Seller.

This limitation on the express assumption of liability was further emphasized in another provision of the contract, that Amsted was "not assuming any liability, debt or obligation of (Bontrager) except those expressly required to be assumed * * * under (the) agreement and that (Bontrager) shall continue to be solely responsible for all its other known or unknown liabilities, debts and obligations arising prior or subsequent to the Closing." The purchase agreement likewise addressed the question of repair of defective products:

> Defective Products. All machines sold by Seller on or prior to the Closing Date shall be deemed for the purpose of this Section 8 to be products of Seller, and Seller alone shall be responsible, to the extent of the warranties heretofore given by Seller to its customers, for all liability for the correction and repair of defects in material or workmanship thereof involving costs and expenses in excess of $50 per machine. Purchaser agrees to perform the necessary work to correct and repair the defects involved in such claims for and on behalf of Seller, and Seller agrees to assume and pay for the costs and expenses occasioned by such work to the extent of the warranties heretofore given by Seller to its customers * * *.

Thus it is clear that Amsted expressly declined to assume liability for any claims arising out of defects in products manufactured by its predecessors.

Following the 1962 acquisition Amsted manufactured the Johnson press line through its wholly-owned subsidiary, South Bend Lathe, Inc. (South Bend I), in the original Johnson plant in Elkhart. The Bontrager assets assigned by Amsted to South Bend I included the single outstanding share of Johnson common stock that had been transferred to Bontrager in 1956. The corporate existence of Johnson was dissolved in July 1965 pursuant to the Indiana General Corporation Act, with Amsted being the sole shareholder. Prior to the dissolution Amsted's officers had served as the officers and directors of the corporate shell that was Johnson Press.

In September 1965 South Bend I, the Amsted subsidiary that had been manufacturing the Johnson product line, was dissolved and its assets and liabilities were assumed by Amsted. * * *

III

Amsted urges this Court to judge its potential liability for defective Johnson products on the basis of the traditional analysis of corporate successor liability. Although not heretofore treated by this Court the general principle has been accepted in New Jersey that "where one company sells or otherwise transfers all its assets to another company the latter is not liable for the debts and liabilities of the transferor, including those arising out of the latter's tortious conduct." * * * However, there are four established exceptions to the general rule of corporate successor nonliability in asset acquisitions. Under the traditional approach the purchasing corporation will be held responsible for the debts and liabilities of the selling corporation, including those arising out of defects in the latter's products, where (1) the purchasing corporation expressly or impliedly agreed to assume such debts and liabilities; (2) the transaction amounts to a consolidation or merger of the seller and purchaser; (3) the purchasing corporation is merely a continuation of the selling corporation, or (4) the transaction is entered into fraudulently in order to escape responsibility for such debts and liabilities. * * * In *McKee supra,* which is presently recognized as the seminal New Jersey case on corporate successor liability in the products context, the court added that "(a) fifth exception, sometimes incorporated as an element of one of the above exceptions, is the absence of adequate consideration for the sale or transfer." 109 N.J.Super. at 561, 264 A.2d 98. Courts applying this traditional corporate law approach have examined the nature and consequences of the asset acquisition in order to determine whether successor liability can be imposed upon the purchasing corporation under one or more of the exceptions to the general rule of nonliability.

In recent years, however, the traditional corporate approach has been sharply criticized as being inconsistent with the rapidly developing principles of strict liability in tort and unresponsive to the legitimate interests of the products liability plaintiff. Courts have come to recognize that the traditional rule of nonliability was developed not in response to the interests of parties to products liability actions, but rather to protect the rights of commercial creditors and dissenting shareholders following corporate acquisitions, as well as to determine successor corporation liability for tax assessments and contractual obligations of the predecessor. * * *

Strict interpretation of the traditional corporate law approach leads to a narrow application of the exceptions to nonliability, and places unwarranted emphasis on the form rather than the practical effect of a particular corporate transaction. The principal exceptions to nonliability outlined in McKee, supra, condition successor liability on a determination of whether the transaction can be labeled as a merger or a de facto merger, or whether the purchasing corporation can be described as a mere continuation of the selling corporation. Traditionally, the triggering of the "de facto merger" exception has been held to depend on whether the assets were transferred to the acquiring corporation for shares of stock or for cash—that is, whether the stockholders of the selling corporation become the stockholders of the purchasing corporation. * * * Under a narrow application of the *McKee* exception of de facto merger no liability is imposed where the purchasing corporation paid for the acquired assets principally in cash. * * *

In like manner, narrow application of *McKee's* "continuation" exception causes liability vel non to depend on whether the plaintiff is able to establish that there is continuity in management, shareholders, personnel, physical location, assets and general business operation between selling and purchasing corporations following the asset acquisition. * * * Where the commonality of corporate management or ownership cannot be shown, there is deemed to have been no continuation of the seller's corporate entity. * * *

We * * * refuse to decide this case through a narrow application of *McKee.* The form of the corporate transaction by which Amsted acquired the manufacturing assets of Bontrager should not be controlling as to Amsted's liability for the serious injury suffered by plaintiff some thirteen years after that transaction. * * *

IV

In an effort to make the traditional corporate approach more responsive to the problems associated with the developing law of strict products liability several courts have broadened the *McKee* exceptions of "de facto merger" and "mere continuation" in order to expand corporate successor liability in certain situations.

* * *

Perhaps the most significant decision expanding the "mere continuation" exception to the traditional rule of corporate successor nonliability is Turner v. Bituminous Cas. Co., 397 Mich. 406, 244 N.W.2d 873 (1976). The defendant in *Turner* contended that where manufacturing assets are acquired by a purchasing corporation for cash rather than for stock, there is no continuity of shareholders and therefore no corporate successor liability. Id. 244 N.W.2d at 879. However, the court looked upon the kind of consideration paid for assets as but "one factor to use to determine whether there exists a sufficient nexus between the successor and predecessor corporations to establish successor liability." Id. at 880.

* * *

We agree with plaintiffs that under *Turner,* * * * Amsted may be held to be the mere continuation of Johnson for the purpose of imposing corporate successor liability for injuries caused by defective Johnson products. However, the Appellate Division actually based its decision below and its ultimate test of successor corporation liability not on the *Turner* analysis but rather on the so-called "product line exception" developed by the California Supreme Court in Ray v. Alad Corp., 19 Cal.3d 22, 560 P.2d 3, 136 Cal.Rptr. 574 (1977), * * *. There are fundamental practical and analytical differences between *Turner's* expanded "mere continuation" exception and *Ray's* "product line" approach. * * * Whereas the *Turner* variation on continuation of the enterprise contemplates such factors as the ownership and management of the successor's corporate entity, its personnel, physical location, assets, trade name, and general business operation, the *Ray* test is concerned not with the continuation of the corporate entity as such but rather with the successor's undertaking to manufacture essentially the same line of products as the predecessor.

Because we believe that the focus in cases involving corporate successor liability for injuries caused by defective products should be on the successor's continuation of the actual manufacturing operation and not on commonality of ownership and management between the predecessor's and successor's corporate entities, and because the traditional corporate approach, even as broadened by *Turner* and its progeny, renders inconsistent results, we adopt substantially *Ray's* product line analysis.

V

* * *

The *Ray* court offered a three-fold justification for its imposition of potential liability upon a successor corporation that acquires the assets and continues the manufacturing operation of the predecessor:

> (1) The virtual destruction of the plaintiff's remedies against the original manufacturer caused by the successor's acquisition of the business, (2) the successor's ability to assume the original manufacturer's risk-spreading role, and (3) the fairness of requiring the successor to assume a responsibility for defective products that was a burden necessarily attached to the original manufacturer's good will being enjoyed by the successor in the continued operation of the business. (19 Cal.3d at 31, 560 P.2d at 9, 136 Cal.Rptr. at 580.)

In our view these policy considerations likewise justify the imposition of potential strict tort liability on Amsted under the circumstances here presented. First, the plaintiff's potential remedy against Johnson, the original manufacturer of the allegedly defective press, was destroyed by the purchase of the Johnson assets, trade name and good will, and Johnson's resulting dissolution. It is true that there was an intermediate transaction involved, namely, the acquisition of the Johnson assets by Bontrager in 1956. But the acquisition of these assets by Amsted in 1962 directly brought about the ultimate dissolution of Bontrager's corporate existence. Accordingly, the Bontrager acquisition destroyed whatever remedy plaintiff might have had against Johnson, and the Amsted acquisition destroyed the plaintiff's potential cause of action against Bontrager. What is most important, however, is that there was continuity in the manufacturing of the Johnson product line throughout the history of these asset acquisitions.

Second, the imposition of successor corporation liability upon Amsted is consistent with the public policy of spreading the risk to society at large for the cost of injuries from defective products.

* * *

By the terms of the 1962 purchase agreement with Bontrager, Amsted acquired the Johnson trade name, physical plant, manufacturing equipment, inventory, records of manufacturing designs, patents and customer lists. Amsted also sought the continued employment of the factory personnel that had manufactured the Johnson presses for Bontrager. "With these facilities and sources of information, (Amsted) had virtually the same capacity as (Johnson) to estimate the risks of claims for injuries from defects in previously manufactured (presses) for purposes of obtaining (liability) insurance coverage or planning self-insurance." Id. at 33, 560 P.2d at 10, 136 Cal.Rptr. at 581. * * *

Third, the imposition upon Amsted of responsibility to answer claims of liability for injuries allegedly caused by defective Johnson presses is justified as a burden necessarily attached to its enjoyment of Johnson's trade name, good will and the continuation of an established manufacturing enterprise. * * *

VI

Defendant contends that the imposition of strict products liability on corporations that purchase manufacturing assets for cash will have a chilling—even a crippling—effect on the ability of the small manufacturer to transfer ownership of its business assets for a fair purchase price rather than be forced into liquidation proceedings. Business planners for prospective purchasing corporations will be hesitant to acquire "a potential can of worms that will open with untold contingent products liability claims." In order to divest itself of its business assets, the small manufacturing corporation will be forced to sacrifice such a substantial deduction from a fair purchase price that it would lose the ability to net a sum consistent with the true worth of the business assets.

These contentions raise legitimate concerns. * * * However, in light of the social policy underlying the law of products liability, the true worth of a predecessor corporation must reflect the potential liability that the shareholders have escaped through the sale of their corporation. Thus, a reduction of the sale price by an amount calculated to compensate the successor corporation for the potential liability it has assumed is a more, not less, accurate measure of the true worth of the business.

Furthermore, a corporation planning the acquisition of another corporation's manufacturing assets has certain protective devices available to insulate it from the full costs of accidents arising out of defects in its predecessor's products. In addition to making adjustments to the purchase price, thereby spreading the potential costs of liability between predecessor and successor corporations, it can obtain products liability insurance for contingent liability claims, and it can enter into full or partial indemnification or escrow agreements with the selling corporation. True, the parties may experience difficulties in calculating a purchase price that fairly reflects the measure of risk of potential liabilities for the predecessor's defective products present in the market at the time of the asset acquisition. Likewise do we acknowledge that small manufacturing corporations may not find readily available adequate and affordable insurance coverage for liability arising out of injuries caused by the predecessor's defective products. However, these concerns, genuine as they may be, cannot be permitted to overshadow the basic social policy, now so well-entrenched in our jurisprudence, that favors imposition of the costs of injuries from defective products on the manufacturing enterprise and consuming public rather than on the innocent injured party. In time, the risk-spreading and cost avoidance measures adverted to above should become a normal part of business planning in connection with the corporate acquisition of the assets of a manufacturing enterprise.

* * *

NOTE

As the discussion in *Ramirez* points out, the structure of the acquisition traditionally has dictated the extent to which the acquirer assumes the target's liabilities. At one extreme lies the statutory merger. Here, the surviving company assumes by operation of law all the disappearing company's obligations. Cal. Corp. Code § 1107; Del. Gen. Corp. Law § 259(a); N.Y. Bus. Corp. Law § 906(b)(3); M.B.C.A. § 11.07(a)(4). Why exactly does this pose any problem? Before giving the facile answer that these liabilities represent sums which the acquirer must then pay, keep in mind, unless the target is insolvent (in other words, its liabilities exceed its assets), the buyer can lower the price it pays the seller to fully reflect the assumed debts. This normally should not matter from the seller's standpoint, since the alternative in a sale of assets transaction in which the buyer does not assume the target's liabilities is for the target to pay off its obligations prior to distributing the proceeds to its shareholders—leaving the target's shareholders the same net return in either case. So, for example, if a target has $1 million in assets and $500,000 in liabilities, the parties end up at the same place if, in a merger, the buyer obtains the assets, assumes the liabilities, and pays the target's shareholders $500,000, or if, instead, the buyer pays the target $1 million for its assets, and the target pays off the $500,000 in liabilities and distributes the remaining $500,000 to its shareholders.

This works well, however, only with known debts. The real problem lies in a situation like *Ramirez*. There, a product manufactured 13 or 14 years before the acquisition involving Amsted, caused an injury 13 years after the transaction. The prospect of such claims makes it much more difficult to reach agreement on an adjustment in the price. Not only are there the burdens of gathering sufficient information upon which to estimate risk—more so in fact if the product has only a limited history than in a situation like *Ramirez*—but also, unlike the case with known liabilities, the seller is no longer neutral concerning a decrease in price to cover future claims. The reason is that in an asset sale as occurred *Ramirez,* often neither the target corporation, which dissolved or became an empty shell years before the claim arose, nor its shareholders, would otherwise ever have paid for the claim. *See, e.g., Pacific Scene, Inc. v. Penasquitos, Inc.,* reprinted later in this chapter. Keep in mind as well, the problem of unknown claims arising years later can occur in other areas beyond products liability—for instance, environmental hazards.

Consider the other alternatives the court suggests to protect the acquirer from unknown debts. Escrows or indemnity agreements, as discussed earlier in this chapter, are one means to try to deal with the difficulty of predicting future events. To the extent, however, claims can arise 13 years later (as in *Ramirez*), the practicality of this solution deteriorates. Moreover, this solution may not help if major disaster strikes and the claims exceed the purchase price paid by the acquirer. At most, the buyer escrows the purchase price, and the target's shareholders could be very reticent to agree to indemnity obligations in excess of what they are to receive. (This would increase the target's shareholders' personal risk in excess of both the worth of the transaction and their risk without the sale.) Liability insurance is certainly a good idea, but its utility may decrease as the uncertainties with respect to future claims increase. The problem is that greater uncertainty can mean both higher premiums, and more danger of purchasing inadequate courage.

One other factor is worth noting with respect to the assumption of liabilities in a statutory merger. What are the respective priorities between the creditors of the merging companies? Presumably, the unsecured creditors from each constituent firm have no priority vis-a-vis each other. Recall the danger this can create for the target's creditors when, as discussed earlier in exploring leveraged buy-outs, the acquiring company is a shell set up simply for the transaction and with little assets. On the other hand, secured creditors retain their liens despite the merger. *E.g.*, Cal. Corp. Code § 1107(c); Del. Gen. Corp. Law § 259(a). The problem here is that loan agreements covering corporate borrowing often call for extending the lien to newly acquired property. How will this impact the creditors' relative positions? See, *e.g.*, Cal. Corp. Code § 1107(b) (liens on property of disappearing corporation extend only to the assets the lien covered before the merger); *Inter Mountain Association of Credit Men v. Villager, Inc.*, 527 P.2d 664 (Utah 1974) (refused to extend lien to cover assets of other constituent corporations in a merger). Notice the premium the California statute places on which company survives the merger. To deal with increased risks creditors might face from a merger, loan agreements sometimes contain provisions requiring the lenders' or bondholders' approval of a merger (as well as of other modes of acquisition).

In contrast to the statutory merger, in a sale of assets transaction the acquirer traditionally only bears those liabilities of the selling company which it agrees to assume. Why would the acquirer agree to assume any liabilities? One factor is simply a comparison of the cost of capital. If the buyer assumes the selling company's debts, and lowers the purchase price accordingly, it may avoid the need to raise added funds at a higher cost (in interest and transaction costs) than the interest rate charged by the selling corporation's creditors. In some cases, moreover, the buyer simply might be unable to raise the added funds. (The selling company's creditors could have the right under their loan agreements to prevent the assumption, however. *See, e.g., Sharon Steel Corp. v. Chase Manhattan Bank*, 691 F.2d 1039 (2d Cir.1982).) As discussed later in this chapter, tax considerations can also favor the buyer's assumption of the selling firm's debts when the parties undertake a tax-free sale of assets transaction.

Nevertheless, for the reasons outlined above, the purchaser often will not want to assume unknown debts of the selling corporation. For example, notice in *Ramirez* how Amsted drafted its contract to exclude any implication it agreed to assume unknown debts. Still, as *Ramirez* shows, a sale of assets transaction is not always a guarantee against successful claims from the selling company's creditors. Some creditor protections which may lead to liability of the buyer are straightforward and easily dealt with. For example, failure to give the notice required by the bulk sale acts (Article 6 of the Uniform Commercial Code) could allow the seller's creditors to follow the seller's assets into the hands of the buyer. Needless to say, if the buyer does not wish to take assets subject to liabilities, any mortgages or liens against the seller's property must be paid off. Also, if the buyer pays the target's shareholders, rather than the target corporation itself, there could be liability for aiding in a fraudulent conveyance. *E.g., Luedecke v. Des Moines Cabinet Co.,* 140 Iowa 223, 118 N.W. 456 (1908). A less tractable threat is the de facto merger doctrine mentioned in *Ramirez.* The problem here from a planning standpoint is knowing precisely when a court would find a de facto merger. Some of the factors involved are the degree to which the buyer picks up the seller's organization, management and personnel, how long and with what activities the selling corporation continues after the sale, and, most critically, whether the sale is for cash or stock in the buyer. *See, e.g., Shannon v. Samuel Langston Co.,* 379 F.Supp. 797 (W.D.Mich.1974). Even less avoidable is the products liability based doctrine followed by cases like *Ramirez.* While other courts have refused to follow this approach (*e.g., Stratton v. Garvey Intern., Inc.,* 9 Kan.App.2d 254, 676 P.2d 1290 (1984)), this may not be a situation in which the buyer can count on its state of incorporation (rather than the plaintiff's home state) providing the applicable law. *E.g., Litarowich v. Wiederkehr,* 170 N.J.Super. 144, 405 A.2d 874 (1979). *But see Brown v. Kleen Kut Mfg. Co.,* 238 Kan. 642, 714 P.2d 942 (1986). Moreover, environmental statutes (such as the Comprehensive Environmental Response, Compensation, and Liability Act (CERCLA), 42 U.S.C. §§ 9601–9657) may impose liability upon the purchaser of property containing hazardous waste, even if an earlier owner—for instance, the selling company in a corporate acquisition—disposed of the waste upon the property. *E.g., New York v. Shore Realty Corp.,* 759 F.2d 1032 (2d Cir.1985). *But see* 42 U.S.C. §§ 9601(f)(35), 9607(b) (creating a possible defense for innocent purchasers who prove they conducted all appropriate inquiry into the previous ownership and uses of the property consistent with good commercial and customary practice and did not discover the waste). Suppose, however, the acquiring corporation does not buy the property containing the hazardous waste; can it then avoid liability under CERCLA? See *United States v. Carolina Transformer Co.,* 978 F.2d 832 (4th Cir.1992) (found liability based upon successor corporation theory).

Traditionally, a purchase of stock transaction has represented a middle ground between the statutory merger and the sale of assets transaction as far as the acquirer's succession to the target's liabilities. Unlike the sale of assets transaction, the acquirer cannot pick and choose which liabilities it will assume and thus eschew the assumption of unknown claims. Instead, in buying the target's stock, the purchaser now owns a corporation which remains subject to all its former debts. This means, if unknown claims prove overwhelming, the acquirer could end up with an insolvent subsidiary and thereby lose its entire investment. In contrast to the statutory merger, however, the acquirer itself does not automatically become liable for the target's debts. Hence, at worst—assuming no grounds for disregarding the subsidiary's separate corporate status—the acquirer stands to lose what it paid for the target (and anything else it thereafter may have pumped into the company), but no more.

Decisions like *Ramirez,* and statutes like CERCLA, however, might lead one to rethink this comparison between the three basic modes of structuring an acquisition. No longer can a planner conclude that an asset sale is best at allowing the acquirer to control what debts it will become liable for. In this light, the stock purchase may become the avenue of choice, as it limits the scope of loss to the purchase price. (On the other hand, might a court willing to reach a result like *Ramirez,* also be inclined to disregard the separate corporate status of a subsidiary and find the parent corporation liable? See, *e.g., Powers v. Baker–Perkins, Inc.,* 92 Mich.App. 645, 285 N.W.2d 402 (1979) (held acquirer liable when it ran the target as a subsidiary for 28 years and then dissolved the target). Suppose, however, the parties, for other reasons, do not wish to undertake a sale of stock transaction. Could a triangular merger (or even an asset acquisition by a subsidiary) accomplish the same result?

National Labor Relations Board v. Burns International Security Services

406 U.S. 272 (1972).

■ MR. JUSTICE WHITE delivered the opinion of the Court.

Burns International Security Services, Inc. (Burns), replaced another employer, the Wackenhut Corp. (Wackenhut), which had previously provided plant protection services for the Lockheed Aircraft Service Co. (Lockheed) located at the Ontario International Airport in California. When Burns began providing security service, it employed 42 guards; 27 of them had been employed by Wackenhut. Burns refused, however, to bargain with the United Plant Guard Workers of America (UPG) which had been certified after a National Labor Relations Board (Board) election as the exclusive bargaining representative of Wackenhut's employees less than four months earlier. The issues presented in this case are whether * * * the National Labor Relations Board could order Burns to observe the terms of a collective-bargaining contract signed by the union and Wackenhut that Burns had not voluntarily assumed. * * *

I

The Wackenhut Corp. provided protection services at the Lockheed plant for five years before Burns took over this task. On February 28, 1967, a few months before the changeover of guard employers, a majority of the Wackenhut guards selected the union as their exclusive bargaining representative in a Board election after Wackenhut and the union had agreed that the Lockheed plant was the appropriate bargaining unit. On March 8, the Regional Director certified the union as the exclusive bargaining representative for these employees, and, on April 29, Wackenhut and the union entered into a three-year collective-bargaining contract.

Meanwhile, since Wackenhut's one-year service agreement to provide security protection was due to expire on June 30, Lockheed had called for bids from various companies supplying these services, and both Burns and Wackenhut submitted estimates. * * * Lockheed * * * accepted Burns' bid * * *. Burns chose to retain 27 of the Wackenhut guards, and it brought in 15 of its own guards from other Burns locations.

* * * [T]he UPG demanded that Burns recognize it as the bargaining representative of Burns' employees at Lockheed and that Burns honor the collective-bargaining agreement between it and Wackenhut. When Burns refused, the UPG filed unfair labor practice charges * * *.

The Board, adopting the trial examiner's findings and conclusions, found the Lockheed plant an appropriate unit and held that Burns had violated §§ 8(a)(5) and 8(a)(1) of the National Labor Relations Act, * * * 29 U.S.C. §§ 158(a)(5), 158(a)(1), by failing to recognize and bargain with the UPG and by refusing to honor the collective-bargaining agreement that had been negotiated between Wackenhut and UPG.[2]

* * *

II

We address first Burns' alleged duty to bargain with the union, and in doing so it is well to return to the specific provisions of the Act, which courts and the Board alike are bound to observe. Section 8(a)(5) as amended by the Labor Management Relations Act, 1947, 29 U.S.C. § 158(a)(5), makes it an unfair labor practice for an employer "to refuse to bargain collectively with the representatives of his employees, subject to the provisions of section 159(a) of this title." Section 159(a) provides that "(r)epresentatives designated or selected for the purposes of collective bargaining by the majority of the employees in a unit appropriate for such purposes, shall be the exclusive representatives of all the employees in such unit for the purposes of collective bargaining. . . ." Because the Act itself imposes a duty to bargain with the representative of a majority of the

2. In regard to this latter finding, the Board stated: "The question before us thus narrows to whether the national labor policy embodied in the Act requires the successor-employer to take over and honor a collective-bargaining agreement negotiated on behalf of the employing enterprise by the predecessor. We hold that, absent unusual circumstances, the Act imposes such an obligation.

"We find, therefore, that Burns is bound to that contract as if it were a signatory thereto, and that its failure to maintain the contract in effect is violative of Sections 8(d) and 8(a)(5) of the Act."

employees in an appropriate unit, the initial issue before the Board was whether the charging union was such a bargaining representative.

The trial examiner first found that the unit designated by the regional director was an appropriate unit for bargaining. The unit found appropriate was defined as "(a)ll full-time and regular part-time employees of (Burns) performing plant protection duties as determined in Section 9(b)(3) of the (National Labor Relations) Act at Lockheed, Ontario International Airport; excluding office clerical employees, professional employees, supervisors, and all other employees as defined in the Act." This determination was affirmed by the Board, accepted by the Court of Appeals, and is not at issue here because pretermitted by our limited grant of certiorari.

The trial examiner then found, inter alia, that Burns "had in its employ a majority of Wackenhut's former employees," and that these employees had already expressed their choice of a bargaining representative in an election held a short time before. Burns was therefore held to have a duty to bargain, which arose when it selected as its work force the employees of the previous employer to perform the same tasks at the same place they had worked in the past.

The Board, without revision, accepted the trial examiner's findings and conclusions with respect to the duty to bargain, and we see no basis for setting them aside. In an election held but a few months before, the union had been designated bargaining agent for the employees in the unit and a majority of these employees had been hired by Burns for work in the identical unit. It is undisputed that Burns knew all the relevant facts in this regard and was aware of the certification and of the existence of a collective-bargaining contract. In these circumstances, it was not unreasonable for the Board to conclude that the union certified to represent all employees in the unit still represented a majority of the employees and that Burns could not reasonably have entertained a good-faith doubt about that fact. Burns' obligation to bargain with the union over terms and conditions of employment stemmed from its hiring of Wackenhut's employees and from the recent election and Board certification. It has been consistently held that a mere change of employers or of ownership in the employing industry is not such an "unusual circumstance" as to affect the force of the Board's certification within the normal operative period if a majority of employees after the change of ownership or management were employed by the preceding employer.

* * *

It would be a wholly different case if the Board had determined that because Burns' operational structure and practices differed from those of Wackenhut, the Lockheed bargaining unit was no longer an appropriate one.[4] Likewise, it would be different if Burns had not hired employees

4. The Court of Appeals was unimpressed with the asserted differences between Burns' and Wackenhut's operations: "All of the important factors which the Board has used and the courts have approved are present in the instant case: 'continuation of the

already represented by a union certified as a bargaining agent,[5] * * *. But where the bargaining unit remains unchanged and a majority of the employees hired by the new employer are represented by a recently certified bargaining agent there is little basis for faulting the Board's implementation of the express mandates of § 8(a)(5) and § 9(a) by ordering the employer to bargain with the incumbent union. * * *

III

It does not follow, however, from Burns' duty to bargain that it was bound to observe the substantive terms of the collective-bargaining contract the union had negotiated with Wackenhut and to which Burns had in no way agreed. Section 8(d) of the Act expressly provides that the existence of such bargaining obligation "does not compel either party to agree to a proposal or require the making of a concession."

* * *

These considerations, evident from the explicit language and legislative history of the labor laws, underlay the Board's prior decisions, which until now have consistently held that, although successor employers may be bound to recognize and bargain with the union, they are not bound by the substantive provisions of a collective-bargaining contract negotiated by their predecessors but not agreed to or assumed by them. * * *

The Board, however, has now departed from this view and argues that the same policies that mandate a continuity of bargaining obligation also require that successor employers be bound to the terms of a predecessor's collective-bargaining contract. It asserts that the stability of labor relations will be jeopardized and that employees will face uncertainty and a gap in the bargained-for terms and conditions of employment, as well as the possible loss of advantages gained by prior negotiations, unless the new employer is held to have assumed, as a matter of federal labor law, the obligations under the contract entered into by the former employer. Recognizing that under normal contract principles, a party would not be bound

same types of product lines, departmental organization, employee identity and job functions.' ... Both Burns and Wackenhut are nationwide organizations; both performed the identical services at the same facility; although Burns used its own supervisors, their functions and responsibilities were similar to those performed by their predecessors; and finally, and perhaps most significantly, Burns commenced performance of the contract with 27 former Wackenhut employees out of its total complement of 42." 441 F.2d 911, 915 (1971) (citation omitted). Although the labor policies of the two companies differed somewhat, the Board's determination that the bargaining unit remained appropriate after the changeover meant that Burns would face essentially the same labor relations environment as Wackenhut: it would confront the same union representing most of the same employees in the same unit.

5. The Board has never held that the National Labor Relations Act itself requires that an employer who submits the winning bid for a service contract or who purchases the assets of a business be obligated to hire all of the employees of the predecessor though it is possible that such an obligation might be assumed by the employer. * * * However, an employer who declines to hire employees solely because they are members of a union commits a § 8(a)(3) unfair labor practice. * * *

to a contract in the absence of consent, the Board notes that in John Wiley & Sons, Inc. v. Livingston, 376 U.S. 543, 550 (1964), the Court declared that "a collective bargaining agreement is not an ordinary contract" but is, rather, an outline of the common law of a particular plant or industry. The Court held in *Wiley* that although the predecessor employer which had signed a collective-bargaining contract with the union had disappeared by merger with the successor, the union could compel the successor to arbitrate the extent to which the successor was obligated under the collective-bargaining agreement. The Board contends that the same factors that the Court emphasized in *Wiley,* the peaceful settlement of industrial conflicts and "protection (of) the employees (against) a sudden change in the employment relationship," id., at 549, require that Burns be treated under the collective-bargaining contract exactly as Wackenhut would have been if it had continued protecting the Lockheed plant.

We do not find *Wiley* controlling in the circumstances here. *Wiley* arose in the context of a § 301 suit to compel arbitration, not in the context of an unfair labor practice proceeding where the Board is expressly limited by the provisions of § 8(d). That decision emphasized "(t)he preference of national labor policy for arbitration as a substitute for tests of strength before contending forces" and held only that the agreement to arbitrate, "construed in the context of a national labor policy," survived the merger and left to the arbitrator, subject to judicial review, the ultimate question of the extent to which, if any, the surviving company was bound by other provisions of the contract. Id., at 549, 551.

Wiley's limited accommodation between the legislative endorsement of freedom of contract and the judicial preference for peaceful arbitral settlement of labor disputes does not warrant the Board's holding that the employer commits an unfair labor practice unless he honors the substantive terms of the pre-existing contract. The present case does not involve a § 301 suit; nor does it involve the duty to arbitrate. Rather, the claim is that Burns must be held bound by the contract executed by Wackenhut, whether Burns has agreed to it or not and even though Burns made it perfectly clear that it had no intention of assuming that contract. *Wiley* suggests no such open-ended obligation. Its narrower holding dealt with a merger occurring against a background of state law that embodied the general rule that in merger situations the surviving corporation is liable for the obligations of the disappearing corporation. * * * Here there was no merger or sale of assets, and there were no dealings whatsoever between Wackenhut and Burns. On the contrary, they were competitors for the same work, each bidding for the service contract at Lockheed. Burns purchased nothing from Wackenhut and became liable for none of its financial obligations. Burns merely hired enough of Wackenhut's employees to require it to bargain with the union as commanded by § 8(a)(5) and § 9(a). But this consideration is a wholly insufficient basis for implying either in fact or in law that Burns had agreed or must be held to have agreed to honor Wackenhut's collective-bargaining contract.

We agree with the Court of Appeals that the Board failed to heed the admonitions of the *H. K. Porter* case. Preventing industrial strife is an important aim of federal labor legislation, but Congress has not chosen to make the bargaining freedom of employers and unions totally subordinate to this goal. * * * Here, Burns had notice of the existence of the Wackenhut collective-bargaining contract, but it did not consent to be bound by it. The source of its duty to bargain with the union is not the collective-bargaining contract but the fact that it voluntarily took over a bargaining unit that was largely intact and that had been certified within the past year. Nothing in its actions, however, indicated that Burns was assuming the obligations of the contract, and "allowing the Board to compel agreement when the parties themselves are unable to agree would violate the fundamental premise on which the Act is based—private bargaining under governmental supervision of the procedure alone, without any official compulsion over the actual terms of the contract." H. K. Porter Co. v. NLRB, 397 U.S., at 108.

We also agree with the Court of Appeals that holding either the union or the new employer bound to the substantive terms of an old collective-bargaining contract may result in serious inequities. A potential employer may be willing to take over a moribund business only if he can make changes in corporate structure, composition of the labor force, work location, task assignment, and nature of supervision. Saddling such an employer with the terms and conditions of employment contained in the old collective-bargaining contract may make these changes impossible and may discourage and inhibit the transfer of capital. On the other hand, a union may have made concessions to a small or failing employer that it would be unwilling to make to a large or economically successful firm. The congressional policy manifest in the Act is to enable the parties to negotiate for any protection either deems appropriate, but to allow the balance of bargaining advantage to be set by economic power realities. Strife is bound to occur if the concessions that must be honored do not correspond to the relative economic strength of the parties.

The Board's position would also raise new problems, for the successor employer would be circumscribed in exactly the same way as the predecessor under the collective-bargaining contract. It would seemingly follow that employees of the predecessor would be deemed employees of the successor, dischargeable only in accordance with provisions of the contract and subject to the grievance and arbitration provisions thereof. Burns would not have been free to replace Wackenhut's guards with its own except as the contract permitted. Given the continuity of employment relationship, the pre-existing contract's provisions with respect to wages, seniority rights, vacation privileges, pension and retirement fund benefits, job security provisions, work assignments and the like would devolve on the successor. Nor would the union commit a § 8(b)(3) unfair labor practice if it refused to bargain for a modification of the agreement effective prior to the expiration date of the agreement. A successor employer might also be deemed to have inherited its predecessor's pre-existing contractual obligations to the union that had accrued under past contracts and that had not been discharged when the business was transferred. * * *

In many cases, of course, successor employers will find it advantageous not only to recognize and bargain with the union but also to observe the pre-existing contract rather than to face uncertainty and turmoil. Also, in a variety of circumstances involving a merger, stock acquisition, reorganization, or assets purchase, the Board might properly find as a matter of fact that the successor had assumed the obligations under the old contract. Cf. Oilfield Maintenance Co., 142 N.L.R.B. 1384 (1963). Such a duty does not, however, ensue as a matter of law from the mere fact than an employer is doing the same work in the same place with the same employees as his predecessor, as the Board had recognized until its decision in the instant case. * * * We accordingly set aside the Board's finding of a § 8(a)(5) unfair labor practice insofar as it rested on a conclusion that Burns was required to but did not honor the collective-bargaining contract executed by Wackenhut.

IV

* * * [T]he Board's opinion also stated that "(t)he obligation to bargain imposed on a successor-employer includes the negative injunction to refrain from unilaterally changing wages and other benefits established by a prior collective-bargaining agreement even though that agreement had expired. In this respect, the successor-employer's obligations are the same as those imposed upon employers generally during the period between collective-bargaining agreements." * * * This statement by the Board is consistent with its prior and subsequent cases that hold that whether or not a successor employer is bound by its predecessor's contract, it must not institute terms and conditions of employment different from those provided in its predecessor's contract, at least without first bargaining with the employee's representative. * * * Thus, if Burns, without bargaining to impasse with the union, had paid its employees on and after July 1 at a rate lower than Wackenhut had paid under its contract, or otherwise provided terms and conditions of employment different from those provided in the Wackenhut collective-bargaining agreement, under the Board's view, Burns would have committed a § 8(a)(5) unfair labor practice. * * *

Although Burns had an obligation to bargain with the union concerning wages and other conditions of employment when the union requested it to do so, this case is not like a § 8(a)(5) violation where an employer unilaterally changes a condition of employment without consulting a bargaining representative. It is difficult to understand how Burns could be said to have changed unilaterally any pre-existing term or condition of employment without bargaining when it had no previous relationship whatsoever to the bargaining unit and, prior to July 1, no outstanding terms and conditions of employment from which a change could be inferred. The terms on which Burns hired employees for service after July 1 may have differed from the terms extended by Wackenhut and required by the collective-bargaining contract, but it does not follow that Burns changed its terms and conditions of employment when it specified the initial basis on which employees were hired on July 1.

Although a successor employer is ordinarily free to set initial terms on which it will hire the employees of a predecessor, there will be instances in which it is perfectly clear that the new employer plans to retain all of the employees in the unit and in which it will be appropriate to have him initially consult with the employees' bargaining representative before he fixes terms. In other situations, however, it may not be clear until the successor employer has hired his full complement of employees that he has a duty to bargain with a union, since it will not be evident until then that the bargaining representative represents a majority of the employees in the unit as required by § 9(a) of the Act, 29 U.S.C. § 159(a). Here, for example, Burns' obligation to bargain with the union did not mature until it had selected its force of guards late in June. It is true that the wages it paid when it began protecting the Lockheed plant on July 1 differed from those specified in the Wackenhut collective-bargaining agreement, but there is no evidence that Burns ever unilaterally changed the terms and conditions of employment it had offered to potential employees in June after its obligation to bargain with the union became apparent. If the union had made a request to bargain after Burns had completed it hiring and if Burns had negotiated in good faith and had made offers to the union which the union rejected, Burns could have unilaterally initiated such proposals as the opening terms and conditions of employment on July 1 without committing an unfair labor practice. * * * The Board's order requiring Burns to make whole its employees for any losses suffered by reason of Burns' refusal to honor and enforce the contract, cannot therefore be sustained on the ground that Burns unilaterally changed existing terms and conditions of employment, thereby committing an unfair labor practice which required monetary restitution in these circumstances. Affirmed.

NOTES

1. The court's discussion in *Burns* recognizes that often a buyer is only willing to acquire a moribund business if the buyer can make changes which lower the target's labor costs. Moreover, the purchaser might contemplate such changes even if acquiring a generally successful business. Achieving this objective, in turn, may depend upon the extent to which the purchaser succeeds to the target's obligations with respect to unionized employees. *Burns* holds that such succession depends upon the obligation involved: specifically, the duty to recognize and bargain with a particular union on the one hand, or adherence to the terms of the preexisting contract between the union and the target on the other. Yet a different analysis may exist with respect to assuming the target's obligations to remedy unfair or discriminatory labor practices. *See, e.g., Golden State Bottling Co. v. N.L.R.B.*, 414 U.S. 168 (1973). With respect to recognizing union representation, courts liberally impose on the acquiring firm the duty to bargain with the union representing the target's employees. After all, the underlying question essentially is whether it is worthwhile to hold a

new election to see if the employees desire representation by this union. The assumption is, if the acquirer hires the target's employees under circumstances in which their working conditions do not substantially change, the election result would be the same. *E.g., N.L.R.B. v. Fall River Dyeing & Finishing Corp.,* 775 F.2d 425 (1st Cir.1985), *aff'd,* 482 U.S. 27 (1987). (Of course, if the target's employees become only a minority of the new work force, this assumption would not apply. *See, e.g., N.L.R.B. v. Band–Age, Inc.,* 534 F.2d 1 (1st Cir.), *cert. denied,* 429 U.S. 921 (1976).) In *Burns,* the willingness to impose the duty to bargain went so far as to cover a situation in which the new employer had not even purchased the former employer's business. Moreover, from a planning standpoint, the buyer's freedom of action to avoid a duty to bargain is rather constrained. As the court notes, refusing to hire individuals because they belong to a union is an unfair labor practice.

Burns holds that the standard is different with respect to abiding by the contract the target entered with the union. After all, here the question is not simply what the employees want, it is whether to bind an employer to an agreement it did not make. To some extent, this analysis involves the same considerations discussed above when dealing with successor liabilities for the target's debts generally. For instance, in an acquisition carried out through a purchase of stock, the shift in the ownership of the target should be irrelevant to the target's obligations under its labor contracts, just as such a change in ownership is irrelevant to the target's obligations under its contracts generally. *See, e.g., United Paperworkers International Union v. Penntech Papers, Inc.,* 439 F.Supp. 610 (D.Me.1977), *aff'd,* 583 F.2d 33 (1st Cir.1978). Similarly, one might assume an acquisition by merger would leave the labor agreement intact, since, under state law, the surviving corporation in a merger assumes all the rights and liabilities of the merging companies. Indeed, *Burns* distinguished the *Wiley* decision, in which the Supreme Court held the successor bound by the target's agreement with the union to arbitrate, partially on the ground *Wiley* involved a merger. (Curiously, however, the *Wiley* decision disclaimed reliance upon state merger law (*see also Golden State Bottling Co. v. N.L.R.B.,* 414 U.S. 168, 182–83 n. 5 (1973)); albeit it is hard to imagine a court not binding the survivor of a merger to the labor contract, as this would mean treating labor contracts worse than contracts generally.) Not surprisingly, the real question is what to do in a sale of assets situation. In *Howard Johnson Co. v. Detroit Local Joint Executive Board,* 417 U.S. 249 (1974), the Supreme Court, in a sale of assets transaction, refused to bind the purchaser to the target's agreement with the union to arbitrate. (This undermines the portion of the *Burns* opinion which, in distinguishing *Wiley,* suggested arbitration agreements might readily bind all successors.) The court emphasized several factors: (i) the lack of any express or implied assumption of the agreement to arbitrate by the purchaser; (ii) the continued existence of the selling company as a viable entity against which the union might seek relief; and, perhaps most importantly, (iii) the fact that the buyer had not hired most of the selling company's work force (indeed, its refusal to do so was the issue the union sought to arbitrate). Note the not unexpected similarities between these factors, and the factors courts sometimes employ in dealing with successor liabilities for debts of the target generally. In this context, however, instead of focusing on the type of consideration paid (stock versus cash) as with the de facto merger doctrine, or on the transfer of goodwill and the continuation of a product line (as with some of the product liability cases), the focus is much more on the continuity in the work force. With respect to this factor, the question is what percentage of the *target's* employees did the buyer continue to employ. This is different than the question for the duty to bargain; when the issue is what percentage of the *buyer's* work force in the applicable unit were former employees of the target, and hence likely to vote for the union. *E.g., Boeing Co. v. International Ass'n of Machinists,* 504 F.2d 307 (5th Cir.1974), *cert. denied,* 421 U.S. 913 (1975).

Finally, suppose the target's contract with the union contains a clause attempting to bind successors. In itself, such a clause will not bind the buyer who makes clear its refusal to assume the contract. *Howard Johnson Co. v. Detroit Local Joint Executive Board,* 417 U.S. 249 (1974). Nevertheless, should the target attempt to sell its business to a buyer who refuses to accept the contract, the union might be able to enjoin the sale for violating the successor term. *Local Lodge No. 1266, IAM v. Panoramic Corp.,* 668 F.2d 276 (7th Cir.1981).

2. One other potential labor cost associated with acquiring a corporation exists if the target firm has adopted a plan—often referred to as a "golden parachute"—to provide severance benefits to senior employees (or to all employees in a "tin parachute") who leave their positions following a change in control. Applying the principles from Chapter IV's discussion of corporate compensation generally, one would expect courts to uphold such plans if they are a reasonable effort to attract and retain personnel and to strike them down if they are not. *See, e.g., International Ins. Co. v. Johns,* 874 F.2d 1447 (11th Cir.1989). Some jurisdictions also have provided such severance rights by statute. *E.g.* Penn. Assoc. Code §§ 2581–83. *But see Simas v. Quaker Fabric Corp.,* 6 F.3d 849 (1st Cir.1993) (holding ERISA preempts a Massachusetts statute providing such severance benefits). Unfortunately for the acquirer, Section 280G of the Internal Revenue Code generally denies the corporation a deduction for golden parachute payments.

Pension Benefit Guaranty Corporation v. Ouimet Corporation

630 F.2d 4 (1st Cir.1980), *cert. denied,* 450 U.S. 914 (1981).

■ BROWNES, CIRCUIT JUDGE.

* * *

The case began with the bankruptcy of a corporation, Avon, and its wholly owned subsidiary, Tenn–ERO, which were part of a larger group of corporations, the Ouimet Group. A brief prefatory explanation of ERISA, and the role in it of the Pension Benefit Guaranty Corporation (PBGC), is necessary to appreciate the issues. Under ERISA, PBGC assumes the administration and payment of benefits of a terminated pension plan whose assets are insufficient to cover all guaranteed benefits. PBGC may recover from the employer 30% of its net worth determined as of a date within one hundred twenty days of the plan termination, or the deficit, whichever is less. The bankrupts, here, had no positive net worth as of the valuation date. This means that, if the term "employer" is limited to the bankrupts, PBGC recovers nothing and a dividend will be paid to the creditors. If, on the other hand, "employer" is construed to mean the Ouimet Group of corporations, including the bankrupts, it is probable that PBGC will receive all of the bankrupts' assets with the creditors receiving nothing.

The Ouimet Group of Corporations

Over forty years ago, Emil R. Ouimet purchased the Brockton, Massachusetts shoe-trim manufacturing concern for which he had worked for several years. * * * He renamed it Ouimet Stay & Leather Company (Stay) when production expanded to include shoe upper strippings as well as other types of shoe findings. In 1950, he founded Ouimet Corporation (Ouimet) * * *. Ouimet manufactures shoe findings, laminations, and vinyl-coated fabrics. * * * In 1968, [Emil] Ouimet purchased the Avon Sole Company (Avon), a shoe sole manufacturing factory located in Holbrook, Massachusetts. In 1972, Avon formed a wholly-owned subsidiary, Tenn–ERO, to operate a nonunion-plant in Lawrenceburg, Tennessee.

* * *

Emil Ouimet * * * owns 80% of Ouimet; and 80% of Stay. He owned all stock in Avon which, in turn, held 100% of Tenn–ERO's stock. * * *

The Plan

Pursuant to a collective bargaining agreement with the Rubber Workers Union and the International Brotherhood of Fireman and Oilers, Avon instituted a pension plan for its hourly workers in 1959. The plan * * * gave the company the right to "amend, modify, suspend or terminate the Plan" and limited the benefits payable upon termination of the plan to "the assets then remaining in the Trust Fund." Avon made all actuarially mandated contributions, but at all times the plan was underfunded. There were three reasons for this. (1) Initial underfunding occurred because credit was given for past years of service while no immediate contribution to the plan for this credit was required. Rather, the deficit was expected to be amortized over thirty years. (2) Ouimet negotiated several benefit increases which were not met by current contributions. (3) A decrease in the value of certain fund investments in 1974 and 1975 led to a devaluation of the plan assets. When Ouimet purchased Avon, the underfunding amounted to $92,000. By March 25, 1975, the day Avon closed its doors, it was $552,339.64.

Prior Proceedings

On June 18, 1975, Avon and Tenn–ERO filed Chapter XI bankruptcy petitions; on March 22, 1976, they were adjudicated bankrupts. When the plant shut-down appeared imminent, Avon notified PBGC of its intent to terminate the pension plan. * * * On March 31, 1976, PBGC filed suit against the Ouimet Group in the United States District Court for the District of Massachusetts.

* * *

[The district court] ruled that ERISA imposes joint and several liability on all members of a controlled group of corporations. After a careful analysis of the statutory and constitutional issues, it granted PBGC's motions for partial summary judgment and for relief from the automatic stay in bankruptcy and remanded the case to the bankruptcy court for a determination of the net worth of the Ouimet Group of corporations.

* * *

Who Is the Employer?

We start with the definition section of subchapter III—Plan Termination Insurance. 29 U.S.C. § 1301(b) provides in part:

> For purposes of this subchapter, under regulations prescribed by the [Pension Benefit Guaranty] corporation, *all employees of trades or businesses (whether or not incorporated) which are under common control shall be treated as employed by a single employer and all such trades and businesses as a single employer.* The regulations prescribed under the preceding sentence shall be consistent and co-extensive with regulations prescribed for similar purposes by the Secretary of the Treasury under section 414(c) of Title 26 (emphasis added).[13]

Section 1301(b) applies, by its terms, only to groups "under common control" as that term is defined in regulations coextensive with the regulations under 26 U.S.C. § 414(c).[14] Those regulations define a group "under

13. 26 U.S.C. § 414(c) states in pertinent part, "all employees of trades or businesses (whether or not incorporated) which are under common control shall be treated as employed by a single employer."

14. Temporary Treasury Regulations promulgated under 26 U.S.C. § 414(c) provide in part:

§ 11.414(c)–2 Two or more trades or businesses under common control * * *.

(a) In general. For purposes of this section, the term "two or more trades or businesses under common control" means any group of trades or businesses which is either a "parent-subsidiary group of trades or businesses" under common control: as defined in paragraph (b) of this section, a "brother-sister group of trades or businesses under common control" as defined in paragraph (c) of this section, or a "combined group of trades or businesses under common control" as defined in paragraph (d) of this section. * * *

(b) Parent-subsidiary group of trades or businesses under common control—(1) General. The term "parent-subsidiary group of trades or businesses under common control" means one or more chains of organizations conducting trades or businesses connected through ownership of a controlling interest with a common parent organization if—

(i) A controlling interest in each of the organizations, except the common parent or-

common control" as a parent-subsidiary group, brother-sister group, or combined group. The regulations go on to define these terms according to the degree and nature of common stock ownership. The Ouimet Group * * * clearly meets the test of stock ownership in the regulations. The group is, therefore, under common control for purposes of section 1301(b).

The apparent meaning of section 1301(b) is that a group under common control is to be treated as a single employer for purposes of subchapter III, which is entitled Plan Termination Insurance. It appears, then, that the term "employer," as used in section 1362(b), which is part of subchapter III, refers, in the case of a group under common control, to all the "trades or businesses" which are members of the group. Under this reading of the statute, all members of the Ouimet Group would be jointly and severally liable to PBGC.

Ouimet argues, however, that section 1301(b) does not mean what it appears to mean. Rather, in Ouimet's view, this language was intended only to prevent employers from avoiding application of ERISA by shifting employees around among various corporate entities. Ouimet maintains that, in the absence of section 1301(b), an employer could avoid application of ERISA by dividing into several corporations, each with less than twenty-five employees. * * *

Ouimet is correct in asserting that Congress intended to prevent such evasion of ERISA. * * * If Congress had intended to limit the application of section 1301(b) to certain purposes * * * it could have done so by referring specifically to the affected sections. Instead, * * * Congress meant, by that phrase, the whole subchapter, including section 1362(b).

* * *

ganization, is owned * * * by one or more of the other organizations; and

(ii) The common parent organization owns * * * a controlling interest in at least one of the other organizations, excluding, in computing such controlling interest, any direct ownership interest by such other organizations.

(2) Controlling interest defined—(i) Controlling interest. For purposes of paragraphs (b) and (c) of this section, the phrase "controlling interest" means:

(A) In the case of an organization which is a corporation, ownership of stock possessing at least 80 percent of the total combined voting power of all classes of stock entitled to vote of such corporation or at least 80 percent of the total value of shares of all classes of stock of such corporation;

* * *

(c) Brother-sister group of trades or businesses under common control—(1) General. The term "brother-sister group of trades or businesses under common control" means two or more organizations conducting trades or business if (i) the same five or fewer persons who are individuals, estates, or trusts own * * *, singly or in combination, a controlling interest of each organization, and (ii) taking into account the ownership of each such person only to the extent such ownership is identical with respect to each such organization, such persons are in effective control of each organization.

(2) Effective control defined. For purposes of this paragraph, persons are in "effective control" of an organization if—

(i) In the case of an organization which is a corporation, such persons own stock possessing more than 50 percent of the total combining voting power of all classes of stock entitled to vote of such corporation or more than 50 percent of the total value of shares of all classes of stock of such corporation;

* * *

We do not think it necessary to track in detail each of Ouimet's other arguments against application of the plain meaning of section 1301(b), since we consider them adequately addressed in the district court's opinion. We hold that the Ouimet Group, as a group under common control, is one employer for purposes of liability under section 1362.

We are not persuaded that, because only one of a group of corporations under common control contributes to a plan, it is unjust to make the group responsible for the plan's deficit. The facts of this case illustrate why such a group should be treated as an integrated whole. Ouimet purchased Avon with full knowledge of the plan and its funding requirements. Ouimet participated in the labor negotiations resulting in greater pension benefits that contributed to the deficit. The Ouimet Group filed a consolidated tax return on which the Avon contributions were deducted. We see nothing unfair in treating the Ouimet Group as a single employer.

* * *

NOTES

1. The acquired firm's obligations with respect to employee pension plans is another area of liability the parties might wish to consider in structuring the acquisition. The law in this area is governed by a complex Federal statute, ERISA. This area is technical enough to probably call for bringing in a specialist. For present purposes, however, *Ouimet* shows how different rules govern liabilities of an acquired company under ERISA, thereby demonstrating the broader point that the lawyer structuring an acquisition must be cognizant of the different types of liabilities that may be involved. *Ouimet* involved a single employer's defined benefit pension plan. Such a plan promises the employees a certain sum upon retirement, in contrast to a defined contribution plan, which only promises a certain contribution by the employer toward retirement benefits. The hazard illustrated by *Ouimet* for a defined benefit plan—which cannot occur by definition for a defined contribution plan—is that the contributions (for the reasons typified by facts in *Ouimet*) may be insufficient to fund the promised benefits. In this event, the employer, upon terminating the plan, faces liability (the cap on which has changed since *Ouimet*) to the Pension Benefit Guarantee Corporation for the shortfall. (Notice incidentally, that ERISA overrides efforts, such as contained in the pension plan in *Ouimet*, to disclaim liability for any benefits in excess of the funds in the trust. *Nachman Corp. v. PBGC,* 446 U.S. 359 (1980).)

The holding in *Ouimet* illustrates a significant difference between pension obligations and other liabilities involved in an acquisition. As discussed above, the normal rule with an acquisition structured as a purchase of stock is that the liability remains solely with the acquired company. By contrast, under ERISA, not only does the acquired company in a purchase of stock transaction retain its obligation with respect to its pension plan, but the acquiring company picks up the liability as well, since ERISA places the obligation on the entire controlled group. *But see PBGC v. Anthony Co.,* 537 F.Supp. 1048 (N.D.Ill.1982) (suggesting that imposing a liability on the parent, which exceeded the benefit the parent received from its subsidiary, might be unconstitutional). On the other hand, there does not appear to be any doctrine under ERISA that would impose liabilities for an underfunded plan upon the buyer in a sale of assets transaction, unless the buyer agreed to assume the obligation. *See, e.g.,* PBGC Opinion Letter 76–111 (Sept. 16, 1976).

2. Additional concerns exist when dealing with pension plans qualified for the favorable tax treatment outlined in Chapter IV. For example, to obtain these advantages, the plan must meet certain tests designed to ensure it does not discriminate in favor of employees who are shareholders, officers, or highly compensated. I.R.C. § 410(b). Acquisition of a business—whether or not the buyer continues the target's pension plan—can alter either the percentage of the acquirer's employees covered by its plans, or the relative benefits enjoyed by various groups of the acquirer's employees. (These effects can occur even if the purchaser keeps the acquired business in a separate subsidiary, since the tests apply on a controlled group basis. I.R.C. § 414(b).) Hence, the buyer may need to amend its plans to ensure their continued qualification after the transaction. Still other considerations concerning qualified plans involve the treatment of the target's employees. If the acquirer maintains the target's plan, it must credit each employee's length of service with the target toward meeting any requirements for minimum time to participate in the plan and minimum years of employment to possess vested benefits. I.R.C. § 414(a). Moreover, the transaction could trigger the vesting of benefits if it results in terminating (or even partially terminating) the plan. I.R.C. § 411(d)(3). Termination, if the plan had only existed for a few years, could also create a challenge to the plan's qualification from the start on grounds of lack of permanence. Treas. Reg. § 1.401–1(b)(2). Finally, can the acquirer, who assumes the target's obligations under a qualified plan, obtain the immediate deduction normally available for making such contributions, or must it—following the usual rule for assumption of liabilities in a purchase—capitalize this expenditure as a part of the cost of the acquisition? *See F. & D. Rentals, Inc. v. Commissioner,* 365 F.2d 34 (7th Cir.1966), *cert. denied,* 385 U.S. 1004 (1967) (stating that payments are immediately deductible).

3. SECURITIES LAW ASPECTS

a. *Registration Requirements Resulting from Issuing Shares to Buy the Business*

The acquisition of a business conducted through a corporation can involve the movement of securities in either, or both, of two directions: from the acquirer, or from the target's shareholders. For example, if the parties structure the acquisition as a sale of stock transaction, then the target's shareholders will sell securities (their shares in the target) to the acquiring company. The issues raised by the target's stockholders selling their shares will be addressed later. The present discussion concerns the flow of securities from the acquirer to either the target or the target's shareholders, which occurs when the purchasing corporation pays with its stock or debt instruments, or pays with the stock or debt instruments of an affiliated firm such as its parent (or might even occur with a cash earn-out, to the extent such a cash earn-out could constitute a "security"). The initial question here is whether the acquirer must register under the 1933 Securities Act if it plans to use securities as payment.

For many years, the answer to this question turned on the mode in which the parties structured the acquisition: sale of stock, sale of assets, or statutory merger. The sale of stock transaction is straightforward. Here, it has always been understood that the acquirer's issuance of stock or debt instruments in exchange for the outstanding stock of the target constitutes a sale by the acquirer of its securities to those of the target's shareholders who participate in the exchange. *E.g., "Disclosure to Investors"—Report and Recommendations to the Securities Exchange Commission From the Disclosure Policy Study* 251 (1969). Hence, the acquiring corporation would need to register this issuance unless it could find an exemption. (For example, if the target was a closely held corporation, the exemptions for small, private or even intrastate offerings might be available, depending upon the value of the target's stock exchanged for the acquirer's securities, the number and sophistication of the target's shareholders, or the residence of both the target's shareholders and the acquirer. If a government agency approved the fairness of the exchange, Section 3(a)(10) might apply.)

A sale of assets transaction presumably also constitutes a sale by the acquiring corporation of the securities it issues—in this case, in exchange for the target's assets. The problem is identifying the purchaser of the securities: the target corporation, or the target's shareholders. This is critical because, if the target corporation is the purchaser, then the private offering exemption should normally apply, whereas if the target's shareholders are the buyers, finding an exemption becomes much more problematic.

The statutory merger involves yet a different analysis. Here, as with the sale of stock transaction, the target's stockholders exchange their shares directly with the corporation issuing the new stock or debt instruments (ignoring, for the present, the possibility of a triangular merger). Hence, there is no question that the target's shareholders, rather than the target company, constitute the purchasers of the acquirer's securities. The difficulty is that the target's shareholders lack an individual choice in making the exchange: If the requisite majority votes to approve the merger, all must go along (unless a shareholder chooses to exercise appraisal rights). Recall, this same lack of individual volition was a troubling point in considering whether a cram-down recapitalization constituted a sale of securities. In fact, even in a sale of assets transaction followed immediately by a dissolution, this same lack of individual choice exists.

Before 1972, the Securities Exchange Commission took the position, in its former Rule 133, that sale of assets transactions and statutory mergers (as well as involuntary recapitalizations) did not constitute a sale of securities to the target's shareholders, because of the lack of individual volition. In 1972, this changed with the repeal of Rule 133, and the adoption of Rule 145. The latter rule identifies three types of transactions which it deems to constitute an offer to sell or a sale to a corporation's security holders, within the meaning of the 1933 Securities Act. Chapter VI dealt with the first category—reclassifications. The second type of transaction is a merger or consolidation on which the security holders vote, and in which they exchange their securities for the securities of any other company. (Note this picks up triangular mergers.) The rule excepts, however, a merger whose sole purpose is to change a company's state of incorporation. On its face, the rule would also seem to exclude a short form merger, since this would not require a shareholder vote. In the release announcing the rule, however, the Securities Exchange Commission took the position that short form mergers, in which the subsidiary's shareholders receive securities in exchange for surrendering their stock, constitute a sale. Sec. Act Rel. 5316 (1972). The rule's approach to sale of assets transactions is a little more complicated. Again, it only reaches transactions on which the target's security holders vote, and in which the acquirer pays with its securities (or the securities of an affiliated firm, such as its parent). However, the rule differentiates between sales of securities to the target corporation itself, and sales to the target's shareholders, by adopting four alternative tests which essentially seek to determine whether, as part of the transaction, the target will distribute to its shareholders the securities it received in exchange for its assets. Application of Rule 145 raises a number of questions, some of which the Securities Exchange Commission answered in the following release.

Securities Act Release No. 5463

Securities and Exchange Commission, February 28, 1974.

DIVISION OF CORPORATION FINANCE'S INTERPRETATIONS OF RULE 145

* * * In order to assist all persons in their understanding of, and their compliance with, Rule 145, the Commission has authorized the publication of this interpretative release setting forth the current views and positions of its Division of Corporation Finance with respect to Rule 145 and related matters.

* * *

I. Relationship of Rule 145 to Exemptions Set Forth in Sections 3 and 4 of the Act * * *

Illustration A

Facts: X Company proposes to issue common stock in exchange for the assets of Y Company after Y Company obtains the approval of its several stockholders, as required by state law, with respect to an agreement setting forth the terms and conditions of the exchange and providing for a distribution of the X company common stock to the Y Company stockholders. X Company has determined that the private offering exemption afforded by Section 4(2) of the Act would be available for the transaction.

Question: In light of Rule 145, may X Company choose between relying upon the private offering exemption available under Section 4(2) and registering the securities to be issued in the transaction * * *?

Interpretative Response: Yes, * * *. Rule 145 does not affect statutory exemptions which are otherwise available. However, * * * X Company may register the securities to be issued in the transaction * * * so that an affiliate of Y Company would be able to resell immediately his securities either pursuant to the registration statement, if [requisite information regarding] such resales [is] disclosed in the registration statement, or subject to the limitations referred to in Rule 145(d).

* * *

II. Application of Rule 145 to Various Types of Reclassifications and Business Combination Transactions.

* * *

Illustration E

Facts: X Company proposes to acquire at least 80% of the outstanding common stock of Y Company by offering its common stock to the stockholders of Y Company in exchange for their Y Company common stock in a transaction intended to qualify as a tax free reorganization pursuant to Section 368(a)(1)(B) of the Internal Revenue Code of 1954, as amended.

Question: Is Rule 145 applicable to such an exchange offer * * * ?

Interpretative Response: No. Rule 145 * * * [is] not applicable to "B" type reorganizations. * * *

Illustration F

Facts: The board of directors of X Company is considering an offer by Y Company whereby a significant portion (but not substantially all) of X Company's assets will be transferred to Y Company in return for shares of Y Company common stock which would be distributed to the stockholders of X Company on a pro-rata basis. Although not required to do so by state law or by Y Company's certificate of incorporation or by-laws, X Company's board of directors will submit the matter to the stockholders of X Company for their authorization.

Question: Assuming that no statutory exemption is available, is Rule 145 applicable to this proposed transaction?

Interpretative Response: Yes. Rule 145(a)(3) states that:

> [a] "sale" shall be deemed to be involved, within the meaning of Section 2(3) of the Act, so far as the security holders of a corporation ... are concerned where, pursuant to statutory provisions ... or similar controlling instruments, *or otherwise,* there is submitted for the

vote or consent of such security holders a plan or agreement for ... transfers of assets. (emphasis added)

Accordingly, inasmuch as the board of directors in its discretion has determined to submit the matter to stockholders, Rule 145 is applicable * * *.

III. Communications Deemed Not to be a "Prospectus" or "Offer to Sell" for Purposes of Rule 145 * * *

Illustration

Facts: X Company and Y Company are about to sign an agreement in principle setting forth their understanding with respect to a proposed merger of the two companies which will be registered pursuant to Rule 145. One condition set forth in the agreement in principle requires that, prior to the consummation of the merger, Y Company divest itself of a significant subsidiary in order to avoid potential problems under the Federal anti-trust laws. Although not set forth in the agreement in principle, it is clear from the preliminary negotiations that, subsequent to the merger, certain assets of Y Company will be liquidated because their book value is materially lower than their market value.

Question: Does Rule 145(b) prohibit the announcement of these facts prior to the filing of a registration statement?

Interpretative Response: No. Rule 145(b)(1) describes communications which will be deemed not to be a "prospectus" or "offer to sell" as defined in the Act. Inasmuch as the divestiture of a significant subsidiary is a material part of the transaction, and will have a material effect on the business of one party, it should be disclosed. To the extent that the assets to be liquidated are material to Y Company's operations, this plan should also be disclosed.

IV. Resales of Securities Acquired in Rule 145 Transactions * * *

Illustration A

Facts: X Company filed a registration statement on Form S–1 covering the proposed issuance of its common stock (but not covering the resale thereof) in connection with a proposed acquisition of Y Company in a Rule 145 type statutory merger which, if approved by Y Company's stockholders, would result in Y Company's stockholders receiving common stock of X Company. * * *

Question A–1: Assuming for the purposes of this question only that A is a controlling person of X Company and also owns common stock of Y Company, would his resales of the X Company common stock which he receives in this transaction be subject to the limitations of Rule 145(d)?

Interpretative Response: No. Inasmuch as A controls X Company, he is already deemed to be an affiliate of X Company and is subject to the provisions of Rule 144. Accordingly, the resale of any additional shares of X Company common stock, which he acquires in a Rule 145 transaction or otherwise, is subject to the provisions of Rule 144.

Question A–2: Assuming for the purposes of this question only that B does not own any common stock of X Company but is a controlling person of Y Company and that after the merger he will become a controlling person of X Company, would his resales of the X Company common stock which he receives in this transaction be subject to the limitations of Rule 145(d)?

Interpretative Response: No. Inasmuch as B will become a controlling person of X Company, he would be deemed to be an affiliate of X Company. By virtue of his becoming an affiliate of X Company, B would become subject to Rule 144 and the resale of all of his X Company common stock would be subject to the provisions of Rule 144.

Question A–3: Assuming for the purposes of this question only that C is an affiliate of Y Company but not of X Company; what restrictions are imposed by Rule 145(d) on C's public resale of the X Company common stock which he receives in the Rule 145 transaction?

Interpretative Response: Rule 145(d) would permit C to resell X Company securities received in the Rule 145 transaction subject to the provisions of paragraphs (c), (e), (f) and (g) of Rule 144. It should be noted that neither the two year holding period requirement nor the notice of sale requirement of Rule 144 would be applicable to C's sales pursuant to Rule 145(d).

Question A–4: Assuming for the purposes of this question only that D is not an affiliate of X Company or of Y Company and that his only relationship to the transaction is that he owns Y Company common stock, some of which was purchased previously in a private offering, would D be immediately free to resell publicly all of the X Company common stock which he receives in the transaction?

Interpretative Response: Yes. Since D is not an affiliate of X Company or Y Company then he is not deemed to be an underwriter with respect to the securities he receives in the Rule 145 transaction. Accordingly, D is immediately free to resell publicly all of the X Company common stock which he receives in the transaction regardless of whether some of his Y Company common stock was restricted.

* * *

The registration requirement potentially triggered by the acquirer paying with its securities raises a number of practical questions from a planning standpoint. To begin with, how much of a burden is this? The discussion of going public in Chapter V noted the time and expense involved with registering an initial public offering under the 1933 Securities Act. The time factor may be as important in the acquisition context as it was to a corporation looking for quick infusions of cash from a public offering. The longer the buyer takes to complete the transaction—even a friendly transaction—the more danger it might face of other bidders entering the scene and upsetting the deal. Mitigating this, however, the SEC allows a buyer to make a tender offer, in which the buyer proposes to pay for the tendered shares with the buyer's securities, upon the filing of the 1933 Act registration statement, rather than waiting until the registration statement takes effect. The target's shareholders can tender their stock before the registration statement becomes effective, but the buyer cannot accept the shares until the registration statement is effective. Sec. Act Rule 162. In contrast to concerns about delay, the added expense of registering the securities used for the acquisition may not present much problem—at least if the buyer and seller are 1934 Securities Exchange Act reporting companies. The acquirer can use Form S–4 to register either a sale under Rule 145 or an acquisition of stock in exchange for its securities. If the acquirer has shares registered under the 1934 Act, Form S–4 allows it to incorporate by reference much of the information in its 1934 Act filings. The same is true for the information which an S–4 filing requires about the target. Moreover, if the target has shares registered under the Securities Exchange Act, it must comply with the proxy rules promulgated pursuant to Section 14 of the Act when soliciting its stockholders' approval of a merger or sale of assets anyway. Here, the parties can avoid duplication by preparing the S–4 prospectus in the form of a proxy statement. As with an initial public offering, registration requires disclosure about the firm issuing the securities. Form S–4, however, also requires disclosure about the target company. This is something of a curious phenomenon: The buyer is supposed to inform the seller's stockholders about their own company. To what extent does this require the purchaser to tip its hand as far as what value it sees (but of which the target's shareholders are unaware) in the target company? *See Feit v. Leasco Data Processing Equip. Corp.*, 332 F.Supp. 544 (E.D.N.Y.1971) (requiring disclosure). *But see Flynn v. Bass Bros. Enterprises, Inc.*, 744 F.2d 978 (3d Cir.1984) (buyer's appraisals of target's assets or business may not be sufficiently reliable to be material). Registration requirements in the acquisition context present one other problem beyond both delay in executing the transaction and the potential burdens of preparing disclosure. This comes from the requirement of silence about a planned offer prior to filing. (Recall the reference to "gun jumping" in the discussion of pre-and post-effective offers in the article on going public by Messrs. Schneider, Manko and Kant in Chapter V.) The need to keep silent could put persons proposing an acquisition for stock at a severe disadvantage in an ongoing contest with another acquirer offering cash. Several rules promulgated by the Securities Exchange Commission address this problem by allowing greater pre-filing communication in the context of a business combination for stock than would otherwise be permissible in a public offering of securities. Exch. Act Rule 135(a)(2)(viii) (permitting publication of basic terms of proposed combination prior to filing registration statement); 165 (permitting pre-filing offers by acquiring firm in a business combination as long as communications are filed with the SEC); 166 (allowing pre-filing communication with analysts and major stockholders about proposed combinations).

One way to avoid registration is to undertake a sale of assets transaction in which the target does not dissolve or otherwise distribute the securities it received to its stockholders. There are, as discussed later in this chapter, a number of practical problems with such an idea. Moreover, tax consequences can discourage this approach. From a securities law standpoint, one danger here is that the target might thereafter need to register as an investment company under the Investment Company Act of 1940.

When acquiring a business in exchange for securities, it is important to consider not only the initial registration, but also resales. If the target's shareholders cannot sell the securities they receive, this obviously lowers the value of the package the buyer pays. (In fact, one of the main motivations for owners of a non-public firm to sell is to obtain marketable securities.) The interpretative release reprinted above explores a number of aspects of the resale question. The Commission points out that an acquirer may wish to register, despite an available exemption, in order to avoid the problems from the resale of unregistered securities. *But see* S.E.C. No Action Letter, St. Ives Holding Co. (July 22, 1987) (unregistered securities received under Section 3(a)(10) exemption may be resold by non-affiliates regardless of Rule 144). As explained when considering this subject in Chapter V, resales of unregistered securities face a question as to whether the selling security holder is a statutory underwriter and thus unable to rely upon the exemption in Section 4(1) for one who is not an issuer, dealer or underwriter. Recall, Rule 144 established a safe harbor allowing resales under certain conditions. Merely registering the issuance of securities for the acquisition, however, will not ensure all the target's former shareholders can resell the securities they received in the transaction. Rather, as the interpretive release illustrates through several examples, it depends upon whether the security-holder (i) is an affiliate (a person having control) of the acquirer (in which event resales through a broker face a statutory underwriter question under the last sentence in Section 2(11)); (ii) was an affiliate of the target (in which case paragraph (c) of Rule 145 will deem the person to be an underwriter if he or she resells the securities, unless he or she complies with the provisions of paragraph (d) of the Rule); or (iii) is and has been a non-affiliate of either firm, in which event he or she can resell registered shares without worry. To avoid the problems created under paragraphs (c) and (d) of Rule 145, affiliates of the target may wish to insist on the acquirer's registration covering their resales. (Incidentally, if the issuer of the securities used in the acquisition is a 1934 Act reporting company, and any of the recipients are statutory insiders of the issuer, they will want to keep in mind the liability Section 16(b) imposes for resales within six months of acquiring stock.)

Finally, what about state securities laws? The Uniform Securities Act has evolved in a manner parallel to the Securities Exchange Commission's movement from Rule 133 to Rule 145. The 1956 Uniform Act defined a sale to exclude any action incident to a class vote by stockholders on a merger, reclassification or sale of assets in exchange for securities. Uniform Securities Act (1956) § 401(j)(6)(C). The 1985 revision of the Act no longer contains this exclusion. *See* Uniform Securities Act (1985) § 101(13)(vi). Nevertheless, even the 1985 revision has eschewed most regulation in this area. It does so by creating an exemption from registration for a distribution of securities in connection with mergers, sales of assets, or even exchanges of securities (thus picking up acquisitions through all the modes) in either of two situations: (i) if the distributed securities are registered under the 1933 Securities Act, or (ii) for securities not registered under the 1933 Act, if, at least 10 days before the transaction, the parties provide the state's administrator with written notice of the proposed acquisition and a copy of all materials used to solicit the shareholders' approval, and the administrator does not disallow the exemption. Uniform Securities Act (1985 rev.) § 402(17). The 2002 revision of the Uniform Securities Act goes even further. It exempts all exchanges of securities pursuant to mergers, exchanges of shares, sales of assets, and the like in which stockholders of one party to the transaction receive shares in another party to the transaction. Uniform Securities Act (2002 rev.) § 202(18).

Other states, most notably California, have been more aggressive in applying their blue sky laws to the issuance of securities in an acquisition. California's statute expressly requires qualification of securities issued in connection with a merger or a sale of assets. Cal. Corp. Code § 25120. (Issuing securities to purchase the target's outstanding stock directly from its shareholders comes within the general provisions covering issuer transactions, Cal. Corp. Code § 25110, *et seq.* 1 Marsh & Volk, *Practice Under the California Securities Laws* § 8.08(6) (rev'd ed. 1989).) The impact of these provisions is to require the California Corporations Commissioner to approve the fairness of the transaction, including, particularly, with respect to the respective values of the securities exchanged. 10 Cal.Code Reg. § 260.140.61. (On the other hand, such fairness approval creates the basis for an exemption from federal registration under Section 3(a)(10). *See* 10 Cal.Code Reg. § 260.140.62 (applicant may request a fairness hearing).) Needless to say, obtaining fairness approval from each state might seem unduly burdensome in a merger involving major corporations with stockholders all over the country. In this regard, it is useful to note that California exempts mergers and sale of assets transactions from qualification unless at least 25 percent of the target's shareholders have, according to the company's records, addresses in California. Cal. Corp. Code § 25103(c). At the other extreme, if the transaction involves a small target company, the limited offering exemption (Cal. Corp. Code § 25102(f)) might apply to a sale of stock type of transaction (but not to a merger or sale of assets transaction). Note the impact of this difference on the question of how to structure the acquisition of a closely held California target company. Conversely, note the fact that the less than 25 percent California residents exclusion applies only to mergers and sale of assets transactions, not to sale of stock transactions—again meaning structure can be important in avoiding the necessity of state qualification. (On the other hand, California cannot block an entire sale of stock transaction—as it could a merger or sale of assets transaction—rather, it can only prevent the participation of California stockholders.) In any event, if the acquirer uses securities listed on the New York or American stock exchanges or the Nasdaq, then federal law precludes state regulation. Sec. Act § 18.

b. *Restrictions on Acquisitions of Shares*

As pointed out above, structuring the acquisition of a business as a purchase by the acquiring company of the target's outstanding stock involves the target's stockholders selling securities (their shares). Section 4(1) should exempt this transaction from registration under the 1933 Securities Act; neither should the sale require registration under various state blue sky laws. *See, e.g.,* Uniform Securities Act (1985 revision) § 402(1), (2), (5), (11); Uniform Securities Act (2002 revision) § 202(1); *Fox v. Ehrmantraut,* 28 Cal.3d 127, 167 Cal.Rptr. 595, 615 P.2d 1383 (1980). (Presumably, the same would be true even if one considered the target's shareholders' surrender of their stock in a merger, or in a dissolution following a sale of assets, to constitute a sale of securities.) Keep in mind, however, because there is a sale of securities, misrepresentations by the target's shareholders to the buyer can create a cause of action under Rule 10b–5, and Section 10(b) of the 1934 Securities Exchange Act. *Landreth Timber Co. v. Landreth,* 471 U.S. 681 (1985).

Typically, however, the securities laws are concurred less with the prospect of the target's shareholders taking advantage of the acquirer, than with the other way around. This brings one back to the Williams Act, introduced when dealing with toehold share purchases earlier in this chapter. As noted in the previous discussion, one aspect of the Williams Act is to require formal disclosure (a Schedule TO) before making a tender offer for shares registered under Section 12 of the Securities Exchange Act—or for certain other specialized types of shares—if the proposed transaction would give the purchaser over five percent ownership of the sought after class. Sec. Exch. Act § 14(d)(1). (The Act also requires disclosure (a Schedule 13D) after an individual acquires five percent or more of such a class of shares, even without a tender offer. Sec. Exch. Act § 13(d).) Several aspects of this disclosure raise questions. Schedule TO (like Schedule 13D) calls for discussion of the purchaser's plans for the company. This again creates the problem of what to say if the buyer has no firm plans. Of course, with a tender offer seeking a controlling amount of stock, the question of whether the buyer is purchasing only for investment, rather than to acquire control, seems answered. Yet, the purchaser, while presumably having some strategy, may not be entirely sure of precisely what it will do with the target—merger, liquidation, other restructuring—until it gains control and gets a first hand look at the company. Hence, a similar sort of hedging disclosure as found in 13D filings often occurs in the tender offer context as well. *E.g., Grumman Corp. v. LTV Corp.,* 527 F.Supp. 86 (E.D.N.Y.), *aff'd on other grounds,* 665 F.2d 10 (2d Cir.1981). One disclosure sometimes demanded by a Schedule TO, but not by a 13D, is financial information about the buyer. The buyer must provide such information (assuming the purchaser is not a natural person) if the information would be material to the target's shareholders in deciding whether to tender or to hold their stock. When would such information be material? Will it be material even if the buyer seeks 100 percent of the shares in exchange for cash? *See* Item 10 of Schedule TO (not requiring disclosure for an all cash, all shares offer unless the offer is subject to a financing condition). As a general proposition, however, it may be easier for a public company to disclose the financial information, rather than worry about whether the information is material. Finally, to what extent must the buyer disclose favorable information concerning the purchaser's perception of the target's worth? Courts have generally not required disclosure concerning the buyer's valuation of the target's business or assets on the grounds that it is too speculative or unreliable to be material. *See, e.g., Flynn v. Bass Bros. Enterprises, Inc.*, 744 F.2d 978 (3d Cir.1984). *But see Feit v. Leasco Data Processing Equip. Corp.*, 332 F.Supp. 544 (E.D.N.Y.1971).

In addition to requiring formal disclosure, Section 14(d) imposes substantive rules on tender offers. The section address three subjects. The first is the right of tendering shareholders to change their minds and get back their stock (Section 14(d)(5)). While the statute allowed this for up to seven days after publication of the tender offer (and again after 60 days if the offer was still open), the Securities Exchange Commission has expanded the right under its rulemaking authority to allow withdrawal for the entire period the tender offer is open (Sec. Exch. Act Rule 14d–7), which must extend at least 20 business days (Sec. Exch. Act Rule 14e–1). *But see* Sec. Exch. Act Rule 14d–11 (allowing tender offers to provide a period after the expiration of the tender offer during which shareholders can tender stock without having the right to withdraw their tender). Notice that this timing rule can make it necessary to determine when exactly a tender offer begins. Generally, under Rule 14d–2, an offer does not commence until the offeror announces the means by which shareholders can tender their stock. The next restriction concerns what happens if stockholders tender more shares than the buyer offered to purchase. Buyers typically would like to use an approach of "first come, first served" in order to create an incentive to tender. Section 14(d)(6), however, requires a pro-rata acceptance of the tendered shares (in other words, purchasing an equal percentage from each tendering stockholder). While the statute only grants this treatment for shareholders who tender within the first ten days of the offer (or after an increase in the offered price), again the Commission has expanded this by rule to cover all shareholders who tender during the life of the offer. Sec. Exch. Act Rule 14d–8. Finally, Section 14(d)(7) requires the buyer who increases the offered price while the tender offer is still open, to give the shareholders who already tendered in response to the offer the benefit of the higher price. In addition to these three statutory areas of control, the S.E.C. has adopted one other substantive rule specifically for Section 14(d) tender offers. As pointed out in the discussion of toehold share purchases, Rule 14d–10 generally requires an offer to be equally open to all holders of the sought after class of shares.

It is useful to keep in mind that the disclosure requirements and substantive regulations in Section 14(d) apply (with a few exceptions) only to tender offers for shares registered under the 1934 Securities Exchange

Act. (In other words, it is the target, not the acquirer, which must be a 1934 Act reporting company, for Section 14(d) to apply.) Still, acquisitions of shares in smaller companies can involve the Williams Act. This is because Section 14(e) of the Securities Exchange Act (added by the Williams Act) proscribes false statements, or fraudulent, deceptive or manipulative acts and practices, in connection with any tender offer—whether or not the offer is for registered shares. *See, e.g., L.P. Acquisition Co. v. Tyson,* 772 F.2d 201 (6th Cir.1985). This is important for two reasons. First, it creates a federal cause of action if the buyer misleads the target's shareholders. *See Schreiber v. Burlington Northern, Inc.*, 472 U.S. 1 (1985). More significantly in terms of planning, the Securities Exchange Commission has used its rulemaking authority granted by Section 14(e) to impose substantive regulations on all tender offers—both for registered shares and for unregistered shares. These requirements include holding the offer open for at least 20 business days from its publication, and 10 additional days from any change in the number of shares sought or in the price paid, as well as public announcement of any extension of a tender offer. Sec. Exch. Act Rule 14e–1. Rules 14e–4 and 14e–5 provide two other regulations applicable to tender offers generally. Rule 14e–4 prohibits short tendering (tendering shares one does not own) in response to a tender offer for less than all of the target's shares. (The concern here is that stockholders can use this technique to get more than their pro-rata share of stock purchased in an oversubscribed offer.) Rule 14e–5 prohibits a person who makes a tender offer from buying or arranging to buy the sought after securities, other than through the tender offer, while the offer is open. (Recall the claim involving this prohibition in the *Wellman* opinion reprinted earlier in this chapter.) These rules again make it critical to determine when share acquisitions constitute a tender offer: Specifically, how do the eight *Wellman* factors apply when dealing with a small corporation for which a sale of stock mode of acquisition presumably involves negotiated purchases with individual shareholders, rather than a general solicitation in the newspaper? See, *e.g., Astronics Corp. v. Protective Closures Co.,* 561 F.Supp. 329 (W.D.N.Y.1983) (not finding a tender offer).

Keep in mind that the tender offer rules apply whether the acquisition is "friendly" or "hostile". In either event, the target's management may wish to issue a statement supporting or opposing the offer. If the management makes a statement about a tender offer which has commenced, it must file a Schedule 14D–9. Sec. Exch. Act Rule 14d–9. The most significant item on this schedule is typically the requirement of disclosing whether any negotiation is underway (for instance, with another buyer) in response to the tender offer—albeit management need not disclose the specifics of the possible transaction (such as price and the identity of the other party) before reaching an agreement in principle if this could upset the negotiations. Suppose the target's management wishes to remain silent. Rule 14e–2 prevents this by requiring a statement in response to a tender offer within 10 days of the offer's publication—although the statement can be one of no opinion or neutrality. Even a neutral opinion, however, triggers the 14D–9 disclosure.

Finally, recall that acquisitions of shares, in contrast to acquisition of assets, can bring into play the margin rules imposed under the 1934 Securities Exchange Act. *See* pp. 951–953 *supra*.

4. TAX ASPECTS

a. *Recognition Upon the Exchange*

As discussed earlier, corporate acquisitions can take a variety of forms. These occasionally include establishing a partnership between the corporations involved, or creating a new corporation to which both existing companies transfer their assets for stock or to which their stockholders transfer their shares for stock. The tax impacts of such transactions entail principles familiar from Chapters III and IV. Typically, however, the acquisition employs the sale of assets, sale of stock, statutory merger, or triangular structures outlined previously. These structures, in turn, can take taxable and tax-free forms.

(i) The Taxable Sale of Assets Transaction

Structuring a transfer of the business as a sale by the target corporation of its assets normally results in the target company recognizing gain (or loss) measured by the difference between its basis in the property conveyed, and the fair market value of what it received in return. I.R.C. § 1001. Moreover, should the buyer assume the target's liabilities, this too constitutes part of the gain. Treas. Reg. § 1.1001–2(a). Typically, the target's shareholders have no business reason to keep the corporation around after it has sold its entire operation, and they would like to get their hands on the proceeds. Hence, they often will liquidate the company. This results in a second taxable event, in which the shareholders must recognize gain (or loss) measured by the difference between their basis in their stock, and the value of what they obtain from the company. *See* I.R.C. § 331(a). This double tax (assuming the business sells at a gain) can make transferring the business through a taxable sale of assets transaction more profitable for the government than for the sellers. (Of course, if the company were an S corporation, the parties could avoid one level of tax—except insofar as the company sold assets with built-in gain from a period when it was a C corporation. I.R.C. § 1374.)

Could the parties improve matters by turning the transaction around; in other words, liquidate the target corporation first, and then have its shareholders sell the assets to the buying firm? This presumably avoids a tax on the actual sale of the property, since the shareholders will obtain a basis equal to the property's fair market value as a result of recognizing gain on the liquidation. I.R.C. § 334(a). The problem is that under Section 336(a), as amended by the Tax Reform Act of 1986, a corporation which distributes an appreciated asset to its shareholders in liquidation must recognize gain, just as if the company had sold the property.

Shareholders can postpone the second tax by not liquidating the target company. Indeed, if the shareholders wait long enough, the stepped-up basis their stock obtains upon death will preclude the second tax if the company then liquidates or redeems the shares. (This is not much fun for the decedent, however.) One tax difficulty with this strategy is that if a closely held company simply invests the proceeds and accumulates the investment income, it could face tax as a personal holding company. See p. 466 *supra*. To avoid this tax, the firm could pay dividends with its investment income, but this means a double tax on passive investments. Perhaps an S election would help; but recall the problem faced by S corporations with accumulated earnings and profits if they make too much passive income. See p. 494 *supra*.

The flip side to the unfavorable treatment of the target company and its shareholders in a taxable asset sale is the favorable treatment of the buyer. The buying company obtains a cost basis in the purchased property. I.R.C. § 1012. (Of course, the purchaser recognizes no income unless it pays using appreciated property other than its own stock. *See* I.R.C. § 1032 (providing non-recognition upon issuing stock for property).) When acquiring an entire business, the sale will include numerous assets. What basis will each specific item of property get? If the basis depends upon what portion of the purchase price the parties allocate to each asset, the buyer can gain an advantage by specifying most of the price as being for inventory and depreciable property. Before 1987, this often would have disadvantaged the seller severely, both because gain on the sale of such property could be ordinary income, and because such income might not qualify for the favorable treatment accorded by former Section 337, which allowed liquidating companies to sell out their assets tax-free. This is much less important after the 1986 Tax Reform Act repealed significantly more favorable capital gains rates as well as tax-free liquidation under former Section 337. (While Congress has resurrected a lower tax rate on capital gains made by individuals, a C corporation selling its assets enjoys no favorable rate on capital gains.) One continuing disadvantage of allocating more purchase price to inventory and depreciable property, however, is that a seller cannot use installment reporting for recapture income. I.R.C. § 453(i). To prevent parties from allocating sale prices among the assets in a manner favorable to the buyer (and no longer of such serious concern to the seller), Section 1060 forces the parties to use the allocation formula imposed for a deemed sale under Section 338 (which is discussed below). (Parties to an agreement allocating the sale price among various assets cannot use Section 1060, however, to back away from the agreed allocation; it is up to the I.R.S. to challenge the allocation. I.R.C. § 1060(a)).

Typically, among the assets sold with a going business will be various intangibles such as goodwill, know-how, customer lists, other trade secrets and licenses. In addition, the buyer may demand the former owners enter into a covenant not to compete or a consulting contract. For many years, this provided the potential for some tax planning, as well for disputes between the Internal Revenue Service and buyers of businesses. Traditionally, buyers were unable to obtain any deduction (through amortization) of sums spent on the goodwill or going concern value of a purchased business. On the other hand, in *Newark Morning Ledger Co. v. United States*, 507

U.S. 546 (1993), the Supreme Court held that if a purchaser could prove both the useful life and the value of an intangible asset—such as a customer list—the taxpayer could take depreciation deductions on the asset. Even better, courts have long held that payments for a covenant not to compete or a consulting contract could produce a write-off over the life of the contract. *E.g., Warsaw Photographic Assoc. v. Commissioner,* 84 T.C. 21, 48 (1985). Needless to say, the result was to create continuous dispute between the Internal Revenue Service and buyers over whether payments ostensibly for covenants not to compete, consulting contracts or other intangibles in fact represented consideration for goodwill (*e.g., Forward Communications Corp. v. United States*, 608 F.2d 485 (Ct.Cl.1979)), as well as over the value assignable to such covenants and other intangibles (*e.g., Beaver Bolt, Inc. v. Commissioner*, T.C. Memo. 1995–549).

In 1993, Congress changed the ground rules concerning the purchase of business intangibles by adding new Section 197 to the Internal Revenue Code. Section 197 allows the buyer of so-called section 197 intangibles to obtain a deduction determined by amortizing the intangible's basis ratably over a fifteen year period from the acquisition. The good news for buyers is that section 197 intangibles include goodwill and going concern value, thereby changing the prior rule of non-deductibility for such assets. I.R.C. § 197(d)(1)(A), (B). The bad news is that customer lists, covenants not to compete and similar contracts also are section 197 intangibles (I.R.C. § 197(d)(1)(E)), thereby precluding any faster deduction. *See* I.R.C. § 197(b). (What about consulting contracts? See H. Rep. No. 103–213, 103d Cong., 1st Sess. 216 (1993) (may treat such contracts as a covenant not to compete to the extent payments are in excess of reasonable compensation).)

Still, while Section 197 has narrowed the scope for controversy between buyers, who wish to treat various payments incurred during and after the acquisition of a business as an immediately deductible expense, and the Internal Revenue Service, who often insists on capitalizing such payments as part of the cost of acquiring the business, the Section has not eliminated all such controversy. For example, in *Illinois Tool Works, Inc. v. Commissioner*, 355 F.3d 997 (7th Cir.2004), the acquiring corporation agreed to assume the selling corporation's liabilities, including a potential liability for patent infringement. When this potential liability later turned into an all too real damage award, the court held that the resulting payment was part of the cost of the acquisition, rather than an immediately deductible expense. By comparison, had the target paid the award itself, or had this been a tax-free sale of assets transaction subject to Section 357(a), then the payment presumably would have been immediately deductible. In any event, regulations issued by the Internal Revenue Service address the need to capitalize, rather than treat as an expense, various costs incurred to facilitate the acquisition of a business. Treas. Reg. § 1.263(a)–5.

If the characterization issue between covenants not to compete, goodwill and other intangibles has lost much of its significance from the buyer's standpoint, what about from the seller's side? Compare the type of income—ordinary income versus capital gains—represented by payments for a covenant not to compete versus payments for goodwill. On the other hand, keep in mind the double tax faced by sales of corporate assets, including the firm's goodwill, when followed by a liquidating distribution to the shareholders, and recall as well that capital gains have no tax advantage when received by a C corporation. Contrast the double tax resulting from a corporate asset sale and liquidation, with the treatment of payments directly to the shareholders in exchange for the shareholders' personal promise not to compete (or to provide consulting services).

(ii) The Taxable Sale of Stock Transaction

Unlike the taxable asset sale, the taxable sale of stock transaction ordinarily produces no recognition of income for the target company; after all, the target company in this transaction does not make any sale or exchange. Instead, the only gain (or loss) normally occurs for the target's stockholders who sell their shares. Offsetting this favorable treatment of the seller (at least relative to the double-taxed asset sale), is the less favorable treatment of the buyer. While the purchaser obtains a cost basis in the stock it acquires, the basis of the target corporation's property remains unaffected by the sale. Moreover, this may not change even if the purchasing company liquidates the target. As discussed later in this chapter, the liquidation of a controlled subsidiary may occur pursuant to Section 332 without recognition of taxable income or loss, and can leave the parent holding assets with a substituted basis under Section 334(b). (Note this disadvantage for the buyer exists even when the target is an S corporation, in which event an asset sale would not have produced (barring a problem under Section 1374) a double tax.)

Section 338 provides a mechanism to gain the advantage of a stepped-up basis for the target's properties. This section comes into play when a corporation, within a 12 month period, acquires stock with at least 80 percent of the total voting power and 80 percent of the total value of all the stock in another corporation. I.R.C. §§ 338(d), 1504(a)(2). (The 80 percent test excludes, however, preferred stock which is non-voting, non-participating and non-convertible. I.R.C. § 1504(a)(4).) The acquisition must occur in purchases which do not involve a substituted basis—in other words, in taxable transactions. I.R.C. § 338(h)(3)(A)(i), (ii). The purchases also cannot be of shares the buyer already constructively owned under Section 318(a) (except if the constructive ownership is only by virtue of an option to purchase the shares). I.R.C. § 338(h)(3)(A)(iii).

Such a purchasing corporation can make an election to apply Section 338 within nine and one-half months of acquiring the stock which put it over the requisite 80 percent. I.R.C. § 338(g)(1). (This election is irrevocable. I.R.C. § 338(g)(3).) If the buyer makes this election, Section 338(a) creates a fictitious conveyance (for tax purposes) in which the target company sells all its assets to itself as a "new" (for tax purposes) corporation. This sale gives the target a basis in its assets equal to the "grossed-up basis" of the purchaser's "recently purchased stock" in the target, plus the purchaser's basis in its "non-recently purchased stock" in the target, plus adjustments for the liabilities of the target. I.R.C. § 338(b)(1), (2).

Taking these items one at time, the purchaser's "grossed-up basis" in the "recently purchased stock" essentially equals the total price the purchaser paid to acquire 80 percent or more of the shares within a 12 month period, extrapolated to include the additional amount the purchaser would have paid at the same average price per share for the remaining stock which it did not buy (and did not already own before the 12 month period). I.R.C. § 338(b)(4). For example, if the purchaser bought 100 percent of the stock in the target within 12 months, the grossed-up basis simply would be the price the buyer paid. If the purchaser bought only 80 percent of the shares (and owned no other stock in the company from before), the grossed-up basis would be 100/80 times the price the buyer paid. (Notice this gives the target the same increase in basis whether or not the buyer purchases 100 percent of the stock.) If, however, the purchaser already owned 20 percent of the stock in the target, then the grossed-up basis would only be the price the buyer actually paid for the newly purchased 80 percent. This is because the target will obtain, as part of its new basis, both the grossed-up basis and the buyer's basis in stock the buyer already had before the qualifying purchases (so-called "non-recently purchased stock"). (The purchaser can, however, make an election to step-up the basis of its earlier acquired stock in the target to a level commensurate with its new purchases—in exchange, of course, for recognizing an immediate gain. I.R.C. § 338(b)(3).) Finally, keep in mind the price of stock should reflect the value of a company's assets less its liabilities. For this reason, the new basis of the target's assets also includes the amount of its debts.

As discussed earlier in connection with the taxable sale of assets transaction, when dealing with the transfer of an entire business, one must figure out how much of the total cost becomes the basis of each individual item of property. This is also true for the imaginary sale under Section 338. The rule is the same in both cases (since Section 1060 cross references Section 338(b)(5)). Under the regulations, each asset receives a basis equal to its fair market value: first to cash and cash equivalents, then to marketable securities and the like, then to receivables and the like, then to inventory, then, whatever of the total basis is left over, to the rest of the specific tangible property, then, if any basis remains, to the Section 197 assets (excluding goodwill), and finally, if anything is still left over of the total basis, it goes to goodwill or going concern value. Treas. Reg. § 1.338–6(b). (If the total basis is not enough to cover the fair market value of all the assets in a category, each item in the category receives a basis in proportion to its relative fair market value.) Notice the potential this scheme creates for disputes between the I.R.S. and the buyer over the fair market value of the specific assets, since the buyer will argue for a high value on depreciable property and inventory.

Naturally, getting the advantage of this increase in basis has a cost. The target corporation must recognize income on the imaginary sale of its assets to itself. I.R.C. § 338(a). The statute deems this fictitious sale to occur at a price equal to the actual fair market value of the target's assets, or the target can employ a formula specified by the regulations (which largely parallels the basis adjustments discussed above). I.R.C. § 338(a)(1), (h)(11); Treas. Reg. § 1.338–4. The result of this recognition, as a general proposition, is to make the Section 338 election more expensive than it is worth. Another factor to consider is that the deemed sale under Section 338(a) results in the target corporation losing all its former tax attributes. On the positive side, this means wiping out all the accumulated earnings and profits. On the negative side, if the target has a net operating loss carryover, the target will lose this too. (On the other hand, the loss carryover can offset the gain on the imaginary sale—which the statute taxes to the preacquisition target—and thus provides an instance in which Section 338 might be a worthwhile election.) Suppose, however, the target company was a subsidiary of another corporation. In this instance, if the former parent was eligible to file a consolidated return with the target, the buying and selling companies might consider making an election under Section 338(h)(10). The effect of this election is to allow the former parent to not recognize its gain on the sale of the subsidiary's stock, and instead to recognize, on a consolidated return with its former subsidiary, the subsidiary's gain on the imaginary Section 338 sale. This gives the buyer the advantage of the step-up in the target's assets at a cost of only one level of tax. The Section 338(h)(10) election may also be handy when the subsidiary has declined rather than appreciated in value. Specifically, a Section 338(h)(10) election (or just a sale of assets transaction by the subsidiary), could produce a loss for the parent to take on its consolidated return in situations in which the parent would not have been able to recognize a loss on the sale of its stock in the subsidiary.

Finally, suppose the selling company possesses some property for which a stepped-up basis is particularly desirable (even at the cost of immediate recognition) and other property for which the basis increase is less useful. Could the purchasing company buy the former assets from the target (thereby obtaining a cost basis) and then buy the stock in the target (thereby avoiding double tax on the acquisition of the latter property)? (As a more complicated variation on this pattern, the target could divide itself into two companies. The purchaser might buy the assets from one and the stock of the other. Alternately, it might buy the stock in both, but attempt to make a Section 338 election for only one.) Section 338 contains various consistency rules to prevent such transactions. I.R.C. § 338(e), (f). These consistency rules created a potential trap by forcing a Section 338 election—which, as discussed above, generally costs more than it is worth—under certain circumstances. For this reason, it is fortunate that the regulations have largely defanged the consistency rules. Treas. Reg. § 1.338–8 (replacing the deemed Section 338 election called for under Section 338(e) and (f) with a carryover basis for the acquirer of assets and limiting the reach of even this mild consistency rule to involve only certain asset acquisitions from subsidiaries in consolidated groups—where the concern exists that the buyer may otherwise obtain a cost basis without the parent in the group facing any real taxable gain from the asset sale (due to the investment basis adjustments)).

(iii) The Tax–Free Sale of Assets Transaction

Certain transfers of a business through a sale of assets followed by a liquidation will not face the costly double tax discussed earlier in dealing with the taxable sale of assets transaction; rather they can be tax-free to the selling corporation and its stockholders. Section 368(a)(1)(C) includes among transactions which constitute a "reorganization" (often referred to as a "C" reorganization), one corporation's acquisition of substantially all the properties of another company solely in exchange for the acquirer's voting stock. Qualifying the sale as a reorganization brings into play Section 361, which generally precludes recognition by the transferor company, both upon the sale of its assets (Section 361(a), (b)(1)), and upon distributing the consideration received for its assets to its shareholders (Section 361(c)). Being a reorganization also makes applicable Section 354(a), which precludes recognition by the shareholders upon exchanging their stock for shares in the buyer. To obtain this tax-free treatment, Section 368(a)(1)(C) outlines two requirements: (1) that the buyer acquire "substantially all" of the selling company's assets, and (2) that the buyer use as consideration solely its voting stock. In addition, Section 368(a)(2)(G) commands that the selling company liquidate as a part of the reorganization, unless the Internal Revenue Service waives this requirement.

Turning to the first prerequisite, how much exactly is "substantially all" of the selling company's assets?

Revenue Ruling 57–518

1957–2 C.B. 253.

* * *

Advice has been requested as to the Federal income tax consequences of a reorganization between two corporations under the circumstances described below.

The *M* and *N* corporations were engaged in the fabrication and sale of various items of steel products. For sound and legitimate business reasons, *N* corporation acquired most of *M* corporation's business and operating assets. Under a plan of reorganization, *M* corporation transferred to *N* corporation (1) all of its fixed assets (plant and equipment) at net book values, (2) 97 percent of all its inventories at book values, and (3) insurance policies and other properties pertaining to the business. In exchange therefor, *N* corporation issued shares of its voting common stock to *M* corporation.

The properties retained by *M* corporation include cash, accounts receivable, notes, and three percent of its total inventory. The fair market value of the assets retained by *M* was roughly equivalent to the amount of its liabilities. *M* corporation proceeded to liquidate its retained properties as expeditiously as possible and applied the proceeds to its outstanding debts. The property remaining after the discharge of all its liabilities was turned over to *N* corporation, and *M* corporation was liquidated.

Section 368 of the Internal Revenue Code of 1954, in defining corporate reorganizations, provides in part:

(a) REORGANIZATION.—

(1) IN GENERAL.—* * * the term "reorganization" means—

* * *

(C) The acquisition by one corporation, in exchange solely for all or a part of its voting stock (or in exchange solely for all or a part of the voting stock of a corporation which is in control of the acquiring corporation), of substantially all of the properties of another corporation, * * *.

The specific question presented is what constitutes "substantially all of the properties" as defined in the above section of the Code. The answer will depend upon the facts and circumstances in each case rather than upon any particular percentage. Among the elements of importance that are to be considered in arriving at the conclusion are the nature of the properties retained by the transferor, the purpose of the retention, and the amount thereof. In *Milton Smith, et al. v. Commissioner,* 34 B.T.A. 702 * * *, a corporation transferred 71 percent of its gross assets. It retained assets having a value of $52,000, the major portion of which was in cash and accounts receivable. It was stated that the assets were retained in order to liquidate liabilities of approximately $46,000. Thus, after discharging its liabilities, the outside figure of assets remaining with the petitioner would have been $6,000, which the court stated was not an excessive margin to allow for the collection of re-receivables with which to meet its liabilities. No assets were retained for the purpose of engaging in any business or for distribution to stockholders. In those circumstances, the court held that there had been a transfer of "substantially all of the assets" of the corporation. The court very definitely indicated that a different conclusion would probably have been reached if the amount retained was clearly in excess of a reasonable amount necessary to liquidate liabilities. Furthermore, the court intimated that transfer of all of the net assets of a corporation would not qualify if the percentage of gross assets transferred was too low. Thus, it stated that, if a corporation having gross assets of $1,000,000 and liabilities of $900,000 transferred only the net assets of $100,000, the result would probably not come within the intent of Congress in its use of the words "substantially all."

The instant case, of the assets not transferred to the corporation, no portion was retained by *M* corporation for its own continued use inasmuch as the plan of reorganization contemplated *M*'s liquidation. Furthermore, the assets retained were for the purpose of meeting liabilities, and these assets at fair market values, approximately equaled the amount of such liabilities. Thus, the facts in this case meet the requirements established in the case of *Milton Smith, supra.*

* * *

NOTE

The Internal Revenue Service will provide an advance ruling that the seller has met the "substantially all" requirement if the seller conveys assets having a fair market value at least equal to 70 percent of the total value of all the seller's properties and at least equal to 90 percent of the net value of its assets over its liabilities. Rev. Proc. 77–37, 1977–2 C.B. 568. When will meeting the substantially all requirement pose a practical problem; put another way, why would the selling corporation ever need to hold back property from the buyer? One reason, noted in the ruling, is to pay off debts upon the seller's liquidation. Along somewhat similar lines, the selling company may need to pay dissenting shareholders who exercise statutory appraisal rights. An alternate reason may be that the buyer does not desire certain assets. To the extent that keeping property which the buyer does not want would constitute too great a retention under the substantially all test, recall the discussion earlier of whether the selling corporation can distribute such property to its shareholders in a transaction preceding the actual transfer of the business. At any event, should the selling company hold back appreciated assets for disbursement to its stockholders, the company must recognize gain upon the distribution, just as if the company sold the property. I.R.C. § 361(c)(2). Moreover, the distributed property will constitute potentially taxable boot to the shareholders. *See* I.R.C. § 356(a)(1). This double tax makes the failure to convey all the target's assets to the buyer potentially expensive, even if the holdback does not violate the substantially all test.

Instead of the seller holding back assets to pay its debts and any dissenting shareholders, suppose the buyer agrees to assume these obligations. This brings one to the requirement that the buyer pay solely with its voting stock. Does this requirement interfere with such an assumption?

Revenue Ruling 73–102

1973–1 C.B. 186.

Advice has been requested whether, under the circumstances described below, the "solely for voting stock" requirement of section 368(a)(1)(C) of the Internal Revenue Code is satisfied.

For valid business reasons, *X* corporation entered into a plan of reorganization with unrelated *Y* corporation. Pursuant to the plan, *X* transferred all of its assets to *Y* in exchange for *Y* voting stock and the assumption by *Y* of the *X* liabilities, including liabilities to pay claims of dissenting shareholders.

Under the plan, *Y* paid 50*x* dollars to dissenting *X* shareholders in satisfaction of their claims, based on the fair market value of their *X* stock surrendered. The dissenting shareholders surrendered all their *X* stock for cash in the transaction. The fair market value of the gross assets transferred by *X* to *Y* was 2,000*x* dollars. The amount of the liabilities assumed by *Y* (other than the liability to pay dissenting shareholders) was 150*x* dollars.

Section 368(a)(1)(C) of the Code defines as a reorganization the acquisition by one corporation, in exchange solely for shares of its voting stock, of substantially all the properties of another corporation. Section 368(a)(1)(C) of the Code further provides that in determining whether the exchange is solely for stock the assumption by the acquiring corporation of a liability of the other will be disregarded.

Section 368(a)(2)(B) of the Code provides that if, in addition to voting stock, the acquiring corporation exchanges money or other property, and if the acquiring corporation acquires, solely for voting stock, property of the other corporation having a fair market value which is at least 80 percent of the fair market value of all the property of the other corporation, then such acquisition will be treated as qualifying under section 368(a)(1)(C) of the Code. For the purpose of the percentage computation of section 368(a)(2)(B) of the Code, liabilities assumed by the acquiring corporation are treated as money.

In *Helvering v. Southwest Consolidated Corp.*, 315 U.S. 194 (1942), * * *, the Supreme Court of the United States held that the "solely for voting stock" requirement of the predecessor of section 368(a)(1)(C) of the Code was violated where the acquiring corporation directly or indirectly transferred to the acquired corporation or its shareholders property other than voting stock in exchange for the equity interest being acquired. The Court stated: " 'Solely' leaves no leeway."

The payment by *Y* of 50*x* dollars to dissenting shareholders of *X* in satisfaction of their claims was, in substance, the same as if *Y* had exchanged cash plus voting stock for the properties of *X*. Therefore, this cash payment is not a payment by *Y* of an assumed liability, but is additional consideration paid by *Y* in the exchange for the properties acquired by *Y*. Thus, the acquisition of the *X* property for the *Y* voting stock and cash cannot qualify under section 368(a)(1)(C) of the Code unless section 368(a)(2)(B) of the Code applies.

For purposes of section 368(a)(2)(B) of the Code, *Y* constructively paid a total of 200*x* dollars in money to *X* (liabilities assumed in the amount of 150*x* dollars, plus 50*x* dollars paid to the dissenting shareholders). Therefore, *Y* received property of *X* having a fair market value of 1,800*x* dollars (gross assets in the amount of 2,000*x* dollars, less 200*x* dollars in money constructively paid to *X*) solely for voting stock of *Y*, which represents 90 percent of the fair market value of all of the *X* property.

Accordingly, in the instant case, since at least 80 percent of all the property of *X* was acquired solely for voting stock of *Y*, it is held that the transaction qualifies as a reorganization under sections 368(a)(1)(C) and (a)(2)(B) of the Code. * * *

NOTES

1. As the ruling states, Section 368 carves out two exceptions to the solely for voting stock requirement for "C" reorganizations. Section 368(a)(1)(C) itself establishes the first one when it allows the parties to disregard the assumption of the seller's liabilities by the purchasing corporation in determining whether the buyer pays solely with its voting stock. Notice, however, the ruling did not treat the payment of the dissenting stockholders as coming within this exception. This is in accordance with the Supreme Court's decision in *Helvering v. Southwest Consolidated Corp.*, cited in the ruling, which held obligations created as part of the reorganization itself are not liabilities within the meaning of the statute. Somewhat inconsistently, the Internal Revenue Service considers other expenses incurred by the selling corporation in carrying out the reorganization (such as legal fees, for example) to constitute liabilities within the meaning of the provision. Rev. Rul. 73–54, 1973–1 C.B. 187. (Expenses incurred by the seller's shareholders in the transaction—as, for example, for legal advice on whether to participate—generally do not qualify. The Service allows the buyer, however, to pick up expenses which the target's stockholders otherwise might pay, if the expenses are "solely and directly related to the reorganization"—albeit, the above-cited ruling taking this position provides no examples of such expenses paid by shareholders rather than by the target. This inability to pay most of the shareholders' expenses can pose some hardship when the shareholders only get voting stock in the transaction—meaning they must come up with the cash out of pocket to cover the expenses.)

Not only may the buyer assume the seller's liabilities without breaking the requirements for reorganization treatment, but Section 357(a) generally precludes recognition by the seller even to the extent of the liabilities assumed. (In other words, the assumption does not constitute potentially taxable boot.) In addition to governing the assumption of liabilities in a Section 351 transaction, as discussed in Chapter IV, Section 357 also applies to a reorganization. Even better, the exception under Section 357(c) for debts in excess of basis does not apply to reorganizations, other than a Section 368(a)(1)(D) reorganization. (In this regard, one should note that if the seller's stockholders have at least 50 percent control of the buyer after the transaction—in other words, an upside-down sale of assets transaction—the sale constitutes a 368(a)(1)(D), rather than a 368(a)(1)(C), reorganization. I.R.C. § 368(a)(2)(A), (H).) The exception in Section 357(b) for assumptions of liabilities motivated by a tax avoidance purpose remains applicable, however, to all reorganizations. With Section 357(a) in mind, it is useful to compare the consequences of the buyer assuming the seller's liabilities, with the tax impact of the selling company holding back enough assets to pay its own debts. The latter may still allow, as discussed above, the transfer of the business to achieve reorganization treatment. Nevertheless, the seller must recognize gain if it uses appreciated assets to pay off its debts. Having the buyer pay the debts generally avoids all gain, at least to the seller.

Several other questions may arise regarding this exception. Suppose the buyer exchanges its debt securities for outstanding debt securities issued by the target company. Can this qualify as an "assumption" of liabilities? See *Southland Ice Co. v. Commissioner,* 5 T.C. 842 (1945) (yes). *But see Stoddard v. Commissioner,* 141 F.2d 76 (2d Cir.1944) (if the new security differs in its terms too much from the original, the debt is no longer assumed, but rather replaced, and the new security constitutes property other than voting stock). Also, can the buyer immediately pay off the seller's debt as part of the closing? *See Stockton Harbor Industrial Co. v. Commissioner,* 216 F.2d 638 (9th Cir.1954), *cert. denied,* 349 U.S. 904 (1955) (yes, if it pays an obligation whose value and amount was fixed prior to the reorganization; but not if the reorganization altered the amount or value of the debt). On the other hand, can the buyer transfer cash to the seller in order for the seller to pay the debts, and still fit within this exception. See Rev. Rul. 73–54, 1973–1 C.B. 187 (giving a negative answer).

2. Section 368(a)(2)(B) provides a second exception to the solely for voting stock requirement. It allows the buyer to also give money or other property, so long as the buyer pays for at least 80 percent of the value of all the seller's property with voting stock. Note, this does not mean the buyer can automatically pay 20 percent of the consideration in cash or other property—it can only pay that much boot if it acquires 100 percent of the seller's assets. If the seller were to retain 20 percent of its property, the buyer could pay no boot. Not only does the "substantially all" requirement impact in this manner how much boot the buyer can give, but the assumption of liabilities exception does as well. For purposes of computing whether the buyer has paid for 80 percent of the seller's assets with voting stock, Section 368(a)(2)(B) treats the purchaser's assumption of the seller's liabilities as if the purchaser paid the seller cash in the amount of the obligations assumed. Hence, if the buyer assumed debts exceeding 20 percent of the value of the target's assets, the buyer could pay no boot. (Keep in mind, Section 368(a)(2)(B) does not impose a limit on the amount of liabilities the buyer can assume; the limit exists only on the buyer's ability also to pay boot.)

Unlike the assumption of liabilities (for which there is no recognition barring a problem under Section 357(b)), payment of cash or other property (in other words, boot) can yield a taxable gain even if the exception under Section 368(a)(2)(B) applies. Interestingly, the selling company does not face gain upon receiving boot, so long as it distributes the boot to its shareholders or creditors in liquidation. I.R.C. § 361(b)(1), (3). This means boot from the buyer generally does not face a double tax. (On the other hand, if the purchasing company includes, among the boot it pays, property whose value exceeds the purchaser's basis in the item, then the purchaser must recognize gain, just as if it sold the property. *See* Rev. Rul. 72–327, 1972–2 C.B. 197. As a result of the purchaser's recognition, the selling company ends up with a basis in the boot equal to the property's fair market value (*see* I.R.C. § 362(b)), and, therefore, will not face recognition under Section 361(c)(2) when it distributes the boot upon liquidation. If, however, the boot consists of the buyer's non-voting stock or debt instruments, then the buyer would not recognize gain in any event. *See* I.R.C. § 1032. Here, Section 361(c) steps in to provide non-recognition for the selling corporation when distributing this type of consideration to its shareholders.)

The brunt of the recognition for receiving boot falls upon those of the seller's stockholders who obtain cash or other property upon the seller's liquidation. (In addition to property received from the buyer and distributed, property retained by the selling company and disbursed in the liquidation also will be boot to the recipient shareholders. *See* I.R.C. § 356(a)(1).) Recognition by the recipient stockholders is a function of Section 356, whose workings Chapter VI discussed when dealing with the receipt of boot in a recapitalization. (A recapitalization is a form of reorganization, just as a sale of assets coming within Section 368(a)(1)(C). I.R.C. § 368(a)(1)(E).) Briefly, under Section 356(a)(1), the shareholders receiving boot must recognize their gain, but not any loss (I.R.C. § 356(c)), up to the amount of the boot received. Section 356(a)(2) will characterize this gain as a dividend (limited to the recipient's rateable share of the corporation's earnings and profits) if the distribution has the effect of a dividend. This effect depends upon whether the recipient incurred a meaningful reduction in his or her proportionate interest in the company's equity (much as under the test for sale versus distribution treatment in redemptions).

With an acquisition, however, there is an added complication in applying this meaningful reduction test. The former shareholders in the selling company now own stock in the buyer. Comparing the boot recipient's percentage ownership in the selling company before the transaction, with his or her percent holding in the buyer after, will normally yield a major reduction—which has little to do, however, with receiving boot rather than stock. One alternate approach would be to hypothesize a redemption, prior to the sale of the business, of those shares for which the former stockholder essentially received boot rather than stock in the buyer. One could then see whether such a prior redemption would satisfy the tests for sale treatment under Section 302. Under this approach, a pro-rata receipt of boot by the seller's former stockholders would face dividend treatment since such a hypothetical pre-sale redemption would not yield a meaningful reduction in proportionate interest. A different approach would be to compare the amount of stock the recipient of boot actually received in the buyer, with the amount he or she would have received if, instead of the cash or other property, he or she had obtained more stock with a fair market value equal to the boot. If this difference would constitute a meaningful reduction, then the boot does not have the effect of a dividend. Under this approach, the receipt of boot by a former shareholder in the target could constitute a sale rather than a dividend, if, for example, receipt of voting stock in the buyer of equivalent value instead of the boot would have given him or her control of the buying company. While the Internal Revenue Service had followed the hypothetical pre-sale redemption approach, the Supreme Court rejected the Service's view in favor of testing dividend equivalence based upon a comparison of boot versus added stock in the acquiring company. *Commis-*

sioner v. Clark, 489 U.S. 726 (1989). In any event, as discussed in Chapter VI, the distinction between sale and distribution treatment under Section 356 has lost the vast majority of its significance with the reduction in the tax rate on dividends to match the rate on capital gains.

Finally, if the property received by the selling company's shareholders includes non-voting stock or debt securities in the buyer, then even the shareholders' recognition of gain becomes uncertain. While such consideration creates a problem with qualifying the transaction as a "C" reorganization, once the exchange so qualifies, Section 354(a) generally allows the tax-free receipt of any stock or securities in a corporation which is a party to the reorganization. There are, however, some exceptions to the tax-free receipt of stock or securities. To begin with, the 1997 Taxpayer Relief Act makes so-called nonqualified preferred stock the equivalent of boot under Section 354. I.R.C. § 354(a)(2)(C). The definition of nonqualified preferred stock is found in Section 351(g), as added by the 1997 Act. Broadly speaking, this is stock which has a dividend preference, does not participate in corporate growth, and is either subject to a redemption right which may be exercised within 20 years and is not subject to a contingency making the redemption unlikely, or has a dividend which varies with interest rates or the like. Moreover, even if the stock does not fit within the definition of non-qualified preferred, preferred stock received in a reorganization may be Section 306 stock whose later sale or redemption will not qualify for capital gains treatment. *See, e.g.,* Rev.Rul. 88–100, 1988–2 C.B. 46. Recall, as well, the potential for recognition created when debt securities change hands in a reorganization, as discussed in Chapter VI in dealing with recapitalizations. For example, receipt of securities with a principal amount in excess of the amount of securities surrendered constitutes taxable boot. I.R.C. § 354(a)(2)(A), 356(d). (Installment reporting may be available to the recipients of debt instruments constituting boot—but only if Section 356(a)(2) does not categorize them as a dividend. *See* I.R.C. § 453(f)(6).)

3. The solely for voting stock requirement raises several other issues. To begin with, what exactly constitutes voting stock? Either common or preferred shares can qualify, so long as the shares have the right to vote for directors. *See, e.g.,* Rev. Rul. 63–234, 1963–2 C.B. 148. Moreover, the stock need not have the same voting power as other shares in the buyer. Fractional shares and various contingent arrangements raise questions under the solely for voting stock requirement. However, these concerns are more typical of the sale of stock than of the sale of assets transaction, and their consideration is deferred until then. Finally, suppose the buyer already owns some stock in the selling corporation. In *Bausch & Lomb Optical Co. v. Commissioner,* 267 F.2d 75 (2d Cir.1959), *cert. denied,* 361 U.S. 835, the buying company already owned 79% of the stock in the target. The buying company then acquired all the target's assets in exchange for voting stock in the buyer; whereupon the target liquidated and returned most of the voting stock back to the buyer. The court held this was not an acquisition solely for voting stock. Rather, the purchaser had acquired only 21% of the assets for voting stock, and 79% for surrendering its stock in the target during the liquidation. Fortunately, the Internal Revenue Service

recently issued a regulation which does away with much of the *Bausch & Lomb* doctrine. Treas. Reg. § 1.368–2(d)(4). The regulation, however, imposes two caveats on this generosity. It will not apply in situations in which the preexisting stock ownership had been acquired as a step toward the overall purchase of the selling corporation's assets. In addition, the amount of boot (including assets held back from the sale) distributed to the shareholders of the selling corporation other than the purchaser, as well as the liabilities of the selling corporation assumed by the purchaser, cannot exceed 20 percent of the value of the selling corporation's assets.

4. One alternative to either holding back assets to pay creditors and dissenting shareholders, or having the acquiring company assume these obligations, is to use some of the stock received in order to meet these needs. In fact, paying creditors with stock or debt instruments from the buyer (if the creditors will accept such consideration) can be tax-free to the target. I.R.C. § 361(c)(3). (Otherwise, the target could recognize gain when it sells the stock.) Suppose the selling company must use most of the stock in this manner? Reconsider this question later after exploring the material concerning the judicially imposed continuity of interest test for reorganization treatment.

(iv) The Tax–Free Sale of Stock Transaction

Chapman v. Commissioner of Internal Revenue

618 F.2d 856 (1st Cir.1980).

■ LEVIN H. CAMPBELL, CIRCUIT JUDGE.

* * * We must decide whether the requirement of Section 368(a)(1)(B) that the acquisition of stock in one corporation by another be solely in exchange for voting stock of the acquiring corporation is met where, in related transactions, the acquiring corporation first acquires 8 percent of the acquiree's stock for cash and then acquires more than 80 percent of the acquiree in an exchange of stock for voting stock. * * *

The Facts

Appellees were among the more than 17,000 shareholders of the Hartford Fire Insurance Company who exchanged their Hartford stock for shares of the voting stock of International Telephone and Telegraph Corporation pursuant to a formal exchange offer from ITT dated May 26, 1970. On their 1970 tax returns, appellees did not report any gain or loss from these exchanges. Subsequently, the Internal Revenue Service assessed deficiencies * * *. Appellees petitioned the Tax Court for redetermination of these deficiencies, and their cases were consolidated with those of twelve other former Hartford shareholders. The Tax Court, with five judges dissenting, granted appellees' motion for summary judgment, and the Commissioner of Internal Revenue filed this appeal.

The events giving rise to this dispute began in 1968, when the management of ITT, a large multinational corporation, became interested in acquiring Hartford as part of a program of diversification. In October 1968, ITT executives approached Hartford about the possibility of merging the two corporations. This proposal was spurned by Hartford, which at the time was considering acquisitions of its own. In November 1968, ITT learned that approximately 1.3 million shares of Hartford, representing some 6 percent of Hartford's voting stock, were available for purchase from a mutual fund. After assuring Hartford's directors that ITT would not attempt to acquire Hartford against its will, ITT consummated the $63.7 million purchase from the mutual fund with Hartford's blessing. From November 13, 1968 to January 10, 1969, ITT also made a series of purchases on the open market totalling 458,000 shares which it acquired for approximately $24.4 million. A further purchase of 400 shares from an ITT subsidiary in March 1969 brought ITT's holdings to about 8 percent of Hartford's outstanding stock, all of which had been bought for cash.

* * * [O]n April 9, 1969 a provisional plan and agreement of merger was executed by the two corporations.

* * * On December 13, 1969, however, the merger plan ground to a halt, as the Connecticut Insurance Commissioner refused to endorse the arrangement. ITT then proposed to proceed with a voluntary exchange offer to the shareholders of Hartford on essentially the same terms they would have obtained under the merger plan. After public hearings and the imposition of certain requirements on the post-acquisition operation of Hartford, the insurance commissioner approved the exchange offer on May 23, 1970, and three days later ITT submitted the exchange offer to all Hartford shareholders. More than 95 percent of Hartford's outstanding stock was exchanged for shares of ITT's $2.25 cumulative convertible voting preferred stock. The Italian bank to which ITT had conveyed its original 8 percent interest [in an attempt to ensure tax-free treatment] was among those tendering shares, as were the taxpayers in this case.

* * *

Taxpayers advanced two arguments in support of their motion for summary judgment. Their first argument related to the severability of the cash purchases from the 1970 exchange offer. Because 14 months had elapsed between the last of the cash purchases and the effective date of the exchange offer, and because the cash purchases were not part of the formal plan of reorganization entered into by ITT and Hartford, the taxpayers argued that the 1970 exchange offer should be examined in isolation to determine whether it satisfied the terms of Section 368(a)(1)(B) of the 1954 Code. The Service countered that the two sets of transactions the cash purchases and the exchange offer were linked by a common acquisitive purpose, and that they should be considered together for the purpose of determining whether the arrangement met the statutory requirement that the stock of the acquired corporation be exchanged "solely for . . . voting stock" of the acquiring corporation. The Tax Court did not reach this argument; in granting summary judgment it relied entirely on the taxpayer's second argument.

For purposes of the second argument, the taxpayers conceded *arguendo* that the 1968 and the 1969 cash purchases should be considered "parts of the 1970 exchange offer reorganization." Even so, they insisted upon a right to judgment on the basis that the 1970 exchange of stock for stock satisfied the statutory requirements for a reorganization without regard to the presence of related cash purchases. The Tax Court agreed with the taxpayers, holding that the 1970 exchange in which ITT acquired more than 80 percent of Hartford's single class of stock for ITT voting stock satisfied the requirements of Section 368(a)(1)(B), so that no gain or loss need be recognized on the exchange under Section 354(a)(1). The sole issue on appeal is whether the Tax Court was correct in so holding.

I.

We turn first to the statutory scheme under which this case arose. * * * Section 354(a)(1) does not apply to an exchange unless the exchange falls within one of the six categories of "reorganization" defined in Section 368(a)(1). The category relevant to the transactions involved in this case is defined in Section 368(a)(1)(B):

"(T)he term 'reorganization' means—

(B) the acquisition by one corporation, in exchange solely for all or a part of its voting stock ... of stock of another corporation if, immediately after the acquisition, the acquiring corporation has control of such other corporation (whether or not such acquiring corporation had control immediately before the acquisition)."

The concept of "control" is defined in Section 368(c) as "the ownership of stock possessing at least 80 percent of the total combined voting power of all classes of stock entitled to vote and at least 80 percent of the total number of shares of all other classes of stock of the corporation." Subsection (B) thus establishes two basic requirements for a valid, tax-free stock-for-stock reorganization. First, "the acquisition" of another's stock must be "solely for ... voting stock." Second, the acquiring corporation must have control over the other corporation immediately after the acquisition.

The single issue raised on this appeal is whether "the acquisition" in this case compiled with the requirement that it be "solely for ... voting stock." It is well settled that the "solely" requirement is mandatory; if any part of "the acquisition" includes a form of consideration other than voting stock, the transaction will not qualify as a (B) reorganization. * * * The precise issue before us is thus how broadly to read the term "acquisition."

* * *

II.

For reasons set forth extensively in section III of this opinion, we do not accept the position adopted by the Tax Court. * * * As explained below, we find a strong implication in the language of the statute, in the legislative history, in the regulations, and in the decisions of other courts that cash purchases which are concededly "parts of" a stock-for-stock exchange must be considered constituent elements of the "acquisition" for purposes of applying the "solely for ... voting stock" requirement of Section 368(a)(1)(B). We believe the presence of non-stock consideration in such an acquisition, regardless of whether such consideration is necessary to the gaining of control, is inconsistent with treatment of the acquisition as a nontaxable reorganization. It follows for purposes of taxpayers' second argument which was premised on the assumption that the cash transactions were part of the 1970 exchange offer reorganization that the stock transfers in question would not qualify for nonrecognition of gain or loss.

Our decision will not, unfortunately, end this case. The Tax Court has yet to rule on taxpayers' "first" argument. * * * The question of what factors should determine, for purposes of Section 368(a)(1)(B), whether a given cash purchase is truly "related" to a later exchange of stock requires further consideration by the Tax Court, as does the question of the application of those factors in the present case. We therefore will remand this case to the Tax court for further proceedings on the question raised by the taxpayers' first argument in support of their motion for summary judgment.

* * *[17]

III.

A.

Having summarized in advance our holdings, and its intended scope, we shall now revert to the beginning of our analysis, and, in the remainder

17. We do not intend to dictate to the Tax Court what legal standard it should apply in determining whether these transactions are related. We would suggest, however, that the possibilities should include at least the following; perhaps others may be developed by counsel or by the Tax Court itself.

One possibility advanced by the taxpayers is that the only transaction which should be considered related, and so parts of "the acquisition," are those which are included in the formal plan or reorganization adopted by the two corporations. The virtues of this approach—simplicity and clarity—may be outweighed by the considerable scope it would grant the parties to a reorganization to control the tax treatment of their formal plan of reorganization by arbitrarily including or excluding certain transactions. A second possibility—urged by the Commissioner—is that all transactions sharing a single acquisition purpose should be considered related for purposes of Section 368(a)(1)(B). Relying on an example given in the legislative history, *see* S.Rep.No. 1622, 83d Cong., 2d Sess. 273, *reprinted in* (1954) U.S. Code Cong. & Admin. News, pp. 4621, 4911 (hereinafter cited as *1954 Senate Report*), the Commissioner would require a complete and thoroughgoing separation, both in time and purpose, between cash and stock acquisitions before the latter would qualify for reorganization treatment under subsection (B).

A third possible approach, lying somewhere between the other two, would be to focus on the mutual knowledge and intent of the corporate parties, so that one party could not suffer adverse tax consequences from unilateral activities of the other of which former had no notice. * * * Such a rule would prevent, for example, the situation where the acquiree's shareholders expect to receive favorable tax treatment on an exchange offer, only to learn later than an apparently valid (B) reorganization has been nullified by anonymous cash purchases on the part of the acquiring corporation. * * *

of this opinion, describe the thinking by which we reached the result just announced. We begin with the words of the statute itself. The reorganization definitions contained in Section 368(a)(1) are precise, technical, and comprehensive. They were intended to define the exclusive means which nontaxable corporate reorganizations could be effected. In examining the language of the (B) provision, we discern two possible meanings. On the one hand, the statute could be read to say that a successful reorganization occurs whenever Corporation X exchanges its own voting stock for stock in Corporation Y, and, immediately after the transaction, Corporation X controls more than 80 percent of Y's stock. On this reading, purchases of shares for which any part of the consideration takes the form of "boot" should be ignored, since the definition is only concerned with transactions which meet the statutory requirements as to consideration and control. To take an example, if Corporation X bought 50 percent of the shares of Y, and then almost immediately exchanged part of its voting stock for the remaining 50 percent of Y's stock, the question would arise whether the second transaction was a (B) reorganization. Arguably, the statute can be read to support such a finding. In the second transaction, X exchanged only stock for stock (meeting the "solely" requirement), and after the transaction was completed X owned Y (meeting the "control" requirement).

The alternative reading of the statute and the one which we are persuaded to adopt treats the (B) definition as prescriptive, rather than merely descriptive. We read the statute to mean that the entire transaction which constitutes "the acquisition" must not contain any nonstock consideration if the transaction is to qualify as a (B) reorganization. In the example given above, where X acquired 100 percent of Y's stock, half for cash and half for voting stock, we would interpret "the acquisition" as referring to the entire transaction, so that the "solely for . . . voting stock" requirement would not be met. We believe if Congress had intended the statute to be read as merely descriptive, this intent would have been more clearly spelled out in the statutory language.

We recognize that the Tax Court adopted neither of these two readings. * * * [T]he Tax Court purported to limit its holding to cases, such as this one, where more than 80 percent of the stock of Corporation Y passes to Corporation X in exchange solely for voting stock. The Tax Court presumably would assert that the 50/50 hypothetical posited above can be distinguished from this case, and that its holding implies no view as to the hypothetical. * * * In order to distinguish the 80 percent case from the 50 percent case, it is necessary to read "the acquisition" as referring to at least the amount of stock constituting "control" (80 percent) where related cash purchases are present. Yet the Tax Court recognized that "the acquisition" cannot always refer to the conveyance of an 80 percent bloc of

Difficulties suggest themselves with each of these rules, and without benefit of thorough briefing and argument, as well as an informed decision by the lower court, we are reluctant to proceed further in exploring this issue. We leave to the Tax Court the task of breaking ground here.

stock in one transaction, since to do so would frustrate the intent of the 1954 amendments to permit so-called "creeping acquisitions."[19]

The Tax Court's interpretation of the statute suffers from a more fundamental defect, as well. In order to justify the limitation of its holding to transactions involving 80 percent or more of the acquiree's stock, the Tax Court focused on the *passage* of control as the primary requirement of the (B) provision. This focus is misplaced. Under the present version of the statute, the *passage* of control is entirely irrelevant; the only material requirement is that the acquiring corporation *have* control immediately after the acquisition. As the statute explicitly states, it does not matter if the acquiring corporation already has control before the transaction begins, so long as such control exists at the completion of the reorganization. * * *

B.

[The court next reviewed the history leading up to Section 368(a)(1)(B).] * * *

As this history shows, Congress has had conflicting aims in this complex and difficult area. * * * At best, we think Congress has drawn somewhat arbitrary lines separating those transactions that resemble mere changes in form of ownership and those that contain elements of a sale or purchase arrangement. In such circumstances we believe it is more appropriate to examine the specific rules and requirements Congress enacted, rather than some questionably delineated "purpose" or "policy," to determine whether a particular transaction qualifies for favorable tax treatment.

To the extent there is any indication in the legislative history of Congress' intent with respect to the meaning of "acquisition" in the (B) provision, we believe the intent plainly was to apply the "solely" requirement to all related transactions. In those statutes where Congress intended to permit cash or other property to be used as consideration, it made explicit provision therefore. *See, e.g.,* 26 U.S.C. § 368(a)(2)(B). * * *

C.

Besides finding support for the IRS position both in the design of the statute and in the legislative history, we find support in the regulations adopted by the Treasury Department construing these statutory provisions. * * *

D.

Finally, we turn to the body of case law that has developed concerning (B) reorganizations to determine how previous courts have dealt with this

19. * * * In the typical creeping acquisition situation, Corporation X acquires a portion of Corporation Y's stock, let us say 40 percent, for cash or other nonstock consideration. If (B) reorganizations were limited to those encompassing 80 percent or more of Y's stock in one transaction, X would thereafter be barred, as a practical matter, from acquiring the remainder of Y's shares in a tax-free (B) reorganization. The 1954 Code, however, clearly permits X to trade voting stock for 40 percent or more of Y's remaining stock so long as the stock acquisition is sufficiently separated from the prior cash purchase. *See 1954 Senate Report, supra* note 17 at 273. In these circumstances, therefore, "the acquisition" must be interpreted as referring to an amount of stock less than 80 percent. * * *

question. Of the seven prior cases in this area, all to a greater or lesser degree support the result we have reached, and none supports the result reached by the Tax Court.

* * *

Our reading of the statute is reinforced by another more recent circuit decision as well. In *Mills v. Commissioner,* 331 F.2d 321 (5th Cir.1964), *rev'g,* 39 T.C. 393 (1962), the issue was whether cash payments for fractional shares in an exchange prevented a nontaxable reorganization. General Gas Corporation, the acquiror, offered the three taxpayers, sole stockholders in three small gas corporations, shares of General common stock in exchange for all of their stock. The number of General shares to be exchanged at a value of $14 per share was to be determined by measuring the net book value of the three small corporations. In the event the purchase price was not evenly divisible by 14, cash was to be paid in lieu of fractional shares. As a result, each taxpayer received 1,595 shares of General stock and $27.36 in cash. The Tax Court held this transaction invalid as a tax-free reorganization, declining to adopt a *de minimis* rule. * * * The Fifth Circuit agreed that cash could not form any part of the consideration in a(B) reorganization, but concluded in reversing the Tax Court that the fractional-share arrangement was merely a bookkeeping convenience and not an independent part of the consideration. * * *

* * * Thus, in the only case raising the issue now before us under the 1954 Code, the Tax Court accepted as a premise that no cash was permissible as consideration in a (B) reorganization, even where the facts showed that control had passed solely for voting stock.

IV.

* * *

Finally, we see no merit at all in the suggestion that we should permit "boot" in a (B) reorganization simply because "boot" is permitted in some instances in (A) and (C) reorganizations. Congress has never indicated that these three distinct categories of transactions are to be interpreted in pari materia. In fact, striking differences in the treatment of the three subsections have been evident in the history of the reorganization statutes.

* * *

Vacated and remanded.

NOTES

1. Section 368(a)(1)(B) grants "reorganization" status—and, hence, tax-free treatment to the exchanging shareholders by virtue of Section 354(a)—to certain sale of stock transactions (known as "B" reorganizations). As the court explains, the section contains two requirements for this treatment: (1) the company purchasing stock must have control of the target company immediately after the acquisition; and (2) the purchasing company must pay for the stock solely with its voting shares.

Notice, these two requirements parallel the two prerequisites under Section 368(a)(1)(C) for a tax-free sale of assets transaction. Instead of demanding acquisition of substantially all assets of the target, now, as befits the different nature of the transaction, the statute demands the purchaser end up holding a controlling interest in the target's stock. The definition of having control immediately after the transaction is familiar from the earlier exploration of Section 351. Here, as with Section 351, one must look to the 80 percent test under Section 368(c). Moreover, as with Section 351, the buyer need not acquire 80 percent in this transaction; it may have owned shares before. In fact, acquisition of stock by a company already holding a controlling amount can be a reorganization under this provision. In this regard, the focus of the requirement is somewhat different from the substantially all assets test under Section 368(a)(1)(C), since Section 368(a)(1)(B) does not concern itself with how much stock the purchaser acquires in the transaction at issue, but only with how much the buyer owns immediately after.

Again, like the tax-free asset sale, the allowed consideration is solely voting stock. For a "B" reorganization, however, the statute does not carve out the two exceptions existing for "C" reorganizations. To begin with, it does not expressly call for disregarding the assumption of the target's liabilities. This may be explainable because there is no reason typically for the buyer to assume the target's liabilities in a sale of stock transaction. More significantly, even if the buyer did assume the target's liabilities, the assumption normally would be irrelevant to the solely for voting stock requirement (without the statute needing to say so) because it is not part of the consideration flowing in exchange for the acquired shares. *E.g.,* Rev. Rul. 69–142, 1969–1 C.B. 107. On the other hand, might there be situations in which the selling shareholders benefit from the buyer's assumption of the target's debts? For example, what would happen if any of the selling shareholders had personally guaranteed some of the liabilities assumed? *Compare* Rev. Rul. 79–89, 1979–1 C.B. 152 (contribution of cash to the target by the acquiring company, in order for the target to pay off a debt guaranteed by a selling stockholder, did not, when it was not a condition of the share exchange, contravene the solely for voting stock requirement), *with* Rev. Rul. 79–4, 1979–1 C.B. 150 (payment of target's debt held to be impermissible boot when shareholder-guarantor was the real debtor). Alternately, suppose some of the selling shareholders also own debt securities in the target; can the buyer exchange new debt securities for the outstanding securities, without the I.R.S. taking the position that the exchange constituted additional consideration for the stock? See Rev. Rul. 98–10, 1998–1 C.B. 643 (divergence in the ownership of the debt securities and the ownership of the target's stock was evidence that the exchange of debt securities was not a disguised attempt to get boot to the shareholders in exchange for their shares). Along similar lines, the acquirer can pay the target's reorganization expenses, but not those incurred by the selling stockholders (unless they are "solely and directly related to the reorganization"). Rev. Rul. 73–54, 1973–1 C.B. 187. One problem, however, with concluding that the assumption of the target's liabilities does not violate the solely for voting stock requirement because this is not part of acquiring the target's stock is to create the basis for an argument that such an assumption (or the exchange of the target's outstanding securities for securities of the acquirer) is also not part of a "B" reorganization for purposes of being tax-free under Sections 354(a) and 357(a). After taking this position for many years (*see, e.g.,* Rev. Rul. 70–41, 1970–1 C.B. 77), the Internal Revenue Service now concedes that the exchange of securities can be part of the plan of a B reorganization and so potentially tax-free under Sections 354(a) and 357(a). Rev. Rul. 98–10, 1998–1 C.B. 643.

A more significant difference from Section 368(a)(1)(C) is that Section 368(a)(1)(B) lacks an accompanying provision allowing the payment of any boot. In *Chapman,* the Tax Court had created a self-help equivalent by interpreting Section 368(a)(1)(B) to only require that the buyer purchase the requisite controlling amount of shares solely in exchange for its voting stock, but allowing the buyer to purchase other shares, which were not needed to meet the control requirement, in exchange for boot. The First Circuit rejected this approach, as did the Third Circuit on a case arising out of the same facts. *Heverly v. Commissioner,* 621 F.2d 1227 (3d Cir.1980).

This absolutely no boot rule creates a number of problems, one of which the facts in *Chapman* illustrate. It makes it hazardous any time toehold share purchases for cash precede an attempt at a tax-free sale of stock transaction. Recall, under the *Bausch & Lomb* decision, even as modified by the recent regulation discussed earlier, toehold share purchases also threaten the availability of tax-free sale of assets treatment. This may make a statutory merger the only safe approach for a tax-free transaction following such purchases. Alternately, if the earlier share purchases are not part of the same transaction as the acquisition of the controlling stock, then the solely for voting stock requirement may not thwart tax-free treatment of the later exchange. Treas. Reg. § 1.368–2(c). This was the issue the court remanded for further trial. Regrettably, from the standpoint of later readers, the Court of Appeals did not resolve what standard the Tax Court should use in determining whether earlier purchases were part of the same transaction. This litigation yielded no further guidance on the issue, as IT & T settled the matter by paying tax on behalf of the various exchanging stockholders. Keep in mind also that the single transaction issue can serve to extend tax-free treatment, rather than just destroy it. Earlier purchases made in exchange for voting stock in the buyer can become tax-free if treated as part of the reorganization with later purchases for voting stock which put the buyer over the 80 percent mark. *See* Treas. Reg. § 1.368–2(c) (treating the purchases as part of the reorganization when made within a relatively short time, such as one year).

Finally, note one other difference from the prerequisites for a tax-free sale of assets transaction. There is no requirement for the target to liquidate following the acquisition of stock.

2. The solely for voting stock requirement creates a number of problems beyond the hazard presented by toehold share purchases (as in *Chapman*). Another concern involves how to deal with fractional shares. Any time the

share exchange is not on a one-for-one basis, or does not otherwise involve receipt of an even multiple of voting stock in the buyer for each share in the target, some of the selling stockholders may be entitled to receive a fraction of a share. (By way of comparison, in a "C" reorganization, presumably the buyer and seller can agree upon a price for the target company's assets which does not require transfer to the target of less than a whole number of shares. Of course, the need to deal with fractional rights may arise when the selling company liquidates and distributes the stock in the buyer to the seller's stockholders. Even then, however, the seller could easily solve the problem by, for instance, retaining a small amount of property to cash out the fractional rights.)

Handling fractional rights in a share exchange could entail giving the selling stockholders scrip representing the fractional shares. (The recipients can then buy and sell the scrip in order to put together enough to trade for whole shares.) Generally, such scrip does not have voting rights, and, therefore, would not seem to be voting stock. *See, e.g.,* Cal. Corp. Code § 407; Del. Gen. Corp. Law § 155; N.Y. Bus. Corp. Law § 509(c); M.B.C.A. § 6.04(c). Nevertheless, the Service allows its use without violating the solely for voting stock requirement. Rev. Rul. 55–59, 1955–1 C.B. 35. Alternately, many times it may be more convenient from both the buying company's and the recipient stockholders' standpoints for the buyer to pay cash in lieu of fractional shares. Clearly, such cash is not voting stock. Despite this fact, the *Mills* decision, discussed in *Chapman,* allowed the payment of cash in lieu of fractional shares. The Service has acquiesced in this result, so long as the cash is not a separately bargained for consideration. Rev. Rul. 66–365, 1966–2 C.B. 116.

3. A more serious problem with the solely for voting stock requirement comes from the common desire to create a flexible or contingent price arrangement along the lines outlined earlier in this chapter. This desire may exist in a sale of assets transaction because of uncertainty as to how much the purchased business will earn in the future. It becomes more pressing in the sale of stock transaction, because the buyer then also picks up the risk of having the value of its purchased stock diminish due to unknown liabilities—the assumption of which it may exclude in a sale of assets. *But see Ramirez v. Amsted Industries,* reprinted earlier in this chapter. To deal with this uncertainty, a buyer may agree to pay the selling stockholders a certain amount of its stock immediately, and more stock in the future if the business performs as expected or no additional liabilities turn up. Alternately, the buyer may pay the full price immediately, but demand some of the shares it pays go into an escrow to be returned to it should earnings or liabilities not turn out as promised. At one time, the Internal Revenue Service took the position that the promise of additional shares in the future (or the release of stock from escrow in the future) constituted consideration other than voting stock. After the courts rebuffed the Service in this view (*e.g., Carlberg v. United States,* 281 F.2d 507 (8th Cir.1960)), the I.R.S. conceded that such arrangements will not automatically destroy tax-free treatment. The Service has provided the following criteria for when it will give an advance ruling favorable to contingent or escrow arrangements:

Revenue Procedure 84–42

1984–1, C.B. 521.

* * *

.01 Section 3.03 of Rev.Proc. 77–37 is amplified to read as follows:

In transactions under sections 368(a)(1)(A), 368(a)(1)(B), 368(a)(1)(C), 368(a)(1)(D), 368(a)(1)(E), and 351 of the Code, it is not necessary that all the stock which is to be issued in exchange for the requisite stock or property, be issued immediately provided (1) that all the stock will be issued within 5 years from the date of transfer of assets or stock for reorganizations under sections 368(a)(1)(A), 368(a)(1)(C), 368(a)(1)(D), and 368(a)(1)(E), or within 5 years from the date of the initial distribution in the case of transactions under sections 368(a)(1)(B) and 351; (2) there is a valid business reason for not issuing all the stock immediately, such as difficulty in determining the value of one or both of the corporations involved in the transaction; (3) the maximum number of shares which may be issued in the exchange is stated; (4) at least 50 percent of the maximum number of shares of each class of stock which may be issued is issued in the initial distribution; (5) the agreement evidencing the right to receive stock in the future prohibits assignment (except by operation of law) or if the agreement does not prohibit assignment, the right must not be evidenced by negotiable certificates of any kind and must not be readily marketable; (6) such right can give rise to the receipt only of additional stock of the corporation making the underlying distribution; (7) such stock issuance will not be triggered by an event the occurrence or nonoccurrence of which is within the control of shareholders; (8) such stock issuance will not be triggered by the payment of additional tax or reduction in tax paid as a result of a Service audit of the shareholders or the corporation either (a) with respect to the reorganization or section 351 transaction in which the contingent stock will be issued, or (b) when the reorganization or section 351 transaction in which the contingent stock will be issued involves persons related within the meaning of section 267(c)(4) of the Code; and (9) the mechanism for the calculation of the additional stock to be issued is objective and readily ascertainable. Stock issued as compensation, royalties or any other consideration other than in exchange for stock or assets will not be considered to have been received in the exchange. Until the final distribution of the total number of shares of stock to be issued in the exchange is made, the interim basis of the stock of the issuing corporation received in the exchange by the shareholders (not including that portion of each share representing interest) will be determined, pursuant to section 358(a), as though the maximum number of shares to be issued (not including that portion of each share representing interest) has been received by the shareholders.

* * *

.02 Section 3.06 of Rev.Proc. 77–37 is amplified to read as follows:

In transactions under sections 368(a)(1)(A), 368(a)(1)(B), 368(a)(1)(C), 368(a)(1)(D), 368(a)(1)(E), and 351 of the Code, a portion of the stock issued in exchange for the requisite stock or property may be placed in escrow by the exchanging shareholders, or may be made subject to a condition pursuant to the agreement, or plan of reorganization or of the transaction, for possible return to the issuing corporation under specified conditions provided (1) there is a valid business reason for establishing the arrangement; (2) the stock subject to such arrangement appears as issued and outstanding on the balance sheet of the issuing corporation and such stock is legally outstanding under applicable state law; (3) all dividends paid on such stock will be distributed currently to the exchanging shareholders; (4) all voting rights of such stock (if any) are exercisable by or on behalf of the shareholders or their authorized agent; (5) no shares of such stock are subject to restrictions requiring their return to the issuing corporation because of death, failure to continue employment, or similar restrictions; (6) all such stock is released from the arrangement within 5 years from the date of consummation of the transaction (except where there is a bona fide dispute as to whom the stock should be released); (7) at least 50 percent of the number of shares of each class of stock issued initially to the shareholders (exclusive of shares of stock to be issued at a later date as described in .01 above) is not subject to the arrangement; (8) the return of stock will not be triggered by an event the occurrence or nonoccurrence of which is within the control of shareholders; (9) the return of stock will not be triggered by the payment of additional tax or reduction in tax paid as a result of a Service audit of the shareholders or the corporation either (a) with respect to the reorganization or section 351 transaction in which the escrowed stock will be issued, or (b) when the reorganization or section 351 transaction in which the escrowed stock will be issued involves persons related within the meaning of section 267(c)(4) of the Code; and (10) the mechanism for the calculation of the number of shares of stock to be returned is objective and readily ascertainable.

* * *

One difference in the tax impact between a contingent promise of additional shares and an escrow arrangement relates to the taxation of the unstated interest presumably exacted whenever a person agrees to accept delayed payment without receiving market rate interest expressly in return. Prior to 1984, it was clear that Section 483 imposed a tax upon such imputed interest in contingent stock arrangements. *E.g.,* Treas. Reg. § 1.483–1(b)(6) Ex. (7). (This imputed interest does not constitute disqualifying boot, however.) As a result of amendments in 1984, it may be that this hidden interest element will now face tax instead under the original issue discount provisions of Sections 1273–1275. (As discussed in Chapter IV, the difference is one of timing of recognition.) In either event, this recognition will not apply to an escrow arrangement in which the selling stockholders can vote and receive dividends on the escrowed shares while the stock is in escrow. Rev. Rul. 70–120, 1970–1 C.B. 124. On the other hand, suppose escrowed shares increase in value before termination of the escrow. Can this lead to any recognition? It can if the agreement measures the obligation of the selling stockholders to give up escrowed shares (for example, because of the discovery of additional liabilities) based upon the value of the escrowed stock at the time of surrender, rather than the value at the time of the original transaction. *Compare* Rev. Rul. 78–376, 1978–2 C.B. 149, *with* Rev. Rul. 76–42, 1976–1 C.B. 102.

Finally, note that warrants (options to buy additional shares) constitute prohibited boot. *E.g., Helvering v. Southwest Consolidated Corp.,* 315 U.S. 194 (1942). On the other hand, suppose that the purchasing corporation exchanges new warrants for outstanding warrants in the target corporation, rather than in exchange for stock in the target. The fact that such warrants do not constitute voting stock does not matter in this case, because Section 368(a)(1)(B) is only concerned with what the target's shareholders receive for their shares. (Recall the same point in the earlier discussion regarding the assumption of the target's debts by the buyer in a "B" reorganization.) Moreover, not only will such a warrant exchange not spoil the "B" reorganization for those exchanging stock, the warrant exchange itself can be tax-free. *See* Treas. Reg. § 1.354–1(e) (warrants issued by a party to a reorganization constitute "securities" for purposes of Section 354(a), with a principal amount of zero); Rev. Rul. 98–10, 1998–1 C.B. 643 (exchange of new for outstanding warrants during a "B" reorganization can be part of the exchange covered by Section 354).

4. Several more fundamental difficulties exist with matching the strict confines of a "B" reorganization to the elements of an agreement which all the parties really want. Some of the target's shareholders may refuse to accept consideration other than cash. At the same time, the buyer may face a practical limit on how many voting shares it can issue, because of concerns with diluting the control of its current owners. The buyer also may not desire all of the target's assets. Perhaps transactions between the target and its shareholders, either preliminary to or following the exchange of shares with the buyer, can help meet these goals. In this regard, recall the discussion earlier of bootstrap transactions by the target. Alternately, perhaps shareholders wishing cash could sell the voting stock they receive. Reconsider this last avenue after exploring the judicially imposed continuity of interest requirement for reorganization treatment.

(v) The Statutory Merger

J.E. Seagram Corp. v. Commissioner of Internal Revenue

104 T.C. 75 (1995).

[This opinion arose out of an unsuccessful effort by J.E. Seagram (referred to in the opinion as JES) to take over Conoco, Inc. (Conoco).]

* * *

On June 25, 1981, JES Holdings, Inc. (JES Tenderor), a wholly owned subsidiary of JES, initiated a tender offer for the purchase of up to 35 million shares (40.76 percent of the 85,864,538 shares outstanding on such date) of Conoco for $73 per share (the JES Tender Offer).

* * *

On June 30, 1981, the Conoco board of directors recommended that Conoco shareholders reject the JES Tender Offer on the ground that it was not "in the best interests of [Conoco] and its subsidiaries."

* * *

On June 24, 1981, Edward G. Jefferson, chairman and chief executive officer of E.I. DuPont de Nemours and Co. (DuPont), called [Ralph] Bailey [the Chairman and CEO of Conoco] to determine whether there was any constructive role DuPont might play in light of public reports [of the JES tender offer]. * * * Beginning on June 28, 1981, Conoco and DuPont representatives discussed a possible merger.

On July 6, 1981, DuPont Holdings, Inc. (DuPont Tenderor), a wholly owned subsidiary of DuPont, signed an agreement with Conoco (the DuPont/Conoco Agreement or, alternatively, the Agreement). The DuPont/Conoco Agreement provided that DuPont Tenderor would offer (the DuPont Tender Offer) to exchange for each share of Conoco common stock at least either (i) 1.6 shares of DuPont common stock, or (ii) $87.50 in cash. The Agreement also provided that "As promptly as practicable following the consummation or termination of the Offer, * * * [Conoco] shall be merged into * * * [DuPont Tenderor] in accordance with the Delaware General Corporation Law" (the Merger) and DuPont Tenderor would thereby acquire any Conoco shares not acquired in the tender offer.

* * *

On July 12, 1981, JES Tenderor increased its tender offer to include the purchase of up to 44,350,000 Conoco shares (slightly over 51 percent of the outstanding Conoco shares not already owned by JES) and increased its offering price from $73 to $85 in cash per Conoco common share. * * *

On July 14, 1981, DuPont Tenderor announced an increase in the cash price of its tender offer from $87.50 to $95 per Conoco common share and in the number of shares of DuPont common stock offered from 1.6 to 1.7 shares per Conoco share.

* * *

On July 23, 1981, JES Tenderor increased its tender offer price from $85 to $92 in cash per Conoco common share. * * *

On August 1, 1981, at 1:00 p.m., the withdrawal rights with respect to shares tendered to JES expired. Immediately thereafter, JES Tenderor began buying tendered Conoco shares. As of midnight on August 1, 1981, JES Tenderor had received tenders of more than 15,500,000 Conoco shares.

* * *

At midnight on August 4, 1981, the withdrawal period for shares tendered to DuPont Tenderor expired. On August 5, 1981, DuPont Tenderor began purchasing Conoco common shares tendered for cash. A press release issued on that day stated that

> The DuPont Company has been tendered a significant majority of the outstanding shares of Conoco Inc., and will move forward as rapidly as possible to effect a merger of the two companies.

* * *

On August 7, 1981, the JES Tender Offer expired with approximately 28 million Conoco shares (32 percent of the Conoco shares outstanding at the commencement of the DuPont Tender Offer) having been tendered to JES Tenderor for cash at $92 per share. JES Tenderor ultimately purchased 24,625,750 shares of Conoco for $92 per share and 3,113,025 shares for $91.35 per share, with an aggregate cost of $2,557,738,302.25.

* * *

A press release dated August 11, 1981, announced that the board of directors of [JES's parent corporation] had authorized the exchange of the Conoco shares held by JES Tenderor pursuant to the terms of the DuPont Tender Offer. The release quoted JES chairman and chief executive officer Edgar Bronfman as stating:

> This is an appropriate time to congratulate the management and Board of DuPont on the success of their offer for Conoco. While Seagram would have been delighted to have won 51 percent of Conoco, we are pleased at the prospect of becoming a large stockholder of the combined DuPont and Conoco. We believe it will be a very strong company, with a fine future.

On August 17, 1981, JES Tenderor tendered its shares of Conoco in exchange for shares of DuPont common stock on the basis of an exchange ratio of 1.7 shares of DuPont for each Conoco share.

* * *

On September 30, 1981, Conoco merged into DuPont Tenderor. The Merger was approved by a shareholder vote in which 99,100,246 Conoco shares (97 percent) were voted in favor and 89,889 Conoco shares (less than 0.1 percent) were voted against the Merger. The 5,491,896 Conoco shares (6 percent of the shares outstanding at the commencement of the DuPont Tender Offer) not tendered were exchanged for DuPont stock pursuant to the Merger.

* * *

DuPont treated the tender offer and merger as a tax-free reorganization for Federal income tax purposes and filed its tax return for its 1981 taxable year accordingly. DuPont and Conoco advised former Conoco shareholders who had exchanged their stock for DuPont stock in either the exchange portion of the tender offer or the merger that they had no taxable gain or loss.

When the dust had settled at the completion of the Conoco–DuPont merger on September 30, 1981, approximately 78 percent of the Conoco stock had changed hands for cash pursuant to the competing JES and DuPont tender offers, yet approximately 54 percent of the Conoco equity * * * remained in corporate solution in the form of DuPont shares received in exchange for Conoco shares.

Petitioner tendered each share of Conoco stock, for which it had paid about $92 per share, in exchange for 1.7 shares of DuPont stock, each share of which had a mean market value on the August 17, 1981, tender date of about $43 or approximately $73.10 for each 1.7 share unit.

* * *

The amount of the loss petitioner claims to have realized (whether or not recognizable) upon the exchange of Conoco stock for DuPont stock was $530,410,896.

Discussion

The ultimate issue for decision is whether, for tax purposes, petitioner had a recognized loss upon the exchange of its Conoco stock for DuPont stock. Whether such a loss is to be recognized depends upon the effect to be given section 354(a)(1) under the above facts. Section 354(a)(1) provides:

> SEC. 354. EXCHANGES OF STOCK AND SECURITIES IN CERTAIN REORGANIZATIONS.
>
> (a) General Rule.—
>
> (1) In General.—No gain or loss shall be recognized if stock or securities in a corporation a party to a reorganization are, in pursuance of the plan of reorganization, exchanged solely for stock or securities in such corporation or in another corporation a party to the reorganization.

* * *

In form, at least, DuPont's acquisition of Conoco (during the course of which petitioner effected the aforementioned exchange) was what the commentators Bittker and Eustice have called a "creeping multistep merger"; that is, a merger which is in their words "the culminating step in a series of acquisition transactions, all looking to the ultimate absorption of the target company's properties when control has been obtained by the acquiring corporation." Bittker & Eustice, Federal Income Taxation of Corporations and Shareholders, par. 14.12.3, at 14–35 (Fifth ed. 1987).

* * *

Section 368(a) provides in relevant part:

SEC. 368. (a) REORGANIZATION.—

(1) In General.—For purposes of parts I and II and this part, the term "reorganization" means—

(A) A statutory merger or consolidation;

* * *

(2) Special Rules Relating To Paragraph (1).—

* * *

(D) Use Of Stock Of Controlling Corporation In Paragraph (1)(A) and (1)(G) Cases.—The acquisition by one corporation, in exchange for stock of a corporation (referred to in this subparagraph as "controlling corporation") which is in control of the acquiring corporation, of substantially all of the properties of another corporation shall not disqualify a transaction under paragraph (1)(A) or (1)(G) if—

(I) no stock of the acquiring corporation is used in the transaction, and

(ii) in the case of a transaction under paragraph (1)(A), such transaction would have qualified under paragraph (1)(A) had the merger been into the controlling corporation.

Section 1.368–2(g), Income Tax Regs., provides:

(g) The term "plan of reorganization" has reference to a consummated transaction specifically defined as a reorganization under section 368(a). The term is not to be construed as broadening the definition of "reorganization" as set forth in section 368(a), but is to be taken as limiting the nonrecognition of gain or loss to such exchanges or distributions as are directly a part of the transaction specifically described as a reorganization in section 368(a). Moreover, the transaction, or series of transactions, embraced in a plan of reorganization must not only come within the specific language of section 368(a), but the readjustments involved in the exchanges or distributions effected in the consummation thereof must be undertaken for reasons germane to the continuance of the business of a corporation a party to the reorganization. Section 368(a) contemplates genuine corporate reorganizations which are designed to effect a readjustment of continuing interests under modified corporate forms.

There appears to be no dispute that the merger of Conoco into DuPont Tenderor complied with the requirements of Delaware law, thus meeting the description of a "reorganization" in section 368(a)(1)(A) in that there was a "statutory merger or consolidation", and that the exchange of DuPont common stock by DuPont Tenderor for Conoco common stock fits within the provisions of section 368(a)(2)(D). Petitioner maintains, however, that the exchange of its Conoco common stock for DuPont common stock was not done in pursuance of a plan of reorganization, as required by section 354, and that therefore a loss is to be recognized on the exchange.

* * * Simply stated, petitioner claims that DuPont's tender offer and the subsequent merger squeezing out the remaining Conoco shareholders were separate and independent transactions. Consequently, petitioner argues that the exchange of Conoco stock for DuPont stock pursuant to DuPont's tender offer rather than pursuant to the merger could not have been in pursuance of a plan of reorganization, as section 354 requires.

* * *

The concept of "plan of reorganization", as described in section 1.368–2(g), Income Tax Regs., quoted above, is one of substantial elasticity. * * * One commentator has stated that

> The courts, and the Service where it has served its purposes, have adopted a functional approach to the problem that is undoubtedly consistent with congressional intent. They have held that a plan of reorganization is a series of transactions intended to accomplish a transaction described as a reorganization in section 368, regardless of how and in what form the plan is expressed and whether the parties intended tax-free treatment. * * * [Faber, "The Use and Misuse of the Plan of Reorganization Concept," 38 Tax L.Rev. 515, 523 (1982–1983).]

The DuPont/Conoco Agreement was the definitive vehicle spelling out the interrelated steps by which DuPont would acquire 100 percent of Conoco's stock. To explain the mechanics of the type of procedure utilized by DuPont and Conoco, respondent submitted an "Expert Affidavit" of Bernard S. Black [a professor of law at Columbia University]. * * *

In the affidavit, Professor Black states that

> In substance, DuPont's bid for Conoco was a minor variant on a standard two-step acquisition, in which the parties sign a merger agreement that contemplates a first-step cash tender offer, to be followed by a second-step merger. The parties to an acquisition often use this transaction form, rather than a single-step merger (without a tender offer), because a tender offer can close faster than a merger, which increases the likelihood that the acquisition will be completed.

* * *

Professor Black goes on to observe that "DuPont added a third step to this transaction form—an exchange offer of DuPont stock for Conoco stock."

The DuPont/Conoco Agreement, which definitively states the terms for "the acquisition of [Conoco] by [DuPont Tenderor] (and thus by DuPont)", sets out the steps referred to by Professor Black in his affidavit—the series of transactions which in their totality were intended to accomplish a section 368 reorganization.

* * *

Petitioner argues that DuPont had a "plan" to engage in a series of transactions that might "ultimately may include a reorganization," but not a "plan of reorganization". For reasons already discussed, we disagree. We hold that, because DuPont was contractually committed to undertake and complete the second step merger once it had undertaken and completed the first step tender offer, these carefully integrated transactions together constituted a plan of reorganization within the contemplation of section 354(a).

Petitioner also argues that even if the DuPont tender offer and merger were to be treated as an integrated transaction, the merger does not qualify as a reorganization because it fails the "continuity of interest" requirement.

In *Penrod v. Commissioner*, [88 T.C.] at 1427–1428, we stated that

> It is well settled that, in addition to meeting specific statutory requirements, a reorganization under section 368(a)(1)(A) must also satisfy the continuity of interest doctrine. See sec. 1.368–1(b), Income Tax Regs. * * * Because the reorganization provisions are based on the premise that the shareholders of an acquired corporation have not terminated their economic investment, but have merely altered its form, the continuity of interest doctrine limits the favorable nonrecognition treatment enjoyed by reorganizations to those situations in which (1) the nature of the consideration received by the acquired corporation or its shareholders confers a proprietary stake in the ongoing enterprise, and (2) the proprietary interest received is definite and material and represents a substantial part of the value of the property transferred. * * *

On the date of the Conoco/DuPont Agreement, July 6, 1981, there were approximately 85,991,896 Conoco shares outstanding. Petitioner is essentially arguing that because it acquired approximately 32 percent of these shares for cash pursuant to its own tender offer, and DuPont acquired approximately 46 percent of these shares for cash pursuant to its tender offer, the combined 78 percent of Conoco shares acquired for cash after the date of the Agreement destroyed the continuity of interest requisite for a valid reorganization. We think petitioner's argument, and the logic that supports it, miss the mark.

Pursuant to its two-step tender offer/merger plan of reorganization, DuPont acquired approximately 54 percent of the "initial" 85,991,896 shares of Conoco stock in exchange for DuPont stock, which included petitioner's recently acquired Conoco shares that it tendered pursuant to DuPont's tender offer. If the 54 percent had been acquired by DuPont from Conoco shareholders in a "one-step" merger-type acquisition, there would be little argument that continuity of interest had been satisfied. Sec. 368(a)(1)(A).

In *Helvering v. Minnesota Tea Co.*, 296 U.S. 378 (1935), the Supreme Court held that an equity interest in the transferee equal to about 56 percent of the value of the transferor's assets was adequate. In *John A. Nelson Co. v. Helvering*, 296 U.S. 374 (1935), the Supreme Court considered 38–percent equity continuity to be sufficient. For advance ruling purposes, the IRS considers a 50–percent equity continuity of interest, by value, to be sufficient. Rev. Proc. 77–37, 1977–2 C.B. 568. On the other hand, the United States Court of Appeals for the Fifth Circuit has held that a 16.4–percent continuing common stock interest, representing less than one percent of the total consideration (consisting of cash, bonds, and common stock) paid by the acquiring corporation, did not evidence sufficient continuity of interest to bring a transaction within the requirements of the predecessor of section 368(a)(1)(A). *Southwest Natural Gas Co. v. Commissioner*, 189 F.2d 332 (1951), affg. 14 T.C. 81 (1950).

* * *

The parties stipulated that petitioner and DuPont, through their wholly owned subsidiaries, were acting independently of one another and pursuant to competing tender offers. Furthermore, there is of course nothing in the record to suggest any prearranged understanding between petitioner and DuPont that petitioner would tender the Conoco stock purchased for cash if petitioner by means of its own tender offer failed to achieve control of Conoco. Consequently, it cannot be argued that petitioner, although not a party to the reorganization, was somehow acting in concert with DuPont, which was a party to the reorganization. If such had been the case, the reorganization would fail because petitioner's cash purchases of Conoco stock could be attributed to DuPont, thereby destroying continuity.

The cases cited by petitioner in support of its argument that DuPont's plan of reorganization failed for lack of continuity of interest are not germane. For example, petitioner quotes *Superior Coach of Fla., Inc. v. Commissioner*, 80 T.C. at 904, as stating that "[the continuity of interest requirement is] based upon the fundamental statutory purpose of providing for the carryover of tax attributes only if the reorganization is distinguishable from a sale." In *Superior Coach of Fla., Inc.*, the majority shareholders of P purchased all of the shares of T and merged T into P. We held that the P shareholders' acquisition of the T stock was "inextricably interwoven" with the intent to effect the merger, and since the "historic shareholders" of T retained no proprietary interest in P, the merger did not qualify as a reorganization under section 368(a)(1)(A). In other words, the reorganization failed because the majority shareholders of P were acting on its behalf when they bought the T stock for cash, and there was no continuity of interest on the part of the acquired corporation's previous shareholders. * * *

Petitioner cites *Yoc Heating Corp. v. Commissioner*, 61 T.C. 168, 177 (1973) for the proposition that continuity requires looking at shareholders "immediately prior to the inception of the series of transactions" in an integrated transaction. Again, we look at the facts: R, the acquiring corporation, purchased for cash over 85 percent of the stock of O, and then caused O to transfer its assets, subject to its liabilities, to R's wholly owned subsidiary, N. N issued one share of its stock to R in exchange for every three shares of O held by R plus cash to be paid to the minority shareholders of O.

The Commissioner argued in *Yoc Heating* that the taxpayer's series of transactions constituted a reorganization within the meaning of section 368(a)(1)(F) or, alternatively, section 368(a)(1)(D). We held, however, that the acquisition by N of O's assets constituted a purchase under the "integrated transaction" (step transaction) doctrine, rather than a reorganization under either section proposed by the Commissioner. *Id.* at 177–178. Thus *Yoc Heating's* comparison of stock ownership immediately prior and immediately after the series of transactions is perfectly appropriate to the facts of that case, where the acquiring corporation acquired control of the target for cash and then effected the corporate combination, because the shareholders of O before the acquisition by R lacked the requisite continuing interest in the affairs of O after the acquisition.

Petitioner also attempts to apply cases involving pre-arranged postacquisition sales of acquiring corporation stock by shareholders of the acquired corporation. Petitioner points out that these cases hold that a sale that was not pursuant to the plan of reorganization was fatal to continuity of interest where the sale "establish[ed an] intent to divest * * * [the old stockholders] of their proprietary interest." *Heintz v. Commissioner,* 25 T.C. 132, 143 (1955). Petitioner also cites *McDonald's Restaurants of Illinois, Inc. v. Commissioner*, 688 F.2d 520 (7th Cir.1982), revg. 76 T.C. 972 (1981), which involved a similar fact pattern and reached a result parallel with that in *Heintz.*

By citing *Heintz* and *McDonald's Restaurants of Illinois*, petitioner is attempting to draw an analogy between the post-reorganization sales of these cases and the sales by Conoco shareholders to petitioner during the course of the reorganization transactions in this case. * * *

We do not believe petitioner's analogy is appropriate, because in a case such as the one before us we must look not to the identity of the target's shareholders, but rather to what the shares represented when the reorganization was completed. In this case, a majority of the old shares of Conoco were converted to shares of DuPont in the reorganization, so that in the sense, at least, that a majority of the consideration was the acquiring corporation's stock, the test of continuity was met. In this aspect of the case step transaction and continuity questions would have arisen only had there been some preexisting intention or arrangement for the disposal of the newly acquired DuPont shares, but there were none.

Respondent points out, correctly we believe, that the concept of continuity of interest advocated by petitioner would go far toward eliminating the possibility of a tax-free reorganization of any corporation whose stock is actively traded. Because it would be impossible to track the large volume of third party transactions in the target's stock, all completed transactions would be suspect. Sales of target stock for cash after the date of the announcement of an acquisition can neither be predicted nor controlled by publicly held parties to a reorganization. A requirement that the identity of the acquired corporation's shareholders be tracked to assume a sufficient number of "historic" shareholders to satisfy some arbitrary minimal percentage receiving the acquiring corporation's stock would be completely unrealistic.

* * *

In the "integrated" transaction before us petitioner, not DuPont, "stepped into the shoes" of 32 percent of the Conoco shareholders when petitioner acquired their stock for cash via the JES competing tender offer, held the 32 percent transitorily, and immediately tendered it in exchange for DuPont stock. For present purposes, there is no material distinction between petitioner's tender of the Conoco stock and a direct tender by the "old" Conoco shareholders themselves. Thus, the requirement of continuity of interest has been met.

* * *

For the reasons stated in this Opinion, we hold that a loss cannot be recognized by petitioner on its exchange of Conoco stock for DuPont stock, made pursuant to the DuPont–Conoco plan of reorganization.

NOTES

1. Section 368(a)(1)(A) provides reorganization treatment for statutory mergers or consolidations. On its face, this type of transaction—often referred to as an "A" reorganization—seemingly allows tax-free status for any acquisition adhering to state law requirements for a merger or consolidation. *But see* Rev. Rul. 2000–5, 2000–1 C.B. 436 (the fact that a state statute calls a transaction a "merger" does not make the transaction a merger for purposes of Section 368(a)(1)(A) when the result of the transaction is not that one corporation acquires the assets of another corporation and the other corporation disappears). This provides tremendous flexibility relative to the strictures of Section 368(a)(1)(B) or (C). For example, in contrast to the solely for voting stock requirement for a tax-free sale of assets or sale of stock transaction, state merger statutes, as discussed earlier, generally contain no limits on allowable consideration. As *Seagram* illustrates, however, the courts and the regulations have imposed additional requirements, beyond those expressed in Section 368, in order to obtain reorganization treatment. These include: (i) The transaction must have a business purpose; (ii) There must be some continuity of the former business enterprise after the reorganization; and (iii) There must be a continuity in the proprietary interest of the former owners after the reorganization. *E.g,* Treas. Reg. § 1.368–1(b), (c). (These requirements apply to "B" and "C", as well as "A", reorganizations—albeit, they are far less likely to pose any problem in sale of stock or sale of assets transactions which meet the express demands of Section 368(a)(1)(B) or (C).)

2. The business purpose requirement was encountered before when dealing with recapitalizations and corporate divisions. In those contexts, the prospect that the transaction was made to bail property out of a corporation without taxable dividends (or otherwise to further the interests of dominant shareholders rather than of the company) meant this prerequi-

site often posed a significant barrier to tax-free treatment. When dealing with the purchase or sale of a business, however, the business purpose is fairly evident, and this requirement rarely poses a problem. (While the selling stockholders may operate from a personal motive, the transaction presumably also serves the corporate purpose of the acquiring company—which is sufficient. On the other hand, the combination of corporations already under common ownership, or for the purpose of obtaining the selling company's net operating loss carryover, might have trouble with this standard. *E.g., Wortham Machinery Co. v. United States,* 521 F.2d 160 (10th Cir.1975).)

3. Normally, the purchaser of a corporate business (at least one which is not insolvent) intends to continue the target's activity. Often, however, if the target engaged in a number of ventures, the purchaser may only wish to pursue some of them. Occasionally, the buyer is not interested in any of the acquired company's lines of business, but rather plans to redeploy the target's assets in the buyer's activities. Finally, some buyers may not acquire a company either for its businesses or its assets. Instead, such a purchaser may see an opportunity to make a profit by liquidating the target. The regulations have long required that there must exist "a continuity of business enterprise under the modified corporate form" in order to obtain reorganization treatment. Treas. Reg. § 1.368–1(b). (The notion behind this regulation is that reorganizations receive tax-free treatment because they describe transactions which are merely changes in form.) How does this requirement impact upon acquisitions in which the buyer does not plan to continue all the target's activities?

At one time, the Internal Revenue Service took the position that the buyer must continue the business of the acquired company in order to obtain tax-free status. After the courts rejected this view (*e.g., Bentsen v. Phinney,* 199 F.Supp. 363 (S.D.Tex.1961)), the Service interpreted its regulation simply to mean the buyer must continue in some business—even if a different one from anything the target did—after the acquisition. *E.g.,* Rev. Rul. 63–29, 1963–1 C.B. 77. This renders the requirement rather negligible. More recently, however, the I.R.S. promulgated a regulation which requires the buyer, after the transaction, either to continue the acquired company's historic business (or, if the acquired firm conducted more than one line of business, to continue at least one significant line of its former businesses), or to use a significant portion of the target's historic business assets in a business, in order to obtain reorganization classification. Treas. Reg. § 1.368–1(d). (The reference to historic business, or historic business assets, is to prevent the target from engaging in pre-reorganization transactions, such as selling off its assets for cash or securities, and then merging. Treas. Reg. § 1.368–1(d)(5) Exs. (3), (4). As a result of this point of reference, the regulation can impact the pre-acquisition cooperative sale of unwanted assets, at least in an extreme case.)

Interestingly enough, this continuity requirement does not extend to the purchasing company's historic business or assets. Rev. Rul. 81–25,

1981–1 C.B. 132. As pointed out previously, it is possible to structure a sale of assets transaction, for example, in such a way that the "real" buyer acts as the company selling its assets (an upside-down transaction). Moreover, in a merger or consolidation, one cannot always say who is the buyer. Does this suggest an exploitable gap in the requirement?

4. The most important extra-statutory limit on tax-free mergers or consolidations—and the one involved in *Seagram*—is the continuity of proprietary interest requirement. This test denies reorganization status to transactions in which the shareholders of a company have substantially cashed out their interests, rather than remaining owners in a continuing firm. *See* Treas. Reg. § 1.368–1(b). The rationale for the limit is that such transactions are inherently inconsistent with the underlying premise for providing non-recognition; this being that reorganizations mark more a change in form, than a sale.

Essentially, there are two ways in which a continuity of proprietary interest problem can arise—or, put another way, in which the shareholders of a company can cash out in the course of what is otherwise a reorganization. The first is to receive money or property other than stock in the merger. (This is not a concern in a "B" or "C" reorganization, because the solely for voting stock requirement rules out the receipt of a substantial amount of other consideration anyway.) The following ruling gives some idea how far shareholders can go in receiving other consideration, and still not fail this test:

Revenue Ruling 66–224

1966–2 C.B. 114.

Corporation *X* was merged under state law into corporation *Y*. Corporation *X* had four stockholders (*A*, *B*, *C*, *D*), each of whom owned 25 percent of its stock. Corporation *Y* paid *A* and *B* each $50,000 in cash for their stock of corporation *X*, and *C* and *D* each received corporation *Y* stock with a value of $50,000 in exchange for their stock of corporation *X*. There are no other facts present that should be taken into account in determining whether the continuity of interest requirement of section 1.368–1(b) of the Income Tax Regulations has been satisfied, such as sales, redemptions or other dispositions of stock prior to or subsequent to the exchange which were part of the plan of reorganization.

Held, the continuity of interest requirement of section 1.368–1(b) of the regulations has been satisfied. It would also be satisfied if the facts were the same except corporation *Y* paid each stockholder $25,000 in cash and each stockholder received corporation *Y* stock with a value of $25,000.

* * *

Several points are worth noting about this ruling. To begin with, it gives no thought to the size of the surviving corporation, "Y". If "Y" was a large company, $50,000 worth of its shares would represent a tiny fraction of its outstanding stock, and the four former shareholders of "X" would not have a significant stake in "Y", at least vis-a-vis the other "Y" stockholders. It does not matter: The continuity of proprietary interest test is concerned with how much the shareholders of a company have cashed out, not with how great an interest they received in the surviving firm. *See, e.g., Helvering v. Minnesota Tea Co.,* 296 U.S. 378 (1935). Next, notice that two of the four former stockholders completely cashed out, but the ruling held the test satisfied. This is an illustration of the rule that the test applies to the stockholders of a company as a group, not individually. *See also Reilly Oil Co. v. Commissioner,* 189 F.2d 382 (5th Cir.1951). In the ruling, the stockholders as a group received 50 percent of the value of their consideration in cash, rather than stock. The favorable holding given for this much cash is in line with the Service's long-time policy that it would give an affirmative advance ruling for an "A" reorganization in which shareholders of the acquired company receive at least half of the value of their consideration in stock in the surviving firm. Rev. Proc. 77–37, 1977–2 C.B. 568 (which the *Seagram* opinion cites). In fact, however, the regulations now contain an example establishing an even lower threshold. Temp. Treas. Reg. § 1.368–1T(e)(2)(v) Ex. 1 (40 percent of consideration in stock was enough for continuity of interest). *But see* Temp. Treas. Reg. § 1.368–1T(e)(2)(v) Ex. 4 (25 percent is insufficient). (Incidentally, since the value of stock received in a merger can change between the date of the deal and the date of the actual merger, and, as discussed before, some consideration may be put in escrow or be subject to contingencies, Treas. Reg. § 1.368–1T(e)(2) also addresses when to measure the value of stock versus money, and how to deal with contingencies, for purposes of the continuity of interest test.) Finally, note the ruling did not specify what type of stock—voting, non-voting, common, preferred—the two shareholders of "X" company received, other than it was stock in "Y" corporation. The moral is that for purposes of this standard (in marked contrast to the voting stock requirement specified in Section 368(a)(1)(B) and (C)) any stock will do. *See, e.g., John A. Nelson & Co. v. Helvering,* 296 U.S. 374 (1935). What about debt instruments: In which camp do they fall? Regardless of whether the instruments constitute securities, the I.R.S. and the courts treat them as cashing out for purposes of the continuity of interest requirement. *E.g., Le Tulle v. Scofield,* 308 U.S. 415 (1940). Hence, this test looks to a fairly bright line: All equity counts; nothing else does. (Things may get somewhat muddy, however, when the ownership interests do not come in the form of stock, as in a mutual savings and loan or other company where depositors or insureds "own" the firm and also are its creditors. *See Paulsen v. Commissioner*, 469 U.S. 131 (1985).)

Seagram involved the second type of continuity of interest problem; that occasioned by sales of shares outside of the merger itself. In *Seagram*, the sales in question—the sales in response to Seagram's tender offer—took place before the merger. Other cases, such as the *Heintz and McDonald's* opinions cited by *Seagram*, involve sales immediately after the merger. In both instances, the underlying problem is the same: Most of the original shareholders of the one of the merging corporations are cashing out. One approach to this problem—that urged by Seagram—would require that the "historic" shareholders of the merging companies receive a sufficient percentage of shares in the survivor corporation to meet the continuity of interest test (and that the historic shareholders retain those shares for some period of time after the merger). As the court noted in *Seagram*, because of the constant turnover in share ownership in a publicly traded corporation, especially around the time of a merger, this interpretation would often preclude tax-free treatment for mergers of publicly traded corporations. At the other extreme, one might argue that any sales outside of the merger itself should not count. Notice the potential that such a formalistic approach would create for parties to avoid the continuity of interest limit: All the parties would need to do is to arrange to have the acquirer or target corporation purchase the shares of those who desire for cash (or other boot) either before or after the merger, leaving only those who wish tax-free treatment to exchange shares in the merger itself. Interestingly, this sort of formalistic approach would have resulted in treating Seagram's (and most of the other) exchanges of Conoco for DuPont shares as not tax-free, because these exchanges technically took place as part of DuPont's tender offer, and not pursuant to the actual merger of Conoco with DuPont's subsidiary.

In fact, at first glance, the court in *Seagram* seems to be employing a curious double standard—integrating Seagram's tendering its Conoco shares to DuPont with the following merger, yet refusing to treat Seagram's purchases as part of the overall transaction in order to find that most of the original Conoco shareholders had cashed out. What explains this result? The answer, as suggested by the way the court distinguished *Superior Coach* and *Yoc Heating*, is to look at where the consideration comes from for those shareholders who cash out. If one of the merging corporations, or a party who is affiliated with, or acting on behalf of, one of the merging corporations, purchases shares for cash or boot, then there can be a problem with continuity of interest, even if the purchase takes place outside of the merger itself. On the other hand, purchases by outsiders, such as Seagram, are irrelevant to the continuity issue. A regulation issued by the Internal Revenue Service after *Seagram* largely confirms this approach. Treas. Reg. § 1.368–1(e). In fact, this regulation goes beyond *Seagram* in a couple of ways. For one thing, the regulation disregards sales to outsiders either before or after the merger. This effectively overrules the post merger sales cases, *McDonald's* and *Heintz*, discussed by the court in *Seagram*. In addition, the regulation narrows the list of parties whose relationship with either of the merging corporations is sufficient to make purchases by those parties relevant to assessing continuity of interest. The regulation only fits corporate, but not individual (as in *Superior Coach*), shareholders within the definition of related parties for this purpose. Suppose the acquiring corporation initiates or continues a program of repurchasing its stock on the market following the acquisition. Will this ruin compliance with the continuity of interest requirement, since now the non-stock consideration going to the target's shareholders who take advantage of these repurchases comes from the acquiring corporation? See Rev. Rul. 99–58, 1999–2 C.B. 701 (not when there was a market for the acquirer's shares anyway, the acquirer did not favor the target's former shareholders nor even know the identity of the sellers in the repurchases, and parties did not negotiate to undertake such repurchases as part of the acquisition).

In any event, keep in mind that the continuity of interest requirement concerns whether the exchanging shareholders will avoid recognition on any of the consideration they received. Even if the transaction satisfies the test, receipt of money or property other than stock and securities in the other party to the merger, as well as securities with a principal amount greater than those surrendered, constitutes taxable boot. I.R.C. §§ 354(a), 356(a). (Recall the treatment of such boot discussed when dealing with the tax-free sale of assets transaction.) Moreover, resale of stock received in a reorganization constitutes a taxable event.

5. In *Seagram*, the I.R.S. argued for reorganization status, and the taxpayer against. This was because Seagram hoped to recognize a loss on the transaction. Another reason to argue against reorganization status lies in the trade-off which goes with non-recognition, this being a substituted basis. The basis rules are generally familiar from dealing with Section 351 transactions, recapitalizations and tax-free corporate divisions. Section 358(a) gives the exchanging stockholders a basis in the shares they receive equal to their basis in the stock they surrendered, increased by any gain recognized, and decreased for any boot received. Section 362(b) gives the purchasing corporation a basis in any property acquired in a tax-free reorganization (in other words, stock in the target in a "B" reorganization, and the target's assets in an "A" or "C" reorganization) equal to the basis the transferring party had in the property, increased for any gain recognized by the transferor. (Note that the transferor(s) are the exchanging shareholders for a "B" reorganization, and the target company in an "A" or "C" reorganization. *Cf.* Rev. Rul. 72–327, 1972–2 C.B. 197. None of these parties normally recognize gain, since boot cannot change hands in a "B" reorganization, and only the shareholders recognize the gain upon receiving boot in an "A" or "C" reorganization—assuming the selling company liquidates in the latter transaction. Hence, the acquiring corporation normally receives simply a substituted basis.)

Incidently, who recognizes gain in a merger or consolidation which is fully taxable because of the failure to meet one of the extra-statutory limits? *Compare West Shore Fuel, Inc. v. United States,* 453 F.Supp. 956 (W.D.N.Y.1978), *aff'd,* 598 F.2d 1236 (2d Cir.1979) (treating the merger as equivalent to a sale of assets by and a liquidation of the disappearing company), *with Home Sav. & Loan Assn. v. United States,* 514 F.2d 1199 (9th Cir.1975), *cert. denied,* 423 U.S. 1015 (treating the merger as equivalent to a sale of stock transaction with a tax-free liquidation of the disappearing company).

6. The reorganization provisions apply solely to combinations between corporations. *See* I.R.C. § 368(a)(1), (b). This includes S corporations. *See*

I.R.C. § 1371(a). These provisions do not apply to acquisitions by individuals, or by, or of, businesses conducted through a partnership. As noted in Chapter II, this can present a disadvantage for those who do business in a non-corporate form. Can persons who do business in a non-corporate form create a corporation and then engage in a tax-free reorganization? See Rev. Rul. 70–140, 1970–1 C.B. 73 (incorporation in anticipation of "B" reorganization treated as a taxable sale of assets for stock rather than a 351 transaction and a "B" reorganization). Because partnerships, limited partnerships, LLPs or LLCs are not corporations (unless they elect to be treated as such under the "check-the-box" regulation), mergers between such entities do not count as an A reorganization, even though effectuated through new statutes allowing for mergers of non-corporate business forms. Suppose, however, that a merger occurs between a corporation and an LLC entirely owned by another corporation. Because an LLC with a single owner is a nullity for tax purposes—since a partnership requires two owners—if a corporation merges into an LLC wholly owned by another corporation, this would be the equivalent, for tax purposes, of the corporation merging into the corporation which owns the LLC, rather than merging into the LLC. Hence, it could be an A reorganization, assuming the non-statutory requirements are met. On the other hand, suppose the wholly-owned LLC merges into the other corporation so that the other corporation is the entity which survives the merger. This would not constitute an A reorganization, because it would leave two corporations surviving the merger, and the Internal Revenue Service takes the position that an A reorganization requires mergers in which only one corporation survives. Treas. Reg. § 1.368–2(b)(1).

(vi) Triangular Transactions

Many times, it may be in the buyer's interest to have a subsidiary acquire the target's business. Indeed, this, in fact, is what occurred in *Seagram*. The buyer can accomplish this in a number of ways which can be part of either a taxable or tax-free transaction. To begin with, a corporation can have a new subsidiary, or an already existing one, purchase the target's assets or stock in a taxable exchange. Alternately, a company could purchase the target's assets or stock in a taxable transaction, and then transfer them to a newly created or existing subsidiary in exchange for the subsidiary's stock (a so-called drop-down transaction). In either event, this transaction generally does not raise any new tax issues beyond those previously explored for taxable sale of assets or sale of stock transactions and Section 351 transfers. There is one exception. Suppose the parent wishes to use its stock as a portion of the consideration for the acquisition; albeit, not a large enough portion to qualify the purchase for tax-free treatment. This would entail no recognition if the parent bought the target's assets or stock, and then dropped them down into a controlled subsidiary. I.R.C. §§ 351, 1032. If the subsidiary buys the assets or shares using the parent's stock, however, must it recognize gain due to any difference between the acquired asset's or stock's fair market value, and the subsidiary's basis in the parent's shares? See Treas. Reg. § 1.1032–3 (subsidiary, which receives stock in its parent corporation in a Section 351 transaction, and immediately uses this stock to make a taxable purchase, will be treated as if the subsidiary had bought the stock for cash at the stock's fair market value, thereby avoiding recognition of gain by the subsidiary due to its lack of basis in the stock).

Use of enough voting stock in the parent or subsidiary begins one thinking of a tax-free sale of assets or sale of stock transaction. If the subsidiary uses voting stock in itself to make the acquisition, then the analysis is no different than for any "B" or "C" reorganization. What if the subsidiary pays for the assets or stock with voting shares in its parent? In fact, Section 368(a)(1)(B) and (C) expressly allow the use of voting shares in a parent. (The language doing so is contained in parentheticals, and, hence, this is sometimes referred to as either a parenthetical "B" or a parenthetical "C" reorganization.) Two points should be noted about these provisions. To begin with, for them to apply, the parent must have control of the acquiring corporation within the meaning of Section 368(c). In addition, the parentheticals allow use solely of voting stock in the parent: In other words, the subsidiary must meet the solely for voting stock requirement by using either entirely stock in itself, or entirely stock in its parent, not a bit of each. Treas. Reg. § 1.368–2(d)(1). This type of transaction also raises questions with respect to assuming liabilities. The language in Section 368(a)(1)(C) disregarding the assumption of liabilities refers only to an assumption by the acquiring corporation. Therefore, if the parent agrees to pick up any of the selling company's debts, this constitutes boot. Rev. Rul. 70–107, 1970–1 C.B. 78. (In a parenthetical "B" reorganization, however, the assumption of the target's liabilities is irrelevant, and so the parent could do it as well as the subsidiary.)

As with taxable asset or stock sales, one could attempt to accomplish a result parallel to a parenthetical "B" or parenthetical "C" reorganization by using a drop-down following a "B" or "C" reorganization by the parent. Will the subsequent transfer of the target's assets or stock endanger reorganization treatment, due to failure to meet the continuity of business or continuity of interest tests? Section 368(a)(2)(C) removes any doubt on this score by stating that the recipient of assets or stock in an "A", "B", or "C" reorganization may transfer the property to a corporation which it controls (within the meaning of Section 368(c)) without disqualifying the reorganization. Moreover, the regulations allow tax-free multi-tier drop downs—in other words, a corporation which receives assets or stock in what would otherwise be an "A", "B", or "C" reorganization can transfer the property to a corporation which it controls (within the meaning of Section 368(c)), and the controlled corporation can then transfer the property to another corporation which the controlled corporation controls (and so on) without upsetting reorganization treatment for the initial acquisition. Treas. Reg. § 1.368–2(k).

Tax-free mergers using subsidiaries are also available. As stated above, Section 368(a)(2)(C) expressly validates the drop-down of assets to a subsidiary following a statutory merger by the parent. Generally, however, the drop-down technique fails to accomplish the purposes for involving a subsidiary in a merger (such as avoiding the need for a vote by the parent's shareholders or the parent's automatic assumption of all the target's liabilities.) Hence, the purchaser may desire to have the target merge into its subsidiary (a forward triangular merger) or its subsidiary merge into the target (a reverse triangular merger). If the target's shareholders were to receive stock in the surviving subsidiary as most of their consideration (or simply retain their stock in the target in a reverse triangular merger), presumably this merger could qualify as an "A" reorganization. Typically, however, both sides would prefer the target's stockholders to give up their shares in the target in exchange for shares in the parent. Indeed, this is what occurred in the forward triangular merger in *Seagram*. If shares in the parent constitute boot, the merger will fail the continuity of interest test. Fortunately, Section 368 contains provisions which expressly qualify both forward and reverse triangular mergers as reorganizations despite employing stock in the parent.

Section 368(a)(2)(D), which the court quoted in *Seagram*, deals with forward triangular mergers. Under this provision, such mergers constitute reorganizations within the meaning of Section 368(a)(1)(A), despite use of stock in the parent, if the transaction meets three prerequisites: (1) the subsidiary must acquire in the merger substantially all the assets of the target corporation; (2) the target's stockholder's cannot receive stock in the subsidiary (in other words, no mixing of stock in the parent and stock in the subsidiary for the target's former shareholders if the merger is to qualify under this provision); and (3) the transaction must otherwise be one which would have qualified as an "A" reorganization (for instance, under the continuity of interest test) had the merger been into the parent. Again, as in the three party sale of assets or sale of stock transactions, the parent must be a corporation which controls the subsidiary within the meaning of Section 368(c).

Section 368(a)(2)(E) allows tax-free reverse triangular mergers using stock in the parent. To come within this provision, the target must emerge from the transaction holding substantially all the assets which both it and the former subsidiary had before the merger. (The regulations exclude from the "substantially all" requirement, however, assets which the parent placed in the disappearing subsidiary solely for use in the merger. Treas. Reg. § 1.368–2(j)(3)(iii).) In addition, the target's former stockholders must give up in the merger an amount of stock constituting control of the target within the meaning of Section 368(c) in exchange for voting stock in the parent. Notice that Section 368(a)(2)(E) is more restrictive than Section 368(a)(2)(D). In both cases, the parent must end up in control of the corporation surviving the merger, and the surviving firm must own, after the transaction, substantially all the assets of the target (or of the target plus the disappearing subsidiary in a reverse triangular merger). Yet, in a reverse triangular merger, the target's former shareholders can receive only voting stock in the parent in exchange for enough of their former shares to constitute control of the target; whereas in the forward triangular merger, the target's former shareholders can receive any consideration, so long as the mix of consideration meets the continuity of interest test, and the consideration excludes any stock in the subsidiary. On the other hand, unlike a "B" reorganization, the target's shareholders in a reverse triangular merger can receive some boot, so long as they surrender 80% of the shares in the target for voting stock in the parent. (This is much like what the Tax Court would have allowed for "B" reorganizations in the decision overruled in *Chapman.*) Hence, a reverse triangular merger allows a buyer to get a similar result as a tax-free sale of stock transaction (i.e. it ends up owning 80 percent or more of the stock in the target), but with the ability to throw in a little bit of boot. Note, however, unlike a "B" reorganization, shares in the target already owned by the parent do not count toward meeting the requirements for a tax-free reverse triangular merger; rather the merger itself must entail the exchange of the requisite controlling amount of shares. Treas. Reg. § 1.368–2(j)(3)(i). *But see* Revenue Ruling 2001–26, 2001–1 C.B. 1297 (treating a tender offer involving an exchange of the acquiring parent's voting stock for a majority of the outstanding stock in the target, followed by a reverse triangular merger, as one transaction in order to find that such a two-step acquisition met the requirements for a tax-free reverse triangular merger, even though the acquiring parent did not obtain the requisite 80 percent of the target's outstanding stock in the merger itself).

The provisions of Section 368 discussed thus far allow parenthetical "B" and parenthetical "C" reorganizations, forward and reverse triangular mergers, and drop downs, to constitute reorganizations despite the solely for voting stock and continuity of interest tests. To complete the prerequisites for tax-free treatment, it is necessary to define all the corporations involved in these transactions as "parties" to the reorganization, since this is the operative key for which firms can obtain tax-free treatment under Section 361, and which firms' stock and securities individuals can receive tax-free under Section 354. Section 368(b) accomplishes this. This just leaves the question of what basis the various exchanging parties obtain in the stock or assets they receive. Introducing exchanges for a parent's stock into the picture renders the application of Sections 358(a) and 362(b) no longer straightforward. For example, does Section 358(a) set the basis for the stock the parent receives in exchange for its stock in a forward or reverse triangular merger—in which case, the parent would probably obtain a basis of zero because it has no basis in stock in itself—or can the parent pick up a basis equal to the what the target's shareholders had in their stock, or what the target had in its assets (following the general rule of Section 362(b))? See Treas. Reg. § 1.358–6 (following the general approach of giving the parent a basis in the stock the parent has after the merger equal to the parent's basis in the stock the parent owned in the subsidiary before the merger, plus an amount equal to the target's basis in the target's assets before the merger (less the amount of the target's liabilities)).

b. *Carryover of Tax Attributes*

(i) Generally

Every corporation, once it starts operating, gains tax attributes—in other words, items in its history which will affect its (or its shareholders') future income tax obligations. For example, a company has a basis and a holding period in each of its assets, dictated by how and when it acquired the property. One of the important questions in structuring (and sometimes even in deciding whether to go through with) the acquisition of a business operating in the corporate form is what will happen to these tax attributes. For instance, as already discussed, the trade-off for avoiding the double tax of a taxable sale of assets transaction, by instead undertaking either a taxable sale of stock (without a Section 338 election) or a tax-free reorganization, is that the acquiring firm does not obtain a cost basis in the target's properties. A host of other tax attributes exist for each corporation besides its basis and holding period in specific assets. (For a list of over twenty such items, see I.R.C. § 381(c).) Two of these items are particularly important. An undesirable attribute (unless it is a deficit) is a corporation's accumulated earnings and profits. A highly prized attribute is a net operating loss (or NOL) carryback or carryover. NOLs result when a taxpayer, during a year, incurs deductions (with certain exceptions) in excess of gross income. I.R.C. § 172(c), (d). Section 172 allows the taxpayer to carry the loss back to use as a deduction against the prior two years' income, and, if this does not exhaust the amount of the loss, the taxpayer can carry the NOL forward to use as a deduction against future income for up to the next twenty years. (A taxpayer may elect to forego the carryback, however, and use the NOL only as a carryover. I.R.C. § 172(b)(3)(C).)

What happens to these attributes of an acquired company? This depends, at least initially, upon which of the previously discussed modes the parties use to structure the acquisition. The simplest result occurs in the taxable sale of assets transaction. Sale of a corporation's properties in a taxable exchange does not transfer any of the selling company's tax attributes to the purchasing corporation. *See* I.R.C. § 381(a). Instead, the attributes remain with the selling firm, and terminate upon its liquidation. (This assumes the selling corporation is not a controlled subsidiary, whose parent will pick up its attributes upon liquidation. I.R.C. § 381(a)(1).) Note the disadvantage here if the selling company possesses substantial NOLs.

A very different scheme follows if the acquisition occurs through either a tax-free sale of assets transaction or a statutory merger (in other words, through a "C" or "A" reorganization). In this event, Section 381 steps in and provides generally that the acquiring corporation succeeds to and must take into account the various tax attributes listed in Section 381(c) of the company whose assets it acquired (i.e. the selling corporation in a "C" reorganization, or the disappearing corporation in an "A" reorganization). Keep in mind when dealing with three party "A" or "C" reorganizations that the attributes go to the corporation acquiring the assets, not its parent. *See* Treas. Reg. § 1.381(a)–1(b)(2). While the list in Section 381(c) includes both earnings and profits, and net operating loss carryovers, the Section prescribes certain limits on their succession.

Section 381(c)(2)(A) carries the selling or disappearing firm's earnings and profits over to the acquiring company (meaning the acquirer's accumulated earnings and profits increases by the amount of the selling or disappearing company's earnings and profits). As a result, one cannot use a tax-free sale of assets or merger to shed the burden of this tax attribute.

On the other hand, Section 381(c)(2)(B) limits the acquirer's ability to gain the advantage of a deficit in the selling or disappearing firm's earnings and profits. Instead of subtracting such a deficit from its accumulated earnings and profits, the acquirer may only use the deficit to offset earnings and profits which it accumulates after the purchase or merger. What this means is that if the acquirer in the future distributes less than its current earnings and profits for a year, it can use up the inherited deficit to slow the growth in its accumulated earnings and profits. However, if the acquirer distributes more than its current earnings and profits during a future year, the excess will remain a dividend until the distribution exhausts the acquirer's accumulated earnings and profits from before the acquisition. (Section 381(c)(2)(B) applies as well to a deficit in the acquiring firm's earnings and profits. Such an acquirer cannot offset its deficit against the accumulated earnings and profits it inherits from the selling or disappearing company under Section 381(c)(2)(A). Hence, there is no advantage in turning the acquisition around.)

Turning to NOLs, Section 381 contains several limitations on their use by the acquiring company. To begin with, suppose the acquiring company incurs a net operating loss after the acquisition. Section 381(b)(3) prevents the acquirer from carrying the NOL back to use as a deduction against the acquired firm's pre-acquisition income. The acquirer, however, can carry the NOL back to use as a deduction against the acquirer's own pre-acquisition income. Treas. Reg. § 1.381(c)(1)–1(b). Consider the planning impact in the case of a combination of a previously profitable and previously unprofitable corporation. If the parties anticipate the possibility of post-combination losses which they would desire to carry back, then the previously profitable firm could be the survivor of the merger, or the buyer in a sale-of-assets reorganization, so it carries back the post-combination losses against its own pre-combination income.

Of typically greater interest, Section 381(c)(1) addresses the use of pre-acquisition NOLs. It provides that the acquiring company succeeds to the pre-acquisition net operating loss carryovers of the selling or disappearing firm. The acquirer, however, cannot use the NOLs as a carryback to deduct against its pre-acquisition income. I.R.C. § 381(c)(1)(A), (B). Applying this rule is simple if the acquisition takes place at the end of the acquirer's tax year; in which case the acquirer can use the NOLs starting against all its next year's income. Often, however, the transaction does not yield itself to such convenient timing. The result is to create a post-acquisition part year consisting of the period between the acquisition and the end of the acquirer's tax year. While the acquirer may apply the NOLs to this part year, in doing so, the acquirer can only offset a portion of its total acquisition year's income. I.R.C. § 381(c)(1)(B). (The ratio of the post-acquisition part year to the whole year dictates this portion. For example, if the acquisition occurred three-quarters of the way through the acquirer's tax year, the acquirer could only deduct the NOLs against one-quarter of the acquisition year's income.) Despite this limitation, this part year counts as a year against the twenty year carryover limit. Treas. Reg. 1.381(c)(1)–1(e)(3). Moreover, Section 381(b)(1) creates a short tax year ending on the date of acquisition for the acquired firm. This short tax year also counts as a year for the NOL carryover limit. Treas. Reg. § 1.381(c)(1)–1(e). As a result, making the acquisition on any date other than the last day of the acquirer's tax year, effectively consumes an extra year against the twenty year maximum. This could become quite significant if the selling or disappearing firm has been running at a loss for some time and so has NOLs in danger of soon expiring. (Needless to say, the acquisition does not start a new twenty year period.) For parties deciding to time their transaction with this fact in mind, it may be useful to point out that the date of the acquisition is generally the date on which the transfer of assets is completed, albeit it may be the date by which substantially all the assets are transferred if all that is left for the selling company to do is to liquidate. I.R.C. § 381(b)(2). Finally, the acquiring firm keeps its own pre-acquisition NOLs unaffected by the transaction, except that if both companies have pre-acquisition NOLs, Section 381(c)(1)(C) sets out fairly complex rules for the order in which the post-acquisition firm uses them up.

A sale of stock transaction—either taxable, or tax-free (a "B" reorganization)—introduces yet another scheme. With the target corporation continuing to exist (only its ownership has changed), at first glance one would presume it will continue to possess its tax attributes undisturbed. Several factors, however, complicate this conclusion. To begin with, the buyer in a taxable exchange could make a Section 338 election. Recall the impact of this election is to create an imaginary sale in which the target emerges as a new (for tax purposes) corporation—thereby wiping out all its previous tax attributes. Alternately, following either a taxable or tax-free sale of stock transaction, the buyer may choose to liquidate the target. In this case, if the buyer owned sufficient stock in the target to allow for a tax-free liquidation under Section 332 (and assuming the purchaser made no Section 338 election), then the purchasing corporation will succeed to the tax attributes of the liquidated subsidiary pursuant to Section 381. This brings back into play the various provisions of Section 381 discussed above dealing with earnings and profits and net loss carryovers. Still another alternative for the buyer, after either a taxable or tax-free sale of stock transaction, could be to file a consolidated return with the target. (Recall the discussion of consolidated returns in Chapter II.) Yet a different result could occur if the target had been a subsidiary of a parent filing a consolidated return. The regulations allow such a parent to reattribute to itself the subsidiary's NOLs to the extent the regulations prevented the parent from recognizing a loss on the sale of its stock in the subsidiary. Treas.Reg. § 1.1502–20(g)(1).

(ii) Uses, Abuses and Limitations

Briarcliff Candy Corp. v. Commissioner of Internal Revenue

54 T.C.M. (CCH) 667 (1987).

This case is before the Court on petitioners' Motion for Summary Judgment. The sole issue for decision is whether section 269 applies to the acquisition by Briarcliff Candy Corporation (Briarcliff), a corporation with substantial net operating losses, of Health–Med Corporation (Health–Med) and its subsidiaries, so as to disallow deduction of the net operating losses against profits from Health–Med and its subsidiaries.

FACTUAL BACKGROUND

* * *

Briarcliff operated a candy factory and a chain of candy shops. It also sold franchises to independent store owners to operate candy shops under the Loft name. Due to competitive pressures, it became increasingly difficult for Briarcliff to profitably operate its candy stores. * * * Therefore, Briarcliff sold many company-owned stores to franchisees and closed shops which it could not sell. Prior to and in the course of selling and closing down its own candy stores, Briarcliff had incurred net operating losses which were available for carryover * * *.

In 1973, Briarcliff entered into negotiations with a group of corporations consisting of Eckmar Corporation (Eckmar), Eckmar HDC Corporation (HDC), Health–Chem Corporation (Health–Chem) and Medallion Leisure Corporation (Medallion). Eckmar owned a majority interest in HDC and 80 percent of the stock of Medallion. HDC owned approximately 82 percent of the stock of Health–Chem.

As a result of these negotiations, on August 10, 1973, Eckmar, HDC, and Briarcliff entered into an agreement whereby HDC agreed to change its name to Health–Med Corporation (Health–Med) and undergo a recapitalization. * * * [As part of the recapitalization,] Eckmar would exchange the 1,000,000 shares of HDC common stock it held prior to the recapitalization for 2,800 shares of Heath–Med junior preferred stock. Eckmar would also transfer its 866,000 shares of preferred and 600,000 shares of common stock in Medallion to Health–Med in exchange for an additional 1,200 Health–Med junior preferred shares. Briarcliff would purchase 40,000 Health–Med common shares for $100,000, which would constitute all of the then outstanding Health-med common shares. Thus, after the closing, Eckmar would own 4,000 shares of Health–Med junior preferred stock and approximately 500 shares of preferred stock, and Briarcliff would own 40,000 shares of Health–Med common stock. As a result, Eckmar would hold stock possessing approximately 10 percent of the total combined voting power of all Health–Med shares entitled to vote and Briarcliff would hold stock possessing approximately 90 percent of the total combined voting power of Health–Med. [Health–Med, in turn, already owned over 80 percent of the stock in Health–Chem and ended up owning the 80 percent of the stock in Medallion previously owned by Eckmar.]

Each share of junior preferred stock would be convertible to Health–Med common stock, at Eckmar's option, after the earliest of: (1) commencement of voluntary or involuntary bankruptcy proceedings by or against Briarcliff; (2) adoption by Briarcliff of a plan of liquidation; or, (3) December 31, 1980. The conversion ratio of the junior preferred stock would give

Eckmar as much as 95 percent of the total combined voting power of all Heath–Med shares entitled to vote. Further, each junior preferred share would be redeemable by Heath–Med for $10,000 per share at Health–Med's option, and commencing in 1988, Health–Med would be required to redeem these shares on an annual basis.

This transaction was closed on August 17, 1973. After the closing, Briarcliff, Health–Med, Health–Chem, and Medallion entered into an agreement to file consolidated Federal income tax returns. Under the terms of the agreement, Health–Med agreed to pay Briarcliff an amount equal to 21 percent of the [tax savings by having] * * * a consolidated return filed with Briarcliff * * *.

Briarcliff joined in the filing of consolidated returns with Health–Med, Health–Chem, and Medallion for the taxable years ended June 30, 1974 and June 30, 1975. On the consolidated returns for 1974 and 1975, they claimed deductions of $9,596,729 and $7,187,915, respectively, attributable to net operating loss carryovers of Briarcliff. * * *

DISCUSSION

* * *

Section 269 as applicable to this transaction provides as follows:

(a) IN GENERAL.—If—

(1) any person or persons acquire, or acquired on or after October 8, 1940, directly or indirectly, control of a corporation,

* * *

and the principal purpose for which such acquisition was made is evasion or avoidance of Federal income tax by securing the benefit of a deduction, credit, or other allowance which such person or corporation would not otherwise enjoy, then the Secretary may disallow such deduction, credit, or other allowance. For purposes of paragraphs (1) and (2), control means the ownership of stock possessing at least 50 percent of the total combined voting power of all classes of stock entitled to vote or at least 50 percent of the total value of shares of all classes of stock of the corporation.

In order for section 269 to apply to this transaction, there must be the acquisition of control of a corporation, and the principal purpose of such acquisition must be the "evasion or avoidance of Federal income tax by securing the benefit of a deduction * * * which such person or corporation would not otherwise enjoy." * * * However, before we consider these requirements, we must address petitioners' argument that section 269 does not apply to a loss corporation's acquisition of a profitable subsidiary.

Petitioners contend that respondent recognizes that section 269 does not apply to a loss corporation's acquisition of a profitable subsidiary, and that respondent stated, in Rev.Rul. 63–40, 1963–1 C.B. 46, that *Libson Shops, Inc. v. Koehler,* 353 U.S. 382 (1957) will not be applied in a situation where there is "no more than a minor change in stock ownership of a loss corporation." Thus, petitioners argue that since there was no change in ownership of Briarcliff, the loss corporation, neither *Libson Shops* nor section 269 apply to the transaction.

Libson Shops did not involve a question of tax avoidance, and thus as expressly noted by the Supreme Court, section 129 of the 1939 code, the predecessor of section 269 of the 1954 Code, was not applicable. * * * In contrast, here respondent has determined that Briarcliff acquired Health–Med for the principal purpose of evading or avoiding Federal income tax, and that section 269 applies. Accordingly, *Libson Shops* is not dispositive of the issue of whether section 269 applies to the transaction involved here.

This court and others have held that section 269 applies where a loss corporation acquires control of a profitable corporation since the acquiring corporation thereby secures the benefit of loss it would not otherwise have enjoyed. *Vulcan Materials Co. v. United States,* 446 F.2d 690, 698 (5th Cir.1971); *Southland Corp. v. Campbell,* 358 F.2d 333, 336 (5th Cir.1966); *F.C. Publication Liquidating Corp. v. Commissioner,* 304 F.2d 779, 781 (2d Cir.1962), affg. 36 T.C. 836 (1961); * * * Further, the legislative history of section 129 of the Internal Revenue Code of 1939 supports the proposition that section 269 is not limited to any particular form of transaction (e.g., the acquisition by a loss corporation of a profitable subsidiary). Rather, this section was broadly drafted to include any type of acquisition which constitutes a device by which one corporation secures a tax benefit to which it is otherwise not entitled.

* * *

Having determined that section 269 can apply to a loss corporation's acquisition of a profitable subsidiary, we must next decide whether under the particular circumstances here, petitioners are entitled to summary judgment. * * *

One requirement under section 269 is that there must be an acquisition of control. It appears that Briarcliff has met the definition of "control" in section 269 in that Briarcliff owns "at least 50 percent of the total combined voting power of all classes of stock entitled to vote." Section 269(a). However, while Briarcliff appears to have met the form of the statute, we believe there exists a material question as to whether the acquisition of control had substance.

Respondent submitted several exhibits with his opposition to petitioners' motion. These exhibits raise the question of whether, notwithstanding the ownership of a majority of the voting power, Briarcliff lacked effective control over the business and management of Health–Med and its subsidiaries. In particular, these exhibits show that at a November 14, 1973 annual meeting of Briarcliff shareholders, the shareholders were informed that because of Eckmar's ownership of convertible securities in Health–Med and other factors, "effective managerial control of Health–Med remains in Eckmar." In a report of Briarcliff's financial condition, the shareholders were again advised that Eckmar retained control over Health–

Med and its subsidiaries due to conversion rights of the preferred stock, the initial composition of Health–Med's board of directors and the respective rights of the various classes of its securities.

* * *

In addition to the acquisition of control, for section 269 to apply, the principle purpose of the acquisition must be the "evasion or avoidance of Federal income tax." This question is a factual one which requires a subjective evaluation of petitioner's motives. * * * Generally, summary judgment is not appropriate in cases where motive or intent is involved, as such a question typically involves a genuine and material factual issue. * * *

Because we find that there are unresolved questions as to material facts, summary judgment is not appropriate here. Accordingly, petitioners' Motion for Summary Judgment will be denied.

NOTES

1. *Briarcliff Candy* illustrates how a marriage between a corporation with substantial NOLs and a corporation (or corporate group) with substantial taxable income might significantly reduce the payment of income tax. At one time, this led corporations with NOLs to advertise, like mail order brides, their availability for such a match. As the court's opinion also illustrates, Congress has adopted statutory provisions designed to limit match-ups in this field where the bonds only run as deep as tax savings.

In *Briarcliff Candy*, the I.R.S. invoked Section 269. Section 269 subjects three types of transactions to scrutiny. The first, and the one involved in *Briarcliff Candy,* is the acquisition of control of a corporation. I.R.C. § 269(a)(1). Notice, Section 269(a) provides a very broad definition of control as compared with the tests applicable to Section 351 transactions, reorganizations and Section 338 elections. Instead of requiring 80 percent ownership, control under Section 269(a) flows from obtaining as little as 50 percent of a company's outstanding shares. Moreover, unlike the conjunctive tests in Sections 368(c) and 1504(a)(2), Section 269(a) finds control if a party obtains either 50 percent of the voting power or 50 percent of the value of all the outstanding stock. Of course, just as with the other control tests, the presence of multiple classes of stock or voting agreements can raise questions as to how to measure the voting power or the value of blocks of shares. *E.g., Hermes Consolidated, Inc. v. United States,* 14 Cl.Ct. 398 (1988). *Briarcliff Candy* shows the willingness of courts to go beyond simply counting shares and instead to look at all the circumstances to see whether, as a practical matter, the requisite control exists. (On the other hand, if Briarcliff Candy Corp. lacked control, then did it meet the criteria for filing a consolidated return with Health–Med? See I.R.C. § 1504(a)(2).) In addition to its broad definition of control, Section 269(a)(1) applies to the acquisition of such control by any person (or persons), even if the acquirer is not a corporation itself. Hence, the provision could apply if, for example, several individuals purchased the stock of a failing company possessing substantial NOL carryovers in order to have the firm undertake a different line of business, whose profit they will thereby shield from tax. *Commissioner v. British Motor Car Distributors,* 278 F.2d 392 (9th Cir. 1960). Moreover, the purchase of stock upon the formation of a company fits the definition of an acquisition of control. Accordingly, as mentioned in Chapter II, Section 269 can apply to persons forming corporations for tax avoidance purposes. *E.g., Bobsee Corp. v. United States,* 411 F.2d 231 (5th Cir.1969) (Section 269 used against multiple corporations formed to gain advantages of multiple surtax exemptions).

The second type of transaction to which Section 269 can apply consists of one corporation's acquiring assets from another corporation, if the acquirer keeps the transferor's basis in the property. I.R.C. § 269(a)(2). This includes "A" and "C" reorganizations—for which, as discussed earlier, Section 381 provides the acquirer with the transferor's tax attributes. It does not include taxable purchases of another company's property. Consider the planning lesson for a company, like Briarcliff Candy Corp., which possesses substantial NOL carryovers and would like to acquire a profitable business in order to use them. Buying stock, or a tax-free acquisition of assets, brings Section 269 into play. Purchasing the profitable firm's property for cash does not. Incidentally, Section 269(a)(2) does not apply if the two corporations involved in the asset transaction are under common control, or one controls the other.

The third type of transaction to which Section 269 can apply is a liquidation of a corporation within two years following another company's acquiring control of it (within the meaning Section 1504(a)(2)'s 80 percent tests) if the acquirer did not make a Section 338 election. I.R.C. § 269(b). (Such a liquidation, as discussed earlier, provides the parent with the subsidiary's tax attributes.)

Given one of the three types of transactions to which Section 269 can apply, the question becomes whether the parties undertook the acquisition or liquidation for the principal purpose of tax avoidance. The principal purpose test raises several questions from a planning perspective: What sort of factors will evidence the forbidden purpose? For example, what facts suggested such a motive in *Briarcliff Candy*? (Notice the temporary nature of Briarcliff's ownership and its lack of any particular business on its own.) Moving beyond transactions wholly motivated by tax advantage, what happens when there are both tax and non-tax objectives at work? Specifically, how much, if at all, can parties consider (or even be aware of) the possible tax advantages of an acquisition or liquidation before these advantages become the principal purpose of the transaction? Assuming a business reason for undertaking an acquisition or liquidation, can choosing a tax-advantaged method to carry out the transaction trigger Section 269? See *United States Shelter Corporation v. United States,* 13 Cl.Ct. 606 (1987):

> While all the FPC and Old Shelter directors who testified denied that tax avoidance was a major reason for the reorganization, it is clear that they were aware of the NOLs and desired to use them if possible. Tuck stated that he would have entered into the First Piedmont

> reorganization even if the NOLs were not available, but added: "[T]here's no question that the NOLs, that if we could use them, were a very important portion of this thing.... We told the lawyers to try and structure the transaction where we could use those tax credits. I'm paid as a CEO of a company to look out for its assets." * * * Such motive or intent is not fatal. It is not inconsistent with the cases which hold Section 269 inapplicable. The principal purpose of a transaction does not become tax avoidance merely because the parties were cognizant of and considered the tax consequences.

Shelter Corp. states that Section 269 does not apply simply because parties used the most tax-advantaged means to structure a business motivated acquisition. Some contrary authority exists, however, at least in situations involving highly convoluted transactions designed to procure a high basis in properties a company desires to buy. *Canaveral International Corp. v. Commissioner,* 61 T.C. 520 (1974).

While *Briarcliff Candy* involves the typical case in which one corporation brings substantial NOLs to the marriage, suppose a company acquires another corporation which it expects will incur losses after the acquisition. Can Section 269 apply? *Compare Borge v. Commissioner,* 405 F.2d 673 (2d Cir.1968), *cert. denied,* 395 U.S. 933 (1969), *with Herculite Protective Fabrics Corp. v. Commissioner,* 387 F.2d 475 (3d Cir.1968).

2. Not satisfied with a provision, like Section 269, which requires litigating over the motives for an acquisition, Congress enacted a far more pervasive barrier to the use of NOLs following an acquisition. This is Section 382. The *Garber Industries* decision in Chapter VI illustrated how a sale of stock between existing shareholders—neither of whom probably gave much thought to the impact of the transaction on the use of NOLs—could trigger Section 382 and thereby severely limit a corporation's ability to use its NOLs.

In *Garber Industries*, the issue before the court was whether an "ownership change" had occurred. As the court there explained, Section 382 comes into play in the event of an "ownership change" of a corporation with NOLs (a "loss" corporation). An ownership change occurs if, immediately after an "owner shift", the percentage of stock owned by one or more shareholders owning five percent or more of the loss corporation (so-called 5 percent shareholders) has increased by more than 50 percentage points over the lowest percentage of stock owned by such persons during the prior three years. I.R.C. § 382(g)(1), (i), (k)(7). An owner shift is any change in corporate ownership affecting the percentage of stock owned by a 5 percent shareholder. I.R.C. § 382(g)(2). Notice, as the brothers probably were surprised to discover in *Garber Industries*, this picks up more than acquisitions of corporations by other corporations as in *Briarcliff Candy*. Fortunately, certain transfers of stock, such as upon death, gift or divorce, are essentially ignored under Section 382. I.R.C. § 382(*l*)(3)(B).

An expansive definition of an owner shift creates an obvious problem for public corporations in which shares constantly change hands. To avoid this problem, Section 382 limits its reach to owner shifts that involve 5 percent shareholders. (While Section 382 seems to demand a review of whether there has been an ownership change whenever there is an "equity structure shift"—in other words, a reorganization (with certain exceptions) within the meaning of Section 368—the regulations limit this to reorganizations that affect 5 percent shareholders. I.R.C. § 382(g)(1), (3); Temp. Treas. Reg. § 1.381–2T(e).) The focus on the 5 percent shareholder is not as straightforward as it, at first, might appear:

> An individual is considered a 5–percent shareholder if he directly or indirectly owns 5% or more of the loss corporation's stock. An individual indirectly owns stock of a loss corporation by virtue of his ownership interest in a "first tier entity" or a "higher tier entity." A first tier entity is an entity which owns a 5% or more direct ownership interest in the stock of the loss corporation. A higher tier entity is an entity which owns a 5% or more direct ownership interest in a first tier entity or another higher tier entity. Example: X Corporation directly owns 20% of Loss Corporation's stock. Y Corporation owns 10% of X Corporation's stock. * * * X Corporation is a first tier entity because it directly owns more than 5% of Loss Corporation's stock. Y Corporation is a higher tier entity as a result of its 10% interest in X Corporation, a first tier entity. * * * An individual who owns a direct interest in X Corporation or Y Corporation would have an indirect ownership interest in Loss Corporation (as a result of his interest in the first tier entity or higher tier entity, respectively).
>
> * * *
>
> [I]n determining whether an individual is a 5–percent shareholder, the individual is treated as owning his proportionate share of the loss corporation stock owned (directly or indirectly) by the first tier entity or higher tier entity, unless the individual directly owns less than 5% of the stock of the first tier entity or higher tier entity. * * * Example: X Corporation owns 90% of Loss Corporation's stock. Z owns 20% of X Corporation's stock. Z indirectly owns 18% (20% × 90% = 18%) of Loss Corporation's stock and is, therefore, a 5–percent shareholder of Loss Corporation.
>
> * * *
>
> Unlike the usual rules of section 318(a) relating to family member attribution, an individual is not considered to own the stock owned by other members of his family. Instead, all members of a family described in section 318(a)(1) are treated as one individual, provided that if a family member would not be a 5–percent shareholder standing alone, then he is not among the members of the family considered to be the 5–percent shareholder. * * *
>
> The stock owned by an individual through a first tier entity or a higher tier entity, directly and indirectly, is not the only stock the individual is considered to own for purposes of determining whether an ownership change has occurred; options held by the individual also may be considered. Likewise, the individuals who directly or indirectly

through first tier or higher tier entities own the loss corporation's stock subject to an option may not be the stockholders taken into account on a testing date.

* * *

After the individual 5–percent shareholders of the loss corporation have been ascertained, it is then necessary to review the corporation's ownership to identify "public groups." A "public group" is a group of individuals, entities, or other persons each of which owns, directly or indirectly, less than 5% of the loss corporation's stock. Each public group is considered to be a separate 5–percent shareholder. A public group may arise at any level in the loss corporation's hierarchy, from direct ownership in the loss corporation to the first tier entity level to any higher tier entity level. A loss corporation may have more than one public group and, under certain circumstances, each first tier entity or higher tier entity may have more than one public group. The purpose for establishing public groups is to disregard corporate ownership and to provide a mechanism for identifying the ultimate beneficial owners of the corporation. * * *

* * * Example: 1000 unrelated individuals own equal interests in X Corporation. X Corporation owns 50% of Y Corporation and 100 unrelated individuals own equal interests in the remaining 50%; Y Corporation owns 20% of Loss Corporation. Since none of the shareholders of X Corporation owns indirectly 5% or more of Loss Corporation, each shareholder is a member of X Corporation's public group. The public group of X Corporation owns 10% of Loss Corporation through X Corporation's shares of Y Corporation (50% × 20% = 10%) and is, therefore, a 5–percent shareholder of Loss Corporation. Any future acquisition within the testing period by X Corporation of Loss Corporation's stock, e.g., by increasing its ownership in Y Corporation, would be an increase of the ownership interest of X Corporation's public group's interest in Loss Corporation and would be considered in any determination of ownership change.

* * *

The direct public group of the loss corporation will be segregated for purposes of determining whether an ownership change has occurred if any of three different types of transaction occur. The first type of transaction includes (i) certain tax-free reorganizations in which the loss corporation is a party. * * * Example: On January 1, 1988, 1% of all of the stock of Loss Corporation is owned by each of 100 unrelated individuals. All the stock of X Corporation is owned similarly by a different 100 unrelated individuals. On January 2, 1989, Loss Corporation merges into X Corporation in a tax-free reorganization under Section 368(a)(1)(A), with the public group of the Loss Corporation prior to the merger receiving 40% of the stock of X Corporation. Since the direct public group which existed before the merger must be segregated from any direct public group which resulted from the merger, the pre-existing public group of Loss Corporation is treated separately from the public group comprised of shareholders of X Corporation. The sixty percentage point increase of X Corporation's public group's interest in Loss Corporation constitutes an ownership change.

The second type of transaction where the direct public group of a loss corporation will be segregated involves redemptions. The public group that exists immediately before the redemption is segregated so that the stock acquired in the transaction is treated as owned by a separate group from each public group that owns the stock which is not acquired in the redemption. Example: One percent of the stock of Loss Corporation is owned by each of 100 unrelated individuals. On January 1, 1988, Loss Corporation redeems the stock of sixty shareholders for cash. The direct public group of Loss Corporation is segregated into two public groups immediately before the redemption, one comprised of the group of redeeming shareholders and one comprised of the group of remaining shareholders. Since the remaining shareholders' public group increased its interest from 40% to 100% as a result of the redemption, an ownership change has occurred.

* * *

New public groups may arise not only from transactions entered into by the loss corporation itself, but also from transactions entered into by direct or indirect owners of the loss corporation's stock.

Davidow, *Limitations Imposed By the Tax Reform Act of 1986 on a Corporation's Use of Net Operating Loss Carryovers After an Ownership Change*, 17 U. Balt. L. Rev. 331 (1988). Incidentally, stock for purposes of Section 382 excludes preferred stock described in Section 1504(a)(4). I.R.C. § 382(k)(6)(A).

Several points are worth noting when computing whether the interest of 5 percent shareholders has increased. To begin with, the examination looks to persons who are five percent shareholders after the owner shift, even if they were not such shareholders before. (Otherwise, the sale of all stock to a new shareholder would not count.) Next, the comparison is against the lowest percentage of ownership by each 5 percent shareholder during the prior three years, even in a case in which the percentage owned by the 5 percent shareholder immediately after the owner shift could be less than what the shareholder owned at earlier times in the three year period. Finally, the question is whether the percentage ownership of all of the 5 percent shareholders, whose ownership increased when measured against their low points during the prior three years, taken as a group, increased by 50 percent points as compared with their low points during the prior three years, even if the increases are due to unrelated events. In other words, the test is a very mechanical one of matching the lowest percentage ownership during the prior three years for each 5 percent shareholder against that shareholder's holdings immediately after the owner shift, and totaling up the increases, while ignoring the decreases. Temp. Treas. Reg. § 1.381–2T(c).

In the event of an ownership change, Section 382 imposes two limits on the use of NOLs. First, the post-ownership change loss corporation (or any corporation that inherits the right to use the loss corporation's NOLs) must continue the business—presumably within the meaning of the continuity of business test for a tax-free reorganization—of the pre-ownership change loss corporation for at least two years after the ownership change. Failure to meet this requirement precludes any use of the pre-ownership change NOLs (except to offset gain from an election under Section 338). I.R.C. § 382(c). Beyond this absolute limit, Section 382 imposes a cap based upon the pre-ownership change value of the loss corporation. Specifically, the post-ownership change loss corporation (or any corporation that inherits the right to use the loss corporation's NOLs) can only utilize pre-ownership change NOLs to offset an amount of post-ownership change taxable income equal to the pre-ownership change value of the loss corporation multiplied by the long-term tax exempt rate. I.R.C. § 382(b), (f).

Section 382 also addresses property in a loss corporation when the property either has a higher or lower value upon an ownership change than the corporation's basis in the property. Section 382 treats the corporation's recognition of a built-in loss (in other words, the amount by which the property's value at the time of the ownership change was less than the corporation's basis in the property) the same as a NOL from before the ownership change. I.R.C. § 382(h)(1)(B). By contrast, the corporation's recognition of a built-in gain (in other words, the amount by which the property's value at the time of the ownership change was greater than the corporation's basis in the property) increases the amount of pre-ownership change NOLs that the loss corporation is entitled to recognize after the ownership change. I.R.C. § 382(h)(1)(A). Notice that these rules make it important to appraise the value of corporate property upon an ownership change. *See* I.R.C. § 382(h)(2)(imposing the burden on the loss corporation to establish existence of built-in gain and to disprove the existence of built-in loss). Mitigating the burden, however, Section 382 places a floor on the amount of built-in gain or loss that triggers the Section's application. I.R.C. § 382(h)(3)(B)(ignore built-in gain or loss if the total is not at least 15 percent of the fair market value of the loss corporation's assets or $10 million).

Finally, a couple of other sections of the Internal Revenue Code exist to fill specific gaps in the reach of Section 382. Section 382 deals only with NOL carryovers, not with other tax attributes which might occasionally make the acquisition of a corporation desirable. Some of these other attributes include net capital loss carryovers under Section 1212, unused business credit carryovers under Section 39, unused minimum tax credits under Section 53, and unused foreign tax credit carryovers under Section 904(c). Section 383, however, authorizes the Internal Revenue Service to promulgate regulations limiting, in a manner consistent with the general approach employed by Section 382, the use of these four carryovers following an ownership change. Moreover, Section 382 does not apply to the acquisition by a corporation with NOL carryovers of a profitable company, at least so long as there is no ownership change in the loss company. Hence, it would not have applied in *Briarcliff Candy*, even if the transaction there occurred after Congress had enacted the modern version of Section 382 in 1986. Section 384 puts one minor crimp on this type of transaction. This section prevents use of pre-acquisition NOLs from one company—regardless of whether it is the acquirer or the acquired—to offset built-in gains from the sale of property of the other company, following an acquisition of stock giving one company control (under the eighty percent tests of Section 1504(a)(2)) of the other, or following a tax-free acquisition of assets in an "A", "C" or "D" reorganization. (An exception exists when the two companies were previously under common control for five years. I.R.C. § 384(b).) The purpose is to prevent the use of NOL carryovers from one company to enable another company to slip around the double tax normally incident to the disposition of appreciated property.

3. *Briarcliff Candy* mentioned the case of *Lisbon Shops v. Koehler*. In its decision in this case, the Supreme Court allowed a company emerging from a merger to use pre-merger NOL carryovers only to offset the post-merger income generated by the business inherited from the firm which produced the NOLs. *Lisbon Shops* involved the 1939 tax code, and substantial doubt existed as to whether it applied to transactions under the 1954 code (since the 1954 code adopted specific provisions in Sections 381 and 382 dealing with the inheritance of NOL carryovers). *Compare Maxwell Hardware Co. v. Commissioner,* 343 F.2d 713 (9th Cir.1965), *with National Tea Co. v. Commissioner,* 793 F.2d 864 (7th Cir.1986). The legislative history of the Tax Reform Act of 1986 may (or may not) end the controversy with its statement that *Lisbon Shops* no longer applies—at least to any situation addressed by Sections 381 and 382. H.R. Rep. No. 841, 99th Cong., 2d Sess. 194 (1986).

4. The consolidated return regulations contain additional rules designed to prevent trafficking in NOLs. The *Wolter Construction* opinion, reprinted in Chapter II, arose out of the limitations which the regulations impose on the group's use of NOLs incurred by a corporation prior to its affiliation with the group. Generally, such NOLs may only offset the cumulative post-consolidation income of the corporation which incurred them (or the cumulative post-consolidation income of the subgroup in which this corporation was a member before the acquisition). Treas. Reg. § 1.1502–21(c). (Note how this follows the *Lisbon Shops* approach, rather than the formula limitation imposed by Section 382. The regulations state, however, that in situations in which Section 382 covers the transaction—in other words, when a corporation becomes a member of the consolidated group within a half year of an ownership change—Section 382 governs the limitation on the use of NOLs. Treas. Reg. § 1.1502–21(g).) The regulations impose the same sort of limit on a group's use of so-called built-in losses from firms entering the group. Treas. Reg. § 1.1502–15. (An example of a built-in loss would be a company's sale, after joining the group, of an asset which had

declined in value prior to the affiliation below the company's basis in the asset.) Suppose it is the group or the common parent (rather than an acquired company) which incurred the pre-affiliation loss. Here, the regulations prevent the use of the pre-affiliation NOLs to offset consolidated income generated by the new arrival to the group by applying Section 382 to groups. Treas. Reg. §§ 1.1502–90–1.1502–99. Keep in mind as well that the limitations contained in Sections 269, 382, 383 and 384 remain applicable even to use of NOLs through consolidated returns. *See also Elko Realty Co. v. Commissioner,* 29 T.C. 1012 (1958), *aff'd,* 260 F.2d 949 (3d Cir.1958) (court denied three corporations the right to file a consolidated return, when one of the three had acquired the stock of the other two without a business purpose, but simply to gain the advantage of setting their losses off against its income).

5. The alternative minimum tax applicable to corporations may create one other set of tax motivated acquisitions. For example, suppose a corporation incurs numerous deductions which lower its taxable income without involving immediate out-of-pocket expenditures (perhaps because the company is involved in heavy industry and thus owns considerable depreciable property). As a result, this company may face a tax on its "alternative minimum taxable income"—broadly speaking, its taxable income, increased by certain types of deductions (such as accelerated rather than straight line depreciation) which the company claimed and which arguably cause the firm's taxable income to differ from its "real" earnings. I.R.C. §§ 55, 56. A firm need not pay the alternate minimum tax, however, except insofar as a 20 percent tax on its "alternative minimum taxable income" would exceed its regular tax liability for the year. I.R.C. § 55(a). Hence, if this company could find another firm (perhaps in a service industry) whose regular tax will substantially exceed the 20 percent rate on the other firm's alternative minimum taxable income—which, at a 34 or 35 percent rate, the regular tax will do when the taxable income and alternative minimum taxable income do not significantly diverge—then the combination of the firms could save the corporation with substantial deductions from the alternative minimum tax.

SECTION C. FOLLOW-UP TRANSACTIONS

1. LIQUIDATING THE SELLING CORPORATION FOLLOWING A SALE OF ASSETS

a. *In General*

After selling its assets, the target corporation could keep or reinvest the proceeds (depending upon whether it received stock or cash) and continue to exist indefinitely. A number of factors, however, will often lead the parties to dissolve the target company and distribute its properties to its shareholders. Two motivations for this exist from the buyer's side, and, as a result, the buyer sometimes demands such dissolution as a term in the contract of sale. *See Hariton v. Arco Electronics, Inc.,* reprinted earlier in this chapter. The buyer may wish to procure the name and goodwill of the selling company, as well as ensure the seller does not later re-enter the field in competition with the purchaser. (A buyer might, however, obtain these objectives without requiring the target to dissolve.) More significantly, if the purchaser pays with its voting stock, the buying firm's management might be worried about the effect on control of leaving the stock concentrated in the selling corporation rather than dispersed among the target's former shareholders. (Cutting against these motivations, the buyer might desire preservation of the selling firm in order lessen the prospects of successor liability, the possible need to follow the corporate merger rules under the de facto merger doctrine, or the requirement of registering securities issued in exchange for the assets.)

Stronger motivations for a post-sale dissolution exist from the seller's side. There is the simple desire of the selling company's shareholders to receive the proceeds. (Not only may some of the stockholders wish to spend rather than reinvest the proceeds, but even those planning reinvestment often prefer to make their own choices.) Tax factors also play a role. Obtaining tax-free treatment under Section 368(a)(1)(C) demands liquidation unless the Internal Review Service waives the requirement. Moreover, while liquidation following a taxable sale triggers a second tax, not liquidating and simply accumulating investment income can create problems with penalty taxes. Other factors include avoiding appraisal rights (*see, e.g.,* N.Y. Bus. Corp. Law § 910(a)(1)(B)), and preventing the need to register under federal law as an investment company. Dissolution can also serve to cut off liabilities the selling company might otherwise have faced.

Pacific Scene, Inc. v. Penasquitos, Inc.

46 Cal.3d 407, 250 Cal.Rptr. 651, 758 P.2d 1182 (1988).

■ MOSK, JUSTICE.—We are called upon in this case to determine whether an action under the equitable "trust fund" theory can be maintained against the former shareholders of a dissolved corporation, to the extent of their distribution of corporate assets, when a defective product manufactured by the corporation causes injury after dissolution. We conclude that the Legislature has barred such an action. Pacific Scene, Inc. (hereafter Pacific) is a corporation producing tract homes. Prior to its dissolution in 1979, Penasquitos, Inc., was a California corporation in the business of developing and finishing residential lots suitable for tract home construction. Pacific purchased a number of lots from Penasquitos in 1974, and in 1975 sold tract homes constructed thereon. In 1982 nine homeowners discovered damage caused by the subsidence of lots sold by Penasquitos. They sued Pacific on various theories, including strict products liability, negligence, and breach of warranty.

Pacific cross-claimed against Penasquitos, which demurred. The court sustained the demurrer without leave to amend and dismissed the cross-complaint, concluding that Corporations Code section 2011 barred suits against dissolved corporations on claims arising after dissolution. Pacific appealed.

* * *

Discussion

Dissolution of a corporation under the common law "terminate[d] its existence as a legal entity, and render[ed] it incapable of suing or being sued as a corporate body or in its corporate name." * * * The trust fund theory was developed to ameliorate the harsh result of this common law rule, which allowed corporations to shield their assets from the reach of creditors through distribution to shareholders pursuant to dissolution. * * *

Under the equitable theory, "a creditor of the dissolved corporation may follow [the distributed assets] as in the nature of a trust fund into the hands of stockholders. The creditors have the right to subject such assets to their debts and for that purpose the stockholders hold them as though they were trustees. In other words, the assets of the dissolved corporation are a trust fund against which the corporate creditors have a claim superior to that of the stockholders. A stockholder who receives only a portion of the assets is liable to respond only for that portion. Where the assets coming into the hands of a stockholder suffer a change in value, the creditor must take the trust fund as he finds it, securing the advantage of any increase and suffering any decrease, unless the stockholder is responsible for the decrease. Where the trust property has been used by the stockholder for his own purpose, or disposed of by him, he may be held personally liable for the full value thereof." (*Koch v. United States* (10th Cir.1943) 138 F.2d 850, 852.) * * *

I.

The shareholders first contend that the Legislature has completely occupied the field concerning the rights and remedies attending corporate dissolution, thus preempting antecedent common law remedies such as the trust fund theory. * * *

Sections 1800 to 2011 of the Corporations Code, enacted as part of a comprehensive statutory revision in 1977, comprise a broad and detailed scheme regulating virtually every aspect of corporate dissolution. * * * Included therein are two sections specifically governing claims asserted by creditors against former shareholders for the recovery of distributed corporate assets. Section 2009 provides: "(a) Whenever in the process of winding up a corporation any distribution of assets has been made ... without prior payment or adequate provision for payment of any of the debts and liabilities of the corporation, any amount so improperly distributed to any shareholder may be recovered by the corporation.... [¶] (b) Suit may be brought in the name of the corporation to enforce the liability under subdivision (a) against any or all shareholders receiving the distribution by any one or more creditors of the corporation, whether or not they have reduced their claims to judgment." Section 2011, subdivision (a) (hereafter section 2011(a)), provides: "In all cases where a corporation has been dissolved, the shareholders may be sued in the corporate name of such corporation upon any cause of action against the corporation arising prior to its dissolution."

* * *

In view of the detailed statutory remedies now encompassing virtually all claims previously asserted in equity against the former shareholders of dissolved corporations, we must similarly conclude that the Legislature has occupied the field and precluded resort to dormant common law doctrines for the provision of extra-statutory relief. This conclusion is especially compelling on the facts before us, insofar as the equitable relief sought by Pacific would require us to confront a variety of intractable policy questions intimately bound up with the provisions and objectives of the existing statutory scheme. Once the Legislature has evinced an intent to comprehensively define the contours of a particular field, however, such complex policy determinations must plainly remain beyond the reach of our equitable jurisdiction.

II.

The shareholders maintain that even if the Legislature did not intend to completely occupy the field with respect to the rights and remedies attending corporate dissolution, the assertion of post-dissolution claims under the trust fund theory nonetheless conflicts with the specific intent of section 2011(a).

Section 2011(a) provides: "In all cases where a corporation has been dissolved, the shareholders may be sued in the corporate name of such corporation upon any cause of action against the corporation arising *prior* to its dissolution. This section is procedural in nature and is not intended to determine liability." (Italics added.) The shareholders argue that this language, by negative implication, evinces an intent to preclude actions against former shareholders for injuries arising after corporate dissolution, and thus that any corresponding equitable action must be similarly barred. * * *

The Court of Appeal reasoned that although section 2011(a) plainly preempts the trust fund theory with respect to predissolution claims, the statute simply fails to address the postdissolution context and therefore need not be read to bar equitable relief for claims then arising.

* * *

The Court of Appeal conceded, however, that its construction of section 2011(a) would subject shareholders to the possibility of "unending liability...." * * *

We are aware, of course, that other interests are reflected in the dissolution provisions of the Corporations Code, not the least of which is payment to corporate creditors. * * * This interest stands in inherent conflict with the final and certain conclusion of a corporation's affairs, as the comment to section 14.07 of the 1985 Model Business Corporations Act explains: "[O]n the one hand, the application of a mechanical ... limitation period to a claim for injury that occurs after the period has expired involves obvious injustice to the plaintiff. On the other hand, to permit these suits generally makes it impossible ever to complete the winding up of the corporation...." * * * The 1985 model act reconciles these conflicting interests by allowing the assertion of claims against former shareholders during a five-year period following corporate dissolution, but barring claims arising thereafter. (Id. § 14.07, * * *) Here we are asked to infer that the Legislature has balanced the same interests entirely on the shoulders of shareholders, who assertedly are required to face such claims in perpetuity.

* * *

We must choose, then, between a construction of section 2011(a) premised on a silent legislative intent to procedurally encumber postdissolution creditors in the unending assertion of their claims, or alternatively a construction precluding postdissolution claims in a manner consistent with the statutory objectives of certainty and finality. We accordingly determine that the statute bars the assertion of postdissolution claims in equity. * * *

Courts in several other jurisdictions construing similar statutory provisions have reached the same result. A number of states have enacted statutes substantially identical to section 105 of the 1969 Model Business Corporations Act, which allows actions against dissolved corporations and their officers, directors, and shareholders on predissolution claims brought within two years of corporate dissolution. * * *[79] Courts considering such statutes in Texas, Illinois, and Iowa have each concluded that the exclusive statutory authorization of predissolution claims bars the assertion of claims arising thereafter. * * * Our analysis of section 2011(a) is thus consistent with the substantial body of precedent construing the parallel statutory provisions of our sister states.

Conclusion

For the reasons stated, we conclude that the Legislature has precluded the assertion of postdissolution claims against the former shareholders of a dissolved corporation under the equitable "trust fund" theory. We emphasize, however, that this determination does not insulate dissolving corporations or their shareholders from actions for the recovery of fraudulently transferred assets. Thus if a corporation were to mass produce defective products and then dissolve to avoid liability, "leaving a multitude of potential claims in its wake" * * *, grave questions would be raised under the Uniform Fraudulent Transfer Act. * * * In the case at bar, no such allegation was made. The judgment of the Court of Appeal is reversed with

79. * * * Significantly, the drafters of the model act itself recently concluded that the emphasized language failed to adequately provide for the assertion of postdissolution claims, and have entirely rewritten the provision to authorize the assertion of such claims during the first five years following dissolution. (See Model Bus.Corp. Act Ann. (1985) § 14.07.)

directions to affirm the judgment of dismissal entered by the superior court.

* * *

NOTES

1. Terminating a corporation after selling its assets involves three basic activities. One is to carry out the formalities specified by statute to dissolve the company. (In this regard, it is useful to differentiate two terms: "dissolution," which refers to the legal process of ending the corporation's existence as an entity, and "liquidation," which refers to the practical process of disposing of the assets of the company. *See, e.g.,* Cal. Corp. Code §§ 1808, 1905. M.B.C.A. § 14.05. Recall a parallel distinction in the partnership area.) Typically, to voluntarily dissolve a corporation, state statutes call for a vote by the company's directors and shareholders (or, under some statutes, just the shareholders), and the filing of an appropriate document (often called a certificate or articles of dissolution; sometimes preceded by a "statement of intent to dissolve") with the Secretary of State (or similar state official). *E.g.,* Cal. Corp. Code §§ 1900, 1901, 1905, 1907; Del. Gen. Corp. Law § 275; N.Y. Bus. Corp. Law §§ 1001, 1003; M.B.C.A. §§ 14.02, 14.03.

2. The second basic activity involved in terminating a company after the sale of its assets is to pay off its creditors. Failure to do so prior to distributing money or property to the stockholders can lead to liability for the recipient shareholders under the equitable or statutory theories outlined in *Pacific Scene,* as well as for the directors approving the distribution. *E.g.,* Cal. Corp. Code § 316(a)(2). *See also* Del. Gen. Corp. Law §§ 281, 282. From a planning standpoint, dealing with creditors' claims upon dissolution raises two problems for the solvent company. To begin with, as noted earlier, often the buyer will agree to assume some or all of the selling company's debts. Does this mean the selling company can go ahead and distribute the proceeds of the sale, and not worry about the obligations the buyer agreed to pick up? *Compare Darcy v. Brooklyn & N.Y. Ferry Co.,* 196 N.Y. 99, 89 N.E. 461 (1909) (creditors must agree to the buyer's assumption of liability), *with* Cal. Corp. Code § 2005(a) (assumption of liability by a person or corporation, reasonably and in good faith determined by the dissolving company's board to be financially responsible, is adequate). *Pacific Scene* involved the second problem: what to do about claims unknown to the corporation or arising after its dissolution. Some corporations statutes contain notice provisions, which, if complied with, can serve to bar later claims—at least after a certain amount of time—or else allow directors to cut off claims by setting aside some funds or otherwise making provision for later arising claims. *E.g.,* Del. Gen. Corp. Law §§ 280–282; N.Y. Bus. Corp. Law § 1007; M.B.C.A. §§ 14.06, 14.07. California's statute had allowed the directors to distribute the remaining assets to the shareholders after payment of known debts (Cal.Corp.Code § 2004), without the shareholders, according to *Pacific Scene*, thereafter normally facing any liability for later claims. In 1991, however, the California

legislature amended Section 2011 of the state's corporation code to make shareholders liable for post dissolution claims to the extent of any assets the shareholders received from the corporation. This amendment would not have changed the result in *Pacific Scene* since, following the approach of other jurisdictions discussed in the court's opinion, Section 2011 now cuts off claims made more than four years after dissolution.

3. Finally, the corporation will distribute what is left of its cash or properties to its stockholders. Needless to say, the company must make the distribution in accordance with any liquidation preferences between classes of shares. *But see* Cal. Corp. Code § 2007 (allowing a distribution upon liquidation to deviate from the liquidation rights of preferred shares if approved by a majority vote of each class of shares; but also granting dissenting shares appraisal rights); *Goldman v. Postal Telegraph, Inc.*, 52 F.Supp. 763 (D.Del.1943) (shareholders approved a proposal to sell the company's assets and dissolve the corporation, which proposal also amended the certificate to alter the liquidation preference of the preferred). If the target sells its assets for stock in the buyer, the existence of liquidation preferences can pose a problem. Often, the articles state the preference as demanding the payment of cash. Possibly, the preferred shareholders might vote to amend the articles (or, for a California corporation, to accept a distribution under Cal. Corp. Code § 2007). Otherwise, in addition to the evident economic problems, recall the tax consequences if the selling corporation in a "C" reorganization must come up with cash for the preferred stockholders. Moreover, even if the preferred can receive a distribution paid in the buyer's stock, this obviously creates a need to value the distributed shares.

b. *Tax Aspects*

The Tax Reform Act of 1986 removed most of the tax complexities formerly associated with liquidating a corporation. For example, the Act renders the outcome now relatively simple when a target company sells all its properties for cash, and has the buyer assume all its liabilities—leaving for the liquidation solely the distribution of the cash to the stockholders. As discussed earlier, the sale constitutes a taxable transaction to the target, regardless—in a major change from the law up to 1986—of the target's intention to liquidate. Upon the liquidation itself, the shareholders recognize gain or loss measured by the difference between the amount of cash they receive, and their basis in their shares. The Code treats the liquidating distribution(s) (with one minor exception) as equivalent to the sale of stock; ordinarily meaning it produces a capital gain or loss. I.R.C. § 331.

Suppose the buyer does not pay all cash, but instead pays in whole or in part with its stock or debt securities. If it pays entirely with voting stock, the transaction becomes a "C" reorganization. I.R.C. § 368(a)(1)(C). As discussed earlier, this renders not only the sale of assets, but also the ensuing liquidation, generally tax-free to both the selling corporation and its shareholders. If the buyer pays with its debt instruments, liquidation will terminate the selling company's ability to take advantage of installment reporting of any gain. I.R.C. § 453B(a). If, however, the selling company adopts a plan of liquidation before the sale, and liquidates within one year, then the shareholders to whom it distributes the debt instruments can use installment reporting to spread the shareholders' (as opposed to the company's) recognition (assuming the conditions for such reporting otherwise apply). I.R.C. § 453(h)(1). *See also* I.R.C. § 453B(h) (preventing recognition in this event by an S corporation; meaning that the owners of an S corporation can avoid recognizing any gain until receipt of payment upon the installment obligation). This suggests, if the selling company is going to liquidate after selling its assets for debt, it adopt a plan making this intention clear before the sale, and not dawdle thereafter.

Often, the buyer will not purchase all of the selling firm's assets, or assume all of its liabilities. This introduces a number of additional considerations when the selling company liquidates. To begin with, now the stockholders must measure their gain or loss by the difference between their basis in their shares, and both the amount of cash and the fair market value of the property they receive from the company. I.R.C. § 1001(b). The liquidating company must also recognize gain, or (with certain exceptions) loss, if the fair market value of the distributed property differs from the company's basis in the assets. I.R.C. § 336(a). (The company's gain under Section 336(a) flows through to the shareholders of an S corporation (unless Section 1374 applies), but, since the recognition raises the stockholders' basis, they will not face a second tax upon the distribution. *See* I.R.C. § 1367(a)(1). *See also* The Technical Correction Act of 1988, Pub.L. 100–647, § 1006(f)(7) (repealing former Section 1363(d) and (e)).)

These factors place a premium upon valuing assets distributed in liquidation. Normally, one might expect the corporation and recipient shareholders to urge a low value (in order to decrease their gain or increase their loss), and the I.R.S. to take a contrary position. Occasionally, however, the positions may flip over, and the taxpayers might seek a high valuation. The reason is that the distributed assets receive a basis equal to their fair market value at the time of distribution. I.R.C. § 334(a). A high basis might decrease later recognition of ordinary income, for example, by providing greater depreciation deductions. At the same time, Sections 331 and 336 generally treat the shareholder's and the corporation's recognition as capital gain. *But see* I.R.C. § 1239 (recharacterizing the corporation's gain as ordinary income if it sells or, presumably, distributes depreciable property to the holder of more than 50 percent of the value of its outstanding stock). Note, however, that corporate capital gains are now taxed at the same rate as corporate ordinary income.

Beyond the possibility of disputes over valuation, sometimes the company may distribute assets—such as a contested claim for payments from a foreign government—which are so speculative as to defy valuation. *See* Rev. Rul. 58–402, 1958–2 C.B. 15 (stating that this problem exists only in rare and extraordinary circumstances). In this event, the taxpayers may obtain open transaction treatment—meaning the recipient will report gain on the transaction as he or she collects upon the speculative claim involved, and only after receiving a return of his or her basis. *E.g., Likins–Foster Honolulu Corp. v. Commissioner,* 840 F.2d 642 (9th Cir.1988). Notice how much more favorable open transaction treatment is to the taxpayer than is immediate recognition of the present fair market value of the claim. Not only does this delay recognition of any gain, but it also can affect the character of the income which the taxpayer recognizes. If the taxpayer recognized immediate gain (or loss) based upon the present fair market value of the claim, later payments upon the claim in excess of the taxpayer's basis might produce ordinary income rather than capital gains. *E.g., Warren v. United States,* 171 F.Supp. 846 (Ct.Cl.1959), *cert. denied,* 361 U.S. 916.

If the value of the distributed assets is below the liquidating company's basis in the property, the firm may recognize a loss. I.R.C. § 336(a). Section 336(d) places two limitations upon this rule in order to prevent abuse. Essentially, the concern is that stockholders owning property with a value less than their basis in it could contribute the asset in a Section 351 transaction to a company they soon plan to liquidate, and thereby double the loss recognized. To stop this from occurring, Section 336(d)(2) precludes the liquidating corporation from recognizing the loss built in to property it received in a Section 351 transaction (or as a capital contribution) when the principal purpose for transferring the property to the company was to enable the firm to recognize the loss upon liquidation. (Section 336(d)(2)(B)(ii) presumes that the transfer of property to the company within two years of the firm adopting a plan of liquidation generally is for the prohibited purpose.) Supplementing this largely subjective approach, Section 336(d)(1) establishes an objective disqualification upon the company's claiming a loss. This disqualification occurs either when the corporation makes a non-pro-rata distribution of property to a related shareholder (within the meaning of Section 267), or when the corporation distributes to such a shareholder property the company received in a Section 351 transaction (or through a capital contribution) within five years of the distribution. What is to prevent, however, the corporation from selling the contributed property at a loss, and then liquidating with a second loss for its stockholders? See I.R.C. § 336(d)(2)(A). In this regard, notice, in contrast to the scope of Section 336(d)(2)(A), the objective barrier of Section 336(d)(1) only reaches distributions, not sales to third parties. Consider the planning implication if a corporation, possessing substantial loss property received less than five years earlier in a Section 351 transaction, receives an offer to buy all its assets. How should the corporation structure the sale: sell the property and liquidate, or liquidate first and have its shareholders sell the property? (Incidentally, Section 267 itself does not apply to prevent recognition of losses in the complete liquidation of a corporation, even if the liquidation involves distributions from the corporation to related parties. I.R.C. § 267(a)(1).)

The existence of corporate debts which the buyer did not assume also impacts the tax effects of a liquidation. If the buyer does not assume all the target company's obligations, the target's shareholders may plan to do so.

This decreases the stockholder's recognition of gain (or increases their recognition of loss). Rev. Rul. 59–228, 1959–2 C.B. 59. On the other hand, it can increase the liquidating company's gain. Specifically, if the liquidating company distributes an asset subject to a liability, the corporation recognizes income or loss equal to the difference between the company's basis in the property, and the greater of the item's fair market value or the obligation encumbering the item. I.R.C. § 336(b). Suppose the liability is contingent or contested. In this event, the liability does not decrease the assuming shareholder's gain; rather it produces a later loss deduction upon payment. *Schneider v. Commissioner,* 65 T.C. 18 (1975). Since this later loss is normally a capital loss (*Arrowsmith v. Commissioner,* 344 U.S. 6 (1952)), and since shareholders who are individuals cannot carry a capital loss back to offset their earlier gain upon the liquidation (*see* I.R.C. § 1212(b)), the result is to make it disadvantageous for shareholders to assume contested or contingent liabilities. Perhaps it may be possible to delay liquidation until the corporation handles these claims.

Suppose some of the corporate debt represents claims owed to its shareholders. If the claims represent items, such as back salary, which will yield ordinary income upon payment, the shareholder-creditors may be tempted to forgive the claim and obtain more as a liquidating distribution in their status as stockholders. If the corporation has only one substantial shareholder, or the stockholders forgive claims which are roughly proportional to their shareholdings, the release has no economic reality. In this event, courts may ignore the release of the claims. *E.g., Dwyer v. United States,* 622 F.2d 460 (9th Cir.1980). If respected, however, will the forgiveness create income for the corporation, or constitute a tax-free capital contribution? See I.R.C. § 108(e)(6) (cancellation of zero basis debt will constitute income for the corporation).

Often, a liquidating corporation may disburse its assets to its stockholders through a series of distributions, rather than all at once. In this event, the recipient shareholders do not recognize gain until the distributions have first recovered their basis in their stock. Rev. Rul. 68–348, 1968–2 C.B. 141. (Contrast this with the proportionate recovery of gain in each payment under Section 453. While one might argue that Section 453 prevents open transaction treatment here—since Section 331 characterizes a liquidation as a sale of stock—the Internal Revenue Service has not pursued this notion. *See* Rev. Rul. 85–48, 1985–1 C.B. 126.) If a shareholder owns several blocks of stock acquired at different times, or at different prices, the stockholder must allocate the liquidating distributions ratably among the blocks, and measure gain or loss separately for each. Treas. Reg. § 1.331–1(e). The open transaction approach of Revenue Ruling 68–348 may not only delay recognition of gain, it could also delay recognition of loss until the last payment to the shareholders. *But see* Rev. Rul. 69–334, 1969 C.B. 98 (allowed earlier recognition of loss when later payment would only be a few cents per share). Moreover, liquidating through a series of distributions, especially when the company adopts no formal plan of liquidation, could result in characterization of the early payments as dividends, rather than distributions in liquidation. *Estate of Maguire v. Commissioner*, 50 T.C. 130 (1968).

2. DEALING WITH THE SUBSIDIARY AND NON-SELLING SHAREHOLDERS FOLLOWING A SALE OF STOCK TRANSACTION

a. *In General*

Alpert v. 28 Williams St. Corp.

63 N.Y.2d 557, 483 N.Y.S.2d 667, 473 N.E.2d 19 (1984).

■ COOKE, CHIEF JUDGE.

The subject of contention in this litigation is a valuable 17-story office building, located at 79 Madison Avenue in Manhattan. In dispute is the propriety of a complex series of transactions that had the net effect of permitting defendants, who were outside investors, to gain ownership of the property and to eliminate the ownership interests of plaintiffs, who were minority shareholders of the corporation that formerly owned the building. This was achieved through what is commonly known as a "two-step" merger: (1) an outside investor purchases control of the majority shares of the target corporation by tender offer or through private negotiations; (2) this newly acquired control is used to arrange for the target and a second corporation controlled by the outside investor to merge, with one condition being the "freeze-out" of the minority shareholders of the target corporation by the forced cancellation of their shares, generally through a cash purchase. This accomplishes the investor's original goal of complete ownership of the target corporation.

Since 1955, the office building was owned by 79 Realty Corporation (Realty Corporation), which had no other substantial assets. About two thirds of Realty Corporation's outstanding shares were held by two couples, the Kimmelmans and the Zauderers, who were also the company's sole directors and officers. Plaintiffs owned 26% of the outstanding shares. The remaining shares were owned by persons who are not parties to this litigation.

Defendants, a consortium of investors, formed a limited partnership, known as Madison 28 Associates (Madison Associates), for the purpose of purchasing the building. In March 1980, Madison Associates began negotiations with the Kimmelmans and the Zauderers to purchase the latter's controlling block of stock at a price equal to its proportion of the building's value, agreed in June 1980 to be $6,500,000. In addition, Madison Associates promised that it would also offer to purchase plaintiffs' stock under the same terms within four months of the closing of the stock purchase agreement in September 1980. Madison Associates formed a separate, wholly owned company, 28 Williams Street Corporation (Williams Street), to act as the nominal purchaser and owner of the Kimmelman and Zauderer interests. The stock purchase agreement was actually signed by

Williams Street and its principal asset was the newly acquired shares of Realty Corporation.

Upon selling their shares, the Kimmelmans and the Zauderers resigned their positions with Realty Corporation and were replaced by four partners of Madison Associates. Now acting as the controlling directors of Realty Corporation on October 17, 1980, the partners of Madison Associates approved a plan to merge Realty Corporation with Williams Street, Realty Corporation being the surviving corporation. Together with a notice for a shareholders meeting to vote on the proposed merger, a statement of intent was sent to all shareholders of Realty Corporation, explaining the procedural and financial aspects of the merger, as well as defendants' conflict of interest and the intended exclusion of the minority shareholders from the newly constituted Realty Corporation through a cash buy-out. Defendants also disclosed that they planned to dissolve Realty Corporation after the merger and thereafter to operate the business as a partnership. The merger plan did not require approval by any of the minority shareholders.

* * *

From the outset, plaintiffs resisted their exclusion from Realty Corporation. First, they rejected overtures by Madison Associates to purchase their shares. Then they unsuccessfully sought to enjoin the sale of the Kimmelman and Zauderer interest to Madison Associates.

The plaintiffs instituted this action on October 31, 1980, initially seeking to enjoin the shareholders meeting called to approve the merger. Failing to temporarily enjoin the Realty Corporation's merger with Williams Street, plaintiffs later amended their complaint to include a request for equitable relief in the form of rescission of the merger.

* * *

Upon retrial, Supreme Court denied plaintiffs' requested relief. It determined that plaintiffs had failed to demonstrate that the merger was not for a legitimate business purpose or that they had been dealt with unfairly and inequitably. The court found that the merger advanced several proper corporate business purposes. It provided a means by which the corporation could attract outside capital investment for extensive repairs and renovations of the building that were needed to produce maximum rents. Certain tax advantages and the distribution of mortgage proceeds would accrue upon the ultimate dissolution of the merged corporation and transfer of the building to the partnership.

The court recognized that because the merger would advance defendants' self-interest and plaintiffs' shares were to be eliminated, it would have been preferable for defendants to have had independent directors or appraisers evaluate whether the merger was fair to all parties. The failure to do so, however, was not deemed fatal to the transaction if, viewed as a whole, it was fair. Thus, the court undertook its own review considering the role that defendants' self-interest played in the merger decision, whether overreaching or bad faith were present, and the extent of disclosure of material information to plaintiffs. It also examined how the price for the minority's shares was established and determined that defendants' arrangement with the Kimmelmans and the Zauderers was arrived at through arm's length negotiations and that it reflected the fair market value of the building at the time. In addition, the court noted that the price offered plaintiffs was many times the amount plaintiffs paid for the stock and greatly exceeded the stock's book value and the corporation's past and present earnings. The court concluded that, as a whole, the transaction was fair.

On this appeal, the principal task facing this court is to prescribe a standard for evaluating the validity of a corporate transaction that forcibly eliminates minority shareholders by means of a two-step merger. It is concluded that the analysis employed by the courts below was correct: the majority shareholders' exclusion of minority interests through a two-step merger does not violate the former's fiduciary obligations so long as the transaction viewed as a whole is fair to the minority shareholders and is justified by an independent corporate business purpose. Accordingly, this court now affirms.

(A)

* * *

Generally, the remedy of a shareholder dissenting from a merger and the offered "cash-out" price is to obtain the fair value of his or her stock through an appraisal proceeding (see Business Corporation Law, § 623). * * * The pursuit of an appraisal proceeding generally constitutes the dissenting stockholder's exclusive remedy (see Business Corporation Law, § 623, subd. (k) * * *). An exception exists, however, when the merger is unlawful or fraudulent as to that shareholder, in which event an action for equitable relief is authorized (Business Corporation Law, § 623, subd. (k); * * *). Thus, technical compliance with the Business Corporation Law's requirements alone will not necessarily exempt a merger from further judicial review.

* * *

(C)

* * * In reviewing a freeze-out merger, the essence of the judicial inquiry is to determine whether the transaction, viewed as a whole, was "fair" as to all concerned. * * *

As a general matter, a principal indicator of fair dealing is the relationship between the parties representing the corporations to be merged * * *. When the directors and majority shareholders of each corporation are independent and negotiate at arm's length, it is more likely that the negotiations will reflect the full exertion of each party's bargaining power and the final terms of the transaction will be the best attainable. When, however, there is a common directorship or majority ownership, the inherent conflict of interest and the potential for self-dealing requires careful scrutiny of the transaction. * * *

* * * The interested parties may attempt to establish this element of fair dealing by introducing evidence of efforts taken to simulate arm's length negotiations. Such steps may have included the appointment of an independent negotiating committee made up of neutral directors or of an independent board to evaluate the merger proposal and to oversee the process of its approval. * * *

Fair dealing is also concerned with the procedural fairness of the transaction, such as its timing, initiation, structure, financing, development, disclosure to the independent directors and shareholders, and how the necessary approvals were obtained. * * * Basically, the courts must look for complete and candid disclosure of all the material facts and circumstances of the proposed merger known to the majority or directors, including their dual roles and events leading up to the merger proposal. * * *

The fairness of the transaction cannot be determined without considering the component of the financial remuneration offered the dissenting shareholders.

* * *

(D)

Fair dealing and fair price alone will not render the merger acceptable. As mentioned, there exists a fiduciary duty to treat all shareholders equally * * *. The fact remains, however, that in a freeze-out merger the minority shareholders are being treated in a different manner: the majority is permitted continued participation in the equity of the surviving corporation while the minority has no choice but to surrender their shares for cash. On its face, the majority's conduct would appear to breach this fiduciary obligation.

Majority shareholders, however, have an overriding duty to provide good and prudent management, which demands that decisions be made for the welfare, advantage, and best interests of the corporation and the shareholders as a whole * * *.

In the context of a freeze-out merger, variant treatment of the minority shareholders—i.e., causing their removal—will be justified when related to the advancement of a general corporate interest. The benefit need not be great, but it must be for the corporation. For example, if the sole purpose of the merger is reduction of the number of profit sharers—in contrast to increasing the corporation's capital or profits, or improving its management structure—there will exist no "independent corporate interest". * * * All of these purposes ultimately seek to increase the individual wealth of the remaining shareholders. What distinguishes a proper corporate purpose from an improper one is that, with the former, removal of the minority shareholders furthers the objective of conferring some general gain upon the corporation. Only then will the fiduciary duty of good and prudent management of the corporation serve to override the concurrent duty to treat all shareholders fairly * * *. We further note that a finding that there was an independent corporate purpose for the action taken by the majority will not be defeated merely by the fact that the corporate objective could have been accomplished in another way, or by the fact that the action chosen was not the best way to achieve the bona fide business objective.

* * *

(E)

As noted, the courts below applied the correct legal standard in concluding that the merger here was proper. * * *

* * * There is evidence in the record to support its conclusion that, viewed as a whole, the transaction was fair. Full disclosure of material information was made in the statement of intent mailed to plaintiffs who also had access to Realty Corporation's books. The stock price was tied to the fair market value of the office building, the corporation's only substantial asset, which was determined in arm's length negotiations.

Without passing on all of the business purposes cited by Supreme Court as underlying the merger, it is sufficient to note that at least one justified the exclusion of plaintiffs' interests: attracting additional capital to effect needed repairs of the building. There is proof that there was a good-faith belief that additional, outside capital was required. Moreover, this record supports the conclusion that this capital would not have been available through the merger had not plaintiffs' interest in the corporation been eliminated. Thus, the approval of the merger, which would extinguish plaintiffs' stock, was supported by a bona fide business purpose to advance this general corporate interest of obtaining increased capital.

Accordingly, the order of the Appellate Division should be affirmed.

NOTES

1. As explained earlier, a sale of stock transaction (unless undertaken pursuant to statutory provisions allowing compulsory share exchanges) can leave the purchaser with less than 100 percent ownership of the target's stock. Why might the presence of minority shareholders pose any problem for the buyer, or, put another way, what advantages can the purchaser obtain by removing the minority? Broadly speaking, the potential benefits usually fall into three camps. To begin with, there are tax advantages to increasing ownership to over 80 percent. For example, as explained in Chapter II, the companies can then file a consolidated return, or, even without such a return, the parent can receive dividends tax free from the subsidiary under I.R.C. § 243(b). Of course, obtaining these advantages does not require removal of all the minority shareholders; indeed, the purchaser might be able to acquire the requisite 80 percent for favorable tax treatment, without forcing any unwilling stockholders to sell, if it can

buy additional shares from the corporation and not trigger preemptive rights.

The second category of benefit is the one the court spoke disparagingly of *Alpert*: increasing the acquirer's return by removing other claimants from the corporation. Obtaining this advantage is a function of the price paid to the minority. If the price is low, then the future profits from the acquisition will make cashing out the minority worthwhile. Moreover, and often of greater significance, the threat of freezing out non-selling shareholders at a low price can induce stockholders to accept the original tender offer—thereby lowering the price paid for the target overall. (This is the theory behind the so-called coercive two-tier tender offer. Recall, however, the discussion earlier in this chapter of the defenses available to the target to combat such techniques.) On the other hand, if the price paid to remove the minority is high, then there is no gain of profit by removing the minority, since the cost of doing so is to pay out a sum equal to or greater than the present value of such profits.

The third area of benefit is the avoidance of the various costs and inhibitions potentially created by the presence of minority shareholders. As explained in Chapter IV, a minority stockholder is generally powerless to dictate corporate policies when faced with a cohesive majority block. Nevertheless, various statutory and judicial protections of the minority might limit the majority's freedom of action to do what it wishes with the corporation, or, at the very least, impose some expense. For example, a company with over 500 shareholders faces the cost of making filings under the 1934 Securities Exchange Act, which it can avoid by cashing out the minority. (This is often referred to as going private.) In addition, removing the minority can enable the acquirer to engage in transactions with its subsidiary without concern as to whether minority shareholders might challenge the conduct as unfair. *See, e.g., Sinclair Oil Corp. v. Levien,* 280 A.2d 717 (Del.1971).

In *Alpert,* the purported business purpose lay in the need to raise more money. At first glance, it is difficult to see why cashing out the plaintiffs—which takes money—advances this goal. Perhaps the thinking was that obtaining new investors required operating the building through a limited partnership, rather than a corporation. Yet, even then, was it really necessary to cash out the plaintiffs?

2. Several methods exist to force out unwilling minority stockholders. One is to dissolve the corporation and transfer its operating assets to the majority and cash to the minority as part of the liquidation. A second method is to undertake a reverse stock split in a sufficiently large ratio so that none of the minority stockholders ends up entitled to more than a fraction of a share. Then, the corporation pays cash to the minority in lieu of issuing fractional shares under statutory provisions allowing such an action. *E.g.,* Cal. Corp. Code § 407; Del. Gen. Corp. Law § 155; N.Y. Bus. Corp. Law § 509(b); M.B.C.A. § 6.04(a)(1). The most popular freeze-out technique, however, is through a merger in which the plan of merger calls for the minority to receive cash (or even debt) from the surviving corpora-

tion in exchange for surrendering their shares. This was the technique used in *Alpert*.

Note some other potential attributes of the dissolution and merger means of removing the minority. If the acquirer itself merges with the target, or if the acquirer itself obtains the operating assets in a liquidation, then the result is to leave only one corporation (assuming the acquirer is a corporation). This may create a possible advantage in terms of simplifying operations by removing the need to have two boards of directors and two sets of officers. On the other hand, in a merger, the acquirer will pick up all the target's liabilities, while in a liquidation, the acquirer must have the target pay off its debts before the distribution of assets. To avoid the assumption of liabilities problem in a freeze-out merger, the acquirer often forms a new subsidiary with which to merge the target. There also can be problems with non-assignable contract rights in a merger or liquidation. Finally, the acquirer may dissolve and liquidate the target, not to remove the minority, but rather because the buyer believes it can make more money by selling off the target's properties piecemeal than it paid to buy the firm. (This is often referred to as a "bust-up" takeover.)

3. The buyer, in evaluating its ability to use these techniques for involuntarily removing minority stockholders, traditionally must consider two problems. To begin with, does the statute or other source relied upon by the purchaser really provide authority for employing the transaction in question as a means to cash out an unwilling minority. Take dissolution for example: While corporations statutes typically authorize the majority to dissolve the company and have the firm distribute to its shareholders the assets remaining after payment of creditors, courts have been very reluctant to interpret these provisions as empowering the company to distribute the operating assets to the majority stockholder, and cash (even of proportionate value) to the minority shareholders. *E.g., Kellogg v. Georgia–Pacific Paper Corp.,* 227 F.Supp. 719 (W.D.Ark.1964). Perhaps the majority shareholders can avoid this problem by having the target corporation first sell all its assets to the majority holder for cash or securities, and then distribute the cash or securities back to all the shareholders (including, mostly, the majority). *See, e.g., Abelow v. Midstates Oil Corp.,* 41 Del.Ch. 145, 189 A.2d 675 (1963) (upholding such a transaction). Could, however, the minority demand a public sale of the assets in this case—open to the minority or to outside bidders—following the model of partnership liquidations? See *Mason v. Pewabic Mining Co.,* 133 U.S. 50 (1890) (yes). Moving beyond the asset distribution problem, some courts have gone so far as to hold that a transaction which results in the continuation of the business unchanged except for the elimination of the minority is simply not a dissolution within the meaning of the statute. *E.g., Theis v. Spokane Falls Gaslight Co.,* 34 Wash. 23, 74 P. 1004 (1904).

Similar questions exist with freeze-out mergers. The technique faces difficulty if the governing state statute does not expressly allow the plan of merger to call for receipt of consideration other than stock in the survivor. In this event, the best the buyer can achieve through a merger is to remove the minority shareholders in the target by making them stockholders in the purchaser itself—which the buyer might not wish to do because of dilution of its existing shareholders' interests. One way around such a problem might be to give shares redeemable at the option of the corporation. *See Matteson v. Ziebarth,* 40 Wash.2d 286, 242 P.2d 1025 (1952). *But see Outwater v. Public Service Corp.,* 103 N.J.Eq. 461, 143 A. 729 (Ch.1928), *aff'd,* 104 N.J.Eq. 490, 146 A. 916 (Err. & App. 1929) (court held it was unfair to force the acceptance of redeemable stock in exchange for non-redeemable shares through a merger). At any event, most statutes now allow use of cash or other consideration in a merger. *E.g.,* Cal. Corp. Code § 1101(d), Del. Gen. Corp. Law § 251(b); N.Y. Bus. Corp. Law § 902(a)(3); M.B.C.A. § 11.02(c)(3). Again, a broader challenge exists under some judicial opinions which simply do not accept the notion that a combination with a shell corporation for the purpose of removing minority stockholders is a transaction contemplated by merger statutes. *E.g., Jutkowitz v. Bourns,* No. CA 000268 (Cal. Super. Nov. 19, 1975). The overwhelming majority of judicial opinions, however, have refused to read merger statutes as so limited. *E.g., Matteson v. Ziebarth,* 40 Wash.2d 286, 242 P.2d 1025 (1952).

The economic impact of removing the minority through a dissolution or through a merger is identical. Yet, courts seem more receptive to the latter approach than they are to the former. Putting aside the policy question of whether this difference makes any sense, from a planning standpoint the lesson is obvious: As with structuring the acquisition, one must be aware of the potential significance of the form employed to accomplish the sought-after result. Moreover, consider the impact of the difference in form if the buyer wishes to cash out preferred shareholders. In a dissolution, the holders of preferred are entitled to receive an amount equal to their liquidation preferences, but they are not so entitled if cashed out in a merger. *E.g., Rothschild Intern. Corp. v. Liggett Group Inc.,* 474 A.2d 133 (Del.1984).

What about freeze-outs through a reverse stock split followed by a cash-out of fractional shares? In *Applebaum v. Avaya, Inc.*, 812 A.2d 880 (Del.2002), the Delaware Supreme Court upheld a freeze-out through a reverse stock split in a situation that may have pushed the envelop. Avaya's board asked its shareholders to authorize a reverse stock split followed by a cash-out of those shareholders who ended up only with fractional shares. Interestingly, shareholders who ended up with a mix of whole and fractional shares would not even have their fractional shares cashed out. Instead, after the cash-out of those shareholders who received only fractional shares, there would be a stock split leaving the remaining shareholders back with the same number of shares they had before the reverse stock split. Despite the unequal treatment of shareholders even with respect to the treatment of fractional interests, and the rather ephemeral nature of the reverse stock split, the Delaware Supreme Court upheld the Chancery Court's refusal to enjoin the transaction. Significantly, however, the Delaware Supreme Court's decision seems motivated, at least in part, by the view that those shareholders who did not wish to be cashed out could avoid this fate by purchasing shares on the market—which could distinguish this case from the more typical freeze-out by a single majority shareholder.

Even if authority exists for involuntarily cashing out minority shareholders through a merger or other mechanism, the minority stockholders might challenge the specific freeze-out confronting them as a breach of the majority's fiduciary duty. This was the challenge made in *Alpert.* (Recall, as well, the *Zahn* opinion reprinted in Chapter VI.) Such an attack raises several issues. To begin with, state corporations statutes typically provide a right of appraisal for stockholders dissenting from a merger (and often for those dissenting from other transactions as well). Do these statutes establish an exclusive remedy? If so, the minority stockholders may be able to demand the corporation pay them more, and pay them cash (rather than debt instruments, for example), but they will not be able to halt their forced removal on the ground it constitutes a breach of fiduciary duty. Both the language of appraisal provisions, and judicial interpretations (which, needless to say, sometimes reach results not expressed by the statute's language), vary between the states. At one extreme lie opinions holding that the appraisal provisions preclude any challenge to the merger (except presumably for failure to comply with statutory requirements (for example, insufficient votes cast in favor), or perhaps for misrepresentations in inducing the shareholder vote). *E.g., Yanow v. Teal Industries, Inc.,* 178 Conn. 262, 422 A.2d 311 (1979). *See also* M.B.C.A. § 13.02(d). Short of this extreme lie a host of variations. *E.g., Steinberg v. Amplica, Inc.,* 42 Cal.3d 1198, 233 Cal.Rptr. 249, 729 P.2d 683 (1986) (appraisal is the exclusive remedy except in a transaction with a controlling shareholder); *Weinberger v. UOP, Inc.,* 457 A.2d 701 (Del.1983) (ordinarily, any monetary remedy should come from appraisal, but appraisal may not be adequate in cases of fraud, self dealing, waste or gross overreaching); *Walter J. Schloss Associates v. Arkwin Industries, Inc.,* 61 N.Y.2d 700, 472 N.Y.S.2d 605, 460 N.E.2d 1090 (1984) (appraisal statute bars an action unless it seeks primarily an equitable remedy rather than money damages). At any event, notice here again the impact of form. If the majority chooses a technique (such as dissolution) not covered by an appraisal statute, the exclusive remedy argument is inapropos.

Assuming the challenging stockholders get past the appraisal statutes, the question becomes upon what grounds will the court upset the transaction. Here, one confronts a basic division between those jurisdictions, like New York, which require a business purpose for removal of the minority, and those that do not. *E.g., Weinberger v. UOP, Inc.,* 457 A.2d 701 (Del.1983). Even within the two camps, however, there exists uncertainty and variation. For example, exactly what business purpose will suffice in jurisdictions requiring this for a freeze-out? *Alpert* holds the purpose must be that of the corporation. Prior to abandoning the business purpose limit in *Weinberger,* the Delaware Supreme Court had held the majority's own business purpose could suffice. *Tanzer v. International Gen. Industries, Inc.,* 379 A.2d 1121 (Del.1977). Looking back at the general reasons for removing minority stockholders outlined earlier, which of them will pass muster? Tax savings would seem to be a legitimate business purpose—at least from a state law standpoint—but which company (parent or subsidiary) will save the taxes? See, *e.g., Case v. New York Central RR. Co.,* 15 N.Y.2d 150, 256 N.Y.S.2d 607, 204 N.E.2d 643 (1965) (allocation agreement gave most of the savings from a consolidated return to the parent). Moreover, as noted above, the tax objective does not require removal of all the minority. The goal of increasing the acquirer's profits by removing other claimants is the example used by the court in *Alpert* of a motive which does not suffice. Suppose, however, the acquirer can make the argument that the minority is free riding on special benefits its efforts will achieve for the target; can this change the result? See *Cross v. Communication Channels, Inc.,* 116 Misc.2d 1019, 456 N.Y.S.2d 971 (1982) (53 percent shareholder personally guaranteed bank loans for the corporation). Finally, what about avoiding the disclosure and fairness obligations created by the presence of minority shareholders? *Compare Tanzer Economic Associates, Inc. v. Universal Food Specialties, Inc.,* 87 Misc.2d 167, 383 N.Y.S.2d 472 (1976), *with Coggins v. New England Patriots Football Club, Inc.,* 397 Mass. 525, 492 N.E.2d 1112 (1986). Turning to the jurisdictions which do not require a business purpose, what else can they review? In *Weinberger,* the Delaware Supreme Court required "fair dealing and fair price." The latter obviously gets into the question of valuation; *Alpert* provides some discussion as to the meaning of the former. Note here the importance of candor; which creates some possible tension with the normal instinct to say things which might mollify the minority holders and not say things which may upset them.

4. In addition to the traditional judicial limitations discussed thus far, the buyer planning to remove the minority stockholders must consider the impact of so-called anti-takeover statutes and article provisions. A number of states have enacted statutes addressing actions the buyer can take following the purchase of a controlling interest in the target. (Some of these statutes were described earlier in discussing toehold share purchases.) For example, Section 203 of Delaware's General Corporation Law prevents a purchaser of 15 percent or more of the corporation's voting stock from entering into a business combination (such as a merger, but also including various other transactions) with the corporation for three years after the purchase. The section, however, does not prevent freeze-out mergers involving Delaware corporations. The purchaser can be patient and wait three years. Alternately, the section creates exceptions for a purchaser who acquires at least 85 percent of the target's voting stock in the same transaction in which it crosses the 15 percent threshold, or who can persuade two-thirds of the other shareholders to vote for the merger or other combination, or whose original acquisition or proposed combination received the approval of the board of directors prior to the acquisition of shares (in other words, a friendly takeover). In addition, the section excludes from coverage companies whose shares are not widely traded, and firms whose certificate of incorporation opts out of the section. New York has a similar provision, which creates a five year moratorium on business combinations (including bust-up liquidations) after a buyer acquires 20 percent ownership of a corporation's voting stock (unless the preacquisition

board approved). N.Y. Bus. Corp. Law § 912. Even after the five years, the New York statute sets a minimum price the cashed out shareholders must receive, unless a majority of the disinterested shareholders vote to allow the combination. A number of other states follow this last pattern of requiring either disinterested or supermajority shareholder approval for the merger or other combination, or payment to the cashed out minority at least equal to a statutory fair price formula—albeit without imposing any delay on the buyer's ability to engage in a merger or other combination with the target. *E.g.,* Ill. Bus. Corp. Act § 7.85. California's corporation code contains a series of provisions limiting the ability of a majority shareholder to force out a minority holding over 10 percent of the corporation's stock. For example, Section 407 of the California Corporations Code precludes cashing out fractional shares constituting more than 10 percent of any class of outstanding stock. Section 1001(d) and (e) requires a sale of substantially all assets to a majority shareholder either (i) to receive approval by a 90 percent vote, (ii) to be in exchange for non-redeemable common shares in the buyer, or (iii) to receive approval by the State Corporation's Commissioner (or other regulatory authority) after a fairness hearing. Similarly, Sections 1101 and 1101.1 prevent a cash-out merger by a majority shareholder unless it has the 90 percent ownership necessary for a short form merger, or it receives approval after a fairness hearing.

Corporate articles also may contain provisions restricting mergers following a purchase of the corporation's shares. This can include supermajority requirements to approve the merger, or minimum payment formulas. Such provisions were among the "takeover defenses" explored at the beginning of this chapter.

5. The surrender by the minority of their shares constitutes the sale of a security. As a result, any misrepresentation or non-disclosure of material facts to them could trigger liability under Rule 10b–5. *E.g., Healey v. Catalyst Recovery of Pennsylvania, Inc.,* 616 F.2d 641 (3d Cir.1980). *But see Santa Fe Industries, Inc. v. Green,* 430 U.S. 462 (1977) (unfairness of a freeze out merger, without misrepresentation or non-disclosure, does not create a violation of Rule 10b–5). In addition, should the merger result in the corporation ceasing to have listed shares or to be subject to 1934 Securities Exchange Act reporting requirements, then the company must make the going private filing required by Rule 13e–3. *But see* Sec.Exch. Act Rule 13e–3(g)(1) (exception for a transaction within one year of a tender offer at the same price as the tender offer and when the tender offer originally was for 100 percent of the shares).

By and large, state blue sky laws exempt this sort of transaction from regulation. *E.g.,* Uniform Securities Act (1985 revision) § 402(1), (2), (5), (11), (17); Uniform Securities Act (2002 revision) §§ 201(1), 18). California, however, provides somewhat of an exception to the extent the transaction involves the issuance of securities (for instance, the whole shares(s) issued to the majority holder in a reverse stock split) in California, and one of the exemptions discussed earlier (see p. 1062 *supra*) does not apply. *See* Cal. Corp. Code §§ 25103, 25120.

b. *Tax Aspects*

As discussed earlier, shareholders ordinarily recognize gain or loss upon the liquidation of their corporation, measured by the difference between their basis in their stock, and the value of what they receive from the company. *See* I.R.C. § 331(a). In a transaction in which an acquiring corporation dissolves the target company, however, a different consequence may occur. This is because Section 332 creates an exception to recognition, when the shareholder, itself, is a corporation, which liquidates its subsidiary. Two requirements exist under the section to come within this exception. The first is that the parent must own an amount of stock meeting the test of Section 1504(a)(2) at the time the subsidiary adopts a plan to liquidate. I.R.C. § 332(b)(1). Recall, Section 338 also points to Section 1504(a)(2), in that case as the measure of how many shares a company must acquire within 12 months in order to make the basis election under Section 338. I.R.C. § 338(d)(3). Unlike Section 338, however, Section 332 does not specify how or when the parent must have acquired the requisite number of shares—just that it owns them by the time the subsidiary adopts a plan of liquidation. In any event, Section 1504(a)(2) calls for ownership of at least 80 percent of the total voting power and 80 percent of the total value of the subsidiary's outstanding shares; albeit, Section 1504(a)(4) excludes preferred stock which is non-voting, non-participating and non-convertible from the test.

What can a parent can do if it falls short of the requisite 80 percent ownership? The parent might buy shares from the minority stockholders. Rev. Rul. 75–521, 1975–2 C.B. 120. In *George L. Riggs, Inc. v. Commissioner*, 64 T.C. 474 (1975), the subsidiary redeemed stock from the minority shareholders. Such a redemption, however, may look suspiciously like the first step in a liquidation—which often entails series of redemptions—meaning the parent lacked the requisite 80 percent ownership until after adoption of the plan of liquidation. *Compare George L. Riggs with* Rev. Rul. 70–106, 1970–1 C.B. 70. Not only must the parent meet the 80 percent ownership test on the date the subsidiary adopts the plan of liquidation, it must continue to maintain that level of ownership until completion of the liquidation. This indicates the need for care when the liquidation involves a series of redemptions—which can change the percentage shareholdings if not made pro-rata from all the stockholders.

The second requirement for tax-free treatment relates to the timing of the liquidation. Section 332(b) provides a choice of two alternative tests: The liquidation must occur all within one taxable year, or it must finish (and the plan of liquidation must so provide) within three years after the close of the taxable year within which the subsidiary made the first distribution. (Taxable year refers to the liquidating subsidiary's tax year, not the parent's. Rev. Rul. 76–317, 1976–2 C.B. 98.) Under either alternative, the time limit does not start running upon adoption of the plan of liquidation. Rather, it starts upon the first distribution of the subsidiary's property (at least if there is a legitimate business reason for the delay). Rev. Rul. 71–326, 1971–2 C.B. 177. Completion requires cancellation or redemption of all the corporation's outstanding stock, and distribution of all but possibly a nominal amount of the company's assets; albeit the corporation does not need to dissolve. Treas. Reg. § 1.332–2(c). What is the impact of having both a one-year and a three-year limit in the statute? Notice the power of the I.R.S. specified by Section 332(b) to require a bond and a waiver of the statute of limitations if the liquidation misses the one-year cut-off.

In addition to the two statutory requirements, a judicial opinion involving a predecessor of Section 332 stated that tax-free liquidation does not apply if the parent does not continue the subsidiary's line of business. *Fairfield Steamship Corp. v. Commissioner,* 157 F.2d 321 (2d Cir.1946), *cert. denied,* 329 U.S. 774. *But see International Investment Corp. v. Commissioner,* 11 T.C. 678 (1948), *aff'd,* 175 F.2d 772 (3d Cir.1949) (confining *Fairfield Steamship* to situations in which the parent also liquidates). The Internal Revenue Service does not appear to follow this extra-statutory limitation. E.g., Rev. Rul. 69–172, 1969–1 C.B. 99.

Non-recognition under Section 332 is a mixed blessing. If the parent's basis in its stock in the subsidiary exceeds the fair market value of the assets it will receive in liquidation, then the effect of the section is to prevent the parent from recognizing a loss. Moreover, as with non-recognition provisions generally, the *quid pro quo* of tax-free treatment is a substituted basis—in this case, mandated by Section 334(b). Note that Section 334(b) gives the parent a basis in the property it receives equal to the subsidiary's basis in the assets, rather than equal to the parent's basis in the surrendered shares. It is entirely possible for the subsidiary to have had a basis in its assets less than their fair market value—meaning the parent receives property with a built-in gain—whereas, at the same time, the parent's basis in the surrendered stock exceeded the distributed property's value—which meant the parent would have recognized a loss in a taxable liquidation.

Unfortunately from the standpoint of the parent faced with these unpleasant consequences, Section 332 is not expressly elective. Nevertheless, it may be possible for the parent to deliberately fail the requirements for the section to apply. For instance, the parent could sell off enough of its shares in the subsidiary to fall below the eighty percent mark. *E.g., Commissioner v. Day & Zimmermann, Inc.,* 151 F.2d 517 (3d Cir.1945). Alternately, the subsidiary may break the timing requirements in carrying out the liquidation. *But see Service Co. v. Commissioner,* 165 F.2d 75 (8th Cir.1948) (a parent corporation could not use its failure to comply with the record keeping provisions in the regulations to avoid application of Section 332's predecessor). To the extent the problem with Section 332 lies in the substituted basis rule (rather than the inability to recognize an immediate loss), the parent might consider a Section 338 election. (This assumes, of course, the parent acquired the requisite shares within 12 months in taxable purchases. I.R.C. § 338(d)(3), (h)(3).)

On the other hand, the basis effect of Section 334(b) can be advantageous when the subsidiary's basis in the distributed assets exceeds the parent's basis in the surrendered stock. In fact, this can give the acquiring company a motive to structure a taxable acquisition as a purchase of stock and liquidation, rather than a purchase of assets, in cases in which the target's basis in its properties exceeds their present worth. (While this deprives the target of the opportunity to incur an immediate loss, a loss may not be useful to a corporation selling all its assets and going out of business.) At one time, courts responded to this strategy by deeming a purchase of stock followed by an immediate liquidation to equal a purchase of the target's assets. E.g., *Kimbell–Diamond Milling Co. v. Commissioner,* 14 T.C. 74 (1950), *aff'd,* 187 F.2d 718 (5th Cir.1951), *cert. denied,* 342 U.S. 827. The legislative history of Section 338, however, indicates the section overrules these holdings. Staff of the Joint Committee on Taxation, *General Explanation, Tax Equity and Fiscal Responsibility Act of 1982,* 133 (1982). Alternatively, such a strategy might run afoul of Section 269(b). This provision allows the Internal Revenue Service to deny tax advantages, such as a carryover of a high basis in assets, in cases when a company acquires stock without making a Section 338 election for which it was eligible and, within two years, liquidates the acquired company for the primary purpose of avoiding tax. It is unclear, however, whether choosing a tax-advantaged route (here, purchase of stock and liquidation) to achieve a business purpose (acquiring property) shows the principal purpose of the liquidation is tax avoidance. Moreover, if the acquirer waits two years to liquidate, the provision does not apply. Finally, Section 382's limitation on the use of built-in losses—including through depreciation deductions (I.R.C. § 382(h)(2)(B))—following an ownership change, curtails the utility of this strategy.

As also discussed earlier, a liquidating corporation normally reorganizes gain or loss upon distributing its property to its shareholders, just as if it sold the property at fair market value. I.R.C. § 336(a). Section 337, as enacted in the Tax Reform Act of 1986, creates an exception to this rule, paralleling the non-recognition principle of Section 332. (This new version of Section 337 should not be confused with the pre–1986 Section 337—which had broadly allowed tax-free liquidations following a taxable sale of assets.) Section 337(a) provides that the liquidating corporation recognizes no gain or loss when it distributes property to its parent in a Section 332 liquidation.

A parent company may not only own stock in its subsidiary, but also could have loaned money to the firm. In order to avoid questions as to what property the subsidiary used to pay debts owed its parent, and what property it distributed to the parent in cancellation of stock, Section 337(b)(1) allows the subsidiary to avoid recognition upon paying with appreciated assets debts owed its parent, so long as the debt existed when the subsidiary adopted the plan to liquidate. Here, however, the parallel between Sections 332 and 337 breaks down. Section 332 only precludes recognition of gain or loss by the parent stemming from payments received in its capacity as a stockholder, not as a creditor. Treas. Reg. § 1.332–7. As a result, a parent might obtain a bad debt deduction, for example, if the subsidiary is insolvent and cannot repay the parent's loans. Rev. Rul. 59–

296, 1959–2 C.B. 87. In fact, Section 332 will not apply at all if the subsidiary is insolvent and, accordingly, distributes nothing in respect of its stock. Treas. Reg. § 1.332–2(b). Hence, the parent can also recognize a loss on its worthless shares. *See H.K. Porter Co. v. Commissioner,* 87 T.C. 689 (1986) (applying the same principle to the subsidiary's failure to do more than pay the liquidation preferences of its outstanding preferred shares).

Finally, one other discontinuity between Sections 332 and 337 is worth noting. Section 332 requires a parent to possess at least 80 percent ownership in order to obtain tax-free distributions from the liquidating subsidiary. This suggests only one corporate shareholder can qualify. The consolidated return regulations, however, allow affiliated companies to aggregate their ownership of stock together for purposes of Section 332; meaning two affiliated corporations making a consolidated return could both be parents of the same subsidiary under Section 332 if between them they possessed the requisite 80 percent of the shares. Treas. Reg. § 1.1502–34. This rule became the genesis of another technique (known as a mirror transaction) for dealing with unwanted assets in a corporate acquisition. The thrust of this strategy was for the purchaser to set up two subsidiaries to acquire the target's stock. The subsidiaries could then liquidate the target—one taking the desired business, the other the unwanted properties—and the purchaser could thereafter sell the subsidiary with the unwanted assets. If Section 337 covered the liquidation of the target, this technique would allow the disposition of unwanted assets without the target or purchaser paying a tax on the appreciation of these properties. Congress amended Section 337(c), however, to exclude liquidating distributions to corporations whose 80 percent ownership exists by virtue of the consolidated return regulations. Hence, the mirror devise can no longer achieve non-recognition for the liquidating company.

Section 332 allows only the parent to receive liquidating distributions tax-free. Minority shareholders of the subsidiary still face tax under the normal principle of Section 331. Treas. Reg. § 1.332–5. Moreover, the liquidating corporation must recognize gain upon the distribution of appreciated property to the minority shareholders under the general principle of Section 336. *See* I.R.C. § 337(a). (To prevent a tempting division of properties, the liquidating company cannot recognize loss upon the distribution to minority shareholders when it does not recognize gain upon the distribution to its parent. I.R.C. § 336(d)(3).)

As discussed earlier, acquiring companies often use follow-up mergers in lieu of liquidations in order to obtain the target's assets or remove minority shareholders. If the acquirer owns at least 80 percent of the target's stock before a follow-up parent-subsidiary merger, then Section 332 still governs the tax impact on the parent despite the transaction following the form of a merger rather than a liquidation. Treas. Reg. § 1.332–2(e). Nevertheless, it can be important that the transaction occurs as a merger rather than a liquidation. If the merger meets the requirements for a tax-free "A" reorganization, the minority shareholders can obtain tax free treatment otherwise only available to the parent company under Section 332. *See, e.g., King Enterprises, Inc. v. United States,* 189 Ct.Cl. 466, 418 F.2d 511 (1969).

The discussion so far has focused on the tax impact of the liquidation (or merger) of the subsidiary, without regard to any preceding step in which the acquirer gains control of the formerly independent target company. The step transaction doctrine, however, may make it necessary to consider the impact of the first step in the acquisition followed by liquidation. In some instances, the step transaction doctrine can create a potentially desired outcome for the taxpayer. So, for example, a purchase of stock that fails to meet the requirements for a tax free B reorganization, or a reverse triangular merger that fails to meet the requirements for tax free treatment under Section 368(A)(2)(E), might obtain tax free treatment as part of an A reorganization if considered under the step transaction doctrine to be part of a follow-on merger of the acquired subsidiary into the acquiring corporation. *King Enterprises, Inc. v. United States,* 189 Ct.Cl. 466, 418 F.2d 511 (1969) (court treated the purchase of stock followed by a merger of the target into the acquirer as all part of an "A" reorganization); Rev. Rul. 2001–46, 2001–42 I.R.B. 321 (treating a reverse triangular merger, which did not meet the requirements for non-recognition under Section 368(A)(2)(E), and a subsequent merger of the target into the acquiring parent, as one transaction in order to create non-recognition as an A reorganization). On the other hand, treating a follow-on merger as part of the same transaction as the initial acquisition of more than 60 percent of the target's stock for cash could preclude minority shareholders, who received stock in the merger, from non-recognition, since viewing the transaction as starting with the initial acquisition causes problems with the continuity of interest requirement for an "A" reorganization. *E.g., Kass v. Commissioner,* 60 T.C. 218 (1973), *aff'd,* 491 F.2d 749 (3d Cir.1974).

As discussed above, the legislative history suggests Congress intended Section 338 to overrule judicial application of the step transaction doctrine in situations in which courts had treated a taxable acquisition of stock immediately followed by a tax-free liquidation as if there was a taxable acquisition of assets. Carrying out this intent, the regulations "turn off" the step transaction doctrine in situations in which the acquiring corporation makes an election under Section 338(h)(10), and thereafter merges or liquidates the acquired subsidiary. Treas. Reg. § 338(h)(10)–1(c)(2). What about a tax-free acquisition of stock (a "B" reorganization) followed by a Section 332 liquidation? Here, Section 338 does not apply (I.R.C. § 338(h)(3)), and the Internal Revenue Service takes the position that the transaction is really an acquisition of the target's assets. Rev. Rul. 67–274, 1967–2 C.B. 141. Generally, this will not make any difference, since the transaction just becomes a tax-free acquisition of assets (a "C" reorganization). If, however, the target distributed a significant amount of its assets in a pre-acquisition dividend or redemption, or if the buyer had acquired its shares in several stages (as in *Bausch and Lomb*), then the transaction may fail the substantially all assets test necessary for tax-free sale of assets treatment. If this risk exists, prudence may council against liquidating the target following a "B" reorganization.

APPENDIX

PROBLEM I

Lysozyme: Start-up

Robert Bender has been a client of your law firm for a number of years (although you have never before personally met him or dealt with any of his transactions). The partner of your firm, who asked you to handle this matter, described Mr. Bender as "a very interesting fellow that you will enjoy working with," and gave you the following background information concerning Mr. Bender. Bender is 50 years old, married and has two children (a 20 year old son at college and an 18 year old daughter living at home). He has a mechanical engineering degree. A few years after graduating college, he went to work as the plant manager of a small manufacturing company in the south. He eventually worked his way to become president and 50 percent shareholder in this company. Eight years ago, he sold his interest for close to two million dollars to the holders of the other 50 percent of the stock and moved into this locality. Since that time, he has invested both his efforts and money in a variety of start-up or turn-around businesses. As the partner explained, "he fancies himself as something of a venture capitalist and has had moderate success." Right now, while he has several "pots boiling," most of his income (last year he reported taxable income of $220,000) is coming from his investment as a limited partner in a firm which purchased and successfully turned around what had been a declining shopping center.

Mr. Bender came to your office with another gentleman who introduced himself as Albert Wise. Bender explained that Wise is Bender's cousin and a professor of biochemistry at Big State University (BSU). During the course of the interview, you learned that Wise is 36 years old, married, and has one daughter (age 5). He has a PhD in biochemistry, is tenured and receives a salary of $75,000 per year. His major assets are his house (purchased some years ago for $300,000 and having a mortgage of $260,000), $45,000 in his TIAA retirement account, and $20,000 in savings at the bank.

Bender and Wise explained to you that last summer, at a wedding reception both attended, they got to chatting. Wise told Bender about a new line of research Wise was hoping to pursue if he received a government or foundation grant to fund the work. Specifically, the research involves an enzyme (called lysozyme) which Wise believes has strong antibacterial properties. If proven out, Wise feels that lysozyme could have dramatic potential as a food preservative and revolutionize food storage—features Wise had been counting on to interest funding sources.

By way of background, Wise explained that lysozyme was first discovered in the 1920s in human tears, where it serves as a natural antibacterial agent. In the 1960s, a research team isolated a form of lysozyme found in chicken egg-whites. Unfortunately, while this provided a plentiful source for the enzyme (in contrast to human tears), the egg-white lysozyme was a much weaker antibacterial agent than the human tear lysozyme. Since that time, various researchers have been seeking ways to increase the strength of the egg-white lysozyme. Now, Wise believes he has discovered a method for processing the egg-white lysozyme which will radically increase its effectiveness. So far, he has only done very crude tests on small batches of egg-white lysozyme processed through his method (since this was all he could do on an unfunded basis using the University laboratory facilities to which he has access). Thus far, the results seem promising.

Intrigued by this initial conversation, Bender had contacted Wise and, after getting more details, convinced Wise that instead of pursuing this research as an academic project on a grant basis, Bender should fund the research as a commercial venture. To obtain legal assistance in setting up this venture is why they have come to see you.

Wise and Bender showed you a budget they prepared for the first phase of their venture, which phase Wise estimates will take around one year. The object of this phase is to test the effectiveness of egg-white lysozyme treated through Wise's process against different types of bacteria, as well as yeast and mold, in a variety of food products; to modify the process as needed; and to develop procedures for producing the treated lysozyme on a commercial scale. Specifically, Wise, aided by a chemist and a laboratory assistant, will prepare batches of the egg-white lysozyme treated using Wise's process. They will then add the treated lysozyme to cultures of various types of bacteria, yeast and mold to determine which microorganisms the treated lysozyme might be effective against and at what levels of concentration. (Wise has already done a little of this at the University.) Next, they will add various concentrations of treated lysozyme to a variety of food products spiked with microorganisms—such as botulinum, salmonella, listeria, and staph aureus—which cause food poisoning or spoilage. They will then leave food with and without the treated lysozyme at room temperature for various lengths of time and send the resulting samples to an outside laboratory to determine the amount of bacteria present. Wise will also observe the food to see if the treated lysozyme otherwise affects it.

Wise and Bender explained that they based the Phase I budget upon the proposal Wise was going to submit for grant funding. Essentially, they substituted the cost of commercially obtaining various services, facilities and equipment the University would have provided (albeit with a charge against any grant) had Wise done the work with the University.

LYSOZYME PROJECT PHASE ONE BUDGET

Personnel (1 year salary plus 1/4 salary for employment tax and benefits)	
Prof. Wise	$ 60,000
Chemist	60,000
Laboratory Assistant (graduate student)	30,000
Office Assistant (part-time)	20,000
Office/Laboratory Space & Utilities (1 year)	24,000

Equipment & Furniture	50,000
Supplies	12,000
Outside Testing	160,000
Legal/Patents	4,000
TOTAL	$420,000

Glancing down the budget, you noted the small amount allocated for legal and patent work. Upon mentioning this to Bender, he replied that he recognized the legal costs could go higher, but hoped your firm would be willing to accept an interest in the venture in lieu of cash fees. You stated you would need to raise this proposal with the partners in your firm, and, in any event, your firm did not do patent law work.

One other item in the budget produced some discussion. The budget item for Wise represents $48,000 salary and $12,000 (25% of salary) for employment tax, insurance and other benefits. $48,000 salary is the minimum Wise feels he can get by on for a year while he takes a leave of absence from the University to work on this project. It is agreeable to Bender.

To cover this budget, Bender will contribute $400,000 (which represents about 10 percent of Bender's net worth), and Wise will contribute the $20,000 Wise has in savings. As to other financial matters, Bender and Wise agreed to share profits equally. Bender added that as far as cash distributions, he should receive his $400,000 back before any distributions (other than salary) to Wise.

As far as the role the two parties will play in the venture, Wise will take a leave of absence from BSU and devote full time to directing the research. Bender will handle the business end. He stated that this will be fairly administrative at the beginning—for example, arranging for a lease of space, purchasing or renting furniture and equipment, and generally monitoring expenditures. In regards to the last item, Bender informs you that he feels any expenditure over $5,000 should require both parties' approval. During the last half of Phase I, Bender stated that his participation should increase substantially as he will need to travel around and start making marketing contacts, as well as develop plans to exploit the process. Specially, Bender will work on making arrangements either to license the process to food processors or other users, to enter a joint venture with such parties to produce the enzyme, or for he and Wise to build a plant and produce and sell the enzyme themselves. (Bender somewhat apologetically noted that he normally likes to have a much firmer business strategy from day one of a new venture; but in this instance, pending the tests to determine in which foods and against which microorganisms the lysozyme is effective, as well as getting a better feel as to what it will take to produce the substance on a commercial scale, that is just not possible.) In response to your noticing that you did not see travel expenses in the budget, Bender explained that he would simply cover them out of his pocket.

Toward the end of the interview, you inquired as to whether Wise had any written contract with the University which specified the school's rights to any ideas Wise came up with while employed by BSU. Wise replied that

Bender and he did not think this would be a problem because Wise had talked this subject over with the Chair of his Department. The Department Chair had stated, according to Wise, that while the final say lay with the BSU's Patent Committee, she (the Chair) was sure the committee would not oppose Wise developing the process as proposed, although the school would no doubt expect some compensation if Wise was successful. The Chair suggested, however, that it would not be politically smart for Wise to go before the Patent Committee until the lawyers organized the venture and there was a firm written commitment to go forward. (This would impress the Committee that Wise was serious, and avoid his looking like a fool before all his colleagues if the deal fell apart.)

At the end of the interview, Bender stated that he had heard great things about you from the partner of the firm who generally handled his business, and therefore he had every confidence in your ability. He requested you to suggest an appropriate legal structure for the venture and to draft whatever documents are necessary to get the venture started.

PROBLEM II

Lysozyme: Incorporating and Financing the Going Venture

It is 16 months since you completed the work to get Wise and Bender's venture started. They now return to your office in order to bring you up to speed on developments and to discuss the next phase of the business. Wise enthusiastically reports that the research end of the project has gone even better than expected. The lysozyme treated with Wise's process has proven to be a very effective agent against a wide variety of bacteria, mold and yeast, and significantly delayed spoilage caused by microorganisms in a large number of foods. To give one dramatic example, the researchers added a very small amount of treated lysozyme to raw hamburger meat spiked with various sorts of bacteria known to cause food poisoning, and left the meat at room temperature. No detectable amounts of the bacteria were present in the meat for periods as long as seven days thereafter. As Wise states, "can you imagine being able to keep unrefrigerated meat fresh for a week." Based upon these results, Bender hired a consulting firm with expertise on the food industry to prepare a market analysis for the treated lysozyme (the executive summary from which Bender brought to the interview for you to see). In response to your inquiry, the parties state that they have applied for a patent on lysozyme treated with Wise's process. Although the application is still pending, Bender states that their patent attorney assured them there should be no problem.

Unfortunately, reports Bender, the parties have run into obstacles from governmental regulation, which will require significant time and money to overcome. Specifically, Bender had hired a Washington D.C. law firm to deal with the Food and Drug Administration. The law firm's strategy, Bender explains, was to get the FDA to put the treated lysozyme on the list of food components which are Generally Recognized As Safe (GRAS). Achieving status as GRAS avoids a substance needing to get FDA approval as a food additive. A substance can obtain GRAS status either by showing it was part of foods safely consumed prior to 1958 by a significant number of Americans or by showing that a consensus exists in the scientific community that the substance is safe. With respect to the treated lysozyme, the argument for GRAS status was that the main component, lysozyme, comes from egg-whites, which are widely eaten. Nevertheless, the FDA rejected GRAS categorization for treated lysozyme (because people who eat egg-whites do not consume lysozyme treated as Wise proposes or mixed with other foods as a preservative, and there is little scientific evidence specifically addressing its safety). (Bender snickered that he was not sure whether the real reason was because of the Washington D.C. law firm's incompetence or because one needs to bribe somebody to get things through the FDA; a remark which you tactfully ignored.) At any event, the upshot is that the parties will need to petition the FDA to approve the treated lysozyme as a food additive. This requires extensive outside testing to prove the safety of the substance and will cost between $8 and $20 million and can take two to four years. (While progress on the use of lysozyme as a food preservative has slowed pending government approval, the parties are conducting investigations into other uses for the treated lysozyme. For example, they found it could be a useful preservative for some types of cosmetics and are looking into its application as an additive to feed grains in order to serve as a natural antibiotic which will keep livestock healthier.)

This brings your discussion with Bender and Wise to where the venture now stands financially. Beyond the initial contributions of $400,000 by Bender and $20,000 by Wise, the firm you helped the parties form—which the parties named "Lysozyme Research, [with the appropriate suffix for the form of business you recommended they form]"—has borrowed $200,000 from the bank (which Bender personally guaranteed). In addition, the firm borrowed $50,000 from Wise's sister-in-law. In response to your questioning, Wise explains that his wife's sister, Cathy Cohn, is a senior account executive—in other words, she takes charge of client relations and designing marketing campaigns for clients—at a large advertising agency. After hearing all about his super-preservative, she wanted to put some money into the venture if the parties could use it. So, at his wife's urging, Wise agreed to give Cohn a five percent share of the firm's profits out of Wise's profit share in exchange for Cohn's loaning the firm $50,000 (to be repaid when the firm's earnings allowed), as well as her paying an additional $20,000 to Wise (who found himself running short of cash during his leave of absence from the university). (This was acceptable to Bender, since Cohn's five percent came out of Wise's profit share and she did not request any say in management.) On the outflow side, the first year/first phase went roughly according to budget—except for incurring much more legal expenses, and paying a significant amount to the consulting firm for the marketing study. Since then, the firm has continued to employ the chemist, research assistant and office assistant it hired (the office assistant now being employed full-time), and has retained the space the firm is renting. Wise, however, has returned to the University and only is doing research on lysozyme part time. Hence, he has ceased to draw any salary.

This leaves the parties with an annual budget of a little over $300,000. All told, the firm presently owes $200,000 to the bank and $50,000 in legal fees to the Washington D.C. law firm retained to aid in dealing with the FDA. In addition, Bender has expended $30,000 out of pocket to cover travel expenses. The business presently has $50,000 in the bank, the laboratory equipment and furniture (purchased at the start of the venture for $50,000), and, of course, the process. In addition, Bender just completed negotiating a contract with Avalon Co., granting Avalon a five-year license to manufacture and use treated lysozyme as a preservative in Avalon's cosmetics. (This does not require the same FDA approval as does use as a food preservative.) This license agreement calls for Avalon to pay Lysozyme Research $100,000 per year. (The first year's installment is due in 90 days.)

Looking to the future, Bender states that the firm has two paths it can take and regarding which he wants your input:

THE INCORPORATED JOINT VENTURE

The first possibility is to enter into a corporate joint venture with the Gilbert Chemical Company. Gilbert Chemical is a large corporation which manufactures a wide variety of chemical products. For example, it is the only producer of sorbates in the United States. Sorbates are one of the four most widely used food preservatives (and are mostly used to combat molds and yeast in cheese). Bender contacted Gilbert Chemical figuring that its knowledge of the preservative industry, as well as its marketing contacts, could allow quick penetration by treated lysozyme into the market following FDA approval (as well as the fact that Gilbert Chemical already had some experience in obtaining FDA approval of products). Bender also calculated that the revolutionary potential of treated lysozyme, as well as the fact that sales of chemical preservatives such as sorbates have grown only slowly in recent years, could make this an interesting opportunity for a firm such as Gilbert Chemical. It seems Bender was correct, since the parties have received the following proposal from Gilbert Chemical:

"(1) Gilbert Chemical Company and Lysozyme Research will form a corporation, 'LysoChem, Inc.' LysoChem will be authorized to issue one million shares of common stock.

"(2) Lysozyme Research will transfer to LysoChem exclusive rights in perpetuity to manufacture and sell or to license others to manufacture and sell lysozyme treated through Dr. Wise's process for use as a food preservative. Lysozyme Research will retain the rights to make any other use of treated lysozyme. In exchange for the transfer of these rights, Lysozyme Research will receive immediately 125,000 shares of LysoChem common stock. Lysozyme Research will also have the right to receive without further payment an additional 375,000 shares of common stock at such time as LysoChem gains FDA approval for the use of treated lysozyme as a food additive. In addition, Dr. Wise will agree without further compensation to hold himself available for such consulting as may be necessary to aid in obtaining FDA approval.

"(3) Gilbert Chemical will produce treated lysozyme necessary for testing, provide all necessary funds (estimated at $15 million) to pay for testing by independent laboratories, and undertake all other activities necessary to obtain FDA approval of treated lysozyme as a food preservative. In exchange, Gilbert Chemical will receive immediately 500,000 shares of LysoChem common stock.

"(4) LysoChem will have a five person board of directors: Dr. Wise, Mr. Bender, and three representatives appointed by Gilbert Chemical.

"(5) After obtaining FDA approval for the use of treated lysozyme as a food preservative, LysoChem and Gilbert Chemical will enter into good faith negotiations for Gilbert Chemical to aid LysoChem in the manufacture and marketing of the treated lysozyme as a food preservative.

"(6) Prior to FDA approval, neither shareholder of LysoChem may sell its shares without the consent of the other shareholder. Thereafter, each shareholder agrees to give the other the right of first refusal prior to any sale."

THE UNDERWRITER'S FINANCING PROPOSAL

The second alternative Bender and Wise are considering stems from conversations Bender has had with Goldie MacMillian, a partner with the underwriting firm of Dreg & Co. Ms. MacMillian, reports Bender, was scornful of accepting any joint venture proposal from a major chemical corporation. Her view is that Wise and Bender should not give up control over the destiny of their enterprise; a view which struck a sympathetic chord especially with Bender. Instead, MacMillian believes, based upon the dramatic results the parties have achieved with the treated lysozyme, they should be able to raise sufficient money through one or two public offerings of stock to fund the testing necessary to gain FDA approval. Thereafter, with FDA approval of the treated lysozyme secured, the parties could either seek to raise more money with an additional public offering in order to build a plant to manufacture treated lysozyme, or else they could license food processors to produce and use the product.

Specifically, MacMillian proposes the following three stage plan:

First, the parties will form a new corporation, "Lysozyme Research, Inc." The current Lysozyme Research firm will transfer to Lysozyme Research, Inc. its patent pending and all rights in the treated lysozyme, as well as all its other assets. In exchange, the new corporation will issue the current owners of Lysozyme Research 2 million shares of common stock in accordance with their interests in the current firm, and agree to assume all the liabilities of the current firm.

Next, MacMillian will conduct a private placement of 50,000 shares of Lysozyme Research, Inc. common stock to a small number of wealthy clients of Dreg & Co. for $12 per share. The $600,000 this raises should cover the out of pocket expenses (attorneys and accountants fees, printing costs, etc.) of the public offering.

Finally, Lysozyme Research, Inc. will make a public offering of 900,000 shares of common stock for $18 per share. Dreg & Co. will underwrite this offering on a best efforts basis in exchange for a 10% commission. Dreg & Co. will also receive warrants to purchase an additional 50,000 shares of common stock at $18 per share.

Bender and Wise would like your opinion on these two proposals, as well as any other ideas you might suggest they consider pursuing at this stage. Bender also raises with you a number of specific questions:

With respect to the Gilbert Chemical proposal, Bender has three broad concerns. Initially, he wants to know why Lysozyme Research cannot receive 50 percent of LysoChem's shares immediately, rather than receiving the bulk only after FDA approval. He wonders whether there could be a legitimate reason for this, or whether Gilbert Chemical is up to something here. He asks whether you see any problems with this aspect of the proposal from "our" side, and, if so, whether you can suggest some alternatives to meet Gilbert Chemical's legitimate interests (assuming there are any).

Next, Bender (and Wise) are very concerned about Gilbert Chemical's proposal to have three of the five directors and hence control. As Bender explains, making a deal like this involves something of a "pact with the devil," since there is always the danger a company like Gilbert Chemical simply may be seeking to squash a product which potentially competes with their existing line. He wants to know what ideas you have for structuring control to deal with this danger.

Lastly with respect to Gilbert Chemical's proposal, Bender asks what you think of the restriction on the sale of shares. He notes that the right of first refusal seems rather one sided because he and Wise probably would not be able to afford to buy Gilbert Chemical's shares.

Turning to MacMillian's idea, she said Bender should discuss with his attorney (you) whether you are aware of any facts which would create special disclosure problems. Along this line, she was perturbed when she heard about the deal with Cathy Cohn, although Bender does not understand what the problem is.

Finally, with respect to both proposals, Bender wonders whether the current firm or the owners should end up holding the stock. If the owners receive the stock, he is not sure how much each should get.

LYSOZYME PRESERVATIVE MARKET POTENTIAL STUDY EXECUTIVE SUMMARY

1. The Product

1.1. Description

Egg-white lysozyme treated through the Wise–Bender proprietary process (hereinafter "treated lysozyme") consists of an enzyme extracted from chicken egg-whites and treated through a proprietary process which increases the enzyme's anti-microorganism activity.

1.2. Use

Test results indicate that treated lysozyme is a highly effective food preservative. (See Appendix A to this report.) A food preservative prevents the deterioration of food caused by the growth and activity of microorganisms which can render the food less acceptable to the ultimate consumer and ultimately unsafe for human consumption. Treated lysozyme, however, does not prevent chemical deterioration of food products (oxidation) which can affect a food's consumer acceptance.

1.3. Critical Specifications

In preparing this report, it is assumed that treated lysozyme will possess the following characteristics:

(1) The product must achieve effectiveness as a preservative generally in accordance with the test results set out in Appendix A, even when produced and used commercially. This includes preventing significant bacterial spoilage of unrefrigerated fresh meat, fish, poultry and milk for a period of up to seven days, and tripling the shelf-life of fresh fruits and vegetables.

(2) The product must be safe for human consumption as recognized by the appropriate governmental authority.

(3) The product must not alter the taste or other attributes of food (other than by preventing microorganism spoilage). Professor Wise has opined that based on the nature of the product this should not be a problem. Actual taste testing must await a finding that the product is safe for human consumption.

(4) The product can come in either a powder or a liquid form and can be easily added by food processors to processed foods and by packers to fresh foods. It is easy to transport and store.

(5) The product is easy to manufacture, requiring only simple equipment and techniques. Accordingly, manufacture will not require an overly large capital outlay nor significant volume to achieve economies of scale. When produced in commercial quantities, an amount of treated lysozyme sufficient to preserve 100 pounds of food will cost approximately 25 cents.

2. Prospective Users

2.1. Categories

Prospective users of treated lysozyme fall into the following categories:

(1) Producers of processed foods including:

Beverages

Fats and oils

Processed fruits and vegetables

Processed meats

Cereals

Snack foods

Other (e.g. condiments)

But not including bakery products (since treated lysozyme kills yeast)

(2) Producers of dairy products including milk, cheese and butter

But not including ice cream (since treated lysozyme provides no advantage in preserving a frozen product)

(3) Packers of fresh meat, fish and poultry

(4) Packers of fresh fruits and vegetables

2.2. Potential Volume of Treated Lysozyme Purchases by Major Market Segments

(1) Processed foods producers

	Year 1	Year 2	Year 3	Year 4	Year 5
Total Unit Sales (000's)	400	2,000	4,000	6,000	8,000

Note: One unit of treated lysozyme is twenty grams, which will preserve 100 pounds of processed food products. The above forecast is based on a total market potential of 40 million units if all present purchasers of sorbates and parabens for use in processed foods replaced all purchases with treated lysozyme. (See Competition.) This market is relatively stable. The unit sales are based on treated lysozyme attaining 1% market share in year one, 5% in year two, and growing by 5% per year up to 20% market share in year five.

(2) Dairy product producers

	Year 1	Year 2	Year 3	Year 4	Year 5
Total Unit Sales (000's)	12,900	25,800	64,500	129,000	258,000

Note: One 20–gram unit of treated lysozyme will preserve 100 pounds of dairy products. The United States produces approximately 139 billion pounds of dairy products per year. The major components of the dairy market include milk (34% of the market), cheese (53% of the market), ice cream (7% of the market) and butter (6% of the market). The dairy market is relatively stable. Unit sales of treated lysozyme are based on 1% of total dairy products (except ice cream) containing treated lysozyme in year one, 2% in year two, 5% in year three, 10% in year four, and 20% in year five.

(3) Fresh meat, fish and poultry packers

	Year 1	Year 2	Year 3	Year 4	Year 5
Total Unit Sales (000's)	6,500	13,000	32,500	65,000	130,000

Note: One 20–gram unit of treated lysozyme will preserve 100 pounds of fresh meat, fish or poultry. The United States produces approximately 65 billion pounds of fresh meat, fish and poultry per year. While the components fluctuate from year to year, the total production remains relatively constant. Total unit sales are based on market usage penetration of 1% in year one, 2% in year two, 5% in year three, 10% in year four, and 20% in year five.

(4) Fresh fruit and vegetable packers

	Year 1	Year 2	Year 3	Year 4	Year 5
Total Unit Sales (000's)	2,400	4,800	12,000	24,000	48,000

Note: One 20–gram unit of treated lysozyme will preserve 100 pounds of fresh fruits or vegetables. The United States produces approximately 24 billion pounds of fresh fruits and vegetables per year. Total unit sales are based on treated lysozyme attaining 1% market usage in year one, 2% in year two, 5% in year three, 10% in year four, and 20% in year five.

(5) Total combined unit sales

	Year 1	Year 2	Year 3	Year 4	Year 5
Total Unit Sales (000's)	22,200	45,600	113,000	224,000	444,000

3. Competition

3.1. Existing Preservatives

Presently there are four major food preservatives in use in the United States:

PRESERVATIVE	EFFECTIVENESS	MAJOR USE	ANNUAL SALES
Benzoates	All microorganisms	Soft drinks	$10.2 Million
Parabens	All microorganisms	Pastries	$ 4.3 Million
Propionates	Mold	Bread	$27.3 Million
Sorbates	Mold and Yeast	Cheese	$26.1 Million

3.2. Comparison with Treated Lysozyme

3.2.1. Price

Assuming treated lysozyme is sold at a price twice its manufacturing costs, it will have a price comparable to sorbates and parabens, which constitute the currently high priced preservatives. It will be significantly more expensive than propionates (approx. 3 times the price) and benzoates (approx. 6 times the price).

3.2.2. Utility

Treated lysozyme will not compete with propionates for use in bread and other bakery goods requiring yeast.

Treated lysozyme exhibits significantly greater effectiveness than other existing preservatives: (1) in the range of microorganisms against which it is effective; (2) in the pH levels at which it can function (which is a significant problem for existing preservatives other than parabens); and (3) in the extent and length of time for which it remains effective. These advantages should allow sale of treated lysozyme where no current preservative is effective. This includes for use on fresh meat, fish and poultry, and in fresh milk.

4. Marketing Strategy

4.1. Generally

It is proposed to sell treated lysozyme directly to the user groups (food processors and packers). Solicitation should be accomplished through direct contact and advertisements in industry literature. Mass media advertising to create demand by the ultimate consumers for foods preserved with treated lysozyme should be considered.

4.2. Product Acceptance Factors

User groups should be encouraged to buy treated lysozyme based upon two principal motivations:

(1) Cost savings due to decreased losses from spoilage of food prior to sale by food processors and packers, and due to less need for expensive refrigeration during storage and transport of food products.

(2) Increased demand for food products containing treated lysozyme from food purchasers—both retailers and the ultimate consumers—who can also achieve savings and added convenience due to less spoilage and less need for refrigeration.

4.3. Product Resistance Factors

Marketing surveys suggest that treated lysozyme might encounter market resistance from two sources:

(1) Disbelief in the claims made for its effectiveness. Presumably, demonstrations can counter this problem.

(2) Concerns over its safety as a food additive despite government approval. One response may be to emphasize the fact that treated lysozyme is an all-natural product; in other words, it largely consists of a material extracted from egg-whites.

It may be necessary to conduct test marketing after the product is actually available in order to weigh the strength of these resistance factors.

5. Financial Projections

	Year 1	Year 2	Year 3	Year 4	Year 5
Unit Sales (000's)	22,200	45,600	113,000	224,000	444,000
Unit Price	$ .50	.50	.50	.50	.50
Total Sales (000's)	11,100	22,800	56,500	112,000	222,000
Unit Cost	.25	.25	.25	.25	.25
Cost of Goods Sold (000's)	5,550	11,400	28,250	56,000	111,000
Other Costs (000's)	4,220	6,560	13,300	24,400	46,400
Profit Before Tax (000's)	1,330	4,840	14,950	31,600	64,600
Tax (000's)	532	1,936	5,980	12,640	25,840
Net Income (000's)	$ 798	2,904	8,970	18,960	38,760

Note: Other costs includes sales and advertising expenses, administrative and overhead, and interest expense. It is based on a minimum of $2 million plus 10 percent of sales.

PROBLEM III

Lysozyme: Corporate Restructuring

It is now five years after the events involved in Problem II. Bender and Wise formed an incorporated joint venture with Gilbert Chemical in order to obtain FDA approval for and thereafter market the treated lysozyme as a food preservative. Bender and Wise continued the firm formed in Problem I (Lysozyme Research) for the purpose of developing and exploiting other uses of the treated lysozyme—which presently include a preservative for cosmetics, an additive to feed grains, and an ingredient for various over-the-counter first aid ointments and sprays. Last year, Lysozyme Research collected license fees in excess of one and one-half million dollars from the producers of such products, as against a research and administration budget of around $400,000.

The problem they now wish your help with concerns the incorporated joint venture, LysoChem, Inc. This corporation has one million shares of common stock outstanding, distributed as follows:

Gilbert Chemical	500,000 shares
Bender	212,500 shares
Wise	202,500 shares
Big State University	75,000 shares
Cathy Cohn	10,000 shares

The company has a six-person board of directors: three representatives of Gilbert Chemical, plus Bender, Wise, and Dorothy Dodd, who is the dean of BSU's business school. (Putting Ms. Dodd on the board represented a key compromise on the management issue, which had been a major stumbling block in forming LysoChem.) One of the Gilbert Chemical representatives serves as president of LysoChem, while Bender is the company's secretary and treasurer.

After three years and $16 million in expenditures, the venture obtained FDA approval of the treated lysozyme as a food additive. Taste tests established that the treated lysozyme did not alter the taste of foods. Armed with FDA approval and these test results, LysoChem began a program to market the product. It hired a sales staff which essentially consisted of Gilbert Chemical personnel "loaned" to LysoChem for a few years. The sales staff and LysoChem's president put together a strategy which targeted meat and fresh produce packers as potential customers and emphasized to them treated lysozyme's benefits of reducing their losses from spoilage. The selling group decided, however, to deliberately downplay treated lysozyme's more revolutionary potential (such as the fact it could at least partially eliminate the need for costly refrigeration at both the supplier and consumer levels). The selling group's professed concern was that most customers will dismiss the more dramatic claims as too good to be true, especially as treated lysozyme does not prevent chemical changes in food (oxidation) which affect appearance (for instance, meat will turn brown). Moreover, those customers who do believe the claims may overreact and allow food to spoil by leaving it out beyond even treated lysozyme's protective potential. Wise and Bender disagreed, but Dodd voted to defer to the expertise of the sales personnel.

The last two years, LysoChem has followed this conservative strategy with what Bender and Wise believe are disappointing results. In the first year, LysoChem had sales of just under $1 million, which, after subtracting $495,000 paid to Gilbert Chemical for producing the treated lysozyme, and $1,000,000 in sales and administrative expenses, resulted in a net loss for the year of $505,000. (Gilbert Chemical contracted with LysoChem to produce the treated lysozyme for LysoChem to sell until LysoChem could reach a sales volume which justified LysoChem undertaking its own manufacturing operation. Gilbert Chemical charged LysoChem a price equal to Gilbert Chemical's cost plus 10 percent. LysoChem sold the treated lysozyme for a 100 percent markup over the price LysoChem paid Gilbert Chemical. LysoChem financed its first year deficit by borrowing from Gilbert Chemical.) Last year saw sales rise to $2.1 million, resulting in just reaching the break-even point. This year, the sales personnel are projecting sales of around $5 million for a net profit of $1.4 million.

Bender and Wise have lost patience with the path LysoChem is taking. They believe if the sales force would promote the advantages of treated lysozyme avoiding food spoilage for the ultimate consumer, pressure from the retail level would force a large portion of meat and produce packers to use treated lysozyme just to stay competitive. This, plus pushing the use of lysozyme in dairy products and some processed foods, should create the sort of sales results reflected in the marketing study prepared by Bender five years earlier. Bender and Wise also suspect that Gilbert Chemical may be deliberately stalling the growth of treated lysozyme so as not to undercut Gilbert Chemical's sales of sorbates (which run $17 million per year). (They note that the sales group has only targeted types of customers which do not use sorbates.) While not suspecting bad faith, Dodd now reluctantly agrees the business needs to take a more aggressive approach. Her switch in position, however, has only produced deadlock on the board, which threatens to worsen the situation.

Bender decided that the only solution was to go to the news media with this story of "a big corporation suppressing a wonderful boon to mankind in order to preserve sales of their existing product." He was able to convince a television newsmagazine to run a story to this effect concerning LysoChem. There followed a stormy meeting of LysoChem's board of directors (with Gilbert Chemical's CEO also present). Gilbert Chemical's CEO taunted Bender and Wise that if they really believed they could do so much better with LysoChem, they should be willing to buy out Gilbert Chemical at a price reflecting the multimillion dollar profits Bender projects. He proposed a price of $50 million for Gilbert Chemical's LysoChem shares, payable over five years, with a lien against all LysoChem's assets to secure Gilbert Chemical against non-payment. Dodd protested that the price was ridiculous and the whole deal struck her as a ploy to take the entire company for Gilbert Chemical. Nevertheless, Wise and Bender expressed their willingness to agree to such a purchase, and stated they would have their attorney (you) contact Gilbert Chemical's counsel to work out the details of the transaction.

After separate telephone conversations with Bender, Dodd and Gilbert Chemical's attorneys to set up a meeting, you jotted down the following agenda items to consider before this meeting occurs:

"(1) Dodd is screaming bloody murder about the price. She says there is no way either the corporation or Bender and Wise individually can afford this under any realistic projection. She also threatened that if LysoChem acts as buyer, the University will demand the company purchase its shares at the same price. Need to carefully look at this and better pull Bender's marketing study from the file.

"(2) Gilbert's attorneys want to structure the deal to avoid Gilbert paying a large capital gain on the sale. Specifically, they want to take advantage of the dividends received deduction of Section 243. Should anticipate how they might seek to accomplish this and make sure there are no problems from our end. How can we get dividends only to them when there is just one class of stock? Should we introduce a class of preferred with redemption rights? How? Alternately, will a sequential purchase of their shares work here?

"(3) Dodd suggests an alternative to the buy-out. Why not split off a second corporation which would also have the right to sell the treated lysozyme food preservative? Gilbert could own all the stock in LysoChem and everybody else gets the stock in the new firm. Let the better marketing plan win. Interesting thought; any legal or other problems with it?

"(4) Anything else I am overlooking?"

PROBLEM IV

Lysozyme: Sale of the Business

THE COMPANY NOW

It is nine years after the events in Problem III. The parties ultimately decided to resolve that situation by following Dodd's split-off suggestion: Gilbert Chemical became the sole owner of LysoChem, while Wise, Bender, BSU and Cathy Cohn became the owners of a new corporation—Lysozyme Preservatives, Inc. The central component of this deal was a three-way contract between Lysozyme Research (the business formed in Problem I, which owned the patent to treated lysozyme), LysoChem, and Lysozyme Preservatives, granting both LysoChem and Lysozyme Preservatives rights to manufacture and sell treated lysozyme for use as a food preservative. The contract provides that these rights are exclusive to LysoChem and

Lysozyme Preservatives and are non-assignable—which provision cannot be waived except by agreement of all three parties to the contract.

Since that time, Lysozyme Preservatives has evolved in its business, ownership, and management.

The Business

Lysozyme Preservatives now owns three manufacturing plants—one in the western United States, one in the eastern United States and one in Europe—which produced and sold $112.5 million worth of treated lysozyme as a food preservative last year. (The only other producer of treated lysozyme for use as a food preservative, LysoChem, reported somewhat smaller sales figures.) Several years ago, the parties changed the name of Lysozyme Research to Lysozyme Products (reflecting the fact that the firm had become less involved in looking for new uses of lysozyme, as opposed to exploiting existing uses), and transferred ownership of Lysozyme Products to Lysozyme Preservatives (in exchange for additional stock in Lysozyme Preservatives to Bender, Wise, Cohn and BSU). Lysozyme Products reported sales last year of around $8 million plus approximately $2.4 million in licensing fees. (Lysozyme Preservatives' most recent consolidated financial statements are attached.)

Ownership

In order to finance Lysozyme Preservatives' manufacturing operation and expansion, the parties took the company public, followed by several subsequent public offerings of shares. The result has been to significantly dilute the ownership of Bender, Wise, BSU and Cathy Cohn (albeit, the transfer of ownership of Lysozyme Products to Lysozyme Preservatives, in exchange for Lysozyme Preservatives stock, reversed a small amount of this dilution). Lysozyme Preservatives presently has ten million shares of common stock outstanding, distributed as follows:

Bender	1,500,000 shares
Wise	1,425,500 shares
BSU	525,000 shares
Cohn	75,000 shares
Employees (in blocks ranging from 50,000 to 500 shares)	350,000 shares
Institutional investors (in blocks ranging from 100,000 to 5000 shares)	1,500,000 shares
Others	4,625,000 shares

In addition, Lysozyme Preservatives has 500,000 shares of $8 cumulative, non-participating preferred shares outstanding. The company issued this preferred at $100 per share, and the shares have a non-participating liquidation preference for the issue price plus any dividend arrearage (of which there presently is none). The company has the option to redeem the shares at $110 per share plus any arrearage. The shares are convertible into four shares of common for each share of preferred. The shares lack voting rights except if the corporation skips four successive dividends, in which event the preferred are entitled to elect two directors.

Both the common and preferred are traded on the NASDAQ. This year, the common traded at prices ranging between a high of $16.5 and a low of $14.25 per share, most recently closing at $15.75. The preferred has traded this year between $102.25 and $96.5 per share (largely depending on prevailing interest rates), closing most recently at $99.

Management

Initially, Bender, who became President and Chief Executive Officer of Lysozyme Preservatives, pretty well ran the company. Wise was not interested in business affairs (although he and Dodd were directors of the company). Pressures from expansion and to maintain credibility with outside investors soon led the hiring of several other senior managers, particularly, Marvin Fein, who became Senior Executive Vice President of Finance and Chief Financial Officer, and Edward Tomara, who became Senior Executive Vice President of Production and Chief Operating Officer. In addition, you left your law firm and joined Lysozyme Preservatives full time as General Counsel.

Several years ago, as Lysozyme Preservatives reached the level of a mature company, Bender began to lose interest in spending full time with it. Earlier this year, he turned 65 and decided to resign as President and Chief Executive Officer. He became Chairman of the Board, while the board, on Bender's recommendation, appointed Tomara to be President and Chief Executive Officer. (Jack Hall, who previously ran the western United States operation, replaced Tomara as Senior Executive Vice President of Production and Chief Operating Officer.)

Lysozyme Preservatives' board of directors presently consists of Bender, Wise, Dodd, Tomara, Fein, you, Goldie MacMillian, Ned Wilder (the CEO of a local bank) and Dr. Olivia Zoeman (a well respected expert on food safety matters).

THE PROSPECTIVE BUYER

Rose Company is a Delaware corporation which started as a producer of dairy products and now makes a wide variety of foods and related items. Rose has sales over $3 billion per year. (Rose Company's most recent financial statements are attached at the end of this problem.) Rose has over 36 million shares of stock outstanding, which are traded on the New York Stock Exchange. The most recent closing price of its shares was $78.75 per share.

Last year, Rose purchased over $5 million worth of treated lysozyme from Lysozyme Preservatives for use in dairy and other products. Rose also has a non-exclusive license from Lysozyme Products to manufacture a derivative of treated lysozyme for use as a natural antibiotic ingredient in feed grains made and sold by Rose. (This five-year license expires and must be renegotiated this year.) These contacts have led Rose's management to become interested in the possibility of acquiring Lysozyme Preservatives. A

Rose management task force has identified several advantages of such an acquisition:

"(1) Acquisition of Lysozyme Preservatives is a natural area of expansion for Rose;

"(2) Added marketing clout of Rose should result in significant increased sales for treated lysozyme food preservative, especially in the dairy field;

"(3) Rose can use control to get an exclusive license to the treated lysozyme feed grain antibiotic, which could give a major boost to sales of Rose feed grains and make Rose the leader in the feed grain industry;

"(4) Current favorable stock price/earnings ratio comparison (Rose at approx. 15 to one; Lysozyme Preservatives at approx. 12.5 to one) allows payment of a substantial premium without too much dilution of Rose per share earnings until achievement of synergies;

"(5) Lysozyme Preservatives has adequate cash flow to service the interest cost of a cash-out acquisition."

Once Rose's management heard that Bender essentially had retired, Rose's management decided it would be an opportune time to explore such an acquisition.

THE DISCUSSIONS THUS FAR

Two weeks ago, Rose began purchasing shares in Lysozyme Preservatives over the market. It now owns 4.5 percent of the outstanding common stock. Several days ago, representatives of Rose contacted Bender. They told Bender that they were meeting him not to present a formal proposal, but rather to explore very generally the possibility of an acquisition by Rose. The representatives stated that Rose was looking at a price in the range of $250 million for the entire company. There was a very broad discussion between them and Bender about the nature of payment—cash, debt securities or stock in Rose. The representatives raised with Bender two alternatives to Rose's acquisition of the entire company: One possibility would be for Rose just to purchase the outstanding common stock in Lysozyme Preservatives. The representatives suggested Rose could pay $22 per share for such an acquisition. Alternately, if Bender felt Lysozyme Preservatives' board of directors would oppose any sale of the company, the representatives stated that Rose was prepared right then to offer Bender, Wise, BSU and any other major shareholders $24 per share for all their common stock. Finally, the representatives outlined the sort of terms Rose, as a matter of policy, typically demanded in its acquisitions:

First, Rose did not want the seller to use it as a stalking horse to obtain higher bids. Hence, Rose normally required a no-shop provision in any merger agreement, as well as a favorable lock-up option on some assets or newly issued shares to compensate Rose should the deal fall apart. (In this case, the representatives thought an option to purchase all patent rights to the treated lysozyme feed grain antibiotic for an amount equal to two years' license fees from all users would be along the lines of what they had in mind. The patent on the feed grain antibiotic still has seven years to run.)

Second, Rose did not wish to acquire product lines too dissimilar from its food oriented focus. Hence, if Rose acquired the Lysozyme Products' operations involving derivatives of treated lysozyme used for various medical purposes, Rose would simply turn around and unload these rights. As a gesture of goodwill, the Rose representative stated that Rose would not lower the price if the parties structured the deal to hold back for the seller the rights to the medical uses and related assets. (Such uses currently produce around $3.5 million of Lysozyme Products' total yearly revenues.)

Third, Rose required any acquisition to follow a structure which gives Rose maximum protection against off-book liabilities ("for example, if ten years from now someone discovers that treated lysozyme causes cancer").

Fourth, Rose would expect to enter consulting and non-competition contracts with key persons like Bender and Wise.

Fifth, Rose did not want to end up leaving any minority voting interests outstanding in any corporation it acquired.

Finally, the agreement should contain the usual warranties.

Shortly after Bender's meeting with the Rose representatives, Bender called a special meeting of Lysozyme Preservatives' board of directors. All the directors were present (in person or by speaker phone). Bender laid out the substance of his conversation with the Rose representatives. He then expressed his opinion that the board should enter into negotiations with Rose with a view toward selling the company. Bender explained that he reached this conclusion based upon the fact that the key patent for the treated lysozyme food preservative would expire in just three years (which, Bender felt, is why Lysozyme Preservatives stock has been underperforming the broader stock market). After then, it would be very useful to be part of a company, like Rose, which is better equipped to fight for market share in the food industry. Moreover, the longer Lysozyme Preservatives delayed a sale from here on out, the less the shareholders could expect to get. Bender concluded by saying that if the board did not vote to proceed with the sale, he would accept Rose's $24 a share offer—a sentiment with which Wise and Dodd expressed concurrence. (In fact, Wise came up to you after this meeting to ask whether he could sell his shares for $24 per share regardless of what the board did.)

Tomara then spoke up in absolute opposition to a sale to Rose. He stated that $250 million was an inadequate price for the company. He explained that upon discovering the recent unusual activity in Lysozyme Preservatives' common stock (Rose's purchases), he, Fein and MacMillian had begun to "run some numbers." They calculated that Lysozyme Preservatives' cash flow could support a management buy-out of the outstanding common stock for $27.50 a share. He requested that, at the least, the board delay any negotiations with Rose until he, Fein and MacMillian had a chance to put together a proposal for a management buy-out and to see if they could line up financing. Tomara also suggested the board should consider taking defensive steps to prevent the sale of Lysozyme Preservatives at an inadequate price. Finally, he commented that while he was not a lawyer, it seemed the Rose transaction might pose some antitrust problems.

Bender responded to Tomara by demurring to the idea of delay. Bender stated that he was due to meet with representatives of Rose the day after tomorrow. (Bender then suggested that you should accompany him to this meeting.)

By this point of the meeting it had become pretty obvious that the board was split between Bender, Wise and Dodd favoring negotiations with Rose; Tomara, Fein and MacMillian opposing such negotiations; with you, Wilder and Zoeman holding the balance. At this point, Zoeman stated that she would like to hear from you as corporate counsel a legal analysis of what the board should do next.

LYSOZYME PRESERVATIVES, INC. And Lysozyme Products

CONSOLIDATED BALANCE SHEET (Dollars in thousands)

December 31	Last Year	Year Before Last
ASSETS		
Current Assets		
Cash	$ 1,918	$ 1,826
Short-term investments, at cost	7,946	7,239
Receivables, less reserve for doubtful accounts of $1,021 and $905	20,420	18,503
Inventories, at lower of cost (first-in, first-out) or market—		
Raw materials and supplies	10,632	9,672
Finished product	13,003	11,110
Prepaid expenses	1,204	1,084
Total current assets	55,123	49,434
Property and Equipment		
Land, buildings, improvements and equipment, less accumulated depreciation of $22,113 and $20,809	46,456	45,748
Patents, Licenses and Goodwill, less accumulated amortization of $4,200 and $3,600	1,100	1,500
	$102,679	$96,682

	Last Year	Year Before Last
LIABILITIES		
Current Liabilities		
Indebtedness to banks	$ 2,858	$ 2,384
Current portion of long-term debt	620	620
Accounts payable	4,466	4,020

	Last Year	Year Before Last
Accrued liabilities		
Salaries and wages	1,586	1,498
Taxes	4,064	3,543
Total current liabilities	13,594	12,065
Long-term Debt	10,440	11,060
Stockholders' Investment		
Preferred stock, no par value, 500,000 shares outstanding	50,000	50,000
Common stock, no par value, 10,000,000 shares outstanding	10,000	10,000
Retained earnings	18,645	13,557
	$102,679	$96,682

CONSOLIDATED STATEMENT OF INCOME
(Dollars in thousands, except per share amounts)

Year ended December 31	Last Year	Year Before Last	2 Years Before Last
Revenue			
Net sales	$120,509	$108,043	$92,112
Licensing fees	2,428	2,209	1,847
Interest on short-term investments	583	548	506
	123,520	110,800	94,465
Costs and Expenses (Note 1)			
Cost of sales	81,103	73,091	61,794
Selling, general and administration expenses	14,031	12,764	11,564
Interest expense	1,193	1,234	1,278
	96,327	87,089	74,636
Income before Income Taxes	27,193	23,711	19,829
Taxes on Income	10,605	9,247	7,733
Net Income	16,588	14,464	12,096
Cash Dividends			
To Preferred	4,000	4,000	4,000
To Common	7,500	7,500	6,250
	11,500	11,500	10,250
Surplus to Retained Earnings	5,088	2,964	1,846

Year ended December 31	Last Year	Year Before Last	2 Years Before Last
Earnings per Common Share (Note 2)	1.26	1.05	.81

Note 1. Includes provision for depreciation and amortization of $1,904 last year, $1,894 the year before last, and $1,884 2 years before last.

Note 2. Net income less dividends to preferred, divided by 10,000,000 shares of common stock outstanding.

CONSOLIDATED BALANCE SHEET
Rose Company and Subsidiaries

December 31	Last Year	Year Before Last
	(in thousands of dollars)	
Assets		
Current Assets:		
Cash	$ 16,399	$ 23,236
Short-term commercial obligations and marketable securities, at cost (approximately market)	360,627	308,322
Accounts and notes receivable, less allowances of $8,747 and $9,183 for uncollectible accounts—		
Trade	313,096	310,970
Miscellaneous	33,619	38,049
Inventories, at lower of cost (principally first-in, first-out) or market—		
Raw materials and supplies	155,468	186,325
Finished goods	291,730	313,478
Prepaid expenses	30,978	30,168
Total current assets	1,201,917	1,210,548
Non-current Receivables and Miscellaneous Investments, at lower of cost or estimated realizable values	15,809	10,451
Investments in Affiliated Companies	17,567	13,507
Plant Assets, at cost less accumulated depreciation of $364,966 and $374,410	421,640	367,213
Excess of Purchase Price of Companies Acquired over Net Assets at Dates of Acquisition, less accumulated amortization of $3,826 and $3,299	55,393	46,643
	$1,712,326	$1,645,362

Liabilities

Current Liabilities:		
Indebtedness to banks and others	$ 54,902	$ 71,132
Current portion of long-term debt	6,171	11,776
Trade accounts payable	134,124	137,302
Accrued liabilities—		
Salaries and wages	25,633	25,735
Taxes, other than income	10,793	12,444
Other	130,175	120,305
Foreign and other taxes measured by income	20,632	25,145
Federal income taxes	26,119	20,821
Total current liabilities	408,549	424,660
Deferred Income Taxes	53,497	44,690
Long-term Debt	108,451	119,528
Obligations under Capitalized Leases	35,423	36,850
Minority Interests in Subsidiaries	769	4,909
Investment of Stockholders		
Common stock, $2.00 par value—Authorized, 50,000,000 shares, Outstanding, 36,578,473 shares last year and 36,730,002 the year before last (excluding 828,454 and 676,925 treasury shares, respectively)	73,157	73,460
Other capital	54,227	49,598
Retained earnings	1,016,379	915,678
Cumulative foreign currency translation	(38,126)	(24,011)
	$1,712,326	$1,645,362

CONSOLIDATED STATEMENT OF INCOME

Year ended December 31	Last Year	Year Before Last	2 Years Before Last
	(in thousands except per share data)		
Net Sales	$3,382,212	$3,354,141	$3,236,222
Interest on Short-Term Investments	40,045	38,279	21,539
Miscellaneous Income	9,166	7,443	5,098
	3,431,423	3,399,863	3,262,859
Costs and Expenses, including provision for depreciation of $46,858, $44,695 and $44,161:			
Cost of sales	2,430,338	2,477,800	2,409,045
Selling, general and administrative expenses	617,255	576,667	542,322
Interest expense	26,388	25,894	26,161
	3,073,981	3,080,361	2,977,528
Income before Provision for Taxes on Income	357,442	319,502	285,331
Taxes on Income	166,875	147,225	133,400

Year ended December 31	Last Year	Year Before Last	2 Years Before Last
Net Income	$190,567	$172,277	$151,931
Net income per share	$5.21	$4.67	$4.08
Cash dividends per share	$2.00	$1.82	$1.66
Average number of shares outstanding	36,570,350	36,853,365	37,254,995

INDEX

References are to Pages.

ACCUMULATED EARNINGS TAX
Generally, 462–466
Repurchase of shares, 787–797, 799–800

ACQUISITIONS
See Sale of Business

ALTERNATIVE MINIMUM INCOME TAX
As factor in choice of entity, 77
As motive for acquisition, 1123

ARTICLES OF INCORPORATION
See Corporate Formation

ASSIGNMENT OF INCOME DOCTRINE
In formation of corporation, 381–384
In formation of partnership, 153

AT-RISK LIMITATION
Generally, 221–222
Impact on choice of entity, 75

ATTORNEYS
See also Legal Opinions
Advice by,
Regarding business decisions, 4, 16, 575
"Spoiling the deal", 17–18, 574
As planners,
Litigation compared, 4
Techniques, 1–4
Ethical responsibilities,
Associating specialists, 39
Conflict of interest, 27–35
Entity as client, 30–33, 40–45
Giving opinion on exemptions from securities registration, 717–720
Investigating accuracy of prospectus, 620–623, 633–634, 645
Position on client's board of directors, 35
Receiving interest in client's business, 33–35
Tax return advice, 35–38
Role in specific transactions,
Financing, 577, 594, 620–623, 633–634, 645, 668, 717–720
Forming corporation, 575
Redemption, 763
Sale of business, 964

BOOTSTRAP ACQUISITION
See Sale of Business, Disposition of unwanted assets

BUY-OUTS
See Cross Purchases; Limited Liability Companies; Limited Liability Partnerships; Limited Partnership; Partnership; Redemptions; Share Transfer Restrictions

BYLAWS
See Corporate Formation

CHECK-THE-BOX REGULATION
See Choice of Entity

CHOICE OF ENTITY
Alternate minimum tax comparison, 77
Appreciated assets, 80–85, 86–87
Available choices, 58, 64, 69–70
Capital structure, 61–62, 66–67
Check-the-box regulation, 70–71
Complexity, 92–93
Default rules, 66–69, 94–99
Dividend received deduction, 79
Double taxation, 71, 77–78
Formalities, 58, 62–63
Fringe benefits, 73, 87
Limited liability, 59-60, 63–65, 97–98
Limited liability partnership versus limited liability company, 94–99
Loss deductions, 74–76
Management, 61, 66, 68, 98–99
Number of investors, 72, 88, 92, 581–582
Partnership basis advantages versus S corporation, 89–92
Passive activity losses, 72, 74–76
Permissible business, 99
Perpetual existence, 60, 65–66
S Corporation eligibility limits, 89
Switching entities, 85–86
Tax rate comparison, 76–77
Tax shelters, 74
Transferability, 61, 65–66

CLOSELY HELD CORPORATIONS, MANAGEMENT OF
Arbitration, 564–565
Cumulative voting, 506–508
Deadlock, 560–564

CLOSELY HELD CORPORATIONS, MANAGEMENT OF—Cont'd
Direct election of officers by shareholders, 525
Dispensing with board of directors, 525
Employment contracts, 527–528
Fiduciary duty, 494–500
Irrevocable proxies, 510–511
Multiple classes of stock with different voting rights, 513–514
Shareholder agreements re corporate decisions, 514–524
"Squeeze outs",
 Causes of, 566–574
 Example, 494–500
Statutory close corporations, 524–525
Supermajority requirements,
 For corporate decisions, 525–527
 For director election, 508
Voting agreements, 500–506, 508–510
Voting trusts, 511–513

CONSOLIDATED TAX RETURNS
See Multiple Corporations; Sale of Business, Net operating loss carryovers

CORPORATE CONTRACTIONS
 See also Redemptions
Sale of assets,
 Bulk transfer acts, 884–885
 Liquidation preferences, 885
 Shareholder approval and appraisal rights, 882–884
Tax aspects,
 Corporation as recipient, 889
 Treatment as partial liquidation, 885–889

CORPORATE DISSOLUTION AND LIQUIDATION
 See also Sale of Business
Dissolution for deadlock or oppression, 560–564
Voluntary dissolution contract, 535–536

CORPORATE DIVISIONS
Mechanics of,
 Fiduciary duty, 865
 Forming subsidiary, 863–864
 Spin-offs, 864
 Split-offs, 864–865
 Split-ups, 865
Purposes for, 862–863
Securities law considerations,
 Sale of securities, 865–868
 State securities laws, 868
Tax aspects,
 Active trade or business requirement, 858–862, 874–879
 Boot, 879–880
 Business purposes versus a devise, 871–874
 "D" reorganization, 868–869
 Divisions in connection with acquisition of control, 881–882, 994–998, 1001–1003
 Net operating loss carryovers, 1110–1111

CORPORATE DIVISIONS—Cont'd
Tax aspects—Cont'd
 Non pro-rata distributions, 880–881
 Nonrecognition requirements, 869–871, 879, 881

CORPORATE FORMATION
 See also Closely Held Corporations, Management of
Allocation of profit,
 By altering shareholdings, 443–444
 Partnership compared, 442–443
 Through dividend preferences, 444–446
Articles of incorporation, 360
Bylaws, 360–361
Corporate debt,
 Advantages and disadvantages,
  Generally, 400–407
  Tax, 423–424, 428–429
 Convertible debt, 407
 Debt-equity classification, 412–413, 419–423, 423–427
 Shareholder guarantees, 428, 489–491
Incorporation of going business,
 Assignment of receivables, 381–384
 Assumption of liabilities, 382–383, 384–389
Incorporation of partnership,
 Tax aspects, 389–397
 Transfer of limited partnership interest, 306–307
Issuance of stock,
 Authorized shares, 435
 Directors' duties, 361, 431–434, 436
 For future services, 362–365
 Impact on existing shareholders, 433–435
 Preemptive rights, 436–437
 Price, 362, 363–364, 433
 Sales tax, 381
 Subscription agreement, 361
 Valuation of property received for, 365
Leasing,
  Generally, 408
 Tax aspects, 428–431
Section 351 exchange,
  Basis impact, 410–411, 414–417
  Control requirement,
   Defined, 374
   Immediately after the exchange, 375–380
   Shares for services problem, 369, 374–375
  Licenses, 374
  Partnership rules compared, 369–370
  Solely for stock,
   Boot, 413
   Debt instruments, 413–414
   Earnouts versus warrants, 380, 1087–1090
   Non-qualified preferred stock, 380–381
  Transfer of property versus services, 365–369, 370–374
Section 1244 stock, 398–399

CORPORATE FORMATION—Cont'd
Section 1202 stock, 399–400
State of incorporation, 359–360
Taxation of stock for services,
  Bargain purchases, 372
  Impact on issuing corporation, 372–373
  Intangible property compared, 365–369, 370–372
  Planning approaches, 373–374

CROSS PURCHASES
Disclosure, 722–726
Fiduciary duties, 528–531
Net operating loss carryovers, 729–730
Tax affects, 726–730

DEBT INSTRUMENTS
  See also Corporate Formation, Corporate debt
Bad debts, deduction for, 427–428
Exchanged in reorganization, 852–854, 1075, 1085–1086, 1102
Installment tax treatment, 414, 416
Original issue discount, 417–419
Notes as securities, 601–606
Terms of loan, 407–408
Trust indenture, 578–580, 581

DEFERRED COMPENSATION
See Employee Compensation
DIVIDENDS
  See also Stock Dividends
Declaring dividends,
  Contractual restrictions, 453–454, 457–458
  Directors' discretion, 438–442, 452–454
  Statutory limits, 454–458
Dividend preferences, 444–447
Qualified Dividends, 461–462
Tax aspects,
  Consequences to corporation, 461
  Constructive dividends, 471–472, 474–475
  Dividend defined for tax purposes, 458–459
  Dividend received deduction, 458–459
  Earnings and profits, 459–461

EMPLOYEE COMPENSATION
Deferred compensation, 479
Fiduciary duty, 475–476
Pension plans, 476–479
Salary, 466–472, 472–473, 475–476
Stock options, 480–481

EMPLOYMENT CONTRACTS
In closely held corporation, 527–528
When selling business, 975–976

ESTATE FREEZE
Generally, 297, 823

FINANCING
  See also Securities Regulation
Attorney's role, 577, 594, 620–623, 633–634, 645, 668, 717–720
Bank loans, 666

FINANCING—Cont'd
Determining financial needs, 11–15, 576–577
Going public,
  Advantages and disadvantages, 609–610
  Class of securities to offer, 578–579
  Premature offerings, 610–612
  Underwriters, 612–616
Internet, 616–617, 696–698
Marketability of type of interest, 578
Placement agents, 667
SBA and SBIC funds, 665–666
Staged financing, 577
State and local aid, 664
Tax impact of new investors,
  On flow-through treatment, 581–582
  On net operating loss carryovers, 582–583, 1110–1111
  On Section 351 exchange, 375–380
Venture capital, 668–673

FREEZE-OUTS
See Redemptions; Sale of Business

INDEMNITY AGREEMENTS
For directors, 481
In sale of business, 933–934, 1035–1036

INTELLECTUAL PROPERTY
Copyrights, 47–48
Patents, 48–51
Trade secrets, 51
Trademarks, 45–47

LEGAL OPINIONS
  Generally, 18–22
In sale of business, 964
Regarding securities exemptions, 717–720

LIMITED LIABILITY COMPANIES
  See also Partnership
Articles of organization, 115–117
Assignment of membership interests, 329–330
Authority of members, 98–99, 264–265
Books and records, 174–175
Contribution to capital,
  Additional contributions, 166–168
  Agreed value, 129, 133–134
  Loans compared, 160
Conversion of partnership into, 353–354
Distribution to members, 283
  Allocation, 175–176
  Buy-out, 306–307
  Coordination with profit allocation, 168–170, 171–175
  Right to demand, 176–177
  Statutory limits, 177–180
Expulsion, 292
Fiduciary duties,
  Non-competition, 120–128
  Partners, compared, 126–127
  Waivers, 120–125, 127
Governing statute, 114, 115–116
Loss allocation, impact,
    Generally, 188–191

LIMITED LIABILITY COMPANIES—Cont'd
Loss allocation—Cont'd
  Tax, 203
Management,
  Drafting issues, 249–255
  Extraordinary actions, 257–269
  Formalities, 264, 266, 268
  Use of managers, 255–257, 255–257
Mergers, 349–353
New members, 329–330
Operating agreement, generally, 117–118, 155–158
Piercing limited liability,
  Formalities, 266–268
  Inadequate capital, 119
Profit allocation, 170–171
Property, partnership compared, 163–164
Salaries, partnership compared, 237–238
Share of liabilities, 219–220
Taxation as a partnership, 70–71
Withdrawal of members,
  Without dissolution, 276–285

LIMITED LIABILITY PARTNERSHIPS
  See also Partnership
Authority of partners, 98–99
Contribution to capital,
  Additional contributions, 167
  Loans compared, 161
Conversion of ordinary partnership into, 349, 354
Distribution to members,
  Buy-out, 306–307
  Statutory limits, 177–180
Governing statute, 114
Loss allocation, impact,
    Generally, 188–191
  Tax, 203
Minimum insurance requirements, 119
Property, ordinary partnership compared, 161
Registration, 115
Share of liabilities, 219–220

LIMITED PARTNERSHIPS
  See also Partnership
Assignment of interest, 329–330
Books and records, 174–175
Certificate of limited partnership, 115–116
Contributions to capital,
  Additional contributions, 166–168
  Agreed value, 129, 133–134
  Loans compared, 160–161
Conversion of ordinary partnership into, 349, 353–354
Corporate general partners,
  Limited partner liability from, 60, 63, 101–102
  Permissibility under corporate law, 102
  Permissibility under partnership law, 102
Distributions to limited partners,
  Allocation, 175–176
  Right to demand, 176–177

LIMITED PARTNERSHIPS—Cont'd
Distributions to limited partners—Cont'd
  Statutory limits, 177–180
General and limited partners, departure of,
  Without dissolution, 281–282
Governing statute, 114
Limited partner's liability for participating in control, 265–266
Loss allocation, impact, 188–189
Mergers, 349
New partners, 329–330
Profit allocation, 170–171
Share of liabilities, 218–219

MERGER
See Sale of Business; Partnership

MUTIPLE CORPORATIONS
Alter ego problem, 107
Consolidated returns,
  Advantages and disadvantages, 104, 110–112
  Eligibility and election, 103–104, 109–110
  Intercorporate transactions, 110–111
  Investment basis adjustments, 111
  Net operating loss carryovers, 102–106, 111–112, 1122–1123
Purposes, for, generally, 106–108
Tax advantages, 108–109

PARTIAL LIQUIDATION
See Corporate Contractions

PARTNERSHIP
  See also Limited Liability Partnerships; Limited Partnerships
Antiabuse regulations, 212
Authority of partners, 265
Basis,
  Partner's basis in property interest, 151, 194–195, 213–222, 343–344
  Partnership's basis in assets, 151, 343–344
Books and records, 174–175
Buy-out agreements,
  Buy-out price, 293–299
  Covenant not to compete, generally, 292
  Expulsion of partners, 292
  Funding the buy-out,
    Installment payments, 304, 307
    Insurance, 299–304
  Handling liabilities, 304–306
  Tax aspects,
    Abandonment compared, 318
    Close of tax year, impact on, 316
    Consequences to remaining partners, 307–318
    Consequences to selling partner, 307–318
    Covenant not to company, 313
    Liabilities, 318
    Payments for interest in partnership property, 314–315
    Sale versus liquidation of interest, 307–318

PARTNERSHIP—Cont'd
Buy-out agreements—Cont'd
Tax aspects—Cont'd
Section 751 impact, 316–317
Termination of partnership, 315–316
Timing of recognition, 315
Triggering events,
Generally, 285–293
Capital accounts,
Explained, 173
Impact on liquidation, 322–323
Tax requirement for, 196–201
Contributions to capital,
Assignment of income, 153
Basis results, 151
Description in agreement, 120, 128
Disguised sales, 154–155
Encumbered property, 152–153
Future obligations, 166–168
Impact of Section 721, 153–154
Intangibles, 151–152
Loans, leases and sale to partnership compared, 159–166
Non-recognition rule, 151
Valuation, 129, 132–133
Withdrawal of, 177–178
Conversions,
R.U.P.A., 342–343
Tax, 342–352
Dissolution,
Avoidability, 274–275
Causes of, 269–272, 274–275
Consequences, 272–274, 275–276
Dissociation compared, 275
Distributions,
Coordination with profit allocation, 171–175
Effect on basis, 173
Gain/loss recognition, 195
Right to demand, 175–177
Distributive shares,
Computation of, 193–194
Distributions compared, 193–194
Expenses paid by partner, 213
Impact on basis, 194–195
Partner's interest in firm, 199, 212–213
Section 704(c) adjustments, 204–209
Special allocations, 194, 196–204
Draws,
Purpose for, 177
Salary compared, 236
Tax treatment, 242
Family partnerships, 210–211
Fiduciary duties,
Contractual waivers, 127
In formation, 135
In liquidation, 270–274, 318–320
Non-competition, 126–128
Goodwill,
As firm property, 164
Tax impact, 314, 970
Valuation, 297
Guaranteed payments, 238–246
Liabilities,

PARTNERSHIP—Cont'd
Liabilities—Cont'd
Of partners,
Effect of dissolution and buy-out, 304–306
New partners, 331
Personal liability, 63
Tax impact,
Assumption of partner's liability by firm, 152
At-risk limitations, 221–222
Effect on basis in partnership interest, 213–219
Nonrecourse loans, 220–221
Partner's share of liabilities, 213–219,
Release from, 218, 318
What constitutes a liability,
Loss allocation,
Adjusting profit allocation to compensate for, 185–186
Impact, 186–188
Partner fault as factor in, 186
Tax factors,
Substantial economic effect, 196–204
Unequal contribution problem, 180–186
Management, 246–249, 255–257
Mergers,
Mechanics, 346–350
Tax, 353–358
New partners,
Assignments of profits interest,
Denial of right to, 330–331
Versus entry as new partner, 326–329
Entry of new partners,
As substitute for buy-out, 331
Bankruptcy trustee, 331–337
Consent required for, 326–329
Executor, 337–340
Interest in existing property, 330–331
Liability for preexisting debts, 331
Tax aspects,
Assignment of profits versus entry as partner, 346
Closing tax year, 344–345
Partnership termination, 345
Revaluation of assets, 345–346
Section 754 election, 340–342, 344
Treatment of selling partner, 342–343
Partner loans,
Right to interest, 159–160, 235–236
Tax impact, 164–166
Partners as employees,
Salaries, generally, 235, 236–237
Tax treatment of salaries,
Characterization of payment, 245–246
Consequences to partnership and other partners, 242–243
Consequences to recipient partner, 242
Equity options, 246
Fringe benefits, 245–246
Passive loss considerations, 243–245
Timing of recognition, 243
Partnership agreement, 113–114
Partnership property,

PARTNERSHIP—Cont'd
Partnership property—Cont'd
Creditor's rights, 163–164
Death of a partner, 162–163
Disposition on liquidation, 160–161
Intangibles, 128, 151–152, 164
Loan property compared, 159–161
Partners' rights to use, 161–162
Sale of, 163
Title to property, 161–162
Profit allocation, 170–171
Publicly traded partnerships, 92, 582
S corporations compared, 87–94
Services,
As capital contribution, 129–133
Taxation of partnership interest received for,
Capital interest, 135–141
Impact of Section 83, 143, 145–147, 149
Impact on other partners, 149–150
Planning approaches, 143–149
Profits interest, 142, 144–145, 147–148
Valuation of interest received for, 140–141, 142–143
Tax year, 192–193
Taxable income, 191–192
Term of partnership, 270–272, 274–275, 292
Tiered partnerships, 102
Unrealized receivables and substantially appreciated inventory, 196, 316–317, 342–343
Winding up partnership,
Capital accounts, 322–323
Distributing proceeds of sale, 322–324
Fiduciary duty, 318–320
In-kind distribution,
Rights of partners, 321, 324
Tax impact of, 325–326
Sale of assets,
Rules governing, 321
Tax impact of, 324–325
Who conducts, 320–321

PASSIVE ACTIVITY LOSSES
Activity, 230
C Corporations, impact on, 74–76
Disposition of passive activities, 76, 232–233
Limited partners, 231
Material participation, 222–232
Planning considerations, 233
Portfolio income, 232, 244
Rental activities, 223–224, 230–231, 244–245
Taxpayers affected, 74–76, 230
Treatment of passive activity losses, 232–233

PERSONAL HOLDING COMPANY
Following sale of business, 1065
Taxation as, 465–466

PIERCING CORPORATE VEIL
Formalities, 59, 62–63, 266–268
Inadequate capitalization, 55, 361–362, 407, 408
Multiple corporations, 107
Successor liability compared, 1038

PREEMPTIVE RIGHTS
See Corporate Formation, Issuance of stock

RECAPITALIZATION
"Cram-down" recapitalization,
By article amendment, 830, 832–833
By merger, 833
Minority shareholder protections, 823–828, 831–832, 833
Definition of, 828
Purposes for, 829–830
Securities registration,
Sale of securities, 833–834
Section 3(a)(9) exemption, 834–835, 837
Section 3(a)(10) exemption, 835–837
State securities laws, 837–838
Tax aspects,
Boot, 849–852
Changes in proportionate interest, 843–844, 845, 848–849
Constructive stock distributions, 843–845
Debt instruments exchanged, 840–841, 852–854
Non-qualified preferred stock, 852
Reorganization treatment, 838–843
Section 306 stock, 854–858
Section 1202 stock, 858
Valuation, 845–849
Voluntary exchanges, 830

REDEMPTIONS
Fiduciary duty,
Equal opportunity in close corporation, 753–759, 763
Greenmail, 752–753, 763
Interested director transactions, 519, 762–763
"Freeze outs", 759–762, 764
Purposes for, 730–731
Securities laws,
Disclosure requirements, 765–766
Manipulative repurchases, 766
Registration requirements, 764, 767
Williams Act rules, 765–766
Statutory requirements,
Funds available, 731–741
Generally, 737–739
Installment acquisitions, 731–737, 739–741
Tax aspects,
Accumulated earnings tax, 787–797, 799–800
Attribution rules, 770–775, 780–781
Complete termination of interest, 770–771, 781–784
Constructive dividend treatment,
Buy-out agreements, 800–802, 804–805
Periodic redemption plans, 802–804, 805
Corporate consequences, generally, 797–798
Dividend equivalence, 771–775, 777–778

REDEMPTIONS—Cont'd
Tax aspects—Cont'd
Divorce, 786–787, 805
Effect on earnings and profits, 798–799
"Greenmail gain", 786
Meaningful reduction in interest, 772–773, 778
Net operating loss carryovers, 798–799
Prohibited interest, 782–784
Sale to controlled corporation, 785–786
Sale versus distribution treatment, 769–770, 776–777
Section 303 redemptions, 784–785
Section 1202 stock, 805
Series of redemptions, 779–780
Substantially disproportionate redemptions, 778–779
Waiver of attribution, 770–771, 774–775, 781–784

REDUCTION OF CAPITAL
Generally, 740–741

S CORPORATIONS
As buyer or seller of business, 1064, 1067, 1104–1105
As partner in partnership, 88, 100
Election, 89, 481–482
Eligibility,
Number of shareholders, 88
One class of stock,
Debt-equity classification, 89, 486–487
Planning impact, 486–487
Voting rights, 487
Types of shareholders, 88
Family corporations, 488–489
Former C corporations, 493–494
Partnership compared, 87–94, 559–560
Revocation of election, 483–484
Shareholder employees, 93–93, 492–493
Share transfers,
Effect on eligibility, 559
Effect on pro-rata shares, 560
State taxation of, 94
Subsidiaries, 112
Treatment of corporation,
Basis in assets, 90–91
Computation of income, 484–485
In-kind distributions, 493–494
Taxation of entity, 90, 493–494
Tax year, 464
Treatment of shareholders,
Basis in stock,
Adjustments to, 91, 485
Effect of debt, 91–92, 489–491
Carryover of losses, 486, 492
Distributions, 92, 485–486
Pro-rata shares, 91, 485

SALE OF ASSETS
See Corporate Contractions; Sale of Business

SALE OF BUSINESS
Acquirer's rights and liabilities,
Assumption of liabilities, 1028–1038

SALE OF BUSINESS—Cont'd
Acquirer's rights and liabilities—Cont'd
CERCLA, 1037
Non-assignable rights, 1023–1028
Products liability, 1028–1035, 1037
Unknown claims, 1035–1038
Agreement in principle, 959
Alternate minimum tax, 1123
Anti-takeover defenses,
Article and bylaw provisions, 900–901
Fiduciary duties regarding, 890–898, 899–900, 905–908
"Pac Man", 903
"Poison Pill", 901–903
Recapitalization, 903–905
"White Knight", 903–904
Antitrust laws,
Department of Justice merger guidelines, 908–917
Hart–Scott–Rodino Act, 993
Appraisal rights, 1010–1011, 1013–1016, 1020–1023
Approval by shareholders, 1009–1010, 1012–1014, 1014–1020, 1021–1022
Bulk sales acts, 1037
Carryover of tax attributes, 1108–1123
Competing bids, 959, 961–962
Contingent or escrow agreements,
Purposes for, 933–934, 1035–1036
Tax consequences, 1087–1090
Creditors' rights, 948, 1036
Deciding whether to sell,
Directors' role, 899–901, 905–908
Owners' role, 898–899
Disposition of unwanted assets,
Generally, 998–999
Bootstrap redemptions, 999–1001
Impact on reorganization treatment, 1003–1006
Mirror transactions, 1147
Pre-sale dividends, 999
Purchase followed by sale, 998–999
Tax-free spin-offs, 994–998, 1001–1003
Division of price among selling shareholders, 934–935, 1023
"Drop-down" transactions, 1105–1107
Employee pension plans, 1047–1052
Employment contracts,
Buyer's reasons for, 975–976, 1027
Fiduciary duty issues, 975–976
Tax advantages, 1065–1067
Form of transaction,
Defacto merger doctrine, 1013, 1014, 1021, 1031, 1037
Forming new corporation or partnership, 1022–1023
Purchase of target stock,
Rights and liabilities of buyer, 1026–1027, 1037–1038, 1046, 1047–1051
Role of target's board, 1014
Shareholder rights, 1014–1016
Tax consequences, 1067–1070, 1078–1090, 1105–1108

SALE OF BUSINESS—Cont'd
Form of transaction—Cont'd
Sale of assets,
Contract of sale, 1012
Rights and liabilities of buyer, 1026–1035, 1036–1038, 1046–1047, 1051–1052
Shareholder rights, 1006–1008, 1012–1014
Tax consequences, 1064–1067, 1070–1078, 1105–1108
Statutory merger,
Impact of pre-acquisition disposition of assets on, 1006
Plan of merger, 1008–1009
Rights and liabilities of survivor, 1023–1026, 1027–1028, 1035–1036, 1046, 1051–1052
Shareholder rights, 1009–1011
Tax consequences, 1090–1105
Triangular merger,
Generally, 1016–1022
Tax consequences, 1105–1108
Upside-down merger, 1022
Fractional shares,
Purposes for, 934
Tax consequences, 1084, 1086–1087
Freeze-outs,
Minority shareholder protections, 1133–1137, 1139–1143
Purposes for, 1137–1138
Securities law limitations, 1143
Techniques, 1138–1139
Golden parachute, 1047
Investigating the target, 963–964
Labor contracts, 1089–1047
Leveraged buy-outs,
Fraudulent conveyance, 936–945, 948–949
Margin rules, 949–951
Structuring, 947–948
Tax advantages, 951–952
Liquidation of subsidiary, tax aspects,
Non-recognition by parent, 1144–1148
Non-recognition by subsidiary, 1146–1147
Parent-subsidiary merger compared, 1147–1148
Parent's basis, 1145–1146
Recognition by minority shareholders, 1147
Step transaction doctrine, 1148
Lock-up, leg-up and no-shop agreements, 952–959, 960–962
Manner of payment, 935–936
Methods of accounting,
Pooling method, 970
Purchase method, 970
Net operating loss carryovers,
Generally, 1109–1111
Consolidated return regulations, 1122–1123
Lisbon Shops, 1122
Section 382 limits, 1117–1122
Tax motivated acquisitions, 1111–1117
Post-sale dissolution,

SALE OF BUSINESS—Cont'd
Post-sale dissolution—Cont'd
Creditors' claims, 1124–1128, 1128–1129
Formalities, 1128
Liquidation preferences, 1129
Purposes for, 1123–1124
Tax aspects,
Recognition, 1129–1132
Pre-acquisition share purchases,
Generally, 970, 974
Looting the corporation, 974–975
Sale following failed bid for control, 994
Sale of control, 970–975, 989
Sale of directorships, 975
Tax impact, 1078, 1078–1084, 1085–1086
Sales taxes, 1027
Section 197 intangibles, 1066
Section 338 election, 1067–1070
Securities regulation,
Disclosure of negotiations, 962–963
Registration requirements, 1052–1059
Resales, 1055, 1056–1057, 1059
State securities laws, 1059–1060
Tender offer rules, 988, 991–992, 1062–1063
Williams Act filings, 976–988, 989–991, 1061–1064
State take-over laws, 992–993, 1056–1057
Tax-free reorganizations,
Basis, 1104, 1108
Boot, 1075–1077, 1086, 1104
Business purpose requirement, 1099–1100
Continuity of business requirement, 1100–1101
Continuity of interest requirement, 1090–1099, 1101–1104
Triangular transactions, 1105–1108
Type "A" reorganization, 109–1105
Type "B" reorganization,
Assumption of liabilities, 1085–1086
Control requirement, 1005–1006, 1084–1085
Solely for voting stock requirement, 1005, 1078–1084, 1085–1090
Type "C" reorganization,
Assumption of liabilities, 1072–1074
Solely for voting stock requirement, 1072–1078
Substantially all assets requirement, 1004, 1070–1072
Valuation, 918–935
Warranties, 933–934, 963–964, 964–969, 1027

SECTION 351 EXCHANGE
See Corporate Formation

SECTION 306 STOCK
Definition, 854–858
Treatment upon sale or redemption, 814–823

SECURITIES REGULATION
See also Corporate Divisions; Recapitalization; Redemptions; Sale of Business; Stock Dividends
Attorney's insurance coverage for, 720

SECURITIES REGULATION—Cont'd
Blue sky laws,
Exemptions from registration,
Generally, 705–707
Listing, 661–663
Merit review,
Common areas of regulation, 654–656
Non-voting stock, 656
Promoter's investment, 655, 655–656
Promotional shares, 655–656, 657
Statutory standards, 654
Underwriter's compensation, 656, 657–660
Uniform Limited Offering Exemption, 707–712
Registration requirements, 652–654
Sale in state defined, 647–652
Definition of a security,
Investment contracts, 597–598, 606–607
Limited liability company interests, 595–601, 607
Notes, 601–606, 607
Partnership interest, 606–607
Stock, 607–608
Federal registration of public offering,
Expenses, 625–626
"Gun jumping", 624, 628
Liability for misstatements, 628–647
Prospectus, 619–620
Registration statement, 617–619
Risk factors, 619, 641–643
Role of attorney, 620–623, 633–634, 645
SEC review, 619, 623
Soft information, 620, 645–646
Waiting period, 624–625
Intrastate offering exemption,
General requirements for, 698, 704
Rule 147 safe harbor, 699–704
1934 Act reporting requirements, 626–628
Private offering exemption,
Criteria for exemption, 674–680, 681–683
Subsequent transfers, 683–684
Regulation A, 698
Regulation D,
Accredited investors, 685–686
Aggregate offering price, 686–687, 691–692, 693–694
Disclosure requirements, 687–689, 693–694
Inadvertent mistakes, 695
Integrated offerings, 689, 694
Manner of offering, 691, 693–698
Notice of sale, 693
Number of purchasers, 690–691, 693–694, 694–695
Qualified purchasers, 687, 695
Resale limits, 691, 693–694
Resale of securities,
Definition of underwriter, 712–713, 714–715
Impact of intrastate offering exemption, 704–705
Impact on private offering exemption, 683–684

SECURITIES REGULATION—Cont'd
Resale of securities—Cont'd
Impact on Regulation D, 691, 692
Registration of secondary offerings, 712
Rule 144, 713–716
Sales by controlling persons, 713–716
"Section 4(1½) exemption", 717
Section 4(6) exemption, 698
Unregistered nonexempt sales, 673, 681
Verification of facts,
In registration statement, 621–622, 628–639
Necessary for exemption, 705, 717–720

SHARE TRANSFER RESTRICTIONS
Buy-out agreements,
Block-busting, 543–548
Location of agreement, 547
Price, 541
Purchaser, 542–543
Successive options or obligations,
Reasons for, 547
Tax-impacts, 800–802, 804–805
Triggering events, 537–541
Types of, 537
Validity, 536
Consent restrictions, 531–534, 535
Notice, 547, 551, 554
Purposes for, 531, 534–535, 536–537
Tax effects under Section 83,
Consequences of delay in recognition, 373–374, 554
"In connection with performance of services", 554–556
Non-lapse restrictions, 558–559
Section 83(b) election, 554, 557–558
Substantial risk of forfeiture, 548–551, 552–554
Transferability, 551–552, 553–554
Valuation of restricted shares, 374, 558
Termination of interest, 547–548

SPIN-OFFS, SPLIT-OFFS AND SPLIT-UPS
See Corporate Divisions

STATE OF INCORPORATION
See Corporate Formation

STOCK
See also Corporate Formation, Issuance of stock
As a security, 711
Convertible shares, 449–451
Dividend preferences,
Cumulative preferences, 445–446
Participating, 446–447
Liquidating preferences, 447–449
Redemption option,
Drafting, 451–452
Exercise of, 759–762, 764
Voting rights,
Classified shares, 513–514
Of preferred, 447
STOCK DIVIDENDS

STOCK—Cont'd
Accounting treatment, 808–809
Purposes of, 806–807
Securities laws, 809–810
Statutory requirements, 807–808
Stock splits, 808
Tax aspects,
  Basis in received shares, 813–814
  Disproportionate distributions, 811–812
  Election to receive stock or property, 810–811
  Non-recognition rule, 811
  Preferred stock, impact of, 812–813
  Section 306 stock, 814–823

STOCK EXCHANGE LISTING REQUIREMENTS
Impact on avoiding blue sky laws, 660–661
Impact on sale of business, 1013, 1021
Impact on securities offered investors, 581
Nasdaq requirements, 661–663

TAX PENALTIES
Substantial underpayment of tax, 38

TAX RULING REQUESTS
Advantages and disadvantages, 24–25
Effect of ruling, 25–26
Preparation of, 25, 26
Types of rulings, 22–23

TENDER OFFERS
See Sale of Business

VALUATION
  See also Recapitalization, Tax aspects; Sale of Business

VALUATION—Cont'd
Appraisal proceedings, 923–930
Assessment of management, 584
Asset valuation, 53, 921–922
"Before the money", 595
Book value, 53, 293–296, 297
Capital asset pricing method, 928, 930–932
Capitalized earnings, 54–57, 588–593, 595, 919–920, 929–930
Discounted cash flow, 924–929, 929–930
Estate freeze valuation rules, 297, 823
Evaluation of new venture, 5–17
Factors used in, 55–57
Financial statement analysis, 583–586
Forecasting, 586–588, 925–927
Market study, 7–11
Market value, 53–54, 83–84, 919
Of closely held business, 52–57, 845–848
Of common stock, 588–594, 848
Of partnership interest, 140, 142–143, 293–299
Of preferred stock, 846–848
Present value computation, 588–593
Product assessment, 583

WARRANTS
Compensation for underwriters, 561–562
Purposes for, 444
Tax impacts,
  In reorganizations, 1090
  In Section 351 Exchanges, 380

†